Lecture Notes in Computer Science 6280

Commenced Publication in 1973
Founding and Former Series Editors:
Gerhard Goos, Juris Hartmanis, and Jan van Leeuwen

Juan A. Garay Roberto De Prisco (Eds.)

Security and Cryptography for Networks

7th International Conference, SCN 2010
Amalfi, Italy, September 13-15, 2010
Proceedings

Springer

Volume Editors

Juan A. Garay
AT&T Labs Research
Florham Park, NJ 07932, USA
E-mail: garay@research.att.com

Roberto De Prisco
Università di Salerno, Dipartimento di Informatica ed Applicazioni
via Ponte don Melillo, 84084 Fisciano (SA), Italy
E-mail: robdep@dia.unisa.it

Library of Congress Control Number: 2010932603

CR Subject Classification (1998): E.3, K.6.5, D.4.6, C.2, J.1, G.2.1

LNCS Sublibrary: SL 4 – Security and Cryptology

ISSN 0302-9743
ISBN-10 3-642-15316-X Springer Berlin Heidelberg New York
ISBN-13 978-3-642-15316-7 Springer Berlin Heidelberg New York

springer.com

Printed in Germany

Typesetting: Camera-ready by author, data conversion by Scientific Publishing Services, Chennai, India
Printed on acid-free paper 06/3180

Preface

The 7th Conference on Security and Cryptography for Networks (SCN 2010) was held in Amalfi, Italy, during September 13-15, 2010. This biennial conference has traditionally been held in Amalfi, with the exception of the fifth edition which was held in nearby Maiori. This year the conference received the financial support of the Department of "Informatica ed Applicazioni" and of the Faculty of Science of the University of Salerno, Italy.

The wide availability of computer networks, and in particular of the global Internet, offers the opportunity to perform electronically and in a distributed way a wide range of transactions. Hence, cryptography and security assume an increasingly important role in computer networks, both as critical enablers of new functionalities as well as warrantors of the mechanisms' soundness and safety. The principal aim of SCN as a conference is to bring together researchers in the above fields, with the goal of fostering cooperation and exchange of ideas in the stunning Amalfi Coast setting.

The conference received 94 submissions—a record-high number for the SCN conference series—in a broad range of cryptography and security areas, out of which 27 were accepted for publication in these proceedings on the basis of quality, originality, and relevance to the conference's scope. At least three Program Committee (PC) members—out of 27 world-renowned experts in the conference's various areas of interest—reviewed each submitted paper, while submissions co-authored by a PC member were subjected to the more stringent evaluation of five PC members.

In addition to the PC members, many external reviewers joined the review process in their particular areas of expertise. We were fortunate to have this knowledgeable and energetic team of experts, and are deeply grateful to all of them for their hard and thorough work, which included a very active discussion phase—almost as long as the initial individual reviewing period. The paper submission, review and discussion processes were effectively and efficiently made possible by the Web-Submission-and-Review software, written by Shai Halevi, and hosted by the International Association for Cryptologic Research (IACR). Many thanks to Shai for his assistance with the system's various features and constant availability.

Given the perceived quality of the submissions, the PC decided this year to give a Best Paper Award, both to celebrate the science and as a general way to promote outstanding work in the fields of cryptography and security and keep encouraging high-quality submissions to SCN. "Time-Specific Encryption," by Kenneth Paterson and Elizabeth Quaglia, was conferred such distinction.

Recent years have witnessed a rapid and prolific development of lattice- and "learning with errors" (LWE)-based cryptographic constructions, given the hardness and versatility of the underlying problems. The program was further enriched by the invited talk "Heuristics and Rigor in Lattice-Based Cryptography" by Chris Peikert (Georgia Institute of Technology), a world authority on the subject.

We finally thank all the authors who submitted papers to this conference; the Organizing Committee members, colleagues and student helpers for their valuable time and effort; and all the conference attendees who made this event a truly intellectually stimulating one through their active participation.

September 2010

Juan A. Garay
Roberto De Prisco

SCN 2010

The 7th Conference on Security and Cryptography for Networks

September 13-15, 2010, Amalfi, Italy

Program Chair

Juan A. Garay	AT&T Labs – Research, USA

General Chair

Roberto De Prisco	Università di Salerno, Italy

Program Committee

Xavier Boyen	University of Liege, Belgium
Christian Cachin	IBM Research, Switzerland
Haowen Chan	Carnegie Mellon University, USA
Jean-Sébastien Coron	University of Luxembourg, Luxembourg
Yevgeniy Dodis	New York University, USA
Marc Fischlin	Darmstadt University of Technology, Germany
Rosario Gennaro	IBM Research, USA
Martin Hirt	ETH Zürich, Switzerland
Dennis Hofheinz	Karlsruhe Institute of Technology, Germany
Ari Juels	RSA Laboratories, USA
Kaoru Kurosawa	Ibaraki University, Japan
Tal Malkin	Columbia University, USA
John Mitchel	Stanford University, USA
David Naccache	ENS Paris, France
Antonio Nicolosi	Stevens Institute of Technology, USA
Jesper Nielsen	University of Aarhus, Denmark
Kobbi Nissim	Microsoft ILDC and Ben-Gurion University, Israel
Krzysztof Pietrzak	CWI, The Netherlands
Christian Rechberger	K.U. Leuven, Belgium
Vincent Rijmen	K.U. Leuven, Belgium and TU Graz, Austria
Guy Rothblum	Princeton University/IAS, USA
Berry Schoenmakers	TU Eindhoven, The Netherlands
Martijn Stam	EPFL, Switzerland
Vinod Vaikuntanathan	IBM Research, USA

Ivan Visconti	Università di Salerno, Italy
Shabsi Walfish	Google Inc., USA
Hoeteck Wee	Queens College, CUNY, USA

Organizing Committee

Aniello Castiglione	Università di Salerno, Italy
Paolo D'Arco	Università di Salerno, Italy

Steering Committee

Carlo Blundo	Università di Salerno, Italy
Alfredo De Santis	Università di Salerno, Italy
Ueli Maurer	ETH Zürich, Switzerland
Rafail Ostrovsky	University of California - Los Angeles, USA
Giuseppe Persiano	Università di Salerno, Italy
Jacques Stern	ENS Paris, France
Douglas Stinson	University of Waterloo, Canada
Gene Tsudik	University of California - Irvine, USA
Moti Yung	Google Inc. and Columbia University, USA

External Reviewers

Divesh Aggarwal
Laila El Aimani
Kfir Barhum
Rikke Bendlin
Allison Bishop
Carl Bosley
Kevin Bowers
Christophe De Cannière
Ashish Choudary
Seung Geol Choi
Sherman Chow
Dana Dachman-Soled
Özgür Dagdelen
Pooya Farshim
Nelly Fazio
Matthias Fitzi
David Freeman
Eiichiro Fujisaki
Robert Granger
Matthew Green
Jens Groth
Mike Hamburg
Kris Haralambiev
Carmit Hazay
Javier Herranz
Sebastiaan Indesteege
Yuval Ishai
Charanjit Jutla
Alexandre Karlov
Jonathan Katz
Shahram Khazaei
Dmitry Khovratovich
Kazukuni Kobara
Chiu Yuen Koo
Anja Lehmann
Benoit Libert
Adriana Lopez-Alt
Christoph Lucas
Philip Mackenzie
Mark Manulis
Breno de Medeiros
Phong Nguyen
Adam O'Neil
Cristina Onete
Claudio Orlandi
Onur Özen
C. Pandu Rangan
Le Trieu Phong
Bartosz Przydatek
Juraj Šarinay
Alessandra Scafuro
Joern-Marc Schmidt
Michael Schneider
Dominique Schröder
Marc Stevens
Björn Tackmann
Aris Tentes
Stefano Tessaro
Tomas Toft
Yevgeniy Vahlis
Vincent Verneuil
Enav Weinreb
Daniel Wichs
Vassilis Zikas

Table of Contents

Encryption I

Invited Talk

Cryptanalysis

Hash Functions

Side Channel Attacks and Leakage Resilience

Encryption II

Cryptographic Protocols I

Authentication and Key Agreement

Cryptographic Primitives and Schemes

Lattice-Based Cryptography

Groups Signatures and Authentication

Cryptographic Protocols II

Anonymity

Time-Specific Encryption

Kenneth G. Paterson and Elizabeth A. Quaglia

Information Security Group,
Royal Holloway, University of London,
kenny.paterson@rhul.ac.uk, e.a.quaglia@rhul.ac.uk

Abstract. This paper introduces and explores the new concept of Time-Specific Encryption (TSE). In (Plain) TSE, a Time Server broadcasts a key at the beginning of each time unit, a Time Instant Key (TIK). The sender of a message can specify any time interval during the encryption process; the receiver can decrypt to recover the message only if it has a TIK that corresponds to a time in that interval. We extend Plain TSE to the public-key and identity-based settings, where receivers are additionally equipped with private keys and either public keys or identities, and where decryption now requires the use of the private key as well as an appropriate TIK. We introduce security models for the plain, public-key and identity-based settings. We also provide constructions for schemes in the different settings, showing how to obtain Plain TSE using identity-based techniques, how to combine Plain TSE with public-key and identity-based encryption schemes, and how to build schemes that are chosen-ciphertext secure from schemes that are chosen-plaintext secure. Finally, we suggest applications for our new primitive, and discuss its relationships with existing primitives, such as Timed-Release Encryption and Broadcast Encryption.

1 Introduction

Time has always played an important role in communication. Information can become useless after a certain point, sensitive data may not be released before a particular time, or we may wish to enable access to information for only a limited period of time. In this context, being able to specify during what time interval a ciphertext can be decrypted by a receiver is a useful and interesting property. In this paper, we introduce and develop a new cryptographic primitive called Time-Specific Encryption (TSE) which addresses this problem.

More specifically, we consider a setting in which we have a semi-trusted Time Server (TS). TS broadcasts a Time Instant Key (TIK) k_t at each time unit or "tick" of its clock, t, where $0 \leq t \leq T-1$. This TIK is available to all users, and we implicitly assume that it contains a description of t. A sender can specify any interval $[t_0, t_1]$, where $t_0 \leq t_1$, when encrypting a plaintext m to form a ciphertext c. In *Plain* TSE, we wish to achieve the property that c can only be decrypted by a receiver to recover m if the receiver is in possession of a TIK k_t for some t with $t \in [t_0, t_1]$. Notice that we cannot enforce the property that the receiver can only decrypt during the decryption time interval (DTI) $[t_0, t_1]$, since

J.A. Garay and R. De Prisco (Eds.): SCN 2010, LNCS 6280, pp. 1–16, 2010.

a receiver can always obtain an appropriate TIK and then use it at any time later on. Achieving this stronger notion could be done using trusted hardware, for example. Yet, as we discuss below, TSE has several intriguing applications exploiting its defining property that a receiver must obtain a suitable TIK before being able to decrypt.

We extend Plain TSE to the public-key and identity-based settings, where receivers are additionally equipped with private keys and either public keys or identities, and where decryption now requires the use of the relevant private key as well as an appropriate TIK. This provides protection against a curious Time Server, as well as ensuring that a ciphertext is decryptable only by a specified party. We introduce security models for the plain, public-key and identity-based settings, considering both chosen-plaintext and chosen-ciphertext adversaries.

We also provide constructions for schemes in the different settings. Firstly, we build Plain TSE schemes by adapting ideas of [25,27] which themselves employ identity-based and tree techniques. Secondly, we show how to combine Plain TSE with public-key and identity-based encryption schemes to obtain chosen-plaintext secure TSE schemes in the public-key and identity-based settings. Thirdly, we show how to adapt the CHK transform [8] to the TSE setting, obtaining a generic construction for a chosen-ciphertext secure TSE scheme in the public-key setting from a chosen-plaintext secure, identity-based TSE scheme. Our focus is on providing generic constructions that are secure in the standard model. Naturally, more efficient constructions and concrete schemes can be obtained by working in the Random Oracle Model (ROM), and we sketch such constructions where appropriate. In our closing section, we discuss possible extensions of our ideas and areas for future work.

1.1 Applications of TSE

TSE generalises Timed-Release Encryption (TRE), a concept first introduced in [22]. In TRE, a user can only decrypt *after* a specified release time. Existing approaches [9,10,19,15,12] to achieving TRE also make use of a trusted Time Server broadcasting time-specific keys, but suffer from the limitation that some back-up mechanism must be provided in case the receiver misses a key broadcast by the server. In this sense, TRE represents the special case of TSE in which the sender can specify only intervals of the form $[t, t]$. Typically in the literature, it is assumed that the Time Server (or some other agency) will make old keys available on a public server. Clearly this may be inconvenient and would require additional infrastructure on top of the broadcast capability. TSE provides an elegant solution to this problem: if the sender specifies an interval of the form $[t, T-1]$ (where $T-1$ is the maximum time supported by the scheme) then a receiver can decrypt using *any* TIK $k_{t'}$ broadcast by the Time Server at time $t' \geq t$. We note that the use of tree techniques to achieve this capability was sketched in [9,12], but without any formal security analysis. TSE, then, provides a useful extension of TRE that can be exploited in any of the many applications that have already been proposed for TRE in the literature, including electronic auctions, key escrow, on-line gaming, timed release of information such as press releases, and so on.

However, TSE is more flexible than this in the range of applications that it supports. For example, the encrypting party may specify an interval of the form $[0, t]$, meaning that a receiver can decrypt the ciphertext as soon as it is received and a TIK has been obtained, but only up to time t. After this time, TIKs issued by the time server will not help in decryption. Yet, a user might obtain a useful TIK from some other user in the system, so this application of TSE only makes sense in situations where users have a vested interest in not sharing TIKs with one another, such as when users are in competition with one another. For example, the ciphertext may encrypt a ticket for accessing a service that is valid up to time t. More generally, TSE can be used to support any application in which a user benefits from accessing plaintext in a timely manner, and where the utility of a TIK becomes limited shortly after its broadcast time. We sketch an example of such an application in the domain of entity authentication next.

Consider a typical time-stamp based network authentication protocol, in which entities A and B share a symmetric key K and in which A sends B messages of the form $\mathrm{MAC}_K(T||B)$ where T is the current time (at A) and MAC_K denotes a secure MAC algorithm using the key K. Such a protocol requires roughly synchronised clocks, and B needs to allow a "window of acceptance" for values T in A's messages, to cater for any loss of accuracy in synchronisation and network delay. In turn, this means that B needs to keep a log of recently received messages to prevent replays by an attacker during the window. How can TSE help? Suppose B generates a nonce N, encrypts it using a TSE scheme with an interval $[t_0, t_1]$, where $t_1 - t_0$ is equal to the width of a suitable window of acceptance (to cater for network delay and clock drift between A and B), and broadcasts the resulting ciphertext. Now A's ability to send a message of the form $\mathrm{MAC}_K(N||B)$ to B before time t_1 is a proof that A obtained a TIK k_t during the interval $[t_0, t_1]$ and decrypted to obtain the nonce N. Thus B obtains a proof of liveness of A within a certain window of acceptance, so authenticating A to B. This basic protocol can be extended in a number of ways. For example, B's ciphertexts can be predistributed to A, giving A a set of tokens which she can use to authenticate to B during specified time intervals. We can also adapt the basic scheme to use pseudorandomly generated nonces, so saving state at B. We can modify it to provide key transport, by replacing the MAC with an authenticated encryption primitive and including a session key in A's message. We can also add mutual authentication in obvious ways. But what is notable about the protocol design is that we no longer require synchronised clocks, and we have a window of acceptance for responses by design. These features arise from the use of TSE.

1.2 Further Related Work

Range queries over encrypted data and related ideas: Shi *et al.* [25] proposed schemes enabling multi-dimensional range queries over encrypted data (MRQED). In the one-dimensional version of this primitive, data is associated with a single value and is encrypted with respect to that value, while users are equipped with keys enabling them to decrypt data whose values are in a given range. In contrast, in TSE, encryption is performed with respect to a range, while the Time Server makes available keys specific to a particular time value. Thus, our notion of Plain TSE is precisely equivalent to the notion of dual MRQED, introduced but not formalised by Shi *et al.* [25]. We note that [25] gives a construction which builds a dual MRQED scheme from a normal MRQED scheme, but this seems to involve a doubling of dimension and, therefore, a significant loss of efficiency, a problem from which our constructions do not suffer. In addition, in our work, we give constructions achieving non-selective security against chosen-ciphertext attackers, whereas [25] only considers selective security notions and chosen-plaintext attackers in any detail (and then in the MRQED setting rather than its dual). Moreover, we consider plain, public-key and identity-based settings, whereas [25] only handles what amounts to the plain setting. In work related to that of Shi *et al.*, Srivatsa *et al.* introduced [27] Trust-and-Identity Based Encryption (TIBE). Replacing "trust" with time in TIBE, and ignoring the identity-based aspects, we recover a special case of MRQED of dimension 1, but handling only intervals of the form $[t, T-1]$. Another related idea is sketched in [4], where it is shown how to transform a hierarchical identity-based encryption scheme into an encryption system that can send messages into the future. Translated into the language of this paper, this yields a Plain TSE scheme that can only support intervals of the form $[t, T-1]$. Unfortunately, because of specific details of the construction used, this approach does not seem capable of being extended to support more general intervals.

ABE and PE: TSE can be seen as arising from a special case of ciphertext-policy Attribute-Based Encryption (ABE) [18,3], itself a special case of Predicate Encryption (PE) [20], for a class of policies which express interval membership and attributes which express specific times, and with the Time Server playing the role of Attribute Authority. We note that most work on ABE and PE to date, with the exception of [21], is limited to the "selective-attribute" case. In the context of TSE, converting to a non-selective security model would incur a cost of roughly $O(\frac{1}{T^2})$ in the tightness of the security reduction. However, our constructions for TSE already achieve fully adaptive security in the standard model with a *tight* reduction to the security of the IBE scheme used in the specific instantiation.

Broadcast Encryption: Broadcast Encryption (BE) is a cryptographic primitive designed to address the issue of broadcasting a message to an arbitrary subset drawn from a universe of users. Although conceptually opposites (in TSE the *keys* are broadcast while the message is sent beforehand), a BE scheme can be used to construct a Plain TSE scheme: assume the users in the BE scheme can be labeled with elements from $[0, T-1]$, consider a DTI as the target subset of addressed users in the BE encryption algorithm, and broadcast the private key for user with label t at time t. The functionality of the algorithms and the security of the schemes are preserved in this transformation. There are however some *caveats* to this approach. First of all, to meet our TSE security requirement, we need the BE scheme to be *fully* collusion resistant. This condition immediately rules out many of the existing schemes. Furthermore, deploying BE schemes, as they are described generically in [6] and [17], requires the specification of the target set (in our case, the DTI) as an input to the decryption algorithm, inherently preventing the resulting Plain TSE scheme from having the DTI confidentiality property. Finally, the advantages and shortcomings of BE over our approach to the realisation of Plain TSE, as developed in Section 4.1, can be cast in a framework of trade-offs between the sizes of public parameters, private keys and ciphertexts, together with computational costs and strength of security achieved. We give a more detailed analysis in the full version, illustrating the value of a dedicated approach when realising Plain TSE.

Temporal access control: Significant related work in the symmetric key setting exists in the area of cryptographically-enabled "temporal access control", see for example [14] and the references therein. In this line of work, a key is associated with each time "point", and a key assignment scheme is used to ensure that an authorized user is able to derive keys for all the points contained in a designated interval. Such schemes generally require the publication of rather large amounts of information in order to achieve the desired functionality, but do allow efficient derivation of keys associated with time points. In contrast, we use public-key techniques, achieving small public parameters and greater flexibility in operation, at the cost of increased computation.

2 Preliminaries

Throughout the paper we will consider time as a discrete set of time units, regarding these as integers between 0 and $T-1$, where T represents the number of time units supported by the system. We denote by $[t_0, t_1]$, where $t_0 \leq t_1$, the interval containing all time units from t_0 to t_1 inclusive. Adversaries $\mathcal{A}$ are probabilistic polynomial-time algorithms. Bits b are selected uniformly at random from the set $\{0,1\}$. We denote by $\Pr_{\mathcal{A},S}[\texttt{Event}]$ the probability that Event occurs when an adversary $\mathcal{A}$ interacts with a scheme S in a specified security game. By $\neg$Event we denote the complement of Event. In particular, we denote by Succ the event that $b' = b$ in the games played in the following sections. We will use the standard definitions of and security notions for public-key encryption, identity-based encryption and signature schemes.

3 Definitions and Security Notions

3.1 Plain TSE

We start by providing the definition and the security models for the basic form of Time-Specific Encryption, namely Plain TSE.

Definition 1. *A* Plain TSE scheme *is defined by four algorithms and has associated message space $\mathcal{MSP} = \{0,1\}^l$, ciphertext space $\mathcal{CSP}$ and time space $\mathcal{T} = [0, T-1]$. The parties involved in the scheme are the Time Server (TS), the sender (S) and a user (U). The four algorithms are as follows:*

$\texttt{Plain.Setup}$. Run by TS, this algorithm takes as input the security parameter κ and T and outputs the master public key TS-MPK and the master secret key TS-MSK.
$\texttt{Plain.TIK-Ext}$. Run by TS, this algorithm takes as input TS-MPK, TS-MSK, $t \in \mathcal{T}$ and outputs the Time Instant Key (TIK) k_t. This is broadcast by TS at time t.
$\texttt{Plain.Enc}$. Run by S, this algorithm takes as input TS-MPK, a message $m \in \mathcal{MSP}$ and a Decryption Time Interval (DTI) $[t_0, t_1] \subseteq \mathcal{T}$ and outputs a ciphertext c, broadcast by S to all users.
$\texttt{Plain.Dec}$. Run by U, this algorithm takes as input TS-MPK, a ciphertext $c \in \mathcal{CSP}$ and a key k_t and outputs either a message m or a failure symbol $\perp$.

The correctness property *requires that if $\texttt{Plain.TIK-Ext}$ outputs k_t on input $t \in [t_0, t_1]$ and $c = \texttt{Plain.Enc}(TS\text{-}MPK, m, [t_0, t_1])$, then $\texttt{Plain.Dec}(TS\text{-}MPK, c, k_t) = m$, and also that if $t \notin [t_0, t_1]$ then the decryption algorithm returns $\perp$.*

We define a model for IND-CPA security of a Plain TSE scheme.

Definition 2. *Consider the following game.*
***Setup.** The challenger $\mathcal{C}$ runs $\texttt{Plain.Setup}(\kappa, T)$ to generate master public key TS-MPK and master secret key TS-MSK and gives TS-MPK to the adversary $\mathcal{A}$.*
***Phase 1.** $\mathcal{A}$ can adaptively issue TIK extraction queries to an oracle for any time $t \in \mathcal{T}$. The oracle will respond to each query with k_t.*
***Challenge.** $\mathcal{A}$ selects two messages m_0 and $m_1 \in \mathcal{MSP}$ and a time interval $[t_0, t_1] \subseteq \mathcal{T}$ with the restriction that $t \notin [t_0, t_1]$ for all of the queries t in Phase 1. $\mathcal{A}$ passes $m_0, m_1, [t_0, t_1]$ to $\mathcal{C}$. $\mathcal{C}$ chooses a random bit b and computes $c^* = \texttt{Plain.Enc}(TS\text{-}MPK, m_b, [t_0, t_1])$. c^* is passed to $\mathcal{A}$.*
***Phase 2.** $\mathcal{A}$ continues to make queries to the TIK extraction oracle with the same restriction as in the Challenge phase.*
***Guess.** The adversary outputs its guess b' for b.*

$\mathcal{A}$'s advantage in the above game is defined as $Adv_{\mathcal{A}}(\kappa) = \left|\Pr[b' = b] - \frac{1}{2}\right|$.

Definition 3. *We say that a Plain TSE scheme is* IND-CPA secure *if all polynomial-time adversaries have at most negligible advantage in the above game.*

We can extend this definition to address IND-CCA security by considering, in addition, a Decrypt oracle that acts as follows. On input the pair (c, t), where c is a ciphertext and $t \in \mathcal{T}$, it passes t to the TIK extraction oracle, which will respond with k_t. The Decrypt oracle will then compute $\texttt{Plain.Dec}(\text{TS-MPK}, c, k_t)$ and return either a message m or a failure symbol $\perp$ to the adversary. The Decrypt oracle can be adaptively issued queries (c, t) in both Phase 1 and Phase 2, but in the latter phase with the restriction that if c^* and $[t_0, t_1]$ are the challenge ciphertext and time interval, respectively, then the adversary cannot make a decryption query (c, t) where $c = c^*$ and $t \in [t_0, t_1]$. This restriction prevents the adversary from winning the game trivially.

3.2 Public-Key TSE

We now define another version of TSE called Public-Key TSE (PK-TSE) in which the sender S encrypts a message m to a *particular* receiver R who holds a key-pair (pk, sk). The message m has an associated decryption time interval $[t_0, t_1]$ specified by S. R can decrypt if he has his private key sk and a Time Instant Key (TIK) issued by TS between time t_0 and time t_1. We next provide a more formal definition of PK-TSE.

Definition 4. *A* PK-TSE scheme *is defined by five algorithms and has associated message space* $\mathcal{MSP} = \{0,1\}^l$*, ciphertext space* $\mathcal{CSP}$ *and time space* $\mathcal{T} = [0, T-1]$*. The parties involved in the scheme are the Time Server* (TS)*, the sender* (S) *and the receiver* (R)*. The five algorithms are as follows:*
`PK.Setup`*. Run by* TS*, this algorithm takes as input the security parameter* κ *and* T *and outputs the master public key TS-MPK and the master secret key TS-MSK.*
`PK.TIK-Ext`*. Run by* TS*, this algorithm takes as input TS-MPK, TS-MSK,* $t \in \mathcal{T}$ *and outputs* k_t*. This is broadcast by* TS *at time* t*.*
`PK.KeyGen`*. Run by* R*, this algorithm takes as input the security parameter* κ *and outputs a key-pair* (pk, sk)*.*
`PK.Enc`*. Run by* S*, this algorithm takes as input TS-MPK, a message* $m \in \mathcal{MSP}$*, a time interval* $[t_0, t_1] \subseteq \mathcal{T}$ *and a public key* pk *and outputs a ciphertext* $c \in \mathcal{CSP}$*.*
`PK.Dec`*. Run by* R*, this algorithm takes as input TS-MPK, a ciphertext* $c \in \mathcal{CSP}$*, a key* k_t *and a private key* sk *and outputs either a message* m *or a failure symbol* $\perp$*.*

The correctness property *requires that if* k_t *is output by* `PK.TIK-Ext` *on input* $t \in [t_0, t_1]$ *and* $c =$ `PK.Enc`$(\text{TS-MPK}, m, [t_0, t_1], pk)$ *where* (pk, sk) *is output by* `PK.KeyGen`*, then* `PK.Dec`$(\text{TS-MPK}, c, k_t, sk) = m$*, and also that if* $t \notin [t_0, t_1]$ *then the decryption algorithm returns* $\perp$*.*

To model the security of a PK-TSE scheme, we consider (as in [15]) the following kinds of adversaries:

- A curious TS who holds TS-MSK and wishes to break the confidentiality of the message.
- An intended but curious receiver who wishes to decrypt the message outside of the appropriate decryption time interval.

We observe that security against an outside adversary (who is not the intended recipient and does not know TS-MSK) trivially follows from security against the two adversaries considered above. We also note that in Plain TSE there is only one type of adversary, i.e. the curious user, since there is no specific receiver and TS can trivially decrypt any message.

In defining security models for PK-TSE we consider a single-user setting. We first define IND-CPA security against a curious TS.

Definition 5. *Consider the following game, which we call* $Game_{PK\text{-}TS}$*.*
Setup. $\mathcal{C}$ *runs* `PK.Setup`(κ, T) *to generate TS-MPK, TS-MSK, and runs*

PK.KeyGen(κ) to get a pair (pk, sk). C gives (TS-MPK, TS-MSK, pk) to the adversary A.
***Challenge.** A selects two messages m_0 and $m_1 \in \mathcal{MSP}$ and a time interval $[t_0, t_1] \subseteq \mathcal{T}$. A passes $m_0, m_1, [t_0, t_1]$ to C. C chooses a random bit b and computes $c^* =$ PK.Enc(TS-MPK, m_b, $[t_0, t_1]$, pk). c^* is passed to A.*
***Guess.** The adversary outputs its guess b′ for b.*

We can extend this definition to address IND-CCA security by considering, in addition, a Decrypt oracle that on input the pair (c, t), where c is a ciphertext and $t \in \mathcal{T}$, returns either a message m or failure symbol $\perp$ to the adversary. The Decrypt oracle can be adaptively issued queries (c, t) before and after the challenge phase, but with the obvious restriction that the adversary cannot make queries of the form (c, t) where $c = c^*$ and $t \in [t_0, t_1]$ after the challenge phase.

We now address IND-CPA security against a curious receiver.

Definition 6. *Consider the following game, which we call $Game_{PK\text{-}CR}$.*
***Setup.** C runs PK.Setup(κ,T) to generate TS-MPK, TS-MSK, and runs PK.KeyGen(κ) to get a pair (pk, sk). C gives (TS-MPK, pk, sk) to the adversary A.*
***Phase 1.** A can adaptively issue TIK extraction queries for any time $t \in \mathcal{T}$. C responds to each query with $k_t =$ KP.TIK-Ext(TS-MPK, TS-MSK, t).*
***Challenge.** A selects two messages m_0 and $m_1 \in \mathcal{MSP}$ and a time interval $[t_0, t_1] \subseteq \mathcal{T}$ with the restriction that $t \notin [t_0, t_1]$ for all of the queries t in Phase 1. A passes $m_0, m_1, [t_0, t_1]$ to C. C chooses a random bit b and computes $c^* =$ PK.Enc(TS-MPK, m_b, $[t_0, t_1]$, pk). c^* is passed to A.*
***Phase 2.** A continues to make TIK extraction queries with the same restriction as in the Challenge phase.*
***Guess.** The adversary outputs its guess b′ for b.*

$\mathcal{A}$'s advantage in the above games is defined as $Adv_{\mathcal{A}}(\kappa) = \left|\Pr[b' = b] - \frac{1}{2}\right|$.

We observe that this chosen-plaintext notion of security is sufficient to capture all realistic attacks that can be mounted by a curious receiver, so that a chosen-ciphertext notion of security is not required for curious receivers. See the full version [23] for further discussion.

Definition 7. *We say that a PK-TSE scheme is* IND-CPA$_{TS}$ secure *if all polynomial-time adversaries have at most negligible advantage in $Game_{PK\text{-}TS}$.*

Definition 8. *We say that a PK-TSE scheme is* IND-CPA$_{CR}$ secure *if all polynomial-time adversaries have at most negligible advantage in $Game_{PK\text{-}CR}$.*

Definition 9. *We say that a PK-TSE scheme is* IND-CPA secure *if it is both is IND-CPA$_{TS}$ and IND-CPA$_{CR}$ secure.*

3.3 Identity-Based TSE

We finally consider an ID-based version of TSE, called ID-TSE, in which the sender encrypts a message m under the *identity* of a particular receiver. The message m has an associated decryption time interval $[t_0, t_1]$ specified by the sender.

The receiver can decrypt if he holds the private key associated with his identity (as issued by a (semi-)trusted authority TA) and a Time Instant Key (TIK) issued by TS between time t_0 and time t_1. We provide a formal definition of ID-TSE in the full version [23].

To model the security of an ID-TSE scheme we will consider adversaries that interact with multiple users. We consider the following two types of adversaries:

- A curious TS who holds TS-MSK, and hence can derive TIKs for any time t, and wishes to break the confidentiality of the message.
- A curious TA who holds ID-MSK, and hence can derive private keys for any identity id, and wishes to break the confidentiality of the message.

We note that the latter adversary is more powerful than the natural analogue of the curious receiver in the ID setting. Since we are mainly interested in using ID-TSE as a building block to obtain PK-TSE schemes, we defer the formal definitions of IND-CPA security to the full version.

4 Constructions for TSE Schemes

4.1 Plain TSE

Our first step towards building TSE schemes is to focus on how to achieve Plain TSE. Our approach will make use of a binary tree of depth d, where we denote with $\mathsf{parent}(x)$ and $\mathsf{child}(x)$ the standard notions of parent and child of a node x in a tree. The input T to `Plain.Setup`, which represents the number of allowed time units, will be of the form $T = 2^d$. The root node of the tree is labelled with $\emptyset$ and the non-root nodes are labelled with binary strings of lengths between 1 and d, as illustrated for the case $d = 3$ in Figure 1. Hence each node is associated with a binary string $t_0 t_1 ... t_{l-1}$ of length $l \leq d$. In particular we will have that the leaves of the tree are binary strings of length d labelled from 0...0 (on the left) to 1...1 (on the right). Each leaf will represent a time instant $t = \Sigma_{i=0}^{d-1} t_i 2^{d-1-i}$ between 0 and $T - 1$.

We now define two particular sets of nodes.

- **Path $\mathcal{P}_t$ to t.** Given a time instant $t = \Sigma_{i=0}^{d-1} t_i 2^{d-1-i}$ we construct the following path $\mathcal{P}_t$ in the tree, where the last node is the leaf corresponding to t:
$$\emptyset, t_0, t_0 t_1, ..., t_0 ... t_{d-1}.$$
- **Set $\mathcal{S}_{[t_0,t_1]}$ covering the interval $[t_0, t_1]$.** $\mathcal{S}_{[t_0,t_1]}$ is the minimal set of roots of subtrees that cover leaves representing time instants in $[t_0, t_1]$. We will call this the *cover set* for $[t_0, t_1]$. Such a set is unique, of size at most $2d$, and easily computed.

It is easy to see that $\mathcal{P}_t$ and $\mathcal{S}_{[t_0,t_1]}$ intersect in a unique node if and only if $t \in [t_0, t_1]$. This property will ensure that the correctness requirement holds for the Plain TSE scheme that we will construct. The key idea, then, is to view

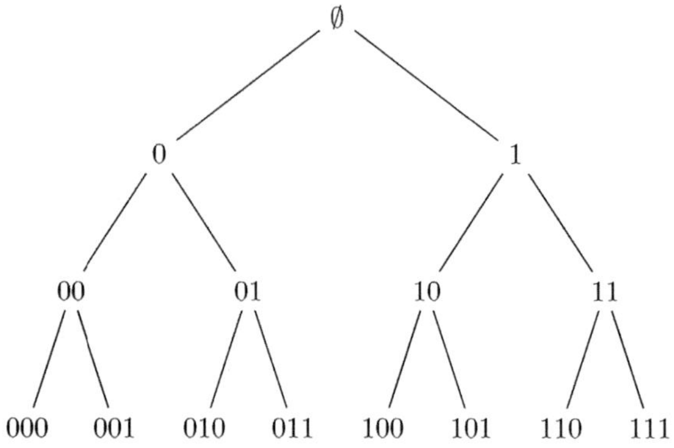

Fig. 1. Example of binary tree of depth $d = 3$ used in our construction

the nodes of the tree as identities and make use of identity-based encryption techniques to instantiate a Plain TSE scheme. Informally, the sender will encrypt under the nodes in the cover set for the Decryption Time Interval (DTI), and the TIK for time t will be the set of private keys associated to the nodes on the path $\mathcal{P}_t$ to t.

More formally, we use an Identity-based Encryption (IBE) scheme $I = (\texttt{Setup}, \texttt{Key-Ext}, \texttt{Enc}, \texttt{Dec})$ with message space $\mathcal{MSP} = \{0,1\}^l$ to construct $X = (\texttt{Plain.Setup}, \texttt{Plain.TIK-Ext}, \texttt{Plain.Enc}, \texttt{Plain.Dec})$, a Plain TSE scheme with the same message space, in the following way:

– $\texttt{Plain.Setup}(\kappa, T)$. Run $\texttt{Setup}$ on input κ to obtain TS-MPK and the master secret key TS-MSK. We set $T = 2^d$, where d is the depth of the tree used in our construction.

– $\texttt{Plain.TIK-Ext}(\text{TS-MPK}, \text{TS-MSK}, t)$. Construct $\mathcal{P}_t$ to obtain the list of nodes $\{\emptyset, p_1, ..., p_d\}$ on the path to t. Run $\texttt{Key-Ext}$ algorithm on all nodes p in $\mathcal{P}_t$ to obtain a set of private keys $\mathcal{D}_t = \{d_p : p \in \mathcal{P}_t\}$. Return $\mathcal{D}_t$ (we implicitly assume that t can be recovered from this set because $\mathcal{D}_t$ will be broadcast at the particular time t).

– $\texttt{Plain.Enc}(\text{TS-MPK}, m, [t_0, t_1])$. Compute a list of nodes $\mathcal{S}_{[t_0,t_1]}$. For each $s \in \mathcal{S}_{[t_0,t_1]}$ run $\texttt{Enc}(\text{TS-MPK}, m, s)$, obtaining a list of ciphertexts $\mathcal{CT}_{[t_0,t_1]} = (c_p : p \in \mathcal{S}_{[t_0,t_1]})$. Output $C = (\mathcal{CT}_{[t_0,t_1]}, [t_0, t_1])$.

– $\texttt{Plain.Dec}(\text{TS-MPK}, C, \mathcal{D}_t)$. Here $C = (\mathcal{CT}, [t_0, t_1])$ denotes a list of ciphertexts for the scheme I together with a time interval. If $t \notin [t_0, t_1]$ return $\perp$. Otherwise generate an ordered list of nodes $\mathcal{S}_{[t_0,t_1]}$ and generate the set $\mathcal{P}_t$; the intersection of these sets is a unique node p. Obtain the key d_p corresponding to p from $\mathcal{D}_t$. Run $\texttt{Dec}(\text{TS-MPK}, c_p, d_p)$, where $c_p \in \mathcal{CT}$ is in the same position in the list $\mathcal{CT}$ as p is in $\mathcal{S}_{[t_0,t_1]}$, to obtain either a message m or a failure symbol $\perp$. Output the result.

For the above construction, the following result holds. The proof is in the full version of the paper [23].

Theorem 1. *Let I be an IND-CPA secure IBE scheme. Then the Plain TSE scheme X constructed from I as above is IND-CPA secure in the sense of Definition 3, and is correct.*

Example: Consider $d = 3$ as in Figure 1. Suppose we wish to decrypt a message that was encrypted using time interval $[2, 6]$. In the tree, these endpoints will correspond to nodes with labels 010 and 110, respectively. We compute $\mathcal{S}_{[2,6]} = \{01, 10, 110\}$. Suppose we obtain the TIK broadcast by TS at time 4 (corresponding to the leaf node labelled 100). This means that we obtain a list of private keys for nodes on the path $\mathcal{P}_4$ from the root to 100. In particular, we have the key corresponding to node 10, the unique intersection of $\mathcal{P}_4$ and $\mathcal{S}_{[2,6]}$. Hence, we are able to decrypt. We observe that for any time t outside of the interval $[2, 6]$, there is no intersection between $\mathcal{P}_t$ and $\mathcal{S}_{[2,6]}$.

In general, ciphertexts in the Plain TSE scheme X consist of up to $2d$ ciphertexts from the IBE scheme I, while private keys consist of at most d private keys from I. The public parameters of X are the same size as those of I. The cost of encryption for the scheme X is up to $2d$ times greater than its cost for the scheme I, while decryption for X costs the same as for I. This compares well with the naive solution of encrypting with a single private key to every time instant in the interval, as it allows for shorter ciphertexts.

A variety of IBE schemes can be used to instantiate the above construction, including Waters' [28] and Gentry's [16] schemes in the standard model, and the Boneh-Franklin scheme [5] and the Sakai-Kasahara scheme (as analysed in [11]) in the ROM. Each of them has various advantages and disadvantages in terms of efficiency and the sizes of public parameters and ciphertexts. For example, Waters' scheme has relatively large public parameters, compact ciphertexts, and depends for its security on the Bilinear Diffie-Hellman Problem, while Gentry's scheme has small public parameters and ciphertexts, but its security depends on a non-standard hardness assumption, the q-Truncated Decisional Augmented Bilinear Diffie-Hellman Exponent (q-TDABDHE) problem.

A potentially more efficient approach would be to use a multi-recipient, single key, ID-based KEM (MR-SK-IBKEM), as defined in [1], which would allow encapsulation of the same key for multiple recipients in an efficient and secure manner. Using an approach similar to that in [27], we can combine an MR-SK-IBKEM with a (symmetric) Data Encapsulation Mechanism (DEM) to produce an multi-recipient IBE scheme in a standard way [2]; if the underlying KEM and DEM satisfy appropriate security notions (IND-CPA and FG-CPA security, respectively), then the resulting multi-recipient IBE scheme will be IND-CPA secure [2]. This primitive perfectly matches our requirement to be able to encrypt the same message to all nodes in a cover set simultaneously, and it is easy to see how to obtain IND-CPA secure Plain TSE from such a primitive. However, current instantiations for IND-CPA secure MR-SK-IBKEMs are only known in the ROM (see for example [1]). To the best of our knowledge, it remains an open problem to find efficient instantiations that are secure in the standard model. We recall that the scheme in [27] actually solves the *dual* of our problem and can only handle intervals of the type $[t, T - 1]$.

4.2 IND-CPA Security

We now wish to address the problem of instantiating IND-CPA secure PK-TSE and ID-TSE schemes. We begin with the PK-TSE case.

Let $\Pi = (\texttt{Gen},\texttt{E},\texttt{D})$ be a public-key encryption (PKE) scheme with message space $\{0,1\}^l$. We will construct a PK-TSE scheme from a Plain TSE scheme $X = (\texttt{Plain.Setup},\texttt{Plain.TIK-Ext},\texttt{Plain.Enc},\texttt{Plain.Dec})$ with $\mathcal{MSP} = \{0,1\}^l$ and Π in the following way:

– $\texttt{PK.Setup}(\kappa, T)$. Run $\texttt{Plain.Setup}$ on the same input to obtain TS-MPK and the master secret key TS-MSK.

– $\texttt{PK.TIK-Ext}(\text{TS-MPK}, \text{TS-MSK}, t)$. Run $\texttt{Plain.TIK-Ext}$ on input $(\text{TS-MPK}, \text{TS-MSK}, t)$ to obtain k_t, broadcast by TS at time t.

– $\texttt{PK.KeyGen}(\kappa)$. Run $\texttt{Gen}(\kappa)$, which will output a key-pair (pk, sk).

– $\texttt{PK.Enc}(\text{TS-MPK}, m, [t_0, t_1], pk)$. Pick a random $r \in \{0,1\}^l$ and set $m' = m \oplus r$. Then run the algorithm $\texttt{Plain.Enc}(\text{TS-MPK}, r, [t_0, t_1])$ to obtain c_0 and $\texttt{E}(pk, m')$ to get c_1. The ciphertext will be (c_0, c_1).

– $\texttt{PK.Dec}(\text{TS-MPK}, (c_0, c_1), k_t, sk)$. Parse c_0 and c_1. Run $\texttt{Plain.Dec}$ on input $(\text{TS-MPK}, c_0, k_t)$ which will output either a message r or a failure symbol $\perp$. Run $\texttt{D}(sk, c_1)$ which will output either a message m' or a failure symbol $\perp$. If either of the decryption algorithms returns $\perp$, then output $\perp$; otherwise output $m = r \oplus m'$.

Lemma 1. *Let Π be an IND-CPA secure PKE scheme. Then the PK-TSE scheme, constructed as above, is IND-CPA$_{TS}$ secure.*

A proof can be found in the full version [23]. We can prove the following result in an analogous way.

Lemma 2. *Let X be an IND-CPA secure Plain TSE scheme. Then the PK-TSE scheme, constructed as above, is IND-CPA$_{CR}$ secure. Moreover, if X is correct, then so is the resulting PK-TSE scheme.*

Hence, the following theorem holds.

Theorem 2. *Let X be an IND-CPA secure Plain TSE scheme and Π be an IND-CPA secure PKE scheme. Then the PK-TSE scheme, constructed as above, is IND-CPA secure. Moreover, if X is correct, then so is the resulting PK-TSE scheme.*

To achieve IND-CPA security in the ID-TSE setting we can adopt an approach similar to the one used above to build a PK-TSE scheme, where instead of a PKE scheme we employ in the obvious manner an IBE scheme $I = (\texttt{Setup}, \texttt{Key-Ext}, \texttt{Enc}, \texttt{Dec})$. In this setting we obtain an analogous result:

Theorem 3. *Let X be an IND-CPA secure Plain TSE scheme and I be an IND-CPA secure IBE scheme. Then the ID-TSE scheme, constructed analogously to the construction of the PK-TSE scheme above, is IND-CPA secure. Moreover, if X is correct, then so is the resulting ID-TSE scheme.*

In particular, we observe that if I is a *selective-id* IND-CPA secure IBE scheme, then it can be shown that the resulting ID-TSE scheme is also secure in the selective sense.

4.3 IND-CCA Security

We will now address the problem of building IND-CCA$_{TS}$ secure PK-TSE schemes, using an approach similar to that of [8].

Suppose we have a selective-id IND-CPA$_{TS}$ secure ID-TSE scheme $I =$ (`TS-Setup`, `ID-Setup`, `ID.TIK-Ext`, `ID.Key-Ext`, `ID.Enc`, `ID.Dec`). Let $\mathcal{MSP} = \{0,1\}^l$ and $\mathcal{IDSP} = \{0,1\}^n$ be the message and the identity space, respectively. We construct an IND-CCA$_{TS}$ secure PK-TSE scheme $\Gamma =$ (`PK.Setup`, `PK.TIK-Ext`, `PK.KeyGen`, `PK.Enc`, `PK.Dec`). In the construction, we use a signature scheme $\Sigma =$ (`G`, `Sign`, `Ver`), whose generation algorithm `G` outputs verification keys of length n. We construct the algorithms of Γ as follows:

- `PK.Setup`(κ, T). Run `TS-Setup`(κ, T) to get TS-MPK, TS-MSK.
- `PK.TIK-Ext`(TS-MPK, TS-MSK, t). To obtain TIK k_t run `ID.TIK-Ext` on input (TS-MPK, TS-MSK, t).
- `PK.KeyGen`(κ). Run `ID-Setup`(κ) to get (ID-MPK, ID-MSK), a key-pair.
- `PK.Enc`(TS-MPK, m, $[t_0, t_1]$, ID-MPK). Run `G`(κ) and obtain $(vk, sigk)$. Compute $c =$ `ID.Enc`(TS-MPK, ID-MPK, m, $[t_0, t_1]$, vk) and $\sigma =$`Sign`$(sigk, c)$. The final ciphertext will be $C = (vk, c, \sigma)$.
- `PK.Dec`(TS-MPK, C, k_t, ID-MSK). Parse C as (vk, c, σ) and check if `Ver`$(vk, c, \sigma) = 1$. If not, output $\perp$. Otherwise, obtain sk_{vk} by running `ID.Key-Ext`(ID-MPK, ID-MSK, vk), and decrypt c by running `ID.Dec` with inputs k_t, sk_{vk}.

Theorem 4. *Let I be a correct, selective-id IND-CPA$_{TS}$ secure ID-TSE scheme and Σ a strongly unforgeable one-time signature scheme. Then Γ, as constructed above, is an IND-CCA$_{TS}$ secure PK-TSE scheme.*

We defer the proof of this theorem to the full version [23]. It is also easy to see that the following result holds.

Theorem 5. *Let I be a selective-id IND-CPA$_{TA}$ secure ID-TSE scheme and Σ a strongly unforgeable one-time signature scheme. Then Γ, as constructed above, is an IND-CPA$_{CR}$ secure PK-TSE scheme.*

We can also use a variant of the more complex Boneh-Katz transform [7] to construct PK-TSE schemes that are IND-CCA secure in the standard model. The resulting schemes generally have improved efficiency. Details are omitted.

We discuss the problem of obtaining IND-CCA secure ID-TSE schemes in the following section, where we discuss future work.

5 Extensions and Future Work

Various extensions of our TSE concept are possible. For example, we could consider TSE schemes (in all three settings) that have the property of hiding the decryption time interval of ciphertexts from adversaries. Our current constructions do not offer this. We call such a property DTIC (Decryption Time Interval

Confidentiality). It will be interesting to explore these properties in conjunction with extensions of key-privacy/recipient-anonymity in the public-key and identity-based settings, to obtain enhanced security properties for TSE.

Another relevant problem is that of constructing TSE schemes allowing the capability of *opening* the message outside of the decryption time interval, a useful feature supporting *break the glass* policies. This extension has already been considered in the setting of TRE [19,15].

Our focus in this paper has been on achieving IND-CCA security of PK-TSE in the standard model. This leaves the problem of constructing IND-CCA secure ID-TSE schemes, in either the standard model or the ROM. It would also be useful to solve the open problem of constructing MR-SK-IBKEMs that are provably secure in the standard model, in order to improve the efficiency of our Plain TSE constructions.

Thinking more broadly, one can envisage the development of the wider concept of Time-Specific Cryptography. This could include, for example, time-specific signatures (where signatures can only be created within certain time intervals). We believe there is much interesting work still to be done in this area.

Acknowledgement

We are grateful to Jason Crampton for suggesting the application of TSE to authentication protocols.

This research was sponsored in part by the US Army Research Laboratory and the UK Ministry of Defense and was accomplished under Agreement Number W911NF-06-3-0001. The views and conclusions contained in this document are those of the authors and should not be interpreted as representing the official policies, either expressed or implied, of the US Army Research Laboratory, the US Government, the UK Ministry of Defense, or the UK Government. The US and UK Governments are authorized to reproduce and distribute reprints for Government purposes notwithstanding any copyright notation hereon.

References

1. Barbosa, M., Farshim, P.: Efficient identity-based key encapsulation to multiple parties. In: [26], pp. 428–441
2. Bentahar, K., Farshim, P., Malone-Lee, J., Smart, N.P.: Generic constructions of identity-based and certificateless KEMs. J. Cryptology 21(2), 178–199 (2008)
3. Bethencourt, J., Sahai, A., Waters, B.: Ciphertext-policy attribute-based encryption. In: [24], pp. 321–334
4. Boneh, D., Boyen, X., Goh, E.-J.: Hierarchical identity based encryption with constant size ciphertext. In: [13], pp. 440–456
5. Boneh, D., Franklin, M.K.: Identity-based encryption from the Weil Pairing. In: Kilian, J. (ed.) CRYPTO 2001. LNCS, vol. 2139, pp. 213–229. Springer, Heidelberg (2001)
6. Boneh, D., Gentry, C., Waters, B.: Collusion resistant broadcast encryption with short ciphertexts and private keys. In: Shoup, V. (ed.) CRYPTO 2005. LNCS, vol. 3621, pp. 258–275. Springer, Heidelberg (2005)

7. Boneh, D., Katz, J.: Improved efficiency for CCA-secure cryptosystems built using identity-based encryption. In: Menezes, A. (ed.) CT-RSA 2005. LNCS, vol. 3376, pp. 87–103. Springer, Heidelberg (2005)
8. Canetti, R., Halevi, S., Katz, J.: Chosen-ciphertext security from identity-based encryption. In: Cachin, C., Camenisch, J.L. (eds.) EUROCRYPT 2004. LNCS, vol. 3027, pp. 207–222. Springer, Heidelberg (2004)
9. Cathalo, J., Libert, B., Quisquater, J.-J.: Efficient and non-interactive timed-release encryption. In: Qing, S., Mao, W., López, J., Wang, G. (eds.) ICICS 2005. LNCS, vol. 3783, pp. 291–303. Springer, Heidelberg (2005)
10. Chan, A.C.-F., Blake, I.F.: Scalable, server-passive, user-anonymous timed release cryptography. In: ICDCS 2005, pp. 504–513. IEEE Computer Society, Los Alamitos (2005)
11. Chen, L., Cheng, Z.: Security proof of Sakai-Kasahara's identity-based encryption scheme. In: [26], pp. 442–459
12. Chow, S.S.M., Roth, V., Rieffel, E.G.: General certificateless encryption and timed-release encryption. In: Ostrovsky, R., et al. (eds.) SCN 2008. LNCS, vol. 5229, pp. 126–143. Springer, Heidelberg (2008)
13. Cramer, R. (ed.): EUROCRYPT 2005. LNCS, vol. 3494. Springer, Heidelberg (2005)
14. Crampton, J.: Trade-offs in cryptographic implementations of temporal access control. In: Jøsang, A., et al. (eds.) NordSec 2009. LNCS, vol. 5838, pp. 72–87. Springer, Heidelberg (2009)
15. Dent, A.W., Tang, Q.: Revisiting the security model for timed-release encryption with pre-open capability. In: Garay, J.A., Lenstra, A.K., Mambo, M., Peralta, R., et al. (eds.) ISC 2007. LNCS, vol. 4779, pp. 158–174. Springer, Heidelberg (2007)
16. Gentry, C.: Practical identity-based encryption without random oracles. In: Vaudenay, S. (ed.) EUROCRYPT 2006. LNCS, vol. 4004, pp. 445–464. Springer, Heidelberg (2006)
17. Gentry, C., Waters, B.: Adaptive security in broadcast encryption systems (with short ciphertexts). In: Joux, A. (ed.) EUROCRYPT 2009. LNCS, vol. 5479, pp. 171–188. Springer, Heidelberg (2010)
18. Goyal, V., Pandey, O., Sahai, A., Waters, B.: Attribute-based encryption for fine-grained access control of encrypted data. In: Juels, A., et al. (eds.) ACM Conference on Computer and Communications Security 2006, pp. 89–98 (2006)
19. Hwang, Y.H., Yum, D.H., Lee, P.J.: Timed-release encryption with pre-open capability and its application to certified e-mail system. In: Zhou, J., López, J., Deng, R.H., Bao, F. (eds.) ISC 2005. LNCS, vol. 3650, pp. 344–358. Springer, Heidelberg (2005)
20. Katz, J., Sahai, A., Waters, B.: Predicate encryption supporting disjunctions, polynomial equations, and inner products. In: Smart, N.P. (ed.) EUROCRYPT 2008. LNCS, vol. 4965, pp. 146–162. Springer, Heidelberg (2008)
21. Lewko, A., Okamoto, T., Sahai, A., Takashima, K., Waters, B.: Fully secure functional encryption: Attribute-based encryption and (hierarchical) inner product encryption. Cryptology ePrint Archive, Report 2010/110 (2010), `http://eprint.iacr.org/`
22. May, T.C.: Time-release crypto (1993) (manuscript)
23. Paterson, K.G., Quaglia, E.A.: Time-Specific Encryption. Cryptology ePrint Archive (2010), `http://eprint.iacr.org/`

24. Pfitzmann, B., McDaniel, P. (eds.): IEEE Symposium on Security and Privacy (S&P 2007). IEEE Computer Society, Los Alamitos (2007)
25. Shi, E., Bethencourt, J., Chan, H.T.-H., Song, D.X., Perrig, A.: Multi-dimensional range query over encrypted data. In: [24], pp. 350–364
26. Smart, N.P. (ed.): Cryptography and Coding 2005. LNCS, vol. 3796. Springer, Heidelberg (2005)
27. Srivatsa, M., Balfe, S., Paterson, K.G., Rohatgi, P.: Trust management for secure information flows. In: Ning, P., et al. (eds.) ACM Conference on Computer and Communications Security 2008, pp. 175–188 (2008)
28. Waters, B.: Efficient identity-based encryption without random oracles. In: [13], pp. 114–127

Public-Key Encryption with Efficient Amortized Updates

Nishanth Chandran[1,⋆], Rafail Ostrovsky[2,⋆⋆], and William E. Skeith III[3]

[1] Department of Computer Science, University of California, Los Angeles
[2] Departments of Computer Science & Mathematics, UCLA
[3] Department of Computer Science, City College, CUNY

Abstract. Searching and modifying public-key encrypted data has received a lot of attention in recent literature. In this paper we re-visit this important topic and achieve improved amortized bounds including resolving a prominent open question posed by Boneh et al. [3].

First, we consider the following much simpler to state problem: A server holds a copy of Alice's database that has been encrypted under Alice's public key. Alice would like to allow other users in the system to replace a bit of their choice in the server's database by communicating directly with the server, despite other users not having Alice's private key. However, Alice requires that the server should not know which bit was modified. Additionally, she requires that the modification protocol should have "small" communication complexity (sub-linear in the database size). This task is referred to as private database modification, and is a central tool in building a more general protocol for modifying and searching over public-key encrypted data. Boneh et al. [3] first considered the problem and gave a protocol to modify 1 bit of an N-bit database with communication complexity $\mathcal{O}(\sqrt{N})$. Naturally, one can ask if we can improve upon this. Indeed, the recent work of Gentry [9] shows that under lattice assumptions, better asymptotic communication complexity is possible. However, current algebraic techniques based on any singly homomorphic encryption, or bilinear maps (which includes for example, all known cryptosystems based on factoring and discrete logs) cannot achieve communication better than $\mathcal{O}(\sqrt{N})$ (see [17]). In this paper we study the problem of improving the communication complexity for modifying L bits of an N-bit database. Our main result is a *black-box* construction of a private database modification protocol to modify L bits of an N-bit database, using a protocol for modifying 1 bit. Our protocol has communication complexity $\tilde{\mathcal{O}}(N^{\beta}L^{(1+\alpha)(1-\beta)})$, where $0 < \alpha < 1$ can be an arbitrary constant and $N^{\beta}, 0 < \beta < 1$ (for constant β) is the communication complexity of a protocol for modifying 1 bit of an N-bit database. We stress that our amortized protocol improves the communication complexity in all cases when the single bit modification protocol uses any known cryptosystem based on factoring or discrete logs.

⋆ Supported in part by NSF grants 0716835, 0716389, 0830803, 0916574.

⋆⋆ Supported in part by IBM Faculty Award, Xerox Innovation Group Award, the Okawa Foundation Award, Intel, Teradata, NSF grants 0716835, 0716389, 0830803, 0916574 and U.C. MICRO grant.

J.A. Garay and R. De Prisco (Eds.): SCN 2010, LNCS 6280, pp. 17–35, 2010.

In addition to our general reduction, we show how to realize an implementation of our amortized protocol under the subgroup decision problem [2]. (We remark that in contrast with recent work of Lipmaa [16] on the same topic, our database size *does not grow* with every update, and stays exactly the same size.)
As sample corollaries to our main result, we obtain the following:

- First, we apply our private database modification protocol to answer the main open question of [3]. More specifically, we construct a public-key encryption scheme supporting PIR queries that allows every message to have a non-constant number of keywords associated with it, which is secure under the subgroup decision problem.
- Second, we show that one can apply our techniques to obtain more efficient communication complexity when parties wish to increment or decrement multiple cryptographic counters (formalized by Katz et al. [15]).

We believe that "public-key encrypted" amortized database modification is an important cryptographic primitive in its own right and will be useful in other applications.

1 Introduction

The problem of private database modification was first studied in the context of public-key encryption supporting private information retrieval (PIR) queries by Boneh et al. [3]. The private database modification protocol of [3] requires communication complexity $\mathcal{O}(\sqrt{N})$ to modify (i.e., change a 0 bit into a 1 and vice-versa) one bit of an N-bit database. Furthermore Ostrovsky and Skeith showed in [17] that using currently known algebraic techniques (which will not increase the database size after an update) with singly homomorphic encryption or bilinear maps, one cannot obtain better communication complexity to modify a single bit. Hence, we turn to the question of modifying multiple bits of the database. Using repeated application of the protocol from [3], one can obtain a private database modification protocol to modify L bits with communication complexity $\mathcal{O}(L\sqrt{N})$.

Lipmaa, in [16], also considered the question of amortizing the communication complexity of private database modification. However, his protocol has a significant drawback. In [16], the size of the database increases with every update made and after only $\mathcal{O}(\frac{\sqrt[4]{N}}{\log^4 N})$ bits have been updated in the database, Alice (the owner of the database) needs to download the entire database and re-send a new encrypted database, for the protocol to have efficient communication complexity thereafter. We shall see a little later that in applications of the private database modification protocol, this drawback is significant.

1.1 Main Result

Let N^β (for constant $0 < \beta < 1$) be the communication complexity of a private database modification protocol for modifying 1 bit of an N-bit database.

Our main contribution in this paper is a *black-box* construction of an amortized protocol (from a protocol that modifies 1 bit) with communication complexity $\tilde{O}(N^{\beta}L^{(1+\alpha)(1-\beta)})$ when modifying L bits of the database (where $0 < \alpha < 1$ is an arbitrary constant), *without ever increasing the size of the database, regardless of the number of updates.* Although we believe the amortized protocol for database modification to be of independent interest, we also describe two results that we obtain as corollaries of our main result.

1.2 Applications

Our first application is an answer to the main open question of [3] (resolving the main drawback of their solution.) Recall that in [3], a private database modification protocol was used to construct a public-key encryption scheme supporting PIR queries. An illustrative example of this concept is that of web-based email. Suppose that Alice stores her email on the server of a storage provider Bob (as is the case for a Yahoo! or Hotmail email account, for example). Bob must provide Alice with the ability to collect, retrieve, search and delete emails but at the same time learn nothing about the contents of the email nor the search criteria used by Alice. For example, a user might send an encrypted email to Alice (via Bob) that is marked with the keyword "Urgent". Bob should store this email without knowing that a user sent an email marked as urgent. Later, Alice should have the ability to retrieve all email messages marked with "Urgent" without Bob knowing what search criteria Alice used. The goal was to obtain communication efficient protocols for this task. This goal was accomplished by making use of a protocol for private database modification in order to mark emails as containing certain keywords. However, in order to keep the communication complexity of the protocol sub-linear, the authors of [3] put constraints on the number of keywords that could be attached to a single message. In particular, this number was forced to be a constant. We can directly apply our batch update protocol to remove this constraint, allowing for non-constant numbers of keywords to be associated to a single message (which may often be the case for large messages). Note, that if we were to use a modification protocol in which the size of the database increased with every update (such as the one in [16]), then Alice needs to frequently download her entire email and send an updated database back to Bob, so that further executions of the modification protocol can have efficient communication complexity. This means that if for example, Alice does not check her mail for a period of time, then users will no longer be able to mark messages with keywords with efficient communication complexity. This defeats the entire purpose of having an email system supporting oblivious collect, retrieve, search and delete queries. Alice could simply achieve all these queries in an oblivious manner when she downloads the entire database. Furthermore, [16] requires that message senders be aware of a certain aspect of the state of the email database (in particular, the number of layers of encryption) before they send a message and perform updates to the database to mark the message with keywords. This would appear to force an interactive protocol for message sending (even for the case of updating a bit with a semi-honest server), which seems undesirable and need not be the case (as shown in [3]).

A second use of our main result is a protocol for amortized updates of cryptographic counters. Cryptographic counters, formalized by [15], allow a group of participants to increment and decrement a public-key encrypted cryptographic representation of a hidden numeric value, stored on a server, in such a way that the server can not observe the value of the counter. The value of the counter can then be determined only by someone with a private key. Cryptographic counters can be used in several electronic voting protocols [5,1,6,7,18,8]. One can imagine a situation in which parties would like to modify not one cryptographic counter but several such counters. For example, there could be a total of N counters and every party could wish to modify at most L of them. This could be seen in situations where every voter must vote for at most L out of N candidates and possibly also specify a ranking of the L selected candidates. We show how to obtain a communication efficient protocol for batch cryptographic counters (better than the batch protocol that is obtained through the trivial repetition of existing protocols). Once again, we cannot use a modification protocol in which the size of the database increases with every update. This is because of the following reason. After every party updates the counters (or casts his or her votes), the party holding the private key, must obtain the value of the counter and send a new "updated" (re-encrypted) value to the server. Clearly, privacy of the protocol would be lost here.

1.3 Our Techniques and High-Level Outline of Our Constructions

Our starting point are the techniques from Ishai, Kushilevitz, Ostrovsky and Sahai [13] on batch codes. Before we explain the main ideas of our construction (and in particular why batch codes do not apply directly) we need to give short background on batch codes.

Recall that batch codes of [13] are used for encoding an N-bit database on M different servers such that a user could read L bits of the N-bit database, by reading at most t bits from every server. The goal is to minimize both the total storage of the M servers as well as minimize t. At a high level, Ishai et al., make D copies of every bit and store each copy on a different server. To decide the server on which the rth copy of a bit should be stored, they use an expander graph for the encoding.

We note that we cannot apply the construction of Ishai et al., in our setting: in the setting of Ishai et al., the problem is to read a bit of the (static) database, and reading any of the D copies of the bit gives the correct value. However, while writing a bit of the database, modifying one copy out of D copies does not yield a correct solution and modifying all eliminates all the efficiency savings.

The setting in our main construction is as follows. Users wish to change L 0-bits of the database on the server, into 1-bits without the server knowing which L bits were changed to 1. Additionally, Alice (the owner of the database) wishes to change L 1-bits of the database on the server, into 0-bits without the server knowing which L bits were changed to 0. We wish to obtain an amortized communication complexity for both these tasks. For solving this, we consider other encodings of a bit of the database. One fruitful approach is to encode every bit of the database through D bits such that the *majority* of the D bits decodes to the bit in the database. The D bits that encode a bit will again be on M different "virtual" databases. However, now in order to modify a bit in the database, one needs to modify a majority of the copies of the bit. Unfortunately, using a generic expander (as in [13]) the encoding *does not* allow us to enjoy the property that a user reads the same number of bits from every virtual database. However, it turns out that the careful use of *lossless* expanders for our encoding achieves the desired savings. This requires us to prove that for every set of L bits, one can modify a majority of each of the bits in the encoding by modifying the same (small) number of bits on each virtual database. The solution that we then obtain gives us an amortization on the communication complexity when we modify a 0 bit into a 1 as well as vice-versa. Finally, we remark that the recent work of Gentry on fully homomorphic encryption [9] could indeed be used to achieve better asymptotic communication complexity under lattice assumptions. However, as shown in [17], current algebraic techniques based on any singly homomorphic encryption, or bilinear maps (which includes for example, all known cryptosystems based on factoring and discrete logs) cannot achieve communication better than $\mathcal{O}(\sqrt{N})$. Furthermore, we note that the techniques for amortizing communication given here are abstract and apply to any protocol which privately updates single bits of a database. We stress that our amortized protocol improves the communication complexity in all cases when the single bit modification protocol uses any known cryptosystem based on factoring or discrete logs.

Organization of the paper. We begin with a brief description of the private database modification protocol of [3] in Section 2. In Section 3, we describe our main result, the private database modification protocol for modifying L bits with amortized communication complexity. In Section 4, we show how to use the amortized private database modification protocol to obtain a public-key encryption scheme supporting PIR queries with non-constant numbers of keywords associated with each message. In Appendix B, we show how to apply the amortized modification protocol to get an amortization of cryptographic counters.

2 Background: Private Database Modification with Sub-linear Communication

Consider the following problem. A server is holding a database of Alice's, which has been encrypted under her public key. Alice would like to allow her friends to use her public key to update a bit (of their choice) in the database by communicating directly with the server. For concreteness, typically what will be meant by "update" or "modify" is translation by a non-identity element in a group (as in the [3] implementation). In some instances where the updates are made by

Alice herself (who has knowledge of pieces of the database contents) the updates can be designed to explicitly write any values of her choice. However all that is required in most cases (where the parties know nothing of the database contents) is that the new value be different than the previous (which is always the case for non-identity element translation in a group). Alice requires the following conditions:

1. The details of each modification are hidden from the server. That is, without the private key, each transaction for an update is computationally indistinguishable from any another.
2. Her friends need only a "small" amount of communication (sub-linear in the database size) in order to perform an update of a single bit.

For a database of size N, we'll call a protocol for privately updating subsets of L bits by $\mathsf{Update}(N, L)$, and protocols for updating a single bit will accordingly be denoted by $\mathsf{Update}(N, 1)$. The first construction of an $\mathsf{Update}(N, 1)$ protocol which satisfied the above requirements was developed in [3]. The [3] protocol made use of a homomorphic cryptosystem that allows computation of polynomials of total degree 2 on ciphertexts (due to Boneh et al. [2]). That protocol has communication complexity $\mathcal{O}(\sqrt{N})$ for updating a single bit.

Given only an $\mathsf{Update}(N, 1)$ protocol, an $\mathsf{Update}(N, L)$ protocol can be constructed simply by running $\mathsf{Update}(N, 1)$ L times sequentially, which will of course come at a $\mathcal{O}(L\sqrt{N})$ cost in communication complexity. Hence, if $\Omega(\sqrt{N})$ updates are to be made at once, the total communication becomes $\Omega(N)$, making the scheme no better than various trivial privacy-preserving solutions[1].

In this work, we present an oblivious database modification protocol that amortizes the communication complexity of modifying L bits of the database. Our $\mathsf{Update}(N, L)$ protocol is obtained using any protocol to modify a single bit, in a black-box manner (for example the $\mathsf{Update}(N, 1)$ protocol from [3]).

3 Private Database Modification with Batches

In this section, we describe how one can amortize the communication complexity when running a private database modification protocol to modify L bits. In other words, let $\mathsf{Update}(N, 1)$ denote any protocol for private database modification to modify 1 bit of an N-bit database and let the communication complexity of $\mathsf{Update}(N, 1)$ be denoted by $C_{N,1} = N^{\beta}$, for constant $0 < \beta < 1$. Let $\mathsf{Update}(N, L)$ denote a private database modification protocol to modify L bits of an N-bit database and let the communication complexity of $\mathsf{Update}(N, L)$ be denoted by $C_{N,L}$. We construct a protocol for $\mathsf{Update}(N, L)$, such that $C_{N,L} =$

[1] E.g., the database could be encrypted under any homomorphic scheme and then Alice's friend could simply request the entire encrypted database, make the updates using homomorphic encryption, re-randomize by translating with encryptions of the identity, and send the resulting database back. A non-interactive version may also be obtained just by communicating an $\Omega(N)$-length vector of ciphertext in a homomorphic scheme.

$\tilde{O}(N^{\beta}L^{(1+\alpha)(1-\beta)})$, where $0 < \alpha < 1$ can be an arbitrary constant. We note that, we can pick α such that $(1+\alpha)(1-\beta) < 1$ and this ensures that the communication complexity of our protocol $< LC_{N,1}$ for sufficiently large values of L.

We first begin with the description of our security game for privacy. We assume a semi-honest adversary $\mathcal{A}$ that runs in probabilistic polynomial time (PPT). Informally, a semi-honest adversarial server should not have any knowledge about which L bits a user modified in the database (changed from 0 to 1). The security game when Alice modifies L 1-bits in the database to 0-bits is exactly the same (except that the protocol requires Alice to know the secret key of the encryption scheme being used). The interface for Update(N, L) is described in Section 2. The security game for privacy is defined through the two experiments (0 and 1) below. Let W_b denote the probability with which $\mathcal{A}$ outputs 1 in Experiment b for $b = 0, 1$.

1. In both experiments,
   (a) The challenger picks the public key of the encryption scheme pk and sends it to $\mathcal{A}$.
   (b) $\mathcal{A}$ sends an N-bit string denoting the database to the challenger.
   (c) The challenger encrypts these N bits using pk and sends it to $\mathcal{A}$.
   (d) $\mathcal{A}$ picks 2 sets S_0 and $S_1 \subseteq [N]$, such that $|S_0| = |S_1| = L$, where at every index in S_0 and S_1, the database contains a 0. Also, for every index in S_0 and S_1, $\mathcal{A}$ specifies if the bit at that index must be changed to a 1 or not. Note that $\mathcal{A}$ can also choose to not change any bit to a 1; this corresponds to the case when $\mathcal{A}$ does not change any bit in the database.
2. In Experiment b, the challenger runs Update(N, L) with $\mathcal{A}$ using S_b as input.
3. $\mathcal{A}$ outputs a bit 0 or 1.

Definition 1. *We say that* Update(N, L) *is L-private, if for all semi-honest PPT adversaries $\mathcal{A}$, we have $|W_0 - W_1|$ is negligible.*

Let Update$^*(N, 1)$ denote a private database modification protocol in which a user runs the modification protocol but does not modify any bit of the database. For example, Update$^*(N, 1)$ could be defined just as Update$(N, 1)$ of [3], but replacing the encryptions of characteristic vectors with encryptions of 0-vectors.

We first begin with some background on expanders in §3.1. In §3.2, we describe our main construction.

3.1 Expander Graphs

Expanders are graphs that are sparse but highly connected. Expanders have had several applications in computer science (see for example the survey of [12]). We define expanders and lossless expanders below and refer the reader to [4,12,20,11] for further details.

Definition 2. *A bipartite multi-graph with* $N = 2^n$ *left vertices and* $M = 2^m$ *right vertices, where every left vertex has degree* $D = 2^d$*, can be specified by a function* $\Gamma : [N] \times [D] \to [M]$*, where* $\Gamma(u, r)$ *denotes the* r^{th} *neighbor of vertex* $u \in [N]$*. For a set* $S \subseteq [N]$*,* $\Gamma(S)$ *denotes the set of neighbors of* S*. That is,* $\Gamma(S) = \{\Gamma(x, y) : x \in S, y \in [D]\}$*. Let* $|\Gamma(S)|$ *denote the size of the set* $\Gamma(S)$*.*

Definition 3. *A bipartite graph* $\Gamma : [N] \times [D] \to [M]$ *is a* (L, A) *expander, if for every set* $S \subseteq [N]$*, with* $|S| = L$*, we have* $|\Gamma(S)| \geq A \cdot L$*.* Γ *is a* $(\leq L_{max}, A)$ *expander if it is a* (L, A) *expander for every* $L \leq L_{max}$*. An expander is unbalanced if* $M << N$*.*

Definition 4. *A* $(\leq L_{max}, A)$ *expander* $\Gamma : [N] \times [D] \to [M]$ *is a* (L_{max}, ϵ) *lossless expander if* $A = (1 - \epsilon)D$*.*

3.2 Main Construction

Our solution, uses techniques from the work of Ishai et al. [13] on batch codes and their applications. Ishai et al. considered the problem of encoding an N-bit database on M different servers such that a user could read L bits of the N-bit database, by reading at most t bits from every server. The goal is to minimize the total storage of the M servers as well as minimize t.

The idea in Ishai et al. is as follows. Make D copies of every bit in the N-bit database. The parameters D and M are picked such that $\Gamma : [N] \times [D] \to [M]$ is a $(\leq L_{\max}, A)$ expander for some $A > 1$. Now, the ND bits are distributed among the M servers according to the expander graph. In other words, the rth copy of bit $i \in [N]$ of the database is stored in database $\Gamma(i, r)$. Now one can show that to read any L bits of the N-bit database (with $L \leq L_{\max}$), one only needs to read at most 1 bit from each of the M servers. So, by reading 1 bit from each of the M servers, t is minimized. The bound on the total storage of the M servers is obtained through the expansion property of Γ, thus satisfying the other required property.

Note that [13], do not consider the problem of modifying bits of a database. The encoding in [13] works because in order to read a bit from the N-bit database, one only needs to read any copy of that bit. The encoding does not directly apply in our setting as modifying 1 bit out of the D bits that encode a bit does not result in a correct modification.

At a high level, our protocol for private database modification to modify $L_{\max}$ bits of an N-bit database is as follows. We encode every bit of the database through D bits. The majority value of these D bits decodes to the original bit in the database. The resulting ND bits from the encoding are distributed into M "virtual" databases according to a (L_{max}, ϵ) *lossless* expander graph Γ. Let the number of bits in each of the M virtual databases be denoted by $a_1, a_2, \cdots, a_M$.

We will then show that to modify a majority of each of the bits in any set of $L_{\max}$ bits of the N-bit database, one only needs to modify at most 1 bit from each of the M virtual databases. One can modify 1 bit from each of the M virtual databases using $\mathsf{Update}(a_i, 1)$ for all $1 \leq i \leq M$. The bound on the communication complexity of the protocol will be obtained through the lossless expansion property of Γ.

While reading a bit from the N-bit database, one reads all D bits that encode this bit from the M virtual databases and takes the majority value. We first describe how to create the virtual databases.

Creating Virtual Databases. Consider a (L_{max}, ϵ) lossless expander $\Gamma : [N] \times [D] \rightarrow [M]$ as defined in §3.1. Let $L = 2^l$ and $L_{max} = 2^{l_{max}}$.

Every node $u \in [N]$ represents a bit in the database and the $D = 2^d$ neighbors of the node u are the encoded bits of u. For bit $u \in [N]$, the rth bit of the encoding of u is present in database $\Gamma(u, r)$. To read the value of bit $u \in [N]$, one reads all D bits of the encoding of u and takes the majority of these values as the value of u. Hence, note that to modify bit u, one has to modify a majority of the bits that encode u. Below, we show that this can be done by modifying at most 1 bit in every virtual database.

By the lossless expansion property, first note that for all sets $S \subseteq [N]$ with $|S| = L \leq L_{\max}$, we have $|\Gamma(S)| \geq (1-\epsilon)LD$. To modify bits from a set S, we show that there is a strategy to modify at least $(1-2\epsilon)D$ bits of the encodings of all the bits in S by modifying at most 1 bit in each of the virtual databases.

Lemma 1. *Let Γ be a lossless expander as above. Then for every subset $S \subseteq [N]$ where $|S| = L \leq L_{max}$, the number of nodes $v \in [M]$ that have exactly one neighbor in S (v is then called a* unique neighbor node *with respect to S) is at least $(1-2\epsilon)LD$.*

Proof. Let $S \subseteq [N]$ where $|S| = L \leq L_{max}$. Let x_1 be the number of nodes $v \in [M]$ that have exactly one neighbor in S and let x_2 be the number of nodes $v \in [M]$ that have at least 2 neighbors in S. Now, $|\Gamma(S)| = x_1 + x_2 \geq (1-\epsilon)LD$ (from the property of lossless expansion). Assume for contradiction that $x_1 < (1-2\epsilon)LD$. That is, let $x_1 = (1-2\epsilon-\delta)LD$ for some $\delta > 0$. This means, that $x_2 = |\Gamma(S)| - x_1 \geq (\epsilon+\delta)LD$. From counting the edges that originate out of S, we have $LD \geq x_1 + 2x_2 \geq (1+\delta)LD$ which cannot be true for $\delta > 0$ and is a contradiction. Hence, the lemma. □

Lemma 2. *Fix any set $S \subseteq [N]$ where $|S| = L \leq L_{max}$. Let $g_S(v)$ for all $v \in [M]$, be a function such that $g_S(v) =$ NIL or $g_S(v) = u$ such that $u \in S$ and there exists $r \in [D]$ such that $\Gamma(u, r) = v$. In other words, $g_S(v)$ is either NIL or a neighbor of v in S. Let $h_S(u) = |g_S^{-1}(u)|$ for all $u \in S$. That is, $h_S(u)$ is the number of $v \in [M]$ such that $g_S(v) = u$. There exists a polynomial time computable function $g_S(\cdot)$, such that $h_S(u) \geq (1-2\epsilon)D$ for all $u \in S$, and furthermore the function $g_S(\cdot)$ can be constructed in polynomial time for any $S \subseteq [N]$.*

Proof. We shall construct $g_S(\cdot)$ as follows:

1. Let $S' = S$. A node $u \in S'$ is *satisfied* if $h_S(u) \geq (1-2\epsilon)D$.
2. For every node $v \in [M]$, let $g_S(v) = u$ if u is the only neighbor of v in S'. Let H denote the set of nodes in S' that are satisfied.

3. Set $S' = S - H$. If S' is not empty, repeat Step 2, otherwise halt, setting $g_S(v)$, for all unassigned nodes v, to NIL.

We will prove that at every iteration of the algorithm, at least one node in S' is satisfied. This means the algorithm will halt in time $\mathcal{O}(L)$. In this case, every node $u \in S$ is satisfied and hence $h_S(u) \geq (1-2\epsilon)D$ for all $u \in S$. Let $|S'| = L'$. We will show that $|H| > 0$. Let $|H| = h$. Let l be the number of unique neighbor nodes with respect to S' in $[M]$. We have that $l \geq (1-2\epsilon)L'D$ (By Lemma 1).

Now, consider a *satisfied* node $u \in S'$. The number of unique neighbor nodes with respect to S' in $[M]$ that have their unique neighbor as u can be at most D, as the degree of every node in $[N]$ is at most D.

Consider a node $u \in S'$ that is not satisfied. The number of unique neighbor nodes with respect to S' in $[M]$ that have their unique neighbor as u is strictly less than $(1-2\epsilon)D$. Otherwise, u would be satisfied. (This is because at no stage of the algorithm did we assign $g_S(v)$ to be u when v was also a neighbor of a node $u' \in S$ that was not already satisfied.)

Hence we have $l < hD + (L'-h)(1-2\epsilon)D$. Since $l \geq (1-2\epsilon)L'D$, we have that $hD + (L'-h)(1-2\epsilon)D > (1-2\epsilon)L'D$, which means $h > 0$. □

We note that the above proof is similar in flavor to the proof of error correction in linear time encodable/decodable expander codes (Refer [19,4] for further details.). Our protocol uses the specific lossless expander explicit construction from [11]. We pick ϵ, such that $1 - 2\epsilon > \frac{1}{2}$. In other words, $\epsilon < \frac{1}{4}$. We state the theorem below.

Theorem 1. [11] *For all constants $\alpha > 0$, every $N \in \mathbb{N}$, $L_{max} \leq N$, and $\epsilon > 0$, there is an explicit (L_{max}, ϵ) lossless expander $\Gamma : [N] \times [D] \rightarrow [M]$ with degree $D = \mathcal{O}((\log\ N)(\log\ L_{max})/\epsilon)^{1+1/\alpha}$ and $M \leq D^2 \cdot L_{max}^{1+\alpha}$. Moreover D is a power of 2.*

Protocol Description. Let $\mathsf{Update}(N, 1)$ denote any private database modification protocol for modifying 1 bit of an N-bit database. We now describe our black-box construction of private database modification protocol $\mathsf{Update}(N, L_{\max})$ from $\mathsf{Update}(N, 1)$.

1. Create M smaller databases according to lossless expander Γ from Theorem 1 and encode the bits of the database into the M smaller databases as described earlier. Let size of database $v \in [M]$ be denoted by a_v.
2. To modify a set $S \subseteq [N]$ of bits of the database with $|S| = L_{max}$, create $g_S(v)$ as described in Lemma 2.
3. Run $\mathsf{Update}(a_v, 1)$ to modify bit $g_S(v)$ in database v for all databases $v \in [M]$. If $g_S(v) =$ NIL, then run $\mathsf{Update}^*(a_v, 1)$ with database v.

Protocol Correctness and Security. Let $\mathsf{Update}(N, 1)$ denote a protocol for privately modifying 1 bit of an N-bit database. The correctness of the protocol $\mathsf{Update}(N, L_{\max})$ follows trivially from Lemma 2 and from the correctness of the $\mathsf{Update}(N, 1)$ protocol. The security is proven below.

Theorem 2. *If* $\mathsf{Update}(N,1)$ *is* 1*-private, then* $\mathsf{Update}(N,L_{\max})$ *is* $L_{\max}$*-private.*

Proof. Lemma 2 shows that the number of bits we modify in each of the M virtual databases is independent of the subset of $L_{\max}$ bits we wished to modify in the original database. In particular, in each virtual database, we either modify 1 bit by running $\mathsf{Update}(a_v,1)$ or do not modify any bits by running $\mathsf{Update}^*(a_v,1)$. Now, since $\mathsf{Update}(a_v,1)$ is 1-private, no adversary can distinguish between the case when we run $\mathsf{Update}(a_v,1)$ and modify a bit and when we run $\mathsf{Update}^*(a_v,1)$. Hence, it follows by a simple hybrid argument that $\mathsf{Update}(N,L_{\max})$ is $L_{\max}$-private. □

Communication Complexity. We now analyze the communication complexity of protocol $\mathsf{Update}(N,L_{\max})$. Let the communication complexity of $\mathsf{Update}(N,1)$ be $C_{N,1}=N^{\beta}$ for some constant $0<\beta<1$. Note that if a_v is the number of bits in the vth smaller database, then the communication complexity of $\mathsf{Update}(N,L_{\max})$ is $C_{N,L_{\max}}=\sum_{i=1}^{M}C_{a_i,1}$. We have $C_{a_i,1}=a_i^{\beta}$. We also have $\sum_{i=1}^{M}a_i=ND$. Now, Hölder's inequality, states the following:

Let $1\le p,q\le\infty$ with $\frac{1}{p}+\frac{1}{q}=1$. Let n be a positive integer. Then,

$$\sum_{i=1}^{n}|x_iy_i|\le(\sum_{i=1}^{n}|x_i|^p)^{\frac{1}{p}}(\sum_{i=1}^{n}|y_i|^q)^{\frac{1}{q}}$$

for all $(x_1,x_2,\cdots,x_n),(y_1,y_2,\cdots,y_n)\in\mathbb{R}^n$. In this inequality, let $n=M$, $x_i=a_i^{\beta}$ for all $1\le i\le M$, $y_i=1$ for all $1\le i\le M$, $p=\frac{1}{\beta}$ and $q=\frac{1}{1-\beta}$. Now, by Hölder's inequality, we get

$$\sum_{i=1}^{M}|a_i^{\beta}|\le(\sum_{i=1}^{M}|a_i|)^{\beta}(\sum_{i=1}^{M}1)^{1-\beta}$$

Now, since $\sum_{i=1}^{M}a_i=ND$, it follows that $C_{N,L_{\max}}\le(ND)^{\beta}M^{1-\beta}$. Next, setting the parameters according to Theorem 1, we get the communication complexity to be $\mathcal{O}(N^{\beta}L_{\max}^{(1+\alpha)(1-\beta)}(\frac{\log N\log L_{\max}}{\epsilon})^{(2-\beta)(1+\frac{1}{\alpha})})$, where $0<\alpha<1$ is an arbitrary constant. Now, we can pick $\alpha<\frac{\beta}{1-\beta}$, giving us $(1+\alpha)(1-\beta)<1$. Hence, we get $C_{N,L_{\max}}=\tilde{\mathcal{O}}(N^{\beta}L_{\max}^{(1+\alpha)(1-\beta)})$. We note that if we use the protocol of [3] for $\mathsf{Update}(N,1)$, we have $\beta=\frac{1}{2}$ and the communication complexity of $\mathsf{Update}(N,L_{\max})$ is $\tilde{\mathcal{O}}(\sqrt{NL_{\max}^{1+\alpha}})$.

Maintaining Consistencies over Different Values of L_{max}. Note that if we run $\mathsf{Update}(N,L_{\max})$ when we wish to modify L bits in the database with $L<L_{\max}$, then the communication complexity is not optimal as the communication complexity depends only on L_{max} and not on L. For example, if we have $L_{max}=\mathcal{O}(\sqrt{N})$ and $C_{N,1}=\sqrt{N}$, then running $\mathsf{Update}(N,L_{\max})$ when we want to modify $L=\mathcal{O}(\sqrt[4]{N})$ bits, will not be optimal. $\mathsf{Update}(N,L_{\max})$ will

then have communication complexity $\mathcal{O}(D^{3/2}\sqrt[4]{N^{3+\alpha}})$, which is more than the communication complexity when running $\mathsf{Update}(N,1)$, $\mathcal{O}(\sqrt[4]{N})$ times.

Now, if we use different lossless expanders for the encoding depending on the number of bits we wish to modify, then the encoding of each bit of the original database will not be consistent. More specifically, since the degree of the graphs are not uniform, we may not modify "enough" copies of a particular bit.

To overcome this difficulty, we pick $W = \mathcal{O}((\log\ N)^2/\epsilon)^{1+1/\alpha}$ bits to encode every bit and store them. Now, for all values of $L_{max} \leq N$, the corresponding value of D is $\leq W$. When we wish to modify $L_{\max}$ bits of the original database, we use the corresponding lossless expander with degree D. We repeat this protocol $\lceil \frac{W}{D} \rceil$ times using a different (disjoint) set of D bits of the encoding of every bit in each iteration. Now, since in each execution we modify at least $(1-2\epsilon)D$ bits of the encoding of a bit, in total we will modify at least $(1-2\epsilon)W$ bits of the encoding of every bit that we modify and hence the decoding of majority still works. Furthermore, note that we do not increase the communication complexity of the protocol.

We note that our protocols for modifying $L < L_{\max}$ bits of the N-bit database, do not attempt to hide the value of $L_{\max}$. Note that any protocol for modifying bits of a database, will reveal an upper bound on the number of bits that are modified. This is because, if we wish to hide the value of $L_{\max}$, then such a protocol must be indistinguishable from a protocol where a user modifies all bits of the N-bit database and this protocol, by an information theoretic argument, must have communication complexity $\Omega(N)$. We assume that the bound, $L_{\max}$, on the number of bits that we wish to modify in the database is public. Note that for optimal communication complexity L must equal $L_{\max}$.

An Important Remark. In the context of the remote mail storage example, consider a scenario in which Alice, the holder of the secret key wishes to update some part of her own database (perhaps she would like to delete a recently read message). In such a situation, the contents of the portion of the database to be modified are known. Say, Alice wishes to modify L bits which maybe either 0 or 1. Alice will know the contents of the database, including that of the encoding (she can learn this through an efficient PIR protocol). Now, the protocol described above gives us an amortization on the communication complexity both while marking messages with keywords as well as when removing marked keywords (when deleting a message). This is because, each bit is encoded through D bits and the majority of the D bits decode to the bit in the N-bit database. Now, irrespective of whether we are changing a 0 bit into a 1, or vice-versa, it will always suffice to modify at most a majority of the D copies of the bit.

Other Encodings. In addition to the majority encoding, other encodings can also prove useful in this context. Rather than using a lossless expander and an encoding where D bits encode a 0 or a 1 through the majority, one could encode every bit through D bits where the sum (modulo 2) of the D bits determines the encoded bit. Now, in order to modify a bit (either from 0 to 1 or vice-versa), one only needs to modify any single bit out of the D bits and can then apply the results of [13] on batch codes more directly. This approach may be of particular use when it is desirable for a party without the secret key to modify 1-bits back to 0-bits (although this is not of utility in the main application of remote mail storage).

4 Applications of Batch Protocols for Database Modification to [3]

The protocol of [3] applies to a scenario that models a somewhat ideal internet-based email service: all email messages are encrypted under the user's public key, yet the user can still perform the common tasks of searching for and retrieving messages via keywords, erasing messages, etc., without revealing any information to the service provider about the messages nor the keywords being searched for. Furthermore, this can be done with "small" (i.e. sub-linear) communication.

The protocols will typically involve a message sender, receiver, and a storage provider. We'll use the following notational conventions to represent the various parties: $\mathcal{X}$ will refer to a message sending party; $\mathcal{Y}$ will refer to the message receiving party (owner of the private key); $\mathcal{S}$ will refer to the server/storage provider.

The protocol of [3] accomplished the basic task outlined above, but in order to maintain sub-linear communication complexity as well as to preserve the correctness of the protocol, several limitations were enforced. The most prominent conditions needed were as follows:

1. The number of messages associated to a single keyword must be bounded by a constant.
2. The number of keywords in use must be proportional to the number of messages.
3. The number of keywords associated to a particular message must be bounded by a constant.

We still enforce conditions 1 and 2 (which apply for the same technical reasons regarding correctness) however using batch protocols for private database modification, we show how to relax the third condition and allow non-constant numbers of keywords to be associated with a single message. Clearly the protocol of [3] cannot have this capability for a keyword set of size $\Omega(\sqrt{N})$: The expected number of bits one is required to update would similarly be $\Omega(\sqrt{N})$, and $\sqrt{N}$ executions of $\mathsf{Update}(N, 1)$ from [3] will yield $\Omega(N)$ communication complexity for sending this single message, violating the requirement of maintaining sub-linear communication.

Protocol Description

The details of the protocol are fairly straightforward. Let $\mathcal{K}, \mathcal{E}, \mathcal{D}$ represent the key generation, encryption and decryption algorithms, respectively, of a public key cryptosystem that allows for the evaluation of polynomials of total degree 2 on ciphertext (e.g., [2]). Adopting the notation of [3], we'll denote the maximum number of keywords that can be associated to a single message by θ. The protocol of [3] requires that this value in fact be constant. We will make no such assumption on θ and demonstrate a protocol that satisfies the same definitions of correctness and of privacy.

For brevity, we direct the reader to [3] for formal definitions of correctness and privacy for such a protocol, and instead provide an intuitive summary here. Roughly speaking, for integers λ, θ and a message database of N messages, a public-key storage with keyword search is said to be (N, λ, θ)-*correct* if the protocol for retrieval of messages by keywords yields the appropriate results after any sequence of executions of the message sending protocol, given that not more than θ keywords are associated to a single message. The work of [3] presents a public-key storage with keyword search that is (N, λ, θ)-correct where θ is a constant, independent of N, and independent of the message size. Below, we extend this protocol to maintain communication efficiency in the case of non-constant θ. In order to simplify the description, we will present the protocol at a high level and refer the reader to the work of [3] for details when needed. The protocol consists of the following three algorithms.

$\mathsf{KeyGen}(s)$ — Run the key generation algorithm $\mathcal{K}$ of the underlying cryptosystem to produce a public and private pair of keys.

$\mathsf{Send}_{\mathcal{X},\mathcal{S}}(M, W)$ — Sender $\mathcal{X}$ wants to send message M marked with the set of keywords W to $\mathcal{Y}$ via $\mathcal{S}$. $\mathcal{X}$ encrypts M and the keywords and then proceeds as in [3] in order to update the keyword-message association structure. However, rather than repeatedly applying $\mathsf{Update}(N, 1)$, $\mathcal{X}$ will use the $\mathsf{Update}(N, \theta)$ protocol described in §3.2 to efficiently perform the updates as a batch. Note that in order to mark a message as having a only single keyword, $\mathcal{X}$ is required to update $\Omega(\log^2 N)$ bits of the Bloom filter structure that holds the keyword-message associations.

$\mathsf{Retrieve}_{\mathcal{Y},\mathcal{S}}(w)$ — $\mathcal{Y}$ wishes to retrieve all messages associated with the keyword w and optionally erase them from the server. This protocol consists of steps similar to [3] in order to decrypt the locations of matching messages and subsequently download and decrypt. However in the case where message erasure is also performed, we will have $\mathcal{Y}$ execute $\mathsf{Update}(N, \theta)$ from §3.2 with $\mathcal{S}$, as opposed to repeated usage of $\mathsf{Update}(N, 1)$ (as found in [3]) which allows us to handle non-constant numbers of keywords to be associated with a single message.

Theorem 3. *The Public-Key Storage with Keyword Search from the preceding construction is (N, λ, θ)-correct according to the definition of [3].*

Remark. The proof of the above theorem follows in much the same way as that of [3]. However, there is a need for one remark on this subject. Recall that in [3] it was required that only a constant number of messages were associated to a particular keyword, since fixed-length buffers were needed to represent sets. As mentioned, we have adopted this same requirement for much the same reason. However, we would like to note that in a practical implementation of our protocol this may be harder to achieve since the increased number of keywords per message will naturally lead to more messages being associated with a particular keyword. That is, if θ is large, it will generally not be possible to have *every* message associated to θ keywords without exceeding λ messages associated to some particular keyword. None the less, we emphasize that our protocol conforms to the very same definitions for correctness as that of [3]; it is just that the antecedent will perhaps not come as easily.

We again leave the formal definitions of privacy for the sender and receiver to [3] for the purposes of brevity. Roughly, they state that the sending and receiving protocols do not reveal any information about the messages nor the keyword associations to a computationally bounded adversary. This is phrased via a standard indistinguishability condition.

Theorem 4. *Assuming CPA-security of the underlying cryptosystem, the Public-Key Storage with Keyword Search from the above construction is* sender-private *as well as* receiver-private*, according to the definitions of [3].*

Proof. This follows almost immediately from the privacy of the $\mathsf{Update}(N, 1)$ protocol, Theorem 2 and the analogous theorem from [3]. □

References

1. Benaloh, J.C., Yung, M.: Distributing the power of a government to enhance the privacy of voters. In: PODC 1986: Proceedings of the fifth annual ACM symposium on Principles of distributed computing, pp. 52–62. ACM, New York (1986)
2. Boneh, D., Goh, E.-J., Nissim, K.: Evaluating 2-DNF formulas on ciphertexts. In: Kilian, J. (ed.) TCC 2005. LNCS, vol. 3378, pp. 325–341. Springer, Heidelberg (2005)
3. Boneh, D., Kushilevitz, E., Ostrovsky, R., Skeith, W.E.: Public key encryption that allows PIR queries. In: Menezes, A. (ed.) CRYPTO 2007. LNCS, vol. 4622, pp. 50–67. Springer, Heidelberg (2007)
4. Capalbo, M.R., Reingold, O., Vadhan, S.P., Wigderson, A.: Randomness conductors and constant-degree lossless expanders. In: IEEE Conference on Computational Complexity, p. 15 (2002)
5. Cohen, J.D., Fischer, M.J.: A robust and verifiable cryptographically secure election scheme. In: Symposium on Foundations of Computer Science, pp. 372–382 (1985)
6. Cramer, R., Franklin, M.K., Schoenmakers, B., Yung, M.: Multi-autority secret-ballot elections with linear work. In: Maurer, U.M. (ed.) EUROCRYPT 1996. LNCS, vol. 1070, pp. 72–83. Springer, Heidelberg (1996)
7. Cramer, R., Gennaro, R., Schoenmakers, B.: A secure and optimally efficient multi-authority election scheme. In: Fumy, W. (ed.) EUROCRYPT 1997. LNCS, vol. 1233, pp. 103–118. Springer, Heidelberg (1997)
8. Damgard, I., Jurik, M.: Efficient protocols based on probabilistic encryption using composite degree residue classes (2000)
9. Gentry, C.: Fully homomorphic encryption using ideal lattices. In: STOC, pp. 169–178 (2009)
10. Goldreich, O.: Foundations of Cryptography: Basic Applications, vol. 2. Cambridge University Press, New York (2004)

11. Guruswami, V., Umans, C., Vadhan, S.P.: Unbalanced expanders and randomness extractors from Parvaresh-Vardy codes. In: IEEE Conference on Computational Complexity, pp. 96–108 (2007)
12. Hoory, S., Linial, N., Wigderson, A.: Expander graphs and their applications. Bull. Amer. Math. Soc. 43, 439–561 (2006)
13. Ishai, Y., Kushilevitz, E., Ostrovsky, R., Sahai, A.: Batch codes and their applications. In: STOC 2004, pp. 262–271 (2004)
14. Ishai, Y., Kushilevitz, E., Ostrovsky, R., Sahai, A.: Cryptography with constant computational overhead. In: STOC 2008, pp. 433–442 (2008)
15. Katz, J., Myers, S., Ostrovsky, R.: Cryptographic counters and applications to electronic voting. In: Pfitzmann, B. (ed.) EUROCRYPT 2001. LNCS, vol. 2045, pp. 78–92. Springer, Heidelberg (2001)
16. Lipmaa, H.: Private branching programs: On communication-efficient cryptocomputing. Cryptology ePrint Archive, Report 2008/107 (2008), `http://eprint.iacr.org/2008/107`
17. Ostrovsky, R., Skeith, W.E.: Communication complexity in algebraic two-party protocols. In: Wagner, D. (ed.) CRYPTO 2008. LNCS, vol. 5157, pp. 379–396. Springer, Heidelberg (2008)
18. Schoenmakers, B.: A simple publicly verifiable secret sharing scheme and its application to electronic. In: Wiener, M. (ed.) CRYPTO 1999. LNCS, vol. 1666, pp. 148–164. Springer, Heidelberg (1999)
19. Sipser, M., Spielman, D.A.: Expander codes. IEEE Transactions on Information Theory 42(6), 1710–1722 (1996)
20. Ta-Shma, A., Umans, C., Zuckerman, D.: Lossless condensers, unbalanced expanders, and extractors. Combinatorica 27(2), 213–240 (2007)
21. Yao, A.C.-C.: Protocols for secure computations (extended abstract). In: FOCS 1982, pp. 160–164 (1982)

A Appendix

A.1 Privacy Game for Batch Cryptographic Counters

The privacy for batch cryptographic counters with respect to server T (modified from [15]) is given through the following two experiments 0 and 1. Let the batch cryptographic counter protocol with N counters, where every party modifies at most L counters, be denoted by $\mathsf{Counter}(N, L)$. Let W_b denote the probability with which $\mathcal{A}$ outputs 1 in Experiment b for $b = 0, 1$.

1. In both experiments,
   (a) The challenger picks the public key of the encryption scheme pk and sends it to $\mathcal{A}$. $\mathcal{A}$ plays the role of the server T here.
   (b) $\mathcal{A}$ sends N values denoting the initial values of the N cryptographic counters to the challenger.
   (c) The challenger encrypts these N values using pk and sends it to $\mathcal{A}$.
   (d) $\mathcal{A}$ picks 2 sets S_0 and $S_1 \subseteq [N]$, such that $|S_0| = |S_1| = L$. Also, for every index in S_0 and S_1, $\mathcal{A}$ denotes the value by which the counter in the index must be incremented or decremented ($\mathcal{A}$ may also specify that this counter not be changed).

2. In Experiment b, the challenger runs $\mathsf{Counter}(N, L)$ with $\mathcal{A}$ using S_b as input.
3. $\mathcal{A}$ outputs a bit 0 or 1.

Definition 5. *We say that* $\mathsf{Counter}(N, L)$ *is L-private with respect to server T (run by $\mathcal{A}$), if for all semi-honest PPT adversaries $\mathcal{A}$, we have $|W_0 - W_1|$ is negligible.*

The privacy of $\mathsf{Transfer}(x, y)$ with respect to party P and server T is defined via standard definitions of two-party computation which guarantees that P does not learn anything other than the final value of the counter and that T does not learn anything.

B Application of Batch Protocols for Database Modification to Cryptographic Counters

Cryptographic counters, formalized by Katz et al. [15], allow a group of participants to increment and decrement a cryptographic representation of a hidden numeric value privately. The value of the counter can then be determined by a specific party only. More formally, there are a set of R parties, $\{P_1, P_2, \cdots, P_R\}$. These parties wish to increment and decrement the value of a specific counter C which is stored by a party T, assumed to be semi-honest. After they have incremented/decremented the counter C, T must reveal the value of the counter to a specific party denoted by P. T is semi-honest and is trusted not to collude with P. At the same time, parties wish only the output of the counter to be revealed to P. One can implement this protocol in the following way. Let P pick a public/private key pair (pk_P, sk_P) of an additively homomorphic encryption scheme over $\mathbb{Z}_n$ with n larger than the maximum value of the counter. Let P_i hold input x_i. Let $\mathcal{E}(pk, m)$ denote the encryption of message m with public key pk. Now, P_i sends $\mathcal{E}(pk_P, x_i)$ to T. Using the additive homomorphic property, T computes $\mathcal{E}(pk_P, \Sigma_{i=1}^R x_i)$ and sends the result to P who can then compute $\Sigma_{i=1}^R x_i$.

Now, suppose there are N such counters $C_1, C_2, \cdots, C_N$ that the parties wish to update. Furthermore, assume that each user updates no more than L of these N counters. No user P_i wishes to reveal to anyone, which of the counters he/she modified. An example of this situation would be a voting protocol which has several candidates (N candidates). Voters have to select L out of these N candidates and rank them. Candidates are then selected according to a weighted sum of their votes.

Now, let $x_i[1], \cdots, x_i[N]$ denote the inputs (or weighted votes) held by P_i (only at most L out of these values are non-zero). Using the solution described above, P_i can send $\mathcal{E}(pk_P, x_i[1]), \cdots, \mathcal{E}(pk_P, x_i[N])$ to T. Using the additive homomorphic property, T can compute $\mathcal{E}(pk_P, \Sigma_{i=1}^R x_i[1]), \cdots, \mathcal{E}(pk_P, \Sigma_{i=1}^R x_i[N])$ and send the result to P. However, this protocol has communication complexity $\mathcal{O}(N)$ for every user P_i.

Let a cryptographic counter protocol between a user and server T, where there are N counters and every party modifies at most L out of the N counters, be denoted by $\mathsf{Counter}(N, L)$. Let the protocol to transfer an encrypted value of the final counter value from the server T and user P be denoted by $\mathsf{Transfer}(x, y)$, where x and y are inputs of T and P respectively. The privacy game for $\mathsf{Counter}(N, L)$ with respect to server T and the privacy game for $\mathsf{Transfer}(x, y)$ with respect to party P and server T is given in Appendix A.1. We do not focus on the other security requirements such as universal verifiability and robustness ([15]). Universal verifiability informally means that any party (including third parties) can be convinced that all votes were cast correctly and that the tally was made correctly. Robustness informally means that the final output can be computed even in the presence of a few faulty parties.

We now describe below two solutions for $\mathsf{Counter}(N, L)$ that have communication complexity $\mathcal{O}(\sqrt{L^{1+\alpha}N}$ poly-log $N)$.

B.1 Protocol Using Lossless Unbalanced Expanders

This protocol, uses the private database modification protocol for modifying L bits of an N-bit database from §3.2. We first note that the additively homomorphic encryption scheme of [2] can be used to encrypt messages from a polynomially large message space (of size n). Choose n such that n is greater than the maximum value of the counter. Now, since the encryption scheme of [2] is additively homomorphic, we can use this scheme in order to encrypt the value of the counter. Every user P_i can update the counter by sending an encryption of their input x_i to T.

Now, we describe below how we can amortize the communication complexity of this protocol. We use the (L_{max}, ϵ) lossless expander Γ from Theorem 1. The protocol requires the number of parties R to be less than $\frac{1}{4\epsilon}$. The protocol $\mathsf{Counter}(N, L)$ is described below.

1. Encode every counter through D different counters. To decode, the simple majority value of all values held in these D counters is the value of the counter. Initially these D counters all hold an encryption of 0 under P's public key according to the encryption scheme of [2].
2. Now, using the protocol from §3.2, each party P_i modifies $(1 - 2\epsilon)$ copies of each of the L counters that he/she wishes to update.

$\mathsf{Transfer}(x, y)$: For each counter, T runs an efficient two-party computation [21,10,14] with P to compute the simple majority value present in these counters and returns the value to P. T's input x is all the D encrypted values of a counter and P's input y is the secret key of the homomorphic encryption scheme.

Protocol Correctness, Security and Communication Complexity. We have $R < \frac{1}{4\epsilon}$. We note that since each party modifies at least $(1 - 2\epsilon)D$ copies of every counter, after the first modification to a counter, at least $(1 - 2\epsilon)D$ copies of every counter hold the correct value. Now, after the second modification to the counter at least $(1 - 4\epsilon)D$ copies of the counter hold the correct value and so on. Since $R < \frac{1}{4\epsilon}$, after all parties have modified the counters, a majority of the counters still hold the correct value of the counter and hence when evaluating the simple majority of the value held in the counter (via the two-party computation protocol between P and T), the output obtained will be correct.

Theorem 5. Counter(N, L) *is L-private with respect to T according to the definition given in §A.1.*

Proof. This theorem follows from Theorem 2, that guarantees that T cannot tell which of the L counters were modified. □

Theorem 6. Transfer(x, y) *is private with respect to P and T according to the definition given in §A.1.*

Proof. This theorem follows from the security of the two-party computation protocol (that guarantees that P learns only the output value of the counter) and that T does not learn the value of the counter. □

The communication complexity of Counter(N, L) for every user is the same as that in §3.2, that is $\mathcal{O}(\sqrt{NL^{1+\alpha}}\text{poly-log } N)$ for some constant $0 < \alpha < 1$. Since, the server can run an efficient two-party computation protocol with P, with inputs of size $\mathcal{O}(\text{poly-log } N)$ to compute the majority value of each counter, the communication complexity of Transfer(x, y) is $\mathcal{O}(N\text{poly}D)$ which is $\mathcal{O}(N\text{poly-log } N)$.

B.2 Protocol Using Unbalanced Expanders

We present a protocol for batch counters in which there is no restriction on the number of parties R. Counter(N, L) is describe below.

1. Encode every counter as D different counters. To decode, compute the sum of all these counters to obtain the value of the counter. Initially these D counters all hold an encryption of 0 under P's public key according to [2].
2. To modify a counter, each party P_i modifies any 1 copy of each of the L counters as follows:
   (a) Following work from Ishai et al. [13], it follows that one can modify 1 out of the D bits that encode every bit in a set of $L_{\max}$ bits of the N-bit database by modifying at most 1 bit in each of the M virtual databases. Using the explicit unbalanced expander from Guruswami et al. [11], one can obtain the same communication complexity as in the protocol described in §3.2. Here, we note that we do not require the expander to be lossless, but only that it is unbalanced.
   (b) P_i modifies one of the D different counters encoding every counter that P_i wishes to modify. This modifies the value of the encoding as well (as the encoding is simply a sum of all the counters).
   (c) Again, in order to use the protocol with different values of $L_{\max}$, we store more copies of each bit and use the same solution as described earlier in §3.2.

Transfer(x, y): For each counter, the server (using the additive homomorphism property of [2]) computes the decoding of the counter and returns the encrypted value of the counter to P.

Protocol Correctness, Security and Communication Complexity. The correctness and privacy of the protocol is easy to show. The communication complexity of each user is the same as that in the protocol for database modification.

Generic Constructions of Parallel Key-Insulated Encryption

Goichiro Hanaoka[1] and Jian Weng[2,3]

[1] National Institute of Advanced Industrial Science and Technology, Tokyo, Japan
[2] Department of Computer Science, Jinan University, Guangzhou, China
[3] State Key Laboratory of Information Security
Institute of Software, Chinese Academy of Sciences, Beijing, China
hanaoka-goichiro@aist.go.jp, cryptjweng@gmail.com

Abstract. Exposure of a secret key is a significant threat in practice. As a notion of security against key exposure, Dodis et al. advocated key-insulated security, and proposed concrete key-insulated encryption (KIE) schemes in which secret keys are periodically updated by using a physically "insulated" helper key. For significantly reducing possibility of exposure of the helper key, Hanaoka et al. further proposed the notion of parallel KIE (PKIE) in which multiple helper keys are used in alternate shifts. They also pointed out that in contrast to the case of the standard KIE, PKIE cannot be straightforwardly obtained from identity-based encryption (IBE). In this paper, we clarify that PKIE can be generically constructed by using a new primitive which we call one-time forward secure public key encryption (OTFS-PKE) and show that it is possible to construct OTFS-PKE from arbitrary IBE or hierarchical IBE (without degenerating into IBE). By using our method, we can obtain various new PKIE schemes which yield desirable properties. For example, we can construct first PKIE schemes from lattice or quadratic residuosity problems (without using bilinear maps), and PKIE with short ciphertexts and cheaper computational cost for both encryption and decryption.

Keywords: key exposure, parallel key-insulated encryption, one-time forward secure public key encryption, identity-based encryption.

1 Introduction

Background. Nowadays, there is a growing tendency for cryptographic systems to be deployed on inexpensive, lightweight and mobile devices. In such a situation, a secret key is more casually and frequently used, and thus, both damage and possibility of key exposure increase significantly.

Key-insulated cryptography, introduced by Dodis, Katz, Xu and Yung [13], is a useful technique to mitigate the potential damage caused by key exposure. In a key-insulated encryption (KIE) scheme, the lifetime of the system is divided into discrete periods, and the pubic key remains fixed throughout the lifetime. Each user keeps two kinds of secrets which are called *user secret key* and *helper key*. The user secret key is used for decrypting ciphertexts, and the helper key is used

J.A. Garay and R. De Prisco (Eds.): SCN 2010, LNCS 6280, pp. 36–53, 2010.

for updating the user secret key. Since the user secret key is periodically updated (without changing the public key), its exposure compromises only security during its corresponding time period, and security of other time periods (including past ones) are still maintained. Furthermore, the helper key is stored in a dedicated device named *helper*, which is kept isolated from the network except when it is used for updating the user secret key, and thus we can assume that possibility of its exposure is very low.

The key-insulation paradigm is an effective solution to the key exposure problem. However, we also notice that it is not easy to simultaneously handle (1) reducing damage by exposure of the user secret key, and (2) reducing possibility of exposure of the helper key. Namely, if we update the user secret key more frequently, then exposure of the user secret key compromises security for only a shorter time period. But, this also increases frequency of the helper's connection to insecure environments, and hence increases the risk of helper key exposure. Note that exposure of the helper key may compromise security of *all* time periods.

To address the above problem, Hanaoka, Hanaoka, and Imai [17] introduced the concept of parallel key-insulated encryption (PKIE), where two (or more) distinct helpers are *alternately* used to update the user secret keys. As indicated in [17], PKIE allows frequent updating of the user secret key, and at the same time reduces the risk of the helper key exposure. Namely, assuming that in some time period, the user secret key is updated by using one of two helper keys, next updating procedure cannot be carried out without using the other helper key. Therefore, even if one of helper keys is exposed, its damage is still very limited.

Based on Boneh-Franklin identity-based encryption (IBE) scheme [7], Hanaoka et al. [17] also proposed a concrete PKIE scheme (referred to as HHI scheme) in the random oracle model [4]. Later, based on Boneh-Boyen IBE scheme [5], Libert, Quisquater and Yung [22] further proposed another PKIE scheme (referred to as LQY scheme) without using random oracles.

Libert et al. also pointed out an important fact that in contrast to the standard KIE, *it is not straightforward to construct PKIE from IBE.* Actually, it has not been known if it is possible to generically construct PKIE from any IBE or not, and therefore, we cannot flexibly design PKIE schemes according to individual system requirement.

Our Results. In this paper, we show that it is possible to generically construct a PKIE scheme from an arbitrary IBE scheme, and give various useful instantiations. Specifically, we first introduce a new primitive named one-time forward secure public key encryption (OTFS-PKE), and then present a generic construction of PKIE from OTFS-PKE. Furthermore, we present two generic constructions of OTFS-PKE: one is from standard IBE, and the other is from two-level hierarchical identity-based encryption (2-HIBE). We note that IBE can be trivially obtained from 2-HIBE, but our generalization based on OTFS-PKE yields more flexibility which results in a wider range of applications.

First examples of instantiations of our generic construction are PKIE schemes from various assumptions. Namely, by converting lattice-based IBE schemes [15, 10, 23] into OTSF-PKE schemes, we immediately have PKIE schemes based on difficulty of lattice problems. These schemes can be considered as the first "post-quantum" PKIE schemes. Similarly, based on the quadratic-residuosity-based IBE schemes [11,8], we can construct PKIE schemes from the same underlying assumptions. These are the first PKIE schemes from a factoring-related problem. We stress that all previously known PKIE schemes rely on pairings, thus the above schemes are also the first PKIE schemes without pairings.

Second examples are PKIE schemes with better efficiency in comparison to existing schemes (e.g. [22]) in some aspects. For instance, based on Boneh-Boyen IBE [5], we can construct a new PKIE scheme with shorter ciphertexts and cheaper computational cost for encryption and decryption. For another instance, based on Boneh-Boyen-Goh HIBE [6], we can also construct a new PKIE scheme which yields cheaper computation for helpers. This scheme is useful when helpers are computationally weak devices (e.g. smart cards). Surprisingly, when our Boneh-Boyen-based scheme is extended to support multiple helpers, its public key size, ciphertext size, encryption cost and decryption cost are all constant and independent with the number of helpers. This scheme can be viewed as a (partial) solution to the open question left by Libert et al. in PKC'07.

Related Works. In their seminal paper, Dodis, Katz, Xu and Yung [13] presented generic constructions as well as direct constructions of KIE schemes. Bellare and Palacio [3] proposed a new KIE scheme based on Boneh-Franklin IBE scheme, and they also presented the generic construction of (non-strong key-insulated) KIE from IBE. We remark that these generic constructions cannot be applied to PKIE systems. Hanaoka et al. [18] studied KIE in the unconditional settings, and proposed a dynamic and mutual KIE scheme.

Phan et al. [24] generalized the notion of PKIE and introduced a new paradigm called key-insulated public key encryption with auxiliary helper. Weng et al. [28] extended PKIE to identity-based scenarios, and proposed an identity-based PKIE scheme without random oracles. However, the efficiency of their scheme also degrades with the number of helpers. Hanaoka et al. [19] introduced the paradigm of hierarchial key-insulation, and presented the constructions of identity-based hierarchial KIE. Weng et al. [29] introduced the notion of threshold key-insulation, and proposed an identity-based threshold KIE scheme.

There exist some other related techniques to deal with the key exposure problem. Forward secure cryptography [1] can ensure that, exposure of the current key does not render usages of previous keys insecure, but security of the future periods is lost. Intrusion-resilient cryptography [20] strengths the key-insulated security in the sense that, the system remains secure even after arbitrarily many compromises of both helper key and user secret keys, as long as the compromises are not simultaneous.

2 Preliminaries

2.1 Public Key Encryption

A public key encryption (PKE) scheme $\mathsf{PKE} = (\mathsf{KGen}, \mathsf{Enc}, \mathsf{Dec})$ consists of three algorithms: The *key generation* algorithm $(pk, sk) \leftarrow \mathsf{KGen}(\lambda)$, taking as input a security parameter λ, outputs a public/secret key pair (pk, sk). The *encryption* algorithm $C \leftarrow \mathsf{Enc}(pk, M)$, on input a public key pk and a message $M \in \mathcal{M}$, outputs a ciphertext C. The *decryption* algorithm $M \leftarrow \mathsf{Dec}(sk, C)$, on input a cipertext C and the secret key sk, outputs a plaintext M (or "$\perp$" if C is invalid).

Next, we review the definition of semantic security [16] for PKE, i.e. IND-ATK [2,14,26] where ATK $\in$ {CPA, CCA}. Let $\mathcal{B}$ be an adversary running in two stages `find` and `guess`. Consider the following experiment:

$$\mathbf{Exp}^{\mathsf{IND\text{-}ATK}}_{\mathcal{B},\mathsf{PKE}}(\lambda)\!:\!\Big[(pk, sk) \leftarrow \mathsf{KeyGen}(\lambda);\ (M_0, M_1) \leftarrow \mathcal{B}^{\mathcal{O}_{\mathrm{d}}(\cdot)}_{\mathtt{find}}(pk);\ \delta \xleftarrow{\$} \{0,1\};$$
$$C^* \leftarrow \mathsf{Enc}(pk, M_\delta);\ \delta' \leftarrow \mathcal{B}^{\mathcal{O}_{\mathrm{d}}(\cdot)}_{\mathtt{guess}}(C^*, pk);\ \text{return } 1 \text{ if } \delta = \delta', \text{ or } 0 \text{ otherwise }\Big],$$

where $\mathcal{O}_{\mathrm{d}}(\cdot)$ is a decryption oracle which for given C returns $M \leftarrow \mathsf{Dec}(sk, C)$ if ATK = CCA, or "$\perp$" if ATK = CPA. It is required that $|M_0| = |M_1|$, and $\mathcal{B}$ cannot issue the query $\mathcal{O}_{\mathrm{d}}(C^*)$.

We define $\mathcal{A}$'s advantage as $\mathrm{Adv}^{\mathsf{IND\text{-}ATK}}_{\mathcal{B},\mathsf{PKE}}(\lambda) = \left|\Pr[\mathbf{Exp}^{\mathsf{IND\text{-}ATK}}_{\mathcal{B},\mathsf{PKE}}(\lambda) = 1] - \frac{1}{2}\right|$.

Definition 1. *We say that a* PKE *scheme is* IND-CCA *(resp.* IND-CPA*) secure, if there exists no probabilistic polynomial time (PPT) adversary $\mathcal{B}$ who has advantage* $\mathrm{Adv}^{\mathsf{IND\text{-}CCA}}_{\mathcal{B},\mathsf{PKE}}(\lambda)$ *(resp.* $\mathrm{Adv}^{\mathsf{IND\text{-}CPA}}_{\mathcal{B},\mathsf{PKE}}(\lambda)$*).*

2.2 Hierarchical Identity-Based Encryption

An hierarchical identity-based encryption (HIBE) scheme consists of four algorithms: The *setup* algorithm $(param, msk) \leftarrow \mathsf{Setup}(\lambda, l)$, run by the private key generator (PKG), on input a security parameter λ and the maximum hierarchy depth l, outputs the public parameters $param$ and the master secret key msk. The *key extraction* algorithm $sk_{\mathsf{ID}} \leftarrow \mathsf{Extract}(param, sk_{\mathsf{ID}_{|k-1}}, \mathsf{ID})$, on input $param$, an identity $\mathsf{ID} = (\mathsf{ID}_1, \cdots, \mathsf{ID}_k)$ of depth $k \le l$, and the secret key $sk_{\mathsf{ID}_{|k-1}}$ of the parent identity $\mathsf{ID}_{|k-1} = (\mathsf{ID}_1, \cdots, \mathsf{ID}_{k-1})$, outputs the secret key sk_{ID} for ID. The *encryption* algorithm $C \leftarrow \mathsf{Enc}(param, \mathsf{ID}, M)$, on input $param$, a message $M \in \mathcal{M}$ and an identity ID with a depth equal or less than l, outputs a ciphertext C. The *decryption* algorithm $m \leftarrow \mathsf{Dec}(sk_{\mathsf{ID}}, C)$, on input a secret key sk_{ID} and a ciphertext C, outputs a plaintext M (or "$\perp$" if C is invalid).

Next, we review the semantic security for HIBE/IBE, i.e. IND-ID-ATK where ATK = {CPA, CCA}. For an adversary $\mathcal{A}$, we consider the following experiment:

$$\mathbf{Exp}^{\mathsf{IND\text{-}ID\text{-}ATK}}_{\mathcal{A},\mathtt{HIBE/IBE}}(\lambda)\!:\!\Big[(param, msk) \leftarrow \mathsf{Setup}(\lambda, l);$$
$$(M_0, M_1, \mathsf{ID}^*) \leftarrow \mathcal{A}^{\mathcal{O}_{\mathrm{ext}}(\cdot), \mathcal{O}_{\mathrm{d}}(\cdot,\cdot)}_{\mathtt{find}}(param);\ \delta \xleftarrow{\$} \{0,1\};\ C^* \leftarrow \mathsf{Enc}(param, \mathsf{ID}^*, M_\delta);$$
$$\delta' \leftarrow \mathcal{A}^{\mathcal{O}_{\mathrm{ext}}(\cdot), \mathcal{O}_{\mathrm{d}}(\cdot,\cdot)}_{\mathtt{guess}}(param, C^*);\ \text{if } \delta = \delta' \text{ return } 1 \text{ else } 0\Big],$$

where $\mathcal{O}_{\mathrm{ext}}(\cdot)$ is a key extraction oracle which for given ID returns $sk_{\mathsf{ID}} \leftarrow \mathsf{Extract}(param, msk, \mathsf{ID})$, and $\mathcal{O}_{\mathrm{d}}(\cdot,\cdot)$ is a decryption oracle which for given (ID, C) returns $M \leftarrow \mathsf{Dec}(sk_{\mathsf{ID}}, C)$ if ATK = CCA, or "$\perp$" if ATK = CPA. It is required that $|M_0| = |M_1|$, $\mathcal{A}$ cannot submit ID^* nor a prefix of ID^* to oracle $\mathcal{O}_{\rm ext}$, and $\mathcal{A}$ cannot submit (ID^*, C^*) to oracle $\mathcal{O}_{\rm d}$. We define $\mathcal{A}$'s advantage as $\mathrm{Adv}^{\mathsf{IND\text{-}ID\text{-}ATK}}_{\mathcal{A},\mathtt{HIBE/IBE}}(\lambda) = \left|\Pr[\mathbf{Exp}^{\mathsf{IND\text{-}ID\text{-}ATK}}_{\mathcal{A},\mathtt{HIBE/IBE}}(\lambda) = 1] - \frac{1}{2}\right|$.

Definition 2. *An* HIBE/IBE *scheme is said to be* IND-ID-CCA *(resp.* IND-ID-CPA*) secure, if there exits no PPT adversary $\mathcal{A}$ who has non-negligible advantage* $\mathrm{Adv}^{\mathsf{IND\text{-}ID\text{-}CCA}}_{\mathcal{A},\mathtt{HIBE/IBE}}(\lambda)$ *(resp.* $\mathrm{Adv}^{\mathsf{IND\text{-}ID\text{-}CPA}}_{\mathcal{A},\mathtt{HIBE/IBE}}(\lambda)$*).*

2.3 Parallel Key-Insulated Encryption

A PKIE scheme consists of the following algorithms:

- $\mathsf{KeyGen}(\lambda)$: The *key generation* algorithm, on input a security parameter λ, outputs a public key pk, an initial user secret key usk_0 and two helper keys $(\mathsf{mst}_1, \mathsf{mst}_0)$. Here usk_0 is kept by the user, while mst_1 and mst_0 are kept by the first and the second helper respectively. We write $(\mathsf{pk}, \mathsf{usk}_0, (\mathsf{mst}_1, \mathsf{mst}_0)) \leftarrow \mathsf{KeyGen}(\lambda)$.
- $\Delta\text{-}\mathsf{Gen}(t, \mathsf{mst}_{t \bmod 2})$: The *helper key-update* algorithm is run by the helpers at the beginning of each period. On input a period index t and the corresponding helper key $\mathsf{mst}_{t \bmod 2}$, it outputs an update key hsk_t for period t. We write $\mathsf{hsk}_t \leftarrow \Delta\text{-}\mathsf{Gen}(t, \mathsf{mst}_{t \bmod 2})$.
- $\mathsf{Update}(t, \mathsf{usk}_{t-1}, \mathsf{hsk}_t)$: The *user key-update* algorithm is run by the user at the beginning of each period. Taking as input a period index t, the user secret key usk_{t-1} for period $t-1$ and the update key hsk_t, it returns the user secret key usk_t for period t. We write $\mathsf{usk}_t \leftarrow \mathsf{Update}(t, \mathsf{usk}_{t-1}, \mathsf{hsk}_t)$.
- $\mathsf{Enc}(\mathsf{pk}, t, m)$: The *encryption* algorithm takes as input the public key pk, a period index t and a message $m \in \mathcal{M}$. It outputs a ciphertext $\mathtt{CT}$. We write $\mathtt{CT} \leftarrow \mathsf{Enc}(\mathsf{pk}, t, m)$.
- $\mathsf{Dec}(\mathsf{usk}_t, \mathtt{CT})$: The *decryption* algorithm takes as input a ciphertext $\mathtt{CT}$ under period index t, and the matching user secret key usk_t. It outputs a plaintext m (or "$\perp$" if $\mathtt{CT}$ is invalid). We write $m \leftarrow \mathsf{Dec}(\mathsf{usk}_t, \mathtt{CT})$.

Key-insulated security. This security notion captures the intuition that, if an adversary does not compromise the helper, exposure of the user secret keys for some periods does not affect other periods; furthermore, if a single helper is broken into while a given period t is exposed, only one other period adjacent to t is exposed (recall that even strong key-insulated KIE schemes collapse in this scenario). We refer to this security as IND-KI-ATK where $\mathsf{ATK} \in \{\mathsf{CCA}, \mathsf{CPA}\}$. For an adversary $\mathcal{A}$, we consider the following experiment:

$$\begin{aligned}&\mathbf{Exp}^{\mathsf{IND\text{-}KI\text{-}ATK}}_{\mathcal{A},\mathsf{PKIE}}(\lambda)\text{:}\big[(\mathsf{pk}, \mathsf{usk}_0, (\mathsf{mst}_1, \mathsf{mst}_0)) \leftarrow \mathsf{KeyGen}(\lambda);\\ &(m_0, m_1, t^*) \leftarrow \mathcal{A}^{\mathcal{O}_{\rm u}(\cdot),\mathcal{O}_{\rm h}(\cdot),\mathcal{O}_{\rm d}(\cdot,\cdot)}_{\mathtt{find}}(\mathsf{pk});\ \beta \xleftarrow{\$} \{0,1\}; \mathtt{CT}^* \leftarrow \mathsf{Enc}(\mathsf{pk}, t^*, m_\beta);\\ &\beta' \leftarrow \mathcal{A}^{\mathcal{O}_{\rm u}(\cdot),\mathcal{O}_{\rm h}(\cdot),\mathcal{O}_{\rm d}(\cdot,\cdot)}_{\mathsf{guess}}(\mathsf{pk}, \mathtt{CT}^*);\ \text{return 1 if } \beta = \beta' \text{ or 0 otherwise}\big],\end{aligned}$$

where $\mathcal{O}_{\rm u}(\cdot)$ is a user secret key oracle which for given a period index t returns the user secret key usk_t, $\mathcal{O}_{\rm h}(\cdot)$ is a helper key oracle which for given an index

$i \in \{0,1\}$ returns the helper key mst_i, and $\mathcal{O}_{\mathrm{d}}(\cdot,\cdot)$ is a decryption oracle which for given (t, CT) returns $m \leftarrow \mathsf{Dec}(\mathsf{usk}_t, \mathsf{CT})$ if $\mathsf{ATK} = \mathsf{CCA}$, or "$\perp$" if $\mathsf{ATK} = \mathsf{CPA}$. It is mandated that $|m_0| = |m_1|$ and the following requirements are satisfied: (1) $\mathcal{A}$ cannot issue the user secret key query $\mathcal{O}_{\mathrm{u}}(t^*)$; (2) $\mathcal{A}$ cannot issue both queries $\mathcal{O}_{\mathrm{u}}(t^*-1)$ and $\mathcal{O}_{\mathrm{h}}(t^* \mod 2)$; (3) $\mathcal{A}$ cannot issue both queries $\mathcal{O}_{\mathrm{u}}(t^*+1)$ and $\mathcal{O}_{\mathrm{h}}((t^*+1) \mod 2)$; (4) $\mathcal{A}$ cannot issue both the helper key queries $\mathcal{O}_{\mathrm{h}}(1)$ and $\mathcal{O}_{\mathrm{h}}(0)$; (5) if $\mathsf{ATK} = \mathsf{CCA}$, $\mathcal{A}$ cannot issue the decryption query $\mathcal{O}_{\mathrm{d}}(t^*, \mathsf{CT}^*)$. We define $\mathcal{A}$'s advantage as $\mathrm{Adv}_{\mathcal{A},\mathtt{PKIE}}^{\mathsf{IND\text{-}KI\text{-}ATK}}(\lambda) = \left|\Pr[\mathbf{Exp}_{\mathcal{A},\mathtt{PKIE}}^{\mathsf{IND\text{-}KI\text{-}ATK}}(\lambda) = 1] - \frac{1}{2}\right|$.

Definition 3. *A* PKIE *scheme is said to be* IND-KI-CCA *(resp.* IND-KI-CPA*) secure, if there exists no PPT adversary $\mathcal{A}$ who has non-negligible advantage* $\mathrm{Adv}_{\mathcal{A},\mathtt{PKIE}}^{\mathsf{IND\text{-}KI\text{-}CCA}}(\lambda)$ *(resp.* $\mathrm{Adv}_{\mathcal{A},\mathtt{PKIE}}^{\mathsf{IND\text{-}KI\text{-}CPA}}(\lambda)$*).*

Strong key-insulated security. Key-insulated security can be further enhanced to cover the compromise of both helper keys. To define this security notion, we first define the notion of strong-IND-KI-ATK security, where $\mathsf{ATK} \in \{\mathsf{CCA}, \mathsf{CPA}\}$. For an adversary $\mathcal{A}$, we consider the following experiment:

$$\mathbf{Exp}_{\mathcal{A},\mathtt{PKIE}}^{\mathsf{strong\text{-}IND\text{-}KI\text{-}ATK}}(\lambda)\colon\big[(\mathsf{pk}, \mathsf{usk}_0, (\mathsf{mst}_1, \mathsf{mst}_0)) \leftarrow \mathsf{KeyGen}(\lambda);$$
$$(m_0, m_1, t^*) \leftarrow \mathcal{A}_{\mathtt{find}}^{\mathcal{O}_{\mathrm{d}}(\cdot,\cdot)}(\mathsf{pk}, \mathsf{mst}_1, \mathsf{mst}_0);\ \beta \xleftarrow{\$} \{0,1\}; \mathsf{CT}^* \leftarrow \mathsf{Enc}(\mathsf{pk}, t^*, m_\beta);$$
$$\beta' \leftarrow \mathcal{A}_{\mathsf{guess}}^{\mathcal{O}_{\mathrm{d}}(\cdot,\cdot)}(\mathsf{pk}, \mathsf{mst}_1, \mathsf{mst}_0, \mathsf{CT}^*);\ \text{return 1 if } \beta = \beta' \text{ or 0 otherwise}\big],$$

where $\mathcal{O}_{\mathrm{d}}(\cdot,\cdot)$ is the same as in $\mathbf{Exp}_{\mathcal{A},\mathtt{PKIE}}^{\mathsf{IND\text{-}KI\text{-}ATK}}(\lambda)$. It is mandated that $|m_0| = |m_1|$, and if $\mathsf{ATK} = \mathsf{CCA}$ then $\mathcal{A}$ cannot issue the query $\mathcal{O}_{\mathrm{d}}(t^*, \mathsf{CT}^*)$. We define $\mathcal{A}$'s advantage as $\mathrm{Adv}_{\mathcal{A},\mathtt{PKIE}}^{\mathsf{strong\text{-}IND\text{-}KI\text{-}ATK}}(\lambda) = \left|\Pr[\mathbf{Exp}_{\mathcal{A},\mathtt{PKIE}}^{\mathsf{strong\text{-}IND\text{-}KI\text{-}ATK}}(\lambda) = 1] - \frac{1}{2}\right|$.

Definition 4. *A* PKIE *scheme is* strong-IND-KI-CCA *(resp.* strong-IND-KI-CPA*) secure, if there exists no PPT adversary $\mathcal{A}$ who has non-negligible advantage* $\mathrm{Adv}_{\mathcal{A},\mathtt{PKIE}}^{\mathsf{strong\text{-}IND\text{-}KI\text{-}CCA}}(\lambda)$ *(resp.* $\mathrm{Adv}_{\mathcal{A},\mathtt{PKIE}}^{\mathsf{strong\text{-}IND\text{-}KI\text{-}CPA}}(\lambda)$*).*

Definition 5. *A* PKIE *scheme is strongly key-insulated secure under chosen-ciphertext attack (resp. chosen-plaintext attack), if it is both* IND-KI-CCA *secure (resp.* IND-KI-CPA *secure) and* strong-IND-KI-CCA *secure (resp.* strong-IND-KI-CPA *secure).*

3 Generic Construction of PKIE

3.1 Difficulties in Generic Constructions of PKIE

Dodis et al. [13] showed that an IBE scheme can be converted to a KIE scheme, by viewing the period index as an "identity" and having the PKG as the helper. However, Hanaoka et al. [17] pointed out that it is non-trivial to construct a PKIE scheme from IBE systems. To illustrate the difficulties, two important facts should first be kept in mind: On the one hand, according to the definition of PKIE, *only one* (not both) of the helper keys are used to update the user secret key in each period. On the other hand, the user secret key should *simultaneously* contain the update keys generated by MSK_0 and MSK_1; otherwise, the compromise of a single helper and some periods will harm other periods.

Next, let's review a unsuccessful solution which was previously discussed by Libert et al. [22]. To construct a PKIE scheme by combining two IBE schemes, this solution uses the two PKGs to alternatively act as the helpers for even and odd periods, taking the period indices as identities. For example, a user secret key for an *even* period index t consists of $\mathsf{usk}_t = (sk_{t-1}, sk_t)$, where sk_{t-1} is the secret key generated by the first PKG in the previous period for identity "$t-1$", and sk_t is the secret key generated by the second PKG in current period for identity "t". At first glance, such a solution appears to be feasible. Unfortunately, this is not necessary true, since the user secret key for period t will be exposed by corrupting periods $t-1$ and $t+1$. More specifically, $\mathsf{usk}_t = (sk_{t-1}, sk_t)$ can be derived by *combining* sk_{t-1}, picked from $\mathsf{usk}_{t-1} = (sk_{t-2}, sk_{t-1})$, and sk_t, picked from $\mathsf{usk}_{t+1} = (sk_t, sk_{t+1})$.

The insecurity of the above solution lies in the fact that, the two components generated by distinct PKGs can be individually extracted from the user secret keys, which enables the adversary to assemble another user secret key. Based on this observation, Libert et al. [22] pointed out an intuitive relation between secure PKIE and a category of IBE systems whose key extraction algorithm can be viewed as a signature supporting *aggregation*. Now, the user secret key of the resulting PKIE scheme is the aggregation of two components generated by distinct helpers, so that the individual component cannot be extracted. In fact, both HHI scheme [17] and LQY scheme [22] follow this intuition. However, both schemes are only concrete, and the aggregation property is not generally satisfied in *all* IBE systems. Thus the above intuition cannot be utilized to generic construction of PKIE from *any* IBE systems.

3.2 A New Primitive: One-Time Forward Secure Public Key Encryption

To present our generic construction of PKIE, we first introduce a new primitive named one-time forward secure public key encryption (OTFS-PKE). Like forward secure public key encryption [21, 9], the lifetime of OTFS-PKE is divided into distinct time periods, and the public key remains fixed throughout the lifetime. However, unlike forward secure public key encryption, the secret key in OTFS-PKE can only be evolved once (this is the reason why we use the terminology "one-time" to name this primitive), and then it needs to be regenerated. For convenience, we shall use a bit $\mathsf{flg} \in \{0,1\}$ to identify whether a secret key of a given period can be evolved or not. Concretely, in the beginning of a period t where $t \mod 2 = \mathsf{flg}$, the user regenerates a new secret key d_t (refer to it as *evolvable* secret key), which can be further evolved in the next period $t+1$. While for a period index t where $t \mod 2 = \overline{\mathsf{flg}}$, the secret key d_t is evolved from the previous secret key, and cannot be further evolved (refer to it as an *evolved* secret key). Formally, an OTFS-PKE scheme consists of five algorithms:

- $\mathsf{Setup}(\lambda, \mathsf{flg})$: The *setup* algorithm takes as input a security parameter λ and a bit $\mathsf{flg} \in \{0,1\}$. It returns a public key PK and a master key MK. We write $(PK, MK) \leftarrow \mathsf{Setup}(\lambda, \mathsf{flg})$. (Without loss of generality, we assume flg is included in PK.)
- $\mathsf{KeyGen}(PK, MK, t)$: The *key generation* algorithm takes as input PK, MK and a period index t where $t \mod 2 = \mathsf{flg}$. It outputs an evolvable secret key d_t for period t. We write $d_t \leftarrow \mathsf{KeyGen}(PK, MK, t)$.
- $\mathsf{Upd}(PK, t, d_{t-1})$: The *key update* algorithm takes as input PK, a period index t where $t \mod 2 = \overline{\mathsf{flg}}$, and the evolvable secret key d_{t-1} of the previous period. It returns the evolved secret key d_t for period t. We write $d_t \leftarrow \mathsf{Upd}(PK, t, d_{t-1})$.
- $\mathsf{Enc}(PK, t, M)$: The *encryption* algorithm takes as input PK, a period index t and a message $M \in \mathcal{M}$. It returns a ciphertext C (or "$\perp$" if C is invalid). We write $C \leftarrow \mathsf{Enc}(PK, t, M)$.
- $\mathsf{Dec}(d_t, C)$: The *decryption* algorithm takes as input the secret key d_t and a ciphertext C. It returns a message M (or "$\perp$" if C is invalid). We write $M \leftarrow \mathsf{Dec}(d_t, C)$.

The correctness of OTFS-PKE means that, for any $M \in \mathcal{M}$ and any periods t_1 (where $t_1 \mod 2 = \mathsf{flg}$) and t_2 (where $t_2 \mod 2 = \overline{\mathsf{flg}}$), it holds that

$$\mathsf{Dec}(\mathsf{KeyGen}(PK, MK, t_1), \mathsf{Enc}(PK, t_1, M)) = M,$$
$$\mathsf{Dec}(\mathsf{Upd}(PK, t_2, \mathsf{KeyGen}(PK, MK, t_2 - 1)), \mathsf{Enc}(PK, t_2, M)) = M.$$

Next, we begin to define the formal semantic security for OTFS-PKE, and we refer to it as IND-FS-ATK where ATK $= \{\mathsf{CCA}, \mathsf{CPA}\}$. For an adversary $\mathcal{B}$, we consider the following experiment:

$$\mathbf{Exp}^{\mathsf{IND\text{-}FS\text{-}ATK}}_{\mathcal{B},\mathsf{OTFS\text{-}PKE}}(\lambda){:}\big[\mathsf{flg} \leftarrow \mathcal{B}(\lambda); (PK, MK) \leftarrow \mathsf{Setup}(\lambda, \mathsf{flg});$$
$$(M_0, M_1, t^*) \leftarrow \mathcal{B}^{\mathcal{O}_{\mathrm{ke}}(\cdot),\mathcal{O}_{\mathrm{d}}(\cdot,\cdot)}_{\mathtt{find}}(PK);\ \theta \xleftarrow{\$} \{0,1\}; C^* \leftarrow \mathsf{Enc}(PK, t^*, M_\theta);$$
$$\theta' \leftarrow \mathcal{B}^{\mathcal{O}_{\mathrm{ke}}(\cdot),\mathcal{O}_{\mathrm{d}}(\cdot,\cdot)}_{\mathtt{guess}}(PK, C^*);\ \text{return 1 if } \theta = \theta' \text{ or 0 otherwise}\big],$$

where $\mathcal{O}_{\mathrm{ke}}(\cdot)$ is a key-exposure oracle which on input index t returns $d_t \leftarrow \mathsf{KeyGen}(PK, MK, t)$ if $t \mod 2 = \mathsf{flg}$ or $d_t \leftarrow \mathsf{Upd}(PK, t, \mathsf{KeyGen}(PK, MK, t - 1))$ if $t \mod 2 = \overline{\mathsf{flg}}$, and $\mathcal{O}_{\mathrm{d}}(\cdot,\cdot)$ is a decryption oracle which on input (t, C) returns $m \leftarrow \mathsf{Dec}(d_t, C)$ if ATK $=$ CCA, or "$\perp$" if ATK $=$ CPA. It is mandated that (1) $|M_0| = |M_1|$; (2) $\mathcal{B}$ cannot issue the key-exposure query $\mathcal{O}_{\mathrm{ke}}(t^*)$; (3) If $t^* \mod 2 = \overline{\mathsf{flg}}$, $\mathcal{B}$ cannot issue the key-exposure query $\mathcal{O}_{\mathrm{ke}}(t^* - 1)$; (4) If ATK $=$ CCA, $\mathcal{B}$ cannot issue the decryption query $\mathcal{O}_{\mathrm{d}}(t^*, C^*)$. We define $\mathcal{B}$'s advantage as $\mathrm{Adv}^{\mathsf{IND\text{-}FS\text{-}ATK}}_{\mathcal{B},\mathsf{OTFS\text{-}PKE}}(\lambda) = \left|\Pr[\mathbf{Exp}^{\mathsf{IND\text{-}FS\text{-}ATK}}_{\mathcal{B},\mathsf{OTFS\text{-}PKE}}(\lambda) = 1] - \frac{1}{2}\right|$.

Definition 6. *We say that an* OTFS-PKE *scheme is* IND-FS-CCA *(resp.* IND-FS-CPA*) secure, if there exists no PPT adversary $\mathcal{B}$ who has non-negligible advantage* $\mathrm{Adv}^{\mathsf{IND\text{-}FS\text{-}CCA}}_{\mathcal{B},\mathsf{OTFS\text{-}PKE}}(\lambda)$ *(resp.* $\mathrm{Adv}^{\mathsf{IND\text{-}FS\text{-}CPA}}_{\mathcal{B},\mathsf{OTFS\text{-}PKE}}(\lambda)$*).*

KeyGen(λ): Given a security parameter λ, 1. choose a PKE scheme PKE and two OTFS-PKE schemes $\mathsf{OTFS\text{-}PKE}_1$ and $\mathsf{OTFS\text{-}PKE}_0$, 2. run $(pk, sk) \leftarrow \mathsf{PKE.KGen}(\lambda)$, $(PK_1, MK_1) \leftarrow \mathsf{OTFS\text{-}PKE}_1.\mathsf{Setup}(\lambda, 1)$, $(PK_0, MK_0) \leftarrow \mathsf{OTFS\text{-}PKE}_0.\mathsf{Setup}(\lambda, 0)$, $d_{1,-1} \leftarrow \mathsf{OTFS\text{-}PKE}_1.\mathsf{KeyGen}(PK_1, MK_1, -1)$, $d_{1,0} \leftarrow \mathsf{OTFS\text{-}PKE}_1.\mathsf{Upd}(PK_1, 0, d_{1,-1})$, $d_{0,0} \leftarrow \mathsf{OTFS\text{-}PKE}_0.\mathsf{KeyGen}(PK_0, MK_0, 0)$, 3. output $\mathsf{pk} = (pk, PK_1, PK_0)$, $\mathsf{usk}_0 = (sk, d_{1,0}, d_{0,0})$, $\mathsf{mst}_1 = MK_1$ and $\mathsf{mst}_0 = MK_0$.
Δ-Gen(t, $\mathsf{mst}_{t \bmod 2}$): To generate the update key hsk_t with the helper key $\mathsf{mst}_{t \bmod 2}$, 1. let $i = t \mod 2$, and run $d_{i,t} \leftarrow \mathsf{OTFS\text{-}PKE}_i.\mathsf{KeyGen}(PK_i, \mathsf{mst}_i, t)$, 2. output the update key for period t as $\mathsf{hsk}_t = d_{i,t}$.
Update(t, usk_{t-1}, hsk_t): In period t, to update the user secret key from usk_{t-1} to usk_t, 1. let $i = t \mod 2$ and $j = (t-1) \mod 2$, 2. parse usk_{t-1} as $(sk, d_{i,t-1}, d_{j,t-1})$ and hsk_t as $d_{i,t}$, 3. run $d_{j,t} \leftarrow \mathsf{OTFS\text{-}PKE}_j.\mathsf{Upd}(PK_j, t, d_{j,t-1})$, and return $\mathsf{usk}_t = (sk, d_{j,t}, d_{i,t})$.
Enc(pk, t, m): In period t, to encrypt a message m under public key pk, 1. let $i = t \mod 2$ and $j = (t-1) \mod 2$, 2. pick $M', M'_j \xleftarrow{\$} \mathcal{M}$, and set $M'_i = m \oplus M'_j \oplus M'$, 3. run $C \leftarrow \mathsf{PKE.Enc}(pk, M')$, $C_j \leftarrow \mathsf{OTFS\text{-}PKE}_j.\mathsf{Enc}(PK_j, t, M'_j)$, $C_i \leftarrow \mathsf{OTFS\text{-}PKE}_i.\mathsf{Enc}(PK_i, t, M'_i)$, 4. return $\mathsf{CT} = (C, C_j, C_i)$.
Dec(CT, usk_t): To decrypt a ciphertext CT with the matching user secret key usk_t, 1. let $i = t \mod 2$ and $j = (t-1) \mod 2$, 2. parse CT as (C, C_j, C_i) and usk_t as $(sk, d_{j,t}, d_{i,t})$, 3. run $M' \leftarrow \mathsf{PKE.Dec}(sk, C)$, $M'_j \leftarrow \mathsf{OTFS\text{-}PKE}_j.\mathsf{Dec}(d_{j,t}, C_j)$, $M'_i \leftarrow \mathsf{OTFS\text{-}PKE}_i.\mathsf{Dec}(d_{i,t}, C_i)$, 4. return $m = M' \oplus M'_j \oplus M'_i$.

Fig. 1. Generic Construction of PKIE from OTFS-PKE and PKE

3.3 Generic Construction of PKIE from OTFS-PKE

Basic Idea. We first explain how to use two OTFS-PKE schemes to construct a PKIE scheme with (non-strong) key-insulated security. We use two OTFS-PKE schemes: $\mathsf{OTFS\text{-}PKE}_1$ with $\mathsf{flg} = 1$ and $\mathsf{OTFS\text{-}PKE}_0$ with $\mathsf{flg} = 0$. The master key MK_1 (resp. MK_0) in $\mathsf{OTFS\text{-}PKE}_1$ (resp. $\mathsf{OTFS\text{-}PKE}_0$) acts as the helper key mst_1 (resp. mst_0) for the resulting PKIE scheme. In a given period t (let $i = t \mod 2$ and $j = (t-1) \mod 2$), the user secret key is of the form $\mathsf{usk}_t = (d_{j,t}, d_{i,t})$, where $d_{i,t}$ is an *evolvable* secret key directly generated by mst_i, and $d_{j,t}$ is an *evolved* secret key evolved from $d_{j,t-1}$, which is directly generated by mst_j in the previous period. In the next period $t+1$, the helper key mst_j generates a new *evolvable* secret key $d_{j,t+1}$, while $d_{i,t}$ evolves into an *evolved* secret key $d_{i,t+1}$. And hence the user secret key for period $t+1$ is $\mathsf{usk}_{t+1} = (d_{i,t+1}, d_{j,t+1})$. Now, unlike the unsuccessful solution mentioned in Section 3.1, even if both $\mathsf{usk}_{t-1} = (d_{i,t-1}, d_{j,t-1})$ and $\mathsf{usk}_{t+1} = (d_{i,t+1}, d_{j,t+1})$ are corrupted, $\mathsf{usk}_t = (d_{j,t}, d_{i,t})$ are still uncorrupted, since it is impossible derive $d_{i,t}$ from $d_{i,t+1}$ due to the "forward security" of the OTFS-PKE scheme. This resulting PKIE scheme cannot achieve the strong key-insulated security, since the corruption of both helper keys means all the periods will be exposed. To achieve the strong key-insulated security, we use an additional PKE scheme. Suppose the secret key of the PKE scheme is sk, then the user secret key for period t is of the form $\mathsf{usk}_t = (sk, d_{j,t}, d_{i,t})$. Now, even if both of the helper keys are corrupted, the security of all the periods are still ensured, since sk is unknown to the adversary. The detailed construction is shown in Figure 1.

Theorem 1. *The* PKIE *scheme shown in Figure 1 is strongly key-insulated secure under chosen-plaintext attack, if the underlying* PKE *scheme is* IND-CPA-*secure and the underlying* OTFS-PKE *schemes are* IND-FS-CPA-*secure.*

Note that the detailed proofs for all the theorems and lemmas in this paper will be given in the full paper.

Chosen-ciphertext Security. In our generic PKIE scheme, the algorithm Enc is a multiple encryption, and only achieves the chosen-plaintext security. Using Dodis et al.'s technique [12], we can readily achieve the chosen-ciphertext security for our scheme. Due to the space limits, we omit the details here.

3.4 Generic Constructions of OTFS-PKE

In this section, we first show that OTFS-PKE can be generically constructed from any IBE scheme. Furthermore, we point out that it is also possible to directly construct OTFS-PKE from any 2-HIBE without degenerating into IBE.

Construction of OTFS-PKE from IBE. In this subsection, we demonstrate a generic construction of OTFS-PKE from arbitrary IBE.

$\mathsf{Setup}(\lambda, \mathsf{flg})$: Given a security parameter λ and a bit $\mathsf{flg} \in \{0,1\}$, 1. run $(param, msk) \leftarrow \mathsf{IBE.Setup}(\lambda)$, and return $PK = (param, \mathsf{flg})$ and $MK = msk$.
$\mathsf{KeyGen}(PK, MK, t)$: To generate an evolvable secret key for period t (where $t \mod 2 = \mathsf{flg}$), 1. run $sk_t \leftarrow \mathsf{IBE.Extract}(PK, MK, t)$, $sk_{t+1} \leftarrow \mathsf{IBE.Extract}(PK, MK, t+1)$, 2. return $d_t = (sk_t, sk_{t+1})$.
$\mathsf{Upd}(PK, t, d_{t-1})$: In period t where $t \mod 2 = \overline{\mathsf{flg}}$, to generate an evolved secret key for period t, 1. parse d_{t-1} as (sk_{t-1}, sk_t), and return $d_t = sk_t$.
$\mathsf{Enc}(PK, t, m)$: In period t, to encrypt a message m under public key PK, 1. run $C \leftarrow \mathsf{IBE.Enc}(PK, t, m)$, 2. return the ciphertext C.
$\mathsf{Dec}(d_t, C)$: To decrypt a ciphertext C using secret key d_t, 1. parse d_t as $d_t = sk_t$ (if $t \mod 2 = \overline{\mathsf{flg}}$) or $d_t = (sk_t, sk_{t+1})$ (if $t \mod 2 = \mathsf{flg}$), 2. return $m \leftarrow \mathsf{IBE.Dec}(sk_t, C)$.

Fig. 2. Generic Construction of OTFS-PKE from IBE

Our basic idea is as follows. We set the public parameter $param$ and the master secret key msk in the IBE scheme as the public key PK and the master key MK in the OTFS-PKE scheme, respectively. In period t where $t = \mathsf{flg}$, the evolvable secret key is $d_t = (sk_t, sk_{t+1})$, which consists of two secret keys for identities "t" and "$t+1$". Encryption is only carried under identity "t", and hence the decryption only involves sk_t while sk_{t+1} is merely used for evolution. That is, in the next period, the secret key evolves to be $d_{t+1} = sk_{t+1}$, where sk_t has been deleted. Observe that from $d_{t+1} = sk_{t+1}$, it is impossible to derive the decryption key sk_t in the previous secret key. Therefore, the security of period t is still ensured even if the period $t+1$ is exposed. Recall that this is exactly the requirement for a *secure* OTFS-PKE scheme. Detailed construction is presented in Figure 2.

Theorem 2. *The* OTFS-PKE *scheme shown in Figure 2 is* IND-FS-ATK *secure, if the underlying* IBE *scheme* IBE *is* IND-ID-ATK *secure, where* $\mathsf{ATK} \in \{\mathsf{CPA}, \mathsf{CCA}\}$.

Construction of OTFS-PKE from 2-HIBE. It is well known that forward secure public key encryption can be obtained by using HIBE [9]. Therefore, our next direction for designing OTFS-PKE is to directly use HIBE as a building block. Since in the previous approach, we can also construct OTFS-PKE from standard IBE (see Sec. 3.4), one might think that our HIBE-based construction is not necessary. However, due to the difference between these two approaches, there are concrete OTFS-PKE schemes with interesting properties which cannot be obtained without using our HIBE-based construction (see Sec. 4.2). Thus, we consider that HIBE-based construction is worth discussing despite of existence of IBE-based one.

$\mathsf{Setup}(\lambda, \mathsf{flg})$: Given a security parameter λ and a bit $\mathsf{flg} \in \{0,1\}$, 1. run $(param, msk) \leftarrow \mathtt{HIBE}.\mathsf{Setup}(\lambda, 2)$, and return $PK = (param, \mathsf{flg})$ and $MK = msk$.
$\mathsf{KeyGen}(PK, MK, t)$: To generate an evolvable secret key for period t where $t \mod 2 = \mathsf{flg}$, 1. run $sk_t \leftarrow \mathtt{HIBE}.\mathsf{Extract}(PK, MK, t)$, and return $d_t = sk_t$.
$\mathsf{Upd}(PK, t, d_{t-1})$: In period t where $t \mod 2 = \overline{\mathsf{flg}}$, to generate an evolved secret key for period t, 1. run $sk_{(t-1,t)} \leftarrow \mathtt{HIBE}.\mathsf{Extract}(PK, d_{t-1}, (t-1, t))$, and return $d_t = sk_{(t-1,t)}$.
$\mathsf{Enc}(PK, t, m)$: In period t, to encrypt a message m under public key PK, 1. if $t \mod 2 = \mathsf{flg}$, run $C \leftarrow \mathtt{HIBE}.\mathsf{Enc}(PK, t, M)$; else run $C \leftarrow \mathtt{HIBE}.\mathsf{Enc}(PK, (t-1, t), M)$, 2. return the ciphertext C.
$\mathsf{Dec}(d_t, C)$: To decrypt a ciphertext C using the secret key d_t, 1. compute $M \leftarrow \mathtt{HIBE}.\mathsf{Dec}(d_t, C)$, and return M.

Fig. 3. Generic Construction of OTFS-PKE from 2-HIBE

Our basic idea is as follows. For a given 2-HIBE scheme, we have its public parameter $param$ and the master secret key msk as the public key PK and the master key MK for the OTFS-PKE scheme, respectively. In the beginning of a period t (where $t \mod 2 = \mathsf{flg}$), taking the index t as a one-level identity, we use the master secret key msk to generate a secret key sk_t, which is viewed as an *evolvable* secret key for period t. In the next period $t+1$, we use sk_t to generate a secret key $sk_{(t,t+1)}$ for the two-level offspring identity "$(t, t+1)$". Here $sk_{(t,t+1)}$ is viewed as an *evolved* secret key for period $t+1$. Note that according to the property of HIBE, from $sk_{(t,t+1)}$, it is impossible to derive the pervious secret key sk_t. This is exactly the requirement for a *secure* OTFS-PKE scheme. The encryption and decryption algorithms can be accordingly designed. Figure 3 gives our construction.

Theorem 3. *The* OTFS-PKE *scheme given in Figure 3 is* IND-FS-ATK *secure, if the underlying* HIBE *scheme* HIBE *is* IND-ID-ATK *secure, where* ATK $\in$ {CPA, CCA}.

4 Instantiations of Our Generic Constructions

Previous section indicates that PKIE schemes can be generically constructed from IBE or 2-HIBE. Thus, from existing IBE and HIBE schemes with specific properties, we can construct PKIE schemes with a variety of features which previous PKIE schemes cannot have. In this section, we show such instantiations. There are mainly two kinds of instantiations: (1) constructions from various assumptions, and (2) constructions with better efficiency in certain aspects.

4.1 Instantiations from Various Assumptions

As mentioned above, by using our generic construction, a PKIE scheme can be immediately obtained from arbitrary IBE. This means that if there exists an IBE scheme which is provably secure under some mathematical assumption, then there also exists a PKIE scheme under the same assumption.

For example, based on the lattice-based IBE schemes [15, 10, 23], we can construct PKIE schemes by assuming only difficulty of certain types of lattice problems, e.g. the learning with error problem [27]. These are considered as the first "post-quantum" PKIE schemes. Furthermore, based on the quadratic-residuosity-based IBE schemes [11, 8], we can construct PKIE schemes under the decisional quadratic residuosity assumption. These are considered as the first PKIE schemes based on the factoring problem.

4.2 Efficient Instantiations from Pairings

For example, our IBE-based construction from Boneh-Boyen IBE [5] yields shorter ciphertexts and cheaper cost for encryption and decryption. Furthermore, our HIBE-based construction from Boneh-Boyen-Goh HIBE [6] yields cheaper cost for Δ-Gen algorithm, and this is useful when a helper is a cheap device, e.g. a smart card. It should be also noticed that in terms of computational cost for Δ-Gen, our Boneh-Boyen-Goh-based scheme is more efficient than both the LQY scheme and our Boneh-Boyen-based scheme, and this implies that our HIBE-based generic construction is still useful despite of existence of our IBE-based generic construction.

In the rest of this paper, we shall use the bilinear groups $(\mathbb{G}, \mathbb{G}_T)$ with prime order $p \geq 2^\lambda$, where λ is the security parameter, and there exists a bilinear map $e : \mathbb{G} \times \mathbb{G} \rightarrow \mathbb{G}_T$.

Efficient Instantiation from Boneh-Boyen IBE. LQY scheme is based on Boneh-Boyen IBE scheme [5]. Interestingly, when our IBE-based generic construction is instantiated with Boneh-Boyen IBE scheme, we can make use of its algebraic property to obtain a PKIE scheme more efficient than LQY scheme.

KeyGen(λ): Given a security parameter λ,
1. pick $\alpha', \alpha_0, \alpha_1 \xleftarrow{\$} \mathbb{Z}_p^*$, $g, g_2, h \xleftarrow{\$} \mathbb{G}$, and set $g' = g_2^{\alpha'}, g_1 = g^{\alpha'+\alpha_0+\alpha_1}$, $\mathsf{mst}_1 = g_2^{\alpha_1}$, $\mathsf{mst}_0 = g_2^{\alpha_0}$,
2. pick a target collision-resistant hash function $H : \mathbb{Z} \to \mathbb{Z}_p^*$, and pick $r_{1,0}, r_{0,0}, r_{0,1} \xleftarrow{\$} \mathbb{Z}_p^*$,
3. set $(a_{0,0}, b_{0,0}) = \left(\mathsf{mst}_1\mathsf{mst}_0 \cdot (g_1^{H(0)}h)^{r_{1,0}+r_{0,0}}, g^{r_{1,0}+r_{0,0}}\right)$, $(a_{0,1}, b_{0,1}) = \left(\mathsf{mst}_0 \cdot (g_1^{H(1)}h)^{r_{0,1}}, g^{r_{0,1}}\right)$,
4. return $\mathsf{pk} = (g, g_1, g_2, h)$, $\mathsf{usk}_0 = (g', (a_{0,0}, b_{0,0}), (a_{0,1}, b_{0,1}))$ and $(\mathsf{mst}_1, \mathsf{mst}_0)$.

Δ-Gen($t, \mathsf{mst}_{t \bmod 2}$): To generate the update key hsk_t with the matching helper key $\mathsf{mst}_{t \bmod 2}$,
1. let $i = t \bmod 2$, and pick $r_{i,t}, r_{i,t+1} \xleftarrow{\$} \mathbb{Z}_p^*$,
2. set $(\hat{a}_{i,t}, \hat{b}_{i,t}) = \left(\mathsf{mst}_i \cdot (g_1^{H(t)}h)^{r_{i,t}}, g^{r_{i,t}}\right)$ and $(\hat{a}_{i,t+1}, \hat{b}_{i,t+1}) = \left(\mathsf{mst}_i \cdot (g_1^{H(t+1)}h)^{r_{i,t+1}}, g^{r_{i,t+1}}\right)$,
3. return $\mathsf{hsk}_t = ((\hat{a}_{i,t}, \hat{b}_{i,t}), (\hat{a}_{i,t+1}, \hat{b}_{i,t+1}))$.

Update($t, \mathsf{usk}_{t-1}, \mathsf{hsk}_t$): In period t, to update the user secret key from usk_{t-1} to usk_t,
1. let $i = t \bmod 2$ and $j = (t-1) \bmod 2$,
2. parse usk_{t-1} as $(g', (a_{j,t-1}, b_{j,t-1}), (a_{j,t}, b_{j,t}))$, and hsk_t as $((\hat{a}_{i,t}, \hat{b}_{i,t}), (\hat{a}_{i,t+1}, \hat{b}_{i,t+1}))$
3. set $a_{i,t} = a_{j,t} \cdot \hat{a}_{i,t}$, $b_{i,t} = b_{j,t} \cdot \hat{b}_{i,t}$, $a_{i,t+1} = \hat{a}_{i,t+1}$ and $b_{i,t+1} = \hat{b}_{i,t+1}$,
4. return $\mathsf{usk}_t = (g', (a_{i,t}, b_{i,t}), (a_{i,t+1}, b_{i,t+1}))$.

Enc(pk, t, m): In period t, to encrypt a message $m \in \mathbb{G}_T$ under public key pk,
1. pick $s \xleftarrow{\$} \mathbb{Z}_p^*$, and compute $C_1 = e(g_1, g_2)^s \cdot m$, $C_2 = g^s$, $C_3 = (g_1^{H(t)}h)^s$,
2. return $\mathsf{CT} = (C_1, C_2, C_3)$.

Dec($\mathsf{usk}_t, \mathsf{CT}$): To decrypt a ciphertext CT with user secret key usk_t,
1. let $i = t \bmod 2$, and parse usk_t as $(g', (a_{i,t}, b_{i,t}), (a_{i,t+1}, b_{i,t+1}))$, and CT as (C_1, C_2, C_3),
2. return $m \leftarrow \dfrac{C_1 \cdot e(C_3, b_{i,t})}{e(C_2, g' \cdot a_{i,t})}$.

Fig. 4. Our Concrete PKIE Scheme Based on Boneh-Boyen IBE

Our concrete PKIE scheme consists of two Boneh-Boyen IBE systems with the same the public parameters g, g_2 and h. The master secret keys of the two systems are $\mathsf{mst}_1 = g_2^{\alpha_1}$ and $\mathsf{mst}_0 = g_2^{\alpha_0}$ respectively, which act as the two helper keys for the PKIE scheme and alternately update the user secret keys. It is worth noting that, Boneh-Boyen IBE system has a distinguished *aggregation* property, i.e., a product of secret keys for the same ID under different master keys also works as the secret key for that ID under another master key (which is the product of these underlying master keys). Based on this observation, we product the parameters (i.e., g^{α_1} and g^{α_0}) of the two systems into a single $g_1 = g^{\alpha_1+\alpha_0}$ (this parameter will be further changed, which will be clear later). Also, two secret keys for the same identity are aggregated into a single one. For example, in the initial user secret key usk_0, the secret key $\left(\mathsf{mst}_1 \cdot (g_1^{H(0)}h)^{r_{1,0}}, g^{r_{1,0}}\right)$, generated by the master secret key mst_1 for identity "0", and the secret key $\left(\mathsf{mst}_0 \cdot (g_1^{H(0)}h)^{r_{0,0}}, g^{r_{0,0}}\right)$, generated by mst_0 for identity "0", are integrated into $(a_{0,0}, b_{0,0}) = \left(\mathsf{mst}_1\mathsf{mst}_0 \cdot (g_1^{H(0)}h)^{r_{1,0}+r_{0,0}}, g^{r_{1,0}+r_{0,0}}\right)$. Note that we do not use a PKE scheme to achieve the strong key-insulated security. Instead, an element $g' = g_2^{\alpha'}$ is included in the user secret key, and the public parameter g_1 is accordingly changed to be $g_1 = g^{\alpha'+\alpha_1+\alpha_0}$. Figure 4 gives our detailed construction.

Theorem 4. *The Boneh-Boyen-based* PKIE *scheme given in Figure 4 is strongly key-insulated secure under chosen-plaintext attack, assuming the decisional bilinear Diffie-Hellman (DBDH) assumption holds in groups* $(\mathbb{G}, \mathbb{G}_T)$.

KeyGen(λ): Given a security parameter λ,
1. pick a collision-resistant hash function $H : \mathbb{Z} \to \mathbb{Z}_p^*$,
2. pick $g, g_2, f, h_0, h_1 \stackrel{\$}{\leftarrow} \mathbb{G}$, $\alpha_0, \alpha_1, \alpha' \stackrel{\$}{\leftarrow} \mathbb{Z}_p^*$. Set $g_1 = g^{\alpha'+\alpha_0+\alpha_1}$, $g' = g_2^{\alpha'}$, $\mathsf{mst}_1 = g_2^{\alpha_1}$, $\mathsf{mst}_0 = g_2^{\alpha_0}$,
3. pick $r_{1,0}, r_{0,0} \stackrel{\$}{\leftarrow} \mathbb{Z}_p^*$, and set $(a_{1,0}, b_{1,0}) = \left(\mathsf{mst}_1 \cdot (g_1^{H(-1)} f^{H(0)} h_1)^{r_{1,0}}, g^{r_{1,0}}\right)$ and $(a_{0,0}, b_{0,0}, c_{0,0}) = \left(\mathsf{mst}_0 \cdot (g_1^{H(0)} h_0)^{r_{0,0}}, g^{r_{0,0}}, f^{r_{0,0}}\right)$,
4. return $\mathsf{pk} = (g, g_1, g_2, f, h_0, h_1)$, $\mathsf{usk}_0 = (g', (a_{1,0}, b_{1,0}), (a_{0,0}, b_{0,0}, c_{0,0}))$, mst_1 and mst_0.

Δ-Gen($t, \mathsf{mst}_{t \bmod 2}$): To generate the update key hsk_t with the matching helper key $\mathsf{mst}_{t \bmod 2}$,
1. let $i = t \mod 2$. Pick $r_{i,t} \stackrel{\$}{\leftarrow} \mathbb{Z}_p^*$, and set $(a_{i,t}, b_{i,t}, c_{i,t}) = \left(\mathsf{mst}_i \cdot (g_1^{H(t)} h_i)^{r_{i,t}}, g^{r_{i,t}}, f^{r_{i,t}}\right)$,
2. return $\mathsf{hsk}_t = (a_{i,t}, b_{i,t}, c_{i,t})$.

Update($t, \mathsf{usk}_{t-1}, \mathsf{hsk}_t$): In period t, to update the user secret key from usk_{t-1} to usk_t,
1. let $i = t \mod 2$ and $j = (t-1) \mod 2$,
2. parse hsk_t as $(a_{i,t}, b_{i,t}, c_{i,t})$, and usk_{t-1} as $(g', (a_{i,t-1}, b_{i,t-1}), (a_{j,t-1}, b_{j,t-1}, c_{j,t-1}))$,
3. pick $r_{j,t} \stackrel{\$}{\leftarrow} \mathbb{Z}_p^*$, and set $a_{j,t} = a_{j,t-1} \cdot c_{j,t-1}^{H(t)} \cdot (g_1^{H(t-1)} f^{H(t)} h_j)^{r_{j,t}}$ and $b_{j,t} = b_{j,t-1} \cdot g^{r_{j,t}}$,
4. return $\mathsf{usk}_t = (g', (a_{j,t}, b_{j,t}), (a_{i,t}, b_{i,t}, c_{i,t}))$.

Enc(pk, t, m): In period t, to encrypt a message m under public key pk,
1. let $i = t \mod 2$ and $j = (t-1) \mod 2$,
2. pick $s \stackrel{\$}{\leftarrow} \mathbb{Z}_p^*$, and set $C_1 = e(g_1, g_2)^s \cdot m$, $C_2 = g^s$, $C_3 = (g_1^{H(t-1)} f^{H(t)} h_j)^s$ and $C_4 = (g_1^{H(t)} h_i)^s$,
3. return $\mathsf{CT} = (C_1, C_2, C_3, C_4)$.

Dec($\mathsf{usk}_t, \mathsf{CT}$): To decrypt a ciphertext CT with user secret key usk_t,
1. let $i = t \bmod 2$, $j = (t-1) \bmod 2$. Parse $\mathsf{CT} = (C_1, C_2, C_3, C_4)$, and $\mathsf{usk}_t = (g', (a_{j,t}, b_{j,t}), (a_{i,t}, b_{i,t}, c_{i,t}))$.
2. return $m \leftarrow \dfrac{C_1 \cdot e(b_{j,t}, C_3) \cdot e(b_{i,t}, C_4)}{e(C_2, g' a_{j,t} a_{i,t})}$.

Fig. 5. Our Concrete PKIE Scheme Based on Boneh-Boyen-Goh 2-HIBE

Efficient Instantiation from Boneh-Boyen-Goh 2-HIBE. Based on Boneh-Boyen-Goh 2-HIBE scheme, we here present an HIBE-based instantiation of PKIE scheme, which is given in Figure 5. Our scheme consists of two HIBE systems. To achieve the strong key-insulated security, we introduce an element $g' = g_2^{\alpha'}$ into the user secret key. To shorten the public key, we use the same public parameters (g, g_2, f) and integrate the parameters $(g^{\alpha'}, g^{\alpha_1}, g^{\alpha_0})$ into a single $g^{\alpha'+\alpha_1+\alpha_0}$. The resulting PKIE scheme is comparable with LQY scheme: the same public key size, ciphertext size, encryption cost and decryption cost, only with slight longer user secret keys and heavier cost for user key-updates.

Theorem 5. *The above Boneh-Boyen-Goh-based* PKIE *scheme is strongly key-insulated secure under chosen-plaintext attack, assuming the 2 decisional bilinear Diffie-Hellman exponentiation (2-DBDHE) assumption holds in groups* $(\mathbb{G}, \mathbb{G}_T)$.

4.3 Extension: PKIE Scheme with n Helpers

In this section, we discuss how to extend our concrete PKIE scheme to obtain a PKIE scheme with n helpers (n-PKIE for short). In such a scheme, these n helpers are *alternately* used to update the user secret key. For example, in period t, the helper with helper key $\mathsf{mst}_{t \bmod n}$ is used to update the user secret key from usk_{t-1} to usk_t. While in the next period $t+1$, the helper key $\mathsf{mst}_{(t+1) \bmod n}$ will be used to update user secret key from usk_t to usk_{t+1}. Similarly to PKIE

$\mathsf{KeyGen}(\lambda)$: Given a security parameter λ,
1. pick $g, g_2, h \xleftarrow{\$} \mathbb{G}$ and $\alpha', \alpha_0, \cdots, \alpha_{n-1} \xleftarrow{\$} \mathbb{Z}_p^*$, and set $g' = g_2^{\alpha'}, g_1 = g^{\alpha' + \sum_{i=0}^{n-1} \alpha_i}$,
2. set $\mathsf{mst}_i = g_2^{\alpha_i}$ for $i = 0$ to $n-1$,
3. pick a collision-resistant hash function $H : \mathbb{Z} \rightarrow \mathbb{Z}_p^*$,
4. for $k = 0$ to $n-1$,, compute $a_{0,k} = \big(\prod_{i=k}^{n-1} \mathsf{mst}_i\big) \cdot (g_1^{H(k)} h)^{\sum_{i=k}^{n-1} r_{i,k}}$ and $b_{0,k} = g^{\sum_{i=k}^{n-1} r_{i,k}}$, where $r_{i,k} \xleftarrow{\$} \mathbb{Z}_p^*$ for $i = k, \cdots, n-1$,
5. return $\mathsf{pk} = (g, g_1, g_2, h)$, $\mathsf{usk}_0 = (g', (a_{0,0}, b_{0,0}), \cdots, (a_{0,n-1}, b_{0,n-1}))$ and $(\mathsf{mst}_0, \cdots, \mathsf{mst}_{n-1})$.

$\Delta\text{-}\mathsf{Gen}(t, \mathsf{mst}_{t \bmod n})$: To generate the update key hsk_t with the matching helper key $\mathsf{mst}_{t \bmod n}$,
1. let $i = t \mod n$,
2. for $k = t$ to $t+n-1$, pick $r_{i,k} \xleftarrow{\$} \mathbb{Z}_p^*$, and set $\hat{a}_{i,k} = \mathsf{mst}_i \cdot (g_1^{H(k)} h)^{r_{i,k}}$, $\hat{b}_{i,k} = g^{r_{i,k}}$,
3. return $\mathsf{hsk}_t = ((\hat{a}_{i,t}, \hat{b}_{i,t}), \cdots, (\hat{a}_{i,t+n-1}, \hat{b}_{i,t+n-1}))$.

$\mathsf{Update}(t, \mathsf{usk}_{t-1}, \mathsf{hsk}_t)$: In period t, to update the user secret key from usk_{t-1} to usk_t,
1. let $i = t \mod n$ and $j = (t-1) \mod n$
2. parse usk_{t-1} as $(g', (a_{j,t-1}, b_{j,t-1}), \cdots, (a_{j,t+n-2}, b_{j,t+n-2}))$, and hsk_t as $((\hat{a}_{i,t}, \hat{b}_{i,t}), \cdots, (\hat{a}_{i,t+n-1}, \hat{b}_{i,t+n-1}))$,
3. for $k = t$ to $t+n-2$, set $a_{i,k} = a_{j,k} \cdot \hat{a}_{i,k}$, and $b_{i,k} = b_{j,k} \cdot \hat{b}_{i,k}$.
4. set $a_{i,t+n-1} = \hat{a}_{i,t+n-1}$ and $b_{i,t+n-1} = \hat{b}_{i,t+n-1}$
5. return $\mathsf{usk}_t = (g', (a_{i,t}, b_{i,t}), \cdots, (a_{i,t+n-1}, b_{i,t+n-1}))$.

$\mathsf{Enc}(\mathsf{pk}, t, m)$: In period t, to encrypt a message m under public key pk,
1. pick $s \xleftarrow{\$} \mathbb{Z}_p^*$, and compute $C_1 = e(g_1, g_2)^s \cdot m$, $C_2 = g^s$, $C_3 = (g_1^{H(t)} h)^s$,
2. return $\mathsf{CT} = (C_1, C_2, C_3)$.

$\mathsf{Dec}(\mathsf{usk}_t, \mathsf{CT})$: To decrypt a ciphertext CT with the matching user secret key usk_t,
1. parse CT as (C_1, C_2, C_3), and usk_t as $(g', (a_{i,t}, b_{i,t}), \cdots, (a_{i,t+n-1}, b_{i,t+n-1}))$,
2. return $m \leftarrow \dfrac{C_1 \cdot e(C_3, b_{i,t})}{e(C_2, g' \cdot a_{i,t})}$.

Fig. 6. n-PKIE Scheme Based on Boneh-Boyen IBE

systems, key-insulated security for an n-PKIE system captures the intuition that, even if up to $n-1$ helpers are broken into while a given period t is exposed, only one other period adjacent to t is exposed. Furthermore, the strong key-insulated security ensures that, even if the n helpers are simultaneously corrupted, all the periods are still secure. Formal definitions and security notions for n-PKIE is given in the full paper.

Our PKIE scheme presented in Figure 4 can be naturally extended to an n-PKIE scheme as presented in Figure 6. We here explain the meanings of the subscripts used in the scheme. For the random numbers $r_{i,k}$ used in algorithms KeyGen and Δ-Gen, its subscript k corresponds to the time period index, and i corresponds to the index of the helper key mst_i. The subscripts in $(a_{i,t}, b_{i,t})$ and $(\hat{a}_{i,t}, \hat{b}_{i,t})$ have the similar meanings.

4.4 Comparisons

In this section, we compare the efficiency of LQY scheme (which is the currently known best scheme in the standard model) and our proposed PKIE schemes in terms of communication overhead and computational cost. In Table 1, $|\mathbb{G}|$ and $|\mathbb{G}_T|$ denote the bit-length of an element in group $\mathbb{G}$ and $\mathbb{G}_T$ respectively,

Table 1. Efficiency comparisons between our concrete schemes and LQY schemes [22]

	LQY PKIE [22]	BB-based PKIE	BBG-based PKIE	LQY n-PKIE [22]	BB-based n-PKIE
public key	$6\|\mathbb{G}\|$	$4\|\mathbb{G}\|$	$6\|\mathbb{G}\|$	$(2n+2)\|\mathbb{G}\|$	$4\|\mathbb{G}\|$
user secret key	$3\|\mathbb{G}\|$	$5\|\mathbb{G}\|$	$6\|\mathbb{G}\|$	$(n+1)\|\mathbb{G}\|$	$(2n+1)\|\mathbb{G}\|$
ciphertext	$3\|\mathbb{G}\|+1\|\mathbb{G}_T\|$	$2\|\mathbb{G}\|+1\|\mathbb{G}_T\|$	$3\|\mathbb{G}\|+1\|\mathbb{G}_T\|$	$(n+1)\|\mathbb{G}\|+1\|\mathbb{G}_T\|$	$2\|\mathbb{G}\|+1\|\mathbb{G}_T\|$
Δ-Gen	$2t_m + 1t_r$	$2t_m + 2t_r$	$1t_m + 2t_r$	$2t_m + 1t_r$	$nt_m + nt_r$
Enc	$2t_m + 1t_r + 1t_T$	$1t_m + 1t_r + 1t_T$	$2t_m + 1t_r + 1t_T$	$nt_m + 1t_r + 1t_T$	$1t_m + 1t_r + 1t_T$
Dec	$3t_p$	$2t_p$	$3t_p$	$(n+1)t_p$	$2t_p$
without RO?	✓	✓	✓	✓	✓

t_r, t_m, t_T and t_p denote the computational cost of one regular exponentiation in $\mathbb{G}$, one multi-exponentiation [25] in $\mathbb{G}$, one regular exponentiation in $\mathbb{G}_T$ and one pairing in $(\mathbb{G}, \mathbb{G}_T)$ respectively, and "without RO" denotes that the security is proved without random oracles. We note that t_m is approximately equal to $1.2t_r$ due to the Pippenger algorithm [25].

We see that our Boneh-Boyen-based scheme is superior to other schemes in many aspects (except for size of user secret key and computational cost for Δ-Gen). In terms of computational cost for Δ-Gen, our Boneh-Boyen-Goh-based PKIE scheme is superior to other schemes, and it is suitable for environments where helpers are computationally weak. LQY scheme is superior to others in terms of size of user secret key. In summary, we have three different PKIE schemes with different advantages, and one can choose an appropriate one from them according to each situation.

As to the extended schemes with n helpers, the advantage of our Boneh-Boyen-based n-PKIE scheme over (the n-PKIE version of) LQY scheme becomes more obvious. The public key size, ciphertext size, encryption cost and decryption cost in the n-PKIE version of LQY scheme grows linearly with the number n of helpers, while ours are independent of the number of helpers. Honestly, we admit that our scheme still has the following limitations: the computation cost in algorithm Δ-Gen is linear with the number of helpers, and its user secret key size is about twice of LQY scheme.

Acknowledgements

The authors would like to thank Yevgeniy Dodis as a part of this work was inspired by discussion with him. The authors would also like to thank Benoît Libert for his valuable comments. This work is supported by the National Science Foundation of China under Grant No. 60903178, and it also supported by the Fundamental Research Funds for the Central Universities.

References

1. Anderson, R.: Two remarks on public-key cryptology (1997), `http://www.cl.cam.ac.uk/users/rja14/` (invited lecture)
2. Bellare, M., Desai, A., Pointcheval, D., Rogaway, P.: Relations among notions of security for public-key encryption schemes. In: Krawczyk, H. (ed.) CRYPTO 1998. LNCS, vol. 1462, pp. 26–45. Springer, Heidelberg (1998)

3. Bellare, M., Palacio, A.: Protecting against key-exposure: strongly key-insulated encryption with optimal threshold. Appl. Algebra Eng. Commun. Comput. 16(6), 379–396 (2006)
4. Bellare, M., Rogaway, P.: Random oracles are practical: A paradigm for designing efficient protocols. In: ACM Conference on Computer and Communications Security, pp. 62–73 (1993)
5. Boneh, D., Boyen, X.: Efficient Selective-ID Secure Identity-Based Encryption Without Random Oracles. In: Cachin, C., Camenisch, J.L. (eds.) EUROCRYPT 2004. LNCS, vol. 3027, pp. 223–238. Springer, Heidelberg (2004)
6. Boneh, D., Boyen, X., Goh, E.-J.: Hierarchical identity based encryption with constant size ciphertext. In: Cramer, R. (ed.) EUROCRYPT 2005. LNCS, vol. 3494, pp. 440–456. Springer, Heidelberg (2005)
7. Boneh, D., Franklin, M.K.: Identity-based encryption from the weil pairing. In: Kilian, J. (ed.) CRYPTO 2001. LNCS, vol. 2139, pp. 213–229. Springer, Heidelberg (2001)
8. Boneh, D., Gentry, C., Hamburg, M.: Space-efficient identity based encryption without pairings. In: FOCS, pp. 647–657. IEEE Computer Society, Los Alamitos (2007)
9. Canetti, R., Halevi, S., Katz, J.: A forward-secure public-key encryption scheme. In: Biham, E. (ed.) EUROCRYPT 2003. LNCS, vol. 2656, pp. 255–271. Springer, Heidelberg (2003)
10. Cash, D., Hofheinz, D., Kiltz, E.: How to delegate a lattice basis. Cryptology ePrint Archive, Report 2009/351 (2009), `http://eprint.iacr.org/`
11. Cocks, C.: An identity based encryption scheme based on quadratic residues. In: Honary, B. (ed.) Cryptography and Coding 2001. LNCS, vol. 2260, pp. 360–363. Springer, Heidelberg (2001)
12. Dodis, Y., Katz, J.: Chosen-ciphertext security of multiple encryption. In: Kilian, J. (ed.) TCC 2005. LNCS, vol. 3378, pp. 188–209. Springer, Heidelberg (2005)
13. Dodis, Y., Katz, J., Xu, S., Yung, M.: Key-insulated public key cryptosystems. In: Knudsen, L.R. (ed.) EUROCRYPT 2002. LNCS, vol. 2332, pp. 65–82. Springer, Heidelberg (2002)
14. Dolev, D., Dwork, C., Naor, M.: Non-malleable cryptography (extended abstract). In: STOC, pp. 542–552. ACM, New York (1991)
15. Gentry, C., Peikert, C., Vaikuntanathan, V.: Trapdoors for hard lattices and new cryptographic constructions. In: Ladner, R.E., Dwork, C. (eds.) STOC, pp. 197–206. ACM, New York (2008)
16. Goldwasser, S., Micali, S.: Probabilistic encryption. J. Comput. Syst. Sci. 28(2), 270–299 (1984)
17. Hanaoka, G., Hanaoka, Y., Imai, H.: Parallel key-insulated public key encryption. In: Yung, M., Dodis, Y., Kiayias, A., Malkin, T.G. (eds.) PKC 2006. LNCS, vol. 3958, pp. 105–122. Springer, Heidelberg (2006)
18. Hanaoka, G., Nishioka, T., Zheng, Y., Imai, H.: A hierarchical non-interactive key-sharing scheme with low memory size and high resistance against collusion attacks. Comput. J. 45(3), 293–303 (2002)
19. Hanaoka, Y., Hanaoka, G., Shikata, J., Imai, H.: Identity-based hierarchical strongly key-insulated encryption and its application. In: Roy, B.K. (ed.) ASIACRYPT 2005. LNCS, vol. 3788, pp. 495–514. Springer, Heidelberg (2005)
20. Itkis, G., Reyzin, L.: Sibir: Signer-base intrusion-resilient signatures. In: Yung, M. (ed.) CRYPTO 2002. LNCS, vol. 2442, pp. 499–514. Springer, Heidelberg (2002)
21. Katz, J.: A forward-secure public-key encryption scheme. Cryptology ePrint Archive, Report 2002/060 (2009), `http://eprint.iacr.org/`

22. Libert, B., Quisquater, J.-J., Yung, M.: Parallel key-insulated public key encryption without random oracles. In: Okamoto, T., Wang, X. (eds.) PKC 2007. LNCS, vol. 4450, pp. 298–314. Springer, Heidelberg (2007)
23. Peikert, C.: Bonsai trees (or, arboriculture in lattice-based cryptography). Cryptology ePrint Archive, Report 2009/359 (2009), `http://eprint.iacr.org/`
24. Phan, T.L.A., Hanaoka, Y., Hanaoka, G., Matsuura, K., Imai, H.: Reducing the spread of damage of key exposures in key-insulated encryption. In: Nguyên, P.Q. (ed.) VIETCRYPT 2006. LNCS, vol. 4341, pp. 366–384. Springer, Heidelberg (2006)
25. Pippenger, N.: On the evaluation of powers and related problems. In: SFCS 1976: Proceedings of the 17th Annual Symposium on Foundations of Computer Science, Washington, DC, USA, pp. 258–263. IEEE Computer Society, Los Alamitos (1976)
26. Rackoff, C., Simon, D.R.: Non-interactive zero-knowledge proof of knowledge and chosen ciphertext attack. In: Feigenbaum, J. (ed.) CRYPTO 1991. LNCS, vol. 576, pp. 433–444. Springer, Heidelberg (1992)
27. Regev, O.: On lattices, learning with errors, random linear codes, and cryptography. In: Gabow, H.N., Fagin, R. (eds.) STOC, pp. 84–93. ACM, New York (2005)
28. Weng, J., Liu, S., Chen, K., Ma, C.: Identity-based parallel key-insulated encryption without random oracles: Security notions and construction. In: Barua, R., Lange, T. (eds.) INDOCRYPT 2006. LNCS, vol. 4329, pp. 409–423. Springer, Heidelberg (2006)
29. Weng, J., Liu, S., Chen, K., Zheng, D., Qiu, W.: Identity-based threshold key-insulated encryption without random oracles. In: Malkin, T.G. (ed.) CT-RSA 2008. LNCS, vol. 4964, pp. 203–220. Springer, Heidelberg (2008)

Heuristics and Rigor in Lattice-Based Cryptography
(Invited Talk)

Chris Peikert

Georgia Institute of Technology

Abstract. Cryptographic schemes based on *lattices* first emerged in the mid-1990s, and have developed rapidly in the past few years. At the outset, works in this area fell into two very distinct types:

- Heuristic proposals such as NTRU, which lacked any formal security justification but were very practical;
- Schemes building on Ajtai's breakthrough work, which were highly impractical but came with provable 'worst-case' security guarantees.

More recently, the line between efficiency and rigorous security has been blurred significantly (though not yet obliterated completely).

This talk will survey several examples of early proposals that lacked any rigorous security analysis — and in some cases, turned out to be completely insecure — but which later inspired theoretically sound and efficient solutions. Even better, these solutions have opened the door to unexpected and far more advanced cryptographic applications than were originally envisioned.

J.A. Garay and R. De Prisco (Eds.): SCN 2010, LNCS 6280, p. 54, 2010.

Differential Fault Analysis of LEX

Jianyong Huang, Willy Susilo, and Jennifer Seberry

Centre for Computer and Information Security Research,
School of Computer Science and Software Engineering,
University of Wollongong, Wollongong NSW 2522, Australia
{jyh33,wsusilo,jennie}@uow.edu.au

Abstract. LEX is a stream cipher based on the round transformation of the AES block cipher, and it was selected for the final phase evaluation of the eSTREAM project. LEX is 2.5 times faster than AES both in software and in hardware. In this paper, we present a differential fault attack on LEX. The fault model assumes that the attacker is able to flip a random bit of the internal state of the cipher but cannot control the exact location of the induced fault. Our attack requires 40 faults, and recovers the secret key with 2^{16} operations.

Keywords: LEX, stream cipher, AES, cryptanalysis, differential fault analysis.

1 Introduction

The aim of the eSTREAM project was to stimulate work in the area of stream ciphers. The call for primitives was released in 2004 and 34 proposals were submitted to the project. The competition was completed in 2008 and seven ciphers were selected in the eSTREAM portfolio.

LEX [4] was one of the candidates of the eSTREAM final phase evaluation. LEX is based on a design principle known as a leak extraction from a block cipher. In this construction, the output key stream is extracted from parts of the internal state of a block cipher at certain rounds (possibly after passing an additional filter function). The extracted parts of the internal state need to be selected carefully because leaking the wrong part of the state may endanger the security of the cipher. The underlying block cipher of LEX is AES [7], and the key stream is generated by extracting 32 bits from each round of AES in the Output Feedback (OFB) mode. LEX has a simple and elegant structure and is fast in software and hardware (2.5 times faster than AES).

There are two types of attacks against the security of cryptosystems: direct attacks and indirect attacks. In direct attacks, the cryptanalyst targets to exploit any theoretical weakness in the algorithm used in the cipher, and examples of direct attacks include differential cryptanalysis [1] and linear cryptanalysis [13]. In indirect attacks, the attacker tries to obtain information from the physical implementation of a cryptosystem, and aims to break the system by making use of the gained information. Instances of indirect attacks include timing attacks [11],

J.A. Garay and R. De Prisco (Eds.): SCN 2010, LNCS 6280, pp. 55–72, 2010.

power attacks [12] and fault attacks [6]. The concept of fault analysis was first introduced by Boneh, DeMillo and Lipton [6] in 1996, and the attack was used to target certain implementations of RSA and Rabin signatures by taking advantage of hardware faults. Fault analysis was also used to attack block ciphers such as DES [2]. It was showed in [10] that a fault attack is a powerful cryptanalytic tool which can be employed to attack stream ciphers.

After LEX was submitted to the eSTREAM project, a few attacks against this cipher have been proposed. The resynchronization of LEX is vulnerable to a slide attack [15], and the attack needs $2^{60.8}$ random IVs and 20,000 keystream bytes generated from each IV. A generic attack, which requires $2^{65.7}$ resynchronizations, was published in [9]. A differential attack [8] can recover the secret key of LEX in time of 2^{112} operations by using $2^{36.3}$ bytes of key stream produced by the same key (possibly under many different IVs). A related key attack was shown in [14], and the attack requires $2^{54.3}$ keystream bytes and can recover the secret key with 2^{102} operations. These four proposed attacks on LEX belong to direct attacks.

In this paper, we describe a differential fault attack on LEX. The fault model assumes that the attacker can flip a random bit of the internal state of the cipher and she can carry out the operation many times for the same internal state. However, the attacker is not supposed to know the exact location of the flipped bit. The proposed attack requires 40 faults and recovers the secret key of LEX with 2^{16} operations.

This paper is organized as follows. Section 2 describes the AES block cipher and the LEX stream cipher. Section 3 provides the details of the differential fault analysis of LEX. The paper is concluded in Section 4.

2 Descriptions of AES and LEX

We briefly describe the AES block cipher in Section 2.1. The LEX stream cipher is described in Section 2.2. We provide the notations used throughout this paper in Section 2.3.

2.1 The AES Block Cipher

The Advanced Encryption Standard [7] is a block cipher with a 128-bit block length and supports key lengths of 128, 192 or 256 bits. For encryption, the input is a plaintext and a secret key, and the output is a ciphertext. The plaintext is first copied to a four-by-four array of bytes, which is called the state. After an initial round key addition, the state array is transformed by performing a round function 10, 12, or 14 times (for 128-bit, 192-bit or 256-bit keys respectively), and the final state is the ciphertext. Each round of AES consists of the following four transformations (the final round does not include the MixColumns operation).

- SubBytes (SB). It is a non-linear byte substitution that operates independently on each byte of the state using a substitution table.
- ShiftRows (SR). The bytes of the state are cyclically shifted over different numbers of bytes. Row i is shifted to the left i byte cyclicly, $0 \le i \le 3$.

- MixColumns (MC). It operates on the state column-by-column. The columns are treated as polynomials and multiplied by a constant 4×4 matrix over $GF(2^8)$.
- AddRoundKey (ARK). A round key is added to the state by a simple bitwise exclusive or (XOR) operation.

The AES round keys are derived from the cipher key by employing the key schedule. The cipher key is first expanded into an expanded key. The round keys are selected from this expanded key in the following way: the first round key consists of the first Nb (the number of columns comprising the state) words, the second one of the following Nb words, and so on. The expanded key is an array of 4-byte words and is denoted by $W[Nb*(Nr+1)]$, where Nr is the number of rounds. The first Nk (number of 32-bit words comprising the cipher key) words contain the cipher key. All other words are defined recursively in terms of words with smaller indices. The pseudocode for key expansion for 128-bit cipher keys is shown below, where Key is the cipher key, $SW(x)$ applies the substitution operation to each byte of the word, $RW(x)$ cyclically shifts the word to the left 8 bits, and $Rcon$ is an array of predefined constants.

```
for(i = 0; i < Nk; i++)
    W[i] = (Key[4*i],Key[4*i+1],Key[4*i+2],Key[4*i+3]);

for(i = Nk; i < Nb * (Nr + 1); i++)
    temp = W[i-1];
    if (i % Nk == 0)
    temp = SW(RW(temp)) ^ Rcon[i/Nk];
    W[i] = W[i-Nk] ^ temp;
```

2.2 The LEX Stream Cipher

Two versions of LEX, the original version [3] and the tweaked version [5], were submitted to the eSTREAM project. We only provide the description of the tweaked version in this paper. LEX uses the building blocks of the AES block cipher. First, a standard AES key schedule for a secret 128-bit key K is performed. Then, a given 128-bit IV is encrypted by a single AES encryption, $S = AES_K(IV)$. The 128-bit result S and the secret key K comprise a 256-bit secret state of the stream cipher. Under the key K, S is repeatedly encrypted in the OFB mode. In each round of the encryption, 32 bits are extracted from the intermediate state to form the key stream. The positions of the extracted 32 bits are shown in Fig. 1. The IV is replaced after 500 encryptions and the secret key is changed after 2^{32} different IVs are used.

2.3 Notations

An AES intermediate state, as well as an AES round key, is represented as a four-by-four array of bytes. A byte of an intermediate state is written as $b_{i,j}$,

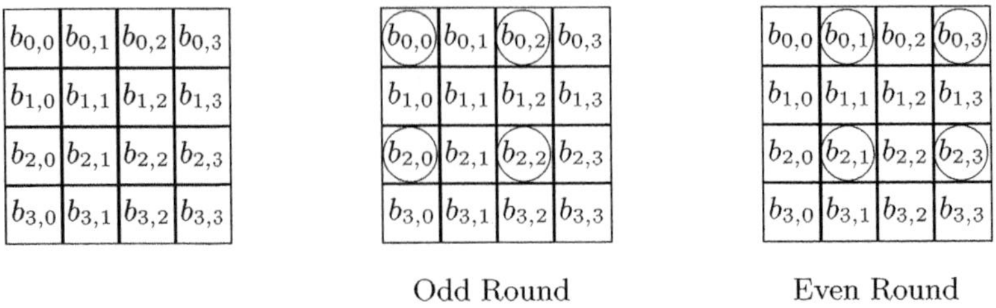

Fig. 1. The positions of the leak in the even and odd rounds

the corresponding faulty byte is denoted by $b'_{i,j}$, and the difference of $b_{i,j}$ and $b'_{i,j}$ is represented as $\Delta b_{i,j}$, $0 \leq i, j \leq 3$. A key byte of Round x is denoted by $K^x_{i,j}$, $0 \leq i, j \leq 3$. The symbol ? stands for an unknown byte. In all figures, a keystream byte of LEX is surrounded by a circle.

3 The Differential Fault Analysis

The fault model used in this paper assumes that the attacker can flip a random bit of the internal state of the cipher during the keystream generation and obtain the corresponding faulty key stream. Another assumption is that the attacker can reset the state back to its original status and repeat the fault injection process many times. However, the attacker is not supposed to know the exact location of the injected fault. Based on the fault model, we first describe a method to determine the fault position and then we show that the attacker can recover the secret key of LEX by analyzing the original and faulty key stream.

3.1 The Fault Position Determination Method

Since the attacker does not know the exact fault position in our fault model, we need to determine the fault location first. The idea is that we can find out the fault position by observing the changes of the key stream after the fault is injected. We show that we can identify into which byte the random bit fault is injected. We divide all possible cases into two categories. In the first category, the fault is injected into the state after the MC or ARK transformation, and in the second category, the fault is injected into the state after the SB or SR transformation.

We use Fig. 2 to describe the position determination method. Suppose the three-round diagram starts with an odd round, i.e., i is an odd number (we can also do the analysis by using the same idea if i is an even number). The keystream bytes are $g_{0,0}$, $g_{0,2}$, $g_{2,0}$ and $g_{2,2}$ in Round i, $l_{0,1}$, $l_{0,3}$, $l_{2,1}$ and $l_{2,3}$ in Round $i+1$ and $s_{0,0}$, $s_{0,2}$, $s_{2,0}$ and $s_{2,2}$ in Round $i+2$.

1. Category 1. The fault is injected into the state after the MC or ARK transformation. We only focus on cases where the fault is injected into the state after the MC transformation, and we can use the same idea to analyze cases

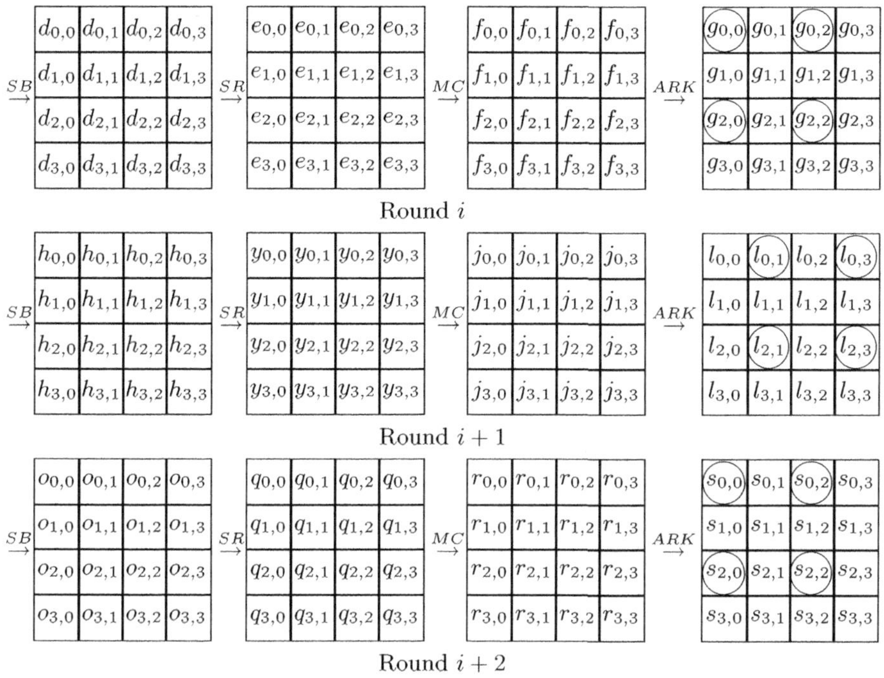

Fig. 2. The three-round diagram

where the fault is injected into the state after the ARK operation. Suppose the fault is induced to the state after the MC transformation in Round i. We further divide all possible cases of this category into four groups and each group contains four bytes.

- Group 1. This group includes four bytes: $f_{0,0}$, $f_{2,0}$, $f_{0,2}$ and $f_{2,2}$.
- Group 2. This group has four bytes: $f_{1,0}$, $f_{2,1}$, $f_{3,2}$ and $f_{0,3}$.
- Group 3. This group comprises four bytes: $f_{3,0}$, $f_{0,1}$, $f_{1,2}$ and $f_{2,3}$.
- Group 4. This group consists of four bytes: $f_{1,1}$, $f_{3,1}$, $f_{1,3}$ and $f_{3,3}$.

The relation between the fault position and the changes of the keystream bytes is summarized in Table 1. For example, if a fault is induced to $f_{0,0}$ (see the first entry of Group 1 in Table 1) in Fig. 2, we can see the change of $g_{0,0}$ from the key stream in Round i. Since $g_{0,0}$ is changed, $h_{0,0}$, $y_{0,0}$, $j_{0,0}$, $j_{1,0}$, $j_{2,0}$, $j_{3,0}$, $l_{0,0}$, $l_{1,0}$, $l_{2,0}$, $l_{3,0}$ are changed in Round $i+1$. However, we cannot see the changes from the key stream in Round $i+1$ because the keystream bytes of this round are $l_{0,1}$, $l_{0,3}$, $l_{2,1}$ and $l_{2,3}$. In Round $i+2$, all 16 bytes are changed after the MC transformation and we can see that all four keystream bytes $s_{0,0}$, $s_{0,2}$, $s_{2,0}$ and $s_{2,2}$ are changed. The difference among Group 1, Group 2, Group 3 and Group 4 is that the changes of the keystream bytes in Round i and Round $i+1$ take place at different positions.

2. Category 2. The fault is injected into the state after the SB or SR transformation. We only concentrate on cases where the fault is injected into the

Table 1. Four groups of fault positions

Group 1			
Fault	i	$i+1$	$i+2$
$f_{0,0}$	$g_{0,0}$	None	$s_{0,0}, s_{0,2}, s_{2,0}, s_{2,2}$
$f_{2,0}$	$g_{2,0}$	None	$s_{0,0}, s_{0,2}, s_{2,0}, s_{2,2}$
$f_{0,2}$	$g_{0,2}$	None	$s_{0,0}, s_{0,2}, s_{2,0}, s_{2,2}$
$f_{2,2}$	$g_{2,2}$	None	$s_{0,0}, s_{0,2}, s_{2,0}, s_{2,2}$

Group 2			
Fault	i	$i+1$	$i+2$
$f_{1,0}$	None	$l_{0,3}, l_{2,3}$	$s_{0,0}, s_{0,2}, s_{2,0}, s_{2,2}$
$f_{2,1}$	None	$l_{0,3}, l_{2,3}$	$s_{0,0}, s_{0,2}, s_{2,0}, s_{2,2}$
$f_{3,2}$	None	$l_{0,3}, l_{2,3}$	$s_{0,0}, s_{0,2}, s_{2,0}, s_{2,2}$
$f_{0,3}$	None	$l_{0,3}, l_{2,3}$	$s_{0,0}, s_{0,2}, s_{2,0}, s_{2,2}$

Group 3			
Fault	i	$i+1$	$i+2$
$f_{3,0}$	None	$l_{0,1}, l_{2,1}$	$s_{0,0}, s_{0,2}, s_{2,0}, s_{2,2}$
$f_{0,1}$	None	$l_{0,1}, l_{2,1}$	$s_{0,0}, s_{0,2}, s_{2,0}, s_{2,2}$
$f_{1,2}$	None	$l_{0,1}, l_{2,1}$	$s_{0,0}, s_{0,2}, s_{2,0}, s_{2,2}$
$f_{2,3}$	None	$l_{0,1}, l_{2,1}$	$s_{0,0}, s_{0,2}, s_{2,0}, s_{2,2}$

Group 4			
Fault	i	$i+1$	$i+2$
$f_{1,1}$	None	None	$s_{0,0}, s_{0,2}, s_{2,0}, s_{2,2}$
$f_{3,1}$	None	None	$s_{0,0}, s_{0,2}, s_{2,0}, s_{2,2}$
$f_{1,3}$	None	None	$s_{0,0}, s_{0,2}, s_{2,0}, s_{2,2}$
$f_{3,3}$	None	None	$s_{0,0}, s_{0,2}, s_{2,0}, s_{2,2}$

state after the SR transformation, and we can use the same idea to analyze cases where the fault is injected into the state after the SB transformation. Assume that the fault is induced to the state after the SR transformation in Round i. We split all possible cases of this category into three groups.

- Group 5. This group has four bytes: $e_{0,0}$, $e_{1,0}$, $e_{2,0}$ and $e_{3,0}$.
- Group 6. This group is made up of four bytes: $e_{0,2}$, $e_{1,2}$, $e_{2,2}$ and $e_{3,2}$.
- Group 7. This group contains eight bytes: $e_{0,1}$, $e_{1,1}$, $e_{2,1}$, $e_{3,1}$, $e_{0,3}$, $e_{1,3}$, $e_{2,3}$ and $e_{3,3}$.

The relation between the fault position and the changes of the keystream bytes is described in Table 2. For instance, if a fault is injected into byte $e_{0,0}$ (see the first entry of Group 5 in Table 2) in Fig. 2, $g_{0,0}$, $g_{1,0}$, $g_{2,0}$ and $g_{3,0}$ are changed and we can observe the changes of $g_{0,0}$ and $g_{2,0}$ from the key stream in Round i. In Round $i+1$, all 16 bytes are changed after the MC transformation and we can see the changes of $l_{0,1}$, $l_{0,3}$, $l_{2,1}$ and $l_{2,3}$ from the key stream. Similarly, all 16 bytes are changed starting from the SB operation in Round $i+2$, and we can see the changes of $s_{0,0}$, $s_{0,2}$, $s_{2,0}$ and $s_{2,2}$ from the key stream.

By watching the changes of the keystream bytes listed in Table 1 and Table 2, we can identify the fault position. In this paper we are only interested in cases where a fault is injected into a byte which is listed in Table 1.

3.2 Recovering 4 Key Bytes of Round $i+2$

We first show that we are able to recover the actual values of 12 bytes after the SR transformation in Round $i+2$ by using 8 faults. Then, we describe the idea of recovering 4 key bytes of Round $i+2$ by using the 12 known values.

We provide an observation which is used to identify the position of a faulty byte in the MC transformation.

Observation 1. *In the MixColumns transformation, for each $0 \leq i \leq 3$, if we know three out of four input differences ($\Delta y_{0,i}$, $\Delta y_{1,i}$, $\Delta y_{2,i}$ and $\Delta y_{3,i}$) are zero and one input difference is non-zero and we also know two output differences ($\Delta j_{0,i}$ and $\Delta j_{2,i}$), the two unknown output differences ($\Delta j_{1,i}$ and $\Delta j_{3,i}$) and the position and the difference of the non-zero input can be uniquely determined.*

Table 2. Three groups of fault positions

Group 5			
Fault	i	$i+1$	$i+2$
$e_{0,0}$	$g_{0,0}, g_{2,0}$	$l_{0,1}, l_{0,3}, l_{2,1}, l_{2,3}$	$s_{0,0}, s_{0,2}, s_{2,0}, s_{2,2}$
$e_{1,0}$	$g_{0,0}, g_{2,0}$	$l_{0,1}, l_{0,3}, l_{2,1}, l_{2,3}$	$s_{0,0}, s_{0,2}, s_{2,0}, s_{2,2}$
$e_{2,0}$	$g_{0,0}, g_{2,0}$	$l_{0,1}, l_{0,3}, l_{2,1}, l_{2,3}$	$s_{0,0}, s_{0,2}, s_{2,0}, s_{2,2}$
$e_{3,0}$	$g_{0,0}, g_{2,0}$	$l_{0,1}, l_{0,3}, l_{2,1}, l_{2,3}$	$s_{0,0}, s_{0,2}, s_{2,0}, s_{2,2}$

Group 6			
Fault	i	$i+1$	$i+2$
$e_{0,2}$	$g_{0,2}, g_{2,2}$	$l_{0,1}, l_{0,3}, l_{2,1}, l_{2,3}$	$s_{0,0}, s_{0,2}, s_{2,0}, s_{2,2}$
$e_{1,2}$	$g_{0,2}, g_{2,2}$	$l_{0,1}, l_{0,3}, l_{2,1}, l_{2,3}$	$s_{0,0}, s_{0,2}, s_{2,0}, s_{2,2}$
$e_{2,2}$	$g_{0,2}, g_{2,2}$	$l_{0,1}, l_{0,3}, l_{2,1}, l_{2,3}$	$s_{0,0}, s_{0,2}, s_{2,0}, s_{2,2}$
$e_{3,2}$	$g_{0,2}, g_{2,2}$	$l_{0,1}, l_{0,3}, l_{2,1}, l_{2,3}$	$s_{0,0}, s_{0,2}, s_{2,0}, s_{2,2}$

Group 7			
Fault	i	$i+1$	$i+2$
$e_{0,1}$	None	$l_{0,1}, l_{0,3}, l_{2,1}, l_{2,3}$	$s_{0,0}, s_{0,2}, s_{2,0}, s_{2,2}$
$e_{1,1}$	None	$l_{0,1}, l_{0,3}, l_{2,1}, l_{2,3}$	$s_{0,0}, s_{0,2}, s_{2,0}, s_{2,2}$
$e_{2,1}$	None	$l_{0,1}, l_{0,3}, l_{2,1}, l_{2,3}$	$s_{0,0}, s_{0,2}, s_{2,0}, s_{2,2}$
$e_{3,1}$	None	$l_{0,1}, l_{0,3}, l_{2,1}, l_{2,3}$	$s_{0,0}, s_{0,2}, s_{2,0}, s_{2,2}$
$e_{0,3}$	None	$l_{0,1}, l_{0,3}, l_{2,1}, l_{2,3}$	$s_{0,0}, s_{0,2}, s_{2,0}, s_{2,2}$
$e_{1,3}$	None	$l_{0,1}, l_{0,3}, l_{2,1}, l_{2,3}$	$s_{0,0}, s_{0,2}, s_{2,0}, s_{2,2}$
$e_{2,3}$	None	$l_{0,1}, l_{0,3}, l_{2,1}, l_{2,3}$	$s_{0,0}, s_{0,2}, s_{2,0}, s_{2,2}$
$e_{3,3}$	None	$l_{0,1}, l_{0,3}, l_{2,1}, l_{2,3}$	$s_{0,0}, s_{0,2}, s_{2,0}, s_{2,2}$

$$\begin{pmatrix} \Delta y_{0,i} \\ \Delta y_{1,i} \\ \Delta y_{2,i} \\ \Delta y_{3,i} \end{pmatrix} \xrightarrow{MC} \begin{pmatrix} \Delta j_{0,i} \\ \Delta j_{1,i} \\ \Delta j_{2,i} \\ \Delta j_{3,i} \end{pmatrix}.$$

Suppose a fault is injected into a byte which is $f_{0,3}$, $f_{1,0}$, $f_{2,1}$ or $f_{3,2}$ (Group 2 in Table 1). We use Fig. 3 to demonstrate the progress. We establish a formula, Formula (1), by using the input and out differences of the MC operation in Round $i+1$. We create another formula, Formula (2), with the input and out differences of the MC transformation in Round $i+2$.

$$\begin{pmatrix} 0 & 0 & 0 & \Delta y_{0,3} \\ 0 & 0 & 0 & \Delta y_{1,3} \\ 0 & 0 & 0 & \Delta y_{2,3} \\ 0 & 0 & 0 & \Delta y_{3,3} \end{pmatrix} \xrightarrow{MC} \begin{pmatrix} 0 & 0 & 0 & \Delta j_{0,3} \\ 0 & 0 & 0 & \Delta j_{1,3} \\ 0 & 0 & 0 & \Delta j_{2,3} \\ 0 & 0 & 0 & \Delta j_{3,3} \end{pmatrix} \tag{1}$$

$$\begin{pmatrix} 0 & 0 & 0 & \Delta q_{0,3} \\ 0 & 0 & \Delta q_{1,2} & 0 \\ 0 & \Delta q_{2,1} & 0 & 0 \\ \Delta q_{3,0} & 0 & 0 & 0 \end{pmatrix} \xrightarrow{MC} \begin{pmatrix} \Delta r_{0,0} & \Delta r_{0,1} & \Delta r_{0,2} & \Delta r_{0,3} \\ \Delta r_{1,0} & \Delta r_{1,1} & \Delta r_{1,2} & \Delta r_{1,3} \\ \Delta r_{2,0} & \Delta r_{2,1} & \Delta r_{2,2} & \Delta r_{2,3} \\ \Delta r_{3,0} & \Delta r_{3,1} & \Delta r_{3,2} & \Delta r_{3,3} \end{pmatrix} \tag{2}$$

1. We use Formula (1) to decide the values of $\Delta l_{1,3}$ and $\Delta l_{3,3}$ by performing the following steps. Since $\Delta j_{0,3}$ is equal to $\Delta l_{0,3}$ and $\Delta j_{2,3}$ is equal to $\Delta l_{2,3}$ ($\Delta l_{0,3}$ and $\Delta l_{2,3}$ can be calculated from the key stream), we know the values of $\Delta j_{0,3}$ and $\Delta j_{2,3}$. In the fourth columns of the input and output, there are 5 known bytes (3 zero bytes, $\Delta j_{0,3}$ and $\Delta j_{2,3}$) and 3 unknown bytes (the non-zero input byte, $\Delta j_{1,3}$ and $\Delta j_{3,3}$). Although we know there are three

zero inputs and one non-zero input, we do not know the exact layout of the four input bytes. We can determine the 2 unknown output bytes ($\Delta j_{1,3}$ and $\Delta j_{3,3}$) and the position and the difference of the non-zero input byte by using Observation 1 (a similar method is described in [8], in which the authors used 4 known bytes to calculate the values of 4 unknown bytes). In Fig 3, we assume the faulty byte is $f_{1,0}$. As $\Delta l_{1,3}$ is equal to $\Delta j_{1,3}$ and $\Delta l_{3,3}$ is equal to $\Delta j_{3,3}$, we know the values of $\Delta l_{1,3}$ and $\Delta l_{3,3}$.

2. In Formula (2), $\Delta q_{3,0}$ and $\Delta q_{1,2}$ can be deduced as follows.
   (a) Because $\Delta r_{0,0}$ is equal to $\Delta s_{0,0}$ and $\Delta r_{2,0}$ is equal to $\Delta s_{2,0}$ ($\Delta s_{0,0}$ and $\Delta s_{2,0}$ can be computed from the key stream), we know the values of $\Delta r_{0,0}$ and $\Delta r_{2,0}$. In the first columns of the input and output, there are 5 known bytes (3 zero bytes, $\Delta r_{0,0}$ and $\Delta r_{2,0}$) and 3 unknown bytes ($\Delta q_{3,0}$, $\Delta r_{1,0}$ and $\Delta r_{3,0}$). Here we know the positions of the three zero inputs and the non-zero input (see the first column of the input in Formula (2)). The 3 unknown bytes can be deduced from the 5 known bytes.
   (b) Similarly, there are 5 known bytes (3 zero bytes, $\Delta r_{0,2}$ and $\Delta r_{2,2}$) and 3 unknown bytes ($\Delta q_{1,2}$, $\Delta r_{1,2}$ and $\Delta r_{3,2}$) in the third columns of the input and output. The values of 3 unknown bytes can be computed by making use of the 5 known bytes.

In Fig. 4, we know the values of $\Delta o_{1,3}$ and $\Delta o_{3,3}$ since we know $\Delta q_{1,2}$ and $\Delta q_{3,0}$ and the SR operation is just a permutation. Now we know the input differences

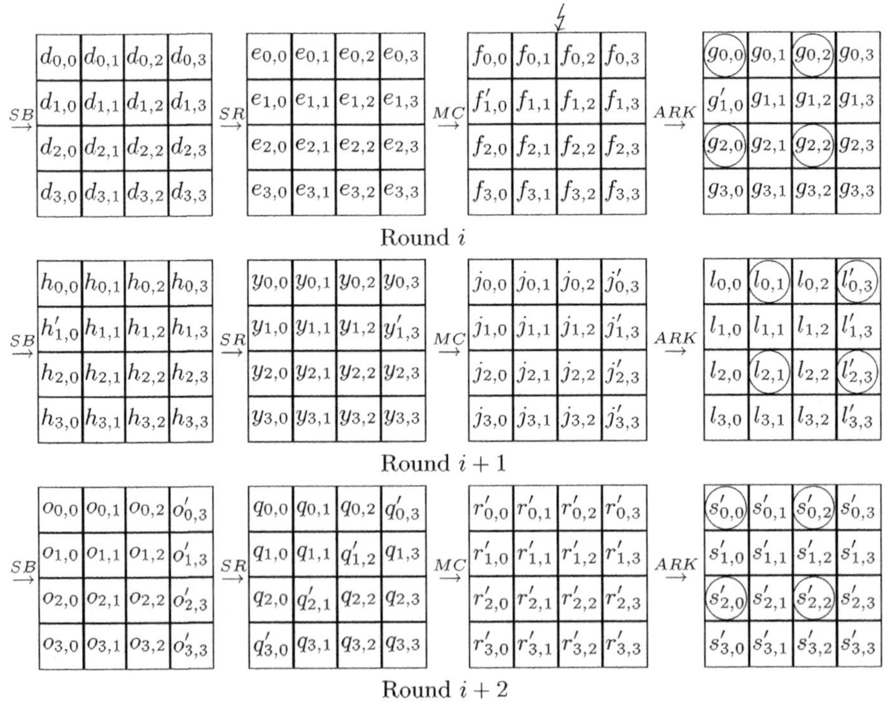

Fig. 3. Computing the values of $\Delta l_{1,3}$, $\Delta l_{3,3}$, $\Delta q_{1,2}$ and $\Delta q_{3,0}$

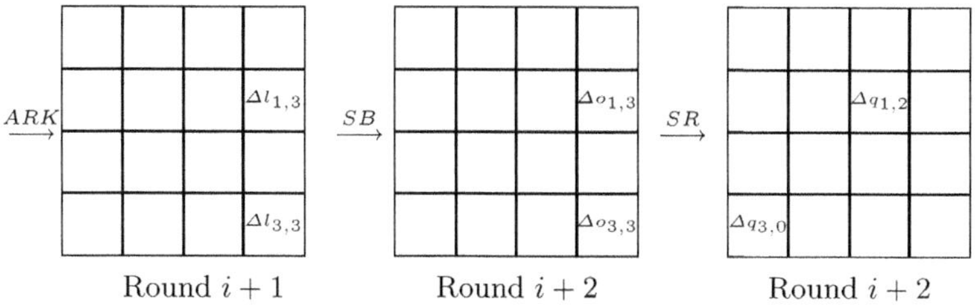

Fig. 4. Deducing the actual values of $q_{1,2}$ and $q_{3,0}$

$(\Delta l_{1,3}, \Delta l_{3,3})$ and the corresponding output differences $(\Delta o_{1,3}, \Delta o_{3,3})$ to the SB operation, and we can deduce 4 actual values for $o_{1,3}$, $o'_{1,3}$, $o_{3,3}$ and $o'_{3,3}$ by using a lookup table, which contains all possible input differences and their corresponding output differences of the SB operation. Here we encounter a 1-in-2 situation: although we already have 4 actual values for $o_{1,3}$, $o'_{1,3}$, $o_{3,3}$ and $o'_{3,3}$, we cannot distinguish the correct values ($o_{1,3}$ and $o_{3,3}$) from the faulty ones ($o'_{1,3}$ and $o'_{3,3}$). To address this problem, we need one more fault injected into $f_{1,0}$ and repeat the above steps since the correct values will appear twice in both keystream processing. After we get the actual values of $o_{1,3}$, $o'_{1,3}$, $o_{3,3}$ and $o'_{3,3}$, we know the actual values of $q_{1,2}$, $q'_{1,2}$, $q_{3,0}$ and $q'_{3,0}$ after the SR operation. As we know the actual values of $l_{0,1}$, $l_{0,3}$, $l_{2,1}$ and $l_{2,3}$ from the key stream, we know the actual values of $q_{0,1}$, $q_{0,3}$, $q_{2,1}$ and $q_{2,3}$ after the SB and SR operations. So far, we know the actual values of 6 bytes, $q_{1,2}$, $q_{3,0}$, $q_{0,1}$, $q_{0,3}$, $q_{2,1}$ and $q_{2,3}$, after the SR transformation in Round $i+2$:

$$\begin{pmatrix} ? & q_{0,1} & ? & q_{0,3} \\ ? & ? & q_{1,2} & ? \\ ? & q_{2,1} & ? & q_{2,3} \\ q_{3,0} & ? & ? & ? \end{pmatrix}.$$

We use the same idea to recover the actual values of $q_{0,0}$, $q_{2,2}$, $q_{1,0}$, $q_{3,2}$, $q_{2,0}$ and $q_{0,2}$. The details are listed as follows.

1. We are able to obtain the actual values of $q_{0,0}$ and $q_{2,2}$ by using 2 faults which are injected into $f_{0,0}$, or $f_{2,2}$. The procedure is shown in Appendix A.
2. We can recover the actual values of $q_{1,0}$ and $q_{3,2}$ by using 2 faults which are induced on $f_{0,1}$, $f_{1,2}$, $f_{2,3}$ or $f_{3,0}$. The steps are described in Appendix B.
3. We can get the actual values of $q_{2,0}$ and $q_{0,2}$ by using 2 faults which are injected into $f_{0,2}$ or $f_{2,0}$. The details are presented in Appendix C.

Since we now know the actual values of the 12 bytes after the SR transformation in Round $i+2$ in Fig. 5, we can compute the actual values of the first column ($r_{0,0}$, $r_{1,0}$, $r_{2,0}$ and $r_{3,0}$) and third column ($r_{0,2}$, $r_{1,2}$, $r_{2,2}$ and $r_{3,2}$) of the MC transformation. By XORing $(r_{0,0}, r_{0,2}, r_{2,0}, r_{2,2})$ with $(s_{0,0}, s_{0,2}, s_{2,0}, s_{2,2})$, we finally recover 4 round key bytes: $K^{i+2}_{0,0}$, $K^{i+2}_{0,2}$, $K^{i+2}_{2,0}$ and $K^{i+2}_{2,2}$.

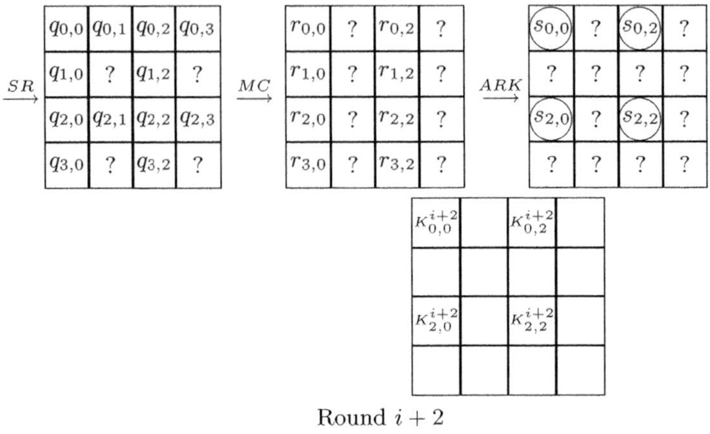

Fig. 5. Recovering 4 key bytes

3.3 Retrieving 16 Key Bytes in Round $i-1$, i, $i+1$ and $i+3$

By using the same techniques as described in Section 3.2, we can recover 16 ($K_{0,1}^{i-1}$, $K_{0,3}^{i-1}$, $K_{2,1}^{i-1}$, $K_{2,3}^{i-1}$, $K_{0,0}^{i}$, $K_{0,2}^{i}$, $K_{2,0}^{i}$, $K_{2,2}^{i}$, $K_{0,1}^{i+1}$, $K_{0,3}^{i+1}$, $K_{2,1}^{i+1}$, $K_{2,3}^{i+1}$, $K_{0,1}^{i+3}$, $K_{0,3}^{i+3}$, $K_{2,1}^{i+3}$ and $K_{2,3}^{i+3}$) more key bytes in Round $i-1$, i, $i+1$ and $i+3$ (see Fig. 7) with 32 faults. The details of recovering these 16 key bytes are provided as follows. We use Fig. 6 to describe the complete details.

3.3.1 Computing $K_{0,1}^{i-1}$, $K_{0,3}^{i-1}$, $K_{2,1}^{i-1}$ and $K_{2,3}^{i-1}$

1. Inject 2 faults into $\theta_{0,1}$ or $\theta_{2,3}$, and use these 2 faulty bytes to determine the actual values of $z_{0,1}$ and $z_{2,3}$.
2. Induce 2 faults on $\theta_{0,2}$ or $\theta_{2,1}$, and employ these 2 faulty values to calculate the actual values of $z_{0,3}$ and $z_{2,1}$.
3. Inject 2 faults into $\theta_{0,0}$, $\theta_{1,1}$, $\theta_{2,2}$ or $\theta_{3,3}$, and use these 2 faulty bytes to decide the actual values of $z_{1,3}$ and $z_{3,1}$.
4. Induce 2 faults on $\theta_{0,2}$, $\theta_{1,3}$, $\theta_{2,0}$ or $\theta_{3,1}$, and employ these 2 faulty values to find out the actual values of $z_{1,1}$ and $z_{3,3}$.
5. Apply the MC operation to ($z_{0,1}$, $z_{1,1}$, $z_{2,1}$, $z_{3,1}$) and ($z_{0,3}$, $z_{1,3}$, $z_{2,3}$, $z_{3,3}$) to get the actual values of $\beta_{0,1}$, $\beta_{1,1}$, $\beta_{2,1}$, $\beta_{3,1}$, $\beta_{0,3}$, $\beta_{1,3}$, $\beta_{2,3}$ and $\beta_{3,3}$. XOR $\beta_{0,1}$ with $\lambda_{0,1}$, $\beta_{0,3}$ with $\lambda_{0,3}$, $\beta_{2,1}$ with $\lambda_{2,1}$, and $\beta_{2,3}$ with $\lambda_{2,3}$ to recover $K_{0,1}^{i-1}$, $K_{0,3}^{i-1}$, $K_{2,1}^{i-1}$ and $K_{2,3}^{i-1}$.

3.3.2 Determining $K_{0,0}^{i}$, $K_{0,2}^{i}$, $K_{2,0}^{i}$ and $K_{2,2}^{i}$

1. Induce 2 faults on $\phi_{0,0}$ or $\phi_{2,2}$, and employ these 2 faulty values to compute the actual values of $e_{0,0}$ and $e_{2,2}$.
2. Inject 2 faults into $\phi_{0,2}$ or $\phi_{2,0}$, and use these 2 faulty values to calculate the actual values of $e_{0,2}$ and $e_{2,0}$.

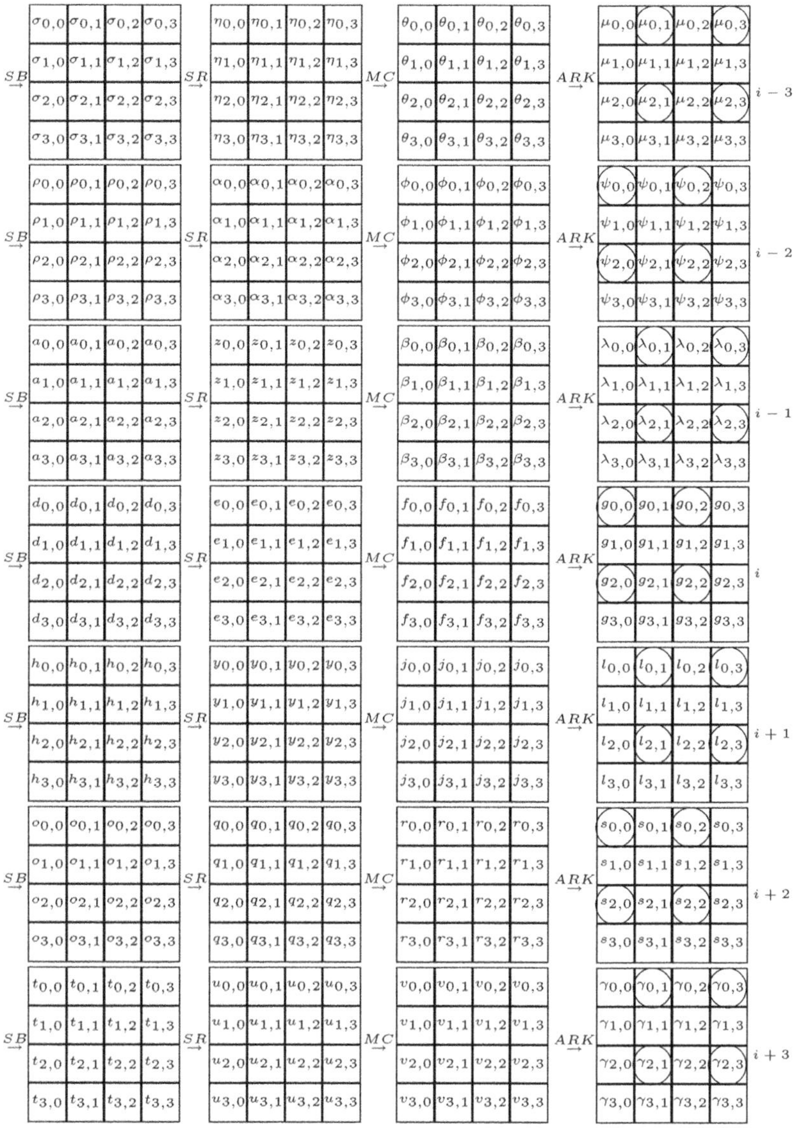

Fig. 6. The seven-round diagram

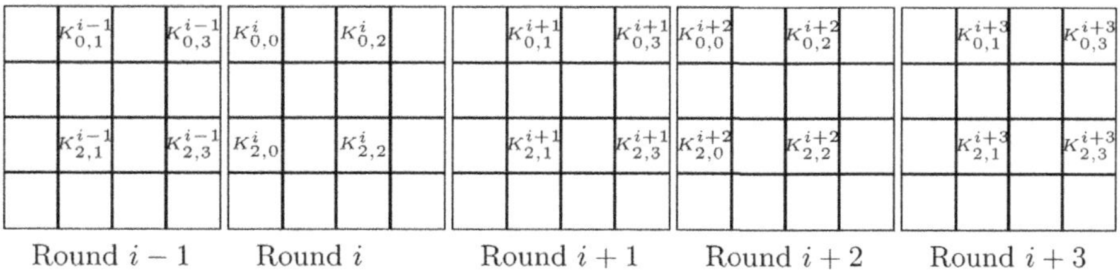

Fig. 7. The recovered key bytes

3. Induce 2 faults on $\phi_{0,3}$, $\phi_{1,0}$, $\phi_{2,1}$ or $\phi_{3,2}$, and use these 2 faulty values to decide the actual values of $e_{1,2}$ and $e_{3,0}$.
4. Inject 2 faults into $\phi_{0,1}$, $\phi_{1,2}$, $\phi_{2,3}$ or $\phi_{3,0}$, and employ these 2 faulty bytes to determine the actual values of $e_{1,0}$ and $e_{3,2}$.
5. Apply the MC operation to $(e_{0,0}, e_{1,0}, e_{2,0}, e_{3,0})$ and $(e_{0,2}, e_{1,2}, e_{2,2}, e_{3,2})$ to get the actual values of $f_{0,0}$, $f_{1,0}$, $f_{2,0}$, $f_{3,0}$, $f_{0,2}$, $f_{1,2}$, $f_{2,2}$ and $f_{3,2}$. XOR $f_{0,0}$ with $g_{0,0}$, $f_{0,2}$ with $g_{0,2}$, $f_{2,0}$ with $g_{2,0}$, and $f_{2,2}$ with $g_{2,2}$ to retrieve the actual values of $K^i_{0,0}$, $K^i_{0,2}$, $K^i_{2,0}$ and $K^i_{2,2}$.

3.3.3 Calculating $K^{i+1}_{0,1}$, $K^{i+1}_{0,3}$, $K^{i+1}_{2,1}$ and $K^{i+1}_{2,3}$

1. Inject 2 faults into $\beta_{0,1}$ or $\beta_{2,3}$, and use these 2 faulty bytes to decide the actual values of $y_{0,1}$ and $y_{2,3}$.
2. Induce 2 faults on $\beta_{0,3}$ or $\beta_{2,1}$, and employ these 2 faulty bytes to compute the actual values of $y_{0,3}$ and $y_{2,1}$.
3. Inject 2 faults into $\beta_{0,0}$, $\beta_{1,1}$, $\beta_{2,2}$ or $\beta_{3,3}$ and use these 2 faulty bytes to determine the actual values of $y_{1,3}$ and $y_{3,1}$.
4. Induce 2 faults on $\beta_{0,2}$, $\beta_{1,3}$, $\beta_{2,0}$ or $\beta_{3,1}$, and employ these 2 faulty bytes to calculate the actual values of $y_{1,1}$ and $y_{3,3}$.
5. Apply the MC transformation to $(y_{0,1}, y_{1,1}, y_{2,1}, y_{3,1})$ and $(y_{0,3}, y_{1,3}, y_{2,3}, y_{3,3})$ to obtain the actual values of $j_{0,1}$, $j_{1,1}$, $j_{2,1}$, $j_{3,1}$, $j_{0,3}$, $j_{1,3}$, $j_{2,3}$ and $j_{3,3}$. XOR $j_{0,1}$ with $l_{0,1}$, $j_{0,3}$ with $l_{0,3}$, $j_{2,1}$ with $l_{2,1}$, and $j_{2,3}$ with $l_{2,3}$ to recover $K^{i+1}_{0,1}$, $K^{i+1}_{0,3}$, $K^{i+1}_{2,1}$ and $K^{i+1}_{2,3}$.

3.3.4 Recovering $K^{i+3}_{0,1}$, $K^{i+3}_{0,3}$, $K^{i+3}_{2,1}$ and $K^{i+3}_{2,3}$

1. Use 2 faulty bytes which are $j_{0,1}$ or $j_{2,3}$ to determine the actual values of $u_{0,1}$ and $u_{2,3}$.
2. Employ 2 faulty bytes which are $j_{0,3}$ or $j_{2,1}$ to retrieve the actual values of $u_{0,3}$ and $u_{2,1}$.
3. Make use of 2 faulty bytes which are $j_{0,0}$, $j_{1,1}$, $j_{2,2}$ or $j_{3,3}$ to calculate the actual values of $u_{1,3}$ and $u_{3,1}$.
4. Employ 2 faulty bytes which are $j_{0,2}$, $j_{1,3}$, $j_{2,0}$ or $j_{3,1}$ to compute the actual values of $u_{1,1}$ and $u_{3,3}$.
5. Apply the MC operation to $(u_{0,1}, u_{1,1}, u_{2,1}, u_{3,1})$ and $(u_{0,3}, u_{1,3}, u_{2,3}, u_{3,3})$ to get the actual values of $v_{0,1}$, $v_{1,1}$, $v_{2,1}$, $v_{3,1}$, $v_{0,3}$, $v_{1,3}$, $v_{2,3}$ and $v_{3,3}$. We can retrieve $K^{i+3}_{0,1}$, $K^{i+3}_{0,3}$, $K^{i+3}_{2,1}$ and $K^{i+3}_{2,3}$ (see Fig. 7) by XORing $v_{0,1}$ with $\gamma_{0,1}$, $v_{0,3}$ with $\gamma_{0,3}$, $v_{2,1}$ with $\gamma_{2,1}$, and $v_{2,3}$ with $\gamma_{2,3}$.

3.4 Deducing 10 More Key Bytes in Round $i + 2$

By employing the definition and the properties of the AES key schedule, we use the 20 recovered key bytes to deduce 10 more key bytes in Round $i+2$ (see Fig. 8). The steps of deducing these 10 key bytes are listed as follows, where SB^{-1} is the inverse of the byte substitution transformation and $Rcon^i$ represents the round constant used to generate round key K^i.

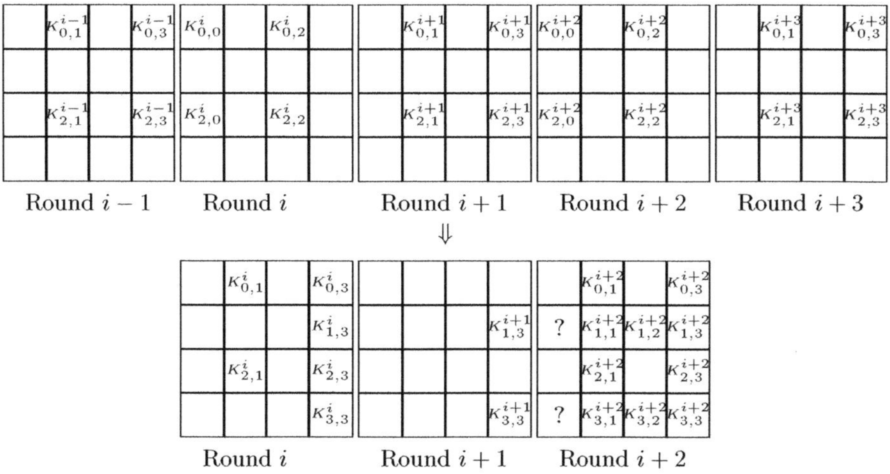

Fig. 8. The deduced key bytes

1. Deduce $K^{i+2}_{0,1}$, $K^{i+2}_{2,1}$, $K^{i+2}_{0,3}$ and $K^{i+2}_{2,3}$.

$$\begin{aligned} K^{i+2}_{0,1} &= K^{i+1}_{0,1} \oplus K^{i+2}_{0,0}, \\ K^{i+2}_{2,1} &= K^{i+1}_{2,1} \oplus K^{i+2}_{2,0}, \\ K^{i+2}_{0,3} &= K^{i+1}_{0,3} \oplus K^{i+2}_{0,2}, \\ K^{i+2}_{2,3} &= K^{i+1}_{2,3} \oplus K^{i+2}_{2,2}. \end{aligned}$$

2. Calculate $K^{i+2}_{3,3}$ and $K^{i+2}_{1,3}$.

$$\begin{aligned} K^{i+3}_{2,1} &= K^{i+3}_{2,0} \oplus K^{i+2}_{2,1} = SB(K^{i+2}_{3,3}) \oplus RCON^{i+3}(2) \oplus K^{i+2}_{2,0} \oplus K^{i+2}_{2,1} \\ &= SB(K^{i+2}_{3,3}) \oplus Rcon^{i+3}(2) \oplus K^{i+1}_{2,1}, \\ K^{i+2}_{3,3} &= SB^{-1}(K^{i+3}_{2,1} \oplus Rcon^{i+3}(2) \oplus K^{i+1}_{2,1}), \\ K^{i+3}_{0,1} &= K^{i+3}_{0,0} \oplus K^{i+2}_{0,1} = SB(K^{i+2}_{1,3}) \oplus Rcon^{i+3}(0) \oplus K^{i+2}_{0,0} \oplus K^{i+2}_{0,1} \\ &= SB(K^{i+2}_{1,3}) \oplus Rcon^{i+3}(0) \oplus K^{i+1}_{0,1}, \\ K^{i+2}_{1,3} &= SB^{-1}(K^{i+3}_{0,1} \oplus Rcon^{i+3}(0) \oplus K^{i+1}_{0,1}). \end{aligned}$$

3. Determine $K^{i+2}_{3,1}$ and $K^{i+2}_{1,1}$.

$$\begin{aligned} K^{i}_{0,3} &= K^{i-1}_{0,3} \oplus K^{i}_{0,2}, \\ K^{i}_{2,3} &= K^{i-1}_{2,3} \oplus K^{i}_{2,2}, \\ K^{i+1}_{2,1} &= K^{i+1}_{2,0} \oplus K^{i}_{2,1} = SB(K^{i}_{3,3}) \oplus Rcon^{i+1}(2) \oplus K^{i}_{2,0} \oplus K^{i}_{2,1} \\ &= SB(K^{i}_{3,3}) \oplus Rcon^{i+1}(2) \oplus K^{i}_{2,0} \oplus K^{i}_{2,0} \oplus K^{i-1}_{2,1} \\ &= SB(K^{i}_{3,3}) \oplus Rcon^{i+1}(2) \oplus K^{i-1}_{2,1}, \end{aligned}$$

$$
\begin{aligned}
K^{i}_{3,3} &= SB^{-1}(K^{i+1}_{2,1} \oplus Rcon^{i+1}(2) \oplus K^{i-1}_{2,1}),\\
K^{i+2}_{3,1} &= K^{i}_{3,3} \oplus K^{i+2}_{3,3},\\
K^{i+1}_{0,1} &= K^{i+1}_{0,0} \oplus K^{i}_{0,1} = SB(K^{i}_{1,3}) \oplus Rcon^{i+1}(0) \oplus K^{i}_{0,0} \oplus K^{i}_{0,1}\\
&= SB(K^{i}_{1,3}) \oplus Rcon^{i+1}(0) \oplus K^{i-1}_{0,1},\\
K^{i}_{1,3} &= SB^{-1}(K^{i+1}_{0,1} \oplus Rcon^{i+1}(0) \oplus K^{i-1}_{0,1}),\\
K^{i+2}_{1,1} &= K^{i}_{1,3} \oplus K^{i+2}_{1,3}.
\end{aligned}
$$

4. Decide $K^{i+2}_{3,2}$ and $K^{i+2}_{1,2}$.

$$
\begin{aligned}
K^{i}_{0,1} &= K^{i-1}_{0,1} \oplus K^{i}_{0,0},\\
K^{i}_{2,1} &= K^{i-1}_{2,1} \oplus K^{i}_{2,0},\\
K^{i+2}_{2,1} &= K^{i+2}_{2,0} \oplus K^{i+1}_{2,1} = SB(K^{i+1}_{3,3}) \oplus Rcon^{i+2}(2) \oplus K^{i+1}_{2,0} \oplus K^{i+1}_{2,1}\\
&= SB(K^{i+1}_{3,3}) \oplus Rcon^{i+2}(2) \oplus K^{i}_{2,1},\\
K^{i+1}_{3,3} &= SB^{-1}(K^{i+2}_{2,1} \oplus Rcon^{i+2}(2) \oplus K^{i}_{2,1}),\\
K^{i+2}_{3,2} &= K^{i+1}_{3,3} \oplus K^{i+2}_{3,3},\\
K^{i+2}_{0,1} &= K^{i+2}_{0,0} \oplus K^{i+1}_{0,1} = SB(K^{i+1}_{1,3}) \oplus Rcon^{i+2}(0) \oplus K^{i+1}_{0,0} \oplus K^{i+1}_{0,1}\\
&= SB(K^{i+1}_{1,3}) \oplus Rcon^{i+2}(0) \oplus K^{i}_{0,1},\\
K^{i+1}_{1,3} &= SB^{-1}(K^{i+2}_{0,1} \oplus Rcon^{i+2}(0) \oplus K^{i}_{0,1}),\\
K^{i+2}_{1,2} &= K^{i+1}_{1,3} \oplus K^{i+2}_{1,3}.
\end{aligned}
$$

In summary, we recover 14 key bytes of Round $i+2$, and the 2 unknown key bytes ($K^{i+2}_{1,0}$ and $K^{i+2}_{3,0}$, represented by a question mark) can be determined by exhaustive search with 2^{16} operations.

4 Conclusions

We described a differential fault attack on LEX in this paper. We presented a method to decide the fault position by observing the changes of the key stream after a fault is injected. The attack makes use of the differential properties of the AES round transformations, the AES key schedule properties and the structural features of LEX. The proposed attack needs 40 faults and recovers the secret key of LEX with 2^{16} time complexity.

References

1. Biham, E., Shamir, A.: Differential Cryptanalysis of the Data Encryption Standard. Springer, Heidelberg (1993)
2. Biham, E., Shamir, A.: Differential Fault Analysis of Secret Key Cryptosystems. In: Kaliski Jr., B.S. (ed.) CRYPTO 1997. LNCS, vol. 1294, pp. 513–525. Springer, Heidelberg (1997)

3. Biryukov, A.: A New 128-bit Key Stream Cipher LEX. ECRYPT stream cipher project report 2005/013 (2005), http://www.ecrypt.eu.org/stream
4. Biryukov, A.: The Design of a Stream Cipher LEX. In: Biham, E., Youssef, A.M. (eds.) SAC 2006. LNCS, vol. 4356, pp. 67–75. Springer, Heidelberg (2007)
5. Biryukov, A.: The Tweak for LEX-128, LEX-192, LEX-256. ECRYPT stream cipher project report 2006/037 (2006), http://www.ecrypt.eu.org/stream
6. Boneh, D., DeMillo, R.A., Lipton, R.J.: On the Importance of Checking Cryptographic Protocols for Faults (Extended Abstract). In: Fumy, W. (ed.) EUROCRYPT 1997. LNCS, vol. 1233, pp. 37–51. Springer, Heidelberg (1997)
7. Daemen, J., Rijmen, V.: The Design of Rijndael: AES - The Advanced Encryption Standard. Springer, Heidelberg (2002)
8. Dunkelman, O., Keller, N.: A New Attack on the LEX Stream Cipher. In: Pieprzyk, J. (ed.) ASIACRYPT 2008. LNCS, vol. 5350, pp. 539–556. Springer, Heidelberg (2008)
9. Englund, H., Hell, M., Johansson, T.: A Note on Distinguishing Attacks. In: Preproceedings of State of the Art of Stream Ciphers workshop (SASC 2007), Bochum, Germany, pp. 73–78 (2007)
10. Hoch, J.J., Shamir, A.: Fault Analysis of Stream Ciphers. In: Joye, M., Quisquater, J.-J. (eds.) CHES 2004. LNCS, vol. 3156, pp. 240–253. Springer, Heidelberg (2004)
11. Kocher, P.C.: Timing Attacks on Implementations of Diffie-Hellman. In: Koblitz, N. (ed.) CRYPTO 1996. LNCS, vol. 1109, pp. 104–113. Springer, Heidelberg (1996)
12. Kocher, P.C., Jaffe, J., Jun, B.: Differential Power Analysis. In: Wiener, M. J. (ed.) CRYPTO 1999. LNCS, vol. 1666, pp. 388–397. Springer, Heidelberg (1999)
13. Matsui, M.: Linear Cryptanalysis Method for DES Cipher. In: Helleseth, T. (ed.) EUROCRYPT 1993. LNCS, vol. 765, pp. 386–397. Springer, Heidelberg (1994)
14. Mondal, M., Mukhopadhyay, D.: Related Key Cryptanalysis of the LEX Stream Cipher (2010), http://eprint.iacr.org/2010/011
15. Wu, H., Preneel, B.: Resynchronization Attacks on WG and LEX. In: Robshaw, M.J.B. (ed.) FSE 2006. LNCS, vol. 4047, pp. 422–432. Springer, Heidelberg (2006)

A Calculating the Actual Values of $q_{0,0}$ and $q_{2,2}$

Assume a fault is induced on $f_{0,0}$ or $f_{2,2}$ (Group 1 in Table 1), and suppose the faulty byte is $f_{0,0}$. We create a formula, Formula (3), by employing the input and out differences of the MC operation in Round $i+1$. We build another formula, Formula (4), with the input and out differences of the MC transformation in Round $i+2$.

$$\begin{pmatrix} \Delta y_{0,0} & 0\ 0\ 0 \\ 0 & 0\ 0\ 0 \\ 0 & 0\ 0\ 0 \\ 0 & 0\ 0\ 0 \end{pmatrix} \xrightarrow{MC} \begin{pmatrix} \Delta j_{0,0} & 0\ 0\ 0 \\ \Delta j_{1,0} & 0\ 0\ 0 \\ \Delta j_{2,0} & 0\ 0\ 0 \\ \Delta j_{3,0} & 0\ 0\ 0 \end{pmatrix} \tag{3}$$

$$\begin{pmatrix} \Delta q_{0,0} & 0 & 0 & 0 \\ 0 & 0 & 0 & \Delta q_{1,3} \\ 0 & 0 & \Delta q_{2,2} & 0 \\ 0 & \Delta q_{3,1} & 0 & 0 \end{pmatrix} \xrightarrow{MC} \begin{pmatrix} \Delta r_{0,0} & \Delta r_{0,1} & \Delta r_{0,2} & \Delta r_{0,3} \\ \Delta r_{1,0} & \Delta r_{1,1} & \Delta r_{1,2} & \Delta r_{1,3} \\ \Delta r_{2,0} & \Delta r_{2,1} & \Delta r_{2,2} & \Delta r_{2,3} \\ \Delta r_{3,0} & \Delta r_{3,1} & \Delta r_{3,2} & \Delta r_{3,3} \end{pmatrix} \tag{4}$$

1. In Formula (3), $\Delta y_{0,0}$ can be computed from the key stream of Round i by using the values of $g_{0,0}$ and $g'_{0,0}$. In the first columns of the input and output, there are 4 known bytes ($\Delta y_{0,0}$ and 3 zero bytes) and 4 unknown bytes ($\Delta j_{0,0}$, $\Delta j_{1,0}$, $\Delta j_{2,0}$ and $\Delta j_{3,0}$). The 4 unknown bytes can be decided by using the 4 known bytes. After $\Delta j_{0,0}$, $\Delta j_{1,0}$, $\Delta j_{2,0}$ and $\Delta j_{3,0}$ are decided, we know the values of $\Delta l_{0,0}$, $\Delta l_{1,0}$, $\Delta l_{2,0}$ and $\Delta l_{3,0}$.
2. In Formula (4), $\Delta r_{0,0}$ can be computed from the key stream of Round $i+2$ by using the values of $s_{0,0}$ and $s'_{0,0}$. Similarly, we get the value of $\Delta r_{2,0}$. In the first columns of the input and output, there are 5 known bytes ($\Delta r_{0,0}$, $\Delta r_{2,0}$ and 3 zero bytes) and 3 unknown bytes ($\Delta q_{0,0}$, $\Delta r_{1,0}$ and $\Delta r_{3,0}$). We get the values of $\Delta q_{0,0}$, $\Delta r_{1,0}$ and $\Delta r_{3,0}$ by using the 5 known bytes. By using the same method to analyze the third columns of the input and output, we can deduce the values of $\Delta q_{2,2}$, $\Delta r_{1,2}$ and $\Delta r_{3,2}$ by employing the 5 known bytes ($\Delta r_{0,2}$, $\Delta r_{2,2}$ and 3 zero bytes).
3. We know $\Delta o_{0,0}$ and $\Delta o_{2,0}$ because $\Delta q_{0,0}$ is equal to $\Delta o_{0,0}$ and $\Delta q_{2,2}$ is equal to $\Delta o_{2,0}$. Now we know the input differences ($\Delta l_{0,0}$, $\Delta l_{2,0}$) and the corresponding output differences ($\Delta o_{0,0}$, $\Delta o_{2,0}$) to the SB operation, and we can deduce 4 actual values for $o_{0,0}$, $o'_{0,0}$, $o_{2,0}$ and $o'_{2,0}$. Although we have 4 actual values for $o_{0,0}$, $o'_{0,0}$, $o_{2,0}$ and $o'_{2,0}$, we are not able to separate the correct values ($o_{0,0}$ and $o_{2,0}$) from the faulty ones ($o'_{0,0}$ and $o'_{2,0}$). To overcome this problem, we need one more fault induced on $f_{0,0}$ and repeat the steps mentioned above to make the correct values emerge twice. After knowing the actual values of $o_{0,0}$, $o'_{0,0}$, $o_{2,0}$ and $o'_{2,0}$, we obtain the actual values of $q_{0,0}$, $q'_{0,0}$, $q_{2,2}$ and $q'_{2,2}$ after the SR operation.

B Computing the Actual Values of $q_{1,0}$ and $q_{3,2}$

Suppose a fault is induced on a byte which is $f_{0,1}$, $f_{1,2}$, $f_{2,3}$ or $f_{3,0}$ (Group 3 in Table 1). By using the input and out differences of the MC operation in Round $i+1$, we establish a formula, Formula (5). By employing the input and out differences of the MC transformation in Round $i+2$, we build another formula, Formula (6).

$$\begin{pmatrix} 0 & \Delta y_{0,1} & 0 & 0 \\ 0 & \Delta y_{1,1} & 0 & 0 \\ 0 & \Delta y_{2,1} & 0 & 0 \\ 0 & \Delta y_{3,1} & 0 & 0 \end{pmatrix} \xrightarrow{MC} \begin{pmatrix} 0 & \Delta j_{0,1} & 0 & 0 \\ 0 & \Delta j_{1,1} & 0 & 0 \\ 0 & \Delta j_{2,1} & 0 & 0 \\ 0 & \Delta j_{3,1} & 0 & 0 \end{pmatrix} \tag{5}$$

$$\begin{pmatrix} 0 & \Delta q_{0,1} & 0 & 0 \\ \Delta q_{1,0} & 0 & 0 & 0 \\ 0 & 0 & 0 & \Delta q_{2,3} \\ 0 & 0 & \Delta q_{3,2} & 0 \end{pmatrix} \xrightarrow{MC} \begin{pmatrix} \Delta r_{0,0} & \Delta r_{0,1} & \Delta r_{0,2} & \Delta r_{0,3} \\ \Delta r_{1,0} & \Delta r_{1,1} & \Delta r_{1,2} & \Delta r_{1,3} \\ \Delta r_{2,0} & \Delta r_{2,1} & \Delta r_{2,2} & \Delta r_{2,3} \\ \Delta r_{3,0} & \Delta r_{3,1} & \Delta r_{3,2} & \Delta r_{3,3} \end{pmatrix} \tag{6}$$

1. In Formula (5), $\Delta j_{0,1}$ can be computed from the key stream of Round $i+1$ by using the values of $l_{0,1}$ and $l'_{0,1}$, and $\Delta j_{2,1}$ can be computed from the key stream of Round $i+1$ by using the values of $l_{2,1}$ and $l'_{2,1}$. In the second columns of the input and output, we employ Observation 1 and use the 5

known bytes ($\Delta j_{0,1}$, $\Delta j_{2,1}$ and 3 zero input bytes) to decide the 2 unknown output bytes ($\Delta j_{1,1}$ and $\Delta j_{3,1}$) and the position and the difference of the non-zero input byte. Assume the recovered non-zero input byte is $\Delta y_{2,1}$.

2. In Formula (6), $\Delta r_{0,0}$ can be computed from the key stream of Round $i+2$ by using the values of $s_{0,0}$ and $s'_{0,0}$. Similarly, we get the value of $\Delta r_{2,0}$. In the first columns of the input and output, we use the 5 known bytes ($\Delta r_{0,0}$, $\Delta r_{2,0}$ and 3 zero bytes) to decide the 3 unknown bytes ($\Delta q_{1,0}$, $\Delta r_{1,0}$ and $\Delta r_{3,0}$). By using the same method to analyze the third columns of the input and output, we can deduce the values of 3 unknown bytes ($\Delta q_{3,2}$, $\Delta r_{1,2}$ and $\Delta r_{3,2}$) by employing the 5 known bytes ($\Delta r_{0,2}$, $\Delta r_{2,2}$ and 3 zero bytes).
3. We know $\Delta o_{1,1}$ and $\Delta o_{3,1}$ because $\Delta q_{1,0}$ is equal to $\Delta o_{1,1}$ and $\Delta q_{3,2}$ is equal to $\Delta o_{3,1}$. We now know the input differences ($\Delta l_{1,1}$, $\Delta l_{3,1}$) and the corresponding output differences ($\Delta o_{1,1}$, $\Delta o_{3,1}$) to the SB operation, and we can deduce 4 actual values for $o_{1,1}$, $o'_{1,1}$, $o_{3,1}$ and $o'_{3,1}$. Although we have 4 actual values for $o_{1,1}$, $o'_{1,1}$, $o_{3,1}$ and $o'_{3,1}$, we cannot distinguish the correct values ($o_{1,1}$ and $o_{3,1}$) from the faulty ones ($o'_{1,1}$ and $o'_{3,1}$). To address this issue, we need one more fault injected into $f_{2,3}$ and repeat the above steps to make the correct values appear twice in both keystream processing. After knowing the actual values of $o_{1,1}$, $o'_{1,1}$, $o_{3,1}$ and $o'_{3,1}$, we know the actual values of $q_{1,0}$, $q'_{1,0}$, $q_{3,2}$ and $q'_{3,2}$ after the SR operation.

C Deducing the Actual Values of $q_{2,0}$ and $q_{0,2}$

Assume a fault is injected into a byte which is $f_{0,2}$ or $f_{2,0}$ (Group 1 in Table 1), and assume the faulty byte is $f_{2,0}$. We create a formula, Formula (7), with the input and out differences of the MC operation in Round $i+1$. We establish another formula, Formula (8), by employing the input and out differences of the MC transformation in Round $i+2$.

$$\begin{pmatrix} 0 & 0 & 0 & 0 \\ 0 & 0 & 0 & 0 \\ 0 & 0 & \Delta y_{2,2} & 0 \\ 0 & 0 & 0 & 0 \end{pmatrix} \xrightarrow{MC} \begin{pmatrix} 0 & 0 & \Delta j_{0,2} & 0 \\ 0 & 0 & \Delta j_{1,2} & 0 \\ 0 & 0 & \Delta j_{2,2} & 0 \\ 0 & 0 & \Delta j_{3,2} & 0 \end{pmatrix} \tag{7}$$

$$\begin{pmatrix} 0 & 0 & \Delta q_{0,2} & 0 \\ 0 & \Delta q_{1,1} & 0 & 0 \\ \Delta q_{2,0} & 0 & 0 & 0 \\ 0 & 0 & 0 & \Delta q_{3,3} \end{pmatrix} \xrightarrow{MC} \begin{pmatrix} \Delta r_{0,0} & \Delta r_{0,1} & \Delta r_{0,2} & \Delta r_{0,3} \\ \Delta r_{1,0} & \Delta r_{1,1} & \Delta r_{1,2} & \Delta r_{1,3} \\ \Delta r_{2,0} & \Delta r_{2,1} & \Delta r_{2,2} & \Delta r_{2,3} \\ \Delta r_{3,0} & \Delta r_{3,1} & \Delta r_{3,2} & \Delta r_{3,3} \end{pmatrix} \tag{8}$$

1. In Formula (7), $\Delta y_{2,2}$ can be computed from the key stream of Round i by using the values of $g_{2,0}$ and $g'_{2,0}$. In the third columns of the input and output, we use 4 known bytes ($\Delta y_{2,2}$ and 3 zero bytes) to decide 4 unknown bytes ($\Delta j_{0,2}$, $\Delta j_{1,2}$, $\Delta j_{2,2}$ and $\Delta j_{3,2}$). The values of $\Delta l_{0,2}$, $\Delta l_{1,2}$, $\Delta l_{2,2}$ and $\Delta l_{3,2}$ are also decided.
2. In Formula (8), $\Delta r_{0,0}$ can be computed from the key stream of Round $i+2$ by using the values of $s_{0,0}$ and $s'_{0,0}$. Similarly, we get the value of $\Delta r_{2,0}$ by

using the values of $\Delta s_{2,0}$ and $\Delta s'_{2,0}$. In the first columns of the input and output, we can use the 5 known bytes ($\Delta r_{0,0}$, $\Delta r_{2,0}$ and 3 zero bytes) to decide the 3 unknown bytes ($\Delta q_{2,0}$, $\Delta r_{1,0}$ and $\Delta r_{3,0}$). Similarly, we can use the 5 known bytes ($\Delta r_{0,2}$, $\Delta r_{2,2}$ and 3 zero bytes) to decide the 3 unknown bytes ($\Delta q_{0,2}$, $\Delta r_{1,2}$ and $\Delta r_{3,2}$) in the third columns of the input and output.

3. We know $\Delta o_{0,2}$ and $\Delta o_{2,2}$ because $\Delta q_{0,2}$ is equal to $\Delta o_{0,2}$ and $\Delta q_{2,0}$ is equal to $\Delta o_{2,2}$. We now know the input differences ($\Delta l_{0,2}$, $\Delta l_{2,2}$) and the corresponding output differences ($\Delta o_{0,2}$, $\Delta o_{2,2}$) to the SB operation, and we can deduce 4 actual values for $o_{0,2}$, $o'_{0,2}$, $o_{2,2}$ and $o'_{2,2}$. Although we have 4 actual values for $o_{0,2}$, $o'_{0,2}$, $o_{2,2}$ and $o'_{2,2}$, we cannot separate the correct values ($o_{0,2}$ and $o_{2,2}$) from the faulty ones ($o'_{0,2}$ and $o'_{2,2}$). To overcome this obstacle, we need one more fault injected into $f_{2,0}$ and repeat the above steps because the correct values will emerge twice in both keystream processing. After knowing the actual values of $o_{0,2}$, $o'_{0,2}$, $o_{2,2}$ and $o'_{2,2}$, we know the actual values of $q_{0,2}$, $q'_{0,2}$, $q_{2,0}$ and $q'_{2,0}$ after the SR operation.

Generalized RC4 Key Collisions and Hash Collisions

Jiageng Chen* and Atsuko Miyaji**

School of Information Science,
Japan Advanced Institute of Science and Technology,
1-1 Asahidai, Nomi, Ishikawa 923-1292, Japan
{jg-chen,miyaji}@jaist.ac.jp

Abstract. In this paper, we discovered that RC4 can generate colliding key pairs with various hamming distances, other than those found by Matsui (with hamming distance one), and by Chen and Miyaji (with hamming distance three). We formalized RC4 colliding key pairs into two large patterns, namely, Transitional pattern and Self-Absorbing pattern, according to the behavior during KSA. The colliding key pairs found in the previous researches can be seen as either subsets of the Transitional pattern or of the Self-Absorbing pattern. We analyzed both patterns and clarified the relations among the probability of key collision, key length and hamming distances which yield the colliding key pairs. Also we show how to make use of the RC4 key collision patterns to find collisions of RC4-Hash function which was proposed in INDOCRYPT 2006. Some concrete experimental results (RC4-Hash collision and RC4 colliding key pairs) are also given in this paper.

1 Introduction

The stream cipher RC4 is one of the most famous ciphers widely used in real world applications such as Microsoft Office, Secure Socket Layer (SSL), Wired Equivalent Privacy (WEP), etc. Due to its popularity and simplicity, RC4 has become a hot cryptanalysis target since its specification was made public on the Internet in 1994 [5]. Various general weaknesses of RC4 have been discovered in some previous works including [6,7,8], etc. Another popular cryptanalysis direction of RC4 is in the WEP environment. Such works include [9,10,11,12], etc.

Our paper focuses on RC4 key collisions, especially the existence of secret key pairs that generate the same initial states after key scheduling algorithm. This is a serious flaw for a stream cipher from the cryptographic point of view, since two encryptions will become the same under two different secret keys. The study of "colliding keys" of RC4 can be dated back to 2000. Grosul and Wallach [1] first pointed out that RC4 can generate near collisions when the key size is close to the full 256 bytes. In [2] first colliding key pairs with hamming distance one were discovered, where hamming distance one means that the two keys differ from

* This author is supported by the Graduate Research Program, JAIST.
** This work is supported by Grant-in-Aid for Scientific Research (B), 20300003.

J.A. Garay and R. De Prisco (Eds.): SCN 2010, LNCS 6280, pp. 73–87, 2010.

each other at one position. Later in [3], other colliding key pairs with hamming distance three were found. Note that these researches can also generate "near colliding keys" of RC4, that generate initial states with small hamming distances after key scheduling algorithm. In a sense, these researches mean that we can control key scheduling algorithm. Recently, a new type of attack, which uses such two initial states with small hamming distances, has been proposed [4].

In this paper, we further analyzed the RC4 colliding key behavior, and we discovered that more colliding key pairs with various hamming distances exist in RC4, in addition to the ones found in [2] and [3]. We also found that all currently known RC4 colliding key pairs can be organized into two patterns, according to the behavior during KSA. We analyze these two generalized patterns and formalize the RC4 key collisions. Collision probability is estimated, and we point out that it is mainly affected by key length and hamming distances between the two keys. By making use of the RC4 key collision, we can also find collisions for RC4-Hash, which is built from RC4 [14] using KSA as a compression function.

Structure of the paper. In Section 2, we briefly describe the RC4 algorithm, followed by some previous works on RC4 key collisions. Section 3 shows the formalized RC4 colliding key patterns and how they work. The probability evaluation is given in Section 4, followed by the RC4-Hash Collisions in Section 5. Some experimental results on RC4-Hash Collisions and RC4 key collisions are given in Section 5 and Appendix.

2 Preparation

2.1 Description of RC4

The internal state of RC4 consists of a permutation S of the numbers $0, ..., N-1$ and two indices $i, j \in \{0, ..., N-1\}$. The index i is determined and known to the public, while j and permutation S remain secret. RC4 consists of two algorithms: The Key Scheduling Algorithm (KSA) and the Pseudo Random Generator Algorithm (PRGA). The KSA generates an initial state from a random key K of k bytes as described in Algorithm 1. It starts with an array $\{0, 1, ..., N-1\}$ where $N = 256$ by default. At the end, we obtain the initial state S_{N-1}. Once the initial state is created, it is used by PRGA. The purpose of PRGA is to generate a keystream of bytes which will be XORed with the plaintext to generate the ciphertext. PRGA is described in Algorithm 2. In this paper, we focus only on KSA.

Algorithm 1. KSA

for $i = 0$ **to** $N-1$ **do**
  $S[i] \leftarrow i$
end for
$j \leftarrow 0$
for $i = 0$ **to** $N-1$ **do**
  $j \leftarrow j + S[i] + K[i \bmod l]$
  swap$(S[i], S[j])$
end for

Algorithm 2. PRGA

$i \leftarrow 0$
$j \leftarrow 0$
loop
  $i \leftarrow i + 1$
  $j \leftarrow j + S[i]$
  swap$(S[i], S[j])$
keystream byte $z_i = S[S[i] + S[j]]$
end loop

2.2 Previous Research on RC4 Key Collisions

Three important previous studies on RC4 key collisions are [1], [2] and [3]. In [1], the authors pointed out that it's possible for two secret keys with length close to 256 bytes to generate similar internal state after KSA, and thus they will generate similar hundred byte output during PRGA. The reason for this is that for two keys K_1, K_2, if we assume $K_1[i] = K_2[i]$ except when $i = t$, then when t is close to 255, the two internal states will be substantially similar. However, this idea cannot generate strict key collisions, and this result only works for key lengths close to 256.

In [2], RC4 key collision was first discovered. The key pattern is almost the same as in [1], namely, two keys differ at only one byte position ($K_1[i] = K_2[i]$ except $i = t$) and the value difference is $1 (K_1[t] = K_2[t] - 1)$. The intuition behind the collision is that from the first time i touches the different position t, the pattern ensures that there are always only two differences in the internal state as the key scheduling process continues. The difference is absorbed when i touches t for the last time. Please refer to [2] for the detailed description.

In [3], colliding key pairs with hamming distance three were first discovered. The key pattern is totally different from [1] and [2], namely, $K_1[d] = K_2[d] - t, K_1[d+1] = K_2[d+1] + t, K_1[d+t+1] = K_2[d+t+1] - t$. This key pattern shows us a more flexible way in which the two keys can differ from each other.

3 Generalized RC4 Colliding Key Pairs

We found out that RC4 can generate many other colliding key pairs with different key relations, other than those found in [2] and [3]. We formalize all the currently known colliding key pairs into two patterns. We describe them in the following section by first giving the key relations, and then explaining how the two keys with these relations can achieve collisions.

3.1 Notation

- K_1, K_2: a secret key pair with some differences between them.
- $S_{1,i}, S_{2,i}$: S-Boxes corresponding to the secret key pair at time i.
- $i, j_{1,i}, j_{2,i}$: internal states of RC4. When $j_{1,i} = j_{2,i}$, we use j_i to denote.
- d: the first index of the key differences.
- h: hamming distances between the two keys (number of different positions where two keys differ from each other).
- k: the lengths (bytes) of the secret keys.
- n: the number of times the key differences appear during KSA. $n = \lfloor \frac{256+k-1-d}{k} \rfloor$.
- $l_1, ..., l_{h-1}$: the intervals between two consecutive key difference indices.
- l: interval between the first and last key difference indices, $l = \sum_{i=1}^{h-1} l_i$.
- Γ: the set of indices at which two keys differ from each other, $|\Gamma| = h$, $\Gamma = \{\gamma_1, ..., \gamma_h\}$ and $d = \gamma_1$.

3.2 Transitional Pattern

Key relations in Transitional pattern: Let $K_2[i] = K_1[i]+1, i \in \Gamma$, namely, two keys differ from each other at h places, and the value differences at these positions all equal 1.

Transitional pattern has the property that after the first internal state differences are generated, which is due to the key difference, the internal state differences are transferred to the later indices of the S-Box, and these differences exist before the last key difference comes into play during KSA.

Figure 1 illustrates the case in which the secret keys are short, so they will appear several times during KSA. When i first touches the key difference, j difference and two S-Box differences are generated. Notice that Transitional pattern requires that one j equal i. Thus the two S-Box differences generated at the beginning are located next to each other, and meanwhile, we require that S-Box value differences also be one. The dotted line area in the figure shows the three internal state differences generated by the first key difference. The next two j return to the same value, due to the effects of previous j difference (▲) and one S-Box difference(★). Meanwhile, the S-Box difference (★) is transferred to the next key difference index, and this transfer will repeat each time when i touches the next key difference index. The situation for the last appearance of the key is a little bit different. In order to achieve collision, we require that the two S-Box differences ♦, ★ be in consecutive positions just before the last key difference index. The two S-Box differences are absorbed by each other and generate a j difference(▲). Finally, the last key difference is there to absorb the previous j difference and the internal states become the same.

The colliding key pairs found in [2] demonstrate a special case of this pattern, where the hamming distance between two keys can only be one ($|\Gamma| = h = 1$). In our generalized Transitional pattern, two keys can have various hamming distances as the probability allows. Here we give a more detailed example of a 128-byte colliding key pair with hamming distance three, to show how key collision can be achieved. Two keys differ from each other at indices $1, 4$ and 8.

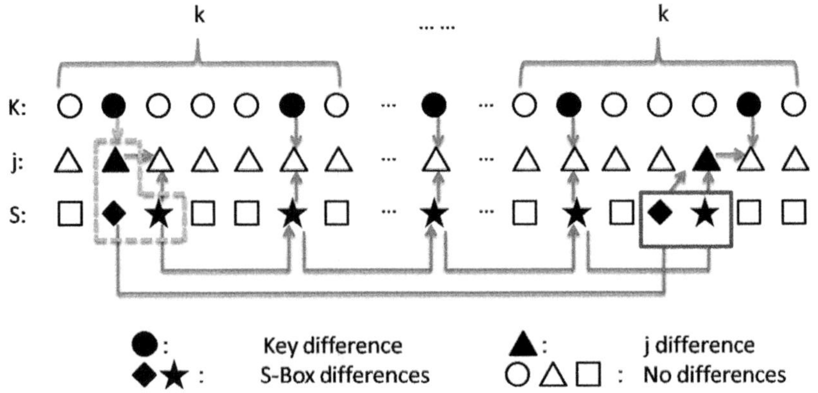

Fig. 1. Transitional Pattern

Table 1. Transitional Pattern, $h = 3, n = 2 (k = 128)$

			Internal State																		Difference
i	$K_1[i]/K_2[i]$	$j_{1,i}/j_{2,i}$	0	1	2	3	4	5	6	7	8	...	129	130	131	132	133	134	135	136	
0	$K_1[0]$	*		1	2																Same
	$K_2[0] = K_1[0]$	*		1	2																
1	$K_1[1]$	1		1	2																j, S-Box
	$K_2[1] = K_1[1] + 1$	2		2	1																
2	$K_1[2]$	4		1			2														S-Box
	$K_2[2] = K_1[2]$	4		2			1														
4	$K_1[4]$	8		1							2										S-Box
	$K_2[4] = K_1[4] + 1$	8		2							1										
8	$K_1[8]$	129		1									2								S-BoX
	$K_2[8] = K_1[8] + 1$	129		2									1								
129	$K_1[1]$	132		1												2					S-Box
	$K_2[1] = K_1[1] + 1$	132		2												1					
132	$K_1[4]$	135		1															2		S-Box
	$K_2[4] = K_1[4] + 1$	135		2															1		
134	$K_1[6]$	1																1	2		S-Box
	$K_2[6] = K_1[6]$	1																2	1		
135	$K_1[7]$	135																1	2		j
	$K_2[7] = K_1[7]$	134																1	2		
136	$K_1[8]$	*																1	2		Same
	$K_2[8] = K_1[8] + 1$	*																1	2		

The S-Box in Table 1 denotes the state after the swap. Notice that when $i = 134$, the other S-Box difference should be swapped to the index 134, but not necessarily from index 1, as shown in the example. The first S-Box difference can be touched by j before 134, to be swapped to other positions. As long as this S-Box difference appears in index 134 when $i = 134$, the pattern works.

3.3 Self-absorbing Pattern

In addition to the above Transitional pattern, we investigate that some of the other RC4 colliding key pairs have the following properties: the internal state differences are generated and absorbed within one key appearance, namely, the differences will not be transferred to the later parts of the S-Box. We can further divide this pattern into two sub-patterns, which are shown in Figures 2(a) and 2(b). Due to the self absorbing property, only one key appearance needs to be illustrated, since the others are the same. The ones found in [3] show a special case of Self-Absorbing pattern 1 ($|\Gamma| = h = 3$).

Key relations in Self-Absorbing pattern 1: $K_2[d] = K_1[d] + t$, $K_2[d+1] = K_1[d+1] - t$ and $K_2[i] = K_1[i] + t$ for $i \in \Gamma \setminus \{\gamma_1, \gamma_2\}$. The value difference t is the same for all h different positions.

Figure 2(a) illustrates the case of hamming distance 4 ($h = 4$) and $t = 2$. The first key difference generates three internal differences (dotted line area). In this illustration, the key value difference is $t = 2$, so the interval between

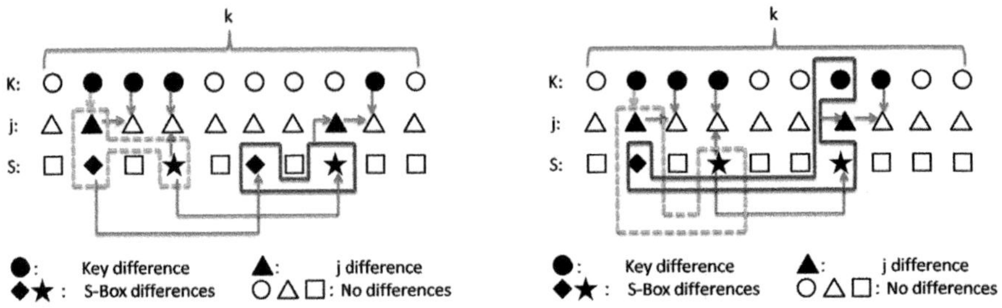

(a) Self-Absorbing Pattern 1 (b) Self-Absorbing Pattern 2

Fig. 2. Self-Absorbing Pattern

two S-Box differences is also required to be t. The second key difference is there to absorb the previous j difference. The third key difference makes the S-Box difference(★) jump to the index just before the last key difference within this key appearance. S-Box difference ♦ should be swapped to the index two intervals from ★ when i touches that index. Then when i touches the S-Box difference ★, two S-Box differences absorb each other and generate a j difference (solid line area). Finally the last key difference is there to absorb the previous j difference, so that the internal states become the same. Table 2 is one example of 128-byte colliding key pair with hamming distance 4. Two keys differ from each other at indices $1, 2, 3$ and 8.

Key relations in Self-Absorbing pattern 2: $K_2[d] = K_1[d] + t$, $K_2[d+1] = K_1[d+1] - t$, $K_2[i] = K_1[i] + t$ for $i \in \Gamma \setminus \{\gamma_1, \gamma_2, \gamma_{h-1}, \gamma_h\}$, $K_2[\gamma_{h-1}] = K_1[\gamma_{h-1}] - t^{'}$, $K_2[\gamma_h] = K_1[\gamma_h] + t^{''}$. For the previous $h-2$ different positions, the value difference t is the same. The last two value differences $t^{'}$ and $t^{''}$, which are determined by the specific key values, can be different values other than t.

Self-Absorbing pattern 2 is almost the same as Self-Absorbing pattern 1, except that in addition to using S-Box differences themselves, it also depends on key differences to absorb the S-Box differences (shown in solid line area in Figure 2(b)) at the final stage. This will allow a more flexible way of how the key value difference can vary, namely, the value difference can choose different values instead of a fixed value, as in the Transitional pattern and Self-Absorbing pattern 1. Table 3 shows a 128-byte colliding key pair example with hamming distance 5. The two keys differ from each other at indices $1, 2, 3, 5$ and 6.

4 Probability Evaluation

In this section, we evaluate the existence probabilities of RC4 colliding key pairs, and give approximate statistics on the scale and distribution of these keys.

4.1 Transitional Pattern

From the previous analysis, we know that colliding key pairs have the property that the key value difference is fixed at one, and the hamming distance can vary.

Table 2. Self-Absorbing Pattern 1, $h = 4, n = 2(k = 128)$

Internal State																					Difference
i	$K_1[i]/K_2[i]$	$j_{1,i}/j_{2,i}$	0	1	2	3	4	5	6	7	8	...	129	130	131	132	133	134	135	136	
0	$K_1[0]$	*		1		3															Same
	$K_2[0] = K_1[0]$	*		1		3															
1	$K_1[1]$	1		1		3															j, S-Box
	$K_2[1] = K_1[1] + 2$	3		3		1															
2	$K_1[2]$	*		1		3															S-Box
	$K_2[2] = K_1[2] - 2$	*		3		1															
3	$K_1[3]$	7		1						3											S-Box
	$K_2[3] = K_1[3] + 2$	7		3						1											
5	$K_1[5]$	1						1		3											S-Box
	$K_2[5] = K_1[5]$	1						3		1											
7	$K_1[7]$	7						1		3											j
	$K_2[7] = K_1[7]$	5						1		3											
8	$K_1[8]$	*						1		3											Same
	$K_2[8] = K_1[8] + 2$	*						1		3											
129	$K_1[1]$	129											129		131						j, S-Box
	$K_2[1] = K_1[1] + 2$	131											131		129						
130	$K_1[2]$	*											129		131						S-Box
	$K_2[2] = K_1[2] - 2$	*											131		129						
131	$K_1[3]$	135											129						131		S-Box
	$K_2[3] = K_1[3] + 2$	135											131						129		
133	$K_1[5]$	129															129		131		S-Box
	$K_2[5] = K_1[5]$	129															131		129		
135	$K_1[7]$	135															129		131		j
	$K_2[7] = K_1[7]$	133															129		131		
136	$K_1[8]$	*															129		131		Same
	$K_2[8] = K_1[8] + 2$	*															129		131		

We divide the whole process into three phases as shown in Figure 1, namely, the starting phase (first appearance of the key), the ending phase (last appearance of the key) and the repeating phase (middle repeating parts).

Starting Phase. First, before i touches d, j can not touch d or $d+1$ with probability $(\frac{254}{256})^d$. When i touches d, $j_1 = d$ and $j_2 = d+1$ with probability $\frac{1}{256}$. For each of the other key difference indices, we will pay the probability $\frac{1}{256}$ each, totally $(\frac{1}{256})^{h-1}$. When i is between two consecutive key difference indices, the pattern requires that j does not touch the later key difference index, otherwise i will never be able to touch the later S-Box difference again. This will add $(\frac{255}{256})^{l_1-2}(\frac{255}{256})^{l_2-1}\cdots(\frac{255}{256})^{l_{h-1}-1}(\frac{255}{256})^{k-l-1} = (\frac{255}{256})^{k-h-1}$ to the total probability cost. Thus, the totally probability in the starting phase is $(\frac{1}{256})^h(\frac{254}{256})^d(\frac{255}{256})^{k-h-1}$.

Repeating Phase. Key will appear $n-2$ times during the repeating phase. For each key, the procedure is as follows. When i touches one key difference index, $\frac{1}{256}$ probability will be paid, $(\frac{1}{256})^h$ in total. When i is between two difference indices, it is not allowed to touch the later one (same as starting phase), this will add probability $(\frac{255}{256})^{k-h}$ in the repeating phase. Thus, the probability that

Table 3. Self-Absorbing pattern 2, $h = 5, n = 2(k = 128)$

Internal State																		Difference
i	$K_1[i]/K_2[i]$	$j_{1,i}/j_{2,i}$	0	1	2	3	4	5	6	...	129	130	131	132	133	134		
0	$K_1[0]$	*		1		3												Same
	$K_2[0] = K_1[0]$	*		1		3												
1	$K_1[1]$	1		1		3												j, S-Box
	$K_2[1] = K_1[1] + 2$	3		3		1												
2	$K_1[2]$	*		1		3												S-Box
	$K_2[2] = K_1[2] - 2$	*		3		1												
3	$K_1[3]$	5		1				3										S-Box
	$K_2[3] = K_1[3] + 2$	5		3				1										
5	$K_1[5]$	5		1				3										j
	$K_2[5] = K_1[5] - 2$	1		1				3										
6	$K_1[6]$	*		1				3										Same
	$K_2[6] = K_1[6] + 4$	*		1				3										
129	$K_1[1]$	129									129		131					j, S-Box
	$K_2[1] = K_1[1] + 2$	131									131		131					
130	$K_1[2]$	*									129		131					S-Box
	$K_2[2] = K_1[2] - 2$	*									131		129					
131	$K_1[3]$	133									129				131			S-Box
	$K_2[3] = K_1[3] + 2$	133									131				129			
133	$K_1[5]$	133									129				131			j
	$K_2[5] = K_1[5] - 2$	129									129				131			
134	$K_1[6]$	*									129				131			Same
	$K_2[6] = K_1[6] + 4$	*									129				131			

one key appearance must pay is $(\frac{1}{256})^h(\frac{255}{256})^{k-h}$. Since the key will repeat $n-2$ times, the total probability is $(\frac{1}{256})^{h(n-2)}(\frac{255}{256})^{(k-h)(n-2)}$.

Ending Phase. We need probability $(\frac{1}{256})^{h-1}$ for the key difference indices except for the last one, and when i touches the index two intervals before the last key difference, the other S-Box difference needs to be swapped here with probability $\frac{1}{256}$. When i touches the index before the last key difference, we need two S-Box differences to swap with each other with probability $\frac{1}{256}$. And as in the repeating and starting phases, j can not touch the later key difference index when i is between the two. In the ending phase, this probability can be easily calculated as $(\frac{255}{256})^{l_1-1}(\frac{255}{256})^{l_2-1}\cdots(\frac{255}{256})^{l_{h-1}-1} = (\frac{255}{256})^{l-h+1}$. Thus the total probability in the ending phase is $(\frac{1}{256})^{h+1}(\frac{255}{256})^{l-h+1}$. By multiplying the probabilities in the three phases, we get the following theorem.

Theorem 1. *The probability of two keys with relations in Transitional pattern forming a colliding key pair, Prob(trans), is given as follows:*

$$Prob(tran) = \left(\frac{1}{256}\right)^{h\times n+1}\left(\frac{254}{256}\right)^{d}\left(\frac{255}{256}\right)^{(k-h)\times(n-3)+l-h} \approx O\left(\left(\frac{1}{256}\right)^{h\times n}\right)$$

4.2 Self-absorbing Pattern 1

We only need to evaluate the probability of one key appearance, the other parts just repeat the first key appearance procedure. The value difference t is the same for all different positions in Self-Absorbing pattern 1.

Before i touches index d, we need $S_d[d] + t = S_d[d+t]$ with probability $\frac{255}{256} \times (\frac{254}{256})^{d-1} + \frac{1}{256}$ (Refer to [3] for the proof). When i touches d, we require $j_d = d$ with probability $\frac{1}{256}$. Then for i between $d+1$ and $d+t-1$, index $d+t$ should not be touched with probability $(\frac{255}{256})^{t-1}$. Then we need one of the differences (★ in Figure 2) to appear at indices $\Gamma \bigcup \{\gamma_h - 1\} \setminus \{\gamma_1, \gamma_2, \gamma_3, \gamma_h\}$ when i touches them, and j cannot touch the later key difference position when i is between the consecutive two of them. The probability can be calculated in the same way as in the repeating phase in Transitional pattern, namely, $(\frac{1}{256})^{h-3}(\frac{255}{256})^{l-t-h+3}$. Also we need the S-Box difference (♦) to be at position $d+l-t-1$ and it cannot be touched when i is between $d+l-t$ and $d+l-1$. So this will give us probability $\frac{1}{256}(\frac{255}{256})^{t-1}$. Finally, when i touches index $d+l-1$, we need $j_{d+l-1} = d+l-1$ with probability $\frac{1}{256}$. By multiplying them together, we get the probability of one key appearance $(\frac{1}{256})^h(\frac{255}{256})^{l+t-h+1}(\frac{255}{256}(\frac{254}{256})^{d-1} + \frac{1}{256})$. Raise this probability to the power of n due to the n times appearance of the key during KSA, we get the following theorem for the total probability of Self-Absorbing pattern 1.

Theorem 2. *The probability of two keys with relations in Self-Absorbing pattern 1 forming a colliding key pair, Prob(self1), is given as follows:*

$$Prob(self1) = \left(\frac{1}{256}\right)^{h\times n} \left(\frac{255}{256}\right)^{n\times(l+t-h+1)} \left(\frac{255}{256}\left(\frac{254}{256}\right)^{d-1} + \frac{1}{256}\right)^n$$
$$\approx O\left(\left(\frac{1}{256}\right)^{h\times n}\right)$$

4.3 Self-absorbing Pattern 2

Self-Absorbing pattern 2 behaves very similarly to Self-Absorbing pattern 1, except at the final stage. Recall Figure 3, which shows that the S-Box differences are absorbed by both key differences and S-Box itself. So in this pattern, we don't need the S-Box difference (♦) to be t intervals from another difference (★) in the final part. So we only need to cut off the probability for ♦ to be transferred to the corresponding position in the final stage in Self-Absorbing pattern 1, namely, $\frac{1}{256}(\frac{255}{256})^{t-1}$. So the total probability for Self-Absorbing pattern 2 is as follows.

Theorem 3. *The probability of two keys with relations in Self-Absorbing pattern 2 forming a colliding key pair, Prob(self2), is given as follows:*

$$Prob(self2) = \left(\frac{1}{256}\right)^{(h-1)\times n} \left(\frac{255}{256}\right)^{n\times(l-h)} \left(\frac{255}{256}\left(\frac{254}{256}\right)^{d-1} + \frac{1}{256}\right)^{n}$$
$$\approx O\left(\left(\frac{1}{256}\right)^{(h-1)\times n}\right)$$

We can conclude that the probabilities of both Transitional pattern and Self-Absorbing patterns are mainly affected by hamming distance h and length of the secret key. The probability decreases as the hamming distance h becomes larger or the key length k becomes shorter (n becomes larger). Table 4 and 5 gives the probability data for different key lengths and hamming distances according to Theorems 1,2 and 3. According to the previous analysis, we know that Self-Absorbing pattern 1 requires $h \geq 3$, and Self-Absorbing pattern 2 requires $h \geq 5$.

Table 4. Probabilities of colliding key pairs in Transitional pattern

h / $n(k)$	1	2	3	4	5
8(32)	2^{-64}	2^{-128}	2^{-192}	2^{-256}	2^{-320}
4(64)	2^{-32}	2^{-64}	2^{-96}	2^{-128}	2^{-160}
2(128)	2^{-16}	2^{-32}	2^{-48}	2^{-64}	2^{-80}
1(256)	2^{-8}	2^{-16}	2^{-24}	2^{-32}	2^{-40}

Table 5. Probabilities of colliding key pairs in Self-Absorbing pattern 1 (Self-Absorbing pattern 2)

h / $n(k)$	3	4	5
8(32)	$2^{-192}(-)$	$2^{-256}(-)$	$2^{-320}(2^{-256})$
4(64)	$2^{-96}(-)$	$2^{-128}(-)$	$2^{-160}(2^{-128})$
2(128)	$2^{-48}(-)$	$2^{-64}(-)$	$2^{-80}(2^{-64})$
1(256)	$2^{-24}(-)$	$2^{-32}(-)$	$2^{-40}(2^{-32})$

5 Application to RC4-Hash Collisions

In INDOCRYPT 2006, a new hash function name "RC4-Hash" based on RC4 was proposed. It followed the "wide pipe" hash function design principle proposed by Lucks [13] and it was claimed to be as efficient as some widely-used hash functions, such as SHA-family and MD-family, while also ruling out all possible generic attacks against those famous hash functions. First hash collision was found in [16] by exploiting the idea of Finney States [15]. We show in this section that totally different from [16], collisions can also be found by making use of previous key collision pattern. First we briefly describe the RC4-Hash algorithm, and then we give the collision analysis. For a more detailed description of the hash function, please refer to [14].

5.1 RC4-Hash

$\{0,1\}^{<2^{64}}$ denotes the set of all messages whose length is at most $2^{64}-1$. l is the output length of the RC4 hash function, $16 \leq l \leq 64$. RC4-Hash function can be described as $\{0,1\}^{<2^{64}} \rightarrow \{0,1\}^{8l}$.

Padding Rule: $\text{pad}(M) = \text{bin}_8(l)||M||1||0^k||\text{bin}_{64}(|M|) = M_1|| \cdots ||M_t$, where M_t is the last 512-bit block. $\text{bin}_{64}(|M|)$ is the 64-bit binary representation of the number of bits of M. k is the least non-negative integer such that $8 + |M| + 1 + k + 64 \equiv 0 \bmod (512)$ and $|M_i| = 512$.

Iteration Phase: Let $(S_0, j_0) = (S^{IV}, 0)$ be an initial value. The compression function C is invoked iteratively as follows:

$$(S_0, j_0) \overset{M_1}{\to} (S_1, j_1) \overset{M_2}{\to} \cdots (S_{t-1}, j_{t-1}) \overset{M_t}{\to} (S_t, j_t)$$

where $(S, j) \overset{X}{\to} (S^*, j^*)$ denotes $C((S, j), X) = (S^*, j^*)$.

Post-Processing: Let (S_t, j_t) be the internal state after the classical iteration. Compute $S_{t+1} = S_0 \circ S_t$ and $j_{t+1} = j_t$. Then compute $HBG_l(OWT(S_{t+1}, j_{t+1}))$.

$C((S,j),X)$	$OWT((S,j))$	$HBG_l((S,j))$
for $i = 0$ **to** 255	Temp1 $= S$	**for** $i = 1$ to l
$j \leftarrow j + S[i] + X[r(i)]$	**for** $i = 0$ to 511	$j \leftarrow j + S[i]$
Swap(S[i],S[j]);	$j \leftarrow j + S[i]$	Swap($S[i], S[j]$)
Return (S,j)	Swap($S[i], S[j]$)	Out $= S[S[i] + S[j]]$
	Temp2 $= S$	
	$S =$ Temp1 $\circ$ Temp2 $\circ$ Temp1	
	Return (S, j)	

$\circ$ denotes the composition of the permutations. Function $r : [256] \to [64]$ reorders the 64-byte message block. There are four r mapping functions(r_0, r_1, r_2, r_3) corresponding to the four iteration processes for each message block. In other words, each message block is reordered three times (r_0 is the identity permutation) during one iteration process. Refer to appendices for S^{IV} and r_i.

5.2 Collisions for RC4-Hash Function

Let's look at the iteration phase carefully. After message is padded, it is cut into 64-byte blocks, and each block is processed by the compression function C four times. The compression function C is actually the KSA in RC4, and the input message block can be seen as a 64-byte secret key, except for two differences. First, the message block is reordered by using r_i functions three times (instead of using the same 64-byte key which appears 4 times during KSA) and second, instead of the identity permutation used at the beginning of KSA, a shuffled S-Box S^{IV} is used as the initial S-Box. The similarities between the compression function and KSA gave us the intuition that we could make use of the RC4 key collision to find collisions for RC4-Hash. Now let's take a look at how these two differences can affect our search. In both Transitional pattern and Self-Absorbing pattern, when i touches the first different position, we need $S_d[d] + t = S_d[d+t]$. This is very easy to achieve when the initial S-Box is an identity permutation (j does not touch index d or index $d+t$ before i touches index d). But still we can make this happen with S^{IV} (Several candidates are available by checking S^{IV} carefully, and we use one of them in the following example). For the transitional pattern, the reordering of the message will not have much effect on finding collisions, because even though the different positions between the two messages change three times, we do not have to pay extra probabilities because there are no restrictions among these different message positions. Thus it works just the same as finding key collisions in the Transitional pattern. However, there are strict relations between the different positions in Self-Absorbing pattern (Self-Absorbing pattern 1: $K_2[d] = K_1[d] + t$, $K_2[d+1] = K_1[d+1] - t$ and $K_2[i] = K_1[i] + t$ for $i \in \Gamma \setminus \{\gamma_1, \gamma_2\}$), and the reordering of the message breaks those relations at the later rounds in the compression function, thus making it difficult to find a collision by using this pattern.

Here we give a concrete collision example by making use of the Transitional pattern. Since the initial S-Box S^{IV} is not an identity permutation, we need to first make two consecutive indices have the value difference one. There are several candidates we can use, by examining the S^{IV} carefully, we choose to let $S^{IV}[24] = 53$ appear in index 27 when i touches it, and $S^{IV}[28] = 54$ should not be touched by j before. Then we have two values, 53 and 54, next to each other at indices 27 and 28 when i touches index 27. The four iterations of the 64-byte message block during the compression function C can be seen as a KSA procedure with a 64-byte key. Since the message will be reordered three times, we need to check the mapping function r_i to identify the different positions. According to the Transitional pattern, in order to achieve a collision, two messages should differ from each other at index 27, and the value difference should be one. According to r_1, r_2 and r_3, the differences between two messages will appear at indices 125, 179 and 213. After i touches 213, the two internal states become the same. Figure 4 describes the above collision by using Transitional pattern during one compression function C (63-byte message plus one padded byte).

From the above analysis, we know the complexity is equal to the key collision complexity in Transitional pattern, which is approximately equal to $O((\frac{1}{256})^{h \times n})$. In RC4-Hash with $k = 64 (n = 4)$, we can find a collision with the smallest complexity $O(2^{32})$ when two messages have the smallest hamming distance $h = 1$. Notice that our method results in higher complexity than in [16], where complexity is $O(2^9)$.

Here is the collision pair we found by using the RC4 key collision Transitional pattern with one day computation on an Intel Core i7 CPU PC (only one core was used). Messages and hash outputs are represented in Hexadecimal form. In our example, we set the output length l to be 16 bytes.

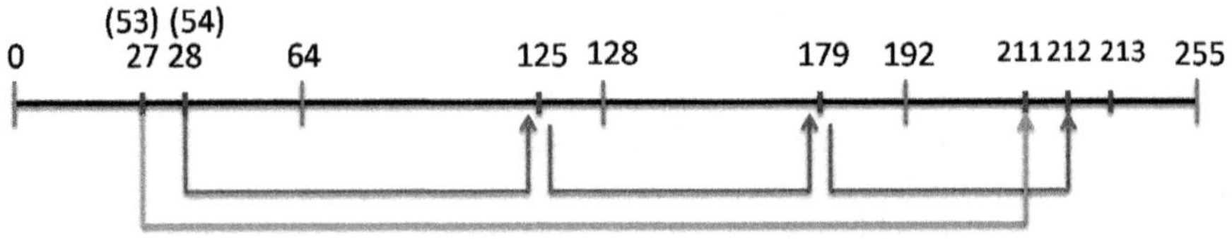

Fig. 3. RC4-Hash collision using Transitional Pattern

Message1(Message2): d8 4b be e4 ac c5 e3 c6 59 16 db b1 c2 7a de c2 62 5e 40 91 2c 7e de 4a f3 55 **8b(8c)** 2c 8f 96 f0 50 f7 54 78 3a 35 f5 ee 7e 76 72 35 83 0a e3 26 b5 06 7f 3b 1e b5 41 1c 1b ec 4e 80 c2 ba 64 9b

Hash Output: 76 54 b9 c6 65 f9 99 83 1b 66 c8 af 5f 0c 68 fa

5.3 Discussion

From the above analysis, we can see that the design of the compression function by modifying KSA using S^{IV} and mapping function r_i cannot eliminate the KSA collision property. Here we propose one method to mitigate the attack by redesigning S^{IV} carefully. Recall in the previous collision example, we need two values with value difference one to be next to each other when i touches the smaller one (Values 53 and 54 at indices 27 and 28 when i touches index 27). If we can prevent this from happening, then we can eliminate the collision. That is to say, if the index of value 54 is greater than 63 in S^{IV}, our Transitional pattern will not work. Generally speaking, design S^{IV} satisfies $|S^{IV}[i]^{-1} - (S^{IV}[i]+1)^{-1}| \geq 64 - \text{MIN}(S^{IV}[i]^{-1}, (S^{IV}[i]+1)^{-1})$ (Transitional pattern) for $0 < i < 64$, where v^{-1} denotes the index of value v. This will eliminate the collisions caused by the RC4 key collision patterns we found.

6 Conclusion

In this paper, we have shown that RC4 can generate many other colliding key pairs with various hamming distances. We analyzed the behavior of these colliding key pairs and formalized them into two patterns, which include the newly discovered colliding key pairs we found, and also the ones found in previous research. We further estimated the collision probabilities for all the RC4 colliding key pairs, and clarified the relations among collision probability, key length and hamming distance. Finally, we showed how the RC4 key collision patterns can be used to find collisions for RC4-Hash which was proposed at INDOCRYPT 2006. We leave how to use the mitigating methods proposed in this paper and [16] to construct secure RC4-Hash function as future work.

References

1. Grosul, A.L., Wallach, D.S.: A Related-Key Cryptanalysis of RC4. Technical Report TR-00-358, Department of Computer Science, Rice University (2000), `http://cohesion.rice.edu/engineering/computerscience/tr/TRDownload.cfm?SDID=126`
2. Matsui, M.: Key Collisions of the RC4 Stream Cipher. In: Dunkelman, O., Preneel, B. (eds.) FSE 2009. LNCS, vol. 5665, pp. 1–24. Springer, Heidelberg (2009)
3. Chen, J., Miyaji, A.: A New Class of RC4 Colliding Key Pairs With Greater Hamming Distance. In: Kwak, J., Deng, R.H., Won, Y., Wang, G. (eds.) ISPEC 2010. LNCS, vol. 6047, pp. 30–44. Springer, Heidelberg (2010)
4. Miyaji, A., Sukegawa, M.: New Analysis Based on Correlations of RC4 PRGA with Nonzero-Bit Differences. IEICE Trans. Fundamentals E93-A(6), 1066–1077 (2010)

5. Anonymous: RC4 Source Code. CypherPunks mailing list (September 9, 1994), http://cypherpunks.venona.com/date/1994/09/msg00304.html, http://groups.google.com/group/sci.crypt/msg/10a300c9d21afca0
6. Roos, A.: A Class of Weak Keys in the RC4 Stream Cipher (1995), http://marcel.wanda.ch/Archive/WeakKeys
7. Mantin, I., Shamir, A.: A Practical Attack on Broadcast RC4. In: Matsui, M. (ed.) FSE 2001. LNCS, vol. 2355, pp. 152–164. Springer, Heidelberg (2002)
8. Paul, S., Preneel, B.: A New Weakness in the RC4 Keystream Generator and an Approach to Improve Security of the Cipher. In: Roy, B., Meier, W. (eds.) FSE 2004. LNCS, vol. 3017, pp. 245–259. Springer, Heidelberg (2004)
9. Fluhrer, S., Mantin, I., Shamir, A.: Weaknesses in the Key Scheduling Algorithm of RC4. In: Vaudenay, S., Youssef, A.M. (eds.) SAC 2001. LNCS, vol. 2259, pp. 1–24. Springer, Heidelberg (2001)
10. Klein, A.: Attacks on the RC4 Stream Cipher. Designs, Codes and Cryptography 48(3), 269–286 (2008)
11. Tews, E., Weinmann, R.P., Pyshkin, A.: Breaking 104 Bit WEP in Less than 60 Seconds. In: Kim, S., Yung, M., Lee, H.-W. (eds.) WISA 2007. LNCS, vol. 4867, pp. 188–202. Springer, Heidelberg (2008)
12. Vaudenay, S., Vuagnoux, M.: Passive-Only Key Recovery Attacks on RC4. In: Adams, C., Miri, A., Wiener, M. (eds.) SAC 2007. LNCS, vol. 4876, pp. 344–359. Springer, Heidelberg (2007)
13. Lucks, S.: A Failure-Friendly Design Principle for Hash Functions. In: Roy, B. (ed.) ASIACRYPT 2005. LNCS, vol. 3788, pp. 19–35. Springer, Heidelberg (2005)
14. Chang, D., Gupta, K.C., Nandi, M.: RC4-Hash: A New Hash Function Based on RC4. In: Barua, R., Lange, T. (eds.) INDOCRYPT 2006. LNCS, vol. 4329, pp. 80–94. Springer, Heidelberg (2006)
15. Finney, H.: An RC4 cycle that can't happen. Newsgroup post in sci.crypt (September 1994)
16. Indesteege, S., Preneel, B.: Collision for RC4-Hash. In: Wu, T.-C., Lei, C.-L., Rijmen, V., Lee, D.-T. (eds.) ISC 2008. LNCS, vol. 5222, pp. 355–366. Springer, Heidelberg (2008)

A RC4-Hash (r_i Functions and S^{IV})

r1 : 0, 55, 46, 37, 28, 19, 10, 1, 56, 47, 38, 29, 20, 11, 2, 57, 48, 39, 30, 21, 12, 3, 58, 49, 40, 31, 22, 13, 4, 59, 50, 41, 32, 23, 14, 5, 60, 51, 42, 33, 24, 15, 6, 61, 52, 43, 34, 25, 16, 7, 62, 53, 44, 35, 26, 17, 8, 63, 54, 45, 36, **27**, 18, 9.

r2: 0, 57, 50, 43, 36, 29, 22, 15, 8, 1, 58, 51, 44, 37, 30, 23, 16, 9, 2, 59, 52, 45, 38, 31, 24, 17, 10, 3, 60, 53, 46, 39, 32, 25, 18, 11, 4, 61, 54, 47, 40, 33, 26, 19, 12, 5, 62, 55, 48, 41, 34, **27**, 20, 13, 6, 63, 56, 49, 42, 35, 28, 21, 14, 7.

r3 : 0, 47, 30, 13, 60, 43, 26, 9, 56, 39, 22, 5, 52, 35, 18, 1, 48, 31, 14, 61, 44, **27**, 10, 57, 40, 23, 6, 53, 36, 19, 2, 49, 32, 15, 62, 45, 28, 11, 58, 41, 24, 7, 54, 37, 20, 3, 50, 33, 16, 63, 46, 29, 12, 59, 42, 25, 8, 55, 38, 21, 4, 51, 34, 17.

S^{IV}:

145, 57, 133, 33, 65, 49, 83, 61, 113, 171, 63, 155, 74, 50, 132, 248, 236, 218, 192, 217, 23, 36, 79, 72, **53**, 210, 38, 59, **54**, 208, 185, 12, 233, 189, 159, 169, 240, 156,

184, 200, 209, 173, 20, 252, 96, 211, 143, 101, 44, 223, 118, 1, 232, 35, 239, 9, 114, 109, 161, 183, 88, 66, 219, 78, 157, 174, 187, 193, 199, 99, 52, 120, 89, 166, 18, 76, 241, 13, 225, 6, 146, 151, 207, 177, 103, 45, 148, 32, 29, 234, 7, 16, 19, 91, 108, 186, 116, 62, 203, 158, 180, 149, 67, 105, 247, 3, 128, 215, 121, 127, 179, 175, 251, 104, 246, 98, 140, 11, 134, 221, 24, 69, 190, 154, 253, 168, 68, 230, 58, 153, 188, 224, 100, 129, 124, 162, 15, 117, 231, 150, 237, 64, 22, 152, 165, 235, 227, 139, 201, 84, 213, 77, 80, 197, 250, 126, 202, 39, 0, 94, 42, 243, 228, 87, 82, 27, 141, 60, 160, 46, 125, 112, 181, 242, 167, 92, 198, 172, 170, 55, 115, 30, 107, 17, 56, 31, 135, 229, 40, 111, 37, 222, 182, 25, 43, 119, 244, 191, 122, 102, 21, 93, 97, 131, 164, 10, 130, 47, 176, 238, 212, 144, 41, 14, 249, 220, 34, 136, 71, 48, 142, 73, 123, 204, 206, 4, 216, 196, 214, 137, 255, 195, 26, 8, 51, 178, 2, 138, 254, 90, 194, 81, 245, 106, 95, 75, 86, 163, 205, 70, 226, 28, 147, 85, 5, 110.

B RC4 Colliding Key Pairs

B.1 Transitional Pattern, h=3, k=128. $K_1(K_2)$

71, **185(186)**, 1, 63, **192(193)**, 206, 161, 132, **114(115)**, 12, 69, 19, 160, 125, 44, 78, 26, 119, 59, 18, 200, 221, 130, 215, 157, 208, 205, 210, 165, 96, 99, 44, 68, 17, 146, 161, 227, 188, 123, 218, 172, 154, 100, 99, 92, 205, 235, 78, 179, 8, 5, 1, 142, 115, 31, 245, 151, 170, 140, 140, 104, 198, 128, 189, 145, 163, 42, 178, 113, 223, 135, 21, 243, 236, 90, 141, 70, 78, 96, 8, 200, 8, 161, 123, 112, 57, 190, 224, 179, 196, 41, 87, 24, 105, 231, 41, 84, 12, 139, 107, 82, 228, 130, 23, 148, 38, 196, 3, 238, 164, 2, 233, 22, 41, 182, 130, 201, 95, 211, 140, 11, 248, 189, 6, 109, 27, 92, 1.

B.2 Self-absorbing Pattern 1, h=4, k=128. $K_1(K_2)$

41, **215(217)**, **60(58)**, **197(199)**, 78, 163, 94, 159, **253(255)**, 76, 84, 228, 174, 159, 214, 86, 52, 146, 24, 235, 130, 98, 91, 117, 23, 44, 155, 55, 136, 46, 182, 76, 55, 200, 20, 25, 171, 59, 184, 240, 6, 178, 173, 29, 33, 126, 49, 151, 200, 185, 218, 219, 60, 188, 14, 49, 51, 215, 123, 58, 26, 222, 26, 96, 177, 14, 13, 175, 9, 90, 106, 179, 57, 183, 103, 183, 55, 51, 40, 163, 193, 93, 187, 151, 209, 145, 42, 10, 70, 166, 179, 136, 166, 206, 153, 21, 100, 241, 226, 120, 165, 74, 159, 125, 18, 14, 77, 151, 79, 129, 201, 19, 23, 109, 75, 14, 29, 96, 118, 87, 75, 225, 31, 28, 248, 126, 161, 148.

B.3 Self-absorbing Pattern 2, h=5, k=128. $K_1(K_2)$

222, **34(36)**, **98(96)**, **157(159)**, 174, **75(73)**, **231(235)**, 9, 221, 154, 135, 215, 175, 166, 27, 58, 91, 226, 252, 225, 7, 164, 124, 198, 65, 132, 222, 132, 205, 184, 196, 21, 86, 41, 124, 121, 115, 138, 108, 2, 26, 137, 55, 224, 46, 92, 109, 63, 15, 156, 104, 144, 101, 3, 41, 224, 98, 15, 185, 198, 152, 226, 148, 111, 2, 136, 35, 69, 159, 211, 250, 47, 130, 40, 200, 19, 97, 205, 250, 226, 34, 243, 45, 120, 86, 175, 52, 157, 145, 214, 138, 107, 182, 50, 247, 20, 121, 20, 144, 40, 172, 236, 150, 77, 196, 200, 158, 198, 44, 206, 73, 90, 169, 64, 152, 1, 82, 163, 192, 235, 246, 24, 121, 185, 234, 158, 48, 200.

On the Indifferentiability of the Grøstl Hash Function

Elena Andreeva, Bart Mennink, and Bart Preneel

Dept. Electrical Engineering, ESAT/COSIC and IBBT
Katholieke Universiteit Leuven, Belgium
{elena.andreeva,bart.mennink,bart.preneel}@esat.kuleuven.be

Abstract. The notion of indifferentiability, introduced by Maurer et al., is an important criterion for the security of hash functions. Concretely, it ensures that a hash function has no structural design flaws and thus guarantees security against generic attacks up to the proven bounds. In this work we prove the indifferentiability of Grøstl, a second round SHA-3 hash function candidate. Grøstl combines characteristics of the wide-pipe and chop-Merkle-Damgård iterations and uses two distinct permutations P and Q internally. Under the assumption that P and Q are random l-bit permutations, where l is the iterated state size of Grøstl, we prove that the advantage of a distinguisher to differentiate Grøstl from a random oracle is upper bounded by $O((Kq)^4/2^l)$, where the distinguisher makes at most q queries of length at most K blocks. This result implies that Grøstl behaves like a random oracle up to $q = O(2^{n/2})$ queries, where n is the output size. Furthermore, we show that the output transformation of Grøstl, as well as 'Grøstail' (the composition of the final compression function and the output transformation), are clearly differentiable from a random oracle. This rules out indifferentiability proofs which rely on the idealness of the final state transformation.

1 Introduction

Hash functions are a basic building block in cryptography. Formally, a hash function maps a bit string of arbitrary length to an output string of fixed length, $\mathcal{H} : \mathbb{Z}_2^* \to \mathbb{Z}_2^l$. An established practice in the design of hash functions is to first construct a fixed input length compression function, e.g. $f : \mathbb{Z}_2^l \times \mathbb{Z}_2^l \to \mathbb{Z}_2^l$, and then iterate it to allow the processing of arbitrarily long strings. The most popular iteration principle is the strengthened Merkle-Damgård [12, 18] design[1]. Common hash functions, such as members of the SHA and MD family, incorporate the Merkle-Damgård method in their design. However, recent attacks on the widely used SHA-1 and MD5 [22, 23] have rendered these designs insecure. This grim situation has triggered the launch of the SHA-3 competition [20] for the selection of a new secure hash function algorithm by NIST (National Institute of Standards and Technology). In the current second round of the competition, 14 candidates are under active evaluation.

[1] Throughout, we will refer to it as the 'Merkle-Damgård design'.

J.A. Garay and R. De Prisco (Eds.): SCN 2010, LNCS 6280, pp. 88–105, 2010.

These 14 candidates use a wide variety of iterative modes. Some of the designs still follow the basic Merkle-Damgård iteration. Others either add new features to it, or simply propose different constructions. Candidates from the latter two classes include iterations based on the chop-Merkle-Damgård [13], HAIFA [7], wide-pipe [16] and Sponge [5] design strategies. The main advantage of the basic Merkle-Damgård construction is its collision security guarantee under the assumption that the underlying compression function is collision resistant [12, 18]. Other important hash function security properties, such as second preimage and preimage security are, however, not preserved by the Merkle-Damgård iteration [1]. Moreover, the extension attack shows that the Merkle-Damgård hash function is clearly differentiable from a monolithic random oracle [11].

A natural question that arises with the emerge of new iterative designs is to identify the security properties achieved by these constructions. Other than the classical collision, second preimage and preimage security properties, the *indifferentiability* property has gained more recent attention due to the advancements in the theoretical differentiability model of Maurer et al. [17] and their further development in the context of hashing [11, 2, 9, 10]. Indifferentiability is an important security criterion because it ensures that the hash function has no structural design flaws in composition. Such a result provides a guarantee that no generic attacks (attacks on the iteration which assume ideal behavior of the underlying primitives) up to the proven bounds are possible.

In this work we analyze the indifferentiability of the Grøstl SHA-3 candidate [15]. Grøstl borrows characteristics mainly from the wide-pipe and the chop-Merkle-Damgård iterations: the iterated state is wider than the final hash output, which classifies it as a type of a wide-pipe design. The iterative message processing together with a final state truncation in Grøstl resemble the chop-Merkle-Damgård hash function with the added difference of an output transformation before truncation. More concretely, Grøstl processes its inputs by first calling the compression function f iteratively, then applying a final output transformation to the state and finally truncating the result to the desired output length. The compression function f is built out of two permutations P and Q and the output transformation is designed on top of the permutation P.

1.1 Our Result

Indifferentiability results on hash functions can be obtained following several different approaches. One way to argue indifferentiability is to assume ideal behavior of the first layer components (i.e., the underlying compression functions), and prove the result for the concrete composition of interest [11, 10]. Dodis et al. [14] relax the assumption on the internal compression functions from a random oracle to preimage awareness. If a composition is preimage aware, which they show is true for the Merkle-Damgård iteration when the compression function is preimage aware itself, then they prove indifferentiability by assuming idealness only of the final extra transformation. Both approaches turn out futile for the Grøstl hash function: fixed points for the compression function can be found easily (as already observed in [15]), and also the final output transformation is clearly differentiable from a random function. Even stronger, if we consider the composition of the final compression function f and the output transformation (with and without truncation), which we refer to as 'Grøstail', then we prove that Grøstail is differentiable from a random function. We do so by demonstrating an attack that tricks any simulator for the indifferentiability of Grøstail in only three oracle queries. This result indicates that Grøstail is highly non-random and therefore the results of [14] could not be applied directly.

The next attempt for an indifferentiability proof for the Grøstl hash function is to refine the level of modularity and to explore the second layer integral components, i.e. the permutations P and Q. In a similar fashion, Coron et al. [11] prove that the chop-Merkle-Damgård construction with Davies-Meyer (DM) [21] compression function is indifferentiable from a random oracle assuming an ideal behavior from the block cipher underlying the DM function. While the Grøstl iteration is a type of a DM chop-Merkle-Damgård construction, the latter result cannot be applied here due to clear design differences, such as the presence of an output transformation. Instead, to prove indifferentiability of the Grøstl hash function we start from scratch by assuming ideal behavior of the underlying permutations.

The proof is constructed following the indifferentiability theoretical framework by [17]. We build a simulator for the permutations P and Q that is granted access to a random oracle. The goal of the simulator is to answer its queries, such that it is hard for a distinguisher to tell apart the interactions with the Grøstl hash functions and truly random permutations from the ones with a random oracle and the simulator. The simulator is also consistent with the outputs of the random oracle. Although our proof is geared towards the concrete design of the Grøstl hash function, we believe its underlying idea can be applied to similar constructions of independent interest. We prove that the advantage of a distinguisher to differentiate Grøstl from a random oracle is upper bounded by $O((Kq)^4/2^l)$, where the distinguisher makes at most q queries of length at most K blocks to its oracles. Here, l is the iterated state size which, for Grøstl, is at least twice as large as the output hash size n. Intuitively, this means that Grøstl behaves like a random oracle up to $q = O(2^{n/2})$ queries.

The JH [6], Keccak [4] and Shabal [8] SHA-3 second round candidates have recently been also proved indifferentiable. All of them claim security beyond the birthday bound (with respect to the output length n). In particular, JH is proven indifferentiable up to $O(q^3/2^{l-m})$, and Keccak and Shabal up to $O((Kq)^2/2^{l-m})$ where l is the size of the chaining value and m the number of message bits compressed in one application of the compression function. We notice, however, that this is an unfair comparison: JH, Keccak and Shabal have iterated state sizes l of $1024, 1600$ and 1408 bits, respectively, which are significantly larger than the state size of Grøstl. For comparison, Keccak-256 is indifferentiable up to bound $O((Kq)^2/2^{512})$, while our result implies that Grøstl-256 would be indifferentiable up to $O((Kq)^4/2^{1600})$, were Grøstl be designed to have the same state size as Keccak. Such an adjustment would, however, decrease the efficiency.

2 Preliminaries

For $n \in \mathbb{N}$, where $\mathbb{N}$ is the set of natural numbers, let $\mathbb{Z}_2^n$ denote the set of bit strings of length n, $(\mathbb{Z}_2^n)^*$ the set of strings of length a multiple of n and $\mathbb{Z}_2^*$ the set of strings of arbitrary length. If x, y are strings, then $x\|y$ is the concatenation of x and y. If $k, l \in \mathbb{N}$ then $\langle k \rangle_l$ is the encoding of k as an l-bit string. If S is a set, then $x \overset{\$}{\leftarrow} S$ denotes the uniformly random selection of an element from S. We let $y \leftarrow \mathsf{A}(x)$ and $y \overset{\$}{\leftarrow} \mathsf{A}(x)$ be the assignment to y of the output of a deterministic and randomized algorithm A, respectively, when run on input x. For a function f, by $\mathrm{dom}(f)$ and $\mathrm{rng}(f)$ we denote the domain and range of f, respectively. Abusing notation, by $(x, y) \in f$, we denote that $x \in \mathrm{dom}(f)$ and $y = f(x)$. A random oracle [3] is a function which provides a random output for each new query. A random l-bit permutation is a function that is taken uniformly at random from the set of all l-bit permutations. A random primitive will also be called 'ideal'.

2.1 Grøstl

On input of a message of arbitrary length, the Grøstl hash function $\mathsf{Gr} : \mathbb{Z}_2^* \to \mathbb{Z}_2^n$ outputs a digest of n bits, with $n \in \{224, 256, 384, 512\}$ [15]. Grøstl is a type of a wide-pipe design where the iterated state size l is significantly larger than the final hash output. More concretely: for $n = 224, 256$, $l = 512$, and for $n = 384, 512$, $l = 1024$. The Grøstl hash function makes use of the Merkle-Damgård construction to process its inputs, then applies an output transformation on the state value and finally truncates (chops) the result from l to n bits. The Grøstl compression function $f : \mathbb{Z}_2^l \times \mathbb{Z}_2^l \to \mathbb{Z}_2^l$ is defined as $f(h, m) = P(h \oplus m) \oplus Q(m) \oplus h$, where $P, Q : \mathbb{Z}_2^l \to \mathbb{Z}_2^l$ are two l-bit permutations. Throughout, P and Q are considered to be independent random permutations.

For a fixed initialization vector IV_n the hash function Gr (see Fig. 1) processes an arbitrary length message M as follows:

$$
\begin{aligned}
(M_1, \ldots, M_k) &= \mathrm{pad}(M), \\
h_0 &= IV_n, \\
h_i &= f(h_{i-1}, M_i) \text{ for } i = 1, \ldots, k, \\
h_{k+1} &= P(h_k) \oplus h_k, \\
\mathsf{Gr}(M) &= \mathrm{chop}_{l-n}(h_{k+1}),
\end{aligned}
$$

where $\mathrm{chop}_{l-n}(x)$ chops off the $l - n$ rightmost bits of x, and the padding function pad is defined as $\mathrm{pad}(M) = M'$, with $M' = M\|1\|0^{-|M|-65 \bmod l}\|\langle\lceil(|M| +$

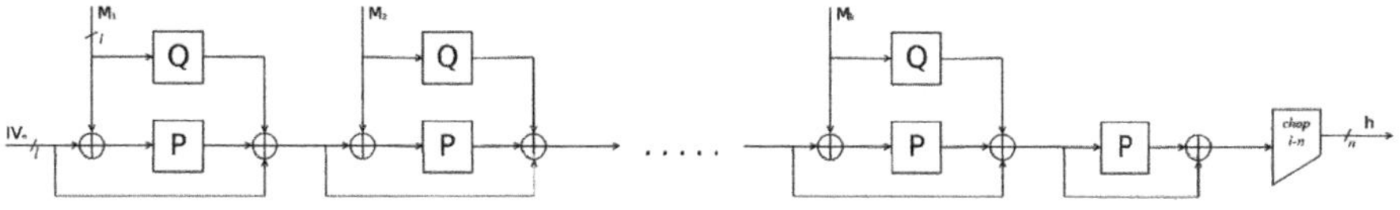

Fig. 1. The Grøstl hash function Gr

$65)/l\rceil\rangle_{64}$, parsed as a sequence of l-bit blocks. On input of a message $M' \in (\mathbb{Z}_2^l)^*$, the function depad$(M')$ is defined as follows: if $M' = \text{pad}(M)$ for some message M, it outputs this M, otherwise it outputs $\perp$. Observe that the output is unique as the padding function is injective[2]. For an $M \in (\mathbb{Z}_2^l)^*$, we denote by $Z(M)$ the set of all values $m \in \mathbb{Z}_2^l$ that make (M, m) a valid padding. Formally: $Z(M) = \{m \in \mathbb{Z}_2^l \mid \text{depad}(M\|m) \neq \perp\}$. Apart from the indifferentiability of the Grøstl hash function, we also consider the Grøstail function $\mathsf{F} : \mathbb{Z}_2^l \times \mathbb{Z}_2^l \to \mathbb{Z}_2^l$, a composition of the last compression function f with the final transformation (i.e., Grøstail is the 'tail' of Grøstl):

$$\mathsf{F}(h, m) = P(f(h, m)) \oplus f(h, m). \tag{1}$$

2.2 Indifferentiability

The indifferentiability framework introduced by Maurer et al. [17] is an extension of the classical notion of indistinguishability. It proves that if a construction $\mathcal{C}^{\mathcal{G}}$ based on an ideal subcomponent $\mathcal{G}$ is indifferentiable from an ideal primitive $\mathcal{R}$, then $\mathcal{C}^{\mathcal{G}}$ can replace $\mathcal{R}$ in any system.

Definition 1. *A Turing machine $\mathcal{C}$ with oracle access to an ideal primitive $\mathcal{G}$ is said to be $(t_\mathcal{D}, t_\mathcal{S}, q, \varepsilon)$ indifferentiable from an ideal primitive $\mathcal{R}$ if there exists a simulator $\mathcal{S}$, such that for any distinguisher $\mathcal{D}$ it holds that:*

$$\text{Adv}^{\text{pro}}_{\mathcal{C},\mathcal{S}}(\mathcal{D}) = \left|\Pr\left(\mathcal{D}^{\mathcal{C}^{\mathcal{G}},\mathcal{G}} = 1\right) - \Pr\left(\mathcal{D}^{\mathcal{R},\mathcal{S}^{\mathcal{R}}} = 1\right)\right| < \varepsilon.$$

The simulator has oracle access to $\mathcal{R}$ and runs in time at most $t_\mathcal{S}$. The distinguisher runs in time at most $t_\mathcal{D}$ and makes at most q queries.

In the remainder, we refer to $\mathcal{C}^{\mathcal{G}}, \mathcal{G}$ as the 'real world', and to $\mathcal{R}, \mathcal{S}^{\mathcal{R}}$ as the 'simulated world'; the distinguisher $\mathcal{D}$ converses either with the real or the simulated world and its goal is to tell both worlds apart. $\mathcal{D}$ can query both its 'left oracle' L (either $\mathcal{C}$ or $\mathcal{R}$) and its 'right oracle' R (either $\mathcal{G}$ or $\mathcal{S}$). In the remainder, R has four interfaces, corresponding to forward and inverse queries to permutations P and Q. These interfaces are denoted by $R_P, R_{P^{-1}}, R_Q, R_{Q^{-1}}$.

3 Differentiability of Grøstail

A recent result by Dodis et al. [14] prescribes how to prove indifferentiability of hash functions by ways of preimage awareness. Loosely speaking, Dodis et al. proved that if $\mathcal{H} : \mathbb{Z}_2^* \to \mathbb{Z}_2^l$ is a preimage aware hash function and $RO : \mathbb{Z}_2^l \to \mathbb{Z}_2^l$ is a random function, then the composition $RO \circ \mathcal{H}$ is indifferentiable from a random oracle. One might be tempted to consider this approach for the indifferentiability analysis of Grøstl, i.e., by assuming that the output transformation is a random oracle and then proving the Grøstl hash function (without

[2] We stress that, for the purpose of the proof, injectivity is the only property required from the padding function.

the output transformation) to be preimage aware. However, the behavior of the output transformation $P(x) \oplus x$ deviates significantly from a random function: similarly to the Davies-Meyer construction [19], fixed points $P(x) \oplus x = x$ are easy to compute by making the inverse query $P^{-1}(0) = x$. A second attempt is to go one step backwards in the iteration and view the last compression function together with the output transformation, i.e., Grøstail (1), as a random function. We show that this approach also fails since Grøstail is easily differentiable from a random function.

Proposition 1. *Let P, Q be two random l-bit permutations, let* F *be the Grøstail compression function (1), and let $RO : \mathbb{Z}_2^l \times \mathbb{Z}_2^l \to \mathbb{Z}_2^l$ be a random function. For any simulator* S *that makes at most q queries to RO, there exists a distinguisher $\mathcal{D}$ that makes at most 3 queries to its oracle, such that* $\mathrm{Adv}^{\mathrm{pro}}_{\mathsf{F},\mathsf{S}}(\mathcal{D}) \geq 1 - q/2^l$.

Proof. Let S be any simulator that makes at most q queries to RO. We construct a distinguisher $\mathcal{D}$ that with overwhelming probability distinguishes Grøstail from a random function in 3 oracle queries. The distinguisher proceeds as follows. First, it makes inverse queries $x_2 = R_{Q^{-1}}(0)$ and $x_1 = R_{P^{-1}}(x_2)$. Then, it makes a query to the left oracle to obtain $y = L(x_1 \oplus x_2, x_2)$. If $\mathcal{D}$ converses with $(\mathsf{F}^{P,Q}, (P, Q))$, then $y = \mathsf{F}^{P,Q}(x_1 \oplus x_2, x_2) = P(x_1) \oplus x_1 = x_1 \oplus x_2$. If $\mathcal{D}$ converses with (RO, S^{RO}), this equation holds only if the simulator can find x_1, x_2 such that $RO(x_1 \oplus x_2, x_2) = x_1 \oplus x_2$, i.e., only if the simulator can find a fixed point for RO. As the probability for the simulator to find fixed points for RO is upper bounded by $q/2^l$, the advantage for $\mathcal{D}$ to distinguish, $\mathrm{Adv}^{\mathrm{pro}}_{\mathsf{F},\mathsf{S}}(\mathcal{D})$, is lower bounded by $1 - q/2^l$. □

If the final truncation is included in Grøstail as well, a lower bound $1 - q/2^n$ can be obtained similarly.

4 Indifferentiability of Grøstl

In this section, we present the main result of this paper: we show that the Grøstl hash function is indifferentiable from a random oracle, under the assumption that the underlying permutations P, Q are ideal. Intuitively, we demonstrate that there exists a simulator such that no distinguisher can differentiate the real world $\mathsf{Gr}^{P,Q}, (P, Q)$ from the simulated world RO, S^{RO}, except with negligible probability.

Theorem 1. *Let P, Q be two random l-bit permutations, let* Gr *be the Grøstl hash function (Sect. 2.1), and let RO be a random oracle. Let $\mathcal{D}$ be a distinguisher that makes at most q_L left queries of maximal length $(K-1)l$ bits, where $K \geq 1$, q_P right queries to P and q_Q right queries to Q, and runs in time t. Then:*

$$\mathrm{Adv}^{\mathrm{pro}}_{\mathsf{Gr},\mathsf{S}}(\mathcal{D}) \leq \frac{58(q_P + (K+1)q_L)^2(q_Q + Kq_L)^2}{2^l}, \tag{2}$$

where S *makes $q_S \leq q_P$ queries to RO and runs in time $O(\max\{q_P, q_Q\}^4)$.*

The simulator S used in the proof mimics the behavior of random permutations P and Q such that queries to S and queries to RO are 'consistent', which means that relations among the query outputs in the real world hold in the simulated world as well. To this end, the construction of the simulator is based on several designing decisions. In what remains, the simulator used in the proof (Fig. 2) is introduced and explained in more detail. Then, Thm. 1 is proven in Sect. 4.3.

4.1 Initialization of the Simulator

The simulator maintains two, initially empty, lists $\mathcal{L}_P, \mathcal{L}_Q$ that represent the permutations it simulates. These lists consist of tuples $(x, y) \in \mathbb{Z}_2^l \times \mathbb{Z}_2^l$, where y denotes the (simulated) image of x under P or Q. Abusing notation, we denote by $\text{dom}(\mathcal{L}_P)$ (resp. $\text{rng}(\mathcal{L}_P)$) the set of first (resp. second) elements in $\mathcal{L}_P$, and similar for $\mathcal{L}_Q$. The simulator has four interfaces, denoted by $\mathsf{S}_P, \mathsf{S}_{P^{-1}}, \mathsf{S}_Q, \mathsf{S}_{Q^{-1}}$, and access to RO. Furthermore, the simulator maintains a graph (V, E), initially $(\{IV\}, \emptyset)$. The edges $e \in E$ are labeled by messages in $\mathbb{Z}_2^l$: any $(x_1, y_1) \in \mathcal{L}_P$ and $(x_2, y_2) \in \mathcal{L}_Q$ define an edge $x_1 \oplus x_2 \xrightarrow{x_2} x_1 \oplus x_2 \oplus y_1 \oplus y_2$ in (V, E). Intuitively, an edge in (V, E) corresponds to an evaluation of the Grøstl compression function f, and if there is a path $IV \xrightarrow{M_1} s_1 \xrightarrow{M_2} \cdots \xrightarrow{M_k} s_k$ in (V, E), then $f(\ldots f(f(IV, M_1), M_2) \ldots, M_k) = s_k$. Abusing notation, we denote by $s \xrightarrow{M} t$ that there is a path from s to t in (V, E) with the edges labeled by $M \in (\mathbb{Z}_2^l)^*$. We say that (V, E) contains *colliding paths* if there exists an $s \in V$ such that $IV \xrightarrow{M} s$ and $IV \xrightarrow{M'} s$ are two paths in (V, E), for different $M, M' \in (\mathbb{Z}_2^l)^*$.

Furthermore, by $V_{\text{out}}, V_{\text{in}}$ we denote the set of vertices in V with an outgoing or ingoing edge, respectively. Observe that if $\mathcal{L}_P, \mathcal{L}_Q$ are of size q_P, q_Q, respectively, the sets $V_{\text{out}}, V_{\text{in}}$ are of size at most $q_P q_Q$. By $r(V)$, we denote the set of all 'rooted' nodes in V, i.e.: $r(V) = \left\{v \in V \mid \exists\, M \in (\mathbb{Z}_2^l)^* \text{ such that } IV \xrightarrow{M} v\right\}$. By construction, $r(V) \subseteq V_{\text{in}}$. Finally, we introduce a specific subset of $r(V)$:

$$\bar{r}(V) = \left\{v \in V \mid \exists\, M \in (\mathbb{Z}_2^l)^* \text{ such that } IV \xrightarrow{M} v \text{ and } \text{depad}(M) \neq \bot\right\}.$$

For simplicity, $V, r(V)$ and $\bar{r}(V)$ are updated by the simulator implicitly.

4.2 Intuition behind the Simulator

In this section we take a closer look at the simulator of Fig. 2 by starting with an example. Consider the case that a node x is a member of both $\bar{r}(V)$ and $\text{dom}(\mathcal{L}_P)$. This means that (1) there exists an M such that $IV \xrightarrow{M} x$ and $\text{depad}(M) \neq \bot$, and (2) there exists a $y \in \text{rng}(\mathcal{L}_P)$, such that $y = \mathsf{S}_P(x)$. In the real world (where the left oracle is the Grøstl hash function), these values satisfy $\mathsf{Gr}(\text{depad}(M)) = \text{chop}_{l-n}(x \oplus y)$ by construction. If the simulator does not answer its queries wisely, this equality would hold with negligible probability in the simulated world. More generally, the simulator can guarantee that this equation holds only if x is added to $\text{dom}(\mathcal{L}_P)$ *after* it was added to $\bar{r}(V)$ (reflected in requirement R3 below)[3]. Maintaining consistency, however, becomes harder when $|\bar{r}(V)|$ and $|\mathrm{dom}(\mathcal{L}_P)|$ increase. The idea behind the simulator is to answer its queries such that it can control the growth of $r(V)$, and in particular the growth of $\bar{r}(V)$ as a subset of $r(V)$, while still maintaining consistency in its answers. Intuitively, the simulator responds to its queries, such that the following requirements are satisfied:

R1. There are no colliding paths in $(r(V), E)$. Observe that two different paths to the same node may lead to distinguishability for $\mathcal{D}$ as the simulator can be consistent with only *one* of the paths. This requirement is satisfied if $r(V)$ is never increased with a node that has two incoming edges in the updated[4] graph;

R2. S increases $r(V)$ only if it is forced to do. In particular, $r(V)$ is never increased with a node that has an outgoing edge in the updated graph. Observe that each path in $(r(V), E)$ leads to a potential node in $\bar{r}(V)$;

R3. S never increases $\bar{r}(V)$ with a node in the updated $\mathrm{dom}(\mathcal{L}_P)$;

R4. S increases $\mathrm{dom}(\mathcal{L}_P)$ with a node in $\bar{r}(V)$ only if it is forced to. Observe that in case of inverse queries to $\mathsf{S}_{P^{-1}}$, the simulator can avoid outputting elements in $\bar{r}(V)$. In forward queries to S_P, the simulator may be forced to increase $\bar{r}(V) \cap \mathrm{dom}(\mathcal{L}_P)$. In this case, it consults its oracle RO to generate the answer.

The first two conditions are regarding the growth of $r(V)$, and the second two concern the growth of $\bar{r}(V) \cap \mathrm{dom}(\mathcal{L}_P)$. We show how these conditions occur in the description of the simulator in Fig. 2. We first consider requirements R1 and R2, then we look at R3 and R4.

Restricting the growth of $r(V)$

INVERSE QUERIES. Consider an inverse query y_1 to $\mathsf{S}_{P^{-1}}$. It is easy to see that both R1 and R2 are satisfied if the simulator outputs its answer x_1, such that none of the newly added vertices $\{x_1 \oplus x_2 \mid x_2 \in \mathrm{dom}(\mathcal{L}_Q)\}$ to V_{out} is already rooted. A similar observation holds for queries to $\mathsf{S}_{Q^{-1}}$. These requirements translate to lines 3e and 4c in the description of the simulator in Fig. 2.

FORWARD QUERIES. In forward queries to $\mathsf{S}_P, \mathsf{S}_Q$, the simulator may be forced to increase $r(V)$. Consider a query x_1 to S_P, and consider any $x_2 \in \mathrm{dom}(\mathcal{L}_Q)$ such that $x_1 \oplus x_2 \in r(V)$. Then, the edge $x_1 \oplus x_2 \xrightarrow{x_2} x_1 \oplus x_2 \oplus y_1 \oplus y_2$ will be added

[3] Observe that $RO(\mathrm{depad}(M)) = \mathrm{chop}_{l-n}(\mathcal{L}_P(x) \oplus x)$ should hold for $IV \xrightarrow{M} x$. If $x \in \mathrm{dom}(\mathcal{L}_P)$ before it is added to $\bar{r}(V)$, this means that $\mathcal{L}_P(x) \oplus x$ is fixed before $RO(\mathrm{depad}(M))$ is known.

[4] This requirement should hold for the 'updated' graph, which can be seen as follows: suppose the distinguisher makes a forward query x_1 to S_P such that $x_1 \oplus x_2, x_1 \oplus x_2' \in r(V)$ for different $x_2, x_2' \in \mathrm{dom}(\mathcal{L}_Q)$, and both $x_1 \oplus x_2 \oplus y_1 \oplus y_2$ and $x_1 \oplus x_2' \oplus y_1 \oplus y_2'$ are not in V yet. By construction, these nodes have zero incoming edges in the non-updated (V, E), but it may accidentally be the case that these nodes are equal, in which case they have two incoming edges in the updated graph.

to (V, E) by construction. Denote by V' the multiset of updated nodes after the query. Then, we require that $x_1 \oplus x_2 \oplus y_1 \oplus y_2$ does not occur twice in V'_{in} (in order to establish R1), and moreover that it does not occur in V'_{out} (in order to establish R2). If we define $V_{\text{new}} = \{x_1 \oplus x'_2, \ x_1 \oplus x'_2 \oplus y_1 \oplus y'_2 \mid (x'_2, y'_2) \in \mathcal{L}_Q\}$ to be the multiset of newly added nodes to V in the query to S_P, both requirements are satisfied if $x_1 \oplus x_2 \oplus y_1 \oplus y_2 \notin V \cup (V_{\text{new}} \backslash \{x_1 \oplus x_2 \oplus y_1 \oplus y_2\})$ holds for all $(x_2, y_2) \in \mathcal{L}_Q$ such that $x_1 \oplus x_2 \in r(V)$. A similar condition can be derived for queries to S_Q. These requirements translate to lines 1k and 2e in the description of the simulator in Fig. 2.

Restricting the growth of $\bar{r}(V) \cap \text{dom}(\mathcal{L}_P)$
INVERSE QUERIES. As explained, S never increases $\bar{r}(V) \subseteq r(V)$ in inverse queries. Hence, requirement R3 is naturally satisfied. Furthermore, R4 is guaranteed if queries to $\mathsf{S}_{P^{-1}}$ are never answered with a node in $\bar{r}(V)$. This requirement translates to line 3c from Fig. 2.

FORWARD QUERIES. First consider requirement R3. Let the distinguisher make a query to S_P or S_Q, such that $\bar{r}(V)$ gets increased. By construction and the fact that requirement R2 is satisfied, this means that an edge $x_1 \oplus x_2 \xrightarrow{x_2} x_1 \oplus x_2 \oplus y_1 \oplus y_2$ is added to (V, E), such that $IV \xrightarrow{M} x_1 \oplus x_2$ for some $M \in \left(\mathbb{Z}_2^l\right)^*$, and $x_2 \in Z(M)$. The simulator needs to be designed such that the newly added value to $\bar{r}(V)$, $x_1 \oplus x_2 \oplus y_1 \oplus y_2$, is not a member of (the updated) $\text{dom}(\mathcal{L}_P)$. This requirement translates to lines 1l and 2f in Fig. 2. Requirement R4 is clearly not applicable to queries to S_Q. Consider a query x_1 to S_P, where $x_1 \in \bar{r}(V)$. Then, the simulator is forced to increase $\bar{r}(V) \cap \text{dom}(\mathcal{L}_P)$. As $x_1 \in \bar{r}(V)$, there exists an M such that $IV \xrightarrow{M} x_1$ and $\text{depad}(M) \neq \bot$. The output of the simulator needs to be consistent with its random oracle, such that $RO(\text{depad}(M)) = \text{chop}_{l-n}(\mathsf{S}_P(x_1) \oplus x_1)$. This requirement translates to lines 1b-1e in the description of the simulator in Fig. 2.

4.3 Proof of Thm. 1

Thm. 1 will be proven via a game-playing argument, where the games are used to simulate one of the worlds (left or right). It is inspired by the proofs of [11], but differs in several aspects. Let S be the simulator of Fig. 2, and let $\mathcal{D}$ be any distinguisher that makes at most q_L left queries of maximal length $(K-1)l$ bits, where $K \geq 1$, q_P right queries to P and q_Q right queries to Q. Recall from Def. 1 that the goal is to bound:

$$\mathbf{Adv}^{\mathrm{pro}}_{\mathsf{Gr},\mathsf{S}}(\mathcal{D}) = \left|\Pr\left(\mathcal{D}^{\mathsf{Gr}^{P,Q},(P,Q)} = 1\right) - \Pr\left(\mathcal{D}^{RO,\mathsf{S}^{RO}} = 1\right)\right|. \quad (3)$$

Game 1 (Fig. 3). The left oracle L_1 of game 1 is a lazily-sampled random oracle, and the four interfaces of the right oracle are the simulator of Fig. 2, except for the inclusion of some failure conditions $\mathbf{bad}_i$ $(i = 0, \ldots, 4)$. In other words, we have $G_1 = (RO, \mathsf{S}^{RO})$, and in particular, $\Pr\left(\mathcal{D}^{RO,\mathsf{S}^{RO}} = 1\right) = \Pr\left(\mathcal{D}^{G_1} = 1\right)$.

On query $\mathsf{S}_P(x_1)$:

1a **if** $x_1 \in \mathrm{dom}(\mathcal{L}_P)$ **ret** $y_1 = \mathcal{L}_P(x_1)$
1b **if** $x_1 \in \bar{r}(V)$ **for** $IV \xrightarrow{M} x_1$:
1c $\quad h \leftarrow RO(\mathrm{depad}(M))$
1d $\quad w \xleftarrow{\$} \mathbb{Z}_2^{l-n}$
1e $\quad y_1 \leftarrow x_1 \oplus (h \| w)$
1f $\quad$ **if** $y_1 \in \mathrm{rng}(\mathcal{L}_P)$:
1g $\qquad$ **GOTO** 1d
1h **else** $y_1 \xleftarrow{\$} \mathbb{Z}_2^l \backslash \mathrm{rng}(\mathcal{L}_P)$
1i $V_{\mathrm{new}} \leftarrow \{x_1 \oplus x_2', x_1 \oplus x_2' \oplus y_1 \oplus y_2' \mid (x_2', y_2') \in \mathcal{L}_Q\}$ multiset
1j $\forall\ (x_2, y_2) \in \mathcal{L}_Q$ **s.t.** $x_1 \oplus x_2 \in r(V)$ **for** $IV \xrightarrow{M} x_1 \oplus x_2$:
1k $\quad$ **if** $x_1 \oplus x_2 \oplus y_1 \oplus y_2 \in V \cup (V_{\mathrm{new}} \backslash \{x_1 \oplus x_2 \oplus y_1 \oplus y_2\})$ **or**
1l $\qquad \big(x_2 \in Z(M)$ **and** $x_1 \oplus x_2 \oplus y_1 \oplus y_2 \in \mathrm{dom}(\mathcal{L}_P) \cup \{x_1\}\big)$:
1m $\qquad$ **GOTO** 1b
1n **ret** $\mathcal{L}_P(x_1) \leftarrow y_1$

On query $\mathsf{S}_Q(x_2)$:

2a **if** $x_2 \in \mathrm{dom}(\mathcal{L}_Q)$ **ret** $y_2 = \mathcal{L}_Q(x_2)$
2b $y_2 \xleftarrow{\$} \mathbb{Z}_2^l \backslash \mathrm{rng}(\mathcal{L}_Q)$
2c $V_{\mathrm{new}} \leftarrow \{x_1' \oplus x_2, x_1' \oplus x_2 \oplus y_1' \oplus y_2 \mid (x_1', y_1') \in \mathcal{L}_P\}$ multiset
2d $\forall\ (x_1, y_1) \in \mathcal{L}_P$ **s.t.** $x_1 \oplus x_2 \in r(V)$ **for** $IV \xrightarrow{M} x_1 \oplus x_2$:
2e $\quad$ **if** $x_1 \oplus x_2 \oplus y_1 \oplus y_2 \in V \cup (V_{\mathrm{new}} \backslash \{x_1 \oplus x_2 \oplus y_1 \oplus y_2\})$ **or**
2f $\qquad \big(x_2 \in Z(M)$ **and** $x_1 \oplus x_2 \oplus y_1 \oplus y_2 \in \mathrm{dom}(\mathcal{L}_P)\big)$:
2g $\qquad$ **GOTO** 2b
2h **ret** $\mathcal{L}_Q(x_2) \leftarrow y_2$

On query $\mathsf{S}_{P\text{-}1}(y_1)$:

3a **if** $y_1 \in \mathrm{rng}(\mathcal{L}_P)$ **ret** $x_1 = \mathcal{L}_P^{-1}(y_1)$
3b $x_1 \xleftarrow{\$} \mathbb{Z}_2^l \backslash \mathrm{dom}(\mathcal{L}_P)$
3c **if** $x_1 \in \bar{r}(V)$:
3d $\quad$ **GOTO** 3b
3e $\forall\ x_2 \in \mathrm{dom}(\mathcal{L}_Q)$: **if** $x_1 \oplus x_2 \in r(V)$:
3f $\quad$ **GOTO** 3b
3g **ret** $\mathcal{L}_P^{-1}(y_1) \leftarrow x_1$

On query $\mathsf{S}_{Q\text{-}1}(y_2)$:

4a **if** $y_2 \in \mathrm{rng}(\mathcal{L}_Q)$ **ret** $x_2 = \mathcal{L}_Q^{-1}(y_2)$
4b $x_2 \xleftarrow{\$} \mathbb{Z}_2^l \backslash \mathrm{dom}(\mathcal{L}_Q)$
4c $\forall\ x_1 \in \mathrm{dom}(\mathcal{L}_P)$: **if** $x_1 \oplus x_2 \in r(V)$:
4d $\quad$ **GOTO** 4b
4e **ret** $\mathcal{L}_Q^{-1}(y_2) \leftarrow x_2$

Fig. 2. The simulator S for P and Q used in the proof of Thm. 1

Game 2 (Fig. 3). Game 2 only differs from game 1 in the left oracle: L_1 is replaced by a relay oracle L_2 that simply passes the queries made by the distinguisher to L_1. The right oracle remains unchanged, and still queries the subroutine L_1. The distinguisher has identical views in G_1 and G_2. Formally, we obtain $\Pr\left(\mathcal{D}^{G_1} = 1\right) = \Pr\left(\mathcal{D}^{G_2} = 1\right)$.

Game 3 (Fig. 4). Game 3 differs from game 2 in the fact that the left oracle L_2 is replaced by the Grøstl hash function, which makes queries to the right oracle. The right oracle itself remains unchanged, and still queries subroutine L_1. It is proven in Prop. 2 that, until $\mathbf{bad} := \bigvee_{i=0}^{4} \mathbf{bad}_i$ occurs in any of the two games, both are identical. Formally, we obtain:

$$\left|\Pr\left(\mathcal{D}^{G_2} = 1\right) - \Pr\left(\mathcal{D}^{G_3} = 1\right)\right| \leq \Pr\left(\mathcal{D}^{G_2} \text{ sets } \mathbf{bad}\right) + \Pr\left(\mathcal{D}^{G_3} \text{ sets } \mathbf{bad}\right).$$

Game 4 (Fig. 5). Game 4 differs from game 3 in the fact that the right oracle does not query subroutine L_1 anymore, but rather, it generates the outcomes itself. Concretely, in line 1c, h is now randomly sampled from $\mathbb{Z}_2^n$. The distinguisher cannot notice the difference: as the padding rule is injective, in game 3 the right oracle R_P will never query its left oracle twice on the same value, and hence it will always receive $h \xleftarrow{\$} \mathbb{Z}_2^n$. Formally, we obtain $\Pr\left(\mathcal{D}^{G_3} = 1\right) = \Pr\left(\mathcal{D}^{G_4} = 1\right)$.

Game 5 (Fig. 5). Game 5 only differs from game 4 in the fact that the **GOTO**-statements are removed. In other words, game 5 and game 4 proceed identically until **bad** occurs. As a consequence:

$$\left|\Pr\left(\mathcal{D}^{G_4} = 1\right) - \Pr\left(\mathcal{D}^{G_5} = 1\right)\right| \leq \Pr\left(\mathcal{D}^{G_4} \text{ sets } \mathbf{bad}\right).$$

On query $R_P(x_1)$:

1a **if** $x_1 \in \mathrm{dom}(\mathcal{L}_P)$ **ret** $y_1 = \mathcal{L}_P(x_1)$
1b **if** $x_1 \in \bar{r}(V)$ **for** $IV \xrightarrow{M} x_1$:
1c $\quad h \leftarrow L_1(\mathrm{depad}(M))$
1d $\quad w \xleftarrow{\$} \mathbb{Z}_2^{l-n}$
1e $\quad y_1 \leftarrow x_1 \oplus (h \| w)$
1f $\quad$ **if** $y_1 \in \mathrm{rng}(\mathcal{L}_P)$:
1g $\quad\quad$ $\mathbf{bad}_0 \leftarrow$ **true**
1h $\quad\quad$ **GOTO** 1d
1i **else** $y_1 \xleftarrow{\$} \mathbb{Z}_2^l \backslash \mathrm{rng}(\mathcal{L}_P)$
1j $V_{\mathrm{new}} \leftarrow \{x_1 \oplus x_2', x_1 \oplus x_2' \oplus y_1 \oplus y_2' \mid (x_2', y_2') \in \mathcal{L}_Q\}$ multiset
1k $\forall\ (x_2, y_2) \in \mathcal{L}_Q$ s.t. $x_1 \oplus x_2 \in r(V)$ **for** $IV \xrightarrow{M} x_1 \oplus x_2$:
1l $\quad$ **if** $x_1 \oplus x_2 \oplus y_1 \oplus y_2 \in V \cup (V_{\mathrm{new}} \backslash \{x_1 \oplus x_2 \oplus y_1 \oplus y_2\})$ **or**
1m $\quad\quad \left(x_2 \in Z(M) \text{ and } x_1 \oplus x_2 \oplus y_1 \oplus y_2 \in \mathrm{dom}(\mathcal{L}_P) \cup \{x_1\}\right)$:
1n $\quad\quad$ $\mathbf{bad}_1 \leftarrow$ **true**
1o $\quad\quad$ **GOTO** 1b
1p **ret** $\mathcal{L}_P(x_1) \leftarrow y_1$

On query $R_Q(x_2)$:

2a **if** $x_2 \in \mathrm{dom}(\mathcal{L}_Q)$ **ret** $y_2 = \mathcal{L}_Q(x_2)$
2b $y_2 \xleftarrow{\$} \mathbb{Z}_2^l \backslash \mathrm{rng}(\mathcal{L}_Q)$
2c $V_{\mathrm{new}} \leftarrow \{x_1' \oplus x_2, x_1' \oplus x_2 \oplus y_1' \oplus y_2 \mid (x_1', y_1') \in \mathcal{L}_P\}$ multiset
2d $\forall\ (x_1, y_1) \in \mathcal{L}_P$ s.t. $x_1 \oplus x_2 \in r(V)$ **for** $IV \xrightarrow{M} x_1 \oplus x_2$:
2e $\quad$ **if** $x_1 \oplus x_2 \oplus y_1 \oplus y_2 \in V \cup (V_{\mathrm{new}} \backslash \{x_1 \oplus x_2 \oplus y_1 \oplus y_2\})$ **or**
2f $\quad\quad \left(x_2 \in Z(M) \text{ and } x_1 \oplus x_2 \oplus y_1 \oplus y_2 \in \mathrm{dom}(\mathcal{L}_P)\right)$:
2g $\quad\quad$ $\mathbf{bad}_2 \leftarrow$ **true**
2h $\quad\quad$ **GOTO** 2b
2i **ret** $\mathcal{L}_Q(x_2) \leftarrow y_2$

On query $R_{P^{-1}}(y_1)$:

3a **if** $y_1 \in \mathrm{rng}(\mathcal{L}_P)$ **ret** $x_1 = \mathcal{L}_P^{-1}(y_1)$
3b $x_1 \xleftarrow{\$} \mathbb{Z}_2^l \backslash \mathrm{dom}(\mathcal{L}_P)$
3c **if** $x_1 \in \bar{r}(V)$:
3d $\quad$ $\mathbf{bad}_3 \leftarrow$ **true**
3e $\quad$ **GOTO** 3b
3f $\forall\ x_2 \in \mathrm{dom}(\mathcal{L}_Q)$: **if** $x_1 \oplus x_2 \in r(V)$:
3g $\quad$ $\mathbf{bad}_3 \leftarrow$ **true**
3h $\quad$ **GOTO** 3b
3i **ret** $\mathcal{L}_P^{-1}(y_1) \leftarrow x_1$

On query $R_{Q^{-1}}(y_2)$:

4a **if** $y_2 \in \mathrm{rng}(\mathcal{L}_Q)$ **ret** $x_2 = \mathcal{L}_Q^{-1}(y_2)$
4b $x_2 \xleftarrow{\$} \mathbb{Z}_2^l \backslash \mathrm{dom}(\mathcal{L}_Q)$
4c $\forall\ x_1 \in \mathrm{dom}(\mathcal{L}_P)$: **if** $x_1 \oplus x_2 \in r(V)$:
4d $\quad$ $\mathbf{bad}_4 \leftarrow$ **true**
4e $\quad$ **GOTO** 4b
4f **ret** $\mathcal{L}_Q^{-1}(y_2) \leftarrow x_2$

On query $L_1(M)$:

5a **if** $M \in \mathrm{dom}(\mathcal{H})$ **ret** $h = \mathcal{H}(M)$
5b $h \xleftarrow{\$} \mathbb{Z}_2^n$
5c **ret** $\mathcal{H}(M) \leftarrow h$

On query $L_2(M)$:

6a **ret** $h \leftarrow L_1(M)$

Fig. 3. Game 1 (with the boxed statement removed) and game 2 (including the boxed statement). In game 1, the distinguisher has access to L_1, R^{L_1}. In game 2, the distinguisher has access to $L_2^{L_1}, R^{L_1}$.

Game 6 (Fig. 6). The left oracle of game 6 is the Grøstl algorithm, and the four interfaces of the right oracle perfectly mimic two lazily-sampled random permutations P and Q. In other words, we have $G_6 = (\mathsf{Gr}^{P,Q}, (P, Q))$, and thus $\Pr\left(\mathcal{D}^{G_6} = 1\right) = \Pr\left(\mathcal{D}^{\mathsf{Gr}^{P,Q},(P,Q)} = 1\right)$. The only difference between games 6 and 5 is in the forward queries to R_P: in game 5, some queries to R_P are answered with uniform random samples from $\mathbb{Z}_2^l$. Therefore, distinguishing game 6 from game 5 is at least as hard as distinguishing a random permutation from a random function. As R_P will be queried at most $q_P + (K+1)q_L =: r_P$ times, we obtain:

$$\left|\Pr\left(\mathcal{D}^{G_5} = 1\right) - \Pr\left(\mathcal{D}^{G_6} = 1\right)\right| \leq \frac{r_P^2}{2^l}.$$

As we have $\Pr\left(\mathcal{D}^{G_2} \text{ sets } \mathbf{bad}\right) \leq \Pr\left(\mathcal{D}^{G_3} \text{ sets } \mathbf{bad}\right) = \Pr\left(\mathcal{D}^{G_4} \text{ sets } \mathbf{bad}\right)$, we conclude that (3) reduces to:

$$\mathbf{Adv}^{\mathrm{pro}}_{\mathsf{Gr},\mathsf{S}}(\mathcal{D}) \leq \frac{r_P^2}{2^l} + 3 \cdot \Pr\left(\mathcal{D}^{G_4} \text{ sets } \mathbf{bad}\right). \tag{4}$$

Game 7 (Fig. 7). Game 7 is used to simplify the computation of the probability that $\mathcal{D}^{G_4}$ sets **bad**. In game 7, the failure conditions for $\mathbf{bad}_0, \ldots, \mathbf{bad}_4$ of game 4 are rewritten into sets $A_0, \ldots, A_4$. By the straightforward definition of A_0, A_3

```
On query R_P(x_1):
1a  if x_1 ∈ dom(L_P) ret y_1 = L_P(x_1)
1b  if x_1 ∈ r̄(V) for IV --M--> x_1 :
1c      h ← L_1(depad(M))
1d      w <-$- Z_2^{l-n}
1e      y_1 ← x_1 ⊕ (h||w)
1f      if y_1 ∈ rng(L_P) :
1g          bad_0 ← true
1h          GOTO 1d
1i  else y_1 <-$- Z_2^l \ rng(L_P)
1j  V_new ← {x_1 ⊕ x'_2, x_1 ⊕ x'_2 ⊕ y_1 ⊕ y'_2 | (x'_2, y'_2) ∈ L_Q} multiset
1k  ∀ (x_2, y_2) ∈ L_Q s.t. x_1 ⊕ x_2 ∈ r(V) for IV --M--> x_1 ⊕ x_2 :
1l      if x_1 ⊕ x_2 ⊕ y_1 ⊕ y_2 ∈ V ∪ (V_new \ {x_1 ⊕ x_2 ⊕ y_1 ⊕ y_2}) or
1m          (x_2 ∈ Z(M) and x_1 ⊕ x_2 ⊕ y_1 ⊕ y_2 ∈ dom(L_P) ∪ {x_1}) :
1n          bad_1 ← true
1o          GOTO 1b
1p  ret L_P(x_1) ← y_1

On query R_Q(x_2):
2a  if x_2 ∈ dom(L_Q) ret y_2 = L_Q(x_2)
2b  y_2 <-$- Z_2^l \ rng(L_Q)
2c  V_new ← {x'_1 ⊕ x_2, x'_1 ⊕ x_2 ⊕ y'_1 ⊕ y_2 | (x'_1, y'_1) ∈ L_P} multiset
2d  ∀ (x_1, y_1) ∈ L_P s.t. x_1 ⊕ x_2 ∈ r(V) for IV --M--> x_1 ⊕ x_2 :
2e      if x_1 ⊕ x_2 ⊕ y_1 ⊕ y_2 ∈ V ∪ (V_new \ {x_1 ⊕ x_2 ⊕ y_1 ⊕ y_2}) or
2f          (x_2 ∈ Z(M) and x_1 ⊕ x_2 ⊕ y_1 ⊕ y_2 ∈ dom(L_P)) :
2g          bad_2 ← true
2h          GOTO 2b
2i  ret L_Q(x_2) ← y_2
```

```
On query R_{P^-1}(y_1):
3a  if y_1 ∈ rng(L_P) ret x_1 = L_P^{-1}(y_1)
3b  x_1 <-$- Z_2^l \ dom(L_P)
3c  if x_1 ∈ r̄(V) :
3d      bad_3 ← true
3e      GOTO 3b
3f  ∀ x_2 ∈ dom(L_Q) : if x_1 ⊕ x_2 ∈ r(V) :
3g      bad_3 ← true
3h      GOTO 3b
3i  ret L_P^{-1}(y_1) ← x_1

On query R_{Q^-1}(y_2):
4a  if y_2 ∈ rng(L_Q) ret x_2 = L_Q^{-1}(y_2)
4b  x_2 <-$- Z_2^l \ dom(L_Q)
4c  ∀ x_1 ∈ dom(L_P) : if x_1 ⊕ x_2 ∈ r(V) :
4d      bad_4 ← true
4e      GOTO 4b
4f  ret L_Q^{-1}(y_2) ← x_2

On query L_1(M):
5a  if M ∈ dom(H) ret h = H(M)
5b  h <-$- Z_2^n
5c  ret H(M) ← h

On query L_3(M):
6a  (M'_1, ..., M'_k) ← pad(M)
6b  h_0 ← IV_n
6c  for i = 1, ..., k :
6d      a ← R_Q(M'_i)
6e      b ← R_P(h_{i-1} ⊕ M'_i)
6f      h_i ← a ⊕ b ⊕ h_{i-1}
6g  d ← R_P(h_k)
6h  h ← chop_{l-n}(d ⊕ h_k)
6i  ret h
```

Fig. 4. Game 3. The distinguisher has access to $L_3^{R^{L_1}}, R^{L_1}$.

and A_4, it is clear that for $i = 0, 3, 4$, $\mathcal{D}^{G_4}$ sets $\mathbf{bad}_i$ if and only if $\mathcal{D}^{G_7}$ sets $\mathbf{bad}_i$. Now, suppose $\mathcal{D}^{G_4}$ sets $\mathbf{bad}_1$. This means that for some $(x_2, y_2) \in \mathcal{L}_Q$ such that $x_1 \oplus x_2 \in r(V)$ either one of the following two cases occurred:

$$y_1 = \begin{cases} x_1 \oplus x_2 \oplus y_2 \oplus s, \text{ for some } s \in V \cup (V_{\text{new}} \backslash \{x_1 \oplus x_2 \oplus y_1 \oplus y_2\}), \\ x_1 \oplus x_2 \oplus y_2 \oplus x_1', \text{ for some } x_1' \in \text{dom}(\mathcal{L}_P) \cup \{x_1\}. \end{cases}$$

By definition of A_1, this means that $y_1 \in A_1$. In other words, $\mathcal{D}^{G_7}$ sets $\mathbf{bad}_1$ if $\mathcal{D}^{G_4}$ sets $\mathbf{bad}_1$. A similar observation holds for $\mathbf{bad}_2$. As a consequence, $\Pr\left(\mathcal{D}^{G_4} \text{ sets } \mathbf{bad}\right) \leq \Pr\left(\mathcal{D}^{G_7} \text{ sets } \mathbf{bad}\right)$, and therefore (4) reduces to:

$$\mathrm{Adv}^{\mathrm{pro}}_{\mathsf{Gr},\mathsf{S}}(\mathcal{D}) \leq \frac{r_P^2}{2^l} + 3 \cdot \Pr\left(\mathcal{D}^{G_7} \text{ sets } \mathbf{bad}_1 \mid \neg \mathbf{bad}_0\right) + 3 \sum_{\substack{i=0 \\ i \neq 1}}^{4} \Pr\left(\mathcal{D}^{G_7} \text{ sets } \mathbf{bad}_i\right).$$

In the remainder, we concentrate on the computation of these probabilities. Observe that the distinguisher makes at most $q_P + (K+1)q_L =: r_P$ queries to $R_P, R_{P^{-1}}$ and $q_Q + Kq_L =: r_Q$ queries to $R_Q, R_{Q^{-1}}$.

```
On query R_P(x1):
1a if x1 ∈ dom(L_P) ret y1 = L_P(x1)
1b if x1 ∈ r̄(V) :
1c     h ←$ Z_2^n
1d     w ←$ Z_2^{l−n}
1e     y1 ← x1 ⊕ (h‖w)
1f     if y1 ∈ rng(L_P) :
1g         bad0 ← true
1h         [GOTO 1d]
1i else y1 ←$ Z_2^l \ rng(L_P)
1j V_new ← {x1 ⊕ x2', x1 ⊕ x2' ⊕ y1 ⊕ y2' | (x2', y2') ∈ L_Q} multiset
1k ∀ (x2, y2) ∈ L_Q s.t. x1 ⊕ x2 ∈ r(V) for IV −M→ x1 ⊕ x2 :
1l     if x1 ⊕ x2 ⊕ y1 ⊕ y2 ∈ V ∪ (V_new \ {x1 ⊕ x2 ⊕ y1 ⊕ y2}) or
1m        (x2 ∈ Z(M) and x1 ⊕ x2 ⊕ y1 ⊕ y2 ∈ dom(L_P) ∪ {x1}) :
1n         bad1 ← true
1o         [GOTO 1b]
1p ret L_P(x1) ← y1

On query R_Q(x2):
2a if x2 ∈ dom(L_Q) ret y2 = L_Q(x2)
2b y2 ←$ Z_2^l \ rng(L_Q)
2c V_new ← {x1' ⊕ x2, x1' ⊕ x2 ⊕ y1' ⊕ y2 | (x1', y1') ∈ L_P} multiset
2d ∀ (x1, y1) ∈ L_P s.t. x1 ⊕ x2 ∈ r(V) for IV −M→ x1 ⊕ x2 :
2e     if x1 ⊕ x2 ⊕ y1 ⊕ y2 ∈ V ∪ (V_new \ {x1 ⊕ x2 ⊕ y1 ⊕ y2}) or
2f        (x2 ∈ Z(M) and x1 ⊕ x2 ⊕ y1 ⊕ y2 ∈ dom(L_P)) :
2g         bad2 ← true
2h         [GOTO 2b]
2i ret L_Q(x2) ← y2
```

```
On query R_P^{-1}(y1):
3a if y1 ∈ rng(L_P) ret x1 = L_P^{-1}(y1)
3b x1 ←$ Z_2^l \ dom(L_P)
3c if x1 ∈ r̄(V) :
3d     bad3 ← true
3e     [GOTO 3b]
3f ∀ x2 ∈ dom(L_Q) : if x1 ⊕ x2 ∈ r(V) :
3g     bad3 ← true
3h     [GOTO 3b]
3i ret L_P^{-1}(y1) ← x1

On query R_Q^{-1}(y2):
4a if y2 ∈ rng(L_Q) ret x2 = L_Q^{-1}(y2)
4b x2 ←$ Z_2^l \ dom(L_Q)
4c ∀ x1 ∈ dom(L_P) : if x1 ⊕ x2 ∈ r(V) :
4d     bad4 ← true
4e     [GOTO 4b]
4f ret L_Q^{-1}(y2) ← x2

On query L_3(M):
5a (M_1', ..., M_k') ← pad(M)
5b h_0 ← IV_n
5c for i = 1, ..., k :
5d     a ← R_Q(M_i')
5e     b ← R_P(h_{i−1} ⊕ M_i')
5f     h_i ← a ⊕ b ⊕ h_{i−1}
5g d ← R_P(h_k)
5h h ← chop_{l−n}(d ⊕ h_k)
5i ret h
```

Fig. 5. Game 4 (including the boxed statements) and game 5 (with the boxed statements removed). In both games, the distinguisher has access to L_3^R, R.

$\Pr\left(\mathcal{D}^{G_7} \text{ sets } \mathbf{bad}_0\right)$. Consider the jth query to R_P, $1 \leq j \leq r_P$. The probability that $\mathbf{bad}_0$ is set in this query, $\mathbf{bad}_0^j$, equals the probability that y_1 hits A_0. But as y_1 is taken uniformly at random from a set of size 2^l, and A_0 is of size at most r_P, $\mathbf{bad}_0^j$ occurs with probability at most $\frac{r_P}{2^l}$. By the union bound, $\Pr\left(\mathcal{D}^{G_7} \text{ sets } \mathbf{bad}_0\right) \leq \frac{r_P^2}{2^l}$;

$\Pr\left(\mathcal{D}^{G_7} \text{ sets } \mathbf{bad}_1 \mid \mathcal{D}^{G_7} \text{ sets } \neg\mathbf{bad}_0\right)$. Consider the jth query to R_P, $1 \leq j \leq r_P$. The probability that $\mathbf{bad}_1$ is set in this query, $\mathbf{bad}_1^j$, equals the probability that y_1 hits A_1. But as y_1 is taken uniformly at random from a set of size at least $2^l - r_P$ (because $\mathcal{D}^{G_7}$ sets $\neg\mathbf{bad}_0$), and A_1 is of size at most $r_Q(2r_Pr_Q + r_P)$, $\mathbf{bad}_1^j$ occurs with probability at most $\frac{r_Pr_Q(2r_Q+1)}{2^l - r_P}$. By the union bound, $\Pr\left(\mathcal{D}^{G_7} \text{ sets } \mathbf{bad}_1 \mid \mathcal{D}^{G_7} \text{ sets } \neg\mathbf{bad}_0\right) \leq \frac{r_P^2r_Q(2r_Q+1)}{2^l - r_P}$;

Analogously, $\mathbf{bad}_2$ is set with probability at most $\frac{r_P^2r_Q(2r_Q+1)}{2^l - r_Q}$, $\mathbf{bad}_3$ with probability at most $\frac{r_P^2r_Q(r_Q+1)}{2^l - r_P}$, and $\mathbf{bad}_4$ with probability at most $\frac{r_P^2r_Q^2}{2^l - r_Q}$. Concluding, under the assumption that $r_P, r_Q < 2^{l-1}$, we obtain:

$$\mathrm{Adv}_{\mathsf{Gr},\mathsf{S}}^{\mathrm{pro}}(\mathcal{D}) \leq \frac{58(q_P + (K+1)q_L)^2(q_Q + Kq_L)^2}{2^l}.$$

On query $R_P(x_1)$:

1a **if** $x_1 \in \mathrm{dom}(\mathcal{L}_P)$ **ret** $y_1 = \mathcal{L}_P(x_1)$
1b $y_1 \xleftarrow{\$} \mathbb{Z}_2^l \backslash \mathrm{rng}(\mathcal{L}_P)$
1c **ret** $\mathcal{L}_P(x_1) \leftarrow y_1$

On query $R_Q(x_2)$:

2a **if** $x_2 \in \mathrm{dom}(\mathcal{L}_Q)$ **ret** $y_2 = \mathcal{L}_Q(x_2)$
2b $y_2 \xleftarrow{\$} \mathbb{Z}_2^l \backslash \mathrm{rng}(\mathcal{L}_Q)$
2c **ret** $\mathcal{L}_Q(x_2) \leftarrow y_2$

On query $R_{P^{-1}}(y_1)$:

3a **if** $y_1 \in \mathrm{rng}(\mathcal{L}_P)$ **ret** $x_1 = \mathcal{L}_P^{-1}(y_1)$
3b $x_1 \xleftarrow{\$} \mathbb{Z}_2^l \backslash \mathrm{dom}(\mathcal{L}_P)$
3c **ret** $\mathcal{L}_P^{-1}(y_1) \leftarrow x_1$

On query $R_{Q^{-1}}(y_2)$:

4a **if** $y_2 \in \mathrm{rng}(\mathcal{L}_Q)$ **ret** $x_2 = \mathcal{L}_Q^{-1}(y_2)$
4b $x_2 \xleftarrow{\$} \mathbb{Z}_2^l \backslash \mathrm{dom}(\mathcal{L}_Q)$
4c **ret** $\mathcal{L}_Q^{-1}(y_2) \leftarrow x_2$

On query $L_3(M)$:

5a $(M'_1, \ldots, M'_k) \leftarrow \mathrm{pad}(M)$
5b $h_0 \leftarrow IV_n$
5c **for** $i = 1, \ldots, k$:
5d $\quad a \leftarrow R_Q(M'_i)$
5e $\quad b \leftarrow R_P(h_{i-1} \oplus M'_i)$
5f $\quad h_i \leftarrow a \oplus b \oplus h_{i-1}$
5g $d \leftarrow R_P(h_k)$
5h $h \leftarrow \mathrm{chop}_{l-n}(d \oplus h_k)$
5i **ret** h

Fig. 6. Game 6. The distinguisher has access to L_3^R, R.

This completes the proof of Thm. 1.

Proposition 2. *Until* **bad** *occurs in game 2 or 3, both games are identical. Formally:* $\Pr\left(\mathcal{D}^{G_2} = 1 \mid \mathcal{D}^{G_2} \textit{ sets } \neg\mathbf{bad}\right) = \Pr\left(\mathcal{D}^{G_3} = 1 \mid \mathcal{D}^{G_3} \textit{ sets } \neg\mathbf{bad}\right)$.

Proof. We need to prove that the query outcomes in game 2 and 3 are identically distributed, until the distinguisher sets **bad** in either one of the games. As the right oracles of the games are the same, $\mathcal{D}$ can differentiate game 2 and 3 only if it discovers any inconsistencies in the answers by the left oracles (L_2 for game 2 and L_3 for game 3), given any list of queries made by $\mathcal{D}$ to the right oracle. Recall that $\mathcal{L}_P, \mathcal{L}_Q$ denote the query history to the right oracles R_P, R_Q, and (V, E) the graph defined by these queries (cf. Sect. 4.1). Denote any query history to L_i ($i = 2, 3$) by $\mathcal{L}$. Furthermore, denote by $\tilde{\mathcal{L}}_P, \tilde{\mathcal{L}}_Q$ the set of queries to the right oracles that are observed by the distinguisher[5], and denote by $(\tilde{V}, \tilde{E})$ the subgraph defined by these. We focus on the outcomes of the left oracle: we need to prove that given the views $\tilde{\mathcal{L}}_P, \tilde{\mathcal{L}}_Q$, and given query history $\mathcal{L}$, the outcomes of new queries to the left oracle are identically distributed in game 2 and 3. Concretely, for $\alpha \in \mathbb{Z}_2^n$, we analyze the probability

$$\Pr\left(L_i(M) = \alpha \text{ in } G_i \mid \tilde{\mathcal{L}}_P, \tilde{\mathcal{L}}_Q, \mathcal{L};\ M \notin \mathrm{dom}(\mathcal{L});\ \mathcal{D}^{G_i} \text{ sets } \neg\mathbf{bad}\right). \quad (5)$$

Define $M' = (M'_1, \ldots, M'_k) = \mathrm{pad}(M)$ to be the padding of M. The query $L_i(M)$ is called 'evaluatable' by $\tilde{\mathcal{L}}_P, \tilde{\mathcal{L}}_Q$ if there exists an h_k in $\bar{r}(\tilde{V})$ such that $IV \xrightarrow{M'} h_k$, and $h_k \in \mathrm{dom}(\tilde{\mathcal{L}}_P)$. We will show that for both games the following holds: if $L_i(M)$ is evaluatable by $\tilde{\mathcal{L}}_P, \tilde{\mathcal{L}}_Q$, the query answer can be obtained deterministically from this history. On the other hand, if it is *not* evaluatable by $\tilde{\mathcal{L}}_P, \tilde{\mathcal{L}}_Q$, (5) holds with probability $1/2^n$ only. In other words, this probability is the same in both games $i = 2, 3$, which proves the claim that the answers by L_2, L_3 are identically distributed.

For the purpose of the proof, we also consider evaluatability by $\mathcal{L}_P, \mathcal{L}_Q$, which is defined similarly as before. Observe that $H_i(M)$ is evaluatable by $\mathcal{L}_P, \mathcal{L}_Q$ if it is evaluatable by $\tilde{\mathcal{L}}_P, \tilde{\mathcal{L}}_Q$. We now analyze (5). First we consider the case $L_i(M)$

[5] In game 3, the right oracles R_P, R_Q are also queried in each call to the left oracle, via lines 6d, 6e and 6g, but the distinguisher does not observe these queries.

```
On query R_P(x_1):
1a if x_1 ∈ dom(L_P) ret y_1 = L_P(x_1)
1b if x_1 ∈ r̄(V) :
1c     h ←$ Z_2^n
1d     w ←$ Z_2^{l-n}
1e     y_1 ← x_1 ⊕ (h||w)
1f     if y_1 ∈ A_0 :
1g         bad_0 ← true
1h         GOTO 1d
1i else y_1 ←$ Z_2^l \ rng(L_P)
1j if y_1 ∈ A_1 :
1k     bad_1 ← true
1l     GOTO 1b
1m ret L_P(x_1) ← y_1

On query R_Q(x_2):
2a if x_2 ∈ dom(L_Q) ret y_2 = L_Q(x_2)
2b y_2 ←$ Z_2^l \ rng(L_Q)
2c if y_2 ∈ A_2 :
2d     bad_2 ← true
2e     GOTO 2b
2f ret L_Q(x_2) ← y_2
```

```
On query R_{P-1}(y_1):
3a if y_1 ∈ rng(L_P) ret x_1 = L_P^{-1}(y_1)
3b x_1 ←$ Z_2^l \ dom(L_P)
3c if x_1 ∈ A_3 :
3d     bad_3 ← true
3e     GOTO 3b
3f ret L_P^{-1}(y_1) ← x_1

On query R_{Q-1}(y_2):
4a if y_2 ∈ rng(L_Q) ret x_2 = L_Q^{-1}(y_2)
4b x_2 ←$ Z_2^l \ dom(L_Q)
4c if x_2 ∈ A_4 :
4d     bad_4 ← true
4e     GOTO 4b
4f ret L_Q^{-1}(y_2) ← x_2
```

```
On query L_3(M):
5a (M'_1, ..., M'_k) ← pad(M)
5b h_0 ← IV_n
5c for i = 1, ..., k :
5d     a ← R_Q(M'_i)
5e     b ← R_P(h_{i-1} ⊕ M'_i)
5f     h_i ← a ⊕ b ⊕ h_{i-1}
5g d ← R_P(h_k)
5h h ← chop_{l-n}(d ⊕ h_k)
5i ret h
```

$$
\begin{aligned}
A_0 &= \mathrm{rng}(\mathcal{L}_P);\\
A_1 &= \textstyle\bigcup_{(x_2,y_2)\in\mathcal{L}_Q}\Big(\ \{x_1\oplus x_2\oplus y_2\oplus s \mid s\in V\cup(V_{\mathrm{new}}\backslash\{x_1\oplus x_2\oplus y_1\oplus y_2\})\ \}\cup\\
&\qquad\qquad \{x_1\oplus x_2\oplus y_2\oplus x_1' \mid x_1'\in\mathrm{dom}(\mathcal{L}_P)\cup\{x_1\}\}\Big),\\
&\qquad \text{where } V_{\mathrm{new}}=\{x_1\oplus x_2',\, x_1\oplus x_2'\oplus y_1\oplus y_2' \mid (x_2',y_2')\in\mathcal{L}_Q\} \text{ is a multiset};\\
A_2 &= \textstyle\bigcup_{(x_1,y_1)\in\mathcal{L}_P}\Big(\ \{x_1\oplus x_2\oplus y_1\oplus s \mid s\in V\cup(V_{\mathrm{new}}\backslash\{x_1\oplus x_2\oplus y_1\oplus y_2\})\ \}\cup\\
&\qquad\qquad \{x_1\oplus x_2\oplus y_1\oplus x_1' \mid x_1'\in\mathrm{dom}(\mathcal{L}_P)\}\Big),\\
&\qquad \text{where } V_{\mathrm{new}}=\{x_1'\oplus x_2,\, x_1'\oplus x_2\oplus y_1'\oplus y_2 \mid (x_1',y_1')\in\mathcal{L}_P\} \text{ is a multiset};\\
A_3 &= \bar{r}(V)\cup\{x_2\oplus s \mid x_2\in\mathrm{dom}(\mathcal{L}_Q),\, s\in r(V)\}\,;\\
A_4 &= \{x_1\oplus s \mid x_1\in\mathrm{dom}(\mathcal{L}_P),\, s\in r(V)\}\,.
\end{aligned}
$$

Fig. 7. Game 7. The distinguisher has access to L_3^R, R.

is evaluatable by $\tilde{\mathcal{L}}_P, \tilde{\mathcal{L}}_Q$. Then we consider the case it is not evaluatable by these views (but it may be evaluatable by $\mathcal{L}_P, \mathcal{L}_Q$).

(1) $L_i(M)$ $(i = 2, 3)$ **is evaluatable by** $\tilde{\mathcal{L}}_P, \tilde{\mathcal{L}}_Q$**.** In both games, this means that there exists an h_k in $\bar{r}(\tilde{V})$ such that $IV \xrightarrow{M'} h_k$, and $h_k \in \mathrm{dom}(\tilde{\mathcal{L}}_P)$. By Claim 2 below, there are no colliding paths and in particular the described path M' is unique. Furthermore, due to Claim 3 below, h_k had been added to $\mathrm{dom}(\tilde{\mathcal{L}}_P)$ in a forward query, *after* it was added to $\bar{r}(\tilde{V})$. Therefore, by line 1c, we have $R_P(h_k) = h_k \oplus (h\|w)$, where $h = L_1(M)$. As a consequence, $L_1(M)$, and thus $L_2(M)$ and $L_3(M)$, is fully determined by $\tilde{\mathcal{L}}_P, \tilde{\mathcal{L}}_Q$, which means that the outcomes in game 2 and 3 are identically distributed;

(2) $L_i(M)$ $(i = 2, 3)$ **is not evaluatable by** $\tilde{\mathcal{L}}_P, \tilde{\mathcal{L}}_Q$**, but it is evaluatable by** $\mathcal{L}_P, \mathcal{L}_Q$**.** This event is excluded for game 2 as $(\tilde{\mathcal{L}}_P, \tilde{\mathcal{L}}_Q) = (\mathcal{L}_P, \mathcal{L}_Q)$ in this game. In game 3, $\mathcal{L}_P, \mathcal{L}_Q$ also includes queries made to the right oracle via the left oracle L_3. We will show, however, that (5) holds with probability $1/2^n$ then. Similarly to case (1), there exists an h_k in $\bar{r}(V) \cap \mathrm{dom}(\mathcal{L}_P)$ such

that $IV \xrightarrow{M'} h_k$ and $R_P(h_k) = h_k \oplus (h\|w)$, where $h = L_1(M)$. But $L_3(M)$ is *not* evaluatable by $\tilde{\mathcal{L}}_P, \tilde{\mathcal{L}}_Q$, which means that h_k had been queried to R_P independently of $\tilde{\mathcal{L}}_P, \tilde{\mathcal{L}}_Q$. Furthermore, $L_3(M)$ is also independent of $\mathcal{L}$.[6] Concluding, (5) holds with probability $1/2^n$ in this case;

(3) $L_i(M)$ **(**$i = 2, 3$**) is not evaluatable by** $\mathcal{L}_P, \mathcal{L}_Q$**.** As a consequence, there either exists *no* $h_k \in \bar{r}(V)$ such that $IV \xrightarrow{M'} h_k$, or there exists such h_k, but it is no element of $\text{dom}(\mathcal{L}_P)$. For game 2, $M \notin \text{dom}(\mathcal{L})$ implies that M had not been queried to L_1 before (L_1 is queried in lines 6a and 1c only). Therefore, in this case $L_2(M)$ outputs a value h randomly sampled from $\mathbb{Z}_2^n$. For game 3, let $j \leq k$ be the maximal index such that $IV = h_0 \xrightarrow{M_1'} \cdots \xrightarrow{M_j'} h_j$ is a path in (V, E). We consider the following cases:
   - (i) $j = k$. Then, there exists an $h_k \in \bar{r}(V)$ such that $IV \xrightarrow{M'} h_k$, but as $L_3(M)$ is not evaluatable, we have $h_k \notin \text{dom}(\mathcal{L}_P)$. In line 6h of the oracle query of $L_3(M)$, $R_P(h_k)$ will then be computed via lines 1b-1e: $R_P(h_k) = h_k \oplus (h\|w)$ for $h \xleftarrow{\$} \mathbb{Z}_2^n$. The outcome $L_3(M)$ thus equals $L_3(M) = \text{chop}_{l-n}(R_P(h_k) \oplus h_k) = h$. As a consequence, the outcomes of L_2 and L_3 are identically distributed in this case;
   - (ii) $j < k$. Then, there exists a path $IV \to h_j$ labeled by $(M_1', \ldots, M_j')$, but (V, E) contains no edge $h_j \to h_{j+1}$ labeled by M_{j+1}'. By virtue of Claim 2, in the $(j+1)^{\text{th}}$ iteration of lines 6c-6f, a new node h_{j+1} will be added to $r(V)$ such that h_{j+1} was not rooted yet and there is no outgoing edge from h_{j+1} in the updated graph. The same holds for all subsequent iterations, and in particular h_k will be newly added to $\bar{r}(V)$ in the kth iteration. Due to Claim 3, this newly added note is not an element of $\text{dom}(\mathcal{L}_P)$ after this last round. Now, the same analysis as in (3i) applies. □

Claim 2. Suppose $\mathcal{D}^{G_i}$ sets $\neg$**bad** (for $i = 2, 3$). Consider a node $s \in r(V)$, and a right oracle query in which an edge (s, t) will be added to (V, E). Denote by (V', E') the updated graph (after the query). Then, t has no incoming or outgoing edge in $(V', E' \backslash \{(s, t)\})$. As a consequence, after the execution of G_i, the final graph contains no colliding paths.

Proof. In a right query to $R_{P^{-1}}$ or $R_{Q^{-1}}$, none of the newly added edges have a rooted node as starting point, by $\neg(\mathbf{bad}_3 \vee \mathbf{bad}_4)$ (lines 3f and 4c). Consider a query x_1 to R_P, and let (V, E) be the graph before the query. An outgoing edge from $s \in r(V)$ will only be added if $s = x_1 \oplus x_2$ for some $x_2 \in \text{dom}(\mathcal{L}_Q)$. By construction, the end node of the edge is $x_1 \oplus x_2 \oplus y_1 \oplus y_2 =: t$. By line 1l and $\neg\mathbf{bad}_1$, we have (a) $t \notin V$, (b) none of the newly added edges will leave from t and (c) apart from (s, t), none of the newly added edges will arrive at t. As a

[6] Observe that in game 3, $\mathcal{L}$ consists of pairs $(\bar{M}, \bar{h})$ such that $\bar{h} = \text{chop}_{l-n}(R_P(\bar{h}_k) \oplus \bar{h}_k)$ for some $\bar{h}_k \in \bar{r}(V) \cap \text{dom}(\mathcal{L}_P)$, where, by Claim 3, $R_P(\bar{h}_k)$ had been generated via lines 1b-1e. As there are no colliding paths in (V, E) by Claim 2, h_k differs from all such $\bar{h}_k$'s, and in particular $\mathcal{L}$ reveals nothing about $L_3(M)$.

consequence, t is an isolated node in $(V', E'\backslash\{(s,t)\})$. A similar argument holds for queries to R_Q, by line 2e and $\neg\mathbf{bad}_2$.

We prove that the final graph contains no colliding paths by mathematical induction. Before the first query is made, $E = \emptyset$ and hence no colliding paths occur. Assume (V, E) contains no colliding paths and consider a right oracle query. We can sequentially apply the above reasoning and discard all newly added edges (s,t) for $s \in r(V)$, in order to observe that colliding paths in (V', E') imply colliding paths in (V, E). By the induction hypothesis, these do not occur. □

Claim 3. Suppose $\mathcal{D}^{G_i}$ sets $\neg\mathbf{bad}$ (for $i = 2, 3$). Consider a right oracle query in which a node t will be added to $\bar{r}(V)$. Then, t is no element of (the updated) $\mathrm{dom}(\mathcal{L}_P)$. Furthermore, $\bar{r}(V) \cap \mathrm{dom}(\mathcal{L}_P)$ will only be increased in forward queries to R_P.

Proof. As a direct consequence of Claim 2, $\bar{r}(V)$ will be increased only if an edge $x_1 \oplus x_2 \xrightarrow{x_2} x_1 \oplus x_2 \oplus y_1 \oplus y_2$ is added such that $IV \xrightarrow{M} x_1 \oplus x_2$ is a path in (V, E), and $x_2 \in Z(M)$. Due to lines 1m and 2f, and by $\neg(\mathbf{bad}_1 \vee \mathbf{bad}_2)$, this newly added node is not an element of (the updated) $\mathrm{dom}(\mathcal{L}_P)$. Furthermore, an inverse query to R_P will never be answered with a node already in $\bar{r}(V)$, by line 3c and $\neg\mathbf{bad}_3$, and therefore $\bar{r}(V) \cap \mathrm{dom}(\mathcal{L}_P)$ will only be increased in forward queries to R_P. □

Acknowledgments. This work has been funded in part by the IAP Program P6/26 BCRYPT of the Belgian State (Belgian Science Policy), and in part by the European Commission through the ICT program under contract ICT-2007-216676 ECRYPT II. The first author is supported by a Ph.D. Fellowship from the Flemish Research Foundation (FWO-Vlaanderen). The second author is supported by a Ph.D. Fellowship from the Institute for the Promotion of Innovation through Science and Technology in Flanders (IWT-Vlaanderen).

References

[1] Andreeva, E., Neven, G., Preneel, B., Shrimpton, T.: Seven-property-preserving iterated hashing: ROX. In: Kurosawa, K. (ed.) ASIACRYPT 2007. LNCS, vol. 4833, pp. 130–146. Springer, Heidelberg (2007)
[2] Bellare, M., Ristenpart, T.: Multi-property-preserving hash domain extension and the EMD Transform. In: Lai, X., Chen, K. (eds.) ASIACRYPT 2006. LNCS, vol. 4284, pp. 299–314. Springer, Heidelberg (2006)
[3] Bellare, M., Rogaway, P.: Random oracles are practical: A paradigm for designing efficient protocols. In: ACM Conference on Computer and Communications Security, pp. 62–73. ACM, New York (1993)
[4] Bertoni, G., Daemen, J., Peeters, M., van Assche, G.: On the indifferentiability of the sponge construction. In: Smart, N.P. (ed.) EUROCRYPT 2008. LNCS, vol. 4965, pp. 181–197. Springer, Heidelberg (2008)
[5] Bertoni, G., Daemen, J., Peeters, M., Van Assche, G.: Sponge functions. In: ECRYPT Hash Workshop 2007 (2007)

[6] Bhattacharyya, R., Mandal, A., Nandi, M.: Security analysis of the mode of JH hash function. In: beyer, I. (ed.) FSE 2010. LNCS, vol. 6147, pp. 168–191. Springer, Heidelberg (2010)
[7] Biham, E., Dunkelman, O.: A framework for iterative hash functions – HAIFA. Cryptology ePrint Archive, Report 2007/278 (2007)
[8] Bresson, E., Canteaut, A., Chevallier-Mames, B., Clavier, C., Fuhr, T., Gouget, A., Icart, T., Misarsky, J.-F., Naya-Plasencia, M., Paillier, P., Pornin, T., Reinhard, J.-R., Thuillet, C., Videau, M.: Indifferentiability with distinguishers: Why Shabal does not require ideal ciphers. Cryptology ePrint Archive, Report 2009/199 (2009)
[9] Chang, D., Lee, S., Nandi, M., Yung, M.: Indifferentiable security analysis of popular hash functions with prefix-free padding. In: Lai, X., Chen, K. (eds.) ASIACRYPT 2006. LNCS, vol. 4284, pp. 283–298. Springer, Heidelberg (2006)
[10] Chang, D., Nandi, M.: Improved indifferentiability security analysis of chopMD hash function. In: Nyberg, K. (ed.) FSE 2008. LNCS, vol. 5086, pp. 429–443. Springer, Heidelberg (2008)
[11] Coron, J.-S., Dodis, Y., Malinaud, C., Puniya, P.: Merkle-Damgård revisited: How to construct a hash function. In: Shoup, V. (ed.) CRYPTO 2005. LNCS, vol. 3621, pp. 430–448. Springer, Heidelberg (2005)
[12] Damgård, I.: A design principle for hash functions. In: Brassard, G. (ed.) CRYPTO 1989. LNCS, vol. 435, pp. 416–427. Springer, Heidelberg (1990)
[13] Dodis, Y., Gennaro, R., Håstad, J., Krawczyk, H., Rabin, T.: Randomness extraction and key derivation using the CBC, cascade and HMAC modes. In: Franklin, M. (ed.) CRYPTO 2004. LNCS, vol. 3152, pp. 494–510. Springer, Heidelberg (2004)
[14] Dodis, Y., Ristenpart, T., Shrimpton, T.: Salvaging Merkle-Damgård for practical applications. In: Joux, A. (ed.) EUROCRYPT 2009. LNCS, vol. 5479, pp. 371–388. Springer, Heidelberg (2010)
[15] Gauravaram, P., Knudsen, L., Matusiewicz, K., Mendel, F., Rechberger, C., Schläffer, M., Thomsen, S.: Grøstl – a SHA-3 candidate (2009)
[16] Lucks, S.: A failure-friendly design principle for hash functions. In: Roy, B. (ed.) ASIACRYPT 2005. LNCS, vol. 3788, pp. 474–494. Springer, Heidelberg (2005)
[17] Maurer, U., Renner, R., Holenstein, C.: Indifferentiability, impossibility results on reductions, and applications to the random oracle methodology. In: Naor, M. (ed.) TCC 2004. LNCS, vol. 2951, pp. 21–39. Springer, Heidelberg (2004)
[18] Merkle, R.: One way hash functions and DES. In: Brassard, G. (ed.) CRYPTO 1989. LNCS, vol. 435, pp. 428–446. Springer, Heidelberg (1990)
[19] Miyaguchi, S., Ohta, K., Iwata, M.: Confirmation that some hash functions are not collision free. In: Damgård, I.B. (ed.) EUROCRYPT 1990. LNCS, vol. 473, pp. 326–343. Springer, Heidelberg (1991)
[20] National Institute for Standards and Technology. Announcing Request for Candidate Algorithm Nominations for a New Cryptographic Hash Algorithm (SHA3) Family (November 2007)
[21] Preneel, B., Govaerts, R., Vandewalle, J.: Hash functions based on block ciphers: A synthetic approach. In: Stinson, D.R. (ed.) CRYPTO 1993. LNCS, vol. 773, pp. 368–378. Springer, Heidelberg (1994)
[22] Wang, X., Yin, Y., Yu, H.: Finding collisions in the full SHA-1. In: Shoup, V. (ed.) CRYPTO 2005. LNCS, vol. 3621, pp. 17–36. Springer, Heidelberg (2005)
[23] Wang, X., Yu, H.: How to break MD5 and other hash functions. In: Cramer, R. (ed.) EUROCRYPT 2005. LNCS, vol. 3494, pp. 19–35. Springer, Heidelberg (2005)

Algorithmic Tamper-Proof Security under Probing Attacks

Feng-Hao Liu* and Anna Lysyanskaya*

Department of Computer Science, Brown University
{fenghao,anna}@cs.brown.edu

Abstract. Gennaro et al. initiated the study of algorithmic tamper proof (ATP) cryptography: cryptographic hardware that remains secure even in the presence of an adversary who can tamper with the memory content of a hardware device. In this paper, we solve an open problem stated in their paper, and also consider whether a device can be secured against an adversary who can both tamper with its memory and probe a few memory locations or wires at a time. Our results are as follows:

- It is impossible to realize a secure cryptographic functionality with a personal identification number (PIN) where a user is allowed to make up to ℓ incorrect consecutive attempts to enter her PIN, with no total limit on incorrect PIN attempts. (This was left as an open problem by Gennaro et al.)
- It is impossible to secure a deterministic cryptographic device against an adversary who is allowed to both tamper with the memory of the device and probe a memory location; it is also essentially infeasible to secure it if the adversary's probing power is restricted to internal wires; it is impossible to secure it against an adversary whose probing power is restricted to internal wires, but who is also allowed to tamper with a few internal wires.
- By extending the results of Ishai et al., we show that a cryptographic device with a true source of randomness can withstand tampering and limited probing attacks at the same time.

1 Introduction

In cryptography, we typically assume that an adversary launching an attack can neither probe bits of a secret key, nor tamper with it; the adversary may only obtain input/output (i.e. black-box) access to a functionality it is trying to attack. However, in practice, adversaries may attack a cryptographic device through other means. For example, in a side-channel attack [AK96, AK97], an adversary can measure the power consumption of the device [KJJ99, CRR03], timing of operations [Koc96], electromagnetic radiation [AARR03], etc. Additionally, an adversary may tamper with the device's memory [BS97] or circuitry [SA03] and check the effect this might have on the device's computation.

There are several lines of work that place these attacks on theoretical foundations. Gennaro et al. [GLM$^+$04] defined security of a cryptographic functionality against an

* Supported by NSF grant CNS-0347661 and CNS-0831293.

J.A. Garay and R. De Prisco (Eds.): SCN 2010, LNCS 6280, pp. 106–120, 2010.

adversary who can tamper with the contents of a device's memory, and showed how to satisfy their definition. Ishai et al. [ISW03], in contrast, defined and realized security for devices where an adversary can probe the memory of the device (more precisely, wires of its circuit), and even fix some of the wires in a circuit under attack.

In this paper, we examine security under a combination of attacks described in these previous papers. Intuitively, it would seem that it should be possible to combine the positive results of the two lines of work and design a device that would withstand an adversary who can both tamper with its memory and probe a few memory locations at a time. Surprisingly, we show that a cryptographic functionality cannot withstand such a combined attack, unless augmented with a true source of randomness. We give an adversary who, given the ability to only probe one memory location at a time, and the ability to tamper with the memory of a deterministic device, retrieves the entire secret content of the device's memory, even though the device may continuously update its secret content (so the trivial attack that just probes memory locations one by one would not work).

Related work. Gennaro et al. [GLM$^+$04] considered the adversary who, in addition to black-box access to a functionality he is trying to attack, also has the ability to tamper with the memory of this device. Their work was motivated by that of Biham and Shamir [BS97] who showed how to break cryptographic schemes by having the memory of a device modified in a certain way. Gennaro et al. gave a definition of algorithmic tamper-proof (ATP) security: this means that the device is programmed in such a way that the underlying cryptographic functionality (e.g., a signature scheme) will remain secure (e.g., existentially unforgeable) even in the presence of such an adversary. They then showed that, unless a device has a self-destruct capability and can be initialized via a trusted setup phase, this notion of security is unattainable. However, they also showed that using self-destruct and trusted setup, it is possible to achieve ATP security.

Ishai et al. [ISW03] considered the adversary who, in addition to black-box access to a circuit implementing a cryptographic functionality, could also probe individual wires of this circuit (we call this a "memory probing adversary"). They showed, surprisingly, that one could tolerate an adversary that probes up to some constant t wires at a time using a transformed circuit where corresponding to every wire of the original circuit, there are $\Theta(t)$ wires, each carrying a share of value of the original wire. Moreover, every time such a circuit is invoked it can redistribute these shares, and so it can be probed again, so over the lifetime of the circuit, the adversary can probe each wire several times. This resharing does not require a continuous source of true randomness: it can be done using a pseudorandom generator seeded by a random string that resides in the circuit's memory and also gets updated at every invocation. In a follow-up paper, Ishai et al. [IPSW06] further extended this model to allow the adversary to tamper with another c wires: to fix them temporarily or permanently. They showed that it was still possible to have a circuit that withstood such an attack.

Micali and Reyzin [MR04] defined security for cryptographic primitives under side channel attacks and show how to use these primitives; their side channel attack is much more general than attacks that are known in the real world [AK96, Koc96, KJJ99, AARR03, CRR03], and also more general than the probing attack of Ishai et al. [ISW03]. In fact, the model of Ishai et al. [ISW03] is a special case of the

Micali-Reyzin model. Micali and Reyzin do not, however, consider an adversary that tampers with the device.

Recently Dziembowski, Pietrzak, and Wichs [DPW10], they also consider security against the algorithmic tamper and probing adversaries. Their main technique is to construct "non-malleable codes" against a certain class of tampering attacks. In the plain model, their positive result holds for a smaller class of tampering functions that do modifications effecting each bit of the memory but independent of other bits. With a random oracle, they are able to extend the results against a broader class of tampering functions, yet the random oracle model is less desirable. We remark this does not contradict our impossibility results since we consider the stronger adversaries who can perform any polynomial-time computable tampering attacks in the plain model, where it is still open that one can extend their positive results in this case.

Our contribution. Our first contribution in the ATP model is to resolve, in the negative, the problem left open by Gennaro et al. of whether it was possible to realize a secure cryptographic functionality with a personal identification number (PIN) where a user is allowed to make up to ℓ incorrect consecutive attempts to enter her PIN, with no total limit on incorrect PIN attempts. (In contrast, Gennaro et al. showed that it was possible to limit the *total* number of incorrectly entered PINs). Along the way, we also showed that no ATP secure functionality can allow a user to change her PIN.

Next, we address the natural question of whether it is possible to achieve ATP security even in the presence of a memory-probing adversary. Here we remark that suppose the adversary can read all the contents in the memory by probing at one shot, then no security can be achieved. Thus in our model of memory-probing adversary, we consider a relaxation of the adversary's power by restricting the number of bits she can probe in a time. However, we do not limit the total number of bits (information) she can gather over time. This approach is similar to the key leakage model where the leakage is bounded at any moment but not over time.

Then, we give a definition of security for this scenario; our definition is a natural generalization of the definition of Gennaro et al. Next, we show that no deterministic circuit can achieve this notion of security: a memory-probing adversary who can also tamper with the memory can retrieve the secret content of the device's memory, even if she can only probe a constant number (very small fraction of the memory) in any moment.

Note that this impossibility applies to the circuit constructed by Ishai et al.: even though their construction uses randomness, ultimately it is the pseudorandom generator supplying it using a random seed in a deterministic fashion, hence their overall circuit is deterministic. The difference is that they only allow up to a certain number of wires to be tampered, while we consider the much more powerful tampering adversary of Gennaro et al., who may apply any polynomial-time computable transformation to the contents of a circuit's memory.

We also consider a variation of the memory probing adversary: one who may not probe memory cells, but only intermediate wires of the circuit. This is to model the idea that perhaps memory cells can be invulnerable to probing. It turns out that such an adversary is almost equally powerful: even though he is only explicitly allowed to read up to a constant t wires of the circuit at a time, he can cause any deterministic circuit to behave in such a way that the contents of every wire in a particular invocation of the circuit (other than the protected memory cells) will become exposed to the adversary, i.e. the adversary can read all the wires at once. Due to impossibility of obfuscation [BGI+01], this leads to insecurity. (On the other hand, since we cannot reverse-engineer a circuit either, it does not necessarily imply that the secret content of the circuit can be computed from this information.)

Finally, we also consider the adversary who is allowed to tamper with wires of a circuit in addition to tampering with its memory and probing additional wires. Here, even if we do not allow the adversary to probe memory cells, the adversary can still retrieve the secret content of any deterministic circuit. Moreover, he can do it even if he chooses the set of wires to probe and tamper with *non-adaptively*.

On the positive side, we show that the Ishai et al.'s randomized construction (i.e. the one that uses true randomness, not a pseudorandom generator), in combination with the Gennaro et al.'s construction, achieves ATP security in the face of the circuit probing and tampering attack (but not memory probing). This is the best positive result we could get: for any other scenario we showed negative results!

Having investigated into the models in both paper, we briefly describe the distinction between those two: for the [GLM+04] model, the adversary can tamper with the whole memory, but cannot do with the circuit. In [IPSW06] model, the adversary can partially tamper and probe every part of the circuit, but cannot tamper with the whole memory in a single clock cycle. Both models have positive results. It is natural to consider if we can combine those models, to give the adversary more power, to see if positive results still remain or where they get stuck.

We show, mostly, that security cannot be achieved under a combination of attacks, for circuits without a source of true randomness. Under some conditions, the circuit with such source can apply the previous techniques to achieve security against the combined attacks. This is a separation for the models that shows a circuit with its randomness stored vulnerably is strictly less secure than that with a source of true randomness.

2 Definitions

2.1 ATP Models

Following Gennaro et al., we consider a system with two components: (1) secret content, sc (containing some secret key, sk, randomness, and possibly state information), and (2) a cryptographic algorithm implemented by a circuit C which uses the secret content.

We say that the system implements a certain function F, if for any input a,$C(sc, a) = F(a)$. We say that C implements a keyed cryptographic functionality $F(\cdot, \cdot)$, if for every key sk (from the appropriate domain) there exists a setting sc_{sk} of the secret data, such that the system (C, sc_{sk}) implements the function $F(\mathsf{sk}, \cdot)$. An algorithm computing sc_{sk} will be called a *software setup algorithm*. Finally, a device setup protocol implementing $F(\cdot, \cdot)$ is a pair of algorithms. The first generates the algorithm C, possibly with some additional state information to be passed to the second algorithm. The second is a software setup algorithm: given input sk and C, and possibly an additional state information input, the algorithm generates an appropriate sc_{sk}. If the software setup algorithm is stateful, we say that the device uses public parameters. We will consider devices with efficient setup algorithms, and all the functionalities the devices compute are polynomially-computable.

Consider C which implements some $F(\cdot,\cdot)$ (e.g., a signature algorithm). Gennaro et al. defined a *tampering adversary* who can request two commands to be carried out: $\mathsf{Run}(\cdot)$ and $\mathsf{Apply}(\cdot)$, and Setup.

- The command $\mathsf{Run}(a)$, invokes the cryptographic computation C using the software content sc on input a. The output is the output of such computation, i.e., $C(sc, a)$. For example, if the cryptographic algorithm is a signature then the output is a signature on the message a using the secret key stored in sc.
- The command $\mathsf{Apply}(f)$ takes as input a function f, and modifies the software content sc to $f(sc)$. From this point on, until a new $\mathsf{Apply}(f)$ is requested, all $\mathsf{Run}(a)$ operations will use $f(sc)$ as the new software content. f can be a probabilistic function. Note that the next invocation of $\mathsf{Apply}(f')$ would change $f(sc)$ to $f'(f(sc))$, i.e. it does not apply f' to the original sc. There is no output for this command.
- The command $\mathsf{Setup}(\mathsf{sk})$ invokes the software setup algorithm, outputting sc such that the device $C(sc,\cdot)$ implements the function $F(\mathsf{sk},\cdot)$.

The device may also have a *self-destruct* capability, called by the circuit C. If this happens, every Run command from then on will always output $\perp$.

As mentioned above, security of smartcards and other portable devices is one of the motivations for considering this model. For convenience, throughout this paper we refer to the system interchangeably as a "card" or a "device".

In the tampering adversary model (referred to in the sequel as the ATP model and the [GLM$^+$04] model), the adversary only applies a polynomial-time computable transformation on the secret memory content sc without reading it directly. On the other hand, the underlying hardware circuit C cannot be tampered with, and results of intermediate computation steps cannot be eavesdropped.

In the following sections, we extend the [GLM$^+$04] model to allow the adversary to not only tamper with the circuit's memory, but also to probe the circuit's wires and gates while the computation is going on, and to tamper with the individual wires in the circuit. We get adversaries of different strengths by allowing various combinations of these attacks. The memory probing adversary is allowed to read one bit at a time of the secret content sc, in addition to being able to tamper with it through the Apply command. The circuit probing adversary will be allowed to retrieve the contents of a wire in the circuit during the execution of a Run command, in addition to being able to issue Apply commands. The wire fixing adversary is allowed to fix a particular wire of the circuit so that for the duration of the Run query it carries a particular bit. We will formalize the definitions of these additional adversarial behaviors in the following sections.

2.2 Memory-Probing Models

In this section, we consider the adversary by allowing the probing attacks on the memory. Besides Run, the adversary can probe several (a constant number of) cells in the memory once, after Run is finished. To formalize that, we make available to the adversary the following capability: Let the memory content $sc \in \{0,1\}^m$ be an m-bit string, and T be a subset of $\{1,2,\ldots,m\}$ The command ProbeMem(T) returns the ith bit of the secret content, sc_i for any $i \in T$.

If $|T| = m$, then we could never achieve security.Therefore, it is natural to limit the size of probing by allowing $|T| = t$ for a constant parameter (that does not grow with m). The command ProbeMem can be executed at most once following an execution of the Run command. We allow the adversary to change the set of indices it queries, T, adaptively.

2.3 Circuit-Probing and Circuit-Tampering Models

In this section, we consider another type of attacks: the adversary can tamper or probe the circuit's wires when Run is operating. To formalize that, we let the wires in the circuit be labeled by $W = \{w_1, w_2, \ldots, w_\ell\}$ for some ℓ, and T be a subset of $\{w_1, w_2, \ldots, w_\ell\}$.

For the Circuit-Probing model, the adversary may issue the following command:

- The commands ProbeWire(T) returns the values of the wires $w_i \in T$.

For the Circuit-Tampering model, the adversary may issue the following commands:

- The commands ChangeWire(T, val) returns nothing but replaces the value in the wire $w_i \in T$ with val_i temporarily.
- The commands FixWire(T, val) returns nothing but replaces the value in the wire $w_i \in T$ with val_i permanently.

The adversary is able to apply any and only one of these commands per clock cycle when the circuit is operating (Run is called.) Since this model inherits the results of [IPSW06], it is reasonable for us to limit the size of T by setting $|T| = t$ for some constant parameter, as they did.

2.4 Combined ATP, Memory-Probing, Circuit-Tampering, Circuit-Probing Models

In the following sections, we will consider a variety of combination of models. In summary, section 4 considers the combination of ATP and Memory-Probing models; section 5 considers the combination of ATP, Circuit-Probing, and Circuit-Tampering models. The details will be explained in the sections respectively.

2.5 Security Definition

Here we give a general definition for the security of the circuit. This definition is an extension of the [GLM+04] definition: it gives the adversary a broader set of capabilities.

Definition 1. *Define $\mathcal{A}_{\mathsf{Ideal}}$ be the set of adversaries that can only obtain the input-output behavior of the device, and $\mathcal{A}_{\mathsf{Model}}$ be the set of adversaries that can perform any attack defined in a particular* Model *(this* Model *can be a combination of attack capabilities described above). Let C be a circuit that implements some functionality.*

We say C is Model*-secure if there exists a probabilistic polynomial time simulator S such that for any $A \in \mathcal{A}_{\mathsf{Model}}$, the following two experiments are computationally indistinguishable:*

1. *$S^A \in \mathcal{A}_{\mathsf{Ideal}}$ outputs a bit after interacting with C.*
2. *$A \in \mathcal{A}_{\mathsf{Model}}$ outputs a bit after interacting with C.*

In the following sections, if we don't specify the Model, we are referring to the model discussed in that section.

3 New Impossibility Result in the ATP Model

Consider the following functionality for a signature device with a personal identification number (PIN). The device has a public key pk, and its secret content sc contains the corresponding sk and a personal identification code pin that must be entered for the device to run properly. The idea is that a user Alice of the device would need to remember a short PIN; if she loses the device and it falls into the adversary's hands, the adversary will still have to correctly guess the PIN before he can use it. We want a device that tolerates a few incorrect PIN attempts (since Alice may occasionally mistype the PIN), but stops working after the number of incorrectly entered PINs exceeds a certain threshold α (a constant that is much smaller than all possible PINs). Gennaro et al. showed that this is possible if we want to tolerate α as the *total* number of incorrectly entered PINs, but left as an open problem the question of whether it was possible to have a functionality that allowed any number of incorrectly entered PINs over the life of the device, but would stop working if the number of *consecutive* incorrect PINs exceeds the threshold α. Here we show that this functionality (referred to in the sequel as "signature with consecutive PIN protection") cannot be ATP-secure. We also show that we cannot achieve ATP security for the functionality that allows Alice to change her PIN (referred to in the sequel as "signature with user changeable PIN").

In the following theorems, we assume that the device computes a polynomial-time function that on input PIN and the secret component outputs $1/0$, denoting the validity of the PIN. Also we assume that the PIN has a polynomial-size support.

Theorem 1. *The signature with user changeable PIN functionality cannot be* ATP *secure, even if a circuit can self-destruct, assuming the device implements a polynomial-time change-pin function $f_{ChangePIN}$ that on input $(sc, NewPIN, OldPIN)$ outputs a new valid secret component sc', and the devices calls $f_{ChangePIN}$ when the user changes her PIN.*

Proof. The adversary will take advantage of the existence of this function $f_{ChangePIN}$ in order to break the ATP security of the device. Recall that the adversary may specify, as input to the Apply command, a polynomial-time computable function f. As a result of Apply(f), our adversary will succeed in replacing the old PIN (which he does not know) with a new PIN. For simplicity, the new PIN will be the all-zero string 0^ℓ where ℓ is the length of the PIN. As a result of Apply(f), the adversary will be able to use the device from now on.

This function f works as follows: for every possible PIN p, it runs the following function f_p: On input secret component sc of the device, f_p first checks whether p is the correct PIN, then it returns $sc' = f_{ChangePIN}(sc, 0^\ell, p)$. Else f_p returns sc. Since f does this for every possible PIN p, we guarantee that in the end, sc will be modified in the same way as if the user changed her PIN to 0^ℓ. f is polynomial-time, because the PIN is a memorizable short number, for which all possibilities can be enumerated in polynomial time (from the assumption). □

Theorem 2. *The signature with consecutive PIN protection functionality cannot be* ATP *secure, even if a circuit can self-destruct, assuming the device implements a polynomial-time reset function $f_{ResetPIN}$ that on input $sc, Input, pin$ outputs a valid sc' for the correct PIN, and every time every time the PIN is correctly entered, the counter of consecutive errors is reset.*

Proof. Our adversary will take advantage of the existence of this function $f_{ResetPIN}$ in order to come up with the function f to give as argument to the Apply command. As a result of Apply(f), the counter for incorrect consecutive PIN attempts will be reset, even though the adversary has not issued Run$(Input, pin)$ for the correct PIN pin.

f will work as follows: for all possible PINs p, it will run the function f_p. f_p (similarly to the proof of Theorem 1) works like this: on input $(sc, Input)$, where $Input$ is any message in the message space of the signature scheme — for simplicity, let $Input$ be the all-zero message 0^n. it first checks whether p is the correct PIN; if so, it returns $sc' = f_{ResetPIN}(sc, Input, p)$; else, it returns sc.

Once again, since PIN is a memorizable short number, f can call every possible f_p in polynomial time. After Apply(f) is executed, the secret content is whatever it would be after Run$(Input, pin)$ is queried with the valid PIN pin. □

4 Impossibility of Deterministic Circuits in the ATP-Memory-Probing Model

Suppose that, after the circuit C executes a Run command, the secret contents sc always remains unchanged, i.e. the same as before the Run command was executed. Then the memory probing adversary can trivially learn the entire string sc by simply probing each bit of sc one by one. Here we show that even if the circuit C updates sc before completing the execution of Run, the memory probing adversary can still compute a candidate sc' that would correspond to the secret contents of the device for some time period.

Let C_{mem} be the function that, on input sc and a outputs the updated version of sc, the secret contents of the device's memory left behind after Run(a) is executed. For a particular a, let $X_0 = sc$, $X_{i+1} := Next_a(X_i)$ be shorthand for $C_{mem}(X_i, a)$. Let sc and a be given; for $i > 0$, if the circuit is deterministic, each X_i is well-defined.

Theorem 3. *A deterministic signature functionality cannot be* ATP-Memory-Probing *secure, even if the circuit can self-destruct: there exists a polynomial-time adversary that outputs X_i for some i.*

Proof. We prove the theorem by giving an adversary that attacks any device that implements the signature functionality. The adversary will get some "useful" information by probing some bits in the memory. The intuition is: the adversary takes advantage of a polynomial-time computable function f that first identifies a good location to probe, signals this location back to the adversary, and then conveys the secret content in that particular location in the memory. To be more specific: for the memory contents $X_0, X_1, \ldots, X_\ell$ for some ℓ, there is either a simple cycle or at least one bit of the memory that has changes with enough regularity. For the former case, the adversary can always fix the memory content to be the same and then probe it bit by bit. For the latter one, the adversary can obtain this location (having changes with enough regularity) and then transmit one X_t for some t through probing at this location.

Let us explain how this function conveys information and how the adversary receives it with the following algorithms. Algorithm 5 describes the function f that the adversary is going to use: f is parameterized by (r, aux, a). r is an integer that depends on how many times the adversary has already modified the memory. aux is a string that depends on what she is trying to do at this stage. a is the index of $Next_a(sc) = C_{mem}(sc, a)$. With the algorithm, we develop the following lemmas for the theorem.

Lemma 1. *The adversarial function is a polynomial-time computable function.*

Proof. Every step in the algorithm is clearly polynomial-time computable. We put a more detailed proof in the full version of this paper.

Lemma 2. *The adversary will find a sc' that $C(sc', \cdot)$ also implements a valid signature function as $C(sc, \cdot)$ does.*

Proof. We consider two cases, (1) there exists a cycle with length no greater than $m^3 + 3m$ on $X_0, X_1, \ldots, X_\ell$, where $X_0 = sc$, $X_i = Next_a(X_{i-1})$, and $\ell = m^3 + 4m - r$, for some $r \in [m]$. (2) there doesn't. For the first case, we let X_0 be the start of the cycle; otherwise the function will first return X_j, where $Next_a(X_j)$ is the start of the cycle, and then we go back to the case where X_0 is the start of the cycle.

1. Suppose there exists a $j < m^3 + 4m < \ell$ such that $X_j = X_0 = sc$, the adversarial function will move the memory to X_{j-1}. After the device runs, it updates the memory from X_{j-1} to $X_j = X_0 = sc$, so the adversary will probe with the same memory contents (sc) in the first m rounds. Also, since $m^3 + 3m \le \ell = m^3 + 4m - r$ for $r \in [m]$, the adversarial function will always find this cycle, and the memory will always be X_0 when the adversary probes it. Therefore the adversary will find sc and construct $C(sc, \cdot)$ as desired.
2. Suppose there doesn't exist such small cycle, then the adversary will most likely not get a good candidate after step 1. (*Note: if she still does get one by luck, then she will be very happy and doesn't need the following procedure. The proof is done.*) Now, she is going to query "Is location k a good place to probe?" for every bit. Since there doesn't exist a cycle or a small cycle in $X_0, X_1, \ldots, X_l$, we assume $X_0, X_1, \ldots, X_{m^3+3m}$ are distinct elements without loss of generality. Then the adversary is going to ask which location is a good place to probe. *Note: a good location is the place which contains a lot of* $0, 1$ *alternations.* So the adversarial

function can use those $0/1$'s to convey sc' when the adversary is probing such location.

3. Now we want to prove *there must be a good location to probe:* if location i is not the place to be probed, then the adversarial function will at most move from X_0 to X_2 after "Give me 0" and "Give me 1", since we can always find a two-bit string in $X_0(i), X_1(i), X_2(i)$ that violates "01" (in any one of the eight combinations of those three bits.) Thus, at each time when the third step of the function is run, there are at least m^3 distinct elements (i.e. $X_0, X_1, \ldots X_{m^3},$) (for a bad location, we waste at most three distinct elements. Thus, every time we have at least $m^3 + 3m - 3m$ distinct elements.)
   Since those elements are distinct, we have $\sum_{j=1}^{j=m} |X_i(j) - X_{i+1}(j)| \geq 1$ for any $i = 1 \ldots m^3 - 1$. This implies $\sum_{i=0}^{m^3-1} \sum_{j=1}^{j=m} |X_i(j) - X_{i+1}(j)| \geq m^3$. This is a finite summation and i, j are independent, so we can change the summation order to get: $\sum_{j=1}^{j=m} \sum_{i=0}^{m^3-1} |X_i(j) - X_{i+1}(j)| \geq m^3$. According to the pigeon hole principle, we must have some k such that $\sum_{i=0}^{m^3-1} |X_i(k) - X_{i+1}(k)| \geq m^3/m = m^2 > 5m+2$. *Note:* $\mathit{diff}_k = \sum_{i=0}^{m^3+4m-r} |X_i(k) - X_{i+1}(k)| \geq \sum_{i=0}^{m^3-1} |X_i(k) - X_{i+1}(k)| \geq 5m + 2 - r$. Thus we must have some k such that $\mathit{diff}_k > 5m + 2 - r$ for $r = 0$ or 1.
   This implies in this case, there must exist a good location to probe. And the adversary will get this one from the function f. After this location is obtained, there are $5m$ alternations of $0/1$ on this bit, and the adversarial function can easily convey the message about sc' through this bit. The remaining argument follows straightforwardly with the algorithm □

Remark 1. A natural question is: what can this attack do to a functionality with a PIN? In such a functionality, the adversary must enter the correct PIN pin to run $\mathsf{Run}(a, pin)$. Recall that we require the PIN to be an easily memorizable string, and so the number of possible choices is not large. Therefore the adversary has a non-negligible probability of guessing it correctly. Once she guesses the correct PIN, she can find out the secret content sc' using the attack above.

Remark 2. This result is not limited to the signature functionality; we used signatures for concreteness. In fact, no deterministic testable (as defined by Gennaro et al.) functionality can be ATP secure in the memory probing model.

5 Impossibility of Deterministic Circuits in the ATP-Circuit-Probing-Tampering-Model

In this section, we are going to consider the model where the adversary can do the probing attacks and tampering attacks on the wires. From the previous section, we have already shown that if the adversary is able to read directly the memory cell (or read from the wires that carry the content into the circuitry) then the deterministic circuit can not achieve ATP security. Those impossibilities are still inherited here. Therefore, we are going to consider further restrictions on the adversary.

Algorithm 1. Description of the Adversary (Theorem 3)

1. Pick an arbitrary a from the message space in the signature scheme.
   for $i = 1$ to m **do**
   Let $r = i$, $aux = \epsilon$, $sc' = \epsilon$.
   Run consecutively $\mathsf{Apply}(f_{r,aux,a})$, $\mathsf{Run}(a)$, and $sc' = sc' \circ \mathsf{ProbeMem}(\{i\})$. I.e. probe location i of the memory and then concatenate the outcome with sc'.
   end for
   Then we have a candidate sc' from the bits we've probed.
   Construct a circuit $C(sc', \cdot)$ and check if this circuit outputs validly for the signature scheme as $C(sc, \cdot)$ does.
2. **if** the constructed circuit does **then**
   Output sc'
   else
   for $i = 1$ to m **do**
   Let $r = 0$, $aux =$"Is location i a good place to probe?"○"Give me 0"
   Run $\mathsf{Apply}(f_{r,aux,a})$, $\mathsf{Run}(a)$ and then $\mathsf{ProbeMem}(\{i\})$. .
   Let $r = 1$, $aux =$"Is location i a good place to probe?"○"Give me 1"
   Run $\mathsf{Apply}(f_{r,aux,a})$, $\mathsf{Run}(a)$ and then $\mathsf{ProbeMem}(\{i\})$.
   If the outcomes of two consecutive probes are anything other than 01, then the adversary knows this is not a good location to probe, so it continues. Otherwise, exit **for** and let bit $pb = i$ be the location to be probed.
   end for
   end if
3. Let $str = \epsilon$
   for $i = 1$ to m **do**
   Let $r = i$, $aux =$"Location pb will be probed."○"I want bit i of the secret." ○"Bits $1, 2, \ldots, i-1$ of the secret are str"
   Run $\mathsf{Apply}(f_{r,aux,a})$, $\mathsf{Run}(a)$, and $b = \mathsf{ProbeMem}(\{pb\})$. (Probe location pb, and get the outcome b.)
   Let $str = str \circ b$ (a concatenation.)
   end for
   Output str.

Before stating them, we first consider some motivations for intuitively understanding. Suppose the adversary has some nano needles that can perform the probing and tampering attacks on wires, but each needle occupies some areas and after placing the needle, the adversary cannot change its position without damaging the original circuit. Thus she should choose a small set of wires which she is going to attack in advance and cannot change them adaptively. In this section, we show that even with the restrictions, the adversary can destroy the ATP security. As a consequence, the adversary with even stronger power that can attack wires adaptively can certainly destroy the ATP security.

Now we state the restrictions explicitly: the adversary needs to select a set of wires to attack before the operation of the device. Note: every wire can be included in this set, and once it is chosen, the adversary can only tamper or probe the wires in this set. Also, after this set has been chosen, the adversary cannot change it. This is called non-adaptive attacks.

Algorithm 2. The adversarial function $f_{r,aux,a}$ (Theorem 3)

On input sc do:

1. Compute $X_0, X_1, \ldots, X_\ell$, for $\ell = m^3 + 4m - r$. *Note: recall* $X_0 = sc, X_i = Next_a(X_{i-1})$ *as defined in the beginning in this section.*
2. If $aux = \epsilon$, then try to determine if the sequence of values $\{X_i\}$ contains a cycle:

   If $aux \neq \epsilon$, goto Step 3: *that is, the adversary already knows that there are no small cycles.*
   Else, check for cycles with its length no greater than $m^3 + 3m$: does there exist an $0 \leq i < j \leq \ell$ such that $X_i = X_j$, and $j - i < m^3 + 3m$, and $X_i, X_{i+1}, \ldots, X_j$ are distinct.

   if NO (i.e. no cycle or there exists a cycle but the length is too large) **then**
   Output X_0.
   else
   consider two cases: (a) $i > 0$: output X_i (b) $i = 0$: output X_{j-1}.
   end if
3. **if** aux contains the string "Location k will be probed." **then**
   go to Step 4. *The adversary already knows which location to probe in the memory to get useful information.*
   else
   aux must contain the string "Is location k a good place to probe?" A good location to probe is one where, as the value of sc changes over time, the bit stored at this memory location keeps changing. Thus, if we want to communicate a bit b to the adversary, we can do so by setting $sc = X_i$ for some X_i whose k^{th} bit is b.
   Let S be the string obtained by concatenating the following bits: $S = X_1(k) \circ X_2(k) \circ \cdots \circ X_l(k)$ where $X_i(j)$ means the j-th bit of X_i. Let $diff_k = \sum_{j=2}^{\ell} |X_j(k) - X_{j-1}(k)|$. I.e., $diff_k$ measures how many times the value stored at the kth memory location changes as sc changes over time.
   if $diff_k > 5m + 2 - r$ **then**
   This is a good location, because $diff_k$ is high. This needs to be communicated back to the adversary. We know that the adversary will be probing the kth memory location to get the answer to this question, and therefore we do as follows:
   consider the two cases:
   (a) aux contains "Give me a 0" then let $t + 1$ be the smallest integer such that $X_{t+1}(k) = 0$. Output X_t.
   (b) aux contains "Give me a 1" then let $t + 1$ be the smallest integer such that $X_{t+1}(k) = 1$. Output X_t.
   else
   k is a bad location.
   consider the two cases:
   (a) aux contains the string "Give me a 0" then if $X_1(k) = 1$ output X_0. If $X_1(k) = 0$, and $X_2(k) = 1$ output X_1. Else if $X_1(k) = 0$,and $X_2(k) = 0$ output X_0.
   (b) aux contains the string "Give me a 1" then output X_0.
   end if
   end if
4. The adversary will probe location k. Among the ℓ possibilities for sc, $X_0, \ldots, X_\ell$, find X_t for a sufficiently large t, consistent with what the adversary already knows, and communicate a bit of X_t by making sure that this bit will be read off from location k. More precisely:

   aux must contain "Location k will be probed", and "I want bit j of the secret.", and "Bits $1, 2, \ldots, j-1$ of the secret are $s_1, s_2, \ldots, s_{j-1}$."
   Find the least $t \geq m^5 - m^3 r$ such that the first $j - 1$ bits of X_t are $s_1, s_2, \ldots, s_{j-1}$. Find the least u such that $X_{u+1}(k) = X_t(j)$. Output X_u.

In the following, we are going to show the adversary only needs to attack a small set of wires to destroy ATP security. Since the construction of the adversary and proofs are similar to theorem 3, we only state the theorem here and leave the details including the formalization of the model and proofs the full version of this paper for the curious readers.

Theorem 4. *A deterministic signature functionality cannot be* ATP-Circuit-Probing-Tampering *secure in the non-adaptive model. That is: the adversary first sets the attack range on the output wires of C_{check} and then will either disable the self-destruct function or find out some valid sc'.*

Note: C_{check} is one part of the components in the circuit, which checks if the memory is valid. The functionality is necessary for every cryptographic device. The precise model can be found in the the full version of this paper.

Remark 3. Gennaro et al. showed there is no ATP secure achieved without self-destruct functionality. Thus, if the adversary disables such functionality, she can retrieve the secret content as the authors did in [GLM+04].

Remark 4. Since the signature functionality cannot be ATP secure under non-adaptive model, it is clearly that it cannot withstand a stronger adversary which can do the adaptive attacks.

6 ATP-Circuit-Probing-Tampering Security from Encoded Randomness Gates

In the previous sections, we see the limitations of deterministic circuits. Thus it seems that the signals in the wires should be made independent of the memory content to defend against probing attacks. And this is where randomness comes in handy. Intuitively, one can think that randomness provides an independent and unpredictable shield that hides each signal (using a secret sharing scheme [ISW03]) which the adversary cannot manipulate by merely tampering with the memory content.

In this section, we consider circuits with a source of true randomness. For this model, the previous results in [IPSW06, ISW03, GLM+04] work. After we rule out yet another class of attacks that makes the circuit entirely vulnerable, we can combine the techniques in those works to achieve ATP security in this new model.

Definition 2 (Randomness gate). *A randomness gate is a gate with no input and one output wire that emits a truly random bit each clock cycle.*

Lemma 3. *In the* ATP-Circuit-Probing-Circuit-Tampering *model, there exists an adversary who, for any keyed cryptographic functionality, either discovers a valid secret sc', or determines all the values of all the internal wires corresponding to the execution of the* Run() *command, even for circuits with randomness gates.*

Proof (sketch). Let $RG = \{rg_1, rg_2, \ldots, rg_r\}$ be the set of randomness gates used by the circuit. Since the adversary can tamper with any internal wire, he can fix the output of every randomness gate. We must make sure that this does not cause the device to self-destruct (for example, a device that remembers the randomness used in previous invocation might detect that something suspicious is going on). To do that, once the output of a randomness gate is fixed, the adversary must run the Apply() command that will make a device that can store m bits of memory "fast-forward" far enough into the future, using true randomness, so that it would no longer remember the fixed randomness. Now the circuit becomes deterministic and we can use a similar attack in the previous section. A formal description is deferred to the full version of this paper.

We see that if all randomness gates are vulnerable under tampering attacks, then the circuit can be made deterministic. Thus, to defend against tampering attacks, we need a more complex gadget: "encoded randomness gate," as proposed in [IPSW06]. Let the encoded randomness gate ERG^k be an element that takes no input and produces a string of output a k-bit string per clock cycle, 1^k representing 1, 0^k representing 0, and others representing the invalid signal. The output distribution is $Pr[ERG^k = 1^k] = Pr[ERG^k = 0^k] = 1/2$. The intuition for this gadget is that the adversary has little probability to fix the entire output of a gadget before causing an invalid signal. From the techniques in [IPSW06], we can design an implementation that if an invalid signal is caused, then it will be passed to the whole circuit and erase the whole output and memory content.

Theorem 5 (main result in [GLM$^+$04]). *Under the assumption of the existence of strong universal unforgeable signature scheme, there exists unforgeable signature scheme that achieves ATP security. That is, there exists a circuit $C(sc, \cdot)$ that implements a signature functionality with secret content sc stored in the* ***Memory*** *and is ATP secure.*

The main idea here is let $sc = sc' \circ \sigma_{\Pi}(sc)$ where σ is a universal unforgeable signature scheme and Π is the secret signing key of the card manufacturer, and sc' contains the signing key of the signature device. In brief, since $\sigma_{\Pi}(sc)$ can be only issued by the manufacturer, the adversary is not able to produce it by himself, and thus she cannot produce any other valid sc' that will pass the verification process. The formal reduction proof can be found in [GLM$^+$04].

Next, we recall the main result of Ishai et al. By "registers" we mean a special component of the circuit into which a portion of memory (and intermediate results of computation steps) can be loaded at execution time.

Theorem 6 (main result in [IPSW06]). *There exists a circuit $C(\cdot)$, using AND, OR, NOT, and "encoded randomness gates," with sc stored in its* ***registers*** *that implements a signature functionality and achieves* Circuit-Probing-Circuit-Tampering *security.*

Theorem 7 (combined result). *Let m be the length of the secret content sc. There exists a circuit $C(\cdot)$, using AND, OR, NOT, "encoded randomness gates," and $\Theta(m)$ "robust wires" which are invulnerable to probing attacks, with sc stored in its* ***memory*** *that implements a signature functionality and achieves* ATP-Circuit-Probing-Tampering *security.*

The idea here is that the circuit first uses the robust wires to load the memory content to the registers. Then during the execution, the device only uses the registers in the circuit for the memorization of internal states, etc. Finally, the circuit updates the memory through the robust wires. Then Theorem 5 and Theorem 6 combine perfectly.

References

[AARR03] Agrawal, D., Archambeault, B., Rao, J.R., Rohatgi, P.: The EM side-channel(s). In: Kaliski Jr., B.S., Koç, Ç.K., Paar, C. (eds.) CHES 2002. LNCS, vol. 2523, pp. 29–45. Springer, Heidelberg (2003)

[AK96] Anderson, R., Kuhn, M.: Tamper Resistance - a Cautionary Note. In: Proceedings of the Second Usenix Workshop on Electronic Commerce, pp. 1–11 (November 1996)

[AK97] Anderson, R., Kuhn, M.: Low cost attacks on tamper resistant devices. In: Lomas, M. (ed.) Security Protocols 1996. LNCS, vol. 1189. Springer, Heidelberg (1997)

[BGI+01] Barak, B., Goldreich, O., Impagliazzo, R., Rudich, S., Sahai, A., Vadhan, S.P., Yang, K.: On the (im)possibility of obfuscating programs. In: Kilian, J. (ed.) CRYPTO 2001. LNCS, vol. 2139, pp. 1–18. Springer, Heidelberg (2001)

[BS97] Biham, E., Shamir, A.: Differential fault analysis of secret key cryptosystems. In: Kaliski Jr., B.S. (ed.) CRYPTO 1997. LNCS, vol. 1294, pp. 513–525. Springer, Heidelberg (1997)

[CRR03] Chari, S., Rao, J.R., Rohatgi, P.: Template attacks. In: Kaliski Jr., B.S., Koç, Ç.K., Paar, C. (eds.) CHES 2002. LNCS, vol. 2523, pp. 13–28. Springer, Heidelberg (2003)

[DPW10] Dziembowski, S., Pietrzak, K., Wichs, D.: Non-malleable codes. In: ICS (2010)

[GLM+04] Gennaro, R., Lysyanskaya, A., Malkin, T., Micali, S., Rabin, T.: Algorithmic tamper-proof (atp) security: Theoretical foundations for security against hardware tampering. In: Naor, M. (ed.) TCC 2004. LNCS, vol. 2951, pp. 258–277. Springer, Heidelberg (2004)

[IPSW06] Ishai, Y., Prabhakaran, M., Sahai, A., Wagner, D.: Private circuits ii: Keeping secrets in tamperable circuits. In: Vaudenay, S. (ed.) EUROCRYPT 2006. LNCS, vol. 4004, pp. 308–327. Springer, Heidelberg (2006)

[ISW03] Ishai, Y., Sahai, A., Wagner, D.: Private circuits: Securing hardware against probing attacks. In: Boneh, D. (ed.) CRYPTO 2003. LNCS, vol. 2729, pp. 463–481. Springer, Heidelberg (2003)

[KJJ99] Kocher, P.C., Jaffe, J., Jun, B.: Differential power analysis. In: Wiener, M. J. (ed.) CRYPTO 1999. LNCS, vol. 1666, pp. 388–397. Springer, Heidelberg (1999)

[Koc96] Kocher, P.C.: Timing attacks on implementations of Diffie-Hellman, RSA, DSS, and other systems. In: Koblitz, N. (ed.) CRYPTO 1996. LNCS, vol. 1109, pp. 104–113. Springer, Heidelberg (1996)

[MR04] Micali, S., Reyzin, L.: Physically observable cryptography. In: Naor, M. (ed.) TCC 2004. LNCS, vol. 2951, pp. 278–296. Springer, Heidelberg (2004)

[SA03] Skorobogatov, S.P., Anderson, R.J.: Optical fault induction attacks. In: Kaliski Jr., B.S., Koç, Ç.K., Paar, C. (eds.) CHES 2002. LNCS, vol. 2523, pp. 2–12. Springer, Heidelberg (2003)

Leakage-Resilient Storage*

Francesco Davì[1], Stefan Dziembowski[1], and Daniele Venturi[2]

[1] Department of Computer Science,
University of Rome "La Sapienza",
via Salaria 113,
00198 Rome, Italy
davi@di.uniroma1.it
stefan@dziembowski.net
[2] INFOCOM Department,
University of Rome "La Sapienza",
via Eudossiana 18,
00186 Rome, Italy
venturi@infocom.uniroma1.it

Abstract. We study a problem of secure data storage on hardware that may leak information. We introduce a new primitive, that we call *leakage-resilient storage* (LRS), which is an (unkeyed) scheme for encoding messages, and can be viewed as a generalization of the *All-Or-Nothing Transform* (AONT, Rivest 1997). The standard definition of AONT requires that it should be hard to reconstruct a message m if not all the bits of its encoding $\mathsf{Encode}(m)$ are known. LRS is defined more generally, with respect to a class Γ of functions. The security definition of LRS requires that it should be hard to reconstruct m even if some values $g_1(\mathsf{Encode}(m)), \dots, g_t(\mathsf{Encode}(m))$ are known (where $g_1, \dots, g_t \in \Gamma$), as long as the total length of $g_1(\mathsf{Encode}(m)), \dots, g_t(\mathsf{Encode}(m))$ is smaller than some parameter c.

We construct an LRS scheme that is secure with respect to Γ being a set of functions that can depend only on some restricted part of the memory. More precisely: we assume that the memory is divided in 2 parts, and the functions in Γ can be just applied to one of these parts. We also construct a scheme that is secure if the cardinality of Γ is restricted (but still it can be exponential in the length of the encoding). This construction implies security in the case when the set Γ consists of functions that are computable by Boolean circuits of a small size.

We also discuss the connection between the problem of constructing leakage-resilient storage and a theory of the compressibility of NP-instances.

Keywords: leakage resilient cryptography, secure storage.

1 Introduction

Some of the most devastating attacks on cryptographic devices are those that break the actual physical implementation of the scheme, not its mathematical abstraction.

* The European Research Council has provided financial support under the EuropeanCommunity's Seventh Framework Programme (FP7/2007-2013) / ERC grant agreement no CNTM-207908.

J.A. Garay and R. De Prisco (Eds.): SCN 2010, LNCS 6280, pp. 121–137, 2010.

These, so-called *side-channel attacks*, are based on the fact that the adversary may obtain some information about the internal data of the device by observing its running-time [27], electromagnetic radiation [35,19], power consumption [28], or even sound that the device is emitting [40] (see [34,32] for more examples of such attacks).

1.1 Memory Leakages — Previous Work

Over the last couple of years there has been a growing interest in the design of schemes that already on the abstract level guarantee that their physical implementation is secure against a large well-defined class of side-channel attacks (the pioneering paper in this area was [30]). The main idea is to augment the standard security definition by allowing the adversary to learn the value of a chosen by him *leakage function* g on the internal data τ used by the cryptographic scheme. The results in this area can be categorized according to the class of leakage functions g that the model covers. Some papers consider very restricted classes (e.g. in [24] the model assumes that the adversary can simply read-off some wires that represent the computation), while other ones consider more general leakages—e.g. [1] allow the adversary to choose any function g that is *input-shrinking* (i.e. such that $|g(\tau)| \ll |\tau|$).

Another popular paradigm is to assume that *only computation leaks information*, i.e. the memory cells that do not take part in the computation (in a given time period) do not leak any information. The first paper to state this assumption is [30] (where it is stated as "Axiom 1", page 283), and the other papers that use it are [17,33]. The schemes of [17,33] are actually secure even if the total amount of information that leaks is greater than the memory size (this is possible since the memory contents is evolving during the computation). The other approach [1,31,25,12,11] is to assume that the memory may simply leak information, independently on the computation performed.

It may be questioned if the "only computation leaks information" paradigm is really relevant to the attack that the adversary can perform in real-life. In many situations memory may actually leak information, even if it is unaccessed. First of all, in modern computer systems it is hard to guarantee that a given part of memory really never gets accessed (for example the memory may be refreshed or moved to cache, etc.). Some practical attacks on unaccessed memory were also demonstrated in [38]. More recently a class of *cold boot attacks* relying on the data remanence property was presented in [20].

A natural question to ask is whether there exist methods for storing data securely in the memory that may leak information. This is the main subject of this paper.

A relation to the Bounded-Retrieval Model. The idea to reason about the partial key leakages by modeling them as input-shrinking functions originates from the *Bounded-Retrieval Model* (BRM) [14,9,15,6,16,2] (that in turn was inspired by the Bounded-Storage Model of Maurer [29]). Originally BRM was proposed as a method for protecting against computer viruses that may steal large amounts of data from the PCs: the main idea of the BRM is to construct schemes where the secret key τ is large and to assume that the adversary can retrieve the value of some input-shrinking function g of τ. The main differences between this setting and the models for the side-channel attack come from the fact that the keys in the BRM are huge and hence: (1) one has to design scheme where the honest user does not need to frequently process the entire τ, and (2) one can allow that some part of τ leaks each time the scheme is used. Nevertheless in [14] it was observed that BRM can be used to model the side-channel attacks.

1.2 Our Contribution

In this paper we introduce a new primitive, that we call *leakage-resilient storage*, which can be viewed as a secure storage scheme in the model where the physical memory may leak some side-channel information. A scheme like this consists of two poly-time algorithms Encode and Decode, where the *encoding* algorithm Encode takes as input a message m and produces as output a string $\tau \stackrel{\text{def}}{=} \mathsf{Encode}(m)$, and the *decoding* algorithm Decode is such that we always have $\mathsf{Decode}(\mathsf{Encode}(m)) = m$ (observe that these algorithms do not take as input any secret key).

Informally speaking, in the security definition we allow the adversary to *adaptively* choose a sequence of leakage functions $g_1, \ldots, g_t$, and learn the values of

$$g_1(\tau), \ldots, g_t(\tau).$$

We require that the adversary, after learning these values, should gain essentially no additional information on m (this is formalized using a standard indistinguishability game, see Sect. 2 for details). We assume that the g_i's are elements of some fixed set Γ (that will be a parameter in the definition). Obviously, the larger Γ, the stronger is our definition, and we should aim at defining Γ in such a way that it covers all the attacks the adversary can launch in real-life. All the Γ's that we consider in this paper contain at least the set of functions that read-off the individual bits of τ, hence we need to require that

$$\sum_{i=1}^{t} |g_i(\tau)| < |\tau| \qquad (1)$$

(as otherwise the functions g_i could be chosen in such a way that $(g_1(\tau), \ldots, g_t(\tau)) = \tau$). This is essentially the input-shrinking property that, as discussed above, was already used in the literature.

LRS can also be viewed as a generalization of the All-Or-Nothing Transform (AONT) introduced in [37]. More precisely: AONT is a special case of LRS, where the leakage functions are projections of the individual bits.

Obviously, if we go to the extreme and simply allow the adversary to choose *any* (poly-time) functions g_i that satisfy (1) then there is no hope for any security, since the adversary could always choose g_1 in such a way that it simply calculates $\mathsf{Decode}(\tau)$ and outputs some information about m (say: its first bit). Therefore Γ cannot contain the Decode function, and hence, we need to restrict Γ in some way.

Note that the assumption that Γ is a restricted class of functions is actually very realistic. In practice, the leakage functions need to be computationally "simple": while it is plausible that the adversary can read-off the individual bits, or learn their sum, it seems very improbable that an attack based on measuring power consumption or electromagnetic radiation can directly give information about some more complicated functions of the secret bits.

In this paper we consider two natural choices of such Γ's and show LRS schemes secure in these settings relying on *deterministic extractors* [43,4,7,8,5]. In Sect. 3.1 we describe a construction where each leakage function can depend only on some restricted part of the memory: either because it consists of two separate blocks, or because it is infeasible for the adversary to choose a function that depends on the memory cells that are physically far from each other. In Sect. 3.2 we construct a scheme that is secure if the cardinality of Γ is restricted (but still it can be exponential in $|\tau|$). This construction implies security in the case when the set Γ consists of functions that are computable by Boolean circuits of a small size. Our construction is an adaptation of the technique already used (in a different context) in [41,3].

The idea to model the leakages as functions from a small complexity class appeared already in [17], and was recently used in an independent work by Faust et al. [18] (we discuss the relationship between our work and [18] in Sect. 5. We also discuss (in Sect. 4) the connection between the problem of constructing leakage-resilient storage and a theory of compressibility of NP-instances [23].

1.3 Preliminaries

Let U_n be a random variable distributed uniformly over $\{0,1\}^n$. Given two random variables X_0, X_1 with values in $\mathcal{X}$, their *statistical distance* is defined as

$$\Delta(X_0; X_1) \stackrel{\text{def}}{=} \frac{1}{2} \sum_{x \in \mathcal{X}} |\mathbb{P}[X_0 = x] - \mathbb{P}[X_1 = x]|.$$

If X assumes values in $\{0,1\}^n$, then we let $d(X) \stackrel{\text{def}}{=} \Delta(X, U_n)$ be the statistical distance[1] between X and the uniform distribution over $\{0,1\}^n$. If $d(X) \leq \epsilon$ we say that X is ϵ-close to uniform. We also define $\Delta(X_0; X_1|Y) \stackrel{\text{def}}{=} \Delta(X_0, Y; X_1, Y)$ and $d(X|Y) \stackrel{\text{def}}{=} \Delta(X, Y; U_n, Y)$.

The following was proven in [16].

Lemma 1 ([16]). *Let A, B be random variables where $A \in \mathcal{A}$. Then $\mathbb{P}[B = A] \leq d(A|B) + 1/|\mathcal{A}|$.*

Given a random variable $X \in \mathcal{X}$, the *min-entropy* of X is $\mathbf{H}_\infty(X) \stackrel{\text{def}}{=} -\log \max_{x \in \mathcal{X}} \mathbb{P}[X = x]$.

We will use the following lemma whose proof appears in Appendix A.

Lemma 2. *For every random variables X, Y and an event $\mathcal{E}$ we have*

$$d(X|Y = y \wedge \mathcal{E}) + \mathbb{P}\left[\overline{\mathcal{E}}\right] \geq d(X|Y). \tag{2}$$

The proofs of the following lemmata appear in the full version of [16].

Lemma 3. *Let A, B be two random variables and let ϕ be any function. Then $d(A|B) \geq d(A|\phi(B))$.*

[1] We will overload the symbols $\Delta(\cdot)$ and $d(\cdot)$ and sometimes apply them to the probability distributions instead of the random variables.

Lemma 4. *Let A, B be independent random variables and consider a sequence $V_1, \ldots, V_i$ of random variables, where for some function ϕ, $V_i = \phi_i(C_i) = \phi(V_1, \ldots, V_{i-1}, C_i)$, with each C_i being either A or B. Then A and B are independent conditioned on $V_1, \ldots, V_i$, i.e. $I(A; B|V_1, \ldots, V_i) = 0$, where I denotes the Shannon's information*[2].

We will also use the following standard fact whose proof appears in Appendix B.

Lemma 5. *Let X be a random variable uniformly distributed over $\{0,1\}^n$, and let W be a random variable that is independent on X. Let $f : \{0,1\}^* \to \{0,1\}^c$. Then for every $k \in \mathbb{N}$ we have*

$$\mathbb{P}_{y:=f(X,W)}\left[\mathbf{H}_\infty(X|f(X,W) = y) \leq k\right] \leq 2^{k+c-n}. \tag{3}$$

A family $\{h_s\}_{s \in \mathcal{S}}$ of functions $h_s : \mathcal{X} \to \mathcal{Y}$ is called a *collection of ℓ-wise independent hash functions* if for every set $\{x_1, \ldots, x_\ell\} \subseteq \mathcal{X}$ of ℓ elements, and a uniformly random $S \in \mathcal{S}$ we have that $(h_S(x_1), \ldots, h_S(x_\ell))$ is distributed uniformly over $\mathcal{Y}^\ell$. Several constructions of such functions exist in the literature. For example if $GF(2^n)$ is the field with 2^n elements, and for $s = (s_0, \ldots, s_\ell) \in GF(2^n)^{\ell+1}$ and every $n' \leq n$ we define

$$h_s(x) = \left(\sum_{i=0}^{\ell} s_i x^i\right)_{1 \ldots n'}$$

(where $z_{1 \ldots n'}$ denotes the set of n' first bits of z) then $\{h_s\}$ is a collection of ℓ-wise independent hash functions.

We will also use the following lemma (proven in [3]):

Lemma 6 ([3]). *Let Y be an n-bit random variable with $\mathbf{H}_\infty(Y) \geq k$. Let $H = \{h_s\}_{s \in \mathcal{S}}$ be a collection of ℓ-wise independent hash functions $h_s : \{0,1\}^n \to \{0,1\}^\alpha$ (for $\ell \geq 2$). For at least $1 - 2^{-u}$ fraction of $s \in \mathcal{S}$, we have $d(h_s(Y)) \leq \epsilon$ for*

$$u = \frac{\ell}{2}(k - \alpha - 2\log(1/\epsilon) - \log \ell + 2) - \alpha - 2. \tag{4}$$

2 The Definition

Formally, a *leakage-resilient storage (LRS)* scheme is a pair $\Phi \stackrel{\text{def}}{=} (\mathsf{Encode}, \mathsf{Decode})$, where

- Encode is a randomized, efficiently computable function $\mathsf{Encode} : \{0,1\}^\alpha \to \{0,1\}^\beta$, and
- Decode is a deterministic, efficiently computable function $\mathsf{Decode} : \{0,1\}^\beta \to \{0,1\}^\alpha$.

Security of such a scheme is defined as follows. Consider the following game between an adversary $\mathcal{A}$ and an oracle $\mathcal{O}$ (a similar game was used to define security of the Forward-Secure Storage (FSS) [15], the main difference being that (1) FSS had a secret key and (2) the FSS game had just one round)

[2] In [16] this lemma is stated in terms of a Markov chain.

1. The adversary chooses a pair of messages $m_0, m_1 \in \{0,1\}^\alpha$ and sends them to $\mathcal{O}$.
2. $\mathcal{O}$ chooses a random bit $b \in \{0,1\}$ and sets $\tau \stackrel{\text{def}}{=} \mathsf{Encode}(m_b)$.
3. The following is executed t times, for $i = 1, \ldots, t$:
   (a) $\mathcal{A}$ selects a function $g_i : \{0,1\}^\beta \to \{0,1\}^{c_i} \in \Gamma$, and sends it to $\mathcal{O}$,
   (b) $\mathcal{O}$ sends $g_i(\tau)$ to $\mathcal{A}$. We say that $\mathcal{A}$ *retrieved* c_i *bits from* τ.
4. The adversary outputs b'. We say that he *won the game* if $b = b'$.

Such an adversary is called a (Γ, c, t)-adversary if $\sum_{i=1}^{t} c_i \leq c$. We say that Φ is (Γ, c, t, ϵ)-*secure* if no (Γ, c, t)-adversary wins the game with probability greater than $\frac{1}{2} + \epsilon$.[3] We will drop t and say that Φ is (Γ, c, ϵ)-*secure* if the parameter t does not matter, i.e. if no (Γ, c, t)-adversary wins the game with probability greater than $\frac{1}{2} + \epsilon$, for any t. Unless explicitly stated otherwise, we will assume that the adversary is computationally-unbounded. In this case we assume that the adversary is deterministic. This can be done without loss of generality, since the unbounded adversary can always compute the optimal randomness. For an adversary $\mathcal{A}$ as above, let $\mathsf{view}_\mathcal{A}$ denote the vector of values that the adversary $\mathcal{A}$ retrieves from τ, i.e. $\mathsf{view}_\mathcal{A} \stackrel{\text{def}}{=} (g_1(\tau), \ldots, g_t(\tau))$. Note that $|\mathsf{view}_\mathcal{A}| \leq c$.

As argued in the introduction, LRS can be viewed as a generalization of the All-Or-Nothing Transform (AONT) introduced in [37] (see also e.g. [5] for a formal definition). In our framework AONT is simply a $(\Gamma_\downarrow, c, \epsilon)$-secure LRS, $\Gamma_\downarrow$ being a set of functions g_i that leak some bits of the memory, i.e. the functions that have a form $g_i(\tau_1, \ldots, \tau_\beta) = \tau_i$, where ϵ is equal to 0 if we consider perfectly-secure AONT, or is some negligible value if we consider statistically-secure AONT.

2.1 A Weaker Definition

In our schemes, the encoding τ of a string $m \in \{0,1\}^\alpha$ is composed of two parts: (1) the randomness τ_{rand} used to encode the message and (2) the result of the encoding process, i. e. some value $f(\tau_{rand})$ xored with the message m (where f is some publicly-known function). More generally, one can assume that m is a member of some group $(\mathbb{G}, +)$ and f has a type $\{0,1\}^* \to \mathbb{G}$. In this case the encoding of a message m is $(\tau_{rand}, f(\tau_{rand}) + m)$.

For the sake of the security proofs in this paper, we will consider a game that we call a *weak attack* in which $f(\tau_{rand}) + m$ is hidden from the adversary, and the g_i's are applied only to τ_{rand}. The adversary in this game will be called a *weak adversary* and denoted $\mathcal{A}_{weak}$, and we will say that the LRS scheme is *weakly* (Γ, c, t, ϵ)-*secure* if $d(f(\tau_{rand}) | \mathsf{view}_{\mathcal{A}_{weak}}) \leq \epsilon$, for any $\mathcal{A}_{weak}$, where τ_{rand} is distributed uniformly over $\{0,1\}^n$. We will say that Γ is *robust* if Γ is closed on the operation of fixing the second part of the input, i.e. if for every $g \in \Gamma$ and every $z \in \mathbb{G}$ we have that $g'(x) := g(x, z)$ is also a member of Γ. The following lemma shows that a weakly-secure scheme is also secure according to the general definition.

Lemma 7. *Let Γ be an arbitrary robust set as above. For any c, t and ϵ, if an encoding scheme is* weakly (Γ, c, t, ϵ)-secure *then it is also $(\Gamma, c, t, \epsilon \cdot 2^\alpha)$-secure.*

[3] We say that Φ is *non-adaptively* (Γ, c, t, ϵ)-*secure* if the adversary wins the game with probability at most $\frac{1}{2} + \epsilon$, with the restriction that his choice of the functions g_i is non-adaptive (i.e. he has to choose all the g_i's in advance).

Proof. Take some adversary $\mathcal{A}$ that wins the game described in Sect. 2 with some probability $0.5 + \delta$. We construct a *weak* adversary $\mathcal{A}_{weak}$ such that

$$d(f(\tau_{rand})|Out_{\mathcal{A}_{weak}}) = \delta \cdot 2^{-\alpha}, \tag{5}$$

where $Out_{\mathcal{A}_{weak}}$ is some value that is a function of $\mathsf{view}_{\mathcal{A}_{weak}}$ (we will think of it as an output of the adversary $\mathcal{A}_{weak}$ at the end of the execution). Therefore, by Lemma 3, we will have that $d(f(\tau_{rand})|\mathsf{view}_{\mathcal{A}_{weak}}) \geq \delta \cdot 2^{-\alpha}$. After showing this we will be done, by setting $\delta := \epsilon \cdot 2^{\alpha}$. The adversary $\mathcal{A}_{weak}$ works by simulating $\mathcal{A}$. First, it chooses a random string $z \in \{0,1\}^{\alpha}$ and it starts $\mathcal{A}$. Let m_0, m_1 be the messages that $\mathcal{A}$ outputs. Then, $\mathcal{A}_{weak}$ handles the requests issued by $\mathcal{A}$ in the following way. Recall that each request of $\mathcal{A}$ is a function $g_i : \{0,1\}^n \times \{0,1\}^{\alpha} \rightarrow \{0,1\}^{c_i}$ that should be applied to τ. Each time such a request is issued, the adversary $\mathcal{A}_{weak}$ constructs a request g'_i defined for every τ_{rand} as follows:

$$g'_i(\tau_{rand}) := g_i(\tau_{rand}, z).$$

(By the robustness of Γ we have that if $g_i \in \Gamma$ then also $g'_i \in \Gamma$.) When the interaction is over and $\mathcal{A}$ outputs b', the adversary $\mathcal{A}_{weak}$ outputs $Out_{\mathcal{A}_{weak}} := z - m_{b'}$. By Lemma 1 we have

$$\mathbb{P}\left[Out_{\mathcal{A}_{weak}} = f(\tau_{rand})\right] \leq 2^{-\alpha} + d(f(\tau_{rand})|Out_{\mathcal{A}_{weak}}). \tag{6}$$

Now suppose that for some $i \in \{0,1\}$ the following event $\mathcal{E}_i$ occurred: $z = m_i + f(\tau_{rand})$. In this case $\mathcal{A}_{weak}$ simply simulated the execution of $\mathcal{A}$ against the oracle $\mathcal{O}$ with $b = i$. Since z is chosen uniformly hence $\mathbb{P}[\mathcal{E}_0] = \mathbb{P}[\mathcal{E}_1] = 2^{-\alpha}$. Therefore the probability that $b' = b (= i)$ is equal to $0.5 + \delta$. Moreover, in this case (i.e. when $\mathcal{E}_0 \cup \mathcal{E}_1$ occurred and $b' = b$) we get that $Out_{\mathcal{A}_{weak}} = m_i + f(\tau_{rand}) - m_{b'}$, and therefore $Out_{\mathcal{A}_{weak}} = f(\tau_{rand})$. Hence we have

$$\begin{aligned}\mathbb{P}\left[Out_{\mathcal{A}_{weak}} = f(\tau_{rand})\right] &\geq \mathbb{P}\left[b = i \mid \mathcal{E}_0 \cup \mathcal{E}_1\right] \cdot \mathbb{P}\left[\mathcal{E}_0 \cup \mathcal{E}_1\right] \\ &= (0.5 + \delta) \cdot 2^{-\alpha+1} \\ &= 2^{-\alpha} + \delta \cdot 2^{-\alpha+1}.\end{aligned}$$

Combining it with (6) we get (5). □

3 The Implementations

In this section we consider two types of leakage functions Γ, and show LRS schemes secure against these Γ's relying on deterministic extractors [43,4,7,8,5]. In Sect. 3.1 we describe a construction where each leakage function can depend only on some restricted part of the memory: either because it consists of two separate blocks, or because it is infeasible for the adversary to choose a function that depends from the memory cells that are physically far from each other. In Sect. 3.2 we construct a scheme that is secure if the cardinality of the set of functions that the adversary can choose is restricted.

3.1 Memory Divided into Two Parts

Suppose that the encoding is stored on some physical storage device that consists of two separate chips, i.e. the memory $\mathcal{M}$ is divided into two parts $\mathcal{M}_0$ and $\mathcal{M}_1$, and each leakage function can be applied to one of the $\mathcal{M}_i$'s separately. In other words, the only restriction is that the adversary cannot choose leakage functions that depend simultaneously on both $\mathcal{M}_0$ and $\mathcal{M}_1$. More precisely, take some $\beta' < \beta$ and let $\tau = (\tau^0, \tau^1)$ where $\tau^0 \stackrel{\mathsf{def}}{=} (\tau_1, \ldots, \tau_{\beta'})$, and $\tau^1 \stackrel{\mathsf{def}}{=} (\tau_{\beta'+1}, \ldots, \tau_\beta)$. Let Γ_2 be the set of all functions g_i that "depend only on τ^0 or τ^1", i. e. they have a form

$$g_i(\tau) = g_i'(\tau^0),$$

or

$$g_i(\tau) = g_i'(\tau^1)$$

(for some g_i'). Of course, τ^0 and τ^1 do not need to be stored on two separate memory chips, and it is enough that it is simply impossible for the adversary to compute any function of τ^0 and τ^1 jointly. This may happen for example if τ^0 and τ^1 are stored on one chip, but are physically far from each other. Observe also that the class Γ_2 includes all the functions $g(\cdot)$ that have communication complexity c (where c is the bound on the total amount of bits that the adversary can retrieve). This includes for example the function that computes sum of the bits in (τ^0, τ^1) (as long as c is at least logarithmic in the length of (τ^0, τ^1)).

The construction. One may observe that this model is very similar to the one of the two-party Intrusion-Resilient Secret Sharing (IRSS) of Dziembowski and Pietrzak (see [16], Sect. 2.1). The main difference is that the scheme of [16] has an additional property that the decoding function needs to access only small part of the encoded message. Since we do not need this property here, we can use in our construction a standard tool called *two source extractors* [7]. A function $\mathsf{Ext} : \{0,1\}^n \times \{0,1\}^n \to \{0,1\}^\alpha$ is a (k_0, k_1, ϵ)-two source extractor if it has the following property: for every two independent random variables R_0 and R_1, such that $\mathbf{H}_\infty(R_0) \geq k_0$ and $\mathbf{H}_\infty(R_1) \geq k_1$ we have that $d(\mathsf{Ext}(R_0, R_1)) \leq \epsilon$. Let $\Phi_2 \stackrel{\mathsf{def}}{=} (\mathsf{Encode}_2, \mathsf{Decode}_2)$. To encode a message $m \in \{0,1\}^\alpha$, we pick two n-bit strings R_0 and R_1 uniformly at random and we set

$$\tau = \mathsf{Encode}_2(m) = (\tau_{rand}, m^*) \stackrel{\mathsf{def}}{=} (R_0, R_1, \mathsf{Ext}(R_0, R_1) \oplus m)$$

and we store R_0 in the first part of the memory ($\mathcal{M}_0$), and $(R_1, \mathsf{Ext}(R_0, R_1) \oplus m)$ in the second part ($\mathcal{M}_1$). To decode it suffices to evaluate

$$\mathsf{Decode}_2(R_0, R_1, m^*) \stackrel{\mathsf{def}}{=} m^* \oplus \mathsf{Ext}(R_0, R_1).$$

We have the following lemma.

Lemma 8. *If* $\mathsf{Ext} : \{0,1\}^n \times \{0,1\}^n \to \{0,1\}^\alpha$ *is a* (k, k, ϵ)*-two source extractor then* Φ_2 *is* $(\Gamma_2, c, 2^\alpha \cdot \epsilon + 2^{1+\alpha+k+c-n})$*-secure.*

Proof. First we show that Φ_2 is weakly secure against the adversary $\mathcal{A}_{weak}$ outlined in Section 2.1 (with $\tau_{rand} = (R_0, R_1)$) and then we use Lemma 7. Let $\mathcal{A}_{weak}$ be an adversary that can apply the leakage functions g_i only to τ_{rand} and denote with $\mathsf{view}_{\mathcal{A}_{weak}} = (g_1(\tau_{rand}), \ldots, g_t(\tau_{rand}))$ the view of the adversary after t queries to the oracle $\mathcal{O}$. We can now apply Lemma 4 (with $A = R_0$, $B = R_1$, $\phi_i = g_i$ and $V_i = g_i(\tau_{rand})^4$) and conclude that R_0 and R_1 are independent given $\mathsf{view}_{\mathcal{A}_{weak}}$, i.e. $I(R_0; R_1|\mathsf{view}_{\mathcal{A}_{weak}}) = 0$. Moreover by Lemma 5 we know that for each $i \in \{0, 1\}$

$$\mathbb{P}_{y:=\mathsf{view}_{\mathcal{A}_{weak}}}\left[\mathbf{H}_\infty(R_i|\mathsf{view}_{\mathcal{A}_{weak}} = y) \leq k\right] \leq 2^{k+c-n}.$$

Thus with probability at least $1 - 2^{1+k+c-n}$ it happens that $y = \mathsf{view}_{\mathcal{A}_{weak}}$ is such that for both $i \in \{0, 1\}$ we have $\mathbf{H}_\infty(R_i|\mathsf{view}_{\mathcal{A}_{weak}} = y) \geq k$. Let $\mathcal{V}$ denote the corresponding event. We clearly have that

$$d(\mathsf{Ext}(R_0, R_1)|\mathsf{view}_{\mathcal{A}_{weak}} = y \wedge \mathcal{V}) \leq \epsilon.$$

Hence, by Lemma 2 we get that $d(\mathsf{Ext}(R_0, R_1)|\mathsf{view}_{\mathcal{A}_{weak}}) \leq \epsilon + \mathbb{P}\left[\overline{\mathcal{V}}\right] = \epsilon + 2^{1+k+c-n}$. Combining it with Lemma 7 we get that Φ_2 is $(\Gamma_2, c, 2^\alpha \cdot \epsilon + 2^{1+\alpha+k+c-n})$-secure. □

Instantiations. Several constructions [7,39,42,10,36] of a two-source extractor exist in the literature, and can be used in our scheme. Let $\mathbb{F}$ be a finite field and denote with $\mathsf{Ext}_{\mathsf{Had}} : \mathbb{F}^n \times \mathbb{F}^n \to \mathbb{F}$ the inner product in $\mathbb{F}$, denoted $\mathsf{Ext}_{\mathsf{Had}}(x, y) = \langle x, y \rangle$. As shown in [36], for any $\delta > 0$, the function $\mathsf{Ext}_{\mathsf{Had}}$ is a $(k_{\mathsf{Had}}, k_{\mathsf{Had}}, \epsilon_{\mathsf{Had}})$-two source extractor, for $k_{\mathsf{Had}} > (1/2 + \delta)n \log |\mathbb{F}|$ and $\epsilon_{\mathsf{Had}} = |\mathbb{F}|^{(n+1)/2} 2^{-k_{\mathsf{Had}}}$ (this generalizes previous results of Chor and Goldreich [7] and Vazirani [42]). Plugging it into the construction described above we get the following LRS scheme $\Phi_{\mathsf{Had}} = (\mathsf{Encode}_{\mathsf{Had}}, \mathsf{Decode}_{\mathsf{Had}})$ for encoding messages $m \in \mathbb{F}$:

$$\begin{aligned} \mathsf{Encode}_{\mathsf{Had}}(m) &= (r_0, r_1, \langle r_0, r_1 \rangle + m) \\ \mathsf{Decode}_{\mathsf{Had}}(r_0, r_1, m^*) &= m^* - \langle r_0, r_1 \rangle. \end{aligned} \tag{7}$$

Observe that above, instead of using the xor we used the group operation in $\mathbb{F}$. This is ok, since, as explained in Sect. 2.1, one can transform a weakly-secure scheme into a standard one by using any group operation (not necessarily xor). Using Lemma 8 we get that Φ_{Had} is $(\Gamma_2, c, |\mathbb{F}| \cdot \epsilon_{\mathsf{Had}} + |\mathbb{F}|^{1-n} 2^{1+k_{\mathsf{Had}}+c})$.

3.2 Functions That Have Small Descriptions

The second case that we consider is when the only restriction on Γ is that it is a small set of robust functions: $|\Gamma| = 2^v$, where v is some parameter (that can be for example quadratic in β). One way to look at this family is to fix some method to describe the leakage functions as binary strings, and observe that the set of functions whose description has length v has exactly size 2^v.

A natural example of such a Γ is a set of *functions computable by Boolean circuits of a fixed size* (see e.g. [44] for an introduction to the complexity of Boolean circuits).

[4] Clearly ϕ_i depends only on the values V_i that the adversary retrieved in the previous rounds.

Recall that the *size* of a Boolean circuit is the number ρ of its gates. Each gate G can be connected with two other gates (G_1, G_2) (and we can assume that G is an AND gate if $G_1 \neq G_2$, and it is a NOT gate otherwise). Hence, for each gate we can have at most $(\rho - 1)(\rho - 1) < \rho^2$ choices. Therefore there are at most $(\rho^2)^\rho = \rho^{2\rho}$ circuits of size ρ. Thus the circuits of size ρ can be described using $2\rho \log_2 \rho$ bits.

Several natural functions can be computed by Boolean circuits of a small size (see Sect. 3 of [44]). For example every symmetric function[5] can be computed by a circuit of a linear size (in its input).

Let Γ_v be any robust set of functions such that $|\Gamma_v| = 2^v$. We will now construct a $(\Gamma_v, c, t, \epsilon)$-secure LRS. Let $H = \{h_s : \{0,1\}^n \to \{0,1\}^\alpha\}_{s \in \mathcal{S}}$ be a collection of ℓ-wise independent hash functions. The scheme is parameterized by a value $s \in \mathcal{S}$. For any $s \in \mathcal{S}$ let $\Phi_s \stackrel{\mathsf{def}}{=} (\mathsf{Encode}_s, \mathsf{Decode}_s)$, being

$$\mathsf{Encode}_s(m) = (R, h_s(R) \oplus m),$$

where $R \in \{0,1\}^n$ is random. Let

$$\mathsf{Decode}_s(R, d) = h_s(R) \oplus d.$$

We point out that also the above construction can be interpreted in terms of deterministic extractors. Indeed, as shown in [41] (and in [3]), ℓ-wise independent hash functions are, with high probability, deterministic extractors for sources (with some min-entropy) that can be generated by an efficient sampling algorithm or circuit of a small size.[6] Stated in other words, an ℓ-wise independent hash function can be viewed as a function $\mathsf{Ext} : \{0,1\}^n \to \{0,1\}^\alpha$ with the following property: for every source $R \in \{0,1\}^n$ with min-entropy k which is samplable by a circuit of a small size, $\mathsf{Ext}(R)$ is close to uniform with high probability. The same construction was also used by Dodis et al. [13] in the context of AONT. Both [41] and [13] consider only the non-adaptive case. Here we show that this scheme is secure in the context of leakage-resilient storage. The following lemma states that with a good probability (over the choice of $s \in \mathcal{S}$) the scheme Φ_s is secure.

Lemma 9. *Fix an arbitrary robust set Γ_v such that $|\Gamma_v| = 2^v$. For a randomly chosen s with probability at least $1 - \xi$ we have that Φ_s is $(\Gamma_v, c, t, 2^\alpha \cdot \epsilon + 2^{\alpha+k+c-n})$-secure, for any $c, k, t, v, \ell, \epsilon$ and ξ such that*

$$\xi = 2^{tv - \frac{\ell}{2}(k - \alpha - 2\log(1/\epsilon) - \log \ell + 2) + \alpha + 2}. \tag{8}$$

In the lemma above k is a parameter, that in the proof will correspond to the min-entropy of R conditioned on the view of the adversary. Observe that we have a trade-off between $2^\alpha \cdot \epsilon + 2^{\alpha+k+c-n}$ and ξ (larger k increases the first term, and decreases the second). The proof of this lemma is more involved and we present it in Sect. 3.2.1. Let us first discuss this lemma for more concrete values of the parameters.

---

[5] A function is *symmetric* if its output does not depend on the permutation of the input bits. For example every function that just depends on the sum of the input bits is symmetric. See Sect. 3.4 of [44].

[6] The approach used in [41] is orthogonal to the one used in [7]: in the latter setting, distributions can be arbitrarily complex, but they have to satisfy a strong independence requirement; in the former setting distributions have to be samplable but can involve arbitrary dependencies.

Corollary 1. *Fix an arbitrary robust set Γ_v such that $|\Gamma_v| = 2^v$. For a randomly chosen s with probability at least $1 - \xi$ we have that Φ_s is $(\Gamma_v, c, t, 2^{-\lambda})$-secure, for any c, t, v, ℓ, λ and ξ such that*

$$\xi = 2^{tv - \frac{\ell}{2}(n-c-3\lambda-4\alpha-\log \ell - 1)+\alpha+2}. \tag{9}$$

Proof. Set $\epsilon := 2^{-\alpha-\lambda-1}$ and let $k := n - \lambda - 1 - \alpha - c$. Take Φ_s from Lemma 9. We have that

$$2^{\alpha} \cdot 2^{-\alpha-\lambda-1} + 2^{\alpha+k+c-n} \leq 2^{-\lambda-1} + 2^{-\lambda-1} \leq 2^{-\lambda},$$

and

$$\xi = 2^{tv - \frac{\ell}{2}((n-\lambda-1-\alpha-c)-\alpha-2(\alpha+\lambda+1)-\log \ell+2)+\alpha+2}$$

which is equal to (9). □

Concrete values If we want to have security against circuits of size χn (for some constant $\chi > 1$) then the size of Γ is equal to $2^{2\chi n \log(\chi n)}$. If we apply it $t = \omega n$ times (for some constant $\omega < 1$) then $tv = 2\chi\omega n^2 \log(\chi n)$. To be more precise set $\lambda := 24$ and $\alpha := 128$, and $n := 1024$. If we set $\chi := 10$, $\omega := 3/25$ then we can allow the adversary to retrieve at most 180 bits by setting $\ell = 278323$. With these settings we get $\xi \leq 4 \cdot 10^{-12}$.
If we consider a non-adaptive scenario, in which the adversary chooses a single leakage function (i.e. $t = 1$) and retrieves at most c bits[7], then we obtain a better value for ℓ: for $\lambda := 24$, $\alpha := 128$, $n := 1024$ and $\chi := 10$, we can allow the adversary to retrieve at most 180 bits by setting $\ell = 2203$. With these settings we get $\xi \leq 2 \cdot 10^{-28}$.

Practical considerations The parameter s can be public. Therefore if ξ is negligible, then for the real-life applications s can be just chosen once and for all by some trusted party. For example, one can assume that $s = H(0)||H(1)|| \cdots$, where H is some hash function (this of course can be proven secure only in the random oracle model).

Alternatively, we could just assume that s is chosen independently each time Encode_s is calculated, and becomes a part of the encoding. In other words we could define

$$\mathsf{Encode}'(m) \stackrel{\text{def}}{=} (s, \mathsf{Encode}_s(m)) \quad \text{and} \quad \mathsf{Decode}'(s, x) \stackrel{\text{def}}{=} \mathsf{Decode}_s(x).$$

Of course, in this way the length β of encoding gets larger, and hence if Γ_v is a family of circuits whose size ρ is some function of β, then v becomes much larger.

3.2.1 Proof of Lemma 9

We first show that Φ_s is weakly secure. Suppose that the adversary $\mathcal{A}_{weak}$ performs a weak attack against Φ_s. Let R be distributed uniformly over $\{0,1\}^n$. Then we show that for any $\epsilon > 0$ and for at least $1 - \xi$ fraction of $s \in \mathcal{S}$ we have

$$d(h_s(R)|\mathsf{view}_{\mathcal{A}_{weak}}) \leq \epsilon + 2^{k+c-n},$$

[7] This is equivalent to consider an adversary who chooses $t > 1$ leakage functions in advance, with the same total number of retrieved bits. Note that this scenario is theoretically weaker than the adaptive one but it is useful from a practical point of view.

where ξ is a function of t, v, ℓ, k, α and ϵ as defined in (8). Consider some fixed adversary $\mathcal{A}_{weak}$. Let $Good_{\mathcal{A}_{weak}}$ denote the event that $\mathbf{H}_\infty(R|\mathsf{view}_{\mathcal{A}_{weak}} = y) \geq k$, where $y := \mathsf{view}_{\mathcal{A}_{weak}}$. By Lemma 5 we get that $\mathbb{P}\left[\overline{Good_{\mathcal{A}_{weak}}}\right] \leq 2^{k+c-n}$. On the other hand, we have

$$\mathbf{H}_\infty(R|\mathsf{view}_{\mathcal{A}_{weak}} = y, Good_{\mathcal{A}_{weak}}) \geq k.$$

Therefore, by Lemma 6 we get that

$$\mathbb{P}_s\left[d(h_s(R)|\mathsf{view}_{\mathcal{A}_{weak}} = y, Good_{\mathcal{A}_{weak}}) \geq \epsilon\right] \leq 2^{-u}, \tag{10}$$

where $\mathbb{P}_s$ means that the probability is taken over the choice of $s \in \mathcal{S}$, and u is defined in (4). From Lemma 2 we get that (10) implies that

$$\mathbb{P}_s\left[d(h_s(R)|\mathsf{view}_{\mathcal{A}_{weak}}) \geq \epsilon + \mathbb{P}\left[\overline{Good_{\mathcal{A}_{weak}}}\right]\right] \leq 2^{-u},$$

which implies that

$$\mathbb{P}_s\left[d(h_s(R)|\mathsf{view}_{\mathcal{A}_{weak}}) \geq \epsilon'\right] \leq 2^{-u}, \tag{11}$$

where $\epsilon' := \epsilon + 2^{k+c-n}$. Of course (11) holds just for a fixed adversary and to complete the proof we need to give a bound on the value

$$\max_{\mathcal{A}_{weak}} \left(\mathbb{P}_s\left[d(h_s(R)|\mathsf{view}_{\mathcal{A}_{weak}}) \geq \epsilon'\right]\right). \tag{12}$$

We will do it by applying a union-bound (over all $\mathcal{A}_{weak}$) to (11). However, since that the total number of different adversaries $\mathcal{A}_{weak}$ is doubly-exponential in c,[8] we cannot do it in a straightforward way. Instead, we first observe that

$$\max_{\mathcal{A}_{weak}} \mathbb{P}_s\left[d(h_s(R)|\mathsf{view}_{\mathcal{A}_{weak}}) \geq \epsilon'\right] = \max_{g_1,\ldots,g_t} \mathbb{P}_s\left[d(h_s(R)|g_1(R),\ldots,g_t(R)) \geq \epsilon'\right]. \tag{13}$$

Since each $g_i \in \Gamma_v$, and $|\Gamma_v| = 2^v$ we get

$$\max_{\mathcal{A}_{weak}} \left(\mathbb{P}_s\left[d(h_s(R)|\mathsf{view}_{\mathcal{A}_{weak}}) \geq \epsilon'\right]\right) \leq (2^v)^t \cdot 2^{-u} = 2^{tv-u}. \tag{14}$$

This completes the proof, since now using Lemma 7 we are done. □

4 Connection with the Theory of Compressibility of NP-Instances

We believe that in general the idea to model the leakage as functions from some low complexity class is worth investigating further, as it may lead to new applications of the circuit lower bounds. Interestingly, this is probably the first scenario ever considered in cryptography in which the computing power of the adversary is smaller than the computing power of the users (during some part of the attack). A similar observation was already made in [17] (footnote 3, page 295).

It may also be worth exploring some interesting connections between this area and the theory of the compressibility of NP-instances of Harnik and Naor [23]. Informally,

[8] This is because after retrieving c_i bits in the ith round the adversary can choose 2^v different functions g_{i+1}, hence in every round there are $2^{v \cdot 2^{c_i}}$.

an NP-language L is *compressible* if every $x \in \{0,1\}^*$ can be "compressed" to a much shorter string compress(x) (where g is some poly-time function, and $c = |\text{compress}(x)| \ll |x|$) such that an infinitely powerful machine M can determine if $x \in L$ just by looking at compress(x). Call this $(PTIME, \infty)$-c-compressibility. As a natural generalization of this concept, one can consider any $(\mathcal{P}_0, \mathcal{P}_1)$-compressibility (where $\mathcal{P}_0$ and $\mathcal{P}_1$ are some complexity classes): in this setting we would require that $g \in \mathcal{P}_0$, and the machine M operates in $\mathcal{P}_1$.

For simplicity in this section consider only the one-round LRS's i.e. $t = 1$ (cf. game in Sect. 2). Moreover, assume that the adversary is poly-time. Informally speaking what we are looking for, when constructing a Γ-secure LRS $\Phi = (\text{Encode}, \text{Decode})$ is a class of problems that are not $(\Gamma, PTIME)$-c-compressible on average. More precisely, consider the language L of all valid encodings of some fixed message M. Of course, if this language is $(\Gamma, PTIME)$-c-compressible with some probability ϵ then Φ cannot be $(\Gamma, c, 1, \epsilon)$-secure (as otherwise the adversary could just choose compress to be his leakage function). We leave investigating these connections as a future research direction.

5 Comparison with [18]

In an independent work Faust et al. [18] consider a problem of leakage-resilient computation. In their work, that can be viewed as an extension of the "private circuits" paper of [24], they provide a formal definition of a circuit computation that is secure against a class of leakages $\mathcal{L}_{TR}$ (cf. Def. 1 of [18]), and for certain classes $\mathcal{L}_{TR}$, they construct (Theorem 1, [18]) a generic transformation that, given any circuit C transforms it into another circuit C' that is secure against the leakages in $\mathcal{L}_{TR}$.

The main ingredient of their construction is a *linear* encoding scheme that is secure against leakages in some class $\mathcal{L}$. *Linearity* of the encoding means that the decoding function can be expressed as $\text{Decode}(x_1, \ldots, x_\beta) = r_1 x_1 + \cdots + r_\beta x_\beta$, where $r_1, \ldots, r_\beta$ are constants from some field. Their definition of an encoding scheme is very similar to ours: essentially their *p-adaptive $(\mathcal{L}, \tau, \epsilon)$-leakage-indistinguishable encoding* is the same as our $(\mathcal{L}, c, t, \epsilon)$-secure LRS scheme. The additional parameter τ, that they use indicates the running time of the adversary (that we do not consider in our paper). On the other hand we use the parameter c, that indicates the total amount of bits retrieved from the encoding, which is absent in [18].

We note that while the work of [18] has an obvious advantage over ours by considering not only secure storage, but also computation, our schemes cover different (and possibly more realistic) classes of leakage functions. In particular, both of the approaches in our paper cover trivially the so-called *Hamming weight attacks* [26], where the adversary is allowed to learn a sum of the bits, while the approach of [18] does not cover them.

Acknowledgments

The authors thank Yevgeniy Dodis for a helpful discussion.

References

1. Akavia, A., Goldwasser, S., Vaikuntanathan, V.: Simultaneous hardcore bits and cryptography against memory attacks. In: Reingold, O. (ed.) TCC 2009. LNCS, vol. 5444, pp. 474–495. Springer, Heidelberg (2009)
2. Alwen, J., Dodis, Y., Wichs, D.: Leakage-resilient public-key cryptography in the bounded-retrieval model. In: Halevi [21], pp. 36–54
3. Barak, B., Shaltiel, R., Tromer, E.: True random number generators secure in a changing environment. In: Walter, C.D., Koç, Ç.K., Paar, C. (eds.) CHES 2003. LNCS, vol. 2779, pp. 166–180. Springer, Heidelberg (2003)
4. Blum, M.: Independent unbiased coin flips from a correlated biased source: A finite state markov chain. In: 25th Annual Symposium on Foundations of Computer Science, 1984, pp. 425–433. IEEE Computer Society, Los Alamitos (1984)
5. Canetti, R., Dodis, Y., Halevi, S., Kushilevitz, E., Sahai, A.: Exposure-Resilient Functions and All-Or-Nothing Transforms. In: Preneel, B. (ed.) EUROCRYPT 2000. LNCS, vol. 1807, pp. 453–469. Springer, Heidelberg (2000)
6. Cash, D., Ding, Y.Z., Dodis, Y., Lee, W., Lipton, R.J., Walfish, S.: Intrusion-resilient key exchange in the bounded retrieval model. In: Vadhan, S.P. (ed.) TCC 2007. LNCS, vol. 4392, pp. 479–498. Springer, Heidelberg (2007)
7. Chor, B., Goldreich, O.: Unbiased bits from sources of weak randomness and probabilistic communication complexity. SIAM J. on Computing 17(2), 230–261 (1988)
8. Chor, B., Goldreich, O., Håstad, J., Friedman, J., Rudich, S., Smolensky, R.: The bit extraction problem of t-resilient functions (preliminary version). In: FOCS, pp. 396–407. IEEE, Los Alamitos (1985)
9. Di Crescenzo, G., Lipton, R.J., Walfish, S.: Perfectly secure password protocols in the bounded retrieval model. In: Halevi, Rabin (eds.) [22], pp. 225–244
10. Dodis, Y., Elbaz, A., Oliveira, R., Raz, R.: Improved randomness extraction from two independent sources. In: Jansen, K., Khanna, S., Rolim, J.D.P., Ron, D. (eds.) RANDOM 2004 and APPROX 2004. LNCS, vol. 3122, pp. 334–344. Springer, Heidelberg (2004)
11. Dodis, Y., Goldwasser, S., Kalai, Y.T., Peikert, C., Vaikuntanathan, V.: Public-key encryption schemes with auxiliary inputs. In: Micciancio, D. (ed.) TCC 2010. LNCS, vol. 5978, pp. 361–381. Springer, Heidelberg (2010)
12. Dodis, Y., Kalai, Y.T., Lovett, S.: On cryptography with auxiliary input. In: STOC 2009: Proceedings of the 41st annual ACM symposium on Theory of computing, pp. 621–630. ACM, New York (2009)
13. Dodis, Y., Sahai, A., Smith, A.: On perfect and adaptive security in exposure-resilient cryptography. In: Pfitzmann, B. (ed.) EUROCRYPT 2001. LNCS, vol. 2045, pp. 301–324. Springer, Heidelberg (2001)
14. Dziembowski., S.: Intrusion-resilience via the bounded-storage model. In: Halevi, Rabin (eds.) [22], pp. 207–224
15. Dziembowski, S.: On forward-secure storage. In: Dwork, C. (ed.) CRYPTO 2006. LNCS, vol. 4117, pp. 251–270. Springer, Heidelberg (2006)
16. Dziembowski, S., Pietrzak, K.: Intrusion-resilient secret sharing. In: FOCS, pp. 227–237 (2007)
17. Dziembowski, S., Pietrzak, K.: Leakage-resilient cryptography. In: FOCS 2008: Proceedings of the 49th Annual IEEE Symposium on Foundations of Computer Science, Washington, DC, USA. IEEE Computer Society, Los Alamitos (2008)
18. Faust, S., Rabin, T., Reyzin, L., Tromer, E., Vaikuntanathan, V.: Protecting circuits from leakage: The computationally-bounded and noisy cases. In: Gilbert, H. (ed.) EUROCRYPT 2010. LNCS, vol. 6110, pp. 135–156. Springer, Heidelberg (2010)

19. Gandolfi, K., Mourtel, C., Olivier, F.: Electromagnetic analysis: Concrete results. In: Koç, Ç.K., Naccache, D., Paar, C. (eds.) CHES 2001. LNCS, vol. 2162, pp. 251–261. Springer, Heidelberg (2001)
20. Halderman, A.J., Schoen, S.D., Heninger, N., Clarkson, W., Paul, W., Calandrino, J.A., Feldman, A.J., Appelbaum, J., Felten, E.W.: Lest we remember: cold-boot attacks on encryption keys. Commun. ACM 52(5), 91–98 (2009)
21. Halevi, S. (ed.): CRYPTO 2009. LNCS, vol. 5677. Springer, Heidelberg (2009)
22. Halevi, S., Rabin, T. (eds.): TCC 2006. LNCS, vol. 3876. Springer, Heidelberg (2006)
23. Harnik, D., Naor, M.: On the compressibility of NP instances and cryptographic applications. In: FOCS 2006: Proceedings of the 47th Annual IEEE Symposium on Foundations of Computer Science, Washington, DC, USA, pp. 719–728. IEEE Computer Society, Los Alamitos (2006)
24. Ishai, Y., Sahai, A., Wagner, D.: Private Circuits: Securing Hardware against Probing Attacks. In: Boneh, D. (ed.) CRYPTO 2003. LNCS, vol. 2729, pp. 463–481. Springer, Heidelberg (2003)
25. Katz, J., Vaikuntanathan, V.: Signature schemes with bounded leakage resilience. In: Matsui, M. (ed.) ASIACRYPT 2009. LNCS, vol. 5912, pp. 703–720. Springer, Heidelberg (2009)
26. Kelsey, J., Schneier, B., Wagner, D., Hall, C.: Side channel cryptanalysis of product ciphers. Journal of Computer Security 8, 141–158 (2000)
27. Kocher, P.C.: Timing attacks on implementations of Diffie-Hellman, RSA, DSS, and other systems. In: Koblitz, N. (ed.) CRYPTO 1996. LNCS, vol. 1109, pp. 104–113. Springer, Heidelberg (1996)
28. Kocher, P.C., Jaffe, J., Jun, B.: Differential power analysis. In: Wiener, M. (ed.) CRYPTO 1999. LNCS, vol. 1666, pp. 388–397. Springer, Heidelberg (1999)
29. Maurer, U.M.: Conditionally-perfect secrecy and a provably-secure randomized cipher. J. Cryptology 5(1), 53–66 (1992)
30. Micali, S., Reyzin, L.: Physically observable cryptography (extended abstract). In: Naor, M. (ed.) TCC 2004. LNCS, vol. 2951, pp. 278–296. Springer, Heidelberg (2004)
31. Naor, M., Segev, G.: Public-key cryptosystems resilient to key leakage. In: Halevi (ed.) [21], pp. 18–35
32. European Network of Excellence (ECRYPT). The side channel cryptanalysis lounge, `http://www.crypto.ruhr-uni-bochum.de/en_sclounge.html` (retrieved on 29.03.2010)
33. Pietrzak, K.: A leakage-resilient mode of operation. In: Joux, A. (ed.) EUROCRYPT 2009. LNCS, vol. 5479, pp. 462–482. Springer, Heidelberg (2010)
34. Quisquater, J.-J., Koene, F.: Side channel attacks: State of the art. In: [32] (October 2002)
35. Quisquater, J.-J., Samyde, D.: Electromagnetic analysis (EMA): Measures and countermeasures for smart cards. In: Attali, S., Jensen, T. (eds.) E-smart 2001. LNCS, vol. 2140, pp. 200–210. Springer, Heidelberg (2001)
36. Rao, A.: An exposition of Bourgain's 2-source extractor. Electronic Colloquium on Computational Complexity (ECCC), 14(034) (2007), `http://eccc.hpi-web.de/eccc-reports/2007/TR07-034/index.html`
37. Rivest, R.L.: All-or-nothing encryption and the package transform. In: Biham, E. (ed.) FSE 1997. LNCS, vol. 1267, pp. 210–218. Springer, Heidelberg (1997)
38. Samyde, D., Skorobogatov, S., Anderson, R., Quisquater, J.-J.: On a new way to read data from memory. In: SISW 2002: Proceedings of the First International IEEE Security in Storage Workshop, Washington, DC, USA, p. 65. IEEE Computer Society, Los Alamitos (2002)
39. Shaltiel, R.: How to get more mileage from randomness extractors. In: CCC 2006: Proceedings of the 21st Annual IEEE Conference on Computational Complexity, Washington, DC, USA, 2006, pp. 46–60. IEEE Computer Society, Los Alamitos (2006)

40. Shamir, A., Tromer, E.: Acoustic cryptanalysis. on nosy people and noisy machines, http://people.csail.mit.edu/tromer/acoustic/ (accessed on 29.03.2010)
41. Trevisan, L., Vadhan, S.P.: Extracting randomness from samplable distributions. In: FOCS, pp. 32–42 (2000)
42. Vazirani, U.V.: Strong communication complexity or generating quasirandom sequences form two communicating semi-random sources. Combinatorica 7(4), 375–392 (1987)
43. von Neumann, J.: Various techniques used in connection with random digits. J. Research Nat. Bur. Stand., Appl. Math. Series 12, 36–38 (1951)
44. Wegener, I.: The Complexity of Boolean Functions. John Wiley and Sons Ltd., B. G. Teubner (1987), http://eccc.hpi-web.de/static/books/The_Complexity_of_Boolean_Functions/

A Proof of Lemma 2

Before showing this lemma let us first prove the following:

Lemma 10. *For every random variable X and events $\mathcal{E}, \mathcal{H}$ we have*

$$d(X|\mathcal{H}) \leq d(X|\mathcal{H} \wedge \mathcal{E}) + \mathbb{P}\left[\overline{\mathcal{E}}|\mathcal{H}\right]. \tag{15}$$

Proof. It is enough to show that

$$\Delta(P_{X|\mathcal{H}}; P_{X|\mathcal{H}\wedge\mathcal{E}}) \leq \mathbb{P}\left[\overline{\mathcal{E}}|\mathcal{H}\right]. \tag{16}$$

After showing this we will be done, since from the triangle inequality we have

$$\overbrace{\Delta(P_{X|\mathcal{H}}; U_{\mathcal{X}})}^{=d(X|\mathcal{H})} \leq \overbrace{\Delta(P_{X|\mathcal{H}\wedge\mathcal{E}}\, ; U_{\mathcal{X}})}^{=d(X|\mathcal{H}\wedge\mathcal{E})} + \Delta(P_{X|\mathcal{H}}; P_{X|\mathcal{H}\wedge\mathcal{E}}),$$

where $U_{\mathcal{X}}$ denotes the uniform distribution over $\mathcal{X}$. Let $\mathcal{F}$ denote the set

$$\{x : \mathbb{P}[X = x|\mathcal{H}] > \mathbb{P}[X = x|\mathcal{H} \wedge \mathcal{E}]\}.$$

We have that the left-hand side of (16) is equal to

$$\sum_{x\in\mathcal{F}} \mathbb{P}[X = x|\mathcal{H}] - \overbrace{\mathbb{P}[X = x|\mathcal{H} \wedge \mathcal{E}]}^{=\frac{\mathbb{P}[X=x\wedge\mathcal{E}|\mathcal{H}]}{\mathbb{P}[\mathcal{E}|\mathcal{H}]}\geq\mathbb{P}[X=x\wedge\mathcal{E}|\mathcal{H}]}. \tag{17}$$

$$\leq \sum_{x\in\mathcal{F}} \mathbb{P}[X = x|\mathcal{H}] - \mathbb{P}[X = x \wedge \mathcal{E}|\mathcal{H}] \tag{18}$$

$$= \sum_{x\in\mathcal{F}} \mathbb{P}[X = x|\mathcal{H}] - \sum_{x\in\mathcal{F}} \mathbb{P}[X = x \wedge \mathcal{E}|\mathcal{H}] \tag{19}$$

$$= \mathbb{P}[X \in \mathcal{F}|\mathcal{H}] - \mathbb{P}[(X \in \mathcal{F}) \wedge \mathcal{E}|\mathcal{H}] \tag{20}$$

$$\leq \mathbb{P}\left[\overline{\mathcal{E}}|\mathcal{H}\right]. \tag{21}$$

□

Proof (of Lemma 2). The right-hand side of (2) is equal to

$$\sum_y d(X|Y=y) \cdot \mathbb{P}[Y=y], \tag{22}$$

and the left-hand side of (2) is equal to

$$\sum_y \left(d(X|(Y=y) \wedge \mathcal{E}) + \mathbb{P}\left[\overline{\mathcal{E}}|Y=y\right]\right) \cdot \mathbb{P}[Y=y]. \tag{23}$$

To finish the proof it suffices to show that for every y we have

$$d(X|(Y=y) \wedge \mathcal{E}) + \mathbb{P}\left[\overline{\mathcal{E}}|Y=y\right] \geq d(X|Y=y).$$

This follows directly from Lemma 10, with $\mathcal{H}$ being the event that $Y=y$. □

B Proof of Lemma 5

Proof. We prove that (3) holds for a fixed w. This clearly implies that (3) holds when W is a random variable independent on X. Since $|f(X,w)| \leq c$, hence the number of all y's is at most equal to 2^c. Therefore the number of x's for which there exists some y such that

$$|x : f(x,w) = y| \leq 2^k \tag{24}$$

holds is at most 2^{c+k}. Hence the probability that for a *random* X we have that (24) holds is at most 2^{c+k-n}. Since clearly if (24) does not hold then $\mathbf{H}_\infty(X|f(X,w)=y) > k$ we get that

$$\mathbb{P}_{y:=f(X,w)}(\mathbf{H}_\infty(X|f(X,w)=y) \leq k) \leq 2^{c+k-n}.$$

Thus we are done. □

Searching Keywords with Wildcards on Encrypted Data*

Saeed Sedghi[1], Peter van Liesdonk[2],
Svetla Nikova[1,3], Pieter Hartel[1], and Willem Jonker[1,4]

[1] Dept. EWI/DIES, University of Twente, Enschede, The Netherlands
s.sedghi@utwente.nl
[2] Dept. Math. and Comp. Science, T.U. Eindhoven, Eindhoven, The Netherlands
p.p.v.liesdonk@tue.nl
[3] Dept. ESAT/SCD-COSIC and IBBT, K.U. Leuven, Heverlee, Belgium
[4] Philips Research Laboratories, The Netherlands

Abstract. A hidden vector encryption scheme (HVE) is a derivation of identity-based encryption, where the public key is actually a vector over a certain alphabet. The decryption key is also derived from such a vector, but this one is also allowed to have "$\star$" (or wildcard) entries. Decryption is possible as long as these tuples agree on every position except where a "$\star$" occurs.

These schemes are useful for a variety of applications: they can be used as a building block to construct attribute-based encryption schemes and sophisticated predicate encryption schemes (for e.g. range or subset queries). Another interesting application – and our main motivation – is to create searchable encryption schemes that support queries for keywords containing wildcards.

Here we construct a new HVE scheme, based on bilinear groups of prime order, which supports vectors over any alphabet. The resulting ciphertext length is equally shorter than existing schemes, depending on a trade-off. The length of the decryption key and the computational complexity of decryption are both constant, unlike existing schemes where these are both dependent on the amount of non-wildcard symbols associated to the decryption key.

Our construction hides both the plaintext and public key used for encryption. We prove security in a selective model, under the decision linear assumption.

1 Introduction

With the growing popularity of outsourcing data to third-party data-centers (the cloud), enhancing the security of such remote data is of increasing interest. In an ideal world such data centers may be completely trustworthy, but in practice they may very well be curious for your secrets. To prevent this all data should be

* This work has been supported in part by the research program Sentinels of STW, under the project SEDAN 07630.

J.A. Garay and R. De Prisco (Eds.): SCN 2010, LNCS 6280, pp. 138–153, 2010.

encrypted. However, this directly results in problems of selective data retrieval. If a data-center cannot read the stored information, it also cannot answer any search queries.

Consider the following scenario about storage of health care records. Assume that Alice wants to store her medical records on a server. Since these medical records are highly sensitive, Alice wants to control the access to these records in such a way that a legitimate doctor can only see specific parts. Now Alice either has to trust the server to honestly treat her records, or she should encrypt her records in such a way that specific information can only be found by specific doctors.

Searchable encryption is a technique that addresses the mentioned problem. In general we will consider the following public-key setting: Bob wants to send a document to Alice, but to get it to her he has to store it on an untrusted intermediary server. Before sending he encrypts the document with Alice's public key. To make her interaction with the server easier he also adds some keywords describing the encrypted document. These keywords are also encrypted, but in a special way. Later, Alice wants to retrieve all documents from this server containing a specific keyword. She uses her secret key to create a so-called trapdoor that she sends to the server. Using this trapdoor the server can circumvent the encryption of all the encrypted keywords that it has stored, but only just enough to learn whether the encrypted keyword was equal to the keyword Alice had in mind. If the server finds such a match it can return the encrypted document to Alice.

In many applications it is convenient to have some flexibility when searching, like searching for a subset of keywords or searching for multiple keywords at once using a wildcard. Existing solutions address searching with wildcards using a technique called *hidden vector encryption* (HVE) [7]. A HVE scheme is a variation of identity-based encryption where both the encryption and the decryption key are derived from a vector. Decryption can only be done if the vectors are the same in every element except for certain positions, which we call wildcard- or "don't care"-positions. The relation with searchable encryption comes by viewing a keyword as a vector of symbols. For every keyword Bob will make a HVE encryption of a public message, using the keyword as a 'public key'. The trapdoor Alice sends to the server is actually a decryption key derived from a keyword. The server can now try to decrypt the HVE encryptions; if the decryption works the server can conclude that two keywords were the same, except for the wildcard positions. Because of this relation this paper will focus on the construction of a HVE scheme.

There have been quite a few proposals for HVE schemes, most notably [3,7,14,16,18,22]. These schemes have in general two drawbacks: Firstly, most of them are using *bilinear groups of composite order*, whereas the few schemes that do use the more efficient bilinear groups of prime order [3,14,18] are only capable of working with binary alphabets. Secondly, in all these schemes the *size of the ciphertext* is linear in the length of the vector it's key is derived from. Thirdly, the *size of the decryption key* grows linearly in the amount of non-wildcard symbols.

This directly influences the number of computations needed for decryption. Therefore, these schemes are inefficient for applications where the client wishes to query for keywords that contain just a few wildcard values.

1.1 Related Work

Searchable data encryption was first popularized by the work of Song, Wagner and Perrig [23]. They propose a scheme that allows a client to create both ciphertexts and trapdoors (resulting is a symmetric-key setting), while a server can test whether there is an exact match between a given ciphertext and a trapdoor. Searchable encryption in the symmetric key setting was further developed by [9,10,12,24] to enhance the security and the efficiency of the scheme. While these schemes are useful when you want to backup your own information on a server, the symmetric key makes them hard to use in a multi-user setting.

In [5], Boneh et. al. consider searchable encryption in an asymmetric setting, called *public key encryption with keyword search* (PEKS). Here everybody can create an encrypted keyword, but only the owner of the secret key can create a trapdoor, thus making it relevant for multi-user applications. This setting has been enhanced in [2,19]. The PEKS scheme has a very close connection to anonymous identity-based encryption as introduced in [6], This connection has been studied more thoroughly by [1]. For this reason, most work (including ours) on asymmetric searchable encryption has a direct use for identity-based encryption, and vice versa. Improved IBE schemes useful for searchable encryption have been proposed in [8,11,17,18].

These schemes are usable for equality search, i.e. a message can be decrypted if the trapdoor keyword and the associated keyword of the message are the same. In [13,20] the concept of attribute-based encryption is introduced. Here, multiple keywords are used at encryption time, but a trapdoor can be made to decrypt using (almost) any access structure. Both schemes lack the anonymity property however, which makes them unusable for searchable encryption.

Adding anonymity results in schemes that offer so-called called *hidden vector encryption*, introduced in [8,21]; in these schemes the trapdoor is allowed to have wildcard symbols "$\star$" that matches any possible keyword in the encryption, They all use rather inefficient bilinear groups of a composite order. The same holds for [16,22], which introduce inner product and predicate encryption. Finally, [14] provides a solution for binary hidden-vector encryption that is based purely on bilinear groups of prime order.

1.2 Our Results

Here, we propose a public-key hidden vector encryption (HVE) scheme, which queries encrypted messages for keywords that contain wildcard entries.

Our contributions in comparison to previous HVE schemes are as follows:

- Our construction uses bilinear groups of prime order, while [7,21] use hardness assumptions based on groups of composite order. Our scheme can also

take keywords over any alphabet, unlike [3,14,18] that only take binary symbols.
- The size of the decryption key and the computational complexity for decrypting ciphertexts is constant, while in earlier papers these grow linearly in the number of *non*-wildcard entries of the vector.
- The size of the ciphertext is approximately limited to one group element for every wildcard we are willing to allow (chosen at encryption time), where in previous schemes the ciphertext needs one group element for every symbol in the vector.

Our construction is proven to be semantically secure and keyword-hiding in the selective-keyword model, assuming the Decision Linear assumption [4] holds.

The rest of the paper is organized as follows: in Section 2 we discuss the security definitions we will use and the building blocks required. In Section 3 we introduce our HVE and prove its security properties. In Section 4 we analyze the performance of our scheme and compare it with previous results.

2 Preliminaries

Below, we review searchable data encryption, its relation to hidden vector encryption and their security properties.. In addition we review the definition of bilinear group and the Decision linear (DLin) assumption.

2.1 Searchable Data Encryption

Our ultimate goal is to provide a technique for searching with wildcards. As a basis we will use the concept of *public key encryption with keyword search* as introduced by Boneh et. al.[5]. Suppose Bob wants to send Alice an encrypted e-mail m in such a way that it is indexed by some searchable keywords $W_1, \ldots, W_k$. Then Bob would make a construction of the form

$$(\mathsf{E}_{pk}(m) \parallel S_{pk}(W_1) \parallel \cdots \parallel S_{pk}(W_k)),$$

where E is a regular asymmetric encryption function, pk is Alice's public key, and S is a special *searchable encryption* function. Alice can now – using her secret key – create a trapdoor to search for emails sent to her containing a specific keyword $\bar{W}$. The e-mail server can now test whether the searchable encryption and the trapdoor contain the same keyword and forward the encrypted mail if this is the case. During this process the server learns nothing about the keywords used.

If the trapdoor-keyword is allowed to have wildcard keywords we can get a much more flexible search. As an example, searching for the word '`ba*`' results in encryptions with '`bat`', '`bad`' and '`bag`'. We can also do range queries: '`200*`' matches '`2000`' up to '`2009`' and '`04/**/2010`' matches the whole of April in 2010. These and other applications were first studied in [7].

Definition 1. *A non-interactive* public key encryption with wildcard keyword search *(wildcard PEKS) scheme consists of four probabilistic polynomial-time algorithms (KeyGen, Enc, Trapdoor, Test):*

- Setup(κ)*: Given a security parameter κ and a keyword-length L output a* secret key sk *and a* public key pk.
- Enc(pk, W)*: Given a keyword W of length at most L characters, and the public key pk output a searchable encryption $S_{pk}(W)$.*
- Trapdoor($sk, \bar{W}$)*: Given a keyword $\bar{W}$ of length at most L characters containing wildcard symbols $\star$ and the secret key sk output a trapdoor $T_{\bar{W}}$.*
- Test($S_W, T_{\bar{W}}$)*: Given a searchable encryption S_W and a trapdoor $T_{\bar{W}}$, return 'true' if all non-wildcard characters are the same or 'false' otherwise.*

Such a scheme can typically be made out of a so-called hidden-vector encryption scheme [7], using a variation of the new-ibe-2-peks transformation in [1]. If the HVE is semantically secure, then the constructed wildcard PEKS is computationally consistent, i.e. it gives false positives with a negligible probability. If the HVE is keyword-hiding, then the constructed wildcard PEKS does not leak any information about the keyword used to make a searchable encryption.

2.2 Hidden Vector Encryption

Let Σ be an alphabet. Let $\star$ be a special symbol not in Σ. This star $\star$ will play the role of a wildcard or "don't care" symbol. Define $\Sigma_\star = \Sigma \cup \{\star\}$. The public key used to create a ciphertext will be a vector $W = (w_1, \dots, w_L) \in \Sigma^L$, called *attribute vector*. Every decryption key will also be created from a vector $\bar{W} = (\bar{w}_1, \dots, \bar{w}_L) \in \Sigma_\star^L$. Decryption is possible if for all $i = 1...L$ either $w_i = \bar{w}_i$ or $\bar{w}_i = \star$.

Definition 2 (HVE). *A* Hidden Vector Encryption *(HVE) scheme consists of the following four probabilistic polynomial-time algorithms (Setup, Extract, Enc, Dec):*

- Setup(κ, Σ, L)*: Given a security parameter κ, an alphabet Σ, and a vector-length L, output a* master secret key msk *and* public parameters $param$.
- Extract($msk, \bar{W}$)*: Given an attribute vector $\bar{W} \in \Sigma_\star^L$ and the master secret key msk, output a decryption key $T_{\bar{W}}$.*
- Enc($param, W, M$)*: Given an attribute vector $W \in \Sigma^L$, a message M, and the public parameters $param$, output a ciphertext $S_{W,M}$.*
- Dec($S_{W,M}, T_{\bar{W}}$)*: Given a ciphertext $S_{W,M}$ and a decryption key $T_{\bar{W}}$, output a message M,*

These algorithms must satisfy the following consistency constraint:

$$\mathsf{Dec}\big(\mathsf{Enc}(param, W, M), \mathsf{Extract}(msk, \bar{W})\big) = M \qquad \text{if } w_i = \bar{w}_i \vee \bar{w}_i = \star \text{ for } i = 1 \dots L. \quad (1)$$

Security Definitions. Here, we define the notion of security for hidden vector encryption schemes. Informally, this security definition states that a scheme reveals no non-trivial information to an adversary. In other words there is a separation between *semantic security* – which formalizes the notion that an adversary cannot learn any information about the message that has been encrypted – and *keyword hiding* – which formalizes the notion that he cannot learn non-trivial information about the keyword or vector used for encryption. These notions are both integrated into our security definition. This definition uses the selective model, in which the adversary commits to the encryption vector at the beginning of the "game".

Definition 3 (Semantic Security). *A HVE scheme* (Setup, Extract, Enc, Dec) *is* semantically secure in the selective model *if for all probabilistic polynomial-time adversaries* $\mathcal{A}$,

$$\left|\Pr\left[\mathbf{Exp}_{\mathcal{A}}(\kappa) = 1\right] - \frac{1}{2}\right| < \epsilon(\kappa)$$

for some negligible function $\epsilon(\kappa)$*, where* $\mathbf{Exp}_{\mathcal{A}}(\kappa)$ *is the following experiment:*

- **Init**. *The adversary* $\mathcal{A}$ *chooses an alphabet* Σ*, a length* L *and announces two attribute vectors* $W_0^*, W_1^* \in \Sigma^L$*, different in at least one position, that it wishes to be challenged upon.*
- **Setup**. *The challenger runs* $\mathsf{Setup}(\kappa, \Sigma, L)$*, which outputs a set of public parameters param and a master secret key msk. The challenger then sends param to the adversary* $\mathcal{A}$*.*
- **Query Phase I**. *In this phase* $\mathcal{A}$ *adaptively issues key extraction queries for attribute vectors* $\bar{W} \in \Sigma_\star^L$*, under the restriction that* $\bar{w}_i \neq w_{0i}^*$ *and* $\bar{w}_i \neq w_{1i}^*$ *for at least one* $\bar{w}_i \neq \star$*. Given an attribute vector* $\bar{W}$ *the challenger runs* $\mathsf{Extract}(msk, \bar{W})$ *which outputs a decryption key* $T_{\bar{W}}$*. The challenger then sends the* $T_{\bar{W}}$ *to* $\mathcal{A}$*.*
- **Challenge**. *Once* $\mathcal{A}$ *decides that the query phase is over,* $\mathcal{A}$ *picks a pair of messages* (M_0, M_1) *on which it wishes to be challenged and sends them to the challenger. Given the challenge message* (M_0, M_1) *and the challenge attribute vectors* (W_0^*, W_1^*)*, the adversary flips a fair coin* $\nu \in_R \{0,1\}$*, and invokes the* $\mathsf{Enc}(param, W_\nu^*, M_\nu)$ *algorithm to output* $S_{W_\nu^*, M_\nu}$*. The challenger then sends* $S_{W_\nu^*, M_\nu}$ *to* $\mathcal{A}$*.*
- **Query Phase II**. *Identical to Query Phase I.*
- **Output**. *Finally, the adversary outputs a bit* ν' *which represents its guess for bit* ν*. If* $\nu = \nu'$ *then return* 1*, else return* 0*.*

Intuitively, this experiment simulates a worst-case scenario attack, where the adversary has access to a lot of information: it knows that the challenge ciphertext is either an encryption of M_0 under W_0^* or an encryption of M_1 under W_1, all of which are chosen by him. In addition, it is allowed to know any decryption key that does not directly decrypt the challenge. Query phase I allows the adversary to choose the challenge messages based on decryption keys it already knows. Query phase II allows the adversary to ask for more decryption keys based on the challenge ciphertext it received.

If the encryption scheme would have a flaw and leak even a bit of information, a smart adversary would choose the message and attribute vector in such a way that this weakness would come to light. Thus the statement that no adversary can do significantly better than guessing implies that the encryption scheme does not leak information.

We wish to note that there is a stronger notion of security – the non-selective model – where the adversary chooses W_0^* and W_1^* in the challenge phase. This allows the adversary to make those dependent on the public parameters and on known decryption keys. Creating a secure HVE in that setting is still an open problem.

2.3 Bilinear Groups

Definition 4 (Bilinear Group). *We say that a cyclic group $\mathbb{G}$ of prime order q with generator g is a* bilinear group *if there exists a group $\mathbb{G}_T$ and a map e such that*

- *$(\mathbb{G}_T, \cdot)$ is also a cyclic group, of prime order q,*
- *$e(g,g)$ is a generator of $\mathbb{G}_T$ (non-degenerate).*
- *e is an bilinear map $e: \mathbb{G} \times \mathbb{G} \rightarrow \mathbb{G}_T$. In other words, for all $u, v \in \mathbb{G}_1$ and $a, b \in \mathbb{Z}_q^*$, we have $e(u^a, v^b) = e(u,v)^{ab}$.*

Additionally, we require that the group actions and the bilinear map can be computed in polynomial time. A bilinear map that satisfies these conditions is called admissible.

Our scheme is proven secure under the Decision Linear assumption (DLin), which has been introduced by [4]:

Definition 5 (Decision Linear Assumption). *There exist bilinear groups $\mathbb{G}$ such that for all probabilistic polynomial-time algorithms $\mathcal{A}$,*

$$\left|\Pr\left[\mathcal{A}(\mathbb{G}, g, g^a, g^b, g^{ac}, g^d, g^{b(c+d)})=1\right] - \Pr\left[\mathcal{A}(\mathbb{G}, g, g^a, g^b, g^{ac}, g^d, g^r)=1\right]\right| < \epsilon(\kappa)$$

for some negligible function $\epsilon(\kappa)$, where the probabilities are taken over all possible choices of $a, b, c, d, r \in \mathbb{Z}_q^*$.

Informally, the assumption states that given a bilinear group $\mathbb{G}$ and elements g^a, g^b, g^{ac}, g^d it is hard to distinguish $h = g^{b(c+d)}$ from a random element in $\mathbb{G}$. The Decision Linear assumption implies the decision bilinear Diffie-Hellman assumption. The best known algorithm to solve the Decision Linear Problem is to compute a discrete logarithm in $\mathbb{G}$.

3 Construction

Before we present our scheme we will first explain the intuition behind it.

3.1 Intuition

A common construction for encryption schemes is to hide a message using a one-time pad construction, i.e. multiplying the message with a random session key. In our HVE scheme we choose a session key based on all the elements of the encryption-vector, while the decryption key contains the information to cancel out the effect of symbols at unwanted wildcard-positions. Ciphertext and decryption key together can thus recover the session key.

Suppose we have an encryption-vector $W = (w_1, \ldots, w_L)$ and a decryption-vector $\bar{W} = (\bar{w}_1, \ldots, \bar{w}_L)$, both consisting of L elements. Let $J = \{j_1, \cdots, j_n\} \subset \{1, \ldots, L\}$ denote the position of wildcards in the decryption key (i.e. $J = \{4, 5\}$ for '04/**/2010'). We now consider the polynomial $\prod_{j \in J}(i - j)$ which equals zero in all the wildcard positions. Now the following statement are equal:

$$w_i = \bar{w}_i \vee \bar{w}_i = \star \text{ for } i = 1 \ldots L \tag{2}$$

$$\sum_{i=1}^{L} w_i \prod_{j \in J}(i - j) = \sum_{\substack{i=1 \\ i \notin J}}^{L} \bar{w}_i \prod_{j \in J}(i - j), \tag{3}$$

Given that we can expand $\prod_{j \in J}(i-j) = \sum_{k=0}^{n} a_k i^k$, where the a_k are coefficients only dependent on J, this is also equivalent with

$$\sum_{k=0}^{n} a_k \sum_{i=1}^{L} w_i i^k = \sum_{\substack{i=1 \\ i \notin J}}^{L} \bar{w}_i \prod_{j \in J}(i - j). \tag{4}$$

Practically we want to hide computations in the exponents of group elements. So instead of w_i we work with $U_i^{w_i}$ for some random group element U_i. Equation (4) still holds if:

$$\prod_{k=0}^{n} (\prod_{i=1}^{L} U_i^{w_i i^k})^{a_k} = \prod_{\substack{i=1 \\ i \notin J}}^{L} U_i^{\bar{w}_i \prod_{j \in J}(i-j)} \tag{5}$$

In the ciphertext we introduce new randomness that can only be removed if Eq. (5) – and thus Eq. (2) – is true. For this to work we put pieces of this equation in the ciphertext and in the decryption key, such that it can be evaluated at decryption time. The whole right side is included in the decryption key The left side of Eq. (5) can be computed using the following two sets of elements

- J is included with the decryption key, which allows for computation of all the coefficients a_k,
- for $k = 1, \ldots, n$, the term $\prod_{i=1}^{L} U_i^{w_i i^k}$ is included in elements of the ciphertext.

The ciphertext has to include n almost similar elements – only different in the value for k – since it is infeasible to compute them from a single source. However, the amount of wildcards n used for decryption is unknown at decryption time. The best we can do is choose an upper bound N to n and include N elements. Choosing a small N results in smaller ciphertexts, but also in less flexibility when creating decryption keys. Choosing $N = L$ results in larger ciphertexts, but also allows for the creation of decryption keys that consist of only wildcards.

We can reconstruct the coefficients a_k of the polynomial $\prod_{j \in J}(x - j)$ that occurs in (4) by using Viète's formulas:

$$a_{n-k} = (-1)^k \sum_{1 \leq i_1 < i_2 < \ldots < i_k \leq n} j_{i_1} j_{i_2} \cdots j_{i_k}, \quad 0 \leq k \leq n \tag{6}$$

where $n = |J|$. If J is clear from the context we will write a_i.

For instance when $J = \{j_1, j_2, j_3\}$ we get for the polynomial $(x - j_1)(x - j_2)(x - j_3)$,

$$\begin{aligned} a_3 &= 1 \\ a_2 &= -(j_1 + j_2 + j_3) \\ a_1 &= (j_1 j_2 + j_1 j_3 + j_2 j_3) \\ a_0 &= -j_1 j_2 j_3 \end{aligned}$$

3.2 Construction

We are now ready to give our construction for a hidden vector encryption scheme. Without loss of generality, we look at vectors of maximum length L over a fixed alphabet $\Sigma \subset \mathbb{Z}_q^*$. Other alphabets – like ASCII characters – can always be mapped onto such a subset. In addition, we need to pick an upper bound N to the number of wildcards that are allowed in a decryption vector. While this upper bound can be equal to L, performance increases if $N \ll L$.

This construction allows for shorter vectors of a length $\ell < L$. Intuitively we'll pad these vectors with zeroes up to a length L, but in practice this padding can be safely ignored in the computations.

Our scheme comprises of the following algorithms:

- $\mathsf{Setup}(\kappa, \Sigma, L)$: First, choose an upper bound $N \leq L$ to the number of wildcard symbols in decryption vectors. Next, given security parameter κ:
  1. Generate a bilinear group $\mathbb{G}$ of a large prime order q and choose a bilinear map $e : \mathbb{G} \times \mathbb{G} \longrightarrow \mathbb{G}_T$.
  2. Pick $L+1$ random elements $V_0, U_1, ..., U_L \in_R \mathbb{G}$.
  3. Pick random exponents $\alpha, \beta_1, \beta_2, (x_1, \ldots, x_N) \in_R \mathbb{Z}_q$.
  4. Let $\Omega_1 = e(g, V_0)^{\alpha\beta_1}$ and $\Omega_2 = e(g, V_0)^{\alpha\beta_2}$.
  5. Let $V_j = V_0^{x_j}$ for $j = 1, \ldots, N$.

  The public parameters are:

  $$param = \Big((V_0, V_1, \ldots, V_N), (U_1, \ldots, U_L\ ), g^\alpha, \Omega_1, \Omega_2, q, \mathbb{G}, \mathbb{G}_T, e(\cdot, \cdot)\Big)$$

  The master secret key is $msk = \big(\alpha, \beta_1, \beta_2, (x_1, \ldots, x_N)\big)$.

- $\mathsf{Extract}(msk, \bar{W})$: Let $\bar{W} = (\bar{w}_1, \ldots, \bar{w}_\ell) \in \Sigma_\star^\ell$, where $\ell \leq L$. Assume that W contains $n \leq N$ wildcards which occur at positions $J = \{j_1, \ldots, j_n\}$. Pick a random $s \in_R \mathbb{Z}_q$ and compute: $s_1 = \beta_1 + s, s_2 = \beta_2 + s$. By means of Viète's formulas a_i for $i = 1, \ldots, n$, first compute $t = \sum_{k=0}^n x_k a_k$ and then the decryption key $T_{\bar{W}}$ (where $x_0 = 1$):

$$T_{\bar{W}} = \begin{pmatrix} T_0 = g^{\frac{\alpha s}{t}} \\ T_1 = V_0^{s_1} \prod_{i=1}^{\ell} U_i^{\frac{s}{t} \prod_{k=1}^n (i-j_k)\bar{w}_i} \\ T_2 = V_0^{\alpha s_2} \prod_{i=1}^{\ell} U_i^{\frac{\alpha s}{t} \prod_{k=1}^n (i-j_k)\bar{w}_i} \\ J = \{j_1, \ldots, j_n\} \end{pmatrix}.$$

- $\mathsf{Enc}(param, W, M)$: Let $W = (w_1, \ldots, w_\ell) \in \Sigma^\ell$, where $\ell \leq L$ and $M \in \mathbb{G}_T$ a message. Pick two random values $r_1, r_2 \in_R \mathbb{Z}_q^*$. The ciphertext $S_{W,M}$ is:

$$S_{W,M} = \left(\hat{C} = M \Omega_1^{r_1} \Omega_2^{r_2}, \begin{pmatrix} C_0 = \left(V_0 \prod_{i=1}^{\ell} U_i^{w_i}\right)^{r_1+r_2} \\ C_1 = \left(V_1 \prod_{i=1}^{\ell} U_i^{i\ w_i}\right)^{r_1+r_2} \\ \vdots \\ C_N = \left(V_N \prod_{i=1}^{\ell} U_i^{i^N\ w_i}\right)^{r_1+r_2} \end{pmatrix}, \begin{pmatrix} g^{\alpha r_1} \\ g^{r_2} \end{pmatrix} \right).$$

- $\mathsf{Dec}(S_{W,M}, T_{\bar{W}})$: Given a decryption key $T_{\bar{W}}$ and a ciphertext $S_{W,M}$, first use J to compute Viète's formulas a_i $i = 1, \ldots, n$, then decrypt the message as:

$$M = \hat{C} \frac{e(T_0, \prod_{k=0}^n C_k^{a_k})}{e(T_1, g^{\alpha r_1}) e(T_2, g^{r_2})}$$

3.3 Correctness

We now show that the Dec algorithm indeed returns the correct message when using a decryption key that should be able to decrypt a given ciphertext. Without loss of generality we assume that the vectors contain l symbols and that there are n wildcards at positions $\{j_1, \ldots, j_n\}$. Then

$$e(T_0, \prod_{k=0}^n C_k^{a_k}) = e(g^{\frac{\alpha s}{\sum_{m=0}^n x_m a_m}}, \prod_{k=0}^n V_k^{a_k(r_1+r_2)})\ e(g^{\frac{\alpha s}{\sum_{m=0}^n x_m a_m}}, \prod_{k=0}^n \prod_{i=1}^{\ell} U_i^{i^k a_k w_i (r_1+r_2)})$$

$$= \prod_{k=0}^n \left(e(g, V_0)^{\frac{\alpha s (r_1+r_2) x_k a_k}{\sum_{m=0}^n x_m a_m}} \prod_{i=1}^{\ell} e(g, U_i)^{\frac{\alpha s (r_1+r_2) w_i i^k a_k}{\sum_{m=0}^n x_m a_m}} \right)$$

$$= e(g, V_0)^{\frac{\alpha s (r_1+r_2) \sum_{k=0}^n x_k a_k}{\sum_{m=0}^n x_m a_m}} \prod_{i=1}^{\ell} e(g, U_i)^{\frac{\alpha s (r_1+r_2) w_i \sum_{k=0}^n i^k a_k}{\sum_{m=0}^n a_m x_m}}$$

$$= e(g, V_0)^{\alpha s (r_1+r_2)} \prod_{i=1}^{\ell} e(g, U_i)^{\frac{\alpha s (r_1+r_2) w_i \prod_{k=1}^n (i-j_k)}{\sum_{m=0}^n a_m x_m}} \quad (7)$$

where for (7) we use that $\sum_{k=0}^{n} i^k a_k = \prod_{k=1}^{n}(i - j_k)$.

$$e(T_1, g^{\alpha r_1}) = e(V_0, g)^{\alpha r_1 s_1} \; e\Big(\prod_{i=1}^{\ell} U_i^{\frac{s\prod_{k=1}^{n}(i-j_k)\bar{w}_i}{\sum_{m=0}^{n} a_m x_m}}, g^{\alpha r_1}\Big)$$

$$= \Omega_1^{r_1}\; e(g, V_0)^{\alpha s r_1} \prod_{i=1}^{\ell} e(g, U_i)^{\frac{\alpha s r_1 \prod_{k=1}^{n}(i-j_k)\bar{w}_i}{\sum_{m=0}^{n} a_m x_m}} \tag{8}$$

$$e(T_2, g^{r_2}) = e(V_0, g)^{\alpha r_2 s_2} \; e\Big(\prod_{i=1}^{\ell} U_i^{\frac{\alpha s\prod_{k=1}^{n}(i-j_k)\bar{w}_i}{\sum_{m=0}^{n} a_m x_m}}, g^{r_2}\Big)$$

$$= \Omega_2^{r_2}\; e(g, V_0)^{\alpha s r_2} \prod_{i=1}^{\ell} e(g, U_i)^{\frac{\alpha s r_2 \prod_{k=1}^{n}(i-j_k)\bar{w}_i}{\sum_{m=0}^{n} a_m x_m}} \tag{9}$$

$$e(T_{n+1}, g^{\alpha r_1}) e(T_{n+2}, g^{r_2}) = \Omega_1^{r_1}\Omega_2^{r_2}\; e(g, V_0)^{\alpha s(r_1+r_2)} \prod_{i=1}^{\ell} e(g, U_i)^{\frac{\alpha s(r_1+r_2)\bar{w}_i \prod_{k=1}^{n}(i-j_k)}{\sum_{m=0}^{n} a_m x_m}} \tag{10}$$

If the decryption key is valid, then $w_i = \bar{w}_i$ when $i \notin \{j_1, \ldots, j_n\}$. Thus

$$\hat{C}\frac{e(T_0, \prod_{k=0}^{n} C_k^{a_k})}{e(T_1, g^{\alpha r_1}) e(T_2, g^{r_2})} = \frac{M\Omega_1^{r_1}\Omega_2^{r_2} e(T_0, \prod_{k=0}^{n} C_k^{a_k})}{e(T_{n+1}, g^{\alpha r_1}) e(T_{n+2}, g^{r_2})} = M \tag{11}$$

3.4 Semantic Security

Theorem 1. *The hidden vector encryption scheme in Section 3 is semantically secure in the selective model assuming that the Decision Linear assumption holds in group $\mathbb{G}$.*

Proof. Suppose there exists a PPT adversary $\mathcal{A}$ that can break the selective semantic security, i.e. $\mathcal{A}$ has an advantage in the experiment of Definition 3 larger than some non-negligible ϵ. We build an algorithm $\mathcal{B}$ that uses $\mathcal{A}$ to solve the Decision Linear problem in $\mathbb{G}$.

The challenger selects a bilinear group $\mathbb{G}$ of prime order q and chooses a generator $g \in \mathbb{G}$, the group $\mathbb{G}_T$ and an efficient bilinear map $e: \mathbb{G} \times \mathbb{G} \rightarrow \mathbb{G}_T$. Then the challenger picks four random values $a, b, c, d \in_R \mathbb{Z}_q^*$, computes $Z_0 = g^{b(c+d)}$ and chooses $Z_1 \in_R \mathbb{G}$. After flipping a fair coin $\nu \in_R \{0, 1\}$ the challenger hands the tuple $(g, g^a, g^b, g^{ac}, g^d, Z_\nu)$ to $\mathcal{B}$. Algorithm $\mathcal{B}$'s goal is to guess ν with a better chance of being correct than $\frac{1}{2}$. In order to come up with a guess, $\mathcal{B}$ interacts with adversary $\mathcal{A}$ in a selective semantic security experiment as follows:

Init. Adversary $\mathcal{A}$ chooses an alphabet $\Sigma \subset \mathbb{Z}_q^*$, a length L and announces two attribute vectors $W_0^* \in \Sigma^{\ell_0}$, $W_1^* \in \Sigma^{\ell_1}$, where $\ell_0, \ell_1 \leq L$, which are different in at least one position. $\mathcal{B}$ flips a coin $\mu \in \{0, 1\}$. Let $W_\mu^* = (w_1^*, \ldots, w_{\ell_\mu}^*)$.

Setup. $\mathcal{B}$ chooses an upper bound $N \leq L$ to the number of wildcard symbols. Then $\mathcal{B}$ picks random values $v_0, u_1, \ldots, u_L, x_1, \ldots, x_N \in_R \mathbb{Z}_q^*$ and sets

$$V_j = (g^b)^{x_j v_0} g^{-\sum_{i=1}^{\ell_\mu} i^j u_i} \quad \text{for } j = 0, \ldots, N$$

$$U_i = \begin{cases} g^{\frac{u_i}{w_i^*}} & \text{for } i = 1 \ldots \ell_\mu \\ g^{u_i} & \text{for } i = \ell_\mu + 1, \ldots, L, \end{cases}$$

where $x_0 = 1$. $\mathcal{B}$ picks $\sigma_1, \sigma_2, \sigma_3 \in_R \mathbb{Z}_q$ and computes $\Omega_1 = e(g^a, V_0)^{\sigma_1 - \sigma_2}$ and $\Omega_2 = e\big(g^{\sigma_3}(g^a)^{-\sigma_2}, V_0\big)$. The public parameters are:

$$param = \Big(\big(V_0, V_1, \ldots, V_N\big), \big(U_1, \ldots, U_L\ \big), g^a, \Omega_1, \Omega_2, q, \mathbb{G}, \mathbb{G}_T, e(\cdot,\cdot)\Big)$$

The master secret key is implicitly given by

$$msk = \big(\alpha = a, t_1 = \sigma_1 - \sigma_2, t_2 = \frac{\sigma_3}{a} - \sigma_2, (x_1, \ldots, x_N)\big).$$

Query Phase I. In this phase $\mathcal{A}$ adaptively issues key extraction queries. Each time $\mathcal{A}$ queries for the decryption key of an attribute vector $\bar{W} = (\bar{w}_1, \ldots, \bar{w}_\ell) \in \Sigma_\star^\ell$, consisting of $\ell \leq L$ symbols and $n \leq N$ wildcards at positions $J = \{j_1, \ldots, j_n\}$, algorithm $\mathcal{B}$ responds by computing

$$T_0 = (g^a)^{\frac{\sigma_2}{\sum_{m=0}^n x_m a_m}},$$

$$T_1 = V_0^{\sigma_1} \prod_{i=1}^{\ell} U_i^{\frac{\sigma_2 \prod_{k=1}^n (i-j_k)\bar{w}_i}{\sum_{m=0}^n x_m a_m}},$$

$$T_2 = (g^b)^{\sigma_3 v_0} g^{-\sigma_3 \sum_{i=1}^{\ell_\mu} u_i} (g^a)^{\frac{\sigma_2 \sum_{i=1}^{\ell_\mu} \frac{u_i}{w_i^*} \prod_{k=1}^n (i-j_k)\bar{w}_i}{\sum_{m=0}^n x_m a_m} + \frac{\sigma_2 \sum_{i=\ell_\mu+1}^{\ell} u_i \prod_{k=1}^n (i-j_k)\bar{w}_i}{\sum_{m=0}^n x_m a_m}},$$

which is basically a correct trapdoor for $\bar{W}$ with $s = \sigma_2$. $\mathcal{B}$ returns to $\mathcal{A}$ the decryption key

$$T_{\bar{W}} = \Big(T_0, T_1, T_2, J\Big). \tag{12}$$

Challenge. Once $\mathcal{A}$ decides that the query phase is over, $\mathcal{A}$ picks a pair of messages $M_0, M_1 \in \mathbb{G}_T$ on which it wishes to be challenged. $\mathcal{B}$ computes $S_{W_\mu^*, M_\mu}$ by first computing

$$\hat{C} = M_\mu \cdot e\big(g^{ac}, g^b\big)^{\sigma_1 v_0} \cdot e\big(g^{ac}, g\big)^{(\sigma_1 - \sigma_2)\sum_{i=0}^{\ell_\mu} u_i} \cdot$$
$$e\big(g^a, g^d\big)^{\sigma_2 \sum_{i=0}^{\ell_\mu} u_i} \cdot e\big(g^b, g^d\big)^{\sigma_3 v_0} \cdot e\big(g^d, g\big)^{\sigma_3 \sum_{i=0}^{\ell_\mu} u_i} \cdot e\big(g^a, Z_\nu\big)^{\sigma_2 v_0} \tag{13}$$

and then computing $C_0 = Z_\nu^{v_0}$ and $C_k = Z_\nu^{x_k v_0}$ for $k = 1, \ldots, N$. $\mathcal{B}$ sends the challenge ciphertext

$$S_{W_\mu^*, M_\mu} = \Big(\hat{C}, \big\{C_k\big\}_{k=0}^N, \big(\begin{smallmatrix} g^{ac} \\ g^d \end{smallmatrix}\big)\Big), \tag{14}$$

to $\mathcal{A}$. When $\nu = 0$ this is actually a correct encryption of M_μ under W_μ^* with $r_1 = c$ and $r_2 = d$.

Query Phase II. In Query Phase II $\mathcal{B}$ behaves exactly the same as in Query Phase I.

Output. Eventually, $\mathcal{A}$ outputs a bit μ'.

Finally, $\mathcal{B}$ outputs 1 if $\mu' = \mu$ and 0 if $\mu' \neq \mu$.

We will now analyze the probability of success for algorithm $\mathcal{B}$. First, note that if $\nu = 0$, then $\mathcal{B}$ will behave correctly as a challenger to $\mathcal{A}$. Thus, $\mathcal{A}$ will have probability of $\frac{1}{2} + \epsilon$ of guessing μ. Next note that if $\nu = 1$, then Z_ν is random in $\mathbb{G}$ and $S_{W^*_\mu, M_\mu}$ is independent from μ, thus $\mathcal{A}$ will have a probability of $\frac{1}{2}$ of guessing μ.

To conclude the proof we have

$$\begin{aligned}
&\left|\Pr\left[\mathcal{B}(\mathbb{G}, g, g^a, g^b, g^{ac}, g^d, g^{b(c+d)}) = 1\right] - \Pr\left[\mathcal{B}(\mathbb{G}, g, g^a, g^b, g^{ac}, g^d, g^r) = 1\right]\right| \\
\geq &\left|\Pr\left[\nu = 0 \ \wedge \ \mu' = \mu\right] - \Pr\left[\nu = 1 \ \wedge \ \mu' = \mu\right]\right| \\
= &\left|\frac{1}{2}\Pr\left[\mu' = \mu \mid \nu = 0\right] - \frac{1}{2}\Pr\left[\mu' = \mu \mid \nu = 1\right]\right| \\
= &\frac{1}{2}\left|\Pr\left[\mathbf{Exp}_{\mathcal{A}}(\kappa) = 1\right] - \frac{1}{2}\right| \\
\geq &\frac{1}{2}\epsilon,
\end{aligned}$$

which is non-negligible, contradicting the Decision Linear Assumption. □

4 Conclusion

We presented a new hidden vector encryption scheme which can work as a wildcard searchable encryption scheme that is a more efficient than existing schemes in some scenarios. The tables below summarize the efficiency of our scheme when compared to other schemes. The scheme is proven selectively secure in the sense of hiding the contents of the message and hiding the keywords associated to the message. This is the same model as the one used in the other schemes in the literature. A hidden vector encryption scheme that is secure in the adaptive standard model is still an open problem, as is finding any other construction for wildcard searchable encryption in that model.

Table 1 compares the performance of our scheme with existing searchable encryption schemes from the point of view of memory requirement. It shows that constructing the decryption key is more efficient than the existing schemes. Moreover, since N is always less than ℓ (depending on the application scenario), the ciphertext can be constructed in a more efficient way.

Notation in this table: ℓ is the length of the (ciphertext or decryption key) vector, L is the maximum allowed number of entries in the ciphertext vector, n is the amount of wildcard entries, N is the maximum allowed amount of wildcard entries.

Table 1. Ciphertext- and key-size of several HVE schemes

Schemes	Size of ciphertext	Size of Decryption key	Size of public parameters	Maximum allowed Wildcards
Boneh, Waters [7] Katz et al. [16]	$2\ell + 2$	$2(\ell - n) + 1$	$3L + 3$	Arbitrary
Shi, Waters [22]	$\ell + 4$	$\ell - n + 3$	$4L + 2$	Arbitrary
Iovino, Persiano [14] Blundo et al. [3]	$2\ell + 2$	$\ell - n + 3$	$2L + 4$	Arbitrary
Nishide et al. [18]	$\ell + 2$	$\ell + 1$	$3L + 1$	Arbitrary
This Work	$N + 4$	3	$L + N + 1$	N

Table 2 compares the performance of our scheme with existing searchable encryption schemes from the point of view of decryption cost. It shows that the decryption cost in our scheme is constant and less than other schemes since only three pairings is required for the decryption.

Notation in this table: ℓ is the length of the (ciphertext or decryption key) vector, and n is the amount of wildcard entries.

Table 2. Decryption speed of several HVE Schemes

Schemes	Number of pairings for decryption	Order of bilinear group	Alphabet of entries
Boneh, Waters [7] and Katz et al. [16]	$2(\ell - n) + 1$	Composite	Arbitrary
Shi, Waters [22]	$(\ell - n) + 3$	Composite	Arbitrary
Iovino, Persiano [14] Blundo et al. [3]	$2(\ell - n)$	Prime	Binary
Nishide et al. [18]	$\ell + 1$	Prime	Binary
This Work	3	Prime	Arbitrary

References

1. Abdalla, M., Bellare, M., Catalano, D., Kiltz, E., Kohno, T., Lange, T., Malone-Lee, J., Neven, G., Paillier, P., Shi, H.: Searchable encryption revisited: Consistency properties, relation to anonymous ibe, and extensions. J. Cryptology 21(3), 350–391 (2008)
2. Baek, J., Susilo, W., Zhou, J.: New constructions of fuzzy identity-based encryption. In: Bao, F., Miller, S. (eds.) ASIACCS, pp. 368–370. ACM, New York (2007)

3. Blundo, C., Iovino, V., Persiano, G.: Private-key hidden vector encryption with key confidentiality. In: Garay, J.A., Miyaji, A., Otsuka, A. (eds.) CANS 2009. LNCS, vol. 5888, pp. 259–277. Springer, Heidelberg (2009)
4. Boneh, D., Boyen, X., Shacham, H.: Short group signatures. In: Franklin, M. (ed.) CRYPTO 2004. LNCS, vol. 3152, pp. 41–55. Springer, Heidelberg (2004)
5. Boneh, D., Di Crescenzo, G., Ostrovsky, R., Persiano, G.: Public key encryption with keyword search. In: Cachin, C., Camenisch, J.L. (eds.) EUROCRYPT 2004. LNCS, vol. 3027, pp. 506–522. Springer, Heidelberg (2004)
6. Boneh, D., Franklin, M.K.: Identity-based encryption from the weil pairing. SIAM J. Comput. 32(3), 586–615 (2003)
7. Boneh, D., Waters, B.: Conjunctive, subset, and range queries on encrypted data. In: Vadhan, S.P. (ed.) TCC 2007. LNCS, vol. 4392, pp. 535–554. Springer, Heidelberg (2007)
8. Boyen, X., Waters, B.: Anonymous hierarchical identity-based encryption (without random oracles). In: Dwork, C. (ed.) CRYPTO 2006. LNCS, vol. 4117, pp. 290–307. Springer, Heidelberg (2006)
9. Chang, Y.-C., Mitzenmacher, M.: Privacy preserving keyword searches on remote encrypted data. In: Ioannidis, J., Keromytis, A.D., Yung, M. (eds.) ACNS 2005. LNCS, vol. 3531, pp. 442–455. Springer, Heidelberg (2005)
10. Curtmola, R., Garay, J.A., Kamara, S., Ostrovsky, R.: Searchable symmetric encryption: improved definitions and efficient constructions. In: Juels, et al. (eds.) [15], pp. 79–88
11. Gentry, C.: Practical identity-based encryption without random oracles. In: Vaudenay, S. (ed.) EUROCRYPT 2006. LNCS, vol. 4004, pp. 445–464. Springer, Heidelberg (2006)
12. Goh, E.-J.: Secure indexes. Cryptology ePrint Archive, Report 2003/216 (2003), `http://eprint.iacr.org/`
13. Goyal, V., Pandey, O., Sahai, A., Waters, B.: Attribute-based encryption for fine-grained access control of encrypted data. In: Juels, et al. (eds.) [15], pp. 89–98
14. Iovino, V., Persiano, G.: Hidden-vector encryption with groups of prime order. In: Galbraith, S.D., Paterson, K.G. (eds.) Pairing 2008. LNCS, vol. 5209, pp. 75–88. Springer, Heidelberg (2008)
15. Juels, A., Wright, R.N., De Capitani di Vimercati, S. (eds.): Proceedings of the 13th ACM Conference on Computer and Communications Security, CCS 2006, Alexandria, VA, USA, October 30 - November 3. ACM, New York (2006)
16. Katz, J., Sahai, A., Waters, B.: Predicate encryption supporting disjunctions, polynomial equations, and inner products. In: Smart, N.P. (ed.) EUROCRYPT 2008. LNCS, vol. 4965, pp. 146–162. Springer, Heidelberg (2008)
17. Kiltz, E.: From selective-id to full security: The case of the inversion-based boneh-boyen ibe scheme. Cryptology ePrint Archive, Report 2007/033 (2007), `http://eprint.iacr.org/`
18. Nishide, T., Yoneyama, K., Ohta, K.: Attribute-based encryption with partially hidden ciphertext policies. IEICE Transactions 92-A(1), 22–32 (2009)
19. Rhee, H.S., Park, J.H., Susilo, W., Lee, D.H.: Improved searchable public key encryption with designated tester. In: Li, W., Susilo, W., Tupakula, U.K., Safavi-Naini, R., Varadharajan, V. (eds.) ASIACCS, pp. 376–379. ACM, New York (2009)
20. Sahai, A., Waters, B.: Fuzzy identity-based encryption. In: Cramer, R. (ed.) EUROCRYPT 2005. LNCS, vol. 3494, pp. 457–473. Springer, Heidelberg (2005)

21. Shi, E., Bethencourt, J., Chan, H.T.-H., Song, D.X., Perrig, A.: Multi-dimensional range query over encrypted data. In: IEEE Symposium on Security and Privacy, pp. 350–364. IEEE Computer Society, Los Alamitos (2007)
22. Shi, E., Waters, B.: Delegating capabilities in predicate encryption systems. In: Aceto, L., Damgård, I., Goldberg, L.A., Halldórsson, M.M., Ingólfsdóttir, A., Walukiewicz, I. (eds.) ICALP 2008, Part II. LNCS, vol. 5126, pp. 560–578. Springer, Heidelberg (2008)
23. Song, D.X., Wagner, D., Perrig, A.: Practical techniques for searches on encrypted data. In: IEEE Symposium on Security and Privacy, pp. 44–55. IEEE Computer Society, Los Alamitos (2000)
24. Waters, B.R., Balfanz, D., Durfee, G., Smetters, D.K.: Building an encrypted and searchable audit log. In: NDSS. The Internet Society (2004)

Threshold Attribute-Based Signcryption

Martin Gagné, Shivaramakrishnan Narayan,
and Reihaneh Safavi-Naini*

Department of Computer Science, University of Calgary, Canada
{mgagne,snarayan,rei}@ucalgary.ca

Abstract. In this paper, we propose a new threshold attribute-based signcryption scheme secure in the standard model. The scheme provides message confidentiality, and authenticity of a message in addition to attesting the attributes of the sender. Such a property is useful in applications such as electronic card, digital prescription carrier devices, secure and authentic email service, etc. Our scheme relies on the intractability of the hashed modified decisional Diffie-Hellman and modified computational Diffie-Hellman assumptions, and is proven secure under adaptive chosen ciphertext attack and chosen message attack security notions of signcryption. Further, we achieve a tight reduction for both the security notions in the standard model.

1 Introduction

Attribute-based cryptography has generated much interest in recent years. Attributed based systems allow security functionalities to be provided based on 'attributes' of users and not their individual identities. Attribute-based encryption (ABE) [30,15,5] can elegantly implement role based access control systems, and Attribute Based Signatures (ABS) [16,32], provides a powerful way for users to control their privacy: in signing a document the user can choose the subset of their attributes that is relevant for the specific scenario (there are other proofs of partial knowledge [10] methods that can be used to obtain a similar functionality, but they are much more costly).

In a basic ABE system a user encrypts a message with a set of n attributes such that users whose decryption key have at least t common attributes with the ciphertext attribute set can decrypt the message. Such schemes, initially called fuzzy identity-based encryption, were first proposed by Sahai and Waters [30]. In basic ABS, a user can sign with a subset of their attributes and the verification succeeds with any set of attribute that has at least t common attributes with the signing attribute set. We refer to these systems as *threshold attribute-based encryption (t-ABE)* and *threshold attribute-based signatures (t-ABS)*, respectively, names which we feel are more descriptive and more representative of the functionality of each scheme.

* Financial support for this research was provided in part by Alberta Innovates - Technology Futures, in the Province of Alberta in Canada.

J.A. Garay and R. De Prisco (Eds.): SCN 2010, LNCS 6280, pp. 154–171, 2010.

Combining ABE and ABS provides an attractive solution for complex authorization and access control problems. For example, a HR manager wants to send a confidential email to all employees of a particular department within an organization such that all employees of that concerned department can read and verify the authenticity of the message against the HR manager's attributes. Using ABS together with an ABE provides a direct solution to this problem.

Signcryption systems [35] provide a more efficient way of providing secrecy and authenticity for communication compared to using a signature and an encryption schemes separately. Signcryption systems also provides an integrated security model that is used to prove security of the combined functions. A natural question is whether an attribute-based signcryption (ABSC) can be constructed with substantial efficiency gain.

We consider threshold attribute-based signcryption (t-ABSC) systems that allow a user to sign a message with an arbitrary subset ω_s of their attribute, and encrypt it with a set of attributes ω_e such that a recipient whose attribute set has an overlap of at least t with ω_e can decrypt the message, and authenticity of the signature can be verified against the claimed attribute set ω_s. Although we only discuss threshold policy, a similar question can be asked for more general policies. We believe that the encryption component of the t-ABSC scheme presented in this paper can be extended to allow for more general key policies.

1.1 Our Contribution

In this work, we define threshold attribute-based signcryption, which combines the functionalities of attribute-based encryption and attribute-based signature, present the security model for this new primitive, construct the first t-ABSC scheme and prove its security in the standard model. The encryption component of our construction is inspired by Sahai and Waters' large universe construction [30], whereas the signature component is a new efficient threshold attribute-based signature scheme. The security of our scheme is based on the intractability of the hashed modified version of the decisional bilinear Diffie-Hellman assumption based on the assumptions in [18] and [1] and modified computational Diffie-Hellman assumption.

When compared to the direct composition of an attribute-based encryption scheme and an attribute-based signature scheme that results in a similar functionality, our scheme enjoys the following advantages:

◇ **Bandwidth Efficiency:** The ciphertexts in our scheme require about half the size of what would be needed in a straightforward combination of the most efficient attribute-based encryption and attribute-based signature schemes known in the literature, without sacrificing any functionality or security. The size of the public and private keys remain comparable.

◇ **Chosen-Ciphertext Security:** Most ABE schemes are proven secure only against chosen-plaintext attack ([14] is the only exception), and obtain security against chosen-ciphertext attack through the use of simulation-sound non-interactive zero-knowledge proofs [29,31]. This method is very inefficient due to its reliance on a generic Karp reduction. Our scheme is proven secure against adaptive chosen-ciphertext attack directly. We can obtain security against chosen-ciphertext attack directly by adapting the techniques of Abdalla et al. [1].

◇ **Tight Reduction:** Our scheme has tight reductions for both indistinguishability against adaptive chosen-ciphertext security and unforgeability against chosen-message attack. Given adversaries against our scheme, we can construct algorithms that solve the underlying computational assumption with $\epsilon_{HmDBDH} \approx \epsilon_{CCA2}$ and $\epsilon_{mCDH} \approx \frac{\epsilon_{CMA}}{n_m}$,[1] where n_m is the length of the message. This is similar to other attribute-based encryption schemes when it comes to confidentiality, but significantly tighter than for other attribute-based signature scheme [32,34].

◇ **CCA-secure Attribute-Based Encryption:** Since the signature component of our signcryption scheme does not play a role in the proof of chosen-ciphertext security, we can obtain a CCA-secure version of the Sahai-Waters scheme [30] simply by removing the signature from the ciphertext.

◇ **Short Attribute-Based Signature:** Similarly, we can separate the signature component of our scheme to obtain an attribute-based signature scheme with shorter signature than any previous scheme and a tight security proof.

Our scheme is proven secure in the selective-set model, in which the adversary has to commit to the attribute set which he wants to attack at the beginning of the scheme. We note that such a scheme can be proven adaptively secure using a technique similar to Boneh and Boyen [6], but the reduction is inefficient. This is discussed in Section 4.5.

1.2 Related Work

Signcryption is a public key primitive [35] providing confidentiality and authenticity for messages and motivated by the efficiency gain in computation and communication when compared to applying encryption and signature separately.

A number of signcryption schemes in public key setting [3,33,27] and identity-based setting [26,7,22,23,9,4] has been proposed. To the best of our knowledge this is the first attribute-based signcryption system proposed in the literature.

Sahai and Waters introduced a new type of identity-based encryption called fuzzy identity-based encryption [30] that allows the identity information to be 'fuzzy' with motivating scenario being biometric information used for identities. The main idea was to view an identity as a set of descriptive attributes such that when a message is encrypted for an attribute set ω_e, a user with private key for the attribute set ω' is able to decrypt if and only if ω' and ω_e have an overlap of at least d attributes. We call this as *threshold ABE.*

Goyal et.al introduced key-policy ABE [15], which is an extension of fuzzy identity-based encryption. The aim was to achieve higher expressiveness in determining the group who can decrypt the message. In this system, a ciphertext is encrypted under a set of attributes and the decryption successful if the access

[1] Here, $HmDBDH$ and $mCDH$ stand for hashed modified decision bilinear Diffie-Hellman problem and modified computational Diffie-Hellman problem.

structure associated with a user's private key is satisfied by the attribute set attached to the ciphertext.

Bethencourt et al. presented the first ciphertext-policy ABE [5] which allows senders to associate access structures with ciphertexts. A user can decrypt the ciphertext if that user's attribute in his decryption key satisfy the access structure attached to the ciphertext. Other notable ABE schemes are hierarchical ABE [21], constant ciphertext ABE [13], distributed ABE [28], attribute-based broadcast encryption [24,2] and multi-authority ABE [8].

Attribute-based signature (ABS) extends identity-based signature wherein a signer is identified by a set of attributes instead of a single identity string. An attribute-based signature attests a set of attributes held by a sender, and proves to the verifier that the sender who holds the attribute set has endorsed the message. Guo and Zeng proposed a key-policy ABS in [16] whose security relies on the intractability of strong extended Diffie-Hellman assumption. In [32], a threshold attribute-based signature construction for small attribute universe and large attribute universe was proposed. Other notable ABS schemes include, attribute-based ring signatures [20], fuzzy attribute-based signature [34], attribute-based group signature [12,17] and policy-based ABS in generic model [25].

The rest of the paper is organized as follows: in Section 2 we present an overview of threshold attribute-based signcryption, its security notions and mathematical preliminaries. Section 3 presents our new signcryption construction, followed by its security details, and Section 4 gives a few additional remarks on the scheme. In Section 5, we provide an efficiency analysis of our scheme against direct combination of t-ABE and t-ABS and in Section 6 presents the conclusion.

2 Model and Definitions

The goal in an attribute-based signcryption scheme is to achieve the combined functionality of attribute-based encryption and attribute-based signature. We first note that, contrary to identity-based schemes - in which the keys are tied to the identity of a user, and where it is therefore natural for the decryption and signature keys be generated at the same time and given together - it is possible for users here to be given different rights for decryption and signature.

We enforce this by having the decryption (unsigncryption) key and signature keys generated by two distinct algorithms, and by requiring that the set of encryption attributes $\mathcal{U}_e$ and the set of signature attributes $\mathcal{U}_s$ be disjoint. In practice, if an attribute, say *student*, should be allowed both as an encryption attribute and a signature attribute, then this attribute will have two 'representations', one ($student_e$) used as an encryption-only attribute, and another ($student_s$) used only for signature.

The algorithms **uExtract** and **sExtract** generate unsigncryption and signature keys respectively. Each algorithm takes a set of (encryption or signature resp.) attributes and a threshold d and output a (unsigncryption or signature resp.) key. The threshold d need not be the same from one execution to the next.

When a user wishes to signcrypt a message M given his signature key $sk_{s,\omega_\sigma,d}$ with encryption attributes ω_e,[2], he must first choose a subset ω_s of ω_σ of size d which will be used to sign the message, and then applies the **Signcrypt** algorithm with input $M, \omega_e, \omega_s, sk_{s,\omega_\sigma,d}$.

The **Unsigncrypt** algorithm should be successful in decrypting a ciphertext C with an unsigncrypt key $sk_{u,\sigma_\mu,d}$ if $|\omega_e \cap \omega_\mu| \geq d$, where ω_e is the set of encryption attributes used to signcrypt the ciphertext, and if C contains a valid signature with attributes ω_s (the signature attributes used in C), assuming threshold $|\omega_s|$. It is assumed here that the sets ω_e and ω_s should somehow be encoded in the ciphertext.

Formally, a threshold attribute-based signcryption scheme consists of four algorithms: Setup, sExtract, uExtract, Signcrypt and Unsigncrypt.

Setup: Given a security parameter 1^k, the algorithm outputs the public system parameters *params* and master secret key *msk*.

Key Generation:

sExtract: Given a set ω_σ of signature attributes, a threshold d, and the system master key *msk* as input, the algorithm outputs the private key $sk_{s,\omega_\sigma,d}$.

uExtract: Given a set ω_μ of encryption attributes, a threshold d, and the system master key *msk* as input, the algorithm outputs the private key $sk_{u,\omega_\mu,d}$.

Signcrypt: Given a message M, public parameters *params*, encryption attribute set ω_e (attributes chosen by the sender for encryption), signing attributes set ω_s (sender's attribute set against which the signature is verified) and the sender's secret key $sk_{s,\omega_\sigma,d}$ such that $\omega_s \subset \omega_\sigma$ and $|\omega_s| = d$, the **Signcrypt** algorithm produces a ciphertext C encrypted with attributes ω_e and signed with attributes ω_s.

Unsigncrypt: The unsigncrypt algorithm takes as input the ciphertext C and the private key $sk_{u,\omega_u,d}$. The algorithm can decrypt the encrypted message if $|\omega_e \cap \omega_u| \geq d$, where ω_e is the encryption attributes in C (note that this condition is independent to signature verification since the verification is performed against the signer's attribute set), and verifies the signature on the message against ω_s. The signcryption either returns the message and sender's attributes, or returns $\perp$.

2.1 Security Notions

Message Confidentiality. This attack scenario is modeled on the indistinguishability of ciphertext under a chosen-ciphertext attack in the selective attribute model.

In this scenario, the adversary commits to a set of encryption attributes ω_e^* which will be used to encrypt the challenge ciphertext. During the attack, the

[2] In the signature key $sk_{s,\omega_\sigma,d}$, the s identifies the key as a signature key, ω_σ is the set of signature attributes with which the user is allowed to sign and d is the threshold of the key.

adversary can ask for the signing key of any signature attribute set and any threshold, and any unsigncrypt key that would not allow him to trivially decrypt the challenge ciphertext - that is, any encryption attribute set ω_μ and threshold d such that $|\omega_e^* \cap \omega_\mu| < d$.

The adversary is also allowed to issue Unsigncrypt queries to obtain the unsigncryption of any ciphertext under any key, with the exception that he cannot ask for the unsigncryption of the challenge ciphertext with a key that could trivially decrypt it.

It is not necessary for the adversary to make signcryption queries since he can obtain the signature key for any signature attribute set, and therefore he can signcrypt on his own.

Message confidentiality against adaptive chosen-ciphertext attacks is defined using the following game between an adversary who attempts to break the scheme and a challenger who provides the environment for the attack:

Commit: The adversary $\mathcal{A}$ selects a set of encryption attributes ω_e^* which will be used to encrypt the challenge ciphertext, and returns ω_e^* to the challenger.

Setup: The challenger runs the **Setup** algorithm of the scheme and sends the global system parameters to the adversary $\mathcal{A}$.

Query Phase 1: The adversary adaptively makes a polynomial number of the following queries, which must be answered by the challenger:

◇ sExtract: the adversary queries a signature attribute set $\omega_{s,i}$ and a threshold d_i. The challenger answers by running algorithm **sExtract**$(msk, \omega_{s,i}, d_i)$.

◇ uExtract: the adversary queries an encryption attribute set $\omega_{u,i}$ and a threshold d_i, subject to $|\omega_{u,i} \cap \omega_e^*| < d_i$. The challenger answers by running algorithm **uExtract**$(msk, \omega_{u,i}, d_i)$.

◇ Unsigncrypt: the adversary queries a ciphertext C, encryption attribute set $\omega_{u,i}$ and a threshold d_i. The challenger answers by first computing an $sk_{u,\omega_{u,i},d_i}$ = **uExtract**$(\omega_{u,i}, d_i)$ and answers the query by running the **Unsigncrypt** $(C, sk_{u,\omega_{u,i},d_i})$ algorithm.

At the end of Phase 1, the adversary outputs two challenge messages M_0^*, M_1^*, a sender attribute set ω_s^*.

Challenge Phase: The challenger chooses a random bit b, computes the signature key $sk_{s,\omega_s^*,|\omega_s^*|}$ = **sExtract**$(msk, \omega_s^*, |\omega_s^*|)$ and computes challenge ciphertext C^* = **Signcrypt**$(params, \omega_e^*, \omega_s^*, sk_{s,\omega_s^*,|\omega_s^*|})$.

Query Phase 2: The adversary adaptively makes a polynomial number of queries as in Query Phase 1, with the additional constraint that he is not allowed to make an Unsigncrypt query (C^*, ω_u, d) such that $|\omega_u \cap \omega_e^*| \geq d$.

Response: The adversary outputs a bit b' and wins the game if $b' = b$.

The adversary's advantage is defined to be $Adv(\mathcal{A}) = |\Pr[b' = b] - 1/2|$.

Definition 1. *We say that a threshold attribute-based signcryption scheme is indistinguishable against adaptive chosen ciphertext attack property under selective attribute model (S-IND-t-ABSC-CCA2), if no polynomially bounded adversary $\mathcal{A}$ has a non-negligible advantage in the above attack game.*

Ciphertext Unforgeability. This attack scenario is based on the definition for existential unforgeability under a chosen-message attack.

The queries the adversary is allowed here are similar to the previous game, except that the role of the signature and encryption attributes are switched. The adversary can ask for the unsigncrypt key for any encryption attribute set and any threshold (making unsigncrypt queries unnecessary), and can ask for the signature key for any signature attribute set and threshold except for those that would enable him to trivially produce a valid ciphertext.

The adversary is also allowed to issue Signcrypt queries to obtain a ciphertext for any message, encryption and signature attribute sets.

The attack game for existential unforgeability property is defined as follows:

Commit: The adversary $\mathcal{A}$ selects a set of encryption attributes ω_s^* for which he will try to forge a signature, and returns ω_s^* to the challenger.

Setup: The challenger runs the **Setup** algorithm of the scheme and sends the global system parameter to the adversary $\mathcal{A}$.

Query Phase 1: The adversary adaptively makes a polynomial number of the following queries, which must be answered by the challenger:
$\diamond$ sExtract: the adversary queries a signature attribute set $\omega_{s,i}$ and a threshold d_i, subject to $|\omega_{s,i} \cap \omega_s^*| < d$. The challenger answers by running algorithm **sExtract**$(msk, \omega_{s,i}, d_i)$.
$\diamond$ uExtract: the adversary queries an encryption attribute set $\omega_{u,i}$ and a threshold d_i. The challenger answers by running algorithm **uExtract**$(msk, \omega_{u,i}, d_i)$.
$\diamond$ Signcrypt: the adversary queries a message M, encryption attribute set $\omega_{e,i}$ and signature attribute set $\omega_{s,i}$. The challenger answers by first computing a signature key $sk_{s,\omega_{s,i}} =$ **sExtract**$(msk, \omega_{s,i}, |\omega_{s,i}|)$, and then returns the ciphertext obtained by running **Signcrypt**$(params, \omega_{e,i}, \omega_{s,i}, sk_{s,\omega_{s,i}})$.

Forgery Phase: The adversary returns a ciphertext C^* and an encryption attribute set ω_e^*.

The adversary wins if the ciphertext is valid and was not obtained from a Signcrypt query. That is $Unsigncrypt(C^*, sk_{u,\omega_e^*}) = M \neq \perp$ where $sk_{u,\omega_e^*} =$ **uExtract**$(\omega_e^*, |\omega_e^*|)$ and $\mathcal{A}$ did not issue a query a Signcrypt query$(M, \omega_e^*, \omega_s^*)$.

The adversary's advantage is defined to be $Adv(\mathcal{A}) = \Pr[\mathcal{A} \text{ wins}]$.

Definition 2. *We say that a threshold attribute-based signcryption scheme is existentially unforgeable against chosen-message attack in the selective attribute model or (S-EUF-t-ABSC-CMA), if no polynomially bounded adversary $\mathcal{A}$ has a non-negligible advantage in the above attack game.*

As we can note that in the above game an adversary is allowed to query for the private key of the receiver's attribute set to whom the forged message is presented in the attack game, this corresponds to insider-security for signature unforgeability.

2.2 Complexity Assumptions

Let $\mathbb{G}$ and $\mathbb{G}_T$ be multiplicative groups of prime order q. Let $\mathbb{Z}_q^*$ denote the set of all non-zero integers modulo prime q. A bilinear map is a map $\hat{e} : \mathbb{G} \times \mathbb{G} \rightarrow \mathbb{G}_T$, satisfying the following properties.
- $\hat{e}$ is bilinear, i.e. for all $g, g_1, g_2 \in \mathbb{G}$ and $a, b \in \mathbb{Z}_q^*$, we have
- $\hat{e}(g_1^a, g_2^b) = \hat{e}(g_1, g_2)^{ab}$.
- $\hat{e}$ is non-degenerate, i.e. given $g_1, g_2 \in \mathbb{G} \setminus 1$, $\hat{e}(g_1, g_2) \neq 1$.
- $\hat{e}$ is efficiently computable.

Hashed Modified Bilinear Diffie-Hellman: Let $H : \mathbb{G}_T \rightarrow \mathcal{R}$ be a hash function. Given the distributions $(g, g^a, g^{a^2}, g^b, g^c, H(\hat{e}(g,g)^{abc}))$ and $(g, g^a, g^{a^2}, g^b, g^c, r)$, where $a, b, c \in_R Z_q^*$, $r \in_R \mathcal{R}$, and $g \in \mathbb{G}, \hat{e}(g,g) \in G_T$. The hashed modified decisional bilinear Diffie-Hellman (HmBDH) problem is to distinguish the two distributions.

We define the advantage ϵ of an adversary $\mathcal{B}$ in solving the modified decisional bilinear Diffie-Hellman problem as,

$$\Pr[\mathcal{B}(\mathbb{G}, \mathbb{G}_T, \hat{e}, q, g, g^a, g^{a^2}, g^b, g^c, H(\hat{e}(g,g)^{abc})) = 1] \\ - \Pr[\mathcal{B}(\mathbb{G}, \mathbb{G}_T, \hat{e}, q, g, g^a, g^{a^2}, g^b, g^c, r) = 1],$$

where the probability is over randomly chosen a, b, c, r. We say that the modified decisional bilinear Diffie-Hellman assumption holds if ϵ is negligible for all adversaries $\mathcal{B}$.

This complexity assumption is inspired from the modified Decisional Bilinear Diffie-Hellman assumption by Kiltz and Vahlis [18] and from the hashed Diffie-Hellman assumption by Abdalla et al. [1]. We discuss this complexity assumption in more details in Appendix A.

Modified Computational Diffie-Hellman: Given $(g, g^a, g^{a^2}, g^b) \in \mathbb{G}$, where g is a generator of $\mathbb{G}$ and $a, b \in \mathbb{Z}_q^*$, the modified computational Diffie-Hellman problem is to compute g^{ab}.

We define the advantage ϵ of an adversary $\mathcal{B}$ in solving the modified decisional bilinear Diffie-Hellman problem as, $\Pr[\mathcal{B}(\mathbb{G}, \mathbb{G}_T, \hat{e}, q, g, g^a, g^{a^2}, g^b) = g^{ab}]$, where the probability is over randomly chosen a, b. We say that the modified computational Diffie-Hellman assumption holds if ϵ is negligible for all adversaries $\mathcal{B}$.

2.3 Collision-Resistant and Target Collision Resistant Hashing

Collision-resistant and target collision resistant (TCR) hash functions [11] are a family of keyed hash functions. Let $\mathcal{F} = (HASH_s)_{s \in \{0,1\}^k}$ be a family of keyed hash functions for a security parameter k and with key $s \in \{0,1\}^k$. $\mathcal{F}$ is said to be collision resistant if, for a hash function $\mathbf{H} = HASH_s$ sampled at random from the family, it is infeasible for an efficient adversary to find two distinct values $x \neq y$ such that $\mathbf{H}(x) = \mathbf{H}(y)$.

For target collision resistant hash functions, it should be infeasible for a polynomial time adversary to find y such that $y \neq x$ and $\mathbf{H}(x) = \mathbf{H}(y)$, given a randomly chosen element x and a randomly drawn hash function **H**. Let **B** denote a polynomial time adversary against TCR hash functions, we define the advantage function of the adversary **B** as follows:

$$Adv_{\mathbf{H},\mathbf{B}}^{TCR}(k) = \Pr[\mathbf{B} \text{ finds a collision to } \mathbf{H}(\mathrm{x})]$$

H is said to be target collision resistant if the advantage function $Adv_{\mathbf{H},\mathbf{B}}^{TCR}(k)$ is a negligible function in k for all polynomial time adversaries **B**, given a randomly chosen element x.

2.4 Message Authentication Codes

A message authentication code is a tuple of three algorithms (**KeyGen**, **MAC**, **Verify**). **KeyGen** takes no input and generates a key, **MAC** takes a key and a message of arbitrary length and outputs a tag, **Verify** takes a key, a message and a tag and outputs a bit, 1 indicating that the tag is valid for the message, 0 indicating that is it invalid.

The security of a message authentication code is defined through a game in which a key k is first chosen by running the **KeyGen** algorithm. The attacking algorithm $\mathcal{A}$ is then given oracle access to $\mathbf{MAC}(k, \cdot)$ and $\mathbf{Verify}(k, \cdot)$, and $\mathcal{A}$ succeeds in breaking the message authentication code if it can output a message-tag pair (M, tag) such that $\mathbf{Verify}(k, M, tag) = 1$ but $\mathcal{A}$ did not receive tag as a response from its **MAC** oracle on input M.

3 t-ABSC Construction

In this section we present our threshold attribute-based signcryption construction. The security of our scheme is based on the intractability of the hashed modified decisional bilinear Diffie-Hellman and modified computational Diffie-Hellman assumptions.

Setup: Let n denote the maximum size of an attribute set. Let n_m denote the plaintext size. The public parameters $params$ are:

$$(g, g_1, h, t_1, \ldots, t_{n+1}, u_1, \ldots, u_{n_m}, u', Y, H, H_1, H_2, MAC),$$

where $\hat{e} : \mathbb{G} \times \mathbb{G} \rightarrow \mathbb{G}_T$ is a bilinear pairing function, $s \in_R \mathbb{Z}_q^*$, $g, g_1, h, t_1, \ldots,$ $t_{n+1}, u', u_1, \ldots, u_{n_m} \in_R \mathbb{G}$, $Y = \hat{e}(g, g_1)^s$, $H : \mathbb{G}_T \rightarrow \{0,1\}^{n_m} \times \mathbb{Z}_q^* \times \mathcal{K}_{MAC}$ is a cryptographic hash function which satisfies the hashed mBDH assumption, $H_1 : \{0,1\}^* \rightarrow \mathbb{Z}_q^*$ is a target collision resistant hash function, $H_2 : \{0,1\}^{2n_m} \rightarrow \{0,1\}^{n_m}$ is a collision-resistant hash function and MAC is a message authentication code. The master secret of the system is s.

We define two functions, $T : \mathbb{F}_q \rightarrow \mathbb{G}$ and $W : \{0,1\}^{n_m} \rightarrow \mathbb{G}$ that will be used throughout our scheme. Let $T(x)$ be the function defined by $T(x) = g_1^{x^n} \prod_{i=1}^{n+1} (t_i^{\Delta_{i,N}(x)})$, where $\Delta_{i,N}(x) = \prod_{j \neq i, j \in N} \frac{x-j}{i-j}$ is the Lagrange coefficient for $i \in \mathbb{Z}_q^*$, N is the set $\{1, \ldots, n+1\}$. Let $W(h_m) = u' \prod_{i=1}^{n_m} u_i^{h_{m,i}}$, where h_m a binary string of length n_m consists of $\overrightarrow{h_m} = (h_{m,1}, h_{m,2}, \ldots, h_{m,n_m})$.

uExtract(ω_e, d)**:** The private key corresponding to a set of encryption attributes ω_e and threshold d is a set $\{D_{u,1_i}, D_{u,2_i}, D_{u,3_i}\}_{i\in\omega_e}$ computed as follows:
- $D_{u,1_i} = (g_1^{f(i)}(T(i))^{r_i})_{i\in\omega}$, where $r_i \in_R \mathbb{Z}_q^*$ and f is a random polynomial of degree $d-1$ such that $f(0) = s$.
- $D_{u,2_i} = g^{r_i}$.
- $D_{u,3_i} = h^{r_i}$.

sExtract(ω_s, d)**:** The private key corresponding to a set of signature attributes ω_s and threshold d is a set $\{D_{s,1_i}, D_{s,2_i}\}_{i\in\omega_s}$ computed as follows:
- $D_{s,1_i} = (g_1^{f(i)}(T(i))^{r_i})_{i\in\omega}$, where $r_i \in_R \mathbb{Z}_q^*$ and f is a random polynomial of degree $d-1$ such that $f(0) = s$.
- $D_{s,2_i} = g^{r_i}$.

Signcrypt$(params, M, \omega_e, \omega_s, sk_{s,\omega_\sigma}, |\omega_s|)$**:** Here, ω_e is a set of encryption attributes, ω_s is a set of signature attributes and $sk_{s,\omega_\sigma,|\omega_s|}$ is a signature key with $\omega_s \subset \omega_\sigma$. The algorithm proceeds as follows:
- Choose random $r, r' \in \mathbb{Z}_q^*$.
- Compute $(h_1, h_2, h_3) = H(Y^r)$.
- Let $t = H_1(g^r)$.
- Compute:

$$Z = g^{h_2} \cdot W(H_2(M||h_1))^{r'} \cdot \prod_{i\in\omega_s} (D_{s,1_i})^{\Delta_{i,\omega_s}(0)}.$$

- The signcryption of M is:

$$(\omega_e, \omega_s, g^r, \{(T(i)h^t)^r\}_{i\in\omega_e}, M \oplus h_1, Z, \{(D_{s,2_i})^{\Delta_{i,\omega_s}(0)}\}_{i\in\omega_s}, g^{r'}, tag),$$

where tag is the MAC of all preceding elements in the ciphertext under key h_3.

Unsigncrypt: Given a ciphertext $C = (A_1, A_2, A_3, (A_{4_i})_{i\in\omega_e}, A_5, A_6, (A_{7_i})_{i\in\omega_s}, A_8, A_9)$ and an unsigncryption key $sk_{u,\omega_m u,d}$ the unsigncryption is performed as follows:
- Chooses a subset $S \subset (\omega_\mu \cap A_1)$ containing d attributes. If no such subset exists, output $\perp$.
- Compute $t = H_1(A_3)$.
- Compute $Y' = \prod_{i\in S} \left(\frac{\hat{e}((D_{1_i} D_{3_i}^t), A_3)}{\hat{e}(D_{2_i}, A_{4_i})}\right)^{\Delta_{i,S}(0)}$.
- Compute $(h_1, h_2, h_3) = H(Y')$ and $Z' = A_6 \cdot g^{-h_2}$.
- Test the following equation:

$$\hat{e}(g, Z') = Y \cdot \hat{e}(A_8, W(H_2((A_5 \oplus h_1)||h_1)) \cdot \prod_{i\in A_2} \hat{e}(A_{7_i}, T(i)).$$

If it holds, and A_9 is equal to the MAC of all preceding elements in the ciphertext under key h_3, output $A_5 \oplus h_1$, otherwise, output $\perp$.

3.1 Security

Due to space restrictions, we only state the theorems describing the security of our scheme. The proofs are given in the full version of this paper.

Theorem 1. *Our signcryption scheme is S-IND-t-ABSC-CCA2-secure if the hashed modified decisional bilinear Diffie-Hellman assumption is hard, if* H_1 *is a target-collision resistant hash function and* MAC *is a secure message authentication code. More precisely, if there exists an algorithm* $\mathcal{A}$ *that attacks our scheme, then we can construct algorithms* $\mathcal{B}$, $\mathcal{B}_1$ *and* $\mathcal{C}$ *that have essentially the same running time as* $\mathcal{A}$ *such that*

$$Adv_{\mathcal{A}}^{S-IND-t-ABSC-CCA2} \leq Adv_{\mathcal{B}}^{mDBDH} + Adv_{H_1,\mathcal{B}_1}^{TCR} + Adv_{MAC,\mathcal{C}}^{UNF}.$$

Theorem 2. *Our signcryption scheme is S-EUF-t-ABSC-CMA-secure if the modified computational Diffie-Hellman assumption is hard. More precisely, if there exists an algorithm* $\mathcal{A}$ *that attacks our scheme, then we can construct algorithms* $\mathcal{B}$ *and* $\mathcal{C}$ *that have essentially the same running time as* $\mathcal{A}$ *such that*

$$Adv_{\mathcal{A}}^{S-EUF-t-ABSC-CMA} \leq n_m \cdot Adv_{\mathcal{B}}^{mCDH} + Adv_{H_2,\mathcal{C}}^{CR}.$$

4 Additional Remarks

4.1 CCA-Secure Attribute-Based Encryption

Since the signature part of our signcryption scheme plays no role in proving it CCA secure, it is easy to obtain a CCA-secure attribute-based encryption scheme from our signcryption scheme by simply removing the signature component. The scheme is essentially a CCA-secure version of the Sahai-Waters large universe construction of [30]. This scheme is given in full details in Appendix B.

4.2 Short Attribute-Based Signature

Similarly, we can separate the signature component of our signcryption scheme to obtain a signature scheme whose signature are about half the size of previous schemes [32,34]. It also has a much tighter security reduction than previous schemes. The details of the scheme are in Appendix C.

4.3 Reducing the Number of Keys

We used two disjoint attribute universes for encryption and signature in order to achieve the same functionality as the combination of an attribute-based encryption and an attribute-based signature scheme. However, since, in our scheme, the private keys used for decryption and signature are essentially identical (one more element is needed for decryption keys), it would be possible, in the event that users are always given the same decryption and signature rights, to use the same attributes (and same key generation algorithm) for both encryption and signature, thereby reducing the number of private keys by half. This results in a more complicated security model, which will be discussed in the complete version of this paper.

4.4 Arbitrary Monotone Access Structure for Encryption

For simplicity of exposition, and to preserve a certain symmetry between the access policy used for encryption and signature, we limited the access policies used for unsigncryption keys to threshold policies. However, we believe it should be straightforward to extend our result to arbitrary monotone access structures by splitting the master key msk using techniques similar to those of Goyal et al. [15].

4.5 A Note on Adaptive Security

Using a method similar to Boneh and Boyen [6], we can prove our scheme adaptively secure using a reduction that simply guesses the set of challenge attributes at the beginning. While this reduction is rather inefficient - the probability of correctly guessing the challenge set is $1/2^N$ where N is the total number of attributes used in the scheme - we note that when N is not too large, say $N \leq 500$, one could increase the order of the group to retain security and still obtain a more efficient scheme than the adaptively secure scheme of Lewko et al. [19], which requires the order of its group to be large enough to be hard to factorize.

5 Efficiency Analysis

We now compare the efficiency of our scheme against the combination of ABE and ABS that provides the same functionality of authenticated encryption. The comparison will be in terms of public parameter size, private key size, ciphertext size, and computational cost for signcryption and unsigncryption. The result of comparison is given in Table 1 below. It can be seen that the new scheme obtains stronger security (CCA versus CPA) with shorter parameter sizes. In particular using our scheme, the ciphertext size when a large number of attributes is used for signcryption, results in a ciphertext with the length almost halved.

Let $|\mathbb{G}|$ and $|\mathbb{G}_T|$ denote the size of the underlying group $\mathbb{G}$ and $\mathbb{G}_T$ respectively in bits, and τ is the size of the tag produced by the message authentication code.

In our t-ABSC scheme the public parameter size is $(n + n_m + 4)|\mathbb{G}| + |\mathbb{G}_T|$, where n is the maximum size of an attribute set and n_m is the size of the messages. The private key size is dependant on the number of attributes held by a user where $1 \leq |\omega| \leq n$. The private key size of our construction is *at most* $5n \cdot |\mathbb{G}|$. The ciphertext size of our scheme depends on the number of attributes used to signcrypt, i.e, $|\omega_e|$ and $|\omega_s|$, where $1 \leq |\omega_e| \leq n$ and $1 \leq |\omega_s| \leq n$ respectively. The ciphertext size in our scheme is *at most* $(2n+3)|\mathbb{G}| + n_m + \tau$.

The number of exponentiations in group $\mathbb{G}$ to signcrypt is *at most* $2n + d + 3$, and additionally, we require on average $\frac{n_m}{2}$ (at most n_m) exponentiations in $\mathbb{G}$ due to the function $W(h_m)$. The cost of unsigncrypt consists of $3d + 3$ pairing computations and $d + \frac{n_m}{2}$ exponentiations in $\mathbb{G}$.

In Table 1, n, n_m denotes the maximum size of an attribute set (we can use for extract/encrypt/sign), and length of the message/Hash output (H_2) respectively. The construction below use the encrypt-then-sign paradigm.

Table 1. Scheme Efficiency

Schemes	*Params* Size	Private Key Size	Ciphertext Size	Security Notion
Ours[‡]	$(n + n_m + 4)\|\mathbb{G}\| + \|\mathbb{G}_T\|$	$5n\|\mathbb{G}\|$	$(2n + 3)\|\mathbb{G}\| + n_m + \tau$	CCA2/CMA
ABE + ABS				
[30]+[32]	$(n + n_m + 7)\|\mathbb{G}\| + \|\mathbb{G}_T\|$	$4n\|\mathbb{G}\|$	$(4n + 5)\|\mathbb{G}\| + \|\mathbb{G}_T\|$	CPA/CMA

We compare our scheme with the combined system of threshold attribute-based encryption (t-ABE) [30] and threshold attribute-based signature(t-ABS) [32].The public parameter of this combined system is $(|\mathbb{G}_T| + (n + n_m + 7)|\mathbb{G}|)$. The signcrypted message size of the combined system is *at most* $(4n + 5)|\mathbb{G}| + |\mathbb{G}_T|$. The private key of the scheme is *at most* $(4n) \cdot |\mathbb{G}|$.

6 Conclusion

We introduced a threshold attribute-based signcryption in the standard model which can be applied to sender identifiable applications wherein the authenticity of message attests sender's attributes. Our scheme can be extended to provide sender privacy, wherein the sender is able to selective disclose his attributes while preserving others. We presented a proof of security under the selective attribute model against both adaptive chosen ciphertext attack and chosen message attack.

References

1. Abdalla, M., Bellare, M., Rogaway, P.: The oracle diffie-hellman assumptions and an analysis of dhies. In: Naccache, D. (ed.) CT-RSA 2001. LNCS, vol. 2020, pp. 143–158. Springer, Heidelberg (2001)
2. Attrapadung, N., Imai, H.: Conjunctive broadcast and attribute-based encryption. In: Shacham, H., Waters, B. (eds.) Pairing-Based Cryptography – Pairing 2009. LNCS, vol. 5671, pp. 248–265. Springer, Heidelberg (2009)
3. Bao, F., Deng, R.H.: A signcryption scheme with signature directly verifiable by public key. In: Imai, H., Zheng, Y. (eds.) PKC 1998. LNCS, vol. 1431, pp. 55–59. Springer, Heidelberg (1998)
4. Barreto, P.S.L.M., Libert, B., McCullagh, N., Quisquater, J.J.: Efficient and provably-secure identity-based signatures and signcryption from bilinear maps. In: Roy, B. (ed.) ASIACRYPT 2005. LNCS, vol. 3788, pp. 515–532. Springer, Heidelberg (2005)
5. Bethencourt, J., Sahai, A., Waters, B.: Ciphertext-policy attribute-based encryption. In: IEEE Symposium on Security and Privacy, SP 2007, pp. 321–334 (2007)
6. Boneh, D., Boyen, X.: Efficient selective-id secure identity based encryption without random oracles. In: Cachin, C., Camenisch, J.L. (eds.) EUROCRYPT 2004. LNCS, vol. 3027, pp. 223–238. Springer, Heidelberg (2004)
7. Boyen, X.: Multipurpose identity-based signcryption: A swiss army knife for identity-based cryptography. In: Boneh, D. (ed.) CRYPTO 2003. LNCS, vol. 2729, pp. 383–399. Springer, Heidelberg (2003)

8. Chase, M.: Multi-authority attribute-based encryption. In: Vadhan, S.P. (ed.) TCC 2007. LNCS, vol. 4392, pp. 515–534. Springer, Heidelberg (2007)
9. Chen, L., Malone-Lee, J.: Improved identity-based signcryption. In: Vaudenay, S. (ed.) PKC 2005. LNCS, vol. 3386, pp. 362–379. Springer, Heidelberg (2005)
10. Cramer, R., Damgaard, I., Schoenmakers, B.: Proofs of partial knowledge and simplified design of witness hiding protocols. In: Desmedt, Y.G. (ed.) CRYPTO 1994. LNCS, vol. 839, pp. 174–187. Springer, Heidelberg (1994)
11. Cramer, R., Shoup, V.: Design and analysis of practical public-key encryption schemes secure against adaptive chosen ciphertext attack. SIAM Journal of Computing 33(1), 167–226 (2004)
12. Emura, K., Miyaji, A., Omote, K.: A dynamic attribute-based group signature scheme and its application in an anonymous survey for the collection of attribute statistics. Journal of Information Processing 17, 216–231 (2009)
13. Emura, L., Miyaji, A., Nomura, A., Omote, K., Soshi, M.: A ciphertext-policy attribute-based encryption scheme with constant ciphertext length (2009)
14. Fang, L., Wang, J., Ren, Y., Xia, J., Bian, S.: Chosen-ciphertext secure multi-authority fuzzy identity-based key encapsulation without rom. In: International Conference on Computational Intelligence and Security, vol. 1, pp. 326–330 (2008)
15. Goyal, V., Pandey, O., Sahai, A., Waters, B.: Attribute-based encryption for fine-grained access control of encrypted data. In: CCS 2006: Proceedings of the 13th ACM conference on Computer and communications security, pp. 89–98. ACM, New York (2006)
16. Guo, S., Zeng, Y.: Attribute-based signature scheme. In: International Conference on Information Security and Assurance, ISA 2008, pp. 509–511 (2008)
17. Khader, D.: Attribute based group signatures. Cryptology ePrint Archive, Report 2007/159 (2007)
18. Kiltz, E., Vahlis, Y.: Cca2 secure ibe: Standard model efficiency through authenticated symmetric encryption. In: Malkin, T.G. (ed.) CT-RSA 2008. LNCS, vol. 4964, pp. 221–238. Springer, Heidelberg (2008)
19. Lewko, A., Okamoto, T., Sahai, A., Takashima, K., Waters, B.: Fully secure functional ecnryption: Attribute-based encryption and (hierarchical) inner product encryption. In: Gilbert, H. (ed.) EUROCRYPT 2010. LNCS, vol. 6110, pp. 62–91. Springer, Heidelberg (2010)
20. Li, J., Kim, K.: Attribute-based ring signatures. Cryptology ePrint Archive, Report 2008/394 (2008)
21. Li, J., Wang, Q., Wang, C., Ren, K.: Enhancing attribute-based encryption with attribute hierarchy. Cryptology ePrint Archive, Report 2009/293 (2009)
22. Libert, B., Quisquater, J.J.: New identity-based signcryption schemes from pairings. In: IEEE Information Theory Workshop, 2003, pp. 155–158 (2003)
23. Libert, B., Quisquater, J.J.: Efficient signcryption with key privacy from gap diffie-hellman groups. In: Bao, F., Deng, R., Zhou, J. (eds.) PKC 2004. LNCS, vol. 2947, pp. 187–200. Springer, Heidelberg (2004)
24. Lubicz, D., Sirvent, T.: Attribute-based broadcast encryption scheme made efficient. In: Vaudenay, S. (ed.) AFRICACRYPT 2008. LNCS, vol. 5023, pp. 325–342. Springer, Heidelberg (2008)
25. Maji, H., Prabhakaran, M., Rosulek, M.: Attribute-based signatures: Achieving attribute-privacy and collusion-resistance. Cryptology ePrint Archive, Report 2008/328 (2008)
26. Malone-Lee, J.: Identity-based signcryption. IACR eprint, report 2002/098 (2002)
27. Malone-Lee, J., Mao, W.: Two birds one stone: Signcryption using rsa. In: Joye, M. (ed.) CT-RSA 2003. LNCS, vol. 2612, pp. 211–226. Springer, Heidelberg (2003)

28. Müller, S., Katzenbeisser, S., Eckert, C.: Distributed attribute-based encryption, pp. 20–36 (2009)
29. Sahai, A.: Non-malleable non-interactive zero knowledge and adaptive chosen-ciphertext security. In: FOCS 1999: Proceedings of the 40th Annual Symposium on Foundations of Computer Science, p. 543. IEEE Computer Society, Los Alamitos (1999)
30. Sahai, A., Waters, B.: Fuzzy identity-based encryption. In: Cramer, R. (ed.) EUROCRYPT 2005. LNCS, vol. 3494, pp. 457–473. Springer, Heidelberg (2005)
31. Santis, A.D., Crescenzo, G.D., Ostrovsky, R., Persiano, G., Sahai, A.: Robust non-interactive zero knowledge. In: Kilian, J. (ed.) CRYPTO 2001. LNCS, vol. 2139, pp. 566–598. Springer, Heidelberg (2001)
32. Shahandashti, S.F., Safavi-Naini, R.: Threshold attribute-based signatures and their application to anonymous credential systems. In: Preneel, B. (ed.) AFRICACRYPT 2009. LNCS, vol. 5580, pp. 198–216. Springer, Heidelberg (2009)
33. Steinfeld, R., Zheng, Y.: A signcryption scheme based on integer factorization. In: Okamoto, E., Pieprzyk, J.P., Seberry, J. (eds.) ISW 2000. LNCS, vol. 1975, pp. 131–146. Springer, Heidelberg (2000)
34. Yang, P., Cao, Z., Dong, X.: Fuzzy identity based signature. Cryptology ePrint Archive, Report 2008/002 (2008)
35. Zheng, Y.: Digital signcryption or how to achieve cost(signature & encryption) $<<$ cost(signature) + cost(encryption). In: Kaliski Jr., B.S. (ed.) CRYPTO 1997. LNCS, vol. 1294, pp. 165–179. Springer, Heidelberg (1997)

A The Hashed Modified Biliear Diffie-Hellman Assumption

The hashed Diffie-Hellman problem was first formally discuss by Abdalla et al. in [1]. In this problem, the adversary is trying to distinguish between $\langle g, g^a, g^b, H(g^{ab})\rangle$ and $\langle g, g^a, g^b, R\rangle$, where a and b are random number between 1 and the order of the group, and R is a random element in the range of the hash function H. When H is the identity function, this is essentially the same as the decisional Diffie-Hellman assumption, and when H is a cryptographic hash function, the hashed Diffie-Hellman assumption is likely to be weaker than the DDH assumption. In the best case, H is a function that extracts hard-core bits, and then the hashed Diffie-Hellman assumption is equivalent to the CDH assumption.

The modified bilinear Diffie-Hellman problem is similar to the traditional bilinear Diffie-Hellman problem (or its decisional counterpart), except that in addition to the elements $g^a, g^b and g^c$, an adversary trying to compute $\hat{e}(g,g)^{abc}$ (or trying to differentiate it from a random group element) is also given g^{a^2}. While this assumption is stronger than the BDH assumption, the additional input to the adversary it not known to reduce the complexity of the problem.

Our hashed modified bilinear Diffie-Hellman assumption is a straightforward adaptation of the hashed Diffie-Hellman assumption to the modified Decisional Bilinear Diffie-Hellman problem of Kiltz and Vahlis [18].

For our scheme, we need the hash function H to be of the form $H : \mathbb{G}_T \rightarrow \{0,1\}^{n_m} \times \mathbb{Z}_q^* \times \mathcal{K}_{MAC}$. Assuming that such a function H exists is not much stronger than assuming that the hash function has the form $H' : \mathbb{G}_T \to \{0,1\}^n$ for some n since one could easily construct H by combining H' with a pseudo-random number generator, using the output of H' as the seed to the PRNG.

B CCA-Secure Threshold Attribute-Based Encryption

The CCA-secure t-ABE scheme is obtained by removing the signature component of our signcryption scheme.

Setup: Let n denote the maximum size of an attribute set. Let n_m denote the plaintext size. The public parameters *params* are:

$$(g, g_1, h, t_1, \ldots, t_{n+1}, Y, H, H_1),$$

where $\hat{e} : \mathbb{G} \times \mathbb{G} \to \mathbb{G}_T$ is a bilinear pairing function, $s \in_R \mathbb{Z}_q^*$, $g, g_1, h, t_1, \ldots, t_{n+1} \in_R \mathbb{G}$, $Y = \hat{e}(g, g_1)^s$, $H : \mathbb{G}_T \to \{0,1\}^{n_m} \times \mathcal{K}_{MAC}$ is a cryptographic hash function which satisfies the hashed mBDH assumption and $H_1 : \{0,1\}^* \to \mathbb{Z}_q^*$ is a target collision resistant hash function. The master secret of the system is s.

Let $T(x)$ be the function defined by $T(x) = g_1^{x^n} \prod_{i=1}^{n+1}(t_i^{\Delta_{i,N}(x)})$, where $\Delta_{i,N}(x) = \prod_{j \neq i, j \in N} \frac{x-j}{i-j}$ is the Lagrange coefficient for $i \in \mathbb{Z}_q^*$, N is the set $\{1, \ldots, n+1\}$.

Extract: The private key corresponding to a set of attributes ω_e and threshold d is a set $\{D_{1_i}, D_{2_i}, D_{3_i}\}_{i \in \omega_e}$ computed as follows:
- $D_{1_i} = (g_1^{f(i)}(T(i))^{r_i})_{i \in \omega_e}$, where $r_i \in_R \mathbb{Z}_q^*$ and f is a random polynomial of degree $d-1$ such that $f(0) = s$.
- $D_{2_i} = g^{r_i}$.
- $D_{3_i} = h^{r_i}$.

Encrypt: Given public parameters *params*, message $M \in \{0,1\}^{n_m}$ and attribute set ω_e, compute the ciphertext as follows:
- Choose a random $r \in \mathbb{Z}_q^*$ and compute $(h_1, h_2) = H(Y^r)$.
- Let $t = H_1(g^r)$.
- The ciphertext for M is:

$$(\omega_e, g^r, \{(T(i)h^t)^r\}_{i \in \omega_e}, M \oplus h_1, tag),$$

where *tag* is the MAC of all preceding elements in the ciphertext under key h_2.

Decrypt: Given a ciphertext $C = (A_1, A_2, (A_{3_i})_{i \in \omega_e}, A_4, A_5)$ and an decryption key $sk_{\omega_m u,d}$ the decryption is performed as follows:
- Chooses a subset $S \subset (\omega_\mu \cap A_1)$ containing d attributes. If no such subset exists, output $\perp$.
- Compute $t = H_1(A_2)$.
- Compute $Y' = \prod_{i \in S} \left(\frac{\hat{e}((D_{1_i} D_{3_i}^t), A_2)}{\hat{e}(D_{2_i}, A_{3_i})} \right)^{\Delta_{i,S}(0)}$.
- Compute $(h_1, h_2) = H(Y')$.
- If A_5 is equal to the MAC of all preceding elements in the ciphertext under key h_2, output $A_4 \oplus h_1$, otherwise, output $\perp$.

The security theorem for this scheme is as follows.

Theorem 3. *The encryption scheme above is S-IND-t-ABE-CCA-secure if the hashed modified decisional bilinear Diffie-Hellman assumption is hard, if H_1 is a target-collision resistant hash function and MAC is a secure message authentication code. More precisely, if there exists an algorithm $\mathcal{A}$ that attacks our scheme, then we can construct algorithms $\mathcal{B}$, $\mathcal{B}_1$ and $\mathcal{C}$ that have essentially the same running time as $\mathcal{A}$ such that*

$$Adv_{\mathcal{A}}^{S-IND-t-ABE-CCA} \leq Adv_{\mathcal{B}}^{mDBDH} + Adv_{H_1,\mathcal{B}_1}^{TCR} + Adv_{MAC,\mathcal{C}}^{UNF}.$$

C Short Attribute-Based Signature

The signature scheme obtained by isolating the signature component of our signcryption scheme.

Setup: Let n denote the maximum size of an attribute set. The public parameters $params$ are:

$$(g, g_1, t_1, \ldots, t_{n+1}, u_1, \ldots, u_{n_m}, u', Y, H),$$

where $\hat{e} : \mathbb{G} \times \mathbb{G} \to \mathbb{G}_T$ is a bilinear pairing function, $g, g_1, t_1, \ldots, t_{n+1}, u', u_1, \ldots, u_{n_m} \in_R \mathbb{G}$, $Y = \hat{e}(g, g_1)^s$, $s \in_R \mathbb{Z}_q^*$, $H : \{0,1\}^* \to \{0,1\}^{n_m}$ is a collision-resistant hash function. The master secret of the system is s.

We define two functions, $T : \mathbb{F}_q \to \mathbb{G}$ and $W : \{0,1\}^{n_m} \to \mathbb{G}$ that will be used throughout our scheme. Let $T(x)$ be the function defined by $T(x) = g_1^{x^n} \prod_{i=1}^{n+1}(t_i^{\Delta_{i,N}(x)})$, where $\Delta_{i,N}(x) = \prod_{j \neq i, j \in N} \frac{x-j}{i-j}$ is the Lagrange coefficient for $i \in \mathbb{Z}_q^*$, N is the set $\{1, \ldots, n+1\}$. Let $W(h_m) = u' \prod_{i=1}^{n_m} u_i^{h_{m,i}}$, where h_m a binary string of length n_m consists of $\overrightarrow{h_m} = (h_{m,1}, h_{m,2}, \ldots, h_{m,n_m})$.

Extract(ω_s, d)**:** The private key corresponding to a set of attributes ω_s and threshold d is a set $\{D_{s,1_i}, D_{s,2_i}\}_{i \in \omega_s}$ computed as follows:
- $D_{s,1_i} = (g_1^{f(i)}(T(i))^{r_i})_{i \in \omega}$, where $r_i \in_R \mathbb{Z}_q^*$ and f is a random polynomial of degree $d-1$ such that $f(0) = s$.
- $D_{s,2_i} = g^{r_i}$.

Sign$(params, M, \omega_s, sk_{s,\omega_\sigma}, |\omega_s|)$**:** Here, ω_s is a set of signature attributes and $sk_{s,\omega_\sigma,|\omega_s|}$ is a signature key with $\omega_s \subset \omega_\sigma$. The algorithm proceeds as follows:
- Choose random $r, r' \in \mathbb{Z}_q^*$.
- Compute $(h_1, h_2, h_3) = H(Y^r)$.
- Let $t = H_1(g^r)$.
- Compute:

$$Z = W(H(M))^{r'} \cdot \prod_{i \in \omega_s} (D_{s,1_i})^{\Delta_{i,\omega_s}(0)}.$$

- The signature on M is:

$$(\omega_s, Z, \{(D_{s,2_i})^{\Delta_{i,\omega_s}(0)}\}_{i \in \omega_s}, g^{r'}).$$

Verify$(params, M, \sigma)$**:** Given a message M and signature $\sigma = (A_1, A_2, (A_{3_i})_{i\in\omega_{A_1}}, A_4)$ the verification is performed as follows:
- Test the following equation:

$$\hat{e}(g, A_2) = Y \cdot \hat{e}(A_4, W(H(M) \cdot \prod_{i\in A_1} \hat{e}(A_{3_i}, T(i)).$$

If it holds, output 1, otherwise, output 0.

Theorem 4. *The signature scheme above is S-EUF-t-ABS-CMA-secure if the modified computational Diffie-Hellman assumption is hard and if H is a collision-resistant hash function. More precisely, if there exists an algorithm $\mathcal{A}$ that attacks our scheme, then we can construct algorithms $\mathcal{B}$ and $\mathcal{C}$ that have essentially the same running time as $\mathcal{A}$ such that*

$$Adv_{\mathcal{A}}^{S-EUF-t-ABS-CMA} \leq n_m \cdot Adv_{\mathcal{B}}^{mCDH} + Adv_{H,\mathcal{C}}^{CR}.$$

Efficiency-Improved Fully Simulatable Adaptive OT under the DDH Assumption

Kaoru Kurosawa[1], Ryo Nojima[2], and Le Trieu Phong[2]

[1] Ibaraki University, Japan
kurosawa@mx.ibaraki.ac.jp
[2] NICT, Japan
{ryo-no,phong}@nict.go.jp

Abstract. At Asiacrypt 2009, Kurosawa and Nojima showed a fully simulatable adaptive oblivious transfer (OT) protocol under the DDH assumption in the standard model. However, Green and Hohenberger pointed out that the communication cost of each transfer phase is $O(n)$, where n is the number of the sender's messages. In this paper, we show that the cost can be reduced to $O(1)$ by utilizing a verifiable shuffle protocol.

Keywords: Adaptive OT, verifiable shuffles, DDH, standard model.

1 Introduction

1.1 Background

Adaptive oblivious transfer is a notion introduced by Naor and Pinkas in [12]. In the scheme, denoted by $\mathrm{OT}^n_{k\times 1}$, a receiver can obtain k messages, *one after the other*, from a sender who has n messages in such a way that: (1) the sender learns nothing on the receiver's selection, and (2) the receiver only learns about the k messages. The key applications of this type of OT are in patent searches, oblivious search, medical databases etc.

The formal security definition for OT schemes capturing the above intuitions gets evolved in the literature. Historically, in half simulation security [14], only the sender security is defined via the real world/ideal world paradigm, while the receiver security is formalized by a *weaker* notion. Many OT schemes in the literature satisfy half simulation security, among which are [18, 3, 9, 11, 13]. However, there is a practical attack against schemes with half simulation security, as realized in [11] and formally emphasized in [1].

To overcome the threat, in 2007, Camenisch, Neven, and shelat introduced a stronger notion called "full simulation security" [1], in which *both* sender and receiver security are defined via the real world/ideal world paradigm. They then constructed a fully simulatable adaptive $\mathrm{OT}^n_{k\times 1}$ in the standard model, relying on the q-strong Diffie-Hellman (q-sDH) and q-power decisional Diffie-Hellman (q-PDDH) assumptions in bilinear groups. Camenisch, Neven, and shelat used signatures as a key ingredient in their approach, which was originally taken in [18] by Ogata and Kurosawa in the random oracle model.

J.A. Garay and R. De Prisco (Eds.): SCN 2010, LNCS 6280, pp. 172–181, 2010.

Table 1. Fully simulatable adaptive OT without random oracles

Scheme	Assumption	Comm. Cost (each transfer)
Camenisch et al [1]	q-strong DH and q-PDDH	$O(1)$
Green-Hohenberger [6]	q-hidden LRSW (UC secure)	$O(1)$
Jarecki-Liu [8]	q-DHI (RSA group)	$O(1)$
Kurosawa-Nojima [10]	DDH	$O(n)$
Green-Hohenberger [7]	decision 3-party DH (3DDH)	O(1)
This work	DDH	$O(1)$

Subsequently, in 2008, Green and Hohenberger, again using signatures, showed a universally composable scheme (and hence fully simulatable), relying on the q-hidden LRSW assumption. In 2009, Jarecki and Liu [8], using pseudorandom function as a component, presented a fully simulatable adaptive OT under the decisional q-Diffie-Hellman inversion (q-DHI) assumption.

We stress that all the above schemes rely on dynamic assumptions (namely, the q-based assumptions in Table 1 where q may depend on n, the number of messages in OT). In 2009, Kurosawa and Nojima [10] built a simple fully simulatable adaptive OT under the DDH assumption. However, Green and Hohenberger [7] pointed out that it has $O(n)$ communication cost in each transfer phase which is much larger than the other schemes. Green and Hohenberger [7] also also proposed a fully simulatable adaptive OT under the decision 3-party Diffie-Hellman (3DDH) assumption, with $O(1)$ communication cost in each transfer phase.

1.2 Our Contribution

In this paper, we show a fully simulatable adaptive OT under the DDH assumption such that each transfer requires only $O(1)$ communication cost in the standard model. (The initialization phase requires $O(n)$ communication cost, which is asymptotically minimal.) Note that the DDH assumption is a more standard assumption than the 3DDH assumption on which the scheme of Green and Hohenberger [7] relies. Furthermore our scheme does not use pairing, while the scheme of Green and Hohenberger [7] does.

Our scheme is obtained by improving the scheme of Kurosawa and Nojima [10] by using a verifiable shuffle protocol. To our knowledge, this is the first time that shuffles are used in building OT protocols. In particular, we employ the shuffle protocol of Neff [16, 17] in this paper. The technique helps greatly reducing the communication cost of each transfer from $O(n)$ in the Kurosawa-Nojima scheme [10] to $O(1)$ as in our proposal.

A comparison between schemes is given in Table 1, and a motivation behind the usage of shuffles is postponed later in Sec.4.

Organization. We begin with some preliminaries in Sec.2, then introduce a verifiable shuffle protocol for our OT construction in Sec.3. We describe our proposal and prove its security in Sec.4.

2 Preliminaries

We will work on a cyclic group G of prime order q, generated by an element g. The symbol " $\xleftarrow{\$}$ " indicates a randomized process.

2.1 Assumption

The DDH assumption claims that for all PPT adversary $\mathcal{A}$, the value

$$\mathbf{Adv}_G^{ddh}(\mathcal{A}) = \left| \Pr\left[b' = b : \begin{array}{c} x, r \xleftarrow{\$} Z_q; b \xleftarrow{\$} \{0,1\}; \\ T_0 \leftarrow g^{xr}; T_1 \xleftarrow{\$} G; \\ b' \xleftarrow{\$} \mathcal{A}(g, g^x, g^r, T_b) \end{array} \right] - \frac{1}{2} \right|$$

is negligible. The well-known ElGamal encryption, which has semantic security under the DDH assumption, produces a ciphertext of a message $M \in G$ as $(g^r, M \cdot (g^x)^r)$ for public key g^x.

2.2 Zero-Knowledge Proof Systems

There exists an efficient 4-round zero-knowledge proof system for knowledge (ZK-PoK) on the discrete log problem. It is obtained by applying the technique of [4] to Schnorr's identification scheme [19].

There also exists an efficient 4-round zero-knowledge proof system for membership (ZK-PoM) on DDH tuples (i.e., $(g, g^x, u, u^x) \in G^4$). It comes from the confirmation protocol of Chaum's undeniable signature scheme [2].

2.3 Security of Adaptive k-Out-of-n Oblivious Transfer

We use almost the same presentation as [10], and consider a weak model of universally composable (UC) framework as follows.

- At the beginning of the game, an adversary $\mathcal{A}$ can corrupt either a sender S or a receiver R, but not both of them.
- $\mathcal{A}$ can send a message, denoted by $\mathcal{A}_{\text{out}}$, to an environment $\mathcal{Z}$ after the end of the protocol. However, $\mathcal{A}$ cannot communicate with $\mathcal{Z}$ during the protocol execution. (This property makes the definitions weaker than standard UC security.)

The ideal functionality of $\text{OT}^n_{k\times 1}$ will be shown below. For a protocol $\Pi = (\mathsf{S}, \mathsf{R})$, define the advantage of $\mathcal{Z}$ as

$$\mathbf{Adv}(\mathcal{Z}) \stackrel{\text{def}}{=} \left| \Pr(\mathcal{Z} = 1 \text{ in the real world}) - \Pr(\mathcal{Z} = 1 \text{ in the ideal world}) \right|$$

where the real and ideal worlds are defined below.

In the ideal world of $\text{OT}^n_{k\times 1}$, there are a few parties: the ideal functionality $\mathcal{F}_{\text{adapt}}$, an ideal world adversary $\mathcal{A}'$, and the environment $\mathcal{Z}$. Also we have dummy sender S' and receiver R'. The parties behave as follows.

Initialization phase

1. The environment $\mathcal{Z}$ sends $(M_1, \ldots, M_n)$ to the dummy sender S'.
2. S' sends $(M_1^*, \ldots, M_n^*)$ to $\mathcal{F}_{\text{adapt}}$, where $(M_1^*, \ldots, M_n^*) = (M_1, \ldots, M_n)$ if S' is not corrupted.

Transfer phase $i = 1, \ldots, k$

1. $\mathcal{Z}$ sends σ_i to the dummy receiver R', where $1 \le \sigma_i \le n$.
2. R' sends σ_i^* to $\mathcal{F}_{\text{adapt}}$, where $\sigma_i^* = \sigma_i$ if R' is not corrupted.
3. $\mathcal{F}_{\text{adapt}}$ sends `received` to $\mathcal{A}'$.
4. $\mathcal{A}'$ sends $b = 1$ or 0 to $\mathcal{F}_{\text{adapt}}$, where $b = 1$ if S' is not corrupted.
5. $\mathcal{F}_{\text{adapt}}$ sends E_i to R', where

$$E_i = \begin{cases} M_{\sigma_i^*}^* & \text{if } b = 1 \\ \perp & \text{if } b = 0 \end{cases}$$

6. R' sends E_i to $\mathcal{Z}$.

After the end of the protocol, $\mathcal{A}'$ sends a message $\mathcal{A}'_{\text{out}}$ to $\mathcal{Z}$. Finally $\mathcal{Z}$ outputs 1 or 0.

On the other hand, in the real world, the protocol $\Pi = (\mathsf{S}, \mathsf{R})$ is executed as specified by its construction (thus without $\mathcal{F}_{\text{adapt}}$). The environment $\mathcal{Z}$ and the real world adversary $\mathcal{A}$ behave in the same way as above.

Definition 1. *Protocol $\Pi = (\mathsf{S}, \mathsf{R})$ is secure against the sender (resp, receiver) corruption if for any real world adversary $\mathcal{A}$ who corrupts the sender S (resp, receiver R), there exists an ideal world adversary $\mathcal{A}'$ who corrupts the dummy sender S' (resp, dummy receiver R') such that for any poly-time environment $\mathcal{Z}$, the advantage* $\mathbf{Adv}(\mathcal{Z})$ *is negligible.*

Definition 2. *Protocol $\Pi = (\mathsf{S}, \mathsf{R})$ is a fully simulatable $OT^n_{k\times 1}$ if it is secure against the sender corruption and the receiver corruption.*

3 Shuffle Protocol

3.1 Honest-Verifier ZK-PoM

Neff [16, Sec.5] showed a seven-round ZK-PoM on L where

$$L = \{(g, g^c, X_1, \ldots, X_n, X^c_{\pi(1)}, \ldots, X^c_{\pi(n)} \mid c \in Z_q,\ \pi \text{ is a permutation on } \{0,1\}^n\}$$

Note that we can extract π if we know c.

It is easy to see that $(g, g^c, X_1, \ldots, X_n, X_1^c, \ldots, X_n^c)$ is indistinguishable from $(g, g^c, X_1, \ldots, X_n, R_1, \ldots, R_n)$ under the DDH assumption, where $R_1, \ldots, R_n$ are random elements of G. This implies that $(g,\ g^c,\ X_1,\ \ldots,\ X_n,\ X^c_{\pi(1)},\ \ldots,\ X^c_{\pi(n)})$ leaks no information on π computationally. Formalizing the intuition, Neff proved that his proof system is honest-verifier computational zero-knowledge under the DDH assumption. The communication cost for the proof system is $O(n)$.

3.2 Any Verifier ZK-PoM

The above protocol (P, V) of Neff is public coin. That is, V sends random elements of Z_q to P. We can transform it into an any verifier ZK-PoM by having V commit the random elements at the beginning of the protocol. (By using the same technique, Goldreich and Kahan [5] showed a constant round ZK-PoM for any NP language under the discrete log assumption. However, as a trade-off against the generality, their protocol is very inefficient.)

For example, suppose that V sends a random $t \in Z_q$ to P in the first round of (P, V). Then we transform it as follows.

1. P sends a random $h \in G$ to V.
2. V chooses random $t_0, r \in Z_q$, and computes
$$\texttt{commit}(t_0, r) = g^{t_0} h^r. \tag{1}$$
He then send it to P.
3. P sends a random $t_1 \in Z_q$ to V.
4. V reveals t_0 and r.
5. If eq.(1) is not satisfied, then P aborts. Otherwise P and V locally compute
$$t = t_0 + t_1 \bmod q.$$

As a result, we obtain a constant round ZK-PoM on L with respect to any verifier. It is computational zero-knowledge under the DDH assumption. The communication cost is still $O(n)$.

4 Proposed Adaptive OT under DDH Assumption

In this section, we show an efficient fully simulatable adaptive $\mathrm{OT}^n_{k\times 1}$ under the DDH assumption. Each transfer phase needs only $O(1)$ communication cost, and the initialization phase requires $O(n)$ communication cost.

The novelty of our protocol is that we use a shuffle protocol in the initialization phase. Namely we use the ZK-PoM shown in Sec.3.2. A problem is that since it is not a ZK-PoK, we cannot extract π from the prover. This problem is solved by having the prover run the ZK-PoK in which P proves that she knows c of g^c. Then π can be extracted from c and $(X_1, \ldots, X_n, X^c_{\pi(1)}, \ldots, X^c_{\pi(n)})$.

4.1 Protocol

As a convention, if proofs or checks are not fulfilled, it is implicitly understood that the protocol immediately stops.

<u>**Initialization Phase**</u>

1. The sender chooses $(r_1, \ldots, r_n, x) \in Z_q^{n+1}$ randomly, and computes $h = g^x$.

2. For $i = 1, \ldots, n$, the sender computes
$$C_i = (A_i, B_i) = (g^{r_i}, M_i \cdot h^{r_i}),$$
where $M_1, \ldots, M_n \in G$.
3. The sender sends $(h, C_1, \ldots, C_n)$.
4. The sender proves by ZK-PoK that he knows the secret key x.
5. The receiver chooses $c \in Z_q$ and sends $C = g^c$. Then he proves in ZK-PoK that he knows c.
6. The receiver chooses $s_i \in Z_q$ randomly and computes $X_i = g^{s_i} A_i$ for every $1 \leq i \leq n$. He sends all X_i and then proves in ZK-PoK that he knows s_i for every i.
7. (Shuffling) The receiver chooses a random permutation π on $\{1, \ldots, n\}$. Then he sends
$$(Y_1, \ldots, Y_n) \stackrel{\text{def}}{=} (X^c_{\pi(1)}, \ldots, X^c_{\pi(n)}).$$
He proves that there exist such π and c by using the ZK-PoM of Sec.3.2. The communication cost is $O(n)$.

The j-th Transfer Phase

1. The receiver obtains an index $1 \leq \sigma \leq n$.
2. The receiver sends $U = Y_{\pi^{-1}(\sigma)}$.
3. The sender checks $U \in \{Y_1, \ldots, Y_n\}$ and sends $V = U^x$.
4. The sender proves that (g, h, U, V) in ZK-PoM that it is a DDH-tuple.
5. Note
$$V = U^x = Y^x_{\pi^{-1}(\sigma)} = X^{cx}_{\pi(\pi^{-1}(\sigma))} = (g^{s_\sigma} A_\sigma)^{cx}$$
so that $V^{1/c} = (g^{s_\sigma} A_\sigma)^x$, and hence $V^{1/c} h^{-s_\sigma} = A^x_\sigma$. The receiver now obtains M_σ via B_σ / A^x_σ.

The ZK-PoKs in the initialization phase are exactly the well-known Schnorr proof [19]. The ZK-PoM in transfer phases can be implemented using Chaum's technique [2].

Relation with Kurosawa-Nojima [10]. In the scheme of Kurosawa and Nojima [10], there are no steps 5-7 of shuffles in the initialization phase. Furthermore, their steps 2 and 3 in each transfer phase are as follows. First, $U = A^u$ for random value $u \in Z_q$ and some $A \in G$, both chosen by the receiver. The receiver is then required to persuade the sender that $A = A_\sigma$ for some $\sigma \in \{1, \ldots, n\}$. Obviously, the receiver cannot reveal A_σ (since otherwise, σ is revealed as well). Kurosawa and Nojima solved in [10] by mixing σ with other indexes in $\{1, \ldots, n\}$. Namely, they forced the receiver to prove in WI-PoK that he knows some $u \in Z_q$ satisfying
$$U = A_1^u \vee \cdots \vee U = A_n^u.$$
The above WI-PoK, unfortunately, makes the communication cost of each transfer become $O(n)$.

In order to have $O(1)$ communication cost for each transfer phase, a possible method is to move the above WI-PoK to the initialization phase. Certainly, since the index σ of each transfer phase may be not chosen in advance, we move the WI-PoKs (each costs $O(n)$) corresponding to all possible n indexes, so that the communication cost of the initialization phase becomes $O(n^2)$. Moving further, we mix the indexes by shuffling, and fortunately, by making use of existing results [16], the cost is better reduced to $O(n)$, which is asymptotically minimal for the initialization phase.

4.2 Security

We now have the following theorems ensuring the security of our adaptive OT protocol.

Theorem 1. *The above adaptive OT protocol is secure against sender corruption under the DDH assumption.*

Proof. For every real-world adversary $\mathcal{A}$ who corrupts the sender, we construct an ideal-world adversary $\mathcal{A}'$ such that the advantage $\mathbf{Adv}(\mathcal{Z})$ is negligible.

We will consider a sequence of games beginning from game G_0, which is the real world experiment, and proceed to the final game, which is the ideal world experiment as in Sec.2.3. For each integer i, let

$$\Pr(G_i) = \Pr(\mathcal{Z} = 1 \text{ in game } G_i),$$

and denote $\Pr(G_i) \approx \Pr(G_j)$ when the two values are negligibly close.

Game G_0: This is the real world experiment such that the sender is controlled by the adversary $\mathcal{A}$. By definition $\Pr(G_0) = \Pr(\mathcal{Z} = 1 \text{ in the real world})$.

Game G_1: This game is the same as the previous one except the following. In the initialization phase, the receiver extracts x from $\mathcal{A}$ by using the knowledge extractor of the ZK-PoK.

If it fails, then the protocol stops. Since the failure occurs with negligible probability, we have $\Pr(G_0) \approx \Pr(G_1)$.

Game G_2: This game is the same as game G_1 except that, in the initialization phase, the game uses the zero-knowledge simulators of the ZK-PoK at steps 5-7. Since the protocol at step 7 is computational zero-knowledge under the DDH assumption, and the others are perfect [4], we have $\Pr(G_1) \approx \Pr(G_2)$.

Game G_3: This game is the same as the previous one except that in the initialization phase, the receiver sends random $(Y_1, \ldots, Y_n) \in G^n$ to the sender.

We will prove $\Pr(G_3) \approx \Pr(G_2)$. Before that, let us state the following established result.

Fact 2 (Naor, Reingold [15]). *There exists a poly-time algorithm* Q *that, on input* (g, g^c, X^*, Y^*), *outputs a random pair* $(X, Y) \in G^2$ *such that* (g, g^c, X, Y) *is a DDH tuple if and only if* (g, g^c, X^*, Y^*) *is.*

Lemma 3. $\Pr(G_3) \approx \Pr(G_2)$ *under the DDH assumption.*

Proof (of Lemma 3). By using $\mathcal{Z}$ and the corrupted sender $\mathcal{A}$, we construct a DDH distinguisher $\mathcal{D}$ as follows. On input $(g, C = g^c, X^*, Y^*)$, $\mathcal{D}$ first runs $\mathsf{Q}(g, C = g^c, X^*, Y^*)$ to generate the pairs $(X_1, Y_1), \ldots, (X_n, Y_n)$.

$\mathcal{D}$ next runs $\mathcal{Z}$ which sends $(M_1, \ldots, M_n)$ to $\mathcal{A}$ (the sender), and an index σ to the receiver. $\mathcal{A}$ and the receiver run the initialization phase until step 4. At step 5, $\mathcal{D}$ sends $C = g^c$ to $\mathcal{A}$, and runs the simulator of the ZK-PoK on c. At step 6, $\mathcal{D}$ sends the above $(X_1, \ldots, X_n)$ to $\mathcal{A}$, and runs the simulator of the ZK-PoK on $s_i (1 \leq i \leq n)$. At step 7, $\mathcal{D}$ sends the above $(Y_1, \ldots, Y_n)$ in random order to $\mathcal{A}$, and runs the zero-knowledge simulator of the shuffle protocol.

$\mathcal{A}$ and the receiver run the transfer phase as it is. Note that $\mathcal{D}$ can extract the secret key from $\mathcal{A}$, and hence extract M_i^* for all i (at the beginning), and $\mathcal{D}$ (playing the receiver) sends M_i^* to $\mathcal{Z}$ if necessary.

Finally, $\mathcal{A}$ sends $\mathcal{A}_{\text{out}}$ to $\mathcal{Z}$. The distinguisher $\mathcal{D}$ outputs what $\mathcal{Z}$ outputs.

One can see that if $\mathcal{D}$'s input $(g, C = g^c, X^*, Y^*)$ is a DDH tuple, then we are in game G_2; otherwise we are in game G_3, finishing the proof.

Game G_4: This game is the same as the previous one except the following. In each transfer phases, the receiver chooses U randomly and distinctly from the set $\{Y_1, \ldots, Y_n\}$. Since the view of $\mathcal{A}$ is unchanged, we have $\Pr(G_4) = \Pr(G_3)$.

Game G_5: This game is the ideal world experiment in which an ideal-world adversary $\mathcal{A}'$ uses $\mathcal{A}$ as a black-box as follows.

1. $\mathcal{A}'$ receives $(M_1, \ldots, M_n)$ from $\mathcal{Z}$, and sends $(M_1, \ldots, M_n)$ to $\mathcal{A}$.
2. $\mathcal{A}'$ runs **Game** G_4 with $\mathcal{A}$, where $\mathcal{A}'$ plays the role of the receiver. She can do this because σ (which is the secret of the receiver) is not used in **Game** G_4.
3. In the initialization phase, $\mathcal{A}'$ computes $M_i^* = B_i/(A_i)^x$ for all i by using x (which is extracted in **Game** G_1), and sends $(M_1^*, \ldots, M_n^*)$ to $\mathcal{F}_{\text{adapt}}$.
4. In each transfer phase, if $\mathcal{A}$ behaved in an acceptable way, then $\mathcal{A}'$ sends $b = 1$ to $\mathcal{F}_{\text{adapt}}$. Otherwise $\mathcal{A}'$ sends $b = 0$ to $\mathcal{F}_{\text{adapt}}$.
5. Suppose that $\mathcal{A}$ sends $\mathcal{A}_{\text{out}}$ to $\mathcal{Z}$ at the end of the game. Then $\mathcal{A}'$ sends $\mathcal{A}'_{\text{out}} = \mathcal{A}_{\text{out}}$ to $\mathcal{Z}$.

We have $\Pr(G_4) = \Pr(G_5)$, and by definition $\Pr(\mathcal{Z} = 1 \text{ in the ideal world}) = \Pr(G_5)$. Summing up all above, we have $\mathbf{Adv}(\mathcal{Z}) = |\Pr(G_0) - \Pr(G_5)|$ is negligible as required. □

Theorem 4. *The above adaptive OT protocol is secure against receiver corruption under the DDH assumption.*

Proof. For every real-world adversary $\mathcal{A}$ who corrupts the receiver, we construct an ideal-world adversary $\mathcal{A}'$ such that the advantage of the environment $\mathbf{Adv}(\mathcal{Z})$ is negligible.

We again consider a sequence of games $G_0, \ldots, G_6$, where G_0 is the real world experiment of Sec.2.3, while G_6 is the ideal world experiment. Again, let $\Pr(G_i) = \Pr(\mathcal{Z} = 1 \text{ in game } G_i)$.

Game G_0: In this game the receiver is controlled by the adversary $\mathcal{A}$, and by definition $\Pr(G_0) = \Pr(\mathcal{Z} = 1 \text{ in the real world})$.

Game G_1: This game is the same as game G_0 except the following. In the initialization phase, the sender extracts c and s_i by using the extractors of the ZK-PoK.

If it fails, then the protocol fails. Since this failure occurs with negligible probability, we have $\Pr(G_1) \approx \Pr(G_0)$.

Game G_2: This game is the same as the previous one except the following. First the sender extracts π by comparing $(X_1^c, \ldots, X_n^c)$ and $(Y_1, \ldots, Y_n)$. Next in each transfer phase, the sender extracts the index σ that $\mathcal{A}$ really used as follows.

$\mathcal{A}$ sends U such that $U \in \{Y_1, \ldots, Y_n\}$. The sender searches the index ρ satisfying $U = Y_\rho$. Recall $U = Y_{\pi^{-1}(\sigma)}$, so $\pi^{-1}(\sigma) = \rho$, and hence $\sigma = \pi(\rho)$. Thus the sender can extract σ that $\mathcal{A}$ really used. Since the change is syntactic, we have $\Pr(G_2) = \Pr(G_1)$.

Game G_3: This game is the same as the previous one except the following. In each transfer phase, the sender computes V as $(B_\sigma M_\sigma^{-1} h^{s_\sigma})^c$. Since the change is syntactic, we have $\Pr(G_3) = \Pr(G_2)$.

Game G_4: This game is the same as the previous one except the following. In each transfer phase, instead of running the ZK-PoM which proves that (g, h, U, V) is a DDH-tuple, the zero-knowledge simulator of the ZK-PoM is run so that $\Pr(G_4) \approx \Pr(G_3)$.

Game G_5: This game is the same as the previous one except the following. In the initialization phase, each B_i is a random element of G. It is easy to see that $\Pr(G_5) \approx \Pr(G_4)$ under the DDH assumption.

Game G_6: This game is the ideal world experiment in which an ideal-world adversary $\mathcal{A}'$ uses $\mathcal{A}$ as a black-box as follows.

1. $\mathcal{A}'$ runs **Game** G_5 with $\mathcal{A}$, where $\mathcal{A}'$ plays the role of the sender.
2. In each transfer phase, $\mathcal{A}'$ sends σ which is extracted as in **Game** G_2 to $\mathcal{F}_{\text{adapt}}$, and obtains M_σ. $\mathcal{A}'$ then computes V as in **Game** G_3.
3. Suppose that $\mathcal{A}$ sends $\mathcal{A}_{\text{out}}$ to $\mathcal{Z}$ at the end of the game. Then $\mathcal{A}'$ sends $\mathcal{A}'_{\text{out}} = \mathcal{A}_{\text{out}}$ to $\mathcal{Z}$.

We have by definition $\Pr(G_6) = \Pr(\mathcal{Z} = 1 \text{ in the ideal world})$. Summing up all above, we have $\mathbf{Adv}(\mathcal{Z}) = |\Pr(G_0) - \Pr(G_6)|$ is negligible as required. □

References

1. Camenisch, J., Neven, G., Shelat, A.: Simulatable adaptive oblivious transfer. In: Naor, M. (ed.) EUROCRYPT 2007. LNCS, vol. 4515, pp. 573–590. Springer, Heidelberg (2007)
2. Chaum, D.: Zero-knowledge undeniable signatures. In: Damgård, I.B. (ed.) EUROCRYPT 1990. LNCS, vol. 473, pp. 458–464. Springer, Heidelberg (1991)

3. Chu, C.-K., Tzeng, W.-G.: Efficient 1-out-of-n oblivious transfer schemes with adaptive and non-adaptive queries. In: Vaudenay, S. (ed.) PKC 2005. LNCS, vol. 3386, pp. 172–183. Springer, Heidelberg (2005)
4. Cramer, R., Damgård, I., MacKenzie, P.D.: Efficient zero-knowledge proofs of knowledge without intractability assumptions. In: Imai, H., Zheng, Y. (eds.) PKC 2000. LNCS, vol. 1751, pp. 354–373. Springer, Heidelberg (2000)
5. Goldreich, O., Kahan, A.: How to construct constant-round zero-knowledge proof systems for np. J. Cryptology 9(3), 167–190 (1996)
6. Green, M., Hohenberger, S.: Universally composable adaptive oblivious transfer. In: Pieprzyk, J. (ed.) ASIACRYPT 2008. LNCS, vol. 5350, pp. 179–197. Springer, Heidelberg (2008)
7. Green, M., Hohenberger, S.: Practical adaptive oblivious transfer from a simple assumption. Cryptology ePrint Archive, Report 2010/109 (2010), `http://eprint.iacr.org/`
8. Jarecki, S., Liu, X.: Efficient oblivious pseudorandom function with applications to adaptive ot and secure computation of set intersection. In: Reingold, O. (ed.) TCC 2009. LNCS, vol. 5444, pp. 577–594. Springer, Heidelberg (2009)
9. Kalai, Y.T.: Smooth projective hashing and two-message oblivious transfer. In: Cramer, R. (ed.) EUROCRYPT 2005. LNCS, vol. 3494, pp. 78–95. Springer, Heidelberg (2005)
10. Kurosawa, K., Nojima, R.: Simple adaptive oblivious transfer without random oracle. In: Matsui, M. (ed.) ASIACRYPT 2009. LNCS, vol. 5912, pp. 334–346. Springer, Heidelberg (2009)
11. Naor, M., Pinkas, B.: Oblivious transfer and polynomial evaluation. In: STOC, pp. 245–254 (1999)
12. Naor, M., Pinkas, B.: Oblivious transfer with adaptive queries. In: Wiener, M. J. (ed.) CRYPTO 1999. LNCS, vol. 1666, pp. 573–590. Springer, Heidelberg (1999)
13. Naor, M., Pinkas, B.: Efficient oblivious transfer protocols. In: SODA, pp. 448–457 (2001)
14. Naor, M., Pinkas, B.: Computationally secure oblivious transfer. J. Cryptology 18(1), 1–35 (2005)
15. Naor, M., Reingold, O.: Number-theoretic constructions of efficient pseudo-random functions. J. ACM 51(2), 231–262 (2004)
16. Neff, C.A.: A verifiable secret shuffle and its application to e-voting. In: ACM Conference on Computer and Communications Security, pp. 116–125 (2001)
17. Neff, C.A.: Shuffles of ElGamal pairs (2004), `http://people.csail.mit.edu/rivest/voting/`
18. Ogata, W., Kurosawa, K.: Oblivious keyword search. J. Complexity 20(2-3), 356–371 (2004), `http://eprint.iacr.org/2002/182`
19. Schnorr, C.-P.: Efficient signature generation by smart cards. J. Cryptology 4(3), 161–174 (1991)

Improved Primitives for Secure Multiparty Integer Computation

Octavian Catrina[1] and Sebastiaan de Hoogh[2]

[1] Dept. of Computer Science, University of Mannheim, Germany
Octavian.Catrina@uni-mannheim.de
[2] Dept. of Mathematics and Computer Science, TU Eindhoven, The Netherlands
S.J.A.d.Hoogh@tue.nl

Abstract. We consider a collection of related multiparty computation protocols that provide core operations for secure integer and fixed-point computation. The higher-level protocols offer integer truncation and comparison, which are typically the main performance bottlenecks in complex applications. We present techniques and building blocks that allow to improve the efficiency of these protocols, in order to meet the performance requirements of a broader range of applications. The protocols can be constructed using different secure computation methods. We focus on solutions for multiparty computation using secret sharing.

Keywords: Secure multiparty computation, secret sharing, secure integer arithmetic, secure comparison.

1 Introduction

The aim of secure computation is to enable a group of mutually distrustful parties to run a joint computation with private inputs. This goal is achieved using cryptographic protocols that carry out the computation without revealing the parties' inputs and ensure that the output is correct.

Applications are found in various areas, including e-voting [10], auctions with secret bids [12], benchmarking with confidential performance indicators [18], collaborative linear programming [25] and supply chain planning [3]. However, the overhead of the cryptographic protocols makes secure computation much slower than usual computation with public data. Improved solutions have emerged for many primitives and application-specific tasks, but meeting the functional, security, and performance requirements of the applications is still a challenge.

In this paper, we focus on improving several related integer computation protocols that support and complement the protocols for fixed-point arithmetic introduced in [6]. The higher level protocols provide accurate truncation (core component for fixed-point arithmetic) and comparison (inequality and equality). These operations are the main performance bottlenecks in complex applications (e.g., multiparty linear programming).

The protocols can be instantiated using secret sharing [8] or homomorphic encryption [9]. We focus on solutions based on secret sharing, semi-honest model, and statistical privacy, which are more suitable for complex applications.

J.A. Garay and R. De Prisco (Eds.): SCN 2010, LNCS 6280, pp. 182–199, 2010.

Our contributions. We specify a collection of related protocols for several operations that determine the performance of secure integer and fixed-point computation, namely comparison and truncation. The protocols are based on few building blocks and the same security model, and thus simplify the development of applications and the analysis of their complexity and security. The main goal of the paper is to present techniques and building blocks that reduce the complexity of these protocols in order to meet the requirements of a broader range of applications. We combine several approaches, improving the efficiency of data encoding (adapted to data type), core tasks (generation of secret random values, inner product), and the main building blocks (k-ary and prefix operations, bitwise comparison). Moreover, we give building blocks for different trade-offs between communication and round complexity, so that the protocols can be adapted to applications and execution environment (network bandwidth and delay).

Related Work. We use standard techniques for multiparty computation based on secret sharing, similar to [5,8,11,24,19,4]. Also, the protocols used for generating shared random values and for share conversions rely on techniques proposed in [7,13,14] in order to reduce the communication overhead. We take, however, a more pragmatic approach, allowing more flexibility in the design of the protocols and focusing on solutions that are more suitable for practical applications, while [11,24] aim at achieving perfect privacy and constant round complexity. Protocols with statistical privacy are often more efficient, while those with logarithmic round complexity often have lower communication complexity.

There is a vast literature on secure integer arithmetic. Our approach is related to a large pool of common techniques and protocols [24,11,19,20,15]. We develop more efficient protocols for k-ary and prefix boolean functions, bitwise comparison, and other building blocks. Efficient but approximate truncation is given in [2]; our protocols offer accurate truncation, required by fixed-point arithmetic.

2 Core Protocols

The protocols presented in Sections 3 and 4 are constructed using abstract primitives that can be instantiated using secret sharing [8] or homomorphic encryption [9]. Solutions based on secret sharing are more efficient and suitable for our target applications. Multiparty computation using secret sharing proceeds as follows. Assume a group of $n > 2$ parties, $P_1, \ldots, P_n$, that communicate on secure channels and run a computation where party P_i, $i \in [1..n]$, has private input x_i and expects output y_i. The parties use a linear secret sharing scheme to create a distributed state of the computation where each party has a share of each secret variable. The secret sharing scheme allows to compute with shared variables and provides controlled access to secret values. Sub-tasks take on input shared data and return shared data, and thus enable secure composition.

The protocols offer perfect or statistical privacy, meaning that the views of protocol execution (all values learned by an adversary) can be simulated such that the distributions of real and simulated views are perfectly or statistically indistinguishable, respectively. Let X and Y be distributions with finite sample spaces V and W and $\Delta(X,Y) = \frac{1}{2}\sum_{v \in V \bigcup W} |Pr(X = v) - Pr(Y = v)|$ the statistical distance between them. We say that the distributions are perfectly indistinguishable if $\Delta(X,Y) = 0$ and statistically indistinguishable if $\Delta(X,Y)$ is negligible in some security parameter. The core of the system consists of protocols for secure arithmetic in a finite field $\mathbb{F}$ using Shamir secret sharing. These protocols provide perfect privacy against a passive threshold adversary that corrupts t out of n parties. In this model, the parties do not deviate from the protocol and any $t+1$ parties can reconstruct a secret, while t or less parties cannot distinguish it from uniformly random values in $\mathbb{F}$. We assume $|\mathbb{F}| > n$ to enable Shamir sharing and $n > 2t$ for multiplication of shared values. We denote $[x]^{\mathbb{F}}$ a Shamir sharing of x in field $\mathbb{F}$; if not specified, the field is $\mathbb{Z}_q$.

Complexity metrics. We use two metrics that reflect different aspects of the interaction between parties. Communication complexity measures the amount of data sent by each party. For our protocols, a suitable abstract metric is the number of invocations of a primitive during which every party sends a share (field element) to the others (Table 1). Round complexity is the number of sequential invocations and is relevant for the network delay, independent of the amount of data. Invocations that can be executed in parallel count as a single round.

Data representation. We consider secure computation with the following data types: binary values, signed integers $\mathbb{Z}_{\langle k \rangle} = \{\bar{x} \in \mathbb{Z} \mid -2^{k-1} \leq \bar{x} \leq 2^{k-1} - 1\}$, and fixed-point rational numbers $\mathbb{Q}_{\langle k,f \rangle} = \{\tilde{x} \in \mathbb{Q} \mid \tilde{x} = \bar{x} \cdot 2^{-f}, \bar{x} \in \mathbb{Z}_{\langle k \rangle}\}$. These data types are encoded in a field $\mathbb{F}$ as follows.

Logical values $false, true$ and bit values $0, 1$ are encoded as 0_F and 1_F, respectively. $\mathbb{F}$ can be a small binary field $\mathbb{F}_{2^m}$ or prime field $\mathbb{Z}_q$. This encoding allows secure evaluation of boolean functions using secure arithmetic in $\mathbb{F}$.

Signed integers are encoded in $\mathbb{Z}_q$ using the mapping $\mathsf{fld} : \mathbb{Z}_{\langle k \rangle} \mapsto \mathbb{Z}_q$, $\mathsf{fld}(\bar{x}) = \bar{x} \bmod q$, $q > 2^k$. Secure arithmetic with signed integers is computed using secure arithmetic in $\mathbb{Z}_q$: for any $\bar{a}, \bar{b} \in \mathbb{Z}_{\langle k \rangle}$ and $\odot \in \{+, -, \cdot\}$ we have $\bar{a} \odot \bar{b} = \mathsf{fld}^{-1}(\mathsf{fld}(\bar{a}) \odot \mathsf{fld}(\bar{b}))$; moreover, if $\bar{b}|\bar{a}$ then $\bar{a}/\bar{b} = \mathsf{fld}^{-1}(\mathsf{fld}(\bar{a}) \cdot \mathsf{fld}(\bar{b})^{-1})$.

A fixed-point rational number $\tilde{x} \in \mathbb{Q}_{\langle k,f \rangle}$ is encoded as an integer $\bar{x} = \tilde{x}2^f \in \mathbb{Z}_{\langle k \rangle}$ and mapped to $\mathbb{Z}_q$ as described above; f and k are public parameters. Secure fixed-point multiplication and division require $q > 2^{2k}$ [6].

Encoding all data types in the same field $\mathbb{Z}_q$ avoids share conversions and thus simplifies the protocols. However, for larger q the running time can be reduced by encoding binary values in small fields.

Notation. We distinguish different representations of a number as follows: we denote $\tilde{x}$ a fixed-point rational number, $\bar{x}$ the integer value of its fixed-point representation, x the field element that encodes $\bar{x}$ (and hence $\tilde{x}$), $[x]$ a sharing of x, and $[x]_i$ the share of party P_i. The notation $x = (\texttt{condition})?\, a : b$ means that the variable x is assigned the value a when `condition`=*true* and b otherwise.

Secret random values. Suppose that the parties want to evaluate a function with secret input $[x]$. The task can often be achieved more efficiently using

Table 1. Complexity of core protocols

Protocol	Rounds	Inv.	Protocol	Rounds	Inv.
$[c]^{\mathbb{F}} \leftarrow [a]^{\mathbb{F}} + [b]^{\mathbb{F}}$	0	0	$[r] \leftarrow \mathsf{PRandFld}(\mathbb{F})$	0	0
$[c]^{\mathbb{F}} \leftarrow [a]^{\mathbb{F}}[b]^{\mathbb{F}}$	1	1	$[r] \leftarrow \mathsf{PRandInt}(k)$	0	0
$[c]^{\mathbb{F}} \leftarrow [a]^{\mathbb{F}}b$; $[c]^{\mathbb{F}} \leftarrow [a]^{\mathbb{F}} + b$	0	0	$[r] \leftarrow \mathsf{PRandBit}()$	1	1 $\mathbb{Z}_q$
$a \leftarrow \mathsf{Output}([a]^{\mathbb{F}})$	1	1	$[r] \leftarrow \mathsf{PRandBitL}()$	2	2 $\mathbb{Z}_{q_1}$
$[z] \leftarrow \mathsf{Inner}([X]^{\mathbb{F}}, [Y]^{\mathbb{F}})$	1	1	$c \leftarrow \mathsf{MulPub}([a], [b])$	1	1 $\mathbb{Z}_q$

Protocol	Rounds	Inv.
$[r''], [r'], [r'_{m-1}], \ldots, [r'_0] \leftarrow \mathsf{PRandM}()$	1	m $\mathbb{Z}_q$
$[r]^{\mathbb{F}_{2^8}}, [r] \leftarrow \mathsf{PRandBitD}()$	2	2 $\mathbb{Z}_{q_1}$
$[b]^{\mathbb{F}_{2^8}} \leftarrow \mathsf{BitZQtoF256}([b]^{\mathbb{Z}_q})$	1	1 $\mathbb{Z}_q$
$[b]^{\mathbb{Z}_q} \leftarrow \mathsf{BitF256ToZQ}([b]^{\mathbb{F}_{2^8}}, [r]^{\mathbb{F}_{2^8}}, [r]^{\mathbb{Z}_q})$	1	1 $\mathbb{F}_{2^8}$

the following technique. The parties jointly generate a shared random value $[r]$, compute $[y] = [x] + [r]$ or $[y] = [x][r]$, and reveal y. Then, they evaluate the function using $[x]$, $[r]$, and y. We obtain $\Delta(x+r, r) = 0$ for $x \in \mathbb{F}$ and uniformly random $r \in \mathbb{F}$ and $\Delta(xr, r) = 0$ for $x \in \mathbb{F}\backslash\{0\}$ and uniformly random $r \in \mathbb{F}\backslash\{0\}$, hence perfect privacy. This is similar to one-time pad encryption of x with key r. Alternatively, for $x \in [0..2^k - 1]$ and random uniform $r \in [0..2^{k+\kappa} - 1]$ we obtain $\Delta(x + r, r) < 2^{-\kappa}$, hence statistical privacy with security parameter κ (only for addition). In this variant, taking $q > 2^{k+\kappa}$ avoids wraparound modulo q when computing $[x] + [r]$ and simplifies certain protocols; the efficiency gain is important (e.g., by eliminating a secure comparison) despite the larger shares.

A shared random integer $r \in [0..2^{k+\kappa} - 1]$ with uniform distribution is usually obtained by generating $k + \kappa$ shared random bits $b_0, \ldots, b_{k+\kappa-1}$ and computing $r = \sum_{i=0}^{k+\kappa-1} 2^i b_i$. However, statistical privacy is also achieved for distributions that can be computed more efficiently and/or have particular properties: (1) $r = \sum_i r_i$, for uniformly random $r_i \in [0..2^{k+\kappa} - 1]$; (2) $r = r' + 2^m r''$, where $r' = \sum_{i=0}^{m-1} 2^i b_i$ and $r'' = \sum_i r_i$, for uniformly random $b_i \in \{0, 1\}$ and $r_i \in [0..2^{k+\kappa-m} - 1]$ (Annex A, Theorems 1, 2). We use the second construction for protocols that need $[r'] = [r \bmod 2^m]$ and/or the binary representation of $[r']$.

Shared random values can be generated without interaction using Pseudo-random Replicated Secret Sharing (PRSS) [7] and its integer variant RISS [13]. We define several protocols that use these techniques. $\mathsf{PRandFld}(\mathbb{F})$ generates a uniformly random element of field $\mathbb{F}$ and $\mathsf{PRandInt}(k)$ a random integer $r = \sum_{i=1}^{N} r_i$, for uniformly random $r_i \in [0..2^{k+\kappa} - 1]$ and $N = \binom{n}{t}$. $\mathsf{PRandInt}$ requires a slightly larger modulus, $q > 2^{k+\kappa+\nu}$, $\nu = \lceil \log(N) \rceil$. $\mathsf{MulPub}([a], [b])$ computes the product of two shared field elements with public output as follows: the parties generate a pseudo-random sharing of zero (PRZS [7]) for a polynomial of degree $2t$; each party P_i computes a randomized product of shares $[c]_i = [a]_i[b]_i + [0]_i$; then they exchange the shares and reconstruct $c = ab$. PRSS reduces the complexity of these protocols by 1 round and 1 invocation. Protocol 2.1, $\mathsf{PRandBit}$, returns a shared random bit encoded in $\mathbb{Z}_q$. It combines the protocol $\mathsf{RandBit}$

in [11] and PRSS. Finally, Protocol 2.2, PRandM, generates the shared random integers $[r']$ and $[r'']$ defined above, together with the shared bits of r'.

Protocol 2.1. $[b] \leftarrow \mathsf{PRandBit}()$

$[r] \leftarrow \mathsf{PRandFld}(\mathbb{Z}_q)$;
$u \leftarrow \mathsf{MulPub}([r],[r])$; // 1 rnd, 1 inv; repeat if $u = 0$, pr $= \frac{1}{q}$
$v \leftarrow u^{-(q+1)/4} \bmod q$; // square root; requires $q \bmod 4 = 3$
$[b] \leftarrow (v[r]+1)(2^{-1} \bmod q)$;
return $[b]$;

Protocol 2.2. $([r''],[r'],[b_{m-1}],\ldots,[b_0]) \leftarrow \mathsf{PRandM}(k,m)$

$[r''] \leftarrow \mathsf{PRandInt}(k+\kappa-m)$;
foreach $i \in [0..m-1]$ **do** $[b_i] \leftarrow \mathsf{PRandBit}(q)$; // 1 rnd, m inv
$[r'] \leftarrow \sum_{i=0}^{m-1} 2^i [b_i]$;
return $[r''],[r'],[b_{m-1}],\ldots,[b_0]$;

Table 1 lists several protocols for generating shared random bits encoded in small fields, $\mathbb{F}_{2^8}$ and $\mathbb{Z}_{q_1}$, $q_1 > 2^{\kappa+\nu}$, and for bit-share conversions using RISS [14]. PRandBitL generates a random bit shared in $\mathbb{Z}_{q_1}$ and then converts its shares to the target field $\mathbb{Z}_q$. PRandBitD uses a similar technique to generate a random bit shared in both $\mathbb{Z}_q$ and $\mathbb{F}_{2^8}$. Bit-shares in $\mathbb{Z}_q$ are used to construct a random uniform integer, while bit-shares in $\mathbb{F}_{2^8}$ are used for binary computation.

Experiments with an implementation of the protocols [22] showed that these techniques reduce significantly the running time for computation with large integers (or fixed-point numbers): PRandM allows to generate a minimum number of shared random bits, while bit encoding in small fields reduces the communication complexity (smaller shares) as well as the computation complexity (the exponentiation in PRandBit becomes expensive for $\log(q) \approx \log(u) > 256$ bits).

We evaluate the complexity of the protocols assuming that all shared random values are precomputed in parallel using the protocols listed in Table 1. Note that the complexity of PRSS grows quite fast with n. A scalable solution is to run the protocols on a small number of semi-trusted servers [7,12]. Our protocols use PRSS only as an optimization for generating shared random values.

Inner product protocol. Given two shared vectors $[X]$ and $[Y]$, $X, Y \in \mathbb{F}^m$, the obvious method for computing the inner product, $[z] = \sum_{i=1}^{m}[X(i)][Y(i)]$, requires m secure multiplications. We present a more efficient method, that reduces the communication complexity to a single invocation. Assume Shamir sharing for n parties with threshold $t < n/2$. Denote $[X(i)]_j$, $[Y(i)]_j$, $i \in [1..m]$, the input shares and $[z]_j$ the output share of party P_j. The protocol, called Inner, proceeds as follows:

1. Party P_j, $j \in [1..n]$, computes $d_j = \sum_{i=1}^{m}([X(i)]_j[Y(i)]_j)$ and then shares d_j sending $[d_j]_k$ to party P_k, $k \in [1..n]$.

2. Party P_k, $k \in [1..n]$, computes the share $[z]_k = \sum_{j \in J} \lambda_j [d_j]_k$, where $J \subseteq [1..n]$, $|J| = 2t+1$, and $\{\lambda_j\}_{j \in J}$ is the reconstruction vector for J.

The protocol is a generalization of the secure multiplication of Shamir-shared field elements [16]. The proofs of correctness and security are similar.

Security. For a passive adversary that can corrupt $t < n/2$ parties, the protocols presented in the following can leak information only in steps where they reconstruct shared values. These values are of the form $y = x + r$, where $x \in [0..2^k - 1]$ is the secret and r is a random value constructed using PRandM as described above. It follows from Theorem 2 (Annex A) that $\Delta(y, r) < 2^{-\kappa}$. Since the sub-protocols provide perfect privacy or statistical privacy with the security parameter κ, we conclude that our protocols provide statistical privacy.

Security against an active adversary that can corrupt $t < n/3$ parties can be achieved using several known methods. A variant of the protocols without PRSS can use any extension of Shamir's secret sharing to verifiable secret sharing (VSS) and an associated multiplication proof (e.g., [16,1,8]). An efficient solution for a variant that uses PRSS can be obtained based on the VSS and multiplication proof in [7,13]. The evaluation of these approaches (in particular, of efficient proofs for the inner product) is the subject of on-going work.

3 Integer Arithmetic and Comparison Protocols

Truncation (division by 2^m). The purpose of the truncation protocols is to compute $\lfloor \bar{a}/2^m \rfloor + u$, where $\bar{a} \in \mathbb{Z}_{\langle k \rangle}$, $m \in [1..k-1]$, and $u \in \{0, 1\}$. The bit u depends on the rounding method: $u = 0$ for rounding down, $u = 1$ for rounding up, and $u = (\bar{a}/2^m - \lfloor \bar{a}/2^m \rfloor \geq 0.5)?\ 1 : 0$ for rounding to the nearest integer. Truncation protocols are core components in secure fixed-point arithmetic. We start by reviewing an efficient protocol introduced in [6].

Protocol 3.1, TruncPR, takes on input a secret-shared signed integer $\bar{a} \in \mathbb{Z}_{\langle k \rangle}$ and a public integer $m \in [1..k-1]$, and returns a sharing of $\bar{d} = \lfloor \bar{a}/2^m \rfloor + u$, where $u \in \{0, 1\}$ is a random bit. The protocol rounds to the nearest integer with probability $1 - \alpha$, where α is the distance between $\bar{a}/2^m$ and that integer.

Protocol 3.1. $[d] \leftarrow \mathsf{TruncPR}([a], k, m)$

$([r''], [r'], [r'_{m-1}], \ldots, [r'_0]) \leftarrow \mathsf{PRandM}(k, m)$; `// 1 rnd, m inv`
$c \leftarrow \mathsf{Output}(2^{k-1} + [a] + 2^m[r''] + [r'])$; `// 1 rnd, 1 inv`
$c' \leftarrow c \bmod 2^m$;
$[d] \leftarrow ([a] - c' + [r'])(2^{-m} \bmod q)$;
return $[d]$;

Correctness: Recall that $\bar{a} \in \mathbb{Z}_{\langle k \rangle}$ is encoded in $\mathbb{Z}_q$ as $a = \bar{a} \bmod q$. Let $b = (2^{k-1} + a) \bmod q$, $b' = b \bmod 2^m$, and $a' = \bar{a} \bmod 2^m$. Observe that $b \in [0..2^k - 1]$ and $b' = a'$ for any $0 < m < k$. The protocol generates a random secret $r = 2^m r'' + r'$, $r \in [0..2^{k+\kappa+\nu} - 1]$ as explained in Section 2, reveals $c = (b + r) \bmod q =$

$b+r$, and then computes $c' = c \bmod 2^m$. From $c' = (b'+r') \bmod 2^m$ it follows that $c'-r' = b'-2^m u = a'-2^m u$, where $u \in \{0,1\}$. Step 4 computes $d' = (\bar{a}-a'+2^m u) \bmod q = (2^m \lfloor \bar{a}/2^m \rfloor + 2^m u) \bmod q$ and then $d = d'(2^{-m} \bmod q) \bmod q = (\lfloor \bar{a}/2^m \rfloor + u) \bmod q$, hence d encodes $\lfloor \bar{a}/2^m \rfloor + u$. Observe that $Pr(u=1) = Pr(r'+a' \geq 2^m)$, which implies the rounding property.

We extend the method used by TruncPR in order to compute $\bar{a} \bmod 2^m$ and $\lfloor \bar{a}/2^m \rfloor$. The additional task is to determine u. Observe that $u = (c' < r')?1:0$ and can be computed using bitwise comparison. This task is achieved by the protocol BitLT (Section 4). We split the computation in two parts: Protocol 3.2, Mod2m, computes $\bar{a} \bmod 2^m$ and Protocol 3.3, Trunc, computes $\lfloor \bar{a}/2^m \rfloor$.

Protocol 3.4, Mod2, handles the case $m = 1$ (extracts the least significant bit). Mod2 is an essential component of the protocols presented in Section 4.

Protocol 3.2. $[a'] \leftarrow \mathsf{Mod2m}([a], k, m)$

$([r''], [r'], [r'_{m-1}], \ldots, [r'_0]) \leftarrow \mathsf{PRandM}(k, m);$ // 1 rnd, m inv
$c \leftarrow \mathsf{Output}(2^{k-1} + [a] + 2^m[r''] + [r']);$ // 1 rnd, 1 inv
$c' \leftarrow c \bmod 2^m;$
$[u] \leftarrow \mathsf{BitLT}(c', ([r'_{m-1}], \ldots, [r'_0]));$ // Tables 3, 4
$[a'] \leftarrow c' - [r'] + 2^m[u];$
return $[a']$;

Protocol 3.3. $[d] \leftarrow \mathsf{Trunc}([a], k, m)$

$[a'] \leftarrow \mathsf{Mod2m}([a], k, m);$ // Table 5
$[d] \leftarrow ([a] - [a'])(2^{-m} \bmod q);$
return $[d]$;

Protocol 3.4. $[a_0] \leftarrow \mathsf{Mod2}([a], k)$

$([r''], [r'], [r'_0]) \leftarrow \mathsf{PRandM}(k, 1);$ // 1 rnd, 1 inv
$c \leftarrow \mathsf{Output}(2^{k-1} + [a] + 2[r''] + [r'_0]);$ // 1 rnd, 1 inv
$[a_0] \leftarrow c_0 + [r'_0] - 2c_0[r'_0];$
return $[a_0]$;

Truncation with deterministic rounding to the nearest integer can be obtained by adding to Protocol 3.3 the following steps: $[v] \leftarrow \mathsf{LTZ}([a'] - 2^{m-1}, m)$ and $[e] \leftarrow [d]+1-[v]$, where LTZ computes $(a' < 2^{m-1})?\,1:0$. However, this solution is much more complex than TruncPR.

Integer division with public divisor. Truncation can be generalized in order to obtain protocols that on input a shared $\bar{a} \in \mathbb{Z}_{\langle k \rangle}$ and a public $x \in [1..2^{k-1}-1]$ compute shares of the quotient $\lfloor \bar{a}/x \rfloor$ and the remainder $\bar{a} \bmod x$. Division can better be handled by secure fixed-point arithmetic [6]. However, integer division with public divisor is relatively simple, and sufficient for some applications [17].

One approach is to adapt Mod2m by replacing 2^m with x. This generalization was first observed in [17]. However, generating a secret r' with uniform distribution in

$[0..x-1]$ instead of $[0..2^m-1]$ is more complex. Let $m = \lceil \log(x) \rceil$. The method used in [17] generates $r' \in [0..2^m-1]$ from random bits and tests if $r' < x$. This method succeeds after $2^m/x < 2$ iterations on average, but the iterations include secure comparisons and are expensive. Protocol 3.5, Mod, avoids the iterative search for r' at the cost of replacing a bitwise comparison by an integer comparison. The protocol for computing the quotient is similar to Trunc.

Correctness: Let $b = (2^{k-1}+a) \bmod q$ and $b' = b \bmod x = \bar{a} \bmod x$. The protocol generates the secret random $r = xr'' + r'$ with $r' \in [0..2^m-1]$, reveals $c = b+r$, and computes $c' = c \bmod x$. Observe that $r \bmod x = r' \bmod x = r' - xv$, where $v = (r' \geq x)?1 : 0$. Furthermore, $c' = (b' + (r' \bmod x)) \bmod x = (b' + r' - xv) \bmod x$, hence $b' = c' - r' + xv + xu$, where $u = (c' < r' - xv)?1 : 0$. Choosing $r' \in [0..2^m-1]$ instead of $r' \in [0..x-1]$ preserves statistical privacy.

Protocol 3.5. $[a'] \leftarrow \mathsf{Mod}([a], k, x)$

$m \leftarrow \lceil \log(x) \rceil$;
$([r''], [r'], [r'_{m-1}], \ldots, [r'_0]) \leftarrow \mathsf{PRandM}(k, m)$; // 1 rnd, m inv
$c \leftarrow \mathsf{Output}(2^{k-1} + [a] + x \cdot [r''] + [r'])$; // 1 rnd, 1 inv
$c' \leftarrow c \bmod x$;
$[v] \leftarrow 1 - \mathsf{BitLT}(([r'_{m-1}], \ldots, [r'_0]), x)$; // Tables 3, 4
$[u] \leftarrow \mathsf{LTZ}(c' - [r'] + x[v], m)$; // Table 5
$[a'] \leftarrow c' - [r'] + x([v] + [u])$;
return $[a']$;

Inequality and equality. The family of secure integer comparison operators with secret inputs and outputs (Table 2) can be constructed based on two primitives: Protocol 3.6, $\mathsf{LTZ}([a], k)$, that computes $(\bar{a} < 0)?1 : 0$, and Protocol 3.7, $\mathsf{EQZ}([a], k)$, that computes $(\bar{a} = 0)?1 : 0$, for $\bar{a} \in \mathbb{Z}_{\langle k \rangle}$.

Table 2. Protocols for integer comparison

Op.	Protocol	Construction	Op.	Protocol	Construction
$a = 0$	$\mathsf{EQZ}(a)$	Primitive	$a = b$	$\mathsf{EQ}(a,b)$	$\mathsf{EQ}(a,b) = \mathsf{EQZ}(a-b)$
$a < 0$	$\mathsf{LTZ}(a)$	Primitive (sign of a)	$a < b$	$\mathsf{LT}(a,b)$	$\mathsf{LT}(a,b) = \mathsf{LTZ}(a-b)$
$a > 0$	$\mathsf{GTZ}(a)$	$\mathsf{GTZ}(a) = \mathsf{LTZ}(-a)$	$a > b$	$\mathsf{GT}(a,b)$	$\mathsf{GT}(a,b) = \mathsf{LTZ}(b-a)$
$a \leq 0$	$\mathsf{LEZ}(a)$	$\mathsf{LEZ}(a) = 1 - \mathsf{LTZ}(-a)$	$a \leq b$	$\mathsf{LE}(a,b)$	$\mathsf{LE}(a,b) = 1 - \mathsf{LTZ}(b-a)$
$a \geq 0$	$\mathsf{GEZ}(a)$	$\mathsf{GEZ}(a) = 1 - \mathsf{LTZ}(a)$	$a \geq b$	$\mathsf{GE}(a,b)$	$\mathsf{GE}(a,b) = 1 - \mathsf{LTZ}(a-b)$

LTZ is based on the following remark: if $\bar{a} < 0$ then $\lfloor \bar{a}/2^{k-1} \rfloor = -1$ and if $\bar{a} \geq 0$ then $\lfloor \bar{a}/2^{k-1} \rfloor = 0$. Therefore, we can determine the sign of a secret integer $\bar{a} \in \mathbb{Z}_{\langle k \rangle}$ by computing $[s] = -\mathsf{Trunc}([a], k, k-1)$.

EQZ starts by computing and revealing $c = 2^{k-1} + a + r$ like the previous protocols. Let $c' = c \bmod 2^k$ and observe that $c' = r'$ if and only if $\bar{a} = 0$. The protocol computes $z = (c' = r')?\ 1 : 0 = \bigvee_{i=0}^{k-1}(c_i \oplus r'_i)$ using the k-ary OR protocol KOr (Section 4). EQZ is similar to a protocol in [19].

Protocol 3.6. $[s] \leftarrow \mathsf{LTZ}([a], k)$

$[s] \leftarrow -\mathsf{Trunc}([a], k, k-1)$; // Table 5
return $[s]$;

Protocol 3.7. $[z] \leftarrow \mathsf{EQZ}([a], k)$

$([r''], [r'], [r'_{k-1}], \ldots, [r'_0]) \leftarrow \mathsf{PRandM}(k, k)$; // 1 rnd, k inv
$c \leftarrow \mathsf{Output}(2^{k-1} + [a] + 2^k[r''] + [r'])$; // 1 rnd, 1 inv
$(c_{k-1}, \ldots, c_0) \leftarrow Bits(c, k)$;
foreach $i \in [0..k-1]$ **do** $[d_i] \leftarrow c_i + [r_i] - 2c_i[r_i]$;
$[z] \leftarrow 1 - \mathsf{KOr}([d_{k-1}], \ldots, [d_0])$; // Tables 3, 4
return $[z]$;

4 Building Blocks

The performance of the protocols presented in the previous section is determined by the complexity of the building blocks for bitwise operations. We discuss in this section protocols for different trade-offs between communication and round complexity, adapted to different types of application and execution environment.

Let $\mathcal{A}$ be a set and $\odot : \mathcal{A} \times \mathcal{A} \rightarrow \mathcal{A}$ an associative binary operator. We consider the following two extensions: a k-ary operation computes $p = \bigodot_{i=1}^{k} a_i$; a prefix operation computes $p_j = \bigodot_{i=1}^{j} a_i$ for $j \in [1..k]$. We focus here on multiplication and simple boolean functions, especially OR and carry propagation.

4.1 Bitwise Operations with Logarithmic Round Complexity

For secure computation with large batches of parallel operations (e.g., large numbers and/or large matrices in linear programming), we can improve the performance by trading off a few rounds for low communication overhead.

Protocols with perfect privacy, low communication, and $\log(k)$ rounds can be obtained by structuring the computation of k-ary and prefix operations as shown in Fig. 1. The protocols for k-ary operations have minimum communication complexity. For prefix operations, the decision is less obvious, since optimal communication complexity requires $2\log(k) - 1$ rounds for $2k - \log(k) - 2$ invocations. The structure in Fig. 1 offers a better trade-off.

Complexity is shown in Table 3, where KOpL and PreOpL are generic protocols for any binary operation computed in 1 invocation, while CarryOutL and CarryAddL compute the carry bits for binary addition (prefix operation, details in [22]). Note that these protocols work for any data encoding (Section 2), in particular for bits encoded in small fields.

Protocol 4.1, BitLTL, is an efficient inequality test in $\log(k)$ rounds for bitwise encoded integers $a, b \in [0..2^k - 1]$. The protocol computes $s = (a < b)?\ 1 : 0$ with perfect privacy. We show the variant used in Section 3, where one integer

Table 3. Complexity of log-rounds bitwise operations

Protocol	Rounds	Invocations ($\mathbb{F}$)
$[p] \leftarrow \mathsf{KOpL}([a_1], \ldots, [a_k])$	$\log(k)$	$k-1$
$[p_1], \ldots, [p_k] \leftarrow \mathsf{PreOpL}([a_1], \ldots, [a_k])$	$\log(k)$	$0.5k\log(k)$
$[c] \leftarrow \mathsf{CarryOutL}(a_k, \ldots, a_1, [b_k], \ldots, [b_1], c')$	$\log(k)$	$2k-2$
$[c_k], \ldots, [c_1] \leftarrow \mathsf{CarryAddL}(a_k, \ldots, a_1, [b_k], \ldots, [b_1])$	$\log(k)$	$k\log(k)$
$[c] \leftarrow \mathsf{CarryOutL}([a_k], \ldots, [a_1], [b_k], \ldots, [b_1], c')$	$\log(k)+1$	$3k-2$
$[c_k], \ldots, [c_1] \leftarrow \mathsf{CarryAddL}([a_k], \ldots, [a_1], [b_k], \ldots, [b_1])$	$\log(k)+1$	$k\log(k)+k$
$[s] \leftarrow \mathsf{BitLTL}(a, [b_k], \ldots, [b_1])$	$\log(k)$	$2k-2$

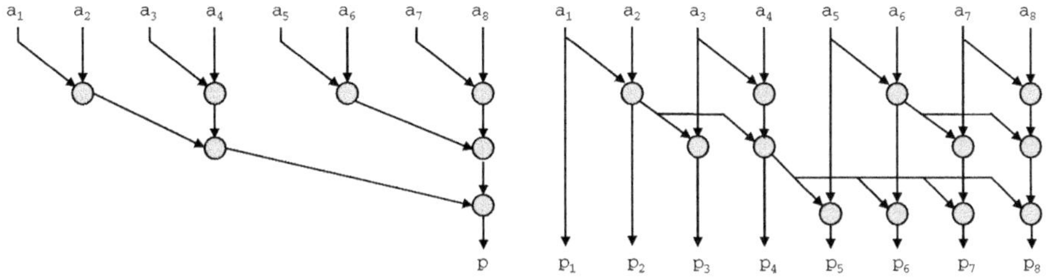

Fig. 1. K-ary (left) and prefix (right) operations in $\log(k)$ rounds (for $k = 8$)

is public. A solution using PreOrL and the algorithm in [11] is less efficient, since it needs $0.5k\log(k)$ invocations (or $2\log(k)$ rounds and $2k - \log(k)$ invocations).

Correctness: Let $d = 2^k + a - b$ and $d_{k+1}, \ldots, d_1$ its binary representation. Observe that $0 < d < 2^{k+1}$ and $d_{k+1} = (a - b < 0)?\ 0 : 1$, hence $s = 1 - d_{k+1}$. On the other hand, $2^k - b = b' + 1$, where $b' = \sum_{i=1}^{k} 2^{i-1} \neg b_i$, and hence $d = a + b' + 1$. The protocol computes d_{k+1} using CarryOutL, for inputs a, b', and carry-in set.

Protocol 4.1. $[s]^{\mathbb{F}} \leftarrow \mathsf{BitLTL}(a, [b_k]^{\mathbb{F}}, \ldots, [b_1]^{\mathbb{F}})$

$(a_k, \ldots, a_1) \leftarrow \mathit{Bits}(a, k)$;
foreach $i \in [1..k]$ **do** $[b'_i]^{\mathbb{F}} \leftarrow 1 - [b_i]^{\mathbb{F}}$;
$[s]^{\mathbb{F}} \leftarrow 1 - \mathsf{CarryOutL}(a_k, \ldots, a_1, [b'_k]^{\mathbb{F}}, \ldots, [b'_1]^{\mathbb{F}}, 1)$; // Table 3
return $[s]^{\mathbb{F}}$;

4.2 Bitwise Operations with Constant Round Complexity

For applications with many sequential operations, the running time is dominated by the network delay (e.g., secure division by functional iteration). It is important, therefore, to reduce the number of rounds of these operations, even at the cost of larger amount of data. Furthermore, precomputation becomes an effective method for reducing the running time, so another design goal is to shift complexity to a precomputation phase. We present new protocols that meet these

Table 4. Complexity of constant-rounds bitwise operations

Protocol	Rounds	Invocations ($\mathbb{Z}_q$)
$[p_1], \ldots, [p_k] \leftarrow \mathsf{PreMulC}([a_1], \ldots, [a_k])$	2	$3k - 1$
After precomputation	1	k
$[p_1], \ldots, [p_k] \leftarrow \mathsf{PreOrC}([a_1], \ldots, [a_k])$	3	$5k - 1$
After precomputation	2	$2k - 1$
$[p] \leftarrow \mathsf{KOrCL}([a_1], \ldots, [a_k])$	3	$4\log(k)$
After precomputation	2	$\log(k) + 1$
$[p_1], \ldots, [p_k] \leftarrow \mathsf{PreOrCS}([a_1], \ldots, [a_k])$	6	$8k + 3\sqrt{k}$
After precomputation	5	$4k + \sqrt{k}$
$[p] \leftarrow \mathsf{KOrCS}([a_1], \ldots, [a_k])$	2	$3k - 1$
After precomputation	1	k
$\mathsf{BitLTC1}(a, [b_k], \ldots, [b_1])$	3	$3k + 1$
After precomputation	2	$k + 1$
$\mathsf{BitLTC2}(a, [b_k], \ldots, [b_1])$	5	$2k - 1$
After precomputation	4	$k + 1$

goals, as well as methods to reduce the complexity of known protocols. Table 4 summarizes the complexity of the protocols discussed in this section. We show the protocols for k-ary and prefix-OR; variants for AND can be obtained using De Morgan's laws. We refer to several known protocols as follows: PreMulC, for prefix multiplication [4]; KOrCS and PreOrCS, for k-ary and prefix OR [11].

We begin with an important building block, PreMulC, that computes in constant-rounds the prefix products $[p_j] = \prod_{i=1}^{j}[a_i]$, $j \in [1..k]$, where $a_1, \ldots, a_k$ are *non-zero* elements of a field $\mathbb{F}$. The protocol follows the method introduced in [4]: the parties compute $[m_i] = [r_i][a_i][r_{i-1}^{-1}]$, $i \in [2..k]$ and $[m_1] = [r_1][a_1]$, where r_i are uniformly random in $\mathbb{F}$; reveal m_i; and then locally compute the prefix products $[p_j] = [r_j^{-1}]\prod_{i=1}^{j} m_i = [r_j^{-1}][r_j][a_j][r_{j-1}^{-1}] \ldots [r_2][a_2][r_1^{-1}][r_1][a_1]$.

Protocol 4.2. $[p_1], \ldots, [p_k] \leftarrow \mathsf{PreMulC}([a_1], \ldots, [a_k])$

foreach $i \in [1..k]$ **do parallel**
  $[r_i] \leftarrow \mathsf{PRandFld}(\mathbb{F})$;
  $[s_i] \leftarrow \mathsf{PRandFld}(\mathbb{F})$;
  $u_i \leftarrow \mathsf{MulPub}([r_i], [s_i])$; `// 1 rnd,` k `inv; repeat if` $u_i = 0$, `pr` $= \frac{2}{|\mathbb{F}|}$
foreach $i \in [1..k-1]$ **do parallel** $[v_i] \leftarrow [r_{i+1}][s_i]$; `//` $k-1$ `inv`
$[w_1] \leftarrow [r_1]$;
foreach $i \in [2..k]$ **do** $[w_i] \leftarrow [v_{i-1}](u_{i-1}^{-1} \bmod q)$;
foreach $i \in [1..k]$ **do** $[z_i] \leftarrow [s_i](u_i^{-1} \bmod q)$;
foreach $i \in [1..k]$ **do parallel** $m_i \leftarrow \mathsf{MulPub}([w_i][a_i])$; `// 1 rnd,` k `inv`
$[p_1] \leftarrow [a_1]$;
foreach $j \in [2..k]$ **do** $[p_j] \leftarrow [z_j](\prod_{i=1}^{j} m_i)$;
return $([p_1], \ldots, [p_k])$;

The variant of prefix multiplication shown as Protocol 4.2 minimizes the number of rounds as follows: steps 1-8 (round 1) compute $[w_1] = [r_1 a_1]$, $[w_i] = [r_i][r_{i-1}]^{-1}$, $i \in [2..k]$, and $[z_i] = [r_i^{-1}]$, $i \in [1..k]$; steps 9-11 (round 2) complete the computation described above. The protocol gains 1 round with respect to the obvious solution by computing in parallel $r_i s_i$ and $r_{i+1} s_i$. The first round can be pre-computed.

The complexity of all the other protocols listed in Table 4 is evaluated assuming that prefix multiplication is optimized as shown in Protocol 4.2, and shared random values are pre-computed in parallel.

The protocol for k-ary symmetric boolean functions proposed in [11] has the same complexity as PreMulC. We can reduce the complexity of k-ary OR (and k-ary AND) from $3k$ to $4\log(k)$ invocations as shown in Protocol 4.3, KOrCL. In particular, this reduces the complexity of the equality test EQZ. KOrCL is based on the remark that $\bigvee_{i=1}^{k} a_i = 0$ if and only if $\sum_{i=1}^{k} a_i = 0$, which can be tested more efficiently (like in EQZ), since $\sum_{i=1}^{k} a_i \leq k$.

Protocol 4.3. $[e] \leftarrow \mathsf{KOrCL}([a_1], \ldots, [a_k])$

$m \leftarrow \lceil \log(k) \rceil$;
$([r''], [r'], [r'_{m-1}], \ldots, [r'_0]) \leftarrow \mathsf{PRandM}(k, m)$; // 1 rnd, m inv
$c \leftarrow \mathsf{Output}(2^m [r''] + [r'] + \sum_{i=1}^{k} [a_i])$; // 1 rnd, 1 inv
$(c_m, \ldots, c_1) \leftarrow Bits(c, m)$;
foreach $i \in [1..m]$ **do** $[d_i] \leftarrow c_i + [r_i] - 2c_i[r'_i]$;
$[e] \leftarrow \mathsf{KOrCS}([d_1], \ldots, [d_m])$; // 2 rnd, $2m-1$ inv
return $[e]$;

Protocol 4.4, PreOrC, computes prefix-OR in 3 rounds, out of which 1 round can be precomputed. PreOrC is more efficient (and much simpler) than the prefix-OR protocol described in [11] (PreOrCS in Table 4).

Correctness: PreOrC computes the prefix products $b_i = \prod_{j=1}^{i}(a_j + 1)$ for $i \in [1..k]$. Observe that if $a_j = 0$ for $j \in [1..i]$ then $b_i = 1$, otherwise b_i is even. Therefore, the complement of the least significant bit of b_i is equal to $\bigvee_{j=1}^{i} a_i$.

Protocol 4.4. $[p_1], \ldots, [p_k] \leftarrow \mathsf{PreOrC}([a_1], \ldots, [a_k])$

$[b_1], \ldots, [b_k] \leftarrow \mathsf{PreMulC}([a_1] + 1, \ldots, [a_k] + 1)$; // 2 rnd, $3k-1$ inv
$[p_1] \leftarrow [a_1]$;
foreach $i \in [2..k]$ **do parallel**
    $[p_i] \leftarrow 1 - \mathsf{Mod2}([b_i], k)$; // 2 rnd, $2k-2$ inv
return $[p_1], \ldots, [p_k]$;

We conclude this section with two constant-rounds variants of the protocol for comparison of bitwise encoded integers. The protocol could be constructed using PreOrC and the method in [11]. However, we can eliminate $2k$ invocations

Protocol 4.5. $[u] \leftarrow \mathsf{BitLTC1}(a, ([b_k], \ldots, [b_1]))$

1 **foreach** $i \in [1..k]$ **do** $[d_i] \leftarrow a_i + [b_i] - 2a_i[b_i]$;
2 $([p_k], \ldots, [p_1]) \leftarrow \mathsf{PreMulC}([d_k] + 1, \ldots, [d_1] + 1)$; // 2 rnd, $3k - 1$ inv
3 **foreach** $i \in [1..k-1]$ **do** $[s_i] \leftarrow [p_i] - [p_{i+1}]$;
4 $[s_k] \leftarrow [p_k] - 1$;
5 $[s] \leftarrow \sum_{i=1}^{k} [s_i](1 - a_i)$;
6 $[u] \leftarrow \mathsf{Mod2}([s], k)$; // 2 rnd, 2 inv
7 **return** $[u]$;

as shown in Protocol 4.5, BitLTC1. This algorithm is also more efficient than the transformation proposed in [20], saving 1 round and k invocations.

Correctness: Step 1 determines the bit differences $d_i = a_i \oplus b_i$ and step 2 computes the prefix products $p_i = \prod_{j=i}^{k}(d_j + 1) = 2^{\sum_{j=i}^{k} d_j}$ for $i \in [1..k]$. Steps 3-4 compute $s_i = p_i - p_{i+1} = d_i p_{i+1}$ for $i \in [1..k-1]$ and $s_k = p_k - 1 = d_k$. Steps 5-6 compute $s = \sum_{i=1}^{k} s_i(1 - a_i) = d_k(1 - a_k) + \sum_{i=1}^{k-1} s_i(1 - a_i)$ and extract the least significant bit of s, denoted u. We distinguish the following cases:

- If $a = b$ then $d_i = 0$, $p_i = 1$, and $s_i = 0$ for $i \in [1..k]$. Therefore, $s = 0$ and hence $u = 0 = (a < b)$. Otherwise, $a \neq b$ and there exists $m \in [1..k]$ such that $a_i = b_i$ for all $i > m$ and $a_m \neq b_m$. Observe that $(a < b) = b_m = 1 - a_m$.
- If $m = k$ then $a_k \neq b_k$, $d_k = 1$, $p_k = 2$, $s_k = 1$, and $s_{k-1} = d_{k-1}p_k = 2d_{k-1}$; for $i \in [1..k-2]$, $s_i = d_i p_{i+1} = d_i 2^{\sum_{j=i+1}^{k} d_j} = 2d_i 2^{\sum_{j=i+1}^{k-1} d_j}$. It follows that $s = (1 - a_k) + 2d_{k-1} + 2\sum_{i=1}^{k-2} d_i(1 - a_i)2^{\sum_{j=i+1}^{k-1} d_j}$, hence $u = 1 - a_k = (a < b)$.
- If $m < k$ then for $i \in [m+1..k]$ we have $a_i = b_i$, $d_i = 0$, $p_i = 1$, and $s_i = p_{i+1}d_i = 0$; if $i = m$ then $d_m = 1$, $p_m = 2$, and $s_m = 1$; for $i \in [1..m-1]$, $s_i = d_i p_{i+1} = 2d_i 2^{\sum_{j=i+1, j\neq m}^{k} d_j}$. It follows that $s = (1 - a_m) + 2\sum_{i=1}^{m-1} d_i(1 - a_i)2^{\sum_{j=i+1, j\neq m}^{k} d_j}$, hence $u = 1 - a_m = (a < b)$.

Protocol 4.6, BitLTC2, is a variant that reduces the communication complexity by splitting the computation of the prefix products in 3 steps, at the cost of 2 additional rounds. We omit the correctness proof which is simple but lengthy.

Protocol 4.6. $[u] \leftarrow \mathsf{BitLTC2}(a, ([b_k], \ldots, [b_1]))$

1 **foreach** $i \in [1..k]$ **do** $[d_i] \leftarrow a_i + [b_i] - 2a_i[b_i]$;
2 $\ell \leftarrow (k - 1)/2$; // Assume that k is odd
3 **foreach** $i \in [1..\ell]$ **do** $[e_i] \leftarrow ([d_{2i-1}] + 1)([d_{2i}] + 1)$; // 1 rnd, $k/2$ inv
4 $[e_{\ell+1}] \leftarrow [d_k] + 1$;
5 $([f_\ell], \ldots, [f_1]) \leftarrow \mathsf{PreMulC}([e_{\ell+1}], \ldots, [e_2])$; // 2 rnd, $3k/2$ inv
6 **foreach** $i \in [1..\ell]$ **do** $[g_i] \leftarrow ([e_i] - 1)(1 - a_{2i-1}) + [d_{2i}](a_{2i-1} - a_{2i})$;
7 $[s] \leftarrow \mathsf{Inner}(([f_1], \ldots, [f_\ell]), ([g_1], \ldots, [g_\ell]))$; // 1 rnd, 1 inv
8 $[s] \leftarrow [s] + [d_k](1 - a_k)$;
9 $[u] \leftarrow \mathsf{Mod2}([s], k)$; // 2 rnd, 2 inv
10 **return** $[u]$;

5 Conclusions

Comparison and truncation are the main performance bottlenecks of applications that involve complex secure computation with integer and fixed-point rational numbers. We focus in this paper on improved solutions for these tasks. We propose efficient protocols for their building blocks, with complexity reduced by a large margin with respect to known protocols. These building blocks are often used in other secure computation tasks. Moreover, we give variants for different trade-offs between communication and round complexity, and thus the protocols can be adapted to applications and the communication network.

Table 5. Complexity of arithmetic and comparison protocols

Protocol	Rounds	Inv. ($\mathbb{Z}_q$)
Mod2mC1($[a], k, m$)	4	$4m + 1$
After prec.	3	$m + 2$
Mod2mC2($[a], k, m$)	6	$3m + 1$
After prec.	5	$m + 3$
Mod2mL($[a], k, m$)	$\log(m) + 2$	$3m - 1$
After prec.	$\log(m) + 1$	$2m - 1$
TruncPR($[a], k, m$)	2	$m + 1$
After prec.	1	1

Protocol	Rounds	Inv. ($\mathbb{Z}_q$)
LTZC1($[a], k$)	4	$4k - 2$
After prec.	3	$k + 1$
LTZC2($[a], k$)	6	$3k - 2$
After prep.	5	$k + 2$
LTZL($[a], k$)	$\log(k) + 2$	$3k - 4$
After prec.	$\log(k) + 1$	$2k - 3$
EQZC($[a], k$)	4	$k + 4\log(k)$
After prec.	3	$\log(k) + 2$

Protocol	Rounds	Inv.	Field
$[s] \leftarrow$ LTZL($[a], k$)	1	1	$\mathbb{Z}_q$
	2	$2k$	$\mathbb{Z}_{q_1}$
	$\log(k) + 1$	$2k - 3$	$\mathbb{F}_{2^8}$
After precomputation	1	1	$\mathbb{Z}_q$
	$\log(k) + 1$	$2k - 3$	$\mathbb{F}_{2^8}$

Table 5 shows the complexity of the main protocols in Section 3. Mod2mC1, Mod2mC2, and Mod2mL are variants of Mod2m constructed with the BitLT variants BitLTC1, BitLTC2, and BitLTL, respectively. The same naming convention is used for LTZ, while EQZC is a variant of EQZ constructed with KOrCL.

Besides the usual setting with all data types encoded in the same field $\mathbb{Z}_q$, we also show a variant of LTZL with bits encoded in small fields ($\mathbb{F}_{2^8}$ for BitLTL, $\mathbb{Z}_{q_1}$ for random bit generation). This variant reduces the amount of data sent from $O(k^2)$ bits to $O(k)$ and thus scales up better for large integers (or fixed-point numbers) and large batches of comparisons. Our measurements for secure linear programming [22] showed that the running time of LTZL is reduced by a factor of 1.6 for $\log(q) = 128$ and 2.5 for $\log(q) = 320$, $\kappa = 48$. On the other hand, using PreOrC and LTZC1 instead of log-rounds protocols reduces the round complexity of the fixed-point division protocol in [6] by 10 rounds (for signed dividend).

From a practical perspective, the comparison protocols (inequality and equality) listed in Table 5 are more efficient than the protocols in [19,24,20]. We note, however, that their work focuses on solutions with perfect privacy, while our protocols offer (only) statistical privacy. Reconciliating these goals, performance and perfect privacy, and finding multiparty comparison and (accurate) truncation protocols with sub-linear complexity, remain open and challenging issues.

Acknowledgements. Part of this work was funded by the European Commission through the grant FP7-213531 to the SecureSCM project.

References

1. Abe, M., Cramer, R., Fehr, S.: Non-interactive Distributed-Verifier Proofs and Proving Relations among Commitments. In: Zheng, Y. (ed.) ASIACRYPT 2002. LNCS, vol. 2501, pp. 206–223. Springer, Heidelberg (2002)
2. Algesheimer, J., Camenish, J., Shoup, V.: Efficient computation modulo a shared secret with application to the generation of shared safe-prime products. In: Yung, M. (ed.) CRYPTO 2002. LNCS, vol. 2442, pp. 417–432. Springer, Heidelberg (2002)
3. Atallah, M., Blanton, M., Deshpande, V., Frikken, K., Li, J., Schwarz, L.: Secure Collaborative Planning, Forecasting, and Replenishment (SCPFR). In: Multi-Echelon/Public Applications of Supply Chain Management Conference (2006)
4. Bar-Ilan, J., Beaver, D.: Non-cryptographic fault-tolerant computing in a constant number of rounds of interaction. In: Proc. 8th ACM Symposium on Principles of Distributed Computing, pp. 201–209. ACM, New York (1989)
5. Ben-Or, M., Goldwasser, S., Wigderson, A.: Completeness theorems for non-cryptographic fault tolerant distributed computation. In: Proc. of 20th ACM Symposium on Theory of Computing (STOC), pp. 1–10 (1988)
6. Catrina, O., Saxena, A.: Secure computation with fixed-point numbers. In: Sion, R. (ed.) FC 2010. LNCS, vol. 6052, pp. 35–50. Springer, Heidelberg (2010)
7. Cramer, R., Damgård, I., Ishai, Y.: Share conversion, pseudorandom secret-sharing and applications to secure computation. In: Kilian, J. (ed.) TCC 2005. LNCS, vol. 3378, pp. 342–362. Springer, Heidelberg (2005)
8. Cramer, R., Damgård, I., Maurer, U.: General Secure Multi-Party Computation from any Linear Secret-Sharing Scheme. In: Preneel, B. (ed.) EUROCRYPT 2000. LNCS, vol. 1807, pp. 316–334. Springer, Heidelberg (2000)
9. Cramer, R., Damgård, I., Nielsen, J.: Multiparty computation from threshold homomorphic encryption. In: Pfitzmann, B. (ed.) EUROCRYPT 2001. LNCS, vol. 2045, pp. 280–300. Springer, Heidelberg (2001)
10. Cramer, R., Gennaro, R., Schoenmakers, B.: A secure and optimally efficient multi-authority election scheme. In: Fumy, W. (ed.) EUROCRYPT 1997. LNCS, vol. 1233, pp. 103–118. Springer, Heidelberg (1997)
11. Damgård, I., Fitzi, M., Kiltz, E., Nielsen, J., Toft, T.: Unconditionally secure constant-rounds multi-party computation for equality, comparison, bits and exponentiation. In: Halevi, S., Rabin, T. (eds.) TCC 2006. LNCS, vol. 3876, pp. 285–304. Springer, Heidelberg (2006)
12. Damgård, I., Nielsen, J., Toft, T., Pagter, J.I., Jakobsen, T., Bogetoft, P., Nielsen, K.: A Practical Implementation of Secure Auctions Based on Multiparty Integer Computation. In: Di Crescenzo, G., Rubin, A. (eds.) FC 2006. LNCS, vol. 4107, pp. 142–147. Springer, Heidelberg (2006)
13. Damgård, I., Thorbek, R.: Non-interactive Proofs for Integer Multiplication. In: Naor, M. (ed.) EUROCRYPT 2007. LNCS, vol. 4515, pp. 412–429. Springer, Heidelberg (2007)

14. Damgard, I., Thorbek, R.: Efficient conversion of secret-shared values between different fields. Cryptology ePrint Archive, Report 2008/221 (2008)
15. Garay, J., Schoenmakers, B., Villegas, J.: Practical and Secure Solutions for Integer Comparison. In: Okamoto, T., Wang, X. (eds.) PKC 2007. LNCS, vol. 4450, pp. 330–342. Springer, Heidelberg (2007)
16. Gennaro, R., Rabin, M., Rabin, T.: Simplified VSS and fast-track multi-party computations with applications to threshold cryptography. In: Proc. of ACM Symposium on Principles of Distributed Computing, PODC 1998 (1998)
17. Guajardo, J., Mennink, B., Schoenmakers, B.: Modulo reduction for paillier encryptions and application to secure statistical analysis. In: Sion, R. (ed.) FC 2010. LNCS, vol. 6052, pp. 375–382. Springer, Heidelberg (2010)
18. Kerschbaum, F.: Building a privacy-preserving benchmarking enterprise system. Enterp. Inf. Syst. 2(4), 421–441 (2008)
19. Nishide, T., Ohta, K.: Multiparty Computation for Interval, Equality, and Comparison Without Bit-Decomposition Protocol. In: Okamoto, T., Wang, X. (eds.) PKC 2007. LNCS, vol. 4450, pp. 343–360. Springer, Heidelberg (2007)
20. Reistad, T.I.: Multiparty comparison - an improved multiparty protocol for comparison of secret-shared values. In: SECRYPT, pp. 325–330. INSTICC (2009)
21. Schoenmakers, B., Tuyls, P.: Efficient Binary Conversion for Paillier Encryptions. In: Vaudenay, S. (ed.) EUROCRYPT 2006. LNCS, vol. 4004, pp. 522–537. Springer, Heidelberg (2006)
22. SecureSCM. Security Analysis. Deliverable D9.2, EU FP7 Project Secure Supply Chain Management, SecureSCM (2009)
23. Shoup, V.: A Computational Introduction to Number Theory and Algebra, 2nd edn. Cambridge University Press, Cambridge (2009)
24. Toft, T.: Primitives and Applications for Multi-party Computation. PhD dissertation, University of Aarhus, Denmark (2007)
25. Toft, T.: Solving Linear Programs Using Multiparty Computation. In: Dingledine, R., Golle, P. (eds.) FC 2009. LNCS, vol. 5628, pp. 90–107. Springer, Heidelberg (2009)

A Annex: Statistical Privacy

The protocols presented in the paper offer two notions of privacy: *perfect* and *statistical*. Some of the protocols provide only statistical security in order to achieve better efficiency. The difference between these notions is discussed below.

Definition 1. *Let X and Y be two random variables, both taking values in some finite set V. The statistical distance between X and Y is defined as*

$$\Delta(X;Y) = \frac{1}{2}\sum_{v \in V} |\mathbb{P}(X = v) - \mathbb{P}(Y = v)|. \tag{1}$$

Intuitively, if $\Delta(X;Y)$ is small (or 0), then the distributions of X and Y are statistically (resp. perfectly) indistinguishable. All our building blocks are based on the following high-level idea. Let x be a random variable denoting a secret integer. We first generate a random secret integer r in some range and reveal $f(x,r)$ for some function f. Let $\delta = \Delta(r, f(x,r))$. The type of security offered by the protocol depends on δ as follows: $\delta = 0$ implies perfect security and $\delta \leq c/2^{\kappa}$ (for some constant c) implies statistical security in security parameter κ.

Following are some basic results about statistical distance. Their proofs can be found in Chapter 8 of [23].

We first show that if U is uniform on some finite set then the statistical distance between $X+U$ and U can be bounded by the size of the domain of U.

Lemma 1. *Let M and K be positive integers with $M \leq K$. Let X, U be random variables in $[0..M-1]$, $[0..K-1]$ respectively such that U is uniform. Then $\Delta(U; X+U) \leq (M-1)/K$ and this bound is tight.*

Proof. This is Lemma 1 in [21, Appendix A].

Remark 1. The result of Lemma 1 implies that $\Delta(U; X+U)$ is small if $M \ll K$. For instance, if one sets $K = M2^k$, we see that the statistical distance between U and $X+U$ is less than $1/2^k$, hence approaches 0 exponentially fast as a function of k. In other words, one can mask an integer value X from a bounded range $\{0, \ldots, M-1\}$ by adding a uniform random integer U from an enlarged range $\{0, \ldots, K-1\}$. This way one can do one-time pad encryption with integers, where X is the message, U is the one-time pad, and $X+U$ is the ciphertext.

In Theorem 1, we show that this holds even if U is not uniform, but a sum of uniform distributions. For this we will use the following lemmas.

Lemma 2. *Let X and Y be random variable taking values in some finite set V and let $f : V \to V'$ be some function mapping to some finite set V'. It holds that*

$$\Delta(f(X); f(Y)) \leq \Delta(X; Y). \tag{2}$$

Proof. This is Theorem 8.32 of [23].

Lemma 3. *Let X,Y and Z be random values, where X and Z are independent and Y and Z are independent, then*

$$\Delta((X, Z); (Y, Z)) = \Delta(X; Y). \tag{3}$$

Proof. This is Theorem 8.33 of [23].

Theorem 1. *Let $X \in [0..2^k-1]$ and U be random variables and let $U = \sum_{i=1}^{n} U_i$ for some finite n, where each U_i is independent and uniform in $[0..2^{k+\kappa}-1]$. Then:*

$$\Delta(X+U; U) < 2^{-\kappa}. \tag{4}$$

Proof. Let $U_i \in_R [0..2^{k+\kappa}-1]$ for $i = 1, \ldots, n$ such that U_i is selected uniformly and let and $X \in [0..2^k-1]$ be with unknown distribution. Let $= \sum_{i=1}^{n} U_i$. Lastly, let $f : [0..(n-1)2^{k+\kappa} - n + 1] \times [0..2^k(1+2^{\kappa}) - 2] \to [0..2^k(1+n2^{\kappa}) - n - 1]$ be defined as $f(x, y) := x + y$. It follows that

$$\begin{aligned}
\Delta(X+U;U) &= \Delta(X+\sum_{i=1}^{n}U_i;\sum_{i=1}^{n}U_i) = \Delta(X+\sum_{i=1}^{n-1}U_i+U_n;\sum_{i=1}^{n-1}U_i+U_n)\\
&= \Delta(f(\sum_{i=1}^{n-1}U_i, X+U_n); f(\sum_{i=1}^{n-1}U_i, U_n))\\
\text{Lemma 2} &\leq \Delta((\sum_{i=1}^{n-1}U_i, X+U_n);(\sum_{i=1}^{n-1}U_i, U_n))\\
\text{Lemma 3} &= \Delta(X+U_n;U_n)\\
\text{Lemma 1} &\leq \frac{2^k-1}{2^{k+\kappa}} < 2^{-\kappa}.
\end{aligned}$$

Theorem 2 is an extension of Theorem 1 where U is constructed in a slightly different manner.

Theorem 2. *Let $X \in [0..2^k-1]$ and U be random variables and let $U = U' + 2^k\sum_{i=1}^{n}U'_i$, where $U' \in_R [0..2^k-1]$ and each U'_i is uniform and independent in $[0..2^\kappa-1]$. Then:*

$$\Delta(X+U;U) < 2^{-\kappa}. \tag{5}$$

Proof. Let $U_n = U' + 2^kU'_n$ and $U_i = 2^kU'_i$ for $i = 1,\ldots,n-1$. Observe that U_n is uniform in $[0..2^{k+\kappa}-1]$, and U_i are independent. Also, let

$$f : [0..(n-1)2^k(2^\kappa-1)] \times [0..2^k(1+2^\kappa)-2] \to [0..2^k(2+n(2^\kappa-1))-2]$$

be defined as

$$f(x,y) := x+y$$

Using the same method as in the proof of Theorem 1 we obtain:

$$\begin{aligned}
\Delta(X+U;U) &= \Delta(X+\sum_{i=1}^{n}U_i;\sum_{i=1}^{n}U_i) = \Delta(X+\sum_{i=1}^{n-1}U_i+U_n;\sum_{i=1}^{n-1}U_i+U_n)\\
&= \Delta(f(\sum_{i=1}^{n-1}U_i, X+U_n); f(\sum_{i=1}^{n-1}U_i, U_n))\\
\text{Lemma 2} &\leq \Delta((\sum_{i=1}^{n-1}U_i, X+U_n);(\sum_{i=1}^{n-1}U_i, U_n))\\
\text{Lemma 3} &= \Delta(X+U_n;U_n)\\
&= \Delta(X+U'+2^kU'_n;U'+2^kU'_n)\\
\text{Lemma 1} &\leq \frac{2^k-1}{2^{k+\kappa}} < 2^{-\kappa}.
\end{aligned}$$

How to Pair with a Human*

Stefan Dziembowski

Department of Computer Science
University of Rome
La Sapienza

Abstract. We introduce a protocol, that we call *Human Key Agreement*, that allows pairs of humans to establish a key in a (seemingly hopeless) case where no public-key infrastructure is available, the users do not share any common secret, and have never been connected by any physically-secure channel. Our key agreement scheme, while vulnerable to the *human*-in-the-middle attacks, is secure against any malicious *machine*-in-the middle. The only assumption that we make is that the attacker is a machine that is not able to break the Captcha puzzles (introduced by von Ahn et al., EUROCRYPT 2003).

Our main tool is a primitive that we call a *Simultaneous Turing Test*, which is a protocol that allows two users to verify if they are both human, in such a way that if one of them is not a human, then he does not learn whether the other one is human, or not.

To construct this tool we use a Universally-Composable Password Authenticated Key Agreement of Canetti et al. (EUROCRYPT 2005).

1 Introduction

One of the main reasons why digital crime is so difficult to combat is the fact that the attacks on digital devices are usually very easy to automatize and repeat for a large number of times. This makes the design of secure digital systems a completely different discipline than the design of physically-secure systems. Just observe that a physical attack on a bank that has probability 0.1% of succeeding may be infeasible, while, an *electronic* attack on a banking system that has the same probability of success may be feasible and profitable for the attacker.

The observation that certain types of malicious behavior are profitable only if they can be performed automatically and efficiently led to a construction of schemes where at some point one of the users has to prove that he is a human. This type of a "proof of being a human" was first proposed in [27], then independently discovered by [25], and finally formalized, and put in a general framework in [37], where it was given a name *Completely Automated Public Turing test to tell Computers and Humans Apart (Captcha)*. In short, a Captcha scheme is a puzzle that is easy to solve by a human and hard to solve by a machine. The most common Captchas are computer-generated images containing a short string of characters written in such a way that they are unreadable

* The European Research Council has provided financial support under the EuropeanCommunity's Seventh Framework Programme (FP7/2007-2013) / ERC grant agreement no CNTM-207908

J.A. Garay and R. De Prisco (Eds.): SCN 2010, LNCS 6280, pp. 200–218, 2010.

for a computer, and still effortlessly readable by a human. Other Captchas that were proposed are based on: recognizing gender of a person on an image [27], understanding facial expression on an image [27], speech recognition [27], recognizing animal pictures [37], etc.

So far, Captcha schemes were mostly used as a method for preventing attacks in which the adversary simply floods the victim with a large number of unwanted requests. Examples of these include email spamming and automated posting to blogs, forums, on-line polls, wikis, etc. [27,37]. Captchas are also used as a for thwarting the dictionary attacks on the password-based systems. Examples include [12] and [31]. Also, some manufacturers of home wifi routers recently started to use Captcha to prevent malicious software from getting access to their machines by simply guessing a password [32].

In this paper we propose a new application of the Captcha schemes. We show how Captchas can be used to construct a session key agreement between two humans that are connected by an insecure link. Our protocol, that we call a *Human Key Agreement* works in a (seemingly hopeless) case where no public-key infrastructure is available, and the users do not share any common secret, have never been connected by any physically-secure channel and do not even know each other personally (so they cannot, e.g., recognize each other's voice). The only assumption that we make is that the attacker is a machine that is not able to break the Captchas generated by the users.

1.1 Related Work

Captcha. Some work on Captchas was already described in Sect. 1. Both designing and breaking Captcha schemes is subject of intensive and active research. One of the interesting new research ideas in this field is the reCaptcha project [38], where the users solving Captchas are helping to digitize old books by deciphering scanned words on which the OCR methods failed. In this case Captcha consists of two images, (a) one that the creator of Captcha can solve himself (this is needed to verify the answer), and (b) one that is unreadable for him. The key point here is that the user who solves the Captcha does not know which image is (a) and which is (b), and hence he has to provide a solution for both.

Typically, the attacks on Captcha use the artificial intelligence methods (see e.g. [22]). An interesting exception is a so-called a *pornography attack*, where the the Captcha puzzles are forwarded to a pornographic web-site, and the web-site users have to solve the Captcha before being allowed to view the web-site contents [39]. For more information and references on Captcha see e.g. the Captcha web-site [35], or the wikipedia article [41].

Key agreement protocols. Key agreement protocols were introduced by Diffie and Hellman in their seminal paper [14]. Informally, a key agreement protocol is a scheme that allows two parties that initially do not share any secret to agree on a common key. The protocol of [14] is secure only against an eavesdropping adversary, i.e. an adversary that can *passively* listen to the messages exchanged between the parties, and is not secure against a more powerful *active* adversary that fully controls the transmission (by modifying, copyng, fabricating or destroying the messages). Such an active adversary is also called a *man-in-the middle*. Subsequently, several methods of protecting against the active attacks were proposed. A common one is to add message authentication to a passively-secure key agreement scheme. For example if the parties already share a common key K, they can authenticate their messages using Message Authentication Codes (see Sect. 3.1 for a definition). It may seem that the assumption that the parties from the beginning share a key trivializes the problem. The main point, however, is that such schemes allow to generate several fresh *session keys* from one long-term key K. An advantage of this method is that it provides *forward-security* [15,19,2], i.e. even if at some point the key K leaks to the adversary, the session keys generated in the past remain secret.

Other popular methods for authenticated key agreement are based on the public-key cryptography, or a trusted third party (for more on this, and for a general introduction to the area of key agreement see e.g. [6]). The drawback of the PKI approach is that it relays on a *public-key infrastructure*, that is usually non-trivial to set-up [17]. Using the trusted third party is often impractical, since it requires the parties to be connected to a party whom they both trust.

Some protocols are also based on the assumption that the agreeing parties share a common *password*, which may not be chosen uniformly at random, but has to be hard to guess for the adversary (we discuss it in more detail later). Yet another method, called *short string comparison*, assumes that the agreeing parties, after the protocol is completed, are able to securely compare, via a trusted channel if two short strings are equal [36,29,24,9]. Such a comparison allows the parties to detect if the adversary performed the man-in-the middle attack, by verifying if both parties have the same view on the set of messages that were exchanged.

Secure pairing schemes. *Secure device pairing* is a term used in the systems security community, referring to protocols whose goal is to establish a secret key between two electronic gadgets (mobile phones, PCs, routers, headsets, cameras and media players, etc.), usually connected with a wireless link. Hence, the meaning is similar to the term *key agreement* described above, and in fact some of the key agreement protocols can be directly used for pairing. The main difference is that the pairing protocols do not assume any shared secrets, trusted parties, or PKI. Moreover, the interfaces of the devices are often so constraint that they do not even permit the use of password protocols (since, e.g., they lack a keyboard or a screen). These protocols usually rely on a human user that is available to assist the pairing.

The first pairing protocol [34] was based on an assumption that a user can actually connect the devices with a secure physical link. Later, several other schemes were proposed. Several of them rely on a so-called "out-of-band" (OOB) channels, which are channels whose security can be verified by the user. For example [3] uses an infrared channel as OOB, and [33] uses human body as the communication medium. Some protocols use essentially the "short string comparison" method. For example the protocol [30] requires the user to verify if the images (that are a graphical representations of the "short strings") displayed on both devices are the same. The protocol used in the *Zfone*, a secure VoIP system (see [42]), requires the users to read out to each other short strings, and to compare them (another example of such a protocol is [43]). The security of this system of course relies on the fact that the users can recognize each other's voice. For more examples of the pairing protocols see e.g. [23].

2 Our Contribution: Human Key Agreement

In this section we describe the *Human Key Agreement* protocol. Informally speaking that, our protocol, while vulnerable to the "man-in-the middle" attacks, is secure against the "*machine*-in-the-middle" attacks (i.e.: an attack in which the adversary in not a human). Moreover, the protocol will be designed in such a way that using a human-in-middle attack, will be very expensive, since it will require the adversary to use humans to constantly monitor the network, solving a large number of Captcha puzzles.

Consider a decentralized protocol for remote communication between the humans. For example, think of an internet instant messaging system, like XMPP[1], or in general, any system where pairs of humans need to establish secure connection. How can the users of such a protocol establish session keys in a way that is secure against the man-in-the-middle attacks, when the the Public-Key Infrastructure is not available? None of the methods described in Sect. 1.1 seems to be applicable in this case. It is usually infeasible for the users to meet in person in order to establish a shared secret password. Sometimes they do not know each other well, so they cannot recognize each other's voice, and hence they cannot use the "short string comparison" method used in the VoIP protocols [42,43] (another reason may be that the voice link may simply not be available). Relying on a trusted server may also be a bad idea, as reported recently in the media [40]. Therefore, the adversary that controls the network can freely monitor, store and analyze all the messages that are transmitted by the users (as described in [40]).

Our *Human Key Agreement* permits the users to significantly increase security of their communication in this situation. The security of our protocol is based on the difficulty of solving the Captcha puzzles by a machine. More precisely the key established between each pair of participants will remain secret assuming that the adversary did not solve the Captcha puzzles that the users generated during the execution of the protocol. In addition, our protocol will be *forward-secure*, which means that, in order to break the security, the adversary will have to solve the Captcha puzzles *during* the execution of the protocol (solving the Captchas *after* the protocol is completed does not help him). Therefore the adversary will have to employ a significant amount of human power in order to decrypt users communication. Although, of course, this does not prevent him from targeting a concrete user, or a pair of users (if he is willing to spend some of his human time), at least it makes it very expensive to monitor and analyze the whole communication in the network. In some sense this is similar to the method based on voice recognition [42], since also there a very determined adversary may actually able to break the security, by using a *voice mimic attack* [43].

The details of the model are a little bit tricky, and we start with presenting them in a very informal way. Consider two parties, Alice (A) and Bob (B), that want to establish a secure connection. Intuitively, our protocol should satisfy the following requirements:

Requirement 1. *If the adversary is passive the protocol is completely secure, even against a human-adversary.*

[1] XMPP stands for Extensible Messaging and Presence Protocol. It was formerly named *Jabber*. For more on XMPP see e.g. a wikipedia article `http://en.wikipedia.org/wiki/Extensible_Messaging_and_Presence_Protocol`

Requirement 2. *If the adversary is performing a machine-in-the middle attack then this attack will be detected by the users.*

Therefore, of course, an active machine-adversary will always be able to prevent the parties from establishing a secure key, but he will not be able to convince the players that the key is secure, while it is not.

It is easy to observe that in order to satisfy Req. 1 both users themselves have to use the fact that they are humans, and demonstrate, during the execution of the protocol, their ability to solve the Captcha puzzles. This is because otherwise a machine-attacker would be completely indistinguishable from the honest users. On the other hand, solving a Captcha each time the protocol is executed would be very cumbersome. Therefore the protocol will have two modes: a *secure* one (during which the users have to solve the Captcha puzzles) and both Req. 1 and 2 hold, and a *normal* one, where only Req. 1 holds.

The secure mode will only be activated if the users need to transmit some secret information, and otherwise they will use the normal mode. More precisely, each user $P \in \{A, B\}$ will be able to decide if he wants to establish a secure connection, or not, by setting his flag $human_P := 1$, or $human_P := 0$, resp. The secure mode will be used only if $human_A \wedge human_B = 1$.

Described this way, it may look like the protocol could actually deteriorate users' security, as the fact that one of the users wants to establish a secure connection could be a signal to the adversary that the user has some secret to hide (and in this case he could quickly call a human to help him solving the Captcha). Thus we introduce the third security condition:

Requirement 3. *A machine-adversary is not able to learn the values of $human_A$ and $human_B$. Moreover the values of $human_A$ and $human_B$ are* forward-secret *in a sense, that the adversary, in order to learn those values, needs to solve the Captcha puzzles* during *the execution of the protocol.*

The reason why the users may be interested in forward-secrecy of $human_P$ is that the fact that some pair of users used the secure mode, could draw the attention of the adversary to them, and hence he could use a human-attacker against them next time when they execute the key-agreement protocol. For this reason, the users should be advised to *always* encrypt their communication with the secret key that they established, no matter if they are in the secure mode or not (since otherwise they would reveal the values to the adversary). Moreover, if $human_P = 1$ and $human_A \wedge human_B = 0$ then P should not interrupt the session (since it could give to the adversary information about the value of $human_P$). The only thing that he has to keep in mind is not to send any secret information in such a session.

Req. 3 implies that the computation of $human_A \wedge human_B$ has to be done in a "covert" way. In particular the parties cannot just send to each other their values $human_A$ and $human_B$, and in general none of them can send it to anyone who did not first prove to him that he is human (since the communication is not authenticated, and one never knows to him he is really talking).

A natural idea for a solution is as follows: let Alice reveal to Bob that $human_A = 1$ only if Bob proves to her that he is human. If we apply this in a naive way, then of course we enter a loop, since in turn Bob will be willing to prove this only if Alice proves to him that she is human. Fortunately, it turns out that we can construct a protocol in which Alice and Bob prove to each other that they are human *simultaneously*, i.e. they will prove to each other that they are human, in such a way that if one of them is *not* a human, he will not learn if the other party is a human or not. We call this a *Simultaneous Turing Test*[2] Moreover, also this proof will be *forward-secure* in the sense, that an adversary that solves the Captcha puzzles *after* the protocol was completed, will not have any information about the inputs $human_A$ and $human_B$. The main tool that we use is called Universally-Composable Password Based-Key Exchange (see Sect. 3.4 for more on this).

While from this description it may seem that our protocol is very complicated, the good news is that in fact from the user point of view the execution of the protocol is quite simple. In particular, each of the users will need to solve the Captcha puzzle only once, during the Simultaneous Turing Test, and the rest of the protocol will be fully automatic. Our protocol may be implemented in the following way. When the users start communicating, each of them has an option to choose a "secure connection" (by pressing some button in his interface, say). In this case his client shows him a Captcha sent from the other user, and the user has 1 minute, say, to solve it. If also the other user solved the Captcha then the client displays an information "secure connection established", and otherwise it says "insecure connection". The user of course does not know if it is because the other user has not chosen "secure connection", or because the adversary interfered in the transmission, but this is unavoidable in our model.

The option to switch to the secure mode may be permanently available for the users (i.e. the clients can, invisibly for the users, execute the key agrement scheme every minute, say). Of course, the users should not explicitly say (over an insecure link) that they want to establish a secure connection, since it would violate Req. 3. The user can, however, indicate it in some non-explicit way, hoping that the other player will understand it, but an inattentive adversary will not.

One of the possible weaknesses of this model is that it does not distinguish between a user that makes an error while solving Captcha, and an adversary. Fortunately, we have an extended version of the protocol (see Sect. 4.5), where the user has a right to a couple of tries when solving Captcha.

3 Tools

3.1 Message Authentication Codes

Message Authentication Codes (MACs) is a tool for guaranteeing integrity of communication between two paries that share a key. An introduction to MACs and a complete

[2] In some sense this is similar in spirit to the problem of secure two-party computation of a conjunction. Recall that a secure evaluation of a two-party function $f : \{0,1\}^* \times \{0,1\}^* \rightarrow \{0,1\}^*$ is a protocol that allows Alice and Bob to learn $f(x_{\mathtt{Alice}}, x_{\mathtt{Bob}})$ without revealing to each other their respective inputs $x_{\mathtt{Alice}}$ and $x_{\mathtt{Bob}}$. This means in particular that if f is a conjunction of two bits then the following security guarantee holds for both $P \in \{\mathtt{Alice}, \mathtt{Bob}\}$: if $x_P = 0$ then P will not know if the input of the other party was 0 or 1. See e.g. [13] for an introduction to this area.

security definition can be found, e.g., in [20]. We will use a following definition of MACs. MAC is a pair of algorithms $(Tag, Vrfy)$, such that Tag takes as an input a random secret key $S \in \{0,1\}^k$ and a message $M \in \{0,1\}^*$. It outputs an *authentication tag* $Tag_S(M)$. We require that always $Vrfy_S(M, Tag_S(M)) = 1$. It is *secure against chosen-message attack* if any polynomial probabilistic time adversary (taking as input 1^k) has negligible[3] (in k) chances of producing a pair (M, T) such that $Vrfy_S(M,T) = 1$, even after seeing an arbitrary number of pairs $(M_1, Tag_S(M_1)), (M_2, Tag_S(M_2))\ldots$ (where $M \notin \{M_1, M_2, \ldots\}$) and even when $M_1, M_2, \ldots$ were adaptively chosen by the adversary.

In our construction we will use a special type of MACs, that have the following non-standard feature: informally, it should be infeasible to discover if two tags were computed with the same key. More precisely, we require that for $S_0, S_1 \in \{0,1\}^k$ chosen uniformly at random, and for any $M_0 \neq M_1$ no polynomial-time adversary that knows $Tag_{S_0}(M_0)$ can distinguish between $Tag_{S_0}(M_1)$ (i.e. M_1 encrypted with the same key) and $Tag_{S_1}(M_1)$ (i.e. M_1 encrypted with a fresh key). This can be formalized as follows: for every polynomial-time machine $\mathcal{A}$ and every M_0 and M_1 we have that

$$\begin{array}{l} |P\left(\mathcal{A}(Tag_{S_0}(M_0), Tag_{S_0}(M_1) = 1)\right) \\ -P\left(\mathcal{A}(Tag_{S_0}(M_0), Tag_{S_1}(M_1) = 1)\right)| \\ \text{is negligible.} \end{array} \tag{1}$$

The standard definition of MACs does not guarantee this. This is because the definition of MACs does not require that no information about the key leaks to the adversary. For example, it may be possible that a MAC is secure, but the first 10 bits of S can be computed from $Tag_S(M)$ (and hence it can be easily checked if two tags were computed with the same key). Luckily, concrete examples of MACs satisfy this extended definition. One example is the standard construction of a MAC from a pseudorandom function (cf. e.g. [20], Sect. 4.4). Recall, that a pseudorandom function (which is essentially the same as a *block-cipher*) is a function f that takes as input some key S, and a (fixed-length) *block* M and outputs a *ciphertext* $C = f_S(M)$ of the same length. Informally speaking, the security of the pseudorandom functions is defined as follows: for every sequence of blocks $M_1, \ldots, M_t$ the string $f_S(M_1), \ldots, f_S(M_t)$ should be indistinguishable from random (even is the blocks $M_1, \ldots, M_t$ are chosen adaptively by the adversary). It is easy to see that a function $Tag_S^{prf}(M) = f_S(M)$ (with $Vrfy^{prf}$ defined in a straightforward way) is a secure MAC that works on messages of fixed length. It can be extended to work on messages of arbitrary length by first hashing a message with a collision-resistant hash function H, and then applying f, i.e. setting $Tag_S^{prf,H}(M) := f_S(H(M))$ (this method is called *hash-and-authenticate*, cf. [20]).

The reason why for any polynomial-time $\mathcal{A}$ the scheme Tag^{prf} satisfies (1) is that, from the definition of a pseudorandom function, both $Tag_{S_0}^{prf}(M_0), Tag_{S_0}^{prf}(M_1)$ and $Tag_{S_0}^{prf}(M_0), Tag_{S_1}^{prf}(M_1)$ are indistinguishable from random strings, and hence, obviously, they are indistinguishable from each other. The same holds for $Tag^{prf,H}$.

---

[3] A $f : \mathcal{N} \to \mathcal{R}$ function is *negligible in* k if for every $c \geq 1$ there exists k_0 such that for every $k \geq k_0$ we have $|f(k)| \leq k^{-c}$.

3.2 Key Agreement

Key Agreement is a scheme that allows two parties, Alice and Bob, that initially share no secret, to establish a common key. For simplicity, in this paper we restrict ourselves to one-round key agreement protocols. Hence, for us a key agreement protocol is a triple of randomized interactive algorithms $(KA_{\texttt{Alice}}, KA_{\texttt{Bob}}, KA_{Key})$. Let $r_{\texttt{Alice}}$ and $r_{\texttt{Bob}}$ denote the respective random inputs of the players. In the first step each algorithm $P \in \{\texttt{Alice}, \texttt{Bob}\}$ sends to the other one a message $m_P = KA_P(r_P)$. Then, Alice calculates her output $K_{\texttt{Alice}} = KA_{Key}(r_{\texttt{Alice}}, m_{\texttt{Bob}})$ and Bob calculates his output $K_{\texttt{Bob}} = KA_{Key}(r_{\texttt{Bob}}, m_{\texttt{Alice}})$. We require that always $K_{\texttt{Alice}} = K_{\texttt{Bob}}$. Security of $(\texttt{Alice}, \texttt{Bob})$ is defined in the following way: for any polynomial time adversary that can see $m_{\texttt{Alice}}$ and $m_{\texttt{Bob}}$ the key $K_{\texttt{Alice}}$ should be indistinguishable from a random string of the same length. Of course, if the adversary is active, then he can cause $K_{\texttt{Alice}} \neq K_{\texttt{Bob}}$, or $K_P = error$ (for $P \in \{\texttt{Alice}, \texttt{Bob}\}$).

An example of a key agreement protocol is the protocol of Diffie and Hellman [14]. Let G be a cyclic group, and let g be its generator. The protocol works as follows: each user P selects a random exponent $r_P \in Z_{|G|}$, calculates $m_P := g^{r_P}$ and sends it to the other player. Then, each player calculates $K := (m_P)^{r_P}$. The protocol is correct, since $(g^{r_{\texttt{Alice}}})^{r_{\texttt{Bob}}} = (g^{r_{\texttt{Bob}}})^{r_{\texttt{Alice}}}$. The protocol is secure under a so-called *Decisional Diffie-Hellman Assumption* in (G, g). See, e.g., [20] for more on this.

Authenticated Key Agreement (AKA) is a protocol between Alice and Bob that share a common key K that allows them to generate a fresh *session key*. It can be constructed from the Key Agreement Scheme described, by asking both users to authenticated their messages with a MAC (using the key K). In our construction we will need a stronger version of this notion, that we call a *Covert-AKA*. This is described below.

3.3 Covert-AKA

As a building-block for our main construction we introduce a scheme that we call *Covert-AKA*. It is a protocol between Alice and Bob. The players have as input two keys sk_A and sk_B. The protocol is executed either with $sk_A = sk_B$ (this is called the "equal keys" case), or with sk_A independent from sk_B (this is called the "independent keys" case). The properties of the protocol are as follows. If the adversary is passive, then

- in the "equal keys" case both parties output the same output: $(secure, K)$,
- in the "independent keys" case both parties output $(normal, K)$.

If the adversary is active then

- in the "equal keys"case he can cause each party (independently) to output $(normal, K')$ (for some K', that can be different for both parties), or $error$
- in the "independent keys" case he can cause each party (independently) to output $error$.

The security conditions are as follows: (1) no polynomial-time adversary that attacks the protocol (even actively) can distinguish between the "equal keys" and "independent keys" case, and (2) whenever one of the parties outputs $(secure, K)$, the key K is indistinguishable from random, for a polynomial-time adversary.

Covert-AKA can be implemented in a similar way to the normal AKA, namely both players execute a passively secure key agreement, authenticating their messages in with the keys sk_A and sk_B, resp. The complete protocol is presented on Fig. 1.

Obviously, if $sk_A = sk_B$ then the players just executed a normal authenticated key agreement, and hence whenever the adversary tampers with the messages he can cause the parties to output $(normal, K')$ (by tampering just with the tag), or *error* (by, e.g., destroying the whole message). If the keys are independent then obviously the verification of the tag will fail.[4] Therefore the adversary cannot force any parties to output *secure*. Moreover, if he is passive, then both parties will always output $(normal, K)$.

Observe, that if the players use a standard MAC scheme for authentication, then the adversary that observes the transcript can in principle see if the keys are equal or independent, since, as explained in Sect. 3.1 a MAC does not even need to hide the entire key. Hence, we use Tag^{prf} constructed in Sect. 3.1, that has exactly the property that the adversary, after seeing the messages $m_{\texttt{Alice}}$ and $m_{\texttt{Bob}}$, and the Tags on them, cannot distinguish (with a non-negligible advantage) if they were authenticated with the same key, or two independent keys.

Alice		Bob
$m_{\texttt{Alice}} := KA_{\texttt{Alice}}(r_{\texttt{Alice}})$ $t_{\texttt{Alice}} := Tag^{prf}_{sk}(\texttt{Alice}, m_{\texttt{Alice}})$	$\xrightarrow{((\texttt{Alice}, m_{\texttt{Alice}}), t_{\texttt{Alice}})}$ $\xleftarrow{((\texttt{Bob}, m_{\texttt{Bob}}), t_{\texttt{Bob}})}$	$m_{\texttt{Bob}} := KA_{\texttt{Bob}}(r_{\texttt{Bob}})$ $t_{\texttt{Bob}} := Tag^{prf}_{sk}(\texttt{Bob}, m_{\texttt{Bob}})$
if $KA_{Key}(r_{\texttt{Alice}}, m_{\texttt{Bob}}) = error$ then output $error$		if $KA_{Key}(r_{\texttt{Bob}}, m_{\texttt{Alice}}) = error$ then output $error$
otherwise:		otherwise:
if $Vrfy^{prf}_{sk}((\texttt{Bob}, m_{\texttt{Bob}}), t_{\texttt{Bob}}) = 1$ then output $(secure, KA_{Key}(r_{\texttt{Alice}}, m_{\texttt{Bob}}))$ otherwise output $(normal, KA_{Key}(r_{\texttt{Alice}}, m_{\texttt{Bob}}))$.		if $Vrfy^{prf}_{sk}((\texttt{Alice}, m_{\texttt{Alice}}), t_{\texttt{Bob}}) = 1$ then output $(secure, KA_{Key}(r_{\texttt{Bob}}, m_{\texttt{Alice}}))$ otherwise output $(normal, KA_{Key}(r_{\texttt{Bob}}, m_{\texttt{Alice}}))$.

Fig. 1. The Covert-AKA scheme. $(KA_{\texttt{Alice}}, KA_{\texttt{Bob}}, KA_{Key})$ is the passively secure key agreement from Sect. 3.2. Tag^{prf} is the Message Authentication Code from Sect. 3.1.

3.4 Universally-Composable Password Authenticated Key Exchange

As briefly mentioned in Sect. 1.1 there exist key-agreement protocols, where it is enough that the users share a *password*. Such schemes, introduced in [5], are called *Password Authenticated Key Exchange* protocols. The main difference between a password, and a cryptographic key is that the latter is usually assumed to have a unform distribution

[4] Actually, here we really need the assumption that the keys are independent, since otherwise the adversary could in principle be able to exploit the correlations between the keys, and launch a related-key attack.

over some set $\{0,1\}^m$, and the distribution of the former can be very far from uniform over $\{0,1\}^m$, e.g., it can be known to the adversary that the password is a word from a dictionary. It is particularly important that such schemes offer protection against the *off-line password guessing attacks*, i.e. the attacks, where the adversary can perform an exhaustive search for a correct password, after he saw the transcript of the communication. The design of such schemes attracted a considerable interest [4,7,26,18,28,21,8] during the last two decades, and has proven to be a challenging task. It has even been non-trivial to come up with the right security definitions. For example, most of the definitions made an unrealistic assumption that the passwords are chosen according to some pre-determined distribution, and that the passwords between different pairs of parties are chosen independently.

In this paper we will use a very strong version of such a protocol, called *Universally-Composable Password Authenticated Key Exchange (UC PAK)*, defined and constructed in [11]. Its definition follows the *Universal Composability* (UC) paradigm of Canetti [10]. There is no space here for a general introduction to the UC framework. Let us just highlight that in the UC framework a protocol Π is defined secure with respect to an *ideal functionality* F which it is supposed to "emulate". The security definition guarantees that if another protocol uses Π as a subroutine one can simply replace each call to Π with a call to F. This holds if the protocols are executed in an arbitrary way, and even if several instances of the same protocol are executed concurrently. To achieve this strong property the security definition has to take into account that the inputs of the honest parties can be chosen in an arbitrary way. This is modeled by introducing a machine called *environment* $\mathcal{Z}$ that is responsible for choosing the inputs.

The ideal functionality of the UC PAK appears in [11]. Informally, the main security guarantees of the UC PAK are as follows. Suppose that the parties are Alice and Bob, each of them holding a password $\pi_{\texttt{Alice}}$, and $\pi_{\texttt{Bob}}$, resp. At the end of the execution both parties obtain either

1. the same uniformly-random session key sk — if $\pi_{\texttt{Alice}} = \pi_{\texttt{Bob}}$ and the adversary did not attempt to compromise the session,
2. two different uniformly-random keys $sk_{\texttt{Alice}}$ and $sk_{\texttt{Bob}}$ (resp.), chosen independently — if $\pi_{\texttt{Alice}} \neq \pi_{\texttt{Bob}}$ or the adversary attempted to compromise the session,

The adversary can compromise the session either by guessing a password (he has a right to *one* such guess), or by corrupting one of the parties. In both cases he has a right to choose the keys that the parties receive. Unless the adversary compromised the session, the only information that he obtains is the fact the the parties executed the protocol. He does not even learn what was the output of the protocol, i.e. if the parties agreed on the same key sk (Case 1 above) or if each of them received a different key chosen independently (Case 2). We will use this property in our construction.[5]

An important feature of the UC framework is that the inputs of the users (in this case: $\pi_{\texttt{Alice}}$ and $\pi_{\texttt{Bob}}$) are chosen by the environment $\mathcal{Z}$ and hence, for example, it may be the case that $\pi_{\texttt{Alice}}$ and $\pi_{\texttt{Bob}}$, although not equal, are in some way correlated. In reality some correlation like this is not an unusual case, since it happens, for example, if a user

[5] In [11] the authors say that they are not aware of any application where this is needed. In fact, it may the first application when this feature is used.

mistypes his password. Another useful feature of the UC PAK is that it provides the *forward-security*, in other words, guessing the password after the session was completed does not give the adversary any additional information.

The first UC PAK was constructed in [11], and proven secure in the common reference string model under the standard number-theoretic assumptions. In [1] the authors prove (in the random oracle model) that one of the existing, more efficient protocols [8] is also UC-secure.

4 The Construction

4.1 Modeling Captchas

It is non-trivial to model Captcha in a proper way. We define a *captcha scheme* to be a pair (G, H), where G is a randomized algorithm called a *captcha generator* that takes as input a string $x \in \{0,1\}^*$ and outputs a *captcha* $G(x)$, and H is a solution function such that we always have $H(G(x)) = x$. We say that (G, H) is secure if for every poly-time adversary $\mathcal{A}$ and for x chosen uniformly at random from $\{0,1\}^m$ we have that

$$|P(\mathcal{A}(G(x)) = x)| \text{ is negligible in } m. \tag{2}$$

Our model is inspired by [12], the main difference being that we explicitly assume that for any solution x one can efficiently generate the Captcha puzzles that have x as their solution (by calculating $y := G(x)$). This makes the description of our protocol a bit simpler, and it also excludes the Captchas where the creator of the puzzle does not know the entire solution to it (an example of such a system is the reCaptcha scheme described in Sect. 1.1). In fact, our protocol works only with the Captchas where the complete solution is known to its creator. Observe that we do not assume anything about the non-malleability of the Captcha puzzles, i.e. it may be possible for the adversary that knows some puzzle $z = G(x)$ to produce (without decoding x) a puzzle that z' such that $H(z')$ is in some way related to x. This corresponds to the real-life situation, where the Captcha puzzles are indeed malleable (for example, removing the first letter from a graphical representation of a text may be easy, even if the whole text is unreadable. Observe also, that the only thing that we require in (2) is that the *whole* solution x is hard to compute, and a Captcha scheme may satisfy our definition even if some part of x is not hidden from the adversary.

To make our model more realistic, we could relax this definition a little bit and require that the probability in (2) is smaller than some $p(m)$ (where p is a function that would be a parameter in the definition, and could be non-negligible). We do not do it since it would complicate our exposition.

A subtle point is how to model the human adversary. As explained in Sect. 2 the adversary can always break the security of some sessions if he uses a human to solve the Captchas, and an important property of our scheme is that only those sessions get broken. Therefore, we need somehow to capture the fact that an adversary "used a human" in some session. To do it, we introduce a *captcha oracle* $\Omega_{G,H}$, which is a machine that accepts requests

- $captcha(x)$ – in this case the oracle replies with $G(x)$,
- $solve(y)$ — in this case the oracle replies with $H(y)$.

In this way we will be able to attach a formal meaning to the expression: "the adversary broke a Captcha of a user P_i": we will say it if the user sent a $solve(y)$ request to the oracle, where y was an output of $G(x)$ and x was $captcha(x)$ was sent to the oracle by P_i. Since we did not assume that Captchas are non-malleable, the adversary could of course "cheat" and send a $solve$ request with a slightly modified y, to circumvent this definition. In order to prevent it, we require that the adversary is only allowed to send $solve(y)$ queries for those y's that in the past were produced as output by the oracle in a response to a $captcha(x)$ query. This restriction may look quite arbitrary, but it is hard to think about any alternative. Observe that, since the Captchas are malleable, in principle there can exist a way to combine several Captchas $y_1 = captcha(x_1), \ldots, y_t = captcha(x_t)$ into one "super-Captcha" whose solution would solve all $y_1, \ldots, y_t$. Therefore to reason formally about it, we would somehow need to be able to measure the "amount of human work" that the adversary invested into breaking the protocol. Since the goal of this paper is to present the protocol, not to introduce a new formal model, we do not investigate it further.

4.2 An Informal Description of the Human Key Agreement Protocol

The high-level description of the model was already presented in Sect. 2. Before defining it formally we give an informal description of the protocol. Recall that the key point of the protocol is the *Simultaneous Turing Test*, which is a procedure that allows two parties to test if they are both human, in such a way that if one of them is not human he will not learn whether the other is human or not. Before defining the model formally, we provide an informal description of the protocol. Consider two players, Alice and Bob, holding inputs $human_{\texttt{Alice}}$ and $human_{\texttt{Bob}}$, resp., where for $P \in \{\texttt{Alice}, \texttt{Bob}\}$ we have $human_P = 1$ if and only if the player P wants to use the secure mode (and hence is willing to solve Captchas).

At the beginning Alice and Bob select randomly two strings $x_{\texttt{Alice}}$ and $x_{\texttt{Bob}}$, resp. Then each of them creates a Captcha whose solution is the string that he has chosen, i.e. Alice calculates $y_{\texttt{Alice}} := captcha(x_{\texttt{Alice}})$ and Bob calculates $y_{\texttt{Bob}} := captcha(x_{\texttt{Bob}})$. Afterwards, they send to each other, over an insecure link, the values $y_{\texttt{Alice}}$ and $y_{\texttt{Bob}}$, together with their identities (Alice and Bob), and a bit indicating their roles in the protocol (Alice sends 0 and Bob sends 1). Now, Alice does the following: if $human_{\texttt{Alice}} = 1$ then she solves the Captcha $y_{\texttt{Bob}}$, and sets $x'_{\texttt{Bob}} := solve(y_{\texttt{Bob}})$, and otherwise she sets $x'_{\texttt{Bob}}$ to be equal to some default value $((0, \ldots, 0)$, say). Bob does a symmetric thing, i.e. he solves $y_{\texttt{Alice}}$ if and only if $human_{\texttt{Bob}} := 1$, setting $x'_{\texttt{Alice}} := solve(y_B)$ and setting $x'_{\texttt{Alice}} := (0, \ldots, 0)$. Denote $\pi_{\texttt{Alice}} = (x_{\texttt{Alice}}, x'_{\texttt{Bob}})$ and $\pi_{\texttt{Bob}} = (x'_{\texttt{Alice}}, x_{\texttt{Bob}})$.

Now, observe that if the adversary did not disturb the communication then we have that $\pi_{\texttt{Alice}} = \pi_{\texttt{Bob}}$ if and only if $human_{\texttt{Alice}} = human_{\texttt{Bob}} = 1$. If this is the case then we will denote the value of $human_{\texttt{Alice}} (= human_{\texttt{Bob}})$ with $\pi_{\texttt{Alice,Bob}}$. If the adversary did disturb the communication then he can always cause $(x_{\texttt{Alice}}, x'_{\texttt{Bob}}) \neq (x'_{\texttt{Alice}}, x_{\texttt{Bob}})$, just by modifying one of the Captchas that were sent over the insecure network, but as long as he is *not* a human it is infeasible for him to cause $(x_{\texttt{Alice}}, x'_{\texttt{Bob}}) = (x'_{\texttt{Alice}}, x_{\texttt{Bob}})$, if $human_{\texttt{Alice}} \neq 1$, or $human_{\texttt{Bob}} \neq 1$, since to do this he would need to solve a Captcha himself.

Observe also that a *machine*-adversary has negligible chances of deciphering $x_{\texttt{Alice}}$ and $x_{\texttt{Bob}}$, and hence, if $human_{\texttt{Alice}} = human_{\texttt{Bob}} = 1$ then the value of $\pi_{\texttt{Alice,Bob}}$ is hidden from him. Moreover, observe that until this point the players did not send to each other the Captcha solutions, and hence the values of $human_P$ remain secret.

In the second phase, the players execute a UC PAK with Alice setting her password to $(\texttt{Alice}, \texttt{Bob}, \pi_{\texttt{Alice}})$, and Bob setting his password to $(\texttt{Alice}, \texttt{Bob}, \pi_{\texttt{Bob}})$. From the properties of UC PAK if $\pi_{\texttt{Alice}} = \pi_{\texttt{Bob}}$ and the execution of the protocol was not disturbed actively by the adversary, then the parties will agree on a common key sk. If $\pi_{\texttt{Alice}} \neq \pi_{\texttt{Bob}}$ then the parties will receive two independent and uniformly-chosen keys sk and sk'. The adversary can cause the same effect by actively disturbing the communication during the execution of PAK. The important thing is, however, that he does not get any information about the inputs $\pi_{\texttt{Alice}}$ and $\pi_{\texttt{Bob}}$, which in turn implies that, no matter what his actions are, he does not know the inputs $human_{\texttt{Alice}}$ and $human_{\texttt{Bob}}$. Hence, after the second phase the players either share the same key sk, or have to independent keys $sk_{\texttt{Alice}}$ and $sk_{\texttt{Bob}}$, resp. Now:

- If $sk_{\texttt{Alice}} \neq sk_{\texttt{Bob}}$ (which happened either because $human_{\texttt{Alice}} \wedge human_{\texttt{Bob}} = 0$, or because the adversary disturbed the communication), then the users will generate a new fresh key for communication. Of course this key will be secure only against a passive adversary (since the users do not share any secret)
- If the users share the same key (i.e. $sk_{\texttt{Alice}} = sk_{\texttt{Bob}}$) then they can use this key to establish a common session key, using an authenticated key agreement.

Of course, the adversary should not be able to distinguish which was the case (since it would give him information about $human_{\texttt{Alice}} \wedge human_{\texttt{Bob}}$). Here we use the Covert-AKA (see Sect. 3.3), that is constructed exactly for this purpose: it allows Alice and Bob, that have keys keys sk_A and sk_B, resp. to establish a common key. If $sk_A = sk_B$ then it is a normal AKA, if sk_A and sk_B are independent, then it is a passively secure key agreement. The users are notified which was the case, while the adversary does not know it. The Human Key Agreement protocol is depicted on Fig. 2.

4.3 A Formal Model

In this section we present a formal definition of our model. An important point is that we have to take into account that several players may execute the protocol concurrently. Since in our model the adversary fully controls the network, we cannot prevent him from hijacking a message that some player P_i to sent to P_j, and forwarding it to some other P_k. Therefore, the players, during the execution of the protocol have to exchange their identities. Of course, if P_k is malicious then he can falsely claim to be P_i (we cannot prevent it). So, from the point of view of P_i the security guarantee is as follows: he knows that either he is talking to P_j, or he is talking to some malicious *human* (since an honest P_k would reveal to him that his identity is P_k, not P_j). Hence, in our model there is no difference between a malicious participant, and a human-adversary. Therefore, for simplicity, we assume that all the players are honest.

	Alice	*Bob*

Phase 1   selects a random $x_{\mathtt{Alice}}$

computes $y_{\mathtt{Alice}} := captcha(x_{\mathtt{Alice}})$

selects a random $x_{\mathtt{Alice}}$

computes $y_{\mathtt{Bob}} := captcha(x_{\mathtt{Bob}})$

$\xrightarrow{(\mathtt{Alice}, y_{\mathtt{Alice}}, 0)}$

$\xleftarrow{(\mathtt{Bob}, y_{\mathtt{Bob}}, 1)}$

if $human_{\mathtt{Alice}} = 1$ then

set $x'_{\mathtt{Bob}} := solve(y_{\mathtt{Bob}})$

otherwise

set $x'_{\mathtt{Bob}} := (0, \ldots, 0)$.

if $human_{\mathtt{Bob}} = 1$ then

set $x'_{\mathtt{Alice}} := solve(y_{\mathtt{Alice}})$

otherwise

set $x'_{\mathtt{Alice}} := (0, \ldots, 0)$.

set $\pi_{\mathtt{Alice}} := (\mathtt{Alice}, \mathtt{Bob}, x_{\mathtt{Alice}}, x'_{\mathtt{Bob}})$

set $\pi_{\mathtt{Bob}} := (\mathtt{Alice}, \mathtt{Bob}, x'_{\mathtt{Alice}}, x_{\mathtt{Bob}})$

Phase 2 $\xrightarrow{\pi_{\mathtt{Alice}}}$ $\xleftarrow{\pi_{\mathtt{Bob}}}$

UC PAK

$\xleftarrow{sk_{\mathtt{Alice}}}$ $\xrightarrow{sk_{\mathtt{Bob}}}$

Phase 3 $\xrightarrow{sk_{\mathtt{Alice}}}$ $\xleftarrow{sk_{\mathtt{Bob}}}$

Covert AKA

$\xleftarrow{out_{\mathtt{Alice}}}$ $\xrightarrow{out_{\mathtt{Bob}}}$

Output $(\mathtt{Bob}, 0, out_{\mathtt{Alice}})$ Output $(\mathtt{Alice}, 1, out_{\mathtt{Bob}})$

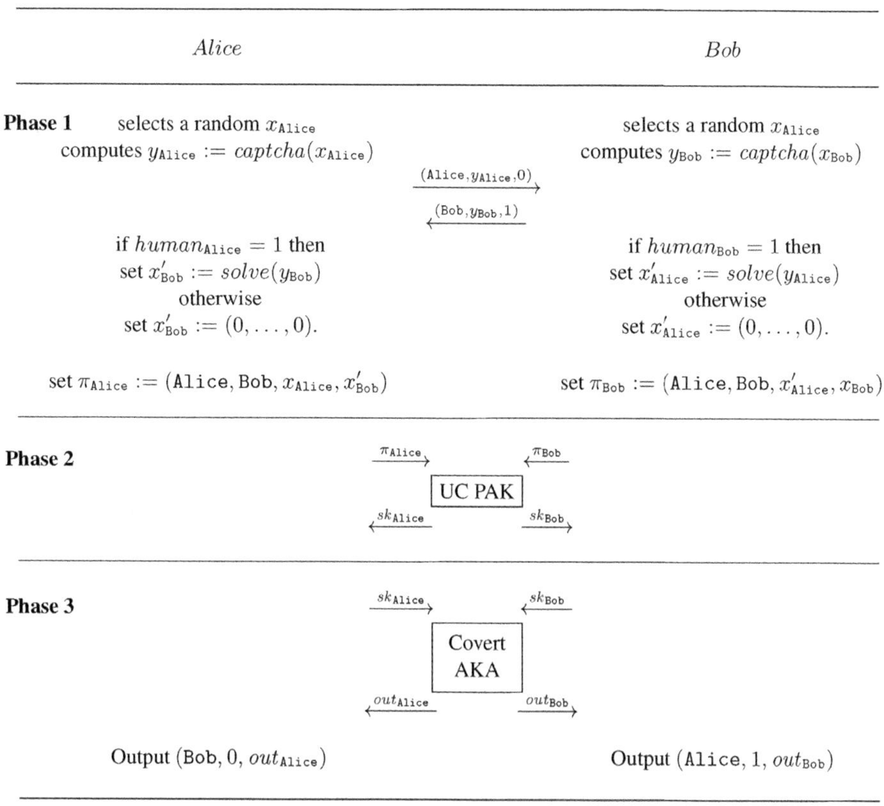

Fig. 2. The Human Key Agreement Protocol. Each out_P is equal to $(secure, K)$, $(normal, K)$ or $error$. The reason why $\mathtt{Alice}$ outputs $(\mathtt{Bob}, 0, out_{\mathtt{Alice}})$ instead of just outputting $out_{\mathtt{Alice}}$ is required by the formal model (that we define in Sect. 4.3) to make sure that the parties have a consistent view on who started the protocol, and what is the identity of the other party.

Other simplifying assumption that we make is that we will consider only two variants of the adversary: *passive* or *active* — in principle the adversary could passively attack some pairs of users, and actively attack the others, but modeling if formally would just complicate the presentation.

We also assume that the each user P_i decides at the beginning of the protocol if he wants to connect securely to all the other users (by setting his flag $human_i := 1$). We in fact assume that $human_i = 1$ with probability $1/2$. This choice is made just not to make the mode too complicated. In fact, our protocol is secure also secure if the users can decide adaptively during the execution of the protocol that to which users they want to connect securely, and to which not.

The adversary in our model is very powerful: he fully controls the network, and he can initiate the sessions between the players by sending request $start(P_i, P_j, role)$ (where $role$ is a bit indicating which party initiates the protocol). For simplicity, we assume that each pair of users generates the key at most one with the same roles (hence, at most twice in total).

Formally, a *Human Key Agreement protocol* is a set of players $\mathcal{P} = \{P_1, \ldots, P_n\}$ represented as interactive randomized machines. An *adversary* is a randomized poly-time interactive machine. The adversary may be *passive* or *active*. Let 1^m be a security parameter that all the players and the adversary take as input. At the beginning each player P_i selects a random bit $human_i \in \{0, 1\}$. Each player P_i is allowed to send to the oracle $\Omega_{G,H}$ the $captcha$ queries. If $human_i = 1$ then P_i is also allowed to send to the oracle the $solve$ queries. The adversary can send to the oracle $captcha$ and $solve$ queries, with the restriction that he can only send a query $solve(y)$, if some player P_i received y as a response to his $captcha$ query. In this case we say that the adversary *solved a captcha of* P_i.

The players start executing the protocol. The execution is divided into rounds. At the beginning of the execution the players are idle. During the execution the players just wait for the requests from the adversary. The adversary can *wake up* each P_i by sending to it a requests $start(P_i, P_j, role)$, where $P_j \in \mathcal{P}$ and $role \in \{0, 1\}$. We assume that $\mathcal{A}$ never sends twice the same message $start(P_i, P_j, role)$. If the adversary is passive then whenever he sends a request $start(P_i, P_j, 0)$ to some P_i in the same round he also sends $start(P_j, P_i, 1)$ to some P_j. After P_i receives a $start(P_i, P_j, role)$ request it wakes up and starts interacting with P_j (we say that P_i *starts a session with* P_j), for a number of rounds. At the beginning of each round P_i can issue a pair (P_j, m) and $m \in \{0, 1\}^*$. These values are passed to the adversary. If the adversary is *passive* then he has to deliver m to P_j, i.e. he has to send a pair (m, P_i) to P_j. If the adversary is *active* he can also prevent m from reaching P_j, modify it, send it to someone else, or fabricate new messages. At the end of the interaction P_i outputs one of the following values (suppose P_i was woken up by a $start(P_i, P_j, role)$ message):

- $(P_j, role, (secure, K_{i,j}))$, where key $K_{i,j} \in \{0, 1\}^m$,
- $(P_j, role, (normal, K_{i,j}))$, where key $K_{i,j} \in \{0, 1\}^m$,
- a message $(P_j, role, error)$.

After producing the output P_i enters again the idle mode (we say that P_i *ended the session*), and waits for the next $start$ message from the adversary. At some point the adversary sends to every player P_i a message end which causes the players to terminate, and a *post-execution game* starts. During this game the adversary can start interacting with an oracle $\Omega_{G,H}$. In particular, he can issue $solve$ requests to the oracle. For every P_i the adversary outputs $human_i^{\mathcal{A}}$. We say that the protocol *human-hiding* if for every P_i such that the adversary did not solve P_i's captcha *before the protocol terminated*, the probability that $human_i^{\mathcal{A}} = human_i$ is at most $1/2 + \epsilon(m)$, where m is negligible.

For each $K_{i,j}$ that was output by some of the players during the execution of the protocol a random bit $b \in \{0, 1\}$ is selected, and the following is calculated and sent to the adversary:

$$K' = \begin{cases} K_{i,j} & \text{if } b = 0 \\ \text{uniformly random } K \in \{0,1\}^m & \text{otherwise.} \end{cases}$$

The adversary outputs $b^{\mathcal{A}} \in \{0, 1\}$. We say that he *distinguished* $K_{i,j}$ *from random* if $b = b^{\mathcal{A}}$. We say that the $K_{i,j}$*-session key is secret* if the probability (taken over the randomness of the adversary and the players) that the adversary distinguishes the $K_{i,j}$ from random is at most $1/2 + \epsilon(m)$, where ϵ is negligible. We say that $(\pi, \Omega_{G,H})$ is *secure* if both following conditions holds

- if the adversary is passive then at the end of a session between P_i and P_j player P_i outputs $(P_j, 0, (secure, K_{i,j}))$, and player P_j outputs $(P_i, 1, (secure, K_{i,j}))$. Moreover, the key $K_{i,j}$ is secret.
- if the adversary is active then whenever some P_i outputs $(P_j, role, (secure, K_{i,j}))$, and the adversary did not solve P_i's captcha during the session that led to producing this output, then:
  - with overwhelming probability in the same round P_j outputs $(P_i, role, (secure, K_{i,j}))$, or $(P_i, role, error)$, and
  - the key $K_{i,j}$ is secret.

Moreover, the protocol has to be human-hiding.

4.4 The Implementation

The implementation was already discussed informally in Sect. 4.2, and depicted on Fig. 2). We now present our protocol in the framework from Sect. 4.3. To make our description consistent with the description in Sect. 4.2 we call the two parties Alice and Bob, instead of P_j and P_j.

The Human Key Agreement protocol

1. Alice receives $start(\texttt{Alice}, \texttt{Bob}, 0)$ message, and Bob receives $start(\texttt{Bob}, \texttt{Alice}, 1)$ message,
2. Alice generates a random $x_{\texttt{Alice}} \in \{0,1\}^m$ and asks the oracle to compute $y_{\texttt{Alice}} = captcha(x_{\texttt{Alice}})$. She sends $(\texttt{Alice}, y_{\texttt{Alice}}, 0)$ to Bob.
3. Bob generates a random $x_{\texttt{Bob}} \in \{0,1\}^m$ and asks the oracle to compute $y_{\texttt{Bob}} = captcha(x_{\texttt{Bob}})$. He sends $(\texttt{Bob}, y_{\texttt{Bob}}, 1)$ to Alice.
4. If $human_{\texttt{Alice}} = 1$ then after receiving this message Alice asks the oracle to compute $x'_{\texttt{Bob}} = solve(x_{\texttt{Bob}})$ (in this case $x'_{\texttt{Bob}} = x_{\texttt{Bob}}$)). Otherwise Alice sets $x'_{\texttt{Bob}} := 0^m$.
   She sets $\pi_{\texttt{Alice}} = (\texttt{Alice}, \texttt{Bob}, x_{\texttt{Alice}}, x'_{\texttt{Bob}})$.
5. If $human_{\texttt{Bob}} = 1$ then after receiving this message Bob asks the oracle to compute $x'_{\texttt{Alice}} = solve(x_{\texttt{Alice}})$ (in this case $x'_{\texttt{Alice}} = x_{\texttt{Alice}}$)). Otherwise Bob sets $x'_{\texttt{Alice}} := 0^m$.
   He sets $\pi_{\texttt{Bob}} = (\texttt{Alice}, \texttt{Bob}, x'_{\texttt{Alice}}, x_{\texttt{Bob}})$.
6. Alice and Bob execute the UC PAK protocol setting their passwords to $\pi_{\texttt{Alice}}$ and $\pi_{\texttt{Bob}}$, resp.
7. Alice and Bob execute the Covert-AKA protocol, let $out_{\texttt{Alice}}$ and $out_{\texttt{Bob}}$ be their respective outputs. Then, Alice outputs $(\texttt{Bob}, 0, out_{\texttt{Alice}})$ and Bob outputs $(\texttt{Alice}, 1, out_{\texttt{Bob}})$.

The following lemma will be proven in the full version of this paper.

Lemma 1. *The Human Key Agreement protocol constructed above is secure.*

4.5 Extensions

One of the common problems with Captcha is that even the human users often fail to solve them correctly. In the protocol presented above, unfortunately, the user cannot distinguish between the case when the other user made a mistake solving Captcha, or the case when he is talking to a malicious machine. In the extended version of this paper [16] we show how to extend our protocol in such a way that it permits the user to attempt to solve the Captchas t times.

References

1. Abdalla, M., Catalano, D., Chevalier, C., Pointcheval, D.: Efficient two-party password-based key exchange protocols in the uc framework. In: Malkin, T.G. (ed.) CT-RSA 2008. LNCS, vol. 4964, pp. 335–351. Springer, Heidelberg (2008)
2. Anderson, R.: Two remarks on public key cryptology. Technical report, University of Cambridge, Computer Laboratory, Technical report (2002)
3. Balfanz, D., Smetters, D.K., Stewart, P., Chi Wong, H.: Talking to strangers: Authentication in ad-hoc wireless networks. In: NDSS. The Internet Society (2002)
4. Bellare, M., Pointcheval, D., Rogaway, P.: Authenticated key exchange secure against dictionary attacks. In: Preneel, B. (ed.) EUROCRYPT 2000. LNCS, vol. 1807, pp. 139–155. Springer, Heidelberg (2000)
5. Bellovin, S.M., Merritt, M.: Encrypted key exchange: Password-based protocols secure against dictionary attacks. In: IEEE Security and Privacy, pp. 72–84 (May 1992)
6. Boyd, C.A., Mathuria, A.: Protocols for Key Establishment and Authentication. Springer, New York (2003)
7. Boyko, V., MacKenzie, P.D., Patel, S.: Provably secure password-authenticated key exchange using diffie-hellman. In: Preneel, B. (ed.) EUROCRYPT 2000. LNCS, vol. 1807, pp. 156–171. Springer, Heidelberg (2000)
8. Bresson, E., Chevassut, O., Pointcheval, D.: Security proofs for an efficient password-based key exchange. In: ACM Conference on Computer and Communications Security, pp. 241–250 (2003)
9. Cagalj, M., Capkun, S., Hubaux, J.P.: Key agreement in peer-to-peer wireless networks. Proceedings of the IEEE 94(2), 467–478 (2006)
10. Canetti, R.: Universally composable security: A new paradigm for cryptographic protocols. In: FOCS, pp. 136–145 (2001), Extended version avaialble at `http://eprint.iacr.org/2000/067`
11. Canetti, R., Halevi, S., Katz, J., Lindell, Y., MacKenzie, P.D.: Universally composable password-based key exchange. In: Cramer, R. (ed.) EUROCRYPT 2005. LNCS, vol. 3494, pp. 404–421. Springer, Heidelberg (2005)
12. Canetti, R., Halevi, S., Steiner, M.: Mitigating dictionary attacks on password-protected local storage. In: Dwork, C. (ed.) CRYPTO 2006. LNCS, vol. 4117, pp. 160–179. Springer, Heidelberg (2006)
13. Cramer, R.: Introduction to secure computation. In: Damgård, I.B. (ed.) EEF School 1998. LNCS, vol. 1561, pp. 16–62. Springer, Heidelberg (1999)
14. Diffie, W., Hellman, M.E.: New directions in cryptography. IEEE Transactions on Information Theory IT-22(6), 644–654 (1976)
15. Diffie, W., van Oorschot, P.C., Wiener, M.J.: Authentication and authenticated key exchanges. Designs, Codes, and Cryptography 2(2), 107–125 (1992)

16. Dziembowski, S.: How to pair with a human. Cryptology ePrint Archive, Report 2009/562 (2009), http://eprint.iacr.org/
17. Ellison, C., Schneier, B.: Ten risks of pki: What you're not being told about public key infrastructure. Computer Security Journal 16(1), 1–7 (2000)
18. Goldreich, O., Lindell, Y.: Session-key generation using human passwords only. J. Cryptology 19(3), 241–340 (2006)
19. Günther, C.G.: An identity-based key-exchange protocol. In: Quisquater, J.-J., Vandewalle, J. (eds.) EUROCRYPT 1989. LNCS, vol. 434, pp. 29–37. Springer, Heidelberg (1990)
20. Katz, J., Lindell, Y.: Introduction to Modern Cryptography. Chapman & Hall/CRC Press, Boca Raton (August 2007)
21. Katz, J., Ostrovsky, R., Yung, M.: Forward secrecy in password-only key exchange protocols. In: Cimato, S., Galdi, C., Persiano, G. (eds.) SCN 2002. LNCS, vol. 2576, pp. 29–44. Springer, Heidelberg (2003)
22. Keizer, G.: Spammers' bot cracks microsoft's captcha. Computerworld (February 2008), http://www.computerworld.com/s/article/9061558/Spammers_bot_cracks_ Microsoft_s_CAPTCHA_
23. Kumar, A., Saxena, N., Tsudik, G., Uzun, E.: A comparative study of secure device pairing methods. Pervasive and Mobile Computing Journal, PMC (2009)
24. Laur, S., Nyberg, K.: Efficient mutual data authentication using manually authenticated strings. In: Pointcheval, D., Mu, Y., Chen, K. (eds.) CANS 2006. LNCS, vol. 4301, pp. 90–107. Springer, Heidelberg (2006)
25. Lillibridge, M., Abadi, M., Bharat, K., Broder, A.: Method for selectively restricting access to computer systems. US patent US6195698 (Filling date: April 13, 1998)
26. MacKenzie, P.D., Patel, S., Swaminathan, R.: Password-authenticated key exchange based on rsa. In: Okamoto, T. (ed.) ASIACRYPT 2000. LNCS, vol. 1976, pp. 599–613. Springer, Heidelberg (2000)
27. Naor, M.: Verification of a human in the loop or identification via the turing test (1996), http://www.wisdom.weizmann.ac.il/~naor/PAPERS/human.pdf
28. Nguyen, M.-H., Vadhan, S.P.: Simpler session-key generation from short random passwords. J. Cryptology 21(1), 52–96 (2008)
29. Pasini, S., Vaudenay, S.: Sas-based authenticated key agreement. In: Yung, M., Dodis, Y., Kiayias, A., Malkin, T.G. (eds.) PKC 2006. LNCS, vol. 3958, pp. 395–409. Springer, Heidelberg (2006)
30. Perrig, A., Song, D.: Hash visualization: A new technique to improve real-world security. In: International Workshop on Cryptographic Techniques and E-Commerce (1999)
31. Pinkas, B., Sander, T.: Securing passwords against dictionary attacks. In: ACM CCS 2002, pp. 161–170 (2002)
32. Reuters Press Release. D-link first to add captcha to its home routers to help prevent against attacks (2009), http://www.reuters.com/article/pressRelease/idUS118678+12-May-2009+MW20090512
33. Soriente, C., Tsudik, G., Uzun, E.: Secure pairing of interface constrained devices. Int. J. Secur. Netw. 4(1/2), 17–26 (2009)
34. Stajano, F., Anderson, R.J.: The resurrecting duckling: Security issues for ad-hoc wireless networks. In: Malcolm, J.A., Christianson, B., Crispo, B., Roe, M. (eds.) Security Protocols 1999. LNCS, vol. 1796, pp. 172–194. Springer, Heidelberg (2000)
35. Carnegie Mellon University. The official captcha site, http://www.captcha.net/
36. Vaudenay, S.: Secure communications over insecure channels based on short authenticated strings. In: Shoup, V. (ed.) CRYPTO 2005. LNCS, vol. 3621, pp. 309–326. Springer, Heidelberg (2005)

37. von Ahn, L., Blum, M., Hopper, N.J., Langford, J.: Captcha: Using hard ai problems for security. In: Biham, E. (ed.) EUROCRYPT 2003. LNCS, vol. 2656, pp. 294–311. Springer, Heidelberg (2003)
38. von Ahn, L., Maurer, B., Mcmillen, C., Abraham, D., Blum, M.: recaptcha: Human-based character recognition via web security measures. Science, 1465–1468 (August 2008)
39. BBC News website. Pc stripper helps spam to spread (October 2007), `http://news.bbc.co.uk/2/hi/technology/7067962.stm` (accessed on June 19, 2007)
40. BBC News website. China spying on skype messages (October 2008), `http://news.bbc.co.uk/2/hi/technology/7649761.stm` (accessed on June 19, 2010)
41. Wikipedia. Captcha, `http://en.wikipedia.org/wiki/CAPTCHA` (accessed on June 19, 2010)
42. Zimmermann, P., Johnston, A., Callas, J.: Zrtp: Media path key agreement for secure rtp. Internet draft available at, `http://zfoneproject.com/docs/ietf/draft-zimmermann-avt-zrtp-16.html`
43. Zisiadis, D., Kopsidas, S., Tassiulas, L.: Vipsec defined. Comput. Netw. 52(13), 2518–2528 (2008)

A New Security Model for Authenticated Key Agreement

Augustin P. Sarr[1,2], Philippe Elbaz-Vincent[2], and Jean-Claude Bajard[3]

[1] Netheos R&D
[2] Institut Fourier – CNRS, Université Grenoble 1
[3] LIP6 – CNRS, Université Paris 6

Abstract. The Canetti–Krawczyk (CK) and extended Canetti–Krawczyk (eCK) security models, are widely used to provide security arguments for key agreement protocols. We discuss security shades in the (e)CK models, and some practical attacks unconsidered in (e)CK–security arguments. We propose a strong security model which encompasses the eCK one. We also propose a new protocol, called Strengthened MQV (SMQV), which in addition to provide the same efficiency as the (H)MQV protocols, is particularly suited for distributed implementations wherein a tamper–proof device is used to store long–lived keys, while session keys are used on an untrusted host machine. The SMQV protocol meets our security definition under the Gap Diffie–Hellman assumption and the Random Oracle model.

Keywords: authenticated key agreement, practical vulnerability, strengthened eCK model, SMQV.

1 Introduction

Much of recent research on key agreement deals with provably secure key exchange. Since this approach was pioneered by Bellare and Rogaway [1], different models were proposed [3,5,30,7,13,16]. Among these models, the Canetti–Krawczyk (CK) [7] and extended Canetti–Krawczyk (eCK) [16] models (which are incomparable [10,33]) are considered as "advanced" approaches to capture security of key agreement protocols; and security arguments for recent protocols are usually provided in the (e)CK models.

Broadly, a security model specifies, among other things, what constitutes a security failure, and what adversarial behaviors are being protected against. The aim is that a protocol shown secure, in the model, confines to the minimum the effects of the considered adversarial behaviors. In the CK and eCK models, session specific information leakages are respectively captured using reveal queries on *session states* and *ephemeral keys*, which stores session specific information; the adversary is supposed to interact with parties, and to try to distinguish a session key from a randomly chosen value. A protocol is secure if an adversary controlling communications between parties, cannot distinguish a session key from a random value, unless it makes queries which overtly reveal the session key.

J.A. Garay and R. De Prisco (Eds.): SCN 2010, LNCS 6280, pp. 219–234, 2010.

Unfortunately, adversaries do not always behave as expected. When leakages on intermediate results in computing session keys are considered, (e)CK–secure protocols often fail in authentication; and the widely accepted principle that *an attacker should not be able to impersonate a party, unless it knows the party's static key* is not achieved. This makes clearly desirable a security model, which captures intermediate results leakages resilience, in addition to the security attributes considered in the (e)CK models.

From [29], we have a hybrid security definition, which considers leakages on intermediate results; however the model cannot be shown to encompass the CK or eCK models. In addition, the security definition from [29] considers intermediate results and ephemeral key leakages in separate settings. In this paper, we propose a strong security definition, the *strengthened* eCK (seCK) model, which encompasses the eCK model, and considers leakages on intermediate results in computing session keys. We also propose a new protocol called Strengthened MQV (SMQV). The SMQV protocol provides the same efficiency as the (H)MQV protocols [17,13]. In addition, because of its resilience to intermediate results leakages, SMQV is particularly suited for implementations using a tamper–resistant device, to store the static keys, together with a host machine on which sessions keys are used. In such SMQV implementations, the non–idle time computational effort of the device can be securely reduced to few non–costly operations.

This paper is organized as follows. In section 2 we discuss security shades in the (e)CK models. The protocol $\mathcal{P}$ [23] is described as an example of protocol that is formally CK–secure, but practically insecure, unless session identifiers are added with further restrictions. We also discuss the vulnerability of the NAXOS type protocols to ephemeral Diffie–Hellman (DH) exponent leakages. In section 3 we present the *strengthened* eCK (seCK) model. In section 4, we describe the SMQV protocol, which meets the seCK security definition, and its building blocks. We conclude in section 5.

The following notations are used in this paper: $\mathcal{G}$ denotes a multiplicatively written cyclic group of prime order q generated by G, $|q|$ is the bit length of q; $\mathcal{G}^*$ is the set of non–identity elements in $\mathcal{G}$. For $X \in \mathcal{G}$, the lowercase x denotes the discrete logarithm of X in base G. The identity of a party with public key A is denoted $\hat{A}$ ($\hat{A}$ is supposed to contain A). If $\hat{A} \neq \hat{B}$, we suppose that no substring of $\hat{A}$ equals $\hat{B}$. H is a λ–bit hash function, where λ is the length of session keys, and $\bar{H}$ is a l–bit hash function, where $l = (\lfloor \log_2 q \rfloor + 1)/2$. The symbol $\in_R$ stands for "chosen uniformly at random in." The Computational Diffie–Hellman (CDH) assumption is supposed to hold in $\mathcal{G}$; namely, given $U = G^u$ and $V = G^v$ with $U, V \in_R \mathcal{G}^*$, computing $CDH(U, V) = G^{uv}$ is infeasible.

2 Practical Limitations in the (e)CK Models

In this section, we discuss security shades in the (e)CK models, and the related unconsidered attacks. (Please, refer to [10,33] for outlines and comparisons of the CK and eCK models, or [7,16] for details.)

Practical Inadequacy of the CK Matching Sessions Definition. In the CK model, two sessions with activation parameters $(\hat{P}_i, \hat{P}_j, s, role)$ and $(\hat{P}_j, \hat{P}_s, s', role')$ are said to be matching if they have the same identifiers ($s = s'$). The requirement about the identifiers (id) used at a party is that *"the session id's of no two KE sessions in which the party participates are identical"* [7]. Session identifiers may, for instance, be nonces generated by session initiators and provided to the peers through the first message in the protocol. In this case, when each party stores the previously used identifiers and verifies at session activation that the session identifier was not used before, the requirement that a party never uses the same identifier twice is achieved.

Protocol 1. The protocol $\mathcal{P}$

I) At session activation with parameters $(\hat{A}, \hat{B}, s)$, $\hat{A}$ does the following:
   (a) Create a session with identifier $(\hat{A}, \hat{B}, s, \mathcal{I})$.
   (b) Choose $x \in_R [1, q-1]$.
   (c) Compute $X = G^x$ and $t_A = H_2(B^a, \mathcal{I}, s, \hat{A}, \hat{B}, X)$.
   (d) Send $(\hat{B}, \hat{A}, s, X, t_A)$ to $\hat{B}$.

II) At receipt of $(\hat{B}, \hat{A}, s, X, t_A)$, $\hat{B}$ does the following:
   (a) Verify that $X \in \mathcal{G}^*$.
   (b) Create a session with identifier $(\hat{B}, \hat{A}, s, \mathcal{R})$.
   (c) Compute $\sigma = A^b$ and verify that $t_A = H_2(\sigma, \mathcal{I}, s, \hat{A}, \hat{B}, X)$.
   (d) Choose $y \in_R [1, q-1]$.
   (e) Compute $Y = G^y$, $t_B = H_2(\sigma, \mathcal{R}, s, \hat{B}, \hat{A}, Y)$, and $K = H(X^y, X, Y)$.
   (f) Destroy y and σ, and send $(\hat{A}, \hat{B}, s, \mathcal{I}, Y, t_B)$ to $\hat{A}$.
   (g) Complete $(\hat{B}, \hat{A}, s, \mathcal{R})$ by accepting K as the session key.

III) At receipt of $(\hat{A}, \hat{B}, s, \mathcal{I}, Y, t_B)$, $\hat{A}$ does the following:
   (a) Verify the existence of an active session with identifier $(\hat{A}, \hat{B}, s, \mathcal{I})$.
   (b) Verify that $Y \in \mathcal{G}^*$.
   (c) Verify that $t_B = H_2(B^a, \mathcal{R}, s, \hat{B}, \hat{A}, Y)$.
   (d) Compute $K = H(Y^x, X, Y)$.
   (e) Destroy x, and complete $(\hat{A}, \hat{B}, s, \mathcal{I})$, by accepting K as the session key.

Unfortunately, when a party, say $\hat{B}$, has no mean to be aware of the sessions initiated at the other parties, and intended to it, apart from receiving the initiator's message, the CK model insufficiently captures impersonations attacks. Consider, for instance, Protocol 1 (wherein H and H_2 are digest functions); it is from [23], and is CK–secure under the Gap Diffie–Hellman assumption [20] and the Random Oracle (RO) model [2]. As the session state is defined to be the ephemeral DH exponent[1], while the protocol $\mathcal{P}$ is (formally) CK–secure, its practical security is unsatisfactory, unless session identifiers are added with further

[1] [23] does not specify the information contained in a session state. But, since the adversary controls communications between parties, we do not see another non–superfluous definition of a session state, with which Protocol $\mathcal{P}$ can be shown CK–secure; as the protocol is insecure if the session state is defined to be $\sigma = A^b$.

restrictions. If session identifiers are nonces generated by initiators, the protocol $\mathcal{P}$ practically fails in authentication. As an illustration, consider Attack 1, wherein the attacker impersonates $\hat{A}$, exploiting a knowledge of an ephemeral DH exponent used at $\hat{A}$.

Attack 1. Impersonation Attack against $\mathcal{P}$ using ephemeral DH exponent leakage

I) At the activation of a session $(\hat{A}, \hat{B}, s, \mathcal{I})$, the attacker $\mathcal{A}$ does the following:
  (a) Intercept $\hat{A}$'s message to $\hat{B}$ $(\hat{B}, \hat{A}, s, X, t_A)$.
  (b) Perform a session *SesssionStateReveal* query on $(\hat{A}, \hat{B}, s, \mathcal{I})$ (to obtain x).
  (c) Send $(\hat{A}, \hat{B}, s, \mathcal{I}, \bar{1}, 0^{|q|})$ to $\hat{A}$, where $\bar{1}$ is the identity element in $\mathcal{G}$ and $0^{|q|}$ is the string consisting of $|q|$ zero bits (as $\bar{1} \notin \mathcal{G}^*$, $\hat{A}$ aborts the session $(\hat{A}, \hat{B}, s, \mathcal{I})$).

II) When $\mathcal{A}$ decides later to impersonate $\hat{A}$ to $\hat{B}$, it does the following:
  (a) Send $(\hat{B}, \hat{A}, s, X, t_A)$ to $\hat{B}$.
  (b) Intercept $\hat{B}$'s message to $\hat{A}$ $(\hat{A}, \hat{B}, s, \mathcal{I}, Y, t_B)$.
  (c) Compute $K = H(Y^x, X, Y)$.
  (d) Use K to communicate with $\hat{B}$ on behalf of $\hat{A}$.

The attacker makes $\hat{B}$ run a session and derive a key with the belief that its peer is $\hat{A}$; in addition, the attacker is able to compute the session key that $\hat{B}$ derives; in practice, this makes the protocol fail in authentication.

The capture of impersonation attacks based on ephemeral DH leakages is insufficient in the CK–model, unless the matching sessions definition is added with further restrictions. The reason is that (in a formal analysis) an attacker$\mathcal{A}$ cannot use the session at $\hat{B}$ (in which it impersonates $\hat{A}$) as a test session, since the matching session is exposed, while there is no guarantee that (in practice) $\hat{B}$ would not run and complete such a session. If matching sessions are defined using matching conversations, it becomes clear that Protocol $\mathcal{P}$ is formally and practically insecure. Indeed, in this case, a leakage of an ephemeral DH exponent in a session allows an attacker to impersonate indefinitely the session owner to its peer in the exposed session.

On the NAXOS Transformation. In the eCK model [16], the ephemeral key of a session is required to contain all session specific information; and all computations performed to derive a session key have to deterministically depend on the ephemeral key, static key, and communication received from the peer.

The design and security arguments of many eCK secure protocols, among which CMQV [32], NAXOS(+, –C) [16,19,23], and NETS [18], use the NAXOS transformation [16], which consists in defining the ephemeral DH exponent as the digest of a randomly chosen value and the static private key (of the session owner), and (unnaturally) destroying it after each use. The ephemeral key is then defined to be the random value. However, from a practical perspective, it seems difficult to see how the NAXOS transformation prevents leakages on the ephemeral DH exponents. And, in any environment, which does not guarantee that leakages on DH exponents cannot occur, the NAXOS type protocols security is at best unspecified.

Consider, for instance, Protocol 2, it is from an earlier version[2] of [10]. If the ephemeral keys are defined to be r_A and r_B (as in the NAXOS security arguments [16]) and the signature scheme is secure against chosen message attacks, Protocol 2 can be shown eCK–secure.

Protocol 2. Signed Diffie–Hellman using NAXOS transformation

I) The initiator $\hat{A}$ does the following:
  (a) Choose $r_A \in_R [1, q-1]$, compute $X = G^{H_1(r_A,a)}$, and destroy $H_1(r_A, a)$.
  (b) Compute $\sigma_A = \mathrm{Sig}_{\hat{A}}(\hat{B}, X)$.
  (c) Send $(\hat{B}, X, \sigma_A)$ to $\hat{B}$.

II) $\hat{B}$ does the following:
  (a) Verify that $X \in \mathcal{G}^*$.
  (b) Verify that σ_A is valid with respect to $\hat{A}$'s public key and the message $(\hat{B}, X)$.
  (c) Choose $r_B \in_R [1, q-1]$, compute $Y = G^{H_1(r_B,b)}$, and destroy $H_1(r_B, b)$.
  (d) Compute $\sigma_B = \mathrm{Sig}_{\hat{B}}(Y, \hat{A}, X)$.
  (e) Send $(Y, \hat{A}, X, \sigma_B)$ to $\hat{A}$.
  (f) Compute $K = H_2(X^{H_1(r_B,b)})$.

III) $\hat{A}$ does the following:
  (a) Verify that $Y \in \mathcal{G}^*$.
  (b) Verify that σ_B is valid with respect to $\hat{B}$'s public key and the message $(Y, \hat{A}, X)$.
  (c) Compute $K = H_2(Y^{H_1(r_A,a)})$.

IV) The shared session key is K.

The protocol is however insecure if the ephemeral keys are defined to contain the ephemeral DH exponents. As an adversary which (*partially*[3]) learns $H_1(r_A, a)$ in a session initiated at $\hat{A}$ with peer $\hat{B}$, can *indefinitely* impersonate $\hat{A}$ to $\hat{B}$. For this purpose, the attacker replays to $\hat{B}$ $\hat{A}$'s message in the session in which $H_1(r_A, a)$ leakage happened (namely $(\hat{B}, X, \sigma_A)$), and computes the session key that $\hat{B}$ derives, using $H_1(r_A, a)$ and the ephemeral public key Y from $\hat{B}$.

3 Stronger Security

In this section, we describe the strengthened eCK model, which considers leakages on intermediate results (the values a party may need to compute between

[2] `http://eprint.iacr.org/cgi-bin/versions.pl?entry=2009/253`, version 20090625.

[3] If an adversary partially learns $H_1(r_A, a)$, it recovers the remaining part, using Shanks' baby step giant step algorithm [31] or Pollard's rho algorithm [31], if the bits it learns are the most significant ones, or tools from [11] if the leakage is on middle–part bits; recovering $H_1(r_A, a)$ from partial leakage requires some extra computational effort.

messages or before a session key), encompasses the eCK model [16], and provides stronger reveal queries to the attacker.

A common setting wherein key agreement protocols are often implemented is that of a server used together with a (computationally limited) tamper–resistant device, which stores the long–lived secrets. In such a setting, safely reducing the non–idle time computational effort of the device, is usually crucial for implementation efficiency. To reduce the device's non–idle time computational effort, ephemeral keys can be computed on the device in idle–time, or on the host machine when the implemented protocol is ephemeral DH exponent leakage resilient.

In many DH protocols, (C, FH, H)MQV–C [17,32,28,13,14] and NAXOS(+, –C) [19,23,16], for instance, the computation of the intermediate results is more costly than that of the ephemeral public key. For these protocols, implementations efficiency is significantly enhanced when the ephemeral keys are computed on the device, while the intermediate results, which require expensive on–line computations and session keys are computed on the host machine. Unfortunately the security of the (e)CK–secure protocols, when leakages on the intermediate results are considered is at best unspecified. A security definition which captures attacks based on intermediate result leakages is clearly desirable. The model we propose captures such attacks, together with the attacks captured in the (e)CK models.

Session. We suppose $n \leqslant \mathcal{L}(|q|)$ (for some polynomial $\mathcal{L}$) parties $\hat{P}_{i=1,\cdots,n}$ supposed to be probabilistic polynomial time machines and a certification authority (CA) trusted by all parties. The CA is only required to verify that public keys are valid ones (i.e., public keys are only tested for membership in $\mathcal{G}^*$; no proof of possession of corresponding private keys is required). Each party has a certificate binding its identity to its public key. A session is an instance of the considered protocol, run at a party. A session at $\hat{A}$ (with peer $\hat{B}$) can be created with parameter $(\hat{A}, \hat{B})$ or $(\hat{B}, \hat{A}, m)$, where m is an incoming message, supposed from $\hat{B}$; $\hat{A}$ is the initiator if the creation parameter is $(\hat{A}, \hat{B})$, otherwise a responder. At session activation, a session state is created to contain the information specific to the session. Each session is identified with a tuple $(\hat{P}_i, \hat{P}_j, \mathfrak{out}, \mathfrak{in}, \varsigma)$, wherein $\hat{P}_i$ is the session holder, $\hat{P}_j$ is the intended peer, $\mathfrak{out}$ and $\mathfrak{in}$ are respectively the concatenation of the messages $\hat{P}_i$ sends to $\hat{P}_j$, or believes to be from $\hat{P}_j$, and ς is $\hat{P}_i$'s role in the session (initiator or responder). Two sessions with identifiers $(\hat{P}_i, \hat{P}_j, \mathfrak{out}, \mathfrak{in}, \varsigma)$ and $(\hat{P}'_j, \hat{P}'_i, \mathfrak{out}', \mathfrak{in}'\varsigma')$ are said to be matching if $\hat{P}_i = \hat{P}'_i$, $\hat{P}'_j = \hat{P}'_j$, $\varsigma \neq \varsigma'$, and at completion $\mathfrak{in} = \mathfrak{out}'$ and $\mathfrak{out} = \mathfrak{in}'$.

For the two–pass DH protocols, each session is denoted with an identifier $(\hat{A}, \hat{B}, X, \star, \varsigma)$, where $\hat{A}$ is the session holder, $\hat{B}$ is the peer, X is the outgoing message, ς indicates the role of $\hat{A}$ in the session (initiator ($\mathcal{I}$) or responder ($\mathcal{R}$)), and $\star$ is the incoming message Y if it exists, otherwise a special symbol meaning that an incoming message is not received yet; in that case, when $\hat{A}$ receives the public key Y, the session identifier is updated to $(\hat{A}, \hat{B}, X, Y, \varsigma)$. Two sessions with identifiers $(\hat{A}, \hat{B}, X, Y, \mathcal{I})$ and $(\hat{B}, \hat{A}, Y, X, \mathcal{R})$ are said to be matching. Notice that the session matching $(\hat{B}, \hat{A}, Y, X, \mathcal{R})$ can be any session $(\hat{A}, \hat{B}, X, \star, \mathcal{I})$; as

$X, Y \in_R \mathcal{G}^*$, a session cannot have (except with negligible probability) more than one matching session.

Adversary and Security. The adversary $\mathcal{A}$, is a probabilistic polynomial time machine; outgoing messages are submitted to $\mathcal{A}$ for delivery ($\mathcal{A}$ decides about messages delivery). $\mathcal{A}$ is also supposed to control session activations at each party via the *Send*($\hat{P}_i, \hat{P}_j$) and *Send*($\hat{P}_j, \hat{P}_i, Y$) queries, which make $\hat{P}_i$ initiate a session with peer $\hat{P}_j$, or respond to the (supposed) session $(\hat{P}_j, \hat{P}_i, Y, \star, \mathcal{I})$. We suppose that the considered protocol is implemented at a party following one of the approaches hereunder. We suppose also that at each party an untrusted host machine is used together with a tamper–resistant device. Basing our model on these implementation approaches does not make it specific; rather, this reduces the gap that often exists between formal models and practical security. Such modeling techniques, which take into account hardware devices and communication flows between components, were previously used in [6].

Approach 1. In this approach, the static keys are stored on the device (a smart–card, for instance) the ephemeral keys are computed on the host machine, passed to the smart–card together with the incoming public keys; the device computes the session key, and provides it to the host machine (application) for use. The information flow between the device and the host machine is depicted in Figure (1a). This implementation approach is safe for eCK–secure protocols when ephemeral keys are defined to be ephemeral DH exponents, as a leakage on an ephemeral DH exponent does not compromise the session in which it is used. In addition, when an attacker learns a session key, it gains no useful information about the other session keys.

Approach 2. Another approach, which has received less attention in the formal treatment of DH protocols, is when the ephemeral keys, and top level intermediate results are computed on the device, and the host machine is provided with some intermediate results IR with which it computes the session key. As the computation of the intermediate results is often more costly than that of the ephemeral public keys, implementation efficiency is often significantly enhanced using this approach. Naturally, this comes with the requirement that leakages on the intermediate results should not compromise any unexposed session. Namely, an adversary may have a malware running on the host machine at a party, and learn all values computed or used at the party, except those stored in the party's tamper–proof device; this should not compromise any unexposed session.

We define two sets of queries, modeling leakages that may occur on either implementation approaches. We consider leakages on ephemeral and static private keys, and also on any intermediate (secret) value which evaluation requires a secret information. As the adversary can compute any information which evaluation requires only public information, considering leakages on such data is superfluous. In Set 1, which models leakages in the first implementation approach, the following queries are allowed.

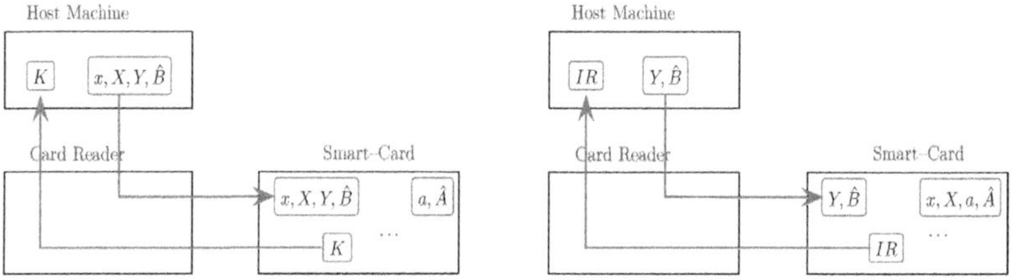

Fig. 1. Implementation Approaches

- *EphemeralKeyReveal(session)*: this query models leakages on ephemeral DH exponents.
- *Corrupt$_{SC}$(party)*: this query models an attacker which (bypasses the eventual tamper protection mechanisms on the device, and) gains read access to the device's private memory; it provides the attacker with the device owner's static private key.
- *SessionKeyReveal(session)*: when the attacker issues this query on an already completed session, it is provided with the session key.
- *EstablishParty(party)*: with this query, the adversary registers a static key on behalf of a party; as the adversary controls communications, from there the party is supposed totally controlled by $\mathcal{A}$. A party against which this query is not issued is said to be *honest.*

In Set 2, which models leakages on the second implementation approach, the following queries are allowed; the definitions remain unchanged for queries belonging also to Set 1.

- For any node in the *intermediate results,* which computation requires a secret value, a reveal query is defined to allow leakage on the information computed in this node. These queries models leakages that may occur on intermediate results in computing session keys.
- *SessionKeyReveal(session).*
- *EstablishParty(party).*
- *Corrupt$_{SC}$(party).*

Before defining the seCK security, we define the session freshness notion. Test queries can only be performed on fresh sessions.

Definition 1 (Session Freshness). *Let Π be a protocol, and $\hat{A}$ and $\hat{B}$ two honest parties, sid the identifier of a completed session at $\hat{A}$ with peer $\hat{B}$, and sid′ the matching session's identifier. The session sid is said to be* locally exposed *if one of the following holds.*

- *$\mathcal{A}$ issues a* SessionKeyReveal *query on sid.*
- *The implementation at $\hat{A}$ follows the first approach and $\mathcal{A}$ issues an* EphemeralKeyReveal *query on sid and a* Corrupt$_{\text{SC}}$ *query on $\hat{A}$.*
- *The implementation at $\hat{A}$ follows the second approach and $\mathcal{A}$ issues an intermediate result query on sid.*

The session sid is said to be exposed *if (a) it is locally exposed, or (b) its matching session sid′ exists and is locally exposed, or (c) sid′ does not exist and $\mathcal{A}$ issues a* $\text{Corrupt}_{\text{SC}}$ *query on $\hat{B}$. An* unexposed *session is said to be* fresh.

Our session freshness conditions match exactly the intuition of the sessions one may hope to protect. In particular, it lowers (more than in the eCK model) the necessary adversary restrictions for any reasonable security definition. Notice that only the queries corresponding to the implementation approach followed by a party can be issued on it.

Definition 2 (Strengthened eCK Security). *Let Π be a protocol, such that if two honest parties complete matching sessions, then they both compute the same session key. The protocol Π is said to be* seCK–secure, *if no polynomially bounded adversary can distinguish a fresh session key from a random value, chosen under the distribution of session keys, with probability significantly greater than 1/2.*

Forward Secrecy. As shown in [13], no two–pass key exchange protocol can achieve *forward secrecy*[4]. Indeed, our security definition captures *weak forward secrecy,* which (loosely speaking) is: *any session established without an active involvement of the attacker remains secure, even when the implicated parties static keys are disclosed.* The seCK security definition can be completed with the session key expiration notion [7] to capture forward secrecy. Although the protocol we propose can be added with a third message, and yield a protocol which (provably) provides forward secrecy, in the continuation, we work with the security definition without forward secrecy, and focus on two–pass DH protocols.

Relations between the seCK and eCK models. In the eCK model, an adversary may compromise the ephemeral key, static key, or session key at a party, independently of the way the protocol is implemented. The seCK model considers an adversary which may (have a malware running at a party's host machine and) learn all information at the party, except those stored in a tamper–resistant device. The seCK approach seems more prevalent in practice, and reduces the gap that often exists between formal arguments and practical implementations security.

The eCK and seCK session identifiers and matching sessions definitions are the same. When the adversary issues the $Corrupt_{SC}$ query at a party, it is provided with the party's static key; the $Corrupt_{SC}$ query is the same as the eCK *StaticKeyReveal* query. For a session between two parties, say $\hat{A}$ and $\hat{B}$, following the first implementation approach, the seCK session *freshness* definition reduces to the eCK freshness. By assuming that all parties follow the first implementation approach, the seCK–security definition reduces to the eCK one; the seCK model encompasses the eCK one.

Proposition 1. *Any seCK–secure protocol is also an eCK–secure one.*

[4] Some authors, [13] for instance, use the term 'perfect forward secrecy', but we prefer 'forward secrecy' to avoid a confusion with (Shannon's) 'perfect secrecy'.

The seCK model also separates clearly from the eCK model. The eCK model does not consider leakages on intermediate results; and this makes many of the eCK secure protocols insecure in the seCK model. For instance, in the CMQV protocol (shown eCK–secure), an attacker which learns an ephemeral secret exponent in a session, can indefinitely impersonate the session owner; the same holds for the (H)MQV(–C) protocols [28,29]. It is not difficult to see that NAXOS cannot meet the seCK security definition. The protocols 1 and 2 from [12, pp. 6, 12] (shown eCK–secure) fail in authentication when leakages one the intermediate results are considered. Indeed an attacker, which learns the ephemeral secret exponents $s_1 = x + a_1$ and $s_2 = x + a_2$ in a session at $\hat{A}$ (see the steps 2 and 3 of the protocols 1 and 2 [12]), can indefinitely impersonate $\hat{A}$ to *any* party. Notice that the attacker cannot compute $\hat{A}$'s static key from s_1 and s_2, while it is not difficult to see that leakages on s_1 (or s_2) *and* the ephemeral key, in the *same session* imply $\hat{A}$'s static key disclosure.

The seCK model is practically stronger than the CK model [7]. Key Compromise Impersonation resilience, for instance, is captured in the seCK model while not in CK model. As shown in [9], and illustrated in section 2 with Protocol $\mathcal{P}$, the CK model is enhanced when matching sessions are defined using matching conversations. In addition, the seCK reveal query definitions go beyond the usual CK session state definition (ephemeral DH exponents). Compared to the CK_{HMQV} model[5] [13], the reveal query definitions are enhanced in the seCK model to capture attacks based on intermediate result leakages. In the HMQV security arguments [13, subsection 7.4], the session state is defined to contain the ephemeral DH exponent[6]; the HMQV protocol does not meet the seCK–security [28,29].

4 The Strengthened MQV Protocol

In this section, we present the *strengthened* MQV protocol, and its building blocks, to show that the seCK security definition is useful, and not limiting; as seCK–secure protocols can be built with usual building blocks. We start with the following variants of the FXCR and FDCR signature schemes [28]. The security of the FXCR–1 and FDCR–1 schemes can be shown with arguments similar to that of the FXCR and FDCR schemes [28,29].

Definition 3 (FXCR–1 Signature). *Let $\hat{B}$ be a party with public key $B \in \mathcal{G}^*$, and $\hat{A}$ a verifier; $\hat{B}$'s signature on a message m and challenge X provided by $\hat{A}$*

[5] CK_{HMQV} is the variant of the CK model in which the HMQV security arguments are provided; however, it seems that the aim of [13] was not to propose a new model, as it refers to [7] for details [13, p. 9], and considers its session identifiers and matching sessions definition (which make the CK and CK_{HMQV} models incomparable) as consistent with the CK model [13, p. 10]. See [10] for a comparison between the CK_{HMQV} and (e)CK models.

[6] In [13, subsection 5.1], the session state is defined to contain the ephemeral public keys, but this definition is superfluous, as the adversary controls communications between parties.

($x \in_R [1, q-1]$ is chosen and kept secret by $\hat{A}$) is $Sig_{\hat{B}}(m, X) = (Y, X^{s_B})$, where $Y = G^y$, $y \in_R [1, q-1]$ is chosen by $\hat{B}$, and $s_B = ye + b$, where $e = \bar{H}(Y, X, m)$. And, $\hat{A}$ accepts the pair (Y, σ_B) as a valid signature if $Y \in \mathcal{G}^*$ and $(Y^e B)^x = \sigma_B$.

Proposition 2 (FXCR–1 Security). *Under the CDH assumption in $\mathcal{G}$ and the RO model, there is no adaptive probabilistic polynomial time attacker, which given a public key B, a challenge X_0 ($B, X_0 \in_R \mathcal{G}^*$), together with hashing and signing oracles, outputs with non–negligible success probability a triple (m_0, Y_0, σ_0) such that:*
(1) (Y_0, σ_0) is a valid signature with respect to the public key B, and the message–challenge pair (m_0, X_0); and
(2) (Y_0, σ_0) was not obtained from the signing oracle with a query on (m_0, X_0).

Definition 4 (FDCR–1 Scheme). *Let $\hat{A}$ and $\hat{B}$ be two parties with public keys $A, B \in \mathcal{G}^*$, and m_1, m_2 two messages. The dual signature of $\hat{A}$ and $\hat{B}$ on the messages m_1, m_2 is $DSig_{\hat{A},\hat{B}}(m_1, m_2, X, Y) = (X^d A)^{ye+b} = (Y^e B)^{xd+a}$, where $X = G^x$ and $Y = G^y$ are chosen respectively by $\hat{A}$ and $\hat{B}$, $d = \bar{H}(X, Y, m_1, m_2)$, and $e = \bar{H}(Y, X, m_1, m_2)$.*

Proposition 3 (FDCR–1 Security). *Let $A = G^a, B, X_0 \in_R \mathcal{G}^*$ ($A \neq B$). Under the RO model, and the CDH assumption in $\mathcal{G}$, given a, A, B, X_0, a message m_{1_0}, a hashing oracle, together with a signing oracle (simulating $\hat{B}$'s role), no adaptive probabilistic polynomial time attacker can output, with non–negligible success probability a triple (m_{2_0}, Y_0, σ_0) such that:*
(1) $DSig_{\hat{A},\hat{B}}(m_{1_0}, m_{2_0}, X_0, Y_0) = \sigma_0$; and
(2) (Y_0, σ_0) was not obtained from the signing oracle with a query on some (m'_1, X') such that $X_0 = X'$ and $(m'_1, m'_2) = (m_{1_0}, m_{2_0})$, where m'_2 is a message returned at signature query on (m'_1, X'); (m_{1_0}, m_{2_0}) denotes the concatenation of m_{1_0} and m_{2_0}.

The strengthened MQV protocol follows from the FDCR–1 scheme; a run of SMQV is as in Protocol 3. The execution aborts if any verification fails.

The shared secret σ is the FDCR–1 signature of $\hat{A}$ and $\hat{B}$, on challenges X, Y and messages $\hat{A}, \hat{B}$ (the representation of $\hat{A}$ and $\hat{B}$'s identities). The parties identities and ephemeral keys are used in the final digest computation to make the key replication resilience security attribute immediate (and also to avoid unknown key share attacks). A run of SMQV requires 2.5 times a single exponentiation (2.17 times a single exponentiation when the multiple exponentiation technique [21, Algorithm 14.88] is used); this efficiency equals that of the remarkable (H, FH)MQV protocols. SMQV provides all the security attributes of the (C, H)MQV protocols, added with ephemeral secret exponent leakage resilience.

Moreover, suppose an implementation of SMQV or (C, H)MQV using an untrusted[7] host machine together with a device; and suppose that the session keys are used by some applications running on the host machine, and that

[7] There are many reasons for not trusting the host machine: bogus or trojan software, viruses, etc.

Protocol 3. The Strengthened MQV Protocol

I) The initiator $\hat{A}$ does the following:
  (a) Choose $x \in_R [1, q-1]$ and compute $X = G^x$.
  (b) Send $(\hat{A}, \hat{B}, X)$ to the peer $\hat{B}$.
II) At receipt of $(\hat{A}, \hat{B}, X)$, $\hat{B}$ does the following:
  (a) Verify that $X \in \mathcal{G}^*$.
  (b) Choose $y \in_R [1, q-1]$ and compute $Y = G^y$.
  (c) Send $(\hat{B}, \hat{A}, Y)$ to $\hat{A}$.
  (d) Compute $d = \bar{H}(X, Y, \hat{A}, \hat{B})$ and $e = \bar{H}(Y, X, \hat{A}, \hat{B})$.
  (e) Compute $s_B = ye + b \mod q$ and $\sigma = (X^d A)^{s_B}$.
  (f) Compute $K = H(\sigma, \hat{A}, \hat{B}, X, Y)$.
III) At receipt of $(\hat{B}, \hat{A}, Y)$, $\hat{A}$ does the following:
  (a) Verify that $Y \in \mathcal{G}^*$.
  (b) Compute $d = \bar{H}(X, Y, \hat{A}, \hat{B})$ and $e = \bar{H}(Y, X, \hat{A}, \hat{B})$.
  (c) Compute $s_A = xd + a \mod q$, and $\sigma = (Y^e B)^{s_A}$.
  (d) Compute $K = H(\sigma, \hat{A}, \hat{B}, X, Y)$.
IV) The shared session key is K.

the ephemeral keys are computed on the device in idle–time. This idle–time pre–computation seems common in practice [27] (and possible in both the (C, H)MQV and SMQV protocols). But, as (C, H)MQV is not ephemeral secret exponent leakage resilient [28,29], the ephemeral secret exponents ($s_A = x + da$ or $s_B = y + eb$) cannot be used on the untrusted host machine. The exponentiation $\sigma = (YB^e)^{s_A} = (XA^d)^{s_B}$ has to be performed on the device *in non idle–time*. In contrast, for SMQV, $\sigma = (Y^e B)^{s_A} = (X^d A)^{s_B}$ can be computed on the host machine, after the ephemeral secret exponent is computed on the device. Because the session key is used on the host machine, and a leakage of only the ephemeral secret exponent, in a SMQV session, does not compromise any other session; there is no need to protect the ephemeral secret exponent more than the session key. In SMQV, the non–idle time computational effort of the device reduces to few non–costly operations (one integer addition, one integer multiplication, and one digest computation), while for (C, H)MQV at least one exponentiation has to be performed on the device in non idle–time.

Table 1 summarizes the comparisons between SMQV and some other DH protocols. All the security reductions are performed using the Random Oracle model [2]; incoming ephemeral keys are validated[8]. KEA1 stands for "Knowledge of Exponent Assumption" [4], CDH and GDH stand respectively for "Computational DH" and "Gap DH" assumptions [25]. The *'A'*, *'D'*, *'E'*, and *'M'* stand respectively for *integer* a*ddition,* d*igest computation,* e*xponentiation, and integer* m*ultiplication.* The NC column indicates the *n*aive *c*ount efficiency (i.e., without optimizations from [21, Algorithm 14.88] and [24]); NICE 1 and NICE 2 indicate the *n*on–*i*dle

[8] Ephemeral key validation is voluntarily omitted in the HMQV design [13], but the HMQV protocol is known to be insecure if ephemeral keys are not validated [22].

Table 1. Security and Efficiency Comparison between SMQV and other DH protocols

Protocol	Security	Assumptions	NC	NICE 1	NICE 2
CMQV [32]	eCK	GDH	3E	1E	1E
FHMQV [29]	CK_{FHMQV}	GDH	2.5E	1E	1D + 1A + 1M
HMQV [13]	CK_{HMQV}	GDH, KEA1	2.5E	1E	1E
MQV [17]	–	–	2.5E	1E	1E
NAXOS [16]	eCK	GDH	4E	3E	3E
NAXOS–C [23]	ceCK	GDH	4E	3E	3E
SMQV	seCK	GDH	2.5E	1E	1D + 1A + 1M

time computational effort of the device in the two approaches (when ephemeral keys are computed in idle–time).

The MQV protocol has no security reduction[9]. The FHMQV security arguments are provided in a model which considers intermediate results and ephemeral key leakages in two separate settings; the model implicitly assumes that all parties follow the same implementation approach, and cannot be shown to encompass the CK or eCK models. In contrast, the seCK model considers also the security of sessions between parties following different implementation approaches, and its matching sessions definition makes it encompass the eCK model. The CMQV and NAXOS protocols are shown eCK–secure, they both use the NAXOS transformation.

The NAXOS–C security arguments are provided in a variant of the eCK model, called *combined eCK model* (ceCK) [23], geared to the post–specified peer model. In the post[10] model, the identity of a peer may be unknown at session activation (it is learned during the protocol execution). It is worthwhile to mention that, the separation between the pre and post models security is unclear. The protocol $\mathcal{P}$ claimed secure in the pre model, and not executable in the post model (unless "modified in a fundamental way") [23, section 3.1], is insecure in the pre model, if the considered security model is strong enough. The HMQV protocol is executable in the post model, but claimed insecure (in the post– model). In fact, the proposed attack [23, section 3.2] cannot be performed in practice; not because it requires an important on–line computational effort (2^{60} operations, when the order of $\mathcal{G}$ is a 160–bit prime), but since the step (2.c) of the attack cannot be performed without changing the $\hat{M}$ found at the step (2.b). In practice, $\hat{M}$ (is a certificate, and) is defined to contain M (which is provided to the certification authority at certificate issuance), and when M is changed,

[9] We are aware of [15], which shows that (under the RO model and the CDH assumption) the MQV variant wherein d and e are computed as $\bar{H}(X)$ and $\bar{H}(Y)$, is secure in a model of their own design. Notice that, for this variant, an attacker which finds $x_0 \in [1, q-1]$ such that $\bar{H}(G^{x_0}) = 0$, can impersonate *any* party to *any other* party. Finding such an x_0 requires $O(2^l)$ digest computations.

[10] The terms 'pre–specified peer' and 'post–specified peer' are respectively shortened to 'pre' and 'post'.

so is $\hat{M}$ (notice also that changing M requires another certificate issuance); and then, after the step (2.c) of the attack, the claimed equality between $\bar{H}(X, \hat{M})$ and $\bar{H}(X, \hat{B})$ does not hold. For the Σ_0 protocol, secure in the post model, while insecure in the pre one [23, section 3.3], the model in which it is shown secure in the post model [8] is not strong enough. It is not difficult to see, for instance, that the Σ_0 protocol is both eCK and ceCK insecure.

The SMQV protocol provides more security attributes than the NAXOS(+, –C), (C, H)MVQ protocols, in addition to allow particularly efficient implementations, in environments wherein a tamper proof device is used to store private keys.

Proposition 4. *Under the GDH assumption in $\mathcal{G}$ and the RO model, the SMQV protocol is seCK–secure.*

The reductionist security arguments are lengthy, and hence is omitted. The full security analysis of SMQV can however be found in the extended version of this paper — report 2010/237 in the Cryptology ePrint Archive.

5 Concluding Remarks

We discussed security shades in the (e)CK moddels. We illustrated the limitations of the CK matching sessions definition; and the insecurity of the NAXOS type protocols when leakages on ephemeral DH exponents are considered. We proposed a new security model, the strengthened eCK model, which encompasses the eCK one, and practically captures the security attributes considered in the CK model. We proposed the Strengthened MQV protocol, which in addition to provide the same efficiency as the (H)MQV protocols, is particularly suited for distributed implementation environments using an untrusted host machine and a tamper–resistant device; in such an environment, the non–idle time computational effort of the device, in a SMQV implementation, reduces to few non–costly operations.

In a forthcoming stage, we will be interested in the enhancement of existing protocols to meet the seCK security definition, and the extension of the strengthened eCK model to consider a wider class of attacks.

References

1. Bellare, M., Rogaway, P.: Entity Authentication and Key Distribution. In: Stinson, D.R. (ed.) CRYPTO 1993. LNCS, vol. 773, pp. 232–249. Springer, Heidelberg (1994)
2. Bellare, M., Rogaway, P.: Random Oracles are Practical: a Paradigm for Designing Efficient Protocols. In: Proc. of the first ACM Conference on Computer and Communications Security, pp. 62–73. ACM, New York (1993)
3. Bellare, M., Rogaway, P.: Provably Secure Session Key Distribution — The Three Party Case. In: Proc. of the twenty–seventh annual ACM symposium on Theory of computing, pp. 57–66. ACM, New York (1995)

4. Bellare, M., Palacio, A.: The Knowledge–of–Exponent Assumptions and 3–round Zero–Knowledge Protocols. In: Franklin, M. (ed.) CRYPTO 2004. LNCS, vol. 3152, pp. 273–289. Springer, Heidelberg (2004)
5. Blake–Wilson, S., Johnson, D., Menezes, A.: Key Agreement Protocols and their Security Analysis. In: Darnell, M.J. (ed.) Cryptography and Coding 1997. LNCS, vol. 1355, pp. 30–45. Springer, Heidelberg (1997)
6. Bresson, E., Chevassut, O., Pointcheval, D.: Dynamic Group Diffie–Hellman Key Exchange under Standard Assumptions. In: Knudsen, L.R. (ed.) EUROCRYPT 2002. LNCS, vol. 2332, pp. 321–336. Springer, Heidelberg (2002)
7. Canetti, R., Krawczyk, H.: Analysis of Key–Exchange Protocols and Their Use for Building Secure Channels. In: Pfitzmann, B. (ed.) EUROCRYPT 2001. LNCS, vol. 2045, pp. 453–474. Springer, Heidelberg (2001)
8. Canetti, R., Krawczyk, H.: Security Analysis of IKE's Signature–based Key–Exchange Protocol. In: Yung, M. (ed.) CRYPTO 2002. LNCS, vol. 2442, pp. 143–161. Springer, Heidelberg (2002)
9. Choo, K.-K.R., Boyd, C., Hitchcock, Y.: Examining Indistinguishability–Based Proof Models for Key Establishment Protocols. In: Roy, B. (ed.) ASIACRYPT 2005. LNCS, vol. 3788, pp. 585–604. Springer, Heidelberg (2005)
10. Cremers, C.: Formally and Practically Relating the CK, CK–HMQV, and eCK Security Models for Authenticated Key Exchange. Cryptology ePrint Archive, Report 2009/253 (2009)
11. Gopalakrishnan, K., Thériault, N., Yao, C.Z.: Solving Discrete Logarithms from Partial Knowledge of the Key. In: Srinathan, K., Rangan, C.P., Yung, M. (eds.) INDOCRYPT 2007. LNCS, vol. 4859, pp. 224–237. Springer, Heidelberg (2007)
12. Kim, M., Fujioka, A., Ustaoglu, B.: Strongly Secure Authenticated Key Exchange without NAXOS' Approach. In: Takagi, T., Echizen, I. (eds.) IWSEC 2009. LNCS, vol. 5824, pp. 174–191. Springer, Heidelberg (2009)
13. Krawczyk H.: HMQV: A Hight Performance Secure Diffie–Hellman Protocol. Cryptology ePrint Archive, Report 2005/176 (2005)
14. Krawczyk, H.: HMQV: A Hight Performance Secure Diffie–Hellman Protocol. In: Shoup, V. (ed.) CRYPTO 2005. LNCS, vol. 3621, pp. 546–566. Springer, Heidelberg (2005)
15. Kunz-Jacques, S., Pointcheval, D.: About the Security of MTI/C0 and MQV. In: De Prisco, R., Yung, M. (eds.) SCN 2006. LNCS, vol. 4116, pp. 156–172. Springer, Heidelberg (2006)
16. LaMacchia, B., Lauter, K., Mityagin, A.: Stronger Security of Authenticated Key Exchange. In: Susilo, W., Liu, J.K., Mu, Y. (eds.) ProvSec 2007. LNCS, vol. 4784, pp. 1–16. Springer, Heidelberg (2007)
17. Law, L., Menezes, A., Qu, M., Solinas, J., Vanstone, S.: An Efficient protocol for authenticated key agreement. Designs, Codes and Cryptography 28(2), 119–134 (2003)
18. Lee, J., Park, C.S.: An Efficient Authenticated Key Exchange Protocol with a Tight Security Reduction. Cryptology ePrint Archive, Report 2008/345 (2008)
19. Lee, J., Park, J. H.: Authenticated Key Exchange Secure under the Computational Diffe–Hellman Assumption. Cryptology ePrint Archive, Report 2008/344 (2008)
20. Maurer, U.M., Wolf, S.: Diffie–Hellman Oracles. In: Koblitz, N. (ed.) CRYPTO 1996. LNCS, vol. 1109, pp. 268–282. Springer, Heidelberg (1996)
21. Menezes, A., van Oorschot, P., Vanstone, S.: Handbook of Applied Cryptography. CRC Press, Boca Raton (1996)

22. Menezes, A., Ustaoglu, B.: On the Importance of Public–Key Validation in the MQV and HMQV Key Agreement Protocols. In: Barua, R., Lange, T. (eds.) INDOCRYPT 2006. LNCS, vol. 4329, pp. 133–147. Springer, Heidelberg (2006)
23. Menezes, A., Ustaoglu, B.: Comparing the Pre– and Post–specified Peer Models for Key Agreement. International Journal of Applied Cryptography 1(3), 236–250 (2009)
24. M'Raïhi, D., Naccache, D.: Batch Exponentiation: A Fast DLP-based Signature Generation Strategy. In: Proc. of the third ACM conference on Computer and communications security, pp. 58–61. ACM, New York (1996)
25. Okamoto, T., Pointcheval, D.: The Gap–Problems: A New Class of Problems for the Security of Cryptographic Schemes. In: Kim, K.-c. (ed.) PKC 2001. LNCS, vol. 1992, pp. 104–118. Springer, Heidelberg (2001)
26. Pointcheval, D., Stern, J.: Security Arguments for Digital Signatures and Blind Signatures. Journal of Cryptology 13, 361–396 (2000)
27. Schnorr, C.P.: Efficient Signature Generation by Smart Cards. Journal of Cryptology 4(3), 161–174 (1991)
28. Sarr, A.P., Elbaz–Vincent, P., Bajard, J.C.: A Secure and Efficient Authenticated Diffie–Hellman Protocol. To appear in Proc. of EuroPKI (2009)
29. Sarr, A.P., Elbaz–Vincent, P., Bajard, J.C.: A Secure and Efficient Authenticated Diffie–Hellman Protocol (extended version). Cryptology ePrint Archive, Report 2009/408 (2009)
30. Shoup V.: On Formal Models for Secure Key Exchange. Cryptology ePrint Archive, 1999/012 (1999)
31. Teske, E.: Square–root Algorithms for the Discrete Logarithm Problem (A survey). In: Public Key Cryptography and Computational Number Theory, pp. 283–301. Walter de Gruyter, Berlin (2001)
32. Ustaoglu, B.: Obtaining a secure and efficient key agreement protocol from (H)MQV and NAXOS. Designs, Codes and Cryptography 46(3), 329–342 (2008)
33. Ustaoglu, B.: Comparing SessionStateReveal and EphemeralKeyReveal for Diffie–Hellman protocols. In: Pieprzyk, J., Zhang, F. (eds.) ProvSec 2009. LNCS, vol. 5848, pp. 183–197. Springer, Heidelberg (2009)

A Security Enhancement and Proof for Authentication and Key Agreement (AKA)*

Vladimir Kolesnikov

Alcatel-Lucent Bell Laboratories, 600 Mountain Ave. Murray Hill, NJ 07974, USA
kolesnikov@research.bell-labs.com

Abstract. In this work, we consider Authentication and Key Agreement (AKA), a popular client-server Key Exchange (KE) protocol, commonly used in wireless standards (e.g., UMTS), and widely considered for new applications. We discuss natural potential usage scenarios for AKA, attract attention to subtle vulnerabilities, propose a simple and efficient AKA enhancement, and provide its formal proof of security.

The vulnerabilities arise due to the fact that AKA is not a secure KE in the standard cryptographic sense, since Client $\mathcal{C}$ does not contribute randomness to the session key. We argue that AKA remains secure in current deployments where $\mathcal{C}$ is an entity controlled by a *single* tamper-resistant User Identity Module (UIM). However, we also show that AKA is *insecure* if several Client's devices/UIMs share his identity and key.

We show practical applicability and efficiency benefits of such multi-UIM scenarios. As our main contribution, we adapt AKA for this setting, with only the minimal changes, while adhering to AKA design goals, and preserving its advantages and features. Our protocol involves one extra PRFG evaluation and no extra messages. We formally prove security of the resulting protocol. We discuss how our security improvement allows simplification of some of AKA security heuristics, which may make our protocol more efficient and robust than AKA even for the current deployment scenarios.

1 Introduction

This work is positioned at the intersection of engineering security and cryptography. We present a security enhancement of an existing heavily deployed protocol (AKA – Authentication and Key Agreement), and analyze it with formal cryptographic tools. We aim this paper for both crypto and security audiences. Therefore, we use the existing AKA notation and some of the corresponding presentation style and, at the same time, we abstract away non-essential protocol details and follow cryptographic formalisms. The result and discussion of the paper is self-contained; standards documents and protocols referenced in this work help put the paper in context for security reader, but are not required for understanding.

---

* Full version of this paper appears in ePrint archive [8].

J.A. Garay and R. De Prisco (Eds.): SCN 2010, LNCS 6280, pp. 235–252, 2010.

Establishment and maintenance of authenticated secure channels is the most used fruit of cryptography today. In particular, wireless and cellular communications critically rely on secure (wired and wireless) channels to exercise control over the network, access, accounting, etc.

In this work, we consider use scenarios (and their security consequences) of one of the most popular wireless protocols – AKA. (Our entire discussion correspondingly applies to AKA-derivative protocols, such as EAP-AKA [4].)

3GPP AKA [2], built as a security enhancement of GSM AKA, is a modern efficient KE protocol, which is based on pre-shared secret key (PSK). It is widely deployed today in GSM and other cellular networks, and is considered for a variety of additional applications.

For logistical reasons (e.g., cellular telephone roaming), there are three players in the protocol: the *user*, user's *home environment* (HE), and the (visited) *serving network* (SN). AKA allows SN to authenticate and exchange keys with the user, without ever being given the user's key. Instead, one-time *authentication vectors* (AV) are issued to SN by the HE. All communication and computation in AKA is very efficient thanks to the use of symmetric-key cryptography. However, because of the complexities of existing SN-to-HE protocols and associated delays, the AVs cannot be retrieved on-demand, are delivered in batches, and, in particular, cannot depend on user-generated nonces[1].

1.1 Related Work

The AKA protocol is proposed and used by the 3rd Generation Partnership Project (3GPP) [2]. EAP-AKA [4], an IETF RFC, is a wrapper around the AKA cryptographic core, to allow for a standard EAP interface to the AKA protocol.

AKA has been extensively debated and scrutinized by the standards bodies, and, less so, in academic research. 3GPP published a technical report [3] containing an (enhanced) BAN-logic [5] proof of security. However, this proof does not operate with rigorous complexity-theoretic notions, and protocol specification contains occasional imprecise security statements, some of which we note in this paper. We note that no serious security vulnerabilities have been discovered in AKA.

In [13], the authors consider a simple Man-in-the-Middle attack that allows an attacker (a "false base station" in their terminology) to redirect the traffic from a legitimate Serving Network to a Serving Network of his choice. The attack relies on the fact, that AV's issued by User's service provider do not cryptographically bind the ID of the Serving Network to which they are issued. The solution of [13] is to do so. We note that this security issue is different from what we are considering in this work.

---

[1] Observe the time it takes to switch on a mobile phone first time after landing in a new country versus switching it on for a second time. In the first case, the authenticators are retrieved from HE. In the second case, they are already cached at the visited SN.

1.2 Our Contributions

In this work, we consider the AKA key exchange protocol. We present a simple and intuitive argument of security of the cryptographic core of AKA in the case when Client $\mathcal{C}$ is an entity, controlled by a *single* User Identity Module (UIM), a tamper-resistant hardware token storing the key and performing KE. We identify the logical steps that rely on the single-UIM assumption.

We then argue that in many settings it is natural, convenient and more efficient to allow for multiple UIMs, issued to the same user, to share the secret key. We show that AKA is *insecure* in the above scenario with multiple UIMs sharing the key[2].

Finally, as our main contribution, we show a simple amendment to AKA that closes this vulnerability, and results in a secure key exchange protocol, which we formally prove. The idea of the proposed modification is to require the client to contribute randomness to the resulting session key. We stress that our modification adheres to the design requirements of AKA, and preserves the underlying data flow structure and patterns, and trust model, which is critical in today's deployment scenario. In particular, no extra communication with Home Environment is required, and batching of authenticators AV is possible (actually is simplified and improved). We discuss how this low-cost amendment (one extra PRFG evaluation and no extra messages) adds robustness, allows new usage scenarios, simplifies complicated AKA nonce generation heuristics, prevents UIM cloning attacks, etc.

1.3 Outline

We start, in §2, with presenting in detail the AKA protocol, and argue its security (in the case when each client is controlled by a corresponding *single* UIM). Then, in §3, we discuss the benefits of having several UIMs contain Client $\mathcal{C}$'s identity and credentials, and show AKA vulnerability in this case. We present our enhanced version of AKA KE protocol in §4, discuss its advantages and sketch a proof. For the lack of space, its formal proof of security is presented in the full version [8]. Finally, we conclude in §5.

2 The AKA Protocol

In this section we present in detail the cryptographic core of the AKA protocol. See Fig. 1 for the players and flow, and Fig. 2 and Fig. 3 for the precise message description.

Notation. For readability, we will introduce and use standard cryptographic KE notation. However, our presentation is based on [2]; therefore, for the benefit of

[2] This scenario is not explicitly disallowed in AKA specification, although the single-UIM setting appears to be implicit in the standards groups. Our discussion of the attacks thus serves to popularize this knowledge and attract attention of potential AKA adopters.

Table 1. Glossary of terms and abbreviations

UIM (User Identity Module) – tamper-proof token	PSK (Pre-shared secret key)
AV (Authentication Vector) – auth. data given to $\mathcal{S}$	SN (Serving Network) – server $\mathcal{S}$
HE (Home Environment) – key server $\mathcal{KS}$	MS (Mobile Station) – client $\mathcal{C}$

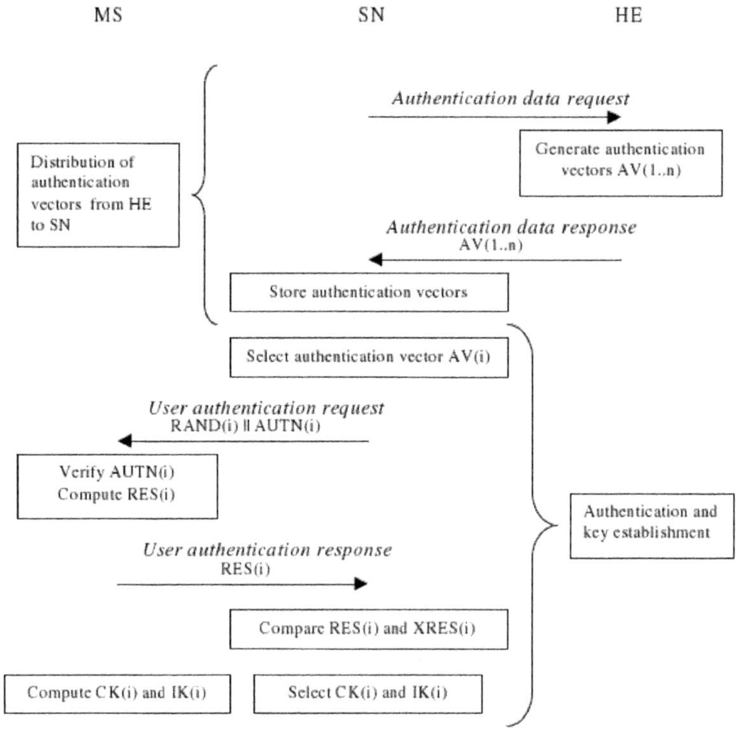

Fig. 1. AKA Flow (HELLOs and other details omitted. See §2 for notation.)

the security reader, we will include its notation for the ease of cross-reference. In particular, the diagrams are presented with notation of [2]. For reference, we provide a glossary of terms and abbreviations we use and their correspondence.

2.1 Players, Credentials, and Communication Flow

Players. There are three participants in AKA:

1. Client $\mathcal{C}$ (i.e., mobile phone, called Mobile Station (MS) in [2] and Peer in [4]) is the party initiating the exchange. In the wireless context, $\mathcal{C}$ is usually a MS requesting to be authenticated and granted access to a resource. $\mathcal{C}$ possesses a secret key k which is the basis for authentication.
2. Key Server ($\mathcal{KS}$) (called Home Environment (HE) in [2]). This player is $\mathcal{C}$'s server (in the wireless context, it is the service provider), who had issued

$\mathcal{C}$'s key k (usually on a secure User Identity Module (UIM)), and securely stores k. Key Server does not directly exchange keys or authenticate $\mathcal{C}$, but facilitates this process by giving one-time credentials to Server (described next).
3. Server $\mathcal{S}$(called Serving Network (SN) in [2]) is the party who directly interacts with and establishes a secure channel with the Client $\mathcal{C}$. In the wireless context, $\mathcal{S}$ grants $\mathcal{C}$ access to resource (network visited while roaming). As noted, $\mathcal{C}$'s credentials (i.e. key k) is not issued by $\mathcal{S}$, and are unknown to him. Instead, $\mathcal{S}$ receives (possibly batched) one-time authentication vectors AV from Key Server.

Credentials. Key exchange in AKA is based on Pre-shared Secret Key (PSK) k. The key is issued by Key Server to client $\mathcal{C}$; thus both $\mathcal{KS}$ and $\mathcal{C}$ have k. We stress that the server $\mathcal{S}$ *does not* have access to k; instead he receives (as needed, possibly batched) one-time authentication vectors AV from Key Server, which allows $\mathcal{S}$ and $\mathcal{C}$ to mutually authenticate and share a session key.

Trust Relationships. Server and Key Server trust each other and are assumed to have established a secure channel. We do not discuss how authentication vectors are delivered to $\mathcal{S}$; we assume this is done in a timely and secure manner. $\mathcal{S}$ and $\mathcal{C}$, on the other hand, do not *a priori* trust each other; it is the goal of KE to establish a secure channel *only* if parties possess matching credentials.

Data Flow. Upon client's initiation of KE, $\mathcal{S}$ contacts $\mathcal{KS}$ and obtains the authentication vector AV (usually, he would have done this in advance). AV (formally presented in the next section), is a vector, consisting of a challenge for $\mathcal{C}$, an expected response, auxiliary security data, and session keys to be used in case of successful authentication. AV's cannot be reused; to enable multiple logins, $\mathcal{KS}$ sends several AV's, indexed by the sequence number. (It is critical that $\mathcal{S}$ contacts $\mathcal{KS}$ as infrequently as possible, due to unacceptable (minutes-long) delays in current deployments. This imposes a rigid requirement on communication patterns; in particular, Client-generated messages (e.g., nonce) cannot be forwarded to $\mathcal{KS}$.)

$\mathcal{S}$ then sends AV's challenge (consisting of a random nonce RAND and its authenticator AUTN) to $\mathcal{C}$. $\mathcal{C}$ uses AUTN and his key k to confirm that the challenge indeed came from $\mathcal{KS}$. If so, $\mathcal{C}$ computes the session keys, computes and sends back response RES, and is ready to securely communicate with $\mathcal{S}$. $\mathcal{S}$ receives $\mathcal{C}$'s response and compares it with expected response XRES, which was sent by $\mathcal{KS}$ as part of AV. If $\mathsf{RES}=\mathsf{XRES}$, $\mathcal{S}$ uses session keys received as part of AV for communication with $\mathcal{C}$.

We do not discuss error handling and other lower level details.

2.2 Authentication and Session Key Derivation

In this section, we present in detail the contents of the exchanged messages, and informally argue the security of AKA in the case when each $\mathcal{C}$ is a *single entity*, such as a securely issued UIM.

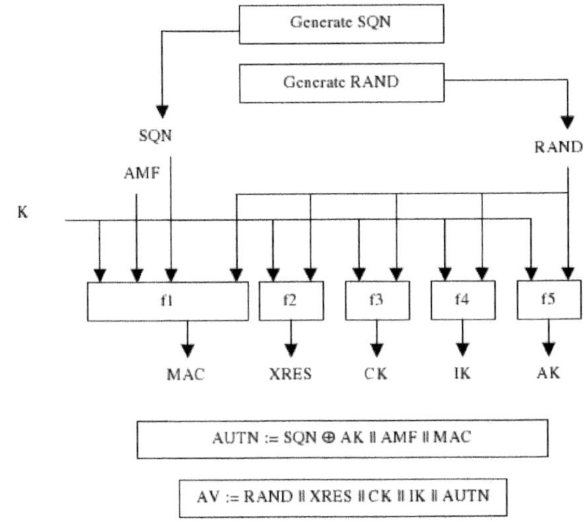

Fig. 2. AKA Authentication Vector

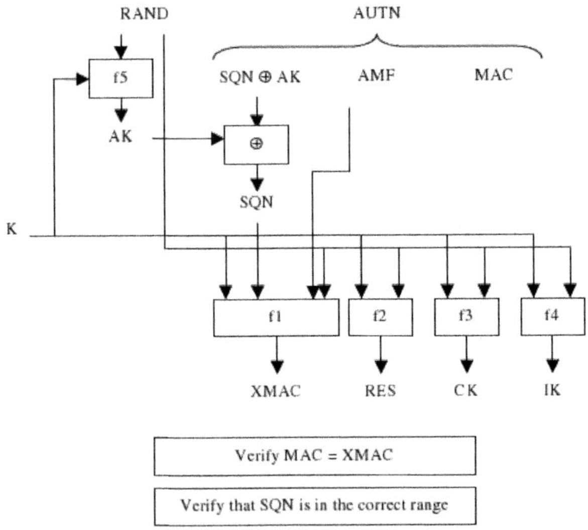

Fig. 3. AKA Client Derivation

As mentioned above, we do not discuss the security of the channel between $\mathcal{KS}$ and $\mathcal{S}$; we assume that the adversary cannot read or interfere with this channel. We concentrate on the channel in control of the adversary – the network (or air) connecting $\mathcal{S}$ and $\mathcal{C}$.

Construction of messages referred to in Fig. 1 and discussed in §2.1, are discussed below and graphically shown on Fig. 2 and Fig. 3.

AV is computed as follows.

First, $\mathcal{KS}$ generates a fresh sequence number SQN and a random challenge RAND[3]. SQN is used to keep track of the usage of the one-time AVs, and to help $\mathcal{C}$ detect and reject replays. SQN need not be sequential; [2] discusses (somewhat involved) selection strategies which allow efficient tracking and re-synchronization in case of failures, which is beyond the scope of this paper. AMF, the Authentication Management Field, is used to select technical parameters, such as timeout values; its use is not relevant for our analysis of the core of AKA.

Then, XRES, CK, IK, AK, AUTN and MAC are derived from PSK k, SQN, RAND, and AMF using message authentication functions f_1, f_2 and key derivation functions $f_3, ..., f_5$. We note that security properties of $f_1, ..., f_5$ are stated insufficiently formally in [2][4]. For simplicity, we assume stronger properties of $f_1, ..., f_5$, namely that they are *pseudorandom*. One can think of these functions as AES evaluated on the argument prefixed with the index of the function, e.g. $f_i(x) = AES(i, x)$. Following the existing notation, we keep the functions $f_1, ..., f_5$ in our presentation.

The derivation proceeds as follows (illustrated on Fig. 2).

- message authentication code MAC
  MAC= f_{1_k}(SQN || RAND || AMF)
- an expected response
  XRES= f_{2_k}(RAND)
- cipher key
  CK= f_{3_k}(RAND)
- integrity key
  IK= f_{4_k}(RAND)
- anonymity key
  AK= f_{5_k}(RAND)
- authentication token
  AUTN = SQN $\oplus$ AK || AMF || MAC

Here, CK and IK are the keys to be used in the event of successful authentication. The use of AK is optional, and when its generating function f_5 is non-zero, AK is used for hiding the sequence number. We do not consider this option, and set $f_5 = 0$, as it is not relevant to the security of AKA core.

Finally, authentication vector AV is the concatenation
AV = RAND || XRES || CK || IK || AUTN.

[3] In [2], depending on the occurrence in text, RAND is required to be either "random" or "unpredictable". We note that actually a weaker requirement of *freshness* is sufficient when derivation functions f_i are pseudorandom (e.g., AES).

[4] In particular, message authentication function f_2, used in the computation of XRES, is allowed to be truncated. We note that, depending on the MAC function, truncation may completely remove its security properties. This is because standard definition of MAC allow for portions of the MAC output to be irrelevant (e.g. always set to 0). Clearly, truncating MAC, leaving only the predictable zeros allows for easy MAC forgery.

Client's computation. $\mathcal{C}$ receives[5] RAND and AUTN = SQN || AMF || MAC. (Recall, AMF is not essential for AKA core security). Since $\mathcal{C}$ has possession of the same PSK k that was used in the derivation of AV, $\mathcal{C}$ is able to derive the respective values: response RES, CK, IK, and expected MAC XMAC, as shown on Fig. 3. Then $\mathcal{C}$ verifies that the received MAC equals to expected MAC (MAC= XMAC) and checks that the sequence number SQN is within the expected (heuristically specified) range. If the checks pass, $\mathcal{C}$ sends his final response RES to $\mathcal{S}$, considers that AKA succeeded, and starts using CK and IK that he derived.

Server's computation. $\mathcal{S}$ receives $\mathcal{C}$'s response RES; if RES = XRES, $\mathcal{S}$ considers that AKA succeeded, and starts using CK and IK that he received from $\mathcal{KS}$.

This completes the description of the cryptographic core of the AKA key exchange.

Security Argument. We present an intuitive argument of security of AKA in the case when each $\mathcal{C}$ is a *single entity*, such as a securely issued UIM. This informal analysis also serves the purpose of identifying the logical steps that use the single-UIM assumption. For simplicity, we assume that each function f_i used is pseudorandom. The analysis of the actual AKA, which relies on MAC, is almost identical.

We proceed with the message flow of AKA, and first consider $\mathcal{C}$ and his actions. Consider the case when $\mathcal{C}$ accepts. (Otherwise $\mathcal{C}$ simply aborts without outputting anything, and, as is easy to see, the adversary $\mathcal{A}$ cannot gain from this. The only information leaked to $\mathcal{A}$ here is the pattern of failures, which he can predict by himself based on the messages he delivers to $\mathcal{C}$.) We first observe that the adversary $\mathcal{A}$ cannot have obtained from $\mathcal{KS}$, $\mathcal{S}$ or $\mathcal{C}$ two vectors AV with the same RAND but different SQN. Since $\mathcal{C}$ accepted, $\mathcal{C}$ must have verified the freshness of SQN (that is that $\mathcal{C}$ had not received AV with this SQN before[6]). We can now see that RAND received by $\mathcal{C}$ is fresh and indeed generated by $\mathcal{KS}$ in the AV with SQN[7]. That is, with overwhelming probability, this RAND had not been used by $\mathcal{KS}$ in other AV's, and it is not replayed[8] or forged by the adversary $\mathcal{A}$. This follows from the unforgeability of PRF (or MAC, if we assume f_1 is a secure MAC, as is done in [2]). Indeed, suppose to the contrary, $\mathcal{C}$ accepted a RAND, SQN pair delivered by $\mathcal{A}$ which was not generated by $\mathcal{KS}$. Then $\mathcal{A}$ must have broken the PRF/MAC property of f_1, by generating a MAC on a new message, since $\mathcal{C}$ must have verified and accepted MAC.

---

[5] Recall we considering the case when AK = 0.

[6] Here is where the assumption of a single instance of $\mathcal{C}$ is critical. If $\mathcal{C}$ is allowed to be instantiated, e.g., on two devices, freshness cannot be guaranteed.

[7] We are also guaranteed that the AMF received by $\mathcal{C}$ was generated by $\mathcal{KS}$ in the same AV as RAND and SQN. However, we are not addressing the AMF issues in this work, and will not discuss this further.

[8] Here the assumption of a single instance of $\mathcal{C}$ comes in again. If $\mathcal{C}$ is allowed to be instantiated, e.g., on two devices, then replays are possible, since both devices will accept the same sequence number SQN.

At this point, we know that $\mathcal{S}$ and $\mathcal{C}$ share the same RAND. Thus $\mathsf{RES} = \mathsf{XRES}$ and $\mathcal{S}$ and $\mathcal{C}$ compute the same IK and CK. Further, RAND is fresh[9], that is, $\mathcal{A}$ had not seen $f_{i_k}(\mathsf{RAND})$. Then, even though $\mathcal{A}$ knows RAND, learning anything about $\mathsf{XRES}= f_{2_k}(\mathsf{RAND})$ or $\mathsf{CK}= f_{3_k}(\mathsf{RAND})$ or $\mathsf{IK}= f_{4_k}(\mathsf{RAND})$, implies that $\mathcal{A}$ can break the pseudorandomness properties of f_i (is thus considered impossible).

Now $\mathcal{C}$ computes and sends out $\mathsf{RES} = f_{2_k}(\mathsf{RAND})$. Both $\mathcal{C}$ and $\mathcal{S}$ had agreed on random and unknown to $\mathcal{A}$ session keys. Now, the most damage $\mathcal{A}$ can do is interfere with the delivery of RES to $\mathcal{S}$, preventing the establishment of the secure channel. However this is not considered a vulnerability in KE, since the same effect can be achieved, e.g., by $\mathcal{A}$ simply jamming the communication channels.

Security Proof. We note that the above security argument can be transformed into a formal proof of security. There are two things that need to be done. First, we need to give a definition of security in the setting with a single-UIM client. Such definition can be derived from existing KE definitions (e.g., [11,6,7,10]) by carefully restricting instance creation in the ideal worlds (simulation-based) or the games (indistinguishability-based) of the definitions. Then, we can transform our argument into a proof based on the proposed definition. We defer these technically involved steps as future work.

3 Multi-UIM Setting and AKA Vulnerabilities

We start with justifying the setting where the client $\mathcal{C}$ would possess several devices provisioned with the same PSK (let's call it the *multi-UIM setting*).

Today, service providers aim to engage the customers as much as possible, and offer bundled services, such as triple play (phone, internet, TV). It is easy to imagine that the next step is to allow customers to have a number of devices, such as laptop, phone, camera, etc., to use the service.

We first observe that it is convenient to decouple the user (i.e. subscriber) from the device (as done, e.g., by GSM and the WiMAX Forum [1]). This allows attractive business scenarios, where one customer may have several subscriptions, and use several devices (e.g., laptop, phone, camera, etc. in case of WiMAX). The convenience factor for the user is that the devices are all linked in one plan, and the service is not linked to the device, but rather to the subscriber identity. A person should be able, e.g., to borrow or buy a new device, plug in his UIM card, and use it. The devices often need to be "swappable", as is done today with the removable UIM cards. The UIM cards should not be tied to the type of service (TV, phone, etc.), but should be interchangeable and mainly serve to authenticate the customer.

In cases as above, it may be convenient (although, of course, not absolutely necessary) to employ multi-UIMs (i.e., UIMs issued to the same $\mathcal{C}$ and initialized with the same PSK). Issuing several *identical* UIM cards to the customer is convenient to the user and the service provider, and it brings significant efficiency gains, as described next.

[9] Again, provided that $\mathcal{C}$ is instantiated on a *single* device, and the adversary $\mathcal{A}$ thus did not replay the AV.

Convenience and efficiency gains with multi-UIM. Clearly, this ensures the swappability as described above, and the associated convenience for the customer. We note that this feature can be emulated by issuing UIMs with different keys, and $\mathcal{KS}$ linking them to the customer's account and keeping track of all the keys. This is a feasible replacement, which, however, comes at a cost. Firstly, $\mathcal{KS}$ must keep track of and *securely store* a much larger number of keys (a factor of 5 to 10 in the near future, depending on the average number of devices per user). Secure storage is expensive, and this is a significant penalty. Further, generating and delivering batched AV is much more convenient with the multi-UIMs, since any of the AV's generated for the customer would work. In contrast, if each of customer's UIMs has a separate key, a separate AV must be requested and delivered to $\mathcal{S}$, causing latencies, additional network load, and increased $\mathcal{S}$ storage.

3.1 Multi-UIM Vulnerabilities of AKA

As already noted, in AKA, $\mathcal{C}$ does not contribute randomness to the resulting session key, and instead relies on the freshness of SQN, which can only be guaranteed if PSK k is stored securely on a UIM and only a *single* UIM is issued per customer identity. At the same time, as discussed above, employing multiple UIMs keyed with the same PSK k is often convenient and more efficient.

Because AKA Client contributes no randomness, the session key is entirely determined by the RAND (and its authenticator AUTN) sent by server. We now show two simple attacks on AKA deployment in the multi-UIM scenario, i.e. if there are two instances (e.g., devices) of $\mathcal{C}$ using the same PSK.

Denote by $\mathcal{C}_1$ and $\mathcal{C}_2$ the two instances/devices of $\mathcal{C}$ sharing the same PSK k.

Attack scenario 1. $\mathcal{C}_1$ and $\mathcal{C}_2$ both wish to connect to the network. $\mathcal{C}_1$ initiates the exchange, and, as prescribed by AKA, $\mathcal{S}$ sends RAND, AUTN to $\mathcal{C}_1$, which $\mathcal{C}_1$ receives, and the adversary $\mathcal{A}$ overhears. $\mathcal{C}_2$ initiates the exchange, which $\mathcal{A}$ blocks from $\mathcal{S}$. Instead, $\mathcal{A}$ replays the RAND, AUTN message to $\mathcal{C}_2$. At this time, both devices $\mathcal{C}_1$ and $\mathcal{C}_2$ derive the same session keys CK,IK, but they both think they are talking to $\mathcal{S}$. Carefully forwarding (presumably secured) messages sent between the two devices and the server may allow $\mathcal{A}$ to create unintended transactions on $\mathcal{C}$'s account. For example, if the transaction performed on $\mathcal{C}_1$ involves a debit on the account maintained by $\mathcal{C}_1$'s UIM, the adversary $\mathcal{A}$ replaying this transaction to $\mathcal{C}_2$ (possible, since $\mathcal{C}_2$ has the same session key as $\mathcal{C}_1$) may effect a corresponding debit on $\mathcal{C}_2$'s UIM – clearly an unintended transaction and a successful attack.

Attack scenario 2. The above attack is strengthened if the adversary $\mathcal{A}$ borrows (or captures or remotely compromises) one of $\mathcal{C}$'s devices containing the PSK k (say, $\mathcal{C}_2$). By good engineering practices, PSK k is securely stored on UIM, which it never leaves. Thus, with k unavailable to $\mathcal{A}$ a secure system should guarantee that the compromised device $\mathcal{C}_2$ should not help $\mathcal{A}$ compromise other devices (e.g., $\mathcal{C}_1$) or their sessions.

Not so with using AKA in this scenario. Indeed, the session keys produced by the UIM are exported into the main memory of the device, which $\mathcal{A}$ can exploit by performing an attack similar to described above. $\mathcal{A}$ simply overhears RAND, AUTN destined to $\mathcal{C}_1$, and forwards it to the UIM in his control. As prescribed by AKA, $\mathcal{A}$'s UIM will generate and export to the device session keys CK,IK, which are the same keys generated on $\mathcal{C}_1$. Clearly, the adversary $\mathcal{A}$ is now in control of the (presumably) secure session established between $\mathcal{S}$ and $\mathcal{C}_1$.

We stress that this attack is especially dangerous if user's devices have different degrees of confidence. Then, the attacker, by remotely hacking an unimportant and weakly protected device, such as child's laptop, may gain access to a high-confidence device on the same account, such as parent's smart phone.

4 Secure Multi-UIM AKA

In this section we present our main contribution – a simple and efficient AKA security enhancement for the multi-UIM case. We formally prove security of our protocol; in particular, we close the multi-UIM vulnerability. The idea of the enhancement is to have the client $\mathcal{C}$'s UIM(s) generate and contribute their randomness to the session key, in a way that preserves AKA message flow.

The most natural (and sufficient!) method to do it is to use the already established CK,IK as *intermediate* keys only, and derive the session keys based on randomness sampled by UIM. For example the actual session keys could be CK' $= f_{\mathsf{CK}}(\mathsf{RANDC})$, IK' $= f_{\mathsf{IK}}(\mathsf{RANDC})$, where RANDC $\in_R \{0,1\}^n$ is sampled by UIM. Now, $\mathcal{C}$ could simply send RANDC to $\mathcal{S}$ to enable server-side derivation. We note that it is critical that UIM never exports to the device anything other than the final session keys.

Intuitively, security now holds since only the parties who possess CK,IK are able to derive the session key by evaluating the prescribed derivation function keyed with CK,IK on argument RANDC. These parties are the (authorized) $\mathcal{C}$ (his UIM sampled RANDC and evaluated on it), and $\mathcal{S}$, who is given CK,IK by $\mathcal{KS}$. The adversary $\mathcal{A}$ is not able to compute session keys CK',IK', even if he compromised $\mathcal{C}$'s additional devices, since UIMs of these devices only evaluate derivation functions on the arguments they (UIM's) sample themselves.

Next, we present our protocol in detail, and give intuition for its security. For the lack of space, we present a formal proof of security in the full version [8].

4.1 The Formal Multi-AKA Protocol

The protocol, informally presented above, demonstrates the step that we need to take to achieve security in the multi-UIM setting. This protocol can be naturally simplified and optimized, which we do in this section. Importantly, we keep the message structure, efficiency, and features of the original AKA protocol.

We observe that there is no need to include two derived keys (CK,IK) into AV. One derivation key KD computed from PSK k and RAND is sufficient to derive CK and IK to be used in the (now secure) session. One simple optimization we perform is using just one key KD in place of CK,IK in AV.

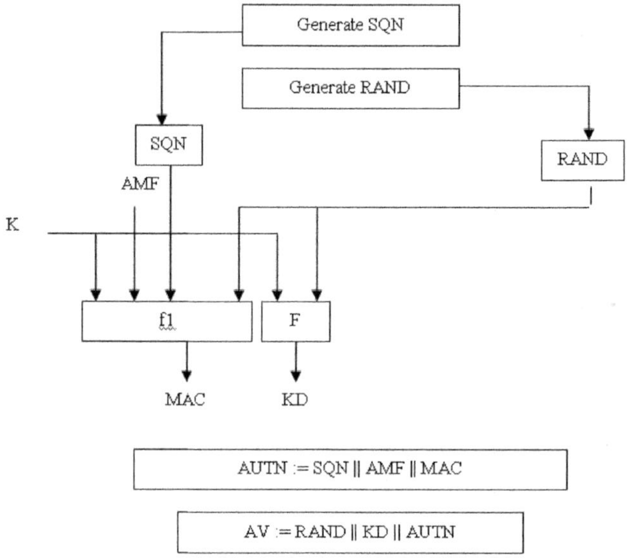

Fig. 4. Multi-AKA Authentication vector

Let $f_1, F, F1, F2$ be pseudorandom function generators, such as AES[10].

Protocol 1. *Multi-AKA*

1. *As follows from the above discussion and examples, in Multi-AKA, $\mathcal{KS}$ will not send the session keys* CK,IK *to $\mathcal{S}$ in the* AV*. Instead, $\mathcal{KS}$ will send to $\mathcal{S}$ the session derivation key* KD*, which is derived from PSK k and the* AV*'s randomness* RAND*:* KD $= F_k$(RAND). MAC *is computed by $\mathcal{KS}$ as before:* MAC$= f_{1_k}$(SQN || RAND || AMF). XRES *is omitted since $\mathcal{S}$ will compute it itself based on* KD *and $\mathcal{C}$'s randomness.* AUTN *is computed as before (*AUTN = SQN || AMF || MAC*)*[11]*, and* AV *is set to* AV = RAND || KD || AUTN*. This step is illustrated on Fig. 4.*
2. *Upon $\mathcal{C}$'s request for authentication, $\mathcal{S}$ forwards* RAND *and* AUTN *to $\mathcal{C}$. $\mathcal{C}$ verifies* MAC *as in AKA, and, if successful, proceeds as follows. First, it computes his version of the derivation key* KD $= F_k$(RAND)*. Then $\mathcal{C}$ samples random* RANDC *and computes* RES $= F_{\mathsf{KD}}$(RANDC)*. $\mathcal{C}$ also computes* CK$=$ $F1_{\mathsf{KD}}$(RANDC)*, and* IK$=$ $F2_{\mathsf{KD}}$(RANDC)*. Then $\mathcal{C}$ sends* RANDC *and* RES *to $\mathcal{S}$ and is ready to communicate over a channel secured by session keys* CK,IK*. This step is illustrated on Fig. 5.*

[10] As already discussed above, these functions can either be different functions, or the same function such as AES. In the latter case, we must ensure differentiation of the evaluation of the functions, e.g. by prepending the (AES) argument with a function-unique prefix.

[11] Recall, we set AK $= 0$.

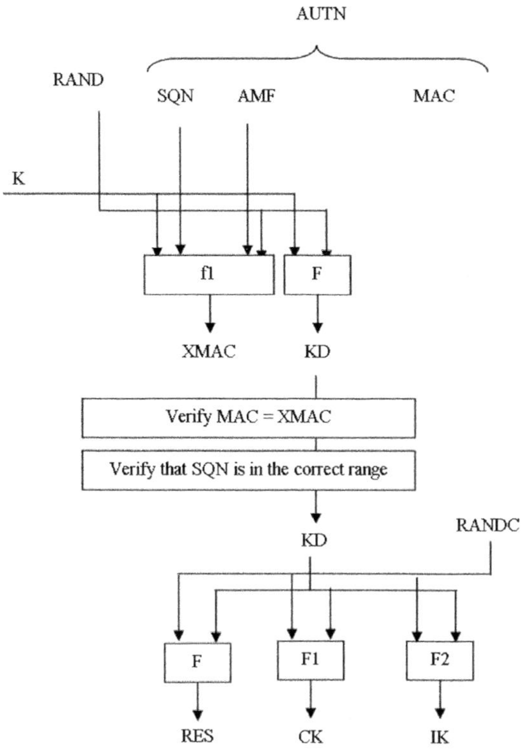

Fig. 5. Multi-AKA Client Computation

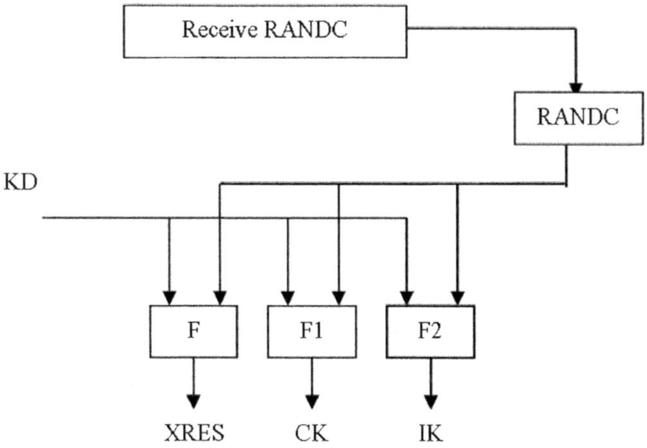

Fig. 6. Multi-AKA Server Computation

3. *Upon receipt from $\mathcal{C}$ the pair* RANDC *and* RES, *$\mathcal{S}$ proceeds as follows. He first computes* XRES= F_{KD}(RANDC), *and checks that* XRES= RES. *If so, $\mathcal{S}$ derives (and uses) the session keys* CK= $F1_{\mathsf{KD}}$(RANDC), *and* IK= $F2_{\mathsf{KD}}$(RANDC). *This step is illustrated on Fig. 6.*

Remark: All actions of $\mathcal{C}$ are performed on a UIM, and only the resulting keys CK,IK *are exported outside of the UIM.*

4.2 Security Argument and Claim

The security proof of Multi-AKA is actually simpler than that of AKA presented above in §2.2. The main reason is that with both $\mathcal{S}$ and $\mathcal{C}$ contributing randomness to session keys, message replays don't matter, since they *always* result in the generation of *unrelated* keys, which cannot help the adversary $\mathcal{A}$ in attacking other sessions.

We proceed with the message flow of Multi-AKA, and first consider $\mathcal{C}$ and his actions. Consider the case when $\mathcal{C}$ accepts (otherwise $\mathcal{C}$ simply aborts without outputting anything, and, as is easy to see, the adversary $\mathcal{A}$ cannot gain from this. The only information leaked to $\mathcal{A}$ here is the pattern of failures, which he can predict by himself based on the messages he delivers to $\mathcal{C}$.) We first observe that $\mathcal{S}$ cannot have received from $\mathcal{KS}$ two vectors AV with the same RAND but different SQN (this is because the probability of collision of two randomly sampled RAND values is negligible). Therefore, there cannot be two instances of $\mathcal{S}$ that generated the same KD. We note that $\mathcal{A}$ can cause different instances of $\mathcal{C}$ (e.g., $\mathcal{C}_1$ and $\mathcal{C}_2$) to generate the same KD simply by replaying $\mathcal{S}$'s message. However, it is easy to see that even in the case when $\mathcal{A}$ controls one of client's instances (say, $\mathcal{C}_1$), the session keys CK,IK output by $\mathcal{C}_2$ cannot be predicted by $\mathcal{A}$, due to the security (namely, pseudorandomness) properties of the function used to generate the keys. This also means that $\mathcal{A}$ cannot arrange for secure channels between unintended parties (e.g., as in our attacks in §3.1, where $\mathcal{S}$ shared session key with two clients). Here, it is critical that UIMs do not export intermediate keys (KD) into the main memory of the device[12].

Similarly, $\mathcal{A}$ cannot learn server keys or mismatch server secure channels (e.g., as in our attacks in §3.1). This is because, firstly, intermediate keys KD generated by any player are unpredictable to $\mathcal{A}$. Further, as noted above, no two servers use the same KD, and thus replaying client's response to $\mathcal{S}$ will cause a verification failure.

Above discussion leads to the following theorem:

Theorem 1. *Protocol 1 (Multi-AKA) is a secure key exchange protocol. In particular, it remains secure if the adversary $\mathcal{A}$ corrupts one or more of $\mathcal{C}$'s instances (devices), but does not get access inside the UIM executing the protocol.*

We approach the proof of Theorem 1 as follows. First, we further abstract away the non-essential messages and concepts and leave only the core message

[12] If in fact KD was exported, then $\mathcal{A}$ could trivially compute the session key established by $\mathcal{C}_2$: CK= $F1_{\mathsf{KD}}$(RANDC).

exchange. Then we recall a KE definition (derived from a more general definition of [10]), and prove security of the abstracted protocol with respect to that definition. Finally, it is easy to see that this implies the statement of Theorem 1.

For the lack of space, we present a formal proof of security in the full version [8].

4.3 Practical Implications and Considerations

We mention several practical implications of our proposed protocol. First, we do not use SQN at all. This means that (at least some of) the complicated heuristics associated with the state maintenance can be avoided or simplified. Further, the persistent AKA problem of UIM cloning goes away in the following sense. Of course, a cloned UIM would be able to access the resource as well as the legitimate UIM, however, he would not be able to mount man-in-the-middle attacks on the legitimate UIM's connection.

Revocation. At the first glance, the issue of revocation would become significantly more complex, since all of $\mathcal{C}$'s UIMs share the same key. However, this does not appear to pose any problems, for the following reasons. One revocation solution can use broadcast encryption techniques, and, upon $\mathcal{C}$'s request, simply update the keys of legitimate UIMs, while excluding the stolen ones. We note, that this would require each UIM storing a small number of keys, depending on the maximum number of user's devices. Other solutions could use out-of-band secure channel (e.g., telephone conversation with an agent or a separately protected web control page) to obtain PIN(s) required to refresh the keys of the authorized UIMs. During refresh, short authenticated string (SAS)-based techniques [12] may prove helpful.

4.4 Performance

As it is easy to see, the costs of added security that we propose are negligible. The final tally would depend on the exact instantiations, but our core protocol has only one (1) additional PRFG evaluation by $\mathcal{S}$, as he now needs to compute XRES himself (however, this offloads the corresponding operation on $\mathcal{KS}$). We do not further calculate these costs, since they are negligible compared to AKA communication costs, in terms of energy consumption and time.

5 Conclusion

We considered a widely used AKA protocol and the issue of its reliance on the uniqueness of the tamper-resistant module, UIM, holding user's key. We presented the intuition for security of AKA in this setting. We noted that issuing multiple UIMs to the user, all of which hold the same user's key is appealing for UIM interchangeability, and allows for protocol efficiency improvement, such as better reuse of authenticating data and reduction of required secure storage.

As AKA turns out to be insecure in this setting, we presented a security enhancement of AKA, along with a formal proof of security. Our protocol has negligible performance premium, and is more robust than AKA, while adhering to AKA design goals. Its robustness offers avenues for simplifications of AKA heuristics. We believe our protocol may be a worthy upgrade for AKA and a candidate for more general scenarios.

Acknowledgements. I would like to thank anonymous reviewers of this paper for many valuable comments, and Simon Mizikovsky for our initial AKA discussion.

References

1. WiMAX Forum, http://www.wimaxforum.org/
2. 3rd Generation Partnership Project. 3GPP Technical Specification 3GPP TS 33.102 V7.1.0: Technical Specification Group Services and System Aspects; 3G Security; Security Architecture (Release 7) (December 2006)
3. 3rd Generation Partnership Project. 3GPP Techical Report TR 33.902: Formal Analysis of the 3G Authentication Protocol (March 2001), http://www.3gpp.org/ftp/Specs/html-info/33902.htm
4. Arkko, J., Haverinen, H.: IETF Network Working Group: Extensible Authentication Protocol Method for 3rd Generation Authentication and Key Agreement (EAP-AKA). RFC 4187 (January 2006), http://tools.ietf.org/html/rfc4187
5. Burrows, M., Abadi, M., Needham, R.: A logic of authentication. ACM Trans. Comput. Syst. 8(1), 18–36 (1990)
6. Canetti, R., Krawczyk, H.: Analysis of key-exchange protocols and their use for building secure channels. In: Pfitzmann, B. (ed.) EUROCRYPT 2001. LNCS, vol. 2045, pp. 453–474. Springer, Heidelberg (2001)
7. Canetti, R., Krawczyk, H.: Universally composable notions of key exchange and secure channels. In: Knudsen, L.R. (ed.) EUROCRYPT 2002. LNCS, vol. 2332, pp. 337–351. Springer, Heidelberg (2002)
8. Kolesnikov, V.: A security enhancement and proof for Authentication and Key Agreement (AKA). Cryptology ePrint Archive, Report 2010/350 (2010), http://eprint.iacr.org/
9. Kolesnikov, V., Rackoff, C.: Key exchange using passwords and long keys. In: Halevi, S., Rabin, T. (eds.) TCC 2006. LNCS, vol. 3876, pp. 100–119. Springer, Heidelberg (2006)
10. Kolesnikov, V., Rackoff, C.: Password mistyping in two-factor-authenticated key exchange. In: Aceto, L., Damgård, I., Goldberg, L.A., Halldórsson, M.M., Ingólfsdóttir, A., Walukiewicz, I. (eds.) ICALP 2008, Part II. LNCS, vol. 5126, pp. 702–714. Springer, Heidelberg (2008)
11. Shoup, V.: On formal models for secure key exchange. Technical Report RZ 3120 (#93166), IBM (1999)
12. Vaudenay, S.: Secure communications over insecure channels based on short authenticated strings. In: Shoup, V. (ed.) CRYPTO 2005. LNCS, vol. 3621, pp. 309–326. Springer, Heidelberg (2005)
13. Zhang, M., Fang, Y.: Security analysis and enhancements of 3gpp authentication and key agreement protocol. IEEE Transactions on Wireless Communications 4, 734–742 (2005)

A Definition of Security of KE

In this section, we present the definition of security we use in our proofs. This definition is a natural adaptation (actually, simplification) of the definitions of Kolesnikov and Rackoff [9,10]. The latter definitions consider a substantially more general setting of multi-factor authenticated KE, where parties possess both long and short keys (e.g. PSK and passwords). The definitions of [9,10] have the graceful degradation property, that is, a compromise of some of the keys results in the security level accorded by the remaining key(s). Naturally (also indirectly implied in [9,10]), omitting the use of short keys results in the definition for our setting.

While one can use one of several KE definitions, we found game-based definition to be the simplest to use. For completeness and the formalization of discussion, we now present the adapted definition that we will use.

We denote by C_i^S the i-th instance of client C who wants to talk to (some instance of) server S. S_j^C is defined symmetrically.

KE definitions rely on the notion of *partners* to specify what constitutes an attack. Informally, two instances of players are partners, if they establish a secure channel. Syntactically, we define partners as follows.

Definition 1. *We say that an instance C_i^S of a client C and an instance S_j^C of a server S are* partners, *if they have output the same session id sid.*

Session id *sid* is an additional (somewhat artificial) output of KE, which need not be used in real execution, but which is needed for syntactic manipulations in the proof. We omit the detailed discussion of the need of *sid* and refer the interested reader to literature, e.g., [9,10] for additional information.

We start by presenting the KE game, which model attacks of a real-life adversary. Recall, we do not address the security aspects of the server (SN in AKA) receiving the authenticating credentials from the key server $\mathcal{KS}$; we assume this is done in a secure manner, e.g. using pre-established channels.

Game KE. *An honest server S is created. Adv then runs players by executing steps 1-6 multiple times, in any order:*

1. *Adv creates an honest client C. C is registered with S, and a randomly chosen key is set up and associated with C. Only one honest client can be created.*
2. *Adv creates a corrupt client B^i. A randomly chosen key is set up and associated with B_i.*
3. *Adv creates an instance C_i of the honest client C. C_i is given (secretly from Adv) as input the key associated with C.*
4. *Adv creates an instance S_j of the honest server S. S_j is given (secretly from Adv) as input the partner client's key*[13].

[13] Other authenticating credentials may be given instead, such as KD in the AKA setting.

5. *Adv delivers a message m to an honest party instance. The instance immediately responds with a reply (by giving it to Adv) and/or, terminates and outputs the result (a sid and either the session key, or the* failure symbol $\perp$*) according to the protocol. Adv learns only the sid part of the output.*
6. *Adv "opens" any successfully completed and checked honest instance – then he is given the session key output of that instance.*

Then Adv asks for a challenge on an instance of an honest player.

The challenge of instance S_j^C of the server S is handled as follows. S_j^C, who has been instantiated to talk to the honest client C, must have completed and output a session key. The challenge is, equiprobably, either the key output by S_j^C or a random string of the same length. Adv must not have opened S_j^C or a partner of S_j^C, and is not allowed to do it in the future.

The challenge of instance C_j^S of the client C is handled symmetrically.

Then Adv continues to run the game as before (execute steps 2-6). Finally, Adv outputs a single bit b which denotes Adv's guess at whether the challenge string was random. Adv wins if he makes a correct guess, and loses otherwise. Adv cannot "withdraw" from a challenge, and must produce his guess.

The above game is almost sufficient for security definition. The only remaining technical aspect is the enforcement of non-triviality. We need to prevent improper partnering (e.g. players unnecessarily outputting same *sid*). Recall, *Adv* is not allowed to challenge parties whose partner has been opened; SID ensures that *Adv* is not unfairly restricted. We handle this by introducing the following game.

Game SID *is derived from game KE by adjusting the win condition. Adv does not ask for (nor answers) the challenge. Adv wins if any two honest partners output different session keys.*

Note, SID allows for one (or both) of the partners to output a failure symbol. *Adv* only wins if two successfully completed parties output different session keys.

We are now ready to present the definition.

Definition 2. *We say that a key exchange protocol Π is secure, if for every polytime adversaries Adv_1, Adv_{sid} playing games KE and SID, their probabilities of winning (over the randomness used by the adversaries, all players and generation algorithms) is at most only negligibly (in security parameter n) better than:*

- *1/2, for KE,*
- *0, for SID.*

Authenticated Key Agreement with Key Re-use in the Short Authenticated Strings Model

Stanisław Jarecki and Nitesh Saxena

[1] University of California, Irvine
[2] Polytechnic Institute of New York University

Abstract. Serge Vaudenay [20] introduced a notion of Message Authentication (MA) protocols in the Short Authenticated String (SAS) model. A SAS-MA protocol authenticates arbitrarily long messages sent over insecure channels as long as the sender and the receiver can additionally send a very short, e.g. 20 bit, *authenticated* message to each other. The main practical application of a SAS-MA protocol is Authenticated Key Agreement (AKA) in this communication model, i.e. SAS-AKA, which can be used for so-called "pairing" of wireless devices. Subsequent work [9,12,10] showed three-round SAS-AKA protocols. However, the Diffie-Hellman (DH) based SAS-AKA protocol of [10] requires choosing fresh DH exponents in each protocol instance, while the generic SAS-AKA construction given by [12] applies only to AKA protocols which have no *shared state* between protocol sessions. Therefore, both prior works exclude the most efficient, although not perfect-forward-secret, AKA protocols that re-use private keys (for encryption-based AKAs) or DH exponents (for DH-based AKAs) across multiple protocol sessions.

In this paper, we propose a novel three-round *encryption-based* SAS-AKA protocol, using non-malleable commitments and CCA-secure encryption as tools, which we show secure (but without perfect-forward secrecy) if each player re-uses its private/public key across protocol sessions. The cost of this protocol is dominated by a single public key encryption for one party and a decryption for the other, assuming the Random Oracle Model (ROM). When implemented with RSA encryption the new SAS-AKA protocol is especially attractive if the two devices being paired have asymmetric computational power (e.g., a desktop and a keyboard).

1 Introduction

Serge Vaudenay [20] introduced a notion of a message authentication protocol (MA) based on so-called short authenticated strings (SAS). Such a protocol allows authenticating messages of arbitrary sizes (sent over insecure channel) making use of an auxiliary channel which can authenticate short, e.g. 20-bit, messages. It is assumed that an adversary has complete control over the insecure channel, i.e., it can eavesdrop, delay, drop, replay, inject and/or modify messages, while the only restriction on the auxiliary channel is that the adversary cannot modify or inject messages on it, but it can eavesdrop, delay, drop, or replay them. Crucially, no other infrastructure assumptions are made, i.e. the players do not share any keys or passwords, and there is no Public Key Infrastructure they can use. The only leverage for establishing security is this

J.A. Garay and R. De Prisco (Eds.): SCN 2010, LNCS 6280, pp. 253–270, 2010.

bandwidth-restricted, public but authenticated "SAS channel" connecting every pair of players.

The primary application of SAS-MA protocols is to enable SAS-based authenticated key agreement (SAS-AKA) between devices with no reliance on key pre-distribution or a public-key infrastructure. A perfectly fitting and urgently needed application of SAS-AKA protocols is establishing secure communication channels between two devices communicating over a publicly-accessible medium (such as Bluetooth, WiFi), which in addition can also send short authenticated messages to each other (and are hence equipped with a SAS channel), given some amount of manual supervision or involvement from the users. (This problem is referred to as "device pairing" in the systems literature.) Implementations of such SAS channels have been proposed for a variety of device types, assuming various user interfaces and different type of manual supervision. In the simplest example of two cell-phones, phone owners can be asked to type a 20 bit string (6 digits) displayed by one phone into the keypad of the other. The systems proposed in [19,1,14,7,16,18,13] show that the same effect can be accomplished with more primitive devices (e.g., with no keypads) or with less user involvement (e.g. relying on sound, blinking LED lights, cameras on the phones, etc). In all of these schemes, it is desirable to have SAS-AKA protocols which are inexpensive both in computation and communication, since the underlying devices might have limited computation and battery power, and which provably achieve an optimal $2^{-k} + \epsilon$ bound on the probability of adversary's attack given a k-bit SAS channel, where ϵ is a negligible factor in the security parameter independent of k. The SAS-AKA protocol we propose in this paper significantly improves upon the first goal compared to the previous work, at the expense of achieving a slightly weaker bound on adversary's attack, namely $2^{-k+1} + \epsilon$.

1.1 Prior Work on SAS-MA Protocols

Following [20,12], we refer to a bi-directional message authentication protocol in the SAS model as SAS-MCA, which stands for "message *cross*-authentication". Note that two instances of a SAS-MA protocol run in each direction always yield such SAS-MCA scheme, but at twice the cost of the underlying SAS-MA scheme. A straightforward solution for a SAS-MCA was suggested by Balfanz, et al. [1]: Devices A and B exchange the messages m_A, m_B over the insecure channel, and the corresponding hashes $H(m_A)$ and $H(m_B)$ over the SAS channel. Although non-interactive, the protocol requires H to be a collision-resistant hash function and therefore it needs at least 160 bits of the SAS bandwidth in each direction. Pasini and Vaudenay [11] showed a non-interactive protocol which weakens the requirement on the hash function to weak (i.e. second-preimage) collision resistance, and reduces the SAS bandwidth to 80-bits. The 'MANA' protocols in Gehrmann et al. [6] reduce the SAS bandwidth to any k bits while assuring the 2^{-k} bound on attack probability,[1] but these protocols require a stronger assumption on the SAS channel, namely the adversary is assumed to be incapable of delaying or replaying

[1] Formally, by "2^{-k} bound on attack probability" we mean that the probability that any adversary that runs in time polynomial in a security parameter n, which is independent of the SAS-bandwidth k, succeeds against a single instance of the protocol is upper-bounded by $2^{-k} + \epsilon(n)$, where $\epsilon(n)$ is negligible in n.

$$\underline{\mathbf{P}_i(m)} \hspace{6cm} \underline{\mathbf{P}_j}$$

Pick $R_i \leftarrow \{0,1\}^k$

$(c,d) \leftarrow \mathsf{com}([m|R_i]) \xrightarrow{\quad m,c \quad}$ Pick $R_j \leftarrow \{0,1\}^k$

$\xleftarrow{\quad R_j \quad}$

$\xrightarrow{\quad d \quad}$

$SAS = R_i \oplus R_j \xRightarrow{\quad SAS \quad}$ $[m|R_i] \leftarrow \mathsf{open}(c,d)$

Output (P_i, m) if $SAS = R_i \oplus R_j$

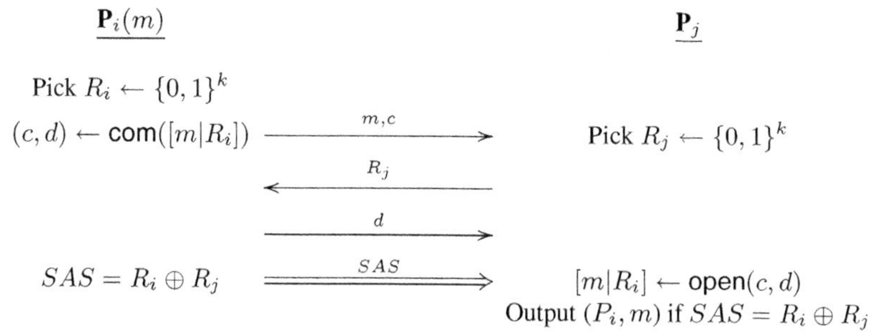

Fig. 1. V-MA : unidirectional SAS-MA authentication (P_i to P_j) of Vaudenay [20]

the SAS messages, which in practice requires synchronization between the two devices, e.g. one device never abandons one session and restarts another session without the other device also doing the same.

In [20], Vaudenay presented the first SAS-MA scheme, called V-MA and depicted in Figure 1, with the analysis that bounds the attack probability by 2^{-k} for a k-bit SAS channel. In [20] this protocol is shown secure under the assumption that the commitment scheme satisfies what Vaudenay refers to as "extractable commitment", and subsequently [9] pointed out that this proof goes through under the more standard and possibly weaker assumption of a non-malleable commitment. The bi-directional SAS-MCA protocol presented in [20] results from running two instances of the V-MA protocol, one for each direction, but with each player $P_{i/j}$ using the same challenge $R_{i/j}$ in both protocol instances. This SAS-MCA scheme requires 4 communication rounds over the insecure channel and was shown to give a 2^{-k} security bound.

In subsequent work, Laur, Asokan, and Nyberg [9,10] and Pasini and Vaudenay [12] independently gave three-round SAS-MCA protocols. Both schemes are modifications of the V-MA protocol of Figure 1, and both employ (although differently) a universal hash function in computation of the SAS message. Both of these protocols make just a few symmetric key operations if the commitment scheme is implemented using a cryptographic hash function modeled as a Random Oracle. Both protocols claim the 2^{-k} security bound at least in the ROM model, although the scheme of [9,10] was analyzed only in a "synchronized" setting where the same pair of players never execute multiple parallel protocol instances with each other[2] (see Theorem 3, Note 5 of [10]).

1.2   Prior Work on SAS-AKA Protocols

Pasini and Vaudenay [12] argue that one can construct a 3-round SAS-based key agreement protocol (SAS-AKA), from any 3-round SAS-based message cross-authentication protocol (SAS-MCA) like the SAS-MCA protocol presented in [12], and any 2-round

---

[2] While in practice it might be the case that a pair of players is not *supposed* to execute several protocol instances concurrently, a man-in-the-middle can cause that several instances of the protocol between the same pair of players are effectively alive, if he manages to force one device to time-out and start a new session while the other device is still waiting for an answer.

key agreement scheme (KA) which is secure over authenticated links, e.g. a Diffie-Hellman or an encryption-based KA scheme. The idea is to run the 2-round KA protocol over an insecure channel, and authenticate the two messages m_1, m_2 produced by the KA protocol using the SAS-MCA protocol. (To achieve a 3-round SAS-AKA protocol, the KA messages m_1, m_2 are piggybacked with the SAS-MCA protocol messages.) This compilation is significantly different from the standard compilation from a protocol secure over authenticated links to a protocol secure over insecure channels, which works by running a separate unidirectional message-authentication sub-protocol (MA) for each message of the underlying protocol, e.g. as in Canetti and Krawczyk's MA + KA $\rightarrow$ AKA compilation in [4]. If the SAS-MA authentication protocol has k rounds then this compilation would result in a $2k$-round SAS-AKA scheme, because the responder cannot, in general, send the second KA message m_2 before successful completion of the SAS-MA sub-protocol that authenticates the first KA message m_1. In contrast, to achieve a $(k+1)$-round SAS-AKA protocol, the compilation given in [12] prescribes that the second message of the KA protocol, m_2, is sent by the responder straight away, i.e. on the basis of the first KA message m_1, which at this moment has not been authenticated yet.

The compilation of Pasini and Vaudenay does result in secure 3-round SAS-AKA schemes, but only when it utilizes a KA scheme which does not keep shared state between different instances of the KA protocol run by the same player. (This was indeed the implicit assumption taken by the proof of security for this compilation given in [12].) Moreover, such SAS-MCA + KA $\rightarrow$ SAS-AKA compilation cannot be applied to KA schemes which *do* share state between instances. For a simple counter-example, consider a 2-round KA protocol secure in the authenticated links model, which is amended so that (1) the computed session key is sent in the last message encrypted using responder P_j's long term public key pk_{ij} chosen for a particular initiator P_i, and (2) the responder P_j reveals the corresponding private key sk_{ij} if the initiator P_i's first message is a special symbol which is never used by an honest sender. Such protocol remains secure in the authenticated links model (in the static corruption case), because only a dishonest sender P_i can trigger P_j to reveal sk_{ij}. However, this protocol is insecure when compiled using the method above, because when P_j computes its response it does not know if the message sent by P_i is authentic, and thus a man-in-the-middle adversary can trigger P_j to reveal sk_{ij} by replacing P_i's initial message in the KA protocol with that special symbol. This way the adversary's interference in a single protocol session leads to revealing the keys on *all* sessions shared between the same pair of players, and thus the compiled protocol is not a secure SAS-AKA. (We elaborate on this counter-example in more detail in Appendix A.)

Independently, Laur and Nyberg also proposed a SAS-AKA protocol [10], based on their own SAS-MCA protocol [9]. In this (Diffie-Hellman based) SAS-AKA protocol, the Diffie-Hellman exponents are picked afresh in each protocol instance, and so this protocol also does not support key re-use across multiple sessions.

1.3 Limitations of SAS-AKA Protocols Without Key Re-use

The key agreement protocols that do not share state between sessions, and thus in particular do not allow for re-use of private keys, are by definition Perfect-Forward Secret

(PFS) but they are also significantly more expensive than non-PFS key agreement protocols. Specifically, the standard Diffie-Hellman PFS KA requires two exponentiations per player, while the encryption-based PFS KA requires generation of a (public,private) key pair and a decryption operation by one player, and a public key encryption by the other player. These are also the dominant costs of the corresponding SAS-AKA schemes implied by the above results of [9,12]. In contrast, the non-PFS Diffie-Hellman with fixed exponents costs only one exponentiation per player, and the encryption-based KA costs one decryption for one player and one encryption for the other. Note that in practice the efficiency of the non-PFS KA schemes often takes precedence over the stronger security property offered by perfect forward secret KA schemes. For example, even though SSL supports PFS version of Diffie-Hellman KA, almost all commercial SSL sessions run the non-PFS encryption-based KA using RSA encryption, since this mode offers dramatically faster client's time (and twice faster server's time). Also, just as the asymmetric division of work in the RSA-encryption based key agreement was attractive for the SSL applications, the same asymmetric costs in the RSA-encryption based SAS-AKA could be attractive for "pairing" of devices with unequal computational power, e.g. a PC and a keyboard, a PC and a cell-phone, or a cell-phone and an earset speaker.

Other applications could also benefit from SAS-AKA protocols which allow for re-use of public keys across multiple protocol sessions. One compelling application is in secure initialization of a sensor network [17]. Sensor initialization can be achieved by the base station simultaneously executing an instance of the SAS-AKA protocol with each sensor. However, since the number of sensors can be large, generating fresh (RSA or DH) encryption keys per protocol instance would impose a large overhead on the base station. An encryption-based SAS-AKA protocol with re-usable public key would be especially handy because it would minimize sensors' computation to a single RSA encryption, and the base station would pick one RSA key pair and then perform one RSA decryption per each sensor. Another application where key re-use in SAS-AKA offers immediate benefits is protection against so-called "Evil Twin" attacks in a cyber-cafe, where multiple users run SAS-AKA protocols to associate their devices with one central access point [15].

1.4 Our Contributions

In this work, we present a provably secure and minimal cost SAS-AKA scheme which re-uses public key pairs across protocol sessions and thus presents a lower-cost but non-PFS alternative to the perfect-forward secret SAS-AKA protocols of [10,12]. Our SAS-AKA relies on a non-malleable commitments just like the SAS-AKA schemes of [20,9,12], but unlike the previous schemes it is built directly on CCA-secure encryption, and it relies on encryption not just for key-establishment but also for authentication security. As a consequence, the new SAS-AKA is somewhat simpler than the previous SAS-AKA's which were built on top of the three-round SAS-MCA's of [9,12], and in particular it does not need to use universal hash functions. However, the most important contribution of the new SAS-AKA scheme is that it remains secure if each player uses a permanent public key, and hence shares a state across all protocol sessions it executes. This leads to two minimal-cost 3-round non-PFS SAS-AKA protocols where the same public/private key pair or the same Diffie-Hellman random contribution is re-used across protocol instances. Specifically, when instantiated with the hash-based commitment and the CCA-secure OAEP-RSA, this implies a 3-round SAS-AKA protocol secure under the RSA assumption in ROM, with the cost of a single RSA encryption for the responder and a single RSA decryption for the initiator. When instantiated with the randomness-reusing CCA-secure version of ElGamal [3] this implies a 3-round SAS-AKA protocol secure under the DH assumption in ROM, with the cost of one exponentiation per player. In other words, the costs of the SAS-AKA protocols implied by our result are (for the first time) essentially the same as the costs of the corresponding basic unauthenticated key agreement protocols. By contrast, previously known *PFS* SAS-AKA protocols require two exponentiations per player if they are based on DH [12,10] or a generation of fresh public/private RSA key pair for each protocol instance if the general result of [12] is instantiated with an RSA-based key agreement.

We note that the SAS-MCA/AKA protocol we show secure is very similar to the SAS-AKA protocols of [20,9,12], and it is indeed only a new variant of the same three-round commitment-based SAS-MA protocol analyzed in [20], which also forms a starting point for protocols of [9,12]. However, prior to our work there was no argument that such SAS-AKA scheme remains secure when players re-use their public/private key pairs across multiple sessions. Moreover, as we explain above, it is unlikely that such result can be proven using a modular argument similar to the one used by [12] for KA protocols that do *not* keep state between protocol instances, which is also why our analysis of the proposed protocol proceeds "from scratch" rather than proceeding in a modular fashion based on already known properties of Vaudenay's SAS-MA scheme. Secondly, our analysis shows that the SAS-AKA protocol can be simpler than even a standard encryption-based KA protocol executed over the 3-round SAS-MCA protocol of [9] or [12]. In fact, our protocol consists of a single instance of the basic *unidirectional* SAS-MA scheme of [20], shown in Figure 1, which authenticates only the initiator's message, but this message includes the initiator's (long-term) public key, which the responder uses to encrypt its message. It turns out that this encryption not only transforms this protocol to a SAS-AKA scheme but also authenticates responder's message, thus yielding not just a cheaper but also a simpler three-round SAS-AKA protocol.

Paper Organization. Section 2 contains our cryptographic tools. Section 3 contains the communication and adversarial models for SAS-MCA and SAS-AKA protocols. We propose our SAS-MCA / SAS-AKA protocol in Section 4. In the same section we argue that this protocol is a secure SAS-MCA scheme, but for lack of space we relegate the (very similar) argument that this protocol is also a secure SAS-AKA scheme protocol) to the full version of this paper [8].

2 Preliminaries

Public Key Encryption. A public key encryption scheme is a tuple of algorithms (KeyGen, Enc, Dec), where KeyGen on input of a security parameter produces a pair of public and secret keys (pk, sk), $\mathsf{Enc}_{pk}(m)$ outputs ciphertext c for message m, and $\mathsf{Dec}_{sk}(c)$ decrypts m from $c = \mathsf{Enc}_{pk}(m)$. In the SAS-MCA/AKA protocol construction, the encrypted messages come from a special space $\mathcal{M}_{\overline{m}} = \{[\overline{m}|R]$ s.t. $R \in$

$\{0,1\}^k\}$ where $\overline{m}$ is some (adversarially chosen) string. Since this message space contains 2^k elements, a chosen-ciphertext secure encryption ensures that an adversary who is given an encryption of a random message in this space can predict this message with probability at most negligibly higher than 2^{-k}. Namely, the following is a simple fact about CCA-secure encryption.

Fact 1. *If an encryption scheme is* (T,ϵ)-SS-CCA *then for every* T*-bounded algorithm* $\mathcal{A}$ *and every* $\overline{m}$*,*

$$\Pr[\mathcal{A}^{\mathsf{Dec}^C_{sk}(\cdot)}(pk,C) = \hat{m} \mid (pk,sk) \leftarrow \mathsf{KeyGen},\ \ m \leftarrow \mathcal{M}_{\overline{m}},$$

$$C \leftarrow \mathsf{Enc}_{pk}(m)] \leq\ 2^{-k} + \epsilon$$

where $\mathsf{Dec}^C_{sk}(\cdot)$ *is a decryption oracle except it outputs* $\perp$ *on* C*.*

Commitment Schemes. Similarly to the SAS-channel message authentication protocols given before by [20,9,12], the protocols here are also based on commitment schemes with some form of non-malleability. In fact, the assumption on commitment schemes we make is essentially the same as in the SAS-MCA protocols of [20,12], but we slightly relax (and re-name) this property of commitment schemes here, so that, in particular, it is satisfied by a very efficient hash-based commitment scheme in the ROM model for a hash function.

The commitment scheme consists of following three functions: gen generates a public parameter K_p on input a security parameter, $\mathsf{com}_{K_p}(m)$, on input of message m, outputs a pair of a "commitment" c and "decommitment" d, and $\mathsf{open}_{K_p}(c,d)$, on input (c,d), either outputs some value m' or rejects. This triple of algorithms must meet a completeness property, namely for any K_p generated by gen and for any m, if (c,d) is output by $\mathsf{com}_{K_p}(m)$ then $\mathsf{open}_{K_p}(c,d)$ outputs m. We assume a *common reference string* (CRS) model, where a trusted third party generates the commitment key K_p and this key is then embedded in every instance of the protocol. Therefore, we will use a simplified notation, and write $\mathsf{com}(m)$ and $\mathsf{open}(c,d)$ without mentioning the public parameter K_p explicitly. For simplicity of notation in the SAS-MCA/AKA protocols, we sometimes use $m_2 \leftarrow \mathsf{open}(m_1,c,d)$ do denote a procedure which first does $m \leftarrow \mathsf{open}(c,d)$ and then compares if m is of the form $m = [m_1|m_2]$ for the given m_1. If it is, the modified open procedure outputs m_2, and otherwise it rejects.

Non-Malleable Commitment Scheme. In our protocols, we use the same notion of non-malleable commitments as in [9], adopted from [5]. An adversary is a quadruple $\mathcal{A} = (\mathcal{A}_1,\mathcal{A}_2,\mathcal{A}_3,\mathcal{A}_4)$ of efficient algorithms interacting with Challenger. $(\mathcal{A}_1,\mathcal{A}_2,\mathcal{A}_3)$ represents an active part of the adversary that creates and afterwards tries to open related commitments and $\mathcal{A}_4$ represents a distinguisher. Challenger is initialized to be in either of two environments, called "World_0" and "World_1". $\mathcal{A}$ succeeds if $\mathcal{A}_4$ can distinguish between these two environments World_0 and World_1.

Challenger first runs gen to produce K_p and sends it to $\mathcal{A}_1$. $\mathcal{A}_1$ outputs a message space $\mathcal{M}$ along with state σ and sends it back to Challenger. Challenger picks two messages m_0 and m_1 at random from $\mathcal{M}$ and computes a challenge commitment $(c,d) = \mathsf{com}_{K_p}(m_1)$ and sends c it to $\mathcal{A}_2$. $\mathcal{A}_2$ in turn responds with a commitment c^*. Challenger aborts if any $c^* = c$, and otherwise sends d to $\mathcal{A}_3$. Now, $\mathcal{A}_3$

must output a valid decommitment d^*. Challenger computes $y^* = \mathsf{open}_{K_p}(c^*, d^*)$. If $y^* = \perp$, then $\mathcal{A}$ is halted. Finally, in the environment World_0, Challenger invokes $\mathcal{A}_4$ with inputs (m_0, y^*), whereas in World_1, it invokes $\mathcal{A}_4$ with inputs (m_1, y^*). A commitment scheme is (T, ϵ)-NM (non-malleable) iff for any t time adversary $\mathcal{A}$ it holds that $Adv_{com}^{\mathsf{NM}}(\mathcal{A}) = |\Pr[\mathcal{A}_4 = 1|\mathsf{World}_1] - \Pr[\mathcal{A}_4 = 1|\mathsf{World}_0]| \leq \epsilon$.

For notational convenience, we use a specialization of this non-malleability notion to message space $\mathcal{M}_{\overline{m}} = \{[\overline{m}|R] \text{ s.t. } R \in \{0,1\}^k\}$, which our SAS-MCA/AKA protocol deals with, and to a particular simple type of tests which our reductions use to distinguish between the two distributions above. Namely, we say that the commitment scheme is (T, ϵ)-NM if for every T-limited adversary $\mathcal{A} = (\mathcal{A}_1, \mathcal{A}_2, \mathcal{A}_3)$, it holds that $Pr[m^* \oplus m = \sigma \mid K_P \leftarrow \mathsf{gen}; (\overline{m}, s) \leftarrow \mathcal{A}_1(K_P); m \leftarrow \mathcal{M}_{\overline{m}}; (c, d) \leftarrow \mathsf{com}_{K_P}(m); (c^*, \sigma) \leftarrow \mathcal{A}_2(c, s); d^* \leftarrow \mathcal{A}_3(c, d, s); m^* = \mathsf{open}_{K_P}(c^*, d^*)] \leq 2^{-k} + \epsilon$

Note that a (T, ϵ)-NM commitment scheme can be created from any (T, ϵ)-SS-CCA encryption scheme (KeyGen, Enc, Dec) [5]. The (K_s, K_p) is a private/public key pair (sk, pk) of the encryption scheme. $\mathsf{com}_{pk}(m)$ picks a random string r and outputs $c = \mathsf{Enc}_{pk}(m; r)$ and $d = (m, r)$, where $\mathsf{Enc}_{pk}(\cdot; r)$ denotes the (randomized) encryption procedure with randomness r. Procedure $\mathsf{open}_{pk}(c, (m, r))$ outputs m if $c = \mathsf{Enc}_{pk}(m; r)$ and $\perp$ otherwise.

Non-Malleable Commitment in the Random Oracle Model (ROM). One can make a fast and simple commitment scheme using a hash function $H : \{0,1\}^* \rightarrow \{0,1\}^{l'}$ modeled as a random oracle, where the adversary's advantage in the NM-Security game can be set arbitrarily low at very little cost. Generator gen in this scheme is a null procedure, $\mathsf{com}(m)$ picks $r \in \{0,1\}^l$ and returns $c = H(m, r)$ and $d = (m, r)$, $\mathsf{open}(c, (m, r))$ returns m if $c = H(m, r)$ and $\perp$ otherwise. This scheme is (T, ϵ)-NM for $\epsilon = q_H 2^{-l} + q_H^2 2^{-l'}$, where q_H is the number of H-function queries that can be made by a T-bounded adversary $\mathcal{A}$. This is because the probability that $\mathcal{A}_2$ learns anything about the value committed by the challenger is $q_H 2^{-l}$ because the only information $\mathcal{A}_2$ can get on m chosen by the challenger is by querying hash function H for some $m \in \mathcal{M}$ and r used by the challenger, but the probability that $\mathcal{A}$ hits the same r as the challenger is bounded by $q_H 2^{-l}$. Moreover, the probability that $\mathcal{A}_3$ is able to decommit to more than one value is bounded by $q_H^2 2^{-l'}$, because this is the probability that within q_H queries to H, the adversary gets a pair of values which collide.

3 Communication and Adversarial Model

3.1 Network and Communication Setting

We consider the same model as in [20,9,12], but we explicitly cast it in the multi-player/multi-session world. In other words, we consider a network consisting of n players $P_1, \cdots, P_n$. Each ordered pair of players (P_i, P_j) is connected by two unidirectional point-to-point communication channels: (1) an insecure channel, e.g. internet or a Bluetooth or a WiFi channel, over which an adversary has complete control by eavesdropping, delaying, dropping, replaying, and/or modifying messages, and (2) a low-bandwidth out-of-band authenticated (but not secret) channel, referred to as a *SAS channel* from here on, which preserves the integrity of messages and also provides source and target authentication. In other words, on the insecure channel, an adversary can behave arbitrarily, but it is *not* allowed to modify (or inject) messages sent on the SAS channel (which we'll call *SAS messages* for short), although it can still read them, as well as delay, drop, or re-order them.

3.2 SAS-MCA and Its Security

Our security model follows the Canetti-Krawczyk model for authenticated key exchange protocols [4], and the earlier work of [2], which allows modeling concurrent executions of multiple protocol instances. While in practice it will very often be the case (e.g. in the device pairing application) that a single player is not *supposed* to execute several protocol instances concurrently, a man-in-the-middle can cause that several instances of the protocol between the same pair of players are effectively alive, if he manages to force device A to time-out and start a new SAS-AKA protocol session, while device B is still waiting for an answer. In this case the adversary can choose which messages to forward to device B among the messages sent on the different sessions started by device A.

A SAS-MCA protocol is a "cross-party" message authentication protocol, executed between two players P_i and P_j, whose goal is for P_i and P_j to send authenticated messages to one another. We denote the τ-th protocol instance run by a player P_i as Π_i^τ, where τ is a locally unique index. The inputs of Π_i^τ are a tuple $(\mathsf{role}_i^\tau, P_j, m_i^\tau)$ where role_i^τ designates P_i as either the initiator ("$init$") or a responder ("$resp$") in this instance of the SAS-MCA protocol, P_j identifies the communication partner for this protocol instance, i.e. it identifies a pair of SAS channels $(P_i \rightarrow P_j)$ and $(P_i \leftarrow P_j)$ with an entity (P_j) with whom P_i's application wants to communicate, and m_i^τ is the message to be sent to P_j in this session. With each session Π_i^τ there is associated a unique string sid_i^τ, which is a concatenation of all messages sent and received on this session, including the messages on the SAS channel. We denote input P_j on session Π_i^τ as $\mathsf{Peer}(\Pi_i^\tau)$. We say that sessions Π_i^τ and Π_j^η executed by two different players are **matching** if $\mathsf{Peer}(\Pi_i^\tau) = P_j$, $\mathsf{Peer}(\Pi_j^\eta) = P_i$, and $\mathsf{role}_j^\eta \neq \mathsf{role}_i^\tau$. We say that the sessions are **partnered** if they are matching and their messages are properly exchanged between them, i.e. $sid_i^\tau = sid_j^\eta$. By the last requirement, and by inclusion of random nonces in the protocol, we ensure that except of negligible probability each session can be partnered with at most one other session. The output of Π_i^τ can be either a tuple $(\mathsf{Peer}(\Pi_i^\tau), m_i^\tau, \hat{m}_i^\tau, sid_i^\tau)$, for some $\hat{m}_i^\tau$, or a rejection. Similarly, Π_j^η can either output $(\mathsf{Peer}(\Pi_j^\eta), m_j^\eta, \hat{m}_j^\eta, sid_j^\eta)$ or reject. The SAS-MCA protocol should satisfy the following **correctness** condition: If sessions Π_i^τ and Π_j^η are partnered then both sessions accept and output the messages sent by the other player, i.e. $\hat{m}_i^\tau = m_j^\eta$ and $\hat{m}_j^\eta = m_i^\tau$.

We model the **security** of a SAS-MCA protocol via a following game between the challenger performing the part of the honest players $P_1, ..., P_n$, and the adversary $\mathcal{A}$. We consider only the *static* corruption model, where the adversary does not adaptively corrupt initially honest players. The challenger and the adversary communicate by exchanging messages as follows: At the beginning of the interaction, the challenger initializes the long-term private state of every player P_i, e.g. by generating a public/private key pair for each player. In the rest of the interaction, the challenger keeps the state of every initialized protocol instance and follows the SAS-MCA protocol on its behalf. $\mathcal{A}$ can trigger a new protocol instance Π_i^τ on inputs (role, P_j, m) by issuing a query $\mathsf{launch}(\Pi_i^\tau, \mathsf{role}, P_j, m)$. The challenger responds by initializing the state of session Π_i^τ and sending back to $\mathcal{A}$ the message this session generates. If $\mathcal{A}$ issues a query $\mathsf{send}(\Pi_i^\tau, M)$ for any previously initialized Π_i^τ and any M, the challenger delivers message M to session Π_i^τ and responds by following the SAS-MCA protocol on its behalf, handing the response of Π_i^τ on M to $\mathcal{A}$. However, if Π_i^τ outputs a SAS message, the challenger hands this message to $\mathcal{A}$ and adds it to a multiset $\mathsf{SAS}(i, j)$, for $P_j = \mathsf{Peer}(\Pi_i^\tau)$, which models the unidirectional SAS channel from P_i to P_j, denoted $\mathsf{SAS}(P_i \rightarrow P_j)$. $\mathcal{A}$ can issue a $\mathsf{SAS\text{-}send}(\Pi_j^\tau, M)$ query for any message M in set $\mathsf{SAS}(i, j)$, where $P_i = \mathsf{Peer}(\Pi_j^\tau)$. The challenger then removes element M from $\mathsf{SAS}(i, j)$ and delivers M on the $\mathsf{SAS}(P_j \rightarrow P_i)$ channel to Π_i^τ. This models the fact that the adversary can see, stall, delete, and re-order messages on each $\mathsf{SAS}(P_i \rightarrow P_j)$ channel, but $\mathcal{A}$ cannot modify, duplicate, or add to any of the messages on such channel.

We say that $\mathcal{A}$ *wins* in attack against SAS-MCA if there exists session Π_i^τ which outputs (P_j, m_i, m_j, sid) but there is no session Π_j^η which ran on inputs $(*, P_i, m_j)$. In other words, if Π_i^τ outputs a message m_j as sent by P_j but P_j did not send m_j to P_i on any session. We call a SAS-MCA protocol (T, ϵ)-**secure** if for every adversary $\mathcal{A}$ running in time T, $\mathcal{A}$ wins with probability at most ϵ. Note that in the SAS-MCA game the adversary can launch multiple concurrent sessions among every pair of players. To make our security results concrete in the multi-player setting, we will consider an (n, τ_t, τ_c)-attacker $\mathcal{A}$ against the SAS-MCA protocol, where the above game is restricted to n players P_i, at most τ_t total number of sessions per player, and at most τ_c sessions that can be concurrently held by any *pair* of players, i.e. $\mathsf{SAS}(i, j) \leq \tau_c$ for all i, j. We note that the τ_c bound is determined by how long the adversary can lag the SAS messages, how many sessions he can cause to re-start at one side, and how long he can keep alive a session waiting for its SAS message on the other side. In many applications it will be rather small, but it is important to realize that in many applications it is greater than 1.

3.3 SAS-AKA and Its Security

SAS-AKA is an Authenticated Key Agreement (AKA) protocol in the SAS model. The inputs to the protocol are as in the SAS-MCA but with no messages. Each instance Π_i^τ outputs either a rejection or a tuple $(\mathsf{Peer}(\Pi_i^\tau), K, sid)$, where K is a fresh, authenticated, and secret key which P_i hopes to have shared with $P_j = \mathsf{Peer}(\Pi_i^s)$, and sid is a locally unique session id. An SAS-AKA scheme protects the secrecy of keys output by honest players on sessions involving other uncorrupted player. The correctness property for a SAS-AKA protocol is that if two sessions Π_i^τ and Π_j^η are partnered then both sessions accept and output the same key $K_i^\tau = K_j^\eta$.

We model **security** of the SAS-AKA protocol similarly as in the SAS-MCA case, by an interaction between the (n, τ_t, τ_c)-attacker $\mathcal{A}$ and the challenger that operates the network of n players $P_1, ..., P_n$. In this game, however, the challenger has a *private input* of bit b. The rules of communication model between the challenger and $\mathcal{A}$ and the set-up of all honest players are the same as in the SAS-MCA game above, and the challenger services $\mathcal{A}$'s requests launch, send, and $\mathsf{SAS\text{-}send}$ in the same way as in the SAS-MCA game, except that there's no message in inputs to the launch request. In addition, $\mathcal{A}$ can issue a query of the form reveal(Π_i^τ) for any Π_i^τ, which gives him the key K_i^τ output by Π_i^τ if this session computed a key, and a null value otherwise. Finally, on one of the sessions Π_i^τ subject to the constraints specified below, the adversary can issue a Test(Π_i^τ) query. If Π_i^τ has not completed, the adversary gets a null value. Otherwise, if $b = 1$ then $\mathcal{A}$ gets the key K_i^τ, and if $b = 0$ then $\mathcal{A}$ gets a random bitstring of the same length. The constraint on the tested session Π_i^τ is that the adversary issues no reveal(Π_i^τ) query *and* no reveal(Π_j^η) query for any Π_j^η which is partnered with Π_i^τ. After testing a session, the adversary can then keep issuing the launch, send, SASsend and reveal commands, except it cannot reveal the tested session or a session that is partnered with it. Eventually $\mathcal{A}$ outputs a bit $\hat{b}$. We say that an adversary has *advantage* ϵ in the SAS-AKA attack if the probability that $\hat{b} = b$ is at most $1/2 + \epsilon$. We say that the SAS-AKA protocol is (T, ϵ)-**secure** if for all $\mathcal{A}$'s bounded by time T this advantage is at most ϵ.

We note that the above model includes only *static* corruption patterns. Indeed, the protocols we present here do *not* have perfect forward secrecy, since we are interested in provable security of minimal-cost AKA protocols in which players re-use their private key material across all protocol sessions.

4 Encryption-Based SAS Message Authentication Protocol

In this section, we present a novel 3-round encryption-based bidirectional SAS-MCA protocol denoted Enc-MCA. The protocol is depicted in Figure 2. It runs between the initiator P_i, who intends to authenticate a message m_i, and the responder P_j, who intends to authenticate a message m_j. (SK_i, PK_i) denotes P_i's private/public key pair of an IND-CCA encryption scheme, which w.l.o.g. we assume to be permanent. The protocol assumes the CRS model where the instance K_P of the CCA-Secure commitment scheme is globally chosen. The protocol is based on the *unidirectional* message-authentication V-MA protocol of Vaudenay [20], Figure 1. The only difference is that P_i adds to its message m_i its public key PK_i and a random nonce $s_i \in \{0,1\}^l$, and the responder P_j sends its randomness R_j *encrypted* under PK_i, together with its message m_j and a random nonce $s_j \in \{0,1\}^l$. In other words, P_i sends (m_i, s_i, PK_i) along with a commitment c_i to (m_i, s_i, PK_i, R_i) where R_i is a random k-bit bitstring. P_j replies with an encryption of m_j, s_j, and a random value $R_j \in \{0,1\}^k$. Finally P_i sends to P_j its decommitment d_i to c_i, and P_i and P_j exchange over the SAS channel values $SAS_i = R_i \oplus R_j$, where P_i obtains R_j by decrypting e_j, and $SAS_j = R_i \oplus R_j$, where P_j obtains R_i by opening the commitment c_i. The players accept if the SAS values match, and reject otherwise. P_i and P_j also output session identifiers sid_i and sid_j, respectively, which are outputs of a collision-resistant hash function H on the concatenation of all messages sent (received resp.) and received (sent resp.) on this session, including the messages on the SAS channel. (This is done only for simplicity of security analysis: In fact the same security argument goes through if $sid_i = sid_j = [s_i|s_j]$.) The following theorem states the security of this protocol against an (n, τ_t, τ_c)-adversary:

Enc-MCA Protocol

(We denote as $\hat{v}$ the value received by P_i/P_j if the value sent by P_j/P_i is denoted as v.)

$\mathbf{P}_i(P_j, (SK_i, PK_i), m_i, init)$		$\mathbf{P}_j(P_i, m_j, resp)$
Pick $R_i \in \{0,1\}^k$, $s_i \in \{0,1\}^l$		Pick $R_j \in \{0,1\}^k$, $s_j \in \{0,1\}^l$
$(c_i, d_i) \leftarrow \mathsf{com}([m_i \vert s_i \vert PK_i \vert R_i])$	$\xrightarrow{m_i, s_i, PK_i, c_i}$	
	$\xleftarrow{e_j}$	$e_j = \mathsf{Enc}_{\hat{PK_i}}([m_j \vert s_j \vert R_j])$
$[\hat{m}_j \vert \hat{s}_j \vert \hat{R}_j] \leftarrow \mathsf{Dec}_{SK_i}(\hat{e}_j)$	$\xrightarrow{d_i}$	$\hat{R}_i \leftarrow \mathsf{open}([\hat{m}_i \vert \hat{s}_i \vert \hat{PK_i}], \hat{c}_i, \hat{d}_i)$
$SAS_i = R_i \oplus \hat{R}_j$	$\xRightarrow{SAS_i}$	$SAS_j = \hat{R}_i \oplus R_j$
$sid_i = H(m_i, s_i, PK_i, c_i, \hat{e}_j, d_i, SAS_i, \hat{SAS}_j)$	$\xLeftarrow{SAS_j}$	$sid_j = H(\hat{m}_i, \hat{s}_i, \hat{PK}_i, \hat{c}_i, e_j, \hat{d}_i, \hat{SAS}_i, SAS_j)$
Output $(P_i, m_i, \hat{m}_j, sid_i)$ if $SAS_j = R_i \oplus \hat{R}_j$		Output $(P_j, m_j, \hat{m}_i, sid_j)$ if $SAS_i = \hat{R}_i \oplus R_j$

Enc-AKA Protocol

The protocol follows Enc-MCA with m_i set to null and $m_j = K$, for random $K \in \{0,1\}^l$ chosen by P_j. If its SAS test passes player P_j, resp. P_i, outputs m_j $[= K]$, resp. $\hat{m}_j$.

Fig. 2. Encryption-based SAS-MCA protocol (Enc-MCA) and SAS-AKA protocol (Enc-AKA)

Theorem 1 (Security of Enc-MCA). *If commitment scheme is (T_C, ϵ_C)-NM and encryption scheme is (T_E, ϵ_E)-SS-CCA, then the Enc-MCA protocol is (T, p)-secure against (n, τ_t, τ_c)-attacker for $p \geq 2n\tau_t\tau_c(2^{-k} + \max(\epsilon_C, \epsilon_E))$ and $T \leq \min(T_C, T_E) - \mu$, for a small constant μ.*

Note on the Security Claim and the Proof Strategy. The $n\tau_t\tau_c 2^{-k}$ security bound would be optimally achievable in the context of (n, τ_t, τ_c)-adversary because this is the probability, for $n\tau_t\tau_c \ll 2^{-k}$, that the k-bit SAS messages are equal on some two matching sessions, even though the adversary substitutes sender's messages on every session, since there are $n\tau_t$ sessions, each of which can succeed if the SAS message it requires to complete is present among τ_c SAS messages produced by the sessions concurrently executed by its peer player. We note that if adversary's goal is to attack any *particular* player and session, the same theorem applies with values $n = \tau_t = 1$.

However, the security bound $n\tau_t\tau_c 2^{-k+1}$ we show is factor of 2 away from the optimal. This factor is due to the fact that the reduction has to guess whether the adversary essentially attacks the encryption or the commitment tool used in our protocol. This also accounts for the essential difference between our proof and those of [9,12]. Even assuming the simplest $n = \tau_t = \tau_c = 1$ case, there are several patterns of attack, corresponding to three possibilities for interleaving messages and other decisions the adversary can make (in our case the crucial switch is whether or not the adversary modifies the initiator's payload m, s, PK). For each pattern of attack, we provide a reduction, which given an attack that breaks the SAS-MCA/AKA scheme with probability $2^{-k}+\epsilon$, *conditioned on this attack type being chosen*, attacks either the commitment or the encryption scheme with probability ϵ. While some of these component reductions are identical to those shown for the same underlying SAS-MA protocol by Vaudenay in [20], others are different e.g. because they attack the encryption scheme. However, it is not clear how to use such reductions to show any better security bound than $q * 2^{-k}$ where q is the number of such attack cases. Fortunately, we manage to group these attack patterns into just two groups, with two reductions, the first translating *any* attack in the first group into an encryption attack, the second translating *any* attack in the second group into a commitment attack. Crucially, both reductions are non-rewinding, and hence they are security-preserving. However, faced with an adversary which adaptively decides which group his attack will fall in we still need to guess which reduction to follow, hence the bound on attacker's probability we show for our SAS-MCA/AKE scheme is a factor of 2 away from the optimal.

Proof: We prove the above by showing that if there exists (n, τ_t, τ_c)-adversary $\mathcal{A}$ which can attack the proposed protocol in time $T < \min(T_C, T_E) - \mu$ and probability $p > 2n\tau_t\tau_c(2^{-k}+\max(\epsilon_C, \epsilon_E))$, then there exists *either* a $T+\mu < T_C$ adversary $\mathcal{B}_C$ which breaks NM security of the commitment scheme with probability better than $2^{-k}+\epsilon_C$, *or* there exists a $T+\mu < T_E$ adversary $\mathcal{B}_\mathcal{E}$ which wins the SS-CCA game for the encryption scheme with probability better than $2^{-k} + \epsilon_E$. $\mathcal{A}$ succeeds if it can find a player P_i and a session Π_i^s with a peer party P_j, such that Π_i^s accepts message $\hat{m_j}^{(s)}$ but the adversary never launches an instance of P_j on message $\hat{m_j}^{(s)}$. To achieve this $\mathcal{A}$ in particular has to route to Π_i^s a SAS message $SAS_j{}^{(s')}$ originated by *some* session $\Pi_j^{s'}$ s.t. $\mathsf{Peer}(\Pi_j^{s'}) = P_i$. By inspection of the protocol, Π_i^s accepts only if $R_i{}^{(s)} \oplus \hat{R}_j^{(s)} = \hat{R}_i^{(s')} \oplus R_j{}^{(s')}$, or equivalently, $SAS_i{}^{(s)} = SAS_j{}^{(s')}$. Note that this condition must hold regardless whether the attacked session Π_i^s is an initiator or a responder. This allows us to simplify the notation and in the remainder of the proof we assume Π_i^s is the initiator, $\Pi_j^{s'}$ is the responder, and we assume that *either* $\hat{m}_i^{(s)} \neq m_i{}^{(s)}$ *or* $\hat{m}_j^{(s')} \neq m_j{}^{(s')}$.

In Figure 3 we show adversary's interactions as a man in the middle between Π_i^s and $\Pi_j^{s'}$. Note that $\mathcal{A}$ can control the *sequence* in which the messages received by these two players are interleaved, and $\mathcal{A}$ has a choice of the following three possible sequences:

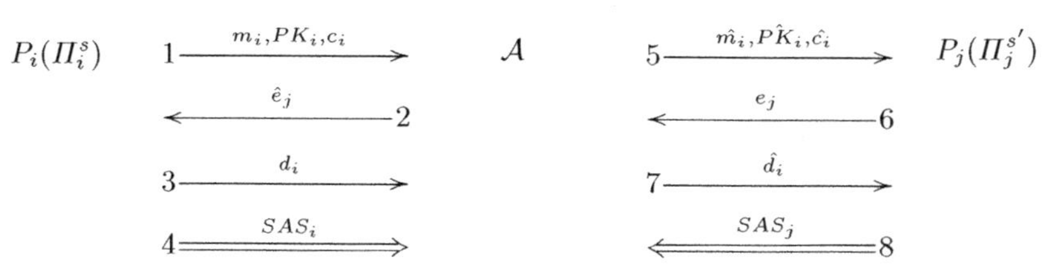

Fig. 3. Adversarial Behavior in the Enc-MCA protocol

$$\text{Interleaving pattern I}: \ (1 \prec 5 \prec 6 \prec 2 \prec 3 \prec 4 \prec 7 \prec 8)$$
$$\text{Interleaving pattern II}: \ (1 \prec 5 \prec 6 \prec 7 \prec 8 \prec 2 \prec 3 \prec 4)$$
$$\text{Interleaving pattern III}: \ (1 \prec 2 \prec 3 \prec 4 \prec 5 \prec 6 \prec 7 \prec 8)$$

In each of these three message interleaving patterns we consider two subcases, depending on whether the pair $(\hat{m}_i, \hat{PK}_i)$ that the adversary delivers to $\Pi_j^{s'}$ in message #5 (see Figure 3) is equal to (m_i, PK_i) that Π_i^s sends in message #1.

We denote the event that adversary succeeds in an attack as AdvSc, the event that $(\hat{m}_i, \hat{PK}_i) = (m_i, PK_i)$ *and* that the attack succeeds as SM, the event that $(\hat{m}_i, \hat{PK}_i) \neq (m_i, PK_i)$ *and* that the attack succeeds as NSM, and we use Int[1], Int[2], Int[3] to denote events when the adversary follows, respectively, the 1st, 2nd, or 3rd message interleaving pattern. We divide the six possible patterns which the successful attack must follow into the following two cases:

$$\text{Case1} = \text{NSM} \vee (\text{AdvSc} \wedge \text{Int}[2]) \quad \& \quad \text{Case2} = \text{SM} \wedge (\text{Int}[1] \vee \text{Int}[3])$$

We construct two reduction algorithms, $\mathcal{B}_\mathcal{C}$ and $\mathcal{B}_\mathcal{E}$, attacking respectively the NM property of the commitment, and the SS-CCA property of the encryption scheme used in the Enc-MCA protocol. Both $\mathcal{B}_\mathcal{C}$ and $\mathcal{B}_\mathcal{E}$ use the Enc-MCA attacker $\mathcal{A}$ as a black box, and both reductions have only constant computational overhead which we denote as μ, hence both $\mathcal{B}_\mathcal{C}$ and $\mathcal{B}_\mathcal{E}$ run in time at most $T - \mu < \min(T_C, T_E)$. We show that if $\Pr[\text{Case1}] \geq p/2$ then $\mathcal{B}_\mathcal{C}$ wins the NM game with probability greater than $2^{-k} + \epsilon_C$, and if $\Pr[\text{Case2}] \geq p/2$ then $\mathcal{B}_\mathcal{E}$ wins the SS-CCA game with probability greater than $2^{-k} + \epsilon_E$. This will complete the proof because $\text{AdvSc} = \text{Case1} \cup \text{Case2}$, and therefore if $\Pr[\text{AdvSc}] = p$ then either $\Pr[\text{Case1}] \geq p/2$ or $n\tau_t\tau_c)$ or $\Pr[\text{Case2}] \geq p/2$.

Both $\mathcal{B}_\mathcal{C}$ and $\mathcal{B}_\mathcal{E}$ proceed by first guessing the sessions Π_i^s and $\Pi_j^{s'}$ involved in $\mathcal{A}$'s attack. The probability that the guess is correct is at least $1/n\tau_t\tau_c$ because $\mathcal{A}$ runs at most $n\tau_t$ sessions and each session can have at most τ_c concurrently running peer sessions. Since the probability of a correct guess is independent of adversary's view, for either $i = 1$ or $i = 2$, the probability that the guess is correct *and* Case$i$ happens is at least $p/2 * 1/n\tau_t\tau_c > 2^{-k} + \max(\epsilon_C, \epsilon_E)$. We show that if $i = 1$ then $\mathcal{B}_\mathcal{C}$ wins in the NM game, and hence its probability of winning is greater than $2^{-k} + \epsilon_C$, and if $i = 2$ then $\mathcal{B}_\mathcal{E}$ wins the SS-CCA game, and hence its probability of winning is greater than $2^{-k} + \epsilon_E$.

It remains for us to construct algorithms $\mathcal{B}_\mathcal{C}$ and $\mathcal{B}_\mathcal{E}$ with the properties claimed above. Algorithm $\mathcal{B}_\mathcal{C}$, depending on the behavior of $\mathcal{A}$, executes one of the three sub-algorithms, $\mathcal{B}_\mathcal{C}$[i] for $i = 1, 2, 3$. These three algorithms correspond to three cases of message interleaving by the adversary. For lack of space we relegate these reductions to the full version [8], but each of these reductions are attacks the non-malleability of the commitment scheme, so each of them is essentially the same as the reduction given by Vaudenay [20] for the corresponding message interleaving pattern for the underlying MCA protocol. More specifically:

If $(\hat{m}_i, \hat{s}_i, \hat{PK}_i) \neq (m_i, s_i, PK_i)$ and $\mathcal{A}$ chooses interleaving pattern I or III, then $\mathcal{B}_\mathcal{C}$ executes sub-algorithms, respectively, $\mathcal{B}_\mathcal{C}[1]$ and $\mathcal{B}_\mathcal{C}[3]$.
If $\mathcal{A}$ chooses interleaving pattern II, $\mathcal{B}_\mathcal{C}$ executes $\mathcal{B}_\mathcal{C}[2]$.
Otherwise, i.e. if $\mathcal{A}$ sends $(\hat{m}_i, \hat{s}_i, \hat{PK}_i) = (m_i, s_i, PK_i)$ and $\mathcal{A}$ follows patterns I or III, $\mathcal{B}_\mathcal{C}$ fails.

Similarly, based on the behavior of $\mathcal{A}$, algorithm $\mathcal{B}_{\mathcal{E}}$ executes one of two sub-algorithms $\mathcal{B}_{\mathcal{E}}$[i] for $i = 1, 2$. In contrast to the original MCA protocol of Vaudenay, these two reductions attack CCA security of encryption. We show reduction $\mathcal{B}_{\mathcal{E}}[1]$ in Figure 4. For lack of space we relegate reduction $\mathcal{B}_{\mathcal{E}}[2]$ to the full version [8], but it is easy to reconstruct given the message interleaving pattern it involves, and it is similar to $\mathcal{B}_{\mathcal{E}}[1]$. The $\mathcal{B}_{\mathcal{E}}$ algorithms proceeds in one of the following ways:

If $(\hat{m}_i, \hat{s}_i, \hat{PK}_i) = (m_i, s_i, PK_i)$ and $\mathcal{A}$ chooses interleaving pattern I, $\mathcal{B}_{\mathcal{E}}$ executes $\mathcal{B}_{\mathcal{E}}[1]$.
If $(\hat{m}_i, \hat{s}_i, \hat{PK}_i) = (m_i, s_i, PK_i)$ and $\mathcal{A}$ chooses interleaving pattern III, $\mathcal{B}_{\mathcal{E}}$ executes $\mathcal{B}_{\mathcal{E}}[2]$.
Otherwise, i.e. if $\mathcal{A}$ sends $(\hat{m}_i, \hat{s}_i, \hat{PK}_i) \neq (m_i, s_i, PK_i)$ or $\mathcal{A}$ follows interleaving pattern II, $\mathcal{B}_{\mathcal{E}}$ fails.

Note that if $(\hat{m}_i, \hat{s}_i, \hat{PK}_i) \neq (m_i, s_i, PK_i)$ then $\mathcal{A}$ essentially attacks the V-MA protocol of Vaudenay, because pair (m_i, PK_i) in the Enc-MCA protocol plays a role of the message in the V-MA protocol, so this event in the Enc-MCA protocol is equivalent to P_j accepting the wrong message in the V-MA protocol. Therefore, the three reduction (sub)algorithms $\mathcal{B}_{\mathcal{C}}[1]$, $\mathcal{B}_{\mathcal{C}}[2]$, and $\mathcal{B}_{\mathcal{C}}[3]$, essentially perform the same attacks on the NM game of the commitment scheme as the corresponding three reductions given by Vaudenay for the V-MA protocol. The only difference is that our reductions put a layer of encryption on the messages sent by P_j, as is done in our protocol Enc-MCA. As in Vaudenay's reductions, the NM game needs to be extended so that the challenger, at the end of the game sends to the attacker the decommitment d corresponding to the challenge commitment c. Since this happens after the attacker sends its R, the difficulty of the NM game remains the same. However, if the $\mathcal{B}_{\mathcal{C}}$ reduction gets the decommitment d from the NM challenger, the reduction can complete the view of the protocol to $\mathcal{A}$, which makes it easier to compare the probability of $\mathcal{A}$'s success with the probability of success of $\mathcal{B}_{\mathcal{C}}$. We refer the reader to the full version [8] for the specification of these three subcases of the reduction to an NM attack. An important feature of these algorithms is that each of these sub-cases of the $\mathcal{B}_{\mathcal{C}}$ reduction at first follows the same protocol with the NM challenger, and that $\mathcal{B}_{\mathcal{C}}$ can decide which path to follow, namely whether to switch to sub-algorithm $\mathcal{B}_{\mathcal{C}}[1,2]$ or $\mathcal{B}_{\mathcal{C}}[3]$, based on the first message it receives from $\mathcal{A}$. Specifically, $\mathcal{B}_{\mathcal{C}}$ switches to $\mathcal{B}_{\mathcal{C}}[3]$ if $\mathcal{A}$ first sends message $\hat{e}_j$, and otherwise $\mathcal{B}_{\mathcal{C}}$ follows $\mathcal{B}_{\mathcal{C}}[1,2]$. Similarly, in the latter case, $\mathcal{B}_{\mathcal{C}}$ switches to either $\mathcal{B}_{\mathcal{C}}[1]$ or $\mathcal{B}_{\mathcal{C}}[2]$ based on $\mathcal{A}$'s next response. Therefore these three algorithms are really just three subcases of a single reduction algorithm $\mathcal{B}_{\mathcal{C}}$. By inspection of these three subcases one can conclude that $\mathcal{B}_{\mathcal{C}}$ wins in its non-malleability attack game with probability at least $\Pr[\text{Case1}]$.

Similarly algorithm $\mathcal{B}_{\mathcal{E}}$ at first follows the same algorithm and then can dispatch into $\mathcal{B}_{\mathcal{E}}[1]$ or $\mathcal{B}_{\mathcal{E}}[2]$ depending on adversary's messages. By inspection of these two subcases one concludes that $\mathcal{B}_{\mathcal{E}}$ wins in its CCA attack game with probability at least $\Pr[\text{Case2}]$, which ends the proof.

Encryption-based SAS Authenticated Key Agreement Protocol. The SAS-AKA protocol Enc-AKA based on the Enc-MCA protocol is just an instance of Enc-MCA where P_i's

$$\mathcal{B}_{\mathcal{E}}[1] \qquad\qquad\qquad \text{SS-CCA Challenger}$$

$$\xrightarrow{\quad m_i, m_j \quad}$$

$$R_i \leftarrow \{0,1\}^k \qquad \xleftarrow{\quad PK_i \quad} \qquad (SK_i, PK_i) \leftarrow \mathsf{KeyGen}$$
$$s_i \leftarrow \{0,1\}^l$$

$$\xleftarrow{\quad m_i, s_i, PK_i, c_i \quad} \quad (c_i, d_i) \leftarrow \mathsf{com}($$
$$[m_i | s_i | PK_i | R_i])$$

$$\xrightarrow{\quad \hat{m}_i, \hat{s}_i, \hat{PK}_i, \hat{c}_i \quad} \quad \text{Fail if } (\hat{m}_i, \hat{s}_i, \hat{PK}_i)$$
$$\neq (m_i, s_i, PK_i) \qquad \xrightarrow{\quad m_j \quad} \qquad R_j \leftarrow \{0,1\}^k$$
$$s_j \leftarrow \{0,1\}^l$$

$$\xleftarrow{\quad e_j \quad} \qquad\qquad \xleftarrow{\quad e_j \quad} \qquad e_j \leftarrow \mathsf{Enc}_{PK_i}([m_j | s_j | R_j])$$

$$\xrightarrow{\quad \hat{e}_j \quad} \quad \text{Fail if } \hat{e}_j \neq e_j \qquad \xrightarrow{\quad \hat{e}_j \quad} \quad [\hat{m}_j | \hat{s}_j | \hat{R}_j] \leftarrow \mathsf{Dec}_{SK_i}(\hat{e}_j)$$

$$\xleftarrow{\quad d_i, SAS_i \quad} \quad SAS_i \leftarrow R_i \oplus \hat{R}_j \qquad \xleftarrow{\quad \hat{m}_j, \hat{s}_j, \hat{R}_j \quad}$$

$$\xrightarrow{\quad \hat{d}_i \quad} \quad \hat{R}_i \leftarrow \mathsf{open}([\hat{m}_i$$
$$| \hat{s}_i | \hat{PK}_i], \hat{c}_i, \hat{d}_i) \qquad \xrightarrow{\quad \hat{R}_j \oplus \hat{R}_i \oplus R_i \quad} \quad \text{Success if } R_j =$$
$$\hat{R}_j \oplus \hat{R}_i \oplus R_i$$

$$\xleftarrow{\quad SAS_j \quad} \quad SAS_j \leftarrow \hat{R}_i \oplus R_j$$

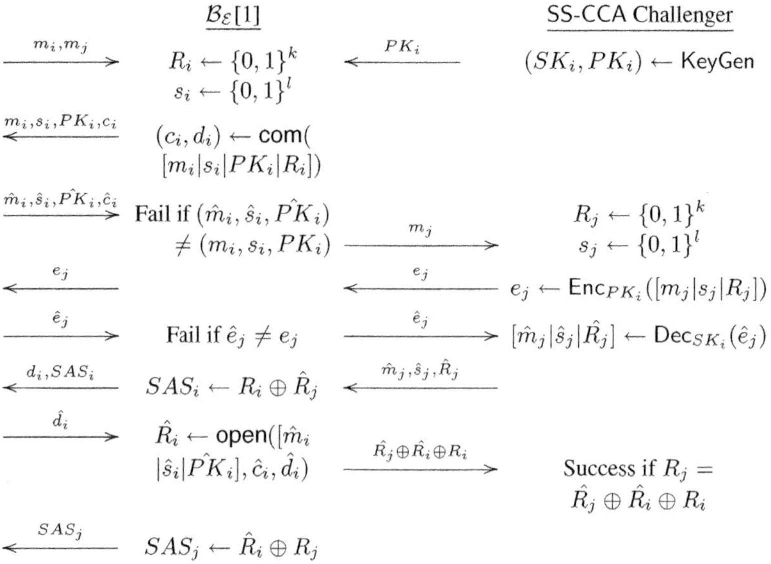

Fig. 4. Construction of $\mathcal{B}_{\mathcal{E}}[1]$ $((m_i, s_i, PK_i) = (\hat{m}_i, \hat{s}_i, \hat{PK}_i)$, interleaving case I)

message m_i is set to null and P_j's message m_j is a fresh random key which P_j picks for each session, as shown in Figure 2. For lack of space we relegate the proof of the following theorem to the full version [8], but it is very similar to the proof of security of the Enc-MCA protocol given above.

Theorem 2 (Security of Enc-AKA). *If commitment scheme is (T_C, ϵ_C)-NM and encryption scheme is (T_E, ϵ_E)-SS-CCA, then the Enc-AKA protocol is (T, p)-secure against (n, τ_t, τ_c)-attacker for $p \geq 2n\tau_t\tau_c(2^{-k} + \max(\epsilon_C, \epsilon_E)$ and $T \leq \min(T_C, T_E) - \mu$, for a small constant μ.*

References

1. Balfanz, D., Smetters, D., Stewart, P., Wong, H.C.: Talking to strangers: Authentication in ad-hoc wireless networks. In: Network and Distributed System Security Symposium (2002)
2. Bellare, M., Canetti, R., Krawczyk, H.: A modular approach to the design and analysis of authentication and key-exchange protocols. In: Symposium on Theory of Computing (2001)
3. Bellare, M., Kohno, T., Shoup, V.: Stateful public-key cryptosystems: How to encrypt with one 160-bit exponentiation. In: ACM Conference on Computer and Communications Security (2006)
4. Canetti, R., Krawczyk, H.: Analysis of key-exchange protocols and their use for building secure channels. In: Pfitzmann, B. (ed.) EUROCRYPT 2001. LNCS, vol. 2045, pp. 453–474. Springer, Heidelberg (2001)
5. Crescenzo, G.D., Katz, J., Ostrovsky, R., Smith, A.: Efficient and non-interactive non-malleable commitment. In: Pfitzmann, B. (ed.) EUROCRYPT 2001. LNCS, vol. 2045, pp. 40–59. Springer, Heidelberg (2001)

6. Gehrmann, C., Mitchell, C.J., Nyberg, K.: Manual authentication for wireless devices. RSA CryptoBytes 7(1), 29–37 (Spring 2004)
7. Goodrich, M.T., Sirivianos, M., Solis, J., Tsudik, G., Uzun, E.: Loud and Clear: Human-Verifiable Authentication Based on Audio. In: International Conference on Distributed Computing Systems, ICDCS (July 2006), `http://www.ics.uci.edu/ccsp/lac`
8. Jarecki, S., Saxena, N.: Authenticated key agreement with key re-use in the short authenticated strings model. Available from the authors (2010)
9. Laur, S., Asokan, N., Nyberg, K.: Efficient mutual data authentication based on short authenticated strings. IACR Cryptology ePrint Archive: Report 2005/424 (November 2005), `http://eprint.iacr.org/2005/424`
10. Laur, S., Nyberg, K.: Efficient mutual data authentication using manually authenticated strings. In: Pointcheval, D., Mu, Y., Chen, K. (eds.) CANS 2006. LNCS, vol. 4301, pp. 90–107. Springer, Heidelberg (2006)
11. Pasini, S., Vaudenay, S.: An optimal non-interactive message authentication protocol. In: Pointcheval, D. (ed.) CT-RSA 2006. LNCS, vol. 3860, pp. 280–294. Springer, Heidelberg (2006)
12. Pasini, S., Vaudenay, S.: SAS-Based Authenticated Key Agreement. In: Yung, M., Dodis, Y., Kiayias, A., Malkin, T.G. (eds.) PKC 2006. LNCS, vol. 3958, pp. 395–409. Springer, Heidelberg (2006)
13. Prasad, R., Saxena, N.: Efficient device pairing using human-comparable synchronized audiovisual patterns. In: Bellovin, S.M., Gennaro, R., Keromytis, A.D., Yung, M. (eds.) ACNS 2008. LNCS, vol. 5037, pp. 328–345. Springer, Heidelberg (2008)
14. Rohs, M., Gfeller, B.: Using camera-equipped mobile phones for interacting with real-world objects. In: Ferscha, A., Hoertner, H., Kotsis, G. (eds.) Advances in Pervasive Computing, Vienna, Austria, pp. 265–271. Austrian Computer Society, OCG (April 2004)
15. Roth, V., Polak, W., Rieffel, E., Turner, T.: Simple and effective defenses against evil twin access points. In: ACM Conference on Wireless Network Security (WiSec), short paper (2008)
16. Saxena, N., Ekberg, J.-E., Kostiainen, K., Asokan, N.: Secure device pairing based on a visual channel (short paper). In: IEEE Symposium on Security and Privacy (S&P 2006) (May 2006)
17. Saxena, N., Uddin, B.: Blink 'em all: Scalable, user-friendly and secure initialization of wireless sensor nodes. In: Garay, J.A., Miyaji, A., Otsuka, A. (eds.) CANS 2009. LNCS, vol. 5888, pp. 154–173. Springer, Heidelberg (2009)
18. Soriente, C., Tsudik, G., Uzun, E.: BEDA: Button-Enabled Device Association. In: International Workshop on Security for Spontaneous Interaction, IWSSI (2007)
19. Stajano, F., Anderson, R.J.: The resurrecting duckling: Security issues for ad-hoc wireless networks. In: Malcolm, J.A., Christianson, B., Crispo, B., Roe, M. (eds.) Security Protocols 1999. LNCS, vol. 1796, pp. 172–194. Springer, Heidelberg (2000)
20. Vaudenay, S.: Secure communications over insecure channels based on short authenticated strings. In: Shoup, V. (ed.) CRYPTO 2005. LNCS, vol. 3621, pp. 309–326. Springer, Heidelberg (2005)

A On the General Compilation Theorem of Pasini-Vaudenay

We claim that the general composition theorem given by Pasini and Vaudenay [12] for transforming KA protocols to SAS-AKA protocols given any SAS-MCA scheme, cannot be applied in general to KA schemes which share state between sessions. The theorem of [12] constructs a SAS-AKA protocol by running any 2-round (non-authenticated) KA protocol and then inputting the two messages generated by this KA, m_i of the initiator P_i and m_j of the responder P_j, into a SAS-MCA protocol, where P_i goes first, and m_j is possibly based on m_i. Known 3-round SAS-MCA protocols allow the responder's message m_j to be picked in the second round, and thus this compilation creates a 4-round SAS-AKA from 2-round KA and 3-round SAS-MCA. Note that at the time P_j computes his response m_j, following the algorithm of the KA protocol on the received message m_i, the message m_i is not yet authenticated by P_j. If the KA protocol does not share state between sessions, having P_j compute m_j on adversarially-chosen $\hat{m}_i$ can endanger only the current session, and since the SAS-MCA subprotocol will let P_j know that $\hat{m}_i$ was not sent by P_i, P_j will reject this session.

However, if P_j keeps a shared state between sessions then the information P_j reveals in m_j, computed on *unauthenticated* message $\hat{m}_i$, could potentially reveal some secret information that endangers all other sessions of player P_j, or at least all other sessions between P_j and P_i. It's easy to create a contrived example of a Key Agreement protocol which is secure in the static adversarial model when implemented over authenticated channels but yields an insecure SAS-AKA protocol when implemented with a SAS-MCA scheme in this fashion. For example, take any Key Agreement protocol, KA, secure over authenticated links, let each player P_j keep an additional long-term secret s_j and compute a per-partner secret $k_{ij} = F_{s_j}(< P_i >)$ where F is a PRF. If the initiator's message m_i contains a special symbol $\perp$, P_j sends $m_j = k_{ij}$ to P_i in the open. Otherwise, P_j follows the KA protocol to compute its response m_j, except that it attaches to it the resulting session key encrypted with a symmetric encryption scheme under k_{ij}. In the authenticated link model, and considering a static adversary, an honest player never sends the $\perp$ symbol. If the encryption is secure, encrypting the session key does not endanger its security. Also, if F is a PRF then learning values of the F function under indices corresponding to the corrupt players does not reveal any information about the values of F on indices corresponding to the honest players. On the other hand, this protocol is an insecure SAS-AKE protocol, because an adversary can inject message $\hat{m}_i =\perp$ on the insecure channel on behalf of any player P_i, and since P_j will reply with k_i, this allows the attacker to compute the keys for *all* sessions, past and future, between P_j and P_i.

This counter-example relies on an admittedly artificial KA protocol with shared session state where interference with a single session between a pair of players trivially reveals the keys on all sessions between the same players. Still, this does show that the compilation technique of [12] can apply only to KA protocols with no shared state. Of course while this general compilation does not apply, a combination of any *particular* SAS-MCA protocol and a KA scheme with shared state can still be shown secure, and that, with some simplifications to the SAS-MCA protocol of Vaudenay [20] made in the process, is exactly what we show in this paper.

Kleptography from Standard Assumptions and Applications

Adam Young[1] and Moti Yung[2]

[1] Cryptovirology.com

[2] Google Inc. and Department of Computer Science, Columbia University

Abstract. Kleptography deals with employing and generating cryptographically secure covert channels as threats to unscrutinized (e.g., tamper-proof) cryptosystems and their applications. A prototypical example is a cryptosystem (or a protocol message employing a cryptosystem) where a cryptogram field (e.g., a public key, an encrypted message, a signature value) hosts an "inner cryptographic field" that is invisible (in the sense of indistinguishability) to all but the attacker, yet it is a meaningful ciphertext to the attacker (who is the designer/producer of the cryptosystem). The technical goal of Kleptography has been to identify "inner fields" as a way to embed cryptographic values in small bandwidth channel/sub-cryptogram inside a hosting system (RSA, DH based systems, etc.)

All asymmetric backdoors to date, that seamlessly embed an inner subliminal crypto field inside a hosting cryptographic value needed random oracle assumptions. This was used to make the inner value look "almost uniformly random" as part of its hosting random field. It was open whether the need for a random oracle is inherent, or, positively put: is there an algebraic cryptographic ciphertext that is embeddable inside another algebraic cryptographic field "as is"? In this work we achieve this goal for small bandwidth fields. To this end we present a new information hiding primitive that we call a "covert key exchange" that permits provably secure covert communications. Our results surpass previous work since: (1) the bandwidth that the subliminal channel needs is extremely small (bit length of a single compressed elliptic curve point), (2) the error probability of the exchange is negligible, and (3) our results are in the standard model. We use this protocol to implement the first kleptographic (i.e., asymmetric) backdoor in the standard model in RSA key generation and point at other applications. Key properties of the covert key exchange are that (1) both Alice's message to Bob and their shared secret appear to all efficient algorithms as uniformly random strings from $\{0,1\}^{k+1}$ and $\{0,1\}^M$, respectively (this is needed for the embedding), and (2) the fastest adversaries of the exchange run in time exponential in k, based on current knowledge (they have to solve DL over e-curves). We achieve this in the standard model based on the ECDDH assumption over a twisted pair of e-curves.

J.A. Garay and R. De Prisco (Eds.): SCN 2010, LNCS 6280, pp. 271–290, 2010.

1 Introduction

Advances in information hiding reveal new threats by parties (e.g., hardware manufacturers, system designers) and uncover trust-related issues in systems. Information hiding in cryptographic algorithms/ protocols, fundamentally requires embedding one cryptographic primitive inside another. Often, kleptographic design is perhaps more demanding than simple cryptosystems (one has usually to prove security of two cryptosystems: one inside the other). In particular, it requires a random element in one cryptosystem to host, as a random substring, an element from another cryptographic primitive, and do so in a hidden (indistinguishable) fashion.

For example, an kleptographic backdoor in RSA key generation has been shown that works for a wide-range of RSA keys (e.g., 768 bits and above) with a complete proof given in [26]. However, the result relies on the random oracle model and ECDDH, thus it does not tell us about an algebraic embedding of a backdoor directly inside an RSA modulus, and is not a "direct relationship" between two algebraic cryptographic distributions. Another example is a highly space-efficient public key stegosystem [17]. But, it relies on the less conventional "Oracle Diffie-Hellman" assumption, which again does not imply feasibility based on a more general assumption such as DDH.

A new approach is needed to advance the state-of-the-art in areas like these, so that we may understand better the direct embedability relationships between algebraic primitives and natural cryptographic assumptions about them (so we get proofs that are not in an idealized world).

Here, we show a new method for the task of "hidden embedding". In our key exchange, the approach balances the entropy in Alice's message to Bob against that of their resulting shared secret, and it permits Alice's message to be subliminally embedded (in a provably indistinguishable sense) and at the same time their shared secret is ready for direct use (no entropy extraction needed). We call the approach "entropy balancing." We further say that such an exchange is *covert* since Alice's trapdoor value looks like a random bit string. This problem is strictly more demanding than simply requiring that one value in the exchange, e.g. the shared secret, appear as a uniformly random bit string.

To make things even more difficult, a covert key exchange is often conducted through a subliminal channel having narrow bandwidth (e.g., in kleptography). First, this implies that if the channel is inside a hosting distribution, one can first determine a random choice of its wishes and can nevertheless sample the hosting distribution (which is a prime property of subliminal channels). Second, the small size necessitates a space-efficient key exchange (e.g., using elliptic curve crypto with point compression). To put it another way, whereas in many cryptographic applications space-efficiency is merely a convenience or an "added benefit", in information hiding space-efficiency is often a mandatory design requirement (this is the case in the asymmetric backdoors that we present).

Our *complete* covert key exchange solution relies on the traditional ECDDH problem in the following sense. We use a twisted pair of elliptic curves that exhibit the following distinguishing characteristic. In one curve the Weierstrass coefficient b is a quadratic residue whereas in the other curve this coefficient is a quadratic non-residue. Both curves in the twist have prime order and half of the upper order bits of p are binary 1s. As we show, an adversary that breaks our scheme is able to solve ECDDH on at least one of these two types of curves.

We employ the notion of entropy balancing to provide the following contributions: (1) *space-efficient covert key exchange* as our building block. We prove the security of the exchange in the standard model using only the traditional ECDDH assumption (as opposed to a newer assumption such as oracle DH). Note that Alice's message size is optimized provided that ECDDH is exponentially hard on both curves in the twist. (2) Kleptographic attack on RSA key generation. This was the first and most researched kleptographic problem, and we give the first complete solution in the standard model. (3) Public key stegosystem secure against chosen plaintext attacks based on ECDDH. (4) We also give the first asymmetric backdoor in SSL in the standard model such that: (a) the backdoor is in effect in each session with overwhelming probability, and (b) there is no state-information for the backdoor stored across sessions (i.e., no key-exposure between sessions).

Organization: In Section 2 we present related work and background material on twisted elliptic curves. The definition of a covert key exchange is presented in Section 3 and a construction for it is given in Section 4. In Section 5 we present our applications. ECDDH is reviewed in Appendix A. The Twisted Decision Diffie-Hellman (TDDH) problem is reviewed in Appendix B. We prove that the key exchange is complete (i.e., terminates in agreement) in Appendix C. The security proofs for the key exchange are given in Appendix D.

2 Background

The background material spans results on key exchange protocols, and asymmetric backdoors in RSA key generation. We review the works in these areas that closely relate to the applications that we present.

Entropy extraction in key exchanges: Previous work has solved the problem of conducting a key exchange in which the shared secret is a uniformly random binary string. The *leftover hash lemma* [12] was used to derive symmetric keys properly from a Diffie-Hellman shared secret [7]. In other words, the symmetric key bits are drawn independently using the uniform distribution. An algebraic approach based on a twisted pair of curves was used to derive a shared secret that is a uniformly random binary string [2]. Related work is [9] that presents a secure hashed Diffie-Hellman transform over a non-DDH group G (a group in which DDH does not hold). Gennaro et al showed that for the hashed DH transform to be secure it is sufficient that G contain a sufficiently large Decision Diffie-Hellman subgroup. Note that unlike the above cases, entropy balancing has the stronger requirement that one of the key exchange messages that is sent in the clear must also be a random binary string. This notion applies to various information hiding applications and we concretely implement this notion in the form of a covert key exchange protocol.

Asymmetric Backdoors in SSL: An asymmetric backdoor in the Secure Sockets Layer (SSL)[1] was shown in [10]. The constructions are heuristic in nature and there are no formal security arguments made. Recent work on the problem also includes [11] that presents general attack ideas. Again, no formal security arguments are made in these works.

An asymmetric backdoor in SSL was presented in [27] that employs Kaliski's elliptic curve pseudorandom bit generator [14]. The construction is based on a key exchange and is proven secure under ECDDH in the standard model. However, key agreement fails with probability very close to 1/2 and this causes the backdoor in SSL to fail to take effect in each session with probability very close to 1/2. However, an extension to the backdoor attack is shown that retains state information across SSL connections (chaining), and the expectation is that the backdoor will remain in effect after the first few SSL sessions. The two problems with the approach are that: (1) completeness of the backdoor is not assured in the first few exchanges, and (2) there is key-exposure in the state information that is stored in the backdoor. We solve these problems.

Asymmetric backdoors in RSA key generation: The notion of an asymmetric (kleptographic) backdoor was introduced in [24,25] along with the first asymmetric backdoor in RSA key generation. The backdoor employs a well-known subliminal channel [21,22] in composites [16,5] to leak the private key. An asymmetric backdoor can only be used by the designer that plants it, even when the full specification of the backdoor is public (confidentiality property). It is applicable in black-box implementations in which the implementation is private. This is relevant, for example, in obfuscated software or tamper-proof hardware or open source code that no one scrutinizes!

An asymmetric backdoor attack is known as a secretly embedded trapdoor with universal protection (SETUP). The embedded trapdoor is the public key of the (malicious) designer. The attack revolves around a reference key generator that has no backdoor (it is a typical public specification of the key generator). An RSA key generation SETUP must satisfy the indistinguishability property. This holds when the ensemble corresponding to the key pair that is output by the backdoor key generator is polytime indistinguishable from the ensemble corresponding to the key pair that is output by the reference key generator. So, RSA key pairs with the backdoor are indistinguishable from key pairs without the backdoor. A secure SETUP satisfies both the confidentiality and indistinguishability properties.

Crépeau and Slakmon presented backdoor designs for RSA key generation in [4]. These designs emphasized speed and were symmetric backdoors as opposed to being asymmetric since the constructions assume that a secret key remains hidden even after reverse-engineering (i.e., when the backdoor is layed bare). The paper presents an approach that is intended to work even when Lenstra's composite generation method is used [16]. The authors made an important observation in RSA key generation backdoor design, namely, that by using Coppersmith's algorithm

[1] Freier, Karlton, and Kocher, Internet Draft "The SSL Protocol Version 3.0," Network Working Group, Nov. 18, 1996.

[3], the amount of information that needs to be leaked is small. In more detail, it is sufficient for the backdoor key generator to leak the upper half of the bits of the RSA prime p instead of (nearly) the whole prime. We employ this observation.

A recent asymmetric backdoor in RSA key generation was proposed that utilizes a twisted pair of binary curves [26]. The backdoor key generator was shown to be secure in the random oracle model under the ECDDH assumption. The backdoor we present, on the other hand, does not use the random oracle model. Note that from a basic research point of view, asymmetric backdoor designs are not merely a warning to users, but represent also properties of cryptographic mechanisms, thus our result establishes a purely algebraic relationship between the two cryptographic distributions.

We point out that straightforward Diffie-Hellman (DH) [6] using twisted curves does not solve our problem of implementing a *space-efficient* covert key exchange. The space-efficiency of ECDH is not the problem, since points can be compressed. However, the problem is making Alice's message to Bob and their shared secret appear as random binary strings. To solve this, the curves could be, e.g. binary or over $\mathbb{F}_p$ with p being a large prime with the upper half of the bits of p being 1. In both cases, a properly chosen twist has the property that a random encoded (compressed) point on it looks like a random binary string. In such a solution, Alice chooses a curve in the twist randomly[2] and uses it for a DH key exchange. The problem is that Alice's trapdoor value to Bob will be on one of the two curves and their shared secret will be on *the same* curve. This correlation causes the solution to fail to solve the problem.

Indeed this key exchange problem was addressed in [27]. As noted, this idea causes Bob to fail to learn the shared secret with probability very close to 1/2. The *partial* covert key exchange solution in [27] is therefore ill-suited for a backdoor in RSA key generation since the backdoor would only take effect with probability very close to 1/2 when a key pair is generated. This is a serious problem since RSA keys are typically generated infrequently (sometimes once every couple of years). It also appears undesirable as a basis for an elliptic curve public key stegosystem since it is not clear how to preserve space-efficiency given that the exchange is prone to fail. In this paper we solve these issues.

2.1 Notation and Conventions

Elliptic Curves: An elliptic curve $E_{a,b}(\mathbb{F}_p)$ is defined by the simplified Weierstrass equation $y^2 = x^3 + ax + b$ where $a, b \in \mathbb{F}_p$ satisfy $4a^3 + 27b^2 \not\equiv 0 \mod p$. Let $\#E_{a,b}(\mathbb{F}_p)$ denote the number of points on the curve $E_{a,b}(\mathbb{F}_p)$. Let $\mathcal{O}$ denote the point at infinity on $E_{a,b}(\mathbb{F}_p)$. We use uppercase to denote a point on an elliptic curve and lowercase to denote a scalar multiplier. So, xG denotes scalar multiplication. Recall that $0G = \mathcal{O}$, $1G = G$, $2G = G + G$, and so on.

In our review of Kaliski's work in [14] (and in particular his Lemma 6.6 that covers embedding using twisted curves) we use his notation $E_{a,b}(\mathbb{F}_p)$ and $E_{a',b'}(\mathbb{F}_p)$. However, we do not use this convention in our constructions. We

[2] In accordance with the number of points on each curve.

define $E_0(\mathbb{F}_p) = E_{a,b}(\mathbb{F}_p)$ and $E_1(\mathbb{F}_p) = E_{a',b'}(\mathbb{F}_p)$. This lets us select between the two curves using a single bit, which we do often. We also define $r_i = \#E_i(\mathbb{F}_p)$ to be the number of points on curve $E_i(\mathbb{F}_p)$ for $i = 0, 1$. Let $\mathcal{O}_i$ be the point at infinity on $E_i(\mathbb{F}_p)$ for $i = 0, 1$.

String Operations: If α is a bit string then $|\alpha|$ denotes the length in bits of α. However, if $\mathcal{S}$ is a set then $|\mathcal{S}|$ denotes the cardinality of $\mathcal{S}$. Let $\alpha||\beta$ denote the concatenation of strings α and β. Let $\texttt{LSB}(\alpha)$ be a function that returns the least significant bit of bit string α. Let $\oplus$ denote the infix bitwise exclusive-or operator that operates on two bit strings of equal length. $\alpha >> b$ denotes the following string operation. The string α is returned but with the rightmost b bits removed from α (this is right shifting).

Selection and Assignment: We use $s \in_R \mathcal{S}$ to denote the selection of an element s uniformly at random from set $\mathcal{S}$. However, unless otherwise stated, an element that is selected randomly is selected using the uniform distribution. The symbol $\leftarrow$ is used for assignment.

Integers vs. Strings: We are careful to treat integers as separate from bit strings. This is to avoid ambiguities that can result from the presence/absence of leading zeros. This is of particular importance in information hiding since the representation of information must be carefully controlled. We define algorithm $\texttt{StrToInt}(x_s)$ to take as input a bit string x_s and return the integer x corresponding to x_s in base-2. We define algorithm $\texttt{IntToStr}(x)$ to take as input a non-negative integer x and return the bit string x_s corresponding to x in base-2 (so the most significant bit is always 1, unless $x = 0$ in which case the output is $x_s = 0$). We define algorithm `Format` as follows.

$\texttt{Format}(x, \ell)$:
1. $x_s \leftarrow \texttt{IntToStr}(x)$
2. if $(|x_s| > \ell)$ then output 0^ℓ else output $0^{\ell - |x_s|}||x_s$

Flow Control: We use logical indentation to show the body of `if` statements, `for` loops, and so on. Also, an algorithm that terminates early uses the keyword `halt` in order to terminate.

2.2 Elliptic Curve Background

Twists using the general class of elliptic curves over $\mathbb{F}_p$ were studied by Kaliski [13,14,15]. Below we give Lemma 6.5 and Definition 6.1 from [14].

Lemma 1. *Let $\beta \neq 0$ be a quadratic nonresidue in the field $\mathbb{F}_p$ and let $E_{a,b}(\mathbb{F}_p)$ be an elliptic curve. Then for every value x, letting $y = \sqrt{x^3 + ax + b}$:*

1. *If y is a quadratic residue, then the points $(x, \pm y)$ are on the curve $E_{a,b}(\mathbb{F}_p)$.*
2. *If y is a quadratic nonresidue, then $(\beta x, \pm\sqrt{\beta^3} y)$ are on $E_{a\beta^2, b\beta^3}(\mathbb{F}_p)$.*
3. *If $y = 0$, then the point $(x, 0)$ is on the curve $E_{a,b}(\mathbb{F}_p)$ and the point $(\beta x, 0)$ is on the curve $E_{a\beta^2, b\beta^3}(\mathbb{F}_p)$.*

A corollary to this lemma is that the number of points *on* the two curves *is* $2p + 2$, two points for each value of x and two identity elements.

Definition 1. *Let $E_{a,b}(\mathbb{F}_p)$ be an elliptic curve of parameter k (i.e., p is k bits long) and let β be a quadratic nonresidue modulo p. A twisted pair $T_{a,b,\beta}(\mathbb{F}_p)$ of parameter k is the union of the elliptic curves $E_{a,b}(\mathbb{F}_p)$ and $E_{a\beta^2,b\beta^3}(\mathbb{F}_p)$.*

A twist may be a multiset, since $E_{a,b}(\mathbb{F}_p)$ and $E_{a\beta^2,b\beta^3}(\mathbb{F}_p)$ may intersect.

Below we review algorithms from [27] (which are built on [14]) that encode/decode points using fixed-length bit strings. Fact 1 is from [14]. The input P to `Encode` is a point originating on E_c where $c \in \{0, 1\}$. `Decode` outputs (P, c) where P resides on E_c where $c \in \{0, 1\}$. X_T, $X_{T,even}^{-1}$, and $X_{T,odd}^{-1}$ are defined in [14]. $\texttt{Encode}(T_{a,b,\beta}(\mathbb{F}_p), P, c) = \texttt{Format}(X_T[T_{a,b,\beta}(\mathbb{F}_p)](P, c), k + 1)$.

$\texttt{Decode}(T_{a,b,\beta}(\mathbb{F}_p), P_s)$:
1. set $ysgn \leftarrow \text{LSB}(P_s)$ and set $\alpha \leftarrow \texttt{StrToInt}(P_s)$
2. if $(ysgn = 0)$ then output $(P, c) \leftarrow X_{T,even}^{-1}[T_{a,b,\beta}(\mathbb{F}_p)](\alpha)$ and `halt`
3. output $(P, c) \leftarrow X_{T,odd}^{-1}[T_{a,b,\beta}(\mathbb{F}_p)](\alpha)$

Fact 1. Let $T_{a,b,\beta}(\mathbb{F}_p)$ be a twisted pair. `Encode` is a polynomial time computable, probabilistic polynomial time invertible mapping between the set of points on the twisted pair $T_{a,b,\beta}(\mathbb{F}_p)$ and all $(k + 1)$-bit strings corresponding to the integers in the set $\{0, ..., 2p + 1\}$ padded with leading zeros as necessary. The inverse function of `Encode` is `Decode`.

3 The Covert Key Exchange

The covert key exchange protocol, denoted by Φ_1, is an implementation of the notion of entropy balancing for secret embeddings. The covert key exchange uses a twisted pair of curves over $\mathbb{F}_p$ where p is a k-bit prime. Informally, when we say that the covert key exchange is *space-efficient* what we mean is that the following properties hold: (1) Alice's message to Bob in the exchange is $k+1$ bits long and (2) the best known cryptanalytic algorithms against the exchange (confidentiality breaking/distinguishing) run in time exponential in k. Currently, the fastest known algorithm for solving ECDDH for curve $E_{a,b}(\mathbb{F}_p)$ runs in time $O(\sqrt{\#E_{a,b}(\mathbb{F}_p)})$ when $\#E_{a,b}(\mathbb{F}_p)$ is prime. It is from this that (2) holds based on current knowledge. This enables Alice to send a small key exchange message to Bob (in the hundreds of bits rather than in the thousands for an algorithm based on DL over a finite field or factoring), based on the state-of-the-art. Property (2) is mandatory to achieve the degree of space-efficiency that we desire (so it is part of the definition below that concretely defines the setting of the key exchange and its constraints).

Definition 2. *Let $\tau = (T_{a,b,\beta}(\mathbb{F}_p), G_0, G_1)$ be agreed upon system parameters where $|p| = k$, let $M \leq 10^4$ be a constant, let $\mathcal{T}_{\tau,\Phi_1}$ denote the probability ensemble corresponding to all possible $(Y_{0,1}, ..., Y_{0,M}, Y_{1,1}, ..., Y_{1,M}, m_A, m_k)$ resulting from Φ_1 and the probability distribution over them resulting from Φ_1, let $\mathcal{T}_{\tau,U}$*

denote $E_0(\mathbb{F}_p)^M \times E_1(\mathbb{F}_p)^M \times \{0,1\}^{k+1} \times \{0,1\}^M$ *and the uniform distribution over it, and let Alice and Bob be probabilistic polytime algorithms. If in a 2-round protocol* Φ_1 *between Alice and Bob, Bob sends* $(Y_{0,1},...,Y_{0,M},Y_{1,1},...,Y_{1,M})$ *to Alice where* $Y_{i,j} \in_R E_i(\mathbb{F}_p)$ *for* $i=0,1$ *and* $j=1,2,...,M$ *(Bob knows the discrete logs* $x_{i,j}$ *of the* $Y_{i,j}$*), and Alice generates a* $(k+1)$*-bit message* m_A *and a* M*-bit shared secret* m_k*, and sends* m_A *to Bob, and*

1. *(completeness) using* m_A *and private information (the* $x_{i,j}$*) Bob computes* m_k *with a probability that is overwhelming (in* k*), and*
2. *(security) the fastest algorithm that distinguishes ensemble* $\mathcal{T}_{\tau,\Phi_1}$ *from ensemble* $\mathcal{T}_{\tau,U}$ *with an advantage that is non-negligible (in* k*) runs in exponential time (*$2^{\epsilon k}$ *for a constraint* $\epsilon > 0$*),*

then Φ_1 *is a* k*-secure* ***space-efficient covert key exchange****.*

The upper bound on M is somewhat arbitrary (10^4 is simply large enough for practical use). Security implies covertness since it establishes that m_A appears as a uniformly random $(k+1)$-bit string. It also implies confidentiality since it establishes that m_k appears as a uniformly random M-bit string.

4 Key Exchange Construction

Alice and Bob agree on TDDH parameters τ. For our reductions to hold and our applications to be secure, they should generate τ using $\texttt{IG}_1$ (see Appendix B for a review of TDDH) where $\texttt{IG}_1$ adheres to the following list of constraints.

1. The prime p in τ is of the form $p = 2^k - \delta$ where δ satisfies $1 \leq \delta < \sqrt{2^k}$. The value δ may be randomly chosen until p of this form is generated.
2. The curves $E_0(\mathbb{F}_p)$ and $E_1(\mathbb{F}_p)$ have prime order. So, r_0 and r_1 are prime.
3. To prevent the attack on prime-field-anomalous curves [19,20,23], it is required that $r_0, r_1 \neq p$.
4. To prevent the Weil and Tate pairing attacks [18,8], it is required that r_0 does not divide $p^\nu - 1$ for $\nu = 1,2,3...$ up to, say, 20. The same holds for r_1.
5. More generally, $E_0(\mathbb{F}_p)$ and $E_1(\mathbb{F}_p)$ *must* provide suitable settings for the ECDDH problem.

From Subsection 2.2 it is the case that $r_0 + r_1 = 2p + 2$. We define $\mathcal{S}_{a,b,\beta,p}$ as follows.

$$\mathcal{S}_{a,b,\beta,p} = \{s : P \in E_0(\mathbb{F}_p), s = \texttt{Encode}(T_{a,b,\beta}(\mathbb{F}_p), P, 0)\} \bigcup \{s : P \in E_1(\mathbb{F}_p), s = \texttt{Encode}(T_{a,b,\beta}(\mathbb{F}_p), P, 1)\}$$

4.1 Intuition Behind the Covert Exchange

By glossing over some details and omitting others, it is possible to describe the covert key exchange algorithm at a high-level. We do so here.

Bob generates $2M$ public keys. Half are points on one curve in the twist and half are on the other. He gives these to Alice. It is her job to generate both her trapdoor value to Bob and their shared secret. Given her trapdoor value he will with overwhelming probability compute their shared secret using his $2M$ private keys.

Alice chooses one of the curves to use randomly. In this choice, the curves are selected in direct proportion to the number of points on them. So, the curve in the twist with the most points is slightly more likely than the other. Let the curve she selects be denoted by $E_u(\mathbb{F}_p)$ where $u \in \{0,1\}$. She generates a scalar multiplier k_1 randomly for this curve and computes her key exchange value to Bob using it. She then generates M shared secrets using k_1 and the M public keys of Bob on $E_u(\mathbb{F}_p)$. She Kaliski encodes them and concatenates the least significant bits of the M encodings together. The resulting string is their shared secret.

We defer to the proofs why the shared secret appears independently random and uniformly distributed. The method that Bob uses to compute the shared secret can be inferred from the above.

4.2 Key Exchange Protocol Φ_1

We define $\texttt{SelCurve}(T_{a,b,\beta}(\mathbb{F}_p))$ to be a randomized algorithm that outputs 0 with probability $\frac{r_0}{2p+2}$ and 1 with probability $\frac{r_1}{2p+2}$. Algorithm DeriveBit and algorithm FillGap are used in the key exchange.

$\texttt{DeriveBit}(T_{a,b,\beta}(\mathbb{F}_p), P)$:
Input: point P on twist $T_{a,b,\beta}(\mathbb{F}_p)$
Output: $b \in \{0,1\}$
1. if $(P \in E_0(\mathbb{F}_p))$ then $c \leftarrow 0$ else $c \leftarrow 1$
2. if $(P = \mathcal{O}_c)$ then output $b \in_R \{0,1\}$ and **halt**
3. output $b \leftarrow \texttt{LSB}(\psi_s)$ where $\psi_s \leftarrow \texttt{Encode}(T_{a,b,\beta}(\mathbb{F}_p), P, c)$

$\texttt{FillGap}(T_{a,b,\beta}(\mathbb{F}_p))$:
Input: twist $T_{a,b,\beta}(\mathbb{F}_p)$
Output: $(y, s_1, s_2) \in \{0,1\} \times \{0,1\}^{k+1} \times \{0,1\}^M$
1. choose $\mu \in_R \{0,1\}^{k+1}$
2. if $(\mu \notin \mathcal{S}_{a,b,\beta,p})$ then
3. choose $\psi \in_R \{2p+2, 2p+3, ..., 2^{k+1}-1\}$ and $s_2 \in_R \{0,1\}^M$
4. compute $s_1 \leftarrow \texttt{Format}(\psi, k+1)$, output $(1, s_1, s_2)$, and **halt**
5. output $(0, 0^{k+1}, 0^M)$

We refer to the following as protocol Φ_1. The value $M \leq 10^4$ is a constant.

Step 1: Bob chooses $x_{i,j} \in_R \{0,1,2,...,r_i-1\}$ and computes $Y_{i,j} \leftarrow x_{i,j}G_i$ for $i = 0,1$ and $j = 1,2,...,M$. Bob sends $(Y_{0,1},...,Y_{0,M},Y_{1,1},...,Y_{1,M})$ to Alice.

Step 2: Alice sends the key exchange message m_A to Bob where $(m_A, m_k) \leftarrow \texttt{ExchAlg}_1(\tau, Y_{0,1},...,Y_{0,M},Y_{1,1},...,Y_{1,M})$.

$\texttt{ExchAlg}_1(\tau, Y_{0,1}, ..., Y_{0,M}, Y_{1,1}, ..., Y_{1,M})$:
Input: TDDH parameters τ, points $Y_{i,j}$ on
$E_i(\mathbb{F}_p)$ for $i = 0, 1$, $j = 1, 2, ..., M$
Output: $(m_A, m_k) \in \{0,1\}^{k+1} \times \{0,1\}^M$
1. $(y, s_1, s_2) \leftarrow \texttt{FillGap}(T_{a,b,\beta}(\mathbb{F}_p))$
2. if $(y = 1)$ then output (s_1, s_2) and halt
3. $u \leftarrow \texttt{SelCurve}(T_{a,b,\beta}(\mathbb{F}_p))$
4. choose $k_1 \in_R \mathbb{Z}_{r_u}$ and compute $U \leftarrow k_1 G_u$
5. $m_A \leftarrow \texttt{Encode}(T_{a,b,\beta}(\mathbb{F}_p), U, u)$
6. for $j = 1$ to M do:
7. compute $P_j \leftarrow k_1 Y_{u,j}$ and
$b_j \leftarrow \texttt{DeriveBit}(T_{a,b,\beta}(\mathbb{F}_p), P_j)$
8. set $m_k \leftarrow b_M || b_{M-1} || ... || b_1$ and output (m_A, m_k)

Step 3: Bob receives the message m_A from Alice. Bob computes $\texttt{Recover}(T_{a,b,\beta}(\mathbb{F}_p), m_A, x_{0,1}, ..., x_{0,M}, x_{1,1}, ..., x_{1,M})$, thereby obtaining (t, m_k).

$\texttt{Recover}(T_{a,b,\beta}(\mathbb{F}_p), m_A, x_{0,1}, ..., x_{0,M}, x_{1,1}, ..., x_{1,M})$:
Input: twist $T_{a,b,\beta}(\mathbb{F}_p)$, $m_A \in \{0,1\}^{k+1}$,
$x_{i,j} \in \mathbb{Z}_{r_i}$ for $i = 0, 1$, $j = 1, 2, ..., M$
Output: $(t, m_k) \in \{0,1\} \times \{0,1\}^M$
1. if $(m_A \notin \mathcal{S}_{a,b,\beta,p})$ then output $(0, 0^M)$ and halt
2. $(U, u) \leftarrow \texttt{Decode}(T_{a,b,\beta}(\mathbb{F}_p), m_A)$
3. for $j = 1$ to M do:
4. compute $P_j \leftarrow x_{u,j} U$ and
$b_j \leftarrow \texttt{DeriveBit}(T_{a,b,\beta}(\mathbb{F}_p), P_j)$
5. set $m_k \leftarrow b_M || b_{M-1} || ... || b_1$ and output $(1, m_k)$

We define *failure* of protocol Φ_1 to be a condition in which any of the following occur:

1. $m_A \in \mathcal{S}_{a,b,\beta,p}$ and the decoding of m_A is on $E_u(\mathbb{F}_p)$ and $\exists\ j \in \{1, 2, ..., M\}$ such that $Y_{u,j} = \mathcal{O}_u$.
2. $m_A \in \{0,1\}^{k+1} \setminus \mathcal{S}_{a,b,\beta,p}$.
3. $m_A \in \mathcal{S}_{a,b,\beta,p}$ and the decoding of m_A is $\mathcal{O}_0$ or $\mathcal{O}_1$ (i.e., $\texttt{ExchAlg}_1$ chooses $k_1 = 0$).

The rationale behind this definition is as follows. These are the conditions that cause one or more bits of m_k to be derived directly from a fair coin flip. So, Bob cannot be certain that he receives m_k correctly in these cases.

An alternate definition is of course possible. For example, we could define success as the raw probability that Bob decides on an m_k that is the same as the m_k that Alice selected (Bob may have to guess 1 or more bits). However, we have decided to use a definition of success that measures Bob's certainty regarding his computation of m_k.

The following Lemma is proven in Appendix C where the definition of a negligible function is reviewed.

Lemma 2. *(completeness) Failure occurs in protocol Φ_1 with a probability that is negligible in k.*

In our failed attempts at designing the exchange we found that the following seemed to occur: when we succeeded in removing the bias in m_A, the construction would introduce bias into m_k in the process, and vice-versa. The two are inextricably linked. $\texttt{ExchAlg}_1$ succeeds in balancing the entropy in m_A and m_k in the sense that they are both random binary strings. This is the origin of our terminology.

We prove Theorem 1 in Appendix D. Theorem 1 establishes Property 2 of Definition 2.

Theorem 1. *(security) The ECDDH problem over $(E_0(\mathbb{F}_p), G_0)$ or ECDDH over $(E_1(\mathbb{F}_p), G_1)$ polytime reduces to the problem of distinguishing $\mathcal{T}_{\tau,\Phi_1}$ from $\mathcal{T}_{\tau,U}$ with an advantage that is non-negligible (in k).*

Lemma 2 establishes property 1 of Definition 2. So, Lemma 2 and Theorem 1 imply Theorem 2.

Theorem 2. *If ECDDH requires exponential time (in k) on $(E_0(\mathbb{F}_p), G_0)$ and $(E_1(\mathbb{F}_p), G_1)$ then Φ_1 is a k-secure space-efficient covert key exchange.*

The above theorem is proven in the appendix. The proof establishes that the exchanged value from Alice is random and that the key established is random and hard to compute to any polynomial time adversary (under the proper decisional DH assumption). The basic intuition of the proof idea is that the exchanged value is random and then the decisional assumption implies that the resulting shared secret is indistinguishable from a random value in the target group, and therefore the shared key extracted itself should not help distinguishing between them and thus is indistinguishable from a pseudorandomly chosen value and thus from a randomly chosen value.

5 Applications

Kleptographic RSA key generation in the standard model: The following describes how to build an asymmetric backdoor in RSA key generation in which the RSA public exponent e can be fixed for all users. The attacker Bob places his public key $(Y_{0,1}, ..., Y_{0,M}, Y_{1,1}, ..., Y_{1,M})$ in Alice's key generation device. Key generation performs Alice's side of the covert key exchange. The shared secret m_k is embedded in the upper order bits of the RSA prime p being generated. The corresponding key exchange value m_A is encoded in the upper order bits of the RSA modulus being generated. Under this constraints an otherwise random public composite is chosen. The attacker obtains Alice's public key from a public channel (e.g., CA, a certificate, etc.). He extracts m_A and uses his private key to compute m_k. Using this and Coppersmith's factoring algorithm [3], he factors the public modulus.

The security adheres to the notion of a SETUP (secretly embedded trapdoor with universal protection). It can be shown that indistinguishability holds provided ECDDH is hard on both curves in the twist. Confidentiality can be shown under this and the assumption that integer factorization is hard.

Public Key Stegosystem: The stegosystem construction is a straightforward implementation of ElGamal based on the covert key exchange. The primary difference between this version of the ElGamal and traditional implementations (ECC and otherwise) is that we exclusive-or the plaintext with the shared secret. Informally, the indistinguishability property dictates that a ciphertext must appear as a fixed-length bit string, where the bits appear as fair coin tosses. We can show that this holds provided ECDDH is hard on both curves in the twist. Furthermore, we can show that if ECDDH is hard on both curves in the twist then the stegosystem is semantically secure against chosen plaintext attacks.

Kleptographic backdoor in SSL: It is well-known that the 28 byte `hello` nonce in SSL is a subliminal channel that is visible in the clear to passive eavesdroppers on the network. The client sends such a nonce to the server and vice-versa. The pre-master secret is 48 bytes and it contains a 46 byte nonce. The pre-master secret nonce is chosen by the client and is sent securely to the server. Knowledge of the two hello nonces and the pre-master secret nonce implies the ability to eavesdrop on the SSL session.

We build an asymmetric backdoor into the client in the SSL protocol. Let $k = 223$ and $M = 368$ for the covert key exchange. The attacker Bob places his elliptic curve public key $(Y_{0,1}, ..., Y_{0,M}, Y_{1,1}, ..., Y_{1,M})$ into Alice's SSL client.

When Alice initiates an SSL session with a server, the asymmetric backdoor takes over the generation of the client hello nonce and the pre-master secret nonce. The backdoor runs $\texttt{ExchAlg}_1(\tau, Y_{0,1}, ..., Y_{0,M}, Y_{1,1}, ..., Y_{1,M})$ to obtain (m_A, m_k). It sets the hello nonce to be m_A and the pre-master secret nonce to be m_k.

Bob passively eavesdrops on the SSL session. He learns both hello nonces since he sees them in the clear. He sets m_A to be Alice's hello nonce. Bob then runs `Recover` and obtains m_k. He is then able to decipher the SSL session.

We note that this attack is a perfect example of the power of our covert key exchange primitive (of Section 4). This is because: (1) the subliminal channel is extremely narrow, a mere 224 bits, and therefore space-efficiency is an obvious requirement, and (2) the kleptographic application is incredibly simple. Observe that the host distribution over (hello nonce,pre-master secret nonce) is exactly the uniform distribution over $\{0, 1\}^{224} \times \{0, 1\}^{368}$. It is not likely to get simpler than this.

For security note that the indistinguishability and confidentiality properties of the asymmetric backdoor in SSL follow from Theorem 1. It is therefore a provable asymmetric backdoor on top of a secure subliminal channel.

References

1. Boneh, D.: The Decision Diffie-Hellman Problem. In: Buhler, J.P. (ed.) ANTS 1998. LNCS, vol. 1423, pp. 48–63. Springer, Heidelberg (1998)
2. Chevassut, O., Fouque, P., Gaudry, P., Pointcheval, D.: The Twist-AUgmented Technique for Key Exchange. In: Yung, M., Dodis, Y., Kiayias, A., Malkin, T.G. (eds.) PKC 2006. LNCS, vol. 3958, pp. 410–426. Springer, Heidelberg (2006)

3. Coppersmith, D.: Finding a small root of a bivariate integer equation; factoring with high bits known. In: Maurer, U.M. (ed.) EUROCRYPT 1996. LNCS, vol. 1070, pp. 178–189. Springer, Heidelberg (1996)
4. Crépeau, C., Slakmon, A.: Simple backdoors for rsa key generation. In: Joye, M. (ed.) CT-RSA 2003. LNCS, vol. 2612, pp. 403–416. Springer, Heidelberg (2003)
5. Desmedt, Y.: Abuses in cryptography and how to fight them. In: Goldwasser, S. (ed.) CRYPTO 1988. LNCS, vol. 403, pp. 375–389. Springer, Heidelberg (1990)
6. Diffie, W., Hellman, M.: New Directions in Cryptography. IEEE Transactions on Information Theory 22(6), 644–654 (1976)
7. Dodis, Y., Gennaro, R., Håstad, J., Krawczyk, H., Rabin, T.: Randomness extraction and key derivation using the CBC, cascade and HMAC modes. In: Franklin, M. (ed.) CRYPTO 2004. LNCS, vol. 3152, pp. 494–510. Springer, Heidelberg (2004)
8. Frey, G., Rück, H.: A remark concerning m-divisibility and the discrete logarithm in the divisor class group of curves. Math. of Computation 62(206), 865–874 (1994)
9. Gennaro, R., Krawczyk, H., Rabin, T.: Secure hashed Diffie-Hellman over non-DDH groups. In: Cachin, C., Camenisch, J.L. (eds.) EUROCRYPT 2004. LNCS, vol. 3027, pp. 361–381. Springer, Heidelberg (2004)
10. Goh, E.-J., Boneh, D., Pinkas, B., Golle, P.: The design and implementation of protocol-based hidden key recovery. In: Boyd, C., Mao, W. (eds.) ISC 2003. LNCS, vol. 2851, pp. 165–179. Springer, Heidelberg (2003)
11. Golebiewski, Z., Kutylowski, M., Zagorski, F.: Stealing secrets with SSL/TLS and SSH—kleptographic attacks. In: Pointcheval, D., Mu, Y., Chen, K. (eds.) CANS 2006. LNCS, vol. 4301, pp. 191–202. Springer, Heidelberg (2006)
12. Impagliazzo, R., Levin, L., Luby, M.: Pseudo-random generation from one-way functions. In: Symp. on the Theory of Comput.—STOC 1989, pp. 12–24 (1989)
13. Kaliski, B.S.: A pseudo-random bit generator based on elliptic logarithms. In: Odlyzko, A.M. (ed.) CRYPTO 1986. LNCS, vol. 263, pp. 84–103. Springer, Heidelberg (1987)
14. Kaliski, B.S.: Elliptic curves and cryptography: A pseudorandom bit generator and other tools. PhD Thesis. MIT (February 1988)
15. Kaliski, B.S.: One-way permutations on elliptic curves. Journal of Cryptology 3(3), 187–199 (1991)
16. Lenstra, A.K.: Generating RSA moduli with a predetermined portion. In: Ohta, K., Pei, D. (eds.) ASIACRYPT 1998. LNCS, vol. 1514, pp. 1–10. Springer, Heidelberg (1998)
17. Möller, B.: A public-key encryption scheme with pseudo-random ciphertexts. In: Samarati, P., Ryan, P.Y.A., Gollmann, D., Molva, R. (eds.) ESORICS 2004. LNCS, vol. 3193, pp. 335–351. Springer, Heidelberg (2004)
18. Menezes, A., Okamoto, T., Vanstone, S.: Reducing elliptic curve logarithms to logarithms in a finite field. IEEE Trans. on Info. Theory 39(5), 1639–1646 (1993)
19. Satoh, T., Araki, K.: Fermat quotients and the polynomial time discrete log algorithm for anomalous elliptic curves. Commentarii Mathematici Universitatis Sancti Pauli 47, 81–92 (1998)
20. Semaev, I.: Evaluation of discrete logarithms in a group of p-torsion points of an elliptic curve in characteristic p. Math. of Computation 67(221), 353–356 (1998)
21. Simmons, G.J.: The prisoners' problem and the subliminal channel. In: McCurley, K.S., Ziegler, C.D. (eds.) Advances in Cryptology—Crypto 1983. LNCS, vol. 1440, pp. 51–67. Springer, Heidelberg (1999)
22. Simmons, G.J.: Subliminal channels: past and present. European Transactions on Telecommunications 5(4), 459–473 (1994)

23. Smart, N.: The discrete logarithm problem on elliptic curves of trace one. Journal of Cryptology 12(3), 193–196 (1999)
24. Young, A., Yung, M.: The dark side of black-box cryptography, or: Should we trust capstone? In: Koblitz, N. (ed.) CRYPTO 1996. LNCS, vol. 1109, pp. 89–103. Springer, Heidelberg (1996)
25. Young, A., Yung, M.: Kleptography: Using cryptography against cryptography. In: Fumy, W. (ed.) EUROCRYPT 1997. LNCS, vol. 1233, pp. 62–74. Springer, Heidelberg (1997)
26. Young, A., Yung, M.: A space efficient backdoor in RSA and its applications. In: Preneel, B., Tavares, S. (eds.) SAC 2005. LNCS, vol. 3897, pp. 128–143. Springer, Heidelberg (2006)
27. Young, A., Yung, M.: Space-efficient kleptography without random oracles. In: Furon, T., Cayre, F., Doërr, G., Bas, P. (eds.) IH 2007. LNCS, vol. 4567, pp. 112–129. Springer, Heidelberg (2008)

A Review of ECDDH

A group family denoted by $\mathcal{G}$ is a set of finite cyclic groups $\mathcal{G} = \{E_{a,b}(\mathbb{F}_p)\}$ where each group has prime order. Let IG_0 be an instance generator for $\mathcal{G}$ that on input k (in unary) generates $(E_{a,b}(\mathbb{F}_p), G)$ where $E_{a,b}(\mathbb{F}_p)$ is from $\mathcal{G}$, G is a generator of $E_{a,b}(\mathbb{F}_p)$, and $r = \#E_{a,b}(\mathbb{F}_p)$. The ECDDH assumption is that no polytime algorithm A_0 exists for $\mathcal{G}$. We define the *superpolynomial* ECDDH assumption to be that no superpolynomial time algorithm A_0 exists for $\mathcal{G}$.

Definition 3. *An ECDDH algorithm A_0 for $\mathcal{G}$ satisfies, for some fixed $\alpha > 0$ and sufficiently large k:*

$$|\Pr[A_0(E_{a,b}(\mathbb{F}_p), G, aG, bG, abG) = 1] - \Pr[A_0(E_{a,b}(\mathbb{F}_p), G, aG, bG, cG) = 1]| > \tfrac{1}{k^\alpha}$$

The probability is over the random choice of $(E_{a,b}(\mathbb{F}_p), G)$ according to the distribution induced by $\mathrm{IG}_0(k)$, the random choice of integers a, b, c satisfying $0 \leq a, b, c \leq r - 1$, and the bits used by A_0.

We now review the ECDDH randomization method from [1] adapted for the case of elliptic curves. Let the $(E_{a,b}(\mathbb{F}_p), G, \mathcal{X}, \mathcal{Y}, \mathcal{Z})$ be an ECDDH problem instance. Algorithm $\mathtt{f}$ chooses scalars u_1, u_2, v randomly satisfying the inequality $0 \leq u_1, u_2, v \leq r - 1$. The function $\mathtt{f}(E_{a,b}(\mathbb{F}_p), G, \mathcal{X}, \mathcal{Y}, \mathcal{Z})$ outputs $(v\mathcal{X} + u_1G, \mathcal{Y} + u_2G, v\mathcal{Z} + u_1\mathcal{Y} + vu_2\mathcal{X} + u_1u_2G)$.

B Review of Twisted DDH

We now review the twisted DDH problem that is covered in [27]. Let TW_k be the set of all twists of parameter k in which both groups (curves) in each twist have prime order. Let IG_1 be an instance generator for TW_k that on input the value k (in unary) generates $\tau = (T_{a,b,\beta}(\mathbb{F}_p), G_0, G_1)$ where G_0 is a generator of $E_0(\mathbb{F}_p)$ and G_1 is a generator of $E_1(\mathbb{F}_p)$ (these curves are defined in Subsection 2.1). Our results in this paper require that $\mathtt{IG}_1$ generate TDDH parameters in accordance with Section 4.

Definition 4. *A TDDH algorithm* $\mathtt{A}_1$ *for* TW_k *satisfies, for some fixed* $\alpha > 0$ *and sufficiently large* k*:*

$$|\Pr[\mathtt{A}_1(\tau, (a_0G_0, b_0G_0, a_0b_0G_0), (a_1G_1, b_1G_1, a_1b_1G_1)) = 1] - \Pr[\mathtt{A}_1(\tau, (a_0G_0, b_0G_0, c_0G_0), (a_1G_1, b_1G_1, c_1G_1)) = 1]| > \frac{1}{k^\alpha}$$

The probability is over the random choice of τ *according to the distribution induced by* $\mathrm{IG}_1(k)$*, the random choice of* $a_0, b_0, c_0 \in \{0, 1, ..., r_0 - 1\}$*, the random choice of* $a_1, b_1, c_1 \in \{0, 1, 2, ..., r_1 - 1\}$*, and the bits used by* $\mathtt{A}_1$*.*

The twisted DDH assumption (TDDH) is that no such polytime $\mathtt{A}_1$ exists for TW_k. The *superpolynomial* TDDH assumption is that no such superpolynomial time $\mathtt{A}_1$ exists for TW_k.

Theorem 3 is straightforward to show. Being able to compute ECDDH for just one of the two curves in the twist breaks TDDH.

Theorem 3. *The TDDH problem polytime reduces to the ECDDH problem over* $(E_0(\mathbb{F}_p), G_0)$ *or the ECDDH problem over* $(E_1(\mathbb{F}_p), G_1)$*.*

Theorem 4. *The ECDDH problem over* $(E_0(\mathbb{F}_p), G_0)$ *or the ECDDH problem over* $(E_1(\mathbb{F}_p), G_1)$ *polytime reduces to TDDH.*

Proof. Suppose there exists a distinguisher $\mathtt{D}$ that solves TDDH. Both $E_0(\mathbb{F}_p)$ and $E_1(\mathbb{F}_p)$ are as defined in Subsection 2.1. Let the values t_0 and t_1 be ECDDH problem instances where $t_i = (E_i(\mathbb{F}_p), G_i, X_i, Y_i, Z_i)$ for $i = 0, 1$.

$\mathtt{M}_0(E_0(\mathbb{F}_p), G_0, X_0, Y_0, Z_0)$:
1. $u_0 \leftarrow \mathtt{f}(E_0(\mathbb{F}_p), G_0, X_0, Y_0, Z_0)$
2. generate a random 3-tuple u_1 over $(E_1(\mathbb{F}_p), G_1)$
3. output (τ, u_0, u_1)

$\mathtt{M}_1(E_1(\mathbb{F}_p), G_1, X_1, Y_1, Z_1)$:
1. $u_1 \leftarrow \mathtt{f}(E_1(\mathbb{F}_p), G_1, X_1, Y_1, Z_1)$
2. generate a random DH triple u_0 over $(E_0(\mathbb{F}_p), G_0)$
3. output (τ, u_0, u_1)

Clearly $\mathtt{M}_0$ and $\mathtt{M}_1$ run in time polynomial in k. Let $S_{i,DH}$ be the set of all DH triples over $(E_i(\mathbb{F}_p), G_i)$ for $i = 0, 1$. Let $S_{i,T}$ be the set of all 3-tuples over $(E_i(\mathbb{F}_p), G_i)$ for $i = 0, 1$.

Without loss of generality we may suppose that the TDDH distinguisher $\mathtt{D}$ outputs 1 with advantage δ_1 in k when both 3-tuples are DH triples and 0 with advantage δ_0 in k when both 3-tuples are random 3-tuples, where δ_1 and δ_0 are non-negligible. Observe that a slightly less powerful distinguisher can be used to construct $\mathtt{D}$, e.g., one in which δ_1 is non-negligible but δ_0 is negligible.

Consider the case that $v_0 \in_R S_{0,DH}$ and $v_1 \in_R S_{1,T}$. There are 3 cases:

Case 1: Consider the case that $\mathtt{D}(\tau, v_0, v_1)$ outputs 0 with probability $1/2 \pm \gamma(k)$ where the function γ is negligible. Let $d \leftarrow \mathtt{D}(\mathtt{M}_0(E_0(\mathbb{F}_p), G_0, X_0, Y_0, Z_0))$. $\mathtt{M}_0$ generates u_1 to be a random 3-tuple over $(E_1(\mathbb{F}_p), G_1)$. Suppose that (X_0, Y_0, Z_0)

is a DH triple. Then by the correctness of f, u_0 is a random DH triple. So, in this case $d = 0$ with probability $1/2 \pm \gamma(k)$ (negligible advantage). Suppose that (X_0, Y_0, Z_0) is not a DH triple. Then by the correctness of f, u_0 is a random 3-tuple. So, $d = 0$ with probability $1/2 + \delta_0(k)$ (non-negligible advantage). There is a polynomial time observable difference in behavior here. Therefore, $\mathtt{D}(\mathtt{M}_0(E_0(\mathbb{F}_p), G_0, X_0, Y_0, Z_0))$ solves the ECDDH problem over $(E_0(\mathbb{F}_p), G_0)$.

Case 2: Suppose that $\mathtt{D}(\tau, v_0, v_1)$ outputs 0 with probability $1/2 - \delta_2(k)$ and 1 with probability $1/2 + \delta_2(k)$ where the value δ_2 is non-negligible. Let $d \leftarrow \mathtt{D}(\mathtt{M}_0(E_0(\mathbb{F}_p), G_0, X_0, Y_0, Z_0))$. Machine $\mathtt{M}_0$ generates u_1 to be a random 3-tuple over $(E_1(\mathbb{F}_p), G_1)$. Suppose that (X_0, Y_0, Z_0) is a DH triple. Then by the correctness of f, u_0 is a random DH triple. So, in this case $d = 1$ with probability $1/2+\delta_2(k)$. Suppose that (X_0, Y_0, Z_0) is not a DH triple. Then by the correctness of f, u_0 is a random 3-tuple. So, $d = 0$ with probability $1/2 + \delta_0(k)$. Therefore, $\mathtt{D}(\mathtt{M}_0(E_0(\mathbb{F}_p), G_0, X_0, Y_0, Z_0))$ solves ECDDH over $(E_0(\mathbb{F}_p), G_0)$.

Case 3: Suppose that $\mathtt{D}(\tau, v_0, v_1)$ outputs 0 with probability $1/2 + \delta_3(k)$ and 1 with probability $1/2 - \delta_3(k)$ where the value δ_3 is non-negligible. Let $d \leftarrow \mathtt{D}(\mathtt{M}_1(E_1(\mathbb{F}_p), G_1, X_1, Y_1, Z_1))$. Algorithm $\mathtt{M}_1$ generates u_0 to be a random DH triple over $(E_0(\mathbb{F}_p), G_0)$. Suppose that (X_1, Y_1, Z_1) is a DH triple. Then by the correctness of f, u_1 is a random DH triple. So, in this case $d = 1$ with probability $1/2+\delta_1(k)$. Suppose that (X_1, Y_1, Z_1) is not a DH triple. Then by the correctness of f, u_1 is a random 3-tuple. So, $d = 0$ with probability $1/2 + \delta_3(k)$. Therefore, $\mathtt{D}(\mathtt{M}_1(E_1(\mathbb{F}_p), G_1, X_1, Y_1, Z_1))$ solves ECDDH over $(E_1(\mathbb{F}_p), G_1)$.

It follows that Theorem 5 holds (equivalence).

Theorem 5. *TDDH is polytime equivalent to ECDDH over $(E_0(\mathbb{F}_p), G_0)$ or ECDDH over $(E_1(\mathbb{F}_p), G_1)$*

C Completeness Proof

Definition 5. *ν is a negligible function if for every constant $c \geq 0$ there exists an integer k_c such that $\nu(k) < \frac{1}{k^c}$ for all $k \geq k_c$.*

The following is the proof of Lemma 2, namely, that failure occurs in Φ_1 with a probability that is negligible in k.

Proof. Let $p_1(k)$ denote the success probability of protocol Φ_1 having security parameter k. Let k_c be 64 (see Definition 5). $p_1(k) =$

$$(\tfrac{r_0-1}{r_0})^M * 1 * \tfrac{2p+2}{2^{k+1}} \tfrac{r_0}{2p+2} \tfrac{r_0-1}{r_0} + 1 * (\tfrac{r_1-1}{r_1})^M \tfrac{2p+2}{2^{k+1}} \tfrac{r_1}{2p+2} \tfrac{r_1-1}{r_1}$$

$$p_1(k) = (\tfrac{r_0-1}{r_0})^M \tfrac{r_0-1}{2^{k+1}} + (\tfrac{r_1-1}{r_1})^M \tfrac{r_1-1}{2^{k+1}}$$

Hasse showed that $|\#E_{a,b}(\mathbb{F}_p) - (p+1)| \leq 2\sqrt{p}$ for an elliptic curve $E_{a,b}(\mathbb{F}_p)$. So, $r_u - 1 \geq p - 2\sqrt{p}$ for $u = 0, 1$.

$$p_1(k) \geq ((\frac{r_0-1}{r_0})^M \frac{p-2\sqrt{p}}{2^{k+1}} + (\frac{r_1-1}{r_1})^M \frac{p-2\sqrt{p}}{2^{k+1}}) = \frac{p-2\sqrt{p}}{2^{k+1}}((\frac{r_0-1}{r_0})^M + (\frac{r_1-1}{r_1})^M)$$

From the Binomial Theorem it follows that,

$$(-\frac{1}{r_u}+1)^M = 1 - \frac{M}{r_u} + \sum_{\ell=2}^{M} \binom{M}{\ell}(-\frac{1}{r_u})^\ell$$

Observe that if M is even, then the last term in the summation above is positive. So, we can get rid of it and use an inequality. So, let $L = M$ if M is odd and set $L = M - 1$ if M is even. Then,

$$(-\frac{1}{r_u}+1)^M \geq 1 - \frac{M}{r_u} + \sum_{\ell=2}^{L} \binom{L}{\ell}(-\frac{1}{r_u})^\ell$$

$$(-\frac{1}{r_u}+1)^M \geq 1 - \frac{M}{r_u} + \sum_{\ell=1}^{\frac{L-1}{2}} (\frac{1}{r_u})^{2\ell}\binom{L}{2\ell}(1 - \frac{1}{r_u}\frac{L-2\ell}{2\ell+1})$$

Since $M \leq 10^4$ and $k \geq k_c = 64$ it follows from Hasse's Theorem that the term $1 - \frac{1}{r_u}\frac{L-2\ell}{2\ell+1} > 0$ for $u = 0, 1$ and $\ell = 1, 2, ..., (L-1)/2$. So,

$$(-\frac{1}{r_u}+1)^M \geq 1 - \frac{M}{r_u}$$

Recall that $p = 2^k - \delta$ and $1 \leq \delta < \sqrt{2^k}$. So, $p - 2\sqrt{p} > 2^k - 3 * 2^{k/2}$. Since $r_0, r_1 > p - 2\sqrt{p}$,

$$p_1(k) \geq \frac{p-2\sqrt{p}}{2^{k+1}}(2 - \frac{2M}{p-2\sqrt{p}}) > \frac{2^k - 3*2^{k/2}}{2^{k+1}}(2 - \frac{2M}{p-2\sqrt{p}}) = (1 - \frac{3}{2^{k/2}})(1 - \frac{M}{p-2\sqrt{p}})$$

It follows from Definition 5 that the failure probability is negligible in k.

D Security Proof

Algorithm $\mathtt{f}_1$ chooses scalars u_1, u_2, v randomly satisfying the inequality $0 \leq u_1, u_2, v \leq r-1$. However, unlike $\mathtt{f}$, algorithm $\mathtt{f}_1$ gives the additional output u_2. $\mathtt{f}_1(E_{a,b}(\mathbb{F}_p), G, \mathcal{X}, \mathcal{Y}, \mathcal{Z}) = (v\mathcal{X} + u_1G, \mathcal{Y} + u_2G, v\mathcal{Z} + u_1\mathcal{Y} + vu_2\mathcal{X} + u_1u_2G, u_2)$ Algorithm $\mathtt{f}_2$ chooses scalars u_1, v randomly satisfying the inequality $0 \leq u_1, v \leq r-1$. Algorithm $\mathtt{f}_2(E_{a,b}(\mathbb{F}_p), G, \mathcal{X}, \mathcal{Y}, \mathcal{Z}, u_2)$ returns the following tuple $(v\mathcal{X} + u_1G, \mathcal{Y} + u_2G, v\mathcal{Z} + u_1\mathcal{Y} + vu_2\mathcal{X} + u_1u_2G)$.

Let $(X, Y, Z) = \mathtt{f}_2(E_{a,b}(\mathbb{F}_p), G, \mathcal{X}, \mathcal{Y}, \mathcal{Z}, u_2)$. We partition the set of possible inputs to $\mathtt{f}_2$ into two sets, DH triples and non-DH triples.

Suppose that $(\mathcal{X}, \mathcal{Y}, \mathcal{Z})$ is a DH triple. Let $\mathcal{X} = xG$, $\mathcal{Y} = yG$ and $\mathcal{Z} = xyG$. So, $X = (vx + u_1)G$, $Y = (y + u_2)G$, and,

$$Z = (vxy + u_1y + vu_2x + u_1u_2)G = (vx + u_1)(y + u_2)G$$

It follows that (X, Y, Z) is $(\mathcal{X}, \mathcal{Y}, \mathcal{Z})$ transformed as follows. The scalar y is replaced by $y + u_2$ and the scalar x is replaced by the random scalar $vx + u_1$. So, (X, Y, Z) is a DH triple. We say that such a DH triple is a *one-scalar randomized* DH triple of $(\mathcal{X}, \mathcal{Y}, \mathcal{Z})$.

Now suppose that $(\mathcal{X}, \mathcal{Y}, \mathcal{Z})$ is not a DH triple. Then $X, Z \in_R E_{a,b}(\mathbb{F}_p)$. This claim needs justification. Let $\mathcal{Z} = zG$. Observe that $z = xy + c$ for some scalar

$c > 0$. So, $Z = (vx + u_1)(y + u_2)G + v(cG)$. Define $X' = (vx + u_1)G$, $Y' = (y + u_2)G$, and $Z' = (vx + u_1)(y + u_2)G$. Then $(X, Y, Z) = (X', Y', Z' + v(cG))$ and cG is a generator since $c > 0$.

We now consider an "exchange" Φ_2 in which Bob really has no hope of recovering m_k (we will show why later on). Let Φ_2 be the same as Φ_1 except that $\texttt{ExchAlg}_1$ is replaced with $\texttt{ExchAlg}_2$.

$\texttt{ExchAlg}_2(\tau, Y_{0,1}, ..., Y_{0,M}, Y_{1,1}, ..., Y_{1,M})$:
Input: TDDH parameters τ, points $Y_{i,j}$ on
  $E_i(\mathbb{F}_p)$ for $i = 0, 1$, $j = 1, 2, ..., M$
Output: $(m_A, m_k) \in \{0,1\}^{k+1} \times \{0,1\}^M$
1. $(y, s_1, s_2) \leftarrow \texttt{FillGap}(T_{a,b,\beta}(\mathbb{F}_p))$
2. if $(y = 1)$ then output (s_1, s_2) and $\texttt{halt}$
3. $u \leftarrow \texttt{SelCurve}(T_{a,b,\beta}(\mathbb{F}_p))$
4. choose $k_1 \in_R \mathbb{Z}_{r_u}$ and compute $U \leftarrow k_1 G_u$
5. $m_A \leftarrow \texttt{Encode}(T_{a,b,\beta}(\mathbb{F}_p), U, u)$
6. for $j = 1$ to M do:
7.   choose $P_j \in_R E_u(\mathbb{F}_p)$ and compute
     $b_j \leftarrow \texttt{DeriveBit}(T_{a,b,\beta}(\mathbb{F}_p), P_j)$
8. set $m_k \leftarrow b_M || b_{M-1} || ... || b_1$ and output (m_A, m_k)

Lemma 3. *In algorithm* $\texttt{ExchAlg}_2$, $m_A \in_R \{0,1\}^{k+1}$.

Proof. Consider the operation of $\texttt{ExchAlg}_2$. Let s be any string in $\{0,1\}^{k+1} \setminus \mathcal{S}_{a,b,\beta,p}$. Then it follows from the definitions of algorithm $\texttt{FillGap}$ and algorithm $\texttt{Format}$ that $\Pr[m_A = s] = \frac{2\delta-2}{2p+2}\frac{1}{2\delta-2}$. Let P be any point on $E_u(\mathbb{F}_p)$. Then it follows from the definitions of $\texttt{FillGap}$, $\texttt{SelCurve}$, and $\texttt{Encode}$ that the probability that m_A is the Kaliski encoding of P is $\frac{2p+2}{2^{k+1}}\frac{r_u}{2p+2}\frac{1}{r_u}$. It follows that each string contained in $\{0,1\}^{k+1}$ is selected by $\texttt{ExchAlg}_2$ and output as m_A with probability $\frac{1}{2^{k+1}}$.

Fact 1: The following is from the Group Law for $E_{a,b}(\mathbb{F}_p)$ when the prime $p \neq 2, 3$. *Negatives*: If $P = (x, y) \in E_{a,b}(\mathbb{F}_p)$ then $(x, y) + (x, -y) = \mathcal{O}$. The point $(x, -y)$ is denoted by $-P$ and is referred to as the *negative* of P. So, $-P$ is in fact a point on $E_{a,b}(\mathbb{F}_p)$. It is also the case that $-\mathcal{O} = \mathcal{O}$.

Lemma 4. *If* $\#E_{a,b}(\mathbb{F}_p)$ *is odd then there are no points with an ordinate of zero on* $E_{a,b}(\mathbb{F}_p)$.

Proof. Let $f(x) = x^3 + ax + b$ with coefficients in $\mathbb{F}_p$. It is well-known that $f(x) = 0$ has 0 solutions, 1 solution x_1, or 3 solutions x_2, x_3, x_4 in $\mathbb{F}_p$. We consider these 3 cases in turn.

Case 1: There are 0 solutions. Let $\mathcal{S} = E_{a,b}(\mathbb{F}_p) \setminus \{\mathcal{O}\}$. Then $|\mathcal{S}| = \#E_{a,b}(\mathbb{F}_p) - 1$. From Fact 1, all points in $\mathcal{S}$ have the following property: $(x, y) \in \mathcal{S} \Leftrightarrow (x, -y) \in \mathcal{S}$ with $(x, y) \neq (x, -y)$. We now make a partitioning argument. Consider the following two sets.

$$\mathcal{S}_0 = \{(x, y) : (x, y) \in \mathcal{S}, y < p/2\} \qquad \mathcal{S}_1 = \{(x, y) : (x, y) \in \mathcal{S}, y > p/2\}$$

Clearly $\mathcal{S} = \mathcal{S}_0 \bigcup \mathcal{S}_1$, $\mathcal{S}_0 \bigcap \mathcal{S}_1 = \emptyset$, and $|\mathcal{S}_0| = |\mathcal{S}_1|$. So, $|\mathcal{S}| = 2|\mathcal{S}_0|$. It follows that $|\mathcal{S}|$ is even, therefore $\#E_{a,b}(\mathbb{F}_p)$ is odd. This supports our claim.

Case 2: There is one solution x_1 and therefore $(x_1, 0)$ is the only point on $E_{a,b}(\mathbb{F}_p)$ with an ordinate of zero. Let $\mathcal{S} = E_{a,b}(\mathbb{F}_p) \setminus \{\mathcal{O}, (x_1, 0)\}$. Then $|\mathcal{S}| = \#E_{a,b}(\mathbb{F}_p) - 2$. From Fact 1, all points in $\mathcal{S}$ have the following property: $(x, y) \in \mathcal{S} \Leftrightarrow (x, -y) \in \mathcal{S}$ with $(x, y) \neq (x, -y)$. Using the partitioning argument it follows that $|\mathcal{S}|$ is even and therefore $\#E_{a,b}(\mathbb{F}_p)$ is even.

Case 3: The integers x_2, x_3, x_4 are solutions to $f(x) = 0$ and therefore the points $(x_2, 0), (x_3, 0), (x_4, 0)$ are the only points with an ordinate of zero on $E_{a,b}(\mathbb{F}_p)$. Let $\mathcal{S} = E_{a,b}(\mathbb{F}_p) \setminus \{\mathcal{O}, (x_2, 0), (x_3, 0), (x_4, 0)\}$. Then $|\mathcal{S}| = \#E_{a,b}(\mathbb{F}_p) - 4$. By a similar argument, $\#E_{a,b}(\mathbb{F}_p)$ is even.

Lemma 5. *For $u = 0, 1$, the ordered execution of, $P_j \in_R E_u(\mathbb{F}_p)$, followed by $b_j \leftarrow$ `DeriveBit`$(T_{a,b,\beta}(\mathbb{F}_p), P_j)$ causes b_j to be a fair coin flip.*

Proof. Let u be any element in $\{0, 1\}$. Since r_u is odd it follows from Lemma 4 that there are no points with an ordinate of zero on $E_u(\mathbb{F}_p)$. So, aside from the point at infinity, if $(x, y) \in E_u(\mathbb{F}_p)$ then $(x, -y) \in E_u(\mathbb{F}_p)$ where $y \neq 0$. It follows from the definition of Kaliski's X_T function that $E_u(\mathbb{F}_p) \setminus \{\mathcal{O}_u\}$ contains exactly $\frac{r_u - 1}{2}$ points with Kaliski encodings that have an LSB of 0. Similarly, $E_u(\mathbb{F}_p) \setminus \{\mathcal{O}_u\}$ contains exactly $\frac{r_u - 1}{2}$ points with Kaliski encodings that have an LSB of 1. `DeriveBit` returns a fair coin flip on input $\mathcal{O}_u$. So, $\Pr[b_j = 1] = \frac{\frac{r_u - 1}{2}}{r_u} + \frac{1}{r_u}\frac{1}{2} = \frac{1}{2}$.

Lemma 6. *In algorithm* `ExchAlg`$_2$, $m_k \in_R \{0, 1\}^M$.

Proof. Consider algorithm `FillGap`. Clearly, $\Pr[\mu \notin \mathcal{S}_{a,b,\beta,p}] = \frac{2\delta - 2}{2^{k+1}}$. If $\mu \notin \mathcal{S}_{a,b,\beta,p}$ then it follows from the definition of `FillGap` that $s_2 = m_k$ is chosen randomly from $\{0, 1\}^M$. Also, $\Pr[\mu \in \mathcal{S}_{a,b,\beta,p}] = \frac{2p+2}{2^{k+1}}$. If $\mu \in \mathcal{S}_{a,b,\beta,p}$ then from Lemma 5, `ExchAlg`$_2$ chooses $m_k \in_R \{0, 1\}^M$. Either $\mu \in \mathcal{S}_{a,b,\beta,p}$ or not and in both cases it follows that $m_k \in_R \{0, 1\}^M$.

Algorithm `InstTrans` transforms an input TDDH problem instance into a tuple that looks like it is from Φ_1 or from Φ_2. `InstTrans` is used in several proofs in this paper.

`InstTrans`(τ, t_0, t_1):
Input: TDDH problem instance (τ, t_0, t_1) where
  $t_i = (\mathcal{X}^{(i)}, \mathcal{Y}^{(i)}, \mathcal{Z}^{(i)})$ are points on $E_i(\mathbb{F}_p)$ for $i = 0, 1$
Output: $(\tau, Y_{0,1}, ..., Y_{0,M}, Y_{1,1}, ..., Y_{1,M}, m_A, m_k)$
1. $(y, s_1, s_2) \leftarrow$ `FillGap`$(T_{a,b,\beta}(\mathbb{F}_p))$
2. if $(y = 1)$ then
3.   choose $Y_{i,j} \in_R E_i(\mathbb{F}_p)$ for $i = 0, 1$, $j = 1, 2, ..., M$
4. $(m_A, m_k) \leftarrow (s_1, s_2)$
5.   **halt** with $(\tau, Y_{0,1}, ..., Y_{0,M}, Y_{1,1}, ..., Y_{1,M}, m_A, m_k)$
6. $u \leftarrow$ `SelCurve`$(T_{a,b,\beta}(\mathbb{F}_p))$

7. $(X, Y, Z, u_2) \leftarrow \mathtt{f}_1(E_u(\mathbb{F}_p), G_u, \mathcal{X}^{(u)}, \mathcal{Y}^{(u)}, \mathcal{Z}^{(u)})$
8. $m_A \leftarrow \mathtt{Encode}(T_{a,b,\beta}(\mathbb{F}_p), Y, u)$
9. for $j = 1$ to M do:
10. $\quad (X_j, Y_j, Z_j) \leftarrow \mathtt{f}_2(E_u(\mathbb{F}_p), G_u, \mathcal{X}^{(u)}, \mathcal{Y}^{(u)}, \mathcal{Z}^{(u)}, u_2)$
11. $\quad$ set $Y_{u,j} \leftarrow X_j$ and choose $Y_{1-u,j} \in_R E_{1-u}(\mathbb{F}_p)$
12. $\quad$ set $P_j \leftarrow Z_j$ and $b_j \leftarrow \mathtt{DeriveBit}(T_{a,b,\beta}(\mathbb{F}_p), P_j)$
13. $m_k \leftarrow b_M || b_{M-1} || ... || b_1$
14. output $(\tau, Y_{0,1}, ..., Y_{0,M}, Y_{1,1}, ..., Y_{1,M}, m_A, m_k)$

Lemma 7. *TDDH polytime reduces to the problem of distinguishing $\mathcal{T}_{\tau,\Phi_1}$ from $\mathcal{T}_{\tau,\Phi_2}$ with an advantage that is non-negligible (in k).*

Proof. Suppose there exists an algorithm D that distinguishes $\mathcal{T}_{\tau,\Phi_1}$ from $\mathcal{T}_{\tau,\Phi_2}$ with an advantage that is non-negligible in k. Consider the polytime (in k) algorithm `InstTrans` that takes as input a problem instance (τ, t_0, t_1) for TDDH.

Suppose that both t_0 and t_1 are DH triples. From the correctness of $\mathtt{f}_1$ and $\mathtt{f}_2$, the (X_j, Y_j, Z_j) for $j = 1, 2, ..., M$ in algorithm `InstTrans` are all one-scalar randomized DH triples of the input Diffie-Hellman triple $(\mathcal{X}^{(u)}, \mathcal{Y}^{(u)}, \mathcal{Z}^{(u)})$ where $u \in \{0, 1\}$ is selected using `SelCurve` in algorithm `InstTrans`. So, the output of algorithm `InstTrans` given by the tuple $(\tau, Y_{0,1}, ..., Y_{0,M}, Y_{1,1}, ..., Y_{1,M}, m_A, m_k)$ is drawn from the same set and probability distribution as in Φ_1.

Suppose t_0 and t_1 are not DH triples. From the correctness of $\mathtt{f}_1$ and $\mathtt{f}_2$, $(X_j, Z_j) \in_R E_u(\mathbb{F}_p) \times E_u(\mathbb{F}_p)$ for $j = 1, 2, ..., M$. So, the output of algorithm `InstTrans` given by the tuple $(\tau, Y_{0,1}, ..., Y_{0,M}, Y_{1,1}, ..., Y_{1,M}, m_A, m_k)$ is drawn from the same set and probability distribution as in Φ_2.

Therefore, D(`InstTrans`(τ, t_0, t_1)) solves TDDH.

Let protocol Φ_3 be the same as protocol Φ_2 except that algorithm $\mathtt{ExchAlg}_2$ is replaced with algorithm $\mathtt{ExchAlg}_3$.

$\mathtt{ExchAlg}_3(\tau, Y_{0,1}, ..., Y_{0,M}, Y_{1,1}, ..., Y_{1,M})$:
Input: TDDH parameters τ, points $Y_{i,j}$ on
$\quad E_i(\mathbb{F}_p)$ for $i = 0, 1$, $j = 1, 2, ..., M$
Output: $(m_A, m_k) \in \{0,1\}^{k+1} \times \{0,1\}^M$
1. choose $m_A \in_R \{0,1\}^{k+1}$ and $m_k \in_R \{0,1\}^M$
2. output (m_A, m_k)

Lemma 8. *$\mathcal{T}_{\tau,\Phi_2}$ is perfectly indistinguishable from $\mathcal{T}_{\tau,\Phi_3}$.*

Lemma 9. *TDDH polytime reduces to the problem of distinguishing $\mathcal{T}_{\tau,\Phi_1}$ from $\mathcal{T}_{\tau,U}$ with an advantage that is non-negligible (in k).*

Lemma 8 follows from Lemmas 3, 6. But, $\mathcal{T}_{\tau,U} = \mathcal{T}_{\tau,\Phi_3}$. So, lemmas 7 and 8 give Lemma 9. Theorem 5 and Lemma 9 imply Theorem 1.

Provably Secure Convertible Undeniable Signatures with Unambiguity

Le Trieu Phong[1], Kaoru Kurosawa[2], and Wakaha Ogata[3]

[1] NICT, Japan
phong@nict.go.jp
[2] Ibaraki University, Japan
kurosawa@mx.ibaraki.ac.jp
[3] Tokyo Institute of Technology, Japan
wakaha@mot.titech.ac.jp

Abstract. This paper shows some efficient and provably-secure convertible undeniable signature schemes (with both selective conversion and all conversion), in the standard model and discrete logarithm setting. They further satisfy unambiguity, which is traditionally required for anonymous signatures. Briefly, unambiguity means that it is hard to generate a (message, signature) pair which is valid for two *different* public-keys. In other words, our schemes can be viewed as anonymous signature schemes as well as convertible undeniable signature schemes. Besides other applications, we show that such schemes are very suitable for anonymous auction.

Keywords: Undeniable signatures, selective/all conversion, anonymous signatures, discrete logarithm, standard model.

1 Introduction

1.1 Background

Undeniable Signatures. Almost twenty years ago, Chaum and van Antwerpen [10] introduced the concept of undeniable signature (US) scheme, where a signature is not publicly verifiable, which is in contrast to ordinary signature schemes. The verification of an undeniable signature requires the cooperation of the signer through the zero-knowledge confirmation protocol (for validity of signatures) and zero-knowledge disavowal protocol (for invalidity of signatures). A mandatory property of a US scheme thus is *invisibility*, namely without interacting with the signer, it is hard to decide whether a signature is valid or not. Also, it is worth noting that either the confirmation or disavowal protocol must be successful if the signer is honest; and the case both protocols fail formally implies that the signer is not cooperating (or cheating).

Undeniable signature is useful when we sign on sensitive data such as software [5], electronic cash [6, 34, 11], confidential business agreement [12]. There have been a wide range of research on the concept [5, 9, 12, 30, 18, 25, 26, 23, 27, 39, 29,

J.A. Garay and R. De Prisco (Eds.): SCN 2010, LNCS 6280, pp. 291–308, 2010.

28, 24], to list just a few. Most of the papers are in the random oracle model, with (even arbitrary) short signatures [29], or extensive security consideration of a classical scheme [30]. In the standard model, the first efficient proposal is that of Laguillaumie and Vergnaud [27] (but relying on a non-standard and strong assumption for invisibility).

In order to link undeniable signature to regular signature, Boyar et al [5] proposed the concept of conversion. In *all conversion*, the signer releases a piece of information so that all issued undeniable signatures can be publicly-verifiable. In *selective conversion*, the signer publishes a piece of information so that a single undeniable signature is publicly-verifiable. The paper [5] gave a generic construction of US scheme with selective and all conversion from one-way function, but the construction is not practical. Note that selectively-convertible undeniable signature schemes play a central role in fair payment protocols [6], so the more efficient the former is, the more practical the latter can be realized. For more applications, the readers may find in [12, 5]. We also note that the above mentioned work of Laguillaumie and Vergnaud [27], while producing very short signatures (of about 170 bits), does not support any kinds of conversion.

In an attempt to realize practical US schemes with conversions, Damgard and Pedersen [12] proposed two dlog-based schemes, but they could not formally prove the invisibility of their schemes, and just conjectured on it. Recently, another attempt was made by Yuen et al [39] using pairings, but their scheme suffers from a big (exponential) loss factor in security reduction, so that the signer is only able to produce very few (less than 128) signatures. The scheme in [39] is claimed to satisfy invisibility, but in the full version of this paper [33], we point out that the claim is incorrect. More recently, El Aimani [13] proposed some generic approaches for building efficient undeniable signature schemes, but with no selective conversion. In the full version [16] of [13], El Aimani claims selective conversion property, but we observe that the claim is correct only if the signer is honest.

However, there exists no convertible undeniable signature scheme which satisfies *unambiguity* which will be explained below.

ANONYMOUS SIGNATURES. The concept is proposed by Yang et al [38] (at PKC '06), and has further study in [17,1,40,35]. Anonymous signatures and undeniable signatures share the same goal of ensuring anonymity (implied by invisibility in this paper) by not revealing the link between signatures and public-keys. However, compared to undeniable signature schemes, anonymous signature schemes do not necessarily have confirmation/disavowal protocols; and yet they have one more security notion called *unambiguity*.

To explain more about anonymous signatures, let us recall its typical application suggested in all previous works, which is anonymous auction where Alice (with pk_A) wishes to place a bid with value bid_A. She wants to be able to claim the bid as hers in case it wins, but otherwise wishes to remain anonymous. The natural solution is to provide, at bidding time, the values bid_A, pk_A, as well as her anonymous signature of bid_A. Later, when the result is announced, and if Alice has won, she can release the relevant opening information to claim her bid.

We however observe that the above usage of anonymous signatures in auction may cause trouble, which is overlooked by previous works. Imagine a situation in which Alice has won, but refuses to provide the opening information. The natural solution for the auctioneer is to choose the second-highest bid_B of Bob as the winning bid. The real trouble now is that, if Alice and Bob cooperate, they will win every auction! Alice places the highest bid just after Bob, and then refuses to open her signature on the bid, so that Bob will be the winner. This is clearly unfair to other players in the auction. All existing works on anonymous signatures have not noticed the situation that either the winner refuses to open, or there is cooperation between two users[1].

To overcome the above trouble, we then suggest that one should use undeniable signature schemes with selective conversion in anonymous auction, *provided that* they meet all security notions of anonymous signatures. Alice then cannot deny her signature of the bid anymore, since the auctioneer can execute the confirmation and disavowal protocols to check.

Let us now explain the unambiguity notion [1] (aka, unpretendability [35]). It intuitively ensures that if Alice has won, and releases the opening information to claim her bid, then no one else can claim that bid. Previously, unambiguity was not considered as a security notion for undeniable signature schemes. However, to serve in the context of anonymous auction as we suggested above, undeniable signature schemes must satisfy unambiguity.

1.2 Our Contribution

We propose two convertible undeniable signature schemes satisfying anonymity, called SCUS_1 and SCUS_2. They have the following properties.

- The schemes support both selective and all conversion. Moreover, they enjoy formally-proven security in the standard model, relying on the strong Diffie-Hellman (sDH) and the decision linear (DLIN) assumption. Their confirmation and disavowal protocols are of (minimal) four moves[2].
- The signature size is about $70 + 3 \cdot |q|$ (resp, $4 \cdot |q|$) bits for SCUS_1 (resp, SCUS_2) where $|q| \approx 170$. The piece of information for all conversion is of $2 \cdot |q|$ bits for both schemes. For each selective conversion, the piece of information is also $2 \cdot |q|$ bits if we accept stateful signers; otherwise, we employ the NIZK proof of Groth and Sahai [20], and need to release a few more bits.

[1] Interestingly, we find that what we discuss for anonymous auction still applies in principle to Yahoo auction in Yapan. Namely, in the Yahoo auction, if two identities (e.g., of one person) cooperate in the way we have described, they will have advantages over ones proceeding honestly. The point is in the Yahoo auction, the winning identity can easily deny contacting the seller for paying process, making the seller to choose the identity with second-highest bid as the winner.

[2] We remark that the 3-move scheme of Kurosawa and Heng [24] is insecure, as shown by Ogata et al in [30] (Sect.V.D, page 2013), who furthermore point out that any 3-move (HVZK) confirmation/disavowal protocols are not secure against active attacks.

- Both SCUS_1 and SCUS_2 additionally meet the unambiguity notion, under the discrete log assumption. Therefore, they can be used in anonymous auction to detect the winner in case she refuses to open (namely, convert) her signature. It is worth noting that it is unknown whether previous undeniable signature schemes with selective conversion have this additional property.

Above, the scheme SCUS_1 produces shorter signatures than SCUS_2, but the public key of SCUS_1 (of $170 \cdot |q|$ bits) is much longer than that of SCUS_2 (of $12 \cdot |q|$ bits). Choosing which one to use thus depends on specific applications.

Let us now look at the ways to obtain the above results. We first focus on the ideas behind SCUS_1.

Sign-then-Encrypt Paradigm. We re-utilize an elegant paradigm introduced by Damgard and Pedersen [12] in which the undeniable signature σ of a message m is of the form $\sigma = \mathsf{Encrypt}_{pk_2}(\mathsf{Sign}_{sk_1}(m))$, where Encrypt and Sign are respectively some regular encryption and signature scheme. For all conversion, the signer publishes the secret key sk_2 of the encryption scheme, so that everyone can decrypt σ to get the regular signature $\mathsf{Sign}_{sk_1}(m)$ and then check its validity. For selective conversion, the signer releases the regular signature $\mathsf{Sign}_{sk_1}(m)$.

Some difficulties when using the above paradigm are: (1) designing efficient zero-knowledge confirmation and disavowal protocols, (2) proving the invisibility of the designed scheme, and (3) releasing $\mathsf{Sign}_{sk_1}(m)$ in a provable way (that it is the signature encrypted in σ). Damgard and Pedersen [12] have overcome (1) but not (2). For (3), they suggested a method of storing all randomness previously used in signing. We suggest another method by using the efficient NIZK proof of Groth and Sahai [20], as seen later.

To overcome (1) (and (3) in an efficient way), one needs to properly choose simple (but-secure-enough) ingredients. To design SCUS_1, we choose the Generic Bilinear Map (GBM) signature [21] and the linear encryption [3] (LE) scheme. A GBM signature on m is of the form $(s, \rho = H(m)^{1/(x+s)})$ for a random s, a standard model hash function H and the secret key $sk_1 = x$. We use the LE scheme to encrypt ρ in the ciphertext $(u_1 = g_1^{r_1}, u_2 = g_2^{r_2}, u_3 = \rho \cdot g^{r_1+r_2})$ for randomness r_1, r_2. The undeniable signature $\sigma = (s, u_1, u_2, u_3)$.

Intuitively, σ seems random-like, unrelated to m, (and thus invisible) because s is random and (u_1, u_2, u_3) is random-like under the decision linear assumption. However, the scheme is in fact *not* invisible. The reason is in the malleability of LE scheme. In particular, if $\sigma = (s, u_1, u_2, u_3)$ is valid on a message m (resp, σ is random), then $\sigma' = (s, u_1 g_1^{\alpha}, u_2 g_2^{\beta}, u_3 g^{\alpha+\beta})$ is also valid on m (resp, σ' is random) for adversarily-chosen randomness α and β. The fact causes a simple attack on the invisibility of (m, σ) as follows: the adversary first asks the signer for converting (m, σ'), so that it knows the validity of the pair, and hence it also is aware of whether the corresponding (m, σ) is valid. (See Definition 3 for a formal definition on invisibility, which also contains some new insights.)

Fortunately, we can overcome the above attack as follows: we authenticate the randomness r_1, r_2 by signing on u_1 and u_2. In our proposed SCUS_1 scheme (in Sect.4), the values $(u_1 = g_1^{r_1}, u_2 = g_2^{r_2})$ are generated first, then the GBM signature on m, u_1, u_2 is created: $\big(s, \rho = H(m \parallel u_1 \parallel u_2)^{1/(x+s)}\big)$. After all, set $u_3 = \rho \cdot g^{r_1+r_2}$ and let the undeniable signature $\sigma = (s, u_1, u_2, u_3)$. With the authentication on the randomness, the adversarily-formed σ' above becomes invalid regardless of whether σ is valid on m, so that the validity of σ' cannot be used to decide that of σ. We succeed in proving the invisibility of our proposed scheme in Theorem 6.

ON CONFIRMATION AND DISAVOWAL PROTOCOL. Now we give ideas on constructing the confirmation and disavowal protocol for SCUS_1. To confirm $(m, \sigma = (s, u_1, u_2, u_3))$, the signer needs to prove for secrets $x_1 (= \mathrm{dlog}_{g_1} g)$, $x_2 (= \mathrm{dlog}_{g_2} g)$, and x:

$$\frac{u_3}{u_1^{x_1} u_2^{x_2}} = H(m \parallel u_1 \parallel u_2)^{\frac{1}{x+s}}.$$

Namely, the LE decryption of (u_1, u_2, u_3) gives the GBM signature on m, u_1, u_2. Or equivalently,

$$u_3^x \cdot u_1^{-x_1(x+s)} \cdot u_2^{-x_2(x+s)} = H(m \parallel u_1 \parallel u_2) \cdot u_3^{-s},$$

which is a proof of representation of public value $H(m \parallel u_1 \parallel u_2) \cdot u_3^{-s}$, and can be realized by standard techniques, using constant moves.

Now we turn to the disavowal protocol. Given $(m, \sigma = (s, u_1, u_2, u_3))$, the signer needs to prove for secrets x_1, x_2, x:

$$\frac{u_3}{u_1^{x_1} u_2^{x_2}} \neq H(m \parallel u_1 \parallel u_2)^{\frac{1}{x+s}},$$

or equivalently,

$$u_3^{x+s} \cdot u_1^{-x_1(x+s)} \cdot u_2^{-x_2(x+s)} \cdot H(m \parallel u_1 \parallel u_2)^{-1} \neq 1.$$

Employing the technique of Camenisch and Shoup [8], we choose $r \xleftarrow{\$} Z_q$ and set

$$U = \left(u_3^{x+s} \cdot u_1^{-x_1(x+s)} \cdot u_2^{-x_2(x+s)} \cdot H(m \parallel u_1 \parallel u_2)^{-1}\right)^r.$$

The signer sends U to the verifier, who checks that $U \neq 1$. Then both execute a proof of representation of U, where the signer holds the secrets r, x, x_1, x_2. The zero-knowledge protocol can also be accomplished via standard techniques, also using constant moves. Moreover, since we will work on a pairing group, the disavowal protocol can be made non-interactive, again thanks to the NIZK proof of Groth-Sahai [20], interestingly yielding a way to efficiently "convert" (namely, make publicly-verifiable) *even invalid* signatures.

MORE SCHEMES. The above ideas work well if we replace the GBM signature by the signature of Boneh and Boyen [2], which is of the form $(s, g_0^{1/(x+H(m)+ys)})$ for random $s \in Z_q$, $g_0 \in G$, and secret signing key x, y. The replacement creates our SCUS_2 described in Sect.5. Furthermore, in the random oracle model, one can use the BLS signature [4] so that the unforgeability of the resulting undeniable signature scheme relies on the CDH assumption in bilinear group. We do not explicitly consider the random oracle scheme in this paper.

More Related Works. Subsequent to a preliminary version of this work [33] on the Eprint, Schuldt, Matsuura [37], and Huang, Wong [22] have suggested some other schemes with interesting additional properties. Both works indicate that, if using NIZK proofs in undeniable signatures, the common reference string must be legitimately set up (say, by a trusted party like the CA in PKI). Unfortunately, the scheme of Huang and Wong [22] turned out not satisfying anonymity, as shown in [37]. The scheme of [37], while relying on a more standard assumption, produces longer signatures (or public keys) than the ones in this paper. Both works [37, 22] do not consider unambiguity.

Independently with us, El Aimani [14] also discovered the usage of the NIZK of Groth and Sahai [20] in the context of confirmer signatures. The sign-then-encrypt approach is also used to build confirmer signatures in [15] in an abstract manner. As a trade-off to its generality, the construction in [15] has to employ the cut-and-choose technique for the confirmation and disavowal protocols, and hence the protocols are not of constant rounds (say, 80 rounds to reach 2^{-80} soundness error). In contrast, we take a concrete approach in this paper, resulting in schemes with minimal 4-round protocols.

The above sign-then-encrypt paradigm has also been successfully re-used in [32] in the RSA-based setting, creating RSA-based US schemes supporting (selective and all) conversions, with signatures of $(80 + 2 \cdot 1024)$ bits, converters of 1024 bits, while the securities rely on the strong RSA assumption and the decisional N-th residuosity (DNR) assumption in the standard model. Note that the RSA-based schemes give longer signatures than dlog-based schemes, as usual.

2 Syntax and Definitions

We begin with the syntax of selectively-convertible undeniable signature (SCUS for short) schemes. We focus on the syntax of schemes with selective conversion here and do not explicitly describe the syntax of all conversion since the latter is very simple in our proposals.

Definition 1 (SCUS scheme). *A selectively-convertible undeniable signature scheme SCUS = (KeyGen, Usign, Convert, Verify, Confirm, Disavowal) consists of four algorithms and two protocols whose descriptions are as follows.*

– KeyGen$(1^\kappa) \to (pk, sk)$: This algorithm generates the public key pk and the secret key (signing key) sk for user.

– USign$(sk, m) \to \sigma$: Using the secret key sk, this algorithm produces a signature σ on a message m.

– Convert$(sk, m, \sigma) \to cvt / \perp$: Using sk, this algorithm releases a converter cvt if the message-signature (m, σ) pair is valid, enabling everyone to check the validity of the pair. If the pair is invalid, the output of the algorithm is $\perp$.[3]

[3] Note that only valid undeniable signatures can be converted, and the signer has no responsibility to convert ill-formed ones. These properties are natural, and sufficient enough for application (e.g., [6]). However, we note in our proposed schemes, the signer can even "convert" invalid signatures by making the disavowal protocol non-interactive (via Groth-Sahai result [20], as seen later).

– *Verify*$(pk, m, \sigma, cvt) \rightarrow 0/1$: *Using the converter* cvt*, everyone can check the validity of* (m, σ) *by this algorithm.*

– *Confirm: This is a protocol between the signer and a verifier, on common input* (pk, m, σ)*, the signer with* sk *proves that* (m, σ) *is a valid message-signature pair in zero-knowledge.*

– *Disavowal: This is a protocol between the signer and a verifier, on common input* (pk, m, σ)*, the signer with* sk *proves that* (m, σ) *is an invalid message-signature pair in zero-knowledge.*

Definition 2 (Unforgeability and strong unforgeability of SCUS). *A selectively convertible undeniable signature scheme SCUS is said to be existential unforgeable under adaptive chosen message attack if no poly-time forger* $\mathcal{F}$ *has a non-negligible advantage in the following game: at the beginning,* $\mathcal{F}$ *is given the public key* pk*. Then* $\mathcal{F}$ *is permitted to issue a series of queries shown below.*

– *Signing queries:* $\mathcal{F}$ *submits a message* m *to the signing oracle and receives a signature* σ *on* m*. These queries are adaptive, namely the next query can depend on the answers of previous ones.*

– *Convert queries:* $\mathcal{F}$ *submits a message-signature pair* (m, σ) *to the convert oracle, and receives a converter* cvt*. These queries are also adaptive.*

– *Confirmation/disavowal queries:* $\mathcal{F}$ *submits a message-signature pair of the form* (m, σ) *to the confirmation/disavowal oracle. We will consider active attack, where the oracle first checks the validity of* (m, σ)*. If it is a valid pair, the oracle returns* 1 *and executes the confirmation protocol with* $\mathcal{F}$ *(acting as a cheating verifier). Otherwise, the oracle returns* 0 *and executes the disavowal protocol with* $\mathcal{F}$*.*

At the end of the game, $\mathcal{F}$ *outputs a pair* (m^*, σ^*)*. In the definition of unforgeability, the forger* $\mathcal{F}$ *wins the game if the pair* (m^*, σ^*) *is a valid message-signature pair, and* m^* *has never been queried to the signing oracle. The advantage of* $\mathcal{F}$ *is defined to be* $\mathbf{Adv}_{SCUS}^{forge}(\mathcal{F}) = \Pr[\mathcal{F}\ wins]$.

In the definition of strong unforgeability, the only different point is that (m^*, σ^*) *does not coincide with any* (m, σ) *at signing queries. We denote* $\mathcal{F}$*'s advantage in this case by* $\mathbf{Adv}_{SCUS}^{sforge}(\mathcal{F}) = \Pr[\mathcal{F}\ wins]$.

The notion of invisibility intuitively ensures that no-one (without contacting the signer) can tell whether a message-signature pair is valid or not, and is formally given below. We note that this definition is new to this work.

Definition 3 (Strong invisibility). *A selectively-convertible undeniable signature scheme SCUS satisfies strong invisibility under adaptive chosen message attack if no poly-time distinguisher* $\mathcal{D}$ *has a non-negligible advantage in the following game. At first,* $\mathsf{KeyGen}(1^\kappa) \rightarrow (pk, sk)$*, and then* $\mathcal{D}$ *is given the public key* pk*. Then* $\mathcal{D}$ *is permitted to issue a series of queries: signing queries, convert queries, confirmation/disavowal queries, as in Definition 2.*

At some point, $\mathcal{D}$ *outputs an arbitrary message* m^**, and requests a challenge signature* σ^* *on* m^**. The challenge signature* σ^* *is generated based on a hidden bit* b*. If* $b = 0$*, then* σ^* *is generated as usual using the signing algorithm; otherwise* σ^*

is chosen randomly from the signature space of the scheme (which only depends on the security parameter κ, and not on pk, sk).

The distinguisher $\mathcal{D}$ may additionally issue signing queries, convert queries, confirmation/disavowal queries with the only restriction that no confirmation/disavowal query and convert query (m^*, σ^*) are allowed.

At the end, $\mathcal{D}$ outputs a bit b' as the guess for b. The distinguisher wins the game if and only if $b' = b$ and its advantage is defined as $\mathbf{Adv}^{inv}_{SCUS}(\mathcal{D}) = |\Pr[b' = b] - 1/2|$.

Remarks 1. *Above, there are some subtleties. First, we do allow the distinguisher to submit convert queries of the form (m^*, σ) with $\sigma \neq \sigma^*$.*

Second, $\mathcal{D}$ can make signing query m^*, even in multiple times, even before and after the challenge query. Intuitively, a scheme meeting the definition enables the signer to sign on the same message many times without any loss in invisibility, so that the scheme is very suitable and easy to use at least in licensing software, which is one of the main applications, where one piece of software may be signed many times. This second subtlety makes our definition differ from and stronger than previous ones (say, that of [30]). A scheme meeting the (weak) definition as in [30] can be turned into another one satisfying our definition by ensuring that the signing messages are pairwise different (via randomness, the time when signing, etc).

Similarly to the second point above, we believe that strong unforgeability is very suitable for undeniable signature schemes, especially in the context of licensing software. Our proposals fortunately meet these strong notions of security.

Another security notion for undeniable signatures is anonymity, intuitively ensuring that given a message-signature pair, it is hard to know who *produces the pair. As pointed out in [18], invisibility implies anonymity if all signers share a common signature space, a condition fulfilled by our proposals. We thus focus on invisibility in the rest of this paper.*

Definition 4 (Standard signature schemes). *A signature scheme S = (Kg, Sign, Vrf) is as follows. On input 1^κ, the key generation algorithm Kg produces the public key pk and the secret signing key sk. On input sk and a message m, the signing algorithm Sign produces a signature σ, which is publicly-verifiable using the verification algorithm Vrf on input pk and σ.*

The unforgeability under chosen message attack (uf-cma security) of a signature scheme S is defined essentially the same as that of SCUS in Definition 2, except that the forger $\mathcal{F}$ against S only issues signing queries. We denote the advantage of $\mathcal{F}$ by $\mathbf{Adv}^{uf-cma}_{S}(\mathcal{F}) = \Pr[\mathcal{F}\ wins]$. The strong unforgeability (suf-cma security) is defined in a similar manner and we have the advantage $\mathbf{Adv}^{suf-cma}_{S}(\mathcal{F}) = \Pr[\mathcal{F}\ wins]$.

3 Preliminaries

PAIRING GROUP. We call $\mathbb{PG} = (G, G_T, q = |G|, g, \hat{e} : G \times G \to G_T)$ a pairing group if G and G_T are cyclic groups of prime order q, where the bit length

$|q| = \kappa \approx 170$. The element g is a generator of G, and the mapping $\hat{e}$ satisfies the following properties: $\hat{e}(g,g) \neq 1$, and $\hat{e}(g^a, g^b) = \hat{e}(g,g)^{ab}$.

Dlog Assumption. The assumption claims that, given $\mathbb{PG}$ as above, and for all poly-time adversary $\mathcal{A}$, $\mathbf{Adv}^{dlog}_{G,\mathbb{PG}}(\mathcal{A}) = \Pr[h = g^x : g, h \stackrel{\$}{\leftarrow} G; x \stackrel{\$}{\leftarrow} \mathcal{A}(g, h, \mathbb{PG})]$ is negligible.

Decision Linear Assumption. Given a pairing group $\mathbb{PG}$, the assumption, first formalized in [3], asserts that the following advantage of a poly-time adversary $\mathcal{A}$ is negligible in the security parameter κ.

$$\mathbf{Adv}^{dlin}_{G}(\mathcal{A}) = \left| \Pr\left[b' = b : \begin{array}{c} \alpha, \beta, \gamma \stackrel{\$}{\leftarrow} Z_q; g_1, g_2, g_3 \stackrel{\$}{\leftarrow} G; \\ T_0 \leftarrow g_3^{\alpha+\beta}; T_1 \leftarrow g_3^{\gamma}; b \stackrel{\$}{\leftarrow} \{0,1\}; \\ b' \stackrel{\$}{\leftarrow} \mathcal{A}(\mathbb{PG}, g_1, g_2, g_3, g_1^{\alpha}, g_2^{\beta}, T_b) \end{array} \right] - \frac{1}{2} \right|.$$

Known Dlog-Based ZKIP. We use known techniques for proving statements about discrete logarithms, such as (1) proof of knowledge of discrete logarithm [36]; (2) proof of knowledge of an element representation in a prime order group [31]; and the $\wedge$ proof of (1) and (2). (The $\wedge$ proof is easily designed by choosing the same challenge while asking the prover to prove both (1) and (2) in parallel.) These proofs need four moves to become zero-knowledge.

When referring to the proofs above, we use the following kind of notation. For instance, $\mathrm{PoK}\{(x_1, x_2)\colon y = g^{x_1} \wedge U = u_1^{x_1} u_2^{x_2}\}$ denotes a zero-knowledge proof of knowledge of x_1 and x_2 such that $y = g^{x_1}$ and $U = u_1^{x_1} u_2^{x_2}$. All values except (x_1, x_2) are assumed to be known to the verifier.

Known NIZK Proof. We utilize the non-interactive zero-knowledge (NIZK) proof for proving that *a system* of equations of the form $g_0 = \Pi_{j=1}^{m} g_j^{X_j}$, over a group G (with pairing as above) is satisfiable, where X_j are variables and $g_0, \ldots, g_m$ are constants in G. This is derived from the result of Groth and Sahai [20]. We will mention more about the NIZK proofs later.

4 Our Proposed SCUS_1

In this section, we describe our first selectively convertible undeniable signature (SCUS) scheme and analyze its securities.

4.1 Building Blocks

We first need the following ingredients, which operate on a common pairing group $\mathbb{PG} = (G, G_T, q = |G|, g, \hat{e} : G \times G \to G_T)$. The pairing group is implicitly included in the public keys of the following schemes.

Generic Bilinear Map Signature Scheme GBM [21]. The signature scheme GBM = (GBM.Kg, GBM.Sign, GBM.Vrf) is briefly recalled with some minor modifications as follows.

$\mathsf{GBM.Kg}(1^\kappa)$: Generate $x \xleftarrow{\$} Z_q$, $X \leftarrow g^x$, and $H : \{0,1\}^* \to G$. Return the verifying key $pk_1 = (X, H, \eta)$ where $\eta = 70$ and the signing key $sk_1 = x$. (The public key size $|pk_1| \approx 162 \cdot \log_2 q$ bits, according to the estimation in [21], due to the concrete description of H.)

$\mathsf{GBM.Sign}(sk_1, m \in \{0,1\}^*)$: $s \xleftarrow{\$} \{0,1\}^\eta$, $\rho \leftarrow H(m)^{\frac{1}{x+s}} \in G$. Return $(s, \rho) \in \{0,1\}^\eta \times G$ as the signature on m.

$\mathsf{GBM.Vrf}(pk_1, m, (s, \rho))$: Check that $(s, \rho) \in \{0,1\}^\eta \times G$ and $\hat{e}(\rho, X \cdot g^s) = \hat{e}(H(m), g)$. Return 1 if all checks pass, else return 0.

The signature scheme is known to be strongly unforgeable (suf-cma secure) under the strong Diffie-Hellman assumption. To be complete, the proof given in [21] is for the uf-cma case, but holds even for suf-cma security.

LINEAR ENCRYPTION [3]. The linear encryption scheme LE= (LE.Kg, LE.Enc, LE.Dec) is as follows.

$\mathsf{LE.Kg}(1^\kappa)$: Generate $x_1, x_2 \xleftarrow{\$} Z_q$ and set $g_1 \leftarrow g^{1/x_1}$, $g_2 \leftarrow g^{1/x_2}$. Return the public key $pk_2 = (g_1, g_2)$ and the secret key $sk_2 = (x_1, x_2)$.

$\mathsf{LE.Enc}(pk_2, m \in G)$: Choose $r_1, r_2 \xleftarrow{\$} Z_q$ and set $u_1 \leftarrow g_1^{r_1}$, $u_2 \leftarrow g_2^{r_2}$, $u_3 \leftarrow m \cdot g^{r_1+r_2}$. Return (u_1, u_2, u_3) as the ciphertext of m.

$\mathsf{LE.Dec}(sk_2, (u_1, u_2, u_3))$: Return $u_3/(u_1^{x_1} u_2^{x_2})$.

The scheme is ind-cpa-secure under the decision linear assumption [3].

4.2 The Scheme SCUS$_1$

The scheme is described as follows.

$\mathsf{KeyGen}(1^\kappa)$: Run $\mathsf{GBM.Kg}(1^\kappa)$ and $\mathsf{LE.Kg}(1^\kappa)$ to get (pk_1, sk_1) and (pk_2, sk_2). Return the public key $pk = (pk_1, pk_2)$ and the signing key $sk = (sk_1, sk_2)$.

$\mathsf{USign}(sk, m)$: First, generate $r_1, r_2 \xleftarrow{\$} Z_q$, and set $u_1 \leftarrow g_1^{r_1}$, $u_2 \leftarrow g_2^{r_2}$, and $\overline{m} = m \parallel u_1 \parallel u_2$. Next, sign on $\overline{m}$ to get $\left(s, \rho = H(\overline{m})^{\frac{1}{x+s}}\right) \xleftarrow{\$} \mathsf{GBM.Sign}(sk_1, \overline{m})$. Then, encrypt ρ in the ciphertext $(u_1, u_2, u_3 = \rho \cdot g^{r_1+r_2})$. Return the undeniable signature $\sigma = (s, u_1, u_2, u_3)$.

$\mathsf{Convert}(sk, m, \sigma)$: Parse σ as $(s, u_1, u_2, u_3) \in \{0,1\}^\eta \times G^3$, and let $\rho \leftarrow u_3/(u_1^{x_1} u_2^{x_2})$. If (s, ρ) is not a GBM signature on $m \parallel u_1 \parallel u_2$ then return $\perp$. Otherwise, return the converter $(\rho, \pi) \in G \times G^{12}$, where π is a NIZK proof proving (with secrets x_1, x_2):

$$g = g_1^{x_1}, g = g_2^{x_2}, u_3/\rho = u_1^{x_1} u_2^{x_2}. \tag{1}$$

Such a NIZK proof π can be efficiently created using the result of Groth and Sahai [20]. See the full version [33] for the concrete description of π.

Another method of converting, inspired by Damgard and Pedersen [12], is to store the randomness r_1, r_2 used in signing and later release them as converter. Then, everyone can check $u_1 = g_1^{r_1}, u_2 = g_2^{r_2}$ and compute ρ as $u_3/g^{r_1+r_2}$.

To do all conversion, release $sk_2 = (x_1, x_2)$ so that everyone can compute $\rho = u_3/(u_1^{x_1} u_2^{x_2})$ and then check whether (s, ρ) is a valid GBM signature on $m \parallel u_1 \parallel u_2$. Note that in this case, our proposal becomes a regular signature scheme equivalent to the GBM scheme.

Verify(pk, m, σ, cvt): Parse σ as $(s, u_1, u_2, u_3) \in \{0,1\}^\eta \times G^3$ and cvt as $(\rho, \pi) \in G \times G^{12}$. Return 1 (meaning, valid) if π is a valid proof of the equations (1), and (s, ρ) is a valid GBM signature on $m \parallel u_1 \parallel u_2$. Otherwise return 0. (We omit details when $cvt = (r_1, r_2)$.)

Confirm: On common input $pk, (m, \sigma)$, the signer and the verifier execute

$$\mathrm{PoK}\Big\{(x, a, b) : g_1^a = (Xg^s)^{-1} \wedge g_2^b = (Xg^s)^{-1} \wedge u_3^x u_1^a u_2^b = H(m \parallel u_1 \parallel u_2) u_3^{-s}\Big\}.$$

Intuitively, the equations first show that $a = -x_1(x+s)$ and $b = -x_2(x+s)$ where $x = \mathrm{dlog}_g(X)$, $x_1 = \mathrm{dlog}_{g_1} g$ and $x_2 = \mathrm{dlog}_{g_2} g$. With the values a, b, the final equation is equivalent to $u_3/(u_1^{x_1} u_2^{x_2}) = H(m \parallel u_1 \parallel u_2)^{1/(x+s)}$. Since $u_1, u_2 \in G$, a cyclic group, there exist r_1, r_2 such that $u_1 = g_1^{r_1}$ and $u_2 = g_2^{r_2}$, and thus $u_1^{x_1} = g^{r_1}$, $u_2^{x_2} = g^{r_2}$. Hence, $u_3 = H(m \parallel g_1^{r_1} \parallel g_2^{r_2})^{1/(x+s)} \cdot g^{r_1+r_2}$, showing that $\sigma = (s, u_1, u_2, u_3)$ is indeed produced by USign on m. The zero-knowledge proof of knowledge can be implemented using known ZKIPs described in Sect. 3.

In the above PoK, the signer must also prove the knowledge of the secret key corresponding to the public key, namely (x, x_1, x_2) satisfying $g^x = X, g = g_1^{x_1} = g_2^{x_2}$. We omit these types of conditions hereafter in all PoKs for clarity.

Disavowal: On common input $pk, (m, \sigma)$, the signer sends a value $U \neq 1$ to the verifier, and both execute

$$\mathrm{PoK}\Big\{(c, d, f, r) : g^c (X^{-1} g^{-s})^r = g_1^d (Xg^s)^r = g_2^f (Xg^s)^r = 1 \\ \wedge\, U = u_3^c \cdot u_1^d \cdot u_2^f \cdot H(m \parallel u_1 \parallel u_2)^{-r}\Big\}.$$

Intuitively, the equations of the first line give us $c = r(x+s)$, $d = -rx_1(x+s)$, and $f = -rx_2(x+s)$. Substituting these values to the second line equation and noting that $U \neq 1$ show $u_3/(u_1^{x_1} u_2^{x_2}) \neq H(m \parallel u_1 \parallel u_2)^{1/(x+s)}$, and thus (m, σ) is invalid. The disavowal protocol is also implemented using known ZKIPs or NIZK proof in Sect. 3. Note that the NIZK proof for the disavowal protocol gives a way to "convert" (namely, make publicly-verifiable) invalid signatures.

Above, if the confirmation protocol fails, then the disavowal protocol is run. If both fails, we conclude that the signer is cheating (or not cooperating). We now consider securities of SCUS_1, which are ensured by the following theorems.

Theorem 5 (Strong unforgeability). *The proposed $SCUS_1$ scheme is strongly unforgeable if the signature scheme GBM is suf-cma-secure. Moreover, given a forger $\mathcal{F}$ against $SCUS_1$, there exists another forger $\mathcal{F}'$ against the GBM signature scheme such that*

$$\mathbf{Adv}^{sforge}_{SCUS_1}(\mathcal{F}) \le \mathbf{Adv}^{suf-cma}_{GBM}(\mathcal{F}'),$$

$$\mathbf{T}(\mathcal{F}') = O(q_{conf/dis}) \cdot \mathbf{T}(\mathcal{F}),$$

where $q_{conf/dis}$ is the total number of confirmation/disavowal queries $\mathcal{F}$ made, and $\mathbf{T}$ expresses the running time.

Proof. Given in [33].

Theorem 6 (Strong invisibility). *The $SCUS_1$ scheme satisfies strong invisibility. Moreover, given a distinguisher $\mathcal{D}$ against $SCUS_1$, there exist an $\mathcal{A}_{dlin}$ against the decision linear assumption, and a forger $\mathcal{F}$ against $SCUS_1$ such that*

$$\mathbf{Adv}^{inv}_{SCUS_1}(\mathcal{D}) \leq \mathbf{Adv}^{dlin}_{G}(\mathcal{A}_{dlin}) + \mathbf{Adv}^{sforge}_{SCUS_1}(\mathcal{F}),$$

$$\mathbf{T}(\mathcal{A}_{dlin}) = O(q_{conf/dis}) \cdot \mathbf{T}(\mathcal{D}), \ \ and\ \mathbf{T}(\mathcal{F}) \approx \mathbf{T}(\mathcal{D}),$$

where $\mathbf{T}$ expresses the running time, and $q_{conf/dis}$ is the total number of confirmation/disavowal queries $\mathcal{D}$ makes.

Proof. We proceed in games as follows.

Game 0: This is exactly the definitional game as in Definition 3. Let W_i $(i = 0, 1)$ be the event that the distinguisher $\mathcal{D}$ wins in Game i, we have $\mathbf{Adv}^{inv}_{\mathsf{SCUS}_1}(\mathcal{D}) = \Pr[W_0]$ by definition.

Game 1: This game is the same as Game 0, except that we consider the following distinguisher: $\mathcal{D}$ never issues a convert or confirmation/disavowal query (m, σ) satisfying (1) the pair is valid (namely, $\perp$ or 0 was not returned), and (2) the pair is different from all previously-issued message-signature pairs at the signing oracle.

Obviously, if $\mathcal{D}$ (in Game 0) issues the pair (m, σ) as above, then we can use (m, σ) as a forgery (in the strong sense) of the SCUS_1 scheme. More precisely, we can use $\mathcal{D}$ to build a forger $\mathcal{F}$ against SCUS_1 with $\mathbf{T}(\mathcal{F}) \approx \mathbf{T}(\mathcal{D})$. Thus, Game 0 and Game 1 are indistinguishable thanks to the strong unforgeability of the scheme, and hence

$$|\Pr[W_0] - \Pr[W_1]| \leq \mathbf{Adv}^{sforge}_{\mathsf{SCUS}_1}(\mathcal{F}).$$

Using the distinguisher $\mathcal{D}$ in Game 1, we now build an adversary $\mathcal{A}_{dlin}$ against the decision linear assumption on G satisfying $\Pr[W_1] \leq \mathbf{Adv}^{dlin}_{G}(\mathcal{A}_{dlin})$. Note that

$$\begin{aligned}\mathbf{Adv}^{inv}_{\mathsf{SCUS}_1}(\mathcal{D}) = \Pr[W_0] &\leq \Pr[W_1] + \mathbf{Adv}^{sforge}_{\mathsf{SCUS}_1}(\mathcal{F}) \\ &\leq \mathbf{Adv}^{dlin}_{G}(\mathcal{A}_{dlin}) + \mathbf{Adv}^{sforge}_{\mathsf{SCUS}_1}(\mathcal{F}),\end{aligned}$$

which completes the proof. Thus the rest is devoted to constructing such $\mathcal{A}_{dlin}$. The input of $\mathcal{A}_{dlin}$ is $(\mathbb{PG}, g_1, g_2, g, g_1^{\alpha}, g_2^{\beta}, T_b)$, where $T_0 = g^{\alpha+\beta}$ and $T_1 = g^{\gamma}$ for $\alpha, \beta, \gamma \xleftarrow{\$} Z_q$. The adversary $\mathcal{A}_{dlin}$ itself sets up the keys for GBM signature scheme: $sk_1 = x \xleftarrow{\$} Z_q$ and $pk_1 = (g^x, H, \eta = 70)$; and generates a simulated crs and a trapdoor t for the NIZK of the equations (1). Then $\mathcal{A}_{dlin}$

gives $pk = (pk_1, g_1, g_2, crs)$ to $\mathcal{D}$ and begins to simulate the environment for the distinguisher as follows:

– Signing query m: $\mathcal{A}_{dlin}$ chooses the randomness $r_1, r_2 \xleftarrow{\$} Z_q$ and $s \xleftarrow{\$} \{0,1\}^\eta$, and computes $\rho \leftarrow H(m \parallel u_1 \parallel u_2)^{1/(x+s)}$ where $u_1 = g_1^{r_1}$ and $u_2 = g_2^{r_2}$. It then lets $u_3 \leftarrow \rho \cdot g^{r_1+r_2}$ and returns $\sigma = (s, u_1, u_2, u_3)$ to $\mathcal{D}$ as the undeniable signature on m. The adversary $\mathcal{A}_{dlin}$ internally keeps a record of the values ρ, and also lets $\mathcal{Q} \leftarrow \mathcal{Q} \cup \{(m, \sigma)\}$ for later use, where $\mathcal{Q}$ is an initially empty set of message-signature pairs appeared so far.

– Convert query (m, σ): If $(m, \sigma) \in \mathcal{Q}$ then return the corresponding recorded ρ and a simulated NIZK proof π_{sim} (of the equations (1)) produced by using the trapdoor t. If $(m, \sigma) \notin \mathcal{Q}$ then return $\perp$ to $\mathcal{D}$. The reasoning behind this simulation is that if $(m, \sigma) \notin \mathcal{Q}$ then the pair must be invalid since we are in Game 1.

– Confirmation/disavowal query (m, σ): Like the simulation for convert query above, if $(m, \sigma) \in \mathcal{Q}$ then return 1 and run the confirmation protocol with $\mathcal{D}$; otherwise return 0 and run the disavowal protocol. The protocols are simulatable using the rewinding technique [19] since they are zero-knowledge.

– Challenge query m^*: Let $u_1^* \leftarrow g_1^\alpha$ and $u_2^* \leftarrow g_2^\beta$. Choose $s^* \xleftarrow{\$} \{0,1\}^\eta$ and then compute $\rho^* \leftarrow H(m^* \parallel u_1^* \parallel u_2^*)^{1/(x+s^*)}$ and $u_3^* \leftarrow \rho^* \cdot T_b$. Return $\sigma^* = (s^*, u_1^*, u_2^*, u_3^*)$ to $\mathcal{D}$.

Note that if $b = 0$ then $T_b = T_0 = g^{\alpha+\beta}$, so that σ^* is a valid undeniable signature on m^*. If $b = 1$ then $T_b = T_1 = g^\gamma$ is a random value over G independent of the other values, so that σ^* is also randomly distributed over the signature space $\{0,1\}^\eta \times G^3$.

At the end, the distinguisher $\mathcal{D}$ outputs a bit b' as a guess of the hidden bit b. The adversary $\mathcal{A}_{dlin}$ in turn outputs b'. The advantage of $\mathcal{A}_{dlin}$ is exactly the probability $\mathcal{D}$ wins in Game 1, namely $\mathbf{Adv}_G^{dlin}(\mathcal{A}_{dlin}) = \Pr[W_1]$. The running time of $\mathcal{A}_{dlin}$ is $O(q_{conf/dis})$ times that of $\mathcal{D}$ due to the rewinding.

5 Our Proposed SCUS_2

In this section, we describe our second scheme SCUS_2, which is also secure under the same assumptions as those of SCUS_1. The scheme SCUS_2 uses the Boneh-Boyen [2] signature scheme as a component. We first recall the Boneh-Boyen signature scheme, basing on a pairing group $\mathbb{PG} = (G, G_T, q = |G|, g, \hat{e} : G \times G \to G_T)$.

BONEH-BOYEN SIGNATURE SCHEME. The (standard) signature scheme $\mathsf{BB} = (\mathsf{BB.Kg}, \mathsf{BB.Sign}, \mathsf{BB.Vrf})$ is as follows.

$\mathsf{BB.Kg}(1^\kappa)$: Generate $g_0 \xleftarrow{\$} G$, $x, y \xleftarrow{\$} Z_q$, $u \leftarrow g^x$, $v \leftarrow g^y$, $z = \hat{e}(g_0, g)$, and a target collision hash $H : \{0,1\}^* \to Z_q$. Return the verifying key $pk_1 = (g_0, u, v, z, H)$ and the signing key $sk_1 = (x, y)$.

$\mathsf{BB.Sign}(sk_1, m)$: $s \xleftarrow{\$} Z_q$, $\rho \leftarrow g_0^{\frac{1}{x+H(m)+ys}} \in G$. Return $(s, \rho) \in Z_q \times G$ as the signature on m.

BB.Vrf$(pk_1, m, (s, \rho))$: Check that $(s, \rho) \in Z_q \times G$ and $\hat{e}\left(\rho, u \cdot g^{H(m)} \cdot v^s\right) = z$. Return 1 if all checks pass, else return 0.

It was proven in [2] that the above signature scheme is suf-cma-secure under the strong Diffie-Hellman assumption.

Our Proposal SCUS$_2$. The scheme, whose security analysis is given the full version [33], is described as follows.

KeyGen(1^κ): Run BB.Kg(1^κ) and LE.Kg(1^κ) to get (pk_1, sk_1) and (pk_2, sk_2). Return the public key $pk = (pk_1, pk_2)$ and the signing key $sk = (sk_1, sk_2)$.

USign(sk, m): First, generate $r_1, r_2 \xleftarrow{\$} Z_q$, and set $u_1 \leftarrow g_1^{r_1}$, $u_2 \leftarrow g_2^{r_2}$, and $\overline{m} = m \parallel u_1 \parallel u_2$. Next, sign on $\overline{m}$ to get $\left(s, \rho = g_0^{\frac{1}{x+H(\overline{m})+ys}}\right) \xleftarrow{\$}$ BB.Sign$(sk_1, \overline{m})$. Then, encrypt ρ in the ciphertext $(u_1, u_2, u_3 = \rho \cdot g^{r_1+r_2})$. Return the undeniable signature $\sigma = (s, u_1, u_2, u_3)$.

Convert(sk, m, σ): The same as that of SCUS$_1$, except now checking whether (s, ρ) is a BB signature or not. Also, for all conversion, release $sk_2 = (x_1, x_2)$, so that our proposal becomes a regular signature scheme equivalent to the BB scheme.

Verify(pk, m, σ, cvt): The same as that of SCUS$_1$, except now checking whether (s, ρ) is a valid BB signature or not.

Confirm: On common input pk, m, $\sigma = (s, u_1, u_2, u_3)$, the signer and the verifier execute

$$\text{PoK}\Big\{(a, b, c):\ g^a = uv^s \wedge g_1^b = g_2^c = \left(uv^s g^{H(m\|u_1\|u_2)}\right)^{-1} \wedge\ u_3^a u_1^b u_2^c = g_0 u_3^{-H(m\|u_1\|u_2)}\Big\}.$$

The first three equations show $a = x + ys$, $b = -x_1\left(x + H\left(m \parallel u_1 \parallel u_2\right) + ys\right)$, and $c = -x_2\left(x + H\left(m \parallel u_1 \parallel u_2\right) + ys\right)$, where $x_1 = \text{dlog}_{g_1} g$ and $x_2 = \text{dlog}_{g_2} g$. With the values a, b, c, the final equation is equivalent to $u_3/(u_1^{x_1} u_2^{x_2}) = g_0^{1/(x+H(m\|u_1\|u_2)+ys)}$, showing that (m, σ) is valid. The zero-knowledge proof of knowledge can be implemented using known ZKIPs or NIZK proofs described in Sect. 3.

Disavowal: On common input pk, m, $\sigma = (s, u_1, u_2, u_3)$, the signer sends a value $U \neq 1$ to the verifier, and both execute

$$\text{PoK}\Big\{(d, e, f, r):\ g^d (ug^{H(m\|u_1\|u_2)}v^s)^{-r} = 1 \wedge\ g_1^e (ug^{H(m\|u_1\|u_2)}v^s)^r = 1 \wedge g_2^f (ug^{H(m\|u_1\|u_2)}v^s)^r = 1 \wedge\ U = u_3^d \cdot u_1^e \cdot u_2^f \cdot g_0^{-r}\Big\}.$$

Intuitively, the first three equations give us $d = r(x + H(m \parallel u_1 \parallel u_2) + ys)$, $e = -rx_1(x + H(m \parallel u_1 \parallel u_2) + ys)$, and $f = -rx_2(x + H(m \parallel u_1 \parallel u_2) + ys)$. Substituting these values to the last equation and noting that $U \neq 1$ show $u_3/(u_1^{x_1} u_2^{x_2}) \neq g_0^{1/(x+H(m\|u_1\|u_2)+ys)}$, and thus (m, σ) is invalid. The disavowal protocol is also implemented using known ZKIPs or NIZK proof in Sect. 3.

6 $\mathsf{SCUS}_{1,2}$ as Anonymous Signature Schemes

The security notions for an anonymous signature scheme are unforgeability, anonymity, and unambiguity. The former two notions are met by SCUS_1 and SCUS_2, as seen in the previous sections. The last notion, unambiguity, intuitively ensures that if one signer releases a converter to convert a signature, then nobody else can convert that signature. We formalize the notion as follows.

Definition 7 (Unambiguity). *A scheme SCUS satisfies unambiguity if for any poly-time adversary $\mathcal{A}$,*

$$\mathbf{Adv}^{unamb}_{\mathsf{SCUS}}(\mathcal{A}) \stackrel{\text{def}}{=} \Pr\left[\begin{array}{c} (pk_A, sk_A) \xleftarrow{\$} \mathsf{KeyGen}(1^\kappa), (pk_B, sk_B) \xleftarrow{\$} \mathsf{KeyGen}(1^\kappa) \\ (m_A, m_B, \sigma, cvt_A, cvt_B) \xleftarrow{\$} \mathcal{A}(pk_A, sk_A, pk_B, sk_B) \\ \mathsf{Verify}(pk_A, m_A, \sigma, cvt_A) = \mathsf{Verify}(pk_B, m_B, \sigma, cvt_B) = 1 \end{array}\right]$$

is negligible in the parameter κ.

If the adversary chooses cvt_A randomly and lets $m_A = m_B$, the above definition essentially becomes that of Saraswat and Yun [35]. On the other hand, the difference with Bellare and Duan [1] is that we require the users indeed hold secret keys corresponding to their public keys (which can be done via efficient zero-knowledge proofs of knowledge). Ours is stronger than [35], weaker than [1]. It is however worth noting that since our schemes are also undeniable signature ones, requiring knowledge of valid secret keys is normal; since otherwise a signer creates a fake pair (sk', pk) (e.g., unrelated values), then all signatures become invalid with respect to pk, so the signer obviously can deny signatures he himself produced.

We now consider the schemes SCUS_1 and SCUS_2, and let the converters of the schemes be the randomness of the LE scheme.

Theorem 8. *The schemes SCUS_1 and SCUS_2 (releasing randomness for selective conversion) satisfy unambiguity, under the discrete-log assumption. In particular, for any adversary $\mathcal{A}$, there is an adversary $\mathcal{B}$ such that*

$$\mathbf{Adv}^{unamb}_{\mathsf{SCUS}_{1,2}}(\mathcal{A}) \leq \mathbf{Adv}^{dlog}_{G}(\mathcal{B}),$$
$$\mathbf{T}(\mathcal{B}) \approx \mathbf{T}(\mathcal{A}).$$

The full proof is given in [33], but the intuition is as follows. From the input g, h of $\mathcal{B}$, we set up the keys (pk_A, sk_A) in base g, and (pk_B, sk_B) in base h and run $\mathcal{A}$. Any ambiguity will lead to the value $\mathrm{dlog}_g(h)$, against the dlog assumption.

Above, we only consider schemes releasing randomness as selective converters. It is interesting to ask whether our schemes with NIZK converters satisfy unambiguity or not. They seem to meet the notion, but we unfortunately cannot prove, so leaving it as an open problem.

Acknowledgements

We thank Dennis Hofheinz for communicating on the strong uf-cma security of the GBM scheme. Many thanks also go to Laila El Aimani, Jacob Schuldt, and

Ryo Kikuchi for fruitful discussions, which sharpened the knowledge of the first author on the topic. We are indebted to the anonymous reviewers for comprehensive comments. Parts of this work was done while the first author was at Tokyo Institute of Technology with a MEXT scholarship.

References

1. Bellare, M., Duan, S.: New definitions and designs for anonymous signatures. Cryptology ePrint Archive, Report 2009/336 (2009), `http://eprint.iacr.org/`
2. Boneh, D., Boyen, X.: Short signatures without random oracles and the sdh assumption in bilinear groups. J. Cryptology 21(2), 149–177 (2008)
3. Boneh, D., Boyen, X., Shacham, H.: Short group signatures. In: Franklin, M. K. (ed.) CRYPTO 2004. LNCS, vol. 3152, pp. 41–55. Springer, Heidelberg (2004)
4. Boneh, D., Lynn, B., Shacham, H.: Short signatures from the weil pairing. J. Cryptology 17(4), 297–319 (2004)
5. Boyar, J., Chaum, D., Damgård, I., Pedersen, T.P.: Convertible undeniable signatures. In: Menezes, A., Vanstone, S.A. (eds.) CRYPTO 1990. LNCS, vol. 537, pp. 189–205. Springer, Heidelberg (1991)
6. Boyd, C., Foo, E.: Off-line fair payment protocols using convertible signatures. In: Ohta, K., Pei, D. (eds.) ASIACRYPT 1998. LNCS, vol. 1514, pp. 271–285. Springer, Heidelberg (1998)
7. Brickell, E.F. (ed.): CRYPTO 1992. LNCS, vol. 740. Springer, Heidelberg (1993)
8. Camenisch, J., Shoup, V.: Practical verifiable encryption and decryption of discrete logarithms. In: Boneh, D. (ed.) CRYPTO 2003. LNCS, vol. 2729, pp. 126–144. Springer, Heidelberg (2003)
9. Chaum, D.: Zero-knowledge undeniable signatures. In: Damgård, I.B. (ed.) EUROCRYPT 1990. LNCS, vol. 473, pp. 458–464. Springer, Heidelberg (1991)
10. Chaum, D., Antwerpen, H.V.: Undeniable signatures. In: Brassard, G. (ed.) CRYPTO 1989. LNCS, vol. 435, pp. 212–216. Springer, Heidelberg (1990)
11. Chaum, D., Pedersen, T.P.: Wallet databases with observers. In: Brickell [7], pp. 89–105
12. Damgård, I., Pedersen, T.P.: New convertible undeniable signature schemes. In: Maurer, U.M. (ed.) EUROCRYPT 1996. LNCS, vol. 1070, pp. 372–386. Springer, Heidelberg (1996)
13. El Aimani, L.: Toward a generic construction of universally convertible undeniable signatures from pairing-based signatures. In: Chowdhury, D.R., Rijmen, V., Das, A. (eds.) INDOCRYPT 2008. LNCS, vol. 5365, pp. 145–157. Springer, Heidelberg (2008)
14. El Aimani, L.: Efficient confirmer signatures from the "signature of a commitment" paradigm. Cryptology ePrint Archive, Report 2009/435 (2009), `http://eprint.iacr.org/`
15. El Aimani, L.: On generic constructions of designated confirmer signatures. In: Roy, B.K., Sendrier, N. (eds.) INDOCRYPT 2009. LNCS, vol. 5922, pp. 343–362. Springer, Heidelberg (2009), `http://eprint.iacr.org/2009/403`
16. El Aimani, L.: Toward a generic construction of convertible undeniable signatures from pairing-based signatures. Cryptology ePrint Archive, Report 2009/362 (2009), `http://eprint.iacr.org/`
17. Fischlin, M.: Anonymous signatures made easy. In: Okamoto, T., Wang, X. (eds.) PKC 2007. LNCS, vol. 4450, pp. 31–42. Springer, Heidelberg (2007)

18. Galbraith, S.D., Mao, W.: Invisibility and anonymity of undeniable and confirmer signatures. In: Joye, M. (ed.) CT-RSA 2003. LNCS, vol. 2612, pp. 80–97. Springer, Heidelberg (2003)
19. Goldreich, O., Oren, Y.: Definitions and properties of zero-knowledge proof systems. J. Cryptology 7(1), 1–32 (1994)
20. Groth, J., Sahai, A.: Efficient non-interactive proof systems for bilinear groups. In: Smart, N.P. (ed.) EUROCRYPT 2008. LNCS, vol. 4965, pp. 415–432. Springer, Heidelberg (2008)
21. Hofheinz, D., Kiltz, E.: Programmable hash functions and their applications. In: Wagner, D. (ed.) CRYPTO 2008. LNCS, vol. 5157, pp. 21–38. Springer, Heidelberg (2008)
22. Huang, Q., Wong, D.S.: New constructions of convertible undeniable signature schemes without random oracles. Cryptology ePrint Archive, Report 2009/517 (2009), http://eprint.iacr.org/
23. Kurosawa, K., Furukawa, J.: Universally composable undeniable signature. In: Aceto, L., Damgård, I., Goldberg, L.A., Halldórsson, M.M., Ingólfsdóttir, A., Walukiewicz, I. (eds.) ICALP 2008, Part II. LNCS, vol. 5126, pp. 524–535. Springer, Heidelberg (2008)
24. Kurosawa, K., Heng, S.-H.: 3-Move undeniable signature scheme. In: Cramer, R. (ed.) EUROCRYPT 2005. LNCS, vol. 3494, pp. 181–197. Springer, Heidelberg (2005)
25. Kurosawa, K., Heng, S.-H.: Relations among security notions for undeniable signature schemes. In: Prisco, R. D., Yung, M. (eds.) SCN 2006. LNCS, vol. 4116, pp. 34–48. Springer, Heidelberg (2006)
26. Kurosawa, K., Takagi, T.: New approach for selectively convertible undeniable signature schemes. In: Lai, X., Chen, K. (eds.) ASIACRYPT 2006. LNCS, vol. 4284, pp. 428–443. Springer, Heidelberg (2006)
27. Laguillaumie, F., Vergnaud, D.: Short undeniable signatures without random oracles: The missing link. In: Maitra, S., Madhavan, C.E.V., Venkatesan, R. (eds.) INDOCRYPT 2005. LNCS, vol. 3797, pp. 283–296. Springer, Heidelberg (2005)
28. Monnerat, J., Vaudenay, S.: Generic homomorphic undeniable signatures. In: Lee, P.J. (ed.) ASIACRYPT 2004. LNCS, vol. 3329, pp. 354–371. Springer, Heidelberg (2004)
29. Monnerat, J., Vaudenay, S.: Undeniable signatures based on characters: How to sign with one bit. In: Bao, F., Deng, R. H., Zhou, J. (eds.) PKC 2004. LNCS, vol. 2947, pp. 69–85. Springer, Heidelberg (2004)
30. Ogata, W., Kurosawa, K., Heng, S.-H.: The security of the FDH variant of Chaum's undeniable signature scheme. IEEE Transactions on Information Theory 52(5), 2006–2017 (2006)
31. Okamoto, T.: Provably secure and practical identification schemes and corresponding signature schemes. In: Brickell [7], pp. 31–53
32. Phong, L.T., Kurosawa, K., Ogata, W.: New rsa-based (selectively) convertible undeniable signature schemes. In: Preneel, B. (ed.) AFRICACRYPT 2009. LNCS, vol. 5580, pp. 116–134. Springer, Heidelberg (2009)
33. Phong, L.T., Kurosawa, K., Ogata, W.: Provably secure convertible undeniable signatures with unambiguity. Cryptology ePrint Archive, Report 2009/394 (2009) (full version of the paper), http://eprint.iacr.org/
34. Pointcheval, D.: Self-scrambling anonymizers. In: Frankel, Y. (ed.) FC 2000. LNCS, vol. 1962, pp. 259–275. Springer, Heidelberg (2001)
35. Saraswat, V., Yun, A.: Anonymous signatures revisited. In: Pieprzyk, J., Zhang, F. (eds.) ProvSec 2009. LNCS, vol. 5848, pp. 140–153. Springer, Heidelberg (2009)

36. Schnorr, C.-P.: Efficient signature generation by smart cards. J. Cryptology 4(3), 161–174 (1991)
37. Schuldt, J.C.N., Matsuura, K.: An efficient convertible undeniable signature scheme with delegatable verification. Cryptology ePrint Archive, Report 2009/454 (2009), http://eprint.iacr.org/
38. Yang, G., Wong, D.S., Deng, X., Wang, H.: Anonymous signature schemes. In: Yung, M., Dodis, Y., Kiayias, A., Malkin, T.G. (eds.) PKC 2006. LNCS, vol. 3958, pp. 347–363. Springer, Heidelberg (2006)
39. Yuen, T.H., Au, M.H., Liu, J.K., Susilo, W.: (Convertible) undeniable signatures without random oracles. In: Qing, S., Imai, H., Wang, G. (eds.) ICICS 2007. LNCS, vol. 4861, pp. 83–97. Springer, Heidelberg (2007)
40. Zhang, R., Imai, H.: Strong anonymous signatures. In: Yung, M., Liu, P., Lin, D. (eds.) Inscrypt 2008. LNCS, vol. 5487, pp. 60–71. Springer, Heidelberg (2009)

History-Free Aggregate Message Authentication Codes

Oliver Eikemeier[1], Marc Fischlin[1], Jens-Fabian Götzmann[1], Anja Lehmann[1,2], Dominique Schröder[1], Peter Schröder[1], and Daniel Wagner[1]

[1] Darmstadt University of Technology, Germany
schroeder@me.com, marc.fischlin@gmail.com
www.minicrypt.de
[2] IBM Research Zurich, Switzerland

Abstract. Aggregate message authentication codes, as introduced by Katz and Lindell (CT-RSA 2008), combine several MACs into a single value, which has roughly the same size as an ordinary MAC. These schemes reduce the communication overhead significantly and are therefore a promising approach to achieve authenticated communication in mobile ad-hoc networks, where communication is prohibitively expensive. Here we revisit the unforgeability notion for aggregate MACs and discuss that the definition does not prevent "mix-and-match" attacks in which the adversary turns several aggregates into a "fresh" combination, i.e., into a valid aggregate on a sequence of messages which the attacker has not requested before. In particular, we show concrete attacks on the previous scheme.

To capture the broader class of combination attacks, we provide a stronger security notion of aggregation unforgeability. While we can provide stateful transformations lifting (non-ordered) schemes to meet our stronger security notion, for the statefree case we switch to the new notion of history-free sequential aggregation. This notion is somewhat between non-ordered and sequential schemes and basically says that the aggregation algorithm is carried out in a sequential order but must not depend on the preceding messages in the sequence, but only on the shorter input aggregate and the local message. We finally show that we can build an aggregation-unforgeable, history-free sequential MAC scheme based on general assumptions.

1 Introduction

Aggregate message authentication codes [5] allow the aggregation of multiple MACs, generated by different senders for possibly different messages, such that the aggregate has the same size as a single MAC. These MACs are especially suited for settings involving resource-constrained devices like mobile ad-hoc networks (MANET). Thereby, the communication is very power-consuming and asymmetric primitives like signatures are prohibitively expensive due to the limited computational power of the devices. In this case, verification of an aggregated tag can be carried out by any receiver that shares all secret keys with the participating senders, e.g., a base station collecting data from the sensors.

J.A. Garay and R. De Prisco (Eds.): SCN 2010, LNCS 6280, pp. 309–328, 2010.

Security Revisited. The unforgeability notions for aggregate MACs follow the known principle for aggregate signature schemes [2]. Basically, it states that an adversary, who controls all aggregating parties except for a single signer, cannot create a valid aggregate for a "fresh" set of messages. Here a set is considered fresh if the designated signer is in this set but has not signed the message before. In other words, the unforgeability of the aggregation scheme is tied to the unforgeability of individual messages.

Aggregation, however, is about combining data, and protection of individual messages may not be sufficient in all settings: deleting parts, re-ordering entries, extending or recombining aggregates to a new valid aggregate may be serious threats for applications. We illustrate our idea with a simple (sequential) network of nodes

$$N_1 \longrightarrow N_2 \longrightarrow N_3 \longrightarrow N_4.$$

The aggregation scheme should be used to authenticate routing paths, where N_i only accepts input from N_{i-1}, augments the aggregate-so-far by a MAC of its own identity before forwarding the new aggregate to N_{i+1}. Then, if one is able to delete for example N_2's contribution from the aggregate, one obtains a valid authentication of an invalid route $N_1 \rightarrow N_3 \rightarrow N_4$. According to the definition of [5], however, the above attack does not constitute a security breach, as no individual MAC has been forged. We discuss similar, concrete attacks of this "mix-and-match" type on the aggregate MAC scheme due to Katz and Lindell [5] in Appendix A.

Aggregation Unforgeability. To cover advanced attacks as discussed above, we introduce our stronger security notion of *aggregation unforgeability*. The attacker's mode of operation is similar to the definitions of [5], i.e., it can make aggregation queries for messages of its choice and should eventually produce a forgery. However, in order to capture attacks on combinations, like the mix-and-match attacks above, our attacker faces multiple honest signers, instead of only a single signer as in all previous works.[1]

Our main modification is the notion of "freshness" for the adversary's forgery attempt. More precisely, we define a "minimal" closure set of all trivial message combinations for which the adversary can easily assemble a valid aggregate out of the data in the attack. For example, the closure contains any message set from an aggregation query but where the adversary trivially adds messages authenticated by corrupt parties. Every message set not appearing in this closure is then declared as fresh. Unlike previous definitions the forgery combination in the mix-and-match attack above is still fresh according to this definition.

History-Free Sequential Aggregation. It is not known how and if our general security models can be satisfied; even if we make the excessive assumption of some

[1] It is tempting to assume that playing against a single honest user would suffice by a standard guessing strategy. However, the mix-and-match attack shows that we may not exploit a weakness in the tagging algorithm, but rather take advantage of the aggregation of tags by several honest parties or of the structure of the aggregate itself.

shared and synchronized information between the nodes, like a counter, we show that we can only achieve a slightly weaker version. Yet, the discussion still shows the limitations of current schemes and we can transfer the main ideas to the important case of *sequential* aggregation where, e.g., a sensor receives some data, performs some operation, and forwards the new data to the next node. With the corresponding adaptations of our security notion —and noting that the attacks above are in fact carried out in the sequential setting— it follows that our security guarantees also go beyond the current models for sequential schemes.

Yet, we even consider a stronger model than pure sequential aggregation. Recall that the proposal of Katz and Lindell supports the aggregation of the data independently of the order of the parties and the aggregating algorithm is key less. The gist of known non-sequential schemes is that the aggregation algorithm computes the new data without inspection of previous messages. To preserve as much of this idea for sequential aggregate MACs we introduce the notion of *history-free* aggregation where the aggregation only depends on the aggregate-so-far and the local message. It is clear that the previous aggregate enters the computation and that this value itself carries (more or less explicit) information about previous messages. Due to the size restriction for aggregates, though, this information is limited. In this sense it is understood that history-free schemes only deny explicit access to previous messages. History-free sequential aggregation is a desirable goal from an efficiency point of view. It allows for example incremental compression of the message sequence without local decompression for each aggregation. This property is especially worthwhile for cases of MANETs where each computation effects on the battery life of the nodes.

In the history-free sequential case we provide solutions meeting our high standards. Our secure construction is based on any pseudorandom permutation (PRP) like AES. The idea here is to carefully chain the tags. In each aggregation step one basically computes a CBC-MAC of the current message concatenated with the previous tag (where we need the properties of the PRP only in the last mixing step). Hence, each aggregation step essentially requires the computation of a MAC plus one invocation of a PRP.

Related Work. Most works about secure aggregation follow the security model of Boneh et al. [2] and Lysyanskaya et al. [6]. The only exception is the recent work by Boldyreva et al. [3] which sketches a possible stronger security notion covering attacks on sequential schemes in which the adversary outputs a prefix of some aggregation query (and then possibly appends further iterations of corrupt players). But their model does not discuss more advanced attacks like "gluing" together aggregates, nor do they provide provably secure solutions for their model, whereas we show how to make schemes secure against very powerful attacks.

We note that the notion of sequential aggregate signed data, recently proposed by Neven [7], also aims at efficiency gains, but focuses on communication complexity instead of computational complexity. For such sequential aggregate signed data only the aggregate (being of roughly the same size as the messages) is passed to the next round. However, according to the definition this aggregate allows to recover the previously signed messages and Neven's solution indeed extracts all these messages for each aggregation step. In this sense, his solution is therefore still not history-free, unlike our construction for MACs.

Organization. In Section 2 we recall the notion of aggregate MACs. We introduce our model for aggregation unforgeability in Section 3. For our constructions we switch to the (history-free) sequential case in Section 4. There, we define history-free sequential aggregate MACs, discuss aggregation unforgeability in this case and finally we present our construction based on the general assumptions.

2 Non-sequential Aggregation of MACs

Roughly speaking, an aggregate MAC is a single tag, called the aggregate, of q different users on q different messages such that the aggregate has nearly the same size as an ordinary tag. The well known definition of MACs and their security are given in Appendix B.

2.1 Definition

Definition 1 (Aggregate MACs). *An aggregate message authentication code* $\mathsf{Agg} = (\mathsf{KGen}, \mathsf{Mac}, \mathsf{Vf}, \mathsf{Agg}, \mathsf{AVf})$ *is a tuple of efficient algorithms such that:*

Key Generation. *The algorithm* KGen *takes the security parameter* 1^λ *and returns for a particular sender a pair* $(sk_{\mathsf{id}}, \mathsf{id})$ *where* sk_{id} *is a key and* id *is an identifier.*

Authentication, Mac Verification. Mac *and* Vf *are defined as in a standard message authentication scheme.*

Aggregation. *Upon input of two sets of message/identifier pairs* $M_1 = \{(m_1^1, \mathsf{id}_1^1), \ldots, (m_{\ell_1}^1, \mathsf{id}_{\ell_1}^1)\}$ *and* $M_2 = \{(m_1^2, \mathsf{id}_1^2), \ldots, (m_{\ell_2}^2, \mathsf{id}_{\ell_2}^2)\}$ *and associated tags* σ_1 *and* σ_2*, algorithm* Agg *outputs a new tag* σ.

Aggregate Verification. *Algorithm* AVf *accepts as input a set of key/identifier pairs* $\mathsf{sk} = \{(sk_1, \mathsf{id}_1), \ldots, (sk_t, \mathsf{id}_t)\}$*, a set of message/identifier pairs* $M = \{(m_1, \mathsf{id}'_1), \ldots, (m_\ell, \mathsf{id}'_\ell)\}$ *and a tag* σ*. This algorithm returns a bit.*

An aggregate message authentication scheme is complete *if the following conditions hold:*

- *For any* $\lambda \in \mathbb{N}$*, any* $(sk_{\mathsf{id}}, \mathsf{id}) \leftarrow \mathsf{KGen}(1^\lambda)$*, any message* $m \in \mathcal{M}_\lambda$*, we have* $\mathsf{Vf}(sk_{\mathsf{id}}, m, \mathsf{Mac}(sk_{\mathsf{id}}, m)) = 1$.
- *Let* M_1 *and* M_2 *be two sets of message/identifier pairs with* $M_1 \cap M_2 = \emptyset$*, let* sk_1 *as well as* sk_2 *be a set of keys, and let* $M = M_1 \cup M_2$ *and* $\mathsf{sk} = \mathsf{sk}_1 \cup \mathsf{sk}_2$*. If* $\mathsf{AVf}(\mathsf{sk}_1, M_1, \sigma_1) = 1$ *and* $\mathsf{AVf}(\mathsf{sk}_2, M_2, \sigma_2) = 1$ *then* $\mathsf{AVf}(\mathsf{sk}, M, \mathsf{Agg}(M_1, M_2, \sigma_1, \sigma_2)) = 1$.

2.2 Security Model and an Instantiation

The security model for aggregate MACs is closely related to the one for aggregate signatures [2]. The only technical difference results from the shared-key setting. Here, an adversary has access to two different oracles. The first oracle, the corruption oracle $\mathsf{Corrupt}(\mathsf{sk}, \cdot)$, returns on input id the corresponding secret key sk_{id}. The second oracle $\mathsf{OMac}(\mathsf{sk}, \cdot)$ allows the adversary to compute MACs for messages and keys of its choice. This oracle is initialized with a set of keys $\mathsf{sk} = ((sk_1, \mathsf{id}_1), \ldots, (sk_\ell, \mathsf{id}_\ell))$ and takes as input a message/identifier pair (m, id), it returns $\sigma \leftarrow \mathsf{Mac}(sk_{\mathsf{id}}, m)$. The adversary is successful if it outputs a set of message/identifier pairs $M = \{(m_1, \mathsf{id}_1), \ldots, (m_\ell, \mathsf{id}_\ell)\}$ and valid tag σ such that there exists at least one pair $(m_{i^*}, \mathsf{id}_{i^*}) \in M$ where id_{i^*} has not been corrupted, nor has $\mathcal{A}$ queried the MAC oracle on input $(m_{i^*}, \mathsf{id}_{i^*})$.

Definition 2 (Unforgeability). *An aggregate message authentication code scheme* $\mathsf{Agg} = (\mathsf{KGen}, \mathsf{Mac}, \mathsf{Vf}, \mathsf{Agg}, \mathsf{AVf})$ *is* unforgeable *if for any efficient algorithm $\mathcal{A}$ the probability that the experiment* $\mathsf{AggForge}_{\mathcal{A}}^{\mathsf{Agg}}$ *evaluates to* 1 *is negligible (as a function of λ), where*

Experiment $\mathsf{AggForge}_{\mathcal{A}}^{\mathsf{Agg}}(\lambda)$
  $(sk_1, \mathsf{id}_1), \ldots, (sk_t, \mathsf{id}_t) \leftarrow \mathsf{KGen}(1^\lambda)$
  $\mathsf{sk} \leftarrow ((sk_1, \mathsf{id}_1), \ldots, (sk_t, \mathsf{id}_t))$
  $(M, \sigma) \leftarrow \mathcal{A}^{\mathsf{Corrupt}(\mathsf{sk},\cdot),\mathsf{OMac}(\mathsf{sk},\cdot)}(\mathsf{id}_1, \ldots, \mathsf{id}_t)$
  Return 1 iff $\mathsf{AVf}(\mathsf{sk}, M, \sigma) = 1$ *and there exists a pair* $(m_{i^*}, \mathsf{id}_{i^*}) \in M$ *such that* $\mathcal{A}$ *never queried* $\mathsf{Corrupt}$ *about* id_{i^*} *and* $\mathcal{A}$ *never invoked* OMac *on input* $(m_{i^*}, \mathsf{id}_{i^*})$.

Instantiation According to Katz-Lindell. The authors also proposed the following provably secure construction, which we call XOR-AMAC. The aggregate message authentication code scheme simply computes XOR of all tags.

Construction 1. *Let* $\mathsf{MAC} = (\mathsf{KGen}, \mathsf{Mac}, \mathsf{Vf})$ *be a deterministic message authentication code and define* $\mathsf{Agg} = (\mathsf{KGen}_{\mathsf{KL}}, \mathsf{Mac}_{\mathsf{KL}}, \mathsf{Vf}_{\mathsf{KL}}, \mathsf{Agg}_{\mathsf{KL}}, \mathsf{AVf}_{\mathsf{KL}})$ *through the following algorithms:*

Key Generation. *Algorithm* $\mathsf{KGen}_{\mathsf{KL}}(1^\lambda)$ *executes for each user independently the key generation algorithm of the underlying MAC scheme* $sk \leftarrow \mathsf{KGen}(1^\lambda)$ *and picks an identifier* $\mathsf{id} \leftarrow \{0,1\}^\lambda$ *at random. It returns the pair* $(sk_{\mathsf{id}}, \mathsf{id})$.

Authentication, Verification. *Defined as in the underlying mac scheme.*

Aggregation. *Upon input two sets* M_1 *and* M_2 *of message/identifier pairs and two tags* σ_1 *and* σ_2 *the algorithm outputs* $\sigma = \sigma_1 \oplus \sigma_2$.

Aggregate Verification. $\mathsf{AVf}_{\mathsf{KL}}$ *takes as input a set of keys* $\mathsf{sk} = ((sk_1, \mathsf{id}_1), \ldots, (sk_\ell, \mathsf{id}_\ell))$*, a set* $M = \{(m_1, \mathsf{id}'_1), \ldots, (m_\ell, \mathsf{id}'_\ell)\}$ *of message/identifier pairs, and a tag* σ*. This algorithm* $\mathsf{AVf}_{\mathsf{KL}}$ *computes* $\sigma' = \bigoplus_{i=1}^{\ell} \mathsf{Mac}(sk_{\mathsf{id}_i}, m_i)$ *and outputs 1 if and only if* $\sigma' = \sigma$.

3 Aggregation Unforgeability for Non-sequential MACs

In this section we first address the non-ordered case of aggregation. As discussed in the introduction, we introduce a security model that captures the broad class of mix-and-match attacks. It is clear that simple countermeasures like prepending the identifier of the user do not prevent theses attacks. Another approach might be to let the sender choose a nonce and have each intermediate user sign this nonce together with the message. The receiver only accepts aggregates for fresh nonces. This approach has some disadvantages, though. First, if the party choosing the nonces is controlled by the adversary, then a nonce may re-appear for several MAC generations.[2] Secondly, ad-hoc networks are highly dynamic. Thus, a node may receive an aggregate more than once (due to undesired loops in the route). Another disadvantage is that the receivers have to keep state. Similar arguments hold also for timing-based or counter-based solution. Nevertheless, we show in Appendix C a counter-based solution.

3.1 Security Model

We propose a stronger definition of unforgeability which we call aggregation-unforgeability. It follows the idea that the adversary is considered successful if he manages to find a valid aggregate for a message set which is not a straightforward combination of previous queries (or aggregates augmented by contributions of corrupt parties).

Regarding aggregate MACs, the main difference to the previous model is manifested in the fact that we grant the adversary in our model an additional *aggregation oracle* returning aggregates for sets of messages. The aggregation oracle, denoted by OAgg, is initialized with the key/identity pairs (sk_i, id_i) of all parties, takes as input a set of message/identifier pairs $\{(M_1, \mathsf{id}_1), \ldots, (M_k, \mathsf{id}_k)\}$ and returns an aggregate MAC σ for these data. We remark that the aggregation oracle only aggregates for honest parties, i.e., where the corresponding keys were not corrupted by the adversary; for corrupted parties the adversary must later add the values himself.

To express that the final output of the adversary is not a trivial combination of the results of the queries, we define a closure of the queries that contains all of these trivial combinations. For this definition we need the following notations. By Q_{Mac} we denote the set of queries of the adversary to the OMac oracle, by Q_{Agg} the set of queries to the aggregation oracle OAgg, and by Q_{Cor} the set of corruption queries. As a very basic example consider the classical unforgeability notion of MACs (one party only). Then the sets Q_{Agg} and Q_{Cor} are empty and Q_{Mac} contains exactly the queries to the MAC oracle. Here, trivial attacks are those where the adversary's forgery is for one of the previously queried messages from Q_{Mac}, i.e., the closure consists exactly of the queried messages.

In the case of aggregation the adversary can assemble more trivial message sets from its data. For example, if the adversary has obtained the aggregated MAC for a pair of messages and identities $\mathsf{id}_1, \mathsf{id}_2$, and knows the MAC for a third honest party id_3, then it can run the public aggregation algorithm to derive a valid MAC for the three messages. Analogously, the adversary can add corrupt parties easily by computing individual MACs for these parties and then aggregating them to a previous result. Our definition follows this idea, basically

[2] Note that letting each party choose a nonce and append it to the aggregate would lead the idea behind aggregation ad absurdum.

saying that the closure of all trivial combinations contains aggregation queries to which we add individual MAC queries and corrupt parties as well as further aggregation queries.

Consider as an instructive example a sensor network monitoring temperature differences, where deviations of 2°F between adjacent sensors would trigger an alarm. Suppose for simplicity that the network only consists of two nodes, one (called 'master') being closer to the base station and forwarding the data from the other node (called 'slave') to the station. When using an aggregation scheme the master sensor receives an aggregate for a temperature from the slave, "inserts" its authentication data for its temperature and forwards the temperatures and the new aggregate to the base.

If the adversary sees the aggregated MACs to the innocuous measurements (70°F, 70°F), (69°F, 70°F), and (70°F, 71°F), then

$$Q_{\mathsf{Agg}} = \{\{(70, \mathsf{id}_1), (70, \mathsf{id}_2)\}, \{(69, \mathsf{id}_1), (70, \mathsf{id}_2)\}, \{(70, \mathsf{id}_1), (71, \mathsf{id}_2)\}\}$$

for identities id_1 = 'slave' and id_2 = 'master'. Assume that there is a third party id_3 which is honest and for which the adversary has obtained an individual MAC $Q_{\mathsf{Mac}} = \{(65, \mathsf{id}_3)\}$ and that there is no corrupt party, $Q_{\mathsf{Cor}} = \emptyset$. Then the closure would be

$$\begin{aligned}
&\mathsf{Closure}(Q_{\mathsf{Mac}}, Q_{\mathsf{Agg}}, Q_{\mathsf{Cor}})\\
&\quad = \{\{(65, \mathsf{id}_3)\},\\
&\quad \{(70, \mathsf{id}_1), (70, \mathsf{id}_2)\},\ \{(69, \mathsf{id}_1), (70, \mathsf{id}_2)\},\ \{(70, \mathsf{id}_1), (71, \mathsf{id}_2)\},\\
&\quad \{(69, \mathsf{id}_1), (70, \mathsf{id}_1), (70, \mathsf{id}_2)\},\ \{(70, \mathsf{id}_1), (70, \mathsf{id}_2), (71, \mathsf{id}_2)\},\\
&\quad \{(70, \mathsf{id}_1), (70, \mathsf{id}_2), (65, \mathsf{id}_3)\}, \{(69, \mathsf{id}_1), (70, \mathsf{id}_2), (65, \mathsf{id}_3)\}, \{(70, \mathsf{id}_1), (71, \mathsf{id}_2), (65, \mathsf{id}_3)\},\\
&\quad \{(69, \mathsf{id}_1), (70, \mathsf{id}_1), (70, \mathsf{id}_2), (71, \mathsf{id}_2)\}, \ldots\}
\end{aligned}$$

Note that we do not treat sets where an identity appears multiple times in any special way. However, such forgery attempts can be easily thwarted by having the verifier check that all identities are distinct. We remark that the pair $\{(69, \mathsf{id}_1), (71, \mathsf{id}_2)\}$ is not a member of the closure (containing only the three originally queries as entries with two elements), but for which the adversary can for example in the Katz-Lindell scheme easily obtain a valid aggregate by adding the aggregates for the three measurements. The aggregate for this pair, even though not forging an individual MAC, would nonetheless trigger an alarm because of the temperature distance.

Definition 3 (Closure of $\mathcal{A}$'s queries). *The closure* Closure *of $\mathcal{A}$'s queries Q_{Mac}, Q_{Agg} and Q_{Cor} is defined as*

$$\mathsf{Closure}(Q_{\mathsf{Mac}}, Q_{\mathsf{Agg}}, Q_{\mathsf{Cor}}) =$$
$$\left\{ \bigcup_{M_A \in A} M_A \cup M_M \cup M_C \;\middle|\; A \subseteq Q_{\mathsf{Agg}},\, M_M \subseteq Q_{\mathsf{Mac}},\, M_C \subseteq \bigcup_{\mathsf{id} \in Q_{\mathsf{Cor}}} \{(m, \mathsf{id}) \mid m \in \mathcal{M}_\lambda\} \right\}$$

with $\mathcal{M}_\lambda$ denoting the message space for the security parameter λ.

With our definition of the closure we get the following definition for aggregation-unforgeable MAC schemes.

Definition 4. *An aggregate message authentication code scheme* $\mathsf{Agg} = (\mathsf{KGen}, \mathsf{Mac}, \mathsf{Vf}, \mathsf{Agg}, \mathsf{AVf})$ *is* aggregation-unforgeable *if for any efficient algorithm* $\mathcal{A}$ *the probability that the experiment* $\mathsf{AggForge}_{\mathcal{A}}^{\mathsf{Agg}}$ *evaluates to* 1 *is negligible (as a function of* λ*), where*

Experiment $\mathsf{AggForge}_{\mathcal{A}}^{\mathsf{Agg}}(\lambda)$
$(sk_1, \mathsf{id}_1), \ldots, (sk_t, \mathsf{id}_t) \leftarrow \mathsf{KGen}(1^\lambda)$
$\mathsf{sk} \leftarrow ((sk_1, \mathsf{id}_1), \ldots, (sk_t, \mathsf{id}_t))$
$(M, \sigma) \leftarrow \mathcal{A}^{\mathsf{Corrupt}(\mathsf{sk},\cdot),\mathsf{OMac}(\mathsf{sk},\cdot),\mathsf{OAgg}(\mathsf{sk},\cdot)}(\mathsf{id}_1, \ldots, \mathsf{id}_t)$
Return 1 iff $\mathsf{AVf}(\mathsf{sk}, M, \sigma) = 1$ *and* $M \notin \mathsf{Closure}(Q_{\mathsf{Mac}}, Q_{\mathsf{Agg}}, Q_{\mathsf{Cor}})$.

3.2 Relationship to the Model of Katz-Lindell

We first prove formally the fact that aggregation-unforgeability implies unforgeability. Then we separate the notion by showing that the aggregate MAC scheme shown in Construction 1 is aggregation-forgeable.

Proposition 1. *Every aggregation-unforgeable message authentication code is also unforgeable.*

Proof. Let $\mathsf{Agg} = (\mathsf{KGen}, \mathsf{Mac}, \mathsf{Vf}, \mathsf{Agg}, \mathsf{AVf})$ be an aggregation-unforgeable message authentication scheme. Suppose towards contradiction that there exists an adversary $\mathcal{A}$ breaking security of Agg. Then we show how to build an algorithm $\mathcal{B}$ against aggregation-unforgeability. This algorithm executes a black-box simulation of $\mathcal{A}$ and answers each oracle query with its own oracles. Finally, $\mathcal{A}$ stops, outputting a pair (M, σ) which $\mathcal{B}$ returns as its forgery.

Algorithm $\mathcal{B}$ performs a perfect simulation from $\mathcal{A}$'s point of view, and since $\mathcal{A}$ is efficient $\mathcal{B}$ is also efficient. To see that the forgery is valid, note that Q_{Agg} is empty because $\mathcal{A}$ performs the aggregation queries locally. Recall that $\mathcal{A}$ only succeeds if there exists at least one pair $(m_{\mathsf{id}_{i^*}}, \mathsf{id}_{i^*}) \in M$ such that $\mathcal{A}$ never queried Corrupt about id_{i^*} and never invoked OMac on $(m_{\mathsf{id}_{i^*}}, \mathsf{id}_{i^*})$. Thus, the forgery is not in the closure and $\mathcal{B}$ succeeds whenever $\mathcal{A}$ returns a valid forgery. □

In the following we separate the notions showing that Construction 1 is "aggregation-forgeable". The basic idea follows the example that we discussed in the previous section and is that $\mathcal{A}$ successfully recombines real subsets of queries to the AMac oracle. Thus, $\mathcal{A}$'s answer M is a set which contains has never been sent to the oracle OAgg.

Proposition 2. *If there exists a deterministic message authentication code where the message-space* $\mathcal{M}_\lambda$ *contains at least four distinct messages, then the aggregate message authentication code defined in Construction 1 is* not *aggregation-unforgeable.*

Proof. The adversary $\mathcal{A}$ forging the aggregate MAC (cf. Definition 4) gets as input $(\mathsf{id}_1, \ldots, \mathsf{id}_t)$ and works as follows: It first picks two identifiers at random from the list, $(\mathsf{id}_1, \mathsf{id}_2)$, chooses randomly four messages $m_1, m_2, m_3, m_4 \leftarrow \mathcal{M}_\lambda$ and sets $M_1 \leftarrow ((m_1, \mathsf{id}_1)(m_2, \mathsf{id}_2))$, $M_2 \leftarrow ((m_1, \mathsf{id}_1)(m_3, \mathsf{id}_2))$ and, $M_3 \leftarrow ((m_4, \mathsf{id}_1)(m_2, \mathsf{id}_2))$. This algorithm then invokes the aggregation oracle three times:

$$\sigma_1 \leftarrow \mathsf{OAgg}(\mathsf{sk}, M_1) \quad \text{and} \quad \sigma_2 \leftarrow \mathsf{OAgg}(\mathsf{sk}, M_2) \quad \text{and} \quad \sigma_3 \leftarrow \mathsf{OAgg}(\mathsf{sk}, M_3).$$

It returns $(M, \sigma) \leftarrow (((m_4, \mathsf{id}_1), (m_3, \mathsf{id}_2)), (\sigma_1 \oplus \sigma_2 \oplus \sigma_3))$.

For the analysis it is easy to see that $\mathcal{A}$ is efficient. The forgery is valid since

$$\begin{aligned}
\sigma = \sigma_1 \oplus \sigma_2 \oplus \sigma_3 &= \mathsf{OAgg}(\mathsf{sk}, M_1) \oplus \mathsf{OAgg}(\mathsf{sk}, M_2) \oplus \mathsf{OAgg}(\mathsf{sk}, M_3) \\
&= \mathsf{Mac}(sk_{\mathsf{id}_1}, m_1) \oplus \mathsf{Mac}(sk_{\mathsf{id}_2}, m_2) \oplus \mathsf{Mac}(sk_{\mathsf{id}_1}, m_1) \oplus \mathsf{Mac}(sk_{\mathsf{id}_2}, m_3) \\
&\quad \oplus \mathsf{Mac}(sk_{\mathsf{id}_1}, m_4) \oplus \mathsf{Mac}(sk_{\mathsf{id}_2}, m_2) \\
&= \mathsf{Mac}(sk_{\mathsf{id}_1}, m_4) \oplus \mathsf{Mac}(sk_{\mathsf{id}_2}, m_3)
\end{aligned}$$

holds. Furthermore $\mathcal{A}$ neither queried the corruption oracle, nor invoked $\mathsf{OAgg}(\mathsf{sk}, \cdot)$ on the tuple $((m_4, \mathsf{id}_1), (m_3, \mathsf{id}_2))$. □

4 History-Free Sequential Aggregate MACs

In this section we introduce the notion of history-free sequential aggregation and adapt the desired security model of aggregation-unforgeability to the new scenario. We then present our sequential aggregate MAC scheme based on an underlying deterministic MAC.

4.1 Definition of Sequential Aggregate MACs

In an aggregate MAC scheme the tags are computed independently by each sender and are then combined into a single aggregate tag. Therefore, the aggregation can be performed even by an unrelated party since the process does not require knowledge of the secret keys. In contrast, in a sequential aggregate MAC schemes the authentication and aggregation is a combined operation. Each sender gets as additional input an aggregate-so-far σ' and transforms that tag into a new aggregate σ which includes the authentication of a message of his choice. We write $M||(m, \mathsf{id})$ for the resulting sequence of message-identifier pairs (where the pair (m, id) is appended to the previous pairs).

Definition 5. *A* sequential aggregate message authentication code *scheme is a tuple of efficient algorithms* $\mathsf{SAGG} = (\mathsf{SKGen}, \mathsf{Mac}, \mathsf{Vf}, \mathsf{SMac}, \mathsf{SVf})$ *such that*

Key generation. SKGen *takes as input the security parameter* 1^λ *and returns a key* sk_{id} *together with an identity* id.

Authentication, Verification. *Defined as in a standard MAC scheme.*

Aggregate Tagging. *Algorithm* SMac *accepts as input a key* sk_{id}*, a message* $m \in \mathcal{M}_\lambda$*, an aggregate-so-far* tag σ' *and a sequence of message/id pairs* $M =$
$((m_1, \mathsf{id}_1), \ldots, (m_t, \mathsf{id}_t))$*. It outputs a new aggregate MAC* σ*.*

Verification algorithm. SVf *takes as input a set of keys* $\mathsf{sk} = \{sk_{\mathsf{id}_1}, \ldots, sk_{\mathsf{id}_\ell}\}$*, a tuple of messages/identifier pairs* $M = ((m_1, \mathsf{id}_1), \ldots, (m_t, \mathsf{id}_t))$ *as well as an alleged sequential aggregate tag* σ *and outputs a bit.*

A sequential aggregate MAC scheme is complete *if*

- *(Single-MAC Correctness) For any pair* $(sk_{\mathsf{id}}, \mathsf{id}) \leftarrow \mathsf{SKGen}(1^\lambda)$*, any message* $m \in \mathcal{M}_\lambda$ *and any* $\sigma \leftarrow \mathsf{Mac}(sk_{\mathsf{id}}, m)$*, it holds that* $\mathsf{Vf}(sk_{\mathsf{id}}, m, \sigma) = 1$*.*
- *(Aggregation Correctness) For all pairs* $(sk_{id}, \mathsf{id}) \leftarrow \mathsf{SKGen}(1^\lambda)$*, all messages* $m \in \mathcal{M}_\lambda$*, for any set of message/identifier pairs* $M = \{(m_1, \mathsf{id}_1), \ldots, (m_\ell, \mathsf{id}_\ell)\}$ *(where* $(m_i, \mathsf{id}_i) \in \mathcal{M}_\lambda \times \{0,1\}^\lambda$ *for all* $i = 1, \ldots, \ell$*), any set of keys* sk *and any tag* $\sigma' \in \mathcal{R}_\lambda$ *with* $\mathsf{SVf}(\mathsf{sk}, M, \sigma') = 1$ *we require that for all* $\sigma \leftarrow \mathsf{SMac}(sk_{\mathsf{id}}, m, \sigma', M)$ *it holds that* $\mathsf{SVf}((\mathsf{sk}||sk_{\mathsf{id}}), M||(m, id_{\mathsf{id}}), \sigma) = 1$*.*

A common approach to build sequential aggregate *signature* schemes is to verify the validity of an received aggregate-so-far before computing the new aggregate. Often, the aggregation algorithm even includes the previous messages in its computations. In the private key setting, however, verification of the aggregate may not be possible as nodes do not share all keys. Moreover, compared with non-sequential schemes, where the aggregation process does not depend on the previous messages, this is a main drawback of sequential schemes (especially from an efficiency point of view). The idea of history-free sequential aggregation is to overcome that restriction by requiring that the aggregation only depends on the aggregate-so-far and the local message.

Definition 6 (History Freeness). *A sequential aggregate message authentication scheme* $\mathsf{SAGG} = (\mathsf{SKGen}, \mathsf{Mac}, \mathsf{Vf}, \mathsf{SMac}, \mathsf{SVf})$ *is called* history-free *if there exists an efficient algorithm* SMac_{hf} *such that* $\mathsf{SMac}_{hf}(\cdot,\cdot,\cdot) = \mathsf{SMac}(\cdot,\cdot,\cdot,M)$ *for all* M*.*

In the sequel we often identify $\mathsf{SMac}_{\mathsf{hf}}$ with SMac and simply omit M from the input of SMac.

4.2 Security Model

A sequential aggregate MAC is called *aggregation-unforgeable*, if any efficient adversary $\mathcal{A}$ succeeds in the following two-phase experiment only with negligible probability. In the first phase, the adversary has access to a corrupt oracle Corrupt, and can obtain the secret keys of senders of his choice. As soon as $\mathcal{A}$ queries its sequential aggregate MAC oracle SeqAgg, the corruption phase has ended and the adversary $\mathcal{A}$ is not allowed to query the corrupt oracle again. The sequential aggregate MAC oracle SeqAgg takes as input a set $\mathsf{sk} = (sk_{\mathsf{id}_1}, \ldots, sk_{\mathsf{id}_\ell})$, an aggregate-so-far tag σ', an ordered set

$M = \{(m_1, \mathsf{id}_1), \ldots, (m_q, \mathsf{id}_q)\}$ of message identifier pairs and returns a (sequentially ordered) tag σ.

Before proposing the formal security model, we define the closure of all trivial combinations. We denote by Q_{Seq} the set of all query/answer tuples $((M, \sigma'), \sigma)$ that occur in $\mathcal{A}$'s interaction with the SeqAgg oracle and by Q_{Cor} we denote the set of all identities' that were queried to the Corrupt oracle.

We stress that in the context of sequential aggregate MACs given the adversary access to a MAC oracle is redundant. Each query to a (single) MAC oracle can easily simulated by calling the sequential aggregate oracle with the empty tag $\sigma_\varnothing$. Thus, the definition of the closure does not need the set Q_{Mac} of queries and responses from the MAC oracle (since this set in contained in Q_{Seq}).

Definition 7 (Sequential Closure of $\mathcal{A}$'s queries). *Let M be a set of message/identifier pairs, let Q_{Cor} and Q_{Seq} be the sets corresponding to the different oracle responses and let $m_\varnothing$ ($\sigma_\varnothing$) be the empty message (empty tag, respectively). Let* $\mathsf{Trivial}_{Q_{\mathsf{Seq}}, Q_{\mathsf{Cor}}}$ *be a recursive function of trivial combinations defined as*

$$\mathsf{Trivial}_{Q_{\mathsf{Seq}}, Q_{\mathsf{Cor}}}(M, \sigma) := \{M\} \cup \bigcup_{((\sigma, M'), \sigma') \in Q_{\mathsf{Agg}}} \mathsf{Trivial}_{Q_{\mathsf{Seq}}, Q_{\mathsf{Cor}}}(M || M', \sigma')$$
$$\cup \bigcup_{\substack{\forall \bar{m}, \bar{\sigma} \\ \wedge id_i \in Q_{\mathsf{Cor}}}} \mathsf{Trivial}_{Q_{\mathsf{Seq}}, Q_{\mathsf{Cor}}}(M || (\bar{m}, id_i), \bar{\sigma}).$$

We can now define the closure Closure *of $\mathcal{A}$'s queries Q_{Agg} and Q_{Cor} by recursively generating the trivial combinations starting from the empty message $m_\varnothing$ and empty tag $\sigma_\varnothing$ as described above:*

$$\mathsf{Closure}(Q_{\mathsf{Agg}}, Q_{\mathsf{Cor}}) := \{\mathsf{Trivial}_{Q_{\mathsf{Seq}}, Q_{\mathsf{Cor}}}(m_\varnothing, \sigma_\varnothing)\}.$$

With the definition of the sequential closure, we propose the following security model for sequential aggregate MACs.

Definition 8. *A sequential aggregate message authentication code scheme* $\mathsf{SAGG} = (\mathsf{SKGen}, \mathsf{Mac}, \mathsf{Vf}, \mathsf{SMac}, \mathsf{SVf})$ *is* aggregation-unforgeable *if for any efficient algorithm $\mathcal{A}$ (working in mode* COR, FOR*) the probability that the experiment* $\mathsf{SeqForge}_{\mathcal{A}}^{\mathsf{Agg}}$ *evaluates to 1 is negligible (as a function of λ), where*

Experiment $\mathsf{SeqForge}_{\mathcal{A}}^{\mathsf{Agg}}(\lambda)$
$(sk_1, \mathsf{id}_1), \ldots, (sk_t, \mathsf{id}_t) \leftarrow \mathsf{SKGen}(1^\lambda)$
$\mathsf{sk} \leftarrow ((sk_1, \mathsf{id}_1), \ldots, (sk_t, \mathsf{id}_t))$
$\mathsf{st} \leftarrow \mathcal{A}^{\mathsf{Corrupt}(\mathsf{sk}, \cdot)}(\text{COR}, \mathsf{id}_1, \ldots . \mathsf{id}_t)$ // *it is understood that $\mathcal{A}$ keeps state* st
$(M, \sigma) \leftarrow \mathcal{A}^{\mathsf{SeqAgg}(\mathsf{sk}, \cdot, \cdot)}(\text{FOR}, \mathsf{st}, \mathsf{id}_1, \ldots, \mathsf{id}_t)$
Return 1 iff $\mathsf{id}_i \neq \mathsf{id}_j$ *for all* $i \neq j$ *and* $\mathsf{SVf}(\mathsf{sk}, M, \sigma) = 1$ *and*
$M \notin \mathsf{Closure}(Q_{\mathsf{Agg}}, Q_{\mathsf{Cor}})$.

Note that in the definition above the adversary $\mathcal{A}$ running in mode FOR has only access to the sequential aggregate MAC oracle an *not* to a tagging oracle Mac. We argue that this is redundant since the attacker is allowed to invoke SeqAgg on tags of its choice. Thus, $\mathcal{A}$ can query SeqAgg on arbitrary messages m together with the empty tag $\sigma_\varnothing$ and yields an ordinary tag for m.

5 Construction of History-Free Sequential MACs

The idea behind our construction is as follows. We again use a "chaining" approach in which we let the next aggregating party (with identity id) compute the next tag over its own message $M \in \{0,1\}^*$ and over the previous tag σ'. That is, $\tau \leftarrow \mathsf{Mac}(sk, M \| \sigma')$ for the deterministic algorithm $\mathsf{Mac}(sk, \cdot) : \{0,1\}^* \rightarrow \{0,1\}^\lambda$. To preserve the order of the aggregating parties we let each party prepend its own identity id to the resulting tag $\sigma \leftarrow \mathsf{id} \| \tau$. Thus, the next party essentially computes a MAC for its own message, the identity of the previous party and the previous tagging result. Formally, prepending id enlarges the tag, yet in most applications the identity of the sending party is known anyway and does not need to be included explicitly.

Proving the security of the above approach leads to some difficulties. Namely, the adversary could potentially gain information from the final tag about an intermediate value, and could thus easily "shorten" such aggregation chains. To prevent this we assume that MAC itself is pseudorandom, ensuring that no such information is leaked.

We also need a special property of the MAC allowing us to "go backwards" in a chain: assume that an adversary successfully outputs a forged sequence by predicting one of the intermediate MACs correctly. Then, in order to break the security of the underlying MAC, we need to be able to undo the MAC computations afterwards and to access the intermediate MAC values. We add this *partial inversion* property as an requirement to the (pseudorandom) MAC and show that standard constructions like CMAC have this property and that one can easily build such MACs from pseudorandom permutations.

5.1 Properties of the MAC

Recall that we need two properties of the underlying MAC in order to make our construction work: pseudorandomness and partial inversion:

Definition 9 (Pseudorandom MAC). *A det. message authentication code* $\mathsf{MAC} = (\mathsf{KGen}, \mathsf{Mac}, \mathsf{Vf})$ *is* pseudorandom *(or a* pseudorandom function*) if for any efficient algorithm $\mathcal{D}$ the value*

$$\left| \mathrm{Prob}\left[\mathcal{D}^{\mathsf{Mac}(sk,\cdot)}(1^\lambda) = 1 \right] - \mathrm{Prob}\left[\mathcal{D}^{f(\cdot)}(1^\lambda) = 1 \right] \right|$$

is negligible, where the probability in the first case is over $\mathcal{D}$'s coin tosses and the choice of $sk \leftarrow \mathsf{KGen}(1^\lambda)$, and in the second case over $\mathcal{D}$'s coin tosses and the choice of the random function $f : \{0,1\}^* \rightarrow \{0,1\}^\lambda$.

A pseudorandom function is called a pseudorandom permutation if it is also a permutation. Note that pseudorandom MACs are unforgeable, too.

Definition 10 (Partial Inversion). *A deterministic message authentication code* $\mathsf{MAC} = (\mathsf{KGen}, \mathsf{Mac}, \mathsf{Vf})$ *is* partially invertible *if there exists an efficient algorithm* $\mathsf{PartInv}$ *which, for any security parameter $\lambda \in \mathbb{N}$, any key $sk \leftarrow \mathsf{KGen}(1^\lambda)$, any $M = M' \| m$ for some $m \in \{0,1\}^\lambda$, and any $\sigma \in \{0,1\}^\lambda$, on input (sk, M', σ) returns a string* $\mathsf{m} \in \{0,1\}^\lambda$ *such that* $\mathsf{Mac}(sk, M' \| \mathsf{m}) = \sigma$.

In the following we present two efficient constructions satisfying the definition of partial inversion. The first construction is CMAC (a security proof is given by Iwata and Kurosawa under the name OMAC in [4]) which can be used for messages of fixed block length. The reason for not using CMAC for arbitrary input-lengths is that the desired block may not be aligned to the final λ bits. The second construction uses a pseudorandom permutation and is applicable for messages of variable length.

A Solution Based on CMAC. If the length of the message/identifier pair is a positive multiple of the block size, then CMAC can be used as the underlying (pseudorandom) message authentication code (when a pseudorandom permutation PRP lies underneath). We first review CMAC briefly and show then that CMAC supports partial inversion.

The key generation algorithm of CMAC generates a pair of keys sk, sk_1 where sk_1 is derived from sk.[3] In order to compute a tag, the tagging algorithm takes as input a message $M = m_1 || \dots || m_k \in \{0,1\}^{k \cdot \lambda}$ and two keys sk, sk_1. It computes

$$c_i \leftarrow \mathsf{PRP}(sk, m_i \oplus c_{i-1}) \text{ for } i = 1, \dots, k-1 \text{ (where } c_0 = 0^\lambda) ,$$

and outputs the final tag as $\sigma \leftarrow \mathsf{PRP}(sk, c_{k-1} \oplus sk_1 \oplus m_k)$. Unforgeability and pseudorandomness follow from the security of CMAC for aligned inputs.

Lemma 1. *CMAC is partially invertible.*

Proof. In the following we describe the algorithm $\mathsf{PartInv}$ which takes as input a message $M' = m_1, \dots, m_{k-1}$ (consisting of $k-1$ blocks $m_1, \dots, m_{k-1}$ of λ bits each) a pair of keys (sk, sk_1), and a tag σ. In the first step, this algorithm emulates the iteration of CMAC but omitting the last step, $c_i \leftarrow \mathsf{PRP}(sk, m_i \oplus c_{i-1})$ for $i = 1, \dots, k-1$. Algorithm $\mathsf{PartInv}$ then decrypts the received tag $\tau \leftarrow \mathsf{PRP}^{-1}(sk, \sigma)$ and returns $\mathsf{m} \leftarrow c_{k-1} \oplus sk_1 \oplus \tau$. It is clear that this recovers an appropriate value m. □

A General Solution. In the following let $M = M' \| m \in \mathcal{M}_\lambda$ be a message whose block length is *not* a positive multiple of the block size. We then present a suitable MAC scheme based on general assumptions. The main idea of the construction is to execute (the underlying deterministic) tagging algorithm $\tau \leftarrow \mathsf{Mac}(sk, M')$ on the first part M' of the message M and to compute a pseudorandom permutation on the value $\tau \oplus m$.

Construction 2. *Let* $\mathsf{MAC} = (\mathsf{KGen}, \mathsf{Mac}, \mathsf{Vf})$ *be a deterministic message authentication code and* $\mathsf{PRP}(\cdot, \cdot)$ *be a pseudorandom permutation (where* Mac *for security parameter* λ *produces* λ*-bit outputs and* PRP *is also over* λ*-bits for security parameter* λ*). We define the procedures* $\mathsf{CKg}, \mathsf{CTag}$ *and* CVf *as follows:*

[3] Note that CMAC deduces two keys sk_1 and sk_2 from sk. As in this construction the second key sk_2 is not required, we omit it here.

KeyGen. *The key generation algorithm* $\mathsf{CKg}(1^\lambda)$ *generates a key* $sk \leftarrow \mathsf{KGen}(1^\lambda)$, *chooses a key* $\mathsf{k}_{\mathsf{PRP}} \in \{0,1\}^\lambda$ *at random and returns* $(sk, \mathsf{k}_{\mathsf{PRP}})$.

Tagging. $\mathsf{CTag}((sk, \mathsf{k}_{\mathsf{PRP}}), M)$ *takes a message* $M = M' \| m$ *with* $M' \in \{0,1\}^*$ *and* $m \in \{0,1\}^\lambda$ *as well as a key pair* $sk, \mathsf{k}_{\mathsf{PRP}}$. *It computes* $\tau \leftarrow \mathsf{Mac}(sk, M')$ *and returns the value* $\mathsf{PRP}(\mathsf{k}_{\mathsf{PRP}}, \tau \oplus m)$.

Verification. *The algorithm* $\mathsf{CVf}((sk, \mathsf{k}_{\mathsf{PRP}}), M, \sigma)$ *returns to* 1 *iff* $\mathsf{CTag}((sk, \mathsf{k}_{\mathsf{PRP}}), M) = \sigma$, *otherwise* 0.

Note that we do not claim to be able to recover the full message $M\|\sigma'$ from a MAC $\tau \leftarrow \mathsf{Mac}(sk, M\|\sigma')$, but it suffices that we recover σ' *given* sk, M *and* σ. The following theorem proves formally the security and the partial inversion property of the construction.

Theorem 3. *If* $\mathsf{MAC} = (\mathsf{KGen}, \mathsf{Mac}, \mathsf{Vf})$ *is an unforgeable message authentication code and* PRP *is a pseudorandom permutation, then Construction 2 is a pseudorandom, partially invertible message authentication code.*

We proof this theorem through the following two proposition, first showing that the resulting MAC scheme is secure and second its partial inversion.

Proposition 3. *If* $\mathsf{MAC} = (\mathsf{KGen}, \mathsf{Mac}, \mathsf{Vf})$ *is an unforgeable message authentication code and* PRP *is a pseudorandom permutation, then Construction 2 is pseudorandom.*

The proof idea is to apply the well-known result that the composition of a (computational) almost universal function and a pseudorandom function remains pseudorandom (see, for example, [1]). This clearly yields a secure MAC. Hence, for our construction it suffices to show that the "inner" part of our MAC algorithm is computational almost universal. Before stating this result, we give a formal definition of computational almost universal MACs.

Definition 11. *A message authentication code* MAC *is called* computational almost universal (cAU) *if for any efficient algorithm* $\mathcal{A}$ *the probability that experiment* cAU *evaluates to 1 is negligible (as a function of* λ*), where*

Experiment $\mathsf{cAU}_{\mathcal{A}}^{\mathsf{MAC}}(\lambda)$
$sk \leftarrow \mathsf{KGen}(1^\lambda)$
$(M_1, M_2) \leftarrow \mathcal{A}(1^\lambda)$
Return 1 iff $M_1 \neq M_2$ *and* $\mathsf{Mac}(sk, M_1) = \mathsf{Mac}(sk, M_2)$.

Lemma 2. *For an unforgeable deterministic message authentication codes* $\mathsf{MAC}' = (\mathsf{KGen}', \mathsf{Mac}', \mathsf{Vf}')$ *the algorithm* $\mathsf{Mac}'(sk, M') \oplus m$ *for* $M = M'\|m$ *is computational almost universal (for key generation* $sk \leftarrow \mathsf{KGen}'(1^\lambda)$*).*

Proof. To prove this lemma first consider the case that we have $M_1' = M_2'$ for a successful adversarial output $M_1 = M_1'\|m_1$, $M_2 = M_2'\|m_2$. Then it must hold that $m_1 \neq m_2$, implying that $\mathsf{Mac}'(sk, M_1') \oplus m_1 \neq \mathsf{Mac}'(sk, M_2') \oplus m_2$ for the deterministic algorithm Mac'. Hence assume from now on that there exists an algorithm $\mathcal{A}$ breaking the almost universal property of the MAC scheme proposed in Construction 2 with noticeable probability for $M_1' \neq M_2'$. We then build an algorithm $\mathcal{B}$, against the underlying MAC scheme MAC', which executes $\mathcal{A}$ in a black-box way and works as follows. $\mathcal{B}$ gets as input the security parameter 1^λ, has access to an tagging oracle $\mathsf{Mac}(sk, \cdot)$ and initiates $\mathcal{A}$ on input 1^λ. At the end of the simulation $\mathcal{A}$ outputs two messages $M_1 = M_1'||m_1$, $M_2 = M_2'||m_2$. $\mathcal{B}$ invokes its MAC oracle $\mathsf{Mac}(sk, \cdot)$ on M_1' and gets σ_1' and outputs $(M_2', \sigma_1' \oplus m_1 \oplus m_2)$.

For the analysis note that $\mathcal{B}$ is efficient since $\mathcal{A}$ is efficient. Furthermore, given that $\mathcal{A}$ produces a collision M_1, M_2 with $M_1' \neq M_2'$, adversary $\mathcal{B}$ succeeds in producing a forgery for a new message since it queries its oracle only once about $M_1' \neq M_2'$ and the derived tag is obviously valid. □

Concerning partial inversion, we have:

Proposition 4. *The message authentication code defined in Construction 2 is partially invertible.*

Proof. The construction supports partial inversion: The algorithm $\mathsf{PartInv}$ takes as input a pair of keys $(sk, \mathsf{k}_{\mathsf{PRP}})$, a string M' and a tag σ. It computes $\tau \leftarrow \mathsf{Mac}(sk, M')$, $c \leftarrow \mathsf{PRP}^{-1}(\mathsf{k}_{\mathsf{PRP}}, \sigma)$ and returns $\mathsf{m} \leftarrow \tau \oplus c$. It is now easy to see that this output is valid. □

5.2 Construction

Construction 4. *Let* $\mathsf{MAC} = (\mathsf{KGen}, \mathsf{Mac}, \mathsf{Vf})$ *be a deterministic MAC. Let* $\mathsf{SAM} = (\mathsf{SeqKg}, \mathsf{SeqAgg}, \mathsf{SeqAggVf})$ *be as follows:*

- **Key Generation.** *The key generation algorithm* SeqKg *takes as input the security parameter* 1^λ, *picks an identifier at random* $\mathsf{id} \in \{0,1\}^\lambda$, *executes the key generation algorithm of the underlying MAC scheme* $sk \leftarrow \mathsf{KGen}(1^\lambda)$ *and returns the pair* (sk, id).
- **Sequential Aggregation.** *The algorithm* $\mathsf{SeqAgg}(sk, M, \mathsf{id}, \sigma')$ *takes as input a private key* sk, *a message* $M \in \{0,1\}^*$, *and a (sequentially aggregated) tag* σ'. *It executes the underlying tagging algorithm* $\tau \leftarrow \mathsf{Mac}(sk, M||\sigma')$ *and outputs* $\sigma \leftarrow \mathsf{id}||\tau$. *(For* $\sigma_0 = \emptyset$ *simply run the MAC algorithm on* M *only.)*
- **Aggregate Verification.** *The input of algorithm* $\mathsf{SeqAggVf}$ *is a sequence of keys* $\mathsf{sk} = (sk_1, \ldots, sk_\ell)$, *a tag* σ *and sequences* $\mathbf{M} = (M_1, \ldots, M_\ell)$ *and* $\mathbf{id} = (\mathsf{id}_1, \ldots, \mathsf{id}_\ell)$ *of messages and identifiers. If any key in* sk *appears twice then return* 0. *Otherwise compute for* $i = 1, \ldots, \ell$, $\sigma_i \leftarrow \mathsf{id}_i||\mathsf{Mac}(sk_i, M_i||\sigma_{i-1})$, *with* $\sigma_0 \leftarrow \emptyset$. *Return* 1 *iff* $\sigma_\ell = \sigma$, *otherwise* 0.

The following theorem captures the security of our construction:

Theorem 5. *If* $\mathsf{MAC} = (\mathsf{KGen}, \mathsf{Mac}, \mathsf{Vf})$ *is a pseudorandom, partially invertible message authentication code then Construction 4 is a history-free, aggregation-unforgeable sequential aggregate message authentication code scheme.*

More precisely, we show that, letting t be the number of parties and Q denote the number of aggregation queries, each of L message-identity pairs at most,

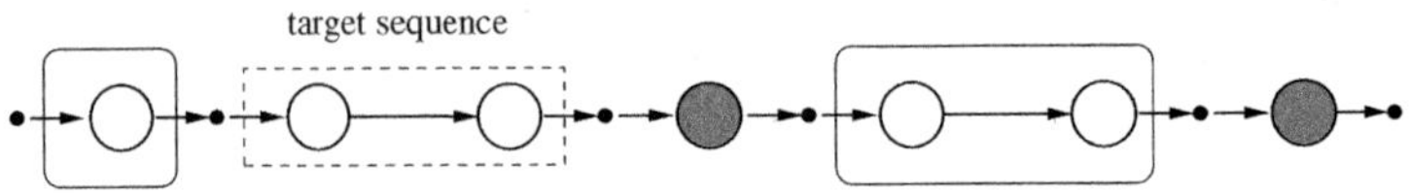

Fig. 1. Example of a target sequence. Shaded circles denote corrupt parties and boxes correspond to aggregation queries such that the input/output aggregates (small filled circles) are known by the adversary.

the probability that an adversary breaks the aggregate MAC scheme is bounded from above by $3t(Q+1)^2L^2$ times the probability of breaking the underlying MAC, plus the advantage of breaking the pseudorandomness of the MAC (in both cases with comparable running time).

The idea of our proof is as follows. When the adversary eventually outputs a forgery attempt there must be a subsequence which is not assembled out of seen values or values of corrupt parties. In particular, this *target sequence* contains only values of honest parties (see Figure 1). We first show that there are no collisions among aggregates output by honest parties (else one could use this collision to forge MACs). It follows that this target sequence cannot be a suffix of an aggregation query because the identity in the forgery attempt must be different from the identity in the corresponding aggregation query (else we would have found a collision when entering the target sequence). The target sequence cannot be a prefix of a previous aggregation query because the pseudorandomness of the MAC hides all information about aggregates in a chain. Hence, the target sequence must be "fresh", implying that one must be able to forge the underlying MAC.

The formal proof that the construction is indeed secure is given in the full version.

Acknowledgments. We thank all the anonymous reviewers for their comments. This work was supported by the Emmy Noether Program Fi 940/2-1 of the German Research Foundation (DFG).

References

1. Bellare, M.: New Proofs for NMAC and HMAC: Security without Collision Resistance. In: Dwork, C. (ed.) CRYPTO 2006. LNCS, vol. 4117, pp. 602–619. Springer, Heidelberg (2006)
2. Boneh, D., Gentry, C., Lynn, B., Shacham, H.: Aggregate and Vericiably Encrypted Signatures from Bilinear Maps. In: Biham, E. (ed.) EUROCRYPT 2003. LNCS, vol. 2656, pp. 416–432. Springer, Heidelberg (2003)
3. Boldyreva, A., Gentry, C., O'Neill, A., Yum, D.H.: Ordered multisignatures and identity-based sequential aggregate signatures, with applications to secure routing. In: ACM Conference on Computer and Communications Security, pp. 276–285. ACM Press, New York (2007)
4. Iwata, T., Kurosawa, K.: OMAC: One-Key CBC MAC. In: Johansson, T. (ed.) FSE 2003. LNCS, vol. 2887, pp. 129–153. Springer, Heidelberg (2003)

5. Katz, J., Lindell, A.Y.: Aggregate Message Authentication Codes. In: Malkin, T.G. (ed.) CT-RSA 2008. LNCS, vol. 4964, pp. 155–169. Springer, Heidelberg (2008)
6. Lysyanskaya, A., Micali, S., Reyzin, L., Shacham, H.: Sequential Aggre- gate Signatures from Trapdoor Permutations. In: Cachin, C., Camenisch, J.L. (eds.) EUROCRYPT 2004. LNCS, vol. 3027, pp. 74–90. Springer, Heidelberg (2004)
7. Neven, G.: Efficient Sequential Aggregate Signed Data. In: Smart, N.P. (ed.) EUROCRYPT 2008. LNCS, vol. 4965, pp. 52–69. Springer, Heidelberg (2008)

A Mix-and-Match Attacks on the Katz-Lindell Scheme

In this section we discuss several attack strategies against the Katz-Lindell [5] aggregate MAC scheme. Note that our attacks do not contradict the security results in [5], because the scheme has only been designed to meet the relaxed unforgeability notion.

The aggregation step in the Katz-Lindell scheme is rather simple: the aggregation algorithm computes the exclusive-or over all (deterministically computed) tags resp. in our routing example of four nodes $N_1 \to N_2 \to N_3 \to N_4$, node N_i adds its MAC for message M_i to the current aggregate value.

Deletion Attack. Given the replies

$$\sigma_1 = \mathsf{Mac}(sk_1, M_1) \oplus \mathsf{Mac}(sk_2, M_2) \oplus \mathsf{Mac}(sk_3, M_3), \qquad \sigma_2 = \mathsf{Mac}(sk_2, M_2)$$

to two aggregation queries for message sets $\{M_1, M_2, M_3\}$, and $\{M_2\}$, where each message M_i is given to node N_i, the adversary is able to delete the element $\sigma_2 = \mathsf{Mac}(sk_2, M_2)$ from the aggregate:

$$\sigma_1^* = \sigma_1 \oplus \sigma_2 = \mathsf{Mac}(sk_1, M_1) \oplus \mathsf{Mac}(sk_3, M_3)$$

and obtains a valid "fresh" aggregate on the set (on the invalid route $N_1 \to N_3$) $\{M_1, M_3\}$.

Re-Ordering Attack. Given the replies

$$\sigma_1 = \mathsf{Mac}(sk_1, M_1) \oplus \mathsf{Mac}(sk_2, M_2), \quad \sigma_2 = \mathsf{Mac}(sk_1, M_3) \oplus \mathsf{Mac}(sk_2, M_2), \quad \sigma_3 = \mathsf{Mac}(sk_1, M_1) \oplus \mathsf{Mac}(sk_2, M_4)$$

to three aggregation queries for message sets $\{M_1, M_2\}$, $\{M_2, M_3\}$ and $\{M_1, M_4\}$, the adversary is able to compute a valid aggregate

$$\sigma^* = \sigma_1 \oplus \sigma_2 \oplus \sigma_3 = \mathsf{Mac}(sk_1, M_3) \oplus \mathsf{Mac}(sk_2, M_4)$$

for the set $\{M_3, M_4\}$.

Extension Attack. Given the replies

$$\sigma_1 = \mathsf{Mac}(sk_1, M_1) \oplus \mathsf{Mac}(sk_2, M_2) \oplus \mathsf{Mac}(sk_3, M_3) \; \sigma_2 = \mathsf{Mac}(sk_A, M_A) \oplus \mathsf{Mac}(sk_B, M_B)$$

to the aggregation queries for message sets $\{M_1, M_2, M_3\}$ and $\{M_A, M_B\}$, the adversary is able to extend the aggregate:

$$\sigma_3^* = \sigma_1 \oplus \sigma_2 = \mathsf{Mac}(sk_1, M_1) \oplus \mathsf{Mac}(sk_A, M_A) \oplus \mathsf{Mac}(sk_3, M_3) \oplus \mathsf{Mac}(sk_B, M_B) \oplus \mathsf{Mac}(sk_2, M_2)$$

and obtains a valid "fresh" aggregate on the set (on the route) $\{M_1, M_A, M_3, M_B, M_2\}$ (for arbitrary M_A, M_B).

Recombination Attack. Given the replies

$$\sigma_1 = \mathsf{Mac}(sk_1, M_1) \oplus \mathsf{Mac}(sk_2, M_2) \oplus \mathsf{Mac}(sk_3, M_3),$$
$$\sigma_2 = \mathsf{Mac}(sk_2, M_2) \oplus \mathsf{Mac}(sk_3, M_3) \oplus \mathsf{Mac}(sk_4, M_4),$$

and

$$\sigma_3 = \mathsf{Mac}(sk_3, M_3) \oplus \mathsf{Mac}(sk_4, M_4) \oplus \mathsf{Mac}(sk_5, M_5),$$

to the aggregation queries for message sets $\{M_1, M_2, M_3\}$, $\{M_2, M_3, M_4\}$, and $\{M_3, M_4, M_5\}$, the adversary is able to recombine the aggregate,

$$\sigma^* = \sigma_1 \oplus \sigma_2 \oplus \sigma_3 = \mathsf{Mac}(sk_1, M_1) \oplus \mathsf{Mac}(sk_5, M_5) \oplus \mathsf{Mac}(sk_3, M_3),$$

and obtains a valid "fresh" aggregate on the set (on the route) $\{M_1, M_5, M_3\}$.

Note also that, if we assume N_i only accepts input from N_{i-1} then replay attacks do not necessarily help, because the adversary can never send a previously obtained tuple $\{M_1, M_2\}$ to the node N_4.

B Preliminaries: MACs and Their Security

Definition 12 (Message Authentication Codes). *A message authentication code scheme* $\mathsf{MAC} = (\mathsf{KGen}, \mathsf{Mac}, \mathsf{Vf})$ *is a triple of efficient algorithms where*

Key Generation. $\mathsf{KGen}(1^\lambda)$ *gets as input the security parameter* 1^λ *and returns a key* sk.

Authentication. *The authentication algorithm* $\sigma \leftarrow \mathsf{Mac}(sk, m)$ *takes as input the key* sk*, a message* m *from a message space* $\mathcal{M}_\lambda$ *and returns a tag* σ *in a range* $\mathcal{R}_\lambda$.

Verification. $\mathsf{Vf}(sk, m, \sigma)$ *returns a bit.*

It is assumed that the scheme is complete*, i.e., for all* $sk \leftarrow \mathsf{KGen}(1^\lambda)$*, any* $m \in \mathcal{M}_\lambda$*, and any* $\sigma \leftarrow \mathsf{Mac}(sk, m)$ *we have* $\mathsf{Vf}(sk, m, \sigma) = 1$.

A message authentication code is called *deterministic* if the tagging algorithm is deterministic. A deterministic MAC is called *canonical* if the verification algorithm recomputes the tag for a given message and checks that it matches the given one. Unforgeability demands that it is infeasible to produce a valid tag for a new message:

Definition 13 (Unforgeability). *A message authentication code* $\mathsf{MAC} = (\mathsf{KGen}, \mathsf{Mac}, \mathsf{Vf})$ *is* (t, q_t, q_v, ϵ)-unforgeable under chosen message attacks *(EU-CMA) if for any algorithm* $\mathcal{A}$ *running in time* t *the probability that the experiment* $\mathsf{Forge}_{\mathcal{A}}^{\mathsf{MAC}}$ *evaluates to* 1 *is at most* $\epsilon(\lambda)$*, where*

Experiment $\mathsf{Forge}_{\mathcal{A}}^{\mathsf{MAC}}(\lambda)$
$sk \leftarrow \mathsf{KGen}(1^\lambda)$
$(m^*, \sigma^*) \leftarrow \mathcal{A}^{\mathsf{Mac}(sk,\cdot),\mathsf{Vf}(sk,\cdot,\cdot)}(1^\lambda)$
Return 1 *if, at some point,* $\mathcal{A}$ *makes a query* m^*, σ^* *to* Vf *such that* $\mathsf{Vf}(sk, m^*, \sigma^*) = 1$ *and* $\mathcal{A}$ *has never queried* $\mathsf{Mac}(sk, \cdot)$ *about* m^* *before.*

and $\mathcal{A}$ *makes at most* q_t *queries to oracle* Mac *and at most* q_v *queries to oracle* Vf. *The probability is taken over all coin tosses of* KGen, Mac, Vf *and* $\mathcal{A}$.

C Counter-Based Aggregation-Unforgeable Schemes

In this section we show that, assuming the existence of a shared counter, we can lift non-ordered aggregate schemes that are unforgeable in the classical sense to achieve a stronger security requirement. However, even such an assumption only allows to prevent some of the mix-and-matching attacks discussed in the introduction, but not attacks aiming to erase subsets of previously queried aggregates. Thus, we introduce a slightly weaker definition of aggregation-unforgeability by considering forgeries that consist of those subsets as trivial. This corresponds to the case that the adversary can remove contributions of honest parties from valid aggregates. Recall that the adversary can query an aggregation oracle, denoted by OAgg, which takes the key/identity pairs (sk_i, id_i) of all honest parties (provided by the system) and a set of message/identity pairs $M = \{(m_1, \mathsf{id}_1), \ldots, (m_k, \mathsf{id}_k)\}$ (chosen by the adversary). The oracle returns an aggregate MAC σ for these data.

To mark subsets of aggregation queries as trivial, we include all message sets that are subsets of queried aggregates into the closure:

$$\mathsf{Closure}^*(Q_{\mathsf{Agg}}, Q_{\mathsf{Cor}}) = \left\{ \bigcup_{M_A \in A} M_A \cup \bigcup_{M_A^* \subseteq A^*} M_A^* \cup M_C \;\middle|\; A^* \in Q_{\mathsf{Agg}}, A \subseteq Q_{\mathsf{Agg}}, M_C \subseteq \bigcup_{\mathsf{id}^* \in Q_{\mathsf{Cor}}} \{(m, \mathsf{id}^*) \,|\, m \in \mathcal{M}_\lambda\} \right\}.$$

We now show how to construct an aggregate tag scheme that is aggregation-unforgeable with respect to the weaker definition.

Given an aggregate MAC scheme $\mathsf{Agg} = (\mathsf{KGen}, \mathsf{Mac}, \mathsf{Vf}, \mathsf{Agg}, \mathsf{AVf})$ that is unforgeable according to the definition of Katz and Lindell [5] we can derive a counter-based aggregate tag scheme that achieves our stronger security requirement of aggregation-unforgeability. To this end, we augment the aggregate tag scheme as follows:

- KGen and AVf remain unchanged
- $\mathsf{Mac}^*(sk, m)$ queries Mac on the string $m^* = (\mathsf{count}, m)$ where count is a synchronized counter shared between all signing parties. It outputs $\sigma^* = (\mathsf{count}, \sigma)$ with $\sigma \leftarrow \mathsf{Mac}(sk, (\mathsf{count}, m))$ and updates the counter.

- $\mathsf{Agg}^*(M, \sigma)$ parses σ as $\{(\mathsf{count}_1, \sigma_1), \ldots, (\mathsf{count}_\ell, \sigma_\ell)\}$ and stops with output $\perp$ if the counter values differ. Else, it computes $\sigma \leftarrow \mathsf{Agg}(M^*, \{\sigma_1, \ldots, \sigma_\ell\})$ for $m_i^* = (\mathsf{count}, m_i)$ and outputs $\sigma^* = (\mathsf{count}, \sigma)$.
- $\mathsf{AggVf}^*(\mathsf{sk}, M, (\mathsf{count}, \sigma))$ sets $M^* = \{(\mathsf{count}, m_1), \ldots, (\mathsf{count}, m_\ell)\}$ for $M = \{m_1, \ldots, m_\ell\}$ and outputs $\mathsf{AggVf}(\mathsf{sk}, M^*, \sigma)$.

Prepending a unique counter value to the messages in each signing request prevents the adversary from recombining several aggregates into a new one, as the verification algorithm first checks that all messages carry the same counter value. Recall that the strength of the adversary in our security model stems from granting an aggregation oracle and considering non-trivial recombinations of aggregates as valid forgeries. However, if the adversary tries to exploit the potential of recombining aggregates into fresh ones, he has to ensure that all counter values are equal. Hence, the adversary can at most delete messages from aggregates or add values by corrupt parties.

More formally, assume that the adversary eventually outputs a valid forgery for message set M and tag (count, σ). Suppose that there is at least one honest party in the corresponding set (else the attempt is trivially in the closure). If the set of augmented messages (count, m_i) contains a value previously not tagged by an honest party, then the security follows from the (basic) unforgeability notion of the underlying scheme.

Hence, suppose all pairs (count, m_i) for honest parties have been tagged before. Since each counter value is used only once, there is a unique aggregation query where tags for these pairs have been computed. It follows that the forgery attempt only contains a subset of this query (and possibly additional contributions by corrupt players). But then the attempt is in the closure.

Recursive Lattice Reduction*

Thomas Plantard and Willy Susilo

Centre for Computer and Information Security Research
School of Computer Science and Software Engineering
University of Wollongong, Australia
{thomaspl,wsusilo}@uow.edu.au

Abstract. Lattice reduction is known to be a very powerful tool in modern cryptanalysis. In the literature, there are many lattice reduction algorithms that have been proposed with various time complexity (from quadratic to subexponential). These algorithms can be utilized to find a short vector of a lattice with a small norm. Over time, shorter vector will be found by incorporating these methods. In this paper, we take a different approach by presenting a methodology that can be applied to any lattice reduction algorithms, with the implication that enables us to find a shorter vector (i.e. a smaller solution) while requiring shorter computation time. Instead of applying a lattice reduction algorithm to a complete lattice, we work on a sublattice with a smaller dimension chosen in the function of the lattice reduction algorithm that is being used. This way, the lattice reduction algorithm will be fully utilized and hence, it will produce a better solution. Furthermore, as the dimension of the lattice becomes smaller, the time complexity will be better. Hence, our methodology provides us with a new direction to build a lattice that is resistant to lattice reduction attacks. Moreover, based on this methodology, we also propose a recursive method for producing an optimal approach for lattice reduction with optimal computational time, regardless of the lattice reduction algorithm used. We evaluate our technique by applying it to break the lattice challenge[1] by producing the shortest vector known so far. Our results outperform the existing known results and hence, our results achieve the record in the lattice challenge problem.

Keywords: Geometry of numbers, Lattice reduction, Hermite factor, Recursive reduction.

1 Introduction

Lattice reduction algorithms have been proposed to solve or approximate the shortest vector problem. In the literature, it has been demonstrated that many cryptosystems can be cryptanalyzed successfully using lattice reduction algorithms. Some of the historical examples include the following[2].

---

* This work is partially supported by The Department of Prime Minister and Cabinet's Research Support for Counter-Terrorism: PR06-0006.

[1] http://latticechallenge.org/

[2] We will refer to [51] for a more specific survey.

J.A. Garay and R. De Prisco (Eds.): SCN 2010, LNCS 6280, pp. 329–344, 2010.

Knapsack Cryptosystems
In 1978, Merkle and Hellman [43] proposed the first public key cryptosystem based on an NP-hard problem, namely the knapsack problem. This is the first practical public key cryptosystem which is the concrete construction of the proposed seminal notion of public key cryptography by Diffie and Hellman [26]. Unfortunately, Merkle-Hellman's first proposition was attacked severely and broken using two different methods: the first attack on the trapdoor itself that was proposed by Shamir [67,68] and the second attack on the knapsack problem using lattice theory that was proposed by Adleman [2]. In 1985, Lagarias and Odlyzko [39] proposed a general attack against knapsack cryptosystems using a lattice reduction algorithm. Their attack does not incorporate the weakness on the trapdoor itself, rather than only using the fact that the knapsack problems produced are generally weaker that a random one. This result was subsequently improved in [25,24,66,58]. Nevertheless, some improvements of knapsack cryptosystems were also proposed (e.g. [16,57]). We refer the reader to [56] for these two faces of knapsack cryptology. Despite many variants that have been proposed in the literature, as mentioned in [55], the knapsack cryptosystem proposed by Okamoto, Tanaka and Uchiyama in 2000 [57] seems to be the only remaining secure knapsack cryptosystem.

SVP-based Cryptosystems
In 1996, Ajtai and Dwork [8] proposed the first lattice cryptosystem where its security is based on a variant of the Shortest Vector Problem (SVP). This cryptosystem received wide attention due to a surprising security proof based on worst-case assumptions. Nonetheless, this cryptosystem is merely a theoretical proposition and it cannot be used in practice. Furthermore, Nguyen and Stern presented a heuristic attack against this cryptosystem [54]. Until then, this initial proposition has been improved [29,14,38] and this result has inspired other cryptosystems based on SVP [60,61,6]. These cryptosystems are based on SVP and are naturally concerned by lattice reduction algorithm.

CVP-based Cryptosystems
There exists a heuristic way introduced by Kannan [36] to solve CVP (Closest Vector Problem) using a lattice reduction algorithm that was originally proposed to solve SVP, namely the *embedding method*. Instead of solving CVP, we solve SVP in a different lattice. Finding the closest vector of v in $\mathcal{L}_B$ can be done by solving the shortest vector of $\mathcal{L}_{B'}$ with $B' = \begin{pmatrix} B & 0 \\ v & 1 \end{pmatrix}$. This method has been successfully applied by Nguyen [50] to develop his first attack against GGH cryptosystem and it seems practically the best way to attack a CVP-based cryptosystem. In 1997, Goldreich, Goldwasser and Halevi (GGH) [30] proposed an efficient way to use lattice theory to build a cryptosystem inspired by McEliece cryptosystem [42] and based on the Closest Vector Problem (CVP). Their practical proposition of a cryptosystem was attacked and broken severely by Nguyen in 1999 [50]. Nonetheless, the general idea is still viable. Until then, the other propositions were made using the same principle [27,44,59].

After the first Nguyen's attack [50], utilization of the initial GGH proposition requires lattices with a big dimension (> 500), to ensure its security. Consequently, the computation of the closest vector even with a "good basis" becomes very expensive. In 2000, Fischlin and Seifert [27] proposed a very intuitive way to build lattices with good basis which can solve the closest vector problem. They used a tensor product of lattice to obtain a divide and conquer approach to solve CVP. In 2001, Micciancio [44] proposed some major improvements of the speed and the security of GGH. In this scheme, the public key uses a Hermite Normal Form (HNF) for the "bad" basis. The HNF basis is better to answer the inclusion question and it also seems to be more difficult to transform to a "good basis" compared to another basis. In 2003, Paeng, Jung and Ha [59] proposed to use some lattices built on a polynomial ring. However, in 2007, Han, Kim, and Yeom [32] used lattice reduction to cryptanalyze this scheme. Their attack can successfully recover the secret key even in a huge dimension (> 1000) and make the Paeng-Jung-Ha scheme [59] unusable. However, there exists a secure (and yet 'unbroken') cryptosystem using polynomial representation, namely the NTRU cryptosystem, for N^{th} degree truncated polynomial ring units. NTRU was originally proposed in 1998 by Hoffstein, Pipher and Silverman [34]. Even this cryptosystem was not modelled initially as a GGH-type cryptosystem, it can actually be represented as one. This has been useful specially for analyzing its security [23].

RSA

In 1996, Coppersmith [20] presented some methods to attack RSA [62] in a special case using lattice reduction. Similar method has been proposed to attack RSA with low exponent [11], RSA with short padding [22] and to factor the RSA public key with or without knowing any partial information [21,12].

Our Contribution

In this paper, we present a methodology that can be applied to *any* lattice reduction algorithms. Our methodology will enable us to find a shorter vector (i.e. a smaller solution) while requiring shorter computation time. The idea of our methodology is as follows. Instead of applying a lattice reduction algorithm to a complete lattice, we work on a sublattice with a smaller dimension obtained in the function of the lattice reduction algorithm that is being used. This way, the lattice reduction algorithm will be fully utilized and hence, it will produce a better solution. Furthermore, as the dimension of the lattice becomes smaller, the time complexity will be better. Hence, our methodology provides us with new direction to build a lattice that is resistant to lattice reduction attacks. Moreover, we also propose a recursive method for producing an optimal approach for lattice reduction with optimal computational time, regardless of the lattice reduction algorithm used. We evaluate our technique by applying it to break the lattice challenge by producing the shortest vector known so far. Our results outperform the existing known results and hence, our results achieve the record in the lattice challenge problem.

Organization of the Paper

The paper is organized as follows. In the next section, we will recall definitions, properties, problems and algorithms of lattice theory required throughout this paper. In Section 3, we will present our methodology. In Section 4, we will present our recursive reduction, followed by analysis of practical tests in Section 5. Finally, Section 6 concludes the paper by showing some results and future works.

2 Lattice Theory

In this section, we will review some concepts of the lattice theory that will be used throughout this paper. For a more complex account, we refer the readers to [45,46].

2.1 Basics of Lattice Theory

The lattice theory, also known as the geometry of numbers, has been introduced by Minkowski in 1896 [49]. A complete discussion on the basic of lattice theory can be found from [15,41,19].

Definition 1 (Lattice). *A lattice $\mathcal{L}$ is a discrete sub-group of $\mathbb{R}^n$, or equivalently the set of all the integral combinations of $d \leq n$ linearly independent vectors over $\mathbb{R}$.*

$$\mathcal{L} = \mathbb{Z} b_1 + \cdots + \mathbb{Z} b_d, \quad b_i \in \mathbb{R}^n.$$

$B = (b_1, ..., b_d)$ is called a basis of $\mathcal{L}$ and d, the dimension of $\mathcal{L}$, noted $dim(\mathcal{L})$. We will refer $\mathcal{L}_B$ as a lattice of basis B.

Definition 2 (Full-rank Lattice). *Let $\mathcal{L} \subset \mathbb{R}^n$ be a lattice. If its dimension d is equal to n then the lattice $\mathcal{L}$ is called full-rank.*

Theorem 1 (Determinant). *Let $\mathcal{L}$ be a lattice. There exists a real value, denoted as $\det(\mathcal{L})$, such that for any basis B of $\mathcal{L}$, we have $\det(\mathcal{L}) = \sqrt{\det(BB^T)}$. $\det(\mathcal{L})$ is called the determinant of $\mathcal{L}$.*

For a given lattice $\mathcal{L}$, there exists an infinite number of basis. However, the Hermite Normal Form basis (Definition 3) is unique [17].

Definition 3 (HNF). *Let $\mathcal{L}$ be an integer lattice of dimension d and $H \in \mathbb{Z}^{d,n}$ be a basis of $\mathcal{L}$. H is a Hermite Normal Form basis of $\mathcal{L}$ if and only if*

$$\forall 1 \leq i,j \leq d \quad H_{i,j} \begin{cases} = 0 & \textit{if } i > j \\ \geq 0 & \textit{if } i \leq j \\ < H_{j,j} & \textit{if } i < j \end{cases}$$

The HNF basis can be computed from a given basis in a polynomial time [37]. For efficient solutions, we refer the readers to [47].

The lattice theory problem is based on distance minimization. The natural norm used in lattice theory is the euclidean norm.

Definition 4 (Euclidean norm). *Let w be a vector of $\mathbb{R}^n$. The euclidean norm is the function $\|.\|$ defined by $\|w\| = \sqrt{<w,w>} = \sqrt{ww^T} = \sqrt{\sum_{i=1}^{n} w_i^2}$.*

Using a norm, we can define some other invariants that are crucial in lattice theory.

Definition 5 (Successive Minima). *Let $\mathcal{L}$ be a lattice and an integer i. The ith Successive Minima, denoted as λ_i, is the smallest real number such that there exist i non zero linear independent vector $v_1, \ldots, v_i \in \mathcal{L}$ with $\|v_1\|, \ldots, \|v_i\| \leq \lambda_i$. If $i = 1$, to find such v_1 is called the Shortest Vector Problem (SVP).*

The determinant and the successive minima of a lattice are connected by an important theorem as follows.

Theorem 2 (Minkowski [49]). *Let $d \in \mathbb{N}^+$. There exists a smallest real, γ_d, such that for any lattice $\mathcal{L}$ of dimension d, $\lambda_1(\mathcal{L}) \leq \sqrt{\gamma_d} \det(\mathcal{L})^{1/d}$. γ_d is called the Hermite Constant.*

The exact value of the Hermite constant is only known for $1 \leq d \leq 8$ and $d = 24$. However, some upper bound are known $\gamma_d \leq 1 + \frac{d}{4}$. We refer to [18] for a better numerical upper bound and to [48,19] for a lower and an upper asymptotical bounds.

2.2 Lattice Reduction Algorithms

Theorem 3 (Ajtai [4]). *SVP is NP-Hard under randomized reductions.*

In 2007, Hanrot and Stehle [33] gave the best known deterministic algorithm to solve SVP in time $O(d^{\frac{d}{2e}})$ where d is the dimension: they used the algorithm proposed by Kannan in 1983 [35] and improved the anlaysis of the worst-case complexity. In 2007, Blömer and Naewe [10] proposed the best known probabilistic algorithm to solve SVP in time $(2 + \frac{1}{\epsilon})^d$. It is an improvement of the initial proposition of Ajtai, Kumar, and Sivakumar in 2001 [9].

As SVP is NP-hard, a relaxation factor has been introduced in the initial SVP to be able to propose and evaluate the quality of polynomial algorithms.

Definition 6 (Hermite-SVP). *Let $\mathcal{L}$ be a lattice of dimension d and $\alpha \in R^+$ be a real positive number. Then, the Hermite-SVP is to find a vector $u \in \mathcal{L}$ such that $0 < \|u\| \leq \alpha \det(\mathcal{L})^{1/d}$. α is called the Hermite Factor.*

Theorem 2 ensures a solution for Hermite-SVP if $\alpha \geq \sqrt{\gamma_d}$.

In 1982 Lenstra, Lenstra and Lovasz [40] proposed a powerful polynomial algorithm, known as the LLL algorithm, which solve Hermite-SVP for a Hermite factor $\alpha_{LLL} = \left(\frac{4}{3}\right)^{\frac{d-1}{4}}$. However, in practice LLL seems to be much more efficient [53]. In addition, a lot of improvements have been proposed on LLL to obtain a better approximation factor and/or a better time complexity. For the recent result on LLL, refer to [52,65].

In 1987, Schnorr [63,64] proposed a method which can be seen as a generalization of LLL, known as LLL with deep insertion (DEEP) and Block Korkin-Zolotarev (BKZ). BKZ allows some exponential computations but only on some block. The length k of the block itself is a parameter. LLL can been seen as BKZ with block length of $k = 2$, whereas the Kannan method can be seen as a BKZ with block length of $k = d$. BKZ$-k$ solves Hermite-SVP for $\alpha_{BKZ-k} = \sqrt{\gamma_k}^{1+\sqrt{\frac{d-1}{k-1}}}$ in theory but the BKZ variant used in practice are difficult to evaluate. Theoretically, DEEP has no best upper bound (cf. LLL), $\alpha_{DEEP-k} = \left(\frac{4}{3}\right)^{\frac{d-1}{4}}$.

BKZ is a very powerful way to attack a cryptosystem and it can be extended to provide a level of security with the block length needed to break a cryptosystem. In [50], Nguyen has successfully broken GGH cryptosystem of dimension 200, 250, 300 using a BKZ-20 and a GGH cryptosystem of dimension 350 using a BKZ-60.

In a recent work [28], Gama and Nguyen presented some tests showing that all of the existing methods seem to solve Hermite-SVP with an average hermite factor α of the form

$$\alpha = bc^d. \tag{1}$$

They also showed that the difference between the theoretical and the practical Hermite factor is huge. We review here those estimations of $\alpha = bc^d$ for different lattice reduction algorithms:

- For LLL, we have $c \sim 1.0219 < 1.0754$.
- For BKZ-20, we have $c \sim 1.0128 < 1.0337$.
- For BKZ-28, we have $c \sim 1.0109 < 1.0282$.
- For DEEP-50, we have $c \sim 1.011 < 1.0754$.

To compare all of these methods practically, Buchmann, Lindner and Rückert [13] proposed a benchmark of lattices created following the paper of Ajtai [3]. Those lattices, denoted as $\mathcal{L}_{m,n,q}$, are characterized using 3 parameters m, n, q. Their basis are as follows

$$\begin{pmatrix} qI & 0 \\ A & I \end{pmatrix}$$

with I the identity matrix and $A \in \mathbb{Z}^{m-n,n}$ a random matrix. The dimension is $\dim(\mathcal{L}_{m,n,q}) = m$ and the determinant is $\det(\mathcal{L}_{m,n,q}) = q^n$.

Those lattices are created such that there exists a vector $v \in \mathcal{L}$ such that $0 < \|v\| \leq \sqrt{m}$. Finding such a vector is the goal of the challenge. However, to find a vector with a norm strictly smaller that q is already difficult[3]. The results of the shortest vector respecting this second condition are presented in the challenge web page http://latticechallenge.org/. There exists a challenge for each dimension with interval 25 between 200 and 2000. However, solutions are accepted only for challenges bigger that 500 (which correspond more to useful dimensions for cryptography).

Remark 1 (Random Lattice). The lattice proposed in this challenge can not be considered as random lattice. Ajtai lattices [3] are lattices for which the solution of SVP implies a solution of SVP in all lattices of a certain smaller dimension. This means that the lattice reduction algorithm solving SVP on those lattice can solve even the worst case of SVP lattices.

Random lattice is a complex notion [5,31,7]. Goldstein and Mayer's characterization of random lattices [31] allows to create random lattices for experiment for example [53]. We will use the same method in our practical section (Section 5) to evaluate our method in the case of random lattices. Practically to respect those criteria, we will create random lattices as $\mathcal{L}_{m,n,q}$ with $n = 1$ and q prime.

3 A Methodology for Lattice Reduction

In this section, we do not propose an algorithm for lattice reduction but rather a methodology applicable to all lattice reduction algorithms with the impact of improving quality and timing of those algorithms.

[3] We note that there exist already some obvious vectors with this norm.

Methodology

Let $\mathcal{A}$ be an algorithm solving Hermite-SVP for a lattice $\mathcal{L}$ of dimension d with a Hermite Factor $\alpha = bc^d$. This means that this algorithm $\mathcal{A}$ will find a vector $v \in \mathcal{L}$ such that $0 < \|v\| \leq bc^d \det(\mathcal{L})^{1/d}$.

The main idea of this methodology can be explained simply in three points as follows.

1. Find d' such that $bc^{d'} \det(\mathcal{L})^{1/d'}$ is minimal.
2. Choose a sublattice $\mathcal{L}' \subseteq \mathcal{L}$ such that $\det(\mathcal{L}') \leq \det(\mathcal{L})$ and $dim(\mathcal{L}') = d'$.
3. Apply $\mathcal{A}$ on $\mathcal{L}'$.

This simple methodology provides several advantages as follows.

a) The quality of the result will be better as $\alpha \det(\mathcal{L})^{1/d'}$ will be smaller.
b) The time and space used will be smaller as $d' \leq d$.

How to Choose a Sublattice $\mathcal{L}' \subseteq \mathcal{L}$

Prior to explaining how to pick d', firstly we develop a simple way to build a sublattice $\mathcal{L}' \subseteq \mathcal{L}$ such that $det(\mathcal{L}') \leq \det(\mathcal{L})$ and $\dim(\mathcal{L}') = d'$. For simplicity, we deal here with a full-rank integer lattice. Nonetheless, this method can be easily modified to accommodate non full-rank and/or non integer lattices.

The first general way is to build a lattice generated by

$$U = \begin{pmatrix} u_1 & 0 & \cdots & 0 & 0 \\ 0 & u_2 & \cdots & 0 & 0 \\ \vdots & & \ddots & & \vdots \\ 0 & 0 & \cdots & u_{d-1} & 0 \\ 0 & 0 & \cdots & 0 & u_d \end{pmatrix}$$

where $u_i = \{0, 1\}$ and $\sum_{i=1}^{d} u_i = d'$. To create $\mathcal{L}'$, we intersect[4] $\mathcal{L}$ and $\mathcal{L}_U$, $\mathcal{L}' = \mathcal{L} \cap \mathcal{L}_U$.

As $\det(\mathcal{L}_U) = 1$ and $\dim(\mathcal{L}_U) = d'$, we obtain $\dim(\mathcal{L}') = d'$ and $\det(\mathcal{L}') \leq \det(\mathcal{L})$[5].

Another simple and practical way is to build the Hermite Normal Form basis of $\mathcal{L}$, and use only the d' last vectors of $\mathcal{L}$ as a basis of $\mathcal{L}'$. Moreover, as all of those vectors will start with zero, we can eventually use only the d' last columns to accelerate some computations. We will need to re-transform the vector to the correct length once the reduction is completed. This method can be generalized using any permutation of the Hermite Normal Form Basis.

How to Find an Optimal d' for a Given Lattice Reduction Algorithm

In this situation, suppose we have a given algorithm $\mathcal{A}$ solving Hermite-SVP for a lattice $\mathcal{L}$ of dimension d with a Hermite Factor $\alpha = bc^d$. This means that this algorithm $\mathcal{A}$ will find a vector $v \in \mathcal{L}$ such that $0 < \|v\| \leq bc^d \det(\mathcal{L})^{1/d}$.

[4] We refer to [45], for the polynomial technique to intersect two lattices.

[5] $\det(\mathcal{L}')$ will be a factor of $\det(\mathcal{L}) \times \det(\mathcal{L}_U) = \det(\mathcal{L})$.

We would like to find d' such that $bc^{d'} \det(\mathcal{L})^{1/d'}$ is minimal or equivalently $\log(b) + d' \log(c) + \frac{\log(\det(\mathcal{L}))}{d'}$ is minimal. To find the minimum value of the function $f(d') = \log(b) + d' \log(c) + \frac{\log(\det(\mathcal{L}))}{d'}$, we compute its derivative $f'(d') = \log c - \frac{\log \det(\mathcal{L})}{d'^2}$ and find d' such that $f'(d') = 0$.

$$\log(c) - \frac{\log(\det(\mathcal{L}))}{d'^2} = 0$$

$$\log(c) = \frac{\log(\det(\mathcal{L}))}{d'^2}$$

$$d'^2 = \frac{\log(\det(\mathcal{L}))}{\log(c)}$$

Finally, we obtain that the best evaluated d' as

$$d' = \sqrt{\frac{\log(\det(\mathcal{L}))}{\log(c)}}. \tag{2}$$

How to Choose Optimally d' to Find a Vector with a Given Norm

In this situation, suppose we have a given lattice in which we want to find a short vector v with a given norm $\|v\|$. Hence, we need an algorithm and a sublattice such that $\|v\| = bc^{d'} \det(\mathcal{L})^{1/d'}$.

In this case, we want to maximize c and therefore, we will use the quicker lattice reduction algorithm.

$$c^{d'} = \frac{\|v\|}{b \det(\mathcal{L})^{1/d'}}$$

$$c = \left(\frac{\|v\|}{b \det(\mathcal{L})^{1/d'}} \right)^{1/d'}. \tag{3}$$

We can apply an equivalent method.

$$\log(c) = \frac{\log(\|v\|) - \log(b)}{d'} - \frac{\log(\det(\mathcal{L}))}{d'^2}$$

To find the maximum of the function $g(d') = \frac{\log(\|v\|)}{d'} - \frac{\log(\det(\mathcal{L}))}{d'^2}$, we need to evaluate its derivative as follows

$$g'(d') = -\frac{\log(\|v\|) - \log(b)}{d'^2} + 2d\frac{\log(\det(\mathcal{L}))}{d'^4}$$

$$g'(d') = -\frac{\log(\|v\|) - \log(b)}{d'^2} + 2\frac{\log(\det(\mathcal{L}))}{d'^3}$$

and find d' such that $g'(d') = 0$.

$$-\frac{\log(\|v\|) - \log(b)}{d'^2} + 2\frac{\log(\det(\mathcal{L}))}{d'^3} = 0$$

$$\frac{\log(\|v\|) - \log(b)}{d'^2} = 2\frac{\log(\det(\mathcal{L}))}{d'^3}$$

$$\log(\|v\|) - \log(b) = 2\frac{\log(\det(\mathcal{L}))}{d'}$$

Finally, we obtain the best evaluated d' for a maximal c as follows

$$d' = 2\left(\frac{\log(\det(\mathcal{L}))}{\log(\|v\|) - \log(b)}\right). \tag{4}$$

Practically, we can ignore $\log(b)$.

This result is important as it demonstrates which are the most difficult lattices for a given bound. Consequently, this result has a great impact on lattice based cryptography.

4 Recursive Lattice Reduction

When attempting to reduce lattices using the two previous methods, some knowledge on the lattices are required, as well as some knowledge on the lattice reduction algorithm. Nevertheless, these knowledge may be imprecise or even missing. For instance, a small error on c can have a huge implication on d'. Henceforth, in this section, we will propose a new technique that incorporates sublattices without requiring any prior knowledge.

Let $\mathcal{A}$ be an algorithm solving Hermite-SVP for a lattice $\mathcal{L}$. We use a *recursive reduction method* as follows.

The main idea of this technique can be explained as follows.

1. Choose d sublattices $\mathcal{L}_i$ such that $\mathcal{L}_1 \subset \cdots \subset \mathcal{L}_i \cdots \subset \mathcal{L}_d = \mathcal{L}$ and $dim(\mathcal{L}_i) = i$.
2. $\mathcal{L}_1$ is already reduced.
3. To reduce each $\mathcal{L}_{i+1}$, apply $\mathcal{A}$ to $\mathcal{L}_{i+1} \cup \mathcal{L}_i$ where $\mathcal{L}_i$ has already been reduced[6].

This technique incorporates the work that has been performed to reduce the previous sublattice, and hence, it simplifies the reduction of the lattice. This will allow reduction on $\mathcal{L}_{d'}$ where d' is optimal, by trying all the possible dimensions without any extra timing cost. We will demonstrate this in our practical test in Section 5 where this method will improve the time complexity, using time computation whenever appropriate.

5 Practical Test

In this section, we present some tests that have been conducted using NTL5.5.2 and GMP4.3.1 libraries [69,1]. We used random lattices that are built according to the definition [31] as used in [53,28] (Remark 1). However, there is no definition for a random basis of a given lattice.

Figure 1 demonstrates some results using 'random' bases that are built with some techniques similar to [30][7]. Each curve represents an average of 10 tests. The determinant is always equivalent to have a proper comparison; only the dimension changes.

[6] Lattice reduction on a lattice corresponds to lattice reduction on its basis.

[7] We multiplied the hermite normal form basis of the lattice by a random unimodular matrix.

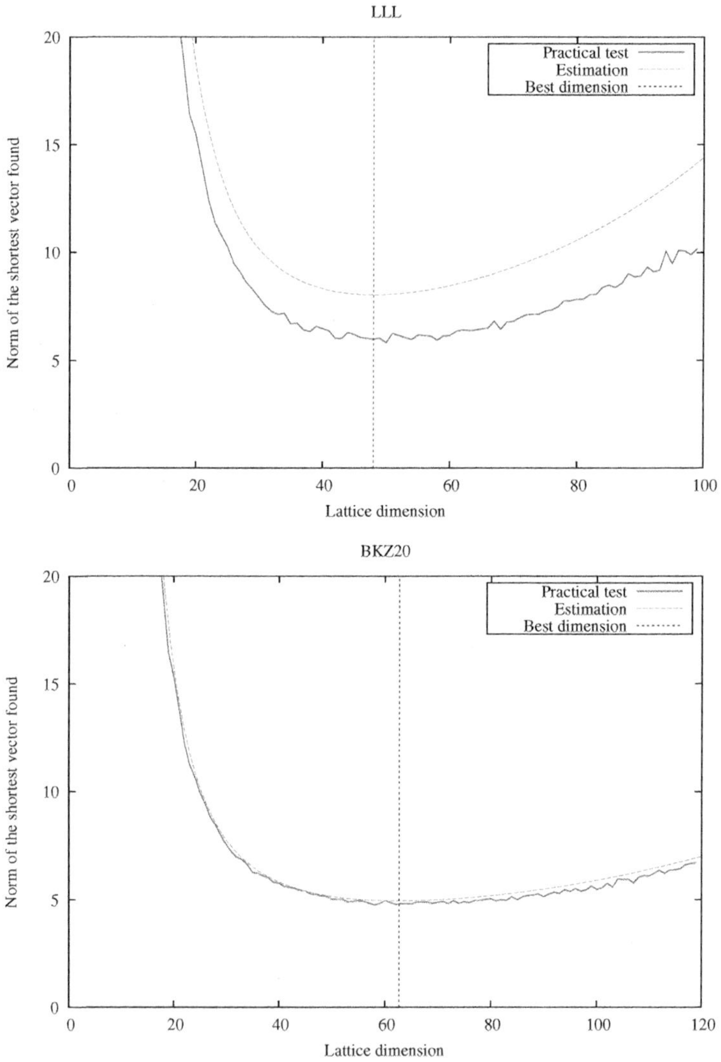

Fig. 1. Result and estimation for LLL and BKZ20

We observed that even if the estimation is not always correct due to the absence of b in its computation, the estimation of the best dimension to use is correct.

After conducting some tests, we observed that instead of using 'random' bases, HNF bases (Definition 3) produce better timing results and avoid the problem to produce a worse result in a bigger dimension as shown in Figure 1. However, the use of HNF basis will still be consistent with the estimation of the best dimension to use (Figure 2).

Figure 2 shows that the recursive reduction will also be consistent with the best dimension to use. Figure 2 clearly demonstrates that the results obtained with the three

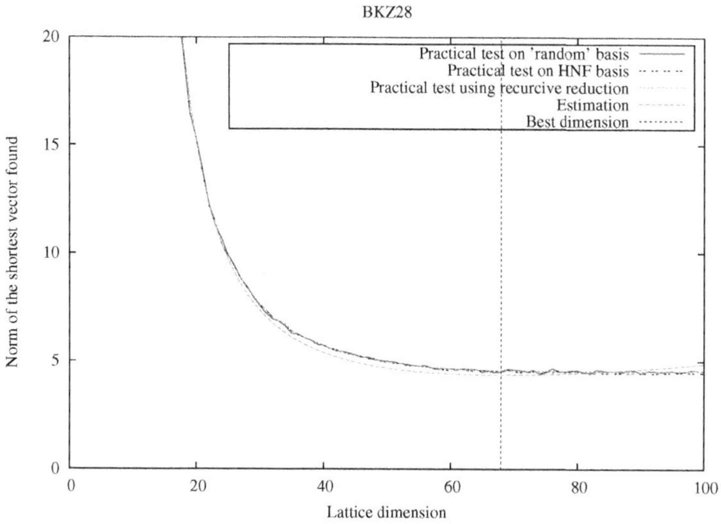

Fig. 2. Result and estimation for BKZ28

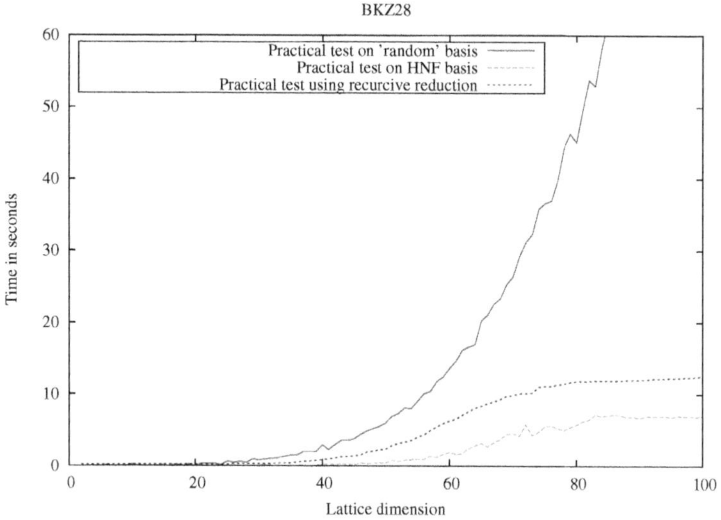

Fig. 3. Time in seconds for BKZ28

different methods are close to each other. However, the main difference is in the timing as shown in Figure 3.

Figure 3 demonstrates that the cost of the recursive method is just a bit higher than the HNF basis if the estimation is correct. However, if the estimation is not precise or unknown, then the non-recursive method will have to do a complete lattice reduction again. In contrast, the recursive method does not need to do so.

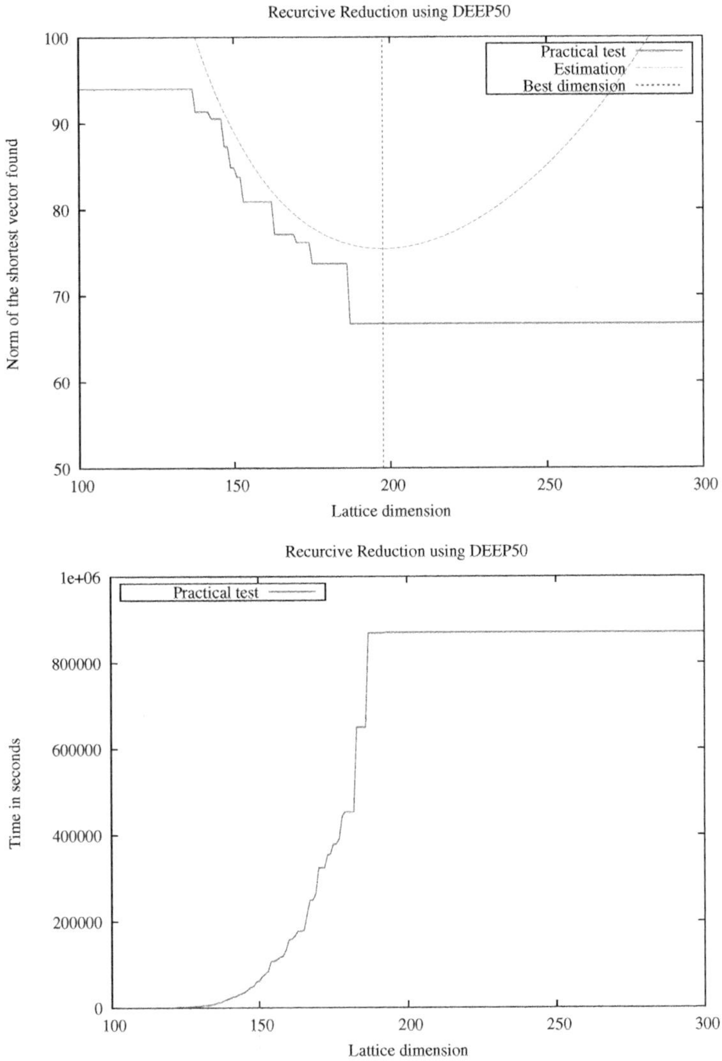

Fig. 4. Result, estimation and time in seconds for DEEP50 with recursive reduction on challenge-650

To finish this section, we present a test performed on lattice of the challenge http://latticechallenge.org/.

Figure 4 demonstrates that the time grows for the recursive reduction only when the quality is improved, and therefore computation is optimally used.

It appears at the end of these practical tests that the recursive technique clearly outperforms the classic application of lattice reduction algorithms, even with a good knowledge of the lattice reduction tool itself. It really simplifies lattice reduction operations as it can be used even if the dimension is not optimal.

6 Conclusion

In this paper, we presented further analysis of lattice reduction algorithms, by presenting a methodology. This methodology offers different consequences, namely better utilization of these algorithms and better level of security of cryptosystems based on or connected to lattices. Using our recursive lattice reduction, we obtained new results in http://latticechallenge.org/ that outperform the previously known results.

Table 1 presents the results we have performed so far on the lattice challenge and outperformed all the previous one. This has been possible only due do the recursive reduction as we have used some reduction techniques (DEEP60,DEEP70, BKZ30, ...) where the estimation is unknown and very difficult to produce with the precision required for such huge lattices.

Table 1. Lattice Challenge Result

Challenge	Previous Best Result	Recurcive Reduction Result
500	25.8457	25.2587
525	35.6651	30.7409
550	39.7995	38.2884
575	50.7149	42.7083
600	57.2975	52.0096
625	61.8061	59.4138
650	69.4478	66.7158
675	82.6015	80.0937
700	89.4315	89.3924
725	103.7208	100.8960
750	-	-

References

1. The GNU multiple precision arithmetic librairy
2. Adleman, L.M.: On breaking generalized knapsack public key cryptosystems (abstract). In: STOC, pp. 402–412 (1983)
3. Ajtai, M.: Generating hard instances of lattice problems (extended abstract). In: Twenty-Eighth Annual ACM Symposium on the Theory of Computing (STOC 1996), pp. 99–108 (1996)
4. Ajtai, M.: The shortest vector problem in l_2 is NP-hard for randomized reductions (extended abstract). In: Thirtieth Annual ACM Symposium on the Theory of Computing (STOC 1998), pp. 10–19 (1998)
5. Ajtai, M.: Random lattices and a conjectured 0 - 1 law about their polynomial time computable properties. In: FOCS, pp. 733–742 (2002)
6. Ajtai, M.: Representing hard lattices with o(n log n) bits. In: STOC, pp. 94–103 (2005)
7. Ajtai, M.: Generating random lattices according to the invariant distribution (2006)
8. Ajtai, M., Dwork, C.: A public-key cryptosystem with worst-case/average-case equivalence. In: Twenty-Ninth Annual ACM Symposium on the Theory of Computing (STOC 1997), pp. 284–293 (1997)

9. Ajtai, M., Kumar, R., Sivakumar, D.: A sieve algorithm for the shortest lattice vector problem. In: 33rd Annual ACM Symposium on Theory of Computing (STOC 2001), pp. 601–610 (2001)
10. Blömer, J., Naewe, S.: Sampling methods for shortest vectors, closest vectors and successive minima. In: Arge, L., Cachin, C., Jurdziński, T., Tarlecki, A. (eds.) ICALP 2007. LNCS, vol. 4596, pp. 65–77. Springer, Heidelberg (2007)
11. Boneh, D.: Twenty years of attacks on the rsa cryptosystem. Notices of the American Mathematical Society (AMS) 46(2), 203–213 (1999)
12. Boneh, D., Durfee, G., Howgrave-Graham, N.: Factoring $n = p^r q$ for large r. In: Wiener, M. (ed.) CRYPTO 1999. LNCS, vol. 1666, pp. 326–337. Springer, Heidelberg (1999)
13. Buchmann, J., Lindner, R., Rückert, M.: Explicit hard instances of the shortest vector problem. In: Buchmann, J., Ding, J. (eds.) PQCrypto 2008. LNCS, vol. 5299, pp. 79–94. Springer, Heidelberg (2008)
14. Cai, J.-Y., Cusick, T.W.: A lattice-based public-key cryptosystem. In: Tavares, S., Meijer, H. (eds.) SAC 1998. LNCS, vol. 1556, pp. 219–233. Springer, Heidelberg (1999)
15. Cassels, J.W.S.: An Introduction to the Geometry of Numbers. Springer, Heidelberg (1959)
16. Chor, B., Rivest, R.L.: A knapsack-type public key cryptosystem based on arithmetic in finite fields. IEEE Transactions on Information Theory 34(5), 901–909 (1988)
17. Cohen, H.: A course in computational algebraic number theory. Graduate Texts in Mathematics, vol. 138. Springer, Heidelberg (1993)
18. Cohn, H., Elkies, N.: New upper bounds on sphere packings i. Annals of Mathematics 157(2), 689–714 (2003)
19. Conway, J.H., Sloane, N.J.A.: Sphere Packings, Lattices and Groups. Springer, Heidelberg (1988)
20. Coppersmith, D.: Finding a small root of a univariate modular equation. In: Maurer, U.M. (ed.) EUROCRYPT 1996. LNCS, vol. 1070, pp. 155–165. Springer, Heidelberg (1996)
21. Coppersmith, D.: Small solutions to polynomial equations, and low exponent rsa vulnerabilities. J. Cryptology 10(4), 233–260 (1997)
22. Coppersmith, D.: Finding small solutions to small degree polynomials. In: Silverman, J.H. (ed.) CaLC 2001. LNCS, vol. 2146, pp. 20–31. Springer, Heidelberg (2001)
23. Coppersmith, D., Shamir, A.: Lattice attacks on ntru. In: Fumy, W. (ed.) EUROCRYPT 1997. LNCS, vol. 1233, pp. 52–61. Springer, Heidelberg (1997)
24. Coster, M.J., Joux, A., LaMacchia, B.A., Odlyzko, A.M., Schnorr, C.-P., Stern, J.: Improved low-density subset sum algorithms. Computational Complexity 2, 111–128 (1992)
25. Coster, M.J., LaMacchia, B.A., Odlyzko, A.M.: An iproved low-denisty subset sum algorithm. In: Davies, D.W. (ed.) EUROCRYPT 1991. LNCS, vol. 547, pp. 54–67. Springer, Heidelberg (1991)
26. Diffie, W., Hellman, M.E.: New directions in cryptography. IEEE Transactions on Information Theory IT-22(6), 644–654 (1976)
27. Fischlin, R., Seifert, J.-P.: Tensor-based trapdoors for cvp and their application to public key cryptography. In: IMA Int. Conf., pp. 244–257 (1999)
28. Gama, N., Nguyen, P.Q.: Predicting lattice reduction. In: Smart, N.P. (ed.) EUROCRYPT 2008. LNCS, vol. 4965, pp. 31–51. Springer, Heidelberg (2008)
29. Goldreich, O., Goldwasser, S., Halevi, S.: Eliminating decryption errors in the ajtai-dwork cryptosystem. In: Kaliski Jr., B.S. (ed.) CRYPTO 1997. LNCS, vol. 1294, pp. 105–111. Springer, Heidelberg (1997)
30. Goldreich, O., Goldwasser, S., Halevi, S.: Public-key cryptosystems from lattice reductions problems. In: Kaliski Jr., B.S. (ed.) CRYPTO 1997. LNCS, vol. 1294, pp. 112–131. Springer, Heidelberg (1997)
31. Goldstein, D., Mayer, A.: On the equidistribution of Hecke points. Forum Mathematicum 15, 165–189 (2003)

32. Han, D., Kim, M.-H., Yeom, Y.: Cryptanalysis of the paeng-jung-ha cryptosystem from pkc 2003. In: Okamoto, T., Wang, X. (eds.) PKC 2007. LNCS, vol. 4450, pp. 107–117. Springer, Heidelberg (2007)
33. Hanrot, G., Stehle, D.: Improved analysis of Kannan's shortest lattice vector algorithm. In: Menezes, A. (ed.) CRYPTO 2007. LNCS, vol. 4622, pp. 170–186. Springer, Heidelberg (2007)
34. Hoffstein, J., Pipher, J., Silverman, J.H.: NTRU: A ring-based public key cryptosystem. In: Buhler, J.P. (ed.) ANTS 1998. LNCS, vol. 1423, pp. 267–288. Springer, Heidelberg (1998)
35. Kannan, R.: Improved algorithms for integer programming and related lattice problems. In: Proceedings of the Fifteenth Annual ACM Symposium on Theory of Computing, Boston, Massachusetts, pp. 193–206 (April 1983)
36. Kannan, R.: Minkowski's convex body theorem and integer programming. Math. Oper. Res. 12(3), 415–440 (1987)
37. Kannan, R., Bachem, A.: Polynomial algorithms for computing the Smith and Hermite normal forms of an integer matrix. SIAM Journal of Computing 8(4), 499–507 (1979)
38. Kawachi, A., Tanaka, K., Xagawa, K.: Multi-bit cryptosystems based on lattice problems. In: Okamoto, T., Wang, X. (eds.) PKC 2007. LNCS, vol. 4450, pp. 315–329. Springer, Heidelberg (2007)
39. Lagarias, J.C., Odlyzko, A.M.: Solving low-density subset sum problems. Journal of the ACM 32(1), 229–246 (1985)
40. Lenstra, A.K., Lenstra, H.W., Lovász, L.: Factoring polynomials with rational coefficients. In: Mathematische Annalen, vol. 261, pp. 513–534. Springer, Heidelberg (1982)
41. Lovász, L.: An Algorithmic Theory of Numbers, Graphs and Convexity. CBMS-NSF Regional Conference Series in Applied Mathematics, vol. 50. SIAM Publications, Philadelphia (1986)
42. McEliece, R.J.: A public-key cryptosystem based on algebraic coding theory. Deep Space Network Progress Report 44, 114–116 (1978)
43. Merkle, R.C., Hellman, M.E.: Hiding information and signatures in trapdoor knapsacks. IEEE Transactions on Information Theory IT-24(5), 525–530 (1978)
44. Micciancio, D.: Improving lattice based cryptosystems using the Hermite normal form. In: Silverman, J.H. (ed.) CaLC 2001. LNCS, vol. 2146, pp. 126–145. Springer, Heidelberg (2001)
45. Micciancio, D., Goldwasser, S.: Complexity of Lattice Problems, A Cryptographic Perspective. Kluwer Academic Publishers, Dordrecht (2002)
46. Micciancio, D., Regev, O.: Lattice-based cryptography. In: Bernstein, D.J., Buchmann, J., Dahmen, E. (eds.) Post-quantum Cryprography. Springer, Heidelberg (2008)
47. Micciancio, D., Warinschi, B.: A linear space algorithm for computing the Hermite normal form. In: International Symposium on Symbolic Algebraic Computation (ISSAC 2001), pp. 231–236 (2001)
48. Milnor, J., Husemoller, D.: Symmetric bilinear forms. Springer, Heidelberg (1973)
49. Minkowski, H.: Geometrie der Zahlen. B. G. Teubner, Leipzig (1896)
50. Nguyen, P.Q.: Cryptanalysis of the Goldreich-Goldwasser-Halevi cryptosystem from crypto 1997. In: Wiener, M. (ed.) CRYPTO 1999. LNCS, vol. 1666, pp. 288–304. Springer, Heidelberg (1999)
51. Nguyen, P.Q.: Public-Key Cryptanalysis. Contemporary Mathematics. AMS–RSME (2008)
52. Nguyen, P.Q., Stehlé, D.: Floating-point LLL revisited. In: Cramer, R. (ed.) EUROCRYPT 2005. LNCS, vol. 3494, pp. 215–233. Springer, Heidelberg (2005)
53. Nguyen, P.Q., Stehlé, D.: LLL on the average. In: Hess, F., Pauli, S., Pohst, M. (eds.) ANTS 2006. LNCS, vol. 4076, pp. 238–256. Springer, Heidelberg (2006)
54. Nguyen, P.Q., Stern, J.: Cryptanalysis of the ajtai-dwork cryptosystem. In: Krawczyk, H. (ed.) CRYPTO 1998. LNCS, vol. 1462, pp. 223–242. Springer, Heidelberg (1998)

55. Nguyen, P.Q., Stern, J.: Adapting density attacks to low-weight knapsacks. In: Roy, B. (ed.) ASIACRYPT 2005. LNCS, vol. 3788, pp. 41–58. Springer, Heidelberg (2005)
56. Odlyzko, A.M.: The rise and fall of knapsack cryptosystems. Cryptology and Computational Number Theory 42, 75–88 (1990)
57. Okamoto, T., Tanaka, K., Uchiyama, S.: Quantum public-key cryptosystems. In: Bellare, M. (ed.) CRYPTO 2000. LNCS, vol. 1880, pp. 147–165. Springer, Heidelberg (2000)
58. Omura, K., Tanaka, K.: Density attack to the knapsack cryptosystems with enumerative source encoding. IEICE Trans Fundam. Electron Commun. Comput. Sci. 87(6), 1564–1569 (2004)
59. Paeng, S.-H., Jung, B.E., Ha, K.-C.: A lattice based public key cryptosystem using polynomial representations. In: Desmedt, Y.G. (ed.) PKC 2003. LNCS, vol. 2567, pp. 292–308. Springer, Heidelberg (2003)
60. Regev, O.: Improved inapproximability of lattice and coding problems with preprocessing. In: IEEE Conference on Computational Complexity, pp. 363–370 (2003)
61. Regev, O.: On lattices, learning with errors, random linear codes, and cryptography. In: STOC, pp. 84–93 (2005)
62. Rivest, R., Shamir, A., Adleman, L.: A method for obtaining digital signatures and public-key cryptosystems. Communications of the ACM 21(2), 120–126 (1978)
63. Schnorr, C.-P.: A hierarchy of polynomial time lattice basis reduction algorithms. Theoretical Computer Science 53(2-3), 201–224 (1987)
64. Schnorr, C.-P.: A more efficient algorithm for lattice basis reduction. Journal of Algorithms 9(1), 47–62 (1988)
65. Schnorr, C.-P.: Fast LLL-type lattice reduction. Information and Computation 204(1), 1–25 (2006)
66. Schnorr, C.-P., Hörner, H.H.: Attacking the chor-rivest cryptosystem by improved lattice reduction. In: Guillou, L.C., Quisquater, J.-J. (eds.) EUROCRYPT 1995. LNCS, vol. 921, pp. 1–12. Springer, Heidelberg (1995)
67. Shamir, A.: A polynomial time algorithm for breaking the basic merkle-hellman cryptosystem. In: McCurley, K.S., Ziegler, C.D. (eds.) CRYPTO 1982. LNCS, vol. 1440, pp. 279–288. Springer, Heidelberg (1999)
68. Shamir, A.: A polynomial-time algorithm for breaking the basic merkle-hellman cryptosystem. IEEE Transactions on Information Theory 30(5), 699–704 (1984)
69. Shoup, V.: NTL: Number theory library

Adaptively Secure Identity-Based Identification from Lattices without Random Oracles*

Markus Rückert

Technische Universität Darmstadt
Department of Computer Science
Cryptography and Computeralgebra
Germany
markus.rueckert@cased.de

Abstract. We propose a concurrently secure, identity-based identification scheme from lattices. It offers adaptive-identity security in the standard model, quasi optimal online performance, optimal leakage resilience, and its security is based on mild worst-case assumptions in ideal lattices. Our scheme uses an ideal-lattice interpretation of the Bonsai tree concept in lattices (EUROCRYPT 2010), which we call *convoluted* Bonsai trees. It allows us to build an identity-based identification scheme in a new "static identity" model that is weaker than the standard "adaptive identity" model. We show that both models are equivalent under the existence of Chameleon hash functions.

Keywords: Lattice cryptography, identification, identity-based cryptography, security model.

1 Introduction

Identification schemes are one of the most important primitives in modern cryptography because typical e-business or e-government applications essentially rely on secure online access control. Their importance is likely to grow in the future as more and more everyday tasks and processes are computerized. With identity-based identification schemes (IBI), motivated by Shamir [Sha84], one can get rid of public-key infrastructures, which are unfavorable in today's widespread decentralized networks. The public key is replaced with a unique identifier string, such as an e-mail address, and the secret key is "extracted" by a trusted party for this identifier. In hierarchical identity-based identification (HIBI), motivated by Gentry and Silverberg [GS02], this concept is generalized so that each party can act as a key extraction authority for its subordinates. Thus, this concept perfectly models organizational structures in, e.g., a company. Currently, we mainly use schemes based on the factoring or discrete logarithm problem.

Our current knowledge suggests that alternatives for the post-quantum era can be based on the hardness of the decoding problem in error correcting codes, on

* This work was supported by CASED (www.cased.de)

J.A. Garay and R. De Prisco (Eds.): SCN 2010, LNCS 6280, pp. 345–362, 2010.

the hardness of solving non-linear multivariate equation systems, or on the hardness of lattice problems. Refer to [BBD08] for an overview of each field. Basically, all three alternatives rely on the hardness of certain *average-case* problems and, at first, it is unclear how to generate hard instances of these problems. More precisely, we always need to know a "hard" distribution of keys that admits efficient key generation. Unlike with multivariate or code-based cryptography, lattice-based constructions have a built-in "trust anchor" in the form of Ajtai's worst-case to average-case reduction [Ajt96]. This reduction is even stronger than a random self reductions in, e.g., the discrete logarithm problem. It states that solving a certain average-case problem, which is relevant in cryptography, implies a solution to a related worst-case problem in *all* lattices. Although this may sound purely theoretical, it is of great practical value as keys that are chosen uniformly at random already provide *worst-case* security guarantees. The hardness of this underlying worst-case problem is also plausible as the best known algorithm to solve it requires exponential time [AKS01, MV10].

It is well-known that identity-based identification schemes can be realized in the standard model with a so-called certification approach due to Bellare, Neven, and Namprempre [BNN09] but these generic, black-box constructions require a certain computational and bandwidth overhead. The only known direct constructions, which are conjectured to resist quantum computer attacks, are the code-based scheme of Cayrel, Gaborit, Galindo, and Girault [CGGG09] and the lattice-based scheme of Stehlé, Steinfeld, Tanaka, and Xagawa [SSTX09]. However, both are only provably secure in the random oracle model and the code-based scheme merely resists passive attacks, where the adversary may not interact with the secret-key holder before his or her impersonation attempt. Another approach is using identity-based signature schemes, e.g., the lattice-based construction due to Rückert [Rüc10], in a challenge-response protocol for identification. This, however, would make the online phase significantly less efficient compared to the solution in this paper.

Therefore, we fill a gap with our proposal, as it is the first direct construction of an adaptive-identity secure identity-based identification scheme that is secure under active attacks without random oracles. We modify the identification scheme of Lyubashevsky [Lyu08a, Lyu08b] to support key extraction via an ideal-lattice interpretation of the Bonsai tree principle, originally due to Cash, Hofheinz, Kiltz, and Peikert [CHKP10]. Our changes make it necessary to re-prove the security of the protocol and we provide a simpler, more modular proof than the one in [Lyu08b] by exploiting the Reset Lemma of Bellare and Palacio [BP02]. This modification also makes the reduction a little tighter. The resulting IBI offers quasi-linear efficiency with respect to secret identification keys, public keys, bandwidth, and computation. The only exception from this quasi-optimality is the quasi-quadratic master public key and the quasi-quadratic complexity of the secret-key extraction procedure. Boyen [Boy10] improves the construction in [CHKP10] to allow for smaller lattice dimensions at the expense of a stronger assumption. We believe that the technique can be adapted for our setting to extract secret identification keys in a smaller dimension.

We also introduce a new, intermediary security model that is akin to the static message attack model for ordinary signatures (SMA), which is sometimes also referred to as "weak unforgeability". It is well-known that such SMA secure schemes are easier to realize than full CMA secure schemes. We demonstrate that the same holds for identity-based "authentication-type" schemes, e.g., for IBI or identity-based signatures. Therefore, we show a generic conversion from static-identity attack security to full adaptive-identity security of identity-based identification schemes. This transformation carries over to identity-based signature schemes and also holds in the hierarchical setting. This transformation does not hold in identity-based encryption-type schemes because the message flow is reversed. For our transformation, it is crucial that the secret key holder can send a message to the public key holder. In encryption schemes, this is not possible. In signature and identification schemes, however, this is exactly what happens.

With our new model, we greatly simplify the security proofs for direct constructions because the simulator has access to all secret-key extraction queries before the actual simulation and it can therefore "rig" the public key accordingly.

Furthermore, as an aside, our identification scheme is leakage-resilient, supporting a per-identity leakage of a $(1-o(1))$ fraction of the identities' secret keys in a model that is inspired by Katz and Vaikuntanathan [KV09].

Organization. After some basic facts about identity-based identification schemes, we introduce our weaker, static-identity security model in Section 2. There, we also provide the necessary background about lattices and Chameleon hash functions. In the next section, Section 3, we explain how static-identity security implies adaptive-identity security if Chameleon hash functions exist. Then, we demonstrate how to construct an identity-based identification scheme from lattices in the weaker model in Section 4. We then conclude the paper in Section 5 and prove additional, supporting lemmas and a result concerning leakage-resilience in the full version.

2 Preliminaries

With n, we always denote the security parameter. The joint execution of two algorithms $\mathcal{A}$ and $\mathcal{B}$ in an interactive protocol with private inputs x to $\mathcal{A}$ and y to $\mathcal{B}$ is written as $b \leftarrow \langle \mathcal{A}(x), \mathcal{B}(y) \rangle$, where b is the result of the interaction. Accordingly, $\langle \mathcal{A}(x), \mathcal{B}(y) \rangle^k$ means that the interaction can take place up to k times. The statement $x \leftarrow_\$ X$ means that x is chosen uniformly at random from the finite set X. When X is an algorithm, it means that X is probabilistic. Recall that the statistical distance of two random variables X, Y over a discrete domain D is defined as $\Delta(X,Y) = 1/2 \sum_{a \in D} |\operatorname{Prob}[X=a] - \operatorname{Prob}[Y=a]|$. A function is negligible if it vanishes faster than $1/p(n)$ for any polynomial p. All logarithms are base 2, we identify $\{1,\ldots,k\}$ with $[k]$, and $\{a_1,\ldots,a_k\}$ with $\{a_i\}_1^k$. With $\omega, \Omega, \mathcal{O}$ we denote the usual Landau symbols for asymptotic growth and $\widetilde{\mathcal{O}}$ is like $\mathcal{O}$ but it hides poly-logarithmic terms. The concatenation of strings, vectors, matrices (column-wise) is done with the operator $||$ and $a \sqsubset b$ means that $b = a||c$ for some, possibly empty, string c.

2.1 Identity-Based Identification

An ID-based identification scheme IBI comprises a triple $(\mathsf{Kg}, \mathsf{Extract}, \mathsf{Protocol})$ of algorithms: The master-key generator Kg outputs a master secret key msk and a master public key mpk; the key extraction algorithm $\mathsf{Extract}$ uses msk to generate a secret key $\mathsf{sk}_{\mathsf{ID}}$ for a given identity ID; and the identification protocol $\mathsf{Protocol}$ is a joint execution of a prover $\mathcal{P}_{\mathsf{ID}}(\mathsf{mpk}, \mathsf{ID}, \mathsf{sk}_{\mathsf{ID}})$ and a verifier $\mathcal{V}(\mathsf{mpk}, \mathsf{ID})$, where $\mathcal{V}$ outputs 1 iff $\mathcal{P}$ could identify itself correctly.

The security model for identity-based identification [Sha84] was first formalized by Kurosawa and Heng [KH05] and it is also discussed in the recent work of Bellare, Neven, and Namprempre [BNN09]. Security is proven against concurrent identity-based impersonation under adaptive identity attacks as described in the $\mathsf{adapt\text{-}id\text{-}imp\text{-}ca}$ experiment in Figure 1, where the adversary (impersonator) $\mathcal{I}^*$ works in two modes: verify and $\mathsf{impersonate}$. In mode verify it has access to mpk, to a secret key extraction oracle $\mathsf{Extract}$ and to provers $\mathcal{P}_{\mathsf{ID}}$ for arbitrary identities ID. At some point, it selects a target identity ID^*, which it tries to impersonate in the second phase. In mode $\mathsf{impersonate}$, $\mathcal{I}^*$ has access to provers and secret keys for all identities different from ID^* and it is supposed to convince a verifier that it knows the secret key for ID^*. Obviously, the secret key for ID^* must not have been among the queries to the extraction oracle in the first phase. Also, note that $\mathcal{I}^*$ is allowed to keep a state $\mathsf{st\_verify}$. The usual security notions for identification schemes, passive (pa), active (aa), and concurrent (ca) apply as well and the experiments can be easily changed to cover these attacks.

In Figure 1, we also propose a relaxed security model, called security against concurrent identity-based impersonation under static identity attacks ($\mathsf{stat\text{-}id\text{-}imp\text{-}ca}$). The model gives $\mathcal{I}^*$ significantly less power as the adversary has to submit all identities (*distinct*) to the oracle $\mathsf{Extract}$ before seeing the master public key. It then receives the extracted secret keys together with mpk. The remaining experiment stays unchanged. This new security model is reminiscent of that for weak unforgeability, or unforgeability under static message attacks, of digital signatures. Via a black-box transformation in Section 3, we show that both models are equivalent if Chameleon hash functions (cf. Section 2.3) exist. This transformation in conjunction with our simplified model enables much simpler designs for identity-based identification and it is also applicable to identity-based signature schemes. The resulting schemes are potentially more efficient and their security proofs are greatly simplified because one can prepare for all key extraction queries before handing over the master public key.

Experiment $\mathsf{Exp}^{\mathsf{adapt\text{-}id\text{-}imp\text{-}ca}}_{\mathcal{I}^*,\mathsf{IBI}}(n)$
$(\mathsf{msk}, \mathsf{mpk}) \leftarrow_{\$} \mathsf{IBI.Kg}(1^n)$
$(\mathsf{ID}^*, \mathsf{st\_verify}) \leftarrow_{\$} \mathcal{I}^{*\langle \mathcal{P}_{\mathsf{ID}}, \cdot\rangle^{\infty}, \mathsf{Extract}(\mathsf{msk}, \cdot)}(\mathsf{verify}, \mathsf{mpk})$
Let $\{\mathsf{ID}_i\}_1^{\ell}$ be the ID's queried to $\mathsf{Extract}$.
$b \leftarrow_{\$} \langle \mathcal{I}^{*\langle \mathcal{P}_{\neq \mathsf{ID}^*}, \cdot\rangle^{\infty}, \mathsf{Extract}_{\neq \mathsf{ID}^*}(\mathsf{msk}, \cdot)}, \mathcal{V}\rangle((\mathsf{impersonate}, \mathsf{st\_verify}), \mathsf{ID}^*)$
Return b

Experiment $\mathsf{Exp}^{\mathsf{stat\text{-}id\text{-}imp\text{-}ca}}_{\mathcal{I}^*,\mathsf{IBI}}(n)$
$(\mathsf{ID}_1, \ldots, \mathsf{ID}_{\ell}, \mathsf{st\_find}) \leftarrow_{\$} \mathcal{I}^*(\mathsf{find})$ for distinct ID_i
$(\mathsf{msk}, \mathsf{mpk}) \leftarrow_{\$} \mathsf{IBI.Kg}(1^n)$
$\mathsf{sk}_i \leftarrow_{\$} \mathsf{Extract}(\mathsf{msk}, \mathsf{ID}_i)$ for $i \in [\ell]$
$(\mathsf{ID}^*, \mathsf{st\_verify}) \leftarrow_{\$} \mathcal{I}^{*\langle \mathcal{P}_{\mathsf{ID}}, \cdot\rangle^{\infty}}(\mathsf{verify}, \mathsf{mpk}, \{\mathsf{sk}_i\}_1^{\ell}, \mathsf{st\_find})$
$b \leftarrow_{\$} \langle \mathcal{I}^{*\langle \mathcal{P}_{\neq \mathsf{ID}^*}, \cdot\rangle^{\infty}}, \mathcal{V}\rangle((\mathsf{impersonate}, \mathsf{st\_verify}), \mathsf{ID}^*)$
Return 1 iff $b = 1 \wedge \mathsf{ID}^* \notin \{\mathsf{ID}_i\}_1^{\ell}$

Fig. 1. Security experiments for identity-based identification

All definitions easily carry over the the hierarchical setting [GS02], where identities can be concatenated to describe a subordinate identity and its relation in an organizational structure. Here, every entity can act as a key extraction authority for its subordinates.

2.2 Lattices

A lattice in $\mathbb{R}^n$ is a discrete set $\Lambda = \{\sum_{i=1}^{d} x_i \mathbf{b}_i \,|\, x_i \in \mathbb{Z}\}$, where $\mathbf{b}_1, \ldots, \mathbf{b}_d$ are linearly independent over $\mathbb{R}^n$. The matrix $\mathbf{B} = [\mathbf{b}_1, \ldots, \mathbf{b}_d]$ is a basis of the lattice Λ and we write $\Lambda = \Lambda(\mathbf{B})$. The dimension of the lattice is d. The main computational problem in lattices is the (approximate) shortest vector problem (SVP^p), where an algorithm is given a description, a basis, of a lattice Λ and is supposed to find the shortest vector $\mathbf{v} \in \Lambda \setminus \{\mathbf{0}\}$ with respect to a certain ℓ_p norm (up to an approximation factor). More precisely, find a vector $\mathbf{v} \in \Lambda \setminus \{\mathbf{0}\}$, such that $\|\mathbf{v}\|_p \leq \gamma \|\mathbf{w}\|_p$ for all $\mathbf{w} \in \Lambda \setminus \{\mathbf{0}\}$ for an approximation factor $\gamma \geq 1$.

In this work, we are interested in a special family of lattices related to ideals in the ring $\mathbf{R} = \mathbb{Z}_q[X]/\langle \mathsf{g} \rangle$, where q is prime and $\mathbb{Z}_q = \{-(q-1)/2, \ldots, (q-1)/2\}$. We focus on $\mathsf{g} = X^n + 1$ and $n =$ "power of two" for efficiency reasons but it may be replaced with any irreducible polynomial over $\mathbb{Z}$. Then, our scheme and the analysis become only slightly more involved. We identify $\mathsf{f} \in \mathbf{R}$ with its coefficient vector $\mathsf{f} = (f_0, \ldots, f_{n-1}) \in \mathbb{Z}_q^n$. Furthermore, we denote elements of the $\mathbf{R}$-module $\mathbf{R}^m$ with $\hat{\mathsf{a}} = (\mathsf{a}_0, \ldots, \mathsf{a}_{m-1})$ or directly with $(a_0, \ldots, a_{mn-1}) \in \mathbb{Z}_q^{mn}$. Consequently, we define $\|\mathsf{f}\|_\infty = \|(f_0, \ldots, f_{n-1})\|_\infty$ for $\mathsf{f} \in \mathbb{Z}[X]$. A lattice corresponds to an ideal $I \subset \mathbf{R}$ if and only if every lattice vector is the coefficient vector of a polynomial in I. The SVP problem easily translates to ideal lattices, where we call it ideal-SVP^p (ISVP^p).

The average-case hardness assumption for our construction relies on the problem finding short vectors in the kernel of the family $\mathcal{H}(\mathbf{R}, m)$ of module homomorphisms $h_{\hat{\mathsf{a}} \in \mathbf{R}^m} : \mathbf{R}^m \to \mathbf{R}, \hat{\mathsf{x}} \mapsto h(\hat{\mathsf{a}}, \hat{\mathsf{x}}) = \hat{\mathsf{a}} \circledast \hat{\mathsf{x}} = \sum_{i=0}^{m-1} \mathsf{a}_i \mathsf{x}_i$, when restricting the domain to $D' \subset \mathbf{R}$, i.e., restricting the coefficients in the input vector to $[-2d, 2d] \cap \mathbb{Z}$.[1] This problem can be stated as a short vector problem in the lattice $\Lambda_{\mathbf{R}}^{\perp}(\hat{\mathsf{a}}) := \{\mathbf{x} \in \mathbb{Z}^{mn} : \mathbf{A}\mathbf{x} \equiv \mathbf{0} \pmod{q}\}$, where $\mathbf{A}$ is structured and represents the multiplication $\circledast$ mod g. Hence, ideal lattices of the form $\Lambda_{\mathbf{R}}^{\perp}(\hat{\mathsf{a}})$ are a special case of q-ary lattices $\Lambda_q^{\perp}(\mathbf{A}) := \{\mathbf{x} \in \mathbb{Z}^{mn} : \mathbf{A}\mathbf{x} \equiv \mathbf{0} \pmod{q}\}$, where $\mathbf{A}$ is unstructured and chosen from $\mathbb{Z}_q^{n \times mn}$.

The main average-case problem is the following collision problem.

Definition 1 (Collision Problem [LM06]). *The problem $Col(\mathcal{H}(\mathbf{R}, m), D)$ asks to find a distinct pair $(\hat{\mathsf{x}}, \hat{\mathsf{x}}') \in D^m \times D^m$ such that $h(\hat{\mathsf{x}}) = h(\hat{\mathsf{x}}')$ for $h \leftarrow_{\$} \mathcal{H}(\mathbf{R}, m)$.*

Obviously, the function is linear over $\mathbf{R}^m$, i.e., $h(\mathsf{a}(\hat{\mathsf{x}} + \hat{\mathsf{y}})) = \mathsf{a}(h(\hat{\mathsf{x}}) + h(\hat{\mathsf{y}}))$ for all $\mathsf{a} \in \mathbf{R}$, $\hat{\mathsf{x}}, \hat{\mathsf{y}} \in \mathbf{R}^m$. In addition, solving $Col(\mathcal{H}(\mathbf{R}, m), D)$ implies being able to solve ISVP^∞ in *every* lattice that corresponds to an ideal in $\mathbf{R}$.

---

[1] For better readability, we use both notations $h_{\hat{\mathsf{a}}}(\cdot)$ and $h(\hat{\mathsf{a}}, \cdot)$.

Theorem 1 (Worst-case to Average-case Reduction, [LM06, Theorem 2]). *Let* $D = \{\mathsf{f} \in \mathbf{R} : \|\mathsf{f}\|_\infty \leq d\}$, $m > \log(q)/\log(2d)$, *and* $q \geq 4dmn\sqrt{n}\log(n)$. *An adversary* $\mathcal{C}$ *that solves the* $Col(h, D)$ *problem, i.e., finds distinct preimages* $\hat{\mathsf{x}}, \hat{\mathsf{y}} \in D^m$ *such that* $h(\hat{\mathsf{x}}) = h(\hat{\mathsf{y}})$, *can be used to solve* ISVP^∞ *with approximation factors* $\gamma \geq 16dmn\log^2(n)$ *in the worst case.*

2.3 Chameleon Hash Functions

Krawczyk and Rabin [KR00] proposed Chameleon hashes to be collision-resistant hash functions with a trapdoor and the following properties. 1) The function $\mathsf{C} : D \times E \to R$ is chosen from a family $\mathcal{C}$ of Chameleon hashes along with a secret trapdoor C^{-1}. 2) The output distribution is indistinguishable from uniform. 3) In order to sample from the distribution $(d, e, \mathsf{C}(d, e)) \in D \times E \times R$, we can do one of two things. Either we run C on the given document d and a randomness $e \sim \Delta(E)$ from an efficiently samplable distribution Δ over E, or we apply an inversion algorithm $e \leftarrow \mathsf{C}^{-1}(d, r)$ on a given image $r \in R$ and a target document $d \in D$. Thus, we obtain a randomness e such that $\mathsf{C}(d, e) = r$. The resulting distributions are indistinguishable. We will require statistical indistinguishability to facilitate a simpler proof in Section 3. Note that whenever we need the Chameleon hash to map to a certain range $\neq R$, we can compose it with an arbitrary collision resistant hash function. As for their realization, Krawczyk and Rabin claim in [KR98] that Chameleon hash functions exist if there are claw-free trapdoor permutations. Interestingly, they can be easily implemented with the lattice-based trapdoor function in [GPV08] as observed in [CHKP10].

3 From stat-id-imp-ca to adapt-id-imp-ca

To simplify the construction of (hierarchical) ID-based identification schemes, we propose a generic, black-box transformation from static-identity security to adaptive-identity security. The transformation is reminiscent of a generic transformation from static message secure digital signature schemes to adaptively chosen message secure schemes as both involve Chameleon hash functions.

In principle, our transform works for all *authentication-type* ID-based cryptography, e.g., ID-based identification or signatures. For encryption this does not work because there is no message-flow from the secret-key holder to the public-key holder. In other words, the encrypter cannot derive the recipients identity as it does not know the randomness for the Chameleon hash.

Suppose we have a scheme $\mathsf{IBI}^{\mathsf{stat}} = (\mathsf{Kg}, \mathsf{Extract}, \mathsf{Protocol})$ that is secure against static identity attacks, we show how to construct a scheme $\mathsf{IBI}^{\mathsf{adapt}} = (\mathsf{Kg}, \mathsf{Extract}, \mathsf{Protocol})$ that is secure against adaptive identity attacks if there is a family of Chameleon hash functions C. Notice that the inversion algorithm C^{-1} is not used in the actual scheme, it is merely necessary to simulate the extraction oracle in the security proof.

Prover $\mathcal{P}(\mathsf{mpk}, \mathsf{ID}, (\mathsf{sk}, e))$		**Verifier** $\mathcal{V}(\mathsf{mpk}, \mathsf{ID})$
$I \leftarrow \mathsf{C}(\mathsf{ID}, e)$	$\xrightarrow{\quad e \quad}$	$I \leftarrow \mathsf{C}(\mathsf{ID}, e)$
$\mathsf{IBI}^{\mathsf{stat}}.\mathcal{P}(\mathsf{mpk}, I, \mathsf{sk})$	$\xleftarrow{\qquad}$ $\xrightarrow{\mathsf{IBI}^{\mathsf{stat}}.\mathsf{Protocol}}$	$\mathsf{IBI}^{\mathsf{stat}}.\mathcal{V}(\mathsf{mpk}, I)$

Fig. 2. Identity-based identification protocol for $\mathsf{IBI}^{\mathsf{adapt}}$

Master-key Generation. $\mathsf{Kg}(1^n)$ runs $(\mathsf{msk}', \mathsf{mpk}') \leftarrow \mathsf{IBI}^{\mathsf{stat}}.\mathsf{Kg}(1^n)$ and select a Chameleon hash function $(\mathsf{C}, \mathsf{C}^{-1}) \leftarrow_{\$} \mathcal{C}(1^n)$. It returns $(\mathsf{msk}, \mathsf{mpk}) \leftarrow (\mathsf{msk}', (\mathsf{mpk}', \mathsf{C}))$.

Key Extraction. $\mathsf{Extract}(\mathsf{msk}, \mathsf{ID})$. The algorithm selects $e \sim \Delta(E)$ and computes $I \leftarrow \mathsf{C}(\mathsf{ID}, e)$. Then, it computes the secret key for I by calling $\mathsf{sk} \leftarrow \mathsf{IBI}.\mathsf{Extract}(\mathsf{msk}, I)$ and returns the pair (e, sk).

Identification Protocol. Whenever a prover $\mathcal{P}$ wants to prove its identity ID to a verifier $\mathcal{V}$, both parties act as per the protocol in Figure 2.

We show a reduction that proves adaptive identity security of $\mathsf{IBI}^{\mathsf{adapt}}$ under two assumptions. First, the underlying $\mathsf{IBI}^{\mathsf{stat}}$ needs to be secure under static identity attacks. Second, the employed Chameleon hash function needs to be collision resistant. Notice that the reduction is property preserving with regard to the identification scheme, i.e., security under passive, active, and concurrent attacks is preserved under the reduction.

Theorem 2 (Adaptive Identity Security). *Suppose Chameleon hash functions exist.* $\mathsf{IBI}^{\mathsf{adapt}}$ *is secure under adaptive identity queries in the imp-{pa, aa, ca} sense if* $\mathsf{IBI}^{\mathsf{stat}}$ *is secure under static identity attacks in the same sense.*

Proof. First of all notice that Chameleon hash functions ensure that there is no efficient adversary that can reuse a given secret key sk for a particular identity ID to impersonate a different identity ID^*. Such an adversary refutes the collision resistance of the family $\mathcal{C}$ of Chameleon hash functions. The reduction is straightforward. Therefore, we focus on the simulation against an impersonator $\mathcal{I}^*$ that does not exploit any weakness in the Chameleon hash function. Suppose that the adversary makes at most Q queries to the extraction oracle.

Setup. On input mpk, the simulator chooses a Chameleon hash function and its trapdoor $(\mathsf{C}, \mathsf{C}^{-1}) \leftarrow_{\$} \mathcal{C}(1^n)$. It prepares a set of random identity strings $I_1, \ldots, I_Q \leftarrow_{\$} R$. Afterwards, the simulator calls its external extraction oracle $\mathsf{IBI}^{\mathsf{stat}}.\mathsf{Extract}$ to obtain the corresponding secret keys $\mathsf{sk}_1, \ldots, \mathsf{sk}_Q$ and sets up a counter $\imath \leftarrow 0$. It runs $\mathcal{I}^*$ on input $(\mathsf{mpk}, \mathsf{C})$.

Extraction Queries. Whenever $\mathcal{I}^*$ queries an identity ID to its extraction oracle, the internal counter $\imath$ is incremented and the reduction calls $e \leftarrow \mathsf{C}^{-1}(\mathsf{ID}, I_\imath)$. It returns $(e, \mathsf{sk}_\imath)$.

Prover Queries. The simulator runs the protocol in Figure 2, by using its external prover oracle.

Impersonation Attempt. At some point, $\mathcal{I}^*$ outputs a challenge identity ID^*, which has not been queried to the extraction oracle before. After that, the extraction oracle answers $\perp$ when queried with ID^*. When the adversary instantiates a verifier to prove its identity ID^* with randomness e^*, the simulation forwards all messages to and from its external verifier oracle for $I^* = \mathsf{C}(\mathsf{ID}^*, e^*)$.

The environment of $\mathcal{I}^*$ is perfectly simulated if the input-output relation of $\mathcal{C}$ can be sampled perfectly. The extraction oracle in the simulation was never called with ID^*, so the simulation never called the external oracle with identity $I^* = \mathsf{C}(\mathsf{ID}^*, e^*)$ (but with negligible probability). If $\mathcal{I}^*$ is successful in the impersonation attempt, so is the simulator in the experiment $\mathsf{Exp}_{\mathcal{I}^*,\mathsf{IBI}}^{\mathsf{adapt\text{-}id\text{-}imp\text{-}ca}}$. □

This transformation can be adapted to work in the hierarchical setting. There, an is identity prefixed with superordinate identities. In the transformation, one simply splits the entire string into sub-identities and computes a Chameleon hash for each of them. The reduction is somewhat looser than in Theorem 2 as the simulator has to prepare identities on all ℓ levels in the hierarchy. In consequence, the reduction only works when $\ell = \widetilde{\mathcal{O}}(1)$.

4 A Construction without Random Oracles

In this section, we show how to instantiate our new static-identity model from lattices. Our construction builds upon Lyubashevsky's identification scheme. By using the Bonsai-tree technique [CHKP10] in the setting of ideal lattices, we show how to realize secret key extraction in the standard model.

The required lattice-based tools are introduced in Section 4.1 and our main construction is in Section 4.2. An additional discussion of leakage-resilience will appear in the full version. For each aspect, we prove a main theorem. Supporting lemmas are stated before the theorems and proven in the full version.

4.1 Convoluted Bonsai Trees

For our main construction, we require a certain toolbox for lattices that goes by the name of "Bonsai trees". In [CHKP10], such a toolbox is constructed from q-ary lattices to implement lattice-based signatures in the standard model as well as identity-based encryption. The authors also point out that Bonsai trees from more efficient ideal lattices seem possible. We confirm this observation by making it explicit, based on a family of trapdoor functions in ideal lattices. Notice that our main construction can be instantiated from q-ary lattices as well and that ideal lattices are merely necessary to achieve quasi-linear efficiency. In addition, making the notion of *ideal Bonsai trees* explicit may be of independent interest.

Preimage-samplable Trapdoor Functions. Gentry et al. [GPV08] introduce a family of preimage samplable functions $\mathsf{GPV} = (\mathsf{TrapGen}, \mathsf{Eval}, \mathsf{SamplePre})$ on lattices, which was later on adapted to ideal lattices by Stehlé et al. [SSTX09].

Its parameters $q, m, \tilde{L}, s = \omega(\sqrt{\log(n)})\tilde{L}$ are functions of n. We define the set $D_d := \{\mathsf{x} \in \mathbf{R} \setminus \{\mathbf{0}\} : \|\mathsf{x}\|_\infty \leq d\}$ for $d > 0$.

The algorithm $\mathsf{TrapGen}(1^n)$ outputs a public description $\hat{\mathsf{a}} \in \mathbf{R}^m$ for the lattice $\Lambda_{\mathbf{R}}^{\perp}(\hat{\mathsf{a}})$ together with a secret trapdoor $\mathbf{T} \in \mathbb{Z}^{mn \times mn}$, $\left\|\tilde{\mathbf{T}}\right\| = \max_{i=1,\ldots,mn} \{\left\|\tilde{\mathbf{t}}_i\right\|_2\} \leq \tilde{L}$, where $\tilde{\mathbf{T}}$ is the Gram-Schmidt orthogonalization of $\mathbf{T}$. Evaluation of the trapdoor function $h_{\hat{\mathsf{a}}} : \mathbf{R}^m \to \mathbf{R}$ is performed by the *convolution* product $\mathsf{Eval}(\hat{\mathsf{a}}, \hat{\mathsf{x}}) = \hat{\mathsf{a}} \circledast \hat{\mathsf{x}}$. The inversion algorithm $\mathsf{SamplePre}(\mathbf{T}, s, \mathsf{Y})$ samples from the set of preimages $\{\hat{\mathsf{x}} \in D_d^m : h(\hat{\mathsf{a}}, \hat{\mathsf{x}}) = \mathbf{y}\}$ for any $d = s\omega(\sqrt{\log(mn)})$. By construction, the function compresses the input and therefore admits collisions, but they are hard to find unless finding short vectors in ideal lattices is easy.

The following proposition is our adaptation of [GPV08] for ideal lattices.

Proposition 1. *Given a basis* $\mathbf{T}$ *for* $\Lambda_{\mathbf{R}}^{\perp}(\hat{\mathsf{a}})$ *with* $\left\|\tilde{\mathbf{T}}\right\| \leq \tilde{T}$ *and a Gaussian parameter* $s = \omega(\sqrt{\log(n)})\tilde{L}$, *there is a polynomial-time algorithm* $\mathsf{SamplePre}$ *that, for any* $\mathsf{Y} \in \mathbf{R}$, *outputs* $\hat{\mathsf{x}} \in \mathbf{R}^m$ *with* $\mathsf{Eval}(\hat{\mathsf{a}}, \hat{\mathsf{x}}) = \mathsf{Y}$ *and* $\hat{\mathsf{x}} \in D_d$ *for* $d = s\omega(\sqrt{\log(mn)})$ *with overwhelming probability. Furthermore,* $\hat{\mathsf{x}}$ *has a conditional min-entropy of* $\omega(\log(n))$, *conditioned on* $h(\hat{\mathsf{a}}, \hat{\mathsf{x}}) = \mathsf{Y}$.

Bonsai Trees from Ideal Lattices. We explicitly describe the functionalities of Bonsai trees in the language of ideal lattices. A central ingredient is the work of Stehlé et al. [SSTX09] because they show how to generate an ideal lattice together with a basis of short vectors of that lattice.

The notion of Bonsai trees on lattices is an analogy to arboriculture. An arborist always starts with a certain amount of *undirected*, i.e., random, natural growth that he cannot control. Then, he applies his tools and starts cultivating individual branches to achieve the desired looks via *directed* growth. The arborist is successful if the resulting tree still looks sufficiently natural to the observer. Once cultivated, a branch can easily be *extended* to form more directed growth without too much additional care. Instead of extending directed growth, the arborist can also generate *randomized* offsprings, which can be given to another arborist that can easily cultivate them by *extending* growth. The offsprings hide the first arborist's work and the employed techniques. We formalize these concepts in the context of ideal lattices. A (binary) bonsai tree is generated out of a root $\hat{\mathsf{a}}^{\star}$ and branches $\hat{\mathsf{b}}_i^{(b)} \in \mathbf{R}^{m_i}, b \in \{0,1\}, i \leq k \leq \mathsf{poly}(n)$, that are statistically close to uniform. The entire tree is the set $\{\hat{\mathsf{a}}^{\star}||\hat{\mathsf{b}}_1^{(x_1)}||\cdots||\hat{\mathsf{b}}_k^{(x_k)} : \mathbf{x} \in \{0,1\}^{\leq k}\}$. The core of the Bonsai-tree technique is that we can append two vectors of polynomials $\hat{\mathsf{a}} \in \mathbf{R}^{m_1}$ and $\hat{\mathsf{b}} \in \mathbf{R}^{m_2}$ to form $\hat{\mathsf{c}} = \hat{\mathsf{a}}||\hat{\mathsf{b}} \in \mathbf{R}^{m_1+m_2}$. Now, knowing a solution $\hat{\mathsf{x}} \in \mathbf{R}^{m_1}$ to the equation $\hat{\mathsf{a}} \otimes \hat{\mathsf{x}} \equiv 0 \in \mathbf{R}$, we immediately obtain a solution $\hat{\mathsf{y}} \in \mathbf{R}^{m_1+m_2}$ to the equation $\hat{\mathsf{c}} \circledast \hat{\mathsf{y}} \equiv 0$ by setting $\hat{\mathsf{y}} = \hat{\mathsf{x}}||\hat{0} \in \mathbf{R}^{m_1+m_2}$ with $\|\hat{\mathsf{x}}\| = \|\hat{\mathsf{y}}\|$ for any norm. To see this, we directly apply the definition of $\circledast$ and obtain $\hat{\mathsf{c}} \circledast \hat{\mathsf{y}} = \hat{\mathsf{a}} \circledast \hat{\mathsf{x}} + \hat{\mathsf{b}} \circledast \hat{0} = 0$.

Proposition 2 (Directed Growth). *Let* $n, \sigma, r \in \mathbb{N}_{>0}$, $q = q(n) \geq 3$ *be a prime,* $\mathsf{f} \in \mathbb{Z}[X]$ *be monic and irreducible over* $\mathbb{Z}$. *Let* $\mathbf{R} = \mathbb{Z}_q[X]/\langle \mathsf{f} \rangle$. *There is a polynomial time algorithm* $\mathsf{ExtLattice}(\hat{\mathsf{a}}, m)$ *that, given a uniformly random*

$\hat{\mathsf{a}} \in \mathbf{R}^{m_1}$, $m = m_1 + m_2 \geq (\lceil \log(q) \rceil + 1)(\sigma + r)$, $m_1 \geq \sigma$, *generates* $\hat{\mathsf{b}} \in \mathbf{R}^{m_2}$ *with* $m_2 = m - m_1$ *together with a basis* $\mathbf{S} = [\hat{\mathsf{s_1}}, \ldots, \hat{\mathsf{s_m}}] \in \mathbf{R}^{m \times m}$ *such that* $(\hat{\mathsf{a}}||\hat{\mathsf{b}}) \circledast \hat{\mathsf{s_i}} \equiv 0$ *for* $i \in [m]$.

Let $\mathsf{f} = \prod_{i \leq t} \mathsf{f}_i$ *be the factorization of* f *over* $\mathbb{Z}_q$. *The algorithm succeeds with probability* $\geq 1 - p(n)$, *where* $p(n) = 1 - \prod_{i \leq t}(1 - q^{-\deg(\mathsf{f}_i)\sigma})$. *When it does, we have 1.* $\Delta(\hat{\mathsf{a}}||\hat{\mathsf{b}}, \mathsf{unif}(\mathbf{R}^m)) \leq p + \frac{m}{2}\sqrt{\prod_{i \leq t}\left(1 + \frac{q}{3^r}^{\deg(\mathsf{f}_i)}\right) - 1}$; *2.* $\|\mathbf{S}\| \leq L = \sqrt{2}\sqrt{n(9r + \sigma)}$; *3.* $\left\|\tilde{\mathbf{S}}\right\| \leq \tilde{L} \leq L$.

The proposition follows [SSTX09, Theorem 3.1].

Given $\mathsf{f} = X^n + 1$ and a prime $q \equiv 3 \bmod 8$, we know that f splits into $\mathsf{f}_1\mathsf{f}_2$ for $\mathsf{f}_i = X^{n/2} + z_i X^{n/4} - 1$, $z_i \in \mathbb{Z}_q$. This seems to be the best choice for q as the success probability and the uniformity of the output in Proposition 2 depend on f having only a small number of factors. But, even if f splits completely over $\mathbb{Z}_q$, it is still possible to find suitable (larger) parameters r, σ. For our choice of q, we can set $\sigma = 1$ and $r = \lceil \log_3(q) + 1 \rceil$ and repeat the process when it fails.

The interpretation in terms of arboriculture is generating "directed growth" out of "undirected growth" because one starts with some random growth $\hat{\mathsf{a}}$ and cultivates a branch $\hat{\mathsf{a}}||\hat{\mathsf{b}}$ along with a trapdoor $\mathbf{S}$, which is the arborist's journal or a trace of his work. However, the observer cannot distinguish undirected growth from directed growth.

Proposition 3 (Extending Control). *There is a polynomial time algorithm* $\mathsf{ExtBasis}(\mathbf{T}, \hat{\mathsf{c}} = \hat{\mathsf{a}}||\hat{\mathsf{b}})$ *that takes a basis* $\mathbf{S}$ *of* $\Lambda_{\mathbf{R}}^{\perp}(\hat{\mathsf{a}})$ *and an extension* $\hat{\mathsf{c}}$ *with* $\mathbf{R}^{m_1} \ni \hat{\mathsf{a}} \sqsubset \hat{\mathsf{c}} \in \mathbf{R}^{m_1+m_2}$ *as input. If* $\hat{\mathsf{a}}$ *generates* $\mathbf{R}$, *the algorithm outputs a basis* $\mathbf{T}'$ *for* $\Lambda_{\mathbf{R}}^{\perp}(\hat{\mathsf{c}})$ *with* $\left\|\tilde{\mathbf{T}}'\right\| = \left\|\tilde{\mathbf{T}}\right\|$.

The proposition is an adaptation of the respective proposition for q-ary lattices. The resulting trapdoor is $\left(\begin{array}{c|c} \mathbf{S} & \mathbf{V} \\ \hline \mathbf{0} & \mathbf{I}_{m_2} \end{array}\right)$, where the columns $\hat{\mathsf{v_i}}$ of $\mathbf{V} \in \mathbf{R}^{m_2 \times m_2}$ are arbitrary (not necessarily short) solutions of the equations $\hat{\mathsf{a}} \circledast \hat{\mathsf{v_i}} \equiv -\mathsf{b}_i$.

Whenever trapdoor delegation is required, one cannot simply use extending control and hand over the resulting basis as it leaks information about the original trapdoor. Here, we can use tree propagation to obtain a *randomized* offspring with a new, random trapdoor.

Proposition 4 (Randomizing Control). *On input a basis* $\mathbf{T}$ *of the lattice* $\Lambda_{\mathbf{R}}^{\perp}(\hat{\mathsf{a}})$ *of dimension* m *and a Gaussian parameter* $s \geq \left\|\tilde{\mathbf{T}}\right\| \omega(\sqrt{\log(n)})$, *the polynomial time algorithm* $\mathsf{RandBasis}(\mathbf{T}, s)$ *outputs a basis* $\mathbf{T}'$ *of* $\Lambda_{\mathbf{R}}^{\perp}(\hat{\mathsf{a}})$ *with* $\left\|\tilde{\mathbf{T}}'\right\| \leq s\sqrt{m}$. *The basis is independent of* $\mathbf{T}$ *in the sense that for any two bases* $\mathbf{T}_0, \mathbf{T}_1$ *of* $\Lambda_{\mathbf{R}}^{\perp}(\hat{\mathsf{a}})$ *and* $s \geq \max\{\left\|\tilde{\mathbf{T}}_0\right\|, \left\|\tilde{\mathbf{T}}_1\right\|\}\omega(\sqrt{\log(n)})$, $\mathsf{RandBasis}(\mathbf{T}_0, s)$ *is within negligible statistical distance of* $\mathsf{RandBasis}(\mathbf{T}_1, s)$.

The proposition is a direct adaptation of the randomizing control algorithm in [CHKP10]. A more efficient alternative is in [Pei10].

For that concept to be used later on, we require a method of transforming a full-rank set of vectors in a lattice into a basis.

Proposition 5 (Full-rank Set to Basis [MG02, Lemma 7.1]). *Let $\Lambda = \Lambda(\mathbf{B})$ be a lattice generated by the basis $\mathbf{B} \in \mathbb{Z}^{m \times m}$. There is a polynomial time algorithm* ToBasis($\mathbf{S}, \mathbf{B}$) *that takes as input a full-rank set of lattice vectors* $\mathbf{S}$ *with* $\mathbf{S} \subset \Lambda(B)$ *and a basis* $\mathbf{B}$. *It outputs a basis* $\mathbf{T}$ *of* Λ *with 1.* $\|\mathbf{T}\| \leq \sqrt{mn}/2 \|\mathbf{S}\|$; *2.* $\left\|\tilde{\mathbf{T}}\right\| \leq \left\|\tilde{\mathbf{S}}\right\|$.

The idea is to use the oblivious sampler for lattices [GPV08, Pei10] to sample mn linearly independent vectors using the set $\mathbf{T}$ as input. The result is a full-rank set of lattice vectors $\mathbf{S}$ that does not reveal any information about $\mathbf{T}$. The final step entails calling ToBasis($\mathbf{S}$, HNF($\mathbf{T}$)) to obtain a basis. HNF is the unique Hermite normal form of $\mathbf{T}$, which is necessary to make the input to ToBasis completely independent of $\mathbf{T}$.

4.2 Our Construction

We construct a lattice-based identity-based identification scheme. It is secure in the standard model under a worst-case assumption in ideal lattices and its time and space complexity is quasi-optimal, i.e., $\widetilde{O}(n)$, in the online phase. The road map for this section is as follows: We describe the 3-move identification scheme IBI, including an informal description of the protocol. Then, we prove completeness and soundness in the static-identity attack model. Full, adaptive-identity security is established by the generic construction in Section 3. Proving completeness is non-trivial as we need to address an inevitable completeness defect. In the course of the discussion, we show that it neither harms security nor efficiency. In particular, the protocol remains statistically witness-indistinguishable and sound unless the collision problem $Col(\mathcal{H}(\mathbf{R}, m), D)$ is easy. Thus, security can be based on the worst-case hardness of the ISVP.

Observe that the scheme requires lots of parameters that need to be carefully worked out. Their definition in Table 1 will be justified later in the analysis.

Informal Description. We give a detailed, slightly informal description of the protocol Steps 1-4 in Figure 3. For each step, we need a set of carefully chosen parameters from Table 2 to achieve completeness and security.

Basically, the protocol follows the structure of the 3-move identification scheme in [Lyu08a, Lyu08b], which provides a witness-indistinguishable proof of knowledge. The prover proves knowledge of $\hat{\mathsf{s}} \in D_s^m$ such that $h(\hat{\mathsf{a}}, \hat{\mathsf{s}}) = \mathsf{S}$ with $(\hat{\mathsf{a}}, \mathsf{S})$ being the public key.

In the *first step*, the prover $\mathcal{P}$ selects the randomness $\hat{\mathsf{y}} \leftarrow_{\$} D_y^m$ for this protocol run, where m depends on the size of the identity space. Then, $\mathcal{P}$ commits to $\hat{\mathsf{y}}$ by sending $Y = h(\hat{\mathsf{a}}_{\mathsf{ID}}, \hat{\mathsf{y}})$ to the verifier $\mathcal{V}$. The key $\hat{\mathsf{a}}_{\mathsf{ID}}$ to h is unique for each identity $\mathsf{ID} \in \{0,1\}^{\lambda}$ and it can be computed from the master public key $(\hat{\mathsf{a}}^{\star}, \left\langle \hat{\mathsf{b}} \right\rangle, \mathsf{S})$.

In the *second step*, $\mathcal{V}$ challenges $\mathcal{P}$ with a challenge c from the set D_c^m.

Table 1. Parameters the identity-based identification scheme IBI

Parameter	**Value**	**Asymptotic bound**
$\mathbf{R}$	$\mathbb{Z}_q[X]/\langle X^n+1\rangle$, q prime	-
n	power of 2	-
m_1, σ	1	$\mathcal{O}(1)$
r	$\lceil \log_3(q)+1\rceil$	$\tilde{\mathcal{O}}(1)$
m_2	$\lceil \log(q)\rceil(\sigma+r)+r$	$\tilde{\mathcal{O}}(1)$
m	$m_1+(\lambda+1)m_2$	$\tilde{\mathcal{O}}(\lambda)$
D_s	$\{\mathsf{f}\in\mathbf{R} : \lVert\mathsf{f}\rVert_\infty \le \tilde{L}\omega(\sqrt{\log(m)}) =: d_s\}$	$\tilde{\mathcal{O}}(\sqrt{n})$
D_c	$\{\mathsf{f}\in\mathbf{R} : \lVert\mathsf{f}\rVert_\infty \le 1 =: d_c\}$	$\mathcal{O}(1)$
ϕ	positive integer constant ≥ 1	$\mathcal{O}(1)$
D_y	$\{\mathsf{f}\in\mathbf{R} : \lVert\mathsf{f}\rVert_\infty \le \phi m n^2 d_s =: d_y\}$	$\tilde{\mathcal{O}}(n^2\sqrt{n})$
G	$\{\mathsf{f}\in\mathbf{R} : \lVert\mathsf{f}\rVert_\infty \le d_y - n d_s d_c =: d_G\}$	$\tilde{\mathcal{O}}(n^2\sqrt{n})$
D	$\{\mathsf{f}\in\mathbf{R} : \lVert\mathsf{f}\rVert_\infty \le d_G + n d_s d_c =: d_D\}$	$\tilde{\mathcal{O}}(n^2\sqrt{n})$
q (prime)	$\ge 4mn\sqrt{n}\log(n)d_D$	$\tilde{\Theta}(n^4)$

The table defines all parameters for our scheme. The parameters $\sigma, r, \tilde{L}, m_1, m_2$ are as per Proposition 2. The constant ϕ governs the completeness error and λ is the bit length of the identities. The third column contains the asymptotic growth for the respective norm bound or parameter with respect to the main security parameter n.

The *third step* entails the computation of the response $\hat{\mathsf{z}}$ and checking whether it falls into a safe set G^m of responses. If the coefficients of $\hat{\mathsf{z}}$ fall outside G, the protocol has to be restarted to ensure witness indistinguishability. Otherwise, $\hat{\mathsf{z}}$ is sent to the verifier.

Finally, the verifier performs the actual verification in the *fourth step*. It involves testing that the coefficients of $\hat{\mathsf{z}}$ are within the correct interval and that the prover has used a correct secret key $\hat{\mathsf{s}}_{\mathsf{ID}}$, such that $h(\hat{\mathsf{a}}_{\mathsf{ID}}, \hat{\mathsf{s}}) = \mathsf{S}$, when computing $\hat{\mathsf{z}}$. This last check is possible due to the linearity of h.

Concerning the abort ($\hat{\mathsf{z}} \leftarrow \bot$) in Step 3, we will show that it happens with probability at most $1 - e^{-1/\phi}$ if the set of D_y is set up properly.

Now, we explain how the secret key $\hat{\mathsf{s}}_{\mathsf{ID}}$ is extracted for a given identity ID. Let $\hat{\mathsf{a}}^\star$ be the root of a Bonsai tree and let $\left\langle\hat{\mathsf{b}}\right\rangle = \left\{(\hat{\mathsf{b}}_i^{(0)}, \hat{\mathsf{b}}_i^{(1)})\right\}_1^\lambda$ be the set of branches. Each identity $\mathsf{ID} = \mathsf{ID}_1||\ldots||\mathsf{ID}_\lambda$ defines a unique path $\hat{\mathsf{a}}_{\mathsf{ID}} := \hat{\mathsf{a}}^\star||\hat{\mathsf{b}}_1^{(\mathsf{ID}_1)}||\ldots||\hat{\mathsf{b}}_\lambda^{(\mathsf{ID}_\lambda)}$ in the tree. Given a trapdoor $\mathbf{S}$ for the master lattice $\Lambda_{\mathbf{R}}^{\perp}(\hat{\mathsf{a}}^\star)$, we can find short vectors in the coset $\{\hat{\mathsf{x}} : h(\hat{\mathsf{a}}_{\mathsf{ID}}, \hat{\mathsf{x}}) \equiv \mathsf{S}\}$ of any super lattice $\Lambda_{\mathbf{R}}^{\perp}(\hat{\mathsf{a}}_{\mathsf{ID}})$. The short elements of the coset correspond $\hat{\mathsf{s}}_{\mathsf{ID}}$.

	Prover $\mathcal{P}(\hat{\mathsf{a}}^\star, \langle\hat{\mathsf{b}}\rangle, \mathsf{S}, \mathsf{ID}, \hat{\mathsf{s}}_{\mathsf{ID}})$		Verifier $\mathcal{V}(\hat{\mathsf{a}}^\star, \langle\hat{\mathsf{b}}\rangle, \mathsf{S}, \mathsf{ID})$
1	$\hat{\mathsf{y}} \leftarrow_\$ D_y^m$ $\mathsf{Y} \leftarrow h(\hat{\mathsf{a}}_{\mathsf{ID}}, \hat{\mathsf{y}})$	$\xrightarrow{\mathsf{Y}}$	
2		$\xleftarrow{\mathsf{c}}$	$\mathsf{c} \leftarrow_\$ D_c$
3	$\hat{\mathsf{z}} \leftarrow \hat{\mathsf{s}}_{\mathsf{ID}}\mathsf{c} + \hat{\mathsf{y}}$ If $\hat{\mathsf{z}} \notin G^m$ $\hat{\mathsf{z}} \leftarrow \perp$ (abort)		
4		$\xrightarrow{\hat{\mathsf{z}}}$	If $\hat{\mathsf{z}} \notin G^m \vee h(\hat{\mathsf{a}}_{\mathsf{ID}}, \hat{\mathsf{z}}) \neq \mathsf{Sc} + \mathsf{Y}$ return 0 Else return 1

Fig. 3. Identity-based identification protocol

The Bonsai trees allow the simulation of the extraction oracle for a polynomial number of identities in the security proof, while the attacked identity is likely to overlap only with branches of uncontrolled growth. There, the simulator will embed the challenge.

The simulation of the provers will be possible by using a single secret key $\hat{\mathsf{s}} \in R^{m_1+m_2}$, such that $h(\hat{\mathsf{a}}^\star, \hat{\mathsf{s}}) = \mathsf{S}$, for all identities. The individual provers only need to pad $\hat{\mathsf{s}}$ with λm_2 zero polynomials to make the objects compatible. The witness indistinguishability hides this deviation. Thus, we demonstrate that sampling from a coset of $\Lambda_{\mathbf{R}}^\perp$ instead of from the lattice itself seems to be much more versatile. A related technique was used in [Rüc10] to achieve *strongly* unforgeable signatures from lattices in the standard model.

Master-key Generation. Let the parameters $q, \mathsf{f}, \tilde{L}, m_1, m_2$ be as per Proposition 2 and let $d = s\omega(\sqrt{\log(nm_1 + (\lambda+1)nm_2)})$ for a Gaussian parameter $s \geq \tilde{L}\omega(\sqrt{\log(n)})$. These parameters may be excluded from the public key as they are the same for all users. Use $\mathsf{ExtLattice}$ to generate a description $\hat{\mathsf{a}}^\star \in \mathbf{R}^{m_1+m_2}$ of the master lattice $\Lambda_{\mathbf{R}}^\perp(\hat{\mathsf{a}}^\star)$ together with a trapdoor $\mathbf{S}^\star$ such that $\left\|\tilde{\mathbf{S}}^\star\right\| \leq \tilde{L}$. Furthermore, generate the sets $\langle\hat{\mathsf{b}}\rangle := \left\{(\hat{\mathsf{b}}_i^{(0)}, \hat{\mathsf{b}}_i^{(1)})\right\}_1^\lambda$ of random elements in $\mathbf{R}^{m_2}$. Then, the algorithm chooses $\mathsf{S} \leftarrow_\$ \mathbf{R}$. Finally, output the secret key $\mathbf{S}^\star$ and the public key $(\hat{\mathsf{a}}^\star, \langle\hat{\mathsf{b}}\rangle, \mathsf{S})$.

Key Extraction. On input $\mathbf{S}^\star$, $\mathsf{ID} \in \{0,1\}^*$, we define the module element $\hat{\mathsf{a}}_{\mathsf{ID}} := \hat{\mathsf{a}}^\star || \hat{\mathsf{b}}_1^{(\mathsf{ID}_1)} || \cdots || \hat{\mathsf{b}}_\lambda^{(\mathsf{ID}_\lambda)} \in \mathbf{R}^{m_1+m_2+\lambda m_2}$. The algorithm samples $\hat{\mathsf{s}}_1, \ldots, \hat{\mathsf{s}}_\lambda$ via $\mathsf{SampleDom}(s)$ and calls $\hat{\mathsf{s}}_0 \leftarrow \mathsf{SamplePre}(\mathbf{S}^\star, s, \mathsf{S} - \sum_{i=1}^\lambda \hat{\mathsf{b}}_i^{(\mathsf{ID}_i)} \circledast \hat{\mathsf{s}}_i)$.
The output is $\hat{\mathsf{s}}_{\mathsf{ID}} \in D_s^m$ with overwhelming probability. In the event that $\hat{\mathsf{s}}_{\mathsf{ID}} \notin D_s^m$, the algorithm re-samples $\hat{\mathsf{s}}_0$.

Identification Protocol. See Figure 3. Let $g(n) = \omega(\log(n))$. Upon an abort, the protocol is repeated, at most $g(n)$ times.

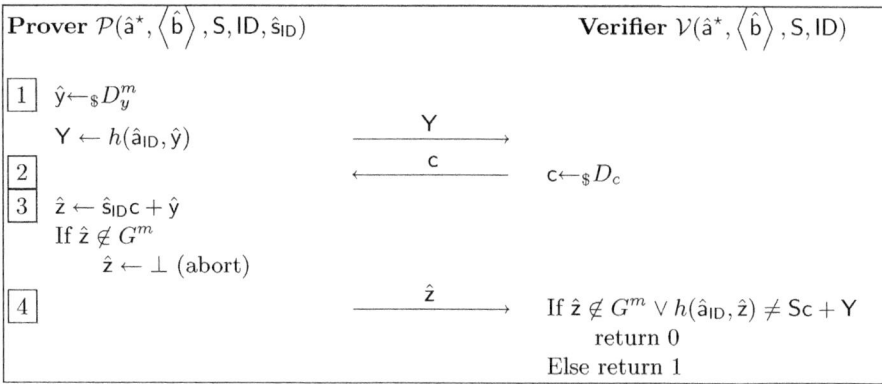

Notice that our scheme can be also be adapted to support a hierarchy of identities, each acting as the key extraction authority for its subordinates. Thus, each user receives a secret key, a trapdoor for a super lattice, that can be used to generate the secret key for the identification scheme. This adaptation involves adding more layers to the Bonsai tree and applying RandBasis during basis delegation to prevent leaking information about the master trapdoor.

Completeness of IBI is a non-trivial issue due to the eventual restarts and the many parameters involved. The next lemma ensures that the number of restarts is small, effectively constant.

Lemma 1. *Let* $k = \Omega(n)$, $\mathbf{a}, \mathbf{b} \in \mathbb{Z}^k$ *with* arbitrary $\mathbf{a} \in \{\mathbf{v} \in \mathbb{Z}^k : \|\mathbf{v}\|_\infty \leq A\}$ *and* random $\mathbf{b} \leftarrow_\$ \{\mathbf{v} \in \mathbb{Z}^k : \|\mathbf{v}\|_\infty \leq B\}$. *Given* $B \geq \phi k A$ *for* $\phi \in \mathbb{N}_{>0}$, *we have* $\operatorname{Prob}_{\mathbf{b}}[\|\mathbf{a} - \mathbf{b}\|_\infty \leq B - A] > \frac{1}{e^{1/\phi}} - o(1)$.

The multiplication of two polynomials modulo $X^n + 1$ plays a major role in the analysis. Therefore, we need the following lemma, which is a special case of [Lyu08b, Lemma 2.8].

Lemma 2. *For any two polynomials* $\mathsf{a}, \mathsf{b} \in \mathbf{R}$, *we have* $\|\mathsf{ab} \bmod (X^n + 1)\|_\infty \leq n \|\mathsf{a}\|_\infty \|\mathsf{b}\|_\infty$.

Theorem 3 (Completeness). *The scheme* IBI *is complete.*

Proof. For all honestly generated master-key pairs $(\mathbf{S}^\star, (\hat{\mathsf{a}}^\star, \langle \hat{\mathsf{b}} \rangle, \mathsf{S}))$, and all identities $\mathsf{ID} \in \{0,1\}^\lambda$, the key extraction algorithm outputs a secret key $\hat{\mathsf{s}}_{\mathsf{ID}} = \hat{\mathsf{s}}_0 \| \ldots \| \hat{\mathsf{s}}_\lambda \in D_s^m$ with $h(\hat{\mathsf{a}}_{\mathsf{ID}}, \hat{\mathsf{s}}_{\mathsf{ID}}) \equiv h(\hat{\mathsf{a}}^\star, \hat{\mathsf{s}}_0) + \sum_{i=0}^{\lambda} h(\hat{\mathsf{b}}_i^{(\mathsf{ID}_i)}, \hat{\mathsf{s}}_i) \equiv \mathsf{S} - \sum_{i=0}^{\lambda} h(\hat{\mathsf{b}}_i^{(\mathsf{ID}_i)}, \hat{\mathsf{s}}_i) + \sum_{i=0}^{\lambda} h(\hat{\mathsf{b}}_i^{(\mathsf{ID}_i)}, \hat{\mathsf{s}}_i) \equiv \mathsf{S}$ and $\|\hat{\mathsf{s}}_{\mathsf{ID}}\|_\infty \leq d_s$ for $d_s = s\omega(\sqrt{\log(m)})$ and $s = \tilde{L}\omega(\sqrt{\log(n)})$ according to Proposition 1.

For all challenges $c \in D_c$ and all random coins $\hat{\mathsf{y}} \in D_y^m$, we have $\|\hat{\mathsf{z}}\|_\infty = \|\hat{\mathsf{s}_{\mathsf{ID}}}\mathsf{c} + \hat{\mathsf{y}}\|_\infty \leq d_y - n \|\hat{\mathsf{s}_{\mathsf{ID}}}\|_\infty \|\mathsf{c}\|_\infty = d_y - n = d_G$ with probability $\geq e^{-1/\phi} - o(1)$ because of Lemma 2 and Lemma 1 ($k = mn, A = n d_s d_c, B = d_y$). Hence, the verifier accepts because $h(\hat{\mathsf{a}}_{\mathsf{ID}}, \hat{\mathsf{z}}) = h(\hat{\mathsf{a}}_{\mathsf{ID}}, \hat{\mathsf{s}}_{\mathsf{ID}})\mathsf{c} + h(\hat{\mathsf{a}}_{\mathsf{ID}}, \hat{\mathsf{y}}) = \mathsf{Sc} + \mathsf{Y}$.

Repeating the protocol $\omega(\log(n))$ times in parallel establishes completeness. In practice, a small and constant number $e^{1/\phi}$ of retries is sufficient. □

Observe that in any case, all operations (including eventual restarts) in IBI.Protocol have $\tilde{O}(n)$ complexity and that private keys, public keys, protocol messages, as well as the master public key have size $\tilde{O}(n)$. The only exceptions from this optimality are the master secret key size, which is $\tilde{O}(n^2)$ bits, and the key extraction algorithm Extract, which requires $\tilde{O}(n^2)$ bit operations. Fortunately, the online phase merely requires quasi-linear operations and a quasi-linear bandwidth.

4.3 Security

Since the function family $\mathcal{H}(\mathbf{R}, m)$ compresses the domain D_s^m, it is easy to show that all secret keys collide with at least one other secret key.

Lemma 3. *Let* m_1 *and* m_2 *as per Proposition 2,* $m \geq m_1 + m_2$, $h_{\hat{\mathsf{a}}} \in \mathcal{H}(\mathbf{R}, m)$, *and* $\mathsf{S} \in \mathbf{R}$. *For every* $\hat{\mathsf{s}} \in D_s^m$, *there is a second* $\hat{\mathsf{s}}' \in D_s^m \setminus \{\hat{\mathsf{s}}\}$ *with* $h(\hat{\mathsf{a}}, \hat{\mathsf{s}}) = h(\hat{\mathsf{a}}, \hat{\mathsf{s}}') = \mathsf{S}$ *(with overwhelming probability).*

The next lemma establishes witness indistinguishability of the protocol. Witness indistinguishability ensures that the malicious verifier cannot distinguish whether the prover uses one of two possible secret keys $\hat{\mathsf{s}}, \hat{\mathsf{s}}' \in h_{\hat{\mathsf{a}}}^{-1}(\mathsf{S}) \cap D_s^m$.

Lemma 4. *Let m_1 and m_2 as per Proposition 2, $m \geq m_1 + m_2$, $h_{\hat{\mathsf{a}}} \in \mathcal{H}(\mathbf{R}, m)$, and $\mathsf{S} \in \mathbf{R}$. For every distinct $\hat{\mathsf{s}}, \hat{\mathsf{s}}' \in D_s^m$ with $h(\hat{\mathsf{a}}, \hat{\mathsf{s}}) = \mathsf{S} = h(\hat{\mathsf{a}}, \hat{\mathsf{s}}')$, the resulting protocol views $(\mathsf{Y}, \mathsf{c}, \hat{\mathsf{z}})$ and $(\mathsf{Y}', \mathsf{c}, \hat{\mathsf{z}})$ are statistically indistinguishable.*

Using lemmas 3 and 4, we can exploit witness indistinguishability to simulate all provers with a single secret key $\hat{\mathsf{s}}$ and at the same time expect the adversary to use a different secret key $\hat{\mathsf{s}}'$ with non-negligible probability. Then, we use the Reset Lemma to extract this knowledge to break the collision problem.

Since the protocol is witness-indistinguishable, we can securely use parallel composition of multiple independent instances.

Theorem 4 (Soundness). *IBI is secure in the stat-id-imp-ca model if the collision problem $Col(\mathcal{H}(\mathbf{R}, m), D)$ is hard.*

Proof. The core idea of the proof is that we can simulate all provers with a single secret key $\hat{\mathsf{s}} = \hat{\mathsf{s}}^\star||\hat{0}||\ldots||\hat{0} \in \mathbf{R}^{m_1+m_2+\lambda m_2}$, where $\hat{\mathsf{a}}^\star \circledast \hat{\mathsf{s}}^\star \equiv \mathsf{S}$, which can be prepared during the simulation.

Extraction queries can be prepared in the static identity attack model. We can prepare the set $\left\langle \hat{\mathsf{b}} \right\rangle$ so that we know a trapdoor for certain branches of the tree, while others are embedded with the external challenge from the collision problem. These "rigged" branches correspond to the target identity in the impersonation attempt of the adversary with non-negligible probability.

During this phase of the attack, we run the knowledge extractor of the underlying proof of knowledge to obtain $\hat{\mathsf{s}}' \neq \hat{\mathsf{s}}$. Hence, we solve the collision problem.

Setup. The reduction receives the input $\hat{\mathsf{a}} = \hat{\mathsf{a}}^\star||\hat{\mathsf{u}}_1^{(0)}||\hat{\mathsf{u}}_1^{(1)}||\cdots||\hat{\mathsf{u}}_\lambda^{(0)}||\hat{\mathsf{u}}_\lambda^{(1)} \in \mathbf{R}^{m_1+(2\lambda+1)m_2}$ together with the parameters $n, q, m = m_1 + m_2$, and the norm bound ν. It invokes $\mathcal{I}^*(\mathsf{find})$ to obtain *distinct* $\mathsf{ID}_1, \ldots, \mathsf{ID}_{q_E} \in \{0,1\}^n$. Let $\langle \pi \rangle := \{\pi_i\}_1^p$ be the set of all strings $\pi \in \{0,1\}^\lambda$ such that $\pi \not\sqsubseteq \mathsf{ID}_j$ for $j \in \{1, \ldots, q_E\}$ and $\pi_i \not\sqsubseteq \pi_j$ for all distinct pairs (π_i, π_j) in $\langle \pi \rangle$. The set $\langle \pi \rangle$ contains at most λq_E elements. Now, randomly select an element $\pi \leftarrow_\$ \langle \pi \rangle$, which represents the challenge subtree. Let $|\pi| = l_\pi$. Setup of the public key:

- $\hat{\mathsf{b}}_i^{(\pi_i)} \leftarrow \hat{\mathsf{u}}_i^{(0)}$ for $i = 1, \ldots, l_\pi$;
- $\hat{\mathsf{b}}_i^{(b)} \leftarrow \hat{\mathsf{u}}_i^{(b)}$ for $b \in \{0,1\}$ and $i = l_\pi + 1, \ldots, \lambda$;
- $\hat{\mathsf{b}}_i^{1-\pi_i}$ and $\mathbf{S}_i$ via $\mathsf{ExtLattice}(\hat{\mathsf{a}}^\star||\hat{\mathsf{b}}_1^{(\pi_1)}||\cdots||\hat{\mathsf{b}}_{i-1}^{(\pi_{i-1})}, m_2)$ for $i = 1, \ldots, l_\pi$.

For the trapdoors, we have $\left\|\tilde{\mathbf{S}}_i\right\| \leq \tilde{L}$. Use $\mathsf{SampleDom}$ with $s = \omega(\sqrt{\log(n)})\tilde{L}$ to sample an element $\hat{\mathsf{s}} \in \mathbf{R}^{m_1+m_2}$ and compute $\mathsf{S} \leftarrow h(\hat{\mathsf{a}}^\star, \hat{\mathsf{s}})$. For each identity $I^{(i)} = \mathsf{ID}_i$, let j be the smallest index with $I_j^{(i)} \neq \pi_j$. Since $\left\|\tilde{\mathbf{S}}_i\right\| \leq \tilde{L}$, we let $s = \omega(\sqrt{\log(n)})\tilde{L}$ and compute the secret key $\hat{\mathsf{s}}_i \leftarrow \mathsf{SamplePre}(\mathsf{ExtBasis}(\mathbf{S}_j, \hat{\mathsf{a}}_{I^{(i)}}), s, \mathsf{S})$. The public key comprises $\hat{\mathsf{A}}^\star$, S, and $\left\langle \hat{\mathsf{b}} \right\rangle := \left\{(\hat{\mathsf{b}}_i^{(0)}, \hat{\mathsf{b}}_i^{(1)})\right\}_1^\lambda$ and the reduction returns the public key and the list of secret keys to $\mathcal{I}^*$.

Prover Queries. $\mathcal{I}^*(\mathsf{verify})$ may challenge the reduction with any identity ID. The simulator acts as per the protocol in Figure 3 but uses the same secret $\hat{\mathsf{s}}$ for all identities.

Impersonation Attempt. At some point, $\mathcal{I}^*$ outputs a challenge identity ID^*, which has not been queried to the extraction oracle before. After that, the extraction oracle answer $\perp$ when queried with ID^*. After the algorithm $\mathcal{I}^*(\mathsf{impersonate})$ submits a commitment Y, it is challenged with a random $\mathsf{c}_1 \leftarrow_\$ D_c$, and outputs $\hat{\mathsf{z}}_1$. Then, the reduction rewinds $\mathcal{I}^*$ to the end of Step 1 and challenges the adversary with a fresh $\mathsf{c}_2 \leftarrow_\$ D_c \setminus \{\mathsf{c}_1\}$ to obtain the answer $\hat{\mathsf{z}}_2$. The reduction suitably rearranges and pads (with $\hat{0}$) the pair $(\hat{\mathsf{z}}_1 - \hat{\mathsf{s}}\mathsf{c}_1, \hat{\mathsf{z}}_1 - \hat{\mathsf{s}}\mathsf{c}_2)$ and outputs the result as its solution to the problem Col.

Analysis. First of all, observe that mpk in the simulation is statistically indistinguishable from mpk in the real scheme. Furthermore, note that the simulator can answer all extraction queries correctly because it knows a trapdoor for a prefix of all requested identities. As for the prover queries, we require that the protocol is witness indistinguishable w.r.t. the secret key (Lemma 4). Let us assume that the reset during $\mathcal{I}^*$'s impersonation attempt yields another valid response without aborting. Then, we certainly have $h(\hat{\mathsf{a}}, \hat{\mathsf{z}}_1 - \hat{\mathsf{s}}\mathsf{c}_1) = \mathsf{Y} = h(\hat{\mathsf{a}}, \hat{\mathsf{z}}_2 - \hat{\mathsf{s}}\mathsf{c}_2)$ with $\max\{\|\hat{\mathsf{z}}_1 - \hat{\mathsf{s}}\mathsf{c}_1\|_\infty, \|\hat{\mathsf{z}}_2 - \hat{\mathsf{s}}\mathsf{c}_2\|_\infty\} \leq d_G + nd_sd_c = d_D$. What is left to show is that $\hat{\mathsf{z}}_1 - \hat{\mathsf{s}}\mathsf{c}_1 \neq \hat{\mathsf{z}}_2 - \hat{\mathsf{s}}\mathsf{c}_2$. Lemma 3 guarantees the existence of at least two distinct valid secret keys $\hat{\mathsf{s}}$ and $\hat{\mathsf{s}}'$. Now, for one of them, we obtain a valid collision. Assuming the contrary, $\hat{\mathsf{z}}_1 - \hat{\mathsf{s}}\mathsf{c}_1 = \hat{\mathsf{z}}_2 - \hat{\mathsf{s}}\mathsf{c}_2$ and $\hat{\mathsf{z}}_1 - \hat{\mathsf{s}}'\mathsf{c}_1 = \hat{\mathsf{z}}_2 - \hat{\mathsf{s}}'\mathsf{c}_2$ yields $\mathsf{c}_1(\hat{\mathsf{s}}' - \hat{\mathsf{s}}) = \mathsf{c}_2(\hat{\mathsf{s}}' - \hat{\mathsf{s}})$ and therfore $(\mathsf{c}_1 - \mathsf{c}_2)(\hat{\mathsf{s}}' - \hat{\mathsf{s}}) = \hat{0}$. This only holds if $\hat{\mathsf{s}}' = \hat{\mathsf{s}}$ because $\max\{\|\hat{\mathsf{s}}\|_\infty, \|\hat{\mathsf{s}}'\|_\infty\} \leq q/2$ and $\mathbb{Z}[X]/\langle X^n + 1\rangle$ is an integral domain.

Thus, with probability $\geq 1/2$, the simulator can use $\mathcal{I}^*$'s output to solve $Col(\mathcal{H}(\mathbf{R}, m), D)$. Concerning the success probability of the reset, assume that $\mathcal{I}^*$ is successful with non-negligible probability $\epsilon(n)$. Then, $\mathcal{I}^*$ is successful with non-negligible probability $\geq (\epsilon(n) - 1/|D_c|)^2$ by the Reset Lemma [BP02] in the second run. Then, we need to account for the inherent completeness defect, which makes the second run abort with probability $\leq (1 - e^{-1/\phi})$. All in all, the success probability of the simulator against the collision problems stays non-negligible if $\epsilon(n)$ is non-negligible. □

5 Conclusions

Using a new, weaker security model for identity-based identification and a generic transformation to full security, we have shown how to construct an identity-based identification scheme from lattices that is secure against concurrent impersonation and adaptive-identity attacks in the standard model. Via a worst-case to average-case reduction, it is provably as hard to break as certain worst-case lattice problems in ideal lattices. Our scheme offers quasi-optimal performance and it is leakage-resilient in an almost optimal sense. Therefore, we expect our construction to withstand even subexponential-time and quantum computers attacks, as well as limited side-channel attacks against the secret key.

Acknowledgments

The author thanks the anonymous reviewers of SCN 2010 for their valuable, detailed, and encouraging comments.

References

[Ajt96] Ajtai, M.: Generating hard instances of lattice problems (extended abstract). In: STOC, pp. 99–108. ACM, New York (1996)

[AKS01] Ajtai, M., Kumar, R., Sivakumar, D.: A sieve algorithm for the shortest lattice vector problem. In: STOC, pp. 601–610. ACM, New York (2001)

[BBD08] Bernstein, D.J., Buchmann, J.A., Dahmen, E. (eds.): PQCrypto 2008. LNCS, vol. 5299. Springer, Heidelberg (2008)

[BNN09] Bellare, M., Namprempre, C., Neven, G.: Security proofs for identity-based identification and signature schemes. J. Cryptology 22(1), 1–61 (2009)

[Boy10] Boyen, X.: Lattice mixing and vanishing trapdoors: A framework for fully secure short signatures and more. In: Nguyen, P.Q., Pointcheval, D. (eds.) PKC 2010. LNCS, vol. 6056, pp. 499–517. Springer, Heidelberg (2010)

[BP02] Bellare, M., Palacio, A.: Gq and schnorr identification schemes: Proofs of security against impersonation under active and concurrent attacks. In: Yung, M. (ed.) CRYPTO 2002. LNCS, vol. 2442, pp. 162–177. Springer, Heidelberg (2002)

[CGGG09] Cayrel, P.-L., Gaborit, P., Galindo, D., Girault, M.: Improved identity-based identification using correcting codes. CoRR, abs/0903.0069 (2009)

[CHKP10] Cash, D., Hofheinz, D., Kiltz, E., Peikert, C.: Bonsai trees, or how to delegate a lattice basis. In: Gilbert, H. (ed.) Advances in Cryptology - EUROCRYPT 2010. LNCS, vol. 6110, pp. 523–552. Springer, Heidelberg (2010)

[GPV08] Gentry, C., Peikert, C., Vaikuntanathan, V.: Trapdoors for hard lattices and new cryptographic constructions. In: Ladner, R.E., Dwork, C. (eds.) STOC, pp. 197–206. ACM, New York (2008)

[GS02] Gentry, C., Silverberg, A.: Hierarchical id-based cryptography. In: Zheng, Y. (ed.) ASIACRYPT 2002. LNCS, vol. 2501, pp. 548–566. Springer, Heidelberg (2002)

[KH05] Kurosawa, K., Heng, S.-H.: Identity-based identification without random oracles. In: Gervasi, O., Gavrilova, M.L., Kumar, V., Laganá, A., Lee, H.P., Mun, Y., Taniar, D., Tan, C.J.K. (eds.) ICCSA 2005. LNCS, vol. 3481, pp. 603–613. Springer, Heidelberg (2005)

[KR98] Krawczyk, H., Rabin, T.: Chameleon hashing and signatures. Cryptology ePrint Archive, Report 1998/010 (1998), http://eprint.iacr.org/

[KR00] Krawczyk, H., Rabin, T.: Chameleon signatures. In: NDSS. The Internet Society (2000)

[KV09] Katz, J., Vaikuntanathan, V.: Signature schemes with bounded leakage resilience. In: Matsui [Mat09], pp. 703–720

[LM06] Lyubashevsky, V., Micciancio, D.: Generalized compact knapsacks are collision resistant. In: Bugliesi, M., Preneel, B., Sassone, V., Wegener, I. (eds.) ICALP 2006, Part II. LNCS, vol. 4052, pp. 144–155. Springer, Heidelberg (2006)

[Lyu08a] Lyubashevsky, V.: Lattice-based identification schemes secure under active attacks. In: Cramer, R. (ed.) PKC 2008. LNCS, vol. 4939, pp. 162–179. Springer, Heidelberg (2008)

[Lyu08b] Lyubashevsky, V.: Towards Practical Lattice-Based Cryptography. PhD thesis (2008)

[Mat09] Matsui, M. (ed.): ASIACRYPT 2009. LNCS, vol. 5912. Springer, Heidelberg (2009)

[MG02] Micciancio, D., Goldwasser, S.: Complexity of Lattice Problems: a cryptographic perspective. The Kluwer International Series in Engineering and Computer Science, vol. 671. Kluwer Academic Publishers, Boston (2002)

[MV10] Micciancio, D., Voulgaris, P.: A deterministic single exponential time algorithm for most lattice problems based on voronoi cell computations. In: Mitzenmacher, M., Schulman, L.J. (eds.) STOC, pp. 351–358. ACM, New York (2010)

[Pei10] Peikert, C.: An efficient and parallel gaussian sampler for lattices (2010) (Manuscript), `http://www.cc.gatech.edu/~cpeikert/`

[Rüc10] Rückert, M.: Strongly unforgeable signatures and hierarchical identity-based signatures from lattices without random oracles. In: Sendrier, N. (ed.) PQCrypto 2010. LNCS, vol. 6061, pp. 182–200. Springer, Heidelberg (2010)

[Sha84] Shamir, A.: Identity-based cryptosystems and signature schemes. In: Blakely, G.R., Chaum, D. (eds.) CRYPTO 1984. LNCS, vol. 196, pp. 47–53. Springer, Heidelberg (1985)

[SSTX09] Stehlé, D., Steinfeld, R., Tanaka, K., Xagawa, K.: Efficient public key encryption based on ideal lattices. In: Matsui [Mat09], pp. 617–635

The Fiat–Shamir Transform for Group and Ring Signature Schemes

Ming Feng Lee, Nigel P. Smart, and Bogdan Warinschi

Dept. Computer Science,
University of Bristol,
Merchant Venturers Building,
Woodland Road,
Bristol, BS8 1UB,
United Kingdom
{lee,nigel,bogdan}@cs.bris.ac.uk

Abstract. The Fiat-Shamir (FS) transform is a popular tool to produce particularly efficient digital signature schemes out of identification protocols. It is known that the resulting signature scheme is secure (in the random oracle model) if and only if the identification protocol is secure against passive impersonators. A similar results holds for constructing ID-based signature schemes out of ID-based identification protocols.

The transformation had also been applied to identification protocols with additional privacy properties. So, via the FS transform, ad-hoc group identification schemes yield ring signatures and identity escrow schemes yield group signature schemes. Unfortunately, results akin to those above are not known to hold for these latter settings and the security of the resulting schemes needs to be proved from scratch, or worse, it is often simply assumed.

In this paper we provide the missing foundations for the use of the FS transform in these more complex settings. We start with defining a formal security model for identity escrow schemes (a concept proposed earlier but never rigorously formalized). Our main result constists of necessary and sufficient conditions for an identity escrow scheme to yield (via the FS transform) a secure group signature schemes. In addition, using the similarity between group and ring signature schemes we give analogous results for the latter primitive.

1 Introduction

Background. A canonical identification scheme is a three-move two-party protocol: the prover first sends a commitment Cmt to the verifier, the verifier picks and returns a random string Ch as a challenge. After receiving the challenge, the prover outputs a response Rsp which is derived from the commitment, the challenge, and the secret of the prover. The verifier checks that the resulting transcript (Cmt, Ch, Rsp) satisfies a certain property, in which case we say that the transcript is accepting and the verifier outputs one, otherwise the verifier outputs zero. The Fiat-Shamir transform [16] takes as input a canonical

J.A. Garay and R. De Prisco (Eds.): SCN 2010, LNCS 6280, pp. 363–380, 2010.

identification protocol and produces a digital signature scheme. The transform essentially removes the interaction in such protocols, and in doing so it involves an arbitrary message M. This results in the following signing algorithm. To sign a message M the signer computes the commitment $\textsc{Cmt}$ as the prover does in the identification scheme, then hashes $\textsc{Cmt}$ and the message M using a hash function H to obtain a challenge $\textsc{Ch} = H(\textsc{Cmt}||M)$. The signer finally computes a response $\textsc{Rsp}$ according to the underlying identification protocol. The resulting signature is $(\textsc{Cmt}, \textsc{Rsp})$. To verify the signature, one recomputes $\textsc{Ch}$ as $H(\textsc{Cmt}||M)$ and verifies that the transcript $(\textsc{Cmt}, \textsc{Ch}, \textsc{Rsp})$ is an accepting identification transcript.

The transform is particularly popular since it yields some of the most efficient digital signature schemes known to date. Unsurprisingly, the transformation had been extensively studied. There are negative results that explain the difficulty of instantiating the hash function used in the transformation in a way that ensures the security of signature scheme in the standard model [15,17]. Also, there are positive results relating the security of the underlying identification protocol to that of the resulting signature scheme in the random oracle model [1,19,20]. The best known such result is due to Abdalla et al. [1] who prove that the resulting signature scheme is secure in the random oracle model, *if and only if* the starting identification protocol is secure against passive impersonators. An important consequence of such general results is that they entail modular security proofs for signature schemes. First, prove the security of the identification protocol (this step is sometimes quite simple – for example it may immediately follow from existing known result, e.g. the identification protocol being honest-verifier zero-knowledge). Then conclude, via the general result, the security of the signature scheme. This path was advocated and used by Bellare, Namprempre, and Neven in a later paper where they prove (among other results) the soundness of the FS transform when applied to ID-based identification schemes to obtain ID-based signature schemes [7].

The Fiat-Shamir transform had been used as a design tool in other contexts where canonical three-move identification protocol occur. Notable examples include the construction of group signature schemes out of group identification schemes and the construction of ring signature schemes out of ad-hoc group identification. Unfortunately, unlike for digital signatures [1] no results formally relate the security of the underlying group/ad-hoc group identification scheme with that of the resulting group/ring signature scheme. In this cases, *e.g.* [2,3,4,5,10,11,12,13], the security of the signature scheme needs to be proved from scratch. Unfortunately, it is simply assumed that the transformation "works". In this paper we investigate the use of the transform in the construction of group and ring signature schemes. We detail our results next.

Our results. We start by formalizing the notion of group identification (or identity-escrow). The primitive had been proposed by Kilian and Petrank [18] but its security had never been rigorously defined. Recall that an identity escrow scheme allows users to (interactively) prove membership in a group in a way that hides their individual identities. In case of misuse however, anonymity can be revoked by a group opener who is in possession of a secret opening key. Such schemes are therefore the interactive counterpart of group signature schemes. We take advantage of progress on security models for group signatures [6,9] and adapt existing security notions for this primitive to group identification. Our models consider the case of monotonic dynamic groups (where users can be added to the group by a group manager). We define three distinct security notions. Two notions refer to adversaries that attempt to impersonate group members and here we distinguish between impersonators that frame other honest group members, and impersonators who produce transcripts that cannot be traced. By analogy with the corresponding notions in group signatures the resulting notions are *non-frameability* and *traceability*. A third requirement, *anonymity* demands that executing the identification protocols hides the user identity: an adversary is not able to tell apart runs of the identification protocol of different users. Finally, we also formalize as a game the correctness of group identification schemes. We give the details of the models for the case of passive adversaries (adversaries that only observe executions of the identification protocols of honest parties, but are not allowed to interact with them). Furthermore, the models are for canonical identification schemes (schemes where the identification protocol has the three-move structure outlined at the beginning of the introduction). We make these restrictions for simplicity: our theorems are only for canonical identification protocols and relate the security of the resulting group signature scheme with that of the underlying identification protocol under passive attacks. Nevertheless, the extension of our definitions to arbitrary group identification schemes and active adversaries is immediate.

Our main result is that the group signature obtained via the FS transform from a canonical identity-escrow scheme is correct, anonymous, traceable, and non-frameable if and only if the underlying group identification is, respectively, correct, anonymous, traceable, and non-frameable under passive (i.e., eavesdropping only) attacks.

Our theorem yields group signature schemes that meet the strongest possible notion of security. However, the literature for group signatures contains a large number of variations on this security model. The reason is that weaker, but still quite reasonable security requirements often allow for significantly more efficient schemes. Examples of restrictions include considering static groups, merging the group opener and the group manager, or disallowing the adversary to ask openings of arbitrary transcripts. These weaker notions are usually obtained by simply imposing restrictions on how the adversary interacts with the oracles defining the security game. In the reduction that proves our main theorem we show how to build an adversary against the underlying group identification scheme out of an adversary for the resulting group signature scheme. In this reduction, the restrictions that the former adversary has on using his oracles translate into similar restrictions on how the latter adversary is allowed to use his own oracles. We therefore obtain analogue versions of our result that relates correspondingly weaker notions of group identification and group signatures by observing how the restrictions between the two settings translate through our reduction.

We take advantage of the similarities between group and ring identification/signature schemes and extend our results to this latter primitive. In this extended abstract we give the theorem that we prove but leave the details for the full version.

In the full version of the paper we also investigate the use of the FS transform to obtain ring signature schemes out of ad-hoc group identification schemes.

NOTATION. We end this introduction by covering some basic notation which will be used throughout this paper. If S is a set then $s \leftarrow S$ means that s is selected uniformly at random from S. Let $\mathcal{A}(\cdot, \cdots, \cdot; R)$ be a randomized algorithm with coins R, then $y \leftarrow \mathcal{A}(x_1, \ldots, x_n R)$ means on input of $x_1, \ldots, x_n$ and coins R, the value y is the unique output of the algorithm. The notation $y \leftarrow \mathcal{A}(x_1, \ldots, x_n)$ is shorthand for first selecting a random R and then setting $y \leftarrow \mathcal{A}(x_1, \ldots, x_n; R)$. We let $\mathsf{Coins}(\mathcal{A})$ denote the space which R is drown from for the algorithm $\mathcal{A}$. An algorithm $\mathcal{A}$ run on input $x_1, \ldots, x_n$ with access to oracles $\mathcal{O}_1, \ldots, \mathcal{O}_m$ will be denoted by $\mathcal{A}(x_1, \ldots, x_n : \mathcal{O}_1, \ldots, \mathcal{O}_m)$, so as to avoid too many superscripts and subscripts.

2 Group Identification Schemes

In this section we formalize group identification schemes. These schemes were introduced by Kilian and Petrank [18] under the name identity escrow schemes. We use these two names interchangeably.

SYNTAX. Group identification schemes allow a user to prove membership in a group in such a way that his personal identity is protected. Using special secret keys, a group manager can add users whereas a group opener can revoke anonymity of any identification transcript. Since group identification schemes are the interactive counterparts of group signature schemes we make use of progress in the formalization of the latter concept. In particular, we follow the model proposed by Bellare, Shi, and Zhang [9].

A group identification scheme is given by the tuple of algorithms $\mathcal{GID} = (\mathsf{GKg}^{\mathcal{GID}}, \mathsf{UKg}^{\mathcal{GID}}, \mathsf{Join}^{\mathcal{GID}}, \mathsf{Iss}^{\mathcal{GID}}, (\mathsf{P}^{\mathcal{GID}}, \mathsf{V}^{\mathcal{GID}}), \mathsf{Open}^{\mathcal{GID}}, \mathsf{Judge}^{\mathcal{GID}})$, where the functionality of these algorithms is as follows:

- $\mathsf{GKg}^{\mathcal{GID}}$: A setup program running a probabilistic key generation algorithm. It takes a security parameter 1^k and outputs the secret-public key pair $(\mathfrak{gmsk}, \mathfrak{gmpk})$ for the group manager $\mathcal{M}$, and a secret key $\mathfrak{osk}$ for the opener $\mathcal{O}p$. The key $\mathfrak{gmpk}$ is the public key for the group.
- $\mathsf{UKg}^{\mathcal{GID}}$: This is a probabilistic algorithm to generate user public/private key pairs. When run by user i, on input of 1^k, this outputs a user's key pair $(\mathfrak{sk}_i, \mathfrak{pk}_i)$.
- $(\mathsf{Join}^{\mathcal{GID}}, \mathsf{Iss}^{\mathcal{GID}})$: This is an interactive protocol between a new group member i and the group manager $\mathcal{M}$. Each of the algorithms take as input a state and produce a new state plus a decision $\{\mathsf{accept}, \mathsf{reject}, \mathsf{cont}\}$. The initial state of $\mathsf{Join}^{\mathcal{GID}}$ is the private key of the user $\mathfrak{sk}_i$, whilst that of $\mathsf{Iss}^{\mathcal{GID}}$ is $\mathfrak{gmsk}$ and the public key of the user. If the issuer group manager (running $\mathsf{Iss}^{\mathcal{GID}}$) accepts then the final output is assigned to $\mathfrak{Inf}_i$ (where i is the index/identity

of the user). This is information that is to be passed to the group opener (who will later use it to open transcripts produced by user i). If the user i accepts then the final state of $\mathsf{Join}^{\mathcal{GID}}$ is assigned to $\mathfrak{gsk}_i$.
- $(\mathsf{P}^{\mathcal{GID}}, \mathsf{V}^{\mathcal{GID}})$: An interactive protocol between a prover and a verifier. The prover's input a value $\mathfrak{gsk}_i$, whereas the verifier's input is $\mathfrak{gmpk}$.
- $\mathsf{Open}^{\mathcal{GID}}$: A deterministic algorithm, on input of a transcript $\mathcal{T}$ of the $(\mathsf{P}^{\mathcal{GID}}, \mathsf{V}^{\mathcal{GID}})$ protocol, the values $\mathfrak{Inf}_*$ and the opening key $\mathfrak{osk}$. The algorithm outputs a pair (i, τ), where $i \geq 0$. If $i = 0$ then the algorithm is claiming that no group member was authenticated using the transcript $\mathcal{T}$, when $i \geq 1$ the algorithm is claiming that the group member with identity i was the prover in the transcript $\mathcal{T}$. In the latter case the value τ is a proof of this claim.
- $\mathsf{Judge}^{\mathcal{GID}}$: This algorithm takes as input $\mathfrak{gmpk}$, an integer j, the public key $\mathfrak{pk}_j$, a transcript $\mathcal{T}$ and a proof τ. It's goal is to check whether τ is a proof that j produced $\mathcal{T}$.

The above syntax is for general group identification scheme. Our results are for a special class of such schemes which we call (following [1]) *canonical*. For ease of exposition we give the security definition for group identification schemes for these class of schemes. The extension to general group identification is immediate.

CANONICAL GROUP IDENTIFICATION SCHEME. A canonical group identification scheme is a group identification scheme as above, except that now the $(\mathsf{P}^{\mathcal{GID}}, \mathsf{V}^{\mathcal{GID}})$ protocol is given by a three-move protocol of the commit-challenge-response variety. In the first move the prover sends a commitment CMT to verifier, the verifier then responds with a random string $\text{CH} \in \{0,1\}^c$ as the challenge. Then the prover outputs a response RSP which is derived from the commitment CMT, the challenge CH and their key $\mathfrak{gsk}_i$. Finally, the verifier verifies the response and outputs a final decision to decide whether i is in the authorized group. In this case a transcript of the execution is given by $\mathcal{T} = (\text{CMT}, \text{CH}, \text{RSP})$. The verifier algorithm is then of the simplified form $\mathsf{V}^{\mathcal{GID}}(\mathcal{T})$ and it returns a single value in $\{0,1\}$.

SECURITY OF CANONICAL GROUP IDENTIFICATION SCHEME. Following the treatment of [9] for group signatures we present notions of security, which we call anonymity, traceability and non-frameability for canonical group identification schemes. All our security models are for *passive* adversaries: while the adversary can obtain transcripts of the identification protocol run by honest users, he cannot directly interact with these users playing the role of the verifier. As explainer earlier, we focus on this setting since our theorems require security in this weaker sense. The extension of the definitions to active adversaries who can also interact with honest users is immediate.

Our definition use a set of oracles which we define in Figure 1. All oracles (and the underlying experiments) maintain the following global variables: a set HU of honest users, a set CU of corrupted users and a set TL of transcripts, all of which are assumed to be initially empty. Figure 1 shows what and how these oracles work in detail. Informally, the adversarial abilities that these oracles model are as follows.

- $\mathsf{AddU}(i)$: The adversary can use this oracle to add an honest user i to the group.
- $\mathsf{CrptU}(i, \mathfrak{pk})$: The adversary can create a corrupt user i and set the users public key to $\mathfrak{pk}$.
- $\mathsf{SndToI}(i, M)$: The adversary can use this oracle to engage as a corrupt user in a group-join protocol with the honest, Iss-executing issuer.
- $\mathsf{SndToU}(i, M)$: This oracle models the situation that the adversary has corrupted the issuer. The adversary can use this oracle to engage in the group-join protocol with the honest, Join-executing user.
- $\mathsf{USK}(i)$: The adversary can call this oracle and obtain both the private secret key and group signing key of an honest user i.
- $\mathsf{Exec}(i)$: This oracle allows the adversary to obtain transcripts of runs of the identification protocol between the honest prover i and an honest verifier.
- $\mathsf{CH}_b(i_0, i_1)$: This oracle is a left-right oracle for defining anonymity. The adversary sends a couple of honest identities (i_0, i_1) to the oracle and gets back a transcript $\mathcal{T}$ of the identification protocol executed by user i_b.
- $\mathsf{Open}(\mathcal{T})$: The adversary can query this oracle to obtain the output of the opening algorithm on $\mathcal{T}$, as long as $\mathcal{T}$ was not returned as a response to the CH_b oracle.

Using these oracles we can now define our security and correctness notions for canonical group identification scheme. We note that we only require security under passive attacks for our application, i.e. the attacker can obtain valid transcripts, but is not able to interact with individual provers. Hence, security is defined for this restricted notion of attack, the generalisation to active attacks is obvious. We also assume that the adversary is not able to read or write the table $\mathfrak{Inf}_*$ which the opener uses to identify provers (this corresponds to the RReg and WReg oracles of [9]). This is purely for syntactic convenience, and this assumption can be removed in the standard way. We do not describe this in detail. To know the detail, please refer to [9].

Correctness. We require that transcripts produced by honest users are accepted by the verifiers, and that the opening algorithm correctly identifies the user that produced a transcript. To formalise this we associate to the group identification scheme $\mathcal{GID}$, any adversary $\mathcal{A}$ and any $k \in \mathbb{N}$ the experiment $\mathsf{Exp}^{corr}_{\mathcal{GID},\mathcal{A}}(k)$ defined in Figure 2 where the adversary may want to make a valid transcript cannot be accepted by the verifiers, or make opener cannot correctly identify the prover, or let the proof τ cannot be correctly judge. We define

$$\mathsf{Adv}^{corr}_{\mathcal{GID},\mathcal{A}}(k) = \Pr[\mathsf{Exp}^{corr}_{\mathcal{GID},\mathcal{A}}(k) = 1],$$

and we say that the scheme is *correct* if $\mathsf{Adv}^{corr}_{\mathcal{GID},\mathcal{A}}(k) = 0$ for all adversaries $\mathcal{A}$ and all $k \in \mathbb{N}$.

Anonymity. Let $\mathcal{A}$ be an adversary performing anonymity experiment given in Figure 2 for $b \in \{0, 1\}$. The goal of the adversary is to determine which of two identities has engaged in a run of the identification protocol. In this experiment,

$\mathsf{AddU}(i)$:
- If $i \in \mathsf{HU} \cup \mathsf{CU}$ then return $\perp$.
- $\mathsf{HU} \leftarrow \mathsf{HU} \cup \{i\}$.
- $(\mathfrak{sk}_i, \mathfrak{pk}_i) \leftarrow \mathsf{UKg}(1^k)$.
- $\mathsf{dec}^i \leftarrow \mathsf{cont}$, $\mathfrak{gsk}_i \leftarrow \perp$.
- $\mathsf{St}_J^i \leftarrow (\mathfrak{gmpk}, \mathfrak{pk}_i, \mathfrak{sk}_i)$.
- $\mathsf{St}_I^i \leftarrow (\mathfrak{gmpk}, \mathfrak{gmsk}, \mathfrak{pk}_i)$, $M_J \leftarrow \perp$.
- $(\mathsf{St}_J^i, M_I, \mathsf{dec}^i) \leftarrow \mathsf{Join}^{\mathcal{GID}}(\S_J^i, M_J)$.
- While $(\mathsf{dec}^i = \mathsf{cont})$ do
  - $(\mathsf{St}_I^i, M_J, \mathsf{dec}^i) \leftarrow \mathsf{Iss}^{\mathcal{GID}}(\mathsf{St}_I^i, M_I, \mathsf{dec}^i)$.
  - If $\mathsf{dec}^i = \mathsf{accept}$ then $\mathfrak{Inf}_i \leftarrow \mathsf{St}_I^i$.
  - $(\mathsf{St}_J^i, M_I, \mathsf{dec}^i) \leftarrow \mathsf{Join}^{\mathcal{GID}}(\mathsf{St}_J^i, M_J)$.
- $\mathfrak{gsk}_i \leftarrow \mathsf{St}_J$.
- Return $\mathfrak{sk}_i$.

$\mathsf{SndToI}(i, M)$:
- If $i \notin \mathsf{CU}$ then return $\perp$.
- $(\mathsf{St}_I^i, M', \mathsf{dec}^i) \leftarrow \mathsf{Iss}^{\mathcal{GID}}(\mathsf{St}_I^i, M, \mathsf{dec}^i)$.
- If $\mathsf{dec}^i = \mathsf{accept}$ then $\mathfrak{Inf}_i \leftarrow \mathsf{St}_I^i$.
- Return M'.

$\mathsf{SndToU}(i, M)$:
- If $i \notin \mathsf{HU}$ then
  - $\mathsf{HU} \leftarrow \mathsf{HU} \cup \{i\}$.
  - $(\mathfrak{sk}_i, \mathfrak{pk}_i) \leftarrow \mathsf{UKg}(1^k)$.
  - $\mathfrak{gsk}_i \leftarrow \perp$, $M \leftarrow \perp$.
  - $\mathsf{St}_J^i \leftarrow (\mathfrak{gmpk}, \mathfrak{pk}_i, \mathfrak{sk}_i)$.
- $(\mathsf{St}_J^i, M', \mathsf{dec}^i) \leftarrow \mathsf{Join}^{\mathcal{GID}}(\mathsf{St}_J^i, M)$
- if $\mathsf{dec}^i = \mathsf{accept}$ then $\mathfrak{gsk}_i \leftarrow \mathsf{St}_J^i$.
- Return (M', dec^i).

$\mathsf{CH}_b(i_0, i_1)$:
- If $i_0 \notin \mathsf{HU}$ or $\mathfrak{gsk}_{i_0} = \perp$ then return $\perp$.
- If $i_1 \notin \mathsf{HU}$ or $\mathfrak{gsk}_{i_1} = \perp$ then return $\perp$.
- $\mathcal{T} \leftarrow \mathsf{Exec}(i_b)$.
- $\mathsf{TL} \leftarrow \mathsf{TL} \cup \{\mathcal{T}\}$.
- Return $\mathcal{T}$.

$\mathsf{CrptU}(i, \mathfrak{pk})$:
- If $i \in \mathsf{HU} \cup \mathsf{CU}$ then return $\perp$.
- $\mathsf{CU} \leftarrow \mathsf{CU} \cup \{i\}$.
- $\mathfrak{pk}_i \leftarrow \mathfrak{pk}$.
- $\mathsf{dec}^i \leftarrow \mathsf{cont}$
- $\mathsf{St}_I^i \leftarrow (\mathfrak{gmpk}, \mathfrak{gmsk}, \mathfrak{pk}_i)$.
- Return 1.

$\mathsf{USK}(i)$:
- If $i \notin \mathsf{HU}$ then return $\perp$.
- Return $(\mathfrak{gsk}_i, \mathfrak{sk}_i)$.

$\mathsf{Open}(\mathcal{T})$:
- If $\mathcal{T} \in \mathsf{TL}$ then return $\perp$
- Return $\mathsf{Open}^{\mathcal{GID}}(\mathcal{T}, \mathfrak{osk}, \mathfrak{Inf}_*)$.

$\mathsf{Exec}(i)$:
- If $i \notin \mathsf{HU}$ or $\mathfrak{gsk}_i = \perp$ then return $\perp$.
- $R \leftarrow \mathsf{Coins}(\mathsf{P}^{\mathcal{GID}})$.
- $\textsc{Cmt} \leftarrow \mathsf{P}^{\mathcal{GID}}(\mathfrak{gsk}_i; R)$.
- $\textsc{Ch} \leftarrow \{0,1\}^c$.
- $\textsc{Rsp} \leftarrow \mathsf{P}^{\mathcal{GID}}(\mathfrak{gsk}_i, \textsc{Cmt}, \textsc{Ch}, R)$.
- $\mathcal{T} \leftarrow (\textsc{Cmt}, \textsc{Ch}, \textsc{Rsp})$.
- Return $\mathcal{T}$.

Fig. 1. Oracles defining security for canonical group identification schemes

the adversary can access the SndToU, CrptU, USK, and Open oracles to get some state information. The adversary uses queries to the CH_b oracle to determine the hidden bit b and hence break the anonymity of $\mathcal{GID}$. We define

$$\mathsf{Adv}^{anon}_{\mathcal{GID},\mathcal{A}}(k) = \left|\Pr[\mathsf{Exp}^{anon\text{-}1}_{\mathcal{GID},\mathcal{A}}(k) = 1] - \Pr[\mathsf{Exp}^{anon\text{-}0}_{\mathcal{GID},\mathcal{A}}(k) = 1]\right| .$$

and we say that the scheme has *anonymity* if $\mathsf{Adv}^{anon}_{\mathcal{GID},\mathcal{A}}(k)$ is a negligible function of k for any polynomial time adversary $\mathcal{A}$.

Experiment $\mathsf{Exp}^{corr}_{\mathcal{GID},\mathcal{A}}(k)$
- $(\mathfrak{gmpk}, \mathfrak{gmsk}, \mathfrak{osk}) \leftarrow \mathsf{GKg}^{\mathcal{GID}}(1^k)$.
- $\mathsf{CU}, \mathsf{HU} \leftarrow \emptyset$.
- $i \leftarrow \mathcal{A}(\mathfrak{gmpk} : \mathsf{AddU}(\cdot))$.
- If $i \notin \mathsf{HU}$ then return 0.
- If $\mathfrak{gsk}_i = \perp$ then return 0.
- $\mathcal{T} \leftarrow \mathsf{Exec}(i)$.
- If $\mathsf{V}^{\mathcal{GID}}(\mathfrak{gmpk}, \mathcal{T}) = 0$ then return 1.
- $(j, \tau) \leftarrow \mathsf{Open}^{\mathcal{GID}}(\mathcal{T}, \mathfrak{osk}, \mathfrak{Inf}_*)$.
- If $i \neq j$ then return 1.
- If $\mathsf{Judge}^{\mathcal{GID}}(\mathfrak{gmpk}, i, \mathfrak{pk}_i, \mathcal{T}, \tau) = 0$ then return 1.
- Return 0.

Experiment $\mathsf{Exp}^{anon\text{-}b}_{\mathcal{GID},\mathcal{A}}(k)$
- $(\mathfrak{gmpk}, \mathfrak{gmsk}, \mathfrak{osk}) \leftarrow \mathsf{GKg}^{\mathcal{GID}}(1^k)$.
- $\mathsf{CU}, \mathsf{HU}, \mathsf{TL} \leftarrow \emptyset$.
- $d \leftarrow \mathcal{A}(\mathfrak{gmpk}, \mathfrak{gmsk} : \mathsf{SndToU}(\cdot,\cdot), \mathsf{CrptU}(\cdot,\cdot), \mathsf{USK}(\cdot), \mathsf{Open}(\cdot), \mathsf{CH}_b(\cdot,\cdot))$.
- Return d.

Experiment $\mathsf{Exp}^{trace}_{\mathcal{GID},\mathcal{A}}(k)$
- $(\mathfrak{gmpk}, \mathfrak{gmsk}, \mathfrak{osk}) \leftarrow \mathsf{GKg}^{\mathcal{GID}}(1^k)$.
- $\mathsf{CU}, \mathsf{HU} \leftarrow \emptyset$.
- $(\textsc{Cmt}, \mathsf{state}) \leftarrow \mathcal{A}_1(\mathfrak{gmpk}, \mathfrak{osk} : \mathsf{AddU}(\cdot), \mathsf{SndToI}(\cdot,\cdot), \mathsf{CrptU}(\cdot,\cdot), \mathsf{USK}(\cdot))$.
- $\textsc{Ch} \leftarrow \{0,1\}^c$.
- $\textsc{Rsp} \leftarrow \mathcal{A}_2(\textsc{Ch}, \mathsf{state} : \mathsf{AddU}(\cdot), \mathsf{SndToI}(\cdot,\cdot), \mathsf{CrptU}(\cdot,\cdot), \mathsf{USK}(\cdot))$.
- $\mathcal{T} \leftarrow (\textsc{Cmt}, \textsc{Ch}, \textsc{Rsp})$.
- If $\mathsf{V}^{\mathcal{GID}}(\mathfrak{gmpk}, \mathcal{T}) = 0$ then return 0.
- $(i, \tau) \leftarrow \mathsf{Open}^{\mathcal{GID}}(\mathcal{T}, \mathfrak{osk}, \mathfrak{Inf}_*)$.
- If $i = 0$ or $\mathsf{Judge}^{\mathcal{GID}}(\mathfrak{gmpk}, i, \mathfrak{pk}_i, \mathcal{T}, \tau) = 0$ then return 1.
- Return 0.

Experiment $\mathsf{Exp}^{non\text{-}frame}_{\mathcal{GID},\mathcal{A}}(k)$
- $(\mathfrak{gmpk}, \mathfrak{gmsk}, \mathfrak{osk}) \leftarrow \mathsf{GKg}^{\mathcal{GID}}(1^k)$.
- $\mathsf{CU}, \mathsf{HU} \leftarrow \emptyset$.
- $(\textsc{Cmt}, \mathsf{state}) \leftarrow \mathcal{A}_1(\mathfrak{gmpk}, \mathfrak{gmsk}, \mathfrak{osk} : \mathsf{SndToU}(\cdot,\cdot), \mathsf{CrptU}(\cdot,\cdot), \mathsf{USK}(\cdot), \mathsf{Exec}(\cdot))$.
- $\textsc{Ch} \leftarrow \{0,1\}^c$.
- $(\textsc{Rsp}, i, \tau) \leftarrow \mathcal{A}_2(\textsc{Ch}, \mathsf{state} : \mathsf{SndToU}(\cdot,\cdot), \mathsf{CrptU}(\cdot,\cdot), \mathsf{USK}(\cdot), \mathsf{Exec}(\cdot))$.
- $\mathcal{T} \leftarrow (\textsc{Cmt}, \textsc{Ch}, \textsc{Rsp})$.
- If $\mathsf{V}^{\mathcal{GID}}(\mathfrak{gmpk}, \mathcal{T}) = 0$ then return 0.
- If the following are all true then return 1 else return 0.
  - $\mathsf{Judge}^{\mathcal{GID}}(\mathfrak{gmpk}, i, \mathfrak{pk}_i, \mathcal{T}, \tau) = 1$ and $i \in \mathsf{HU}$ and $\mathfrak{gsk}_i \neq \perp$.
  - $\mathcal{A}$ did not query $\mathsf{USK}(i)$ and $\mathcal{T}$ was not produced by $\mathsf{Exec}(i)$.

Fig. 2. Security experiments for canonical group identification schemes

Traceability. Let $\mathcal{A}$ be an adversary, running in two stages, performing the traceability experiment given in Figure 2. The goal of the adversary is to produce a transcript that is either declared by the opener to be un-openable, or the opener believes they have identified the opener but they cannot produce a valid proof of this. In this experiment, the adversary can first access the AddU, SndToI, CrptU, USK oracles to obtain state information and then output a commitment CMT. After the verifier has outputted the challenge CH, the adversary queries the above oracles and finally outputs a response RSP associated with CMT and RSP. The transcript $\mathcal{T}$ is (CMT, CH, RSP). We define

$$\mathsf{Adv}^{trace}_{\mathcal{GID},\mathcal{A}}(k) = \Pr[\mathsf{Exp}^{trace}_{\mathcal{GID},\mathcal{A}}(k) = 1],$$

and we say that the scheme has *traceability* if $\mathsf{Adv}^{trace}_{\mathcal{GID},\mathcal{A}}(k)$ is a negligible function of k for any polynomial time adversary $\mathcal{A}$.

Non-Frameability. Let $\mathcal{A}$ be an adversary, also running in two stages, performing the non-frameability experiment given in Figure 2. The goal of the adversary is to output a new transcript which the judge will accept as belonging to an honest user i, where i did not produce this transcript. In this experiment, the adversary can first access the SndToU, CrptU, USK and Exec oracles to obtain state information and it then outputs a commitment CMT. After the verifier has outputted the challenge CH, the adversary queries the above oracles and finally outputs a response RSP associated with CMT and RSP. The transcript $\mathcal{T}$ is (CMT, CH, RSP). We define

$$\mathsf{Adv}^{non\text{-}frame}_{\mathcal{GID},\mathcal{A}}(k) = \Pr[\mathsf{Exp}^{non\text{-}frame}_{\mathcal{GID},\mathcal{A}}(k) = 1],$$

and we say that the scheme has *non-frameability* if $\mathsf{Adv}^{non\text{-}frame}_{\mathcal{GID},\mathcal{A}}(k)$ is a negligible function of k for any polynomial time adversary $\mathcal{A}$.

MODEL VARIATIONS. Our main results relate the security of group signature schemes with the security of the group identification schemes from which they are obtained via the FS transform. The notions that we use are those defined above.

The group signature literature contains other, still reasonable security notions that we weaker. Our results extend to this setting. Via the FS transform one obtains group signature schemes that satisfies weaker notions of security from, correspondingly weakend group identification schemes. Below we sketch these weaker notions by analogy with those for group signatures.

First we note that the above definitions capture the notion of dynamic groups. In the case of a static groups we may have no $\mathsf{UKg}^{\mathcal{GID}}$ algorithm and no $(\mathsf{Join}^{\mathcal{GID}}, \mathsf{Iss}^{\mathcal{GID}})$ protocol for joining a group. Instead, the generation of user secret keys $\mathfrak{gsk}_i$ is assumed to be done by the setup algorithm $\mathsf{GKg}^{\mathcal{GID}}$, and is done once and for all on system setup. The experiments then need to be altered slightly in the obvious way, mainly to remove adversarial calls to the AddU, SndToU and SndToI oracles. In analogy with the definitions from [6] in many schemes the openers secret key $\mathfrak{osk}$ is identical to the group managers secret key $\mathfrak{gmsk}$. We say that such system have an *opener-manager*. In another variant, also considered in [6], the algorithm Open^{GID} does not output a proof of correctness of the opening (to be verified by a judge) but simply outputs the identity i. These are schemes with *non-verified opening.* Again the security experiments need to be slightly modified with respect to how $\mathsf{Open}^{\mathcal{GID}}$ and $\mathsf{Judge}^{\mathcal{GID}}$ work, since there is now no proof and so no need of the $\mathsf{Judge}^{\mathcal{GID}}$ algorithm.

Finally, a scheme which does not allow the adversary to query the opening oracle in the anonymity experiment is said to be weakly secure, or simply CPA secure. One can think of the identity information within the transcript used by the opener as an encryption of this identity. Thus giving the adversary access or not to the opening oracle is akin to giving access to a decryption oracle in the security model for encryption schemes – hence the name.

3 Group Signature Schemes

In this section we describe the syntax and security notions for group signature schemes. The presentation follows closely [9], which also served as guidance for our model for group identification schemes. As such, there is a lot of commonality between the two presentations so we only stress the main differences.

SYNTAX. A group signature scheme is given by a tuple of algorithms: $\mathcal{GS} = (\mathsf{GKg}^{\mathcal{GS}}, \mathsf{UKg}^{\mathcal{GS}}, \mathsf{Join}^{\mathcal{GS}}, \mathsf{Iss}^{\mathcal{GS}}, \mathsf{GSig}, \mathsf{GVf}, \mathsf{Open}^{\mathcal{GS}}, \mathsf{Judge}^{\mathcal{GS}})$. The functionality the algorithms $\mathsf{GKg}^{\mathcal{GS}}$, $\mathsf{UKg}^{\mathcal{GS}}$, $\mathsf{Join}^{\mathcal{GS}}$ and $\mathsf{Iss}^{\mathcal{GS}}$ is identical to those for the group identification schemes considered earlier. What is different is that the prover and verifier interactive algorithms are replaced with a signing algorithm GSig and a verification algorithm GVf. The syntax demanded from the algorithms for opening and judging $\mathsf{Open}^{\mathcal{GS}}$ and $\mathsf{Judge}^{\mathcal{GS}}$ is slightly modified to take this into account. Specifically:

- GSig: Is a probabilistic signing algorithm taking input a group signing key $\mathfrak{gsk}_i$ and a message m, returning a signature σ.
- GVf: Is a deterministic verifying algorithm which takes input the group public key $\mathfrak{gmpk}$, a group signature σ a message m. It then returns a Boolean decision to demonstrate whether the group signature is accepted or rejected.
- $\mathsf{Open}^{\mathcal{GS}}$: This is as before except it takes as input a message and a signature instead of a transcript.
- $\mathsf{Judge}^{\mathcal{GS}}$: Again, this is as before except it takes as input a message and a signature instead of a transcript.

SECURITY NOTIONS. The games that define correctness, anonymity, traceability and non-frameability for group signature schemes are essentially the non-interactive versions of the games we have defined for identification schemes. The schemes make use of a modified set of oracles. The modifications are as follows:

The oracles used by the adversary are changed from that for canonical group identification schemes in the following ways:

- $\mathsf{Open}(\sigma, m)$: This oracle takes as input a signature σ and a message m and returns the result of running the opening algorithm (i.e. the identity of the user plus the associated proof).

- $\mathsf{CH}_b(i_0, i_1, m)$: This oracle is a left-right oracle for defining anonymity. The adversary sends a couple of honest identities (i_0, i_1) and a message m to the oracle and gets back a signature σ of the signature scheme executed by signer i_b. In addition, in CH_b and the game for anonymity we replace the list of transcripts TL by a list of signatures SL issued by the oracle CH_b.
- $\mathsf{Sign}(i, m)$: This oracle allows the adversary to obtain signatures of the signature scheme executed by a valid group member. This oracle takes as input the identity of the group member i and message m, and finally outputs a group signature of the member i.

The changes in games account for the fact that we replace identification with signing. In addition, we are only concerned with schemes secure in the random oracle model (as those obtained via the FS transform) so the algorithms and the adversary have access to oracle H defined in the standard way. Specifically, the oracle $\mathsf{H}(\cdot)$ maintains an internal list, H-List, of pairs (x, h) with the meaning that h was the answer that the oracle returned when it was previously queried with input x. When H receives an input x, it then returns h if (x, h) in H-List. Otherwise, it selects a random $h \in \{0,1\}^c$, adds the entry (x, h) to H-List, and returns h.

The formal games for security are in Figure 3, with the associated advantage functions being defined in the obvious manner.

As for group identification, one can define weaker notions of security for group signature schemes by appropriate restrictions and syntactic modifications. The standard examples from the literature include moving to static groups, CPA security, non-verified opening and schemes with an opener-manager.

4 From Group Identification to Group Signature Schemes

In this section we formally define the Fiat-Shamir transform for group signature and prove that it leads to secure schemes.

THE FIAT-SHAMIR TRANSFORM. The Fiat-Shamir transform for standard digital signature schemes works if the underlying identification protocol is such that the first message (the commitment) has sufficient entropy. To make the transformation applicable to a larger class of identification protocols, one workaround is to "artificially" append a random string to the commitment. Abdalla et al. [1] call this the extended Fiat-Shamir transform. We adapt this more general transformation to the setting of group identification/signatures. Similarly to [1], our security results would then subsume the case when the commitment of the original scheme has sufficient entropy.

The transformation essentially removes the interaction in the identification protocol of the group identification scheme, very much like it does when applied to standard identification protocols.

Let $\mathcal{GID} = (\mathsf{GKg}^{\mathcal{GID}}, \mathsf{UKg}^{\mathcal{GID}}, \mathsf{Join}^{\mathcal{GID}}, \mathsf{Iss}^{\mathcal{GID}}, (\mathsf{P}^{\mathcal{GID}}, \mathsf{V}^{\mathcal{GID}}), \mathsf{Open}^{\mathcal{GID}}, \mathsf{Judge}^{\mathcal{GID}})$ be a canonical group identification scheme, and $s : \mathbb{N} \to \mathbb{N}$ be a function which defines a *seed length* $s(k)$ given the security parameter k. We

Experiment $\mathsf{Exp}^{corr}_{\mathcal{GS},\mathcal{A}}(k)$
- $(\mathfrak{gmpk}, \mathfrak{gmsk}, \mathfrak{osk}) \leftarrow \mathsf{GKg}^{\mathcal{GS}}(1^k)$.
- $\mathsf{CU}, \mathsf{HU} \leftarrow \emptyset$.
- $(i, m) \leftarrow \mathcal{A}(\mathfrak{gmpk} : \mathsf{AddU}(\cdot))$.
- If $i \notin \mathsf{HU}$ then return 0.
- If $\mathfrak{gsk}_i = \perp$ then return 0.
- $\sigma \leftarrow \mathsf{GSig}(\mathfrak{gsk}_i, m)$.
- If $\mathsf{GVf}(\mathfrak{gmpk}, \sigma, m) = 0$ then return 1.
- $(j, \tau) \leftarrow \mathsf{Open}^{\mathcal{GS}}(\sigma, m, \mathfrak{osk}, \mathfrak{Inf}_*)$.
- If $i \neq j$ then return 1.
- If $\mathsf{Judge}^{\mathcal{GS}}(\mathfrak{gmpk}, i, \mathfrak{pk}_i, \sigma, m, \tau) = 0$ then return 1.
- Return 0.

Experiment $\mathsf{Exp}^{anon\text{-}b}_{\mathcal{GS},\mathcal{A}}(k)$
- $(\mathfrak{gmpk}, \mathfrak{gmsk}, \mathfrak{osk}) \leftarrow \mathsf{GKg}^{\mathcal{GS}}(1^k)$.
- $\mathsf{CU}, \mathsf{HU}, \mathsf{SL} \leftarrow \emptyset$.
- $d \leftarrow \mathcal{A}(\mathfrak{gmpk}, \mathfrak{gmsk} : \mathsf{H}(\cdot), \mathsf{SndToU}(\cdot,\cdot), \mathsf{CrptU}(\cdot,\cdot), \mathsf{USK}(\cdot), \mathsf{Open}(\cdot), \mathsf{CH}_b(\cdot,\cdot))$.
- Return d.

Experiment $\mathsf{Exp}^{trace}_{\mathcal{GS},\mathcal{A}}(k)$
- $(\mathfrak{gmpk}, \mathfrak{gmsk}, \mathfrak{osk}) \leftarrow \mathsf{GKg}^{\mathcal{GS}}(1^k)$.
- $\mathsf{CU}, \mathsf{HU} \leftarrow \emptyset$.
- $(\sigma, m) \leftarrow \mathcal{A}(\mathfrak{gmpk}, \mathfrak{osk} : \mathsf{H}(\cdot), \mathsf{AddU}(\cdot), \mathsf{SndToI}(\cdot,\cdot), \mathsf{CrptU}(\cdot,\cdot), \mathsf{USK}(\cdot))$.
- If $\mathsf{GVf}(\mathfrak{gmpk}, \sigma, m) = 0$ then return 0.
- $(i, \tau) \leftarrow \mathsf{Open}^{\mathcal{GS}}(\sigma, m, \mathfrak{osk}, \mathfrak{Inf}_*)$.
- If $i = 0$ or $\mathsf{Judge}^{\mathcal{GS}}(\mathfrak{gmpk}, i, \mathfrak{pk}_i, \sigma, m, \tau) = 0$ then return 1.
- Return 0.

Experiment $\mathsf{Exp}^{non\text{-}frame}_{\mathcal{GS},\mathcal{A}}(k)$
- $(\mathfrak{gmpk}, \mathfrak{gmsk}, \mathfrak{osk}) \leftarrow \mathsf{GKg}^{\mathcal{GS}}(1^k)$.
- $\mathsf{CU}, \mathsf{HU} \leftarrow \emptyset$.
- $(\sigma, m, i, \tau) \leftarrow \mathcal{A}(\mathfrak{gmpk}, \mathfrak{gmsk}, \mathfrak{osk} : \mathsf{H}(\cdot), \mathsf{SndToU}(\cdot,\cdot), \mathsf{CrptU}(\cdot,\cdot), \mathsf{USK}(\cdot), \mathsf{Sign}(\cdot))$.
- If $\mathsf{GVf}(\mathfrak{gmpk}, \sigma, m) = 0$ then return 0.
- If the following are all true then return 1 else return 0.
  - $\mathsf{Judge}^{\mathcal{GS}}(\mathfrak{gmpk}, i, \mathfrak{pk}_i, \sigma, m, \tau) = 1$ and $i \in \mathsf{HU}$ and $\mathfrak{gsk}_i \neq \perp$.
  - $\mathcal{A}$ did not query $\mathsf{USK}(i)$ and σ was not produced by a call to $\mathsf{Sign}(i, m)$.

Fig. 3. Security experiments for group signature schemes

select a hash function $H : \{0,1\}^* \to \{0,1\}^c$ at random from the set of all maps $\{0,1\}^* \to \{0,1\}^c$, where c is the bit length of the challenge CH in the canonical group identification scheme we will be using. From these we construct a group signature scheme $\mathcal{GS} = (\mathsf{GKg}^{\mathcal{GS}}, \mathsf{UKg}^{\mathcal{GS}}, \mathsf{Join}^{\mathcal{GS}}, \mathsf{Iss}^{\mathcal{GS}}, \mathsf{GSig}, \mathsf{GVf}, \mathsf{Open}^{\mathcal{GS}}, \mathsf{Judge}^{\mathcal{GS}})$ as follows. We let $\mathsf{GKg}^{\mathcal{GS}} = \mathsf{GKg}^{\mathcal{GID}}$, $\mathsf{UKg}^{\mathcal{GS}} = \mathsf{UKg}^{\mathcal{GID}}$, $\mathsf{Join}^{\mathcal{GS}} = \mathsf{Join}^{\mathcal{GID}}$ and $\mathsf{Iss}^{\mathcal{GS}} = \mathsf{Iss}^{\mathcal{GID}}$. The functions $\mathsf{GSig}, \mathsf{GVf}, \mathsf{Open}^{\mathcal{GS}}$ and $\mathsf{Judge}^{\mathcal{GS}}$ are defined as in Figure 4. We call the resulting group signature scheme $FS(\mathcal{GID})$.

$\mathsf{GSig}(\mathfrak{gsk}_i, m)$:
- $R_P \leftarrow \mathsf{Coins}(\mathsf{P}^{\mathcal{GID}})$.
- $\textsc{Cmt} \leftarrow \mathsf{P}^{\mathcal{GID}}(\mathfrak{gsk}_i; R_P)$.
- $R \leftarrow \{0,1\}^{s(k)}$.
- $\textsc{Ch} \leftarrow H(R \| \textsc{Cmt} \| m)$.
- $\textsc{Rsp} \leftarrow \mathsf{P}^{\mathcal{GID}}(\mathfrak{gsk}_i, \textsc{Cmt}, \textsc{Ch}, R_P)$.
- $\sigma \leftarrow (R, \textsc{Cmt}, \textsc{Rsp})$.
- Return σ.

$\mathsf{GVf}(\mathfrak{gmpk}, \sigma, m)$:
- Parse σ as $(R, \textsc{Cmt}, \textsc{Rsp})$.
- $\textsc{Ch} \leftarrow H(R \| \textsc{Cmt} \| m)$.
- $\mathcal{T} \leftarrow (\textsc{Cmt}, \textsc{Ch}, \textsc{Rsp})$.
- Return $\mathsf{V}^{\mathcal{GID}}(\mathfrak{gmpk}, \mathcal{T})$.

$\mathsf{Open}^{\mathcal{GS}}(\sigma, m, \mathfrak{osk}, \mathfrak{Inf}_*)$:
- Parse σ as $(R, \textsc{Cmt}, \textsc{Rsp})$.
- $\textsc{Ch} \leftarrow H(R \| \textsc{Cmt} \| m)$.
- $\mathcal{T} \leftarrow (\textsc{Cmt}, \textsc{Ch}, \textsc{Rsp})$.
- Return $\mathsf{Open}^{\mathcal{GID}}(\mathcal{T}, \mathfrak{osk}, \mathfrak{Inf}_*)$.

$\mathsf{Judge}^{\mathcal{GS}}(\mathfrak{gmpk}, i, \mathfrak{pk}_i, \sigma, m, \tau)$:
- Parse σ as $(R, \textsc{Cmt}, \textsc{Rsp})$.
- $\textsc{Ch} \leftarrow H(R \| \textsc{Cmt} \| m)$.
- $\mathcal{T} \leftarrow (\textsc{Cmt}, \textsc{Ch}, \textsc{Rsp})$.
- Return $\mathsf{Judge}^{\mathcal{GID}}(\mathfrak{gmpk}, i, \mathfrak{pk}_i, \mathcal{T}, \tau)$.

Fig. 4. Construction of a group signature scheme from a group identification scheme

Security results. Since the security of the resulting group signature schemes relies on the entropy of the commitment we recall the necessary notion. Security of the above construction relies on the random oracle model. In addition it relies on the values of the constants $s(k)$ and c. In particular the associated min-entropy, defined below, of the commitment generated by the prover needs to be large enough.

Definition 1 (Min-Entropy of Commitments). *Let $\mathcal{GID}$ be a canonical group identification scheme. Let $k \in N$ and $(\mathfrak{sk}_i, \mathfrak{pk}_i)$ be the key pair generated by key generation algorithm $\mathsf{UKg}^{\mathcal{GID}}$ on input of 1^k. We denote by $\mathcal{C}(\mathfrak{sk}_i) = \{\textsc{Cmt} = \mathsf{P}^{\mathcal{GID}}(\mathfrak{sk}_i, R_P)\}$ be the set of all possible commitments associated with $\mathfrak{sk}_i$. We define the maximum probability that a commitment takes on a particular value via*

$$\alpha(\mathfrak{sk}_i) = \max_{\textsc{Cmt} \in \mathcal{C}(\mathfrak{sk}_i)} \left\{ Pr\left[\mathsf{P}^{\mathcal{GID}}(\mathfrak{sk}_i, R_P) = \textsc{Cmt} : R_P \leftarrow \mathsf{Coins}(\mathsf{P}^{\mathcal{GID}})\right]\right\}.$$

Then the min-entropy function associated with $\mathcal{GID}$ is defined as follows:

$$\beta(k) = \min_{\mathfrak{sk}_i} \left\{ \log_2 \left(\frac{1}{\alpha(\mathfrak{sk}_i)} \right) \right\}$$

where minimum is taken over all key pairs $(\mathfrak{sk}_i, \mathfrak{pk}_i)$ generated by $\mathsf{UKg}^{\mathcal{GID}}(1^k)$. We say that $\mathcal{GID}$ is non-trivial if $\beta(\cdot) = \omega(\log(\cdot))$ is super-logarithmic.

Our results show a tight connection between the security of the underlying group identification schemes and the group signature scheme obtained via the FS transform. If the starting group signature scheme is secure (it has the four properties that we have defined earlier), then the resulting group signature scheme is also secure. This result is captured by the following theorem.

Theorem 1. *(Secure $\mathcal{GID} \Rightarrow$ secure $\mathcal{GS}$) Let $\mathcal{GID}$ be a canonical group identification scheme and $\mathcal{GS} = FS(\mathcal{GID})$. If $\mathcal{GID}$ has the properties of correctness, anonymity, traceability and non-frameability under passive attacks, then $\mathcal{GS}$ also has the above properties.*

We also show that security against passive adversaries for the underlying group identification scheme is also necessary. Specifically, we have the following theorem.

Theorem 2. *(Secure $\mathcal{GID} \Leftarrow$ secure $\mathcal{GS}$) Let $\mathcal{GID}$ be a canonical group identification scheme and $\mathcal{GS} = FS(\mathcal{GID})$. If $\mathcal{GS}$ has the properties of correctness, anonymity, traceability and non-frameability, then $\mathcal{GID}$ is correct, anonymous, traceable and non-frameable under passive attacks.*

MODEL VARIATIONS. As remarked earlier different authors have used different notions of security for group signature schemes. Each of these different notions is obtained by appropriate restrictions on the powers of the adversary in the standard security games. Unsurprisingly for both group identification and signature schemes, the restrictions are essentially the same (modulo the parts that are different). For example, in both cases, CPA-security is obtained by not providing the adversary with an oracle for opening transcripts and signatures, respectively. Since this is true for all of the oracles which our reductions preserve essentially unchanged, our proofs easily extend to these variations in models. Specifically, we have the following: If X is one of the properties in the set $\{\mathsf{correctness}, \mathsf{anonymity}, \mathsf{traceability}, \mathsf{non\text{-}frameability}, \mathsf{CPA\text{-}secure}, \mathsf{CCA\text{-}secure}\}$ then, if $\mathcal{GID}$ has property X, then $\mathcal{GS} = FS(\mathcal{GID})$ has property X. This is true for both static and dynamic groups.

5 Proof of the Construction

5.1 Proof of Theorem 1

The concept of our proof for **Theorem 1** is as follow: if $\mathcal{GS} = FS(\mathcal{GID})$ is insecure (i.e., there exists an algorithm $\mathcal{A}$ which can break the security of $\mathcal{GS}$ with non-negligible advantage), then there exists a algorithm $\mathcal{B}$ which can break the security of $\mathcal{GID}$ with non-negligible advantage. We now prove **Theorem 1** via Lemma 1 to Lemma 4. The proofs for the following Lemmas can be found in the full version of the paper.

Lemma 1. *Let $\mathcal{GID}$ be a group identification scheme and $\mathcal{GS} = FS(\mathcal{GID})$. Let $\mathcal{A}$ be an adversary attacking the correctness of the group signature in the random oracle model. Then there is an adversary $\mathcal{B}$ against the correctness of $\mathcal{GID}$ such that $\mathsf{Adv}^{corr}_{\mathcal{GID},\mathcal{B}} \geq \mathsf{Adv}^{corr}_{\mathcal{GS},\mathcal{A}}$.*

Lemma 2. *Let $\mathcal{GID}$ be a group identification scheme and $\mathcal{GS} = FS(\mathcal{GID})$. Let $s(\cdot)$ be a seed length and $\beta(\cdot)$ be the min-entropy function associated with $\mathcal{GID}$. Let $\mathcal{A}$ be an adversary attacking the anonymity of the group signature in the random oracle model, making q_h hash-oracle queries. Then there is an adversary $\mathcal{B}$ against the anonymity of $\mathcal{GID}$ such that $\mathsf{Adv}^{anon}_{\mathcal{GID},\mathcal{B}} \geq \mathsf{Adv}^{anon}_{\mathcal{GS},\mathcal{A}} - \frac{q_h}{2^{s(k)+\beta(k)}}$.*

Lemma 3. *Let $\mathcal{GID}$ be a group identification scheme and $\mathcal{GS} = FS(\mathcal{GID})$. Let $s(\cdot)$ be a seed length and $\beta(\cdot)$ be the min-entropy function associated with $\mathcal{GID}$. Let $\mathcal{A}$ be an adversary attacking the traceability of the group signature in the random oracle model, making q_h hash-oracle queries. Then there is an adversary $\mathcal{B}$ against the traceability of $\mathcal{GID}$ such that* $\mathsf{Adv}^{trace}_{\mathcal{GID},\mathcal{B}} \geq \mathsf{Adv}^{trace}_{\mathcal{GS},\mathcal{A}} - \frac{q_h}{2^{s(k)+\beta(k)}}$.

Lemma 4. *Let $\mathcal{GID}$ be a group identification scheme and $\mathcal{GS} = FS(\mathcal{GID})$. Let $s(\cdot)$ be a seed length and $\beta(\cdot)$ be the min-entropy function associated with $\mathcal{GID}$. Let $\mathcal{A}$ be an adversary attacking the non-frameability of the group signature in the random oracle model, making q_h hash-oracle queries and q_s signature oracles. Then there is an adversary $\mathcal{B}$ against the non-frameability of $\mathcal{GID}$ such that* $\mathsf{Adv}^{non\text{-}frame}_{\mathcal{GID},\mathcal{B}} \geq \mathsf{Adv}^{non\text{-}frame}_{\mathcal{GS},\mathcal{A}}(k) - \frac{1}{q_h} \cdot \frac{q_s(q_h+q_s-1)}{2^{s(k)+\beta(k)}}$.

By combining Lemmas 1, 2, 3 and 4, **Theorem 1** is proved.

5.2 Proof of Theorem 2

The idea behind the proof for **Theorem 2** is as follow: if $\mathcal{GID}$ is insecure (i.e., there exists an algorithm $\mathcal{A}$ which can break the security of $\mathcal{GID}$ with non-negligible advantage), then there exists a algorithm $\mathcal{B}$ which can break the security of $\mathcal{GS} = FS(\mathcal{GID})$ with non-negligible advantage. We now prove **Theorem 2** via Lemma 5 to Lemma 8. Again we leave the proofs of these Lemmas to the full version of the paper.

Lemma 5. *Let $\mathcal{GID}$ be a group identification scheme and $\mathcal{GS} = FS(\mathcal{GID})$. Let $\mathcal{A}$ be an adversary attacking the correctness of the group identification in the random oracle model. Then there is an adversary $\mathcal{B}$ against the correctness of $\mathcal{GS}$ such that* $\mathsf{Adv}^{corr}_{\mathcal{GS},\mathcal{B}} \geq \mathsf{Adv}^{corr}_{\mathcal{GID},\mathcal{A}}$.

Lemma 6. *Let $\mathcal{GID}$ be a group identification scheme and $\mathcal{GS} = FS(\mathcal{GID})$. Let $\mathcal{A}$ be an adversary attacking the anonymity of the group identification. Then there is an adversary $\mathcal{B}$ against the anonymity of $\mathcal{GS}$ such that* $\mathsf{Adv}^{anon}_{\mathcal{GS},\mathcal{B}} \geq \mathsf{Adv}^{anon}_{\mathcal{GID},\mathcal{A}}$.

Lemma 7. *Let $\mathcal{GID}$ be a group identification scheme and $\mathcal{GS} = FS(\mathcal{GID})$. Let $\mathcal{A}$ be an adversary attacking the traceability of the group identification. Then there is an adversary $\mathcal{B}$ against the traceability of $\mathcal{GS}$ such that* $\mathsf{Adv}^{trace}_{\mathcal{GS},\mathcal{B}} \geq \mathsf{Adv}^{trace}_{\mathcal{GID},\mathcal{A}}$.

Lemma 8. *Let $\mathcal{GID}$ be a group identification scheme and $\mathcal{GS} = FS(\mathcal{GID})$. Let $\mathcal{A}$ be an adversary attacking the non-frameability of the group identification. Then there is an adversary $\mathcal{B}$ against the non-frameability of $\mathcal{GS}$ such that* $\mathsf{Adv}^{non\text{-}frame}_{\mathcal{GS},\mathcal{B}} \geq \mathsf{Adv}^{non\text{-}frame}_{\mathcal{GID},\mathcal{A}}$.

By combining Lemmas 5, 6, 7 and 8, **Theorem 2** is proved.

6 From Ad-Hoc Group Identification to Ring Signatures

An ad hoc group identification scheme is an identification protocol in which a prover can anonymously prove she is a valid number of an ad hoc group.

Based on the underlying PKI, arbitrary ad hoc groups of a user population can be formed without the help of a group manager. In [14], the authors give a formal model of an ad hoc identification scheme which is a six-tuple of algorithms ($\mathsf{Setup}, \mathsf{Register}, \mathsf{Make\text{-}GPK}, \mathsf{Make\text{-}GSK}, \mathsf{Anon\text{-}ID}^{\mathsf{P}}, \mathsf{Anon\text{-}ID}^{\mathsf{V}}$). However, in this paper, we slightly modify the notations of the model of [14] in order to suit with the model and notations of our ring signature $\mathcal{RS}$.

An ad hoc group identification scheme is given by the tuple of algorithms $\mathcal{AHID} = (\mathsf{UKg}^{\mathcal{AHID}}, \mathsf{GPKg}^{\mathcal{AHID}}, \mathsf{GSKg}^{\mathcal{AHID}}, (\mathsf{P}^{\mathcal{AHID}}, \mathsf{V}^{\mathcal{AHID}}))$. The functionality of these algorithms is as follows:

- $\mathsf{UKg}^{\mathcal{AHID}}$: This is a probabilistic algorithm to generate user public/private key pairs. When run by user i, on input of 1^k, this outputs a user's key pair $(\mathfrak{sk}_i, \mathfrak{pk}_i)$.
- $(\mathsf{GPKg}^{\mathcal{AHID}}, \mathsf{GSKg}^{\mathcal{AHID}})$: The ad hoc group public key generation algorithm and the ad hoc group secret key generation algorithm. The algorithm $\mathsf{GPKg}^{\mathcal{AHID}}$ is a deterministic algorithm which combines a set of user public keys S into a single ad hoc group public key $\mathfrak{gpk}$. The deterministic algorithm $\mathsf{GSKg}^{\mathcal{AHID}}$ takes as input a user secret/public key pair $(\mathfrak{sk}_i, \mathfrak{pk}_i)$ and a set of user public keys S, it outputs an ad hoc group secret key $\mathfrak{gsk}_i$ which associates with the ad hoc group public key $\mathfrak{gpk}$.
- $(\mathsf{P}^{\mathcal{AHID}}, \mathsf{V}^{\mathcal{AHID}})$: An interactive protocol between a prover and a verifier. The prover's input is a value $\mathfrak{gsk}_i$, whereas the verifier's input is $\mathfrak{gpk}$.

As before we shall focus purely on canonical ad hoc group identification schemes, where the $(\mathsf{P}^{\mathcal{AHID}}, \mathsf{V}^{\mathcal{AHID}})$ protocol is given by three-move protocol of the commit-challenge-response variety.

In the full version we present a security model for such ad-hoc group identification schemes, and an analogous model for ring signatures. We then formalise the construction of ring signatures from ad-hoc group identification schemes via the Fiat–Shamir transform. Finally, an analogous theorem to the earlier one can be proved, namely:

Theorem 3. *Let $\mathcal{AHID}$ be a canonical ad-hoc group identification scheme and $\mathcal{RS} = FS(\mathcal{AHID})$. The derived ring signature scheme $\mathcal{RS}$ has the properties of correctness, anonymity and unforgeability against chosen-message attacks if and only if $\mathcal{AHID}$ has the properties of correctness, anonymity, and non-impersonation under passive attacks.*

Acknowledgements

The work in this paper was partially funded by the European Commission through the ICT programme under contract ICT-2007-216676 ECRYPT II FP7. The second author was supported by a Royal Society Wolfson Merit Award and a grant from Google.

References

1. Abdalla, M., An, J.H., Bellare, M., Namprempre, C.: From identification to signatures via the Fiat–Shamir transform: Minimizing assumptions for security and forward-security. In: Knudsen, L.R. (ed.) EUROCRYPT 2002. LNCS, vol. 2332, pp. 418–433. Springer, Heidelberg (2002)
2. Ateniese, G., Camenisch, J., Joye, M., Tsudik, G.: A practical and provably secure coalition-resistant group signature scheme. In: Bellare, M. (ed.) CRYPTO 2000. LNCS, vol. 1880, pp. 255–270. Springer, Heidelberg (2000)
3. Ateniese, G., de Medeiros, B.: Efficient group signatures without trapdoors. In: Laih, C.-S. (ed.) ASIACRYPT 2003. LNCS, vol. 2894, pp. 246–268. Springer, Heidelberg (2003)
4. Abe, M., Ohkubo, M., Suzuki, K.: 1-out-of-n signatures from a variety of keys. In: Zheng, Y. (ed.) ASIACRYPT 2002. LNCS, vol. 2501, pp. 415–432. Springer, Heidelberg (2002)
5. Boneh, D., Boyen, X., Shacham, H.: Short group signatures. In: Franklin, M. (ed.) CRYPTO 2004. LNCS, vol. 3152, pp. 41–55. Springer, Heidelberg (2004)
6. Bellare, M., Micciancio, D., Warinschi, B.: Foundations of group signatures: Formal definitions, simplified requirements, and a construction based on general assumptions. In: Biham, E. (ed.) EUROCRYPT 2003. LNCS, vol. 2656, pp. 614–629. Springer, Heidelberg (2003)
7. Bellare, M., Namprempre, C., Neven, G.: Security proofs for identity-based identification and signature schemes. In: Cachin, C., Camenisch, J.L. (eds.) EUROCRYPT 2004. LNCS, vol. 3027, pp. 268–286. Springer, Heidelberg (2004)
8. Boneh, D., Shacham, H.: Group signatures with verifier-local revocation. In: Proceedings of ACM CCS 2004, pp. 168–177 (2004)
9. Bellare, M., Shi, H., Zhang, C.: Foundations of group signatures: The case of dynamic groups. In: Menezes, A. (ed.) CT-RSA 2005. LNCS, vol. 3376, pp. 136–153. Springer, Heidelberg (2005)
10. Camenisch, J.: Efficient and generalized group signatures. In: Fumy, W. (ed.) EUROCRYPT 1997. LNCS, vol. 1233, pp. 465–479. Springer, Heidelberg (1997)
11. Camenisch, J., Michels, M.: A group signature scheme with improved efficiency. In: Ohta, K., Pei, D. (eds.) ASIACRYPT 1998. LNCS, vol. 1514, pp. 160–174. Springer, Heidelberg (1998)
12. Chen, L., Pedersen, T.P.: New group signature schemes (extended abstract). In: De Santis, A. (ed.) EUROCRYPT 1994. LNCS, vol. 950, pp. 171–181. Springer, Heidelberg (1995)
13. Camenisch, J., Stadler, M.: Efficient group signature schemes for large group. In: Kaliski Jr., B.S. (ed.) CRYPTO 1997. LNCS, vol. 1294, pp. 410–424. Springer, Heidelberg (1997)
14. Dodis, Y., Kiayias, A., Nicolosi, A., Shoup, V.: Anonymous identification in ad hoc groups. In: Cachin, C., Camenisch, J.L. (eds.) EUROCRYPT 2004. LNCS, vol. 3027, pp. 609–626. Springer, Heidelberg (2004)
15. Dwork, C., Naor, M., Reingold, O., Stockmayer, L.: Magic Functions. Journal of the ACM 50, 852–921 (2003)
16. Fiat, A., Shamir, A.: How to prove yourself: Practical solutions to identification and signature problems. In: Damgård, I.B. (ed.) EUROCRYPT 1990. LNCS, vol. 473, pp. 481–486. Springer, Heidelberg (1991)

17. Goldwasser, S., Tauman, Y.: On the (in)security of the Fiat-Shamir paradigm. In: IEEE Symposium on Foundations of Computer Science – FOCS 2003, pp. 102–115 (2003)
18. Kilian, J., Petrank, E.: Identity escrow. In: Hand, D.J., Kok, J.N., Berthold, M. R. (eds.) IDA 1999. LNCS, vol. 1642, pp. 169–185. Springer, Heidelberg (1999)
19. Ohta, K., Okamoto, T.: On concrete security treatment of signatures derived from identification. In: Krawczyk, H. (ed.) CRYPTO 1998. LNCS, vol. 1462, pp. 223–242. Springer, Heidelberg (1998)
20. Pointcheval, D., Stern, J.: Security arguments for digital signatures and blind signatures. Journal of Cryptology 13, 361–396 (2000)

Get Shorty via Group Signatures without Encryption

Patrik Bichsel[1], Jan Camenisch[1], Gregory Neven[1], Nigel P. Smart[2], and Bogdan Warinschi[2]

[1] IBM Research – Zurich, Switzerland
{pbi,jca,nev}@zurich.ibm.com
[2] Dept Computer Science, Univeristy of Bristol, United Kingdom
{nigel,bogdan}@cs.bris.ac.uk

Abstract. Group signatures allow group members to anonymously sign messages in the name of a group such that only a dedicated opening authority can reveal the exact signer behind a signature. In many of the target applications, for example in sensor networks or in vehicular communication networks, bandwidth and computation time are scarce resources and many of the existent constructions simply cannot be used. Moreover, some of the most efficient schemes only guarantee anonymity as long as no signatures are opened, rendering the opening functionality virtually useless.

In this paper, we propose a group signature scheme with the shortest known signature size and favorably comparing computation time, whilst still offering a strong and practically relevant security level that guarantees secure opening of signatures, protection against a cheating authority, and support for dynamic groups. Our construction departs from the popular sign-and-encrypt-and-prove paradigm, which we identify as one source of inefficiency. In particular, our proposal does not use standard encryption and relies on re-randomizable signature schemes that hide the signed message so as to preserve the anonymity of signers.

Security is proved in the random oracle model assuming the XDDH, LRSW and SDLP assumptions and the security of an underlying digital signature scheme. Finally, we demonstrate how our scheme yields a group signature scheme with verifier-local revocation.

Keywords: Group signatures, pairings, group signature security definition.

1 Introduction

Group signatures, introduced in 1991 by Chaum and van Heyst [18], allow members of a group to anonymously sign messages on behalf of the whole group. For example, they allow an employee of a company to sign a document in such a way that the verifier only learns that it was signed by an employee, but not by which employee. Group membership is controlled by a *Group Manager*, who can add users (called *Group Members*) to the group. In addition, there is an *Opener* who can reveal the identity of signers in the case of disputes. In some schemes, such as the one we propose, the tasks of adding members and revoking anonymity are combined into a single role. In the systems proposed in [3,15,33], group membership can be selectively revoked, i.e., without affecting the signing ability of the remaining members.

J.A. Garay and R. De Prisco (Eds.): SCN 2010, LNCS 6280, pp. 381–398, 2010.

Security notions. Since 1991 a number of security properties have been developed for group signatures including unforgeability, anonymity, traceability, unlinkability, and non-frameability. In 2003 Bellare, Micciancio, and Warinschi [4] developed what is now considered the standard security model for group signatures. They propose two security properties for static groups called *full anonymity* and *full traceability* and show that these capture the previous security requirements of unforgeability, anonymity, traceability, and unlinkability. Bellare, Shi, and Zhang [7] extended the notions of [4] to dynamic groups and added the notion of *non-frameability* (or exculpability), by which the Group Manager and Opener together cannot produce a signature that can be falsely attributed to an honest Group Member.

Boneh and Shacham [10] proposed a relaxed anonymity notion called *selfless anonymity* where signers can trace their own signatures, but not those of others. This weakening, however, leads to the following feature: if a group member signed a message but forgot that she signed it, then she can recover this information from the signature itself. Other schemes [9,11,12] weaken the anonymity notion by disallowing opening oracle queries, providing only so-called CPA-anonymity. This is a much more serious limitation: in practice it means that all security guarantees are lost as soon as a single signature is opened, thereby rendering the opening functionality virtually useless. As we've witnessed for the case of encryption [8], CCA2-security is what can make it into practice.

In this work, we consider a hybrid between the models of [7] and [10] that combines the dynamic group setting and the non-frameability notion of [7] with the selfless anonymity notion and the combined roles of Group Manager and Opener of [10]. We stress however that we prove security under the practically relevant CCA2-anonymity notion, rather than the much weaker CPA-anonymity notion. Yet still, our scheme compares favourably with all known schemes that offer just CPA-anonymity.

Construction paradigms. Many initial group signature schemes were based on the Strong-RSA assumption [2,3,15]. In recent years the focus has shifted to schemes based on bilinear maps [9,10,16,25,32], which are the most efficient group signatures known today, both in terms of bandwidth and computational efficiency.

Most existing group signature schemes follow the construction paradigm where a group signature consists of an anonymous signature, an encryption of the signer's identity under the Opener's public key, and a non-interactive zero-knowledge (NIZK) proof that the identity contained in the encryption is indeed that of the signer. While very useful as an insight, this construction paradigm seems to stand in the way of more efficient schemes. In this paper, we depart from the common paradigm and construct a group signature scheme that consists solely of an anonymous signature scheme and a NIZK proof, removing the need to encrypt the identity of the signer. We thereby obtain the most efficient group signature scheme currently known, both in terms of bandwidth and computational resources (see Section 6).

It is surprising that we can do without a separate encryption scheme, given that group signatures as per [4] are known to imply encryption [1]. This implication however does not hold for group signatures with selfless anonymity, giving us the necessary slack to construct more efficient schemes while maintaining a practically relevant security level.

Our scheme. In our construction each Group Member gets a Camenisch-Lysyanskaya (CL) [16] signature on a random message as a secret key. To produce a group signature, the Group Member re-randomizes this signature and produces a NIZK proof that she knows the message underlying the signature. The novel feature is that the Opener (alias Group Manager) can use information collected during the joining phase to test which user created the signature, without the need for a separate encryption.[1] A disadvantage is that opening thereby becomes a linear operation in the number of Group Members. Since opening signatures is a rather exceptional operation and is performed by the Group Manager who probably has both the resources and the commercial interest to expose traitors, we think that this is a reasonable price to pay.

CL signatures and NIZK proofs have been combined before to produce "group-like" signatures, most notably in the construction of pairing-based DAA schemes [13,20,21]. DAA schemes are not genuine group signatures, however, as there is no notion of an Opener.

Finally, we note that from a certain class of group signature schemes as per our definitions (that includes our scheme), one can build a group signature scheme with verifier-local revocation (VLR) [10]. Such a scheme allows verifiers to check whether a signature was placed by a revoked group member by matching it against a public revocation list. The converse is not true, i.e., a VLR scheme does not automatically yield a group signature as per our definitions, as it does not provide a way to open individual signatures (rather than revoking all signatures by one signer). We refer to Section 3.2 for details.

2 Preliminaries

Notation. If S is a set, we denote the act of sampling from S uniformly at random and assigning the result to the variable x by $x \leftarrow S$. If S consists of a single element $\{s\}$, we abbreviate this to $x \leftarrow s$. We let $\{0,1\}^*$ and $\{0,1\}^t$ denote the set of binary strings of arbitrary length and length t respectively, and let ε denote the empty string. If A is an algorithm, we denote the action of obtaining x by invoking A on inputs $y_1, \ldots, y_n$ by $x \leftarrow A(y_1, \ldots, y_n)$, where the probability distribution on x is determined by the internal coin tosses of A. We denote an interactive protocol P as $P = (P_0, P_1)$. Executing the protocol on input in_0 and in_1, resulting in the respective output out_0 and out_1, we write as $\langle out_0; out_1 \rangle \leftarrow \langle P_0(in_0); P_1(in_1) \rangle$. If $\mathbf{arr}$ is an array or list we let $\mathbf{arr}[i]$ denote the ith element in the array/list.

Digital Signature Scheme. We will use a digital signature scheme consisting of three algorithms, namely a key generation algorithm DSKeyGen, a signing algorithm DSSign, and a signature verification algorithm DSVerify. In our setting the key generation will be executed between a user and a certification authority (CA). It might be an interactive algorithm leading to the user getting a secret key sk and the CA as well as the user get

[1] If the random messages were known to the Group Manager, he could open group signatures simply by verifying the re-randomized signatures against the issued random messages. To achieve non-frameability, however, the random message is only known to the Group Member, so opening in our scheme is slightly more involved.

the public key pk corresponding to the secret key. The signing algorithm accepts a secret key sk and a message m as input and returns a signature $\bar{\sigma} \leftarrow \mathsf{DSSign}(sk, m)$. The signature is constructed such that the verification algorithm upon input a message m', a public key pk, and a signature $\bar{\sigma}$ returns $\mathsf{DSVerify}(pk, m', \bar{\sigma})$, which is true if both $m' \equiv m$, and sk corresponds to pk and false otherwise. The signature scheme must satisfy the notion of unforgeability under chosen-message attacks [28].

Number-Theoretic Background. Our construction will make extensive use of asymmetric pairings on elliptic curves. In particular we will use the following notation, for a given security parameter η,

- $\mathbb{G}_1$, $\mathbb{G}_2$ and $\mathbb{G}_T$ are cyclic groups of prime order $q = \Theta(2^\eta)$.
- We write the group operations multiplicatively, and elements in $\mathbb{G}_1$ will generally be denoted by lower case letters, elements in $\mathbb{G}_2$ by lower case letters with a "tilde" on them, and elements in $\mathbb{Z}_q$ by lower case Greek letters.
- We fix a generator g (resp. $\tilde{g}$) of $\mathbb{G}_1$ (resp. $\mathbb{G}_2$).
- There is a computable map $\hat{e} : \mathbb{G}_1 \times \mathbb{G}_2 \to \mathbb{G}_T$ with the following properties:
  - For all $x \in \mathbb{G}_1$, $\tilde{y} \in \mathbb{G}_2$ and $\alpha, \beta \in \mathbb{Z}_q$ we have $\hat{e}(x^\alpha, \tilde{y}^\beta) = \hat{e}(x, \tilde{y})^{\alpha\beta}$.
  - $\hat{e}(g, \tilde{g}) \neq 1$.

Following [27] we call a pairing of Type-1 if $\mathbb{G}_1 = \mathbb{G}_2$, of Type-2 if $\mathbb{G}_1 \neq \mathbb{G}_2$ and there exists a computable homomorphism $\psi : \mathbb{G}_2 \to \mathbb{G}_1$, and of Type-3 if $\mathbb{G}_1 \neq \mathbb{G}_2$ and no such homomorphism exists. In addition, in [19,31] a further Type-4 pairing is introduced in which $\mathbb{G}_2$ is a group of order q^2, namely the product of $\mathbb{G}_1$ with the $\mathbb{G}_2$ used in the Type-3 pairing setting. In practice Type-3 pairings offer the most efficient implementation choices, in terms of both bandwidth and computational efficiency.

Associated to pairings are the following computational assumptions, which we shall refer to throughout this paper:

Assumption 1 (LRSW). *With the notation above we let $\tilde{x}, \tilde{y} \in \mathbb{G}_2$, with $\tilde{x} = \tilde{g}^\alpha$, $\tilde{y} = \tilde{g}^\beta$. Let $O_{\tilde{x},\tilde{y}}(\cdot)$ be an oracle that, on input of a value $\mu \in \mathbb{Z}_q$, outputs a triple $A = (a, a^\beta, a^{\alpha+\mu\alpha\beta}) \in \mathbb{G}_1^3$ for a randomly chosen $a \in \mathbb{G}_1$. Then for all probabilistic polynomial time adversaries $\mathcal{A}$, the quantity $\nu(\eta)$, defined as follows, is a negligible function:*

$$\nu(\eta) := \Pr[\alpha \leftarrow \mathbb{Z}_q; \beta \leftarrow \mathbb{Z}_q; \tilde{x} \leftarrow \tilde{g}^\alpha; \tilde{y} \leftarrow \tilde{g}^\beta; (\mu, a, b, c) \leftarrow \mathcal{A}^{O_{\tilde{x},\tilde{y}}(\cdot)}(\tilde{x}, \tilde{y}) : \\ \mu \notin Q \wedge a \in \mathbb{G}_1 \wedge b = a^\beta \wedge c = a^{\alpha+\mu\alpha\beta}]$$

where Q is the set of queries passed by $\mathcal{A}$ to its oracle $O_{\tilde{x},\tilde{y}}(\cdot)$.

This assumption was introduced by Lysyanskaya et al. [29], in the case $\mathbb{G} = \mathbb{G}_1 = \mathbb{G}_2$ for groups that are not known to admit an efficient bilinear map. The authors showed in the same paper, that this assumption holds for generic groups, and is independent of the decisional Diffie-Hellman (DDH) assumption. However, it is always applied in protocols for which the groups admit a pairing, and the above asymmetric version is the version that we will require.

Assumption 2 (XDDH; SXDH). *We say XDDH to hold in the pairing groups if DDH is hard in* $\mathbb{G}_1$*, i.e., if given a tuple* $(g, g^{\mu}, g^{\nu}, g^{\omega})$ *for* $\mu, \nu \leftarrow \mathbb{Z}_q$ *it is hard to decide whether* $\omega = \mu\nu \mod q$ *or random. We say SXDH holds if DDH is hard in both* $\mathbb{G}_1$ *and* $\mathbb{G}_2$.

Note that neither XDDH nor SXDH hold in the case of Type-1 pairings. For the others types of pairings XDDH is believed to hold, and only for Type-3 pairings SXDH is believed to hold.

To demonstrate the non-frameability of our scheme we require an additional assumption, which we call the symmetric Discrete Logarithm Assumption (SDLP).

Assumption 3 (SDLP). *Given the tuple* $(g^{\mu}, \tilde{g}^{\mu}) \in \mathbb{G}_1 \times \mathbb{G}_2$ *computing* μ *is a hard problem.*

This is a non-standard assumption which, however, implicitly underlies many asymmetric pairing versions of protocols in the literature that are described in the symmetric pairing setting only. Note that the input to the SDLP problem can always be checked to be a valid input, as given $(h, \tilde{h})$ one can always check whether $\hat{e}(g, \tilde{h}) = \hat{e}(h, \tilde{g})$.

CL Signatures. Our group signature scheme is based on the pairing-based Camenisch-Lysyanskaya (CL) signature scheme [16] (Scheme A in their paper), which is provably secure under the LRSW assumption. The scheme assumes three cyclic groups $\mathbb{G}_1$, $\mathbb{G}_2$, and $\mathbb{G}_T$ of prime order $q = \Theta(2^{\eta})$, with a pairing $\hat{e} : \mathbb{G}_1 \times \mathbb{G}_2 \rightarrow \mathbb{G}_T$, and two generators $g \in G_1$ and $\tilde{g} \in \mathbb{G}_2$.

The secret key of the CL signature scheme consists of $\alpha, \beta \leftarrow \mathbb{Z}_q$ and the public key is defined as $(\tilde{x}, \tilde{y}) \leftarrow (\tilde{g}^{\alpha}, \tilde{g}^{\beta}) \in \mathbb{G}_2^2$. Computing a signature $s \in \mathbb{G}_1^3$ on a message $m \in \mathbb{Z}_q$ is done by choosing $a \leftarrow \mathbb{G}_1$, calculating $b \leftarrow a^{\beta}$ and $c \leftarrow a^{\alpha+m\alpha\beta}$, and setting $s \leftarrow (a, b, c)$. Finally, a tuple $(a, b, c) \in \mathbb{G}_1^3$ is a valid signature on a message $m \in \mathbb{Z}_q$ if both $\hat{e}(a, \tilde{x}) = \hat{e}(b, \tilde{g})$ and $\hat{e}(a, \tilde{x}) \cdot \hat{e}(b, \tilde{x})^m = \hat{e}(c, \tilde{g})$ hold.

Theorem 1 ([16]). *The CL signature scheme A is existentially unforgeable against adaptive chosen message attacks [28] under the LRSW assumption.*

CL signatures are re-randomizable, i.e., given a valid signature $(a, b, c) \in \mathbb{G}_1^3$ on a message m, the signature $(a^r, b^r, c^r) \in \mathbb{G}_1^3$ will also be valid for any $r \in \mathbb{Z}_q^*$. This re-randomization property is central to our new group signature scheme.

Sigma Protocols. We will use a number of protocols to prove knowledge of discrete logarithms (and, more generally, of pre-images of group homomorphisms) and properties about them. This section recaps some basic facts about such protocols and the notation we will use.

Let $\phi : \mathbb{H}_1 \rightarrow \mathbb{H}_2$ be a group homomorphism with $\mathbb{H}_1$ and $\mathbb{H}_2$ being two groups of order q and let $y \in \mathbb{H}_2$. We will use additive notation for $\mathbb{H}_1$ and multiplicative notation for $\mathbb{H}_2$. By $PK\{(x) : y = \phi(x)\}$ we denote the Σ-protocol for a zero-knowledge proof of knowledge of x such that $y = \phi(x)$ [14,17]. Σ-protocols for group homomorphisms are three-move protocols where the prover chooses $\mathsf{rnd} \leftarrow \mathbb{H}_1$ and sends $\mathsf{Comm} \leftarrow \phi(\mathsf{rnd})$ to the verifier; the verifier sends back a random $\mathsf{Cha} \leftarrow \mathbb{H}_1$; the prover then sends $\mathsf{Rsp} = \mathsf{rnd} - \mathsf{Cha} \cdot x$; and the verifier checks that $\phi(\mathsf{Rsp})\phi(x)^{\mathsf{Cha}} = \mathsf{Comm}$.

It is well-known that basic Σ-protocols for group homomorphisms are honest-verifier zero-knowledge proofs of knowledge of the pre-image of the group homomorphism. There is a number of different ways to turn any honest-verifier Σ-protocol into a protocol that is full zero-knowledge with perfect simulation and negligible soundness error (e.g., [22,24]). We denote the full zero-knowledge variant of a Σ-protocol $PK\{\ldots\}$ as $FPK\{\ldots\}$.

The well-known Schnorr identification protocol is the special case $PK\{(x) : y = g^x\}$, i.e., $\phi(x) = g^x$ where g is a generator of a subgroup of order q of $\mathbb{Z}_p$. Let $\phi_1 : \mathbb{H}_1 \rightarrow \mathbb{H}_2$ and $\phi_2 : \mathbb{H}_1 \rightarrow \mathbb{H}_2$. We often write $y_1 = \phi_1(x_1) \wedge y_2 = \phi_2(x_2)$ to denote $\phi(x_1, x_2) := (\phi_1(x_1), \phi_2(x_2))$ or $y_1 = \phi_1(x) \wedge y_2 = \phi_2(x)$ to denote $\phi(x) := (\phi_1(x), \phi_2(x))$.

The "signature" variant of a Σ-protocol is obtained by applying the Fiat-Shamir heuristic [26] to the above Σ-protocol. We denote such a "signature-proof-of-knowledge" on a message $m \in \{0,1\}^*$ by, $SPK\{(x) : y = \phi(x)\}(m)$. That is, when we say that $\Sigma \leftarrow SPK\{(x) : y = \phi(x)\}(m)$ is computed, we mean that a random $\mathsf{rnd} \leftarrow \mathbb{H}_1$ is chosen and the pair $\Sigma \leftarrow (\mathsf{Cha}, \mathsf{Rsp})$ is computed where $\mathsf{Cha} \leftarrow \mathcal{H}(\phi\|y\|\phi(\mathsf{rnd})\|m)$, $\mathsf{Rsp} \leftarrow \mathsf{rnd} - \mathsf{Cha} \cdot x$ and $\mathcal{H} : \{0,1\}^* \rightarrow \mathbb{Z}_q$ is a suitable hash function. Note that $\Sigma \in \mathbb{Z}_q \times \mathbb{H}_1$. We say that $\Sigma = (\mathsf{Cha}, \mathsf{Rsp})$ is valid with respect to y and ϕ if $\mathsf{Cha} = \mathcal{H}(\phi\|y\|y^{\mathsf{Cha}}\phi(\mathsf{Rsp})\|m)$ holds; typically y and ϕ will be clear from the context and we will just say that "Σ is valid." We further note that a unique specification of the statement (e.g., $(x) : y = \phi(x)$) that SPK "proves" needs to be included as an argument to the hash function, i.e., here $\phi\|y$, where ϕ stands for the description of the whole algebraic setting. In the random oracle model [6], one can use the forking lemma [30,5] to extract the secrets from these SPKs if correct care is taken that the prover can indeed be efficiently rewound. Moreover, in the random oracle model one can simulate SPKs for unknown secrets by choosing $\mathsf{Cha}, \mathsf{Rsp} \leftarrow \mathbb{Z}_q$ at random and programming the random oracle so that $\mathcal{H}(\phi\|y\|y^{\mathsf{Cha}}\phi(\mathsf{Rsp})\|m) = \mathsf{Cha}$.

3 Definitions

As mentioned in the Introduction, we propose a notion that builds a hybrid between [7] and [10]. Consequently, our definitions describe a dynamic group signature scheme with a combined role of Group Manager and Opener that obtains selfless anonymity, traceability, and non-frameability.

3.1 Syntax

A group signature scheme consists of a set of users with a unique index i who can produce signatures on behalf of the group. Initially users must interact with a trusted party to establish a public key pair. Users can become Group Members via an interaction with the Group Manager. After the interaction the user obtains a secret signing key that she can use to produce signatures on behalf of the group. The Group Manager obtains a piece of information that he can later use to identify signatures created by the user. In addition, both parties obtain some piece of publicly available information, which certifies the fact that the particular user has joined the group.

As remarked earlier, in our models we put more trust in the Group Manager by requiring that he is also in charge of opening signatures. The syntax that we require is as follows.

Definition 1. *A group signature scheme* GS *extended by a PKI is given by a tuple*

$$(\mathsf{GSetup}, \mathsf{PKIJoin}, (\mathsf{GJoin}_U, \mathsf{GJoin}_M), \mathsf{GSign}, \mathsf{GVerify}, \mathsf{GOpen}, \mathsf{GJudge})$$

where:

1. GSetup *is a setup algorithm. It takes as input a security parameter* 1^η *and produces a tuple* $(gpk, gmsk)$*, where* gpk *is a group public key and* $gmsk$ *is the Group Manager's secret key. To simplify notation we assume that* $gmsk$ *always includes the group public key. Note that the group public key contains system parameters, which need to be checked by all entities not involved in there generation.*
2. PKIJoin *is an algorithm executed by a user to register with a certification authority (CA). It takes as input the index of the user* i *and the security parameter* 1^η*. The output of the protocol is the key pair* $(\mathbf{usk}[i], \mathbf{upk}[i])$ *consisting of user secret key and user public key or* $\perp$ *in case of a failure. The user public key* $\mathbf{upk}[i]$ *is sent to the CA, who makes it available such that anyone can get an authentic copy of it.*
3. GJoin $=$ $(\mathsf{GJoin}_M, \mathsf{GJoin}_U)$ *is a two-party interactive protocol used to add new users to the group. The input for the user is* $(i, \mathbf{usk}[i], gpk)$*, i.e., the index of the user, the user secret key, and the group public key. The input for the Group Manager is* $(i, \mathbf{upk}[i], gmsk)$*, i.e., the user index, the user public key, and the Group Manager's secret key.*

   As a result of the interaction, the user obtains her group signing key $\mathbf{gsk}[i]$*, and the Group Manager obtains some registration information* $\mathbf{reg}[i]$ *(which will later be used to trace signatures of* i*). If the protocol fails, the output of both parties is set to* $\perp$*.*
4. GSign *is the algorithm users employ to sign on behalf of the group. It takes as input an individual user signing key* $\mathbf{gsk}[i]$ *and the message* $m \in \{0,1\}^*$ *to be signed, and outputs a signature* σ*. We write* $\sigma \leftarrow \mathsf{GSign}(\mathbf{gsk}[i], m)$ *for the process of obtaining signature* σ *on* m *with secret key* $\mathbf{gsk}[i]$*.*
5. GVerify *is the signature verification algorithm. It takes as input* (gpk, m, σ)*, i.e., the group public key, a message and a group signature, and returns* 0 *if the signature is deemed invalid and* 1 *otherwise.*
6. GOpen *is the algorithm for opening signatures. It takes as input* $(gmsk, m, \sigma, \mathbf{reg})$*, i.e., the Group Manager's secret key, a message, a valid group signature on the message, and the registration information table* $\mathbf{reg}$*, and returns a user index* $i \in [n]$ *and a proof* π *that user* i *produced signature* σ*, or it returns* $\perp$*, indicating that opening did not succeed.*

   We assume that the opening algorithm, before outputting (i, π)*, always checks that the user* i *is registered, i.e., that* $\mathbf{reg}[i] \neq \perp$*, and that the proof* π *passes the judging algorithm (see the next item). If either of these checks fails, the opening algorithm outputs* $\perp$*.*
7. GJudge *is the judging algorithm. It takes as input a message* m*, a group signature* σ *on* m*, the group public key* gpk*, a user index* i*, the user public key* $\mathbf{upk}[i]$*, and a*

proof π *and outputs* 1 *or* 0*, expressing whether the proof shows that user* i *created signature* σ *or not.*

We assume that the judging algorithm verifies the signature using the GVerify *algorithm on input* gpk, m, *and* σ.

3.2 Security Notions

In this section we give the security definitions that we require from group signature schemes. We describe the oracles that are involved in our definitions, as well as the restrictions that we put on their uses. These oracles use some shared global state of the experiments in which they are provided to the adversary. In particular, at the time of their use, the sets of honest and corrupt users are defined. Also the oracles have access to the global information contained in $\mathbf{upk}$. For honest users the oracles have access to $\mathbf{gsk}$ and if the Group Manager is uncorrupted they also have access to $\mathbf{reg}$. We assume that at the beginning of the execution, the content of each entry in these arrays is set to $\perp$ (uninitialized).

We consider a setting with n users divided (statically) into sets $\mathcal{HU}$ and $\mathcal{DU}$ of honest and dishonest users, respectively. Even though our definitions appear to consider static corruptions only, one can easily see (by taking an upper bound on the number of users for n and guessing the indices of "target" users upfront) that they actually imply security in the dynamic case. However, the latter comes at the cost of losing a factor n in reduction tightness for traceability and non-frameability, and of $n^2/2$ for anonymity. For some notions the adversary $\mathcal{A}$ is actually a pair of algorithms $(\mathcal{A}_0, \mathcal{A}_1)$; we implicitly assume that $\mathcal{A}_0$ can pass state information to $\mathcal{A}_1$. Our security notions make use of the following oracles:

- $\mathsf{Ch}(b, \cdot, \cdot, \cdot)$ is the challenge oracle for defining anonymity. It accepts as input a triple formed from two identities $i_0, i_1 \in \mathcal{HU}$ and a message m, and returns a signature $\sigma^* \leftarrow \mathsf{GSign}(\mathbf{gsk}[i_b], m)$ under the signing key of user i_b, where b is a parameter of the experiment. This oracle can only be called once.
- $\mathsf{SetUPK}(\cdot, \cdot)$ takes an input the index of a user $i \in \mathcal{DU}$ and a value upk. If $\mathbf{reg}[i] \equiv \perp$ it sets the user's public key $\mathbf{upk}[i] \leftarrow upk$. The oracle can only be called before user i joins the group.
- $\mathsf{GJoin}_{UD}(\cdot)$ is an oracle that takes as input an honest user index $i \in \mathcal{HU}$ and executes the user side of the join protocol for i, i.e., $\mathsf{GJoin}_U(i, \mathbf{usk}[i], gpk)$. The local output of the protocol is stored in $\mathbf{gsk}[i]$. This oracle can be used by an adversary to execute the registration protocol with an honest user, the adversary playing the role of the Group Manager (when the latter is corrupt).
- $\mathsf{GJoin}_{DM}(\cdot)$ is an oracle that takes as input the index of a corrupt user $i \in \mathcal{DU}$ and simulates the execution of the join protocol for the (honest) Group Manager, i.e., $\mathsf{GJoin}_M(i, \mathbf{upk}[i], gmsk)$. The local output of the protocol is stored in $\mathbf{reg}[i]$. This oracle can be used by an adversary to execute the registration protocol with the (honest) Group Manager on behalf of any corrupt user.
- $\mathsf{GSign}(\cdot, \cdot)$ accepts as input pairs $(i, m) \in \mathcal{HU} \times \{0,1\}^*$ and obtains a signature on m under $\mathbf{gsk}[i]$ if the user is not corrupt, and its signing key is defined.

– $\mathsf{GOpen}(\cdot,\cdot)$ accepts as input a message-signature pair (m,σ) and returns the result of the function call $\mathsf{GOpen}(gmsk, m, \sigma, \mathbf{reg})$. The oracle refuses to open the signature attained through a call to the Ch oracle, i.e., $\sigma \equiv \sigma^*$.

Note that, depending on the precise group signature scheme, the oracles $\mathsf{GJoin}_{UD}(\cdot)$ and $\mathsf{GJoin}_{DM}(\cdot)$ may require multi-stages, i.e., interaction between the oracle and the adversary to complete the functionality. If this is the case we assume that these stages are executed by the adversary in a sequential order, as if the oracles are a single stage. Thus, we do not allow the adversary to interleave separate executions of the GJoin protocol, or execute multiple of them in parallel.

Correctness. We define the correctness of a group signature scheme GS through a game in which an adversary is allowed to requests a signature on some message by any of the honest players. The adversary wins if either (1) the resulting signature does not pass the verification test, (2) the signature is opened as if it were produced by a different user, or (3) the proof produced by opening the signature does not pass the judging algorithm. The experiment is detailed in Figure 1. We say that GS is correct if for any adversary $\Pr[\mathbf{Exp}^{\mathrm{corr}}_{\mathsf{GS},A}(\eta) = 1]$ is 0.

Anonymity. *Anonymity* requires that group signatures do not reveal the identity of the signer. In the experiment that we consider, the adversary controls all of the dishonest users. The adversary has access to a challenge oracle $\mathsf{Ch}(b,\cdot,\cdot,\cdot)$, which he can call only once with a triple (i_0, i_1, m), where i_0 and i_1 are the indices of two honest signers, and m is some arbitrary message. The answer of the oracle is a challenge signature $\sigma^* \leftarrow \mathsf{GSign}(\mathbf{gsk}[i_b], m)$. During the attack the adversary can (1) add corrupt users to the group of signers (via the $\mathsf{SetUPK}(\cdot,\cdot)$ and $\mathsf{GJoin}_M(\cdot)$ oracles), (2) require signatures of honest users on arbitrary messages via the GSign oracle, and (3) require opening of arbitrary signatures (except the signature σ^* obtained from the challenge oracle) via the GOpen oracle. The experiment is described in Figure 1. For any adversary that obeys the restrictions described above we define its advantage in breaking the anonymity of GS by

$$\mathbf{Adv}^{\mathrm{anon}}_{\mathsf{GS},A}(\eta) = \Pr[\mathbf{Exp}^{\mathrm{anon}\text{-}1}_{\mathsf{GS},A}(\eta) = 1] - \Pr[\mathbf{Exp}^{\mathrm{anon}\text{-}0}_{\mathsf{GS},A}(\eta) = 1]$$

We say that the scheme GS satisfies the anonymity property if for any probabilistic polynomial-time adversary, its advantage is a negligible function of η.

Traceability. Informally, *traceability* requires that no adversary can create a valid signature that cannot be traced to some user that had already been registered. We model the strong but realistic setting where all of the signers are corrupt and work against the group manager. In the game that we define, the adversary can add new signers using access to the GJoin_{DM} oracle and can request to reveal the signers of arbitrary signatures via the GOpen oracle. The goal of the adversary is to produce a valid message-signature pair (m,σ) that cannot be opened, i.e., such that the opening algorithm outputs $\perp$. For any adversary A we define its advantage in breaking traceability of group signature scheme GS by:

$$\mathbf{Adv}^{\mathrm{trace}}_{\mathsf{GS},A}(\eta) = \Pr[\mathbf{Exp}^{\mathrm{trace}}_{\mathsf{GS},A}(\eta) = 1]$$

We say that GS is traceable if for any probabilistic polynomial-time adversary, its advantage is a negligible function of the security parameter.

$\mathbf{Exp}^{\mathrm{corr}}_{\mathsf{GS},\mathcal{A}}(\eta)$
$\mathcal{HU} \leftarrow \{1,\ldots,n\}$; $\mathcal{DU} \leftarrow \emptyset$
$(gpk, gmsk) \leftarrow \mathsf{GSetup}(1^\eta)$
For $i \in \mathcal{HU}$
$(\mathbf{usk}[i], \mathbf{upk}[i]) \leftarrow \mathsf{PKIJoin}(i, 1^\eta)$
$\langle \mathbf{reg}[i]; \mathbf{gsk}[i] \rangle \leftarrow \langle \mathsf{GJoin}_M(i, \mathbf{upk}[i], gmsk); \mathsf{GJoin}_U(i, \mathbf{usk}[i], gpk) \rangle$
$(i, m) \leftarrow \mathcal{A}^{\mathsf{GSign}(\cdot,\cdot),\mathsf{GOpen}(\cdot,\cdot)}(gpk)$
If $i \notin \mathcal{HU}$ then return 0
$\sigma \leftarrow \mathsf{GSign}(\mathbf{gsk}[i], m)$
If $\mathsf{GVerify}(gpk, m, \sigma) = 0$ then return 1
$(j, \pi) \leftarrow \mathsf{GOpen}(gmsk, m, \sigma, \mathbf{reg})$
If $i \neq j$ or $\mathsf{GJudge}(m, \sigma, gpk, i, \mathbf{upk}[i], \pi) = 0$ then return 1
Return 0

$\mathbf{Exp}^{\mathrm{anon}\text{-}b}_{\mathsf{GS},\mathcal{A}}(\eta)$
$\mathcal{DU} \leftarrow \mathcal{A}_0(1^\eta)$
$\mathcal{HU} \leftarrow \{1,\ldots,n\} \setminus \mathcal{DU}$
$(gpk, gmsk) \leftarrow \mathsf{GSetup}(1^\eta)$
For $i \in \mathcal{HU}$
$(\mathbf{usk}[i], \mathbf{upk}[i]) \leftarrow \mathsf{PKIJoin}(i, 1^\eta)$
$\langle \mathbf{reg}[i]; \mathbf{gsk}[i] \rangle \leftarrow \langle \mathsf{GJoin}_M(i, \mathbf{upk}[i], gmsk); \mathsf{GJoin}_U(i, \mathbf{usk}[i], gpk) \rangle$
$b' \leftarrow \mathcal{A}_1^{\mathsf{Ch}(b,\cdot,\cdot,\cdot),\mathsf{SetUPK}(\cdot,\cdot),\mathsf{GJoin}_{DM}(\cdot),\mathsf{GSign}(\cdot,\cdot),\mathsf{GOpen}(\cdot,\cdot)}(gpk)$
Return b'

$\mathbf{Exp}^{\mathrm{trace}}_{\mathsf{GS},\mathcal{A}}(\eta)$
$\mathcal{DU} \leftarrow \{1,\ldots,n\}$; $\mathcal{HU} \leftarrow \emptyset$
$(gpk, gmsk) \leftarrow \mathsf{GSetup}(1^\eta)$
$(m, \sigma) \leftarrow \mathcal{A}^{\mathsf{SetUPK}(\cdot,\cdot),\mathsf{GJoin}_{DM}(\cdot),\mathsf{GOpen}(\cdot,\cdot)}(gpk)$
If $\mathsf{GVerify}(gpk, m, \sigma) = 1$ and $\mathsf{GOpen}(gmsk, m, \sigma, \mathbf{reg}) = \perp$ then return 1
Else return 0

$\mathbf{Exp}^{\mathrm{nf}}_{\mathsf{GS},\mathcal{A}}(\eta)$
$(\mathcal{DU}, gpk) \leftarrow \mathcal{A}_0(1^\eta)$
$\mathcal{HU} \leftarrow \{1,\ldots,n\} \setminus \mathcal{DU}$
For $i \in \mathcal{HU}$
$(\mathbf{usk}[i], \mathbf{upk}[i]) \leftarrow \mathsf{PKIJoin}(i, 1^\eta)$
$(i, m, \sigma, \pi) \leftarrow \mathcal{A}_1^{\mathsf{SetUPK}(\cdot,\cdot),\mathsf{GJoin}_{UD}(\cdot),\mathsf{GSign}(\cdot,\cdot)}(1^\eta)$
If $i \notin \mathcal{HU}$ or $\mathsf{GVerify}(gpk, m, \sigma) = 0$ then return 0
If σ was oracle output of $\mathsf{GSign}(i, m)$ then return 0
If $\mathsf{GJudge}(m, \sigma, gpk, i, \mathbf{upk}[i], \pi) = 0$ then return 1
Return 0

Fig. 1. Experiments for defining the correctness and security of a group signature scheme. The particular restrictions on the uses of the oracles are described in Section 3.2.

Non-Frameability. Informally, *non-frameability* requires that even a cheating Group Manager cannot falsely accuse an honest user of having created a given signature. We model this property through a game that closely resembles that for traceability. The difference is that the adversary has the Group Manager's secret key (who is corrupt). During his attack the adversary can require honest users to join the group via the oracle GJoin_{UD}, and can obtain signatures of honest users through oracle GSign. The goal of the adversary is to produce a signature and a proof that this signature was created by an honest user (who did not actually create the signature). For any adversary A we define its advantage against non-frameability of group signature scheme GS by

$$\mathbf{Adv}^{\mathrm{nf}}_{\mathsf{GS},A}(\eta) = \Pr[\mathbf{Exp}^{\mathrm{nf}}_{\mathsf{GS},A}(\eta) = 1]$$

We say that scheme GS is non-frameable if for any probabilistic polynomial-time adversary, its advantage is a negligible function of η.

Remarks. The security definitions that we present depart from the more established ones in several ways that we describe and justify now. First, we repeat that even though our definitions appear to consider static corruptions only, they imply security in a dynamic setting.

Second, we borrow the *selfless anonymity* notion from [10] that departs from the one of [4] in that it does not allow the adversary access to the signing keys of the two signers involved in the query to the challenge oracle. Thus, we cannot grant the adversary access to the secret information of any honest user. This is a natural, mild restriction which, as discussed in the introduction, may lead to significantly more efficient schemes.

Third, our notion of traceability seems different than the notion of traceability of [4]. Indeed, according to our definition an attacker that creates a signature that opens as some honest identity is not considered an attack! We look at this scenario as a framing attack, however, and it is therefore covered under our non-frameability notion, a notion that was not modeled in [4].

Fourth, a detailed comparison of our security notion with the notion of [7] reveals that we do not provide a read and write oracle for the registration table $\mathbf{reg}$. This follows from the fact that we combine the Group Manager with the opening authority. Thereby, the entities cannot be corrupted individually, thus, the adversary has either full access (i.e., when the Group Manager is corrupted) or he does have no access.

Group Signatures with Verifier-Local Revocation. Let us discuss the relation of our scheme and definition with the group signature scheme with verifier-local revocation by Boneh and Shacham [10]. They define a group signature scheme with verifier-local revocation (VLR) as a scheme that has the additional feature of a revocation list. Essentially, VLR-verification of a group signature contains, in addition to the signature verification as described before, a check for each item in the revocation list whether or not it relates to the group signature at hand. If it does, then the signature is deemed invalid.

The scheme and definitions of Boneh and Shacham (1) do not have an open (or tracing) procedure and (2) assume that the group manager is fully trusted. The latter makes sense because if there is no open procedure, it is not possible to falsely blame a user for having produced a specific group signature. However, Boneh and Shacham point out that any VLR scheme has an implicit opening algorithm: one can make a revocation list consisting of only a single user and then run the VLR group signature verification algorithm. Thus, the verification fails only in the case where the user who generated the signature is (the only) entity in the revocation list, which leads to her identification. This shows that we can convert a VLR-scheme into a group signature scheme with an Opener, however, we stress that the obtained scheme does not satisfy non-frameability.

We now point out that the opposite direction also works: for a sub-class of group signature schemes according to our definition one can construct a group signature scheme with verifier local revocation. The subclass is the schemes for which the GOpen algorithm takes as input $(gpk, m, \sigma, \mathbf{reg})$ instead of $(gmsk, m, \sigma, \mathbf{reg})$ as per our definition (i.e., it does not need to make use of the group manager's secret key). We note that the scheme we propose in this paper falls into this sub-class. Now, the idea for obtaining a VLR group signature scheme is as follows. The new key generation consists of the GSetup, PKIJoin, and $(\mathsf{GJoin}_U, \mathsf{GJoin}_M)$ where the group manager runs the users' parts as well and then just hands them their keys. The VLR group signing algorithm is essentially GSign. To revoke user i, the group manager adds $\mathbf{reg}[i]$ to the revocation list. Finally, the VLR-verification consist of GVerify and GOpen, i.e., it accepts a signature if GVerify accepts and if GOpen fails for all entries $\mathbf{reg}[i]$ in the revocation list. The security notions for VLR group signatures, namely selfless anonymity and traceability, follow from our notions of anonymity and traceability for group signatures. We do not give the precise formulation, but we note that a security model for VLR dynamic group signatures follows by combining our dynamic security model above, with the static VLR model from [10]. We also note that VLR group signatures do not provide forward-anonymity: a new revocation list can also be used on old signatures.

4 Our Group Signature Scheme

Overview of Our Scheme. Our group signature scheme is based on two special properties of CL signatures, namely on their re-randomizability and on the fact that the signature "does not leak" the message that it authenticates. Intuitively, a user's group signing key is a CL signature on a random message ξ that only the user knows. To create a group signature for a message m, the user re-randomizes the CL signature and attaches a signature proof of knowledge of ξ on m.

If non-frameability were not a requirement, we could simply let the Group Manager choose ξ, so that he can open group signatures by checking for which of the issued values of ξ the re-randomized CL signature is valid. To obtain non-frameability, however, the Group Manager must not know ξ itself. Hence, in our scheme ξ is generated jointly during an interactive GJoin protocol between the user and the Group Manager. Essentially, this protocol is a two-party computation where the user and the Group Manager jointly generate ξ, a valid CL signature on ξ, and a key derived from ξ that allows the Group Manager to trace signatures, but not to create them.

System Specification. We now present the algorithms that define our efficient group signature scheme. We assume common system parameters for a given security parameter η. Namely, we assume that an asymmetric pairing is fixed, i.e., three groups $\mathbb{G}_1$, $\mathbb{G}_2$, $\mathbb{G}_T$ of order $q > 2^\eta$ with an efficiently computable map $\hat{e} : \mathbb{G}_1 \times \mathbb{G}_2 \to \mathbb{G}_T$, together with generators g and $\tilde{g}$ of $\mathbb{G}_1$ and $\mathbb{G}_2$, respectively. Further, two hash functions $\mathcal{H} : \{0,1\}^* \to \mathbb{Z}_q$, $\mathcal{G} : \{0,1\}^* \to \mathbb{Z}_q$ are defined.

$\mathsf{GSetup}(1^\eta)$: The Group Manager chooses random $\alpha, \beta \leftarrow \mathbb{Z}_q$, and computes $\tilde{x} \leftarrow \tilde{g}^\alpha$ and $\tilde{y} \leftarrow \tilde{g}^\beta$. It then sets the group public key of the scheme to $gpk \leftarrow (\tilde{x}, \tilde{y})$ and the group secret key to $gmsk \leftarrow (\alpha, \beta)$.

$\mathsf{PKIJoin}(i, 1^\eta)$: The CA certifies public keys of a digital signature scheme as defined in Section 2. The user generates $(\mathbf{upk}[i], \mathbf{usk}[i]) \leftarrow \mathsf{DSKeyGen}(1^\eta)$ and sends $\mathbf{upk}[i]$ to the CA for certification.

$\mathsf{GJoin} = (\mathsf{GJoin}_M(i, \mathbf{upk}[i], gmsk), \mathsf{GJoin}_U(i, \mathbf{usk}[i], gpk))$: When a user i wants to join the group, she must have already run the PKIJoin algorithm. Then she runs the following protocol with the Group Manager. We assume that this protocol is run over secure channels and, for simplicity, that the parties only run one instance at a time. We also assume that if a verification for a party fails, the party informs the other party about the failure and the protocol is aborted.

1. The Group Manager chooses a random $\kappa \leftarrow \mathbb{Z}_q$, computes $t \leftarrow \mathcal{G}(\kappa)$, and sends t to the user.
2. The user i chooses $\tau \leftarrow \mathbb{Z}_q$, computes $s \leftarrow g^\tau$, $\tilde{r} \leftarrow \tilde{x}^\tau$, $k \leftarrow \hat{e}(g, \tilde{r})$, as well as $\bar{\sigma} \leftarrow \mathsf{DSSign}(\mathbf{usk}[i], k)$, sends $(s, \tilde{r}, \bar{\sigma})$ to the Group Manager and executes $FPK\{(\tau) : s = g^\tau \wedge \tilde{r} = \tilde{x}^\tau\}$ with the Group Manager.
3. The Group Manager uses $\mathsf{DSVerify}(\mathbf{upk}[i], \hat{e}(g, \tilde{r}), \bar{\sigma})$ to verify the signature. If it verifies correctly he computes $z \leftarrow s \cdot g^\kappa$ and $\tilde{w} \leftarrow \tilde{r} \cdot \tilde{x}^\kappa$, stores $(\tilde{w}, \tilde{r}, \kappa, \bar{\sigma})$ in $\mathbf{reg}[i]$, chooses $\rho \leftarrow \mathbb{Z}_q$, computes $a \leftarrow g^\rho$, $b \leftarrow a^\beta$, and $c \leftarrow a^\alpha \cdot z^{\rho\alpha\beta}$, and sends (a, b, c, κ) to the user. In addition, he executes
$$FPK\{(\alpha, \beta, \rho, \gamma) : c = a^\alpha z^\gamma \wedge a = g^\rho \wedge \tilde{x} = \tilde{g}^\alpha \wedge \tilde{y} = \tilde{g}^\beta \wedge 1 = b^\alpha / g^\gamma\}$$
with her, where $\gamma = \rho\alpha\beta$. Note that this proof allows the user to verify that $\alpha, \beta \neq 0$.
4. The user computes $\xi \leftarrow \tau + \kappa \bmod q$, and checks whether $t = \mathcal{G}(\kappa)$. She also verifies $\hat{e}(a, \tilde{y}) = \hat{e}(b, \tilde{g})$ and, if the verification is successful, stores the entry $\mathbf{gsk}[i] \leftarrow (\xi, (a, b, c))$.

Remarks: The value of ω stored in $\mathbf{reg}[i]$ allows the Opener to identify a user within the group signature scheme. In addition, the Opener can provably attribute this ω to $k = \hat{e}(g, \tilde{r})$. Consequently, a group signature can be provably attributed to k. By the unforgeability of the external signature scheme, the signature on k allows to attribute a group signature to a user public key $\mathbf{upk}[i]$. Furthermore, the FPK protocol that the Group Manager and the user execute in Step 3 of the protocol indeed proves that c was computed correctly w.r.t. a, b, $\tilde{x}$, and $\tilde{y}$. To this end, note that because of $\hat{e}(a, \tilde{y}) = \hat{e}(b, \tilde{g})$, we know that $b = a^\beta$ and thus $b = g^{\beta\rho}$. Subsequently, from $1 = b^\alpha / g^\gamma$ we can conclude that $\gamma = \rho\alpha\beta$ and hence that c was computed correctly by the Group Manager.

$\mathsf{GSign}(\mathbf{gsk}[i], m)$: Let a user i with signing key $\mathbf{gsk}[i] = (\xi, (a, b, c))$ sign the message m. She first re-randomizes the signature by choosing $\zeta \leftarrow \mathbb{Z}_q$ and computing $d \leftarrow a^\zeta$, $e \leftarrow b^\zeta$, and $f \leftarrow c^\zeta$, and then computes the SPK
$$\Sigma \leftarrow SPK\{(\xi) : \frac{\hat{e}(f, \tilde{g})}{\hat{e}(d, \tilde{x})} = \hat{e}(e, \tilde{x})^\xi\}(m)$$
proving that she knows the "message" for which (d, e, f) is a valid CL-signature. Finally, she outputs $\sigma \leftarrow (d, e, f, \Sigma) \in \mathbb{G}_1^3 \times \mathbb{Z}_q^2$ as the group signature on m.

GVerify(gpk, m, σ): To verify a signature $\sigma = (d, e, f, \Sigma)$ on the message m, the verifier first checks that $\hat{e}(d, \tilde{y}) = \hat{e}(e, \tilde{g})$, where $\tilde{g}, \tilde{y}$ are retrieved from gpk. Secondly, the verifier checks that the proof Σ is valid. If either of the checks fail, output 0; otherwise output 1.

GOpen$(gmsk, m, \sigma, \mathbf{reg})$: Given signature $\sigma = (d, e, f, \Sigma)$ on m, the Group Manager verifies the signature using GVerify. Then, for all entries $\mathbf{reg}[i] = (\tilde{w}_i, \tilde{r}_i, \kappa_i, \bar{\sigma}_i)$ he checks whether $\hat{e}(f, \tilde{g}) = \hat{e}(d, \tilde{x}) \cdot \hat{e}(e, \tilde{w}_i)$ holds. For the $\tilde{w}_i$ where the equation holds, the Group Manager retrieves κ_i and $\bar{\sigma}_i$, computes $k_i \leftarrow \hat{e}(g, \tilde{r}_i)$ and the SPK

$$\Pi \leftarrow SPK\{(\tilde{w}_i, \kappa_i) : \frac{\hat{e}(f, \tilde{g})}{\hat{e}(d, \tilde{x})} = \hat{e}(e, \tilde{w}_i) \wedge k_i = \frac{\hat{e}(g, \tilde{w}_i)}{\hat{e}(g, \tilde{x})^{\kappa_i}}\} ,$$

and outputs $(i, \pi = (k_i, \bar{\sigma}_i, \Pi))$.

Note that $\phi(\tilde{w}) := (\hat{e}(e, \tilde{w}), \hat{e}(g, \tilde{w}))$ is a group homomorphism from $\mathbb{G}_2$ to $\mathbb{G}_T \times \mathbb{G}_T$ and therefore π can be obtained from applying the Fiat–Shamir transform to the underlying Σ-protocol as discussed earlier. Also note that the opening operation is linear in the number of users in the system, but we consider this reasonable as in most practical applications opening is a rather exceptional operation performed by a resourceful Group Manager.

GJudge$(gpk, m, \sigma, i, \mathbf{upk}[i], \pi)$: The signature of the external signature scheme is verified using the signature verification algorithm DSVerify$(upk[i], k, \bar{\sigma})$. If the signature verifies, use input gpk, m, $\sigma = (d, e, f, \Sigma)$, and π, to output 1 if algorithm GVerify$(gpk, m, \sigma) = 1$ and Π is valid. Otherwise output 0.

Remarks. Following the explanations in Section 3.2, we can build a VLR scheme as follows. Transformation of the key generation and the signing algorithm are straightforward. To revoke a user i, the Group Manager publishes the corresponding entry $\tilde{w}_i$ from $\mathbf{reg}[i]$ to the revocation list $\mathbf{rlist}$. Finally, we modify the GVerify algorithm so that it checks not only that $\hat{e}(d, \tilde{y}) = \hat{e}(e, \tilde{g})$ and the proof Σ is valid, but also whether

$$\hat{e}(f, \tilde{g}) = \hat{e}(d, \tilde{x}) \cdot \hat{e}(e, \tilde{w}_i)$$

for any entry $\tilde{w}_i$ in $\mathbf{rlist}$. If this is the case, it rejects the signature. Thus, the verifier performs what has been a part of the tasks of the Opener in our basic group signature scheme.

5 Security Results

Verifying our scheme's correctness is not hard from its description (and the comments we made there). We now present our results that the scheme satisfies our anonymity, traceability, and non-frameability requirements. Proofs of the following theorems can be found in the full version of the paper.

Theorem 2. *In the random oracle model the group signature scheme is anonymous under the XDDH and the SDLP assumptions.*

Theorem 3. *In the random oracle model the group signature scheme is traceable under the LRSW assumption.*

Theorem 4. *In the random oracle model the group signature scheme is non-frameable under the SDLP assumption and the unforgeability of the underlying digital signature scheme.*

Security of our scheme as a VLR group signature scheme, in the random oracle model, follows from the above theorems.

6 Comparison with Previous Schemes

We compare efficiency of several schemes with respect to (1) signature size, (2) computational costs of signature generation, and (3) computational costs of signature verification. We denote the computational cost with the following type of expression $1 \cdot P^2 + 2 \cdot P + 3 \cdot \mathbb{G}_T^2 + 1 \cdot \mathbb{G}_1$, which stands for one product of two pairing values, two pairings, three multi-exponentiations in $\mathbb{G}_T$ with two terms, and one exponentiation in $\mathbb{G}_1$.

We now compare our scheme with the current best schemes w.r.t. signature length. We only consider pairing-based schemes as RSA-based schemes need much larger groups to attain the same security level. Consequently, we can focus on just a small number of schemes.

- The CL scheme from [16] shares many similarities with our own. The basic security is based on the LRSW and the DDH assumption in $\mathbb{G}_T$. The basic construction is in the case of Type-1 pairings, and combines the CL-signature scheme with a Cramer-Shoup encryption, where the latter creates the main divergence from our scheme. Translating the construction to the Type-2 or Type-3 setting we obtain a more efficient construction based on the LRSW and the XDDH assumption.
- The DP scheme of Delerablée and Pointcheval [25] is based on the XDDH assumption and q-SDH. It is shown to provide full-anonymity under the XDDH assumption w.r.t. the so-called CCA attack, which is achieved by combining two ElGamal encryptions. The scheme is also shown to provide full-traceability under the q-SDH assumption.
- The BBS group signature scheme [9] is similar to the DP scheme [25]. However, it provides full-anonymity under the DLIN assumption only w.r.t. the so-called CPA attack (i.e., the adversary is not allowed to make any Open oracle queries). As we strive to provide a comparison between systems that have similar security guarantees, we consider a variant of the BBS scheme that we call BBS* and describe in Section 7.

We summarize the efficiency discussion in Table 1. Note that all schemes provide anonymity w.r.t. the CCA attack, are based on the random oracle model, and provide strong exculpability. As pointed out in the discussion before, they use slightly different underlying assumptions, namely q-SDH or LRSW. A further difference is that our scheme, as opposed to the schemes we compare against, combines Group Manager and Opener into one entity.

Table 1. Comparison of signature lengths, signature generation costs and signature verification costs. Note that we change the computation of the hash in the SPK to reduce the number of computations. For our scheme the changes simplify the security proof.

Scheme	Size of Sig.		Sign Cost						Verification Cost							
	$\mathbb{G}_1$	$\mathbb{Z}_q$	$\mathbb{G}_T^5$	$\mathbb{G}_T^3$	$\mathbb{G}_T^2$	$\mathbb{G}_T$	$\mathbb{G}_1^2$	$\mathbb{G}_1$	P^2	P	$\mathbb{G}_T^3$	$\mathbb{G}_2^2$	$\mathbb{G}_1^4$	$\mathbb{G}_1^3$	$\mathbb{G}_1^2$	$\mathbb{G}_1$
Ours	3	2				1		3	2						1	1
CL	7	4			1		1	11	2			1		2	2	1
DP	4	5		1			1	6		1	1	1		1	2	
BBS*	4	5	1				3	5	1				1	1	4	

Table 1 shows that our scheme compares favourably with the other schemes, especially in the signature length and the signature generation operation. In particular, it reduces the signature size by almost a factor of two. Comparing verification costs shows all schemes on an approximately equal level. Note that short signatures and small signature computation costs are particularly interesting as there are many scenarios where the group signature has to be generated and communicated by a resource constrained device.

7 Sketch of BBS*

This variant of the BBS group signature scheme is based on remarks by Boneh et al. [9] (general scheme and non-frameability) and [32] (CCA anonymity). In particular, the variant we consider attains exculpability by an interactive protocol between Group Manager and user for the joint computation of a triple (A_i, x_i, y_i) such that $A_i^{x_i+\gamma} h^{y_i} = u$. Here y_i is secret to the user, γ is the Group Manager's secret, and $u, h \in \mathbb{G}_1$ are public parameters. Given all schemes we compare are secure under XDDH, we employ standard Cramer-Shoup encryption [23] instead of the linear Cramer-Shoup encryption proposed by Shacham [32].

In more detail, the setup and key generation algorithms produce $u, v \leftarrow \mathbb{G}_1$ and $c \leftarrow u^{\chi_1} v^{\chi_2}, d \leftarrow u^{\mu_1} v^{\mu_2}$, as well as $e \leftarrow v^{\iota}$. As a result of the join protocol, each user gets a tuple (A_i, x_i, y_i) fulfilling $A_i^{x_i+\gamma} h^{y_i} = u$ and the Group Manager uses his secret γ to compute $w \leftarrow v^{\gamma}$. The group public key consists of (u, v, c, d, e, h, w) and the secret key of the Opener contains $(\chi_1, \chi_2, \mu_1, \mu_2)$.

To sign a message, user i chooses $r \leftarrow \mathbb{Z}_q$, $\delta \leftarrow r \cdot x_i$, and computes $T_1 \leftarrow u^r$, $T_2 \leftarrow v^r, T_3 \leftarrow e^r A_i, T_4 \leftarrow c^r d^{r\mathcal{H}(T_1,T_2,T_3)}$. Moreover, she computes the proof

$$\Sigma \leftarrow \mathrm{SPK}\{(r, x_i, \delta, y_i) : T_1 = u^r \wedge T_2 = v^r \wedge T_4 = c^r d^{r\mathcal{H}(T_1,T_2,T_3)} \wedge$$
$$1 = T_1^{x_i} u^{-\delta} \wedge \frac{\hat{e}(u,v)}{\hat{e}(T_3,w)} = \frac{\hat{e}(T_3,v)^{x_i} \hat{e}(h,v)^{y_i}}{\hat{e}(e,w)^r \hat{e}(e,v)^{\delta}}\} \ ,$$

and outputs the signature $\sigma \leftarrow (T_1, T_2, T_3, T_4, \Sigma)$.

The verification of a signature consists of checking the validity of the proof Σ. Opening a signature can be performed by the Opener using his secret key to decrypt the Cramer-Shoup encryption of the value A_i.

Acknowledgements

The work described in this paper has been supported in part by the European Commission through the ICT programme under contract ICT-2007-216676 ECRYPT II and ICT-2007-216483 PRIMELIFE. The fourth author was supported by a Royal Society Wolfson Merit Award and a grant from Google. All authors would like to thank the referee's of a prior version of this paper.

References

1. Abdalla, M., Warinschi, B.: On the minimal assumptions of group signature schemes. In: López, J., Qing, S., Okamoto, E. (eds.) ICICS 2004. LNCS, vol. 3269, pp. 1–13. Springer, Heidelberg (2004)
2. Ateniese, G., Camenisch, J., Joye, M., Tsudik, G.: A practical and provably secure coalition-resistant group signature scheme. In: Bellare, M. (ed.) CRYPTO 2000. LNCS, vol. 1880, pp. 255–270. Springer, Heidelberg (2000)
3. Ateniese, G., Song, D.X., Tsudik, G.: Quasi-efficient revocation in group signatures. In: Blaze, M. (ed.) FC 2002. LNCS, vol. 2357, pp. 183–197. Springer, Heidelberg (2003)
4. Bellare, M., Micciancio, D., Warinschi, B.: Foundations of group signatures: Formal definitions, simplified requirements, and a construction based on general assumptions. In: Biham, E. (ed.) EUROCRYPT 2003. LNCS, vol. 2656, pp. 614–629. Springer, Heidelberg (2003)
5. Bellare, M., Neven, G.: Multi-signatures in the plain public-key model and a general forking lemma. In: ACM CCS 2006, pp. 390–399 (October/November 2006)
6. Bellare, M., Rogaway, P.: Random oracles are practical: A paradigm for designing efficient protocols. In: ACM CCS 1993, pp. 62–73 (November 1993)
7. Bellare, M., Shi, H., Zhang, C.: Foundations of group signatures: The case of dynamic groups. In: Menezes, A. (ed.) CT-RSA 2005. LNCS, vol. 3376, pp. 136–153. Springer, Heidelberg (2005)
8. Bleichenbacher, D.: Chosen ciphertext attacks against protocols based on the RSA encryption standard PKCS #1. In: Krawczyk, H. (ed.) CRYPTO 1998. LNCS, vol. 1462, pp. 1–12. Springer, Heidelberg (1998)
9. Boneh, D., Boyen, X., Shacham, H.: Short group signatures. In: Franklin, M. (ed.) CRYPTO 2004. LNCS, vol. 3152, pp. 41–55. Springer, Heidelberg (2004)
10. Boneh, D., Shacham, H.: Group signatures with verifier-local revocation. In: ACM CCS 2004, pp. 168–177 (October 2004)
11. Boyen, X., Waters, B.: Compact group signatures without random oracles. In: Vaudenay, S. (ed.) EUROCRYPT 2006. LNCS, vol. 4004, pp. 427–444. Springer, Heidelberg (2006)
12. Boyen, X., Waters, B.: Full-domain subgroup hiding and constant-size group signatures. In: Okamoto, T., Wang, X. (eds.) PKC 2007. LNCS, vol. 4450, pp. 1–15. Springer, Heidelberg (2007)
13. Brickell, E., Chen, L., Li, J.: A new direct anonymous attestation scheme from bilinear maps. In: Lipp, P., Sadeghi, A.-R., Koch, K.-M. (eds.) Trust 2008. LNCS, vol. 4968, pp. 1–20. Springer, Heidelberg (2008)
14. Camenisch, J., Kiayias, A., Yung, M.: On the portability of generalized schnorr proofs. In: Joux, A. (ed.) EUROCRYPT 2009. LNCS, vol. 5479, pp. 425–442. Springer, Heidelberg (2010)
15. Camenisch, J., Lysyanskaya, A.: Dynamic accumulators and application to efficient revocation of anonymous credentials. In: Yung, M. (ed.) CRYPTO 2002. LNCS, vol. 2442, pp. 61–76. Springer, Heidelberg (2002)

16. Camenisch, J., Lysyanskaya, A.: Signature schemes and anonymous credentials from bilinear maps. In: Franklin, M. (ed.) CRYPTO 2004. LNCS, vol. 3152, pp. 56–72. Springer, Heidelberg (2004)
17. Camenisch, J., Stadler, M.: Efficient group signature schemes for large groups (extended abstract). In: Kaliski Jr., B.S. (ed.) CRYPTO 1997. LNCS, vol. 1294, pp. 410–424. Springer, Heidelberg (1997)
18. Chaum, D., van Heyst, E.: Group signatures. In: Davies, D.W. (ed.) EUROCRYPT 1991. LNCS, vol. 547, pp. 257–265. Springer, Heidelberg (1991)
19. Chen, L., Cheng, M., Smart, N.P.: Identity-based key agreement protocols from pairings. International Journal of Information Security 6, 213–241 (2007)
20. Chen, L., Morrissey, P., Smart, N.P.: Pairings in trusted computing (invited talk). In: Galbraith, S.D., Paterson, K.G. (eds.) Pairing 2008. LNCS, vol. 5209, pp. 1–17. Springer, Heidelberg (2008)
21. Chen, L., Morrissey, P., Smart, N.P.: DAA: Fixing the pairing based protocols. Cryptology ePrint Archive, Report 2009/198 (2009)
22. Cramer, R., Damgård, I., MacKenzie, P.D.: Efficient zero-knowledge proofs of knowledge without intractability assumptions. In: Imai, H., Zheng, Y. (eds.) PKC 2000. LNCS, vol. 1751, pp. 354–372. Springer, Heidelberg (2000)
23. Cramer, R., Shoup, V.: Design and analysis of practical public-key encryption schemes secure against adaptive chosen ciphertext attack. SIAM Journal on Computing 33(1), 167–226 (2003)
24. Damgård, I.: Efficient concurrent zero-knowledge in the auxiliary string model. In: Preneel, B. (ed.) EUROCRYPT 2000. LNCS, vol. 1807, pp. 418–430. Springer, Heidelberg (2000)
25. Delerablée, C., Pointcheval, D.: Dynamic fully anonymous short group signatures. In: Nguyên, P.Q. (ed.) VIETCRYPT 2006. LNCS, vol. 4341, pp. 193–210. Springer, Heidelberg (2006)
26. Fiat, A., Shamir, A.: How to prove yourself: Practical solutions to identification and signature problems. In: Odlyzko, A.M. (ed.) CRYPTO 1986. LNCS, vol. 263, pp. 186–194. Springer, Heidelberg (1987)
27. Galbraith, S.D., Paterson, K.G., Smart, N.P.: Pairings for cryptographers. Discrete Applied Mathematics 156, 3113–3121 (2008)
28. Goldwasser, S., Micali, S., Rivest, R.L.: A digital signature scheme secure against adaptive chosen-message attacks. SIAM Journal on Computing 17(2), 281–308 (1988)
29. Lysyanskaya, A., Rivest, R.L., Sahai, A., Wolf, S.: Pseudonym systems. In: Heys, H.M., Adams, C.M. (eds.) SAC 1999. LNCS, vol. 1758, pp. 184–199. Springer, Heidelberg (2000)
30. Pointcheval, D., Stern, J.: Security arguments for digital signatures and blind signatures. Journal of Cryptology 13(3), 361–396 (2000)
31. Shacham, H.: New Paradigms in Signature Schemes. PhD thesis, Stanford University (2005)
32. Shacham, H.: A Cramer-Shoup encryption scheme from the linear assumption and from progressively weaker linear variants. Cryptology ePrint Archive, Report 2007/074 (2007)
33. Tsudik, G., Xu, S.: Accumulating composites and improved group signing. In: Laih, C.-S. (ed.) ASIACRYPT 2003. LNCS, vol. 2894, pp. 269–286. Springer, Heidelberg (2003)

Group Message Authentication*

Bartosz Przydatek[1] and Douglas Wikström[2]

[1] Google Switzerland
przydatek@google.com
[2] KTH Stockholm
dog@csc.kth.se

Abstract. Group signatures is a powerful primitive with many practical applications, allowing a group of parties to share a signature functionality, while protecting the anonymity of the signer. However, despite intensive research in the past years, there is still no fully satisfactory implementation of group signatures in the plain model. The schemes proposed so far are either too inefficient to be used in practice, or their security is based on rather strong, non-standard assumptions.

We observe that for some applications the full power of group signatures is not necessary. For example, a group signature can be verified by any third party, while in many applications such a universal verifiability is not needed or even not desired. Motivated by this observation, we propose a notion of *group message authentication*, which can be viewed as a relaxation of group signatures. Group message authentication enjoys the group-oriented features of group signatures, while dropping some of the features which are not needed in many real-life scenarios. An example application of group message authentication is an implementation of an *anonymous* credit card.

We present a generic implementation of group message authentication, and also propose an efficient concrete implementation based on standard assumptions, namely strong RSA and DDH.

1 Introduction

A typical sequence of events in an offline credit card purchase is as follows: A card holder authenticates himself using his card and leaves a receipt of purchase to the merchant. The merchant then gives the receipt to the bank and the bank transfers money from the card holder's account to the merchant's account.

A natural way to improve the security of this scheme is to use smartcards and let a smartcard digitally authenticate each purchase transaction on behalf of the card holder. Message authentication can be achieved using a digital signature scheme. A drawback of this approach, and also of the original scheme, is that it reveals the identity of the card holder to the merchant.

Chaum and van Heyst [9] introduced group signatures to resolve this, and other similar privacy problems. When using a group signature scheme the signatures computed by different signers are indistinguishable, i.e., they provide

* Work done in part at ETH Zurich. The full version of this paper is available on Cryptology ePrint Archive [29].

J.A. Garay and R. De Prisco (Eds.): SCN 2010, LNCS 6280, pp. 399–417, 2010.

unlinkability and anonymity within the group of signers. On the other hand a special party, called the group manager, has the ability to open any valid signature and identify the signer. In the application described above, the bank would play the role of the group manager and each credit card would use a unique signing key. This solution still reveals the correspondence between purchases and card holders to the bank, but in practice this is not a serious problem. Not only would customers leave a bank if it did not treat customer information carefully, but in most countries banks are required to do so by law and they are typically under supervision of some authority.

In principle, group signatures can be constructed under general assumptions [3], but these constructions are prohibitively inefficient for practical purposes. There are efficient schemes, e.g., Ateniese *et al.* [1] or Boyen and Waters [5], but the security of these schemes rests on non-standard pairing-based assumptions, which are still controversial in the cryptographic community. There are also efficient and provably secure realizations of group signatures in the random oracle model, e.g., the scheme given by Camenisch and Groth [6], but the random oracle model is not sound [7]. Thus, a proof of security in this model does not necessarily imply that the scheme is secure when the random oracle is instantiated by an efficiently computable function.

To summarize, despite intensive research there is still no *efficient* group signature scheme provably secure in the *plain model* under *standard* assumptions. This motivates the study of relaxed notions for special applications of group signatures that allows for a simpler solution.

A closer look at our motivating anonymous credit cards problem reveals that group signatures provide several features that are not essential in this setting:

- Signatures are publicly verifiable, while in our setting only the merchant and the bank must be able to verify the authenticity of a transaction, as no other party even receives a signature.
- Group signatures are non-interactive. This is crucial for the bank, since it may receive a large number of transactions from the numerous senders. However, in many applications it is not essential that the merchant is able to verify the authenticity of a transaction without interacting with the sender.
- Although there are exceptions, it is typically required from a group signature scheme that the group manager is unable to frame signers, i.e., he cannot compute signatures on their behalf. This property is not essential in a credit card system, since the bank is trusted to manage all the transactions properly anyway, and would quickly lose all customers if it framed a few of them.

Contributions. Our main contribution is threefold:

- Motivated by our observation that in some classical applications of group signatures a fully blown group signature scheme is not really needed, we formalize a relaxed notion that we call *group message authentication*.
- We give a generic construction of a group message authentication scheme that satisfies our relaxed security definitions.

– We instantiate the generic construction efficiently and in a provably secure way in the plain model under the decision Diffie-Hellman assumption and the strong RSA assumption.

Thus, for an important special case of the original motivating application of group signatures we give the first fully satisfactory solution. We also give the first reduction of the security of the Cramer-Shoup cryptosystem with labels over a cyclic group of composite order to its security over each subgroup. A direct proof can be achieved by adapting the original proof due to Cramer and Shoup (cf. [26]), but we think our analysis is of independent interest.

In group signatures in the random oracle model (cf. [6]), the signer encrypts a token and gives a non-interactive Fiat-Shamir [15] proof, with the message as a prefix to the hashfunction, that the ciphertext was formed in this way. It is tempting to conclude that if we skip the Fiat-Shamir transform, we get a secure group message authentication scheme, but this does not work, since the random oracle is used for three purposes: (a) to embed the message and provide unforgeability, (b) to prove that a ciphertext contains a token, and (c) to prove knowledge of an encrypted valid token and thereby provide the CCA2-like security needed in group signature schemes. One can use a CCA2-secure cryptosystem to avoid (c), but without the Fiat-Shamir proof there is nowhere to embed the message. We could (along the lines of [3]) encrypt a *standard* signature of the message along with the signer's public key and a certificate thereof, but no *efficient* proof that a plaintext has this form is known. We instead use a CCA2-secure cryptosystem with labels and *embed the message in the label.*

Even taken as a group signature scheme (using Fiat-Shamir to eliminate interaction), our construction is novel and, interestingly, its security holds in the *plain* model where the group manager plays the role of the verifier, i.e., he can detect signatures forged due to the failure of Fiat-Shamir heuristic.

Related Work. In addition to the intensive work on group signatures mentioned above, there has been substantial interest in other aspects of group-oriented cryptography.[1] In particular, many researchers have explored numerous variations of group signatures with additional properties such as: traceable signatures [21], multi-group and subgroup signatures [2,24], or hierarchical group signatures [33]. In contrast to these various extensions of group signatures, group message authentication is actually a relaxation of group signatures.

Another related primitive is identity escrow [23], which applies key-escrow ideas to the problem of user identification. In contrast to group signatures or group message authentication, identity escrow does not allow any form of signing a message. More precisely, identity escrow employs an identity token that allows the holder to anonymously authenticate itself as a member of a group, but it does not allow the holder to sign any messages. Furthermore, identity escrow introduces an additional party, *escrow agent*, and requires separability: the agent remains dormant during normal operation of the identification system, and is

[1] In independent work, Laur and Pasini [25] use the term "group message authentication" in a different context.

"woken up" only when there is a request to revoke anonymity. This feature and the requirement of resistance to impersonation imply that not every group signature scheme can be used as an identity escrow scheme.

Other notions related to group message authentication include designated verifier signatures [20] and designated confirmer signatures [8]. Recently, Kiayias *et al.* [22] and Qin *et al.* [30] proposed a group-oriented notion of cryptosystems.

Notation. We denote the set $\{j, j+1, j+2, \ldots, k\}$ of integers by $[j, k]$. We write: $\mathbb{Z}_N$ for the integers modulo N, $\mathbb{Z}_N^*$ for its multiplicative group, and SQ_N for the subgroup of squares in $\mathbb{Z}_N^*$. We say that a prime q is safe if $(q-1)/2$ is prime. We use n as our main security parameter and say that a function $\epsilon(n)$ is negligible if for every constant c, $\epsilon(n) < n^{-c}$ for every sufficiently large n. We say that the probability of an event is overwhelming if it is at least $1 - \epsilon(n)$, where $\epsilon(n)$ is negligible. Given a public key cpk of a cryptosystem we denote the plaintext space by $\mathcal{M}_{cpk}$, the ciphertext space by $\mathcal{C}_{cpk}$, and the randomizer space by $\mathcal{R}_{cpk}$. We use PT to denote the set of deterministic polynomial time algorithms, PPT the set of probabilistic polynomial time algorithms, and IPPT the set of interactive, probabilistic polynomial time algorithms (sometimes with oracles). Given $P, V \in$ IPPT, we denote by $\langle P(w), V(z)\rangle(x)$ the output of V when executed on input (z, x) and interacting with P on input (w, x). We write $V[\![(P_i(w_i))_{i\in[1,k]}]\!]$ when V interacts over separate communication tapes with k copies of $P_i(w_i)$ running on inputs $w_1, \ldots, w_k$ respectively, i.e., it has "oracle access" to these machines.

2 Group Message Authentication Schemes

To avoid confusion with group signatures and related notions we refer to the parties in a group message authentication (GMA) scheme as the *receiver*, *proxies*, and *senders*, and we say that a sender computes an *authentication tag*. Compared to a group signature scheme the role of the receiver is similar to the group manager. It can verify and open an authentication tag, but in a GMA scheme it may need its secret key also to verify a tag. Thus, we combine these two operations into a single *checking algorithm* that outputs an identity if the authentication tag is valid, and outputs $\perp$ otherwise. The role of a sender is similar to a signer, except that when it hands an authentication tag to a proxy, it also executes an interactive *authentication protocol* that convinces the proxy that the receiver will accept it. The role of a proxy corresponds to the holder of a signature, except that it can not hand the signature to anybody but the receiver.

Definition 1 (Group Message Authentication Scheme). *A* group message authentication scheme *consists of four algorithms* $(\mathsf{RKg}, \mathsf{AKg}, \mathsf{Aut}, \mathsf{Check})$ *and a protocol* π_a*, associated with a polynomial* $\ell(\cdot)$*:*

1. *A receiver key generation algorithm* $\mathsf{RKg} \in$ PPT*, that on input* 1^n *outputs a public key* pk *and a secret key* sk*.*
2. *An authentication key generation algorithm* $\mathsf{AKg} \in$ PPT*, that on input* 1^n*, a receiver key* sk*, and an integer* $i \in [1, \ell(n)]$ *outputs an authentication key* ak_i*.*

3. *An authentication algorithm* $\mathsf{Aut} \in \mathrm{PPT}$, *that on input a public receiver key* pk, *an authentication key* ak_i, *and a message* $m \in \{0,1\}^*$ *outputs an authentication tag* σ.
4. *A checking algorithm* $\mathsf{Check} \in \mathrm{PT}$, *that on input the secret receiver key* sk, *a message* $m \in \{0,1\}^*$, *and a candidate authentication tag* σ, *outputs an integer* $i \in [1, \ell(n)]$ *or* $\perp$.
5. *An interactive 2-party authentication protocol* $\pi_a = (P_a, V_a) \in \mathrm{IPPT}^2$, *such that the output of the verifier* V_a *is a bit.*

For every $n \in \mathbb{N}$, *every* $(pk, sk) \in \mathsf{RKg}(1^n)$, *every integer* $i \in [1, \ell(n)]$, *every authentication key* $ak_i \in \mathsf{AKg}_{sk}(1^n, i)$, *every message* $m \in \{0,1\}^*$, *and every* $r \in \{0,1\}^*$ *the following holds: if* $\sigma = \mathsf{Aut}_{ak_i,r}(pk, m)$, *then* $\mathsf{Check}_{sk}(m, \sigma) = i$ *and the probability* $\Pr[\langle P_a(ak_i, r), V_a\rangle(pk, m, \sigma) = 1]$ *is overwhelming.*

2.1 Definition of Security

Conceptually, the security requirements of a GMA scheme must guarantee: that authentication tags are indistinguishable, that it is infeasible to forge an authentication tag, that the receiver can always trace the sender, and that the proxy is never convinced that an invalid authentication tag is valid. We formalize these properties with two experiments similarly as is done in [3] for group signatures.

Experiment 1 (Anonymity, $\mathsf{Exp}^{\mathsf{anon}-b}_{\mathsf{GMA},A}(n)$**).**

$$
\begin{aligned}
(pk, sk) &\leftarrow \mathsf{RKg}(1^n) && \textit{// receiver key}\\
ak_i &\leftarrow \mathsf{AKg}_{sk}(1^n, i) \ \textit{for } i \in [1, \ell(n)] && \textit{// auth. keys}\\
(m, i_0, i_1, \mathrm{state}) &\leftarrow A^{\mathsf{Check}_{sk}(\cdot,\cdot)}(pk, ak_1, \ldots, ak_{\ell(n)}) && \textit{// choose ids}\\
\sigma &\leftarrow \mathsf{Aut}_{ak_{i_b},r}(pk, m), \ \textit{with random } r \in \{0,1\}^* && \textit{// challenge}\\
d &\leftarrow \langle P_a(ak_{i_b}, r), A^{\mathsf{Check}_{sk}(\cdot,\cdot)}(\mathrm{state})\rangle(pk, \sigma, m) && \textit{// guess}
\end{aligned}
$$

If the $\mathsf{Check}_{sk}(\cdot,\cdot)$*-oracle was never queried with* (m, σ), *then output* d, *otherwise output* 0.

Anonymity. We define one experiment for each value of $b \in \{0,1\}$ and then require that the distributions of the two experiments are close. The adversary is given the receiver's public key and all authentication keys. Then it chooses two identities of senders and a message, and hands these to the experiment. The bth experiment chooses the bth of the identities and computes an authentication tag of the given message using the authentication key of this identity. Then it hands the authentication tag to the adversary and executes the authentication protocol on behalf of the chosen identity. Finally, the adversary must guess which of the two authentication keys was used to authenticate the message and execute the authentication protocol. During the experiment the adversary also has access to a checking oracle to which it may send any query, except the challenge message-and-authentication tag pair.[2]

Definition 2 (Anonymity). *A group message authentication scheme* GMA *is anonymous if* $\forall A \in \mathrm{IPPT}$ *the following expression is negligible*

$$\left|\Pr[\mathsf{Exp}^{\mathsf{anon}-0}_{\mathsf{GMA},A}(n) = 1] - \Pr[\mathsf{Exp}^{\mathsf{anon}-1}_{\mathsf{GMA},A}(n) = 1]\right| .$$

Experiment 2 (Traceability, $\mathsf{Exp}^{\mathsf{trace}}_{\mathsf{GMA},A}(n)$).

$$(pk, sk) \leftarrow \mathsf{RKg}(1^n) \qquad // \textit{ receiver key}$$

$$ak_i \leftarrow \mathsf{AKg}_{sk}(1^n, i) \textit{ for } i \in [1, \ell(n)] \qquad // \textit{ auth. keys}$$

$$\textit{Define } ak(i) = \begin{cases} ak_i & \textit{if } i \in [1, \ell(n)] \\ \bot & \textit{otherwise} \end{cases} \qquad // \textit{ auth. key oracle}$$

$$(m, \sigma, \mathrm{state}) \leftarrow A^{ak(\cdot), \mathsf{Check}_{sk}(\cdot,\cdot)}[\![(P_a^+(pk, ak_i))_{i \in [1,\ell(n)]}]\!](pk) \qquad // \textit{ forge auth. tag...}$$

$$d \leftarrow \langle A^{ak(\cdot), \mathsf{Check}_{sk}(\cdot,\cdot)}(state), V_a\rangle(pk, m, \sigma) \qquad // \textit{ ..or authenticate}$$

$$// \textit{ an invalid tag}$$

Let C *be the set of queries asked by* A *to the* $ak(\cdot)$*-oracle. If* $\mathsf{Check}_{sk}(m, \sigma) \in [1, \ell(n)] \setminus C$ *and* P_a^+ *has never output* σ*, or if* $\mathsf{Check}_{sk}(m, \sigma) = \bot$ *and* $d = 1$*, then output* 1*, otherwise output* 0.

Traceability. The adversary is given the receiver's public key, and during the experiment it has access to a checking oracle, it may interact with honest senders, and it may corrupt any sender to acquire its authentication key. To succeed, the adversary must either forge an authentication tag that checks to the identity of an uncorrupted sender, or it must output an authentication tag that checks to $\bot$ and convince the honest verifier of the authentication protocol that the tag checks to an identity.[3]

Denote by $P_a^+ \in \mathrm{IPPT}$ the machine that accepts (pk, ak_i) as input and repeatedly waits for messages on its communication tape. Given an input (Aut, m) on its communication tape P_a^+ computes and outputs $\sigma = \mathsf{Aut}_{ak_i,r}(pk, m)$, and then executes P_a on common input (pk, m, σ) and private input (ak_i, r). In the traceability experiment the adversary has "oracle access" to several copies of P_a^+. We stress that although the "oracle access" to each copy P_a^+ running on some input (pk, ak_i) is sequential by the definition of P_a^+, the adversary may

[2] No oracle for authentication or running the authentication protocol is needed, since the adversary can simulate these using the authentication keys $ak_1, \ldots, ak_{\ell(n)}$. A standard hybrid argument then shows that it suffices to consider a single invokation of the authentication protocol as in the definition.

[3] Traceability could alternatively be formalized by two separate experiments, where each experiment captures one type of attack, but we think this is less natural.

interact concurrently with different copies.[4] This is essential for the definition to be realistic, as we can not assume that different senders are aware of each other.

Definition 3 (Traceability). *A group message authentication scheme* GMA *is traceable if for* $\forall A \in \mathrm{IPPT}$ *the probability* $\Pr[\mathsf{Exp}^{\mathsf{trace}}_{\mathsf{GMA},A}(n) = 1]$ *is negligible.*

Definition 4 (Security). *A group message authentication scheme* GMA *is secure if it is anonymous and traceable.*

We stress, that while the new notion is related to variants of group signatures, it is essentially different from previous work. In particular, in contrast to various enhancements of group signatures, like traceable signatures [21] or identity escrow [23] (cf. Sect. 1), group message authentication it is a *relaxation* of group signatures, aiming at typical applications, and improved efficiency and security.

3 Tools

To construct the algorithms of the group message authentication scheme we use two basic primitives: a bounded signature scheme secure against chosen message attacks and a CCA2-secure cryptosystem with labels. The authentication protocol is loosely speaking a "zero-knowledge proof", but we use relaxed notions that allows efficient instantiation.

Bounded Signature Schemes. Each sender in a GMA scheme is given a unique authentication key that it later uses to authenticate messages. In our construction an authentication key is a signature of the identity of the holder, but a fully blown signature scheme is not needed. Note that standard signature schemes can be used to sign any message from an exponentially large space of strings, but in our setting we only need to sign a polynomial number of different integers. We call a signature scheme with this restriction *bounded.*

Definition 5 (Bounded Signature Scheme). *A* bounded signature scheme *consists of three algorithms* $(\mathsf{SKg}, \mathsf{Sig}, \mathsf{Vf})$ *associated with a polynomial* $\ell(n)$*:*

1. *A key generation algorithm* $\mathsf{SKg} \in \mathrm{PPT}$*, that on input* 1^n *outputs a public key* spk *and a secret key* ssk*.*
2. *A signature algorithm* $\mathsf{Sig} \in \mathrm{PPT}$*, that on input a secret key* ssk *and a message* $m \in [1, \ell(n)]$ *outputs a signature* s*.*
3. *A verification algorithm* $\mathsf{Vf} \in \mathrm{PT}$*, that on input a public key* spk*, a message* $m \in [1, \ell(n)]$*, and a candidate signature* s*, outputs a bit.*

For every $n \in \mathbb{N}$*, every* $(spk, ssk) \in \mathsf{SKg}(1^n)$*, every message* $m \in [1, \ell(n)]$*, and every* $s \in \mathsf{Sig}_{ssk}(m)$*, it must hold that* $\mathsf{Vf}_{spk}(m, s) = 1$*.*

The standard definition of security against chosen message attacks (CMA) [19] is then directly applicable. The existence of an ordinary signature scheme clearly implies the existence of a bounded one.

[4] This is a benign form of concurrency, since each copy of P_a^+ executes using its own independently generated private input (only the public inputs are dependent). Thus, our setting is the sequential setting in disguise.

Cryptosystems With Labels. Cryptosystems with labels were introduced by Shoup and Gennaro [31]. The idea of this notion is to associate a label with a ciphertext without providing any secrecy for the label. One simple way of constructing such cryptosystems is to append to the plaintext before encryption a collision-free hash digest of the label, but there are simpler constructions in practice. As a result, the input to the cryptosystem is not only a message, but also a label, and similarly for the decryption algorithm. Below we recall the definition, with a small modification — in the standard definition the decryption algorithm outputs only the message, without the label. Clearly, this is a minor modification, but we need it to allow certain joint encodings of the label and message in the analysis.

Definition 6 (Public Key Cryptosystem With Labels [31]). *A* public key cryptosystem with labels *consists of three algorithms* $(\mathsf{CKg}, \mathsf{Enc}, \mathsf{Dec})$*:*

1. *A key generation algorithm* $\mathsf{CKg} \in \mathrm{PPT}$*, that on input* 1^n *outputs a public key* cpk *and a secret key* csk*.*
2. *An encryption algorithm* $\mathsf{Enc} \in \mathrm{PPT}$*, that on input a public key* cpk*, a label* l*, and a message* $m \in \mathcal{M}_{cpk}$ *outputs a ciphertext* c*.*
3. *A decryption algorithm* $\mathsf{Dec} \in \mathrm{PT}$*, that on input a secret key* csk*, a label* l*, and a ciphertext* c *outputs the label and a message,* $(l, m) \in \{0,1\}^* \times \mathcal{M}_{cpk}$*, or* $\perp$*.*

For every $n \in \mathbb{N}$*, every* $(csk, cpk) = \mathsf{CKg}(1^n)$*, every label* $l \in \{0,1\}^*$*, and every* $m \in \mathcal{M}_{cpk}$ *it must hold that* $\mathsf{Dec}_{csk}(l, \mathsf{Enc}_{cpk}(l, m)) = (l, m)$*.*

Security against chosen ciphertext attacks is then defined as for standard cryptosystems except for some minor changes. In addition to the challenge messages, the adversary outputs a label to be used in the construction of the challenge ciphertext c. The adversary may also ask any query except the pair (l, c).

Experiment 3 (CCA2-Security With Labels [31], $\mathsf{Exp}^{\mathsf{cca2}-b}_{\mathsf{CSL},A}(n)$).

$$
\begin{aligned}
(cpk, csk) &\leftarrow \mathsf{CKg}(1^n)\\
(l, m_0, m_1, \mathrm{state}) &\leftarrow A^{\mathsf{Dec}_{csk}(\cdot,\cdot)}(\mathsf{choose}, cpk)\\
c &\leftarrow \mathsf{Enc}_{cpk}(l, m_b)\\
d &\leftarrow A^{\mathsf{Dec}_{csk}(\cdot,\cdot)}(\mathsf{guess}, \mathrm{state}, c)
\end{aligned}
$$

If $\mathsf{Dec}_{csk}(\cdot,\cdot)$ *was queried on* (l, c)*, then output 0, otherwise output* d*.*

Definition 7 (CCA2-Security). *Let* CSL *denote a public key cryptosystem with labels. We say that the cryptosystem* CSL *is CCA2-secure if for every adversary* $A \in \mathrm{PPT}$ *the quantity* $\left|\Pr[\mathsf{Exp}^{\mathsf{cca2}-0}_{\mathsf{CSL},A}(n) = 1] - \Pr[\mathsf{Exp}^{\mathsf{cca2}-1}_{\mathsf{CSL},A}(n) = 1]\right|$ *is negligible.*

A Relaxed Notion of Computational Soundness. Another tool used in our constructions, allowing for more efficient protocols, is a relaxed notion of soundness. In contrast to the standard (computational) soundness [18,28], we do not require that the protocol is sound for all inputs, but only when a part of the input is chosen according to a specific distribution, and the rest of the input is chosen by the adversary. Such a relaxation allows to capture scenarios where it is safe to assume that some parameters are chosen according to some prescribed distribution. For example, a bank will usually pick faithfully the keys guarding its transactions. A similar notion (without the oracle) has been used implicitly in several papers and is sometimes called a "computationally convincing proof", see e.g., [13]. In fact, non-interactive computationally sound proofs may be viewed as an instance of this notion.

Definition 8 (**(T,O)-Soundness**). *Let* $T \in \mathrm{PPT}$ *and let* $O \in \mathrm{PT}$ *be an oracle. Define a random variable* $(t_1, t_2, t_3) = T(1^n)$. *A 2-party protocol* $(P, V) \in \mathrm{IPPT} \times \mathrm{IPPT}$ *is* (T,O)*-sound for language* L *if for every instance chooser* $I \in \mathrm{PT}$ *and prover* $P^* \in \mathrm{PT}$ *the following holds: If* $(y, z) = I^{O(t_3,\cdot)}(t_1, t_2)$ *and* $x = (t_1, y)$, *then* $\Pr[x \notin L \wedge \langle P^{O(t_3,\cdot)*}(z), V\rangle(x) = 1]$ *is negligible.*

In the above definition we use generic names T, I, O and t_1, t_2, t_3, y, z to denote abstractly the involved algorithms and the information exchanged between them. The actual meaning and function of these parameters depends on a concrete scenario. For example, in the context of group message authentication algorithm T generates keys for both a signature scheme and a public-key encryption scheme, algorithm O computes signatures, and the parameters t_1, t_2, t_3 correspond to public and secret keys generated faithfully by the receiver (bank) using algorithm T: t_1 denotes (signature and encryption) public keys, t_2 denotes encryption secret key, and t_3 denotes signature secret key (cf. Construction 1). Obviously, if a protocol is sound in the standard sense, it is (T,O)-sound for any T, O. In a slight abuse of notation, we write (X, O)-sound also when X is a polynomially samplable random variable.

A Relaxed Notion of Computational Zero-Knowledge. Recall that a protocol is zero-knowledge if it can be simulated for *every* instance. Goldreich [17] introduced the notion of uniform zero-knowledge to capture the fact that for uniform adversaries it is sufficient to require that no instance for which the protocol leaks knowledge can be found. Wikström [36] generalized this idea to capture settings where the choice of instance is somehow restricted by an instance compiler F and randomized by some sampling algorithm T out of control of the adversary. We generalize Wikström's definition. As in the case of relaxed computational soundness, we use generic names T, I, O, F and t_1, t_2, y, z to denote the involved algorithms and the information exchanged between them. In the concrete context of group message authentication these names gain concrete meaning, e.g., T is a key generation algorithm of a public-key cryptosystem, O is a decryption oracle, and t_1, t_2 denote the public and secret keys, respectively, generated faithfully by the receiver using algorithm T (cf. Construction 1).

A sampling algorithm T outputs a sample $t = (t_1, t_2)$. The first part, t_1, is given to an instance chooser I which outputs a tuple (y, z), where y influences the choice of instance x, and z is an auxiliary input. An instance compiler F takes (t_1, y) as input and forms an instance (x, w) according to some predefined rule. A protocol is said to be (T, F, O)-zero-knowledge, for some oracle O, if for every malicious verifier V^* and every constant $c > 0$ there is a simulator M such that for every instance chooser I as above no distinguisher D can distinguish a real view of V^* from the view simulated by M with advantage better than n^{-c}, when all of these machines have access to the oracle $O(t_2, \cdot)$. Thus, the algorithms T, F, and O represent a class of environments in which the protocol remains zero-knowledge in the ϵ-zero-knowledge sense of Dwork, Naor, and Sahai [14]. We use the following experiment to define our notion formally.

Experiment 4 (Zero-Knowledge, $\mathsf{Exp}^{(T,F,O)-\mathsf{zk}-b}_{\pi,R,I,V^*,M,D}(n)$).

$$
\begin{aligned}
(t_1, t_2) &\leftarrow T(1^n) \\
(y, z) &\leftarrow I^{O(t_2,\cdot)}(1^n, t_1) \\
(x, w) &\leftarrow F(t_1, y) \\
d &\leftarrow \begin{cases} D^{O(t_2,\cdot)}(x, z, \langle P(w), V^{*O(t_2,\cdot)}(z)\rangle(x)) & \text{if } b=0 \\ D^{O(t_2,\cdot)}(x, z, M^{O(t_2,\cdot)}(z, x)) & \text{if } b=1 \end{cases}
\end{aligned}
$$

If $R(x, w) = 0$ or if the output of V_a^* or M respectively does not contain the list of oracle queries as a postfix, then output 0, otherwise output d.

The requirement that the list of queries made is output is quite natural. It captures that the simulator should not be able to ask more queries, or more powerful queries than the real verifier.

Definition 9 ((T, F, O)-Zero-Knowledge). *Let $\pi = (P, V)$ be an interactive protocol, let $T \in \mathrm{PPT}$ be a sampling algorithm, let $F \in \mathrm{PT}$ be an instance compiler, let $O \in \mathrm{PT}$ be an oracle, and let R be a relation. We say that π is (T, F, O)-zero-knowledge for R if for every verifier $V^* \in \mathrm{PPT}$ and every constant $c > 0$ there exists a simulator $M \in \mathrm{PPT}$ such that for every instance chooser $I \in \mathrm{PPT}$ and every distinguisher $D \in \mathrm{PPT}$:*

$$
\left| \Pr[\mathsf{Exp}^{(T,F,O)-\mathsf{zk}-0}_{\pi,R,I,V^*,M,D}(n) = 1] - \Pr[\mathsf{Exp}^{(T,F,O)-\mathsf{zk}-1}_{\pi,R,I,V^*,M,D}(n) = 1] \right| < n^{-c} .
$$

In our security proof we exploit that a protocol that satisfies the definition can be simulated polynomially many times sequentially, where the instance chooser chooses a new common and private input for each execution (see [29] for details).

4 A Generic Construction

The idea of our GMA scheme is simple. The group manager generates a key pair (spk, ssk) of a bounded signature scheme $\mathsf{BSS} = (\mathsf{SKg}, \mathsf{Sig}, \mathsf{Vf})$, and a key pair

(cpk, csk) of a CCA2-secure cryptosystem with labels $\mathsf{CSL} = (\mathsf{CKg}, \mathsf{Enc}, \mathsf{Dec})$. The ith user is given the authentication key $ak_i = \mathsf{Sig}_{ssk}(i)$. To compute an authentication tag σ of a message m, the user simply encrypts its secret key using the message m as a label, i.e., he computes $\sigma = \mathsf{Enc}_{cpk}(m, ak_i)$.

We assume that SKg is implemented in two steps SKg_1 and SKg_2: on input 1^n the algorithm SKg_1 outputs a string spk_1, that is given as input to SKg_2, which in turn outputs a key pair (spk, ssk), where $spk = (spk_1, spk_2)$. We also assume that CKg can be divided into CKg_1, and CKg_2 in a similar way and that $\mathsf{CKg}_1(1^n)$ is identically distributed to $\mathsf{SKg}_1(1^n)$. Note that any pair of a signature scheme and a cryptosystem can be viewed in this way by letting $\mathsf{SKg}_1(1^n) = \mathsf{CKg}_1(1^n) = 1^n$. This allows the signature scheme and the cryptosystem to generate dependent keys which share algebraic structure.

Construction 1 (Group Message Authentication Scheme GMA). Given a polynomial $\ell(n)$, a bounded signature scheme $\mathsf{BSS} = ((\mathsf{SKg}_1, \mathsf{SKg}_2), \mathsf{Sig}, \mathsf{Vf})$ associated with $\ell(n)$, and a cryptosystem with labels $\mathsf{CSL} = ((\mathsf{CKg}_1, \mathsf{CKg}_2), \mathsf{Enc}, \mathsf{Dec})$, the group message authentication scheme $\mathsf{GMA} = (\mathsf{RKg}, \mathsf{AKg}, \mathsf{Aut}, \mathsf{Check}, \pi_a)$ is constructed as follows:

Receiver Key Generation. On input 1^n the algorithm RKg computes $spk_1 = \mathsf{SKg}_1(1^n)$, $(spk, ssk) = \mathsf{SKg}_2(spk_1)$, and $(cpk, csk) = \mathsf{CKg}_2(spk_1)$, where spk_1 is a prefix of both spk and cpk, and outputs $(pk, sk) = ((cpk, spk), (csk, ssk))$.

Authentication Key Generation. On input $(1^n, sk, i)$ the algorithm AKg outputs an authentication key $ak_i = \mathsf{Sig}_{ssk}(i)$.

Authentication Algorithm. On input (pk, ak_i, m) the algorithm Aut outputs the authentication tag $\sigma = \mathsf{Enc}_{cpk}(m, ak_i)$.

Checking Algorithm. On input (sk, m, σ) the algorithm Check returns the smallest[5] $i \in [1, \ell(n)]$ such that $\mathsf{Vf}_{spk}(i, \mathsf{Dec}_{csk}(m, \sigma)) = 1$ or $\perp$ if no such i exists.

Authentication Protocol. Let R_a denote the relation consisting of pairs $((pk, m, \sigma), (ak_i, r))$, s.t. $\mathsf{Vf}_{spk}(i, ak_i) = 1$ and $\sigma = \mathsf{Enc}_{cpk}(m, ak_i, r)$, and let L_a denote the language corresponding to R_a, i.e., $L_a = \{x : \exists y \text{ s.t. } (x, y) \in R_a\}$ are the honestly encrypted valid tags. Let $F_{\mathsf{Enc}} \in \mathrm{PT}$ take as input a tuple $(cpk, (s, m, i, s', r))$. First F_{Enc} computes $(spk, ssk) = \mathsf{SKg}_2(cpk, s)$ and $ak_i = \mathsf{Sig}_{ssk}(i, s')$, where s resp. s' specify the randomness[6] to be used by SKg_2 resp. Sig_{ssk}. If $i \in [1, \ell(n)]$ holds, then the oracle F_{Enc} outputs $(((cpk, spk), m, \mathsf{Enc}_{cpk}(m, ak_i, r)), (ak_i, r))$, and otherwise it outputs $\perp$.

The authentication protocol π_a must be overwhelmingly complete, $(\mathsf{CKg}, F_{\mathsf{Enc}}, \mathsf{Dec})$-zero-knowledge for R_a, and $(((cpk, spk), csk, ssk), \mathsf{Sig})$-sound for the language L_a.

Proposition 1. *The construction* GMA *associated with a polynomial $\ell(n)$ is a group message authentication scheme. If* CSL *is CCA2-secure, and if* BSS *associated with $\ell(n)$ is CMA-secure, then* GMA *is secure.*

[5] In our concrete instantiation at most one index i has this property.

[6] Note that requiring explicit randomness as input ensures that the signature public key spk and the signature ak_i are correctly formed.

A proof is given in [29], but we outline the main ideas of the proof here. The functional property of the scheme is clear by inspection. For anonymity and traceability we argue as follows.

Anonymity. The idea of the proof is to turn a successful adversary A in the anonymity experiment into a successful adversary A' against the CCA2-security of the cryptosystem CSL. We do this in two steps:

1. We replace the invokation of the authentication protocol π_a in the anonymity experiment by a simulation. Due to its $(\mathsf{CKg}, F_{\mathsf{Enc}}, \mathsf{Dec})$-zero-knowledge property this changes the success probability of the adversary by an arbitrarily small amount. This allows simulation of the experiment without using the secret key of the cryptosystem.
2. We construct a new adversary A' that simulates the modified experiment and breaks the CCA2-security of the cryptosystem. When A outputs (m, i_0, i_1), A' hands (m, ak_{i_0}, ak_{i_1}) to its CCA2-experiment and forwards the challenge ciphertext σ it receives as a challenge authentication tag to A. All checking queries are computed by A' using its decryption oracle, and A' outputs the result of the simulated modified experiment. Thus, when A guesses correctly in the anonymity experiment, A' guesses correctly in the CCA2-experiment.

Traceability. The idea of the proof is to turn a successful attacker A against the traceability of GMA into a successful attacker A' against the CMA-security of the bounded signature scheme BSS. We do this in four steps:

1. We replace each invokation of P_a by a simulation. Due to the $(\mathsf{CKg}, F_{\mathsf{Enc}}, \mathsf{Dec})$-zero-knowledge of π_a and the sequential composition lemma [29] this changes the advantage of the adversary by an arbitrarily small amount.
2. We replace the authentication tags computed by P_a^+ by encryptions of 0. This only reduces the advantage of A negligibly, since CSL is CCA2-secure. The CCA2-security is essential for this argument, since we must be able to simulate the $\mathsf{Check}_{sk}(\cdot,\cdot)$-oracle to A without the secret decryption key csk.
3. We use the $(((cpk, spk), csk, ssk), \mathsf{Sig})$-soundness of π_a to argue that the probability that A convinces the honest verifier V_a that an invalid authentication tag is valid is negligible.
4. We show that the adversary in the modified traceability experiment can be used to break the CMA security of the bounded signature scheme. To see this, note that in the modified experiment we may postpone the computation of any authentication key ak_i until the adversary requests it, and to be successful in the modified experiment, A must produce an authentication tag that checks to an uncorrupted sender, i.e., A must produce an encrypted forged bounded signature of a sender's identity, and the simulator holds the secret decryption key.

5 An Efficient Instantiation

We give an efficient instantiation of the above generic scheme and prove its security under the strong RSA assumption and the decision Diffie-Hellman assumption. The strong RSA assumption says that given a modulus $N = pq$, where p and q are random safe primes of the same bit-size, and a random $g \in SQ_N$, it is infeasible to compute (g', e) such that $(g')^e = g \bmod N$ and $e \neq \pm 1$. Let G_q be a prime order q subgroup of $\mathbb{Z}_N^*$ generated by g such that $\log q = O(\log N)$, i.e., the subgroup has "large order". The decision Diffie-Hellman (DDH) assumption for G_q says that if $a, b, c \in \mathbb{Z}_q$ are randomly chosen, then it is infeasible to distinguish the distributions of (g, g^a, g^b, g^{ab}) and (g, g^a, g^b, g^c), where we compute modulo N (cf. full version [29] for formal definitions).

5.1 A Bounded Signature Scheme

We construct a bounded signature scheme $\mathsf{BSS}^{\mathrm{rsa}} = (\mathsf{SKg}^{\mathrm{rsa}}, \mathsf{Sig}^{\mathrm{rsa}}, \mathsf{Vf}^{\mathrm{rsa}}, \ell(n))$ for every polynomial $\ell(n)$, that some readers may recognize as a component of several cryptographic constructions based on the strong RSA-assumption. Denote by n_p an additional security parameter, whose value is determined by the authentication protocol.

Construction 2 (Bounded Signature Scheme $\mathsf{BSS}^{\mathrm{rsa}}$).

Key Generation. On input 1^n the algorithm $\mathsf{SKg}_1^{\mathrm{rsa}}$, i.e., the first step of the key generator, picks two random $n/2$-bit safe primes p and q, then defines and outputs $spk_1 = N = pq$. The key generator $\mathsf{SKg}_2^{\mathrm{rsa}}$ on input spk_1 picks a random $g' \in SQ_N$, and defines $g = (g')^{2\prod_{i=1}^{\ell(n)} \rho_i}$, where ρ_i is the ith positive prime integer larger than 2^{n_p} with $\rho_i = 3 \bmod 8$. This allows for computing roots of g, as required for the computation of signatures (see next step). Finally $\mathsf{SKg}_2^{\mathrm{rsa}}$ outputs the key pair $(spk, ssk) = ((N, g), g')$.

Signature Algorithm. On input a secret key ssk and a message $m \in [1, \ell(n)]$, the signature algorithm $\mathsf{Sig}^{\mathrm{rsa}}$ computes $\omega = g^{1/(2\rho_m)} \bmod N$ and outputs ω. More precisely, ω is computed as $(g')^{\prod_{i=1, i \neq m}^{\ell(n)} \rho_i} \bmod N$.

Verification Algorithm. On input a public key spk, a message $m \in [1, \ell(n)]$, and a candidate signature ω, the verification algorithm $\mathsf{Vf}^{\mathrm{rsa}}$ verifies that $|\rho_m| > 2$ and $\omega^{2\rho_m} = g \bmod N$ or $\omega^{-2\rho_m} = g \bmod N$.

Equivalently, we could define the keys of $\mathsf{BSS}^{\mathrm{rsa}}$ as $(spk, ssk) = ((N, g), (p, q))$, where $g \in SQ_N$ is picked at random. Then to compute a signature on a message m we would just compute the $2\rho_m$-th root of g modulo N directly, using the factorization of N. This would give exactly the same functionality and the same distribution of the signatures, but would not fit our framework with the two-step key generation, which is why we present the above variant. A simple proof of the proposition below, following older work [12,16], is given in [29].

Proposition 2. *For every polynomial $\ell(n)$, the scheme $\mathsf{BSS}^{\mathrm{rsa}}$ is a CMA-secure bounded signature scheme under the strong RSA assumption.*

5.2 A Cramer-Shoup Cryptosystem

The original cryptosystem of Cramer and Shoup [11] was given over a group of prime order, but this is not essential. We may view the key generation as consisting of first choosing a group with a generator and then running the key generation of the cryptosystem as described in [11] using these parameters. Denote by n_r an additional security parameter such that 2^{-n_r} is negligible.

Construction 3 (Cramer-Shoup Cryptosystem CSL^{cs} in SQ_N).

Key Generation. On input 1^n, the first key generator CKg_1^{cs} runs exactly as $\mathsf{SKg}^{\mathrm{rsa}}(1^n)$, and outputs N, i.e., a product of two random safe primes. The group is defined as the group SQ_N of squares modulo N. The second key generator CKg_2^{cs} is the original key generator of Cramer and Shoup with some minor modifications. It chooses $g_1, g_2 \in SQ_N$ and $z, x_1, x_2, y_1, y_2 \in [0, N2^{n_r}]$ randomly, and computes $h = g_1^z$, $c = g_1^{x_1} g_2^{x_2}$, and $d = g_1^{y_1} g_2^{y_2}$. Then a collision-free hash function $H : \{0,1\}^* \to [0, \sqrt{N}/2]$ is generated and $(cpk, csk) = ((N, H, g_1, g_2, h, c, d), (z, x_1, x_2, y_1, y_2))$ is output.

Encryption. On input a public key cpk, a label $l \in \{0,1\}^*$, and a message $m \in SQ_N$, the encryption algorithm Enc^{cs} chooses a random $r \in [0, N2^{n_r}]$ and outputs $(u_1, u_2, e, v) = (g_1^r, g_2^r, h^{2r}m, c^r d^{rH(l,u_1,u_2,e)})$.

Decryption. On input a secret key csk, a label $l \in \{0,1\}^*$, and a ciphertext (u_1, u_2, e, v), the decryption algorithm Dec^{cs} checks if

$$u_1^{2x_1} u_2^{2x_2} (u_1^{y_1} u_2^{y_2})^{2H(l,u_1,u_2,e)} = v^2 .$$

If so, it outputs eu_1^{-2z} and otherwise it outputs $\perp$.

We view (u_1, u_2, e, v) and (u_1', u_2', e', v') as encodings of the *same* ciphertext if $(u_1, u_2, e) = (u_1', u_2', e')$ and $v^2 = (v')^2$. A maliciously constructed, but valid, ciphertext may have $u_1, u_2, e \notin SQ_N$, but this is not a problem as explained in the proof of the proposition [29].

Proposition 3. *The cryptosystem* CSL^{cs} *is CCA2-secure under the decision Diffie-Hellman assumption.*

5.3 An Efficient Authentication Protocol

Given our implementations of a bounded signature scheme and of a cryptosystem with labels, the authentication protocol boils down to convincing the proxy that the plaintext of a Cramer-Shoup ciphertext is a non-trivial root. The basic idea is to first show that the ciphertext is valid, i.e., that the ciphertext (u_1, u_2, e, v) satisfies $u_1^{2x_1} u_2^{2x_2} (u_1^{y_1} u_2^{y_2})^{2H(m,u_1,u_2,e)} = v^2$, and then show that (u_1, e) is on the form $(g_1^r, h^{2r}\omega)$ for some 2ρth root ω. The latter is equivalent to showing that $(u_1^{2\rho}, e^{2\rho}/g)$ is on the form (g_1^s, h^{2s}), for some $|\rho| \geq 3$. Standard methods for proofs of logarithms over groups of unknown order, e.g. [4], could be used to construct a protocol for the above, but that would give an unnecessarily costly solution, involving an additional independently generated RSA-modulus and generators. We exploit the relaxed notions of soundness and zero-knowledge to significantly reduce this cost. We use a joint RSA-modulus of the cryptosystem and signature scheme to avoid the need for additional RSA-parameters, i.e., soundness holds even given a signature oracle. Our simulation of an interaction is indistinguishable from a real interaction only over the randomness of the public keys of the cryptosystem, but even given a decryption oracle. We identify which exponents need to be extracted to prove soundness and settle for existence of the other exponents, i.e., the witness is only partly extractable using standard rewinding techniques. Finally, we use special tricks, e.g., we use exponents of the form $(\rho - 3)/8$ to avoid proving that $|\rho| \geq 3$ using an interval proof [4].

Below we give an explicit protocol and state its security properties. Let n_r and n_b be additional security parameters such that 2^{-n_r} and 2^{-n_b} are negligible, and $2^{n_b} < \sqrt{N}/2$. Choose some n_p such that $n_p > n_b + n_r$. Denote by G_Q a subgroup of $\mathbb{Z}_P^*$ with generator G of prime order Q for some prime P, where $\log Q = n$.

Protocol 1 (Authentication Protocol).
common input: $cpk = (N, H, g_1, g_2, h, c, d)$, $g \in SQ_N$, $m \in \{0,1\}^*$, $u_1, u_2, e, v \in \mathbb{Z}_N^*$.
private input: $\rho > 2^{n_p}$ such that $\rho = 3 \bmod 8$, ω, and $r \in [0, N2^{n_r}]$ such that $\omega^{2\rho} = g \bmod N$ and $(u_1, u_2, e, v) = \mathsf{Enc}^{cs}_{cpk}(m, \omega, r)$.

Set $\hat{u}_1 = u_1^2$, $\hat{e} = e^2$, $\hat{u}_2 = u_2^2$, $\hat{v} = v^2$, and $f = (cd^{H(m,u_1,u_2,e)})^2$.

1. V_a picks a random $X \in \mathbb{Z}_Q$, hands $Y = G^X$ to the P_a, and proves the knowledge of X using the zero-knowledge proof of knowledge of a logarithm from [10].
2. P_a chooses $b_{P_a} \in [0, 2^{n_b} - 1]$, $R \in \mathbb{Z}_Q$, $s, k \in [0, 2^{n+n_r} - 1]$, $l_r, l_s, l_k \in [0, 2^{n+n_b+2n_r} - 1]$, $l_\rho \in [0, 2^{n_p+n_b+n_r} - 1]$, and $l_t \in [0, 2^{n+2n_b+3n_r} - 1]$ randomly and hands to V_a:
$$C = G^{b_{P_a}} Y^R, \quad (\alpha_1, \alpha_2, \beta) = (g_1^{l_r}, g_2^{l_r}, f^{l_r}), \quad (\delta_1, \delta_\rho) = (g_1^{l_t}, h^{l_t}),$$
$$(\gamma_1, \gamma_\rho, \gamma) = (g_1^{l_s} \hat{u}_1^{2l_\rho}, h^{l_s} \hat{e}^{l_\rho}, g_1^{l_k} g_2^{l_\rho}), \text{ and}$$
$$(\nu_1, \nu_\rho, \nu) = (g_1^s \hat{u}_1^{(\rho-3)/8}, h^s e^{(\rho-3)/8}, g_1^k g_2^{(\rho-3)/8}) .$$
3. V_a chooses $b_{V_a} \in [0, 2^{n_b} - 1]$ randomly and hands it to P_a.
4. P_a sets $b = b_{P_a} \oplus b_{V_a}$, and hands $(b_{P_a}, R, a_r, a_s, a_k, a_\rho, a_t)$ to V_a, where
$$a_r = 2rb + l_r \qquad a_\rho = ((\rho - 3)/8)b + l_\rho$$
$$(a_s, a_k) = (2sb + l_s, kb + l_k) \qquad a_t = (16s + 4r\rho)b + l_t .$$
5. V_a first checks if $C \stackrel{?}{=} G^{b_{P_a}} Y^R$, $b_{P_a} \in [0, 2^{n_b} - 1]$, and $a_\rho \in [0, 2^{n_p+n_b+n_r} - 1]$. Then it sets $\hat{\nu}_1 = \nu_1^2$ and $\hat{\nu}_\rho = \nu_\rho^2$, $\tilde{\nu}_1 = \hat{\nu}_1^8 \hat{u}_1^6$, $\tilde{\nu}_\rho = \hat{\nu}_\rho^8 \hat{e}^3$, and $b = b_{P_a} \oplus b_{V_a}$, and checks that
$$(\hat{u}_1^b \alpha_1, \hat{u}_2^b \alpha_2, \hat{v}^b \beta) \stackrel{?}{=} (g_1^{a_r}, g_2^{a_r}, f^{a_r})$$
$$(\hat{\nu}_1^b \gamma_1, \hat{\nu}_\rho^b \gamma_\rho, \nu^b \gamma) \stackrel{?}{=} (g_1^{a_s} \hat{u}_1^{2a_\rho}, h^{a_s} \hat{e}^{a_\rho}, g_1^{a_k} g_2^{a_\rho})$$
$$(\tilde{\nu}_1^b \delta_1, (\tilde{\nu}_\rho / g)^b \delta_\rho) \stackrel{?}{=} (g_1^{a_t}, h^{a_t}) .$$

Proposition 4. *The authentication protocol (Protocol 1) is overwhelmingly complete,* $(\mathsf{CKg}^{cs}, F_{\mathsf{Enc}^{cs}}, \mathsf{Dec}^{cs})$*-zero-knowledge for the relation* R_a*, and* $(((cpk, spk), csk, ssk), \mathsf{Sig})$*-sound for the language* L_a*, under the strong RSA assumption and the decision Diffie-Hellman assumption.*

Proposition 4 is proved the full version of this paper [29]. It seems impossible to prove that the protocol is zero-knowledge, since the pair (ν_1, ν_ρ) may be viewed as an El Gamal ciphertext of part of the witness, namely $g^{\frac{1}{8}-\frac{3}{8\rho}}$, using a public key h which is part of the common input. Hence it is conceivable that the auxiliary input contains sufficient information to check if this is the case, without allowing any simulator to produce a correct view. The protocol is only sound as long as no adversary can reduce modulo the order of the group SQ_N.

5.4 Efficiency of the Concrete Scheme

An authentication tag requires 5 exponentiations to compute and 6 exponentiations to verify. Unique prefixes of authentication keys can be tabulated to speed up identification. The authentication protocol requires 7 rounds, since the subprotocol from [10] requires 4 rounds, but this can be reduced to 5 rounds by interlacing the last two rounds of the subprotocol with the first rounds of the main protocol. For practical parameters, $n = 1024$ and $n_r = 30$, $n_b = 50$, and $n_p = 85$ the complexity of the prover and verifier in the authentication protocol corresponds to 19 and 17 exponentiations [29].

Furthermore, the complexity of our scheme can be reduced by using standard techniques such as simultaneous exponentiation and fixed-base exponentiation [27], but for typical applications this is not practical for the sender. A simpler way to reduce complexity of a sender is to pre-compute most exponentiations in an offline phase. It is immediate that this reduces the complexity in the online phase to less than one exponentiation. This approach is feasible even on weak computational devices.

The protocol can also be simplified in an other direction by letting the receiver choose the commitment parameters G and Y to be used by all parties. This reduces the number of rounds to 3, and also decreases the number of exponentiations by 6 for the prover and 7 for the verifier. However, it seems hard to abstract this version in a natural way and keep the description of the generic scheme reasonably modular. Hence, to keep the exposition clear we have chosen not to present the most efficient solution.

6 Conclusion

We remind the reader that performing an exponentiation in a bilinear group used for the provably secure group signature schemes corresponds to roughly 6-8 modular exponentiations for comparable security levels. Thus, our scheme is in fact competitive with these schemes, but under a better understood assumption.

The standard group signature schemes, analyzed in the random oracle model, clearly out-perform our scheme, but the random oracle model is not sound [7]. This is sometimes considered a purely theoretical nuisance, but we think that the recent attacks on hashfunctions, e.g., the collision-attacks on SHA-1 of Wang [34], show that even in practice it is prudent not to model a hashfunction as a random function.

Furthermore, the strong RSA assumption is arguably the most trusted assumption under which a provably secure ordinary signature scheme is known to exist with sufficiently low complexity for practical use, and the decision Diffie-Hellman assumption is the most studied assumption used in practice for public key cryptography.

In this work we have formalized the new notion of group message authentication, which relaxes some of the requirements of group signatures and has applications to anonymous credit cards, and we have constructed a provably secure scheme under the above two assumptions.

References

1. Ateniese, G., Camenisch, J., Hohenberger, S., de Medeiros, B.: Practical group signatures without random oracles. Cryptology ePrint Archive, Report 2005/385 (2005), `http://eprint.iacr.org/`
2. Ateniese, G., Tsudik, G.: Some open issues and directions in group signatures. In: Franklin, M.K. (ed.) FC 1999. LNCS, vol. 1648, pp. 196–211. Springer, Heidelberg (1999)
3. Bellare, M., Micciancio, D., Warinschi, B.: Foundations of group signatures: Formal definitions, simplified requirements, and a construction based on general assumptions. In: Biham, E. (ed.) EUROCRYPT 2003. LNCS, vol. 2656, pp. 614–629. Springer, Heidelberg (2003)
4. Boudot, F.: Efficient proofs that a committed number lies in an interval. In: Preneel, B. (ed.) EUROCRYPT 2000. LNCS, vol. 1807, pp. 431–444. Springer, Heidelberg (2000)
5. Boyen, X., Waters, B.: Compact group signatures without random oracles. In: Vaudenay, S. (ed.) EUROCRYPT 2006. LNCS, vol. 4004, pp. 427–444. Springer, Heidelberg (2006)
6. Camenisch, J., Groth, J.: Group signatures: Better efficiency and new theoretical aspects. In: Blundo, C., Cimato, S. (eds.) SCN 2004. LNCS, vol. 3352, pp. 120–133. Springer, Heidelberg (2005)
7. Canetti, R., Goldreich, O., Halevi, S.: The random oracle model revisited. In: 30th ACM STOC, pp. 209–218 (1998)
8. Chaum, D.: Designated confirmer signatures. In: De Santis, A. (ed.) EUROCRYPT 1994. LNCS, vol. 950, pp. 86–91. Springer, Heidelberg (1995)
9. Chaum, D., van Heyst, E.: Group signatures. In: Davies, D.W. (ed.) EUROCRYPT 1991. LNCS, vol. 547, pp. 257–265. Springer, Heidelberg (1991)
10. Cramer, R., Damgård, I., MacKenzie, P.D.: Efficient zero-knowledge proofs of knowledge without intractability assumptions. In: Imai, H., Zheng, Y. (eds.) PKC 2000. LNCS, vol. 1751, pp. 354–372. Springer, Heidelberg (2000)

11. Cramer, R., Shoup, V.: A practical public key cryptosystem provably secure against adaptive chosen ciphertext attack. In: Krawczyk, H. (ed.) CRYPTO 1998. LNCS, vol. 1462, pp. 13–25. Springer, Heidelberg (1998)
12. Cramer, R., Shoup, V.: Signature schemes based on the strong RSA assumption. In: 6th ACM CCS, pp. 46–51 (1999)
13. Damgård, I., Fujisaki, E.: A statistically-hiding integer commitment scheme based on groups with hidden order. In: Zheng, Y. (ed.) ASIACRYPT 2002. LNCS, vol. 2501, pp. 125–142. Springer, Heidelberg (2002)
14. Dwork, C., Naor, M., Sahai, A.: Concurrent zero-knowledge. In: 30th ACM STOC, pp. 409–418. ACM Press, New York (1998)
15. Fiat, A., Shamir, A.: How to prove yourself. practical solutions to identification and signature problems. In: Odlyzko, A.M. (ed.) CRYPTO 1986. LNCS, vol. 263, pp. 186–189. Springer, Heidelberg (1987)
16. Gennaro, R., Halevi, S., Rabin, T.: Secure hash-and-sign signatures without the random oracle. In: Stern, J. (ed.) EUROCRYPT 1999. LNCS, vol. 1592, pp. 123–139. Springer, Heidelberg (1999)
17. Goldreich, O.: A uniform-complexity treatment of encryption and zeroknowledge. Journal of Cryptology 6(1), 21–53 (1993)
18. Goldwasser, S., Micali, S., Rackoff, C.: The knowledge complexity of interactive proof systems. SIAM J. Comput. 18(1), 186–208 (1989)
19. Goldwasser, S., Micali, S., Rivest, R.: A digital signature scheme secure against adaptive chosen-message attacks. SIAM J. Comput. 17(2), 281–308 (1988)
20. Jakobsson, M., Sako, K., Impagliazzo, R.: Designated verifier proofs and their applications. In: Maurer, U.M. (ed.) EUROCRYPT 1996. LNCS, vol. 1070, pp. 143–154. Springer, Heidelberg (1996)
21. Kiayias, A., Tsiounis, Y., Yung, M.: Traceable signatures. In: Cachin, C., Camenisch, J.L. (eds.) EUROCRYPT 2004. LNCS, vol. 3027, pp. 571–589. Springer, Heidelberg (2004)
22. Kiayias, A., Tsiounis, Y., Yung, M.: Group encryption. Cryptology ePrint Archive, Report 2007/015 (2007), `http://eprint.iacr.org/2007/015`
23. Kilian, J., Petrank, E.: Identity escrow. In: Krawczyk, H. (ed.) CRYPTO 1998. LNCS, vol. 1462, pp. 169–185. Springer, Heidelberg (1998)
24. Kim, S., Park, S., Won, D.: Group signatures for hierarchical multigroups. In: Okamoto, E. (ed.) ISW 1997. LNCS, vol. 1396, pp. 273–281. Springer, Heidelberg (1998)
25. Laur, S., Pasini, S.: Sas-based group authentication and key agreement protocols. In: Cramer, R. (ed.) PKC 2008. LNCS, vol. 4939, pp. 197–213. Springer, Heidelberg (2008)
26. Lucks, S.: A variant of the cramer-shoup cryptosystem for groups of unknown order. In: Zheng, Y. (ed.) ASIACRYPT 2002. LNCS, vol. 2501, pp. 27–45. Springer, Heidelberg (2002)
27. Menezes, A., Oorschot, P., Vanstone, S.: Handbook of Applied Cryptography. CRC Press, Boca Raton (1997)
28. Micali, S.: Computationally sound proofs. SIAM J. Comput. 30(4), 1253–1298 (2000)
29. Przydatek, B., Wikström, D.: Group message authentication. Cryptology ePrint Archive (2010) (The full version of this paper), `http://eprint.iacr.org/`
30. Qin, B., Wu, Q., Susilo, W., Mu, Y.: Group decryption. Cryptology ePrint Archive, Report 2007/017 (2007), `http://eprint.iacr.org/2007/017`

31. Shoup, V., Gennaro, R.: Securing threshold cryptosystems against chosen ciphertext attack. In: Nyberg, K. (ed.) EUROCRYPT 1998. LNCS, vol. 1403, pp. 1–16. Springer, Heidelberg (1998)
32. Trolin, M., Wikström, D.: Hierarchical group signatures. Cryptology ePrint Archive, Report 2004/311 (2004), `http://eprint.iacr.org/`
33. Trolin, M., Wikström, D.: Hierarchical group signatures. In: Caires, L., Italiano, G.F., Monteiro, L., Palamidessi, C., Yung, M. (eds.) ICALP 2005. LNCS, vol. 3580, pp. 446–458. Springer, Heidelberg (2005) (Full Version [32])
34. Wang, X., Yin, Y.L., Yu, H.: Finding collisions in the full sha-1. In: Shoup, V. (ed.) CRYPTO 2005. LNCS, vol. 3621, pp. 17–36. Springer, Heidelberg (2005)
35. Wikström, D.: Designated confirmer signatures revisited. Cryptology ePrint Archive, Report 2006/123 (2006), `http://eprint.iacr.org/2006/123`
36. Wikström, D.: Designated confirmer signatures revisited. In: Vadhan, S.P. (ed.) TCC 2007. LNCS, vol. 4392, pp. 342–361. Springer, Heidelberg (2007) (Full Version [35])

Fast Secure Computation of Set Intersection

Stanisław Jarecki and Xiaomin Liu

University of California, Irvine

Abstract. A secure set intersection protocol between sender S and receiver R on respective inputs X and Y s.t. $|X|, |Y| \leq n$, allows R to learn $X \cap Y$ while S learns nothing about R's inputs. In other words it is a secure computation of functionality $\mathcal{F}_{\mathsf{SI}}^{n \times n} : (X, Y) \rightarrow (\perp, X \cap Y)$ on sets of size at most n. A variant we call *adaptive* set intersection implements an interactive version of this functionality, which on senders S's input X allows the receiver R to *adaptively* make up to n queries y_i and learn whether or not $y_i \in X$.

We show that a simple protocol using $|X| + 4|Y|$ modular exponentiations and one round of interaction is a secure computation of the adaptive set intersection functionality against malicious adversaries in the Random Oracle Model (ROM) under a *One-More Gap Diffie-Hellman* (OMGDH) assumption, i.e. assuming the One-More Diffie-Hellman problem is hard even when the DDH problem is easy. Even though the protocol has only a single round, the corresponding ideal functionality is adaptive because receiver's queries are efficiently extractable only eventually, rather than during protocol execution. However, under the OMGDH assumption in ROM the set of queries any efficient receiver can make is *committed* at the time of protocol execution, and hence no efficient adversary can benefit from the adaptive feature of this functionality.

Finally we show that this protocol easily extends to Set Intersection with Data Transfer, which is equivalent to the "Keyword Search" problem, where sender S associates each item x_i in X with a data entry d_i, and R learns all (x_i, d_i) pairs such that $x_i \in Y$.

1 Introduction

Secure Protocol for Computing Set Intersection and Extensions. Secure computation of set intersection (or secure evaluation of a set intersection function) is a protocol which allows two parties, sender S and receiver R, to interact on their respective input sets X and Y in such a way that R learns $X \cap Y$ and S learns nothing. Secure computation of set intersection has numerous useful applications: For example, medical institutions could find common patients without learning any information about patients that are not in the intersection, different security agencies could search for common items in their databases without revealing any other information, the U.S. Department of Homeland Security can quickly find if there is a match between a passenger manifest and its terrorist watch list, etc.

A natural extension of the set intersection problem which seems useful in any such application is what we call *Set Intersection with Data Transfer*, which

J.A. Garay and R. De Prisco (Eds.): SCN 2010, LNCS 6280, pp. 418–435, 2010.

allows the sender to associate each item x_i in its set X with a data entry d_i (e.g. the medical records of a given patient, the dossier the security agency holds for a suspect, etc), and the receiver with input set Y learns not only all x_i's s.t. $x_i \in Y$, but also the data entries d_i associated with these matching x_i's. Note that an adaptive version of this problem, where the receiver can query the sender on adaptively chosen items y_j, and each time learns if there exists $x_i \in X$ s.t. $x_i = y_j$, and if so it learns the associated entry d_i, was introduced as the "Oblivious Keyword Search" problem in [FIPR05, OK04], or "Private Matching" in [FNP04], and it is also sometimes called "Keyword OT" (or "Keyword PIR"), since it is a generalization of Oblivious Transfer to oblivious access of sender's data entries using associated keywords rather than indexes.

Prior Work on Set Intersection Protocols. Apart of generic results on two-party secure computation (or secure function evaluation), the first special-purpose protocol for secure computation of set intersection appeared in [EGS03]. It was shown secure against honest-but-curious adversaries under the DDH assumption in ROM, and if only R gets the output then the total computation cost of this protocol is $|X| + 2|Y|$ modular exponentiations.

In the standard model, i.e. without recourse to ROM, Freedman et al. [FNP04] showed a protocol based on oblivious polynomial evaluation secure against honest-but-curious adversaries at the cost of $O(n \log \log n)$ exponentiations, for $|X|$ and $|Y|$ bounded by n. Modifications of this protocol secure against malicious adversaries appeared in several recent papers, by [CZ09], [DSMRY09], and [HN10], at the cost of increasing the protocol bandwidth to $O(n^2)$ group elements and computation to $O(n^2)$ exponentiations in the case of [CZ09], $O(nk^2 \log^2(n))$ and $O(n^2k^2 \log^2(n))$ respectively in [DSMRY09], and $O(nt)$ and $O(n(t + \log \log n))$ respectively in [HN10], where $X, Y \subset \{0,1\}^t$, all secure under DDH.

Another approach for secure computation of set intersection was proposed in [FIPR05], based on *Oblivious Pseudo-Random Function* (OPRF), i.e. a secure computation protocol for a functionality which lets R compute value $f_k(x)$ for a pseudo-random function f given S's input k and R's input x. The idea is simple: S picks k and sends to R the set of values $\tilde{X} = \{f_k(x)\}_{x \in X}$. Then S and R interact in n instances of the OPRF protocol on S's input k and R's input y, for each $y \in Y$. R outputs the set $\{y \in Y \text{ s.t. } f_k(y) \in \tilde{X}\}$. Note that this set is equal to $X \cap Y$ if f is a one-to-one function. This idea was revisited in [HL08] who utilized a non-injective PRF, which could introduce collisions for a maliciously chosen PRF key, and therefore it was not secure against malicious adversaries. Subsequently [JL09] and [BCC$^+$09] proposed secure computation protocols for injective PRF's with $O(1)$ exponentiations, leading to secure set intersection in the standard model with $O(n)$ modular exponentiations. However, the protocols of [JL09, BCC$^+$09] require a Common Reference String which includes a safe RSA modulus – required by a Paillier Encryption [Pai99, CS03] these protocols utilize – which must be securely generated. Moreover, the protocols of [JL09, BCC$^+$09] involve several exponentiations modulo N^2, where N is at least 1024-bit long, with $|N|$-bit exponents, and each such exponentiations is about 24 times slower than a 160-bit exponentiation modulo a 1024-bit modulus.

Main Contribution. Our main contribution is a protocol for set intersection secure against malicious adversaries under the *One-More Gap Diffie-Hellman* (OMGDH) assumption in ROM. This protocol is a very close variant of the protocol of Evfimievski et al. [EGS03], and our contribution is really a security analysis of this modification rather than the protocol itself. This protocol is attractive because it takes only one round of interaction, and its total computational cost is under $3(|X|+|Y|)$ exponentiations. Moreover, since these exponentiations can use 160-bit exponents, this protocol could be on the order of $20-100$ times less expensive than the protocols of [JL09, BCC+09]. Furthemore, the OMGDH assumption and ROM model might be an attractive alternative to the assumptions required by the latter works, which consist of the DCR assumption on $Z^*_{N^2}$ and the DDH assumption on QR_N, for safe RSA modulus N, and the Decisional q-SDH assumption on either $Z^*_{N^2}$ [JL09] or a prime-order group [BCC+09]. While the original protocol of [EGS03] used only $|X|+2|Y|$ exponeniations, it was shown secure only in the honest-but-curious model, which is clearly not satisfying in practice. Thus the significance of our analysis is that assuming ROM one can get a set intersection protocol secure against malicious players at a small overhead over [EGS03], and the resulting solution is an order of magnitude faster than currently fastest standard model solutions, which moreover rely on strong assumptions of DCR, DDH, and q-SDH [JL09, BCC+09].

An important disclaimer is that unlike the protocols of [JL09, BCC+09], the protocol we propose is only shown to implement secure computation of an *adaptive* variant of the set intersection functionality, denoted $\mathcal{F}_{\mathsf{ASI}}^{n\times n}$, which on S's input a set X of at most n elements, allows the receiver R to make n adaptive queries $y_1, ..., y_n$, each time revealing whether or not item y_i belongs to set X. However, we also show that under OMGDH in ROM all efficient adversaries are committed at the time of the protocol execution to the set of at most n distinct queries they can ever make. In other words, even though the protocol achieves only an adaptive version of the set intersection functionality, any efficient adversary is committed to all its inputs at the execution time, and hence it is not clear what advantage an adversary could obtain by not making all these queries straight away at the time of protocol execution, in which case the $\mathcal{F}_{\mathsf{ASI}}^{n\times n}$ functionality is equivalent to the standard set intersection functionality $\mathcal{F}_{\mathsf{SI}}^{n\times n}$.

Closely Related Prior Work. Several prior works on set intersection protocol or adaptive oblivious transfer protocols [EGS03, CNS07, OK04, CT05] consider very close variants of the protocol presented in this paper. In particular the protocol we analyze varies from the protocol shown honest-but-curious secure by [EGS03] in only the following aspects: (1) We change the description of this protocol so that to emphasize that it is a case of the OPRF-based set intersection protocol of [FIPR05, HL08] for the ROM-based PRF function $f_k(x) = (H(x))^k$; (2) we add the outer layer hashing to this function, i.e. we use $f_k(x) = H'(H(x), (H(x))^k)$ instead of $f_k(x) = (H(x))^k$, which facilitates more efficient extraction of inputs x on which a malicious party evaluates this function; (3) to enforce consistency of S's computation we add a zero-knowledge proof of correct exponentiation to S's response; and (4) we change the procedure to blind

R's inputs to make R's privacy perfect instead of computational. The security analysis we provide for this modification of the protocol of [EGS03] shows that (1) getting malicious security for the [FIPR05, HL08]-style OPRF-based $\mathcal{F}_{\mathsf{SI}}^{n \times n}$ protocol which uses the ROM-based PRF shown above requires a *One More DH* assumption, and not just CDH required by the honest-but-curious protocol; (2) the reduction seems to go through only assuming access to the DDH oracle (otherwise it's unclear how to extract adversarial receiver's inputs), so the security of this protocol against malicious players requires the One-More *Gap* DH assumption; and as we explained in a paragraph above, (3) the resulting protocol is a secure computation of $\mathcal{F}_{\mathsf{ASI}}$, and not $\mathcal{F}_{\mathsf{SI}}$, but no efficient receiver can take advantage of the adaptive interface of $\mathcal{F}_{\mathsf{ASI}}$ other than by delaying its committed queries (or foregoing them entirely), assuming OMGDH in ROM.

Another group of papers which considered protocols closely related to the one we consider are Adaptive OT protocols of [OK04] and [CT05], secure under One-More RSA and One-More DH respectively, as well as [CNS07] which generalizes both of them with a generic construction of secure computation of adaptive OT from unique blind signatures. The underlying idea of the set intersection we propose is very similar to these Adaptive OT protocols because unique signature scheme can also be thought of as *verifiable* unpredictable function, and in a sense we enable such verifiability in the security reduction by allowing the reduction to have access to the DDH oracle. However, the difference between our work and [OK04, CT05, CNS07] lies in the following: (1) [CNS07, CT05] provide "index" OT protocols, i.e. R enters an index i to get the i-th data item from the sender who enters a sequence of n items, while our construction is a "keyword" OT, as in [OK04], where S contributes a set of keyword/data pair which R retrieves by also contributing keywords; (2) [CNS07, OK04] are based on unique blind signatures which have efficient verification, unlike our PRF, while (3) [CT05], which does not use blind signatures is only shown secure according to game-based security notions instead of secure computation; and last but not least (4) all of these works target an *adaptive* oblivious transfer, while for us adaptivity is a problem! As we discussed above, our goal is a minimal-round computation of standard set intersection functionality, which is non-adaptive, and although we fall (slightly) short of that goal because we do not guarantee extraction of all n queries made by R *during* protocol execution time, we show that there is a very limited amount of adaptivity in the way an efficient receiver can make these queries: It can only choose to forego or delay making any query in a set of n queries Y to which it is committed at the execution time.

Finally, in parallel with our work, [CT10] proposed a close variant of the protocol analyzed here, with blind RSA signature replacing blinded exponentiation, and analyzed its security against honest-but-curious adversaries. Compared to our protocol the computational cost of S's increases by a factor of two, but R's cost is reduced to four group multiplications. Hence it would be practically relevant to analyze the security of that variant in the malicious adversarial setting.

Extension to Set Intersection with Data Transfer. We also extend the secure computation of set intersection to secure computation of Set Intersection with

Data Transfer, i.e. computation of functionality $\mathcal{F}_{\mathsf{SIwDT}}^{n\times n} : ((X, D), Y) \rightarrow (\perp, \{(x_i, d_i) : x_i \in Y\})$, where $X = (x_1, \ldots, x_N)$ and $D = (d_1, \ldots, d_N)$. As in the set intersecton case, the protocol we present computes securely, under the OMGDH assumption in ROM, the adaptive variant of this functionality, $\mathcal{F}_{\mathsf{ASIwDT}}^{n\times n}$, defined similarly as $\mathcal{F}_{\mathsf{ASI}}$ is defined in relation to $\mathcal{F}_{\mathsf{SI}}$, and as in the set intersection case an efficient adversary is committed to the set of n queries Y it can ever make at the protocol execution time. As a side technical contribution, we also point out a simple oblivious computation protocol for the unpredictable (under CDH) or pseudorandom (under DDH) function $f_k(x) = (H(x))^k$, secure in ROM according to a game-based definition.

Technical Roadmap. [FIPR05] proposed the idea of constructing a set intersection protocol from the oblivious pseudo-random function. Since for any unpredictable function $f_k(x)$, $H'(f_k(x))$ is a pseudo-random function in ROM, a set intersection protocol can be constructed from an oblivious computation of a simple function $f_k(x) = (H(x))^k$ which is unpredictable under CDH in ROM. An oblivious computation of f_k is just a "blind exponentiation" protocol: The receiver R picks a random exponent α, sends $y = (H(x))^\alpha$ to the sender S, upon which S replies with $z = y^k$, so that R can recover $f_k(x) = z^{1/\alpha}$. Receiver's privacy follows from the fact that what R sends are random group elements. Security against malicious receiver is defined in the following way: After (parallel) interaction in Q instances of this protocol, the malicious receiver cannot output $Q + 1$ pairs $(x_i, f_k(x_i))$. This property directly follows from the One-More DH assumption: Given a set of n group elements $(g_1, \ldots, g_N)$, it's hard to output $Q + 1$ pairs of $(g_{i_j}, (g_{i_j})^x)$ if one is allowed only at most Q queries to an oracle which returns h^x for any input h. Note that this simple protocol is not a secure function evaluation of $f_k(x)$, because information is leaked about S's key k in addition to just the function value $f_k(x)$, but as we show it still leads to a secure set intersection protocol.

Using the idea of [FIPR05] we convert this simple OPRF into a set intersection protocol: S computes $u_i = f_k'(\mathsf{s}_i) = H'(f_k(\mathsf{s}_i))$ for each s_i in S's private set, and sends the set of u_i's to the receiver. Then S and R interact to allow R to learn $v_j = f_k'(\mathsf{r}_j))$ for each r_j in R's private set, while leaking no information about any r_j to S. (In our actual protocol we use $f_k'(x) = H'(H(x), f_k(x))$, which allows for better security reduction.) This is done by using the simple protocol above to obliviously compute $f_k(\mathsf{r}_j)$. Because function f_k' is collision-resistant even for maliciously chosen k, with overwhelming probability the receiver can recover the intersection between s_i's and r_j's from the intersection between u_i's and v_j's, while S learns nothing from the protocol.

The one technical difficulty remaining is that it appears difficult to extract a malicious receiver R*'s input together *during* the protocol execution, which is necessary for a secure computation of set intersection. Instead we show that when the hash functions are modeled as random oracles then the simulator can use a DDH oracle to extract R*'s input r_j whenever R* itself learns the $f_k'(\mathsf{r}_j)$ value, which can happen at any time after protocol execution. Thus this protocol achieves secure computation of *Adaptive* Set Intersection functionality

$\mathcal{F}_{\mathsf{ASI}}^{n\times n}$ under the One-More Gap Diffie-Hellman assumption. However, as we show in Section 4.1, the same OMGDH guarantees that for any efficient receiver, its inputs $\mathsf{r}_1, ..., \mathsf{r}_n$ are committed when R^* sends its first protocol message.

Organization. We list the cryptographic assumptions and tools we need in Section 2. A simple oblivious computation of the unpredictable function under OneMore DH in ROM is described in 3, followed by the constructions of Set Intersection protocol and Set Intersection with Data Transfer respectively in Section 4 and Section 5.

2 Assumptions and Tools

- **CDH assumption**: Let g be a generator of a group $\mathbb{G}$ of order q. *CDH problem is (t, ϵ)-hard* if for any t-time algorithm $\mathcal{A}$, $Pr[g^{ab} \leftarrow \mathcal{A}(g^a, g^b)] \leq \epsilon$, for the probability going over random a and b in $\mathbb{Z}_q$.
- **(N, Q)-One-More (Non-Adaptive) DH Assumption:** [BNPS03] shows the *adaptive* One-More RSA Inversion assumption and One-More Discrete Log assumption. Here we give a non-adaptive variant of the One-More problem, One-More DH assumption, where the algorithm $\mathcal{A}$ must prepare all the queries to the One-More DH oracle together. Let $\mathbb{G}$ be a multiplicative group of order q. We say that *(N, Q)-one-more DH problem is (t, ϵ)-hard* if for any t-time algorithm $\mathcal{A}$,

$$Pr\left[\{(g_i, (g_i)^x)\}_{i=1,\ldots,Q+1} \leftarrow \mathcal{A}^{(\cdot)^x}(g_1, \ldots, g_N)\right] \leq \epsilon$$

  where the probability goes over random $(g_1, \ldots, g_N)$ in $\mathbb{G}^N$ and the random x in $\mathbb{Z}_q$, oracle $(\cdot)^x$ on any $h \in \mathbb{G}$ returns h^x, and $\mathcal{A}$ makes at most Q *parallel* query to the oracle $(\cdot)^x$.

  We show a proof of the hardness of the $(Q + 1, Q)$-One-More (Non-Adaptive) DH problem in the generic group model in the full version of this paper [JL10], which implies the hardness of (N, Q)-One-More (Non-Adaptive) DH problem by Lemma 3.3 of [BNPS03], which relates in corresponding way with the *adaptive* One-More *RSA* assumptions.
- **(N, Q)-One-More (Non-Adaptive) Gap DH Assumption:** Informally, we say that (N, Q)-One-More (Non-Adaptive) Gap DH problem is hard if (N, Q)-One-More (Non-Adaptive) DH problem is hard while DDH problem is easy. Formally let $\mathbb{G}$ be a multiplicative group of order q. We say that *(N, Q)-one-more (Non-Adaptive) Gap DH problem is (t, ϵ)-hard* if for any t-time algorithm $\mathcal{A}$,

$$Pr\left[\{(g_i, (g_i)^x)\}_{i=1,\ldots,Q+1} \leftarrow \mathcal{A}^{(\cdot)^x, \mathcal{DDH}(\cdot,\cdot,\cdot,\cdot)}(g_1, \ldots, g_N)\right] \leq \epsilon$$

  where the probability goes over random $(g_1, \ldots, g_N)$ in $\mathbb{G}^N$ and the random x in $\mathbb{Z}_q$, $\mathcal{DDH}(\cdot, \cdot, \cdot, \cdot)$ on tuple (g, h, u, v) returns 1 if there exists a $w \in \mathbb{Z}_q$, s.t. $h = g^w$ and $v = u^w$ and 0 otherwise, and $\mathcal{A}$ makes at most Q parallel queries to the oracle $(\cdot)^x$. Here we don't limit the number of queries made by $\mathcal{A}$ to the oracle $\mathcal{DDH}$.

A weaker version of this assumption replaces the $\mathcal{DDH}$ oracle with $\mathcal{DL}_x(\cdot,\cdot)$ which on pair (g,h) returns 1 if $h = g^x$ and 0 otherwise. We indeed only need this weaker assumption in the security proof for our set intersection protocol in Section 4. This is a simplification of the $\mathcal{DDH}$ oracle, because one can view it as $\mathcal{DDH}(h_1, y_1, \cdot, \cdot)$, where h_1 and y_1 is the query and answer from the $(\cdot)^x$ oracle.

- **An Unpredictable Function under CDH in ROM:** A function (family) $(\mathcal{K}, \mathcal{D}, \mathcal{R}, \mathcal{F})$ for $\mathcal{F} = \{f_k(\cdot) : \mathcal{D} \to \mathcal{R}\}_{k \leftarrow \mathcal{K}}$ is an (t, q_f, ϵ)-*unpredictable function* if for any t-time algorithm $\mathcal{A}$, any auxiliary information z

$$Pr[(x^*, f_k(x^*) \leftarrow \mathcal{A}^{f_k(\cdot)}(z)) \ \wedge \ x^* \notin \mathsf{Q}] \leq \epsilon$$

where $\mathcal{A}$ makes at most q_f queries to $f_k(\cdot)$, Q is the set of these queries, and the probability goes over the random k in $\mathcal{K}$.

Consider a multiplicative group $\mathbb{G}$ of prime order q, a hash functions $H : \{0,1\}^{n_1} \to \mathbb{G}$, and the function $f_k(x) = (H(x))^k$, for $k \in \mathbb{Z}_q$. It is a simple fact that this function $f_k(x)$ is unpredictable in random oracle model under CDH assumption and we give the formal proof of this fact in [JL10].

3 Parallel Oblivious Unpredictable Function

Let $f_k(\cdot)$ be an unpredictable function. A *Parallel Oblivious Unpredictable Function (POUF)* is a protocol between a sender S and a receiver R on common input n, and respective private input key k and arguments $(x_1, \ldots, x_n)$, and at the end of the protocol, S learns nothing, while R learns $(f_k(x_1), \ldots, f_k(x_n))$. The POUF protocol should satisfy *sender security* and *receiver security* defined below:

- **Sender Privacy.** The POUF is (t,ϵ)-*sender-secure* if for any t-time receiver R^*, for any auxiliary information z,

$$Pr\left[\{(x_i, f_k(x_i))\}_{i=1,\ldots,n+1} \leftarrow \mathsf{R}^{*\mathsf{S}(k)}(z)\right] \leq \epsilon$$

where R^* makes at most a single oracle access to $\mathsf{S}(k)$ and the probability goes over randomness of S.

- **Receiver Privacy.** The POUF is (t,ϵ)-*receiver-secure* if for any X_0 and X_1, where $X_b = (x_{b,1}, \ldots, x_{b,n})$ for $b = 0$ and 1, for any t-time sender S^*,

$$\left|Pr\left[\mathsf{S}^{*\mathsf{R}(X_0)} = 1\right] - Pr\left[\mathsf{S}^{*\mathsf{R}(X_1)} = 1\right]\right| \leq \epsilon$$

where the probability goes over the randomness of R. We call a POUF *perfectly receiver-private* if it's (t,ϵ)-receiver-private for all t and ϵ.

3.1 Construction of Parallel Oblivious Unpredictable Function

Here we depict the construction of an Parallel Oblivious Unpredictable Function (POUF) in Figure 1, from the unpredictable function $f_k(x) = (H(x))^k$, and show that this POUF protocol is secure under one-more DH assumption in random oracle model. It also gives an intuition why the protocol shown in Section 4 below is a secure set intersection protocol.

Fact 1: *If the (q_H, n)-One-More DH problem is (t, ϵ)-hard in the group $\mathbb{G}$ of order q, then the POUF protocol constructed in Figure 1 is (t, q_H, ϵ')-sender private, where $\epsilon' = \epsilon + n/q$, q_H is the number of queries to the hash function H.*

Proof. **(sketch)** With the challenge tuple $(g_1, \dots, g_{q_H})$, reduction algorithm Red replies to the i-th hash query with g_i. On the R*'s message $(y_1, \dots, y_n)$ Red queries the one-more DH oracle, gets back $(z_1, \dots, z_n) = ((y_1)^k, \dots, (y_n)^k)$, and passes $(z_1, \dots, z_n)$ to R*. Now when R* returns $\{(x_i, v_i)\}_{i=1,\dots,n+1}$, Red returns $\{(H(x_i), v_i)\}_{i=1,\dots,n+1}$ to the One-More DH challenger.

Denote evt as the event that R* did not query H on x_i, while (x_i, v_i) is a pair in R*'s output and $v_i = (H(x_i))^k$. Then $Pr[\mathsf{evt}] = n/q$. The probability that Red breaks the (n, q_H)-One-More DH assumption is the advantage of R* over the sender privacy game minus n/q.

Fact 2: *The POUF Protocol in Figure 1 is perfectly receiver-private.*

Proof. For any $X \in (\{0,1\}^{n_1})^n$, S*'s view when interacting with R(X) is identical to the uniform distribution in $\mathbb{G}^n$. Hence the protocol is perfectly receiver-private.

S's private input: $k \in \mathbb{Z}_q$		R's private input: $(x_1, \dots, x_n) \in (\{0,1\}^{n_1})^n$
	$\xleftarrow{(y_1,\dots,y_n)}$	$\forall_{i=1,\dots,n}$ $h_i \leftarrow H(x_i)$, $\alpha_i \leftarrow \mathbb{Z}_q$, $y_i \leftarrow (h_i)^{\alpha_i}$
for $i = 1, \dots, n$, $z_i \leftarrow (y_i)^k$	$\xrightarrow{(z_1,\dots,z_n)}$	output $\forall_{i=1..n}$ $f_k(x_i) = z_i^{1/\alpha_i}$

Fig. 1. Construction of POUF under One-More DH in ROM

4 Construction of the Set Intersection Protocol

A set intersection protocol is a protocol between a sender S with input $\mathcal{S} = (\mathsf{s}_1, \dots, \mathsf{s}_{n_s})$, and a receiver R with input $\mathcal{R} = (\mathsf{r}_1, \dots, \mathsf{r}_{n_r})$, and at the end of the protocol, the receiver learns $\mathcal{S} \cap \mathcal{R}$. Secure computation of set intersection is a protocol that securely implement the functionality $\mathcal{F}_{\mathsf{SI}}^{n_s \times n_r} : (\mathcal{S}, \mathcal{R}) \to (\perp, \mathcal{S} \cap \mathcal{R})$. Here we allow dummy items in $\mathcal{S}$ and $\mathcal{R}$.

We introduced an adaptive variant of this functionality, namely $\mathcal{F}_{\mathsf{ASI}}^{n_s \times n_r}$, which allows adaptive queries from R, i.e. $\mathcal{F}_{\mathsf{ASI}}^{n_s \times n_r}$ takes a set $\mathcal{S}$ from sender S at input, for each query on input r_i made by R, for $i = 1, \dots, n_r$, $\mathcal{F}_{\mathsf{ASI}}^{n_s \times n_r}$ returns yes or no for whether $\mathsf{r}_i \in \mathcal{S}$. We allow dummy items in $\mathcal{S}$ and $\mathcal{R}$ for $\mathcal{F}_{\mathsf{ASI}}^{n_s \times n_r}$ too. Below we show a protocol illustrated in Figure 2 that securely computes $\mathcal{F}_{\mathsf{ASI}}^{n_s \times n_r}$, assuming the hardness of the One-More (non-adaptive) Gap DH problem, where $H_1 : \{0,1\}^{n_1} \to \mathbb{G}$ and $H_2 : \mathbb{G}^2 \to \{0,1\}^{n_2}$ are hash functions modeled as random oracle in the security analysis. Although the protocol in Figure 2 is only proven as a secure computation of the functionality $\mathcal{F}_{\mathsf{ASI}}^{n_s \times n_r}$, we argue in Section 4.1 that the receiver's input set is *committed* in the first message $(y_1, \dots, y_{n_r})$, i.e.

the next query of the ideal-world receiver is *independent* of the answers to the previous queries it gets. (Moreover, it is also independent of the randomness feeding to the real-world receiver after the message $(y_1, \ldots, y_{n_r})$ is sent.)

The intuitive reason why the protocol is only proven to be a secure computation of $\mathcal{F}_{\mathsf{ASI}}^{n_s \times n_r}$ instead of $\mathcal{F}_{\mathsf{SI}}^{n_s \times n_r}$ lies in the difficulty in extracting R's input all together *during* the protocol execution. As shown in the proof of Theorem 1 below, the simulator extract R's input one by one by controlling the hash functions H_1 and H_2 (as well as using the DDH oracle). When a pair of (h, t) queried to H_2 satisfy that (1) $t = h^k$ (which can be verified using the DDH oracle) and (2) there exists a query x to H_1, s.t. $H_1(x) = h$, then the simulator concludes that x is in the set $\mathcal{R}$ (with negligible error probability), but at the same time, simulator has to assign the value $H_2(h, t)$, so R immediately learns whether or not $x \in \mathcal{S}$ based on whether there exists $u_i \in U$ s.t. $u_i = H_2(h, t)$.

S's private input: $\mathcal{S} = (\mathsf{s}_1, \ldots, \mathsf{s}_{n_s})$		R's private input: $\mathcal{R} = (\mathsf{r}_1, \ldots, \mathsf{r}_{n_r})$
$k \leftarrow \mathbb{Z}_q$ $(\hat{\mathsf{s}}_1, \ldots, \hat{\mathsf{s}}_{n_s}) \leftarrow \Pi(\mathcal{S})$, where Π is a random permutation	$\xleftarrow{(y_1, \ldots, y_{n_r})}$	for $i = 1$ to n_r $h_i \leftarrow H_1(x_i)$ $\alpha_i \leftarrow \mathbb{Z}_q$, $y_i \leftarrow h_i^{\alpha_i}$
for $i = 1, \ldots, n_r$, $z_i \leftarrow (y_i)^k$ $\pi = PoK\{k \mid \forall_{i=1,\ldots,n}\ z_i \leftarrow (y_i)^k\}$[a]	$\xrightarrow{(z_1, \ldots, z_{n_r}),\ \pi}$	Abort if π doesn't verify.
for $j = 1$ to n_s $u_j \leftarrow H_2\left(H_1(\hat{\mathsf{s}}_j), (H_1(\hat{\mathsf{s}}_j))^k\right)$	$\xrightarrow{U = (u_1, \ldots, u_{n_s})}$	$v_i = H_2\left(h_i, (z_i)^{1/\alpha_i}\right)$ Let $V = (v_1, \ldots, v_{n_r})$ output $\{\mathsf{r}_i \mid \mathsf{r}_i \in \mathcal{R}\ \wedge\ v_i \in U \cap V\}$

[a] S and R interacts in a zero-knowledge proof of knowledge $\pi = PoK\{k \mid z_i \leftarrow (y_i)^k, i = 1, \ldots, n_r\}$, where S performs the prover and R performs the verifier. Here for simplicity, we put non-interactive proof system instead.

Fig. 2. Construction of Set Intersection Protocol under One-More DH in ROM

Remark on Optimizing the Online Computational Cost. We notice that the online cost of this set intersection protocol illustrated in Figure 2 can be reduced by letting S publish a pair (g, pk) at the beginning, s.t. $pk = g^k$, and g is the generator of the group $\mathbb{G}$. Then we modify the protocol as follows: R computes $y_j = H(\mathsf{r}_j) \cdot g^{\alpha_j}$, and computes $w_j \leftarrow z_j \cdot (pk)^{-\alpha_j}$. The online cost of the receiver is then reduced from $2n_r$ exponentiations with variable bases plus n_r inversions mod q, to $2n_r$ exponentiations with fixed bases (Here we did not count the computation in the proof π). However, this modification requires a stronger version of the One-More Gap DH assumption: adversary $\mathcal{A}$, in addition to the challenge tuple $(g_1, \ldots, g_N)$, is also given a pair $(g, pk = g^k)$ as input. Here we make a security claim only for the basic protocol in Figure 2.

Theorem 1. *If the (N, Q)-One-More Non-Adaptive Gap DH problem is hard, and if the proof system π is a zero-knowledge proof of knowledge, our set*

intersection protocol in Figure 2 is a secure computation of the functionality $\mathcal{F}_{\mathsf{ASI}}^{n_s \times n_r}$ *described above in the random oracle model.*

Proof. Constructing an ideal-world SIM_s *from a malicious real-world sender* S^*.

The simulator SIM_s is constructed as follows:

1. SIM_s builds two tables $T_1 = (x, \phi)$ and $T_2 = ((h,t), \psi)$ to answer the hash queries to H_1 and H_2 respectively. To answer an H_1-query on x that has never been queried before, SIM_s picks random ϕ in $\mathbb{G}$, adds an entry (x, ϕ) to T_1, and returns ϕ as $H_1(x)$. Similarly, to answer an H_2-query on the pair (h,t) which has never been queried before, SIM_s picks random $\psi \in \{0,1\}^{n_2}$, adds an entry $((h,t), \psi)$ to T_2, and returns ψ as $H_2(h,t)$.
2. SIM_s sends random $(y_1, \ldots, y_{n_r}) \in \mathbb{G}^{n_r}$ to S^*.
3. After getting the tuple $(z_1, \ldots, z_{n_r})$ and interacting with S^* as verifier in the proof π, if the proof π does not verify SIM_s aborts. Otherwise, SIM_s runs the extractor algorithm for π to extract k.
4. On getting $U = (u_1, \ldots, u_{n_s})$, for each $u_l \in U$, SIM checks if $\exists\ (x_i, \phi_i) \in T_1$ and $\exists\ ((h_j, t_j), \psi_j) \in T_2$, s.t. $\phi_i = h_j$, $t_j = (h_j)^k$ and $\psi_j = u_l$. If so, add x_i to the set $\mathcal{S}$ (initially set to $\emptyset$); otherwise, add a dummy item into $\mathcal{S}$. Then SIM sends $\mathcal{S}$ to $\mathcal{F}_{\mathsf{ASI}}^{n_s \times n_r}$, which uses $\mathcal{S}$ to respond to ideal receiver $\bar{\mathsf{R}}$'s queries.

It is easy to see that S^*'s views when interacting with the real receiver R and with the simulator SIM_s are identical, because $(y_1, \ldots, y_{n_r})$ sent by the real receiver R is uniformly random in $\mathbb{G}^{n_r}$, and the answers to the H_1 and H_2 are all picked at random in the respective ranges.

Now we look at the output of the honest receiver R in the real world interacting with S^*. First, because the proof π is sound, if R doesn't abort the protocol, then with overwhelming probability, every z_i sent by S^* is $(y_i)^k$ for the y_i's sent by R. Now if $z_i = (y_i)^k$ for $i = 1, \ldots, n_r$, then R's final output is a set containing all the r_i's s.t. $H_2(H_1(\mathsf{r}_i), (H_1(\mathsf{r}_i))^k) \in U$, which is equivalent to say that R outputs, for each $i \in \{1, \ldots, n_r\}$, yes if there exists a $u_j \in U$, s.t. $H_2(H_1(\mathsf{r}_i), (H_1(\mathsf{r}_i))^k) = u_j$, and no otherwise. Since H_2 is random oracle, if $H_2(H_1(\mathsf{r}_i), (H_1(\mathsf{r}_i))^k) = u_j$, there are two possibilities: (1) S^* computed u_j from $H_2(H_1(\mathsf{s}_j), (H_1(\mathsf{s}_j))^k)$ for $\mathsf{s}_j = \mathsf{r}_i$; and (2) S^* did not query H_1 on r_i or did not query H_2 on $(H_1(\mathsf{r}_i), (H_1(\mathsf{r}_i))^k)$, but $H_2(H_1(\mathsf{r}_i), (H_1(\mathsf{r}_i))^k)$ happens to be equal to u_j. In case (1) SIM_s described above extracts $\mathsf{s}_j = \mathsf{r}_i$, puts s_j in $\mathcal{S}$, and the ideal world receiver $\bar{\mathsf{R}}$ output yes on r_i. In case (2), S^* either (a) did not query H_1 on r_i or (b) did not query H_2 on $(H_1(\mathsf{r}_i), H_1(\mathsf{r}_i))^k$. If S^* did not query H_2 on $(H_1(\mathsf{r}_i), H_1(\mathsf{r}_i))^k)$, then $Pr[\exists\ u_j \in U,\ \exists\ \mathsf{r}_i \in \mathcal{R},\ \text{s.t. } u_j = H_2(H_1(\mathsf{r}_i), (H_1(\mathsf{r}_i))^k)] \leq n_s \cdot n_r \cdot 2^{-n_2}$. If S^* did not query H_1 on r_i, then $Pr[\exists\ u_j \in U,\ \exists\ \mathsf{r}_i \in \mathcal{R},\ \text{s.t. } u_j = H_2(H_1(\mathsf{r}_i), (H_1(\mathsf{r}_i))^k)] = n_s \cdot n_r \cdot Pr[H_1(\mathsf{r}_i) = h \wedge H_2(h, h^k) = u_j] = n_s \cdot n_r \cdot q \cdot Pr[H_1(\mathsf{r}_i) = t] \cdot Pr[H_2(t^k) = u_j] = n_s \cdot n_r \cdot 2^{-n_2}$. Hence case (2) happens with probability at most $(n_s \cdot n_r \cdot 2^{-n_2+1})$. Therefore, except with probability $(n_s \cdot n_r \cdot 2^{-n_2+1})$, the real world receiver R and the ideal world receiver $\bar{\mathsf{R}}$ output identically.

Constructing an ideal-world SIM_r *from a malicious real-world receiver* R^*.

We construct SIM_r as follows.

1. SIM_r builds two table $T_1 = (x, \phi)$ and $T_2 = ((h,t), \psi, b)$ to answer the H_1 and H_2 queries respectively. The bit b should be set to 1 if $t = h^k$ and there exists an entry $(x, \phi) \in T_1$ such that $h = \phi$, and 0 otherwise. SIM_r first responds with random value to the H_1 and H_2 queries made by S^* while maintaining consistency, and records $(x_i, H_1(x_i))$ in T_1 for every query to H_1 on x_i, $((h_j, t_j), H_2(h_j, t_j), 0)$ for every query to H_2 on (h_j, t_j).
2. On R^*'s message $(y_1, \ldots, y_{n_r})$, SIM_r picks random $k \in \mathbb{Z}_q$, computes $z_i = (y_i)^k$ for $i = 1, \ldots, n_r$, replies to R^* with $(z_1, \ldots, z_{n_r})$ to R^*, and interacts with R^* as prover in the proof π. SIM_r also sends $U = (u_1, \ldots, u_{n_s})$ to R^*, random in $(\{0,1\}^{n_2})^{n_s}$.
3. After $(z_1, \ldots, z_{n_r})$ is sent, SIM_r initializes set $\mathcal{R} = \emptyset$ and $\mathcal{H} = \emptyset$, and answers the H_1 and H_2 queries as follows:

   – For each query x to H_1 not having been queried before, SIM_r picks a random $\phi \in \mathbb{G}$, and checks if $\exists\ ((h_i, t_i), \psi_i, b_i) \in T_2$, s.t. $h_i = \phi$ and $t_i = h^k$. If so, SIM_r outputs fail_1 and aborts. Otherwise, it adds (x, ϕ) to T_1, and returns ϕ to R^* as $H_1(x)$.
   – For each query (h, t) to H_2 that has not been queried before, SIM_r checks if $\exists\ (x_i, \phi_i) \in T_1$, s.t. $h = \phi_i$ and $t = h^k$. If not, then SIM_r answers the H_2 queries in as in item 1 above. Otherwise, SIM_r checks if $\exists\ (h_l, t_l, \psi_l, b_l) \in T_2$, s.t. $h_l = h$ and $t_l = t$.

     • If such an entry exists and $b_l = 0$ then SIM_r outputs fail_2 and aborts. This happens when R^* queried H_2 on some (h, t) for $t = h^k$, before sending the message $(y_1, \ldots, y_{n_r})$ and getting back $(z_1, \ldots, z_{n_r})$ with $z_i = (y_i)^k$ for each $i = 1, \ldots, n_r$, i.e. before seeing any information about k.
     • If such an entry exists and $b_l = 1$, then SIM_r returns ψ_l as $H_2(t)$;

     If such an entry doesn't exist for either $b_l = 0$ or 1, then SIM_r adds x to $\mathcal{R}$. If $|\mathcal{R}| > n_r$, SIM_r outputs fail_3 and aborts. Otherwise, SIM_r sends x to $\mathcal{F}_{\mathsf{ASI}}^{n_s \times n_r}$. If $\mathcal{F}_{\mathsf{ASI}}^{n_s \times n_r}$ returns yes, then SIM_r picks random $u_j \in U \setminus \mathcal{H}$, adds u_j to $\mathcal{H}$, adds $((h,t), u_j, 1)$ to T_2, and returns u_j as $H_2(h,t)$ to R^*. If $\mathcal{F}_{\mathsf{ASI}}^{n_s \times n_r}$ returns no, then SIM_r sets $H_2(t)$ as a random value $\psi \in \{0,1\}^{n_2}$, adds $(h, t, \psi, 1)$ to T_2, and returns ψ to R^*.

This finishes the construction SIM_r. The ideal-world $\bar{\mathsf{S}}$ that interacts with $\mathcal{F}_{\mathsf{ASI}}^{n_s \times n_r}$, which answers the queries from SIM_r as the ideal-world receiver $\bar{\mathsf{R}}^*$, gets $\perp$ from $\mathcal{F}_{\mathsf{ASI}}^{n_s \times n_r}$, and the real-world sender S which interacts with R^* in the real protocol also outputs $\perp$. Now we argue that R^*'s views in the real game with honest real-world sender S and in the interaction with the simulator SIM_r constructed above are indistinguishable. R^*'s view when interacting with the real sender S differs from that when interacting with SIM_r only if one of the following happens:

• fail_1 happens. fail_1 happens if R^* queries x to H_1 which returns ϕ for the entry $((\phi, \phi^k), \psi, b)$ already existing in T_2. I.e. R^* made the query (ϕ, ϕ^k) before knowing that $H_1(x) = \phi$. This happens with probability at most $q_{H_1} \cdot q_{H_2} \cdot 1/q$, for q_{H_1} and q_{H_2} being the number of queries R^* made to H_1 and H_2 respectively.

• fail_2 happens. As explained above, this happens when R^* queried H_2 on (h,t) for $t = h^k$, before seeing any information about k. Since k is random in $\mathbb{Z}_q$, this happens with probability at most q_{H_2}/q.

• fail_3 happens. If fail_3 happens then a reduction can be constructed to break the (q_{H_1}, n_r)-One-More (Non-Adaptive) Gap DH assumption. The reduction Red does everything as SIM_r does, except (1) Red answers all the queries to H_1 using the One-More Gap DH challenge, i.e. $(g_1, \ldots, g_{q_{H_1}})$; (2) after getting $(y_1, \ldots, y_{n_r})$ from R^*, Red queries the One-More DH oracle on $(y_1, \ldots, y_{n_r})$ and gets back $(z_1, \ldots, z_{n_r})$, which it returns to R^*; (3) Red simulates the proof for π. Because the proof system π is zero-knowledge, R^* cannot distinguish the real prover and the simulation except with negligible probability; (4) when SIM_r checks the hash table for whether $\exists\,(x,h) \in T_1$ and $\exists\,(t,h',b) \in T_2$, s.t. $t = h^k$, Red queries the oracle $\mathcal{DL}_k(\cdot,\cdot)$ on (h,t); (5) Red initializes a set $\mathcal{R}' = \emptyset$ at the beginning. Whenever SIM_r decides to add an x into $\mathcal{R}$, which happens only if R^* makes a query on (ϕ,t) such that $\mathcal{DL}_k(\phi,t) = 1$, and there exists (x,ϕ) in T_1, SIM_r also adds (ϕ,t) to $\mathcal{R}'$. If $|\mathcal{R}| > n_r$ then so is $|\mathcal{R}'|$, and SIM_r simply returns all the pairs in $\mathcal{R}'$, hence breaking the (q_{H_1}, n_r)-One-More DH assumption. Therefore, the probability that fail_3 happens is bounded by the probability to break (q_{H_1}, n_r)-One-More DH assumption plus the probability that R^* distinguishes the real proof π from the simulated one.

Since all of the 3 evens happen with negligible probability, R^*'s views in the real game with the real-world sender S and in the interaction with SIM_r are indistinguishable.

4.1 The Committing Property of Our Set Intersection Protocol

We only showed above that our set intersection protocol is a secure computation of the functionality $\mathcal{F}_{\mathsf{ASI}}^{n_s \times n_r}$. Indeed, the receiver in our protocol *cannot* change its input set after sending the message $(y_1, \ldots, y_{n_r})$. In this subsection, we are going to prove the property that the receiver's input set is committed in the message $(y_1, \ldots, y_{n_r})$. Intuitively, if a receiver *can* change its input set with non-negligible probability, then we rewind this receiver to the point when it just finished sending the tuple $(y_1, \ldots, y_{n_r})$. Denote $\mathcal{R}_i$ as the set extracted in the i-th rewinding. We keep rewinding this receiver until $|\bigcup \mathcal{R}_i| > n_r$, which implies breaking the One-More Gap DH assumption (using the same technique as in the proof of Theorem 1). We claim the committing property of the receiver in our set intersection protocol in Figure 2 in terms of the following property of the constructed ideal-world receiver $\bar{\mathsf{R}}$ which is SIM_r in the proof of Theorem 1 with oracle access to the real-world receiver R^*.

Theorem 2. *Let $\gamma = (\gamma^{(1)}, \ldots, \gamma^{(l)})$ be randomness used by $\bar{\mathsf{R}}$ sequentially. (We can assume that $\bar{\mathsf{R}}$ uses $\gamma^{(i)}$ in the i-th step.) If the (N, n_r)-One-More Gap DH problem is $(t_{omdh,\epsilon_{omdh}})$-hard, and if the proof system π is $(t_D, t_{sim}, \epsilon_{zk})$-zero-knowledge, then for any t_{R^*}-time R^*, for at least $(1-\epsilon')$ fraction of γ values, there exists a set $\mathcal{R}$ of size at most n_r and an integer i s.t. $\gamma^{(i)}$ is used* before $\bar{\mathsf{R}}$ *makes the first query to $\mathcal{F}_{\mathsf{ASI}}^{n_s \times n_r}$, for any set $\mathcal{S}$,*

$$Pr\left[\mathsf{r} \leftarrow \bar{\mathsf{R}}(\gamma^{(i+1)}, \ldots, \gamma^{(l)}) \;\wedge\; \mathsf{r} \notin \mathcal{R}\right] \leq \epsilon$$

for the probability going over random $(\gamma^{(i+1)}, \ldots, \gamma^{(l)})$, $t_{\mathsf{R}^*} = \min\{t_{omdh}, t_D\} \cdot (1 + \frac{\kappa(n_r+1)}{\epsilon})^{-1} - t_{sim}$, $\epsilon' = \frac{\epsilon_{omdh}+\epsilon_{zk}}{1-(n_r+1)e^{-\kappa}}$, *and* $N = q_{H_1} \cdot (1 + \frac{\kappa(n_r+1)}{\epsilon})$.

This theorem intuitively claims that for the ideal-world receiver $\bar{\mathsf{R}}$, there exists a point before it makes any query to $\mathcal{F}_{\mathsf{ASI}}^{n_s \times n_r}$, upon which $\bar{\mathsf{R}}$ decides the set $\mathcal{R}$, and then all the queries made by $\bar{\mathsf{R}}$ afterwards must be in the set $\mathcal{R}$. Readers might not get convinced of the committing property for malicious receiver, as we only claim it for a particular ideal-world receiver $\bar{\mathsf{R}}$. However, since this $\bar{\mathsf{R}}$ fully simulates R^*'s view and its behavior, the committing property of $\bar{\mathsf{R}}$ does guarantee that R^*'s inputs are also committed.

Proof. Let's first consider the POUF protocol in Section 3, where the receiver with a set of $(x_1, \ldots, x_n)$ as input wants to interact with the sender, which has a random key $k \in \mathbb{Z}_q$ as input, and finally outputs pairs of $(x_i, (H_1(x_i))^k)$ for $i = 1, \ldots, n$. This protocol is indeed the essential part of our set intersection protocol, while in the set intersection protocol the receiver needs to make another series of H_2 queries to compute $H_2(H_1(x_i), (H_1(x_i))^k)$ (where x_i's are denoted as r_i's in the set intersection Protocol), and it is also given the values $H_2(H_1(\mathsf{s}_i), (H_1(\mathsf{s}_i))^k)$ for every s_i in the sender's set. We claim here the receiver's input set $(x_1, \ldots, x_n)$ is committed in $(y_1, \ldots, y_n)$.

Lemma 1. *Consider any (potentially adversarial)* deterministic *receiver* R^*. *Let* $h = (h_1, \ldots, h_{q_{H_1}}) \in (\mathbb{G})^{q_{H_1}}$ *be the vector used to answer the* H_1 *queries made by* R^* *and let* $\mathcal{I}(\mathsf{R}^*, h)$ *be the index of the* H_1 *query after which* R^* *sent the message* $(y_1, \ldots, y_n)$. *Note that* $(h_1, \ldots, h_{I^*})$ *with* $I^* = \mathcal{I}(\mathsf{R}^*, h)$ *are the only possible randomness for* R^* *to determine the message* $(y_1, \ldots, y_n)$. *Now we define a distribution* $\mathcal{D}$ *for the vector* h *and the receiver* R^* *as follows*

$$\mathcal{D}(\mathsf{R}^*, h) = \{h' = (h'_1, \ldots, h'_{q_{H_1}}) \mid h'_i = h_i \text{ for } 1 \le i \le \mathcal{I}(\mathsf{R}^*, h)\}$$

We now define the set $\mathsf{GoodH}_{\mathsf{R}^*,\epsilon}$ *for our POUF protocol with receiver* R^* *having* n *inputs as the following set.*

$$\mathsf{GoodH}_{\mathsf{R}^*,\epsilon} \triangleq \left\{ h \;\middle|\; \begin{array}{l} \exists\, X = \{(x_j, t_j)\},\ s.t.\ |X| \le n\ \wedge \\ Pr\left[\begin{array}{l} (\mathsf{R}^*)^{h',(\cdot)^k} \to (x,t)\ \wedge\ (x,t) \notin X\ \wedge \\ \exists\, h'_i \in h'\ s.t.\ H_1(x) = h'_i\ \wedge\ t = (h'_i)^k \end{array}\right] \le \epsilon \\ \text{for the probability going over random } k \text{ in } \mathbb{Z}_q \\ \text{and random } h' \in \mathcal{D}(\mathsf{R}^*, h) \end{array} \right\}$$

We claim that for security parameter κ, *if the* (N, n)*-One-More Gap DH problem is* $(t_{omdh}, \epsilon_{omdh})$*-hard, then for every* t_{R^*}*-time deterministic receiver* R^*

$$Pr\left[h \notin \mathsf{GoodH}_{\mathsf{R}^*,\epsilon}\right] \le \epsilon'$$

for the probability going over random h *in* $(\mathbb{G})^{q_{H_1}}$, *where* $t_{\mathsf{R}^*} = t_{omdh} \cdot (1 + \frac{\kappa(n+1)}{\epsilon})^{-1}$, $\epsilon' = \frac{\epsilon_{omdh}}{1-(n+1)e^{-\kappa}}$, *and* $N = q_{H_1} \cdot (1 + \frac{\kappa(n+1)}{\epsilon})$.

Note that ϵ and ϵ' satisfy the following relation: If ϵ (resp. ϵ') is inverse polynomial in the security parameter κ, then ϵ' (resp. ϵ) must be negligible in κ

assuming the hardness of the One-More DH assumption. Intuitively, this lemma claims that a set $\mathcal{X} = (x_1, \ldots, x_{n'})$ for $n' \leq n$ is committed in the message $(y_1, \ldots, y_n)$, i.e. R^* *cannot* compute any $(H_1(x))^k$ for any x outside the set $\mathcal{X}$ except with negligible probability under the One-More Gap DH assumption.

Proof. If there exists a deterministic receiver R^*, s.t. $Pr[h \notin \mathsf{GoodH}_{\mathsf{R}^*,\epsilon}] = \epsilon^* > \epsilon'$, then we show a t_{omdh}-time reduction algorithm Red solving the (N, n)-One-More Gap DH problem with oracle access to R^* with advantage greater than ϵ_{omdh} , where $N = q_{H_1} \cdot (1 + \frac{\kappa(n+1)}{\epsilon})$.
Getting the One-More Gap DH challenger tuple $(g_1, \ldots, g_N)$, Red first sets $h = (g_1, \ldots, g_{q_{H_1}})$ and answer the H_1-queries from R^* using h. With probability ϵ^*, $h \notin \mathsf{GoodH}_{\mathsf{R}^*,\epsilon}$. We now assume h picked by Red is *not* in the set $\mathsf{GoodH}_{\mathsf{R}^*,\epsilon}$. Let $I^* = \mathcal{I}(\mathsf{R}^*, h)$. When R^* sends $(y_1, \ldots, y_n)$, Red queries the One-More DH oracle and gets back $(z_1, \ldots, z_n)$, which satisfies $z_i = (y_i)^k$ for some random $k \in \mathbb{Z}_q$ and all $i = 1, \ldots, n$. Then R^* does the following.

Repeat the following steps $n + 1$ times starting with an empty set $X' = \emptyset$, a flag $\mathsf{found} = \mathsf{false}$, and a integer $j = q_{H_1} + 1$, where X' is supposed to contain triples of $(x, H_1(x), (H_1(x))^k)$, and j is supposed to point to a chunk of the N-tuple $(g_1, \ldots, g_N)$ used for answering the H_1-queries in each iteration:

- Set the flag found to false. Repeat the following steps for κ/ϵ times or until $\mathsf{found} = \mathsf{true}$:
  - Let $l = j + q_{H_1} - I^* - 1$. Set $h' = (g_1, \ldots, g_{I^*}, g_j, \ldots, g_l)$ and answer the H_1-queries from R^* using h'; Set $j \leftarrow j + q_{H_1} - I^*$.
  - Pick a random α in $\mathbb{Z}_q$ and perform the role of the sender with input $k' = \alpha k$, i.e. reply to R^*'s message $(y_1, \ldots, y_n)$ with $((z_1)^\alpha, \ldots, (z_n)^k)$ where the tuple $(z_1, \ldots, z_n)$ was returned by the One-More Gap DH oracle above.
  - If at the end of the interaction between Red simulating S and R^*, R^* outputs a pair (x, t), s.t. $H_1(x) \in h'$, $t = (H_1(x))^{k'}$ (which can be verified by querying the $\mathcal{DL}_k$ oracle on the pair $((H_1(x))^\alpha, t)$), and $(x, t) \notin X'$, then add the triple $(x, H_1(x), t)$ to X' and set the flag found to true.

Now we analyze the advantage that Red breaks the One-More Gap DH assumption. First, note that every h' in the above execution are random in $\mathcal{D}(\mathsf{R}^*, h)$ for the $h = (g_1, \ldots, g_{H_1})$. For each assignment of h' in the i-th iteration and for the random key $k' = \alpha k$ for the unknown key k picked by the One-More Gap DH challenger, the probability that R^* outputs a pair (x, t) s.t. $H(x) \in h'$, $t = (H(x))^{k'}$ is greater than ϵ (because $h \notin \mathsf{GoodH}_{\mathsf{R}^*,\epsilon}$), and hence if this is repeated κ/ϵ times, the probability R^* fails to find such a pair after all the κ/ϵ iterations is $(1 - \epsilon)^{\kappa/\epsilon} \approx e^{-\kappa}$. Therefore the probability that Red fails to find $n + 1$ triples of $(x, H_1(x), (H_1(x))^k)$ is bounded by $(n + 1) \cdot e^{-\kappa}$. All the above probability are conditioned on the fact that $h = (g_1, \ldots, g_{q_{H_1}})$ is *not* in $\mathsf{GoodH}_{\mathsf{R}^*,\epsilon}$, which happens with probability ϵ^* as assumed at the beginning of this proof. Therefore, the probability that Red solves the One-More Gap DH problem is $\epsilon^* \cdot (1 - (n + 1)e^{-\kappa})$ which is greater than ϵ_{omdh} if $\epsilon^* > \epsilon'$, causing a contradiction to the (N, n)-One-More Gap DH assumption.

Now we consider our set intersection protocol. Instead of outputting pairs of $(x, (H_1(x))^k)$ as in the POUF protocol, the (malicious) receiver in the set intersection protocol tries to learn more information about the sender's input than necessary. Since the only information sent by the sender about its own input is $H_2(H_1(\mathsf{s}_i), (H_1(\mathsf{s}_i))^k)$ for every s_i in its input set, the receiver tries to distinguish the value $H_2(H_1(\mathsf{s}_i), (H_1(\mathsf{s}_i))^k)$ from random. We claim the following for the malicious receiver in the protocol in Figure 2.

Lemma 2. *Consider any deterministic receiver* R^*. *Let* $h = (h_1, \ldots, h_{q_{H_1}}) \in (\mathbb{G})^{q_{H_1}}$, $\psi = (\psi_1, \ldots, \psi_{q_{H_2}}) \in \{0,1\}^{n_2 \times q_{H_2}}$ *be the two vectors to answer the* H_1 *and* H_2 *queries made by* R^* *respectively. Let* $(I_1^*, I_2^*) = \mathcal{I}(\mathsf{R}^*, h, \psi)$ *be the numbers of the* H_1 *and* H_2 *queries respectively before* R^* *sending the message* $(y_1, \ldots, y_{n_r})$. *Note that* $(h_1, \ldots, h_{I_1^*})$ *and* $(\psi_1, \ldots, \psi_{I_2^*})$ *with* $(I_1^*, I_2^*) = \mathcal{I}(\mathsf{R}^*, h)$ *are the only possible randomness for* R^* *to determine the message* $(y_1, \ldots, y_{n_r})$. *Now we define a distribution* $\mathcal{D}$ *for the vectors* h *and* ψ *and the receiver* R^* *as follows*

$$\mathcal{D}(\mathsf{R}^*, h, \psi) = \left\{ \begin{array}{l|l} h' = (h'_1, \ldots, h'_{q_{H_1}}) & \forall_{i \in [1..I_1^*]}\ h'_i = h_i,\ \forall_{j \in [1..I_2^*]}\ \psi'_j = \psi_j \\ \psi' = (\psi'_1, \ldots, \psi'_{q_{H_2}}) & \textit{where } (I_1^*, I_2^*) = \mathcal{I}(\mathsf{R}^*, h, \psi) \end{array} \right\}$$

Let $\mathsf{S}(\mathcal{S}; k)$ *denotes the sender taking input set* $\mathcal{S}$ *and randomness* k. *We now define* $\mathsf{GoodH\Psi}_{\mathsf{R}^*,\epsilon}$ *for our set intersection protocol with receiver* R^* *having* n_r *inputs as the following set:*

$$\mathsf{GoodH\Psi} \triangleq \left\{ h, \psi \left| \begin{array}{l} \exists\ \mathcal{R} = \{(\mathsf{r}_j, t_j)\} \textit{ s.t. } |\mathcal{R}| \le n_r, \forall\ \mathsf{r}^* \textit{ s.t.} \\ \forall\ t \textit{ s.t. } (\mathsf{r}^*, t) \notin \mathcal{R} \wedge \forall\ \mathcal{S} \textit{ s.t. } |\mathcal{S}| \le n_s \\ \left| \begin{array}{r} Pr\left[(\mathsf{R}^*)^{h',\psi',\mathsf{S}(\mathcal{S};k)}\left(H_2(H_1(\mathsf{r}^*), (H_1(\mathsf{r}^*))^k)\right) \to 1\right] \\ -Pr\left[(\mathsf{R}^*)^{h',\psi',\mathsf{S}(\mathcal{S};k)}(u) \to 1\right] \end{array} \right| \le \epsilon \\ \textit{where the probability goes over random } k \textit{ in } \mathbb{Z}_q, \textit{ random } u \\ \textit{in } \{0,1\}^{n_2} \textit{ and random } (h', \psi') \textit{ in } \mathcal{D}(\mathsf{R}^*, h, \psi), H_1 \textit{ and } H_2 \\ \textit{queries are answered by } h' \textit{ and } \psi' \textit{ respectively.} \end{array} \right. \right\}$$

We claim that for security parameter κ, *if the* (N, n_r)*-One-More Gap DH problem is* $(t_{omdh}, \epsilon_{omdh})$*-hard, and if the proof system* π *is* $(t_D, t_{sim}, \epsilon_{zk})$*-zero knowledge, then for every* t_{R^*}*-time deterministic receiver* R^*,

$$Pr\left[(h, \psi) \notin \mathsf{GoodH\Psi}_{\mathsf{R}^*,\epsilon}\right] \le \epsilon'$$

for the probability going over random h *in* $(\mathbb{G})^{q_{H_1}}$, *random* ψ *in* $\{0,1\}^{n_2 \times q_{H_2}}$, *where* $t_{\mathsf{R}^*} = \min\{t_{omdh}, t_D\} \cdot (1 + \frac{\kappa(n_r+1)}{\epsilon})^{-1} - t_{sim}$, $\epsilon' = \frac{\epsilon_{omdh} + \epsilon_{zk}}{1-(n_r+1)e^{-\kappa}}$, *and* $N = q_{H_1} \cdot (1 + \frac{\kappa(n_r+1)}{\epsilon})$.

We will not show the detailed proof of this lemma because it is a simple extension of the proof of Lemma 1. Intuitively, if there exists r^* s.t. R^* distinguishes $H_2\left(H_1(\mathsf{r}^*), (H_1(\mathsf{r}^*))^k\right)$ from random u in $\{0,1\}^{n_2}$, then R^* must have queried H_1 on r^* and H_2 on the pair $\left(H_1(\mathsf{r}^*), (H_1(\mathsf{r}^*))^k\right)$. We can use the extractor algorithm Ext as in the security proof of Theorem 1 for malicious receiver to extract $\left(\mathsf{r}^*, H_1(\mathsf{r}^*), (H_1(\mathsf{r}^*))^k\right)$, and add it to the set $\mathcal{R}'$ containing triples of

$(\mathsf{r}, H_1(\mathsf{r}), (H_1(\mathsf{r}))^k)$. As in the proof of Lemma 1, we iterate this procedure until $|X| > n_r$ and we break the One-More Gap DH assumption. □

Let the randomness γ used by $\bar{\mathcal{R}}$ be the random vector h and ψ, as well as the random key k in Lemma 2, ordered by R*'s hash queries and its interaction with real-world sender S, then Theorem 2 is immediately implied by Lemma 2.

5 Set Intersection with Data Transfer

A natural generalization of the set intersection protocol problem is for the receiver not only to learn which of its items $(\mathsf{r}_1, \ldots, \mathsf{r}_{n_r})$ is shared with the sender, but in case an item is shared, the receiver would receive some data which the sender associates with this item. In other words, consider sender's input $(\mathsf{s}_1, \ldots, \mathsf{s}_{n_s})$ as a set of (distinct) *indexes*, denoted $(\mathsf{sID}_1, \ldots, \mathsf{sID}_{n_s})$, where each index sID_i is accompanied by some data entry D_i. The receiver inputs is a set of indexes $(\mathsf{rID}_1, \ldots, \mathsf{rID}_{n_r})$, and the goal of the protocol is to transfer all data entries D_i s.t. $\mathsf{sID}_i = \mathsf{rID}_j$ for some $j \in \{1, \ldots, n_r\}$. More precisely, the receiver should compute a sequence $(D'_1, \ldots, D'_{n_r})$ s.t. for each j, $D'_j = D_i$ if $\mathsf{rID}_j = \mathsf{sID}_i$ for some i, and $D'_j = \perp$ otherwise, while the sender learns nothing from the protocol (except of the size n_r of the receiver's query set, which we treat as a public parameter).

Clearly, Set Intersection with Data Transfer is a generalization of the set intersection problem. It is also a generalization of the "Keyword" Oblivious Transfer problem [FIPR05]: Keyword OT is the same problem restricted so that the receiver has only one query rID. Conversely, Set Intersection with Data Transfer can be thought of as a (n_r, n_s)-Keyword-OT, where the receiver has n_r queries and n_s is the size of the sender's database. One can consider a stronger version of this problem, corresponding to the *adaptive* keyword OT [OK04], defined similarly as adaptive OT [NP99], in which the receiver R can choose the n_r items $(\mathsf{rID}_1, \ldots, \mathsf{rID}_{n_r})$ *adaptively*, i.e. the j-th query rID_j is determined by $(D'_1, \ldots, D'_{j-1})$ where $D'_i = D_l$ if $\mathsf{rID}_i = \mathsf{sID}_l$, and $D'_i = \perp$ otherwise.

Construction of Set Intersection with Data Transfer Protocol. Let $\mathsf{sSet} = \{(\mathsf{sID}_i, D_i)\}_{i=1,\ldots,n_s}$ and $\mathsf{rSet} = \{\mathsf{rID}_i\}_{i=1,\ldots,n_r}$. As described above, Set Intersection with Data Transfer protocol is a secure computation of the functionality $\mathcal{F}_{\mathsf{SIwDT}}$: $(\mathsf{sSet}, \mathsf{rSet}) \rightarrow (\perp, \{D_i \mid \exists\ (\mathsf{sID}_i, D_i) \in \mathsf{sSet}\ \wedge\ \exists\ \mathsf{rID}_j \in \mathsf{rSet}\ \wedge\ \mathsf{sID}_i = \mathsf{rID}_j\})$, where n_s and n_r are the public parameters. The adaptive variant of the $\mathcal{F}_{\mathsf{SIwDT}}$ functionality, called $\mathcal{F}_{\mathsf{ASIwDT}}$ on the public parameters n_s and n_r and S's private input sSet, allows R to make n_r adaptive queries on rID_j and get back $(1, D_i)$ if $\exists\ (\mathsf{sID}_i, D_i) \in \mathsf{sSet} \wedge \mathsf{sID}_i = \mathsf{rID}_j)$; and $(0, \perp)$ otherwise. We show a construction of a secure computation of the functionality $\mathcal{F}_{\mathsf{ASIwDT}}$ in Figure 3. The idea of constructing this protocol is the same as the constructing our set intersection protocol in Section 4. In addition to the unpredictable function $f_k(x) = (H_1(x))^k$ for $H_1 : \{0,1\}^{n_1} \rightarrow \mathbb{G}$ being a hash function, and $\mathbb{G}$ being a multiplicative group of order q, in which we assume the One-More Non-Adaptive Gap DH assumption holds, we need the hash function H_2 to take one more bit as input, i.e. $H_2 : \mathbb{G}^2 \times \{0,1\} \rightarrow \{0,1\}^{n_2}$. Both H_1 and H_2 are modeled as random oracle. tag and data are bit values 0 and 1 respectively.

S		R
S's private input: $\{(\mathsf{sID}_i, D_i)\}_{i=1,\dots,n_s}$		R's private input: $\{\mathsf{rID}_i\}_{i=1,\dots,n_r}$
$k \leftarrow \mathbb{Z}_q$		
for $i = 1, \dots, n$		
$u_i \leftarrow H_2(H_1(\mathsf{sID}_i), (H_1(\mathsf{sID}_i))^k, \mathsf{tag})$		for $j = 1, \dots, n_r$
$v_i \leftarrow H_2\left(H_1(\mathsf{sID}_i), (H_1(\mathsf{sID}_i))^k, \mathsf{data}\right)$		$h_j = H_1(\mathsf{rID}_j)$
$e_i \leftarrow v_i \oplus D_i$	$\xleftarrow{(y_1,\dots,y_{n_r})}$	$\alpha_j \leftarrow \mathbb{Z}_q,\ y_j \leftarrow (h_j)^{\alpha_i}$
$\forall_{j=1,\dots,n_r}\ z_j \leftarrow (y_j)^k$		
$\pi \leftarrow PoK\{k \mid \forall_{j=1,\dots,n_r}\ z_j = (y_j)^k\}$		
	$\xrightarrow{(z_1,\dots,z_{n_r}),\ \pi}$	Abort if π doesn't verify.
	$\xrightarrow{\{(u_i,e_i)\}_{i=1,\dots,n_s}}$	for $j = 1, \dots, n_r$
		$w_j \leftarrow (z_j)^{1/\alpha_j},\ u'_j \leftarrow H_2(h_j, w_j, \mathsf{tag})$
		if $\exists\ i$, s.t. $u_i = u'_j$
		$v'_j \leftarrow H_2(h_j, w_j, \mathsf{data}),\ D'_j \leftarrow v'_j \oplus e_i$
		else $D'_j \leftarrow \perp$
		output $(D'_1, \dots, D'_{qt})$

Fig. 3. Illustration of the Set Intersection with Data Transfer Protocol

As in the set intersection protocol in Figure 2, the receiver here in the Set Intersection with Data Transfer protocol illustrated in Figure 3 also commits to all its queries in its first message $(y_1, \dots, y_{n_r})$. This follows from the same argument as Theorem 2 in Section 4.1.

Theorem 3. *If the (N, Q)-One-More (Non-Adaptive) Gap DH problem is hard, and if the proof system π is a zero-knowledge proof of knowledge, then the Set Intersection with Data Transfer Protocol in Figure 3 is a secure computation of the Adaptive Set Intersection with Data Transfer functionality $\mathcal{F}_{\mathsf{ASIwDT}}$ in the random oracle model.*

Proof idea: For malicious sender, the proof is exactly the same as in the proof of Theorem 1; For malicious receiver, simulator SIM_r sets u_i and e_i at random in $\{0,1\}^{n_2}$, then it controls the hash functions H_1 and H_2 and extracts each rID_j as how the simulator does in the proof of Theorem 1. Then SIM_r sends rID_j to $\mathcal{F}_{\mathsf{ASIwDT}}$, and gets back either $(1, D'_j)$ or $(0, \perp)$. If the answer is $(0, \perp)$, then SIM_r sets $H_2(H_1(\mathsf{rID}_j), (H_1(\mathsf{rID}_j))^k, \mathsf{tag})$ as a random number in $\{0,1\}^{n_2}$ different from all the u_i's. Otherwise, if the answer is $(1, D'_j)$, SIM_r sets $H_2(H_1(\mathsf{rID}_j), (H_1(\mathsf{rID}_j))^k, \mathsf{tag})$ to some u_i that has not been picked before, and $H_2(H_1(\mathsf{rID}_j), (H_1(\mathsf{rID}_j))^k, \mathsf{data}) = e_i \oplus D'_j$. By similar analysis as in the proof of Theorem 1, the malicious receiver's views in the real game and in the interaction with SIM_r are indistinguishable.

References

[BCC+09] Belenkiy, M., Camenisch, J., Chase, M., Kohlweiss, M., Lysyanskaya, A., Shacham, H.: Randomizable proofs and delegatable anonymous credentials. In: Halevi, S. (ed.) CRYPTO 2009. LNCS, vol. 5677, pp. 108–125. Springer, Heidelberg (2009)

[BNPS03] Bellare, M., Namprempre, C., Pointcheval, D., Semanko, M.: The one-more-rsa-inversion problems and the security of chaum's blind signature scheme. J. Cryptology 16(3), 185–215 (2003)

[CNS07] Camenisch, J., Neven, G., Shelat, A.: Simulatable adaptive oblivious transfer. In: Naor, M. (ed.) EUROCRYPT 2007. LNCS, vol. 4515, pp. 573–590. Springer, Heidelberg (2007)

[CS03] Camenisch, J., Shoup, V.: Practical verifiable encryption and decryption of discrete logarithms. In: Boneh, D. (ed.) CRYPTO 2003. LNCS, vol. 2729, pp. 126–144. Springer, Heidelberg (2003)

[CT05] Chu, C.-K., Tzeng, W.-G.: Efficient -out-of- oblivious transfer schemes with adaptive and non-adaptive queries. In: Vaudenay, S. (ed.) PKC 2005. LNCS, vol. 3386, pp. 172–183. Springer, Heidelberg (2005)

[CT10] De Cristofaro, E., Tsudik, G.: Practical set intersection protocols with linear complexity. In: Sion, R. (ed.) FC 2010. LNCS, vol. 6052, pp. 143–159. Springer, Heidelberg (2010)

[CZ09] Camenisch, J., Zaverucha, G.M.: Private intersection of certified sets. In: Dingledine, R., Golle, P. (eds.) FC 2009. LNCS, vol. 5628, pp. 108–127. Springer, Heidelberg (2009)

[DSMRY09] Dachman-Soled, D., Malkin, T., Raykova, M., Yung, M.: Efficient robust private set intersection. In: Abdalla, M., Pointcheval, D., Fouque, P.-A., Vergnaud, D. (eds.) ACNS 2009. LNCS, vol. 5536, pp. 125–142. Springer, Heidelberg (2009)

[EGS03] Evfimievski, A.V., Gehrke, J., Srikant, R.: Limiting privacy breaches in privacy preserving data mining. In: PODS, pp. 211–222 (2003)

[FIPR05] Freedman, M.J., Ishai, Y., Pinkas, B., Reingold, O.: Keyword search and oblivious pseudorandom functions. In: Kilian, J. (ed.) TCC 2005. LNCS, vol. 3378, pp. 303–324. Springer, Heidelberg (2005)

[FNP04] Freedman, M.J., Nissim, K., Pinkas, B.: Efficient private matching and set intersection. In: Cachin, C., Camenisch, J.L. (eds.) EUROCRYPT 2004. LNCS, vol. 3027, pp. 1–19. Springer, Heidelberg (2004)

[HL08] Hazay, C., Lindell, Y.: Efficient protocols for set intersection and pattern matching with security against malicious and covert adversaries. In: Canetti, R. (ed.) TCC 2008. LNCS, vol. 4948, pp. 155–175. Springer, Heidelberg (2008)

[HN10] Hazay, C., Nissim, K.: Efficient set operations in the presence of malicious adversaries. In: Nguyen, P.Q., Pointcheval, D. (eds.) PKC 2010. LNCS, vol. 6056, pp. 312–331. Springer, Heidelberg (2010)

[JL09] Jarecki, S., Liu, X.: Efficient oblivious pseudorandom function with applications to adaptive ot and secure computation of set intersection. In: Reingold, O. (ed.) TCC 2009. LNCS, vol. 5444, pp. 577–594. Springer, Heidelberg (2009)

[JL10] Jarecki, S., Liu, X.: Fast secure computation of set intersection (2010) (full version manuscript)

[NP99] Naor, M., Pinkas, B.: Oblivious transfer with adaptive queries. In: Wiener, M. (ed.) CRYPTO 1999. LNCS, vol. 1666, pp. 573–590. Springer, Heidelberg (1999)

[OK04] Ogata, W., Kurosawa, K.: Oblivious keyword search. J. Complexity 20(2-3), 356–371 (2004)

[Pai99] Paillier, P.: Public-key cryptosystems based on composite degree residuosity classes. In: Stern, J. (ed.) EUROCRYPT 1999. LNCS, vol. 1592, pp. 223–238. Springer, Heidelberg (1999)

Distributed Private-Key Generators for Identity-Based Cryptography*

Aniket Kate and Ian Goldberg

Cheriton School of Computer Science
University of Waterloo, Canada
{akate,iang}@cs.uwaterloo.ca

Abstract. An identity-based encryption (IBE) scheme can greatly reduce the complexity of sending encrypted messages. However, an IBE scheme necessarily requires a private-key generator (PKG), which can create private keys for clients, and so can passively eavesdrop on all encrypted communications. Although a distributed PKG has been suggested as a way to mitigate this key escrow problem for Boneh and Franklin's IBE scheme, the security of this distributed protocol has not been proven. Further, a distributed PKG has not been considered for any other IBE scheme.

In this paper, we design distributed PKG setup and private key extraction protocols for three important IBE schemes; namely, Boneh and Franklin's BF-IBE, Sakai and Kasahara's SK-IBE, and Boneh and Boyen's BB_1-IBE. We give special attention to the applicability of our protocols to all possible types of bilinear pairings and prove their IND-ID-CCA security in the random oracle model against a Byzantine adversary. Finally, we also perform a comparative analysis of these protocols and present recommendations for their use.

1 Introduction

In 1984, Shamir [2] introduced the notion of identity-based cryptography (IBC) as an approach to simplify public-key and certificate management in a public-key infrastructure (PKI) and presented an open problem to provide an identity-based encryption (IBE) scheme. After seventeen years, Boneh and Franklin [3] proposed the first practical and secure IBE scheme (BF-IBE) using bilinear maps. After this seminal work, in the last few years, significant progress has been made in IBC (for details, refer to a recent book on IBC [4] and references therein).

In an IBC system, a client chooses an arbitrary string such as her e-mail address to be her public key. With a standardized public-key string format, an IBC scheme completely eliminates the need for public-key certificates. As an example, in an IBE scheme, a sender can encrypt a message for a receiver knowing just the identity of the receiver and importantly, without obtaining and verifying the receiver's public-key certificate. Naturally, in such a system, a client herself is not capable of generating a private key for her identity. There is a trusted party called a *private-key generator* (PKG) which performs the system setup, generates a secret called the *master key* and provides private

* An extended version of this paper is avaiable [1].

J.A. Garay and R. De Prisco (Eds.): SCN 2010, LNCS 6280, pp. 436–453, 2010.

keys to clients using it. As the PKG computes a private key for a client, it can decrypt all of her messages passively. This inherent *key escrow* property asks for complete trust in the PKG, which is difficult to find in many realistic scenarios.

Importantly, the amount of trust placed in the holder of an IBC master key is far greater than that placed in the holder of the private key of a certifying authority (CA) in a PKI. In a PKI, in order to attack a client, the CA has to actively generate a fake certificate for the client containing a fake public key. In this case, it is often possible for the client to detect and prove the malicious behaviour of the CA. The CA cannot perform any passive attack; specifically, it cannot decrypt a message encrypted for the client using a client-generated public key and it cannot sign some document for the client, if the verifier gets a correct certificate from the client. On the other hand, in IBC, 1) knowing the master key, the PKG can decrypt or sign the messages for any client, without any active attack and consequent detection, 2) the PKG can make clients' private keys public without any possible detection, and 3) in a validity-period-based key revocation system [3], bringing down the PKG is sufficient to bring the system to a complete halt (*single point of failure*), once the current validity period ends. Therefore, the PKG in IBC needs to be far more trusted than the CA in a PKI. This has been considered as a reason for the slow adoption of IBC schemes outside of closed organizational settings.

Boneh and Franklin [3] suggest distributing a PKG in their BF-IBE scheme to solve these problems. In an *(n,t)-distributed PKG*, the master key is distributed among n PKG nodes such that a set of nodes of size t or smaller cannot compute the master key, while a client extracts her private key by obtaining private-key shares from any $t+1$ or more nodes; she can then use the system's public key to verify the correctness of her thus-extracted key. Boneh and Franklin [3] propose *verifiable secret sharing* (VSS) [5] of the master key among multiple PKGs to design a distributed PKG and also hint towards a completely distributed approach using the distributed (shared) key generation (DKG) schemes of Gennaro et al. [6]; however, they do not provide a formal security model and a proof. Further, none of the IBE schemes defined after [3] consider the design of a distributed PKG.

Although various proposed practical applications using IBE, such as pairing-based onion routing [7] or verifiable random functions from identity-based key encapsulation [8], require a distributed PKG as a fundamental need, there is no distributed PKG available for use yet. This practical need forms the motivation of this work.

Related Work. Although we are defining protocols for IBE schemes, as we are concentrating on distributed cryptographic protocols and due to space constraints, we do not include a comprehensive account of IBE. We refer readers to [9] for a detailed discussion on the various IBE schemes and frameworks defined in the literature. Pursuant to this survey, we work in the random oracle model for efficiency and practicality reasons.

None of the IBE schemes except BF-IBE considered distributed PKG setup and key extraction protocols in their design. Recently, Geisler and Smart [10] defined a distributed PKG for Sakai and Kasahara's SK-IBE [11]; however, their solution against a Byzantine adversary has an exponential communication complexity and a formal security proof is also not provided. We overcome both of these barriers in our distributed PKG for SK-IBE: our scheme is secure against a Byzantine adversary and has the same polynomial-time communication complexity as their scheme, which is secure only against an honest-but-curious adversary; we also provide a formal security proof.

Other than [10], there have been a few other efforts in the literature to counter the inherent key escrow and single point of failure issues in IBE. Al-Riyami and Paterson [12] introduce *certificateless public-key cryptography* (CL-PKC) to address the key escrow problem by combining IBC with public-key cryptography. Their elegant approach, however, does not address the single point of failure problem. Although it is possible to solve the problem by distributing their PKG using a VSS (which employs a trusted dealer to generate and distribute the key shares), which is inherently cheaper than a DKG-based PKG by a linear factor, it is impossible to stop a dealer's active attacks without completely distributed master-key generation. Further, as private-key extractions are less frequent than encryptions, it is certainly advisable to use more efficient options during encryption rather than private-key extraction. Finally, with the requirement of online access to the receiver's public key, CL-PKC becomes ineffective for systems without continuous network access, where IBC is considered to be an important tool. Lee et al. [13] and Gangishetti et al. [14] propose variants of the distributed PKG involving a more trustworthy key generation centre (KGC) and other key privacy authorities (KPAs). As observed by Chunxiang et al. [15] for [13], these approaches are, in general, vulnerable to passive attack by the KGC. In addition, the trust guarantees required by a KGC can be unattainable in practice. Goyal [16] reduces the required trust in the PKG by restricting its ability to distribute a client's private key. This does not solve the problem of single point of failure. Further, the PKG in his system still can decrypt the clients' messages passively, which leaves a secure and practical implementation of distributed PKGs wanting.

Threshold versions of signature schemes obtained from some IBE schemes using the Naor transform have been proposed and proved previously [17,18]. However, these solutions do not work for the corresponding IBE scheme. This is due to the inherent secret nature of a client's private keys and corresponding shares as compared to the inherent public nature of signatures and corresponding signature shares. While designing IBE schemes with a distributed PKG, we have to make sure that a PKG node cannot derive more information than the private-key share it generates for a client and that private-key shares are not available in public as commitments.

Our Contributions. We present distributed PKGs for all three important IBE frameworks: namely, full-domain-hash IBEs, exponent-inversion IBEs and commutative-blinding IBEs [9]. We propose distributed PKG setups and distributed private-key extraction protocols for BF-IBE [3], SK-IBE [11], and Boneh and Boyen's (modified) BB_1-IBE [9,19] schemes. The novelty of our protocols lies in achieving the secrecy of a client private key from the generating PKG nodes without compromising the efficiency. We realize this with an appropriate use of non-interactive proofs of knowledge, pairing-based verifications, and DKG protocols with and without the uniform randomness property. Based on the choice of the DKG protocol, our distributed PKGs can work in the synchronous or asynchronous communication model. In terms of feasibility, we ensure that our protocols work for all three pairing types defined by Galbraith et al. [20].

We prove the adaptive chosen ciphertext security (IND-ID-CCA) of the defined schemes in the random oracle model. Interestingly, compared to the security proofs for the respective IBE schemes with a single PKG, there are no additional security reduction factors in our proofs, even though the underlying DKG protocol used in the distributed PKGs does not provide a guarantee about the uniform randomness for the generated master secrets. To the best of our knowledge, there is no threshold cryptographic protocol available in the literature where a similar tight security reduction has been proven while using a DKG without the (more expensive) uniform randomness property. Finally, using operation counts, key sizes, and possible pairing types, we compare the performance of three distributed PKGs we define.

2 Preliminaries

2.1 Cryptographic Background

Bilinear Pairings. For three cyclic groups $\mathbb{G}$, $\hat{\mathbb{G}}$, and $\mathbb{G}_T$ (all of which we shall write multiplicatively) of the same prime order p, an *admissible bilinear pairing* e is a map $e : \mathbb{G} \times \hat{\mathbb{G}} \to \mathbb{G}_T$ with the *bilinearity*, *non-degeneracy* and *admissibility* properties. For a detailed mathematical discussion of bilinear pairings refer to [21]. We consider all three types of pairings [20] for prime order groups: namely, type 1, 2, and 3. In *type* 1 or *symmetric* pairings, an isomorphism $\phi : \hat{\mathbb{G}} \to \mathbb{G}$ as well as its inverse ϕ^{-1} are efficiently computable. In *type* 2 pairings, only the isomorphism ϕ, but not ϕ^{-1}, is efficiently computable. In *type* 3 pairings, neither ϕ nor ϕ^{-1} can be efficiently computed. The efficiency of the pairing computation improves from type 1 to type 2 to type 3 pairings. For a detailed discussion of the performance aspects of pairings refer to [20,22].

Non-interactive Proofs of Knowledge. As we assume the random oracle model in the paper, we can use non-interactive zero-knowledge proofs of knowledge (NIZKPK) based on the Fiat-Shamir methodology [23]. In particular, we use a variant of NIZKPK of a discrete logarithm (DLog) and one for proof of equality of two DLogs.

We employ a variant of NIZKPK of a DLog where given a DLog commitment ($\mathcal{C}_{\langle g \rangle}(s) = g^s$) and a Pedersen commitment [24] ($\mathcal{C}_{\langle g,h \rangle}(s,r) = g^s h^r$) to the same value s for generators $g, h \in \mathbb{G}$ and $s, r \in \mathbb{Z}_p$, a prover proves that she knows s and r such that $\mathcal{C}_{\langle g \rangle}(s)$ and $\mathcal{C}_{\langle g,h \rangle}(s,r)$. We denote this proof as

$$\text{NIZKPK}_{\equiv Com}(s, r, \mathcal{C}_{\langle g \rangle}(s), \mathcal{C}_{\langle g,h \rangle}(s,r)) = \pi_{\equiv Com} \in \mathbb{Z}_p^3. \quad (1)$$

It is nearly equivalent to proving knowledge of two DLogs separately.

We use another NIZKPK (proof of equality) of discrete logs [25] such that given commitments $\mathcal{C}_{\langle g \rangle}(s) = g^s$ and $\mathcal{C}_{\langle h \rangle}(s) = h^s$, a prover proves equality of the associated DLogs. We denote this proof as

$$\text{NIZKPK}_{\equiv DLog}(s, \mathcal{C}_{\langle g \rangle}(s), \mathcal{C}_{\langle h \rangle}(s)) = \pi_{\equiv DLog} \in \mathbb{Z}_p^2. \quad (2)$$

Note that g and h can belong two different groups of the same order. Refer to the extended version of the paper [1] for the descriptions of the above proofs.

There exists an easier way to prove this equality of DLogs if a pairing between the groups generated by g and h is available. Using a method due to Joux and Nguyen [26] to solve the decisional Diffie-Hellman (DDH) problem over pairing-friendly groups, given g^x and $h^{x'}$ the verifier checks if $e(g, h^{x'}) \stackrel{?}{=} e(g^x, h)$. However, when using a type

3 pairing, in the absence of an efficient isomorphism between $\mathbb{G}$ and $\hat{\mathbb{G}}$, if both g and h belong to the same group then the pairing-based scheme does not work. NIZKPK$_{\equiv DLog}$ provides a completely practical alternative there.

2.2 Assumptions

System Assumptions. Except for the steps involving DKG in some form, all other steps in our distributed PKG protocols are independent of the communication model used. As distributedness of PKG is important in IBC outside closed organizational settings, we suggest the asynchronous communication model as it closely models the Internet. In particular, we follow the system model of the DKG protocol in [27]. In a synchronous communication network, it is straightforward to replace this asynchronous DKG with a more efficient protocol such as the Joint Feldman DKG (JF-DKG) [28].

We assume a standard t-Byzantine adversary in a system with $n \geq 3t + 1$ nodes $P_1, P_2, \ldots, P_n$, where any t nodes are compromised or crashed by the adversary. In the synchronous communication model, the above resiliency bound becomes $n \geq 2t + 1$. Further, when the communication model is synchronous, we assume a *rushing* adversary. It can wait for the messages of the uncorrupted players to be transmitted, then decide on its computation and communication for that round, and still get its messages delivered to the honest parties on time. The adversary is also *static* as all of the efficient VSS and DKG schemes that we use are proved secure only against a static adversary, which can choose its t compromisable nodes before a protocol run. They are not considered secure against an adaptive adversary because their security proofs do not go through when the adversary can corrupt nodes adaptively. [28, §4.4] Canetti et al. [29] presented a DKG scheme provably secure against adaptive adversaries with at least two more communication rounds as compared to JF-DKG. Due to the inefficiency of adaptive (provably) secure DKG protocols, we stick to protocols provably secure only against a static adversary. However, it possible to easily use the DKG protocol in [29] and obtain security against the adaptive adversary.

Cryptographic Assumptions. Our adversary is computationally bounded with a security parameter κ. We assume an instance of a pairing framework e of groups $\mathbb{G}$, $\hat{\mathbb{G}}$ and $\mathbb{G}_T$, whose common prime order p is such that the adversary has to perform 2^κ operations to break the system. Let $\mathcal{G} = \langle e, \mathbb{G}, \hat{\mathbb{G}}, \mathbb{G}_T \rangle$. Following [9], we work in the random oracle model for efficiency reasons. For the security of the IBE schemes, we use the *bilinear Diffie-Hellman* (BDH) [30] and *bilinear Diffie-Hellman inversion* (BDHI) [31,32] assumptions. Here, we recall their definitions for asymmetric pairings from [9].

BDH Assumption: Given a tuple $(g, \hat{g}, g^a, \hat{g}^a, g^b, \hat{g}^c)$ in a bilinear group $\mathcal{G}$, the BDH problem is to compute $e(g, \hat{g})^{abc}$. The BDH assumption then states that it is infeasible to solve a random instance of the BDH problem, with non-negligible probability, in time polynomial in the size of the problem instance description.

BDHI Assumption: Given two tuples $(g, g^x, g^{x^2}, \ldots, g^{x^q})$ and $(\hat{g}, \hat{g}^x, \hat{g}^{x^2}, \ldots, \hat{g}^{x^q})$ in a bilinear group $\mathcal{G}$, the q-BDHI problem is to compute $e(g, \hat{g})^{1/x}$. The BDHI assumption for some polynomially bounded q states that it is infeasible to solve a random instance of the q-BDHI problem, with non-negligible probability, in time polynomial in the size of the problem instance description.

2.3 Distributed Computation

We next describe the distributed computation primitives that are required to design our distributed PKGs in an network of n nodes with a t-limited Byzantine adversary. Note that these distributed computation primitives are the efficient versions of the their original forms in [33,34,35,28,36,27] that utilize the presence of random oracles and the pairing-based DDH problem solving technique [26].

DKG over $\mathbb{Z}_p$**.** Pedersen [24] introduced the concept of DKG and developed a DKG protocol. Unlike VSS, where a dealer chooses a secret and distributes its shares among the nodes, DKG requires *no trusted dealer*. In an (n, t)-*DKG* protocol over $\mathbb{Z}_p$, a set of n nodes generates an element $s \in \mathbb{Z}_p$ in a distributed fashion with its shares $s_i \in \mathbb{Z}_p$ spread over the n nodes such that any subset of size greater than a threshold t can reveal or use the shared secret, while smaller subsets cannot. We mandate the following correctness and secrecy properties for a DKG protocol.

Correctness (DKG-C). There exists an efficient algorithm that on input shares from $2t + 1$ nodes and the public information, outputs the same unique value s, even if up to t shares are submitted by malicious nodes.

Secrecy (DKG-S). The adversary with t shares and the public parameters cannot compute the secret s.

In the synchronous and asynchronous communication models, respectively JF-DKG in [28] and the DKG protocol in [27] achieve these properties and are suitable for our use. For ease of exposition, we avoid crash-recoveries used in the DKG protocol in [27].

The shared secret in the above DKG protocols may not be *uniformly* random; this is a direct effect of using only DLog commitments having only computational secrecy. (See [28, §3] for a possible adversary attack.) In many cases, we do not need a uniformly random secret key; the security of these schemes relies on the assumption that the adversary cannot compute the secret. Most of our schemes similarly only require the assumption that it is infeasible to compute the secret given public parameters and we stick with DLog commitments those cases. However, we do indeed need a uniformly random shared secret in few protocols. We mandate the following stronger correctness and secrecy properties based on the DKG correctness and secrecy defined in [28, §4.1].

Strong Correctness (DKG-sC). Along with the DKG-C property, s is now uniformly distributed in $\mathbb{Z}_n$.

Strong Secrecy (DKG-sS). No information about s can be learnt by the adversary except for what is implied by the public parameters.

In this case, we use Pedersen commitments, but we do not employ the methodology defined by Gennaro et al. [6], which increases the number of rounds in the protocol. We observe that with the random oracle assumption at our disposal, the communicationally demanding technique by Gennaro et al. can be replaced with the much simpler computational non-interactive zero-knowledge proof of equality of committed values $\text{NIZKPK}_{\equiv Com}$ described in Eq. 1. The simulator-based proof for the above is similar to that in [28, §4.3] and is included in [1]. We represent DKG protocols using the DLog and Pedersen commitments as $\mathsf{DKG}_{\mathsf{DLog}}$ and $\mathsf{DKG}_{\mathsf{Ped}}$ respectively. For node P_i,

$$\left(\mathcal{C}^{(s)}_{\langle g\rangle}, s_i\right) = \mathsf{DKG}_{\mathsf{DLog}}(n, t, \tilde{t}, g, \alpha_i) \tag{3}$$

$$\left(\mathcal{C}^{(s,s')}_{\langle g,h\rangle}, [\mathcal{C}^{(s)}_{\langle g\rangle}, \text{NIZKPK}_{\equiv Com}], s_i, s'_i\right) = \mathsf{DKG}_{\mathsf{Ped}}(n, t, \tilde{t}, g, h, \alpha_i, \alpha'_i) \tag{4}$$

Here, $\tilde{t}$ is the number of VSS instances to be chosen ($t < \tilde{t} \leq 2t+1$), $g, h \in \mathbb{G}$ are commitment generators and $\alpha_i, \alpha'_i \in \mathbb{Z}_p$ are respectively a secret and randomness shared by P_i. For $\psi, \psi' \in \mathbb{Z}_p[x]$ of degree t with $\psi(0) = s$ and $\psi'(0) = s'$, $\mathcal{C}^{(s)}_{\langle g\rangle} = [g^s, g^{\psi(1)}, \cdots, g^{\psi(n)}]$ and $\mathcal{C}^{(s,s')}_{\langle g,h\rangle} = [g^s h^{s'}, g^{\psi(1)} h^{\psi'(1)}, \cdots, g^{\psi(n)} h^{\psi'(n)}]$ are respectively DLog and Pedersen commitment vectors. The optional $\text{NIZKPK}_{\equiv Com}$ is a vector of proofs that the entries of $\mathcal{C}^{(s)}_{\langle g\rangle}$ and $\mathcal{C}^{(s,s')}_{\langle g,h\rangle}$ commit to the same values.

In the most basic form of DKG, nodes generate shares of a secret z chosen jointly at random from $\mathbb{Z}_p$. Here, every node generates a random $r_i \in \mathbb{Z}_p$ and shares that using the DKG protocol with DLog or Pedersen commitments as $\mathsf{DKG}(n, t, \tilde{t} = t+1, g, [h], r_i, [r'_i])$ where the generator h and randomness r'_i are only required if Pedersen commitments are used. We represent the corresponding protocols as follows:

$$\left(\mathcal{C}^{(z)}_{\langle g\rangle}, z_i\right) = \mathsf{Random}_{\mathsf{DLog}}(n, t, g) \tag{5}$$

$$\left(\mathcal{C}^{(z,z')}_{\langle g,h\rangle}, [\mathcal{C}^{(z)}_{\langle g\rangle}, \text{NIZKPK}_{\equiv Com}], z_i, z'_i\right) = \mathsf{Random}_{\mathsf{Ped}}(n, t, g, h). \tag{6}$$

Distributed Addition over $\mathbb{Z}_p$. Let $\alpha, \beta \in \mathbb{Z}_p$ be two secrets shared among n nodes using the DKG protocol. Let polynomials $f(x), g(x) \in \mathbb{Z}_p[x]$ be the respectively associated degree-t polynomials and let $c \in \mathbb{Z}_p$ be a non-zero constant. Due to the linearity of Shamir's secret sharing [37], a node P_i with shares α_i and β_i can locally generate shares of $\alpha+\beta$ and $c\alpha$ by computing $\alpha_i+\beta_i$ and $c\alpha_i$, where $f(x)+g(x)$ and $cf(x)$ are the respective polynomials. $f(x)+g(x)$ is random if either one of $f(x)$ or $g(x)$ is, and $cf(x)$ is random if $f(x)$ is. Commitment entries for the resultant shares respectively are $\left(\mathcal{C}^{(\alpha+\beta)}_{\langle g\rangle}\right)_i = \left(\mathcal{C}^{(\alpha)}_{\langle g\rangle}\right)_i \left(\mathcal{C}^{(\beta)}_{\langle g\rangle}\right)_i$ and $\left(\mathcal{C}^{(c\alpha)}_{\langle g\rangle}\right)_i = \left(\mathcal{C}^{(\alpha)}_{\langle g\rangle}\right)_i^c$.

Distributed Multiplication over $\mathbb{Z}_p$. Local distributed multiplication of two shared secrets α and β looks unlikely. We use a distributed multiplication protocol against a computational adversary by Gennaro et al. [36, §4]. However, instead of their interactive zero-knowledge proof, we utilize the pairing-based DDH problem solving technique to verify the correctness of the product value shared by a node non-interactively. For shares α_i and β_i with DLog commitments g^{α_i} and $\hat{g}^{\beta_i}$, given a commitment $g^{\alpha_i\beta_i}$ of the shared product, other nodes can verify its correctness by checking if $e(g^{\alpha_i}, \hat{g}^{\beta_i}) \stackrel{?}{=} e(g^{\alpha_i\beta_i}, \hat{g})$ provided the groups of g and $\hat{g}$ are pairing-friendly. We observe that it is also possible to perform this verification when one of the involved commitments is a Pedersen commitment. However, if both commitments are Pedersen commitments, then we have to compute DLog commitments for one of the values and employ $\text{NIZKPK}_{\equiv Com}$ to prove its correctness in addition to using the pairing-based verification. In such a case, the choice between the latter technique and the non-interactive version of zero-knowledge proof suggested by Gennaro et al. [36] depends upon implementation efficiencies of the group operation and pairing computations.

In our IBC schemes, we always use the multiplication protocol with at least one DLog commitment. We denote the multiplication protocol involving two DLog commitments as $\mathsf{Mul}_{\mathsf{DLog}}$ and the one involving a combination of the two types of commitments as $\mathsf{Mul}_{\mathsf{Ped}}$. For the protocol correctness, along with recoverability to a unique value (say s), protocol Mul also requires that $s = \alpha\beta$. For the protocol secrecy, along with the secrecy of $\alpha\beta$, the protocol should not provide any additional information about the individual values of α or β once $\alpha\beta$ is reconstructed.

$$\left(\mathcal{C}^{(\alpha\beta)}_{\langle g^*\rangle}, (\alpha\beta)_i\right) = \mathsf{Mul}_{\mathsf{DLog}}(n, t, g^*, \left(\mathcal{C}^{(\alpha)}_{\langle g\rangle}, \alpha_i\right), \left(\mathcal{C}^{(\beta)}_{\langle \hat{g}\rangle}, \beta_i\right)) \tag{7}$$

$$\left(\mathcal{C}^{(\alpha\beta,\alpha\beta')}_{\langle \hat{g},\hat{h}\rangle}, (\alpha\beta)_i, (\alpha\beta')_i\right) = \mathsf{Mul}_{\mathsf{Ped}}(n, t, \hat{g}, \hat{h}, \left(\mathcal{C}^{(\alpha)}_{\langle g\rangle}, \alpha_i\right), \left(\mathcal{C}^{(\beta,\beta')}_{\langle \hat{g},\hat{h}\rangle}, \beta_i, \beta'_i\right)) \tag{8}$$

For $\mathsf{Mul}_{\mathsf{DLog}}$, $g^* = g$ or $\hat{g}$. For $\mathsf{Mul}_{\mathsf{Ped}}$, without loss of generality, we assume that β is distributed with the Pedersen commitment. If instead α uses Pedersen commitment, then the Pedersen commitment groups for $(\alpha\beta)$ change to g and h instead of $\hat{g}$ and $\hat{h}$.

Briefly, the protocol works as follows. Every honest node runs the $\mathsf{DKG}(n, t, 2t + 1, \hat{g}, [\hat{h}], \alpha_i\beta_i, [\alpha_i\beta'_i])$ from Eq. 3 or 4. As discussed above, pairing-based DDH solving is used to verify that the shared value is equal to the product of α_i and β_i.[1] At the end, instead of adding the subshares of the selected VSS instances, every node interpolates them at index 0 to get the new share $(\alpha\beta)_i$ of $\alpha\beta$.

The above Mul protocols can be seamlessly extended for distributed computation of any expression having binary products (BPs). For ℓ shared secrets $x_1, \cdots, x_\ell$, and their DLog commitments $\mathcal{C}^{(x_1)}_{\langle g\rangle}, \cdots, \mathcal{C}^{(x_\ell)}_{\langle g\rangle}$, shares of any binary product $x' = \sum_{i=1}^{m} k_i x_{a_i} x_{b_i}$ with known constants k_i and indices a_i, b_i can be easily computed by extending the protocol in Eq. 7. We denote this generalization as follows.

$$\left(\mathcal{C}^{(x')}_{\langle g^*\rangle}, x'_i\right) = \mathsf{Mul}_{\mathsf{BP}}(n, t, g^*, \{(k_i, a_i, b_i)\}, \left(\mathcal{C}^{(x_1)}_{\langle g\rangle}, (x_1)_i\right), \cdots, \left(\mathcal{C}^{(x_\ell)}_{\langle g\rangle}, (x_\ell)_i\right)) \tag{9}$$

Node P_j shares $\sum_i k_i (x_{a_i})_j (x_{a_i})_j$. For a type 1 pairing, the correctness of the sharing is verified by other nodes as $e(g^{\sum_i k_i (x_{a_i})_j (x_{b_i})_j}, g) \stackrel{?}{=} \prod_i e((g^{(x_{a_i})_j})^{k_i}, g^{(x_{b_i})_j})$. For type 2 and 3 pairings, $\mathrm{NIZKPK}_{\equiv DLog}$ is used to provide DLog commitments to the $(x_{b_i})_j$ with generator $\hat{g}$, and then a pairing computation like the above is used. We use $\mathsf{Mul}_{\mathsf{BP}}$ in Eq. 9 during distributed private-key extraction in the BB_1-IBE scheme in §3.5.

Sharing the Inverse of a Shared Secret. Given an (n, t)-distributed secret α, computing shares of its inverse α^{-1} in distributed manner (without reconstructing α) can be done trivially but inefficiently using a distributed computation of α^{p-1}; this involves $O(\log p)$ distributed multiplications. However, using a technique by Bar-Ilan and Beaver [33], this can be done using just one Random and one Mul protocol. This protocol involves interpolation of the product of the secret α with a distributed random element z. If z is created using DLog commitments and is not uniformly random, the product αz may leak some information about α. We avoid this by using Pedersen commitments while generating z. For a generator g^*, we represent this protocol as follows:

$$\left(\mathcal{C}^{(\alpha^{-1})}_{\langle g^*\rangle}, (\alpha^{-1})_i\right) = \mathsf{Inverse}(n, t, \hat{g}, \hat{h}, \left(\mathcal{C}^{(\alpha)}_{\langle g\rangle}, \alpha_i\right)) \tag{10}$$

[1] For type 3 pairings, a careful selection of commitment generators is required to make the pairing-based verification possible.

The protocol secrecy is the same as that of DKG except it is defined in the terms of α^{-1} instead of α; for the correctness property, along with recoverability to a unique value s, this protocol additionally mandates that $s = \alpha^{-1}$. For a distributed secret $\left(\mathcal{C}^{(\alpha)}_{\langle g\rangle}, \alpha_i\right)$, protocol Inverse works as follows: Every node P_i runs $\left(\mathcal{C}^{(z,z')}_{\langle \hat{g},\hat{h}\rangle}, z_i, z'_i\right) = \mathsf{Random}_{\mathsf{Ped}}(n, t, \hat{g}, \hat{h})$ and computes shares of $(w, w') = (\alpha z, \alpha z')$ as $\left(\mathcal{C}^{(w,w')}_{\langle \hat{g},\hat{h}\rangle}, w_i, w'_i\right) = \mathsf{Mul}_{\mathsf{Ped}}\left(n, t, \hat{g}, \hat{h}, \left(\mathcal{C}^{(\alpha)}_{\langle g\rangle}, \alpha_i\right), \left(\mathcal{C}^{(z,z')}_{\langle \hat{g},\hat{h}\rangle}, z_i, z'_i\right)\right)$. It then sends (w_i, w'_i) to each node and interpolates w using the correct received shares. If $w = 0$, repeats the above two steps, else locally computes $(\alpha^{-1})_i = w^{-1} z_i$. Finally, it computes the commitment $\mathcal{C}^{(\alpha^{-1})}_{\langle g^*\rangle}$ using w^{-1}, $\mathcal{C}^{(z,z')}_{\langle \hat{g},\hat{h}\rangle}$, and if required, any of the NIZKPK techniques. A modified form of this protocol is used in the distributed PKG for SK-IBE in §3.4.

3 Distributed PKG for IBE

We present distributed PKG setup and private key extraction protocols for three IBE schemes: BF-IBE [3], SK-IBE [11], and modified BB_1-IBE [9]. Each of these schemes represents a distinct important category of an IBE classification defined by Boyen [38]. They respectively belong to *full-domain-hash* IBE schemes, *exponent-inversion* IBE schemes, and *commutative-blinding* IBE schemes. The distributed PKG architectures that we develop for each of the three schemes apply to every scheme in their respective categories. Our above choice of IBE schemes is influenced by a recent identity-based cryptography standard (IBCS) [19] and also a comparative study by Boyen [9], which finds the above three schemes to be the most practical IBE schemes in their respective categories. In his classification, Boyen [38] also includes another category for quadratic-residuosity-based IBE schemes; however, none of the known schemes in this category are practical enough to consider here.

The role of a PKG in an IBE scheme ends with a client's private-key extraction and the distributed form of the PKG does not affect the encryption and decryption steps of IBE. Consequently, we define only the distributed PKG setup and private-key extraction steps of the three IBE schemes under consideration. We recall the original encryption and decryption steps in the extended version of the paper [1].

3.1 Bootstrapping Procedure

Each scheme under consideration here requires the following three bootstrapping steps.

1. Determine the node group size n and the security threshold t such that $n \geq 3t + 1$ (the asynchronous case) or $n \geq 2t + 1$ (the synchronous case).
2. Choose the pairing type to be used and compute groups $\mathbb{G}$, $\hat{\mathbb{G}}$, and $\mathbb{G}_T$ of prime order p such that there exists a pairing e of the decided type with $e : \mathbb{G} \times \hat{\mathbb{G}} \rightarrow \mathbb{G}_T$. The security parameter κ determines the group order p.
3. Choose two generators $g \in \mathbb{G}$ and $\hat{g} \in \hat{\mathbb{G}}$ required to generate public parameters as well as the commitments. With a type 1 or 2 pairing, set $g = \phi(\hat{g})$.

Any untrusted entity can perform these offline tasks. Honest DKG nodes can verify the correctness of the tuple (n, t) and confirm the group choices $\mathbb{G}$, $\hat{\mathbb{G}}$, and $\mathbb{G}_T$ as the first step of their distributed PKG setup. If unsatisfied, they may decline to proceed.

3.2 Formal Security Model

An IBE scheme with an (n, t)-distributed PKG consists of the following components:

- A *distributed PKG setup protocol* for node P_i that takes the above bootstrapped parameters n, t and $\mathcal{G}$ as input and outputs a share s_i of a master secret s and a public-key vector K_{pub} of a master public key and n public-key shares.
- A *distributed private key-extraction protocol* for node P_i that takes a client identity $\mathtt{ID}$, the public key vector K_{pub} and the master-secret share s_i as input and outputs a verifiable private-key share $d_{\mathtt{ID}i}$. The client computes the private key $d_{\mathtt{ID}}$ after verifying the received shares $d_{\mathtt{ID}i}$.
- An *encryption algorithm* that takes a receiver identity $\mathtt{ID}$, the master public key and a plaintext message M as input and outputs a ciphertext C.
- A *decryption algorithm* for client with identity $\mathtt{ID}$ that takes a ciphertext C and the private key $d_{\mathtt{ID}}$ as input and outputs a plaintext M.

Note that the above distributed PKG setup protocol does not require any *dealer* and that we mandate verifiability for the private-key shares rather than obtaining robustness using error-correcting techniques. During private-key extractions, we insist on minimal interaction between clients and PKG nodes—transferring identity credentials from the client at the start and private-key shares from the nodes at the end.

To define security against an IND-ID-CCA attack, we consider the following game that a challenger plays against a polynomially bounded t-limited Byzantine adversary.

Setup: The adversary chooses to corrupt a fixed set of t nodes and the challenger simulates the remaining $n-t$ nodes to run a distributed PKG setup protocol. At the end of the protocol execution, the adversary receives t shares of a shared master secret for its t nodes and a public key vector K_{pub}. The challenger knows the remaining $n-t$ shares and can derive the master secret as $n-t \geq t+1$ in any communication setting.

Phase 1: The adversary adaptively issues private-key extraction and decryption queries to the challenger. For a private-key extraction query $\langle \mathtt{ID} \rangle$, the challenger simulates the distributed key extraction protocol for its $n-t$ nodes and sends verifiable private-key shares for its $n-t$ nodes. For a decryption query $\langle \mathtt{ID}, C \rangle$, the challenger decrypts C by generating the private key $d_{\mathtt{ID}}$ or using the master secret.

Challenger: The adversary chooses two equal-length plaintexts M_0 and M_1, and a challenge identity $\mathtt{ID}_{ch}$ such that $\mathtt{ID}_{ch}$ does not appear in any private-key extraction query in Phase 1. The challenger chooses $b \in_R \{0, 1\}$ and encrypts M_b for $\mathtt{ID}_{ch}$ and K_{pub}, and gives the ciphertext C_{ch} to the adversary.

Phase 2: The adversary adaptively issues more private-key extraction and decryption queries to the challenger except for key extraction query for $\langle \mathtt{ID}_{ch} \rangle$ and decryption queries for $\langle \mathtt{ID}_{ch}, C_{ch} \rangle$.

Guess: Finally, the adversary outputs a guess $b' \in \{0, 1\}$ and wins the game if $b = b'$.

Security against IND-ID-CCA attacks means that, for any polynomially bounded adversary, $b' = b$ with probability negligibly greater than $1/2$.

3.3 Boneh and Franklin's BF-IBE

BF-IBE [3] belongs to the full-domain-hash IBE family. In a BF-IBE setup, a PKG generates a master key $s \in \mathbb{Z}_p$ and a public key $g^s \in \mathbb{G}$, and derives private keys for clients using their identities and s. A client with identity $\mathtt{ID}$ receives the private key $d_{\mathtt{ID}} = (H_1(\mathtt{ID}))^s = h_{\mathtt{ID}}^s \in \hat{\mathbb{G}}$, where $H_1 : \{0,1\}^* \to \hat{\mathbb{G}}^*$ is a full-domain cryptographic hash function. ($\hat{\mathbb{G}}^*$ denotes the set of all elements in $\hat{\mathbb{G}}$ except the identity.)

Distributed PKG Setup. This involves generation of the system master key and the system public-key tuple in the (n,t)-distributed form among n nodes. Each node P_i participates in a common DKG over $\mathbb{Z}_p$ to generate its share $s_i \in \mathbb{Z}_p$ of the distributed master key s. The system public-key tuple is of the form $\mathcal{C}_{\langle g \rangle}^{(s)} = [g^s, g^{s_1}, \cdots, g^{s_n}]$. We obtain this using our $\mathsf{Random}_{\mathsf{DLog}}$ protocol from Eq. 5 as $\left(\mathcal{C}_{\langle g \rangle}^{(s)}, s_i\right) = \mathsf{Random}_{\mathsf{DLog}}(n,t,g)$.

Private-key Extraction. As a client needs $t+1$ correct shares, it is sufficient for her to contact any $2t+1$ nodes (say set $\mathcal{Q}$). The private-key extraction works as follows.

1. Once a client with identity $\mathtt{ID}$ contacts every node in $\mathcal{Q}$, every honest node $P_i \in \mathcal{Q}$ authenticates the client's identity and returns a private-key share $h_{\mathtt{ID}}^{s_i} \in \hat{\mathbb{G}}$ over a secure and authenticated channel.
2. Upon receiving $t+1$ valid shares, the client can construct her private key $d_{\mathtt{ID}}$ as $d_{\mathtt{ID}} = \prod_{P_i \in \mathcal{Q}} (h_{\mathtt{ID}}^{s_i})^{\lambda_i} \in \hat{\mathbb{G}}$, where the Lagrange coefficient $\lambda_i = \prod_{P_j \in \mathcal{Q} \setminus \{i\}} \frac{j}{j-i}$. The client can verify the correctness of the computed private key $d_{\mathtt{ID}}$ by checking $e(g, d_{\mathtt{ID}}) \stackrel{?}{=} e(g^s, h_{\mathtt{ID}})$. If unsuccessful, she can verify the correctness of each received $h_{\mathtt{ID}}^{s_i}$ by checking if $e(g, h_{\mathtt{ID}}^{s_i}) \stackrel{?}{=} e(g^{s_i}, h_{\mathtt{ID}})$. An equality proves the correctness of the share, while an inequality indicates misbehaviour by the node P_i and its consequential removal from $\mathcal{Q}$.

In asymmetric pairings, elements of $\mathbb{G}$ generally have a shorter representation than those of $\hat{\mathbb{G}}$. Therefore, we put the more frequently accessed system public-key shares in $\mathbb{G}$, while the occasionally transferred client private-key shares belong to $\hat{\mathbb{G}}$. This also leads to a reduction in the ciphertext size. However, for type 2 pairings, an efficient hash-to-$\hat{\mathbb{G}}$ is not available for the group $\hat{\mathbb{G}}$ [20]; in that case we compute the system public key shares in $\hat{\mathbb{G}}$ and use the more feasible group $\mathbb{G}$ for the private key shares.

Proof of Security. Using the encryption and decryption steps of the FullIdent version of BF-IBE [3, §4.2] along with the above distributed setup and key extraction protocols, we prove the IND-ID-CCA security of BF-IBE with the (n,t)-distributed PKG ((n,t)-FullIdent) based on the BDH assumption. Hereafter, q_E, q_D and q_{H_i} denote the number of extraction, decryption and random oracle H_i queries respectively.

Theorem 1. *Let H_1, H_2, H_3 and H_4 be random oracles. Let $\mathcal{A}_1$ be an IND-ID-CCA adversary that has advantage $\epsilon_1(\kappa)$ in running time $t_1(\kappa)$ against (n,t)-FullIdent making at most q_E, q_D, q_{H_1}, q_{H_2}, q_{H_3}, and q_{H_4} queries. Then, there exists an* *algorithm $\mathcal{B}$ that solves the* BDH *problem in $\mathcal{G}$ with advantage roughly equal to $\epsilon_1(\kappa)/(q_{H_1}q_{H_2}(q_{H_3}+q_{H_4}))$ and running time $O(t_1(\kappa), q_E, q_D, q_{H_1}, q_{H_2}, q_{H_3}, q_{H_4})$.*

For their proof, Boneh and Franklin define two additional public key encryption schemes: BFBasicPub [3, Sec. 4.1], and its IND-CCA secure version BFBasicPub^{hy} [3, Sec. 4.2] and prove the security of FullIdent in the following proof sequence: FullIdent $\rightarrow$ BFBasicPub^{hy} $\rightarrow$ BFBasicPub $\rightarrow$ BDH. We use distributed versions of these encryption schemes: (n,t)-BFBasicPub^{hy} and (n,t)-BFBasicPub respectively, and prove the proof sequence (n,t)-FullIdent $\rightarrow$ (n,t)-BFBasicPub^{hy} $\rightarrow$ (n,t)-BFBasicPub $\rightarrow$ BDH. For the complete proof, refer to the extended version of the paper. [1]

3.4 Sakai and Kasahara's SK-IBE

SK-IBE [11] belongs to the exponent-inversion IBE family. Here, the PKG generates a master key $s \in \mathbb{Z}_p$ and a public key $g^s \in \mathbb{G}$ just as in BF-IBE. However, the key-extraction differs significantly. Here, a client with identity $\mathtt{ID}$ receives the private key $d_{\mathtt{ID}} = \hat{g}^{\frac{1}{s+H_1'(\mathtt{ID})}} \in \hat{\mathbb{G}}$, where $H_1' : \{0,1\}^* \rightarrow \mathbb{Z}_p$.

Distributed PKG Setup. The distributed PKG setup remains the exactly same as that of BF-IBE, where $s_i \in \mathbb{Z}_p$ is the master-key share for node P_i and $\mathcal{C}^{(s)}_{\langle g \rangle} = [g^s, g^{s_1}, \cdots, g^{s_n}]$ is the system public-key tuple.

Private-key Extraction. The private-key extraction for SK-IBE is not as straightforward as that for BF-IBE. We modify the Inverse protocol described in §2.3; specifically, here a private-key extracting client receives w_i from the node in step 3 and instead of nodes, the *client* performs the interpolation. In step 4, instead of publishing, nodes forward $\hat{g}^{z_i}$ and the associated NIZKPK$_{\equiv Com}$ directly to the client, which computes $\hat{g}^z$ and then $d_{\mathtt{ID}} = (\hat{g}^z)^{w^{-1}}$. The reason behind this is to avoid possible key escrow if the node computes both $\hat{g}^z$ and w. Further, the nodes precompute another generator $\hat{h} \in \hat{\mathbb{G}}$ for Pedersen commitments using $\left(\mathcal{C}^{(r)}_{\langle \hat{g} \rangle}, r_i\right) = \mathsf{Random}_{\mathsf{DLog}}(n,t,\hat{g})$, and set $\hat{h} = \left(\mathcal{C}^{(r)}_{\langle \hat{g} \rangle}\right)_0 = \hat{g}^r$.

1. Once a client with identity $\mathtt{ID}$ contacts all n nodes the system, every node P_i authenticates the client's identity, runs $\left(\mathcal{C}^{(z,z')}_{\langle \hat{g},\hat{h} \rangle}, z_i, z_i'\right) = \mathsf{Random}_{\mathsf{Ped}}(n,t,\hat{g},\hat{h})$ and computes $s_i^{\mathtt{ID}} = s_i + H_1'(\mathtt{ID})$ and for $0 \le j \le n$, $\left(\mathcal{C}^{(s^{\mathtt{ID}})}_{\langle g \rangle}\right)_j = \left(\mathcal{C}^{(s)}_{\langle g \rangle}\right)_j g^{H_1'(\mathtt{ID})} = g^{s_j + H_1'(\mathtt{ID})}$. $\mathsf{Random}_{\mathsf{Ped}}$ makes sure that z is uniformly random.
2. P_i performs $\left(\mathcal{C}^{(w,w')}_{\langle \hat{g},\hat{h} \rangle}, w_i, w_i'\right) = \mathsf{Mul}_{\mathsf{Ped}}(n,t,\hat{g},\hat{h}, \left(\mathcal{C}^{(s^{\mathtt{ID}})}_{\langle g \rangle}, s_i^{\mathtt{ID}}\right), \left(\mathcal{C}^{(z,z')}_{\langle \hat{g},\hat{h} \rangle}, z_i, z_i'\right))$, where $w = s^{\mathtt{ID}}z = (s + H_1'(\mathtt{ID}))z$ and $w' = (s + H_1'(\mathtt{ID}))z'$ and sends $\left(\mathcal{C}^{(w,w')}_{\langle \hat{g},\hat{h} \rangle}, w_i\right)$ along with NIZKPK$_{\equiv Com}(w_i, w_i', \left(\mathcal{C}^{(w)}_{\langle \hat{g} \rangle}\right)_i, \left(\mathcal{C}^{(w,w')}_{\langle \hat{g},\hat{h} \rangle}\right)_i)$ to the client, which upon receiving $t+1$ verifiably correct shares (w_i) reconstructs w using interpolation. If $w \neq 0$, then it computes w^{-1} or else starts again from step 1.
3. Node P_i sends $\left(\mathcal{C}^{(z)}_{\langle \hat{g} \rangle}\right)_i = \hat{g}^{z_i}$ and $\mathcal{C}^{(z,z')}_{\langle \hat{g},\hat{h} \rangle}$ along with NIZKPK$_{\equiv Com}(z_i, z_i', \left(\mathcal{C}^{(z)}_{\langle \hat{g} \rangle}\right)_i, \left(\mathcal{C}^{(z,z')}_{\langle \hat{g},\hat{h} \rangle}\right)_i)$ to the client.

4. The client verifies $\left(\mathcal{C}^{(z)}_{\langle \hat{g} \rangle}\right)_i$ using the received NIZKPK$_{\equiv Com}$, interpolates $t+1$ valid $\hat{g}^{z_i}$ to compute $\hat{g}^z$ and derives her private key $(\hat{g}^z)^{w^{-1}} = \hat{g}^{\frac{1}{(s+H(\mathrm{ID}))}}$.

This protocol can be used without any modification with any type of pairing. Further, online execution of the $\mathsf{Random}_{\mathsf{Ped}}$ computation can be eliminated using batch pre-computation of distributed random elements $\left(\mathcal{C}^{(z,z')}_{\langle \hat{g}, \hat{h} \rangle}, z_i, z'_i\right)$.

Proof of Security. The security of SK-IBE with a distributed PKG ((n,t)-SK-IBE) is based on the BDHI assumption.

Theorem 2. *Let H'_1, H_2, H_3 and H_4 be random oracles. Let $\mathcal{A}_1$ be an IND-ID-CCA adversary that has advantage $\epsilon_1(\kappa)$ in running time $t_1(\kappa)$ against (n,t)-SK-IBE making at most q_E, q_D, $q_{H'_1}$, q_{H_2}, q_{H_3}, and q_{H_4} queries. Then, there exists an algorithm $\mathcal{B}$ that solves the BDHI problem in $\mathcal{G}$ with advantage roughly equal to $\epsilon_1(\kappa)/(q_{H'_1} q_{H_2}(q_{H_3} + q_{H_4}))$ and running time $O(t_1(\kappa), q_E, q_D, q_{H'_1}, q_{H_2}, q_{H_3}, q_{H_4})$.*

Chen and Cheng [39] prove the security of the original SK-IBE protocol in a proof sequence: SK-IBE $\to$ $\mathsf{SKBasicPub}^{hy}$ $\to$ $\mathsf{SKBasicPub}$ $\to$ BDHI, where $\mathsf{SKBasicPub}$ and $\mathsf{SKBasicPub}^{hy}$ [39, §3.2] are public key encryption schemes based on SK-IBE. We prove Theorem 2 by showing (n,t)-SK-IBE $\to$ $\mathsf{SKBasicPub}^{hy}$. For the complete proof, refer to the extended version of the paper [1].

3.5 Boneh and Boyen's BB$_1$-IBE

BB$_1$-IBE belongs to the commutative-blinding IBE family. Boneh and Boyen [32] proposed the original scheme with a security reduction to the decisional BDH assumption [40] in the standard model against selective-identity attacks. However, with a practical requirement of IND-ID-CCA security, in the recent IBCS standard [19], Boyen and Martin proposed a modified version, which is IND-ID-CCA secure in the random oracle model under the BDH assumption. In [9], Boyen rightly claims that for practical applications, it would be preferable to rely on the random-oracle assumption rather than using a less efficient IBE scheme with a stronger security assumption or a weaker attack model. We use the modified BB$_1$-IBE scheme as described in [9] and [19].

In the BB$_1$-IBE setup, the PKG generates a master-key triplet $(\alpha, \beta, \gamma) \in \mathbb{Z}_p^3$ and an associated public key tuple $(g^\alpha, g^\gamma, e(g, \hat{g})^{\alpha\beta})$. A client with identity ID receives the private key tuple $d_{\mathrm{ID}} = (\hat{g}^{\alpha\beta + (\alpha H'_1(\mathrm{ID}) + \gamma)r}, \hat{g}^r) \in \hat{\mathbb{G}}^2$.

Distributed PKG Setup. In [9], Boyen does not include the parameters $\hat{g}$ and $\hat{g}^\beta$ from the original BB$_1$ scheme [32] in his public key, as they are not required during key extraction, encryption or decryption (they are not omitted for security reasons). In the distributed setting, we in fact need those parameters to be public for efficiency reasons; a verifiable distributed computation of $e(g, \hat{g})^{\alpha\beta}$ becomes inefficient otherwise. To avoid key escrow of clients' private-key components ($\hat{g}^r$), we also need $\hat{h}$ and $\mathcal{C}^{(\beta)}_{\langle \hat{h} \rangle}$; otherwise, parts of clients' private keys would appear in public commitment vectors. As in SK-IBE in §3.4, this extra generator $\hat{h} \in \hat{\mathbb{G}}$ is precomputed using the $\mathsf{Random}_{\mathsf{DLog}}$ protocol. Distributed PKG setup of BB$_1$ involves distributed generation of the master-key tuple (α, β, γ). Distributed PKG node P_i achieves this using the following three $\mathsf{Random}_{\mathsf{DLog}}$ protocol invocations: $\left(\mathcal{C}^{(\alpha)}_{\langle g \rangle}, \alpha_i\right) = \mathsf{Random}_{\mathsf{DLog}}(n, t, g)$, $\left(\mathcal{C}^{(\beta)}_{\langle \hat{g} \rangle}, \beta_i\right) = \mathsf{Random}_{\mathsf{DLog}}(n, t, \hat{g})$, and $\left(\mathcal{C}^{(\gamma)}_{\langle g \rangle}, \gamma_i\right) = \mathsf{Random}_{\mathsf{DLog}}(n, t, g)$.

Here, $(\alpha_i, \beta_i, \gamma_i)$ is the tuple of master-key shares for node P_i. We also need $\mathcal{C}^{(\beta)}_{\langle \hat{h} \rangle}$; each node P_i provides this by publishing $\left(\mathcal{C}^{(\beta)}_{\langle \hat{h} \rangle}\right)_i = \hat{h}^{\beta_i}$ and the NIZKPK$_{\equiv DLog}$ $(\beta_i, \hat{g}^{\beta_i}, \hat{h}^{\beta_i})$. The tuple $\left(\mathcal{C}^{(\alpha)}_{\langle g \rangle}, e(g, \hat{g})^{\alpha\beta}, \mathcal{C}^{(\gamma)}_{\langle g \rangle}, \mathcal{C}^{(\beta)}_{\langle \hat{h} \rangle}\right)$ forms the system public key, where $e(g, \hat{g})^{\alpha\beta}$ can computed from the public commitment entries. The vector $\mathcal{C}^{(\beta)}_{\langle \hat{g} \rangle}$, although available publicly, is not required for any further computation.

Private-key Extraction. The most obvious way to compute a BB_1 private key seems to be for P_i to compute $\alpha_i\beta_i + (\alpha_i H'_1(\texttt{ID}) + \gamma_i)r_i$ and provide the corresponding $\hat{g}^{\alpha_i\beta_i + (\alpha_i H'_1(\texttt{ID}) + \gamma_i)r_i}, \hat{g}^{r_i}$ to the client, who now needs $2t+1$ valid shares to obtain her private key. However, $\alpha_i\beta_i + (\alpha_i H'_1(\texttt{ID}) + \gamma_i)r_i$ here is not a share of a random degree-$2t$ polynomial. The possible availability of $\hat{g}^{r_i}$ to the adversary creates a suspicion about secrecy of the master-key share with this method. For private-key extraction in BB_1-IBE with a distributed PKG, we instead use the $\mathsf{Mul}_{\mathsf{BP}}$ protocol in which the client is provided with $\hat{g}^{w_i}$, where $w_i = (\alpha\beta + (\alpha H'_1(\texttt{ID}) + \gamma)r)_i$ is a share of random degree t polynomial. The protocol works as follows.

1. Once a client with identity $\texttt{ID}$ contacts all n nodes the system, every node P_i authenticates the client's identity and runs $\left(\mathcal{C}^{(r,r')}_{\langle \hat{h}, \hat{g} \rangle}, [\mathcal{C}^{(r)}_{\langle \hat{h} \rangle}, \text{NIZKPK}_{\equiv Com}], r_i, r_i\right) = \mathsf{Random}_{\mathsf{Ped}}(n, t, f, \hat{h}, \hat{g})$. $\mathsf{Random}_{\mathsf{Ped}}$ makes sure that r is uniformly random.
2. P_i computes its share w_i of $w = \alpha\beta + (\alpha H'_1(\texttt{ID}) + \gamma)r$ using $\mathsf{Mul}_{\mathsf{BP}}$ in Eq. 9.
$$\left(\mathcal{C}^{(w)}_{\langle g^* \rangle}, w_i\right) = \mathsf{Mul}_{\mathsf{BP}}(n, t, f, g^*, desc, \left(\mathcal{C}^{(\alpha)}_{\langle g \rangle}, \alpha_i\right), \left(\mathcal{C}^{(\beta)}_{\langle \hat{h} \rangle}, \beta_i\right), \left(\mathcal{C}^{(\gamma)}_{\langle g \rangle}, \gamma_i\right), \left(\mathcal{C}^{(r)}_{\langle \hat{h} \rangle}, r_i\right)).$$
Here, $desc = \{(1, 1, 2), (H'_1(\texttt{ID}), 1, 4), (1, 3, 4)\}$ is the description of the required binary product under the ordering $(\alpha, \beta, \gamma, r)$ of secrets. To justify our choices of commitment generators, we present the pairing-based verification in protocol $\mathsf{Mul}_{\mathsf{BP}}$: $e(g^{\alpha_i\beta_i + (\alpha_i H'_1(\texttt{ID}) + \gamma_i)r_i}, \hat{h}) \stackrel{?}{=} e(g^{\alpha_i}, \hat{h}^{\beta_i})e((g^{\alpha_i})^{H'_1(\texttt{ID})}g^{\gamma_i}, \hat{h}^{r_i})$. For type 2 and 3 pairings, $g^* = g$, as there is no efficient isomorphism from $\mathbb{G}$ to $\hat{\mathbb{G}}$. For type 1 pairings, we use $g^* = \hat{h} = \phi^{-1}(h)$. Otherwise, the resultant commitments for w (which are public) will contain the private-key part $g^{\alpha\beta + (\alpha H'_1(\texttt{ID}) + \gamma)r}$.
3. Once the $\mathsf{Mul}_{\mathsf{BP}}$ protocol has succeeded, Node P_i generates $\hat{g}^{w_i}$ and $\hat{g}^{r_i}$ and sends those to the client over a secure and authenticated channel.
4. The client generates her private key $(\hat{g}^{\alpha\beta + (\alpha H'_1(\texttt{ID}) + \gamma)r}, \hat{g}^r)$ by interpolating the valid received shares. For type 1 and type 2 pairings, the client can use the pairing-based DDH solving to check the validity of the shares. However, for type 3 pairings, without an efficient mapping from $\hat{\mathbb{G}}$ to $\mathbb{G}$, pairing-based DDH solving can only be employed to verify $\hat{g}^{w_i}$. As a verification of $\hat{g}^{r_i}$, node P_i includes a NIZKPK$_{\equiv DLog}$ $(r_i, \hat{h}^{r_i}, \hat{g}^{r_i})$ along with $\hat{g}^{w_i}$ and $\hat{g}^{r_i}$.

As in SK-IBE in §3.4, online execution of the $\mathsf{Random}_{\mathsf{DLog}}$ computation can be eliminated using batch precomputation of distributed random elements $\left(\mathcal{C}^{(r)}_{\langle \hat{h} \rangle}, r_i\right)$.

Proof of Security. Along with the above distributed setup and private-key extraction protocols, we prove IND-ID-CCA security of BB_1-IBE with the (n,t)-distributed PKG ((n,t)-BB_1-IBE) based on the BDH assumption. To the best of our knowledge, an IND-ID-CCA security proof for the modified BB_1-IBE scheme has not been published yet.

Theorem 3. *Let H_1', H_2, H_3 and H_4' be random oracles. Let $\mathcal{A}$ be an IND-ID-CCA adversary that has advantage $\epsilon(\kappa)$ in running time $t(\kappa)$ against (n,t)-BB_1-IBE making at most q_E, q_D, $q_{H_1'}$, q_{H_2}, $q_{H_3'}$, and q_{H_4} queries. Then, there exists an algorithm $\mathcal{B}$ that solves the BDH problem in $\mathcal{G}$ with advantage roughly equal to $\epsilon(\kappa)/(q_{H_1'}q_{H_3'})$ and running time $O(t(\kappa), q_E, q_D, q_{H_1'}, q_{H_2}, q_{H_3'}, q_{H_4})$.*

For the proof, refer to the extended version of the paper [1].

Using a more expensive DKG protocol with uniformly random output, all of our proofs would become relatively simpler. However, note that our use of DKG without uniformly random output does not affect the security reduction factor in any proof. This is something not achieved for the known previous protocols with non-uniform DKG such as threshold Schorr signatures [28]. Further, we do not discuss the liveness and agreement properties for our asynchronous protocols as liveness and agreement of all the distributed primitives provides liveness and agreement for the distributed PKG setup and distributed key extraction protocols. Finally, for simplicity of the discussion, it would have been better to combine three proofs. However, that looks difficult, if not impossible, as the distributed computation tools used in these distributed PKGs and the original IBE security proofs vary a lot from a scheme to scheme.

Finally, observing the importance of proactiveness and a capability to handle group dynamics in any practical system, we also discuss the proactive security and group modification primitives for our distributed PKGs in the extended version of the paper [1].

4 Comparing Distributed PKGs

In this section, we discuss the performance of the setup and key extraction protocols of the above three distributed PKGs. For a detailed comparison of the encryption and decryption steps of BF-IBE, SK-IBE and BB_1-IBE, refer to [9]. The general recommendations from this survey are to avoid SK-IBE and other exponent-inversion IBEs due to their reliance on the strong BDHI assumption, and that BB_1-IBE and BF-IBE both are good, but BB_1-IBE can be a better choice due to BF-IBE's less efficient encryption.

Table 1 provides a detailed operation count and key size comparison of three distributed PKGs. We count DKG instances, pairings, NIZKPKs, interpolations and public and private key sizes. We leave aside the comparatively small exponentiations and other group operations. As mentioned in §3.5, for BB_1-IBE, with pairings of type 1 and 2, there is a choice that can be made between using n NIZKPKs and $2n$ pairing computations. The table shows the NIZKPK choice (the only option for type 3 pairings), and footnote b shows where NIZKPKs can be traded off for pairings. An efficient algorithm for hash-to-$\hat{\mathbb{G}}$ is not available for type 2 pairing curves and we interchange the groups used for the public key and client private-key shares. Footnote c indicates how that affects the key sizes.

In Table 1, we observe that the distributed PKG setup and the distributed private-key extraction protocols for BF-IBE are significantly more efficient than those for SK-IBE and BB_1-IBE. Importantly, for BF-IBE, distributed PKG nodes can extract

Table 1. Operation count and key sizes for distributed PKG setups and distributed private-key extractions (per key)

	BF-IBE		SK-IBE		BB_1-IBE	
	Setup	Extraction	Setup	Extraction	Setup	Extraction
Operation Count						
Generator h or $\hat{h}$	X		✓		✓	
DKG[a] (precomputed)	-	0	-	1^P	-	1^P
DKG (online)	1^D	0	1^D	1^P	3^D	1^D
Parings @PKG Node	0	0	0	$2n$	1^b	$2n$
Parings @Client	-	$2(2t+2)$	-	0	-	$2n^b$
NIZKPK	0	0	0	$2n$	n^b	$2n^b$
Interpolations	0	1	0	2	1	2
Key Sizes						
PKG Public Key	$(n+2)\mathbb{G}^c$		$(n+3)\mathbb{G}$		$(2n+3)\mathbb{G}$, $(n+2)\hat{\mathbb{G}}$, $(1)\mathbb{G}_T$	
Private-key Shares	$(2t+1)\hat{\mathbb{G}}^c$		$(3n)\mathbb{Z}_p$, $(3n+1)\hat{\mathbb{G}}$		$(2n)\mathbb{Z}_p{}^b$, $(2n)\hat{\mathbb{G}}$	

[a] For DKG, D indicates use of DLog commitments, while P indicates Pedersen commitments.
[b] For type 1 and 2 pairings, $2n$ extra pairings replace n NIZKPKs. Further, the $2n$ $\mathbb{Z}_p$ elements are omitted from the private-key shares.
[c] For type 2 parings, the groups used for the PKG public key and the private-key shares are interchanged.

a key for a client without interacting with each other, which is not possible in the other two schemes; both BB_1-IBE and SK-IBE require at least one DKG instance for every private-key extraction; the second required instance can be batch precomputed. Therefore, for IBE applications in the random oracle model, we suggest the use of the BF-IBE scheme, except in situations where private-key extractions are rare and efficiency of the encryption step is critical to the system. For such applications, we suggest BB_1-IBE as the small efficiency gains in the distributed PKG setup and extraction protocols of SK-IBE do not well compensate for the strong security assumption required. BB_1-IBE is also more suitable for type 2 pairings, where an efficient map-to-group hash function H_1 is not available. Further, BB_1-IBE can also be proved secure in the standard model with selective-identity attacks. For applications demanding security in the standard model, our distributed PKG for BB_1-IBE also provides a solution to the key escrow and single point of failure problems, using pairings of type 1 or 2.

5 Concluding Remarks

We have designed and compared distributed PKG setup and private key extraction protocols for BF-IBE, SK-IBE, and BB_1-IBE. We observed that the distributed PKG protocol for BF-IBE is the most efficient among all and we suggest its use when the system can support its relatively costly encryption step. For systems requiring a faster encryption, we suggest the use of BB_1-IBE instead. However, during every distributed private key extraction, it requires a DKG and consequently, interaction among PKG nodes. That being said, during private-key extractions, we successfully avoid any interaction between clients and PKG nodes except the necessary identity at the start and key share transfers at the end. Finally, each of the above schemes represents a separate IBE framework and our designs can be applied to other schemes in those frameworks as well.

Acknowledgements. This work is supported by NSERC, MITACS, and a David R. Cheriton Graduate Scholarship. We specially thank Sanjit Chatterjee for his suggestions regarding the pairing types and the IBE literature. We also thank Alfred Menezes, Kenny Paterson and the anonymous reviewers for helpful discussions and suggestions.

References

1. Kate, A., Goldberg, I.: Asynchronous Distributed Private-Key Generators for Identity-Based Cryptography. Cryptology ePrint Archive, Report 2009/355 (June 2010), `http://eprint.iacr.org/2009/355`
2. Shamir, A.: Identity-Based Cryptosystems and Signature Schemes. In: Blakely, G.R., Chaum, D. (eds.) CRYPTO 1984. LNCS, vol. 196, pp. 47–53. Springer, Heidelberg (1985)
3. Boneh, D., Franklin, M.K.: Identity-Based Encryption from the Weil Pairing. In: Kilian, J. (ed.) CRYPTO 2001. LNCS, vol. 2139, pp. 213–229. Springer, Heidelberg (2001)
4. Joye, M., Neven, G.: Identity-Based Cryptography. Cryptology and Information Security Series, vol. 2. IOS Press, Amsterdam (2008)
5. Feldman, P.: A Practical Scheme for Non-interactive Verifiable Secret Sharing. In: FOCS 1987, pp. 427–437 (1987)
6. Gennaro, R., Jarecki, S., Krawczyk, H., Rabin, T.: Secure Distributed Key Generation for Discrete-Log Based Cryptosystems. In: Stern, J. (ed.) EUROCRYPT 1999. LNCS, vol. 1592, pp. 295–310. Springer, Heidelberg (1999)
7. Kate, A., Zaverucha, G.M., Goldberg, I.: Pairing-Based Onion Routing. In: PETS 2007, pp. 95–112 (2007)
8. Abdalla, M., Catalano, D., Fiore, D.: Verifiable Random Functions from Identity-Based Key Encapsulation. In: Joux, A. (ed.) EUROCRYPT 2009. LNCS, vol. 5479, pp. 554–571. Springer, Heidelberg (2010)
9. Boyen, X.: A Tapestry of Identity-based Encryption: Practical Frameworks Compared. IJACT 1(1), 3–21 (2008)
10. Geisler, M., Smart, N.P.: Distributing the Key Distribution Centre in Sakai-Kasahara Based Systems. In: Parker, M.G. (ed.) Cryptography and Coding. LNCS, vol. 5921, pp. 252–262. Springer, Heidelberg (2009)
11. Sakai, R., Kasahara, M.: ID based Cryptosystems with Pairing on Elliptic Curve. Cryptology ePrint Archive, Report 2003/054 (2003)
12. Al-Riyami, S.S., Paterson, K.G.: Certificateless Public Key Cryptography. In: Laih, C.-S. (ed.) ASIACRYPT 2003. LNCS, vol. 2894, pp. 452–473. Springer, Heidelberg (2003)
13. Lee, B., Boyd, C., Dawson, E., Kim, K., Yang, J., Yoo, S.: Secure key issuing in ID-based cryptography. In: ACSW Frontiers 2004, pp. 69–74 (2004)
14. Gangishetti, R., Gorantla, M.C., Das, M., Saxena, A.: Threshold key issuing in identity-based cryptosystems. Computer Standards & Interfaces 29(2), 260–264 (2007)
15. Chunxiang, X., Junhui, Z., Zhiguang, Q.: A Note on Secure Key Issuing in ID-based Cryptography. Technical report (2005), `http://eprint.iacr.org/2005/180`
16. Goyal, V.: Reducing Trust in the PKG in Identity Based Cryptosystems. In: Menezes, A. (ed.) CRYPTO 2007. LNCS, vol. 4622, pp. 430–447. Springer, Heidelberg (2007)
17. Boldyreva, A.: Threshold Signatures, Multisignatures and Blind Signatures Based on the Gap-Diffie-Hellman-Group Signature Scheme. In: Desmedt, Y.G. (ed.) PKC 2003. LNCS, vol. 2567, pp. 31–46. Springer, Heidelberg (2002)
18. Wang, H., Zhang, Y., Feng, D.: Short Threshold Signature Schemes Without Random Oracles. In: Johansson, T., Maitra, S. (eds.) INDOCRYPT 2003. LNCS, vol. 2904, pp. 297–310. Springer, Heidelberg (2003)

19. Boyen, X., Martin, L.: Identity-Based Cryptography Standard (IBCS) (Version 1), Request for Comments (RFC) 5091 (2007), http://www.ietf.org/rfc/rfc5091.txt
20. Galbraith, S.D., Paterson, K.G., Smart, N.P.: Pairings for cryptographers. Discrete Applied Mathematics 156(16), 3113–3121 (2008)
21. Blake, I., Seroussi, G., Smart, N.P. (eds.): Advances in Elliptic Curve Cryptography. London Mathematical Society Lecture Note Series, vol. 317, pp. 183–252 (2005)
22. Chatterjee, S., Menezes, A.: On Cryptographic Protocols Employing Asymmetric Pairings - The Role of Ψ Revisited. CACR 2009-34 (2009), http://www.cacr.math.uwaterloo.ca/techreports/2007/cacr2009-34.pdf
23. Fiat, A., Shamir, A.: How to Prove Yourself: Practical Solutions to Identification and Signature Problems. In: Odlyzko, A.M. (ed.) CRYPTO 1986. LNCS, vol. 263, pp. 186–194. Springer, Heidelberg (1987)
24. Pedersen, T.P.: Non-Interactive and Information-Theoretic Secure Verifiable Secret Sharing. In: Feigenbaum, J. (ed.) CRYPTO 1991. LNCS, vol. 576, pp. 129–140. Springer, Heidelberg (1992)
25. Chaum, D., Pedersen, T.P.: Wallet Databases with Observers. In: Brickell, E.F. (ed.) CRYPTO 1992. LNCS, vol. 740, pp. 89–105. Springer, Heidelberg (1993)
26. Joux, A., Nguyen, K.: Separating Decision Diffie-Hellman from Computational Diffie-Hellman in Cryptographic Groups. Journal of Cryptology 16(4), 239–247 (2003)
27. Kate, A., Goldberg, I.: Distributed Key Generation for the Internet. In: ICDCS 2009, pp. 119–128 (2009)
28. Gennaro, R., Jarecki, S., Krawczyk, H., Rabin, T.: Secure Distributed Key Generation for Discrete-Log Based Cryptosystems. Journal of Cryptology 20(1), 51–83 (2007)
29. Canetti, R., Gennaro, R., Jarecki, S., Krawczyk, H., Rabin, T.: Adaptive Security for Threshold Cryptosystems. In: Wiener, M. (ed.) CRYPTO 1999. LNCS, vol. 1666, pp. 98–115. Springer, Heidelberg (1999)
30. Joux, A.: A One Round Protocol for Tripartite Diffie-Hellman. In: ANTS-IV, pp. 385–394 (2000)
31. Mitsunari, S., Sakai, R., Kasahara, M.: A New Traitor Tracing. IEICE Transactions E85-A(2), 481–484 (2002)
32. Boneh, D., Boyen, X.: Efficient Selective-ID Secure Identity-Based Encryption Without Random Oracles. In: Cachin, C., Camenisch, J.L. (eds.) EUROCRYPT 2004. LNCS, vol. 3027, pp. 223–238. Springer, Heidelberg (2004)
33. Bar-Ilan, J., Beaver, D.: Non-Cryptographic Fault-Tolerant Computing in Constant Number of Rounds of Interaction. In: PODC 1989, pp. 201–209 (1989)
34. Ben-Or, M., Goldwasser, S., Wigderson, A.: Completeness theorems for non-cryptographic fault-tolerant distributed computation. In: STOC 1988, pp. 1–10 (1988)
35. Cachin, C., Kursawe, K., Lysyanskaya, A., Strobl, R.: Asynchronous Verifiable Secret Sharing and Proactive Cryptosystems. In: ACM CCS 2002, pp. 88–97 (2002)
36. Gennaro, R., Rabin, M.O., Rabin, T.: Simplified VSS and Fact-Track Multiparty Computations with Applications to Threshold Cryptography. In: PODC 1998, pp. 101–111 (1998)
37. Shamir, A.: How to Share a Secret. Commun. ACM 22(11), 612–613 (1979)
38. Boyen, X.: General Ad Hoc Encryption from Exponent Inversion IBE. In: Naor, M. (ed.) EUROCRYPT 2007. LNCS, vol. 4515, pp. 394–411. Springer, Heidelberg (2007)
39. Chen, L., Cheng, Z.: Security Proof of Sakai-Kasahara's Identity-Based Encryption Scheme. In: IMA Int. Conf., pp. 442–459 (2005)
40. Joux, A.: The Weil and Tate Pairings as Building Blocks for Public Key Cryptosystems. In: Fieker, C., Kohel, D.R. (eds.) ANTS 2002. LNCS, vol. 2369, pp. 20–32. Springer, Heidelberg (2002)

Solving Revocation with Efficient Update of Anonymous Credentials

Jan Camenisch[1], Markulf Kohlweiss[2], and Claudio Soriente[3]

[1] IBM Research – Zurich, Switzerland
jca@zurich.ibm.com
[2] KU Leuven, Belgium
markulf.kohlweiss@esat.kuleuven.be
[3] Universidad Politécnica de Madrid, Spain
csoriente@fi.upm.es

Abstract. Anonymous credential system promise efficient, ubiquitous access to digital services while preserving user privacy. However, their diffusion is impaired by the lack of efficient revocation techniques. Traditional credential revocation measures based on certificate revocation lists or online certification authorities do not provide privacy and cannot be used in privacy-sensitive contexts. Existing revocation techniques specifically geared towards anonymous credential systems are more involved – for the credential issuer, users, as wells as credential consumers – as users have to prove that their credential is still valid, e.g., not included in a revocation list.

We introduce a novel, non-interactive technique to update issuer-controlled attributes of anonymous credentials. Revocation is implemented by encoding the validity time of a credential into one of these attributes. With the proposed protocol, credential issuers can periodically update valid credentials off-line and publish a small per-credential update value on a public bulletin-board. Users can later download their values and re-validate their credentials to prove possession of a valid credential for the current time period. Our solution outperforms all prior solutions for credential revocation in terms of communication and computational costs for the users and credentials consumers and the issuer's effort is comparable to the best prior proposals.

1 Introduction

The increasing number of ubiquitous digital services calls for efficient and pervasive means of authentication. User-centric identity management solutions like for instance Cardspace [1] do not only provide such an authentication mechanism, but also allow for the exchange of user attributes. To promote a global deployment of such systems and in order to maximize their benefit for democratic societies, authentication and authorization systems must offer a good balance between security, privacy, and performance. Anonymous credential systems as introduced by Chaum [24] offer strong authentication and the best possible privacy protection. The recent efficient realizations such as *idemix* [15] and *U-Prove* [10] are well suited to be used in practice even when using smart cards as authentication tokens [6].

J.A. Garay and R. De Prisco (Eds.): SCN 2010, LNCS 6280, pp. 454–471, 2010.

In an anonymous credential system, the credential issuer provides a user with credentials that certify her attributes and permissions. The issued credentials allow the users in turn to perform transactions in which they disclose only the minimum amount of information required to obtain a service. Moreover, credential issuers do not learn which certified information are shown to which credential consumers, and issuers and consumers cannot link any transactions.

When using credentials to access a service it is of course crucial to ensure their validity and the information they carry. In particular, the support for revocation is essential for any credential or certification system, independent of what privacy protecting features it offers. There are many reasons why a credential needs to be revoked. The user might have lost her right to carry the credential, the secret key underlying the credential might have been compromised, or just because the attributes stated in the credential became outdated. Also, sometimes the application scenario might require a *rich revocation semantic* where a credential might only need to be "partially revoked": for instance, an expired European passport can still be used to travel within Europe but not to travel to the USA, or a driver's license revoked because of speeding could still be valid to prove the owner's age or address. Thus the validity checks that need to be done and therefore the means to use for revocation depend on the particular application scenario.

A possible solution to revocation in the case of non-anonymous credentials is to "blacklist" all serial numbers of revoked credentials in a so-called *certificate revocation list* [26] that can be queried on- or off-line. This solution does not work as such for anonymous credentials, as revealing a unique serial number of a credential would violate the unlinkability requirement. However, the general principle of publishing a list of all valid (or invalid) serial numbers can still work if, rather than revealing the serial number of their credential, users leverage the minimum disclosure feature of anonymous credentials to prove that it is among the list of valid serial numbers, i.e., that this number is not among the invalid ones. A number of protocols that work along these lines have been proposed [8,12,13,30,33] where the solution by Nakanishi, Fujii, Hira and Funabiki [30] seems to be the most elegant one.

A solution inspired by revocation lists is the use of so-called dynamic accumulators [18,16]. Here, all valid serial numbers are accumulated (i.e., compressed) into a single value that is then published. In addition, dynamic accumulators provide a mechanism that allows the user to prove that the serial number of her credential is contained in the accumulated value. Whenever a credential is revoked, a new accumulator value is published that no longer contains the revoked serial number. Accumulator based schemes require, however, that users keep track of the changes to the accumulator to be able to execute their validity proofs. Camenisch, Kohlweiss and Soriente [16] proposed another accumulator where updates only require multiplications; moreover, computing the credential update information for the users can be performed by any party as it requires no secrets. They achieve this at the cost of a very large state, linear in the overall number of issued credentials. Moreover, accumulator-based solutions allow only to invalidate a credential as a whole and do not enable a rich revocation semantic for scenarios where partial revocation is required.

A common drawback of the solutions described so far is that they all make proving and verifying ownership of credentials less efficient (typically about a factor of 2 or worse), as not only possession of the credential has to be proven but also that it is still valid w.r.t. the revocation list/accumulator.

Another solution to revocation of credentials is to limit their lifetime by means of an expiration date and periodically re-issue non-revoked credentials. Here credentials are made valid only for a specific period of time (epoch), such as, only for a week, a couple of days, or hours, depending on the revocation requirements. This requires of course that the credentials are re-issued periodically. As for anonymous credentials, issuing is an interactive protocol between the user and the issuer, this puts quite a burden on the infrastructure, not only in terms of bandwidth and computational power, but also in terms of availability. Indeed, an issuing of credentials such as electronic ID cards does typically not happen via the Internet but only in secured environments (as to protect the signing key) and often involves physical interactions with the user such as visiting a postal office.

In this paper we study to what extent existing credential systems allow for a non-interactive update of credentials. The issuing protocol of an anonymous credential systems typically consists of a protocol between the user and the issuer at the end of which the user gets a signature on a number of attributes, some of them chosen by and secret to the user and some of them chosen by the issuer. The idea we follow here is that the users and the issuer need to run an initialization protocol only once and thereafter the issuer can just update some values and publish them. Users can then retrieve these values and then recompute their credentials to make them valid again for the new time period. In fact, the period for which a credential is valid is only one of the attributes that a credential can hold; the issuer might want to update other attributes as well and enable richer revocation semantic. Our solution has the advantage that the verifier does not need to check any revocation lists and furthermore that the showing and verification of credentials are as efficient as possible, i.e., there are *no* extra work or space incurred by enabling revocation. Moreover the costs for updating credentials are minimal for users and are comparable to other solutions for the issuer. In fact, the issuer can (pre-) compute the update off-line and then periodically published the update values.

Performance and tradeoffs. Different applications have very diverse revocation requirements. The number of total users, the ratio of revoked users to unrevoked ones, the frequency of credential use, and the speed with which revocation has to take effect are just some of the parameters that influence the design of a revocation system for anonymous credentials. In order for the system to scale, the issuer must be able to handle a large number of users. At the same time, computational resources of user devices may be limited.

Our solution does not support immediate revocation or very short epochs (e.g., one hour) as it requires the issuer to provide credential updates for all non-revoked user. Accumulator-based revocation solutions are better suited for short revocation epochs as the issuer is not required to provide per-user updates, i.e., each non-revoked user can update her own witness. However, in application scenarios with infrequent credential usage such as the Belgian electronic identity card (eID) system with large number of issued (2,25 million per year) and revoked users (375.000 per year)[1] witness updates

[1] See `http://godot.be/eidgraphs`

become exorbitantly expensive, e.g., 10 minutes for the CL accumulator [18], according to Lapon et al. [29].

While lacking the feature of immediate revocation, our solution only requires the user to download a short public credential update value and allows for rich revocation semantic at no additional cost for the show protocol. Hence, it is currently the most suitable system for the large scale deployment of anonymous credential systems.

As validity period based revocation mechanisms cannot revoke credentials immediately, they can be combined with accumulator-based solutions for time-critical applications such as for instance passport control. In the example for the Belgian eID scenario, one could set the validity period to a day and use accumulators for immediate revocation. Thus, users would have to process about 1000 revocation updates per day while the computational load of the issuer to compute credential updates is still feasible. In addition, for some less critical uses of the eID, the verifier might not have to check for immediate revocation and hence relieve the user of the accumulator-proof in the show protocol.

Organization. Instead of considering a whole credential system, we first isolate the problem by looking at the core building block of many anonymous credential schemes, i.e., a signature scheme with efficient protocols [19]. We recall this and other cryptographic building blocks in Section 2. In particular we look at the issuing protocol of these signatures. In Section 3 we propose a new mechanism for the issuing of such signatures: it consists of an interactive part run once and a non-interactive part that can be repeated arbitrarily many times and that allows the issuer to change the messages (attributes) of the resulting signature to their current values. We give a definition of these protocols and procedures and their security requirements in Section 3.1. We then provide a sample construction of these protocols for a signature scheme based on bilinear maps in Section 3.2. In Section 4 we discuss how our new protocols can be used to construct an anonymous credential system with efficient revocation and attribute updates. Finally, in Section 5 we discuss for which other signature and credential schemes similar constructions can be developed. We conclude in Section 6.

2 Preliminaries

In this section we recall the cryptographic tools used by our scheme. After discussing efficient zero-knowledge proofs for prime order groups, we look at signature and commitment schemes that operate in the same setting. In particular, aforementioned zero-knowledge proofs will allow us to prove possession of a signature and to prove that a blindly issued signature signs a committed messages.

2.1 Discrete-Logarithm-Based Zero-Knowledge Proofs for Prime Order Groups

In the common parameters model, we use several previously known results for proving statements about discrete logarithms, such as (1) proof of knowledge of a discrete logarithm modulo a prime [32], (2) proof of knowledge of equality of some element of representations different elements [25], (3) proof that a commitment opens to the product of two other committed values [21,23,9], and also (4) proof of the disjunction or conjunction of any two of the previous [28].

When referring to the proofs above, we will follow the notation introduced by Camenisch and Stadler [22] for various proofs of knowledge of discrete logarithms and proofs of the validity of statements about discrete logarithms. For instance,

$$PK\{(\alpha, \beta, \delta) : y = g^{\alpha} h^{\beta} \wedge \tilde{y} = \tilde{g}^{\alpha} \tilde{h}^{\delta}\}$$

denotes a "*zero-knowledge Proof of Knowledge of integers* α, β, *and* δ *such that* $y = g^{\alpha} h^{\beta}$ *and* $\tilde{y} = \tilde{g}^{\alpha} \tilde{h}^{\delta}$ *holds*" where $y, g, h, \tilde{y}, \tilde{g}$, and $\tilde{h}$ are elements of some groups $G = \langle g \rangle = \langle h \rangle$ and $\tilde{G} = \langle \tilde{g} \rangle = \langle \tilde{h} \rangle$ that have the same order. (Note that the some elements in the representation of y and $\tilde{y}$ are equal.) The convention is that variables in parenthesis, such as "(α, β, δ)", denote quantities of which knowledge is being proven, while all other values are known to the verifier. For prime-order groups which include all groups we consider in this paper, it is well known that there exists a knowledge extractor which acts as a verifier and can extract these quantities from a successful prover, if the latter can be rewinded. Also, these proofs can all be done efficiently (in four rounds and $O(k)$ communication, where k is a security parameter) by using the transformation by Cramer, Damgård and MacKenzie [27].

2.2 CL-Signature Schemes

A CL-signature scheme CLS [19] extends a conventional signature scheme and consists of five procedures (KGen, CLSig, CLSVer, CLSProof, CLSPrVer). The procedure KGen generates the public and secret key of the signer, CLSig produces a signature σ on a block of messages $m_1, \ldots, m_n$ on input the secret key, and CLSVer outputs 1 iff σ is a valid signature on $m_1, \ldots, m_n$ w.r.t. the signer's public key. Finally, (CLSProof $\leftrightarrow$ CLSPrVer) is an interactive protocol where a user can prove to a verifier knowledge of a valid signature on some message $m_1, \ldots, m_n$ such that the verifiers does not learn any information about the signatures and messages apart from the set $\{m_j\}_{j \in R}$, where $R \subset \{1 \ldots n\}$ is arbitrarily chosen by the user. The security requirements are that the signature scheme be unforgeable and that the (CLSProof $\leftrightarrow$ CLSPrVer) be a zero-knowledge proof of knowledge.

Camenisch and Lysyanskaya have presented a scheme secure under the Strong RSA assumption [19], one under the LRSW assumption [20], and one that is based on the Boneh, Boyen and Shacham [7] group signature scheme under the Strong Diffie-Hellman assumption [20]. In the following we described a variant of the latter that was proposed and proved secure by Au, Susilo and Mu [2].

A CL-signature scheme based on the Au et al. signature scheme. The signature scheme assumes a non-degenerate bilinear map $\hat{e} : G \times G \rightarrow G_T$ of prime order q with generators $h, h_0, h_1, \ldots, h_n$, where n is a system parameter. The signer's secret key is $x \in \mathbb{Z}_q$ while the public key is $y = h^x$.

A signature on messages $m_1, \ldots, m_n \in \mathbb{Z}_q$ is a tuple $(A, r, \hat{r}, s)$ where $r, s \stackrel{\$}{\leftarrow} \mathbb{Z}_q$ are values chosen at random by the signer. The value $\hat{r} \in \mathbb{Z}_q$ is a value that can be chosen at random by the user in an interactive issuing protocol. For non-interactive signature generation, i.e., the CLSig procedure, we assume that $\hat{r} = 0$. The original signature scheme aggregates r and $\hat{r}$ into one value. We keep the two values separate to ease exposition in the following protocols. The value A is computed by the signer as $A = (hh_0^{r+\hat{r}} h_1^{m_1} \cdots h_n^{m_n})^{1/(x+s)}$. A signature is verified by checking if $\hat{e}(A, h^s y) = \hat{e}(hh_0^{r+\hat{r}} h_1^{m_1} \cdots h_n^{m_n}, h)$ holds.

We now show how to implement the (CLSProof $\leftrightarrow$ CLSPrVer) protocol. In this protocol the user proves knowledge of a signature on messages $m_1 \ldots m_n$ but only reveals an arbitrary subset $\{m_j\}_{j \in R}$, $R \subset \{1 \ldots n\}$ to the verifier. Given a signature $(A, r, \hat{r}, s)$ on messages $m_1 \ldots, m_n \in \mathbb{Z}_q$, we want to prove that we indeed possess such a signature. To this end, we need to augment the public key of the signature with values $u, v \in G$ such that $\log_h u$ and $\log_h v$ are unknown. Proving knowledge of a signature can be done by choosing random values $w, w' \stackrel{\$}{\leftarrow} \mathbb{Z}_q$, computing $\tilde{A} = Au^w$, $B = v^w u^{w'}$ and executing the following proof of knowledge:

$$PK\{(\alpha, \beta, s, w, w', \{m_j\}_{j \in \{1 \ldots n\} \setminus R}, r') : B = v^w u^{w'} \wedge 1 = B^{-s} v^{\alpha} u^{\beta} \wedge \frac{\hat{e}(\tilde{A}, y)}{\hat{e}(h \prod_{j \in R} h_j^{m_j}, h)} = \hat{e}(\tilde{A}^{-s} u^{\alpha} h_0^{r'} \prod_{j \in \{1 \ldots n\} \setminus R} h_j^{m_j}, h) \hat{e}(u, y)^w\} ,$$

where $r' = r + \hat{r}$, $\alpha = sw$, and $\beta = sw'$.

Let us explain this proof protocol. The first statement proves the prover's knowledge of values w and w' such that $B = v^w u^{w'}$. The next statement asserts the prover's knowledge of values α, β, and s such that $\alpha = sw$ and $\beta = sw'$. Let us consider the last line. It asserts the prover's knowledge of further values $\{m_j\}_{j \in \{1 \ldots n\} \setminus R}$ such that

$$\begin{aligned} \hat{e}(\tilde{A}, y) =& \hat{e}(h \prod_{j \in R} h_j^{m_j}, h) \hat{e}(\tilde{A}^{-s} u^{\alpha} h_0^{r'} \prod_{j \in \{1 \ldots n\} \setminus R} h_j^{m_j}, h) \hat{e}(u, y)^w \\ =& \hat{e}((\frac{u^w}{\tilde{A}})^s h h_0^{r'} \prod_{j=1}^{n} h_j^{m_j}, h) \hat{e}(u, y)^w \end{aligned}$$

holds, where we have made use of the relation $\alpha = sw$. We can further reformulate this equation into the following one

$$\hat{e}(\frac{\tilde{A}}{u^w}, y) \hat{e}((\frac{\tilde{A}}{u^w})^s, h) = \hat{e}((\frac{\tilde{A}}{u^w})^{s+x}, h) = \hat{e}(hh_0^{r'} \prod_{j=1}^{n} h_j^{m_j}, h) ,$$

where x is the secret key of the signer. Thus we must have

$$(\frac{\tilde{A}}{u^w})^{s+x} = hh_0^{r'} \prod_{j=1}^{n} h_j^{m_j} ,$$

i.e., that the prover knows a signature $(\tilde{A}u^{-w}, r', s)$ on the messages $m_1, \ldots, m_n$.

It was proved by Au et al. [2] that the above signature is unforgeable under adaptively chosen message attack if the Q-SDH assumption [7] holds, where Q is the number of signature queries. The authors also showed that the associated proof of knowledge is perfect honest-verifier zero-knowledge.

2.3 Commitment Scheme

A *commitment scheme* is a two-phase scheme that allows a user to *commit* to a hidden value, while preserving the ability of the user to *reveal* the committed value at a later stage. The standard definition of a non-interactive commitment scheme consists of a setup algorithm ComSetup, and an algorithm Com that is used both in the commit and reveal stage. $\mathsf{ComSetup}(1^k)$ outputs public parameters $params_{\mathsf{Com}}$ for the commitment scheme. $\mathsf{Com}(params_{\mathsf{Com}}, x, open)$ is a deterministic algorithm that computes C, a commitment to x, using randomness $open$. One opens a commitment C by revealing x and $open$ and verifying that $\mathsf{Com}(params_{\mathsf{Com}}, x, open) = C$.

A secure commitment scheme is *hiding*: the value committed to must remain undisclosed until the reveal stage, and *binding*: the only value that may a commitment can be opened to is the one that was chosen in the commit stage. In our protocols we make use of a commitment scheme that is computationally binding and perfectly hiding:

Definition 1 (Computational Binding). *For all probabilistic polynomial time (p.p.t.) algorithms that on input* $params_{\mathsf{Com}} \leftarrow \mathsf{ComSetup}(1^k)$ *output* $x, x', open, open'$, $x \neq x'$, *the probability that* $\mathsf{Com}(params_{\mathsf{Com}}, x, open) = \mathsf{Com}(params_{\mathsf{Com}}, x', open')$ *is a negligible function* ν *in* k.

Definition 2 (Perfectly Hiding). *Let* U_k *be the uniform distribution over the opening values under public parameters* $params_{\mathsf{Com}} \leftarrow \mathsf{ComSetup}(1^k)$. *A commitment scheme is* perfectly *hiding if for all* $x \neq x'$ *the probability ensembles* $\{\mathsf{Com}(\mathsf{ComSetup}(1^k), x, U_k)\}_{k\in\mathbb{N}}$ *and* $\{\mathsf{Com}(\mathsf{ComSetup}(1^k), x', U_k)\}_{k\in\mathbb{N}}$ *are equal.*

Pedersen commitments. We use the perfectly hiding commitment scheme proposed by Pedersen [31], that is binding under the discrete logarithm (DL) assumption. For the parameters $params_{\mathsf{Com}}$ we will reuse generators u, v of a group G of prime order q from the CL-signature scheme's public key. These values fulfill the property that $\log_u(v)$ is unknown. A commitment C to $x \in \mathbb{Z}_q$ is generated by choosing at random $open \xleftarrow{\$} \mathbb{Z}_q$ and computing $C = \mathsf{Com}(params_{\mathsf{Com}}, x, open) = u^x v^{open}$. The commitment is opened by revealing x and $open$.

In the issuing protocol we also use a generalized of Pedersen commitments computed as $C = h_0^{open} h_1^{x_1} \cdots h_n^{x_n}$ that allows to commit to multiple values.

3 Issue Protocol for CL-Signatures with Updates

We formalize the security properties required from a CL-signature scheme with updates, and give an exemplary construction based on the Au et al. signature scheme.

3.1 Definitions

Let $\mathsf{CLS} = (\mathsf{KGen}, \mathsf{CLSig}, \mathsf{CLSVer}, \mathsf{CLSProof}, \mathsf{CLSPrVer})$ be a secure CL-signature scheme and let $\mathsf{C} = (\mathsf{ComSetup}, \mathsf{Com})$ be a secure commitment scheme. *A blind issuing and update scheme* for CLS and C consists of five additional procedures SKeygen, SObtSig, SIssSig, SIssUpd, and SObtUpd that are defined as follows.

Let ℓ be the number of blindly signed messages. We write $m_{1..n}$ as a shorthand for $m_1, \ldots, m_n$, similarly for $m_{1..\ell}$,$m_{\ell+1..n}$, $open_{1..\ell}$ and $C_{1..\ell}$.

$\mathsf{SKeygen}(1^k)$. This procedure combines the functions of KGen and $\mathsf{ComSetup}$. On input the security parameter k, the algorithm generates the secret and public keys for the signature scheme and the parameters for the commitment scheme. It then augments these keys with all the parameters needed for the issue, and update procedures. It outputs the augmented secret sk_I and public key pk_I of the issuer. The latter also includes the commitment parameters $params_{\mathsf{Com}}$.

$\mathsf{SObtSig}(pk_I, m_{1..n}, open_{1..\ell}) \leftrightarrow \mathsf{SIssSig}(sk_I, C_{1..\ell}, m_{\ell+1..n})$ is a protocol between the user and the issuer. Before running the protocol, the user commits to the messages $m_1, \ldots, m_\ell$ that are to be signed blindly. The opening information $open_{1..\ell}$ is part of the user's input, while the commitments $C_{1..\ell}$ are part of the issuer's input. The user's part $\mathsf{SObtSig}$ outputs the signature σ on messages $m_1, \ldots, m_n$, and the issuer's part $\mathsf{SIssSig}$ outputs the signature state $state_\sigma$ that will be later used to update signatures.

$\mathsf{SIssUpd}(sk_I, state_\sigma, m'_{\ell+1..n})$ on input the state value $state_\sigma$ for blinded messages $m_1, \ldots, m_\ell$, this procedure outputs a value $update_\sigma$ that allows to obtain an updated signature on messages $m_1, \ldots, m_\ell, m'_{\ell+1}, \ldots, m'_n$.

$\mathsf{SObtUpd}(pk_I, m_{1..n}, m'_{\ell+1..n}, \sigma, update_\sigma)$ combines the signature σ on messages $m_1, \ldots, m_n$ (those for which the user ran the issuing protocol initially) and the value $update_\sigma$ to obtain the signature σ' on messages $m_1, \ldots, m_\ell, m'_{\ell+1}, \ldots, m'_n$.

We require that the additional procedures do not damage the security of the original signatures scheme. We formulate this as the following two security requirements: *signer privacy* and *user privacy*. Informally, *signer privacy* requires that the user does not learn anything from interacting with the issuer via $\mathsf{SIssSig}$ and the updates from the issuer via $\mathsf{SIssUpd}$ other than signatures on the list of messages on which these protocols and procedures are run. In particular, this includes that the user shall not be able to forge signatures on other lists of messages.

The *user privacy* requirement states that the issuer does not learn anything about the messages $m_1, \ldots, m_\ell$ when interacting with via $\mathsf{SObtSig}$ with the user.

Signer privacy. The idea here is that no p.p.t. adversary $\mathcal{A}$ can tell if it is obtaining signatures from an honest issuer $\mathcal{I}$ running $\mathsf{SIssSig}$ and receiving signature updates via $\mathsf{SIssUpd}$ or whether it interacts with a simulator $\mathcal{S}$ with algorithms $\mathsf{SSimIssSig}$ and $\mathsf{SSimUpd}$ for issuing and updating signatures that does not know the issuer's secret key but only has access to a signing oracle. We formalize this using two experiments:

Experiment $\mathbf{Real}^{\mathsf{SP}}_{\mathcal{A}}(\mathbf{k})$ proceeds as follows:

1. Run $\mathsf{SKeygen}(1^k)$ and hand the secret and public keys to $\mathcal{A}$. Receive messages $m_1, \ldots, m_n$ and openings $open_1, \ldots, open_\ell$ from $\mathcal{A}$. Compute commitments $C_1 \leftarrow \mathsf{Com}(params_{\mathsf{Com}}, m_1, open_1); \ldots; C_\ell \leftarrow \mathsf{Com}(params_{\mathsf{Com}}, m_\ell, open_\ell)$. Run algorithm $\mathsf{SIssSig}(sk_I, C_{1..\ell}, m_{\ell+1..n})$ with $\mathcal{A}$. The experiment stores the value $state_\sigma$ output by $\mathsf{SIssSig}$.
2. Repeat until $\mathcal{A}$ stops with output b. Receive messages $m'_{\ell+1}, \ldots, m'_n$ from $\mathcal{A}$. Retrieve $state_\sigma$. Otherwise run $\mathsf{SIssUpd}(sk, state_\sigma, m'_{\ell+1..n})$, hand $update_\sigma$ to $\mathcal{A}$.

Experiment $\mathbf{Simulated}_{\mathcal{A}}^{\mathsf{SP}}(\mathbf{k})$ proceeds as follows:

1. Run $\mathsf{SKeygen}(1^k)$ and hand the secret and public keys to $\mathcal{A}$. Receive messages $m_1, \ldots, m_n$ and openings $open_1, \ldots, open_\ell$ from $\mathcal{A}$. Compute commitments $C_1 \leftarrow \mathsf{Com}(params_{\mathsf{Com}}, m_1, open_1); \ldots; C_\ell \leftarrow \mathsf{Com}(params_{\mathsf{Com}}, m_\ell, open_\ell)$. Compute $\sigma \leftarrow \mathsf{CLSig}(sk_I, (m_{1..n}))$ and run $\mathsf{SSimIssSig}(\sigma, comm_{1..\ell}, m_{\ell+1..n})$ with $\mathcal{A}$. The experiment stores the output $state_{\mathcal{S}}$ of SIssSig and messages $m_1, \ldots, m_\ell$.
2. Repeat until $\mathcal{A}$ stops with output b. Receive messages $m'_{\ell+1}, \ldots, m'_n$ from $\mathcal{A}$. Compute $\sigma' \leftarrow \mathsf{CLSig}(sk_I, m_{1..\ell}, m'_{\ell+1..n})$ and run $\mathsf{SSimUpd}(\sigma', state_{\mathcal{S}}, m'_{\ell+1..n})$, hand $update_\sigma$ to $\mathcal{A}$.

The simulator is allowed to rewind the adversary. Let the adversary's advantage in distinguishing between the two experiments be $Adv_{\mathcal{A}}^{\mathsf{SP}}(k) = |Pr[\mathbf{Real}_{\mathcal{A},\mathcal{I}}^{\mathsf{SP}}(\mathbf{k}) = 1] - Pr[\mathbf{Simulated}_{\mathcal{A},\mathcal{S}}^{\mathsf{SP}}(\mathbf{k}) = 1]|$. Signer privacy requires that $Adv_{\mathcal{A}}^{\mathsf{SP}}(k)$ is a negligible function in k.

We have defined *signer privacy* in terms of the issue and update sequence of a single signature, but our definition is strengthened by the fact that the adversary is given the issuers secret key sk_I. A simple hybrid argument can be used to show that this definition implies privacy for many credentials as long as the signature issue protocols are executed sequentially.

User privacy. No p.p.t. adversary $\mathcal{A}$ can tell if it is issuing signatures to an honest user $\mathcal{U}$ running SObtSig or to a simulator $\mathcal{S}$ running SSimObtSig that does not know the users secret inputs. We formalize this using two experiments:

Experiment $\mathbf{Real}_{\mathcal{A}}^{\mathsf{SP}}(\mathbf{k})$ proceeds as follows:

1. Receive a signature public key pk_I, messages $m_1, \ldots, m_\ell$, and openings $open_1, \ldots, open_\ell$ from $\mathcal{A}$.
2. Run $\mathsf{SObtSig}(pk_I, m_{1..\ell}, open_{1..\ell})$ with $\mathcal{A}$. The experiment outputs the adversary's output b.

Experiment $\mathbf{Simulated}_{\mathcal{A}}^{\mathsf{SP}}(\mathbf{k})$ proceeds as follows:

1. Receive a signature public key pk_I, messages $m_1, \ldots, m_\ell$, and openings $open_1, \ldots, open_\ell$ from $\mathcal{A}$. Compute $C_1 \leftarrow \mathsf{Com}(params_{\mathsf{Com}}, m_1, open_1); \ldots; C_\ell \leftarrow \mathsf{Com}(params_{\mathsf{Com}}, m_\ell, open_\ell)$.
2. Run $\mathsf{SSimObtSig}(pk_I, comm_{1..\ell})$ with $\mathcal{A}$. The experiment outputs the adversary's output b.

Again, the simulator is allowed to rewind the adversary. Let the adversary's advantage in distinguishing the two experiments be $Adv_{\mathcal{A}}^{\mathsf{UP}}(k) = |Pr[\mathbf{Real}_{\mathcal{A},\mathcal{U}}^{\mathsf{UP}}(\mathbf{k}) = 1] - Pr[\mathbf{Simulated}_{\mathcal{A},\mathcal{S}}^{\mathsf{UP}}(\mathbf{k}) = 1]|$. User privacy requires that $Adv_{\mathcal{A}}^{\mathsf{UP}}(k)$ is a negligible function in k.

Note that we require that only the user's input $m_1, \ldots, m_\ell$ be hidden from the issuer, but not necessarily the user's output σ. The reason that this is sufficient is that in actual applications (for example, in anonymous credentials), a user would never show σ in the clear; instead, she would just prove that she knows σ.

Definition 3. *We say that* $\mathsf{UCLS} = \mathsf{SKeygen}, \mathsf{CLSig}, \mathsf{CLSVer}, \mathsf{CLSProof}, \mathsf{CLSPrVer}, \mathsf{Com}, \mathsf{SKeygen}, \mathsf{SObtSig}, \mathsf{SIssSig}, \mathsf{SIssUpd}, \mathsf{SObtUpd})$ *is a secure CL-signature scheme* *with updates if the algorithms* ($\mathsf{SKeygen}, \mathsf{CLSig}, \mathsf{CLSVer}, \mathsf{CLSProof}, \mathsf{CLSPrVer}$) *constitute a secure CL-signature scheme, the algorithms* ($\mathsf{SKeygen}, \mathsf{Com}$) *constitute a secure commitment scheme, and* $\mathsf{SKeygen}, \mathsf{SObtSig}, \mathsf{SIssSig}, \mathsf{SIssUpd}, \mathsf{SObtUpd}$ *fulfill the* signer privacy *and* user privacy *properties.*

3.2 Construction

The main insight that leads to our construction is that issuing credential based on CL-signatures typically consists of two stages: 1) the user sends to the issuer some form of commitment to the messages that she wants to be included in the credential and 2) the issuer extends that commitment into one that covers all the message to be signed and then computes the signature of all these messages. As the second stage essentially consists only of computations by the issuer followed by sending the user the signature, this stage can be repeated any number of times with new messages chosen by the issuer and instead of sending the result on-line to the user, it can be provided as an update by any form of communication (e.g., provided for download at a website).

This approach of two stages is possible because for all the CL-signature schemes that we consider [17,19,20] and in particular for the signature scheme by Au, Susilo and Mu [2] on which we base our explicit construction, signing consists of computing a group element from a number of bases where the message to be signed are used as exponents. Hence, this group element can also be considered as a Pedersen commitment to all the message. This holds even for the group element computed by the user for the messages that are hidden from the issuer provided that the user proves to the issuer that she did do these computations correctly.

We describe a construction for CL-signatures with updates and prove the security of the issuing protocol and the update algorithms.

$\mathsf{SKeygen}(1^k)$. On input 1^k, pick a non-degenerate efficiently computable bilinear map $\hat{e} : G \times G \rightarrow G_T$ of prime order q with $G = \langle h \rangle$. Pick additional bases $h_0, h_1, \ldots,$ $h_\ell, h_{\ell+1}, \ldots, h_n \xleftarrow{\$} G$. The signer's secret key is $x \xleftarrow{\$} \mathbb{Z}_q$ while the public key is $y = h^x$. Publish $pk_I = (q, G, G_T, e, h, h_0, h_1, \ldots, h_\ell, h_{\ell+1}, \ldots, h_n, y, u, v)$. The secret key sk_I includes the public key material and x. To speed up computation the issuer can choose values $x_1, \ldots, x_n \leftarrow \mathbb{Z}_q$ and compute $h_i = h^{x_i}$ for $i = 1..n$. This allows to compute a product $\prod_{i=1}^n h_i^{m_i}$ as $h^{\sum_{i=1}^n x_i m_i}$.

$\mathsf{SObtSig}(pk_I, m_{1..n}, open_{1..\ell}) \leftrightarrow \mathsf{SIssSig}(sk_I, comm_{1..\ell}, m_{\ell+1..n})$.

1. $\mathcal{U}$ picks $\hat{r} \xleftarrow{\$} \mathbb{Z}_q$, computes $P = h_0^{\hat{r}} \prod_{i=1..\ell} h_i^{m_i}$ and sends it to $\mathcal{I}$.
2. $\mathcal{U}$ engages with $\mathcal{I}$ in the following proof of knowledge to convince $\mathcal{I}$ that P is correctly formed.

$$PK\{(\hat{r}, m_{1..\ell}, open_{1..\ell}) \bigwedge_{i=1}^{\ell} C = \mathsf{Com}(params_{\mathsf{Com}}, m_i, open_i) \wedge P = h_0^{\hat{r}} \prod_{i=1..\ell} h_i^{m_i}\} .$$

3. $\mathcal{I}$ picks $s, r \xleftarrow{\$} \mathbb{Z}_q^*$, computes $A = (hPh_0^r \prod_{i=\ell+1}^n h_i^{m_i})^{1/(x+s)}$ and sends (A, r, s) to $\mathcal{U}$.
4. $\mathcal{I}$ outputs $state_\sigma = P$.
5. $\mathcal{U}$ outputs $\sigma = (A, r, \hat{r}, s)$.

$\mathsf{SIssUpd}(sk_I, state_\sigma, m'_{\ell+1..n})$. This algorithm is periodically run by $\mathcal{I}$ to update a signature with state $state_\sigma$. $\mathcal{I}$ proceeds with the following steps.

1. $\mathcal{I}$ picks $s', r' \xleftarrow{\$} \mathbb{Z}_q^*$, computes $A' = (hPh_0^{r_i} \prod_{i=\ell+1}^{n} h_i^{m'_i})^{1/(x+s)}$.
2. $\mathcal{I}$ outputs $update_\sigma = (A', r', s')$.

If the issuer chooses $h_i = h^{x_i}$ the computation of A only requires two exponentiation (or rather one two-base multi-exponentiation).

$\mathsf{SObtUpd}(pk_I, m_{1..n}, m'_{\ell+1..n}, \sigma, update_\sigma)$. Given a signature $\sigma = (A, \hat{r}, r, s)$ and $update_\sigma = (A', r', s')$ output $\sigma' = (A', r', \hat{r}, s')$, if $\mathsf{CLSVer}(pk_I, \sigma', m_{1..\ell}, m'_{\ell+1..n}) = 1$ and $\perp$ otherwise.

Theorem 1. *Under the Strong Diffie-Hellman assumption (that implies the Discrete Logarithm assumption), the algorithm above together with the Au et al. CL-signature scheme and the Pedersen constitute a secure CL-signature scheme with updates.*

Lemma 1. *The* SIssSig *and* SIssUpd *algorithms above together with the Au et al. CL signature scheme and the Pedersen commitment scheme fulfill the* signer privacy *property assuming the security of the zero-knowledge proof of knowledge and commitment scheme.*

Proof. Given a list of commitments $C_{1..\ell}$ messages $m_1, \ldots, m_n$ and a signature $\sigma = (A, \tilde{r}, 0, s)$ as input SSimIssSig simulates the adversaries view. Upon receiving the value P, it interacts with the adversary in a proof of knowledge. The adversary proves that she knows messages $m_1, \ldots, m_\ell$ corresponding to $C_{1..\ell}$ and the randomness $\hat{r}$ used to create P. The simulator uses the knowledge extractor of the proof of knowledge to obtain $\hat{r}$, and returns $(A, \tilde{r} - \hat{r}, s)$ to the adversary. The state $state_{\mathcal{S}}$ of the simulator corresponds to $\hat{r}$.

For each request to generate a signature update, SSimUpd receives messages $m'_{\ell+1}, \ldots, m'_n$ and a signature $\sigma' = (A', \tilde{r}', 0, s')$ as input. The simulator uses $\hat{r}$ to returns $update_\sigma = (A', \tilde{r}' - \hat{r}, s')$.

We proof using a sequence of games that $\mathbf{Real}_{\mathcal{A}}(\mathbf{k})$ and $\mathbf{Simulated}_{\mathcal{A}}(\mathbf{k})$ are indistinguishable.

Game 1 corresponds to the $\mathbf{Real}_{\mathcal{A},\mathcal{I}}(\mathbf{k})$ experiment.

Game 2 is the same as Game 1, but the knowledge extractor of the proof of knowledge is used to extract $\hat{r}, \tilde{m}_{1..\ell}, open_{1..\ell}$. If extraction succeeds proceed as in Game 1, otherwise abort. *The probability $\nu_1(k)$ to distinguish between Game 1 and Game 2 is bounded by the knowledge extraction error of the proof of knowledge protocol.*

Game 3 is the same as Game 3, except that the game aborts, if the values $\tilde{m}_{1..\ell}$ extracted from the proof of knowledge differ from the values $m_{1..\ell}$ output by the adversary. *The probability $\nu_2(k)$ to distinguish between Game 2 and Game 3 is bounded based on the security of the commitment scheme.*

Game 4 computes the response of the issuing protocol and all update protocols, by first computing a signature $\sigma = (A, \tilde{r}, 0, s)$ for messages $m_1, \ldots, m_n$ and $m_{1..\ell}$,$m'_{\ell+1,n}$ respectively, and then replying with $(A, \tilde{r} - \hat{r}, s)$. Game 4 is identically distributed to Game 3 and corresponds to experiment $\mathbf{Simulated}_{\mathcal{A},\mathcal{S}}(\mathbf{k})$.

The adversaries advantage in distinguishing the games is bounded by $Adv_{\mathcal{A}}(k) < \nu_1(k) + \nu_2(k)$.

Lemma 2. *The* SObtSig *algorithm above together with the Au et al. CL-signature scheme and the Pedersen commitment scheme fulfill the* user privacy *property.*

Proof. Given the issuers public key pk_I and commitments $comm_{1..\ell}$ as input, the simulator SSimObtSig picks a random value P. Then it uses the zero-knowledge simulator to interact with the adversary in the following proof protocol:

$$PK\{(\hat{r}, m_{1..\ell}, open_{1..\ell}) : \bigwedge_{i=1}^{\ell} C = Commit(params_{\mathsf{Com}}, m_i, open_i) \wedge P = h_0^{\hat{r}} \prod_{i=1..\ell} h_i^{m_i}\} .$$

As both the commitments $C_{1..\ell}$ and P are perfectly hiding Pedersen commitments, this is a proof of a true statement, and the simulation is perfect.

4 Anonymous Credential Systems with Efficient Revocation and Attribute Update

In this section we will show how to use CL-signatures with updates to design an anonymous credential system where credential revocation is accomplished through an efficient, non-interactive protocol for updating credentials. The considered scenario consists of three types of players:

A credential issuer ($\mathcal{I}$) that issues and manages anonymous credentials. *One or more credential verifiers* that provide services to users upon show of valid credentials. *A set of users* that anonymously obtain credentials from $\mathcal{I}$ and show them in a privacy preserving way to verifiers in order to access their services.

Several research papers describe how to construct anonymous credential schemes from CL-signatures. The efficient anonymous credential scheme of Camenisch and Lysyanskaya [17] made use of CL-signatures as an implicit building block that the same authors later formalized in [19]. Their basic system, however, does not support attributes. A non-interactive variant of such a credential system was also proposed by Belenkiy, Chase, Kohlweiss and Lysyanskaya in [5]. Bangerter, Camenisch and Lysyanskaya [3] describe a flexible anonymous certification framework that allows for blind issuing and selective show of credentials that certify multiple user and issuer chosen attributes. CL-signatures also form the basis for direct anonymous attestation (DAA) [14]. The DAA protocol makes use of a blindly certified user secret sk_U. This value never leaves the trusted platform module and protects the credential against theft and abuse.

We describe a credential system that combines the features in the above schemes. In addition, we allow for efficient revocation through the inclusion of time period information. The anonymous credential system uses the SObtSig $\leftrightarrow$ SIssSig protocol to issue a credential with the following information to the user: the users secret sk_U, the credential serial number id, the time period for which the credential is valid t, and d attributes $a_1, \ldots, a_d$ chosen by the issuer. The key sk_U is only known to the user and is certified blindly. The update feature of our CL-signature scheme allows the issuer to publish update information for new time periods. As an added benefit, the issuer can update the users attribute. The latter allows rich revocation semantic as credential can be partially (i.e., only some of the credential attributes) revoked and/or updated.

More formally, our anonymous Credential System with efficient revocation and updates consists of the following algorithms:

$\mathsf{IssuerKeygen}(1^k)$ This algorithm is run once by $\mathcal{I}$ to setup system parameters. It runs $\mathsf{SKeygen}(1^k)$ to create sk_I and pk_I of a CL-signature with Updates scheme. It also outputs an empty set *state* where to store issued credentials.

$\mathsf{UserKeygen}(1^k)$ This algorithm is run only once for each $\mathcal{U}$ before she interacts with the $\mathcal{I}$ to obtain any credential. $\mathcal{U}$ obtains her secret key sk_U and the corresponding public key pk_U that might be advertised as the user identity.

$\mathsf{ObtainCert}(\mathcal{U}(pk_U, sk_U), \mathcal{I}(pk_I, sk_I, a_{1..d}, state, t)$ In this protocol, $\mathcal{U}$ obtains a certified credential with unique serial number id. The latter is arbitrarily chosen by $\mathcal{I}$. For example, given *state* as the set of all issued credentials, $\mathcal{I}$ might set id to the next available serial number.

1. The user commits to her secret key as $C = \mathsf{Com}(params_{\mathsf{Com}}, sk_U, open)$ and user sends her public key and the commitment to the issuer. The user does a proof of knowledge that the public key corresponds to the commitment. This provides the issuer with the guarantee that the credential will be issued to the correct user.
2. Now the issuer sends the attributes $id, t, a_1, \ldots, a_d$ to the user.
3. The user and the issuer run $\mathsf{SObtSig}(pk_I, sk_U, id, t, a_{1..d}, open) \leftrightarrow \mathsf{SIssSig}(sk_I, C, id, t, a_{1..d})$, respectively. Note that sk_U is the only blindly signed message, and $n = d + 3$. The user obtains the signature σ and the issuer obtains $state_\sigma$.
4. The issuer adds record $(1, id, state_\sigma, a_1, \ldots, a_d)$ to *state*; the first element of the record flags the credential as currently valid.
5. The users output is the certificate $cert = (\sigma, id, t, a_1, \ldots, a_d)$.

$\mathsf{InvalidateCerts}(state, id)$ This algorithm is periodically run by $\mathcal{I}$ to revise validity status of issued credentials. For each credential to be revoked, let id be its serial number, $\mathcal{I}$ replaces record $(1, id, state_\sigma, a_1, \ldots, a_d)$ in *state* with record $(0, id, state_\sigma, a_1, \ldots, a_d)$; the first element of the record flags the credential as revoked.

$\mathsf{UpdateAttributes}(state, id, a'_{1..d})$ This algorithm is run by $\mathcal{I}$ before producing the updates of each valid credential. It is used to update credential attributes for valid credentials. The issuer replaces $(1, id, state_\sigma, a_1, \ldots, a_d)$ in *state* with $(1, id, state_\sigma, a'_1, \ldots, a'_d)$ to reflect the changes to the credential attributes for the current time period.

$\mathsf{CertUpdate}(pk_I, sk_I, state, t)$ This algorithm is periodically run by $\mathcal{I}$ to update credentials that are still valid. For each record $(1, id, state_\sigma, a_1, \ldots, a_d)$ in *state*, the issuer runs $\mathsf{SIssUpd}(sk_I, state_\sigma, id, t, a_{1..d})$ and publishes the resulting update value together with the new attribute values as $update_{id,t} = (update_\sigma, a_1, \ldots a_d)$. Note that revoked credentials in *state* do not get updated.

$\mathsf{ProveCert}(\mathcal{U}(sk_U, cert, update_{id,t}, R), \mathcal{V}(pk_I, t, R)$ This algorithm is run at time t by an user $\mathcal{U}$ and a verifier $\mathcal{V}$ before the latter grants any service to the former. At the end of the protocol, $\mathcal{V}$ only learns that $\mathcal{U}$ has a credential issued by $\mathcal{I}$ with attributes

$\{a_i\}_{i\in R}$ that is valid at time t. First, $\mathcal{U}$ parses $update_{id,t}$ as $(update_\sigma, a_1, ...a_d)$ and updates her credential running $\mathsf{SObtUpd}(pk_I, a_{1..d}, \sigma, update_\sigma)$. The updated certificate is $cert = (\sigma', id, t, a_1, \ldots, a_d)$. Where $t, a_1, \ldots, a_d$ correspond to the current time period and the updated attribute values. Later, she can show her credential an arbitrary number of time to any verifier. At each show, the user sends messages $\{a_i\}_{i\in R}$ to the issuer, and performs the following zero-knowledge proof of knowledge:

$$\mathsf{PK}\{(\sigma, sk_U, \{a_i\}_{i\in\{1,\ldots,d\}\setminus R}) : 1 = \mathsf{CLSVer}(pk_I, \sigma, sk_U, id, t, a_{1..d}) \wedge \ldots\} \ .$$

Note that in the above example, credentials are revoked as a whole. Partial revocation can be achieved using multiple flags per credential. To use the driving licence example of Section 1, each credential would have a flag to define credential validity for driving permissions and an additional flag to define its validity for owner identification purposes. Flags could be encoded in the credential and updated independently as required.

Security discussion. In [17] a secure anonymous credentials scheme is defined using an ideal functionality. The authors show that the extraction and zero-knowledge properties of the proof system and the unforgeability of the signature scheme guarantee that an adversary attacking the real world anonymous credential system cannot do more damage than an adversary interacting with the ideal functionality. The signer privacy and user privacy properties introduced by Belenkiy et al. [5] formalize the needed properties for the issuing protocol. In addition to what is shown in [5] we show that the non-interactive signature updates do not leak additional information about the issuers secret key. The credential show protocol is unchanged and relies on the security of the zero-knowledge proof of knowledge of signature possession.

5 Efficient Updates for Other Signatures and Anonymous Credential Schemes

The construction we give in this paper employs a signature scheme based on bilinear maps. There are however a number of other constructions for signature schemes with efficient protocols and constructions for group signatures and credential systems. In this section we discuss whether the approach of introducing validity time periods and publishing credential/signature update information also applies to other schemes.

CL-signatures. Camenisch and Lysyanskaya have proposed a number of different signature schemes that allows efficient proofs of knowledge of a signature. Apart from the one we have already used in our construction, they have proposed a scheme based on the strong RSA assumption [19] and one based on the LRSW assumption [20]. As all of these schemes follows the same principles, they can all be extended in the same way as what we did in our construction. We quickly sketch this for the widely used CL-signature scheme based on the strong RSA assumption:

The signature σ consists of a tuple (A, r, e) with $A = (hh_0^r h_1^{m_1} \ldots h_n^{m_n})^{-e} mod\ \mathfrak{m}$, where $\mathfrak{m}$ is an RSA modulus. Similarly to our construction based on bilinear maps, the issue protocol starts with the user sending a value $P = h_0^{\hat{r}} h_1^{m_1} \ldots h_\ell^{m_\ell}$ that is then extended by the issuer to compute a signature on blinded values $m_1, \ldots, m_\ell$ and issuer chosen messages $m_{\ell+1}, \ldots, m_n$. This last step can be repeated for different messages $m'_{\ell+1}, \ldots, m'_n$ to implement the update.

Blind-signatures based schemes. The credential schemes by Brands [10,11] employ a blind Schnorr signature scheme to achieve anonymity. This signature scheme uses hash functions in a crucial way to achieve unforgeability.

Conceptually, a Schnorr blind signature protocol consists of three steps. The *commitment* step, the *challenge* step, and the *response* step. The first and the last step are computed by the signer. To achieve blindness, the user (signature receiver) needs to compute the challenge as a hash value on the values of the commitment step and the user's public key $h' = g_0^\alpha \prod_{i=1}^n g_i^{m_i}$, that encodes his attributes (see Chapter 4 of [11]). The user then blinds (randomizes) the challenge before the signer can compute signature values in the final response step using its signing secret key. It thus seems inherent that the user needs to do this hash function computation for every signature and thus, signature updates cannot be done non-interactively. A solution that works partially is as follows. The user could prepare many blind signatures and then send them all at once to the signer. The signer could then finish the individual protocols as needed (e.g., one in each epoch). This, however, works only if all the messages (e.g., attributes of a credential) are fixed at the time the user prepares all these blind signatures. Thus, the signer would not be able to update any of the messages in the update phase which seems to be a severe limitation. Furthermore, the user would have to store all the blinding values of all the prepared blind signatures (or to regenerate them from a seed using a suitable pseudo-random function).

Other schemes. Belenkiy el al. [5,4] have proposed so-called P-signatures that are based on bilinear maps and allow one to use Groth-Sahai non-interactive proofs for proving knowledge of a signature. However, issuing signatures in their schemes is highly interactive and it seems not possible to apply our approach to these schemes as they are now.

An approach that works for all interactive and non-interactive CL and P-signature schemes is to combine an interactively issued signature that contains the attribute values that should be blindly signed and the credential identifier id, with a plain signature that contains the same identifier, the time period t, and all issuer attributes. The disadvantage of this approach is that the prove protocol becomes twice as expensive, as the user now has to prove possession of two signatures.

When considering related schemes such as group signatures and identity escrow, we see that our approach can in general not be used as they do not have a means to include a validity time period identifier. However, many of them are constructed along the lines of using a CL-signature to sign a group member's secret key and then defining a group-signature to be a non-interactive proof of knowledge of a CL-signature by the group manager on a secret key. For these schemes, it is of course not hard to extend them such that the group manager signs also a second message being an epoch identifier and hence our approach can be used.

6 Conclusion

Despite a growing concern for user privacy in a cyber-world, the diffusion of Anonymous Credential Systems is impaired by the lack of efficient protocols. Use of non-interactive protocols, rich revocation semantic and minimal overhead at show time are key features to enable the adoption of Anonymous Credential Systems in privacy-preserving scenario with large number of users.

In this paper we have introduced a signature scheme with updates that can be used in anonymous credential systems to enable efficient, semantically rich revocation. Our scheme allows for non-interactive credential update as well as partial revocation/update. Moreover, it enjoys no overhead in the show protocol to prove that a credential is non-revoked. Updates can be performed off-line and later published on a public bulletin board for users to download them. Also, users can miss an arbitrary number of updates, that is, the latest update to their original credential suffices to prove its possession. Compared to previous solutions for revocation, our approach is much more efficient for showing and verifying credentials (there is no additional cost), more flexible (it addresses even updates of attributes), and has a similar overhead for managing revocation status as previous solutions.

Acknowledgements. Markulf Kohlweiss was supported in part by IBBT, the Concerted Research Action (GOA) Ambiorics 2005/11 of the Flemish Government, and by the IAP Programme P6/26 BCRYPT of the Belgian State (Belgian Science Policy). This work was further supported in part by the European Commission through the ICT and IST programmes under the following contracts: ICT-216483 PRIMELIFE and ICT-216676 ECRYPT II. Claudio Soriente has been partially funded by the Spanish National Science Foundation (MICINN) under grant TIN2007-67353-C02 and by the Madrid Regional Research Council (CAM) under grant S2009/TIC-1692 and and by the European Commission under project NEXOF-RA (FP7-216446).

References

1. Windows cardspace (2010), `http://www.microsoft.com/windows/products/winfamily/cardspace/` (accessed April 2010)
2. Au, M.H., Susilo, W., Mu, Y.: Constant-size dynamic k-TAA. In: De Prisco, R., Yung, M. (eds.) SCN 2006. LNCS, vol. 4116, pp. 111–125. Springer, Heidelberg (2006)
3. Bangerter, E., Camenisch, J., Lysyanskaya, A.: A cryptographic framework for the controlled release of certified data. In: Christianson, B., Crispo, B., Malcolm, J.A., Roe, M. (eds.) Security Protocols 2004. LNCS, vol. 3957, pp. 20–42. Springer, Heidelberg (2006)
4. Belenkiy, M., Camenisch, J., Chase, M., Kohlweiss, M., Lysyanskaya, A., Shacham, H.: Randomizable proofs and delegatable anonymous credentials. In: Halevi, S. (ed.) CRYPTO 2009. LNCS, vol. 5677, pp. 108–125. Springer, Heidelberg (2009)
5. Belenkiy, M., Chase, M., Kohlweiss, M., Lysyanskaya, A.: P-signatures and noninteractive anonymous credentials. In: Canetti, R. (ed.) TCC 2008. LNCS, vol. 4948, pp. 356–374. Springer, Heidelberg (2008)
6. Bichsel, P., Camenisch, J., Groß, T., Shoup, V.: Anonymous credentials on a standard Java Card. In: ACM Conference on Computer and Communications Security (2009) (to appear)

7. Boneh, D., Boyen, X., Shacham, H.: Short group signatures. In: Franklin, M. K. (ed.) CRYPTO 2004. LNCS, vol. 3152, pp. 41–55. Springer, Heidelberg (2004)
8. Boneh, D., Shacham, H.: Group signatures with verifier-local revocation. In: Atluri, V., Pfitzmann, B., McDaniel, P. (eds.) ACM CCS 2004, pp. 168–177. ACM, New York (2004)
9. Brands, S.: Rapid demonstration of linear relations connected by boolean operators. In: Fumy, W. (ed.) EUROCRYPT 1997. LNCS, vol. 1233, pp. 318–333. Springer, Heidelberg (1997)
10. Brands, S.: Rethinking Public Key Infrastructure and Digital Certificates — Building in Privacy. PhD thesis, Eindhoven Institute of Technology, Eindhoven, The Netherlands (1999)
11. Brands, S.: Rethinking Public Key Infrastructures and Digital Certificates. MIT Press, Cambridge (2000)
12. Brands, S., Demuynck, L., De Decker, B.: A practical system for globally revoking the unlinkable pseudonyms of unknown users. In: Pieprzyk, J., Ghodosi, H., Dawson, E. (eds.) ACISP 2007. LNCS, vol. 4586, pp. 400–415. Springer, Heidelberg (2007)
13. Brands, S., Demuynck, L., De Decker, B.: A practical system for globally revoking the unlinkable pseudonyms of unknown users. In: Pieprzyk, J., Ghodosi, H., Dawson, E. (eds.) ACISP 2007. LNCS, vol. 4586, pp. 400–415. Springer, Heidelberg (2007)
14. Brickell, E., Camenisch, J., Chen, L.: Direct anonymous attestation. In: Proc. 11th ACM Conference on Computer and Communications Security, pp. 225–234. ACM Press, New York (2004)
15. Camenisch, J., Van Herreweghen, E.: Design and implementation of the *idemix* anonymous credential system. In: Proc. 9th ACM Conference on Computer and Communications Security, ACM Press, New York (2002)
16. Camenisch, J., Kohlweiss, M., Soriente, C.: An accumulator based on bilinear maps and efficient revocation for anonymous credentials. In: Jarecki, S., Tsudik, G. (eds.) PKC 2009. LNCS, vol. 5443, pp. 481–500. Springer, Heidelberg (2009)
17. Camenisch, J., Lysyanskaya, A.: Efficient non-transferable anonymous multi-show credential system with optional anonymity revocation. In: Pfitzmann, B. (ed.) EUROCRYPT 2001. LNCS, vol. 2045, pp. 93–118. Springer, Heidelberg (2001)
18. Camenisch, J., Lysyanskaya, A.: Dynamic accumulators and application to efficient revocation of anonymous credentials. In: Yung, M. (ed.) CRYPTO 2002. LNCS, vol. 2442, pp. 61–76. Springer, Heidelberg (2002)
19. Camenisch, J., Lysyanskaya, A.: A signature scheme with efficient protocols. In: Cimato, S., Galdi, C., Persiano, G. (eds.) SCN 2002. LNCS, vol. 2576, pp. 268–289. Springer, Heidelberg (2003)
20. Camenisch, J., Lysyanskaya, A.: Signature schemes and anonymous credentials from bilinear maps. In: Franklin, M.K. (ed.) CRYPTO 2004. LNCS, vol. 3152, pp. 56–72. Springer, Heidelberg (2004)
21. Camenisch, J., Michels, M.: Proving in zero-knowledge that a number n is the product of two safe primes. In: Stern, J. (ed.) EUROCRYPT 1999. LNCS, vol. 1592, pp. 107–122. Springer, Heidelberg (1999)
22. Camenisch, J., Stadler, M.: Efficient group signature schemes for large groups. In: Kaliski Jr., B.S. (ed.) CRYPTO 1997. LNCS, vol. 1294, pp. 410–424. Springer, Heidelberg (1997)
23. Camenisch, J.L.: Group Signature Schemes and Payment Systems Based on the Discrete Logarithm Problem. PhD thesis, ETH Zürich, Diss. ETH No. 12520. Hartung Gorre Verlag, Konstanz (1998)
24. Chaum, D.: Security without identification: Transaction systems to make big brother obsolete. Communications of the ACM 28(10), 1030–1044 (1985)
25. Chaum, D., Pedersen, T.P.: Wallet databases with observers. In: Brickell, E.F. (ed.) CRYPTO 1992. LNCS, vol. 740, pp. 89–105. Springer, Heidelberg (1993)

26. Cooper, D., Santesson, S., Farrell, S., Boeyen, S., Housley, R., Polk, W.: Internet X.509 Public Key Infrastructure Certificate and Certificate Revocation List (CRL) Profile. RFC 5280 (Proposed Standard) (May 2008)
27. Cramer, R., Damgård, I., MacKenzie, P.D.: Efficient zero-knowledge proofs of knowledge without intractability assumptions. In: Imai, H., Zheng, Y. (eds.) PKC 2000. LNCS, vol. 1751, pp. 354–372. Springer, Heidelberg (2000)
28. Cramer, R., Damgård, I., Schoenmakers, B.: Proofs of partial knowledge and simplified design of witness hiding protocols. In: Desmedt, Y.G. (ed.) CRYPTO 1994. LNCS, vol. 839, pp. 174–187. Springer, Heidelberg (1994)
29. Lapon, J., Kohlweiss, M., De Decker, B., Naessens, V.: Performance analysis of accumulator-based revocation mechanisms. In: Proceedings of the 25th International Conference on Information Security (SEC 2010), Brisbane, AU. IFIP Conference Proceedings, p. 12. Springer, Heidelberg (2010)
30. Nakanishi, T., Fujii, H., Hira, Y., Funabiki, N.: Revocable group signature schemes with constant costs for signing and verifying. In: Jarecki, S., Tsudik, G. (eds.) PKC 2009. LNCS, vol. 5443, pp. 463–480. Springer, Heidelberg (2009)
31. Pedersen, T.P.: Non-interactive and information-theoretic secure verifiable secret sharing. In: Feigenbaum, J. (ed.) CRYPTO 1991. LNCS, vol. 576, pp. 129–140. Springer, Heidelberg (1992)
32. Schnorr, C.P.: Efficient signature generation for smart cards. Journal of Cryptology 4(3), 239–252 (1991)
33. Tsang, P.P., Au, M.H., Kapadia, A., Smith, S.W.: Blacklistable anonymous credentials: blocking misbehaving users without ttps. In: CCS 2007: Proceedings of the 14th ACM conference on Computer and communications security, pp. 72–81 (2007)

Author Index

GPSR Compliance

The European Union's (EU) General Product Safety Regulation (GPSR) is a set of rules that requires consumer products to be safe and our obligations to ensure this.

If you have any concerns about our products, you can contact us on ProductSafety@springernature.com

In case Publisher is established outside the EU, the EU authorized representative is:

Springer Nature Customer Service Center GmbH
Europaplatz 3
69115 Heidelberg, Germany

Batch number: 09490872

Printed by Printforce, the Netherlands